A Century of Theatre (with Ruth Leon)
Spectator at the Theatre: London Theatres 1990–1999

As editor:

The Noël Coward Diaries (with Graham Payn)
Noël Coward and His Friends (with Graham Payn and Cole Lesley)
Theatre 71, 72, 73, 74
The Theatre Addict's Archive
The Autobiographies of Noël Coward
Punch at the Theatre
The Stephen Sondheim Songbook
The Theatregoer's Quiz Book
Bull's Eyes
Out in the Midday Sun
The Methuen Book of Theatrical Short Stories
The Methuen Book of Film Stories
Raymond Mander and Joe Mitchenson's Theatrical Companion
to Coward (with Barry Day)

For the stage:

Noël and Gertie
Spread a Little Happiness
If Love Were All (with Leigh Lawson)

JOHN GIELGUD

The Authorized Biography

SHERIDAN MORLEY

SIMON & SCHUSTER

New York London Toronto Sydney Singapore

SIMON & SCHUSTER
Rockefeller Center
1230 Avenue of the Americas
New York, NY 10020

Designed by Jeanette Olender
Insert Design by Leslie Phillips
Manufactured in the United States of America

1   3   5   7   9   10   8   6   4   2

Library of Congress Cataloging-in-Publication Data
Morley, Sheridan, date.
John Gielgud : the authorized biography / Sheridan Morley.
p. cm.
1. Gielgud, John, Sir, 1904–   2. Actors—Great Britain—Biography.   I. Title.
PN2598.G45 M67 2002   792'.028'092—dc21
[B]   2001055031
ISBN 0-7432-2242-3

Frontispiece photo by Snowdon / Camera Press Ltd.

For information regarding special discounts for bulk purchases,
please contact Simon & Schuster Special Sales at 1-800-456-6798 or
business@simonandschuster.com.

ACKNOWLEDGMENTS

A word or two of explanation about how this book came to be written. About twelve years ago, back in 1989, John Gielgud rang me one morning. We were not perhaps close friends, but in a way I had known him almost all my life; he had directed my grandmother Gladys Cooper in *The Chalk Garden*, and Robert, my father, in *Halfway Up the Tree*, and my mother, Joan, had been an early friend of his own first great love, John Perry. Another of his great friends and colleagues for almost fifty years was the actor Robert Hardy who married my Aunt Sally, who became a close friend. John had also been wonderfully helpful to me in many of my earlier biographies, writing several prefaces to them and filling in, as only he could, a wealth of theatrical detail and gossip for such lives as those I had written of Noël Coward, David Niven, Sybil Thorndike, and Robert and Gladys themselves. I had also very frequently interviewed him for radio and television, newspapers and magazines, and had spent some happy hours with him at Wotton Underwood as well as in California when he was out there filming *The Loved One* with my father for Tony Richardson in the early 1960s. I had even once been assigned to greet him at Honolulu Airport when I was teaching there and he was en route to play his solo *Ages of Man* in Australia; he had the grace to look only mildly surprised as I covered him in a flowered kind of necklace, a local tradition that I think we somehow failed to explain to him.

By the time we began our telephonic life in, I suppose, the early 1980s, he had already acquired the habit of starting his phone calls with no kind of preemptive greeting or introduction, as if aware that his voice alone would be enough. "My biographer," this particular 1989 conversation began, partly wistful and partly almost accusatory, as though it were somehow my fault, "seems to have died."

The biographer in question was Richard Findlater, a distinguished and long-serving arts editor of *The Observer*, who had indeed been engaged for several years on the project for Ion Trewin, then an editor at Hodder & Stoughton and an old friend of mine from the years we spent together as journalists on *The Times*. Richard's death, although at an eminently respectable age, left John and Ion in something of a quandary. Ion wanted the authorized biography, and John wanted at least an answer with which to fend off the many other writers who were now beginning to approach him asking for permission to write his life.

They decided that I might prove a suitable candidate, and it took me all of about ten seconds to agree. Thanks to Richard's widow, I was able to buy all his research notes with my original advance and discovered that although he had not yet started to write John's life, he had interviewed several crucial witnesses, from Olivier to Redgrave, and Vivien Leigh to Sybil Thorndike, whose subsequent deaths made them unavailable to me. He had also painstakingly annotated John's own volumes of theatrical memoirs, and what was already a small bookcase full of other books about him and his remarkable career.

There were two immediate issues to be resolved: would it be possible to write an authorized biography that would add sufficiently to what already existed in print (and on tape, since John had given both radio and television interviewers remarkably long and detailed accounts of his working life)? And could we agree on precisely when the book should appear—for John's ninetieth birthday, which was already close, or his ninety-fifth, or at the time of his death, which was somewhat harder to predict, since almost throughout John's last decade he gave every indication of planning to live forever?

I soon realized that the issues were inextricably linked: the only way of writing fully about John's life, as opposed to his work, which had already been handsomely chronicled elsewhere, was to confront the issue of his arrest for homosexual soliciting in 1953, and that was precisely what John wanted me to avoid. His argument was eminently understandable: he knew that the arrest was on file and public knowledge at least to those who were around at the time. But such was the devotion in which he was held toward the end of his long life that there had grown up an unspoken, and in my experience unprecedented, agreement among those of us who wrote about him that we would simply not mention it. What John feared was not a straightforward account of the facts, such as I have tried to write in what is, I believe, unique detail after years of research in police and other files, but the interest this would arouse in an old case. He feared not so much my book, but the phone calls and the prurient enquiries that it would doubtless elicit from gossip columnists eager to get a paragraph or two out of his apparently scandalous past.

This then became the major problem; I realized very early on that my book could not appear in his own lifetime, but he also realized what I was up to and became increasingly eager to see, if not to censor, the text. He would ring on a regular basis: "How old am I now, dear boy?" he would ask, and for several years I was able to pretend that he was still in his twenties. Along the way I also wrote some other books, always taking care to explain that they were secondary to his, but I think we both knew that I was playing for time.

"I suppose you want me dead?" was the start of another phone call, and I had to explain that although it might technically make my book easier to write and publish, the thought of living without his voice, unquestionably the greatest of the twentieth century, either begging or imparting some new and splendid gossip about the actors we both knew and sometimes loved, would be far too high a price to pay. For the first and (I hope) only time in my life, I had backed myself into a biographer's cul-de-sac. Although I spent the last ten years doing literally hundreds of interviews about John at home and abroad, watching again and again his every film and television appearance, listening to every radio broadcast and even (thanks to John Miller and John Powell) the unbroadcast recordings, I couldn't actually bring myself to start writing the book, because that would have been in my own mind some kind of acknowledgment that John was on the way out, given that we had already come to the reluctant conclusion that it wouldn't be published in his lifetime without hurting the actor whom above all others outside my immediate family I had come to love most, with a love that encompassed the knowledge that the truth about him eventually had to be told.

Other books about him began to appear with increasing frequency and sometimes even his cautious blessing, but none was able to deal in any detail with his private life, not least because by now John had given me all his own letters and private papers, boxes and boxes of them neatly stored by his mother. But again, we never could bring ourselves to discuss precisely what use I was to make of these; John must have known what was in them, and that by showing them to me he was offering a considerable time bomb that would destroy the secrecy in which he had managed to shroud his past. On reflection, I think I know now what he knew: that in his lifetime I would never publish anything that he might in his late nineties consider damaging to his reputation. This meant, logically, that I must be working on a book designed to appear after his death, but even that was not entirely satisfactory, since he clearly wished to read it.

One issue on which we did agree was that of the Bricks. John had, from a very early age, been famous for saying the wrong thing as almost a reflex action, covering a curious, unworldly shyness that years of fame never quite erased. But just as all the best one-liners eventually end up being ascribed to Oscar Wilde or Dorothy Parker or Noël Coward (and having written two of these biographies I have some evidence of this), rightly or wrongly, John was eventually lumbered with all the clangers ever made backstage, and we agreed that I would only include in the book those that could be accurately documented. The only one of these that I have failed to find room for is the morning he rang me in some horror: "You'll never believe this; in America they are actually about to name a theatre after a drama critic. Oh my God, you are one. Good-bye."

So that, more or less, was the state of play when he died on May 21, 2000, soon after his ninety-sixth birthday. That Sunday night, when I was first told of his death, I began for the first time to write the opening of chapter one, as if somehow I could at last see how to do it and even perhaps keep him with me for a few more months. I wrote this book every day and many nights from May to December, drawing on almost two decades of my own and Richard Findlater's research, and papers of John's going back to the early 1920s. I owe many tremendous debts to John himself and his immediate and extended family; to my own darling Ruth Leon, who has lived with me in a house that effectively became the Gielgud Archives for several years; to Mrs. Richard Findlater, for allowing me to acquire her late husband's meticulous pioneering work; to Ion Trewin, who first gave me the assignment and, from his subsequent desk as managing editor at Weidenfeld, has kept a watchful eye over it ever since, wondering like me if we would ever manage to get it together or simply sink under a mountain of memories; to Roland Philipps at Hodder who never once (in all the ten years during which I failed to hand over even an outline) pointed out that I was somewhat late in delivery; to Michael Korda, who picked up the American rights with commendable speed once I had a book to show him; to Paul Webb, who did much of the research and for the last year and more has kept the book in some kind of computerized shape, living patiently from day to day with my increasing technophobia; to my agent Michael Shaw, whose patience has also been far above and beyond what I had any right to expect; and to all of the following, living and sometimes alas now dead, who have helped me in some way to complete the Gielgud jigsaw. Many of them gave me their time and their memories; others simply let me read what they had written about John or hear what they had said about him on the air. Since a comprehensive bibliography would consist of virtually every theater book written in the twentieth century, I have simply listed the authors here who were most immediately helpful, including those who directly or indirectly answered questions about John from Richard Findlater, many of whom therefore now appear in somewhat ghostly form.

I also wish here to record my deep gratitude to Barbra Paskin (herself now a distinguished biographer) for indexing all of John's letters; Angela Herlihy at Hodder; Sydney Cohen for the index; Natalie Goldstein for her wonderful work on the photographs; and to the librarians and archivists at many research centers here and in the United States, principal among them Sandra Archer at the Library of the Academy of Motion Picture Arts and Sciences in Los Angeles, Alan Pally at the New York Public Library for the Performing Arts at Lincoln Center, Cathy Haill at the British Theatre Museum, Richard Mangan at the Mander-Mitchenson Collection, and the keepers of the archives of the British Film Institute, the Royal Shakespeare Company, the National Theatre, the Garrick Club, the Players Club (New

York), the BBC, Colindale, the British Museum, and the British Library. My thanks also go to Peter Coller, Sally-Anne Pinnington and Mark Gold for holding off the rest of the world for long enough to let me get this eventually to press.

Biography is, I have always believed, a form of pentimento: just as, in days when artists could seldom afford new canvas, they would paint over existing pictures, which would eventually break through to the surface in shadow; so you start a biography with one picture and end up with quite another. Let me thank here all the people, listed or not, who helped me to find the Gielgud beneath the surface of his remarkable and historic career; after a decade in all their various and very varied company, I am going to miss them almost as much as I already miss John himself.

In Los Angeles: John Houseman, Roddy McDowall, Dudley Moore. In Mexico: Brian Bedford, Peter Glenville. In Switzerland: Adrianne Allen, Noël Coward, Graham Payn. In Sydney: John McCallum, Greta Scacchi, Googie Withers. All other interviews were conducted in London or New York in the last twenty years, either by Richard Findlater or Paul Webb or the author; the following list includes many now sadly no longer with us, and several who supplied written or recorded material over the same period:

Edward Albee, Mark Amory, Peggy Ashcroft, Frith Banbury, Keith Baxter, Simon Russell Beale, Richard Bebb, Alan Bennett, Michael Billington, Kitty Black, Claire Bloom, Dirk Bogarde, Gyles Brandreth, Peter Brook, Michael Bryant, Peter Bull, Barry Burnett, Richard Burton, Sally Burton, Simon Callow, Judy Campbell, Humphrey Carpenter, John Casson, Michael Coveney, Hume Cronyn, Rosalie Crutchley, Constance Cummings, Milly Daubeny, Judi Dench, Michael Denison, Edith Evans, Laurie and Mary Evans, Ralph Fiennes, Richard Findlater, Bryan Forbes, Meriel Forbes, Clive Francis, David Frost, Christopher Fry, Patrick Garland, Eleanor Gielgud, Maina Gielgud, Marius Goring, Martin Gottfried, Morton Gottlieb, Derek Granger, Dulcie Gray, Hubert Gregg, George Grizzard, Valerie Grove, Alec Guinness, Piers Haggard, Peter Hall, Edward Hardwicke, Robert Hardy, Sally Hardy, Margaret Harris, Ronald Harwood, Frank Hauser, Ronald Hayman, David Hemmings, Jocelyn Herbert, John

Higgins, Wendy Hiller, Clive Hirschhorn, Michael Hordern, Sue Hyman, Barry Ingham, Julie Kavanagh, Rachel Kempson, Gavin Lambert, Anna Massey, Geraldine McEwan, Ian McKellen, Sarah Miles, John Miller, John Mills, Liza Minnelli, Julian Mitchell, Adriana Mnuchin, Tanya Moiseiwitch, Joan Morley, Robert Morley, Cathleen Nesbitt, John Neville, Benedict Nightingale, Garry O'Connor, Laurence Olivier, Tarquin Olivier, Tony Palmer, Michael Pennington, John Perry, Margot Peters, Eric Phillips, Robin Phillips, Harold Pinter, Joan Plowright, John Powell, Anthony Quayle, Corin Redgrave, Michael Redgrave, Vanessa Redgrave, Ralph Richardson, James Roose-Evans, Daniel Rosenthal, Millie Rowland, Peter Sallis, John Schlesinger, Paul Scofield, Marian Seldes, Michael Shaw, Ned Sherrin, Donald Sinden, Lord Snowdon, John Standing, Marguerite Steen, Robert Tanitch, Elizabeth Taylor, Sybil Thorndike, Wendy Toye, Ion Trewin, J. C. Trewin, Wendy Trewin, Dorothy Tutin, Kathleen Tynan, Peter Ustinov, Hugo Vickers, Alexander Walker, Mavis Walker, Eli Wallach and Anne Jackson, Susannah Walton, Geoffrey Wansell, Irving Wardle, John Warner, Elizabeth Welch, Brook Williams, Hugh Whitemore, Audrey Williamson, Irene Worth, Michael York.

For my darling Ruth Leon,

who has been living with John nearly as long as I have;

for my mother, Joan Morley, who once shared a stage with Ellen Terry;

and for my lifelong friend Ion Trewin, who commissioned

this book and then had to wait a decade to read it.

This American edition is also dedicated with love

to Marian Seldes, whose talent as a Broadway historian is only matched

by her splendor as an actress; to Don Smith, who has always

meant to me the very best of New York; and not least

to Annie Jackson and Eli Wallach, my transatlantic friends

for all of half a century.

S.M.

Contents

1. An Edwardian Youth (1904–1921)   21

2. Waterloo Road to Gower Street (1921–1923)   45

3. An Abandoned Museum on the Woodstock Road (1923–1925)   55

4. Noël and the Nymph (1925–1929)   69

5. To the Vic (1929–1930)   83

6. The Importance of Being Richard (1930–1932)   93

7. Vintage Bordeaux (1933–1934)   115

8. The Readiness Is All (1934–1935)   131

9. Hamlet Goes to Broadway (1935–1937)   147

10. Gielgud and Company (1937–1938)   171

11. The West End at War (1938–1940)   185

12. War Weary (1940–1948)   197

13. The Unkindness of Strangers (1948–1949)   219

14. Shakespeare at Stratford (1950–1951)   231

15. Cassius and California (1952)   241

16. Annus Horribilis (1953)   253

17. King Lear Goes to Japan (1954–1955)   287

18. Back on the Avenue (1956–1957)   299

19. The Ages of Man (1958–1960)   313

20. Othello's Occupation Gone (1961–1964)   333

21. All's Welles (1964–1967)   349

22. Into the Valley of Death (1967–1969)   363

23. Home, Sweet Home (1970–1973)   379

24. Bleak House (1974–1977)   397

25. Gored by Vidal (1977–1984)   417

26. The Best of Friends (1984–1994)   441

27. Goodnight, Sweet Prince (1995–2000)   469

CHRONOLOGY   483   BIBLIOGRAPHY   502   INDEX   507

John Gielgud

1. An Edwardian Youth

(1904–1921)

If your great-aunt happens to be Ellen Terry, your great-uncle Fred Terry, your cousins Gordon Craig and Phyllis Neilson-Terry, and your grandmother the greatest Shakespearean actress in all Lithuania, you are hardly likely to drift into the fish trade.

Whatever other achievements may yet be claimed for the twentieth century, one is already beyond all doubt or dispute: it produced in Britain the greatest generation of classical actors that the world has ever known. It took almost eighty years to get from David Garrick to Edmund Kean, and then at least another fifty to get to Henry Irving, and they were essentially on their own, loners unchallenged by any immediate rivals. Yet in the middle of this past century it was possible to see, in the same city and sometimes even the same stage or screen productions or acting companies, Laurence Olivier, Ralph Richardson, Michael Redgrave, Paul Scofield, Alec Guinness, Peggy Ashcroft, Edith Evans, and Sybil Thorndike. And, of course, the greatest survivor of them all, John Gielgud.

The coming together in the same lifetime of this classical galaxy is unlikely ever to be repeated; those of us lucky enough to have witnessed it will just have to be content to describe it to anyone who will listen, illustrating only by often inadequate film or television records, aware that, like any of the magic kingdoms from Prospero's to Peter Pan's, it was just there for a while and then, suddenly, it wasn't. Like the boy Thomas Malory, who is sent by King Arthur behind the lines at the end of *Camelot* to spread the word of what once was, we just have to be aware that, for one brief shining moment, from approximately 1925 to 1975, the British classical theater was at an all-time zenith.

Kenneth Tynan, the greatest theater critic of this midcentury period, and the one lucky enough to be writing about this amazing generation in its prime, once suggested the following analogy:

"You have to imagine the English stage as a vast chasm, with two great cliffs either side towering above a raging torrent. Olivier gets from side to side in one great animal leap; Gielgud goes over on a tightrope, parasol elegantly held aloft, while down there in the rapids you can just discern Redgrave, swimming frantically against the tide."

This, then, is the story of the man on the tightrope: although written with his approval and active cooperation in the last decade of his long life, it is intended as a critical biography of an actor who indeed spent much of that life working on the high wire without a net. And although in retrospect it now seems to have been a charmed life, that of a man from a theatrical family who simply carried on its tradition all the way to solo supremacy, we need to recall at the outset that we are also attempting to record the life of the only leading actor of the twentieth century to have come to the very edge of a prison sentence for homosexual soliciting; a man who then, albeit briefly, considered suicide; a man who had no real financial security until he was well into his sixties; a man who had constantly to cope with the frantic jealousy of his only acknowledged rival, Laurence Olivier; a man who only really learned to live happily in his own skin once he realized that, against all early odds and forecasts, he had outlasted and outperformed all the competition.

But this was also the man who, with his beloved brother Val, virtually invented radio drama and remained, both on stage and radio, his century's longest-running Hamlet, a role he played for almost thirty years at home and abroad. Long before the coming of the Royal Shakespeare Company or the National Theatre in the early 1960s, Gielgud alone in the West End effectively invented what we think of now as the classical repertory company. He was the actor and director who dragged Shakespeare out of the

Victorian era of his own theatrical ancestors and toward something vastly more psychologically complex. His early partnerships with his cousin Edward Gordon Craig, the ground-breaking Russian director Komisarjevsky, and the Harris sisters, who made up the radical costume and set-design team of Motley, meant that he was at the cutting edge of all the revolutionary 1930s changes in how Shakespeare was staged. With Ralph Richardson, in a late-life partnership dubbed by Ralph himself "the broker's men," after a well-known British vaudeville skit, Gielgud was also the first classical stage actor to excel in Harold Pinter and Alan Bennett and David Storey, and the first player king ever to hold the Order of Merit as well as the title Companion of Honour.

Knighted far later in life than he deserved, overlooked for the theatrical peerages that have thus far gone only to Olivier and (amazingly) Bernard Miles, John G. yet managed to end the century having not just outlived but also overtaken all his competition. There is a lot to be said for sheer survival. Gielgud spent his ninety-sixth birthday in April 2000 working with Harold Pinter and David Mamet on a play by Samuel Beckett. He died peacefully on a Sunday afternoon, at home, barely a month later, and only then was the sound of what Alec Guinness once called "the silver trumpet muffled in silk" silenced for the first and last time, just three months before Sir Alec himself died at eighty-six, thereby ending the generation of stage and screen giants of which Gielgud was the first and Guinness the last.

In many ways, John G.'s death was as perfectly timed and placed as his life; his lover Martin Hensler, with whom John had lived for the last forty years of his life, had died of cancer in considerable agony almost sixteen months earlier, and John was appalled by the prospect of a hospital end. With Martin's death, just before Christmas 1998 soon after John himself had been in the same local Aylesbury hospital with a sprained ankle, something in Gielgud also started to die; until then, he had been happily going out to film small but richly paid and showy roles in critical hits like *Shine* and *Elizabeth,* as well as several more obscure parts in minor television movies. He would only accept two or three days' work at a time, knowing now his own fragility, but he loved the gossipy life of a film set, catching up on the lives of those actors whose names he could still recall, and escaping (albeit briefly) Martin's dominant, craggy, reclusive demands at home. Theirs was not, as we shall see, a marriage made in heaven, and toward the end Martin was by no means an easy, or even a very suitable, partner for the older John. Still, there is no doubt that Hensler's death was the moment when John himself started to die.

He also became convinced that, although he still wanted to take every role that came his way (and indeed in the last few months of his life hired a new young agent, Paul Lyon Maris, on the retirement of his old friend Laurie Evans), he must avoid even the possibility of sudden death on the set. John became hilariously obsessed with the idea that, if he were to die in mid-shot, they would send for Michael Denison to replace him, and that was not precisely how Gielgud wished to have his seventy-year career come to an end. Sadly, Denison died a few months before him, but ironically enough it was his widow, Dulcie Gray, who alone took to visiting John almost daily when Martin was no longer around.

John left strict instructions that there was to be no memorial service, according to a pact he had once made with an old friend and colleague Emlyn Williams, and that even his funeral was to be held as privately as possible. His estate was eventually valued for probate in November 2000 at rather more than a million pounds, of which a large proportion would be accounted for by the sale of South Pavilion in Wotton Underwood, where John and Martin had lived for almost thirty years, having bought the magnificently theatrical property from the historian Sir Arthur Bryant.

A few days after his death, John's niece and principal heiress, the dancer and choreographer Maina Gielgud, talked about his last few months:

> I had grown up with John and Martin, and although I know that many found Martin dour and difficult, I got on with him very well, and I knew how much John loved him, even though of course they often irritated each other tremendously. They were like an old married couple, mutually dependent, but also sometimes aching for their individual freedom. Martin was very eccentric, kept all kinds of exotic animals like iguanas in cages in the bathroom, and was obsessed

Gielguds: "The Terrys lay all about us in our infancy . . . a toy playhouse, pillared and elaborately gilded, was the pride and joy of our nursery . . . but John was to owe his career to nothing but his own persistence. Our parents looked distinctly sideways at the stage as a means of livelihood, and when John showed some talent for drawing, our father spoke crisply of the advantages of an architect's office. One of our more managing aunts even extolled the Navy, saying that John would look very nice in the white tabs of a youthful cadet.

"What John possessed from the very beginning was singleness of heart and mind, together with a remarkable capacity for hard work. When he was not acting in the theater, going to the theater or talking about the theater, he was to all intents and purposes not living. All through his life, he was only to experience genuine happiness either on stage or in a dressing-room."

On the other hand, "If I had been a pure Terry," John said later, "my acting talents might have developed in a much more conventional way, especially as at first I never thought that my father's ancestry had any influence on my work. But now I realise that I've always had a tremendous feeling for Russian plays and ballets and music, and it may well be that my Eastern European background gave me a real understanding of Chekhov."

The year of John's birth was the year of the first productions of not only *Peter Pan* but (in Moscow) *The Cherry Orchard,* and it could be argued that these two plays neatly represented the twin poles of what came to be Gielgud's theater—on the one hand a kind of magic sentimentality, and on the other a Russian regret for another type of never-never-land alienation. The year 1904 also saw the births of Graham Greene, Christopher Isherwood, George Balanchine, and Cecil Beaton, all of whose lives were at some point to cross John's.

John and Val shared a bedroom and a bed at the top of the house, and with all the authority of his four-year seniority, Val used to insist that John should get into the bed first, thereby making it nice and warm for him. Relations were not improved between the brothers when Val took to writing acid reviews of John's earliest childhood theatrical endeavors, centered on their toy theater, of which John took instant control. His early directorial efforts were usually dramatic epics starring Val's toy soldiers, despite his early-developed and strong distaste for all things military.

In Gledhow Gardens, where number seven is in fact on the corner of the Old Brompton Road, the young Gielguds led, as Marguerite Steen has noted in her writings about the Terrys:

> a rarefied life, initially controlled by a German governess, a staff of servants, an elder brother at public school, and strict parental conventions. . . . John was a nervous and neurotic little boy, brought up (at least to start with) in privileged conditions. . . . Naturally he was also to become a conceited little boy, yet he never appeared to be spoiled—he was far too serious for that. . . . His grandmother Kate, his parents and aunts, knew everybody; so he grew up, not in the limited world of the theatre, but against a broad and impressive background of Important People. His parents were deeply and intellectually interested in the arts—his father in music, his mother in theatre and literature. The Gielguds moved in a wide social circle of cultured friends, whose means kept pace with their tastes. There always seemed to be enough money, but above all there was always security. . . . John was indubitably an artist, from the time he played with his first toy theater—which to him was not a toy at all, but an intrinsic part of his childish life, and the foundation of his career. Later, he would often retire into a private world of books and music.

Christmas provided the annual opportunity for yet more family drama. Every year, on the feast day itself, Ellen Terry and her sister Marion would arrive for a family lunch and then encourage charades around the fireside, as John was later to recall:

> Ellen was of course the great star of our family, and I fell madly in love with her the first time she ever came to our house. But she had led, to say the least, a somewhat irregular social and sexual life, and

Mother always found her rather restless and fidgety. When I first saw her act, I realised that restlessness was part of her glory because although she was then an old lady, deaf and rather blind and very vague in mind, when she came onstage you really believed that she was either walking on the flagstones of Venice or in the fields of Windsor. I remember her so well, moving with extraordinary swiftness and grace, though of course Shaw said that she also had a genius for standing still. She was a pre-Raphaelite actress, and she had known all the great men of her time, from Browning and Ruskin to Rossetti and Wilde. And although she had learned so much from them, she also had a marvellous humility—she was ready to learn from us children, and she had a wonderful sense of humour, which the rest of my family rather lacked. I think Marion and Fred and Kate all considered Ellen to be the scapegrace—she was the one who had been received into all the great houses in England and America, despite having two illegitimate but enormously talented children [Edith and Edward Gordon Craig]. I have always believed that in my childhood I saw only three great actresses—Sarah Bernhardt, Eleonora Duse, and my own Aunt Ellen. They were all old and infirm, but they could still stop the traffic and form queues right down Shaftesbury Avenue.

The Ellen Terry that John remembered had been born in 1847, herself also the child of a theatrical family. After a brief and unhappy marriage to the artist George Frederick Watts—"He wanted a model, not a wife"—she had joined Henry Irving's company at the Queen's in 1867, and within a year went to live with the married architect E. W. Godwin. This alliance led to her two remarkable children, and to a deeper relationship with them than any Ellen was to achieve in her three marriages.

At the Lyceum, from 1878 to 1900, she was Irving's Ophelia, Portia, Desdemona, Juliet, Beatrice, Viola, Cordelia, Imogen, and Lady Macbeth; in 1906 Bernard Shaw wrote for her the role of Lady Cicely in his *Captain Brassbound's Conversion*. In the years that John knew her, she was making a series of five silent films and also giving solo lectures on the heroines of

Shakespeare, as well as returning intermittently to the stage. Because of her somewhat scandalous extramarital affairs, she had to wait until 1925 to be made a Dame, only the second actress to receive such an honor after the distinguished classical actress Genevieve Ward. Ironically, Irving had overcome the scandal of his marital breakdown to get the first theatrical knighthood; but this was still a time when women were expected to follow a higher moral code—at least in public—and although Ellen Terry was, before Peggy Ashcroft and after Mrs. Siddons, the dominant actress of her age, this elderly and much loved public figure remained, so far as her family was concerned, something of a black sheep.

But if, in John's early years, Ellen was the shining (albeit still somewhat distant) star of the family, there was no shortage of lesser players closer to home. Both John's parents had come from unorthodox backgrounds with strong European connections, and although on his father's side the relatives included a number of professional soldiers and a former chief justice of Lithuania, his mother could deliver at least five working Terrys, as well as Gordon and Edith Craig. Life in Gledhow Gardens was, therefore, never less than theatrical: one year, the boys' audience for their Christmas show even included G. K. Chesterton. A handwritten program survives for just one of the Gielguds' homemade entertainments, a play written by John himself, entitled *The Nightingale* and subtitled "A Set of China in Five Pieces from the Famous Fairy Tale of Hans Andersen." The many scenes and settings included: The Lake, The Palace, A Corridor, The Fisherman's Hut, and (most intriguingly) The Emperor's Bed. The cast list for *The Nightingale* included: Death, A Spiteful Geisha, The Voice of the Nightingale, and The Mother of the Fisherman.

Surprisingly, given all the theatricality around the house, it wasn't until he was seven that Gielgud was first taken to the theater. As for most London children, the play was *Peter Pan*, and it could well be argued that for this stagestruck child to get his first glimpse of real theater in a play about a strange, sexless boy forever trying to coerce his friends into joining him on a magical never-never island was an entirely fitting start for his life in the theater.

As John himself was later to recall:

I was thrilled by the first entrance of the Pirates, drawn on a kind of trolley with Hook enthroned at the centre of the group, and the sinister song that heralded them as they approached from behind the scenes. I loved Nana taking the socks in her mouth from the nursery fender. Was she a real St. Bernard, I wondered, or a man dressed up and walking on all fours? But I resented the wires on the children's backs, which I could see glittering in the blue limelight, and guessed that their night gowns had bunched-up material on the shoulders to hide the harnesses they had to wear underneath. And I wished the wallpaper at the top of the scenery didn't have to split open, as well as the tall windows, when the time came for them to fly away. The doors immediately fascinated me—the one in *Peter Pan*, through which the little house rose slowly at the end of the play, with Peter and Wendy waving to the audience from its windows, and the one in *Where the Rainbow Ends*, which suddenly whisked the wicked aunt and uncle to the nether regions. And of course I loved the fights in both plays: Peter and Hook, St. George and the Dragon King, and the double scene above and below ground in *Peter Pan*, and the hollow tree with stairs inside it, with Hook in a green limelight, leaning over the low door at the bottom, leering at the children as they lay asleep.

For the young Gielgud, the most important place to be was already "the second star to the right," in the immortal line from *Peter Pan*, and to find that you had to keep straight on 'til morning. But there was already a curious contradiction at the heart of John's childhood. Whereas most of his great-aunts and uncles on the Terry side were deeply involved in theater, his own parents were really not at all enthusiastic about it, except in the abstract:

My mother talked about it a good deal, but my father was never keen on the gossipy side of theatre; he was a much more serious and intellectual character than my mother. He liked music very much and would take us to concerts on the very hard seats behind the organ at the Albert Hall, which gave me my appetite for music. He also took us to museums and galleries, which bored me rigid. I think you could say that my two brothers and young sister and I were intelligently brought up, but we were not encouraged ever to play games, because my parents had no interest in that—neither did they swim, or ride, or shoot, or fish, so if we ever went away, it was always just to the seaside.

We had three or four servants, a nurse and a governess, although my father never made more than £2000 a year, but in those pre-war days of course that was all quite possible. I do remember, very clearly, the London of my early youth—the straw thrown down outside houses to muffle the noise of horses when people were ill, and the muffin man with the green baize apron, and the coal-man who carried great sacks on his head, like Doolittle in *Pygmalion*, and would throw the coal down the manhole in front of your house with a terrible crash. In those days, the horses made far more noise than the cars which came later, and everything was for me a kind of excitement and an exhibition.

As soon as I was able to, I started exploring London on foot and fell totally in love with the West End, the marquees, the queues at the Stage Doors and the photographs in front of theaters, all very discreet, with none of the blaring advertisements and quotes from newspapers that you see today. How elegant and dignified it all was.

There followed other theater treats, mostly involving members of the Terry family, and among John's earliest memories were his cousin, Phyllis Neilson-Terry as Queen Elizabeth in *Drake*, which had real white horses onstage, and his uncle, Fred Terry, swashbuckling his way through *Henry of Navarre*. John was already completely obsessed by the theater and there was, from this time forward (despite a brief flirtation with architecture and stage design), to be no real career alternative.

But now, everything was about to change abruptly. In the autumn of

1912, when he was just eight, he was sent away by his parents to Hillside, a preparatory school near Godalming where both his elder brothers had been Head Boy. Aldous Huxley had also been a pupil there, as, in John's time, was the future playwright Ronald Mackenzie in whose work Gielgud was later to appear onstage.

The fraternal tradition was not at first one that John seemed likely to sustain. As he noted later, "It was an altogether ghastly place; a great deal of bullying went on, the Headmaster was far too old, and between lunch and the next morning's breakfast, all we ever got were three chunks of bread, thinly buttered, with a scraping of jam."

If John's early years had come straight out of *The Forsyte Saga* (which, when he read it a few years later, seemed to him to be an amazingly accurate account of his own family life), he now appeared to be moving rapidly into *Tom Brown's Schooldays*. But here, as so often in John's recollection, one has to allow for a certain theatrical exaggeration.

Most important of all, it was at Hillside that he first decided he really might like to be an actor, after giving a duly tearful Mock Turtle in *Alice in Wonderland* ("I sang 'Soup of the Evening' with increasing volume and shrillness in each verse"), followed by an equally successful *Humpty Dumpty*. At the same time that the acting first became important, he also discovered a strong talent for sketching. Every week, the boys of Hillside had to write compulsory letters home, and either because John did not want to betray his loneliness and unhappiness, or because he simply had very little to report, he took to filling the pages of his letters with ink and crayon drawings of the staff and fellow pupils.

John stayed at Hillside until almost the end of World War I. In these five years, he found that Divinity and English were the subjects he liked best, and he especially enjoyed singing in the choir at Sunday services, already working out how to make his voice louder and more identifiable. Gradually, life at Hillside ceased to seem so terrible. As his height and stage experience increased, he was entrusted with Shylock in *The Merchant of Venice*, a production that he also stage-managed, allowing him, for the first time, to incorporate some design ideas of his own. He was also able to send his mother an ink sketch of himself as Shylock, although there was at this time the very real feeling that art rather than drama would be his eventual career.

The year 1917, John's final year at Hillside, was surprisingly successful for the boy who had so hated being there. Although by his own admission "always a funk at games," he had managed to score in football, rugby, and cricket; but the real joy of these last few terms was when he was allowed to follow his brothers as Head Boy. This meant that at cricket matches he could appoint himself scorer, thus giving himself time to prepare for his last Hillside dramatic role as Mark Antony in *Julius Caesar*.

In this summer of 1917, Zeppelin raids were apt to interrupt the school curriculum with increasing regularity, though at first John was inclined to find them fascinating rather than frightening. When nearby Guildford was bombed, resulting in a lot of flying glass, he felt inspired to write a poem, which here makes its first appearance in print:

The Zeppelin Raid on Guildford

A. J. Gielgud

One fine evening (so 'twas said)
While we boys were all in bed
Zeppelins passed overhead
Out to show us "kultur"
    Back to Germany went they
    (They don't like the light of day)
    Leaving bombs about this way
    'Specially at Guildford
We, excited, rushing round
All believing every sound
"Martha's Chapel's on the ground"
said our music master.
    This was not quite true, I fear
    We the real truth did not hear
    'Til the riders with a jeer,
    Said; "It's standing happy"

On the Sunday there we went,
Tried to get some bomb, all bent,
But the Guildford men had sent
All *their* boys to get it.
    Back to Hillside went we sad
    Not a bit of bomb *we* had
    But we saw some houses had
    Had some bombs inside 'em

Back at Gledhow Gardens, as at so many other addresses, the long summer of the prewar world had been abruptly ended by telegrams bearing news of young men killed at the front. For the Gielgud family the bad news was of Lewis, who had been seriously wounded at the Battle of Loos. After several weeks in the hospital in Boulogne, it was suggested by the Red Cross that Kate herself should go out to nurse her son, and it was here that, like so many of John's female relatives, she really came into her own. While Frank stayed nervously at his desk in London, Kate became the life and soul of the Red Cross hospital where Lewis was forced to stay for several months. As soon as she could, Kate brought him home to England and Lewis was transferred to a small clinic for convalescent officers, which had just been opened in a wing of Kensington Palace. There, Kate noted proudly, his first visitors included two of his prewar Oxford contemporaries, the writer Aldous Huxley and the scientist J.B.S. Haldane.

A few months later still, Lewis was allowed to return home, classified "Permanently Disabled," although by the end of 1918 he was sufficiently recovered to be back in France as a cypher clerk at the signing of the Armistice. Lewis's war ended in a blaze of glory, as he was variously attached to the staffs of Clemenceau, Marechal Foch, and Field Marshal Lord Haig.

The atmosphere back home at Gledhow Gardens was rather less victorious; Frank was no longer having much success on the Stock Exchange, there were still school fees to be paid for the younger children, domestic staff had to be let go, and the house now seemed, like so many others, to be in mourning for its prewar life.

John, with all the single-minded selfishness of the adolescent, was meanwhile discovering a whole new world for himself, blithely ignorant of the fact that his parents' social universe was in some ways coming to an end. Whenever possible, on holidays or weekends, he would hang around Shaftesbury Avenue, greedily gobbling up every production for which he could afford a stool in the gallery queue. In these wartime years, he saw every kind of performance from *Chu Chin Chow* (no less than five times), to *Peg o' My Heart*. A year earlier he had also seen the Drury Lane gala celebration of the Shakespeare tercentenary, which brought together every star in the West End firmament, from Henry Ainley and Gerald du Maurier to Genevieve Ward and, from his own family, Ellen, Fred, and Marion Terry.

The Edwardian theatre of my boyhood was dominated by the great actor-managers like George Alexander, Beerbohm Tree and Gerald du Maurier. At the time, I accepted their style of acting completely, and I suppose I longed to be like them. I thought that was the way to act. I much preferred the panache of Fred Terry or Robert Loraine in *Cyrano* to the naturalistic but brilliant acting of Du Maurier or Charles Hawtrey . . . but I had no conception of the various methods necessary to achieve such fine results. Du Maurier often put on rubbish, just as Fred did—they both catered to the public taste for sentimental dramatists like J. M. Barrie. Ibsen and Chekhov had only just arrived in translation, but they certainly weren't what most theatregoers then wanted. Actors in those days read very little, did not like to be taken too seriously, and had little faith in foreign writing. People were also still curiously snobbish about the theatre. My aunt Mabel was very close to Gerald du Maurier's brother Guy, who was killed in the First War, and I once asked her if she had been in love with him. "In love? With an actor?"

As World War I came to its close, the Gielguds' life in South Kensington was slipping into a kind of genteel poverty. Essentially, theirs had been an

Edwardian household, and like so many of its kind, it had undergone during the war an almost imperceptible downgrading. The prewar seaside holidays and large family Christmas parties had of course come to an abrupt end in 1914, and as the four children began to move away, to go to war or public school, the house took on the faintly ghostly air of a theater just after the audience has gone home. Where before there had been servants and warmth and hospitality, now there was a general air of decay, ameliorated by Kate Gielgud's theatrical determination not to let any family problems show "from the front."

Because the family was now in considerable economic difficulty, it had been imperative for John to get a scholarship to his senior school. After he failed both Eton (to which Lewis had won a scholarship) and Rugby (where Val had enjoyed a similar triumph), the nearby Westminster School, though very much a third choice, proved willing to accept the young John on a fee-paying basis, but only after some tough coaching.

No sooner had he arrived, at the age of thirteen, for the September term of 1917, than John knew it was the place to be. More important, had he in fact gone to either Eton or Rugby, he would effectively have become a prisoner within the school grounds. Westminster by contrast, less than a mile away from his home or Shaftesbury Avenue, meant that the whole of central London could now become his playground.

Even so, John only survived a couple of terms as a weekly boarder at Grant's House before he was writing home in desperation to his mother: "Please, dearest Mama, let me become a day boy. All I feel inclined to do is either cry or shriek, and it is so awful trying to fight such unhappiness and homesickness. I feel vilely rotten. Woke up this morning with a deadly fear of getting up, the day, the house, the work, the play, the meals and then going to bed again. I shiver and shake and think and worry. It is all too beastly. One can't enjoy a moment."

Even allowing for schoolboy exaggeration and John's already highly developed sense of drama, this plea sounded ominously like a premature nervous breakdown, and John soon got his way, through an appeal not to his mother's rather unsentimental nature, but to her sense of the practical.

Soon after her son's arrival at Westminster, the now almost nightly air raids would force the whole school to run through the cloisters into one of the oldest Abbey vaults.

By using these air raids and the consequent loss of sleep as an alibi, he persuaded his parents to recast him as a day boy, a move that also represented a considerable economic saving, which came in useful as his father was by now a special constable patrolling Chelsea and, specifically, guarding the Lot's Road power station while awaiting the "all-clear" signal. John also joined a Westminster Cadet group and, hating it deeply, was at least reassured to find that he looked and felt better in uniform than in the top hat and stiff collar that Westminster pupils were still required to wear.

What appealed to John about Westminster was not the education, which he could take or leave, and usually left, but the sheer sense of drama; as a young teenager, he began to experience his lifelong fascination with tombs and statues and weddings and funerals and memorial services, all of which had a theatricality utterly central to his character.

Like Noël Coward, whom he was to understudy and replace in his first West End engagement less than ten years later, John was now finding in religion a kind of musical theatricality, which much appealed to the showman already in his childhood nature. But where Coward had to content himself with appearances as a boy soprano in the suburban churches of Teddington and Battersea, John's stage was Westminster Abbey itself, where the school choir was often to be found in twice-daily performance, albeit without the applause that he already craved.

Of course, it was by no means clear at this stage that John was cut out to be any kind of an actor. His extramural interests at Westminster were still painting and architecture; at home, he set up an easel in what was now his own bedroom and soon paintings displaced the model theater. As he later wrote, "I have always had such a love of the pictorial side of theatre that the very first things in a production that really strike me are always the scenery and costumes. If they delight me, I am already halfway towards enjoying myself."

Although he was not to meet him for several more years, there is no doubt that by the time John was fifteen, the relative who most intrigued him was no longer Ellen Terry but her illegitimate son, Edward Gordon Craig, already perceived as a great and revolutionary stage designer.

While going through his temporary religious phase, John was unsure whether his Church of England background gave him enough emotional support. One possibility would have been High Church or even Roman Catholicism, and he often went to smell the incense at Brompton Oratory, just around the corner from Gledhow Gardens. What he was always searching for was a sense of ceremony and ritual, and one of the few things that made up for his hatred of the Westminster Cadet training was being allowed to play a very small part, as an usher's attendant, at the 1919 Burial of the Unknown Soldier in the Abbey itself.

At Westminster many of his friends were Jewish, and he became aware of their segregation at prayers and mealtimes. Mostly, he admired and felt comfortable with their almost theatrical openness and their unashamed love for the arts, an interest often either dormant or suppressed in more conventional English schoolboys. One of his best friends, Arnold Haskell, was already a fervent ballet addict, and he took John to see such classic events as the Bakst *Sleeping Beauty* and the dancing of great prima ballerinas like Karsavina, Lopokova, and Tchernicheva, all of whom were working in London in 1914 to 1918, during the war. This was also the heyday of the Ballets Russes at the Alhambra, and John was soon able to make the connection with his own partly Russian background: "Haskell, who of course became a leading ballet critic, and I used to save all our pocket money and, after school on wet Saturday afternoons we would stand for hours together in queues—that first production of *Boutique Fantasque,* the exquisite blue backcloth for *Carnaval,* the enchanted tower in *Thamar* and the glory of Bakst's rococo palaces in *The Sleeping Princess* were all early ecstasies. . . . "

Many years later Gielgud was to write of the first time he saw the Ballets Russes: "The entrancing mixture of music, mime and spectacle enraptured me immediately. . . . For *Boutique,* the scenery was extremely avant-garde . . . I was able to appreciate the acting as well as the dancing, which seemed to merge together with incredibly skilful ease and grace. . . . The elegance of *Carnaval,* the high spirits of *Boutique* . . . the savage dances in

Prince Igor, as the music crashed out and the curtain fell to tumultuous applause."

For John G. this experience was not just an artistic revelation, but the rite of passage of another sort: "I left the theatre in a dream. Soon I was to become an aficionado of all the Diaghilev seasons that were to follow. . . . Standing in the Promenade beside my father, and walking about with him in the intervals among the cigar smoke and clinking glasses in the bar, I felt I had really grown up at last."

The influence of the Ballets Russes was not restricted to just this stagestruck public schoolboy. Its explosive combination of the best of modern design, dance, and music had an enormous impact on the English cultural scene, inspiring a generation of ballet dancers, choreographers, and patrons, and appealing to a wider audience of artists and actors. The Edwardian age is now looked back on as a golden Eden, removed from the modern world; culturally, at least, it was, in large measure thanks to Diaghilev's extraordinary ability to conjure up new talent (particularly in the work of Vaslav Nijinsky, his lover and protégé and arguably the most famous male ballet dancer of all time), an age of enormous excitement and change, led not from Paris but from what was then St. Petersburg.

From now on, as a would-be artist and even as a theatergoer, John was to be constantly torn between the ornate grandeur of Diaghilev and the avant-garde minimalism of Gordon Craig. He was still by no means certain precisely what he was going to do with the rest of his life, but at this late teenage moment if you had asked him, the answer would certainly have been designing scenery rather than appearing in front of it:

I think at this time I was tempted by the idea of being a designer, at least partly because I was terrified of the thing I most wanted, which was to be an actor. At home and in school plays, I really hadn't got much further than wandering around with a rug draped over my shoulder, thinking I was a King or something. Years later, when my friends got bored of all my theatrical chat, they used to say, "Oh, for God's sake, put a crown on his head and send him on," which always mortified me, but I suppose was good for my ego.

I was always very vain, and very fond of my voice and my looks, so it took me years to break free and learn to be a real actor; at first, what frightened me was that I moved very badly. I have always hated sport, I played no games, I couldn't swim, I couldn't really do anything. Later, when I learned to drive a car, I even had to give that up because I was so clumsy. I've always dropped things, and it was only on stage that I eventually found my confidence; but I was still very conceited and rather effeminate, and much too fond of the sound of my own voice. It took me an amazingly long time to stop showing off, and start acting.

His lack of interest in sport was in strong contrast to his love of walking around London, and especially into the theater district: "These walks around theatreland allowed me to examine minutely all the photographs and bills outside the theatres, while I tried to decide which of them seemed most likely to encourage me to invest my pocket-money, and to savor the never-ending delight of standing in a queue for several hours waiting for the pit doors to open.

"I was still a boy, but lucky enough to have been born just in time to touch the fringe of the great nineteenth-century of theatre. I saw Sarah Bernhardt die in battle, I saw Adeline Genée dance, I heard Albert Chevalier sing 'My Old Dutch,' and I saw Vesta Tilley and Marie Lloyd in their last days. I also stood in the gallery, ridiculous and mocked in my Westminster school uniform, to see Duse make her farewell appearance in *Ghosts* . . . what impressed me most was the tremendous reception the audience gave her, their breathless silence during her performance, and the air of majestic weariness with which Duse seemed to accept it all. There was something poignant and ascetic about her when she was old and ill, quite different from the indomitable gallantry of the crippled Bernhardt, and the ageless beauty and fun that Ellen Terry still brought with her upon a stage."

1921 was John's last year at Westminster, and clearly decisions now had to be made. Lewis, after his wartime service and rehabilitation, had returned to win a scholarship to Magdalen College, Oxford, and Val had just gotten into Trinity. Visiting them there, John fell in love with both the city and the university, but he was still woefully unacademic. The problem, as usual, was his utter inability to cope with math, and despite some expensive private coaching, he humiliatingly failed his college entrance no less than three times.

Putting the bravest possible face on his failure, his mother Kate recalled, "John declined the university course we had planned for him. He declared that it would be a waste of his time and his father's money, as he wished to spend those three years studying for the stage. . . . I think he always realised that he had my wholehearted backing. I was always certain that there was too much of the artist in him to let him settle down on an office stool, and though an architect's office was offered as a halfway concession, his very poor records at school in math and geometry did not hold out much promise in that direction."

Ironically, this left him in a rather stronger bargaining position with his reluctant parents, and they rapidly came to an understanding: John would apply to Lady Benson, who ran a private drama school close to his grandmother's house on Cromwell Road. If accepted, he would be allowed to train with her for the theater on the strict understanding that if, by the age of twenty-five, he had not become self-supporting, he would turn to a career in art or architecture.

Meanwhile, at Gledhow Gardens, the toy theater was put away in the attic for the very last time, and John was about to find a real one just around the corner.

2. WATERLOO ROAD TO GOWER STREET

(1921–1923)

*Lady Benson was a very bad actress but a splendid teacher. She ran her school
in a ramshackle little drill hall, and on my very first day told me that I walked
like a cat with rickets.*

*J*ohn was now seventeen. His early years had been a curious mixture of
privilege and fading gentility; despite his interest in the theater and his evident artistic interests, there was as yet no indication that he would have
any measure of the success of his eminent relatives. He did not, unlike Noël
Coward, have to fight his way out of South London boarding houses, but
neither did he have the great advantage of Sybil Thorndike and Laurence
Olivier, both born into the Church and therefore accustomed to hearing
their fathers declaiming from the pulpit every Sunday. By contrast, John's
father was still a shy, retiring figure, so starting John's theatrical education
was left to his numerous aunts and distant cousins.

Life at Gledhow Gardens had been enriched by the number of famous
theatrical guests who visited regularly; but money had become tight, and
from an early age John knew his only real assets were a famous family and
a passionate desire to be in the theater.

By the time he arrived at Lady Benson's, where he was one of only four
boys in a class of thirty, he had already progressed from the early family
plays in the attic and his school productions to a couple of amateur ap-

pearances. The first of these was a production of a World War I drama at a theater on King's Road, Chelsea. The cast included not only John as a young Greek officer, but playing a British prisoner of war, the scientist Julian Huxley who, like his brother Aldous, had by now become a friend of all the Gielgud brothers.

John had also played a couple of very minor roles for Rosina Filippi's drama school in Chelsea and made his Shakespearean debut, somewhat disastrously, in an amateur production of *As You Like It*, played in the open air at Battle Abbey. Aged sixteen, and cast as Orlando, he proudly went to the local barbershop demanding to have his hair waved—for a play, he added cautiously. "Certainly, sir," said the barber, "I assume Sir is with the Pierrots on the Pier this week?" He might as well have been. As a duly coiffed Orlando, he strode onto the lawn, drew his sword, declaimed his opening line, "Forbear and eat no more," and promptly fell over a large log. Thus it was that the greatest Shakespearean actor in history made his stage debut by falling flat on his face.

Even during his time at Lady Benson's, John still thought he might prefer to be a designer rather than an actor. He had a deep dislike of the fencing, dancing, and gesture classes that were central to the acting course. He was interested in text, but terrified of the physical side of acting: "As a young man, I was vain and foppish; I pranced around, looking very self-conscious. Then I became too graceful and posed; later I had to control my physical mannerisms by having them checked by others but, at this age, I was still far too shy to ask anyone about them."

Though his parents still had grave doubts about allowing their youngest boy to go into the family business, Kate Lewis Terry, his grandmother, was overjoyed: "Dear old Jack," she wrote him in 1921, "I am delighted to hear of your intended real start in a profession you love, and wish you every success. You must not anticipate a bed of roses, for on the stage, as in every other profession, there are 'rubs and arrows' to contend with. 'Be kind and affable to all your co-mates, but if possible be intimate with none of them.' This is a quotation of my parents' advice to me, and I pass it on, as I have proved it to be very sound. Theatrical intimacy breeds jealousy of a petty kind which is very disturbing. I hope you may have many chances with your various studies and prove yourself worthy."

By John's own admission, he was a talented but conceited pupil at Lady Benson's, yet he now began to develop serious doubts about whether he could ever really make it as an actor: "I became acutely self-conscious, knowing that my laziness and my dislike of games had prevented me from learning, when I was a boy, to move freely and naturally. I walked from the knees instead of from the hips, and bent my legs when I was standing still, instead of holding them straight. I am sure that if I had been forced to run and swim when I was a child, I should not have developed these mannerisms so badly, but it was too late to think of that now. Such a discovery in my first term at Lady Benson's was extremely depressing; however, it dealt a severe blow to my conceit, which was a good thing."

As a result of all these insecurities, John now decided that the only way he might get by as an actor was in wheelchair roles, or those that required him to lie in bed, but he soon worked out that this would mean a severely limited career. He did, however, appear during term-time in a couple of charity matinees, one in Noël Coward's first play *I'll Leave It to You,* and the other in the play that was later to become almost his own personal property, Wilde's *The Importance of Being Earnest.*

The other good thing that emerged from Lady Benson's was his discovery that the Old Vic on Waterloo Road, then as always strapped for cash, was in the habit of using drama students as its extras. Thus it was that, still only seventeen, on November 7, 1921, Gielgud made his first professional, albeit unpaid, appearance onstage as the Herald in *Henry V,* directed by Robert Atkins, who kept shouting to "that boy in the brown suit, for God's sake, take your hand out of your pocket when holding a spear."

For John, susceptible, romantic, uneasy, but convinced by his Terry heritage of the absolute magic of the theater, the Old Vic came as a rude awakening. The rehearsal room was filthy, extras had to change in a box above the stalls with only a curtain to hide them from the audience, and John had said his one line, "Here is the number of the slaughtered French," so badly that for the rest of the season he was not given another word to speak. So unpromising did he seem to the "real" actors in the company that many of them, including Ernest Milton and Sybil Thorndike's brother, Russell, took the trouble to come over and tell him that despite his theatrical heritage, he would be well advised to give up any thought of the professional stage. Curiously, it was this opposition that finally tipped the balance and made him now, for the first time, determined to be an actor.

Daunted but not defeated, John returned for two more terms to Lady Benson and got his first review, playing a vicar in an end-of-term farce called *Lady Huntsworth's Experiment.* True, he wasn't mentioned by name, but the critic of *The Stage* noted, "The worthy parson, unctuously played by quite a beginner, drew much laughter from a critical audience."

By the end of the year's course, John was not really much further along. Lady Benson's was not regarded as a full-fledged drama school, and as for his family, although they had shown polite and loyal interest in his teenage endeavors as both actor and artist, they were not now exactly falling over themselves to find him work. On the other hand, he did already have a few credits, a little humility, and a now unshakable determination to make his future in the theater.

When help did come, it was inevitably from one of the Terrys, albeit one he hadn't seen since early childhood. Phyllis Neilson-Terry was the daughter of Fred, and therefore John's second cousin. She had been on the road in America for several years, and on her return, hearing of his interest in the theater, she wrote offering him four pounds a week for a long tour of fifteen weeks around the provinces to understudy and speak a few words at the end of *The Wheel.* He would also, for the money, be required to work as an assistant stage manager, and after a very few rehearsals (because most of the cast had already done the play in London), they opened at the Theatre Royal in Bradford on September 4, 1922.

The idea of Bradford was to John the height of romantic theatricality; it was, after all, the city where Irving had died, a few hours after giving his last performance as *Becket* in 1905. Seventeen years later, when John got there, he found, to his surprise, an infinitely depressing vista of smokestacks and the universal grayness of northern factory life. He stayed in a small back room in digs largely occupied by the singers and dancers working at the local music hall and felt—this young boy from a classical royal family—rather out of his element amid the rough and tumble of vaudville entertainers. Even in the theater, he found he still had a lot to learn, especially about greasepaint; most nights he would arrive on stage as a British naval officer, but bizarrely resembling a Cherokee Indian, because he kept forgetting to powder his make-up before going under the lights.

The tour proceeded to Sheffield, Hanley, Preston, and Leeds, where John was not best pleased to find in his digs a sign reading "Lav in pub opposite." Things could only improve, and they did so at Aberdeen, where one of the principals fell ill and John had to go on in his place. Phyllis was so pleased with her cousin's achievement that a couple of weeks later, when the tour reached Oxford, she asked the now-recovered leading man to stand down for one night so that John's parents might be invited to come and see him. Something about their presence destroyed his performance, however, and Frank and Kate returned sadly to London, convinced that their boy had made an unwise choice of career. Salvation came in the form of another young actor on the tour, Alexander Sarner, who gently suggested to John that a year with Lady Benson was not exactly the ultimate in theatrical training, and perhaps he would now be wise to apply to RADA (the Royal Academy of Dramatic Art) for a more advanced theatrical education.

By now much more experienced than any of the other applicants, John easily achieved the scholarship that had eluded him everywhere else. His contemporaries during the year 1922 to 1923, which John spent in Gower Street at RADA, included its star pupil, Robert Harris, and other future classical players of the British theater such as Beatrix Lehmann, Veronica Turleigh, George Howe, and Mervyn Johns, all of whom were to work in John's companies in later years. Their principal teachers were Elsie Chester, a formidable and disabled old bat who used to hurl her crutch at students who displeased her, and Claude Rains who went on to an extremely starry Hollywood career in such classics as *Casablanca* and Hitchcock's *Notorious*.

Forty years later, the actor and raconteur Peter Ustinov was to find himself in St. Louis, Missouri, where John was playing his solo Shakespeare recital *The Ages of Man* at a local theater. To publicize it, he had agreed to give a television interview to a local college professor, and it was this that Ustinov caught: "'One final question,' said the interviewer, 'Sir . . . Sir Gielgud . . . did you . . . oh, you must have had . . . we all did . . . at the start of your very wonderful . . . very wonderful and very meaningful . . . let me put it this way . . . did you have someone . . . a man . . . or even a woman . . . at whom you could point a finger and say yes! this person helped me when I . . . ?' By now John seemed to have grasped the question. 'Yes,' he replied thoughtfully, 'there was somebody who taught me a very great deal at drama school, and I am certainly grateful to him for his kindness and consideration. His name was Claude Rains,' and then, as an afterthought, John added, 'I don't know whatever happened to him. I think he failed, and had to go to America.'"

Certainly, at RADA, Rains was more to Gielgud than a failed actor; he was a significant teacher, and it was through his encouragement that John at last began to lose some of his acute self-consciousness. At the end of the first term, Gielgud played the title role in the academy's production of *The Admirable Crichton,* J. M. Barrie's classic comedy about the butler and the aristocrats stranded on a desert island, and he was seen by Nigel Playfair, one of the most revered and adventurous producers and directors of his day. So keen was Playfair to have John join his company that a deal was reached whereby, while continuing at the academy, he would also play the Poet Butterfly in Karel Kapek's *The Insect Play,* a revolutionary piece that flopped badly, because the sexual content that had made it such a success on the continent had been removed by the puritanical Lord Chamberlain (a member of the royal household who had been appointed to censor plays in the eighteenth century and was, amazingly, to go on doing so until 1968), in order to save the blushes of an English audience.

"Looking back, I am amazed that the audience refrained from throwing things at me. . . . I wore white flannels, a silk shirt, a green laurel wreath and a golden shuttlecock. . . . The production was a disaster, and I certainly didn't help it."

At this early stage, it would have been a brave critic who forecast that John really had any future at all as a leading player. Still very frail and sensitive, sheltered even now by a dominant mother, and always having been allowed to escape any kind of physical activity at school, he was deeply uneasy in his own skin—awkward, ungainly, physically inhibited, and already aware that he had to be careful about appearing in any way homosexual, since this was still reckoned anathema to most audiences and, of course, still against the law, even for consenting adults in the privacy of their own homes.

At this time, John G. was about as unlikely an actor as could have been found. Here was no Olivier, eager to appear before an audience; instead, John's magically lyrical voice and artistic inclinations suggested a poet or a painter rather than a public performer. He seemed more likely to be found at the top of an ivory tower than pinned under a spotlight.

Even so, Gielgud already had his supporters, a group not limited to his relatives. Nigel Playfair, for instance, retained such faith in the young RADA student, still only nineteen, that he kept him on at the Regent Theatre for the next and very different production, a staging of *Robert E. Lee* by the poet John Drinkwater, who had just scored a huge success with *Abraham Lincoln*. But his second stab at American Civil War history was by no means as popular as the first, and John's only role was that of an orderly, following Felix Aylmer around the stage and trying not to count the empty seats through his field glasses. He did, however, get to understudy Claude Rains and went on for him in a couple of performances in the title role where he found he was very good on the first night and very bad on the second:

"I seemed at this time always to lose confidence after I had played a part once, but people were agreeably surprised at my ability in the emotional scenes. The feeling of them came to me without much difficulty, and the sincerity of that feeling got over to the audience, despite my lack of technical accomplishment, whereas in the other part, as the orderly, my clumsiness and slovenly movement were conspicuous, and there were no moments of emotion or drama in which I could atone."

But back at RADA, Rains was still giving the young Gielgud what amounted to a series of master classes, putting him through everything from Tolstoy to Shakespeare and even a scene from *L'Aiglon*, which he played in French. With money still very tight, and a constant awareness that under the deal he had made with his father he had only until the age of twenty-five to establish himself in the acting profession, John decided at the end of his first RADA year that the academy had taught him enough and it was time to head out into the real theatrical world. At this point, the only advice on which teachers and pupils at RADA were agreed was that John would certainly have to change his surname, since no one seemed able to pronounce or spell it with any degree of accuracy, and he was usually to be found on theater posters and programs as "Mr Guilguid," suggesting a Scots background rather than an Eastern European one.

John G., however, already had attracted the attention of one important admirer: "I was," recalled the distinguished and veteran actress Dame Sybil Thorndike some years later, "doing a little teaching at RADA and I was horrified by the students—they all acted like governesses, with no power—and I said 'You are all terrible, no fire, no guts, you've none of you got anything in you except that boy over there, the tall one—what's your name?' And he said 'It's John Gielgud' and I said 'Well, you're the only one with possibilities.' None of the rest of them had any voices or style of their own, they were all trying to be Gerald du Maurier, and that's no way to approach Greek tragedy."

John was soon to discover that a mere year at RADA was not in fact nearly enough, but he did now have the experience of a range of college and semiprofessional roles which, although none too successful, at least had given him the feeling of what it was like to go out in front of an audience in a series of vastly different and rapidly learned and rehearsed plays. He also had begun to keep a critical first-night diary, which suggests that he could have had an entirely other career as a sharp, not to say waspish, Fleet Street reviewer. Among his earliest notices, neatly inscribed on the covers of programs he was to keep for more than three-quarters of a century, are reflections on *The Beggar's Opera, Ghosts,* John Barrymore's *Hamlet,* and O'Neill's *The Emperor Jones,* as well as such lightweight productions as *White Cargo* and *Advertising April.* Gielgud notes that at *Mary Rose* he "wept buckets"; *Heartbreak House* he found "dull and ill-constructed"; *The Second Mrs. Tanqueray* "far more dramatic and less dated than I had thought from reading it"; *Anna Christie* "a very fine play, sordid but intensely dramatic." Duse in *Ghosts* "seemed to be somewhat selfish in her playing," and Coward in *London Calling* "definitely not good, lacked charm and personality." As for *The Sleeping Prince* at the Alhambra in November 1921, with a score by Tchaikovsky and a production by Leon Bakst, "far too long and under-rehearsed; disappointing scenery, marvellous clothes, some good dancing but some very dull, wants pulling together, very enjoyable apart from that."

3. An Abandoned Museum on the Woodstock Road

(1923–1925)

"Your name and college, Sir?"
"I fear I am not a member of this University."

*L*eaving RADA behind, John now went on the inevitable rounds of agents' and managers' outer offices in search of a job. Unlike most aspiring actors of his time, however, and perhaps abetted by the Terry connection and the enthusiasm of such influential figures as Rains and Playfair, he was almost immediately able to find work, and indeed hardly ever out of it again for almost exactly three-quarters of a century.

To this day, it is still debatable whether a famous theatrical family background (and Gielgud was, of course, not nominally a Terry) is generally an advantage. The widespread view seems to be that it can help you to get the work, but not necessarily to keep it, and in John's case, there was the added problem of his extreme social and sexual nervousness. He was, in every sense but the most immediately theatrical, a late developer. Innately shy, he also was possessed of the feeling that he was somehow not like other hopeful young actors of his time.

His background was therefore at once an asset and a hindrance; he did not mix easily, and on the rare occasions when he found a real friend, he was somehow embarrassed to admit the grandeur of his connections—a grandeur that had nothing at all to do with money or even class, but everything to do with talent. His family members were always outsiders, not only because the Terrys had first chosen to act at a time when this was still widely considered socially scandalous, but also because a name like Gielgud scarcely suggested reliable British stock. Once again, the timing was against him; actors had begun to become respectable while he was still in his teens, but they did so only by desperately trying to acquire the manners and even the clothing of the squirearchy. Something about John was irredeemably foreign and artistic, at a time around the First War when to be one or the other was suspect, and to be both little short of intolerable.

Nevertheless, his first job after drama school came easily and quickly enough, even if it wasn't quite the beginning that might have been hoped for one who was to become a leading classical actor of the future. The role he was offered was a Christmas season in *Charley's Aunt* at the Comedy Theatre. The play had already become an annual fixture in London and on the road since 1892, and neither the author, Brandon Thomas, nor his daughter Amy, who was now the director, would allow any changes. John's dreams, therefore, of playing Charley in a rather more "modern" manner were rapidly defused in rehearsal, and he was told simply to act it as it always had been acted, move by move, intonation by intonation. It was not a happy engagement, but it only lasted six weeks, and what came next was something altogether more satisfactory.

J. B. Fagan was the Irish author, producer, and director who had already done some very distinguished work at the Royal Court, including Sir Godfrey Tearle's *Othello* (Tearle was a distinguished leading man of the day), and had founded the first Oxford Playhouse Company in an abandoned big-game museum on Woodstock Road, affectionately known as The Red Barn. This soon became one of the most respected regional repertory companies in the country, and by the time John joined it during that first season, early in 1924, Fagan had already gathered an amazing team of young players, including Raymond Massey, Flora Robson, Tyrone Guthrie, Reginald Denham, Richard Goolden, and Glen Byam Shaw.

Over the next eighteen months, John was to appear in a total of eighteen different productions for Fagan. Frequently, however, his parts were just walk-ons, and he seems to have made so little impression on the company that neither walk-ons Raymond Massey nor Tyrone Guthrie in their memoirs indicate any recollection of having met him until years later.

But for John himself this was to be a magical time: "It was very pleasant to be living in Oxford, having meals in college and drinks with the OUDS [Oxford University Dramatic Society], everything I had of course missed by not being a student there. The Playhouse was indeed terribly cramped, there was no foyer, and the stalls groaned and squeaked when anyone got up or sat down or even moved their legs. On the other hand, we did a very interesting season of plays by Congreve, Sheridan, Wilde, Pinero, Shaw, Ibsen, Chekhov and Pirandello."

The first production of the new season was *Captain Brassbound's Conversion*, and although John was only one of the pirate crew, with barely half a dozen lines, *The Times* reported that "He showed both imagination and restraint in the small part of Johnson." He also showed considerable ingenuity when, one night, all the lights failed and the last act had to be played in the beams of two car lamps, held proudly aloft by Gielgud like follow spots.

He got his reward in the second production: "Our big success in my first season was Congreve's *Love for Love*." John was cast as Valentine with Guthrie as his servant, Jeremy. For the actor who had so recently been told that he walked like "a cat with rickets" and that his voice sounded consumptive, surely here was the chance to establish some real credentials.

In the audience one night was an undergraduate who was later to become very important to John.

"I saw, in his first leading role, in *Love for Love*," recalled Emlyn Williams, "a youth whose name in the programme caused a woman behind me to say, 'Poor boy! How does he pronounce it? John Jeel-gud?' ... When he got going, all nose and passion and dragging calves, and unbridled oboe of a voice ... the tall, haughty creature held the stage all right."

John was now living in a tiny flat in the High, earning all of eight pounds a week, a reasonable salary for the time. He was also getting more and more involved with the undergraduates who ran an active drama society under the celebrated Oxford student actor Gyles Isham and fervently began to make up for what he now realized had been his first great lost opportunity: becoming an Oxford student when that university was at its most theatrical in the high-camp early twenties.

When he was not needed in rehearsal at the Red Barn, it was suddenly possible to lead the life he had only ever managed to play in *Charley's Aunt*, that of a languid student in chambers. Thanks to his new friend Gyles Isham, who was then living in college, John almost persuaded himself that he, too, was a student, at least until he was one night stopped by proctors, the university police, for singing bawdy songs in the High after hours. "Your name and college, Sir?" "Alas," replied John with considerable regret, "I fear I am not a member of this University."

On another occasion, Gyles invited John to lunch in his rooms at Magdalen, rooms which had once been occupied by Oscar Wilde, to tell him that he had an ambitious plan to play Romeo in London during the next vacation. On his way home that night, John's neck began to swell and it became clear that he had mumps. He was immediately expelled from the Playhouse Company for the duration. Guthrie was deputed to fumigate his dressing room and take over his roles, "while Mother took me home in a hired car with large pillows on which to rest my face, which now looked so like Humpty Dumpty's that I had to laugh every time I caught sight of myself in the window."

When John returned to the Oxford Playhouse Company, he discovered that Isham had caught his mumps and, through gritted teeth, now had to ask John to take over not only the rehearsals but also the leading role in his *Romeo and Juliet*. To John's fury, Isham recovered in time for the first night, but Gielgud was asked to stay on in the role of Paris, after which (as the first Playhouse season was now at an end) he returned to London where, in April 1924, he received a letter from the agent Akerman May: "Dear Mr. Gielgud," it read, "If you would like to play the finest lead among all the plays by the late William Shakespeare, will you please call upon Mr. Ayliff at the Regent Theatre on Friday at 2.30 pm. Here is an opportunity to become a London Star in a night."

As it happened, Gwen Ffrangcon-Davies was in desperate need of a Romeo for her Juliet, and although John was still only nineteen, and she had been less than impressed by his performance as the Poet Butterfly in *The Insect Play* in which they had both appeared, she decided, after three long auditions, that he would have to do.

Rehearsals went reasonably well because both were word perfect at the outset, John having learned the role for Gyles Isham and Gwen having just played it in Birmingham: "She was wonderfully helpful, extraordinarily keen and unself-conscious. From the very first rehearsal she threw herself wholeheartedly into every moment of her part, running the whole gamut of emotions and telling me not to be frightened of our 'clinches.' So when the moment came to embrace her passionately, I was amazed to find how naturally she slipped into my arms, sweeping her draperies in the most natural and yet artful way so that they should not lose their line or impede her movement, and arranging her head and arms in a position in which we could both speak and breathe in comfort."

It began to look as though John was at last losing some of his physical inhibitions, but shortly before the first night he began to develop severe stage fight: "I was given white tights with soles attached to them underneath and no shoes. My feet looked enormous, and it was most uncomfortable to fight or run around. My wig was coal-black and parted in the middle. Wearing an orange make-up and a very low-necked doublet, my Romeo looked like a mixture of Ramses of Egypt and a tetchy Victorian matron."

Not surprisingly, the reviews were very mixed. Gwen's child-Juliet was warmly acclaimed, but Ivor Brown considered that "Mr. Gielgud is niminy-piminy and from the waist downwards he looks absolutely nothing. He has the most meaningless legs imaginable, a sort of hysterical laugh and generally lacks experience . . . he is also scant of virility."

As was the custom of the time, John and Gwen were also engaged to play special nights at the London Coliseum, doing the balcony scene on a vaudeville bill. As John remembered, "They gave us a terrible set, with a sort of cardboard balcony, which made it look as if Juliet was standing in a picnic box. The audience never knew what to make of it, but one of the stagehands was kind enough to say to me, during the last performance, 'You are doing it a bit better now.'"

They were preceded on the bill by Teddy Brown on his xylophone, and followed by the Houston Sisters, one of whom, Renee, was to spend much of the rest of her life at parties doing a lethal parody of the young Gielgud.

And the worst was still to come. Two weeks into an unhappy run, in which the oversensitive young actor knew he was not being remotely good enough, John developed pneumonia and neither of his understudies, Ion Swinley and Ernest Milton, managed to fill in without carrying the book. The run therefore came to an ignominious end after six weeks, and it was with some relief that John returned for a second season to the Oxford Playhouse.

He had regained some measure of confidence by dint of simply being invited back to rejoin Fagan, since both Flora Robson and Tyrone Guthrie had been unceremoniously dumped after the previous season. This second Oxford stint, in 1924–1925, proved considerably more successful than the first. The reason was a major production of *The Cherry Orchard* in which John made his first real success as Trofimov: "It was the first time I ever went out on stage feeling that perhaps, after all, I could really be an actor." All the same, this was not an altogether easy time for him: "We had only a week to rehearse, and I did not understand the play at all, but there was no time for the director to explain it, so it was all rather clumsy and tentative."

It is hard, seventy years later, to recall that at this time Chekhov was virtually unknown in Britain and his plays, when performed, invariably divided both audiences and critics. Of the new Oxford production, James Agate wrote in *The Sunday Times,* "I suggest that *The Cherry Orchard* is one of the great plays of the world, and young Gielgud as Trofimov is perfection itself."

Audiences were still far from certain, but the *succes de scandale* inspired a new management, that of Nigel Playfair, to transfer *The Cherry Orchard* to his Lyric Theatre, Hammersmith. Here John again played Trofimov. The first performance was well received and there were even cries of "author"; but the reviews were hostile and audiences were poor, at least until the critic James Agate made a very early radio broadcast urging listeners to go and see it. Playfair also printed a poster quoting radically different reviews of the play, including, "This imperishable masterpiece" (Agate) and "This fatuous drivel" (MacDonald Hastings).

Yet it was precisely because of this controversy that John G. now became one of the most talked-about actors in town. The BBC, barely five years old, offered him Malcolm in a live wireless production of *Macbeth,* and John was thrilled to be in at the beginning of a new medium, which he was to make his own for the next seventy years, while his brother Val became the founding father of BBC radio drama.

A few weeks later, John got in at the start of another new medium, though one in which he was always to be much less at home. He was unexpectedly offered a leading role in a silent film, called *Who Is the Man?* The script was based on a play he had seen performed on the Paris stage by his idol, Sarah Bernhardt. Her godson, Louis Verneuil, had written it for her soon after her leg was amputated, so she could play while lying on a divan, covered in rugs. This clearly was not going to do for the film, in which John was required to play an opium-addicted sculptor undergoing a series of frantic emotional tantrums. The studio hired a violinist and piano player to get him into the right mood, but the results were, by all accounts, deeply embarrassing. The film does exist, or at least it is listed in *The British Film Catalogue;* and yet it would seem to have vanished, a fate to which all too many silent films have been consigned, some more happily than others.

It was now clear that, with John's natural affinity for Chekhov and his tentative success in *The Cherry Orchard,* he was ready at last to leave Oxford for the brighter lights of the big city with some confidence. Fagan let him go, having neatly arranged that his brother, Val, would take on some of his roles at the Playhouse, and John was to leave, later looking back at the days spent there as some of the happiest of his entire professional career. It had been a good time to be around Oxford: undergraduates of the period included Oliver Messel, Evelyn Waugh, Graham Greene, Claud Cockburn, and John Betjeman, all of whom were later to write or talk about the first time they had seen John act, however tentatively, in the Red Barn.

But the ambitious plan (by the impresario Philip Ridgeway) to run a complete Chekhov season in London fell rapidly apart. After *The Cherry Orchard,* a nervous hit, they moved on to *The Three Sisters* at the tiny Q theater in Barnes, whose budget was appropriately small—John was to be paid only £1 a week. He recalled this as

a beautiful production, very simply done, and with a lot of very good actors. Komis's [Komisarjevsky, the director] main idea for me was that I should play Tusenbach as a very handsome young man, although in the text Chekhov calls him ugly. Komis believed that English audiences were now badly in need of a romantic hero, and he was an enormous influence in teaching me not to act from outside, not to seize on obvious, showy effects and histrionics, not so much to exhibit myself, as to be within myself trying to impersonate a character who is not aware of the audience, to try to absorb the atmosphere of the play and the background of the character, to build it outwards so that it came to life naturally. This was something I had never thought of, and it seemed to me a great relaxing exercise . . . relaxation which is the secret of good acting. I remember our first rehearsals in someone's Bloomsbury flat, with the floor marked out in bewildering lines of coloured chalk—the groupings, entrances and exits were all most accurately planned, though at first we could none of us imagine why we were being shuffled about in such intricate patterns of movement.

During the brief run of *The Three Sisters,* Gielgud also played for Komisarjevsky a Sunday night performance of another, now much less familiar, Russian drama, Andreyev's *Katarina,* in which he appeared as a jealous husband of fifty, whose wife dances almost naked in front of him during a party, to the despair of both him and his host.

The Three Sisters was not a success, but it had at least introduced Gielgud to the legendary Russian director and Stanislavsky disciple Komisarjevsky, who was soon to marry Peggy Ashcroft and was already widely known in rehearsal as "Come and Seduce Me" on account of his passion for young actresses.

In more recent theatrical times, perhaps only Lee Strasberg at the Actors Studio in New York has had the same revolutionary impact on players as that of Komisarjevsky in the London theater of the early 1920s. Komis was, at least in John's experience, one of the very first directors to exist, and certainly the first ever to free his cast from the simple instruction to learn their lines and not crash into the furniture. In that sense, Komis was also the first psychologist of the British theater and John, who had always been fascinated by Russian theater, was among the first to pick up on what had until then been a very foreign concept: "For the first time, working for Komisarjevsky, I realised that I need no longer worry whether I was moving gracefully or looking handsome. I had not to declaim or die or express violent emotions in fine language. Instead, I must try to create a character utterly different from myself, and then behave as I imagined the creature would behave, whose odd appearance I suddenly saw in my looking glass."

It was during the break between leaving Fagan early in 1925 and joining the Ridgeway season at Barnes that John took what many have seen as one of the most curious career decisions of his early life. Sensing perhaps that the future for an Oxford actor specializing in Chekhov was bound to be limited, John was acutely aware that he had as yet played no part in the West End, which was at this time all-important. Accordingly, he took up an offer to understudy Noël Coward in *The Vortex,* Coward's first major playwriting hit, with the understanding that when Noël took it to America a few months later, John would inherit the role of Nicky Lancaster, the drug-addicted son, in the West End transfer from Hampstead. It was, after all, the nearest he could then get to a modern-dress *Hamlet,* complete with a bedchamber scene and at least the suggestion of incest. Intriguingly, the mother-obsessed Nicky is also probably gay, although this, for 1924, had to remain unspoken in front of an audience that seems to have had no trouble with drug-taking, but were not yet up for homosexuality in their drawing-room dramas.

John had first met Noël a few months earlier at a party given near his home in South Kensington by their mutual friend, Betty Chester. Both Noël and John were also now taken up by the wealthy Earl of Lathom, a stagestruck homosexual aristocrat who was to spend most of his inheritance putting money into Noël Coward's plays and giving country-house parties of extraordinary extravagance, at which footmen would welcome the West End guests by pouring perfume into heated spoons to fill the entrance hall with a thick scent. Gielgud later described him as "a delightful friend who gave me the first expensive gift I ever received—a silver clock from Asprey." For him, as for Coward, this was an introduction to a world of unimaginable opulence, which came to an end in the 1930s, by which time Lathom had run through his considerable fortune—not the least of his extravagances was building a Greek swimming pool and a bowling alley inside the house, where he also created his own personal perfumery. On one occasion he also sent a footman down to London on the night train to return in time for luncheon the next day with a special brand of chocolate almonds. In his short reign as the playboy of the West End world, Lathom was more than generous to both John and Noël.

John's initial impression of Noël, before their weekends with Lathom became a regular feature, had been of someone "dreadfully precocious and rather too keen to show off at the piano." But when, a few weeks later, John went with his parents to see *The Vortex* at the little Everyman Theatre in Hampstead, in October of 1924, he abruptly changed his mind: "In that tiny auditorium the atmosphere was extraordinarily tense, and the curtain of the second act, with Noël sitting in profile to the audience, his white face lifted, chin jutting forward, head thrown back, playing that infuriating little tune over and over, louder and louder, until the curtain fell, was one of the most effective things I had ever seen in the theatre . . . after the performance, clattering back in the half-empty tube on the long journey home to South Kensington, my parents and I all sat silent in that state of flushed exhaustion that only a really exciting evening in the theatre can produce."

A few months later, when *The Vortex* transferred to the West End, it was essential for Coward to have an understudy who could play the piano, and John was therefore asked to audition. He was still not quite twenty-one.

Understudying Coward proved, however, to be both an irritating and a thankless task. Noël, who (unlike John) was already leading an extremely active social life as not only a writer but also a party entertainer to the upper classes, was in the habit of arriving at the stage door only moments before his first entrance. This meant that, almost every night, John had to get into full costume and make-up, only to see Noël rush on stage with seconds to spare. Although John's recollection was that Coward was always charming to him and offered any help he could, it wasn't until almost six months into the London run, when Noël wanted to go to Manchester to see the opening night of his new revue, *On with the Dance,* that John was able to take over the role: "There are few occasions more nerve-racking than playing a leading part in the absence of a principal. Before I went on that evening, some kind person knocked at my door to tell me that several people had asked for their money back because they had seen the notice, posted at the box office, announcing that Noël was not appearing. But audiences are extraordinarily fair and well-disposed towards young understudies, especially if the play is an interesting one, and by the end of the evening the applause was just as warm as it had been on other nights."

Although they were four years apart in age, and Noël was already far better established in the West End than John (not only as an actor, but as a director, playwright, and songwriter), the two men had a great deal in common and were indeed to go on working together across the next half century, in such plays as *Nude with Violin,* and Mike Todd's all-star travelogue, *Around the World in Eighty Days.* But at this much earlier point, their relationship was not particularly close, despite the fact that they were working in the same theater, and both were coming to realize that their innate homosexuality was going to create considerable personal and professional problems, unless carefully guarded from all but their most reliable friends.

At twenty-five, Noël was already far more socially and sexually confident, and even world-weary, than John. For Gielgud, just turning twenty-one, sex was still largely an undiscovered country, but it did not take long for both the actor himself and his closest friends to realize that women were seldom, if ever, going to be a part of his offstage life. And if, in later life, either actor did allow himself to fall in love, it was usually an experience of short, sharp shock from which he fled to the arms of a much lower-maintenance male lover, so that most of his energies could still be reserved for what happened across the footlights.

Sitting in the understudy dressing room night after night, especially after the brief glory of giving two almost flawless performances while Noël was otherwise engaged in Manchester, proved a depressing time for John, especially in the weeks around his twenty-first birthday in April. It did, however, allow him a considerable pause for thought, as well as the chance to look closely at the state of the commercial theater on and around Shaftesbury Avenue.

At this time, far more evidently than later, there were essentially two British theaters: that of the commercial West End and the all-important touring circuit; and that of the small club theaters and Sunday societies and university venues like Fagan's, or summer festivals like Stratford's, where either classic Shakespeare or revolutionary Chekhov and Ibsen could be experimentally staged on minimal budgets. Essentially, John's heart was with the former, and his intellect with the latter. Though always unworldly with money, he rapidly came to realize that Noël's was the most desirable of lives. To be the "shock boy" of the West End, already making two if not three salaries as star, director, and writer, was also to be the latest wonder of theatrical London society, and John immediately came to envy Noël his facility both on and off the boards, his ability to play leading roles in restaurants and at parties as well as in his own plays.

John still came from the unfashionable theater; it was around this time that the greatest of West End stars, Sir Gerald du Maurier, had to explain to an eager fan that he would not be playing Richard III because "my audience would find my appearance in such a play embarrassing," and certainly the gentlemen actors of Gerald's time were not expected to inflict anything intellectual, in either translation or verse, on their loyal followers.

Reflecting on all this backstage at *The Vortex,* John came to realize that if he was to achieve the first and principal dream of his working life, to make classical and even foreign drama acceptable to mainstream, chauvinistic, and still very conservative audiences, then first of all he would have to make his own name, one that many people were still having considerable trouble either spelling or pronouncing correctly. At this time, the only hope for an "intellectual theater" was the rapidly proliferating Sunday night play societies, where new or difficult or even dangerous work would be given an often full-fledged performance, though for one night only, frequently by actors and actresses such as Edith Evans and Esme Percy, who were already tiring of their mindless Monday-to-Saturday West End runs and aching to do more serious and demanding work.

Thus it was that, even while he was understudying Noël, John gave his next performance for the Phoenix Society in May 1925, a few weeks after his coming of age. He appeared in Thomas Otway's *The Orphan* for one Sunday only, a performance caught by the critic Desmond MacCarthy who noted prophetically that "Mr Gielgud, with his charming voice and pleasing vivacity, is sure to make his mark quickly." John was now making a habit, whenever possible, of making himself available for one-night productions whether for play-reading societies or school productions, or anywhere else that he could get the experience of another role.

At Oxford, he had already briefly appeared in Shaw, Congreve, A. A. Milne, and Oliver Goldsmith, not to mention Synge, Ibsen, and Maugham during the 1924–1925 seasons, and his long stay backstage at *The Vortex* only served to make him hungrier for the classical roles that he already knew were his home territory, even if they were not likely to make him as instantly rich or famous as Coward.

4. Noël and the Nymph

(1925–1929)

Although by now I was beginning to get some quite promising reviews, I also received a good deal of personal criticism from my family and a few discriminating friends, who told me that my mannerisms were becoming extremely pronounced, my walk as bad as ever, and my diction slovenly and affected.

*B*y the time John finally replaced Coward in *The Vortex*, he had in less than five years on the stage already played thirty-four roles, admittedly many of them in college, semiprofessional, or Sunday-only productions. No other actor of his time had done so much so fast, but as John's more discriminating friends were beginning to warn him, facility and theatricality alone were by no means enough. He had begun to play the shadows, but not the substance, and yet he was already too old and too experienced to complete the three-year training that he had abandoned at RADA.

Even his regional repertory apprenticeship at Oxford had stopped abruptly before he was twenty-one, and there was now a strong feeling (among those few who really cared about his future) that he was running dangerously fast before he could really walk with any confidence onstage. But at least his next engagement took him back to Chekhov; it was in fact a transfer of *The Cherry Orchard* that he had first played in the previous year at Oxford.

The producer, Nigel Playfair, had been so impressed by the production that he now took it into his Lyric, Hammersmith, with Gielgud still playing Trofimov in a play that he admitted he found "absolutely bewildering," although he had managed to hide himself behind rimless spectacles and a make-up closely based on his brother Val.

But London audiences were still not yet ready for Chekhov, and when John came on at the first night to utter the line, "All these clever people are so stupid," a woman in the stalls shouted back, "How very true!" Unlike the Oxford producer J. B. Fagan, who was inclined to take refuge in the academic theater, Nigel Playfair was a showman, and he realized at once that he had a controversial production to sell when, on the first Sunday of the Hammersmith run, James Agate, for *The Sunday Times*, declared it "the best production in London," and Basil MacDonald Hastings for *The Observer* thought it "the worst." By then, though, Playfair had already decided to fall back on a revival of his ever-popular *Beggar's Opera* and, as a result, when business improved drastically for *The Three Sisters*, Playfair and Fagan had no alternative but to move it into the more cavernous Royalty Theatre. As John recalled:

"Before *The Cherry Orchard* I just felt I could exhibit myself, and I rather enjoyed the business of going to the theatre and walking about on stage. . . . I suppose I always used it as an escape. To go through a stage door, shut myself up in a dressing-room, and come out as somebody else gave me tremendous pleasure. I was always living in some sort of fantasy world, and I was still very englamoured by the older members of my own family. The great thing about Playfair and Fagan was that they were wonderful talent-spotters. I know I must have been very clumsy and conceited as a young actor, silly and vain, but those two men never made me feel hopeless or wretched as a beginner."

John's Trofimov ("Perfection itself," according to Agate) led him back to Fagan's Oxford company for two last appearances in the late summer of 1925, first as the Stranger in Ibsen's *Lady from the Sea*, and then as the title character in Pirandello's *The Man with the Flower in His Mouth*. But by the autumn of that year John was back in London, again performing Chekhov. Cast as Konstantin in *The Seagull* at the Little Theatre, he confirmed his reputation as what *The Times* called "an unequalled interpreter" of Russian drama.

Writing to Gabrielle Enthoven, the theatergoer and longtime Gielgud fan whose unrivaled collection of programs was to form the basis of the Theatre Museum collection, John said how glad he was that she had noticed the way that "I am getting rid of a few of the bad tricks. It's a difficult part, and the producer wasn't much use as a helper, so I have had to go tentatively about my own improvements and developments since the first night. I hope it's getting better by degrees, but it's so irritating to realise suddenly, after one has been playing for some time, some perfectly obvious thing that one has been missing all along."

It was now that John began to take an increasing interest in the idea of directing as well as acting; although it was Valerie Taylor whose performance as Nina made her a star overnight, it was not long before John was back with Komisarjevsky, planning yet another season of Chekhov at Barnes.

Gielgud continued to pick up other work whenever and wherever he could; during the run of *The Seagull* he also turned up for special matinees as the Good Angel in *Doctor Faustus,* Harrington in Gwen John's *Gloriana* pageant, and the hero of *L'Ecole des Cocottes* opposite Gladys Cooper. He even appeared as Ferdinand in Shakespeare's *The Tempest,* though none of these roles made any special impression on audiences or passing critics. What they did was to keep John in permanent rehearsal, unable or unwilling to form any lasting relationships in his private life, but ready and eager to join whatever production or company was up and running for a few days or weeks.

In one sense London was ready for a new classical star, but just how unprepared Gielgud was for that role had become all too clear in 1925 when John Barrymore first brought his swashbuckling *Hamlet* to England from its Broadway triumph, thereby exposing John G. as the clenched, over-introverted player Prince up against the sheer, starry magnetism of Barrymore's New York bravura turn. Some years later, John was to fight his *Hamlet* out on Broadway in sharp competition with Leslie Howard; but at this time Barrymore was the marker for any British Shakespearean, and John missed that mark by a mile. Everything that Barrymore did, and perhaps above all his easy, relaxed relationship with the audience, was something that Gielgud could only wonder at from a seat in the gallery.

But even John, by now, was able to feel part of the community of London theater players; on Sunday nights and Monday afternoons he would turn up in a range of non-Chekhovian roles, everything from Valentine in *Two Gentlemen of Verona* to Rosencrantz in an uneasy modern-dress *Hamlet,* though the most notable of these performances was as the young lover Armand in the first London staging of Dumas's *La Dame aux camélias.* This in turn led him to another long run, although here, once again, he was to be overshadowed by Noël Coward.

Early in 1926 there was no doubt around the West End that the big hit of the season was likely to be Basil Dean's staging of *The Constant Nymph,* Margaret Kennedy's play based on her own best-seller about the Bohemian Sanger family, leading lives of elegant artistic degradation in the Tyrol. The obvious casting for the role of the romantic, pipe-smoking Lewis Dodd, a musical genius who spends most of the play strumming the piano and uttering witty one-liners, was either Coward or the other great matinee idol of the time, Ivor Novello. Basil Dean eventually opted for Noël, on the grounds that he was currently hotter than Ivor after the London and Broadway success of *The Vortex.* At first, however, Noël seemed unenthusiastic about the role, and Dean, always a man to cover his options, quietly offered it to Gielgud, who was understandably less than thrilled to overhear Noël a few days later, at the then-as-now theatrically fashionable Ivy restaurant, announce that he would after all be opening as Lewis Dodd, despite the fact that the author had already come out in favor of John.

As is often the way, all three actors eventually had their turn as Lewis Dodd: Noël opened it, John succeeded him for the bulk of the first run, and two years later Novello made the silent movie. But Noël had been right to approach *The Constant Nymph* with misgivings; the role of Lewis required him to grow his hair long, smoke a pipe, and generally behave onstage as he never had in any of his own work. Dean was determined in rehearsal to get him away from familiar "Noël Coward mannerisms," and

Noël spent a fair amount of his time setting fire to his hair, since he had never before worn it long or indeed smoked a pipe. Asked why he had agreed to take on the role, since it was the first in five years not also written by Coward, Noël replied, "to see if I am any good in other people's work," and the short answer was that he wasn't, or at least not yet. At the end of a long and tough rehearsal period, during which Noël threatened to resign roughly twice a week (and Dean therefore kept Gielgud on a kind of semi-permanent standby), Mrs. Patrick Campbell rang him to beg for dress-rehearsal tickets on the grounds that she was a poor, lonely, unwanted old woman who couldn't afford to buy any; she duly arrived at the final run-through half an hour late, bearing a yapping dog, but in ample time to tell Noël afterward that although she thought Edna Best quite good in her role, he was deeply miscast, lacked the necessary glamour for the character, and should anyway be wearing a beard.

His first-night reviews were not a lot better, and barely three weeks into the run, an already overtired and stressed Noël Coward suffered the first of his three major nervous breakdowns, played one entire performance in floods of tears, and was promptly told by his doctor to retire immediately from the role.

John, who had been half-prepared for the takeover for several weeks now, duly stepped in at the following matinee, and played the part of Lewis Dodd in London and then on the road for the whole of the following year. He too, though, was initially very unhappy; Dean refused to rehearse him for his first three months at the New Theatre and—a situation which was very much more hurtful—insisted on leaving Noël's name on the posters and his face on the front-of-house publicity photographs, as if to imply that he was planning to return to the production at some future date.

Of course he wasn't, but in these uneasy working conditions John took a long time to find his feet:

My performance was far too closely modelled on Noël's, especially as I had been understudying him in *The Vortex* only a few months ear-lier, and although I felt at last that I was getting established in the West End and learning how to play a major contemporary role, I got no particular credit for it. The cast were very kind to me, and seemed to understand I had been badly treated by Dean, but of course the critics never came back, and when Basil Dean did finally come to see me, all he said was, "Not bad for an understudy, but I need something rather better than that." The next day he called a full rehearsal, at which he told me to use my mind on stage instead of just my emotions, which I did find rather good advice later on; but it still took me a long time to get over my nerves at following Noël in two plays, and I rather think that delayed me in finding a style of my own as an actor. When you start out as an actor, though, you do need a model and Noël was certainly mine; he knew how to hold the stage, and I was somehow aware even then that he was going to be a great star.

Once John had settled into the long run at the New Theatre, he too began to enjoy some of the perks of being a West End leading man; he was now twenty-two, and the weekly salary from *The Constant Nymph* allowed him for the first time to move out of the parental home in South Kensington and into a flat of his own near Seven Dials.

"There was," John recalled, "no proper kitchen, and the bathroom had a rather erratic geyser down a flight of stairs that was very draughty in winter. But otherwise the place was charming; the actor Frank Vosper had covered the sitting-room walls with brown hessian, and there was a Braque-like ceiling in one of the bedrooms, with a lot of large nudes sprawling about, which I thought very modern and original indeed."

And there were soon to be one or two more nudes sprawled on the bed below; freed rather later than most from any parental supervision, and flush for the first time with a regular weekly income, John quickly began to lead a discreetly homosexual life around Shaftesbury Avenue, which was now at his doorstep. It was also during the run of *The Constant Nymph* that he took into the flat his first real partner, a young Irishman named John Perry who was to remain a lifelong friend and colleague, even after their sexual relationship had ended.

These were the years when the whole concept of stage and screen celebrity first became identifiable. Although stardom was certainly not comparable to the present day, on either side of the Atlantic, small groups of fans could now be seen for the first time clustering around stage doors in the hope of an autograph from their favorite matinee idol. More so then than now, the London theater was, however, an extraordinarily closed world in which actors met only other actors—either in rehearsal or at one or two late-night drinking clubs where the social and sexual rules of polite London society in the 1920s could safely be abandoned. As many actors were homosexual then as now, but they managed to maintain a remarkable level of secrecy, largely because their fans still behaved like household servants—always respectful, knowing their place, and happy to keep their distance.

The truth about Gielgud's homosexuality is that although it conditioned his life, eventually led to a court conviction, and undoubtedly caused him considerable uneasiness in an era when a homosexual act was still a penal offense even among consenting adults, he (like Noël Coward) was always determined to find low-maintenance partners who would not get in the way of his theatrical obsessions and ambitions.

John Perry, an amiable and very good-looking if none too successful young actor, then working as a florist, fit this bill admirably. Although he was later to write, with the novelist Molly Keane, a couple of successful West End comedies, his true love was really hunting in Ireland. He discovered very early on that he had no real talent as an actor; but he was more than happy to share John's flat, his bed, and his life as an elegant companion with a constant interest in all things theatrical.

Perry died in the mid-1990s, leaving precious little behind him; but his writing partner Molly Keane (who signed her plays M. J. Farrell) made a remarkable return to the best-seller charts in very late life with a 1981 novel called *Good Behavior*. In it there is a remarkable likeness of John Perry, in the character of a young homosexual who fakes a relationship with a young girl rather than face his parents with the truth of a long Cambridge affair with another young man, one whose sudden death gives the novel its tragic quality. The background of Irish country life, prolonged house parties, and a kind of decaying aristocracy is precisely the one from which John Perry came, and where he first met Molly.

In London and later at a country house they shared for weekends, located in the hills above Henley-on-Thames, Perry and Gielgud now became inseparable. To some extent they were an odd couple, and they formed a male partnership not unlike that in later years of Noël Coward and Graham Payn. Where Gielgud was hardworking and obsessive about theater, Perry was boyish, very good-looking, and always ready for a game of tennis or poker. Their gay circle was soon to include such elegant Oxford undergraduates of the period as Terence Rattigan and Giles Playfair.

Behind closed doors, theirs was an unashamedly homosexual world, but we need to recall the very real danger that they all recognized in their increasingly public lives. This was still the time when E. M. Forster could not publish his gay stories, when the Lord Chamberlain was still refusing to license even cautiously gay plays and, worse still, when the rise of fascism all over Europe was leading to sustained bouts of gay-bashing. In Britain every year, more than three hundred people were being convicted and often imprisoned for "acts of gross indecency," even when committed in the privacy of their own homes among consenting adults.

So although the theater was far more tolerant than the rest of society, it was still necessary for its workers to form a kind of secret network, behaving rather like spies. Although Oscar Wilde had been dead for nearly thirty years, the gulf between gay and straight actors was as wide as ever, and this was to condition the lives of Gielgud and all his friends.

At the very end of his life, I asked John Perry to think back to his earliest impressions of John G. Even at a distance of half a century, Perry, still remarkably good-looking—tall, willowy, fair-haired, and with theatrical charm—maintained the discretion about his private life that was partly a matter of his upbringing and partly an ingrained self-defense in a country that had criminalized his sexual behavior for most of his adult life, but he did remember his fascination with what he termed John's "sheer theatricality": "There was something very sexy about his passion for the theatre, but it made him difficult to live with; John never really understood relaxation, and I think that although we enjoyed a few foreign holidays together, he was only really ever happy in rehearsal or performance. Like Coward, he regarded private life as something of an interruption to the rehearsing day, and he could never understand how I seemed happy doing nothing very much—except of course making sure that John had somewhere to come home to, and a place for the week-ends."

It was the run of *The Constant Nymph*, though John soon found it unrewarding theatrically, that allowed him to take his place at the heart of the West End acting community and put him on equal terms with its other young stars. His brother Val had also briefly taken up acting and was in Edgar Wallace's *The Ringer* at a neighboring theater. John soon became friendly with my grandmother, the actress Gladys Cooper, then managing the Playhouse, as well as with Leslie Faber and other players who always proved eager to involve him in their Sunday and charity shows.

There was also, during the run, the excitement of the General Strike in May 1926, chiefly recalled by John Perry for the sight of Gielgud, "immaculate in a large gray Trilby and pearl-gray flannel trousers so wide you could hardly see the patent leather shoes beneath," putting in an appearance at a rally near Hyde Park Corner. Always bleakly uninterested in politics, John was yet eager to be a part of the London life all around him, and it was during the run of *The Constant Nymph* that he truly began to find his feet as a gay actor and a social figure, able for the first time to find his way around the nightclubs and late-night restaurants of London in the mid-twenties, even though his grasp of politics was, to say the least, unworldly.

But it was as Lewis Dodd that Gielgud effectively came of age. His value to the production was still apparently minimal, however, because when Dean decided that the play should go out on the road after nearly a year in the West End, he began to offer the leading role around to several other players—all of them having declined the long tour—before grudgingly agreeing that John could continue in the part, with a derisory salary increase to just thirty-five pounds a week, for the next four months.

All in all, John was to spend fourteen months in *The Constant Nymph*, in London and on tour, and although it gave him the regular income with which to buy his first car, a snub-nosed Morris in which he and John Perry explored the countryside around each of the tour dates, there was no doubt that playing Lewis Dodd, sometimes for nine performances a week, was a considerable strain: "I learned the hard way how to carry this very long and exhausting part for more than a year . . . I felt that I was just beginning to know how to act, but I got no particular credit for it. The director Basil Dean did not even come to see me play it until twelve weeks after I had taken over from Noël, and although my social life around the West End improved hugely, I was always aware that I still lacked the proper repertory company training which would have made me so much more confident and less tricksy onstage."

The two Johns, John and Johnnie as they were always known, could now even afford a cook and they began to give a series of lunch parties, to one of which they invited John's brother Val, now playing the small part of a policeman in *The Ringer,* which was just across St. Martin's Court at Wyndham's, while John was still at the New Theatre. Val in turn brought the star of his show, Leslie Faber, with whom John had played a couple of Sunday-night "specials," and Faber now became his greatest fan.

No sooner had the tour of *The Constant Nymph* come to an end than Leslie suggested that John should take over, at the last minute, the role of the czarevitch in a play called *The Patriot,* which was about to open in New York on Broadway. With only forty-eight hours to pack, John set off to join the rest of the company who were already in the U.S. rehearsing. With a good salary, and a six-week guarantee, he set sail on New Year's Eve 1926 on a small German boat, which had only two other English-speaking passengers—just as well, as he had to learn the role while at sea.

He arrived barely in time for the dress rehearsal. At the theater, he found a superb costume (a blue cloak with an ermine cape, silver and red facings, white breeches and boots), but no great enthusiasm for his acting. Indeed, the producer, Gilbert Miller, and the legendary designer Norman Bel Geddes, spent much of their limited time shouting at John about his voice, movement, and pace onstage.

After all that haste and anxiety, the play (though later a big success for Emil Jannings on film, and onstage in London under the title *Such Men Are Dangerous*) did not exactly take New York by storm. It closed after only eleven performances to a loss of forty thousand dollars, which for 1927 was a considerable shock. But like Noël Coward a couple of years earlier, John did not allow an initial Broadway flop to color his fascination with the city itself: "We were there in icy weather but Fagan, my old Oxford producer, was playing at a theater next door and I went to lots of backstage parties and even to 'speakeasies,' descending steep flights of slippery area steps to little doors, where there would be passwords and faces peering through the gratings, before we could be admitted."

John also found now, as had Noël, an American patron in the columnist and critic Alexander Woollcott, who noted "a young newcomer from the English stage named John Gielgud gave a good account of himself," an opinion not, alas, shared by Brooks Atkinson, who wrote in *The New York Times* of "an appallingly earnest young Prince." Gielgud quickly decided that, despite one or two quite promising offers in New York, including one from Constance Collier who thought she might be able to put him into a revival of Maugham's *Our Betters,* he could not really afford to stay too long away from home, and he therefore chose to return on the next boat to London, once again to try his luck there.

By March 1928, John had come home to the flat in St. Martin's Lane, to John Perry, and to the life of a West End actor: "Over the next eighteen months, I was to appear in ten different plays in London. Not one was a notable success, and they were all in fact pretty terrible, but I took everything that was offered to me. I was the leading man, which was a new experience for me; I was getting good billing and usually a good salary, and I had decided that acting was really a matter of staying in work, doing whatever came along."

And of course, at twenty-four, he was already sure that he wouldn't have to honor the promise that he had made his father about going back to architecture if all else failed.

It was therefore with a real sense of pride and excitement that, a few months later, he opened his dressing-room door to find his uncle Fred Terry, "the Golden Terry" as he was always called, coming toward him exclaiming, "My dear boy, you are one of the family now!"

Back from Broadway, John's first engagement was a double bill of Spanish plays (*Fortunato* and *The Lady from Alfaqueque*), which had been translated by Harley Granville-Barker and was to be directed by James

Whale—later to make his name in Hollywood with such films as *Journey's End* and *Frankenstein*, before becoming, long after his death, the central figure in the movie *Gods and Monsters*.

But Whale, like John, a gay and radical theatrical actor and director, was in fact fired in rehearsal, and the Royal Court season came to a close just in time for John to be free for a series of special matinees of *Ghosts* to celebrate the centenary of Ibsen's birth. This was to be his first meeting with one of the legendary grandes dames of the British theater, Mrs. Patrick Campbell, and it was to stay in John's memory forever. Although both Marion and Ellen Terry had been her rivals, she took an instant liking to John, who was mesmerized by her stage technique. In the one scene where Pastor Manders threatens to take the lead, Mrs. Pat would focus attention on herself by first unpacking, and then hanging, a complete set of drawing-room curtains.

Her advice to John, playing Oswald, was simply "to keep still, gaze at me, empty your voice of meaning, and speak as if you are going to be sick." But the audiences were not good, and to add to their difficulties, there were pneumatic drills laying tarmac in the Charing Cross Road just outside the theater, with deafening results. "I see," whispered Mrs. Pat to John as she came on to play yet another bad matinee, "that the Marquis and Marchioness of Empty are in front again."

Reviews here were good for John ("His Oswald will be as memorable as the play itself," said *The Times*), but James Agate, although finding John "extremely fine," wrote memorably of Mrs. Campbell that she was "like the Lord Mayor's coach, only with nothing inside it."

John's next two engagements, while about as far from Ibsen as he could get, were no more successful: *Holding Out the Apple* was a comedy entirely financed by its author, and *The Skull* was an American thriller in which, some thirty years before *The Mousetrap*, John played a detective who was also the murderer.

Gielgud's last appearance in 1928 was again for an American author, this time Don Marquess. In *Out of the Sea*, he was cast as a young American poet who played Wagner at the piano, and the heroine and villain were reincarnations of Isolde and King Mark. Most critics found it pretentious beyond belief, and the public did not find it at all: "In the last act," recalled John, "the heroine threw herself off a cliff while I sat glooming in a raincoat on a neighbouring rock. We lasted less than a week."

As if to set the seal on a bad season, this was also the year when Ellen Terry died, and John was one of the hundreds who flocked to St. Paul's, Covent Garden:

> The floor of the church was strewn with sweet-smelling herbs, and in the middle of the aisle was a catafalque covered by a golden pall, with candles burning around it, but there was no coffin, and nobody was allowed to wear mourning. By the time I knew her, she was finding it very hard to sustain the success she had always enjoyed with Irving at the Lyceum, but her memory, as with all us Terrys, was treacherously uncertain, and her concentration easily disturbed, though she had continued, to the end of her life, to enchant the public whenever they were lucky enough to see her on or off the stage. She had, like all of her family, a healthy appetite, enormous courage, and longevity, poor eyesight and intermittently indifferent health. She drew her characters with instinctive genius in broad strokes and generously flowing lines, but she was too restless to be confined within the walls of modern drawing-room comedy, and her loyalty to Irving meant that she listened too late to Shaw's entreaties and stayed too long at the Lyceum, with its fading fortunes. In her old age, I heard her at lecture readings, speaking Shakespeare as if she had only just left him in the next room.

Still unable to get back into the kind of classical or repertory company that Gielgud now knew was his only real way forward, John opened 1929 safely enough, by reviving his Konstantin in *The Seagull,* in the production he had first played four years earlier at the Little Theatre. Valerie Taylor was again his Nina, but the repetition bored John and he was happy to move on to his next role, in the short-lived *Red Rust* where Ion Swinley usefully taught him how to break chairs over actors' heads without causing any real damage. The interest here was that it was the first post-revolutionary play to have reached London from Moscow, albeit not for very long.

There followed a takeover in a play about Florence Nightingale, *The Lady with the Lamp*, which, although not entirely distinguished, brought him together with two of his great idols, Edith Evans and Gwen Ffrangcon-Davies. As was now his habit during any long West End run, John spent most of his Sundays in one-night performances of everything from J. M. Barrie (*Shall We Join the Ladies*) to *The Return of the Soldier Ulysses*. Additionally, his ceaseless workload also meant that he would spend his occasional non-matinee days filming at local London studios. After his silent film debut in *Who Is the Man ?* (1924) he also played the title role in Komisarjevsky's Jules Verne silent, *Michael Strogoff* (1926), and the lead in an early Edgar Wallace thriller *The Clue of the New Pin* (1929), in all of which John found himself so embarrassingly inept that he could not ever bear even to watch the rushes, let alone the finished films.

He also returned to Komisarjevsky, to play Trotsky in *Red Sunday*. Again, he made himself up to look remarkably like his brother Val, and took some delight in having to play a club theater because the Lord Chamberlain considered it thoroughly impertinent to show Trotsky, Lenin, and Rasputin on the same stage as the czar, barely a decade after his assassination.

It was during this run, in June 1929, when John happened to be lunching in the restaurant of the Arts Theatre, that he received the unexpected offer of a return to the classical theater repertory on which he had always set his heart.

5. To the Vic

(1929–1930)

Was it for this that I had forsaken a good salary in the West End, a comfortable dressing room for myself, good billing, new suits, late rising, and suppers at the Savoy?

*I*f, at the end of the twentieth century, John Gielgud is to be remembered for any single achievement, it would surely have to be the way in which he redefined and recreated the resident classical repertory company. Because of his interest and involvement in every aspect, from casting to costumes, from production to publicity, both the National Theatre and the Royal Shakespeare Company came into postwar existence still heavily influenced by John's prewar work.

But this is not to suggest that John was immediately happy at the Old Vic of 1930. The man who had invited him to join, at that brief and unplanned Arts Theatre lunchtime encounter, was Harcourt Williams, then a forty-nine-year-old actor-director who had himself just been invited, by the redoubtable Lilian Baylis, to become the director of productions on Waterloo Road.

Baylis had inherited the Vic from her aunt Emma Cons in 1914, and she had turned it from a Victorian Temperance Music Hall into a classical theater so rapidly that by 1923 her first director, Robert Atkins, had already staged all thirty-seven plays in the Shakespeare canon, working on a minimal budget with very little scenery, but attracting such talents as those of Sybil Thorndike, her brother Russell, and Edith Evans. By 1929, however, Baylis had decided that the time had come for a change.

Williams initially had not been at all impressed by Gielgud's work, but seeing him in *Ghosts*, he drastically revised his opinion and offered John an open-ended contract to play at least three major Shakespearean roles in the 1929–1930 season. Williams wanted to revolutionize Shakespeare at the Vic, to have it played faster, with more realistic settings, and to bid a belated farewell to the red-plush Victorian fustian that had hallmarked the group under Atkins.

For John, whose only other offer had been to replace Leslie Howard in *Berkeley Square*, this was not a hard decision to make, although at first he began to wonder what on earth he had gotten himself into:

"There was a faint smell of size from the paint dock, and of steak and tomatoes from the office where Lilian Baylis's lunch was being cooked. I was ushered in through the glass door, and found her sitting behind her big roll-top desk, surrounded by vases of flowers, photographs, two dogs and numerous unwashed cups of tea. I had on my best suit, and tried to look rather arrogant, as I always do when money has to be discussed. 'How nice to see you, dear,' said Lilian, 'of course we would love to have you at the Vic. I knew your dear aunt, you know, but we can never afford stars.' By the end of the interview, I was begging her to let me join the company, and we both evaded any question of payment for as long as possible. In the end it came down to ten pounds a week for leading roles, and five for all others."

Although the top salary at the Vic was now £10 a week, most of the company members were still on £6. Moreover, each production only played an average of thirteen performances, because the Vic was still also being used for opera and ballet.

His first three parts were to be Romeo, Antonio in *The Merchant of Venice*, and Richard II, to which would be added both Oberon, and Cléante in Molière's *Le Malade Imaginaire* (*The Imaginary Invalid*), before Christmas. In the rehearsal room, John found two other refugees from the West End, Martita Hunt (whom he had insisted should also be invited to join the company) and Adele Dixon, as well as much more experienced Shakespeareans such as Donald Wolfit, Leslie French, and Russell Thorndike:

> From the first day of rehearsal in August, we were kept constantly busy; both Gordon Craig and Granville-Barker sent us messages of good luck, and among what you might call the more intellectual theatre community, there was the very real sense that we were a new company starting on something very exciting. Baylis was her usual motherly self, never knew her arse from her elbow when it came to Shakespeare, but our great strength and rallying point was Harcourt Williams, whom I knew Ellen Terry had recognised as one of the best actors and directors of his generation. His main ambition was to preserve the continuity of the plays by natural and speedy delivery of the verse and very light settings which would allow quick changes of scene. He always ruled by trust, and any sign of selfishness or disloyalty to the Vic or Shakespeare would throw him into a mood of amazed disbelief. He would take dress rehearsals with a stop-watch and if the text called for 'two hours traffic of our stage,' that was precisely what Williams tried to deliver.

But despite such good and radical intentions, Harcourt Williams's first residency at the Vic got off to a very poor start. Critics, accustomed as they were to the more declamatory style of the Robert Atkins school, were less than happy with the new regime, and as the total budget for any one production was still only twenty pounds, the feeling of the church hall was still not easily overcome. The actress, and later director, Margaret Webster, a lifelong friend of John's, recalled once being given an entire roll of cloth by the wardrobe mistress and told to wrap it around her, but not to cut it in any way, as it would be needed for the next production by the Vic's sister company at Sadler's Wells, which was opened in 1931.

John was to play Romeo on three subsequent occasions, and often called it his milestone; still this first attempt made him deeply unhappy. As Harcourt Williams himself was later to write, "This was the least interesting performance of John's two years at the Vic. He never touched the last scenes. He failed to bring off the distracted boy, jolted by disaster into full manhood. The ecstasy, too, of Romeo's last moments transcending death, totally escaped him."

The Times noted acidly that "England won another world speed record last Saturday night, when at the Old Vic, Shakespearean blank verse was spoken faster than ever before." Donald Wolfit, playing Tybalt, was also convinced that speed was the problem: "We were all blamed for taking the play at such a lick that the verse and poetry were entirely lost; as Tybalt I scraped past the post, but this was a deeply unpopular opening night, and traditional Vic audiences felt that we had somehow betrayed them with our new style."

The critic of *Punch* concurred: "Gielgud is not, I think, quite the ardent, love-sick stripling of our imagination. He is adequate in elocution, occasionally a little noisy, and spirited in movement; but there is no quality of rapture in his wooing while the rash Tybalt (Mr. Donald Wolfit) is more plausibly Italianate than the rest, spitting the venom of vendetta through passionately compressed lips."

John's second role in this 1929 season at the Vic was Antonio, the title figure in *The Merchant of Venice,* but this, as Harcourt Williams recalled, met with an equally hostile press: "How well I remember the cast hiding from me the newspapers containing the worst notices. They must have been terrible, because I was so overwhelmed by an inferiority complex that I virtually tendered my resignation to Lilian Baylis. . . . Gielgud played Antonio with real sympathy and distinction, he was far less solemn than most Antonios, and never dreary; one felt, for once, that this Merchant had the right to carry the title of the play. However, our only real fan seemed to be Harley Granville-Barker, who sent both John and me pages of very useful criticism. His main advice was to let the verse seem to be carrying the actors along, instead of them carrying it, and above all not to be so damned explanatory."

All through this first season, it was widely known among the company that the role John already coveted was that of Hamlet, and Baylis, far more politically astute than was the impression she gave, would periodically dangle it in front of him, before adding, "But of course, dear Gyles Isham is also very keen, and he has been in the company a little longer than you."

John's third role was Cléante in *Le Malade Imaginaire* (*The Imaginary Invalid*), a production that required him to sing with Adele Dixon, an experience made bearable only because by day John was now rehearsing his first *Richard II*. Although it is arguable that the role of John's career was Hamlet, and he himself was to call Romeo his "milestone," there are those who believe that it was in the role of Richard that he was able to establish his greatest claim to Shakespearean immortality. As with his subsequent Hamlet, he was to go on playing Richard for the best part of the next thirty years, not only in the original text but also in what would be his greatest West End triumph, *Richard of Bordeaux*.

All the same, this first attempt was less than triumphant, despite the fact that, as its director Harcourt Williams was to recall, "In my time I have seen some half a dozen Richards, some shining in other ways than John's brilliance in the part, but none have touched his poetic imagery and emotional power. His playing of the abdication scene will live in my mind as one of the greatest things I have ever seen in the theatre."

Critics remained deeply unimpressed, but one junior member of the company, Eric Phillips, had a vivid recollection of John "sniffing at an orange stuck with cloves, or striding petulantly about the stage with a riding whip . . . the turn of his head, the curve of his body, the movement of his hands, each told a story of their own, and were beautiful to watch . . . at the end of the deposition scene Gielgud tottered down the steps and moved slowly toward the exit, dragging his feet behind him and tilting his chin upwards in a last exhibition of majesty."

As for John himself, he was well aware that much was still wrong with this first, basic, under-rehearsed and poorly financed *Richard II*, even though it was here that for the very first time he felt he was finding his feet in Shakespeare:

I seemed to be immediately in sympathy with that strange mixture of weakness and beauty in the character. I had already seen both Leslie Faber and Ernest Milton play Richard, but although their pictorial qualities had impressed me greatly in the part of the King, I had taken in nothing of the intellectual or poetic beauties of the play. But as soon as I began to study the part myself, the subtlety of Shakespeare's characterisation began to fascinate and excite me. I felt sure I could do justice to some of the imagery and pathos of the character. Richard was such a shallow, spoiled young man, vain of his looks with lovely things to say. I found myself no end in the part, but even that seemed to help my acting of it. I could see from the company's attitude that at last they thought I was going to be good, and I felt a great sense of elation. We only ran three weeks and there were hardly any good reviews, but I began to feel that I had made a real personal success.

The main advantage of this 1929–1930 season was the sheer range of work available to John. Immediately after *Richard II* came a Jacobean *Midsummer Night's Dream* (Gielgud as Oberon, Adele Dixon as Titania, with Martita Hunt and Donald Wolfit among the young lovers), which was mainly notable for the night when a twelve-year-old Wendy Toye, playing one of the fairies and later to become one of England's greatest choreographers and pioneer female filmmakers, managed to set John's flowing Oberon cape alight with her lantern. Within six weeks of that came his first *Macbeth* and a totally uncut *Hamlet*.

The *Macbeth* was less than triumphant, but years later John recalled James Agate (then already the leading drama critic of *The Sunday Times,* and a renowned stage-door gossip) wandering into his dressing room after the murder of Duncan and saying, "You were very good in that scene but I know you won't be able to manage the rest of the play, so I just thought I'd come round and tell you now."

The general feeling among other critics was that John had made a brave stab at a part for which he was still vastly too young, but when, less than a month later, he played his first Hamlet—a role to which he would return more than half a dozen times in the next fifteen years—Agate was the first to cheer: "At twenty-six, Gielgud is the youngest Hamlet in living memory, and I have no hesitation whatsoever in saying that it is the high-water mark of English Shakespearean acting in our time. This actor is young, thoughtful, clever, and sensitive. His performance is subtle, brilliant, vigorous, imaginative, tender and full of the right kind of ironic humour."

This production included several performances of the complete text, known to the cast as the Eternity Version, and John was the first actor in a couple of centuries, since the prodigal child actor of the early nineteenth century, Master Betty, to play Hamlet so young. Indeed the production closed the 1929–1930 season so triumphantly that it transferred to the Queen's Theatre, despite the fact that there were already two other Hamlets in the West End—Henry Ainley, the Edwardian matinee idol, was playing it at the Haymarket, and Alexander Moissi was playing it in German at the Globe.

Donald Wolfit, already at loggerheads with Gielgud, whom he wrongly accused of having the director Harcourt Williams cut his role of Claudius down to the bone, did not improve their relationship by telling John how much better Moissi was than him. Because of John's age, the youthful tantrums and despair of the opening scenes were more poignant than in Gielgud's later and more famous revivals, and he was also the first actor to bring out a dark and ugly streak in the prince's nature.

But divided by three, the West End audience proved very thin for John's version, especially in the stalls. As one critic sourly noted, "Pit, Upper Circle and Gallery are crowded at every performance while the more expensive parts of the house decline to be filled. It is a horrible thing to have to say, but the rich have no taste in matters of the theatre, and those who have theatrical taste have no money. In other words the serious theatre in this country is entirely supported by people who can barely afford to support themselves."

Of all the letters that John was now getting about his Hamlet, those that meant most to him came from his illustrious family. As his uncle Fred

Terry wrote, "I have in the past forty years seen many Hamlets, but none, I think, which Shakespeare himself would have liked as much as yours." In a rare letter to his son, Frank Gielgud wrote, "You must be thrilled with at least some of your notices, but what gave me the greatest pleasure last night was to see you in such command of the role. I do think you are speaking too fast still, and sometimes we lose some of the words, especially at the beginning of 'The Readiness is All.' Your quiet moments are very moving, and your mother was in tears by the end. Much love, and keep up the good work, from your critical old father."

His mother added, "I have told you far too little of the delight I feel at your great success, and I can't tell you of the joy it gives me to have you give up your spare time and forsake your many new friends to come home to me, and let me share your interests, weigh the pros and cons of your future, show me your laurels and to be ever my dear and sympathetic and loving son as well as a brilliant actor. You can dominate the stage but you never step out of the canvas to distort the picture. You do not demand the centre of the stage, but can hold your audience spellbound by a whisper, and their eyes with a gesture—not with mere tricks but with the breadth and truth of your imagination. Hamlet is many men in one and the wholeness, dignity, beauty, breadth, and simplicity of your delivery fills my heart with admiration and wonder."

Among the many non-family letters John received was one from one of the finest actresses of her generation, Sybil Thorndike, who wrote, "Yours is the Hamlet of my dreams and I never hope to see it played better. I was swept off my feet into another world, and moved beyond words." A young actress named Diana Wynyard, with whom John was to score some of his postwar Shakespearean triumphs, now wrote to him for the first time: "I came to the matinee on Saturday, and want to thank you not only for the most completely satisfying and lovely acting I have ever seen, but also for the way you made me think about the play. Your performance seems to me to justify the decision we have made to go into the theatre, because you never drag acting down to the usual shoddy game of whose going to be next up the ladder."

Another young actor, Alan Webb, later to be a lover of Noël Coward's, wrote, "I came especially to London from the Liverpool Playhouse to see your Hamlet—it puts all others in the shade, and I am so glad that old theatrical bores now have something new to discuss. Most of them don't seem to have seen a *Hamlet* since Irving's."

The West End transfer of *Hamlet* having proved to be more of a stagger than a run, John still had several summer months to fill in before he could go back to the Vic as its now-unchallenged leading man.

6. THE IMPORTANCE OF BEING RICHARD
(1930–1932)

Between the two Old Vic seasons, I was asked to play John Worthing in The
Importance of Being Earnest *with my aunt, Mabel Terry-Lewis as Lady
Bracknell. The production was entirely in black and white, in the manner of
Beardsley drawings, and was a great success in a very hot summer, except for
one matinee when I glanced at the audience and saw about six old ladies in
different parts of the theatre all hanging out of their seats, fast asleep. I became
quite hysterical, and was threatened with the sack for giggling so disgracefully.*

*J*ohn's first performance as John Worthing, in what was to become
(with *Hamlet* and *Richard II*) one of his three signature roles, was, on this
first occasion, directed by Nigel Playfair; and after his recent disappointment with the transfer of *Hamlet*, Gielgud was now able to enjoy the luxury of a commercial hit at the Lyric, Hammersmith. He was also secure in
the knowledge that he had the Old Vic to go back to in the autumn, and
the fact that Baylis had granted his request for a small raise in salary suggested that, at long last, she had become aware of his value at the box
office.

There was even, as John recalled, a useful link between John Worthing
and Hamlet: "It was amusing to change the black weeds of the Prince of
Denmark for the top hat and black crepe band of John Worthing, in
mourning for his imaginary brother, and my recent association with the
tragedy gave further point to Wilde's joke. I was very proud to be appearing for the first time with my Aunt Mabel, who shared with Marie Tempest
and Irene Vanbrugh that rare distinction of style, deportment and carriage
which was to vanish with them."

The last time that Gielgud had worked with Nigel Playfair, he had been way down the cast list; now he was appearing, albeit still in Hammersmith, as a leading man, and it was Playfair who for the very first time made John aware, a decade after he had come into the business, that he really might have the capacity to be a classical star.

The summer revival of *The Importance of Being Earnest* had to be cut short because of John's commitment to a second season at the Vic; but it is arguable that the Wilde connection first established Gielgud within the gay community as one of their own. Certainly by then, thirty years after Wilde's death, Oscar's reputation had escaped the stigma of his imprisonment, but it was to be another quarter of a century before John himself was to discover that outside the theater, England was still remarkably and even dangerously intolerant of homosexuality. If there is a subliminal, gay reading of *The Importance of Being Earnest*, with the idea that John Worthing's secret other life (what he calls "Bunburying") may be a metaphor for Wilde's own bisexuality, then John would have been the first to make this connection clear over the footlights.

As the critic Ronald Hayman has noted, "John Gielgud, with his slim, straight back, his meticulous elegance and his air of nobility tilted into a lordly languor, had all the qualities for Wilde's mannered comedy . . . as in *Hamlet*, he conveyed the impression of being quite capable of inventing for himself the perfect lines which the author had given him." But as so often in John's career, other critics were sharply divided; for *The Sunday Times*, James Agate thought that John was "a tragic actor who should never attempt comedy," yet the playwright and critic Charles Morgan wrote in *The Times*, of Gielgud "standing out as the model for the true interpretation of Wilde."

John was now so well established as the leading man of the Old Vic, to which he returned in September of this year, that both the director Harcourt Williams and the manager Lilian Baylis consulted him over the constitution of the company. Undoubtedly the most interesting of the newcomers he chose was Ralph Richardson, with whom John was now to work for the first time at the start of a stage partnership that would last well into the 1970s.

Their first meeting, in the rehearsal room of the Vic, was not, however, exactly auspicious, as Richardson recalled: "I sprang at the opportunity of going to the Vic not only because Johnny Gielgud was a kind of miracle, but also because I stood a really good chance of staying on there when he left at the end of the season. But when we first met, I found his clothes extravagant and his conversation flippant. He was the New Young Man of his time, and I didn't like him at all in rehearsal, although on stage you had to admire him because he was so brilliant, he shone, he was so handsome and his voice was so splendid."

The two actors who were, along with Olivier and Redgrave, to dominate the British theater for most of the rest of the century, had in fact fleetingly met a couple of years earlier, when they were both in a Sunday night performance of *Prejudice,* but it wasn't until they got to the Vic that they really made any impression on each other, as John was later to recall: "When we first acted together at the Old Vic in 1930, I little thought that we might ever become friends. At first we were inclined to circle round each other like suspicious dogs. In our opening production, I played Hotspur to his Prince Hal in *Henry IV Part I,* and was relieved though somewhat surprised to discover that he was as reluctant as I was to engage in the swordplay demanded in the later, under-rehearsed scenes at Shrewsbury. On the first night I was amazed to hear him whispering, loudly enough surely for the audience to hear, 'Now you hit me, cocky; now I hit you!'"

What was going on here was the attraction of opposites; Richardson was a year older than Gielgud, but he would have to wait until 1933 for his first taste of stardom. Gielgud, by contrast, had already played eight leading roles at the Vic and begun to make his name elsewhere, if not yet in the West End then certainly at Hammersmith. Richardson had also unwisely announced to his friends that "Gielgud's acting often keeps me out of the theatre," and yet, precisely because they were so different, they achieved a remarkable kind of odd-couple success. Ralph was deeply embarrassed by any discussion of John's private life, and at first they met only in rehearsal. "I was always," said Ralph, "rather amazed at him, he was a kind of brilliant butterfly, while I was always a gloomy sort of boy."

For his part, Gielgud noted, "Unlike me, Ralph was intensely interested in machinery and all the intimate details of science and engineering, but he despised the petty accessories of theatrical life, all the gossip and the theatre columns in the newspapers which always appealed so strongly to me."

Their first Vic production, directed as usual by Harcourt Williams, got off to a bad start when Ralph brought a bottle of champagne, which he then managed to explode all over the dressing room, and it wasn't until they began working together on *The Tempest*, a few days later, that John found the courage to suggest to Ralph that they might like to take some time out for private rehearsals. Ralph immediately agreed, and thus began an initially wary friendship of fifty years.

In *The Tempest*, Ralph was Caliban to John's first Prospero; later in the season, Ralph was Sir Toby Belch to Gielgud's Malvolio and, in Shaw's *Arms and the Man*, Bluntschli to John's Sergius. John's first Prospero, half a century before he was finally to film it for Peter Greenaway, was a slender and shaky affair, and Gielgud's backstage mood was not helped by his first and very difficult meeting with his celebrated cousin, Edward Gordon Craig.

With Ellen Terry, his mother, Craig was of course the most famous member of John's family, but whereas Ellen was always encouraging and loving toward John, Craig proved at first distinctly prickly. He sent a note backstage to John at the Vic, reading simply, "Perhaps, as we are related, we ought to get to know each other, and you seem to be quite popular here in London." Craig then announced that he had stayed only for the opening scene of *The Tempest*, despite the fact that Harcourt Williams, the director, was one of his oldest friends. Taking John out to dinner, Craig delivered a vitriolic dismissal of Williams, Lilian Baylis, and everything that the Old Vic stood for. Although a somewhat chastened and disappointed John was to remain considerably in awe of Gordon Craig's radical theatrical philosophy, the two cousins did not meet again until 1953, by which time Craig had become considerably more avuncular.

A far easier relationship was that which, through their working together, was now developing between John and Ralph. Richardson always knew, said John once, that of every twelve suggestions I made to him, two would be of some use, and the rest could be thrown in the dustbin. We were neither of us wildly intellectual, but whereas I really adored the billing, the advertisements, the fan letters and the somewhat unbalanced adulation of certain people whose admiration was extravagant and often insincere, Ralph had enormous dignity and reserve where the public was concerned. I would think to myself, "A jolly good house tonight, went marvellously and I made a lot of stunning effects, must remember to put them in again tomorrow night." That was not Ralph's way; he was a realistic actor, labouring to find the core of a character, and until he had time to study a role, he didn't want to be looked at, or even criticised. By contrast, I would conceitedly jump in and take a wild dash at a part from the first rehearsal. I find it difficult to work by myself at home; I develop a part in rehearsal with the company, make mad suggestions, then throw them out and try some more. I am featherheaded, where Ralph was always far more thorough.

During these two seasons at the Vic, John was often miscast, not least as Antony in *Antony and Cleopatra*. But the experience, now at £20 a week, of playing many different roles in front of an enthusiastic but broadly uneducated audience, gave him useful experience in sheer Shakespearean survival against the odds.

When it came to his *Macbeth*, toward the end of this second season, "I had rather more success than when I came to study the part more thoroughly, twelve years later . . . I simply went for the broad lines of the character, without worrying about all the technical, intellectual and psychological difficulties. With only three weeks to rehearse, there was no time to do more than play it from scene to scene, but I do think one should dare to fly high when one is young. One may sometimes surprise oneself, and it is wonderful to give the imagination full play, hardly realising what an exciting danger is involved."

Harold Nicolson wrote in his diary for October 4, 1930: "Talk to Gielgud, who is a fine young man. He does not want to specialise in juvenile parts, since they imply rigidity. He takes a high view of his calling. I think he may well be the finest actor we have had since Irving. His voice and figure are excellent."

It was also at the Vic in this season that Gielgud discovered another of the roles that were to be central to his later career. Benedick in *Much Ado About Nothing* was far more suited to his romantic, mercurial temperament than the soldier Antony, in which role John could only recall "wearing a false beard and shouting and booming a lot." When it came to Benedick, and later both *The Winter's Tale* and *Measure for Measure*, John found far more complex but closely fitting characters, and it was here that for the first time, "I began to trust the sweep of Shakespeare's verse, concentrating at last on the commas, full stops and semicolons. I found that if I kept to them, and breathed with them, like an inexperienced swimmer, the verse seemed to hold me up, and even, at last, to disclose its meaning."

But no sooner had he finally conquered Shakespeare and begun to take an active part in both the direction and the design of the Vic's low-budget productions, than he began to yearn once again for some commercial success. Reluctantly, he therefore told Baylis and Harcourt Williams that he would be leaving the Vic forever at the end of the current season. Williams offered him a choice of farewell roles; he could either revive his now celebrated *Hamlet* or, at the age of just twenty-seven, he could tackle his first *King Lear.*

Unable to resist the challenge, John opted for *Lear,* and as usual he was his own best critic: "I was wholly inadequate in the storm scenes, having neither the voice nor the physique for them. Lear has to *be* the storm, but I could do no more than shout against the thunder sheet. The only scene I thought I did at all well was the one with the Fool, when Lear leaves Goneril to go to Regan: 'O let me not be mad, not mad, sweet heaven ... '"

Critics generally agreed with John's verdict on himself. Peter Fleming, writing for *The Spectator,* also picked up on the scene with the Fool: "I have never seen a better bit of acting than Mr Gielgud's 'O fool, I shall go mad.' He says the words in a voice become suddenly flat and toneless, quickened only with a chilling objective interest in their no longer contestable truth . . . but in general, the performance has the deliberate threat of distant gunfire, rather than the unpredictable menace of a volcano."

John in fact opened his first *Lear* not only at the Old Vic but also Sadler's Wells, which Lilian Baylis had also now bravely started to run as a second stage. Richardson was his Duke of Kent, and Leslie French was the Fool. Sometimes breaking with their usual tradition, the audience would applaud John's first entrance, and sometimes they would not: "If I failed to get the round of applause as I mounted my throne, the expression of amused triumph on Ralph's face would be almost too much for me, and I used to have to turn away for a moment before I began 'Attend the Lords of France and Burgundy.'"

However patchy this first *Lear*, the idea of an actor of twenty-seven playing a king of eighty attracted considerable attention, even abroad. As the *New York Post* wrote at the time, "There is a young actor in London, named John Gielgud, who has taken the town by storm the way John Barrymore first took New York, when he was known as Jack and was knocking the flappers out of their seats. Gielgud's pictures now sell like mad among the earnest young students who flock to his performances."

A rather more thoughtful appraisal of precisely where Gielgud now stood in the British theatrical hierarchy came from the director Harcourt Williams in his farewell speech to John at the Vic, handing over to him a glove that Henry Irving had once worn as Benedick: "I know, from the foundations that stand beneath your power as an actor, that you will grow and expand until you shatter that theatre falsely termed 'commercial' (all good theatres must function commercially) and create one of your own, either of brain or brick, that we shall all be proud of."

Peggy Ashcroft and the publisher Rupert Hart-Davis, then at the start of the affair which was to lead to their marriage, were in the Old Vic audience one night to see John perform. As Rupert later wrote to John, "Peggy and I were so swept away by your magnificent Lear that we couldn't come backstage. Beforehand I could not believe that you would manage it, but my God I was wrong! It is far and away the best thing I have seen you do, vastly better than your Prospero or Malvolio. Your voice, your variety, and your physique are splendid. And although Regan looks like a cook in a sack-race, I thought Richardson was excellent. I'm afraid I thought Leslie French as the Fool wrong in every way—he should not be a maddeningly bright boy, but an ageless and weary man, desperately making jokes against Time. I doubt I shall ever see a better Lear, except of course when you play the part again in twenty years time."

Leaving Ralph to lead the Vic through the next season, John now returned to the West End in Edward Knoblock's adaptation of J. B. Priestley's bestselling novel *The Good Companions,* which he was subsequently also to film, a year later, with Jessie Matthews. Knoblock, one of the most successful dramatists of his time, specialized in adaptations and years later was on the receiving end of one of John's most celebrated conversational gaffes. The two men were lunching alone, when John described a friend as "nearly as boring as Eddie Knoblock, no, no, not you of course, I mean the other Eddie Knoblock."

The character that John played for nearly a year in the West End, Inigo Jollifant, is the young preparatory schoolmaster who, always theater-struck, turns professional pianist and composer to join Priestley's band of wandering players. Several critics, while noting John's uneasiness at the piano, also took the view that after his Old Vic triumphs he should have been doing something rather more cerebral and serious than this unashamed crowd-pleaser. For John himself, the problem was rather different: "This kind of play was quite a new departure for me, and demanded a considerable readjustment of my style of acting. The scenes were very short and sketchy, and there was hardly any development of character . . . Jollifant was a very ordinary juvenile, who had to carry off a few very slight love scenes and a couple of effective comedy situations with the aid of a pipe, undergraduate clothes, and his catch-word 'Absolutely' . . . I had to attract the audience's interest with his first word and sweep my little scenes along to a climax in a few short minutes . . . I was playing with actors of several different schools, and I had to learn tricks of upstaging if I was to survive in a commercial environment."

The success of *The Good Companions* was to change John's private life forever. He could now afford late suppers at the Savoy, and a large number of scripts, some from very established authors, were finding their way to his dressing room. Two of these, Gordon Daviot's *Richard of Bordeaux* and Ronald Mackenzie's *Musical Chairs,* were soon to give him two more of his early West End successes.

John was also, albeit very hesitantly, starting on a film career which, unlike Olivier, Richardson, and Redgrave, all of whom had established lucrative movie careers with Alexander Korda, Alfred Hitchcock, or (in Olivier's case) Hollywood well before the war, he was not really to consolidate until much later. As noted earlier, his first film appearance was in 1924, in, *Who Is the Man?* adapted from one of Sarah Bernhardt's last stage hits:

"I was a sculptor in a beautiful smock, flinging clay at a half-finished nude lady. I had not then yet sat to Epstein, and therefore had no idea of how sculptors really worked, but I made great play with a sweeping thumb and a wire tool, and hoped for the best . . . there was a sofa draped with shawls, on which I flung myself at intervals, smoking a pipe of opium in close-up. I exhausted myself acting in a highly melodramatic manner, and we had to do some scenes over one week-end on location at Le Touquet. I suffered acute embarrassment marching around in yellow make-up and attempting to drive a car, which is not one of my accomplishments. When I finally saw the film there was just a strip of sand, which could have been photographed equally well at Margate. However, we all had a very jolly week-end."

His second, another silent, was an Edgar Wallace thriller *The Clue of the New Pin,* filmed in 1929. "In this, I played the villain, fantastically disguised in a long black cloak, black wig, spectacles and false teeth, and always photographed from the back so that I could by no possible chance be recognised (even by the most adept villain spotter in the audience) as the bright young juvenile whom I had to impersonate during the rest of the film."

His first talking picture, *Insult,* made during the run of *The Good Companions,* was adapted from a long-running stage hit of which John's only recollection was that

the film was set in the Far East, and shot through clouds of smoke. There was a donkey, a monkey, and several horses, one of which I rode gingerly in close-up down a narrow studio-village street, while my double stood close at hand to mount and dismount my fiery steed in long-shot. I was fascinated and horrified by my acting in these three early pictures. Fascinated because seeing one's own back and profile is an interesting experience usually limited to one's visits to the tailor, and horrified at the vulturine grimaces on my face, and the violent and affected mannerisms of my walk and gestures. It was to be a very long time before I came to terms with the camera, and I think my embarrassment, at how bad I was, made me sound very snobbish and superior when I talked about not wanting to leave the stage for the screen. The truth is that unlike Larry and Ralph and Michael, it took me years to learn the difference between stage and screen acting.

As John began to enjoy his first real taste of West End stardom, there were also some subtle changes to his private life. He and John Perry were still effectively locked into what would now be called a gay marriage, and still sharing the flat on St. Martin's Lane, but for the first time their partnership now began to open up; John Perry had amiably abandoned his initial plans to be an actor and was now spending a fair amount of his time in his native Ireland, where he was a keen rider and hunter.

Back in London, John G. was by no means averse to the occasional sexual attentions of the many good-looking, and sometimes ambitious, young men who now began to cluster around his stage door. Moreover, just arrived in London from his native Cardiff, was yet another gorgeous young man, Hugh "Binkie" Beaumont, who, taken under the wing of the much older impresario Harry (H. M.) Tennent, would soon become not only the most successful West End theater manager of the 1930s and forties, but in time also the man who would break up the sexual (and for a short time even social) partnership of the two Johns.

During the run of *The Good Companions,* John became more and more determined not to lose the cultural and critical edge that he had achieved in his seasons at the Old Vic. He was therefore more than delighted, in the opening weeks of 1932, to receive an invitation from the then president of the OUDS (Oxford University Dramatic Society), George Devine, to direct *Romeo and Juliet* at New College, Oxford.

Devine's idea was, as his biographer Irving Wardle has noted, extremely astute. Although Gielgud now had ten years of classical work behind him and was emerging as the dominant London star, one who moreover had already appeared in three productions of *Romeo*, at the age of twenty-eight he had never actually directed anything, and in that sense, by asking John to direct a production of Shakespeare's play about those star-crossed lovers, Devine was offering him something very attractive. Not that John was initially that impressed; Devine struck him as "rather ungainly and gross. Very greasy, spotty and unattractive. But he had great humour and charm, and was immediately very intelligent."

In later years, Devine was to direct John in the controversial Noguchi *King Lear* and, as director of the Royal Court, to open up the English Stage Company, which was to bring John into contact for the first time with post-Osborne playwriting and thereby rescue his postwar stage career when it had fallen to its lowest level.

The OUDS had been as all-male as the university itself until 1927; from then on female undergraduates were theoretically allowed to take part in productions, but it was still the tradition to invite young professional actresses down from London, as much for their talent as for the edification and entertainment of the young gentlemen. Peggy Ashcroft had indeed first played with the OUDS a year earlier in Flecker's *Hassan*. John had not seen this performance, but he had been hugely impressed by her Desdemona to Paul Robeson's Othello at the Savoy Theatre in 1930, so he was greatly pleased to have her playing Juliet. Playing the nurse was Edith Evans, with whom John had already worked in the short-lived *The Lady with the Lamp*.

The Romeo was to be Christopher Hassall (who later found his true vocation as the lyricist for most of Ivor Novello's enormously successful musicals), and also in that amazing student cast were George Devine himself, Hugh Hunt (for many years director of the Bristol Old Vic theater school), and William Devlin, later a distinguished classical and modern actor who was to work with Gielgud frequently. Indeed, only one student was really unhappy in this production, and he was an eighteen-year-old Terence Rattigan, who in the last act was so inept at announcing the death of Juliet, almost his only line, that the audience would regularly fall about with laughter on his line, "Faith, we may put up our pipes and be gone." Many years later, Rattigan's classic backstage comedy, *Harlequinade*, was to feature a small-part player with precisely the same problem.

Inevitably John had to focus most of his rehearsal time on the undergraduates, leaving Edith and Peggy to their own devices. He had arrived in Oxford, as the OUDS historian Humphrey Carpenter relates, to find the student drama group torn apart by internecine warfare between the old guard and Devine's new men, all of whom were determined to drag a somewhat Edwardian society into the twentieth century. Gielgud's first production of *Romeo and Juliet* was to be the barest outline for his subsequent triumph with Olivier in the West End three years later, but for now it would be naïve to pretend that John was commuting from *The Good Companions* to Oxford merely for the sake of his art. The OUDS at that time was a distinctly gay society with some very good-looking young men, among them Peter Glenville, Robert Flemyng, and Rattigan himself, all of whom were keen to cluster around the visiting star. John G. even started a brief affair with James Lees-Milne, subsequently a distinguished architectural historian and diarist, and although this did not continue beyond Gielgud's weeks in Oxford, the two men were to remain distant friends for the rest of their lives. "For six weeks," recalled Lees-Milne, "I was infatuated with him. Then it passed like a cloud; it was a very short-lived affair."

The weekend cottage that the two Johns now shared at Harpsden, just outside Henley on Thames, was also a very gay retreat, though as always there was the vague threat of danger and exposure, one which was to come into sharp focus a year or two later when the young Beverly Nichols, incensed by a hostile review by James Agate for one of his early plays, seriously threatened to make Agate's homosexuality public. Nothing came of this, however, and for a few more years Gielgud and Perry were to sleep with each other in comparative safety.

But the most important connection that John made during his Oxford *Romeo and Juliet* was with the three set and costume designers, Elizabeth

Montgomery and the sisters Margaret and Sophia Harris, who were collectively known as Motley. The three of them had as yet no stage experience, beyond coming up from family homes in Kent to the Old Vic where they would produce character drawings which they would sell to the actors for three guineas. As John was later to recall: "When I was at the Vic they made some drawings of me as Richard II, Macbeth and Lear, which they shyly brought to my notice. In those days they were three silent and retiring young women, and it was some time before I could get them to speak about themselves in their gentle, hesitating voices . . . they later told me that my sudden unexpected arrivals in their tiny Kensington home would throw them all into paroxysms of shyness, as I hurled remarks at them, speaking so fast that they barely understood a word."

Devine himself was not initially keen to bring in outside designers, but he was taken by John to visit "the girls" at Kensington and immediately offered them the job. As Elizabeth recalled, "We rushed out and hired a couple of people to do the sewing for us. But we did almost everything else ourselves. That was really how we started—before that, we had only been making fancy dresses for the shops at Christmas."

This meeting was in fact to be the start of two great partnerships; from now on, John was seldom to work without the Motleys, and Devine was later to marry their Sophie Harris. Hardly surprisingly, Peggy and Edith and the Motleys took Oxford by storm at a time when the undergraduates seldom enjoyed the benefit of any female company at all, let alone that of five radical, intellectual Shakespeareans. John, commuting every night back to *The Good Companions,* also immediately found his feet as a director, bringing to the OUDS a touch of professionalism that society was not to see again until long after the war. John was given one night off to run the first dress rehearsal: "The lights, the scenery and the orchestra were all being used together for the first time. I sat alone in the dress circle, with my notebook and a torch. The house lights went down, the music began to play, and there was a faint glow from the footlights. A wonderful play was about to be performed, and it was for me alone. I felt like Ludwig of Bavaria."

Nevertheless, by the end of the first night, his nerves had gotten the better of him, and at the curtain call John G. memorably referred to Edith and Peggy as "Two leading ladies, the like of whom I hope I shall never meet again." Several years later, introducing the female members of one of his wartime touring companies, he announced to a somewhat amazed military audience: "And now, the ladies I have brought to give you pleasure."

This *Romeo*, of course, was still only a pro-am student production, playing for a few nights in New College, Oxford; it did not attract national attention, although W. A. Darlington, covering for *The Daily Telegraph*, noted, "Although he is not present, it happens again and again in this production that one seems to hear Mr. Gielgud's voice on the stage—which means not that the undergraduates are slavish imitators, but simply that they are indeed learning to speak the verse, and are sensitive enough to recognise a master when they hear him. . . . Above all, Miss Ashcroft's Juliet is not rehearsing phrases, but passionately in love."

Peggy herself later added, "I see Romeo and Juliet as, in themselves, the most glorious, life-giving people . . . I discovered playing Juliet that the essential thing is youth, rather than being tragic. I think she's a victim of circumstance. The tragedy is simply something that happens to her."

As the critic and biographer Michael Billington was to write, "This OUDS *Romeo* was in every sense a momentous production: one that forged vital links between a group of people whose professional lives were to be inter-connected over the next three decades. If there was a sense of family in the upper echelons of British theater, it had its origins in this production."

But it was John's original host at the OUDS, George Devine, who, in a personal letter to him, best captured what had been achieved here: "I don't know how much other people realise it, but to my mind this whole success belongs to you. Some of the glory also goes to me, because I was the President who had the luck to invite you. But the ideas, the actresses, the costumes, the sets, the spirit and the acting are all your contribution. For your lessons in verse-speaking alone we should be more than grateful, and suffice it to say, you have made my OUDS Presidency everything I wanted it to be. I only hope you feel compensated for all the time and hard work which you have devoted to us. I have just managed to extract some money from the box office, and I have bought you a cigarette lighter, as I don't think I ever saw you with one. It's a silly thing to buy, but I can't think of a book about the theatre that you would not already have."

With *Romeo* safely up and running in Oxford (the young Lord David Cecil thought it "easily the best production of the play I have ever seen—straightforward in interpretation, but fresh with youthful, lyrical rapture"), John returned to *The Good Companions* and to his determination to find something more radical to play next.

A backstage letter from the playwright Ronald Mackenzie reminded John G. that they had been together at the same prep school, Hillside. Since then, Mackenzie had not been so fortunate, and no less than six West End managements had turned down a play of his called *The Discontents*, a Chekhovian tragicomedy set amid the oil fields of Galicia in Poland. John, however, always quick to respond to his own Polish ancestry, loved the script on first reading, and especially the central role of a cynical and consumptive pianist whose German fiancée had been killed during the World War I bombing of Dusseldorf, an air raid in which the pianist had himself participated.

John felt that this was the best contemporary role he had ever been offered, above all because it neatly combined the two sides of his nature—the pianist was really a modern Hamlet, and yet the background was indisputably Russian. In its complexity and its challenge, *The Discontents* was a world away from the Shaftesbury Avenue safety of *The Good Companions*.

Immediately befriending Mackenzie, John made two suggestions. Firstly, that an off-putting title be changed to *Musical Chairs*, and secondly that the great Russian director Komisarjevsky be invited to direct. Ever since they had first met on *The Three Sisters* in 1925 at Barnes, Gielgud had been desperately eager to work again with the "Komis" who he felt alone could move the British classical theater forward into the new century. The son of an operatic tenor and a Russian princess, Komisarjevsky had succeeded Meyerhold as artistic director of the major theater in what was then still St. Petersburg, after which he had gone on to run both the Imperial and the State Theaters in Moscow. In 1920, at the age of thirty-seven, he had fled the new communist regime to work first in Paris, then in New York before coming to London on a contract to produce operas for Sir Thomas Beecham.

Like Gielgud, a man of many theatrical talents, he also designed his own sets and costumes, arranged the music, and lit all his own productions with a revolutionary eye on what lighting could do for a play. He was also an architect, responsible for the Phoenix Theatre, which opened on Charing Cross Road in 1930, and several suburban cinemas. As Ronald Hayman has noted, "Komisarjevsky was a near-genius, phenomenally versatile, and violently moody, dynamic and charming, but liable to bouts of depression when he would sulk in silence for hours on end. He was a born rebel, and in each country where he worked he soon became resentful of the prevailing conditions. A man of great sensitivity, he was also capable of being extremely insensitive and even ruthless."

Nevertheless, he was a perfect match for both the play and John G., who he even allowed to take several rehearsals. John, however, found the emotional strain of this production nearly intolerable, and his playing of a consumptive began to look all too realistic. As a friend of Ralph Richardson's said, "I went to see Gielgud the other night—is he really as thin as all that?" Not everyone was thrilled with the play, or indeed the production. Noël Coward left at the end of the first act, later writing to John, "I thought you were overacting badly, and using voice tones and elaborate emotional effects—as I seriously think you are a grand actor, it upset me very much. I also thought that Frank Vosper [playing John's father] had a wig with such a bad join that it looked like a yachting cap."

James Agate, for *The Sunday Times*, wrote one of his rare raves: "I am now ready to burn my boats. *Musical Chairs* is, in my view, the best first play written by any English playwright during the last forty years—better than *Widowers' Houses*, *Journey's End* or *Hindle Wakes*. My reasons for regarding this play as a small masterpiece are as follows: 1) It tells a credible and tragic story. 2) That story is enlivened by a magnificent sense of humour. 3) It is as taut and spare as a barrel, which means it is perfectly made and put together with maximum economy. 4) The characters are real, vivid, and do not overlap each other. 5) As parts they are magnificently laid out for actors. 6) This work of art has its own atmosphere, compounded of strangeness, melancholy and the wildest fun, and Mr. Gielgud plays it with every nerve in his body and brain."

During this hot summer, the company was given two weeks off, and John, on holiday with John Perry in France, was horrified to pick up an English newspaper and read that Ronald Mackenzie, also on holiday in France, had been killed when a burst tire overturned his car. This tragedy hastened the end of *Musical Chairs,* not least because John now had another new play on offer, one that he was really keen to direct.

By chance the play also came from a radical young dramatist, already intent on revolutionizing the British theater using techniques either learned or borrowed from Chekhov. Rodney Ackland's *Strange Orchestra* was a distant forerunner of Rattigan's *Separate Tables,* though on this occasion the paying guests were all sharing a rather run-down Bloomsbury flat. John's first idea for the leading role was the redoubtable and legendary actress Mrs. Patrick Campbell, who from the very first rehearsal took an immediate dislike to the play: "Who," she demanded imperiously of John, "are all these extraordinary characters? Where do they live? Would Gladys Cooper know them?"

It was soon abundantly clear that Mrs. Pat was, neither for the first nor last time, unable to make it through to the first night, and her role was duly taken over by the more reliable if less charismatic Laura Cowie. This was to be Gielgud's first production of a modern play, and he found its characters infinitely engrossing: "They are uncertain of their jobs, they quarrel, make love, indulge in scenes of hysteria, behave abominably to one another, and perform deeds of unselfish heroism, all the while dancing to a gramophone."

Strange Orchestra received mixed reviews, and only survived a few short weeks, but James Agate reckoned that it was "As much superior to the ordinary stuff of theater as tattered silk is to unbleached calico." And Gielgud himself pinpointed what made Ackland special: "The moods and subtleties of his characters are woven together in a very distinctive pattern—his vision is apt to be limited to his own particular type of atmosphere, but at least he deals with real people." One thing most critics were agreed on was that since the tragic death of Ronald Mackenzie, only Ackland seemed interested in pursuing his dramatic line of what might be called "English Chekhov," a line that was really only to reach a happy conclusion in the late 1940s work of N. C. Hunter, in which John was sometimes to star and would also direct.

This demand for reality, at a time when the West End was generally at its most artificial, characterized John's constant search for a new kind of theater, one with which he and Komisarjevsky and the Motleys could break down the old Shaftesbury Avenue certainties with plays that either would disturb an audience or at the very least make it think. On the other hand, he was quick to recognize commercial necessities—having become a star and begun to enjoy the good life, John wasn't about to throw it all up for that of a penniless theatrical revolutionary, condemned always to work in attics and basements for very little money.

As a result, he eagerly took up the offer of filming *The Good Companions* in which he was joined by Max Miller, Jessie Matthews, and the young Jack Hawkins.

During the shooting John was embarrassingly required to do the usual round of fan-magazine interviews, in one of which he even had to pretend that he was on the search for a loving wife: "My trouble is that as my work is my life, I have no real interests outside it. I therefore find it rather difficult to make friends with anyone who is not connected with the theater. For me, age doesn't count at all. For example, Mrs. Patrick Campbell, Edna Best, Gwen Ffrangcon-Davies, Lillian Braithwaite and Adele Dixon have all been the best of 'good companions' to me, and a supreme necessity of good companionship is understanding my need for solitude. I also think good temper and a sense of humour would be vital, more important than actual beauty. I would like a girl who was well-groomed and always appropriately dressed, a good reader and someone who could talk intelligently about pictures and music. I would also like her to be a good cook for, like all my Terry family, I have a thoroughly healthy appetite. I would also hope that she would be devoted to children and not give all her attention to pets, at least not when I am about."

Having thus dealt, as well as any gay man could, with the requirements of popular movie magazines, he returned to the film itself, which the critic C. A. Lejeune thought "suggests a long screen career for John Gielgud."

But he himself was still uneasy with his performance and the life on a film set: "I hate the early rising, the long, endless days of spasmodic work, and I loathe to be patted and slapped and curled and painted, while I lie supine and helpless in the make-up equivalent of a dentist's chair . . . I detest the lack of continuity which insists I should idiotically walk twenty times down a corridor with a suitcase in my hand, to enter the door of a room in which I played some important scene three weeks ago . . . I hate the meals in films, and the heat of the lights which makes them still more disgusting. Above all, I get muddled by all the details, and I hate the close-ups when the heroine is not called, and you play the big moment of your emotional scene to nothing but a camera, a yard away."

John might have been more enthusiastic about film at this time if he had been able to make rather better scripts. Sadly, two projects for the cinema that really did intrigue him both now fell through. One was an Elisabeth Bergner *Saint Joan* in which he would have played the Dauphin (thirty years later, he was to be the Earl of Warwick to Jean Seberg), and the other was Jerome K. Jerome's *Passing of the Third Floor Back,* a role that he lost to Conrad Veidt, who was also to film *The Jew Suss,* another Gielgud favorite.

John's brief encounter with a film camera led the drama critic of *The Evening News* to reflect on the precise nature of his current standing in the profession:

To the best of my knowledge, Mr. Gielgud is the only real star of the British theatre, under thirty. Many others are now in their forties and, unlike Gielgud, were all on the stage either during or before the First War. Mr. Ivor Novello and Herr Richard Tauber are already in their forties, and Mr. Charles Laughton and Mr. Noël Coward are thirty-five. Stardom is a quality above and beyond sheer acting ability; it is a personal, even an emotional quality, and it has undeniably a great deal to do with sex appeal, which in turn has very little to do with good looks. Mr. Gielgud has this quality of stardom, not so much by virtue of possessing wonderfully delicate features and colouring, as because he has that most priceless of all theatrical gifts, the Terry voice at its loveliest. His other great quality is his agelessness; he can be anything from 19 to 90, from Romeo to Prospero, Konstantin to King Lear. I passionately hope that he will prove all this in one evening by playing Peer Gynt.

This in fact was one of the few great classical roles that was always to elude John, but the *News* critic was surprisingly percipient: the actors under thirty that he now tipped for triumph by 1950 included Ralph Richardson, Robert Donat, Maurice Evans, and Jack Hawkins.

As so often happened, the filming of *The Good Companions* overran, which meant that John had to miss the early rehearsals of his first professional production of a Shakespeare play, *The Merchant of Venice*, due to open at the Old Vic in December 1932, with Peggy Ashcroft as Portia and Malcolm Keen as Shylock. Harcourt Williams stood in for him and Gielgud took no fee as director, because he wanted it to go instead to the Motleys for the first Old Vic production in which costumes were specifically designed. In fact, the total décor budget was less than £100 and Shylock's robe was made out of dishcloth at three pence a yard. Nevertheless, Baylis was predictably appalled at this extravagance and less than thrilled with Gielgud's decision to use music from Peter Warlock to give the whole production an air of mystery and fantasy, instead of the usual penny-pinching Old Vic drabness.

Anthony Quayle, then a very junior member of the Vic company, recalled that with John, for the very first time, he felt he was involved in a production "behind which there was a brain and a consistent point of view, whether it was one you liked or not; at least it was coherent. I remember being struck in rehearsal by the elegance of John's clothes—his suede shoes, his beautifully cut suits, his immaculate shirts, the long gold key chain that went around his waist before diving into his trouser pocket; I had never seen the like. I also remember how unfailingly courteous he always was to the older and more distinguished members of the company, although to me he himself already seemed godlike in his eminence."

One of the most detailed reviews of this *Merchant* came not in the press, but in a private letter to John from the young Tyrone Guthrie: "I was entranced, many thanks and congratulations—the casket scene is exquisitely pretty and amusing and the trial scene is perfect. Top marks to Motley, especially for the women's clothes, though some of the men's are rather feminine. Antonio seems nice and worthy but rather dull. And surely he, rather than Shylock, should dominate the trial scene until Portia arrives? Malcolm Keen is over-doing his exit shamefully, and Peggy Ashcroft, just right in personality, like a school prefect, but barely adequate vocally. Why does the Duke of Venice look like a provincial lady mayoress planting a tree? Harcourt Williams was perfect as Aragon, and if you have read this far you will know that I for one found the whole thing stimulating and gay, and I do want to congratulate you."

As for Peggy, although her Portia attracted some wonderful reviews (*The Times* praised her for being the first actress ever to play the "quality of mercy" speech quite naturally, with her hands behind her back, instead of as an oration), she herself had grave doubts about what Gielgud was trying to do: "I think John at the time was very influenced by Komis and all his innovations, but I wasn't too sure about this production because I felt it was fancy-dress, and John could never tell us what period we were supposed to be in."

What John most loved about both Peggy and Edith was that their faces had what he was to call "enigmatic originality," meaning that they both almost cultivated their features into an impersonal canvas, onto which any character could be painted.

Unlike Edith, who spent most of her life in mourning for a husband who had died much too young, Peggy's private life was a constant source of backstage gossip, not least because she herself remained so secretive about it. What is known is that within less than a year of *The Merchant* she had married Komisarjevsky, and then divorced him on finding a series of his love letters to other actresses. In one of his superbly indiscreet and supposedly off-the-record comments, discussing the rival merits of Peggy Ashcroft and Celia Johnson, who were almost of an age, John once said, "Look at Celia, totally happy, lots of money, nice husband, lovely daughters, beautiful house, big success, yet she looks like the back of a London bus. Whereas Peggy has been in and out of every bed in London, and not a line on her face. That must be what a really active sex life can do for a woman."

What John now knew was that he wanted to bring *The Merchant* to an audience that was usually accustomed to an altogether lighter kind of theater, as the young Tyrone Guthrie reported: "Here, for the first time in my limited experience, was Shakespeare done with elegance and wit, light as a feather, and so gaily sophisticated that it makes Maugham and Coward seem like two non-conformist pastors from the Midlands."

John made another of his famously uneasy curtain speeches on the first night, on this occasion thanking Harcourt Williams for "doing all the donkey work," and thus ended a year in which he had played the nine-month run of *Musical Chairs,* appeared in two films, directed both *The Merchant of Venice* and *Strange Orchestra,* and started to work on what was to be his next great West End success, *Richard of Bordeaux.*

7. VINTAGE BORDEAUX

(1933–1934)

Richard of Bordeaux was the success of the season. From the window of my flat, I could look down St. Martin's Lane and see the queues coiled like serpents around the theatre. I was photographed, painted, caricatured, interviewed. I signed my autograph a dozen times a day, and received letters and presents by every post.

*T*he author of *Richard of Bordeaux* was in fact three people. Her real name was Elizabeth Mackintosh, but she had already written several successful historical novels as Josephine Tey and was now to choose her third identity as Gordon Daviot for the play she sent to John because, as she was later to admit, she had been inspired to write her greatest hit after having seen Gielgud at the Old Vic in what might be called "the original" *Richard II*. His playing of Richard made him the obvious casting for Daviot's urbane, romantic, and often witty retread of Shakespeare; and to find another example of the rewriting of medieval history in light-hearted modern language, you would have to go forward thirty years to James Goldman's very similar treatment of Henry II and his quarrelsome family in *The Lion in Winter*.

The Richard of Daviot's play had a non-Shakespearean life of his own. Although his homosexuality could only be suggested through the character of his friend Robert (a kind of amalgam of Shakespeare's Bushy, Bagot, and Green), he was given a sort of weary cynicism in lines like,

"The only people I can trust are my two thousand archers, paid regularly every Friday."

From the moment John first read *Richard of Bordeaux* backstage at the Vic, he realized that not only was it a wonderful vehicle for his talents but also, rather in the manner of Shaw's *Saint Joan,* that there was something very attractive in the still revolutionary idea of great kings and warriors from history now behaving and talking like modern human beings. He was able to insist on directing the play himself and duly brought in his beloved Motley sisters to do the sets and costumes.

They tried it out for a couple of semi-staged Sunday nights at the Arts Theatre while John was still in his last season at the Vic, but as soon as they went into rehearsal for the West End, he decided to go for such epic Edwardian stage effects as the burning down of Sheen Palace. It wasn't until a catastrophic dress rehearsal, at which the fire nearly spread throughout the theater, that John realized his mistake and cut back the production at the last minute to very much more manageable proportions. His costar was once again to be Gwen Ffrangcon-Davies as the unlucky Princess Anne, but also joining the strong cast were such established character actors as Francis Lister, Richard Ainley (son of the matinee idol, Henry Ainley), and Donald Wolfit, who was to start here a lifelong enmity with John. Fifty years later, Gielgud found himself in Tuscany with John Mortimer (filming *Summer's Lease*), when their conversation turned to the missing Lord Lucan. Mortimer suggested that the vanished peer had been the victim of a contract killing for three thousand pounds. "Good Lord," said John, "is that all it costs to have a man killed? If Wolfit had known that, he would have taken out a contract on me, years ago. He really loathed me, you know, and the feeling was always entirely mutual."

At the time of *Richard of Bordeaux,* Wolfit was already unhappily married, with a small child and a career that seemed to be going nowhere. He viewed Gielgud with violent jealousy, as a man who, unlike himself, had come from a privileged and charmed theatrical background and who apparently had never been out of work since leaving drama school. Wolfit, as his biographer Ronald Harwood has noted, had none of Gielgud's graces: "Donald was always blinded to Gielgud's exceptional gifts—his superb voice, his grace of interpretation, his perceptive intelligence and, above all, a soulfulness that was capable of encompassing noble passion in the finest sense . . . as men, they had only their love of the theatre in common, and it would never be enough to form the foundation of anything more than chilly politeness, and sometimes not even that. Disagreements were plentiful and throughout his life, Wolfit would, at the very mention of Gielgud's name, inhale deeply and noisily through his nose, like an enraged bull, which was always his way of signifying enmity."

And there was yet another problem: Wolfit was virulently antihomosexual (as was revealed at the time of John's arrest in 1953) and already suspected him to be at the heart of a gay Mafia that would, as Donald saw it, be specifically determined to keep his own old-fashioned virility in a state of semi-unemployment.

The two men had of course already worked together on a couple of Sunday night readings, and also in two or three productions at the Old Vic, but their tricky and volatile relationship on stage in *Richard of Bordeaux* made for some difficult rehearsals, followed by a curiously subdued first night, attended by few critics since it clashed with a major ballet opening across town.

Yet *Richard of Bordeaux* was to be one of those plays that nobody liked except the public. The morning after it opened was so quiet at the box office that the manager let his assistant go for a long lunch, only then to look through his window and see, to his utter amazement, a queue forming the length of St. Martin's Lane. From that first matinee for the next fourteen months, there was scarcely a seat to be had.

Among those who now flocked to the play was the then Chancellor of the Exchequer, Stanley Baldwin, who wrote afterward to John: "I should like, if I may, to thank you and your admirable team for the delightful evening I spent on Saturday night in your theatre. I forgot all my own difficulties and became immersed in those of poor Richard. How little he realised the extraordinary times through which he was living, and how much you must have enjoyed working up the play."

The actors Herbert Marshall and Edna Best wrote to John of "a glorious evening and a superb play," and Hugh Walpole told him, "I especially admired the way in which you never ceased to be Richard, even while taking your curtain call. This is great acting, and better still great poetic oration." As for Ivor Novello: "What is there to say? I am so grateful for your beauty, imagination and utterly touching loveableness." And from the Shavian actor Esme Percy, "Having been born in an age that now seems legendary, my memory houses many splendours, but your Richard shall be added to my first sight of Henry Irving, to the sound of Bernhardt's voice, and Duse's extraordinary personality among the greatest and most poignant nights of my life."

Clearly this was the most successful historical play since Bernard Shaw's *Saint Joan,* and, historically closer to the facts than was the Shakespeare, it remains an even more revealing assessment of the king's profligate character. Daviot's play starts with Richard at eighteen, an idealist poised for disaster, and then traces the course of his life, leading up to the late bitterness and defeat. As the historian Audrey Williamson was to write: "Dressed in cream or cloth of gold, the sculptured cheekbones and proud poise of his head nobly accentuated beneath his red-gold flame of hair, Gielgud was a royal figure with the hereditary Terry radiance. It was perhaps his romantic tenderness which consolidated his popularity with audiences, but the temper and irony were also superbly presented, his intelligence was never in doubt, and his playing of the last scenes showed a fine appreciation of the sharp springs of disillusion. His characterisation grew in strength with its bitter quietude, and if any one detail of the performance remains clearer than the rest, it is the simple one of Richard allowing his handkerchief to flutter to the ground like a dead leaf at the realisation of Anne's fatal illness. It was a key to the subtlety of his entire performance, one which dominates all memories of the play, and will become the Golden Legend of our age."

In later years, Gielgud was to be very dismissive of his original Old Vic *Richard II:* "When I listen to the old recordings, they sound to me very voice-conscious, and I am rather ashamed to think that I was so contented with that kind of acting." For *Richard of Bordeaux,* however, he found a kind of release into an altogether more contemporary style. The king in Gordon Daviot's play was less self-pitying and had a sharper wit than in

Shakespeare's, and when the critics did catch up with what was already a huge popular hit, they found in John a marvelous combination of vacillation, nobility, and embittered disillusion. For Desmond MacCarthy of *The Times,* John was now "right at the top of his profession, having acquired all the marks of the great actor." For *The Daily Telegraph,* W. A. Darlington noted at the curtain fall "a glorious, full-throated roar of approval, such as the West End seldom hears in these sophisticated days."

But as so often, the most thoughtful review of both the play and the actor came in *The New Statesman,* from the critic Desmond MacCarthy:

> When I first went to the play, historical drama was all the rage, from Lewis Waller to the endless revivals of *The Scarlet Pimpernel* by Fred Terry. But since the War, the high cost of productions has made pageantry impractical, while the popularity of new naturalistic plays has consigned the drama of swagger and duel to the shelf. Failing supply has accompanied diminished demand. But now, Mr. Gielgud brings it all back. His Richard is quite remarkable; there is a morbid, feline elegance about his bearing and careful movements. He changes from the leader of a country in arms to a vain, selfish disillusioned man—an artist who has lost the desire to share delightful things, and can no longer put his faith in his friends. Mr. Gielgud never allows pathos to sink into sentiment, and he triumphs with an economy of gesture. In my opinion he is now the first among English actors. Ours is far from being an age of great acting, but the range of his emotional scope, and the intelligence with which he conceives his role, put him right at the top of his profession. Mr. Gielgud uniquely combines histrionic temperament with interpretative intelligence and that is very rare. Now his temptations will begin. He has the power to charm large audiences, but will he choose only plays which delight them?

Considering that on the first night the box-office takings were only £77, the immediate turnaround in the fortunes of *Richard of Bordeaux* was nothing short of a miracle; John himself, although he had characteristically turned down an offer to invest in the play (such was his terror of any business dealing), was now earning £100 per week, more than twice his most recent salary at the Vic.

The morning after *Richard of Bordeaux* opened, the director Victor Saville summoned John back to Lime Grove for retakes of some of the close-ups in *The Good Companions:* "I congratulated him on the applause and extravagant praise, and all he said was 'What is the good of success in such an unhappy world?'" Even John now seemed to have awoken to the fact that, with the rise of Hitler and Mussolini, some kind of reality was about to invade his closed and closeted theatrical environment.

Still not yet thirty, John had, for the first time, become a star and began now to bask in the adulation that resulted from his newfound fame; as he explained to one of his many new friends: "After the show every night I sit signing hundreds of post-cards in my costume as people come round backstage. Yes, I know it's vulgar, but I can't resist it. I am a star!" As Gordon Daviot was to write in her preface to the published edition of her play, which is dedicated to John, "I like to think that, in time to come, whenever *Richard of Bordeaux* is mentioned, it is your name that will spring to people's lips."

Daviot's hope was to become more of a reality than even she could have wished. Although indeed the fame of her play was always linked to Gielgud's performance, it was effectively only to exist in London for the length of that first production. Although initially much revived and toured around the regions, the play (with Maurice Evans) achieved only a brief Broadway life and has never been given a major postwar revival anywhere, perhaps because its unashamed, flamboyant, poetic sentimentality has never again suited the mood of the moment as it did so perfectly in 1933.

At this moment, a gossip writer in the *Evening News* began for the first time to profile John in some depth:

Inside the theatre he is always fiery, youthful and impetuous, a man of easy and gallant bearing, guaranteed to sweep even the most cynical and sophisticated modern girl right off her feet. Outside the theatre, however, he is just shy John, carefully signing autographs and warmly shaking every hand placed before him:

"These people are the galleryites and the pittites of the Old Vic, the kind of people whose support of Shakespeare makes you glad to be alive . . . they often send me lovely letters and presents of flowers and books. But I draw the line at any personal acquaintance. I do not believe in personal contact between an actor and his audience. The most difficult audiences are always the schoolchildren, but I usually go out first to explain to them that Shakespeare is really much more thrilling than Edgar Wallace. I also tell them not to giggle when two people kiss, or at any reference to magic and fairies. The other really difficult audience are the Old Vic veterans who hate anything fresh. They tell me that a part has always been played in a red wig, and how dare I now choose black?"

By the end of the run, several members of the company, recognizing perhaps that this was little more than a one-man show with extras, had gone off in search of more rewarding work, leading to yet another of John's foot-in-mouth curtain speeches: "What a wonderful audience you have been, and some of you have come again and again, in spite of all the changes in the cast."

Not until the Olivier-Richardson wartime seasons at the Old Vic and then this same New Theatre was any classical actor to take the town by any comparable kind of storm. *Richard of Bordeaux* was the making of John's career and also inevitably something of a millstone around his neck. Forty years later, when he was with some difficulty trying to move into the modern theater of David Storey and Harold Pinter, he once said to me, rather sadly, about his older fans, "If they had it their way, I would have gone on being Richard of Bordeaux for the rest of my life. And theirs."

Even during the extended run of this first production, John rapidly tired of playing nothing but the doomed king; over the next few months while acting eight shows a week, he was to direct two other plays and make his first tentative stab at being a producer. The first of the plays he directed was

Somerset Maugham's *Sheppey,* for which he assembled a magical cast led by Ralph Richardson, Angela Baddeley, and Eric Portman. Overawed by Maugham's presence at the later rehearsals, however, Gielgud declined to make any of the changes that could have solved the problems of *Sheppey,* which essentially were that the first act was a Pinero-like comedy, the second a Shavian kind of drama, and the third a flight of tragic fantasy. The result was not a success, although Maugham later dedicated the published text to John.

As John commented on the experience: "I felt tremendously flattered by his [Maugham's] charming gesture, but I realised that I had found it very hard to get on intimate terms with any living playwright. I suppose my actor's egotism is to blame. I am not clever at drawing people out, and my friends tell me that I have no real interest in anyone but myself. I hope this is not the exact truth, but I rather fear that it may be."

His relationship with Maugham was not helped by the fact that the novelist was already living on Cap Ferrat in the south of France, forced into exile by the fact that his lover, the American Gerald Haxton, had been declared an undesirable alien in Britain after several homosexual scandals. Maugham had, however, handed over all authority to John, as he wrote from the Villa Mauresque on August 19, 1933: "I am very glad indeed to hear that you want to produce my play. It needs to be done with a mixture of imagination and realism and I know no-one who can do that better than you. I am not in the least sensitive about cuts, and I hope you will not hesitate to shorten wherever the play seems to you to drag, or wherever I have made a point at greater length than is needed to bring it home. I have a house full of guests, and do not see how I can abandon them to attend rehearsals. But please remember not to be too kind about firing people if they seem unsuitable when you start work. My own experience in the theatre was that people who are not right for their roles at once never really get any better, no matter how much time the producer devotes to them."

The other play that John directed during the run of *Richard of Bordeaux* was *Spring 1600* by Emlyn Williams, the young Welsh actor and playwright whom he had first met at the Oxford Playhouse while he was still a starstruck undergraduate. In the intervening ten years, Williams had begun to make his name as a somewhat sinister West End actor, notably in such thrillers as Edgar Wallace's *On the Spot,* and *The Case of the Frightened Lady.* This last play had taken him to New York, and while he was there Emlyn wrote *Spring 1600,* a swashbuckling backstage play about the Elizabethan world of such original Shakespearean actors as Richard Burbage and Will Kemp, during their dress rehearsals for the first-ever staging of *Twelfth Night.* In later years, Ned Sherrin and Caryl Brahms were also to explore this world in their *No Bed for Bacon,* but it wasn't until the late 1990s, with Nicholas Wright's play *Cressida* and, far more successfully, Tom Stoppard's script *Shakespeare in Love,* that the idea really came to fruition. At the time of *Spring 1600,* Emlyn Williams was not yet thirty, and still two years away from his first great hit as an actor-dramatist with the thriller *Night Must Fall.*

So although they were of an age, and to become lifelong friends with a good deal in common, not only a passion for all aspects of theater, but also a cautious awareness that their homosexuality still had to be kept carefully hidden from their audiences, and even from some of their friends, John was still inclined to treat Emlyn with a tolerant patronage, insisting that if he was to direct *Spring 1600,* certain changes would have to be made. Accordingly, on his return from Broadway, Williams was summoned to a meeting: "At Number 7, Upper St Martin's Lane, I climbed the steep, narrow stairs to a top flat . . . Gielgud, on our occasional previous meetings, had seemed affable but a little haughty, and though he was less than two years older than me, I always felt in awe of him. I therefore expected, knowing of his fanatical dedication to his work, an impeccable room with perhaps one good painting, a classical bust and lofty talk about Shakespeare, with a couple of reverent acolytes hanging about . . . it was nothing of the sort, being unpretentiously small with good furniture and family pictures, comfortably lived in by the two bachelors who shared the flat. John Perry was my age, tall, gauntly handsome with thinning hair, and a mocking manner which contrived, as I later discovered, to hide a kind heart . . . it was all rather like being in digs on tour. Gielgud hurried in, bare-legged, in a shabby old dressing gown, suggesting a toga."

In the years that followed, Emlyn was frequently to revisit the

Perry/Gielgud flat, recalling "John G eating scrambled eggs before going off to another packed house, and the gramophone always playing Vivaldi. It was, in a way, like coming home. One evening, when I arrived, sitting having a drink was a tall, strikingly handsome boy who looked like an Oxford undergraduate, which is what he had been until very recently. But he had written a first play which was about to be produced in the West End, and from his pocket he gave me a throwaway post-card. It read 'First Episode, by Terence Rattigan.' On another occasion the three of us all changed in John's bedroom into hired Tyrolean outfits, with leather shorts, for the Chelsea Arts Ball."

Rattigan now was a regular visitor, not only to the flat on St. Martin's Lane, but also to the country cottage near Henley, which the two Johns had rented for weekend house parties, as Rattigan's biographer Geoffrey Wansell notes:

> There was poker and Ping-Pong, a great many famous faces and frequent Sunday lunches, as well as elegant and sometimes outrageous parties. This was the magical, star-studded world which Rattigan had longed to be part of. It was also a world of homosexuals, which the theatre accepted more readily and more consistently than any other profession. Gielgud's theatre company was certainly more welcoming to homosexuals than some of the more conventional managements and impresarios of that time; nevertheless, every homosexual knew only too well the dangers that confronted them if they dared to reveal themselves. Any homosexual act between adults over the age of twenty-one was still punishable by months of imprisonment, while the punishment for an affair with a minor was even harsher—and Rattigan at this time was not even twenty-one . . . like every homosexual of his time, he was always on guard, preoccupied with preserving appearances at all costs, conscious of the need to protect his secret world. With Perry and Gielgud, however, he could relax in an atmosphere which delighted him and which he never really wanted to leave.

Not far from John's London flat, at 67 St. Martin's Lane, almost opposite the New Theatre, the Motleys (who had taken their professional name from Jacques' line "Motley's the only wear" in *As You Like It*) had by now set up their design business in a derelict third-floor studio, last used by the revue star Douglas Byng as a gay nightclub. It had also once been the workshop of Thomas Chippendale, and like him the Motleys now combined the studio with a kind of theatrical club where, as John recalled, "Guinness and Ashcroft and Guthrie and I would turn up most evenings, to drink their tea and gossip with George Devine who I remember looking very Bohemian, like an artist from the Latin Quarter with pipe and corduroys—always shock-headed, and twinkling and agreeable. I threw a first-night party for *Richard of Bordeaux* in the studio, and we managed to fuse all the lights by tampering with a very elaborate model theatre which George had just begun to build in one of the corners. Sometimes we would have all-white evenings—white food, white wine and the Motleys all in long white dresses. Their studio really became our powerhouse, where all the new plans were hatched out." When Gielgud later took Devine into his Old Vic company, it was as much for his companionship as his talent.

But unlike the relationship with Devine, which had started very well at Oxford, John and Emlyn failed to hit it off straight away; they had gotten off to a bad start, with John insisting on more and more changes to *Spring 1600*, and Emlyn torn between wanting to have his play directed by the hottest young theater star in the business while already being uneasily aware that not all John's changes were for the better. Under Gielgud's own management, no expense was to be spared. There were elaborate sets, designed, of course, by the Motleys, a large orchestra in the pit for the incidental music, a dozen madrigal singers, and nearly twenty extras. Isabel Jeans, playing a wealthy patron of the Globe, had a black attendant and a monkey that she carried on her shoulder, at least until it gave her a nasty bite. The budget was an almost unprecedented £4,000, most of which John had raised himself, but the first night ran nearly four hours and was, to say the least, not a great success.

John, of course, still playing *Richard of Bordeaux* could not be there, and

Emlyn was in such a high state of nerves in the dress circle that he suddenly became convinced that he was in danger of imminently becoming the first playwright who had ever pissed over his own play.

His terror was needless, at least as far as some critics were concerned. Ivor Brown, for *The Observer,* wrote, "A world's great age begins anew, and we are all party to its pulsing life and the mood of the madrigal." For *The Sunday Times,* James Agate labeled it "choice entertainment for the fastidious"; but there clearly were not enough of them, and despite some drastic cutting by the author and director on the second night, the production barely survived two weeks. The sets and costumes were sold off in job lots, and John wrote to Emlyn: "Oh dear, I am so sad for you; we don't seem to have quite got away with it, all that work and love, and then it just evaporates."

Despite this, and the initial awkwardness that had existed between the two men, in the long term they were to become friends, although in the future Williams was careful, whenever possible, to direct his own work. There had only been one terrible moment during the dress rehearsal when, thinking that Emlyn was not present, John told the cast, through a megaphone from the stalls, "This last act is very thin, but we must try to make the best of it." A quiet voice at his elbow, that of the author, murmured, "I think we all know the act is thin, John, but you need perhaps not have announced it to the entire cast. Why don't we just wait for the critics to do that?"

Unlike John, Emlyn had always been bisexual, and a few years later Gielgud was a principal guest at his wedding to the ex-wife of a barrister, Mary Carus-Wilson. "I'm so glad for Emlyn," John told her at the wedding. "People keep telling me I ought to marry Peggy Ashcroft, but, much as we love each other, I don't think she'd have me; Gwen is such a darling, I suppose she might, at a pinch, but oh dear . . . " Lying behind this characteristically unfortunate summary was of course the fact that Peggy Ashcroft was famously promiscuous and hardly likely to settle for John as a husband, despite the fact that the *Evening Standard* announced their betrothal in 1935, and Gwen Ffrangcon-Davies was a lifelong lesbian. If John was drawn to women at this time, or ever, it was only really for the sake of his public image in a still intolerant world, and he was careful always to associate himself, both onstage and off, with precisely those actresses who were least likely to have any designs on him as a possible sexual or even marital partner.

From this very early stage, John was now beginning to direct as often as possible; he had realized, at the Old Vic, the immediate advantage of a semipermanent group of actors who could start rehearsals over and over again, without the time-wasting need for constant introductions and allowances having to be made for often clashing temperaments:

> My greatest good fortune was that, over the years, I was able to bring together wonderful companies, part with them on excellent terms, and then a few years later come back to work with them again. I find myself so much at home that I can then start work much more quickly than if I have to break the ice with players I do not know at all, and in my first years as a director, I was lucky enough to have three or four elderly actors in minor roles who had started out with Tree, Benson, Fagan or Playfair. They obeyed me without question, and had beautiful manners; even if they were not very fond of each other, their discipline and good behaviour were unfailing. This meant that I was able, on the one hand, to have some highly experienced players and, on the other, to bring on some very enthusiastic young people like Anthony Quayle, Glen Byam Shaw, Alec Guinness, Harry Andrews, actors who were just beginning. The young people matched with their youthful enthusiasm what the older ones had in experience—it seemed to me an ideal situation.

Richard of Bordeaux came to the end of its long London run in the spring of 1934; but almost immediately, it went out on the road, initially with John himself, and subsequently with Glen Byam Shaw, as John began to get more and more involved in what he hoped would be its triumphant sequel. Gordon Daviot had decided during the run that, having given John one of his greatest roles, it would now be only fair to try to do the same for his costar Gwen Ffrangcon-Davies. *Queen of Scots* was therefore the story of the doomed Mary, and her affairs with Bothwell and Darnley. Sadly, although both Frederick Schiller and Robert Bolt scored considerable successes with this historical period, it proved somehow beyond the talents of Gordon Daviot, and *Queen of Scots* enjoyed only the briefest of West End runs.

Characteristically, by the time it closed, John was already into another and rather more promising project. He had discovered that just before Ronald Mackenzie had been killed in the car crash, he had completed another play, this one called *The Maitlands,* which he had given to Komisarjevsky in the hope of repeating the success they had all enjoyed with *Musical Chairs.*

Because of that success, it was now easier to assemble a strong cast, and joining Gielgud here were the young Jack Hawkins, the future Hollywood dowager May Whitty, and the poet and actor Stephen Haggard, in whom many were already seeing a still younger Gielgud. The odds were now very high: Gielgud would be appearing in the West End for the first time since his triumph in *Bordeaux* and had been given massive star billing. The first-night audience therefore expected to see him in another flamboyantly charismatic performance and was thus somewhat shocked to find him in shabby modern dress and a mustache, dressed for the carnival with which the play opened.

He was playing a schoolmaster, trying to bring a mentally disturbed young man (Stephen Haggard) back to health; May Whitty was the worried mother, and Jack Hawkins a flashy and heartless actor, brother to the schoolmaster.

The Maitlands was again a new play of some fascination, not only because Mackenzie pointed the way forward to such other "lost" dramatists as Rodney Ackland and John Whiting, but also because of the violence with which it was greeted. Early in the first act, on the first night, voices from the gallery yelled, "Rubbish!" while others shouted, "Idiots!" leaving it unclear whether this referred to the characters onstage or the gallery first-nighters.

At the curtain call, the jeering from the gallery first-nighters persisted; John, aware that Mackenzie's widow was in the audience, stepped forward to make a speech referring to his recent death, whereupon, unsurprisingly, the jeers died rapidly away.

However, *The Maitlands* was doomed; James Agate accused the play of "taking elegant umbrage at our crude world" and suggested that John was "much too romantic an actor to be happy away from rhetoric and robes— if this fine actor must be modern, it should only be in a Russian blouse. All that goes with a bowler hat utterly defeats him." It was left to Ivor Brown alone, in *The Observer,* to mourn Mackenzie's early death and commend his "new muscularity of attack."

8. THE READINESS IS ALL

(1934–1935)

I was always being told by well-meaning friends (like Emlyn) how jealous Larry was of me, but I could never quite understand why; he had a great advantage over me in his commanding vitality, striking looks, brilliant humour and passionate directness. When we alternated as Romeo and Mercutio, he seemed to be holding all the cards except one. I was of course the director.

*T*he Maitlands, largely because of the advance bookings that had been made on John's name before the reviews came out, staggered on at Wyndham's Theatre for nearly twelve weeks, and toward the end of the run Sir Bronson Albery, who owned that theater as well as a family chain of others, came backstage one night to offer John the production he had really wanted all along. What Albery suggested was a West End *Hamlet* that John could play and direct, design with the Motleys, and on a budget far beyond the wildest dreams of the *Hamlets* he had played at the Old Vic and the Royal Court.

This was, in other words, to be the big one, and although initially it was only meant to run six weeks, it in fact lasted more than six months, to become one of the longest-running West End revivals of Shakespeare at this time. To it, in what was then a generous rehearsal period of four weeks, John brought all the influences that had conditioned his early Shakespearean work. Using not only the Motleys, but a set heavily indebted to both Gordon Craig and Komisarjevsky, he created a production in which he would again try to combine the talents of a generation older than his, with those of some very promising newcomers.

His Ophelia was to be the young Jessica Tandy; as Claudius and Gertrude, he had Frank Vosper and Laura Cowie, looking, he recalled, "like two sleek, evil cats." Jack Hawkins, soon to marry Jessica Tandy, was Horatio; Glen Byam Shaw was Laertes; and George Howe was Polonius. But perhaps the most intriguing member of this company was a young actor of twenty, who had been haunting Gielgud's stage door in the hope of an understudy job. Failing that, John gave him £20 to survive and a few weeks later, impressed by one student production, he offered Alec Guinness the role of Osric. Once again a long and loving friendship, which was to extend across the next sixty years, got off to a catastrophic start when early in rehearsal John decided he had made a terrible mistake.

Alec's recollection of these early rehearsals is one of the best surviving records of John in action as a director at this time: "'Come on from the left. No! No! The other left—oh, someone make him understand! Why are you so stiff? Why don't you make me laugh? Motleys! Would it be pretty to paint the whole thing gold? Perhaps not. Don't fidget, Guinness; now you are gabbling. Now turn upstage. No, not you. You! Turn the other way. Oh, why can't you all act? Get someone to teach you how to act! Why is your voice so harsh? It really is quite ugly. Do just do something about it.'"

And there was worse to come. Guinness, ten years younger than Gielgud, and on £7 per week, finally drove John to distraction: "What on earth has happened to you? You were so good as a student. You're terrible. Do go away. I don't ever want to see you again." But Alec, who had already learned at least a little about the volatility of John's moods, knew enough to hang about until the end of that day's rehearsal. "Excuse me Mr. Gielgud, but am I really fired?"

"No! Yes! No, of course not. But do go away. Come back in a week. Get someone to teach you how to act. Try Martita Hunt—she'll be glad of the money."

Guinness decided not to go anywhere near Martita, whose teaching was, to say the least, a little eccentric, but instead to walk around London's parks for a week and then to report back to Gielgud at the New Theatre. "He seemed delighted to have me back, heaped praise on my Osric and laughed at everything I said. I couldn't swear that I was doing anything I had not done a week earlier. But suddenly and briefly I had become teacher's pet, and John told the Motleys that I should have a hat with a lot of feathers, just like the Duchess of Devonshire."

Another member of this *Hamlet* company was Frith Banbury, later to become one of the most distinguished of West End directors and the one who first discovered such playwrights as Robert Bolt and N. C. Hunter, the author of *A Day by the Sea:* "John was himself such a brilliant actor that he failed to understand those of us who were less good; he would sit with his feet on the railing of the dress circle, yelling at us to be better in some way. I think that something about me always irritated him; I had only a very small part, but he kept taking lines away from me and giving them to Jack Hawkins. At the dress-rehearsal, I somehow missed an entrance, clambered over the bloody revolving stage, only to hear John scream, 'Banbury, I don't mind you being late, but what I can't forgive is you standing about like that when you do arrive.'" It was not so very long after this experience that Frith began to think about the possibilities of becoming a director himself.

During the run, Alec and Frith and the other younger members of the cast would gather in the wings every night to watch what they already seemed to know, intuitively—that this was to be the *Hamlet* of their time. At Christmas, Gielgud gave Guinness a volume of Ellen Terry's letters, in which he inscribed what became Alec's lifelong motto: "The Readiness Is All." But even now, the critics were still divided. Several of them noticed how exhausted John G. had become as actor and director, and Agate thought it was "Everest only half-scaled." In contrast, J. C. Trewin found it "the key Shakespearean revival of its period."

In the view of the critic A. E. Wilson: "Mr. Gielgud has many qualifications for Hamlet. He is an artist, he is intelligent, he is handsome. He still has the slim figure of youth and a romantic profile which he allows us frequent opportunities to admire. He has an agreeable voice with good lungs behind it, although under the stress of passion it becomes high and throaty instead of a full-throated roar. He has a personality which in young people seems to induce hero-worship. He speaks his lines with exceptional intelligence, his diction is elegant and his delivery is unexceptionable except when he falls sometimes into inaudibility. But, he lacks passion or any kind of real emotion. He seems aloof and abstracted from everyone and everything. He is no more excited after the ghost has spoken to him than he was before; there is no bitterness in his disdain, no rage in his hatred, no affection in his friendship and no wildness in his melancholy."

For Audrey Williamson, however, "Gielgud has always achieved his finest effects when surrounded by a cast of high distinction; his performances shine better for their setting. And though he always stressed the sensitivity of Hamlet, his range was remarkable. The mobile beauty of his hands and voice bespoke the prince and the poet; but there was a taut inner fibre in this *Hamlet,* expressed in sudden flashes of steel at moments of active crisis.... There had been a gap of over a generation between Gielgud and the finest classical actors of the past, so audiences had never seen a young Hamlet. And the special charm of this one was that it welded together the best of the old and the new."

In these years, Shakespearean productions were not quite as academically humorless as they were later to become; John was a famous onstage giggler, never more so than on the night when Frank Vosper, as Claudius, had been chatting backstage to an old army friend. A few minutes later, coming on for the duel scene, instead of saying, "Cousin Hamlet, you know the wager," Vosper solemnly enquired, "Cousin Hamlet, you know the Major?"

Looking back, John was to write that he had never been happier than during the run of this *Hamlet.* Not only was he playing, eight times a week, the role that alone would have justified his whole career, but he had made (largely from *Richard of Bordeaux* in London and on the road) enough money to buy, for a thousand pounds, a little weekend cottage in Essex, where he and John Perry would often welcome such young friends as Terence Rattigan and Binkie Beaumont.

The general critical enthusiasm for this production was reflected in hundreds of letters written to John at the theater. From the novelist Rosamund Lehmann, whose actress sister Beatrix had already become a friend: "Your scenes with Ophelia are a revelation, and I felt all through the production that this was exactly what Shakespeare would have wanted. For the first time I felt really satisfied by the play because your acting conveyed the sense of a colossal, overpowering Fate at the back of all the speculation and intellectual beating-about. I really was excited, and I never expect to see a better Hamlet—nor, for that matter, a better Ophelia or Polonius." Emlyn Williams, no longer an undergraduate, wrote from Hertford College, Oxford, "Last night was the best that I have ever spent in a theatre, and I hope you will not misunderstand me when I say that I have never been less conscious of a great actor's interpretation, never more aware of the beauty and unity of the play."

As for George Devine, recently down from Oxford and starting to make his own way in the theater as an actor-director, "I can't help feeling that most of the critics are men of a generation past. . . . They keep comparing you to Irving, Tree, and Forbes-Robertson, whereas the whole point of your ideas and acting is surely that it is designed for a modern theatre audience with a much quicker perception. The general spread of culture and knowledge in our time makes it unnecessary for Hamlet to underline everything as he goes along. What you are doing is crediting us in the audience with a kind of intelligence and although I have some reservations about the other casting, I do think you have shown us the future for Shakespeare instead of, as usual, the past."

Godfrey Tearle, always a rather more flamboyant actor than most, sent John a telegram reading: "Would I were Horatio, to support the finest Hamlet I have ever seen. May God in thy good cause make thee prosperous!"

The Queen Mother, then Duchess of York, sent a message via her lady-in-waiting noting how much she would have liked John to come to the royal box during the performance she and the future George VI attended, but, continued the letter, "when she saw you had but one interval in such a long and exhausting evening, she thought it kinder to refrain."

In addition to all the encouragement and praise from these letters, John also received thanks from within the cast. A particularly grateful member of the company was Alec Guinness, who wrote:

"I could write you a very long letter thanking you not only for giving me a part, but also for your countless little kindnesses, which have made working with you so delightful, but I will spare you all that. It was very courageous of you to give an inexperienced person a part like Osric, and knowing how bad I was even at the end of the run, and how much you said I had improved, I shudder to think what I must have been like at the beginning. I suppose one never forgets one's first part—I certainly shall never forget how happy I have been during these last six months. I am not a very gay or happy person by nature, but I find the confidence you have in me a great source of happiness. I want to write this because it's one of those things which mean a lot to me, but I find very hard to speak."

In sharp contrast, an "unknown fan" who declined to sign the letter sent John a detailed, typewritten, four-page analysis of his current standing in the theater, which was an often devastatingly accurate review:

Most critics shower superlatives on you, and those who like to be different treat you as a mere matinee idol. I consider you one of the great hopes of the English theatre, but there are times when you simply don't quite come off. In the long run of *Richard of Bordeaux* your performance deteriorated badly, showing signs of wear and tear when you spoke too fast and too loud. In moments of strong emotion, something always goes wrong and you become unnatural. You tend to rant and cry far too often without much conviction. I felt that you were always terribly sorry for Hamlet, and you played it with a kind of self-pity which made the emotion ring false. In *The Maitlands* your mannerisms stuck out a mile, and there is always the problem of "the Gielgud voice." I suspect, although you often listen to it, that you have never really heard it. Listen next time, and you will hear the exaggerations. I am neither a schoolgirl nor a flapper, nor a fussy old lady. I don't want you to write back, but do please think about what I have to say, I am not alone.

In fact, with a budget of only £1,500 this *Hamlet* played to an average of £2,000 a week, and its eventual profit at the end of 155 performances, the longest London run of the play in sixty years, was just over £30,000. John himself was asked to explain his success: "There is plenty to account for it. For one thing, I notice that the audience is full of young people. Many of them have probably never seen the play, and they genuinely want to know how it ends. Another thing is that we have gone back to the old tradition of the actor who is also the producer. In this way, during the run of the play, I have been able continually to change and build up and improve the production in small details from night to night. The old school of actor-managers built up a company around them, who knew them and worked continually with them, and would do anything for them. But nowadays, when an outside producer comes in to direct the play, he does so and then goes away again. He usually only comes in once or twice later during the run and terrifies everybody; but there can be no sense of this continual and communal building up of a production."

As the run of *Hamlet* was coming to an end, the playwright Rodney Ackland (for whom John had directed *Strange Orchestra* a couple of years earlier) now brought him an adaptation of Hugh Walpole's best-selling novel, *The Old Ladies*. This was a macabre piece for four actresses, one of whom never spoke, and another of whom came to an ugly and unexpected death in what could be considered one of the first great psychological thrillers of this period. Gielgud assembled a magnificent cast (Edith Evans, Jean Cadell, and Mary Jerrold) and devised, with the Motleys, a brilliant and radically new cutaway set in which the different bedrooms of a boarding house, as well as the downstairs lounge, could all be seen and used simultaneously, like an exaggerated dolls' house.

Unfortunately, the production clashed with King George V's Silver Jubilee celebrations of 1935, and the business suffered accordingly. Still, *The Old Ladies* has frequently been revived and owes a considerable debt to John's pioneering original production. Just when he has become the greatest Hamlet of his time, he also turns out to be a modernist stage director, far ahead of his contemporaries in realizing that although he himself was still very unhappy with the new medium, some of the close-up techniques of cinema now needed to be borrowed back for the live theater. And his unhappiness with the screen only affected him as an actor; it was around now that he began to develop the habit of going to the cinema once or twice a week, the only kind of regular relaxation he was to allow himself in a workaholic lifetime.

As Hugh Walpole himself wrote to John after the opening night of *The Old Ladies,* "You really have done a brilliant job, and I do congratulate you on your genius as a producer. Everything seems to have gone without a hitch, and the best thing is that the play seems to have fulfilled so many different tasks."

John was also, at a time when the London theater was still shamefully parochial, fascinated by the occasional visits of foreign companies. One of these, Michel Saint-Denis's Compagnie des Quinze, had recently played London with Andre Obey's *Noah,* a biblical drama that intrigued John because it was produced in an endearing and stylized way, with animals portrayed by actors in exquisite masks, and all the sound effects performed by the company—in essence an amazing forerunner of the Theatre de Complicite, which was to take London by storm half a century later.

Pierre Fresnay had already taken *Noah* to Broadway, where it had enjoyed limited success, but John was still very eager to play it in London, under the direction of Saint-Denis himself: "We did not really hit it off at first. Michel made me feel, in rehearsal, intensely lazy, ignorant and self-satisfied, and I in turn was terrified that perhaps he was right, and that my talents really were negligible. But in later years we got on very well." They last worked together at the Aldwych in the 1961 RSC *Cherry Orchard:* "But I was really very unhappy as Noah. I suddenly realised that the part really belonged to an actor like Charles Laughton or Cedric Hardwicke, and for some reason I was dressed in velveteen trousers and a fur cap, which made me look bizarrely like a jungle explorer who had suddenly arrived at the North Pole.

"The critics as usual preferred it in the original French, and London audiences seemed embarrassed by our mixture of comedy, mime and religion. On the very last night of a rather brief run, the always purist St. Denis came backstage to tell me that, at last, I was perhaps beginning to find a way of playing at least the very first scene."

Peggy Ashcroft, in the first of her many letters to John, wrote: "I was so moved by your performance last night that I fear I did not make any sense in the dressing-room afterwards. It is very rare now to see a great performance such as yours, so big and moving and yet never breaking through to overbalance the production. I can't tell you how much I admire you for your courage in doing *Noah,* and I long to see it again."

But the last word on this weird adventure should perhaps go to Ivor Brown in *The Observer:* "Mr. Gielgud plays Noah as a six-hundred-year-old man with a prodigious mixture of Lear, Job, Tolstoy and the Old Man of the Sea."

Noah ran for only three months in a scorchingly hot summer that was an agony to the company, most of whom were heavily clothed. But thanks to Gielgud and Saint-Denis, an amazing collection of young actors was here able to play some of their earliest roles; among them were Jack Hawkins; Jessica Tandy, his future wife; Marius Goring and (heavily disguised as wolves and sheep) Alec Guinness and his future wife Merula Salaman; and playing the Lion was Harry Andrews and, as John commented, "obvious casting as a bear," George Devine.

It was Tyrone Guthrie who unfavorably contrasted this new production with the original by the Compagnie des Quinze: "The magic somehow disappeared; originally the production was like a glamorous but rather faded woman in a big shady hat and heaps of tulle. The Gielgud version was the same lady but now in a cold, hard north-east light, a raincoat and no hat."

As Irving Wardle was later to note, what this venture proved was that there was going to be no grand alliance between the director and the star: "For St-Denis, it was a compromised excursion into alien boulevard territory; for Gielgud, it was an instructive digression from his natural line of work. Temperamentally the two were as elementally opposed as earth and air. If Gielgud was a bird, St-Denis was his cage. So although the two men were pushing for similar reforms, they retreated to their separate centres of power and viewed each other's work with respect but from a distance in future."

Not content with being an actor, director, and (in all but name) designer, John now decided to try his hand as a playwright; he had for some time been interested in the idea of a stage version of Dickens's *A Tale of*

Two Cities, one which would allow John not only Sidney Carton's great guillotine speech about the "Far, far better thing," but also, in a typically Gielgud twist, the idea would be for him to double as the wicked Marquis de St. Evremonde. There were, however, initially two major problems. One was that the veteran Sir John Martin-Harvey, hearing of the plan, wrote Gielgud a sharp note to the effect that he was still on the road in his own version of the story, the long-running *The Only Way,* and would be therefore grateful if the young Gielgud would keep his hands off the property.

The second problem was that John was not, of course, really a dramatist at all, and for several months the project was also stalled by his simple inability to get on with it. Eventually, it was John Perry who thought of the solution. Terence Rattigan, a frequent weekend guest to whom they had both taken a considerable fancy, was a young dramatist looking for work, and he willingly went ahead unpaid with the actual writing of the adaptation while John began to engage himself in a still more ambitious project.

The success that he had as Hamlet on Shaftesbury Avenue, following as it did hard upon both the Shakespeare and the Gordon Daviot *Richard*s, clearly indicated that another glossy classic would be the obvious thing to do next. Ever since he had directed that first undergraduate *Romeo and Juliet* at Oxford, three years earlier with Peggy Ashcroft and Edith Evans, he had longed to direct them again in a professional production. He also now decided that rather than just play Romeo (as he had already done at the Old Vic and at the Coliseum), it might be rather more of a challenge to alternate Romeo and Mercutio with another star actor, night on, night off.

With this in mind, Gielgud approached one of his very few romantic rivals, Robert Donat, who had the characteristic grace to reply that he had in fact been planning his own *Romeo and Juliet;* this, he said, he was now willing to abandon in view of what he felt was Gielgud's innate superiority in Shakespeare, but he was still not prepared to alternate roles with John. It must have been the year of *Romeo* in 1935, because when John approached his second idea of a costar, Laurence Olivier, it turned out that he too had been planning a production to star himself and his first wife, Jill Esmond. Ivor Novello was also thought to be in the running.

Olivier was, however, unlike Donat, prepared to do the whole deal—he would abandon his own production and agree to alternate Romeo and Mercutio with John and, more important, under John's direction. There was still just one little calendar problem. John had already contracted to start making a film with Alfred Hitchcock, *The Secret Agent,* at the end of October, which left them by now barely three weeks to get *Romeo* up and running.

Again, John quickly resorted to the Motleys, who with their usual sense of theatrical economy even agreed to convert the sets they had designed for the currently abortive *Tale of Two Cities,* so that in some amazing way the scaffold for the guillotine now became Juliet's balcony. Always a great believer in relying on past strengths, he also repeated the scenic effect from *The Old Ladies* whereby a whole interior scene could be viewed by an audience through windows.

Because they were so tight for time, the production that brought together the two greatest stars of their century for the first and only time got off to an uncertain and rather scrambled start. Years later, Gielgud was to reflect: "Larry found me far too verse-conscious, an exhibitionist in my acting and directing Shakespeare . . . of course, he was a great exhibitionist himself, but in quite a different way—daring, flamboyant and iconoclastic." For his part, Olivier admitted that he was "constantly rebellious against John's power and gifts." The conflict was understandable enough; Gielgud was only three years older than Olivier, but at this time he was the most famous and respected classical actor in England. Olivier, who since his school days had wanted "to knock their bloody eyes out" with his acting, came from an altogether less theatrically privileged background. And although he, too, had already scored considerable hits at the Royal Court, in the West End, and on Broadway (in *Journey's End* and *The Rats of Norway* and *Private Lives,* as well as the controversial closet-homosexual *Green Bay Tree*), he still regarded himself as the defiant outsider: "I will show them, I will show them, I will show them . . . I'm going to be a simply smashing actor."

This was not in fact the first time that Olivier and Gielgud had worked together: Olivier had played the lover Bothwell in Gielgud's short-lived production of *Queen of Scots* in the previous year, but now, for the only time, they were face to face onstage, and the critics were less than enthusi-astic. For the first six weeks Olivier was to play Romeo with Gielgud as Mercutio, and though the reviews were excellent for Peggy Ashcroft, Edith Evans, and Gielgud, Olivier's notices were scathing about his "gabbling in-expertness" while many suggested that he had neither the lyrical voice nor the poetic diction required of a great Romeo.

Olivier's rage and depression at these reviews was such that he even threatened not to play the second night, a threat rapidly defused by Giel-gud. But Larry's ire was not assuaged by the knowledge that precisely those qualities he was being accused of lacking were the ones in which John most excelled, and in which he would soon be seen to advantage.

But nothing is ever that simple, and Olivier already had some influential admirers, not least the critic St. John Ervine who wrote in *The Observer:* "I have seen few sights so moving as the spectacle of Olivier's Romeo . . . an impetuous boy, struggling to be articulate. I think Shakespeare's eyes would have shone had he seen this Romeo, young, and ardent and full of clumsy grace." J. C. Trewin also noted that "Olivier almost sprang on the stage, and I can still remember the gasps of admiration around me in the theatre."

Most interestingly of all, those few American critics reviewing from London all recognized in Olivier the quality that was to ensure that in later years he, rather than Gielgud, had the majority of Broadway and Holly-wood hits. Unlike more traditional and conservative local audiences, the Americans recognized that Olivier was emotionally accessible and came across as a really passionate lover, in a way that Gielgud could never chal-lenge. As for their respective talents, it was a comparatively neutral ob-server, Alec Guinness, who as usual got it right from the sidelines: "Olivier did not have a bad way of reciting the verse; it was just a new and very dif-ferent way to the one which Gielgud had made his own."

"I wanted," recalled Olivier, "at that time to bring a new kind of 1930s re-ality and earthiness and immediacy to Shakespeare, regardless of the verse, but they all wanted still to hear it musically, and I felt that Johnnie was sim-ply encouraging old-fashioned attitudes."

Olivier, never the most generous of actors, husbands, fathers, or men, was unwilling ever to forgive Gielgud this early, albeit unintentional, victory over him. "John always had a preoccupation with the beautiful and the poetic at the expense of reality . . . he was always conscious of his gifts, of music and lyricism. At this time I was always the outsider, and John was always the jewel; everything and everybody was in his favour."

For his part, Gielgud was always saddened by Olivier's often overt enmity, but could never really understand it; Gielgud was above all a company man who (while not averse to stardom) took the view that the production mattered rather more than the performance, and there was, in his character, a genuine lack of envy or rivalry. Moreover, Shakespeare aside, Olivier and Gielgud were seldom up for the same roles, and although Gielgud certainly tired of endlessly being told that he was the best actor in the world from the neck up, and Olivier from the neck down, he genuinely wanted Olivier to succeed and always regretted his failures. The same could not be said in reverse, and indeed in Olivier's memoirs he cannot even bring himself to discuss Gielgud's performance, or his production, of their one great shared stage adventure.

In later years, their relationship was to become still more tortured for other reasons. Olivier was never at his best in the company of gay men, despite bizarre rumors of very brief backstage homosexual liaisons with the likes of Danny Kaye, and was nearly as quick as his definitive Richard III to believe that plots were being laid against him on all sides. In this instance, his second wife, Vivien Leigh, formed a near-lifelong attachment to Gielgud and would use him as a refuge and as a sounding board in the many bleak and black moments of that marriage. Olivier then decided, perhaps not entirely unnaturally, that not only was Gielgud a dangerous rival onstage, but that offstage he was threateningly close to his own troublesome and manic-depressive wife.

But these issues are never quite as clear-cut as they may seem; Laurence (Laurie) Evans, who was Olivier's production manager on the 1940s film of *Henry V,* and then for nearly thirty years agent to both Olivier and Gielgud, recalls that Gielgud, too, could behave somewhat treacherously on occasion: "I never saw evidence of Larry being in any way hostile to John, and he certainly had no problem with homosexuality, unlike Ralph Richardson, who until the 1970s always found John's private life a barrier to real friendship. When I later began negotiating for John, I found him often willing to go back on a deal, or to change his mind about playing a role when contracts were virtually signed. Larry, in my experience, never did that, and I think finally the truth is that Vivien [Leigh] loved John deeply, and that Larry didn't really feel that strongly about him either way."

When it came time for them to switch the roles, John was just about to start filming for Hitchcock, but he was already more than familiar with Romeo, and Olivier seemed much happier as the boisterous Mercutio, all dash and swagger, and gave what he himself later called "a really good music-hall performance." Indeed, his reviews now were the first really good ones he had ever received in Shakespeare, so good that while he was still playing the role, he was invited to star as Orlando in the film of *As You Like It*, thereby beating Gielgud to a Shakespearean film by fully twenty years.

This production of *Romeo and Juliet* broke all the play's box-office records by running at the New Theatre for 189 performances, and John was to recall happier times later in the run. "Peggy and Larry, Glen (Byam Shaw) and I were always visiting each other's dressing rooms or congregating in Edith's, which was the largest of them. She herself would sit in the middle of her sofa, dressed up in her voluminous padded garments as the Nurse, and wondering a little what sort of madhouse this was in which she had suddenly found herself."

Perhaps the best summary of the difference between the two leading men came in retrospect from the critic Herbert Farjeon: "As Romeo, Mr. Olivier was about twenty times as much in love with Peggy Ashcroft's Juliet as Mr. Gielgud was. But Mr. Gielgud spoke most of the poetry far better than Mr. Olivier. Yet, I must out with it, the fire of Mr. Olivier's passion carried the play along in a way that Mr. Gielgud's could never quite manage."

The American critic and broadcaster Alexander Woollcott wrote to John:

I came last night to your *Romeo and Juliet*. At intervals, I have been going to see that lovelorn, tear-stained piece since long before you were so much as contemplated. Some of my first Romeos are now either dead, or shuffling, toothless gaffers. Come to think of it, many of them were when they played it. In my country, what usually happens is that some lovely actress suddenly gets the uncontrollable impulse to play Juliet. There is vast publicity, a hasty assemblage of scenery, and then someone remembers at the last moment that they have to have a Romeo, so some unlucky passer-by is flagged into the stage door and plays it as though he obviously had not been expecting to be called upon. One calamitous revival here was assembled rather too hastily by Ethel Barrymore, at a time when she had a vast bust. The public stayed away in droves. Rows and rows of orchestra seats gaped from the dusk of the auditorium. But, as I cruelly observed at the time, the balcony was full.

John's first drama teacher, Lady Benson, who had started her career as Juliet to Henry Irving's Romeo, wrote, "For once the romance of the play came through perfectly. You are gifted with so beautiful a voice that the love notes are utterly charming. You are also unusually young in the part, and you deserve a high place in our theatre. I am so proud of having once taught you."

Surprisingly, not only was this the only time in their long and often parallel careers that Olivier was to work with Gielgud onstage, it was also the only time that Olivier would appear in a play with Peggy Ashcroft. Their London run was followed by a long and triumphant tour, but John began to notice a new problem with his own performance: "The curious thing is that, after you have played Hamlet, it is very hard to go back to Romeo, not only because he is supposed to be a boy of sixteen, which of course no actor ever manages, but also because the part is oddly badly placed within the play. The big banishment scene is inclined to go for nothing after Juliet with her Nurse, and the Apothecary scene, in which Irving was always said to have made his name, comes immediately after the lamentation over Juliet's body. Irving, it was said, always cut back Juliet and the Nurse as far as he dared, but in our day the fashion was for restoring all the cuts."

Intriguingly, some of Olivier's supporters in the great *Romeo* controversy were those who might temperamentally have been thought to side with Gielgud. Ralph Richardson wrote admiringly, "When Larry stood under the balcony you knew the whole character of Romeo in a moment, because the pose he took was so natural, so light, so animally correct that you just felt the whole quality of Italy, and of the character of Romeo, and of Shakespeare's impulse." The director Tyrone Guthrie added that it didn't matter if Olivier never got the measure of the verse, because his performance had such terrific vitality, speed and intelligence, gusto and muscularity.

In the end, this double production did nothing but good for most of its cast, even though it could be argued that Peggy Ashcroft and Edith Evans got rather short critical shrift, so eager were critics to compare and contrast the two men. But most important for Olivier, the word now spread that for the first time a real classical challenger had arrived on the Shakespearean scene to threaten Gielgud's hitherto undisputed lead; and Olivier himself grudgingly admitted, years later, that had it not been for Gielgud, he might never have become a classical actor. For him at least, the challenge was half the fun of the contest.

Ironically, John's newfound fame now meant another change in his private life: St. Martin's Lane had to be abandoned when too many autograph hunters simply moved camp from the stage doors across the road, and he took refuge in the comparative tranquillity of a flat in St. John's Wood.

9. Hamlet Goes to Broadway

(1935–1937)

By rights, I should have been thrilled with the offer to take my Hamlet to Broadway. But my usual feelings of despair soon took over; I was certain that I should be a failure, and, what's more, extremely sea-sick on the voyage to New York.

*N*o sooner had an uneasy truce been established between Olivier and Gielgud backstage at the New Theatre, with John G. safely back to his Romeo and Olivier cheerfully recast as the swashbuckling Mercutio, than John had to spend all his days honoring his commitment to act in a film for Alfred Hitchcock.

With the coming of talking pictures, the director had moved effortlessly from silents like *The Lodger* through semi-talkies like *Blackmail* to the full sound of *Rich and Strange,* and he was now riding high on the success of *The 39 Steps* (1935). Looking for another thriller in this genre, he decided to merge two of Somerset Maugham's Ashenden adventure stories, originally entitled *The Traitor* and *The Hairless Mexican.*

Hitchcock had also developed, in these last years before going to Hollywood, a tradition of using London stage actors as often as possible, because for them the coming of sound presented no terrors. Thus, for instance, he had already cast Robert Donat (and Peggy Ashcroft as the sinister crofter's wife) in his *The 39 Steps.* For what was now to be called *The*

Secret Agent, Hitch turned to John Gielgud, at the height of his Shakespearean fame, to play Ashenden himself, an intelligence agent who is assigned to Switzerland to kill a spy and by mistake kills an innocent tourist instead. Robert Young, later to achieve considerable Hollywood stardom, played the real spy, but the picture was swiftly hijacked from them both by Peter Lorre, already internationally famous as the child-murderer of Fritz Lang's *M* (1931), and now beginning to develop a line of neurotic villains that would see him safely through to the end of his Hollywood career, thirty years later.

Gielgud also had some small say in the casting of minor roles here, bringing in the director Michel Saint-Denis to play a bystander, and also the veteran Lady Tree, as well as one or two of the sword carriers from his Old Vic days. This is also the film in which Lilli Palmer makes her screen debut, albeit very fleetingly.

But John was deeply unhappy with the shooting, as he frequently told two old Westminster schoolfriends, the producer Ivor Montagu and the writer Angus McPhail, both of whom were also now gainfully employed by Gaumont-British Studios at the moment when the British film industry was entering one of its most active periods.

John's worries were that in the screenplay the character of Ashenden, complex and interesting in the Maugham stories, had been reduced to little more than a cipher. He was also terrified of his costar Madeleine Carroll, who was a creature of film and therefore unlike most of the actresses he knew, and moreover one of those ice maidens always adored by Hitchcock. To make things worse, he had to contend with Peter Lorre, also a film animal, and readily experienced in the art of stealing every scene in which he appeared. John's characteristically nervous attempts to befriend Lorre were not made any easier by the fact that after almost every scene they shared, Peter would rapidly vanish onto the studio lighting grid, there to inject himself with the morphine to which he had already become deeply addicted.

And Lorre wasn't his only problem, as John explained to an interviewer on the set:

The trouble is, that I don't know the first thing about film acting, although I've always been a terrific film fan. In the days when no respectable people ever went to the pictures, I used to go regularly to that little cinema in Windmill Street, just behind Shaftesbury Avenue, to see all the German and Russian silents. My real problem is that on the stage you are part of a big and rather remote picture, and your defects can be hidden under make-up. You seem much more attractive and heroic than you really are. But on the screen you've got no alibis—every detail is in close-up and the more make-up you wear, the more you emphasise your own defects. Of course, the money is a great inducement; I can make more in six weeks on a film than I can in eighteen months on the stage. Real screen actors, like Peter Lorre, can come out at any time and joke to their hearts' content, or even make up some dialogue to fill an awkward moment, but we stage actors are terribly bad at doing anything impromptu. And we are so used to three or more weeks' rehearsal that doing something just once, for a take, and knowing it might be on the screen forever, is really frightening.

But the stage is necessarily limited in scope, whereas film is so much more elastic. Can you imagine, for instance, how thrilled Shakespeare would have been if he could actually have filmed "the vasty fields of France," instead of having to apologise to his theatre audience for having nothing more than "this wooden O"? The problem with screen stories at present is that they are made by mass production, so the result is quantity but never quality. Meanwhile, our theatre is being sapped as both actors and writers go to Hollywood in search of better salaries. Producers over here only cast their artists from that very small group of us who have always played Shakespeare; surely they should now be looking at modern actors who may never have done it before, but might be much more interesting?

As for me, I have no wish to risk my stage Shakespearean reputation by appearing in what might be very unsatisfactory film versions of the same plays. I have occasionally had rather vague offers from

Hollywood, but it's a long way to go if you are not sure of being successful. For instance, I cannot see how anybody would ever manage to make a totally satisfactory film of *Hamlet*.

However wary John might have been about film, he was among the very first stage stars to welcome radio, where he now began to work regularly in new and classic dramas, all the time, of course, encouraged by his brother Val who, from the very early 1930s, had begun to carve out a notable career as the first great BBC radio drama director. Early in these 1930s John was frequently to be heard on the air in *Scenes from Shakespeare*, and then in 1932 he broadcast a two-hour *Othello*, with Peggy Ashcroft as Desdemona and Henry Ainley, one of John's greatest classical heroes, as Iago.

But then again, back at the film studios, Gielgud was not helped by Hitchcock deliberately making the villain (Robert Young) far more charming and amusing and attractive than the picture's moody and indecisive hero. Throughout the shooting, Gielgud was also made to feel thoroughly insecure by Hitchcock's usual chilliness on the set ("Actors are cattle," the director once said, "and should be treated as such") and the realization that with so many other stars around him, all of them more familiar with film, he was unlikely to make much of an impression: "I also had to lie for several days under iron girders and rubbish for the scene of a train wreck. Another day I sat for hours before a blank screen, while a short length of Lake Como was unrolled before me in 'back-projection' . . . a wonderful process, but utterly boring for actors to endure."

When the film *The Secret Agent* opened, audiences and critics alike were disconcerted by a thriller in which the villain (Robert Young) is so much more charming and cinematic than the apparent hero. Hitchcock himself later noted: "A comparative stranger to the screen, Gielgud was rather on the nervous side, but I think his performance is remarkable when you consider that throughout the whole production he was rushing away every evening to play in *Romeo and Juliet*—and declaiming Shakespeare on the stage is in direct contrast to playing such a matter-of-fact, natural part as that of Ashenden."

John's recollections of that time were mainly of sheer exhaustion:

"While playing on stage every night I had to get up at dawn, and then was always fidgeting by 5 or 6 about getting away for the evening performance, which was how I grew so to dislike acting for the screen. Of course, I was paid much more money than in the theatre, but I had the feeling that no one thought I was sufficiently good-looking to be very successful. Hitchcock was naturally inclined to give Madeleine Carroll the best advantage of the camera, while I was seen mostly from the back of my head—which fortunately in those days still had some hair on it . . . Hitchcock was a great joker, and I don't think he had much confidence in my talent as a film actor. When I saw the film I thought I was rather poor, but at least I was not over-acting as grotesquely as I had been in my three or four silents."

At the time, neither Gielgud nor Hitchcock were in fact as generous about each other as in subsequent interviews; on the set, Gielgud once said, "Hitchcock often makes me feel like a jelly, and I am sick with nervousness." Hitchcock responded, "John's stage experience is of absolutely no use to him here. I have had to make him rub out everything and start again from scratch."

Considering the tremendous success that another classical actor steeped in Shakespeare, Michael Redgrave, was to have in Hitchcock's *The Lady Vanishes* only two years later, there is no doubt that John missed an opportunity here; but so unhappy was the experience that he did not work in film again until 1940, and even then it was to be in the character role of Benjamin Disraeli.

As the filming of *The Secret Agent* and the London run of *Romeo and Juliet* were simultaneously coming to an end, in the late spring of 1936, John had a backstage visitor at the New Theatre, the American producer and director Guthrie McClintic, husband of the great American actress Katharine Cornell. Guthrie's idea was hugely welcome: that John should take his *Hamlet* to New York, with an otherwise all-Broadway supporting cast, among whom would be the Australian actress Judith Anderson, and as Ophelia, the great silent star Lillian Gish, whom Guthrie brought backstage with him.

As John remembers the encounter: "Lillian was enchantingly dressed in a summer frock with short sleeves, her fair hair crowned with a big white straw hat with black velvet ribbons. When I saw her, I remembered the advertisements that I used to scan so eagerly on the Piccadilly Underground in the old days of silent films—the backs of two little girls, both wearing straw hats with velvet ribbons, and a big question-mark with an intriguing caption underneath: 'Two Little Strangers About Whom All the World Will Soon Be Talking.' When I mentioned this to Lillian at the first meeting, she said that she had been afraid that I would think her too old now for Ophelia, and had dressed the part to make a good impression on me. I felt sure at once that I should enjoy acting with her."

But before he set off for the New World, John had two last commitments to honor: a return to Oxford to direct the OUDS in *Richard II,* and a production of *The Seagull* in which he would play Trigorin under the direction of Komisarjevsky. The Oxford Richard was to be David King-Wood, who had succeeded George Devine as president of the OUDS, and the Motleys were again to design the sets, but this college production was mainly notable for the young actress whom John imported (as he had Peggy Ashcroft and Edith Evans for *Romeo*) to play Richard's queen. She was Vivien Leigh, then just twenty-three and at the start of the affair with Laurence Olivier, which was to end both their first marriages and establish them as the starriest couple of the mid-century British stage and screen. This was also where John began a lifelong friendship with Vivien, one which was to outlive her Olivier marriage; like Robert Helpmann and Noël Coward, he was always to be there for Viv, even in the depths of her manic-depression.

This production was not as remarkable as John's 1932 OUDS *Romeo,* not least because Vivien, for all her considerable charm, was no Peggy Ashcroft, although Michael Denison, an undergraduate at the time, recalled Leigh descending on Oxford, "bringing ecstasy to those undergraduates whose invitations she accepted, and anguish to those whom, perforce, she had to refuse. It was in fact Glen Byam Shaw who did the donkey work of this production, while John, who was still alternating Romeo and Mercutio at the Vic, gave us all his Sundays and Mondays till mid-afternoon. What an introduction this was for me to the very best in the contemporary theatrical scene, and what a privilege to see such professionalism at work, and assess how far it all was from the carefree fun of the amateurs. My own share in this production was very small, a herald and two minor noblemen in unlikely beards, but I was sufficiently involved and exhilarated by all I saw around me to know that I need seek no further for a career."

The Times praised Vivien's stunning beauty, but thought her "ill at ease with Shakespearean verse," and even the student critic of Isis called her "no more than adequate." For John, the lasting memory of this production was his decision to cast Max Beerbohm's wife, the American actress Florence Kahn, as the Duchess of Gloucester: "She was a formidable lady, who played the Duchess with an old-fashioned declamatory passion. The unfortunate and very short young undergraduate who was playing John of Gaunt shrank back from her in dismay whenever she started to speak, and I can still see the incomparable Max, in the wings, shaking with disloyal but irrepressible mirth."

After these amateur shenanigans, John was able to return to the real theatrical world of The Seagull. He had been encouraged to take on the challenge of appearing in this, the first Chekhov ever performed in the West End, by having Komisarjevsky as designer as well as director, and by the granting of an unprecedented budget of a thousand pounds by their landlord and producer Bronson Albery, whom Komis referred to ever afterward as "that tradesman." Nor did the director endear himself to the cast, on the first day of rehearsal, by delivering a lengthy speech about the dreadful state of the English theater, with its appalling actors, so completely lacking in style compared to those he had known in Russia.

John, having already played Konstantin, was delighted now to be cast as the older Trigorin, with Stephen Haggard in his original role. He had also persuaded Komis to reassemble several of his Romeo company—Edith Evans would play Arkadina, and Peggy Ashcroft was to be Nina.

But this time the real triumph was to be Edith's. "She dressed the part," John remembered, "like a Parisienne, with a high, elegant coiffure, sweeping fashionable dresses, hats and scarves and parasols. On her first entrance she was all smiles and graciousness, but one could see from the angle of her head, as she sat with her back to the audience, watching Konstantin's play, that underneath all the sweetness she was a selfish woman in a very bad temper. Her performance was full of the most subtle touches of comedy, alternating with passages of romantic nostalgia."

Given John's lifelong devotion to Komisarjevsky, and the gathering once again of all his classical clan (Martita Hunt was Masha, George Devine the bailiff, and Alec Guinness the silent estate worker who operates Konstantin's curtain), this should have been a very happy production. Peggy Ashcroft, however, was already at the end of her brief marriage to Komisarjevsky, whose infidelity she found intolerable, and John knew that he could only play for the first six weeks because of his new American commitment to Guthrie McClintic.

Nevertheless, most reviews were ecstatic. *The Times* said, "This is the first time that Chekhov has been produced on the grand scale. And everything is *de luxe*. People may not want to see this play, but they will want to see this cast, one which achieves an atmosphere of brooding melancholy, alleviated by gleams of humour." Another critic wrote of "an exquisite exhibition of sensitive Gielgudry, his Trigorin pining after Nina as Dante did after Beatrice."

Bernard Shaw, however, remained deeply unimpressed: "I went to *The Seagull* and disliked it extremely... Komisar has lost his old Russian touch. He filled the last act with pauses of the sort that are only bearable in a first act when there is no hurry, and the audience is willing to speculate a little on dumb shows. And anyhow, the dumb shows were unintelligible and uninteresting. Somehow it is all a little too careful, too elaborate, too beautiful. There is no waywardness, no rawness, nothing that is not competent and controlled."

For John's faithful chronicler Audrey Williamson, however, "His Trigorin was remarkable, no longer the experienced seducer but a weak, impressionable character absorbed in his work, lazily acquiescent in his comfortable alliance with Arkadina, only to be jolted unexpectedly out of his groove by the fresh, abandoned intensity of Nina's flattering hero-worship. . . . Gielgud subtly suggested the man's cultivated distinction, weak vanity and consciousness of being torn apart by forces suddenly out-

side his own control. His speaking of Trigorin's explanation of the professional life of the writer seemed new-minted from the brain, and in the
scene where Arkadina persuades him not to leave her, a futile gesture of
the hand illuminated the man's whole tragedy—his Trigorin was always
clay in the hands of a stronger personality."

Soon after this, the ever restless Komisarjevsky went off to make a new
life in America where, years later in 1947, he would again direct John, this
time in *Crime and Punishment.*

The directors Margaret Webster and Gordon Craig wrote John ecstatic
letters about *The Seagull,* as did the actress Marie Tempest. As for Komisarjevsky, writing privately to John, "I saw many of the early productions of
The Seagull at the Moscow Art Theatre, and I can honestly say that yours is
by far the best Trigorin. We still need to make some improvements in the
pace, but when we have I think we will have achieved a perfect production,
and I feel very happy to have been associated with you again—this is not
flattery."

Komis was also eager to clear himself of critical charges that he had
made his production far too elegant: "What do English critics know? I saw
with my own eyes the original productions of the Moscow Art Theatre,
and they were always very beautiful." He was to comment rather more
waspishly to a friend, "Of course the trouble with John and Edith now is
that they are so famous they only want to play themselves."

Before starting to work on the Broadway *Hamlet,* John G. and John
Perry took a short holiday in the south of France. With, naturally, John
Perry driving, they went down toward Nice and rented an old farmhouse
with a vine-covered verandah and a swimming pool. There they were
joined by Guthrie McClintic and his Broadway designer, Jo Mielziner. John
was already eager to get as far away as possible from the memory of the last
great New York *Hamlet,* John Barrymore, and they settled for the idea of
scenery and costumes heavily influenced by Rembrandt.

John's holiday, however, was spoiled by the fact that he was already getting increasingly nervous about his first starring role in New York, especially because only Harry Andrews and Malcolm Keen were to join him in
what would otherwise be, apart from Judith Anderson, an all-American

cast. Keen had first played Claudius to John Barrymore's London Hamlet, and Harry Andrews was initially cast as Fortinbras, only to graduate to Horatio (and ten more dollars a week) when an American actor was fired early on.

John sailed over on the *Normandie* and was immediately interviewed on the New York dockside by an alarmingly large number of reporters, sent there by McClintic to drum up some early *Hamlet* bookings:

> They asked me at once what I thought of New York, and at the time of course, I had almost nothing to say. But looking back I am still stimulated by the unpredictable, electric liveliness of the city, despite the extremes of heat and cold, cramped taxis and sweltering buses, the squalor of the subways, the steam-heat and air-conditioning, the friendliness and politeness and occasional rudeness, the foreignness, mixed with familiarity. I love the brilliant qualities of the New York lights, from twinkling towers as they begin to glitter on Central Park South round six o'clock on a winter evening, and the strip of sky which one can always see in four directions, even from the deep canyons of the Avenues. The vista of Fifth Avenue from St. Patrick's Cathedral to the Plaza Hotel is to me one of the finest sights in the world. . . . American theatres dismayed me at first, with their extreme width of auditorium and shallow stages—no bars or proper lounges (save for those cavernous, over-heated cellars with queues lining up for the single telephone in the intervals) and the very disagreeable men who tear up one's ticket as one passes through the doors in the narrow entrance-halls.
>
> And yet, the sense of expectation in an American audience—especially at matinees when the women predominate, screaming and waving greetings across the aisles and wildly applauding every entrance and exit, song or dance—is wonderfully infectious and finally rewarding, both for actors and spectators alike, and infinitely preferable to the scene in London, where trays of tea are shuffled in and out over people's heads, and elderly ladies sit munching with dogged indifference, often slumbering and even snoring as the afternoon wears on.

Having appeared only once previously on Broadway (in the unsuccessful 1928 production *The Patriot*), John was delighted to be back eight years later in considerably starrier and more luxurious circumstances. There was just one little problem: Leslie Howard, already a far bigger star than John on that side of the Atlantic, had also suddenly announced a forthcoming *Hamlet*, and at first, John decided not to risk the competition. Howard had just filmed *Romeo and Juliet* opposite Norma Shearer (a role for which Gielgud had declined even to test, on the grounds that he could not leave the theater for Hollywood), and although the film had been disastrously reviewed by most critics, he had somehow managed to escape relatively unscathed, not least because he had already established a strong Broadway career apart from such hit movies as *Of Human Bondage, The Scarlet Pimpernel,* and *The Petrified Forest.* Although the son of Hungarian immigrants, Howard was now known to stage and screen audiences on both sides of the Atlantic as the perfect English gentleman, and his profile was, even more than John's, classically well suited to the noble prince.

But Gielgud was eventually persuaded by McClintic that Howard could still be successfully challenged when it came to Shakespearean intellect, knowledge, and verse-speaking, and the reckoning was that the supposed rivalry might even be very good news at the box office in terms of publicity. For a while, it looked as though Howard was going to withdraw from the race, but like John he was eventually persuaded by his managers to take up the challenge, especially as there had not been a notable *Hamlet* in America since that of the great John Barrymore almost a decade earlier.

To calm John's considerable nervousness, McClintic had agreed to open their *Hamlet* in Toronto, thereby allowing Gielgud to start somewhere safely removed from the New York critics. As so often with John, however, the first rehearsals had been something of a disaster. The formidable Judith Anderson, playing Gertrude, had gone to considerable trouble to have her hair elaborately dyed and styled for the role. "Why not just wear a wig?" asked John, with his usual tact. "It would look so much better, and be a lot less trouble."

He spent the rest of the rehearsals desperately trying not to put his foot in his mouth again as usual, and trying to adjust his performance until it matched those of the others who were, of course, considerably less experienced. There was also, as usual, the problem of John's fencing; he was arguably, and by his own admission, the worst fencer ever to play Shakespeare, and in London he had already managed to wound, quite seriously, Glen Byam Shaw in *Hamlet,* and Geoffrey Toone in *Romeo and Juliet.* In America, he was unwisely entrusted with a real Elizabethan sword, though on this occasion—for a change—it was he who sustained a nasty gash in his arm, thereby missing three or four days of rehearsal.

Despite such setbacks, however, the Toronto tryout, in a climate far colder than any John had ever known, was hugely successful, and it was here that the American critic Rosamund Gilder, longtime editor of the great *American Theatre Arts* magazine, first started to make the backstage notes that were to result in an entire book called *John Gielgud's Hamlet,* the first and almost the last of its kind ever to be entirely devoted to a single production. Published in 1937 by the Oxford University Press, it takes us scene by scene through the play, describing, in the most intimate and informed and intelligent and intricate detail, precisely where John stood on the stage at any moment, and exactly how he delivered the text. It is, perhaps, the most remarkably detailed account of any one actor in any one role that has ever been published, and John himself added a lengthy, scholarly essay on the history of the play, commenting on other Hamlets that he had himself seen (such as those of Raymond Massey and Laurence Olivier), as well as delving back into his beloved theater history to quote everyone from Sarah Bernhardt to Henry Irving on the trials and tribulations of this, the greatest of all classical roles.

It is, of course, to be regretted that (though unsurprising in 1936) no film or radio record of this production was ever made, but the book, though shamefully out of print these many years, has detailed drawings and photographs, not just of the actors, but also of the sets and costumes, and remains the most minutely detailed and descriptive account ever written of John at work. To read it is, even now, to come as close as has ever been possible to watching John at the height of his Shakespearean powers.

Another insight into John's character and spirit at this time comes from a series of long letters, hitherto unpublished, which he wrote from Canada to his mother, back in London:

> We had two dress rehearsals on Tuesday, with the usual hitches and disasters because the scenery was not ready . . . however the first night went very well, but last night I played abominably—bad anti-climax and exhausting in consequence. It is very difficult to judge the production now it is finished; I hate a lot of it, especially as they have no music at all. The Polonius is poor, and the Rosencrantz and Guildenstern rotten, Horatio only so-so, and the Sentinels and Fortinbras really terrible. This makes it all the harder for me, and what is maddening is that I know if I was the director, and had a few hours with them, I could bully them all into giving me something of what I want . . . outwardly I remain enthusiastic about everything and everybody, so that when I want my own way desperately about some scene, they all agree with a good grace. When McClintic has good actors (Gish, Anderson, and even old Malcolm Keen) he does very well by them, but of course the rest are cheap and inexperienced, and he hasn't the knowledge or experience to teach them how to speak Shakespeare . . . Toronto is a one-horse town, rather like the ones we used to see in early films; I keep expecting cowboys to ride past the theatre shooting their guns.

While they were still in Toronto, Leslie Howard opened his production in Boston, but as he had opted for a longer tour, it was John who, by six weeks, was the first to open as Hamlet in New York. A decade or so earlier, John had in fact been briefly employed in London to understudy Howard in a revival of *Berkeley Square*, for which he never had to go on, but now the two men were locked into what Broadway theater columns eagerly called "The Battle of the Hamlets," and John was only mildly amused to find cab drivers asking him, "So, which Hamlet are you, buddy?"

Contrary to popular belief, John did not open to universally good reviews. Noël Coward led the cheers of the audience at a very elegant first night, but the following morning the two most important papers at the time, *The New York Times* and *The Herald Tribune,* were surprisingly cool. McClintic had gone for a very traditional production, but John's view of the minor casting was less than flattering: "They all seemed cheap and rather inexperienced, and I hadn't the heart to try and teach them how to do it. It would have made me seem so arrogant and English." Nearly twenty years later, he was to make the same mistake during the filming of *Julius Caesar,* when, although James Mason and Marlon Brando begged him to share his expertise, he was again too shy and embarrassed to do so for fear of seeming better at it than they were, which, of course, in this instance he was.

The word of mouth was initially much better than many of the *Hamlet* reviews; but it wasn't until Howard opened to a catastrophic press six weeks later that John's supremacy and success were finally confirmed, and he was seen to have won the battle. Indeed, at Christmas they even had to move from the Empire to a larger theater (the St. James) to accommodate the crowds of people who were by now trying to get in. Old friends over from London and new friends from New York thronged to John's dressing room every night, among them Emlyn Williams, then also working on Broadway, and Mrs. Patrick Campbell, who sent round a note before the performance reading, "I am in front tonight. Give me the beauty I long for!" She was not, however, hugely impressed by the closet scene. As she told a somewhat abashed Judith Anderson, "A great mistake to sit on the bed, dear. Only housemaids sit on beds."

Comparing the two productions, the critic John Mason Brown felt that Howard had a better set, but that "unlike Mr. Gielgud's, Mr. Howard's performance can scarcely be described as an interpretation—it avoids what lies behind the lines, where Mr. Gielgud is always eager to let us see everything."

Gielgud was now the toast of the town; Alexander Woollcott, who had given up his high-rated radio show a couple of years earlier, went back on the air for one night, expressly to enthuse about John, and other backstage visitors now included the Lunts, Helen Hayes, Ruth Gordon, Katharine Cornell, Burgess Meredith, and the playwright Thornton Wilder (*Our*

Family Album, 1912: Kate Gielgud with her four children, Lewis (standing), Val (right), John and Eleanor (seated). *(Private collection)*

John feeding the chickens, 1907. *(Private collection)*

With his sister, Eleanor, in family charades, 1912. *(Private collection)*

The four Gielgud children with their father, Frank, and Lewis now in World War One uniform, 1915. *(Private collection)*

John's cousin, Edward Gordon Craig, son of Ellen Terry, circa 1889. *(Hulton Getty)*

John's great-aunt, Ellen Terry, circa 1870, one of the English theater's legendary leading ladies. *(H.S. Mendelssohn/Hulton Getty Images)*

John, age nine, at home in Little-hampton, 1913. *(Hulton Getty)*

John in *The Insect Play,* Regent Theatre, 1923. *(Mander & Mitchenson Theatre Collection)*

John with Gwen Ffrangcon-Davies in *Romeo and Juliet,* 1924. *(Sasha/Hulton Getty Images)*

An early publicity photograph, 1928. *(Sasha/Hulton Getty Images)*

John as *Richard II*, 1929. *(Gordon Anthony/Hulton Getty Images)*

John donning makeup for the role of Prospero in the Old Vic's opening performance of *The Tempest*, 1930. *(Sasha/Hulton Getty Images)*

With Adele Dixon in the West End production of J. B. Priestley's *The Good Companions. (Mander & Mitchenson Theatre Collection)*

With Jessie Matthews in the film *The Good Companions. (The Kobal Collection)*

Laurence Oliver as Romeo, Edith Evans as the nurse, and John as Mercutio in *Romeo and Juliet*, 1935. *(Mander & Mitchenson Theater Collection)*

With Madeleine Carroll in *Secret Agent*. (*The Kobal Collection*)

John, Alfred Hitchcock, and Peter Lorre; a moment of apparent levity on the set of *Secret Agent,* 1936. (*The Kobal Collection*)

FOLLOWING PAGE

With Gwen Ffrangcon-Davies and Edith Evans in the 1939 revival of *The Importance of Being Earnest*. (*Mander & Mitchenson Theatre Collection*)

John with Judith Anderson in the New York production of *Hamlet,* 1936. (*Mander & Mitchenson Theatre Collection*)

As Will Dearth in *Dear Brutus* at the Globe Theatre, 1941. (*Gordon Anthony/Hulton Getty Images*)

As King Lear in the 1940 Old Vic production. (*Mander & Mitchenson Theatre Collection*)

John as Othello, with Ian Bannen as Iago, at Stratford-upon-Avon, 1961. *(Pix Inc./ TimePix)*

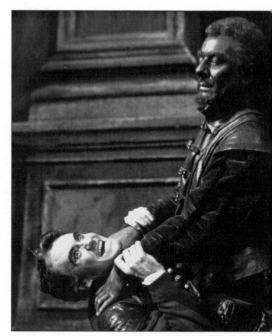

As Valentine in *Love for Love*, 1943. *(Hans Oswald Wild/TimePix)*

John with Peggy Ashcroft in *Much Ado About Nothing*, 1950. *(Mander & Mitchenson Theatre Collection)*

Town), whom John memorably described as "a funny, little, nervous man, like a dentist turned professor, shy at first and then suddenly incoherently explosive, like a soda siphon." Thirty years later the two men were to have one of their rare disasters, when John played Julius Caesar in Wilder's *The Ides of March*, which closed embarrassingly rapidly at the Haymarket in London.

John had never known celebrity like this: the crowds at the stage door, the hundreds of fan letters, and the applause whenever he went into a restaurant were something quite new to an actor who, in London, was already in some danger of being taken for granted. In New York he was not only the new boy in town, but also the greatest Shakespearean performer since Barrymore. As John wrote to his mother: "It is all very exhausting, but immensely gratifying. We are playing to new house records of $21,000 a week, and sometimes we have three hundred people standing, even at the matinees. I have had countless messages and backstage visitors—Mrs. Pat, Helen Hayes, Stravinsky, Gloria Swanson, Dorothy Parker and Elsa Maxwell. Helen Hayes told Mrs. Pat in my dressing room that she wore her years like a crown, a compliment Mrs. Pat as usual spoiled by asking, 'Is it on straight, dear?' I have really seen very little of New York, as whenever I am not playing I am trying to help Rosamund Gilder with her book which will, I think, be a really detailed account of my performance. . . .

"I see a lot of Emlyn (who is also playing here), with his wife and an enchanting new baby. Our flats, or apartments as they call them, all seem rather big and dark, but I keep being taken out to lunch, the other day by Maxwell Anderson, one of their most important authors out here, who wants me to do his new play about Rudolph of Austria; but it's all written in ponderous blank verse, so I am going to turn it down. The weather here is loathsome—warm and muggy and torrents of rain, and although I am longing for John P. to come for Christmas I am already afraid of how homesick I shall feel when he leaves. Harry Andrews and I are both beginning to feel that we can't wait to come home, and in our spare time we have had to nurse Peggy through a very difficult first night."

Ashcroft was making her Broadway debut in Maxwell Anderson's *High Tor*, in which she was cast as a three-hundred-year-old Dutch ghost called

Lisa, engaged in a somewhat tenuous love affair with a young landowner on a rock above the Hudson River. Peggy, characteristically, had started an immediate and tempestuous affair with her costar Burgess Meredith, who later idly wondered whether, had he married her, he could have had a totally different career in the British theater as "Sir Burgess." He was, however, at this time married to Paulette Goddard, and in order to keep their affair secret, Peggy took care to be photographed more often with John G. than with her new lover. Apart from these romantic complications, she was also just getting her divorce from Komisarjevsky, but nights on the town with John led at least one New York showbiz columnist to announce that Gielgud was himself about to marry Ashcroft.

This caused considerable surprise, not only to them, but also to Lilian Baylis, their Old Vic mentor back in London: "I could not be more surprised," declared Baylis, "than if Oxford won the Boat Race."

Perhaps trying to dampen any hopes his parents might have had in this area, John's letters home dealt only with Peggy's health, and that of his parents:

You don't say anything in your letters about how you are—I do hope you and father are taking care of yourselves. Last weekend Peggy and I went to stay with the McClintics in their wonderful country house—in front of a log fire with the rain pouring down outside, we listened to the news from Europe about the Spanish situation [the Civil War], which nobody here, including me, seems to understand. I miss all the news from London, and have had to give up smoking and drinking as I have an awful cold, but I have been offered $1,000 to do a speech from *Hamlet* on the *Rudy Vallee Radio Hour*, all made up and dressed, in front of a studio audience, so naturally I turned it down. I hear, however, that Reggie Gardiner is doing a parody of me as Hamlet in the new Bea Lillie revue, and they tell me that is a sure sign that I have arrived. Poor Leslie Howard is really having a terrible time, one critic said he was "more an antique Romeo than a Dane," and another said that I could cross the Giel out of my name and just be known as the "Gud Hamlet." The trouble is that I have so many English friends in his cast, that I suspect I may become very unpopular with them.

Whatever potential embarrassments this may have set in train, Gielgud was to recall two mortifying backstage visits that actually occurred during his run. The first came when Maria Ouspenskaya, the great Russian tragedienne who was now making a late-life Hollywood success, was announced at the stage door.

She came into the dressing room, a formidable and striking personality with a long cigarette holder in her hand, looking immensely distinguished and escorted by an elegant young man who leaned gracefully against the wall behind her. "Oh, Madame Ouspenskaya," I burst out, clutching my dressing gown around me and wondering if I ought to kiss her hand, "I am so sorry to think that you were in front tonight. I was dreadfully tired and I know I played so badly." At this, Madame nodded her head twice, in profound agreement, turned around and left the room without a word.

On another evening, Judith Anderson brought a friend of hers round to see me, a Swedish countess beautifully bejewelled and dressed. She seemed greatly moved by my performance, and as she was leaving, murmured, "I would like to give you something in remembrance of this great experience." At that, putting out her hand, she began to take off a most beautiful square-cut emerald ring that she was wearing. I, nervously, began to put out my own hand, but just as I did so, she hastily drew her ring back onto her finger and made a graceful exit.

Several local hostesses and theater groups tried to bring Gielgud and Howard together while they were on Broadway, but they both behaved with admirable discretion, declining to see each other's productions and merely exchanging courteous first-night telegrams. Howard closed his

Hamlet as soon as he decently could, as John wrote to his mother: "Leslie Howard closed his *Hamlet* last night with his usual twenty-minute speech at the end, denouncing his critics. He has bluffed very cleverly, and appeared a great deal on the radio, and giving club lectures, which I am refusing to do. He has not been especially dignified over his failure, and I am glad to have avoided meeting him, though some people say he crept in to one of our matinees wearing dark glasses."

By contrast, on January 5, 1937, John broke the Barrymore record of 101 performances, to become the all-time longest-running Broadway *Hamlet*. On that night, for the very first time, he made a curtain speech. That record was to stand until 1964, when it was in its turn broken by Richard Burton, ironically in a production of which John was both the director and the Ghost. Gielgud himself was not to give up the role until well into World War II, and when he returned to London in 1937 to find Olivier playing it at the Vic, he went backstage to offer not only polite congratulations but also the sharp warning that "This is still *my* role."

At the end of the New York run, McClintic was eager to make some more money on the road, and John agreed to a brief tour, which took him to Washington, where they played before the president's wife, Mrs. Eleanor Roosevelt, who seemed, thought John, "gracious, if a bit vague—a very plain, keen-faced woman with a rather grating laugh." On the road as in New York, Gielgud was getting almost a hundred fan letters every week, but one in Washington must have been especially welcome. It came from an old Catholic priest, Father Dawson Byrne: "Before becoming a priest, I was an actor for more than forty years, playing over three hundred productions, all over America. In that time I played with many great actors and saw the best of them—Henry Irving, Tree, E. H. Sothern and John Barrymore. But never had I seen a real Hamlet until I saw yours this week. You were made for the part. You are ideal, and your acting excels all others. You are still very young, and I have in my mind the thought that Ellen Terry must have trained you from your infancy to play Hamlet, otherwise I cannot see how you could give such a reading of the part, but I advise you to take great care of your health: you put so much energy and emotion into the role that it must leave you totally exhausted. Thank you for the best performance of my long life."

The broadcaster Albert Payson Terhune wrote: "My Hamlet memories go back to Edwin Booth, whom I often saw in the role. He played it with almost no make-up and wearing his own hair. Irving's Hamlet was more mannered and less tremendous than Booth's, although Irving's Shylock was infinitely better. Since then I have seen them all—Tree's, played in a yellow wig and beard, Sarah Bernhardt's, which was ghastly except in her scenes with Polonius, Barrymore's, Sothern's and Walter Hampden's. If a tired old man may say so without fulsomeness, yours turns all of theirs to water."

Following this extraordinary reaction to his interpretation of Shakespeare, John suggested to McClintic that, after their triumph in *Hamlet*, it might be clever to go on to the *Richard II*, which he had already made his own in London. McClintic was horrified: "A pansy King will never go down well in America," was his brief reply, before urging John to continue the *Hamlet* tour. It was Maurice Evans who made his name on Broadway with *Richard II*, and John, on his way home, crept into the back of the New York theater feeling somewhat embittered as the cheering began to ring out.

In another of John's weekly letters home to his mother at this time, he wrote:

In what little spare time I have, I am reading a very technical but fascinating new book about acting by Stanislavsky. Like Komis and Michel [St Denis] and of course Uncle Ted [Gordon Craig], he really is trying to revolutionise the theatre, and I feel very proud that in some way I have been able to associate myself with what they are all attempting.

Yesterday I had lunch with Mrs. Pat, who is, I fear, now very mad, living in Hollywood most of the time but grand and majestic as ever, and of course quarrelling with everyone as usual. Aleck Woollcott told me that she was like a sinking ship, firing on all her rescuers, which I thought very good. Everyone here is getting very hysterical about the Abdication crisis. I took Mrs. Pat to see the Laughton film of *Rembrandt* on Friday, and afterwards we went to the Plaza Hotel and heard the King's farewell broadcast very distinctly. Mrs. Pat kept saying it reminded her of *Antony and Cleopatra* but I just feel so sorry for the man and wonder what kind of life he will be able to lead. His frankness and obvious sincerity play very well over here, and it is a pity that the old men of the Church and State will now be crowing over their triumph. No wonder Edward was made bitter and cynical after going through the War and then finding that nothing had really changed. I don't think this business will send anyone flocking back to the Church.

Toward the end of the Broadway run, there had been some good news from home. John's agent had been attempting to sue Gaumont-British for an outstanding but disputed £500 in his contract for *The Secret Agent,* and the studio now settled out of court. When John heard of this, he wrote to his mother:

This was an unexpected pleasure, so in a fit of extravagance I went out and bought a charming water-colour for myself by Dufy for £300. It is the square at Versailles, with the Roi Soleil on his horse in the foreground, and looks so well in my rented room. Dufy is thought a lot of just now, and his pictures are all the rage.

A fat pianist called Copland, who looks like James Agate and plays Spanish music, gave a very good performance for me at a dinner party which had been especially arranged in my honour. On Sunday night there was another dinner in my honour at the Players' Club— delightful telegrams from Barrymore and Forbes-Robertson and wonderful speeches about me from the British consul and Maurice Evans and Cedric Hardwicke. It really was all very moving, and I wish you could have been here to see the love and respect in which they all hold our family. They really are mad about the British theatre, and seem to know as much about it as we do. John Barbirolli was also there, a nice little man, much thrilled by working with American orchestras.

I have at last got rid of all my colds and am just beginning, now it [is] almost time to leave, to appreciate New York—bridges, river, skyscrapers and sky just like the ones we have all seen in films. It is funny to meet film stars like Ruth Chatterton and Kay Francis in the flesh, though they are never as interesting as in their films. Mrs. Pat came again to the play last night, and wanted to know afterwards why Hamlet had a Jewish mother with her bosoms falling out, which I don't think would have pleased Judith Anderson. I am sending you some photographs, which I hope give you some idea of the set and costumes.

This newfound, if rather belated, discovery of Manhattan social life led him to use his usually buried skills as a pianist to entertain fellow partygoers—something one associates more with Noël Coward than with John G. "Just before we closed in New York, Elsa Maxwell, the famous cosmopolitan party queen, gave a party—I went there and played jazz till nearly 3 am, by which time my thumbs were nearly scraped off. It was a thoroughly bizarre affair—we were told to come in barnyard fancy dress, and they had real animals, cows, sheep and goats, in cages around the ballroom. At midnight, six hogs rushed into the room, but I found it all rather unedifying."

John was present when Coward played the piano on another occasion, but didn't enjoy that much, either. He was luckier with Noël's stage partner, Gertrude Lawrence, who was appearing with him on Broadway in the nine plays that made up Coward's *Tonight at 8:30:* "I went to see Noël doing one of his midnight cabarets, but they were all songs I had heard before. On one spectacular night last week, for a charity pageant, Gertie Lawrence appeared as Day and I as Night, she on a white horse and I on a black. Amazingly, they behaved very well, and I just about managed not to fall off."

John had an ambivalent approach to the festive season around Broadway, again best expressed in his letters home:

Christmas here was very strange and wonderful—the city very gay and pretty, but absurdly warm, like late Spring. I have never seen such decorations—laurel wreaths with red ribbons on every door, and dozens of lighted Christmas trees in the windows of restaurants, hotels and churches. . . . I can hardly move in my flat or dressing room for the cards, flowers and presents—I shall need a crate to bring them all home, especially as I have been buying lots of records and books. This afternoon, Mrs. Pat took me to see Edward Sheldon, who wrote one or two famous American plays before being stricken with blindness and an appalling, petrifying paralysis. All the well-known stage people go to see him and act scenes from plays for him. He lies on a bed like a catafalque, his head bent right back, unable to move his limbs, a black bandage over his eyes. But he is beautifully shaved, wears a collar and tie, and talks to you with consummate ease and charm, as if he had known you all your life. He has all the papers read to him, and knows everything about Broadway, he is entirely composed, alive, and yet removed from life, like some extraordinary human oracle. Though the spectacle is so painful and appalling, when you think of the incredible courage of it afterwards, the man himself is so magnificently powerful in his conquest that one longs to give him all the life and vitality he craves, and accept his philosophy and wisdom with wonder and awe. Like Mrs. Pat, Helen Hayes, Kit Cornell and the others, I am going to read Shakespeare to him, as that seems to be what he likes best.

New Year's Eve, on the other hand, was perfectly horrible. Our theatre is on the main Broadway street, and the hooters and penny whistles began almost as soon as we were under way, and never stopped all evening—not a pleasant accompaniment for *Hamlet*. I have, however, survived very well, the only one of my company not to get flu. Yesterday Lillian Gish took me out to Helen Hayes's country place at Nyack. An amazing house with gold-encrusted pelmets, marble fireplaces and an extraordinary number of Renoirs and Vlamincks and Chiricos.

More positively, John was by now being inundated with offers to go to Hollywood at the height of the period when English actors were most in demand out there, not least for their voices and their ability to play something other than cowboys or criminals. But his experience with Hitchcock had so discouraged his hopes of ever becoming a film star anywhere that John swiftly ended the *Hamlet* tour and returned to London, there to direct and star in a brand new play, written especially for him by Emlyn Williams. Somewhat unfortunately for modern sensibilities, and considering the private lives of its two leading figures, it was to be called *He Was Born Gay*.

10. GIELGUD AND COMPANY

(1937–1938)

My experiences at the Old Vic had already made me a firm believer in the importance of a permanent company. The only question in my mind was whether I could make it work commercially in the West End.

*H*e Was Born Gay dramatized the tragedy of the "lost" son of Louis XVI, supposedly brought up in England following the French Revolution, only to come out of hiding at the time of Waterloo, whereupon, disguised as a music teacher, he finds two other men claiming to be him, both determined to prevent his return to a reborn Royalist France. John and Emlyn Williams codirected, with John appearing as the real Dauphin, and Emlyn as one of the impostors. In rehearsal, and even on the road, the project looked promising enough, but when it came in to the Queen's Theatre it ran up against some savage notices, not least from Charles Morgan on *The Times,* who reviewed it with "an embarrassed, incredulous and uncomprehending blush. What made Mr. Williams write this play, or Mr. Gielgud play it, will never be understood."

He Was Born Gay survived only twelve West End performances, and later Emlyn worked out what had gone so wrong: "I had meant it to be the study of a romantic, historical personage in very ordinary circumstances, but he remained a character of tragedy, both vague and unconvincing, while the people around him seemed to have stepped out of a modern farce."

John took the play's failure very hard, coming as it had so swiftly after the greatest triumph of his life with the Broadway *Hamlet*. In fact, the flop made him reconsider his whole career. He was now just thirty-three and could be said to have achieved his initial ambition; he was beyond doubt the leading classical actor of his generation, and nothing that Olivier was doing at the Vic had really threatened his leadership. But, with that leadership, there now came real problems; as Olivier and Redgrave and Richardson, his only real challengers, all began at relatively early ages to sign lucrative long-term film contracts with Alexander Korda, John remained convinced that option remained closed to him. What he wanted was quite simply to continue in stage classics, because his own experience with new plays, from *He Was Born Gay* back to *The Old Ladies* and *Noah,* had been far from happy.

On the other hand, the classics at this time were really only available to him if he returned to the Old Vic. And although money for himself was never an issue, he was painfully aware that the Waterloo Road budget would never allow him the freedom to develop his Shakespearean ideas any further. Like a student leaving college, Gielgud had now graduated from the Old Vic, and there was to be no going home.

In his private life, the relationship with John Perry, although still comfortable, had begun to lose any real sexual energy, and in his professional life he had reached a point where he had simply run out of mentors. With Gordon Craig maintaining a chilly distance because he was somehow disconcerted that John, rather than himself, had become the star of the family, and Komisarjevsky now living in America, the great radical gurus of his earlier years had begun to fall away, and John was now too established to need the help of his original Old Vic teachers. At this precise moment, he wrote to Harley Granville-Barker, now living and teaching in America but still the man who, with Bernard Shaw, had first revolutionized the Royal Court, asking essentially how he could move not only his career but the whole idea of classical theater forward in London.

Granville-Barker's characteristically thoughtful reply served to clarify at least some of the issues that John had raised:

You are distracted by rival aims; one, which is really forced on you, has to do with your personal career; the other has to do with the establishing of the kind of theatre without which your career will not be all you proudly wish it to be. This was Irving's dilemma; he clung on to one horn of it for many glorious years, then he was impaled on the other and it killed him. Beerbohm Tree would have died bankrupt had it not been for *Chu Chin Chow.* George Alexander felt that all he had achieved was paying salaries every Friday night without fail. The question is now, have times changed? Could you hope to establish, if not a blessed National Theatre (names mean nothing), at least a company like that of Stanislavsky or even Max Reinhardt? Could there be some kind of compromise? Everyone in England always likes this, just because they are English. All I can really tell you is this: don't expect to pick more than a few grapes from the thistles, and don't expect them always to be of the best quality.

While taking Barker's rather gloomy advice to heart, John realized now that if he was, with the Motleys, to progress with his ideas as a director and play the rest of the great roles in the canon, he would have to form his own company on Shaftesbury Avenue. Accustomed as we now have become to forty years of the National Theatre and the Royal Shakespeare Company, it is almost impossible to conceive how revolutionary John's idea was for the West End of 1937, where there had simply been nothing like it since the heyday of Henry Irving and the actor-managers more than fifty years earlier. Certainly there had been, in the interim, modern companies run in their own theaters by the likes of Gerald du Maurier and Gladys Cooper; but these had seldom if ever focused on any kind of a classical repertoire, and the general feeling in the late thirties was that this kind of highbrow thing was best left to occasional London visits by La Comédie-Française from Paris.

The first issue to be resolved was that of the National Theatre itself. At the turn of the century, a publisher called Effingham Wilson had begun to campaign for such a building, and several foundation stones had already

been laid in various parts of West London, without, unfortunately, anything above them. In June 1937, Leon Quartermaine, who was to join
John's first permanent company, had written urging him to open a National Theatre as "the only member of our profession who could possibly
do so." But that was easier said than done, and it was in fact to be almost
another forty years before Olivier finally realized the dream. In the meantime, John published in *The Daily Telegraph* a kind of manifesto. "Britain's
National Theatre," he wrote, "should not waste money on a vast new building; it should not limit itself to just Shakespeare and popular hits, and,
thirdly, it should unite Sadler's Wells, the Old Vic, and the Stratford
Memorial Theatre as interchangeable companies, all of whom would form
a part of the National."

Surprisingly, there was already a National Theatre committee, made up
of the great and the good, but as usual without many actual artists. This
committee, which had so far failed to raise any kind of a budget or a building, now saw John as an awkward, external troublemaker and published a
reply demanding that the first priority should indeed be the building of a
"Temple of Drama."

At that point the whole matter was returned to limbo and, seeing no action there, John decided to invest £5,000 of his own money, virtually all his
New York profits from *Hamlet,* and another £5,000 of John Perry's family
legacy in forming a company that would present four classical plays at the
Queen's Theatre, each to be given an unprecedented seven to nine weeks of
rehearsal. Peggy Ashcroft, with whom John had formed a firm offstage
friendship the previous winter in New York, was to be the leading lady.
Around them both, Gielgud managed to build a company of amazing
strength, consisting largely of people with whom he had already worked,
and in some cases those he had actually discovered.

Alec Guinness was to be among them, and George Devine, Glen Byam
Shaw, Harry Andrews, the young Michael Redgrave, and Dennis Price;
John was also careful once again to include such comparatively veteran tal-
ents as those of Harcourt Williams and George Howe, and the budget
would even allow for "guest stars" such as Glen's wife Angela Baddeley and
Gwen Ffrangcon-Davies to come in for one production only.

Having established his team, John decided they should play it safe by opening with *Richard II*, though this was to be followed by *The School for Scandal*, *The Three Sisters*, and *The Merchant of Venice*. Rehearsals got off to a traditionally uneasy start when John was reminiscing about his triumphant New York *Hamlet* to the new company: "Of course, I had a really terrible Horatio . . . Oh, it was you, Harry, isn't it wonderful how much better you've got since?" As Andrews had barely had time to come home, unpack, and start with the new company, he was perhaps less than thrilled with Gielgud's attempted retrieval of yet another brick.

But there was now a great deal more at stake than just another opening of another Shakespearean show. John was betting his savings, and his reputation, on an ensemble the likes of which had simply never been seen in the West End in the twentieth century. Each production was to run for between eight and ten weeks, and the team of geniuses was to include not only Gielgud himself but also Tyrone Guthrie and Michel Saint-Denis, both of whom had already established their reputations as among the most adventurous and unpredictable directors in town. What the critic Harold Hobson was to call "One of the rarest blazes of theatrical light this century," started with Peggy Ashcroft ("the Spring Queen of her time," as Anthony Quayle said) playing the Queen to John's Richard. And although he was the producer of this first production, as well as director and star, he was now determined, because of his company ethic, to make this revival very different from the usual solo-star show that it had been when he previously played the role in both its Shakespeare and Gordon Daviot interpretations.

Thus Michael Redgrave, who had only recently come into the theater from being a public schoolmaster, was encouraged to prove a formidable Bolingbroke: "I felt proud to be a member of such a company; Gielgud himself was only three or four years my senior, but he had been a leading actor for more than a decade while I was still a newcomer. Indeed, when I played Richard at Stratford, fourteen years later, many critics thought they could find traces of Gielgud in my performance. I do not see how it could have been otherwise—if you have seen a performance which you consider definitive, you cannot help but be influenced by it. Even at the first reading,

John was as near perfect as I could wish or imagine. Ninety percent of the beauty of his acting was the beauty of his voice, and to this day I can see no way of improving on the dazzling virtuosity of the phrasing or breathing which was Gielgud's."

Ironically, while by night Redgrave was making his name as a comparatively junior member of Gielgud's company, by day he was doing precisely what John had a few years earlier failed to manage—successfully working for Alfred Hitchcock in the thriller that was to make him a star, *The Lady Vanishes.*

But the whole survival of the new company was riding on this first production, and the reviews were not in fact as ecstatic as John could have wished. Perhaps because critics had now seen his Richard, both ancient and modern, so often, or perhaps because they were already growing weary of Motley's over-decorative sets, there was a slightly grudging reaction typified by Harley Granville-Barker, who sent a sharp note suggesting that John should play the lines and not between them. Others, however, were more enthusiastic; James Agate, after complaining that the set looked like a West End florist's shop, added, "Gielgud's Richard has gained in depth, subtlety, insight and power since he first played it at the Old Vic eight years ago," and Peter Fleming, for *The Spectator,* wrote the review that John must have been dreaming of: "This might almost be a Russian company, so compact and smooth is the texture of a large cast, even in all the bad parts."

The critic of *The Tatler* was in no doubt about the importance of this opening production: "Mr. Gielgud is always incomparable when handling neurosis and instability. What he gives us here is the idea of Richard as a young man bathed in luxury and preciosity, concerned not for his realm, but for the figure that he cuts in it. It is futile, at this time of day, to write of the rich range of melody in Mr. Gielgud's voice, but his memorable performance now shares the limelight with half a dozen others that are nearly as satisfying. Mr. Gielgud, having surrounded himself with a team of unusually expert actors, sees to it, as producer, that their roles are never whittled down to the advantage of his own."

The second of the four plays at the Queen's Theatre was to be *The School for Scandal,* and for this production John brought in Tyrone Guthrie, a young director who was also still moonlighting as an actor; this duality presented several problems when Guthrie not only got a strong role in a Charles Laughton film called *The Beachcomber,* leaving John to take most of the rehearsals, but also unexpectedly had to return to the Old Vic, where the sudden death of Lilian Baylis had left the company in chaos. This was thus not the best time for the company to be starting on a Restoration comedy, considering how many of them (Gielgud, Redgrave, Guinness, and Ashcroft) had all been deeply devoted to "The Lady" who had given most of them their first real opportunities.

As Gielgud later noted, "I fear relations between Guthrie and me deteriorated rapidly, especially as he only gave us about six rehearsals. I also began to realise, here, the problems of having a repertory company of players, because many of them weren't in fact very well suited to the high comedy of *The School for Scandal.* I also found that Tony had devised some very gimmicky scenery, for instance playing the picture scene in a front cloth using the audience for the pictures—stunts like this I really didn't like at all, so in the end I just shut my eyes to his production, or lack of it, and tried to play my own part of Joseph as well as I could. I remember, typically, Guthrie taking great pains with a dance at the curtain calls. One critic wrote that the production really wasn't good enough, which must have been why at the end we all appeared to be going off to join the Russian Ballet. I learned there and then never again to do elaborate curtain calls."

An additional problem was that Guthrie's sets and costumes were characteristically anachronistic, and the third major difficulty was that when Guthrie did manage to spend some time with the cast, his main objective was to have several small-part players doing their own things in odd corners of the stage. John was thus not pleased, playing the relatively small role of Joseph Surface, to find that during his only good scene with Lady Sneerwell, a maid upstage was not only making a double bed, but then, for the wrong kind of laugh, clambering into it. In trying to get away from the mundane revivals of the past, Guthrie finished up with a manic farce, altogether too busy and contrived, although Laurence Olivier, in the first-night audience, was to recall John's Surface as "The best light comedy performance I ever have, or ever shall, see."

Two down, two to go. The next production at the Queen's Theatre was the one on which John was secretly banking all his hopes—a staging by Michel Saint-Denis of *The Three Sisters*. With this, the company at last came into its own; as Herbert Farjeon wrote, "If Mr. Gielgud's season at the Queen's had produced nothing but this, it would have more than justified itself. There is a tenderness in the acting so exquisite that it is like the passing of light . . . Here in short is a production of the very first order, of one of the very great masterpieces of dramatic literature."

But even this production was not without its problems in rehearsal. Michael Redgrave had wanted to play Andrei, the brother, but Saint-Denis insisted on George Devine, relegating Redgrave to the Baron Tuzenbach, where he remained deeply unhappy, mumbling the lines, and casting envious glances at Devine.

In direct contrast to the careless Guthrie, Saint-Denis arrived at the first rehearsal having already planned every move, every line, and every piece of stage business. John, although unhappy as Vershinin, the battery commander, was still delighted with the way in which the company now seemed at last to be coming together. And as the sisters of the title, Carol Goodner, Peggy Ashcroft, and Gwen Ffrangcon-Davies all attracted brilliant reviews. "They seem," wrote the critic Lionel Hale, "to have embraced their characters finally and naturally; they grow in them like flowers bedded in good earth."

Yet below the surface the company was not in fact as happy as Gielgud could have wished, and the moment that *The Three Sisters* made way for *The Merchant of Venice,* Redgrave abruptly left to embark on a film career. But it was eventually Harold Hobson who understood precisely why this *Three Sisters* made such a remarkable and lasting impression on anyone who saw it: "We should remember that at precisely this moment, at the very beginning of 1938, war with Hitler was becoming increasingly certain, despite all the attempts at appeasement. Michael Redgrave as Tuzenbach and Peggy Ashcroft as the youngest of the three sisters made a very poignant thing out of their shy, embarrassed parting on a note of forced cheerfulness in the last act, just before the duel; and the fading music of the marching regiment, dying away into silence at the end of the play, was a sadly sufficient comment on the vanishing hopes of the entire Russian bourgeoisie before their sky darkened into revolution. This was the last evening of tranquil beauty that the British theatre was to know for many years to come, if indeed it was ever to know such a thing again."

As for the translator, Constance Garnett, she wrote that ever since she had begun translating Chekhov, twenty years earlier, she had hoped and longed for an adequate production of his plays in Britain. At last, she told John, "this has been achieved, and I just want to thank you for the great pleasure of seeing my dreams fulfilled."

Tyrone Guthrie, still feeling somewhat ashamed of the shambles he had made of *School for Scandal,* wrote to John, "This is the most articulate and accomplished Chekhov that I have ever seen. Naturally I don't agree with all of it—and I don't suppose you do. St-Denis always overdoes his offstage noises, and all those bloody trilling birds and the wind simply take one's mind off the play. But the company is at its absolute best. Peggy is exquisitely moving and real, and Gwen really excellent. I am not sure the last act set is quite right, but Redgrave seems to me as near perfection as one has any right to expect and you are very distinguished, although some of your stuff in act two is a bit of a cliché."

So successful was this production that John borrowed an idea he had been much taken with on Broadway—that of a special midnight matinee at which actors from all the other West End productions could, if they wished, come to see this one, bringing with them members of their own companies. This resulted in more than a hundred letters written to John, some from actors who knew and had worked with him elsewhere, but many from those who had simply always been working when he was, and therefore were now coming to see Gielgud for the very first time. At the very end of the run, a "tribute dinner" was given by the Garrick Club, which John had only recently joined. This again was to prove a signally rare honor.

But the repertory system, just as it meant advantageously that the company could move swiftly on from a poor *School for Scandal* to a great *Three*

Sisters, also relentlessly meant that no sooner was this established but they all had to start work on the last production of the season, a revival of *The Merchant of Venice.*

John and Peggy Ashcroft were the only two leading players to appear in all four of the plays in Gielgud's season at the Queen's Theatre, and as Ashcroft later noted, "I had never before had such a long contract, and I feared that we might all get very stale, working together for almost a year, but in fact the reverse was true—it changed one's whole attitude to working in the theatre."

After their triumph with *The Three Sisters,* however, the last of Gielgud's four chosen plays was to be something of an anticlimax. He was already feeling the strain of managing the season virtually unaided, and his production of *The Merchant of Venice* (in which he played Shylock to Peggy's Portia) was a considerable disappointment to critics, as indeed to John himself. At this historical time, given what was happening in Germany, audiences in London would probably have been happy to accept a heroic Shylock standing up for his Jewish identity. Instead, John played him as a shuffling, morose, and malignant outsider, ridiculous in his villainy. John's Shylock, wrote Ronald Hayman, "was a Venetian ghetto-Jew, a mean little rat of a money-lender, lacking any dignity, a scavenger . . . this Shylock was a very strange shape, robes spreading like a gypsy's, hunching, crouching, lamenting and scrabbling about. Gielgud looked rather young, though almost bald, with straggling hair and beard, and a ring in his ear. In no characterisation since Noah had John got further away from his own personality."

Some critics approved of this interpretation, but many felt that he had been unwise to direct and play Shylock. Some reviews indicated that John had simply miscast himself. "He is," wrote *The Times,* "as incapable of portraying evil as he is of understanding it as a director."

As this season came to its end, John began to have mixed feelings about the experiment. On the one hand, it had come in fractionally under budget, with only *The Three Sisters* costing more than £2,000 to produce. In critical terms, two of the productions (*Richard II* and *The Three Sisters*) had achieved mostly good reviews, and even with the other two (*The*

School for Scandal and *The Merchant of Venice*) John had been applauded for the courage of the venture. He had also surrounded himself with most of the best classical and modern actors in the business and taught them precisely what it meant to be members of a permanent company. It was an experience many of them would not have again until the 1960s' creation of resident companies at the National and the RSC. As Margaret Harris of the Motley design partnership was later to remark: "John's season changed the point of view by showing that the classics could be a box-office draw, that an identifiable team of actors could be held together in a freelance world, and that great plays repaid minute examination. John has never been given credit for what he did. He single-handedly put the English theatre back on the world map. He led Peggy into doing the sort of work she was best at; he found Olivier as a classical actor, and encouraged people like Alec Guinness, Harry Andrews, and Anthony Quayle. He also encouraged George Devine and Glen Byam Shaw to find their way as directors. He really did the most amazing work, but because of his innate modesty, it was to be Olivier, after the war, who took all the credit for doing everything that John had done before it."

Not surprisingly, John had been depressed at the way in which some members of the company would drift off in mid-season as soon as a better or starrier offer came their way (Redgrave's departure to work in movies being perhaps the most distressing), and he was utterly exhausted himself by the strain of producing, directing, starring, and generally acting as the company's only figurehead and driving force. More important still, he personally had made very little out of the venture and was therefore now easily tempted back onto the moneymaking side of Shaftesbury Avenue, first to direct *Spring Meeting*, a play by the Irish novelist Molly Keane (writing as M. J. Farrell) and his lover John Perry, and almost immediately after that to star with Marie Tempest in *Dear Octopus*, another new play, this one by the prolific and highly successful dramatist, Dodie Smith.

Both these offers had come to him from Hugh ("Binkie") Beaumont, the young Welsh producer who had by now taken over the running of H. M. Tennent and was already forming the third corner of a triangular friendship involving Gielgud and Perry. Binkie and John had first met more than ten years earlier, when John had been acting in the Chekhov season at Barnes, and Beaumont just starting out as its box-office manager. But by now the balance of power had subtly shifted, and Beaumont, at the beginning of a long partnership with John that would stretch into the 1960s, was able not only to send regular work his way, but also from time to time to make it possible for John to pursue his lifelong desire for at least semipermanent companies.

Yet it was to be a double-edged alliance: Binkie was not only to steal John's lover, he was also to keep him for the next thirty or so years on such an extremely tight salary that it wasn't until Gielgud first escaped to Hollywood in 1953 that he began to earn the kind of money that Olivier and Richardson and Redgrave had earned for decades.

Binkie, however, had invested (with John Perry) in the season at the Queen's Theatre, and while John was occupied day and night with its creation and management, his two backers found themselves falling in love. Away from the theater, John Perry had rather more in common with Binkie than with John G.; they both loved racing, gambling, visiting card clubs and casinos and would happily spend whole nights playing bridge or poker with other card players. None of these pastimes had ever interested Gielgud, and it perhaps was not until John Perry actually moved out of their shared flat and into Binkie's in Piccadilly, that John finally focused on what was happening in his private life.

Even then, he was remarkably forbearing; Binkie had already insinuated himself into the lives of the two Johns, and professionally Gielgud now saw him as his only regular employer. As Keith Baxter explains,

> John was clearly shocked by Perry moving in with Binkie, but it is possible that their relationship had not been sexual for some time; the theatre was always much more important to John G. than any private relationship, and very soon he was able to restore his friendship with both the others, and would frequently go to stay with them at their weekend cottage. John Perry really was everything that Binkie was not—jovial, outgoing, always interested in something new. It was

he who encouraged Binkie to take on much riskier plays in later years. And, until he was effectively banished from John G.'s life by his last lover, Martin Hensler, Perry was to remain closer to John G. than anybody else.

You have to remember also that John was always like a chameleon. He took on the character of whoever he was living with at the time, so Cowley Street, when he first moved there with John Perry, was like a very elegant theatrical lodging, whereas when, in much later life, he moved out to the country with Martin Hensler, the décor suddenly became almost Hungarian and Polish, to suit their family back-grounds. In fact, a little touch of the Austro-Hungarian empire, just outside Aylesbury.

Proving that there really were no hard feelings, John G. continued all through their break-up to work for H. M. Tennent as both director and actor, starting with John Perry's own play.

Spring Meeting was a boisterous Irish farce about a family obsessed with racehorses, and although that milieu was very foreign to John G., he nonetheless delivered an immaculate production built around Margaret Rutherford, who made her name here as the eccentric spinster with a genius for backing winners. The play ran for over a year, during which time John Perry not only set up house with Binkie, but also became his partner in H. M. Tennent; as Bryan Forbes wittily wrote, "Perry thus became Mason to Binkie's Fortnum, purveyors of quality theatrical goods to the carriage trade."

No sooner was *Spring Meeting* established than John G. started rehearsals, under Glen Byam Shaw's direction, for another long-running H. M. Tennent comedy success. This one was *Dear Octopus,* a sentimental story about relatives gathering together to celebrate a golden wedding anniversary, at which the toast is "to the family, that dear octopus from whose tentacles we never escape, nor ever really wish to." Although it ran almost a year, *Dear Octopus* (like *Richard of Bordeaux*) was never really to achieve any kind of a postwar life; but at this moment of Munich and the approach of World War II, audiences in London (and around the country during its tour) found in Dodie Smith's domestic homilies something both touching and reassuring. If the middle classes were to have to go to war, this was precisely the world for which they would be fighting. John's role here was inevitably secondary to that of Dame Marie Tempest, and it may seem curious that he was willing to stay for so long in a comercially triumphant but intellectually rather barren and even wooden characterization.

There are various explanations: one is that, at a time of considerable upheaval in his private life, he welcomed the relative security of the same dressing room and eight performances a week, even if the play was being produced by the man for whom his longtime lover had just left him. Beyond this, John was also well aware that Binkie Beaumont might well be persuaded to invest again in a season of classics, if John proved amenable to Binkie's more commercial and pedestrian needs. Bridges were not to be burned, and if possible, life was to continue on its usual course; in this last year of peace, that was precisely what John most sought, at whatever cost to his pride or private emotions.

11. The West End at War

(1938–1940)

The outbreak of the Second War naturally transformed everything in the theatre. I was extremely lucky not to be called up, the authorities taking the view that I could do a better job by staying in the theatre. But I found myself living somewhat precariously, always moving from one production to another and never quite knowing what was going to happen next.

During the ten months that John played *Dear Octopus*, through 1938 and into 1939, he and Binkie and John Perry were naturally concerned about what they should do next in an unusually volatile season. John's idea was that they should go for T. S. Eliot's *The Family Reunion*, a characteristically brave adventure, which he even began to cast with Sybil Thorndike, Martita Hunt, and May Whitty. But both Binkie and John Perry were cautious in their enthusiasm for a verse drama several years ahead of its time, one that introduced the Eumenides into a modern family gathering, and the whole project came to a shuddering halt when John went out to lunch with the author at the Reform Club.

During an uneasy meal, Eliot made it clear that he would only allow his new play to be directed by Martin Browne, who had looked after his *Murder in the Cathedral* a few years earlier, and that he was extremely reluctant to answer any of John's questions about the real meaning of a family drama that brought the Greek fates into a latter-day living room. Soon afterward, Eliot noted that as Gielgud clearly lacked faith in the play and the leading character of Harry Monchensey, he would rather take it else-where, which is what he duly did.

It was therefore with some relief that Binkie and John Perry persuaded John G. to go back to a play and a role in which he had triumphed almost ten years earlier at the Lyric, Hammersmith. John now directed and starred in a series of eight charity matinees of *The Importance of Being Earnest,* so successfully that Binkie decided it should be their next West End project. Before that, however, there was to be another return to a safe harbor. During the previous summer while Gielgud was otherwise occupied with *Dear Octopus* but nonetheless furious at having missed the chance, Laurence Olivier had become the first British actor of modern times to take his Hamlet (directed by Tyrone Guthrie, with Vivien Leigh as Ophelia) back to the battlements of Elsinore itself. John was now determined to follow suit. For this production, which went into rehearsal as he was leaving *Dear Octopus,* John reassembled some familiar members of his old company, together with a few newcomers. Fay Compton was now his Ophelia, with Jack Hawkins and Laura Cowie as Claudius and Gertrude. George Howe, Glen Byam Shaw, and Marius Goring were also in the cast, and the Motleys were again to design the sets.

These sets had to be suitable not only for the courtyard at Elsinore, but also for the Lyceum Theatre on the Strand where John had arranged a week of previews, just as the theater itself was due for demolition. In fact it survived, only to be badly blitzed in the war a few years later; John's *Hamlet* was the last production to be seen there until the 1970s, when Bill Bryden took his Miracle plays in from the National. For Gielgud, the real excitement of this production was the arrival in London of his old mentor Harley Granville-Barker, on a rare visit from America.

"He agreed to come to a run-through, on condition that there would not be any press or publicity. His name was not to be used in any way. We acted the whole play for him, and the following morning he sent for me to the Ritz Hotel. He sat on the sofa with a new edition of *Hamlet* in his hand, cutting the pages with a paper-knife as he went along, and giving me notes at a great rate. I scribbled away with all my might, determined not to let him get away until he had finished. The next day was a Sunday, but we spent all of it putting in his cuts and changes."

Barker's main advice was that John should be stronger in the first half of the play, and then wilder and more despairing and disturbed after the killing of Polonius. He saw Fortinbras and Laertes as the twin poles of what Hamlet could have been, and he recommended an altogether leaner and less busy characterization than John had hitherto opted for onstage.

The production at Elsinore, however, was not a great success. The weather was stormy and terrible, audiences were duly deterred from sitting in the stone courtyard, and the hotel where the company stayed was already full of Nazi naval officers on leave. Marius Goring, to his credit, cut up all their swastika banners and flushed them down one of the hotel lavatories. By now the company had become somewhat hysterical, throwing each other into the sea and putting live chickens in each other's beds. The feeling was that with war due at any minute this was the end of an era, and John's "regulars" (among them Jack Hawkins, Glen Byam Shaw, and Anthony Quayle) were already aware that this was to be the last time for the foreseeable future that they would all be acting together as a unit. The Elsinore production was, however, to be the start of a lifelong friendship for John with the Baroness Blixen, better known as the author Isak Dinesen (*Out of Africa*), who had come to the production and was to stay in touch with him regularly afterward, across both decades and continents.

Audrey Williamson, writing of this Elsinore revival, noted: "The unique quality of Gielgud's Hamlet has always been its radiant, nerve-tossed beauty. Fair and slender, it has the presence of a roi soleil; but the sun is always fitfully shadowed by the wings of demons . . . this is a fey, fairy prince hedged about with the powers of darkness, and Gielgud's performance has flashes of venom and bitter humour as well as sensitiveness and sweetness . . . this Hamlet cares not a jot for Ophelia or Yorick, but the distinctive features of Gielgud's Prince have always been intellect and poetry; there is music and cogency, and nobody has ever spoken the role so exquisitely."

Back in London, John remained resolutely uninterested in the darkening skies; he seems to have believed that if he ignored the threat of war it might simply go away, and with the radio news from Germany getting worse by the hour, he went for a weekend to stay with the journalist and biographer Beverly Nichols: "On the Sunday morning, John walked into the village to get the papers and came back looking devastated. 'Have they declared war yet?' I asked, nervously. 'Oh, I don't know anything about that, but Gladys Cooper has just got the most terrible reviews!'"

The plan now was for John to stage his *Importance of Being Earnest*, with Edith Evans as the definitive Lady Bracknell, and Angela Baddeley and Joyce Carey as Cecily and Gwendolen. Binkie spared no expense on lavish Motley sets and *The Times* went so far as to note that "if the past theatrical decade had to be represented by a single production, then this is the one that a good many judges would choose." The Motleys had moved the period forward to about 1906 from the original 1895, but this did not worry Lord Alfred Douglas who came backstage to tell Gielgud that he was the best John Worthing he had ever seen, and how Oscar would have approved. For Tyrone Guthrie, this was the staging "which established the high water mark in the production of artificial comedy in our epoch."

Even though all those who could afford to were now starting to move out of London in fear of the bombing, *The Importance of Being Earnest* sold out all through the summer of 1939, taking more than £2,000 a week at the box office and confirming (as later did Coward with *Blithe Spirit*) that in time of crisis there is nothing audiences need more than to be taken out of themselves and to another time and place, one where they could, as both plays did, look death in the eye with nothing more threatening than a giggle. A few years later Edith was, of course, to film her Lady Bracknell with Michael Redgrave and Michael Denison, but this was where her performance, with its cascading, multisyllabic "A handbag?" first began to be set in stone as the upper-class gorgon of all time. The role that was both to characterize and imprison Edith had been played in John's first *Importance of Being Earnest*, back in 1930, by his own aunt Mabel Terry, but as John admitted, she was a lady remarkably lacking in a sense of humor, who would whisper under her breath to her nephew onstage, "What is so funny about this play? Why are they all laughing at me?"

Edith knew exactly what Wilde had been about, and it was her performance, built upon a lifetime's hatred of the grandes dames who had kept her mother's family in domestic service for so many years, rather than John's production that was to guarantee the success here. It was still running to packed houses when war was declared on September 3; that Sunday morning, at a crisis meeting with Binkie and John Perry onstage, it was decided to close the production down. At this moment, John had also just started to direct the first ever staging of Daphne du Maurier's best-selling *Rebecca*, but that, too, was immediately abandoned by Binkie, as was a double-staging by Noël Coward of his two new plays, *This Happy Breed* and *Present Laughter.*

The H. M. Tennent theatrical troops now began rapidly to disperse; Michel Saint-Denis went home to fight for his native France; Coward went to Paris on a secret-service mission; Alec Guinness and Anthony Quayle and John Perry were among the many to enlist, and even Binkie now began to carry a gas mask around the office. Immediately following the declaration that morning, the first official wartime executive order had been that all cinemas and theaters in Britain should close for the duration, for fear of air raids. But in the days that followed, there having been no raids of any kind, Binkie presented himself at Downing Street and won, within less than a week, a complete reversal of the order and the concession that theaters and cinemas could reopen in what were designated "safe areas," though nobody specified precisely which these were.

John G. and Binkie duly designated Golders Green the first such "safe" area, and reopened their *Importance of Being Earnest* at the local Hippodrome only ten days after they had been forced to close it on Shaftesbury Avenue. One of John's most faithful chroniclers, the theater historian Audrey Williamson, was in the audience: "This was the first London theatre to reopen after the outbreak of war, and both audience and players felt terribly courageous, although of course there was really no immediate danger. Mutual admiration and sympathy nevertheless crackled across the footlights."

After several more months on the road, they brought *The Importance of Being Earnest* back to the Globe where it ran happily into 1940. John meanwhile had decided that his contribution to the war would be a series of

Shakespearean lectures, originally outlined by the critic Ivor Brown, in which he would talk about the major plays and perform extracts from the roles he had already made his own, from Richard II to Hamlet. These early and somewhat stilted talks still exist, on a series of shellac 78 RPM recordings issued commercially early in the war.

Ten or so years after the war, no longer aided by Ivor Brown but by the Cambridge professor George "Dadie" Rylands, John was to adapt these lectures into the more colloquial *The Ages of Man,* the most successful of all Shakespearean solo shows. Proceeds from these wartime lectures were equally divided between the Red Cross and the Polish Relief Fund, to which John felt a strong familial loyalty.

As soon as war was declared, John, although thirty-five, volunteered for active service only to be told that his age group would not be called up for at least six months. For actors of his generation, there was now something of a problem; they all wished to be seen to be doing their best for the war effort, despite official belief that, in fact, most actors would be far better employed playing to the troops than involving themselves in military activities for which most were hopelessly ill-suited. There were, of course, exceptions. Of John's "regulars," Alec Guinness fought a brave war in the navy and Anthony Quayle was to play a crucial role with the Yugoslav resistance, but by and large the experience of actors in battle dress was more akin to that of Laurence Olivier and Ralph Richardson who, after insisting on being called up to the Fleet Air Arm, were somewhat ignominiously sent back to the Old Vic, not least because their sense of direction was so terrible that they managed to crash several planes even before they were airborne, so careless was their runway technique.

As for John, the actual declaration of war found him not only playing in *The Importance of Being Earnest,* but also rehearsing for the stage the role that Olivier had just filmed as the sinister Maxim de Winter in Daphne du Maurier's *Rebecca.* But as Margaret Rutherford (implausibly now cast as the villainous Mrs. Danvers) recalled, John immediately decided that this was altogether too lightweight a role in which to start World War II. Accordingly, he abandoned it to Owen Nares and, rather like Noël Coward, vowed that his wartime theater would be suitably solemn.

His next engagement, however, came from an unlikely and unexpected source. The conductor Rudolph Bing, then running the young Glyndebourne Festival for John Christie, wanted a London production of John Gay's *The Beggar's Opera,* one for which he had already engaged Michael Redgrave as MacHeath and Christie's wife, Audrey Mildmay, as Polly Peachum. John, whose first production of an opera this was to be, brought in his usual Motley designs and decided to go for a very much more squalid and satirical staging than the classic and still familiar Nigel Playfair production from the Lyric, Hammersmith.

This *Beggar's Opera* did not, however, get off to a very good start, when Michael Redgrave lost his voice and John had to go on as a somewhat implausible MacHeath for four nerve-racked performances at which his singing had to be heard to be believed. "Someone," as John ruefully told the *Daily Mail,* "had to step in and play the part, and I'm afraid the someone had to be me." Redgrave rapidly recovered, but was to remain deeply unhappy throughout the run, not least with John's direction: "I had been much too pre-occupied with the problem of singing to lay the proper foundations for my character, and John had muddled me horribly in rehearsal, giving me one direction one day, and countermanding it the next. . . . He also told Edith Evans [with whom Michael had now started a long affair] that my work was suffering, which was not exactly helpful. And my mood was not improved during an early matinee, when I came on for Act Two to hear a voice in the circle whisper loudly 'And who might this be?'"

Putting *The Beggar's Opera* swiftly behind him, John decided that the time had come to do something rather more serious for the war effort. He and Tyrone Guthrie now formed a plan to reopen the Old Vic with two productions, *King Lear* and *The Tempest,* for which they were able to reassemble a strong team led by Jessica Tandy, her then husband Jack Hawkins, Fay Compton, Marius Goring, and such Old Vic veterans—all now too old to be called up for military service—as Harcourt Williams, Lewis Casson, and Nicholas Hannen.

John immediately went back to Harley Granville-Barker, now living in a Paris not yet invaded by the Germans. Barker agreed to come to London, although again he insisted that his involvement should never be publicized. Lewis Casson was to codirect this *Lear* with Guthrie, and the three men duly presented themselves at his hotel where they read through the play. Barker listened impassively until John got to the very end. "You read exactly two lines correctly. Now we will begin to work. Your main trouble is that whereas Lear is an oak, you are an ash. We must see what we can do with you."

From the very first rehearsal at the Vic, John remembered later, "Barker inspired and dominated everyone like a master craftsman, and everybody in the theatre recognised this at once. . . . He began to work with the actors, not using any notes, but sitting on the stage with his back to the footlights, a copy of the play in his hand, tortoise-shell spectacles well forward on his nose, dressed in a black business suit, his bushy red eyebrows jutting forward, quiet-voiced, seldom moving, coldly humorous, shrewdly observant, infinitely patient and persevering."

Barker had long known precisely how he wanted this *Lear* to look and sound: not mad from the beginning, but gradually overtaken by events that he has set in motion and now cannot control. Barker also wanted the audience to understand the journey that Lear undertakes and wanted him at the end of the play to revert to a kind of second childhood. Asked later to summarize the difference that Barker had made to this Gielgud *Lear,* John said, "He encouraged me to characterise more, while being less declamatory, holding my emotional power in reserve for where it was needed."

But Barker was still curiously determined not to be the director of record. Characteristically, he abruptly returned to Paris the day of the first dress rehearsal, leaving John only a brisk backstage note: "My dear Gielgud, Lear is now in your grasp. Forget all the things I have bothered you about. Let your own now well self-disciplined instincts carry you along and up, while allowing the checks and changes to prevent your being carried away. I happily prophesy great things for you."

Cathleen Nesbitt, whose life was to span a romantic pre–World War I affair with the poet Rupert Brooke through to the role of Rex Harrison's mother in *My Fair Lady,* and who had been Perdita for Granville-Barker as long ago as 1912, was cast here as Goneril, with Fay Compton as Regan and

Jessica Tandy as Cordelia. As Nesbitt remembered, "We were all being paid £10 a week, and any profits were to go to rebuilding the Old Vic after its bombing; outside of his performance, John had a great deal to do with the atmosphere of harmony backstage. He was a wonderful person to be on stage with, less arrogant or egotistic than any actor of his stature that I have ever met. He and Granville-Barker had the same gift for making everyone seem equally important to the play . . . between them, in scene after scene, they achieved effects which were absorbing and moving to watch, night after night . . . I would stand in the wings watching John's *Lear,* its biting irony, its tender, moving gaiety, and a sense of grief too deep for tears."

But once again the critics were divided: "We feel for the words Lear speaks," wrote Herbert Farjeon, "rather than for Lear himself." Desmond MacCarthy thought the role needed a voice of much greater compass than Gielgud's; and *The Times* added that John "acts with a nervous force, but is inclined at times to fall something short on physical toughness." During the run, John's backstage visitors included such admiring writers as Hugh Walpole and the poet Stephen Spender, who wrote afterward, "It seems to me that you have made such a profound study of the part that your acting transcends itself, so one forgets altogether the sense of a performance and has instead an impression of the poetry itself come to life. To me, this was something much more valuable than a star performer, because I now feel I understand the meaning of *Lear* so much better than from the many times I have read it."

It was left to Audrey Williamson to sum up for the defense: "This was a Renaissance *King Lear,* but with enough barbaric force to make the action seem authentically placed in time . . . Gielgud's Lear on his first entrance was no senile, uncombed chieftain dressed in a nondescript nightgown, but a great King, still proud in person and mind, robed in blue satin and rich furs with white hair [and] a carefully curled beard. The emphasis therefore was on an active octogenarian, rashly dividing his kingdom and divesting himself of the cares of state before he was ready to relinquish his authority. Gielgud's superb head, with its high marked cheekbones and forcible nose, had the regal poise of one accustomed to rule without question and the voice held possibilities of thunder. . . . The scenery and costumes for this production were beautifully designed by Roger Furse and over and over again, during the performance, one felt the unseen impact of Granville-Barker's dramatic vision in gesture, pose and inflection."

This time around, Gielgud's Fool was Stephen Haggard, the actor whom he had first discovered in his undergraduate days at Oxford. Tragically, this was to be his last performance. A few months later he mysteriously died, falling from a moving train, having written a letter to his young sons headed by the last words he ever spoke onstage, the Fool's "I'll go to bed at noon."

As soon as they had opened this *King Lear*, John went into rehearsal for Prospero, another role he had first played when rather too young, a decade earlier. This time it was to be codirected at the Vic by George Devine and Marius Goring, who persuaded John to get as far away as possible from the kind of manic conjurer he had first played in 1930. This time Oliver Messel, who had first attracted John as an Oxford undergraduate, was to be the designer, and according to *The Times*, John's Prospero was "a scholarly Italian nobleman of middle age, lightly bearded and well-preserved, even though now accustomed to wearing spectacles . . . his voice is always attuned to the royal note of the verse, and he is never the preaching patriarch."

Another critic added, "Gielgud is a younger Prospero than most; he gives the character a certain wry humour and scholastic irony, and seems always surrounded by the invisible walls of his own enchantment."

By the time this Old Vic season came to an end, on June 22, 1940, there was a plan to take both the productions to Paris; but the fall of France, coming as it did that very weekend, made that project untenable, and the Vic itself was now to go dark until it was hit by a bomb some months later and unable to reopen until well after the war.

It was clear, even to John, that the war had at last become a reality, and that he should join several of his fellow actors on tours of military camps around the country. Shakespeare was hardly likely to be well-suited to audiences of soldiers, sailors, and airmen, who might at any moment be ordered to the front, and he decided therefore to go for a couple of short comedies, *Fumed Oak* and *Hands Across the Sea*, both from Noël Coward's triumphant 1936 *Tonight at 8:30*, although he would add to them his own adaptation of Chekhov's *Swan Song,* a play about an old actor in a deserted theater with only an equally ancient stage manager for company. While playing these parts every night at the head of a company that also starred the eccentric comedienne Bea Lillie, he also regularly repeated his lecture, now ending it topically enough with Henry V's "Once more unto the breach . . ."

The triple bill did not play well. John was never really at home in the brittle, comic dialogue of Coward, and Bea Lillie usually ended up having to retrieve the evening by leading the troops in mass singalongs of "Keep the Home Fires Burning" and "Lily of Laguna." Matters were also not exactly helped by their having to share the bill with an American jazz band, which the troops were impatient to hear. Bea, by now desperate to grab whatever attention she could, suddenly announced to one surprised audience, and John G.'s amazement, in the midst of one of the Coward plays, "I shall now go to the piano and play Ravel's *Concerto for the Left Hand,* all the while smoking a cigarette with my right!" John was left watching gratefully from the side of the set.

While they were playing army camps in Scotland, John was offered the role of Disraeli in Thorold Dickinson's new film *The Prime Minister,* one of many being made at this early stage of the war largely to remind cinemagoers of the highlights of the history of the nation for which they were now being asked to fight. Robert Donat's *Young Mr. Pitt* and the Olivier/Leigh vehicle, *That Hamilton Woman,* about the romance between Nelson and Lady Hamilton, were other examples of the genre.

This was the first but not the last time John ever got to play the title role in a film, and it had been almost a decade since his unhappy experience with Hitchcock on *The Secret Agent.* But now, John was on very much more familiar territory, playing a character part that required him to age from thirty to seventy in a decidedly stagey House of Commons setting. Around him, Dickinson had gathered some starry support, not least from Diana Wynyard as his wife, but also from Fay Compton as Queen Victoria. Gielgud was here, in fact, challenging the memory of George Arliss who had twice filmed Disraeli's life, once as a silent in 1921, and then again in a more lavish 1929 talkie. John, working on a much more limited budget, managed, however, to be rather more convincing, despite having to abandon the shooting for several days when the heavy make-up, consisting largely of fish paste, gave him a terrible skin rash. It is here for the first time, especially in the scenes when Disraeli is alone reading his wife's letters after her death, that Gielgud seems at last to be comfortable with the camera, though (apart from a couple of wartime shorts) it was to be another ten years before he worked in film again.

12. WAR WEARY

(1940–1948)

I kept remembering how marvellous Du Maurier had been as the painter
Dearth in the first 1917 production of Dear Brutus. *I could never touch him*
in the part.

*N*o sooner had John finished filming as Disraeli than he began
to think about a production of *Macbeth*, another of those roles that he
had first played when far too young, at the Old Vic, and that he now
wanted to revisit. At first, it seemed that the new wartime climate was
against any major full-length Shakespeare, especially as John's old enemy
Donald Wolfit was now triumphing in a series of cut-down Shakespearean classics that would run for only an hour for lunchtime patrons
who needed to get home well before the blackout, in a rough-and-ready
Shakespearean equivalent of the Myra Hess wartime concerts at the National Gallery.

Casting around therefore for something rather lighter to appeal to audiences whose minds were often on something else, Gielgud now remembered a play he had first seen and greatly loved as a teenager during World
War I. This was *Dear Brutus*, by J. M. Barrie, a weird and whimsical variant
of *A Midsummer Night's Dream*, in which characters wander into an enchanted wood, there to discover that they can, after all, achieve a second
chance in life. (Though it was never credited, this revival of *Dear Brutus*

was where Alan J. Lerner and Frederick Loewe a few years later got the idea for their first hit Broadway musical, *Brigadoon.*)

Gielgud as director and star now brought this play back as a considerable hit, one which encouraged other theater managers to light up Shaftesbury Avenue again if only for matinees, although John himself was always convinced that he had totally failed to capture Gerald du Maurier's original charm in the role of the lonely, failed, middle-aged artist. For *The New Statesman,* Desmond MacCarthy agreed: "In the first act, Gielgud appears far too well pulled-together, too smart and attractive. In the scene in the wood between the painter and his dream daughter, his charm lacks the crispness of Gerald du Maurier's personality and acting, so necessary in counteracting the sentimentality."

Yet this remained a clever choice in terms of wartime casting, in that there are very few leading male roles in *Dear Brutus,* but enough female parts to allow John a starry line-up: Zena Dare, Mary Jerrold, Margaret Rawlings, Nora Swinburne, Ursula Jeans, and Muriel Pavlow, who made her name here as the young child. A four-month London run was followed by a two-month regional tour, during which other companies were forever meeting up in blackouts on Crewe Station on Sundays as they crisscrossed the land. One especially dark evening, John threw open a carriage only to see, through the gloom, that it was already occupied by Donald Wolfit. "My God," he told Zena Dare, "the enemy has already landed."

During the six-month run of *Dear Brutus,* John decided to tackle another play by the Irish writer Molly Keane (M. J. Farrell), but lightning did not strike twice in that direction. The new play *Ducks and Drakes* lacked the innocent charm of *Spring Meeting* and survived only very briefly at the Apollo.

As always, John was still finding precious little time for a private life, and his grasp of the unfolding events of World War II was to remain tenuous, to say the least. Alec Guinness once recalled walking with John over Waterloo Bridge and seeing a couple of barrage balloons, high above their heads. "Oh!" said John, "I do feel so sorry for those little men up there in the sky, with nothing to eat and no way of keeping warm!" It took Alec some time to explain to John that by their very nature barrage balloons were always unmanned. But John continued, despite some distinguished war work, to consider the hostilities only in the light of what they meant to him, and, of course, to the box-office receipts of wherever and whatever he was playing at the time. As he wrote in June 1942 to Lillian Gish in New York: "I can't begin to tell you all that has happened here since the war began. It has been an extraordinary, timeless kind of nightmare. All one's friends scattered, and turning up again at odd times in uniform, and then gone again before there is any time to settle down and enjoy their company. I have been working continuously in London and on troop tours, where we always have to contend with illness and blitzes and German bombs, which they considerately only seem to drop towards the end of the evening. Everything is at sixes and sevens, and we have no idea when it will all come to an end. I so long to come back to America and see all my New York friends, but of course that is impossible, and sometimes I fear that I will never see any of you ever again. So please give everyone my love."

John's next semipermanent relationship, with the actor and antique dealer Paul Anstee, was still some years into the future, and in the meantime he contented himself with occasional cottaging (random homosexual pickups involving strangers) around the public rest rooms of Chelsea and Westminster, depending as often as not on the kindness of strangers, and thereby falling into a sexual pattern that was, in barely ten years' time, to bring about the greatest crisis of his personal and professional life.

The critic Harold Hobson once told John that he had given himself to the theater just as, in the Middle Ages, men and women gave themselves to monasteries and nunneries, and perhaps for the same reason. Monks and nuns were frequently people who had heard the voice of God summoning them to a life of remote piety. But often, too, the monastery or nunnery was a refuge for those who had no gift or dowry for marriage—people, that is, whose family had failed to provide a life for them. Hobson said, "Gielgud's career has certainly been erratic; it could well have done with that bit of steadying and of common sense which a wife usually brings. He has reached tremendous heights more than once, and also fallen to some sickening depths. A touch of regularity would have saved him a lot of unhappiness."

But for now, John's thoughts were essentially on the *Macbeth* with which he firmly intended to reintroduce major full-length Shakespeare to wartime London, despite the fact that the murderous Scots thane had not proved one of his most natural roles. With the Old Vic now closed for the duration, and many of the younger members of his Queen's Theatre company already in uniform, Gielgud had to rely on a somewhat scratch cast, though he was able to reunite with Gwen Ffrangcon-Davies and give a start to the young Alan Badel, not yet of military age.

John and Binkie, by now his regular manager, decided that they should open in a bitterly cold Manchester early in January of 1942, prior to a long regional tour. In many ways this production was more notable for its backstage than onstage contributors: the music was by William Walton, and the sets and costumes—a deliberate mixture of Aubrey Beardsley and Burne-Jones—were codesigned by Michael Ayrton and another radical young artist of the period, John Minton. According to the critic Ronald Hayman, "John devised a mask-like make-up for himself, with spidery eyebrows, derived partly from Alexander Nevsky in Eisenstein's film."

But the alliance with Michael Ayrton, already one of England's finest painters and sculptors, was not an easy one, as Ayrton's biographer Justine Hopkins chronicled: "Director and potential designer found themselves much in agreement over preliminary conceptions, and a contract was drawn up specifying that Ayrton should be paid fifty pounds as an initial fee for costume drawings and set designs, with a further one percent of the gross weekly box-office takings, up to a total of one hundred and fifty pounds. At the time, this seemed like riches to the young designer, all too well aware of his inexperience and lowly status in the world of stage design; later, as costs snowballed and tempers flared, it was to be yet another bone of contention between himself and his harrassed employer. It took only a few meetings to convince Michael that the burden of work and responsibility was too daunting to be borne alone, and less than a moment for him to fix on the ideal collaborator in John Minton."

Both Ayrton and Minton were, however, called up on active service during the run-up to this *Macbeth,* and although Gielgud secured Ayrton's brief release from the Royal Air Force for the final rehearsals and tour, the strain was evident in his behavior backstage, at least according to an irate letter from John: "Your ungraciousness of manner and lack of charm and generosity [is notable] toward the work people in every department . . . flinging up your hands at intervals, and announcing either that things have been done which you don't approve of and so you wash your hands of the whole thing, or else savagely resenting that there can possibly be still any improvements or adjustments to be made . . . if only you would appear more modest, you would find everyone ready to cooperate rather than oppose, to the great easing of every situation."

By the time they opened on tour, John was still deeply unhappy, not only with Ayrton's backstage behavior but also his work on the scenic design:

> The surrealist things in the scenery are distracting, and must go. The hands on the throne, and the drapery in the trees . . . at the risk of you thinking me unpleasant, I must say I intend to carry out some changes whether you agree [to] them or not. . . . You will I am sure agree that I gave you as free a hand as possible in the beginning, and allowed you to finish in the theatre almost everything you had conceived. Now you must trust to my greater experience. . . . If a man as experienced as Walton can show such modesty, and collaborate with such complete unselfishness, I feel you should do the same, and I do deplore the fact that you haven't got on better with all the people you have come into contact with on this production, which has made the atmosphere sometimes lacking in constructiveness and ease. You will find if you want to go on working in the theatre (which perhaps you don't), that a capacity for extemporising in an emergency, tolerance and patience are three of the most essential qualities.
>
> After this somewhat disagreeable paragraph, I can only add that the big interiors and general atmosphere of the production are really a great success . . . and I am sure that if the changes are carried out, you will have a valuable and deserved success.

On the road, several of Gielgud's now-regular supporters (among them Alec Guinness, Tyrone Guthrie, and the critics Ivor Brown and Alan Dent) all came backstage to offer often conflicting advice about a role in which John, by his very stage presence, was never going to be entirely happily cast.

The famous curse of *Macbeth* struck early, when one of the witches (the veteran Beatrix Fielden-Kay) died during the first week of the tour, and as they trekked on through Scotland, England, and Wales, they very often came up against audiences of schoolchildren or troops who could hardly wait to either giggle or jeer at a somber tragedy, not exactly designed as cheerful wartime entertainment. And there was worse to come. The actor playing Duncan, Marcus Barron, also died during the tour, and Milton Rosmer (playing Banquo) had to leave due to ill health. But when they finally reached London's Piccadilly Theatre in June 1942, the reviews were surprisingly good. True, Agate thought that both John and Gwen were deeply miscast, and Darlington thought that this *Macbeth* rated way below *Hamlet* in the hierarchy of Gielgud's Shakespeare, but another critic wrote of John's success in achieving "the terrible feat of interpreting the most poetical of all murderers; Gielgud may not be bold or resolute, but he has a subtlety in Macbeth's quieter moments and an unusual sardonic intensity."

"Though not as good as Olivier's prewar *Macbeth*," wrote the critic and Old Vic historian Audrey Williamson, John's "airborne dagger seared the eyeballs, and his imaginative impulse was never wholly lost until it dwindled into the yellow flicker of brief candle and the autumn sere. Surprisingly, our most lyrical actor caught the soldier and the murderer too; this was a lithe and virile figure, combining the mud-stained practicability of the warrior with the golden eloquence of the poet; a haunted and haunting performance, with a twilit bitterness at the last."

It was at this time that W. A. Darlington of *The Daily Telegraph* made a useful list of Shakespearean roles that John should and should not tackle. On the forbidden list were Othello, Mark Antony, and Richard III, and the list of desirables included Hamlet, Richard II, Coriolanus, and King Lear. The critic of *The New Statesman*, however, thought that this Macbeth should be added to John's no-go list: "His voice is a magnificent organ, but he treats it here like a Wurlitzer, pulling out different stops for every other word. These ornamentations vulgarise the harmony, just as his pauses and syncopations wreck the melody. There is hardly a line in which the rise and fall of the verse are preserved, and never a passage in which an attempt is not made to improve upon Shakespeare's incomparably varied versifications. Mr. Gielgud can, we know, speak blank verse very finely; but all too often in this production, one seemed to be listening to a cruel revue sketch about his mannerisms."

As for the quarrels about the set, these seemed to calm down once the production reached London, and Ayrton was able to celebrate with a solo show of his paintings at the Leicester Gallery, including one of Gielgud as Macbeth, which the actor himself bought and cherished. The artist was, however, never again invited to design any Gielgud production, and John returned with a certain sense of relief to the comforting arms of the Motleys.

Despite its somewhat mixed reviews, *Macbeth* ran in the West End until the beginning of October, whereupon, with only a week out, John went straight back into a short season of his ever-reliable *The Importance of Being Earnest,* with Gwen Ffrangcon-Davies now replacing an otherwise occupied Edith Evans, thereby becoming the first actress to try to escape from Edith's all-dominating rendering of the handbag scene. No sooner had this revival come to an end, in early December, than John led a troop-concert tour, starting in Gibraltar and playing through Christmas to army camps all over the Rock.

Gielgud had by now begun to adapt himself to these uniformed audiences, which were so very different from those to which he had become accustomed at home, and this time he had strong support since his ENSA company (the Entertainment National Services Association) now also included not only Beatrice Lillie but Edith Evans, Michael Wilding, and the torch singer Elisabeth Welch. John had opted for an incredibly mixed bill of songs, poems, and extracts from *The Way of the World* and *The Importance of Being Earnest;* he also amazingly sang in a trio with Lillie and Wilding and graciously allowed Lillie's manic sense of comedy to win over an audience that was not exactly his natural constituency.

Over the next four weeks they played two shows a day, including Sundays, not only in Gibraltar's hospitals and cinemas, but also onboard the warships and aircraft carriers anchored in the harbor. Though they never came under direct enemy attack, the dangers of their situation were brought home to the company when the news came through that Leslie Howard (John's great rival Broadway Hamlet) had been shot down over the Bay of Biscay, while returning from a somewhat mysterious propaganda visit to Portugal.

John was, throughout his career, always in awe of the way that Edith Evans could silence a large and initially hostile crowd by the strength of her personality, and the way in which Bea Lillie could do the same through laughter: "I always envied stars who could suddenly walk out onto the stage quite alone and enrapture an audience by their sheer talent and originality. Somehow on these occasions my nerve always fails me. I need a set and costumes and other actors around me; I was never cut out for a variety bill."

Gibraltar was to feature more than once on John's wartime tour itinerary, and for a very good reason. His old friend and lover John Perry, now known as Wingless Victory on account of his inability to learn how to fly, was stationed there as an assistant division commander to the governor. So whenever any of the old Tennent team were in the area, they could relay to him the latest West End gossip.

It was then with some relief that, once back home, John answered, in March 1943, a panic call from one of the actresses to whom he was always closest and most devoted, Vivien Leigh. Two weeks earlier, she and the young Cyril Cusack had opened a triumphant revival of *The Doctor's Dilemma* at the Haymarket, but now Cusack had returned violently to the bottle, so disastrously that he had assaulted Vivien onstage one night while quoting to the audience's amazement several speeches from an altogether different play, *The Playboy of the Western World*. This was clearly a sacking offense. Unfortunately, however, in wartime conditions there were not enough understudies, and nobody, apart from Cusack himself, had actually learned the part. Olivier, on behalf of his wife Vivien Leigh, told Binkie that something drastic would have to be done, and thus it was that Gielgud, who managed to learn the long role over one weekend at Binkie's insistence, stepped into the breach for the two weeks that it took for Peter

Glenville to be rehearsed into the part of the dying artist. All the same, during Louis Dubedat's long death scene, John kept a script in his lap for safety, concealing it under the rug that covered his knees in the wheelchair. As for Cusack, he returned to his native Ireland in considerable alcoholic disgrace and did not return to the London stage for all of twenty years.

Once Gielgud had seen Peter Glenville, another gay friend from Oxford, safely into the role, he embarked on a rather more ambitious project. There had been no London revival of Congreve's *Love for Love* for more than seventy years, but back in 1924 John had acted the role of Valentine in that play at the Oxford Playhouse and always longed to return to it. Binkie, as was always the case now, agreed to support him, although the casting was (as usual in wartime) somewhat problematic. Several actors, including Robert Morley, declined the crucial role of Tattle, which went eventually to Leslie Banks, and Gielgud only took over the production himself when his first choice of director, Leon Quartermaine, declared that he could never make it work.

Again, however, the female casting proved a great deal easier, and John managed to round up Yvonne Arnaud, Angela Baddeley, and Rosalie Crutchley. After a five-week regional tour, *Love for Love* opened at the Phoenix to rave reviews, not least for the sets created by Rex Whistler who sadly was very soon to be killed on active service in France. The production then moved to the Haymarket where it ran for over a year, during which time John managed to do a great deal of other work. With his brother Val now installed as head of BBC Radio Drama, John performed a broadcast of *Hamlet* and also a performance as Christian in a radio version of *The Pilgrim's Progress*. He also recorded the commentary for a wartime film *Unfinished Journey*, about General Sikorski (the Polish general killed in an air crash), and then directed two short-lived new plays in the West End, *Landslide* and the Spanish *The Cradle Song* (with Wendy Hiller and Yvonne Mitchell), both of which rapidly came and went, to lukewarm reviews.

In spite of the uncertainties of war, the Gielgud family managed during the run of *Love for Love* one of its last great family gatherings, to celebrate the golden wedding anniversary of Frank and Kate. All four of their children (Lewis at the War Office, Val at the BBC, and Eleanor in the box office at the Globe, where she would stay until becoming John's secretary a few years later) gave them a lunch, which also included the dowager aunts and great-aunts Mabel Terry-Lewis and Julia Neilson.

It was also during the run of *Love for Love* that John made one of his greater mistakes. The movie mogul Alexander Korda and the director Gabriel Pascal now approached him to see whether, at Shaw's recommendation, John would consent to play the lead opposite his beloved Vivien Leigh in a film of *Caesar and Cleopatra*. "I suppose," reflected John, "I should have taken this, and I did get quite excited when Shaw wrote to me saying that I'd be much better off playing his role 'than a poor second-rate part in that eighteenth-century rubbish *Love for Love*.'"

Unfortunately, when John met Pascal for the first time, he so disliked the flamboyant Hungarian that he turned down the film, and the role eventually went to his old RADA tutor Claude Rains. Although John was in later life to play the Inquisitor in a film of *Saint Joan,* and also Shotover in a television production of *Heartbreak House,* his only real encounter with Shaw was to have been the brief takeover in *The Doctor's Dilemma,* and rather to his own surprise, Shaw was to remain one of the great gaps on Gielgud's career chart. He even once refused an invitation to tea with the legendary dramatist at Ayot St. Lawrence, on the grounds that he would have to be driven there and back by the somewhat overbearing Nancy Astor, and John simply chickened out of the long car journey.

He had by now moved, at least for the duration of the war, into the Park Lane flat where his former lover John Perry and Binkie Beaumont had set up as the resident couple, only to be joined by John in a distinctly curious but undoubtedly loving ménage à trois on those rare occasions when Perry came home on leave from Gibraltar.

Binkie, as always keeping a watchful eye on his box-office takings, now decided to subdivide his H. M. Tennent production company into a not-for-profit subsidiary called Tennent Productions; this was to cause considerable opposition from those rival West End managements that merely saw it as a clever tax dodge, a kind of shelter company within which

Binkie could continue producing expensive, prestigious revivals on a much healthier and virtually tax-free basis. Lewis Casson, then heading CEMA (the Council for the Encouragement of Music and the Arts, essentially the forerunner of the Arts Council, and in receipt of a government grant of £150,000), also saw Binkie's diversionary tactic for what it was, and the subsequent argument spread to the House of Commons, where questions were soon being asked about the salaries that Binkie was paying, and the rather dubious nature of his theoretically tax-exempt second company.

John as usual kept well away from all this managerial bickering, central though it always was to the argument about funding for the arts. Casson was now automatically asked to serve on the advisory panel of any theater requesting tax exemption, and although he came out firmly against *Love for Love*, Binkie still managed to get this set up on a tax-exempt basis, one with which he hoped to reinvent John's prewar permanent company.

It was, however, John who for once recognized the immediate problems. First, he had already played, at least once, most of the major Shakespearean roles that really interested him and was unlikely now to make a convincing Richard III or Antony or Othello; second, most of the prewar company at the Queen's Theatre, in which he had his greatest triumphs, were now otherwise engaged in World War II. However, having overcome the opposition from Lewis Casson, Binkie now insisted that John should set up a season of *Hamlet, A Midsummer Night's Dream,* and Somerset Maugham's *The Circle.*

But this was not a good time for John; his old rival Laurence Olivier was already filming the classic wartime *Henry V,* for which he had pointedly refused to offer John any of the numerous leading roles, including the Chorus that John ached to play and which went instead to Leslie Banks. Still worse, Olivier and Ralph Richardson were setting up their Old Vic company at the New Theatre, from which John was again pointedly excluded by Olivier. Richardson did once suggest that John should join the Vic, but Gielgud declined, noting only, "You would have to spend your whole time as a referee between Larry and me." Merely to return to Hamlet, a role he had already played in at least three major productions, would hardly prove an answer to the challenge that Olivier and Richardson now presented. Moreover, John's wayward decision to have two nonprofessional directors, the Cambridge University professors George Rylands and Nevill Coghill, direct the second and third productions in this season was nothing short of foolhardy.

And at last, with the war almost over, John was pressed into service as a firewatcher, which meant clambering onto the roof of the Haymarket and watching out for buzz bombs: "I saw Garland's Hotel totally destroyed, and I dreaded that my beloved theatre, all made of wood and plaster, would also be destroyed, but happily it survived."

The *Hamlet*, under Rylands's direction, soon fell apart, not least because Dadie Rylands had always been accustomed to obedient students in his many Cambridge productions and was thus totally unprepared for an intelligent, middle-aged company that challenged virtually his every decision. John therefore had to play peacemaker and go-between as well as the leading role, and, at almost forty, he was now having a certain amount of trouble with the student prince he had first played in his early twenties. His performance thus became a tired anthology of everything he had done in the past, and although this was where a young Richard Burton, on a school trip from Wales, first came into contact with the role he would one day make his own under Gielgud's direction, most of the reviews noted the difference between now and then.

"Not so much," wrote Darlington in *The Daily Telegraph*, "a sensitive youth aghast at the wickedness of the world, this Hamlet now becomes a sophisticated man to whom wickedness was no surprise."

Nonetheless, some thought this was Gielgud's finest *Hamlet*, based as it was on fifteen years' experience in the role. It was Tyrone Guthrie (who had already directed the stage Hamlets of Laurence Olivier, Robert Helpmann, and Alec Guinness) who now summed up: "The new production is good, but curiously lacking in courage . . . it is a compromise in good taste . . . you stand quite alone, in my opinion, as a speaker of verse. Yours is a distinguished, sophisticated, masterful, gracious and imaginative performance of this majestic concerto. Your lack of youth is more than coun-

terpoised by the new authority and sophistication of maturity, but I don't
think you were sufficiently directed for mannerism of movement, and the
funny bits are awfully unfunny."

As touring was still a wartime priority, and the principal requirement of
any not-for-profit company, John opened this *Hamlet* on the road, and
then brought in a revival of *Love for Love,* before adding *A Midsummer
Night's Dream,* coming in with all three to the Haymarket where the season
was also to take in new productions of Maugham's *The Circle,* Webster's
The Duchess of Malfi, and Wilde's *Lady Windermere's Fan.*

Amazingly, this was to be the first major revival of that play since
Wilde's death, and it was also the production with which Binkie Beaumont
was to celebrate the ending of the war; they opened at the Haymarket just
two days after the atom bomb was dropped on Hiroshima. As Binkie's biographer Richard Huggett has noted: "The timing of this revival was suddenly perfect. After six years of war, Nissen huts, ARP, sandbags, gas masks,
spam, fried eggs, clothes rationing, death, destruction, dreariness, discomfort and all the miseries of food shortages and the black-out, the theatre-
going public was ripe and ready for a truly breathtaking visual experience."

But this experience came not in fact from John, or any of his immensely
starry cast (Isabel Jeans, Dorothy Hyson, Athene Seyler, and Griffith
Jones), but from the newest celebrity in the Tennent circle, the designer
Cecil Beaton. When the Wilde play first opened on the road in Sheffield, a
local critic wrote, "The hero of this glorious evening is Mr Beaton, who has
mounted the play in an Edwardian French set which surpasses the richest
of period fantasies, while his costumes must be the most brilliant and
striking that have been seen on the stage these many years."

But not everything went according to plan. For Lord Darlington, John
had wanted Rex Harrison, who at the last minute pulled out in favor of a
film (*The Rake's Progress*), and his first replacement, Dennis Price, resigned
after a week, saying that he could not deal with Gielgud's changeable and
unpredictable methods of directing. The role was eventually played by
Griffith Jones. John had further trouble with his old aunt, Mabel Terry-
Lewis, whom he hoped to bring out of retirement to play the booming,
dowager Duchess of Berwick. She found the part impossible to learn,

sadly, and had to be replaced by Athene Seyler. Nor was John entirely happy with Beaton, who was clearly now about to usurp his own long-held place as Binkie's favorite. John recalled him as "a terrible prima donna," and had been less than impressed when, meeting Cecil backstage, staggering under an armful of pink flowers for the set, he asked, "Can I help at all, Cecil?" "No, no!" replied Beaton. "Just congratulate me!"

The Haymarket first night in August was a truly prewar affair, attended by such ghosts of the Oscar Wilde past as his son, Vyvyan Holland, and the veteran Lady Alexander, widow of Wilde's most frequent producer. Of all the critics, only Philip Hope-Wallace, in *The Guardian,* thought that this *Lady Windermere's Fan* "is just like a walk through a dusty old museum." The enthusiasm of all the others was such that the production was to run for almost five hundred performances, and Cecil Beaton, in his diaries, was to leave a detailed if characteristically waspish portrait of John at this time:

In his appearance off-stage, John Gielgud looks, at first glance, anything but an artist. But by degrees, one senses his poetic quality, his innate pathos. The large bulbous nose is a stage asset; the eyes, always tired, have a watery blue wistfulness that is in the Terry tradition of beauty. He is not altogether happy that he has inherited so many family characteristics, and praise of his mellifluous voice and superb diction always embarrasses him. But with the good manners that come from his true spirit, and not only on the stage, he has the grand manner. Unlike his rivals, he does not know the sensation of jealousy; he will always plan to do the best for the project as a whole, rather than as a means of shining brightly himself. This has often led him to obliging someone else, by doing the wrong thing for himself - ... something about John appeals very directly to one's sympathy. Often he appears to be deeply unhappy, and seems to make life hard for himself. Then one wonders if he does not take, from the parts he plays on the stage, the compensatory life he misses in private. One of his most disarming aspects is his knowledge and devilish enjoyment of his own shortcomings. "I'm spoiled, I'm niggardly and I'm prissy. I come home in the evening and count the books on the shelf to see if one is missing." John is the first to admit that actors are often vapid and stupid people, yet he spends most of his time, perfectly happily, retelling on the telephone unworthy Green Room gossip.

Beaton also recalled a memorable night on the last of John's wartime tours, when Gielgud found himself sharing a bedroom with both John Perry and Binkie. John G. kept them awake until dawn talking about a prospective theatrical venture. When complete exhaustion ended the conversation, they managed a couple of hours sleep, only to hear John again at daybreak, "But who will do the wigs?"

The success of *Lady Windermere* luckily overshadowed the fact that the other three productions in this Haymarket season had not really worked as well as they should have. Although *The Circle* was strongly built around the high comedy of Yvonne Arnaud, and *The Duchess of Malfi* gave Peggy Ashcroft one of her greatest roles, *A Midsummer Night's Dream* was not helped by John as Oberon wearing a Greek helmet and bright green make-up—looking, said one critic, "more like the ghost of Hamlet's father than the Prince of Fairies." Once again, he was going back to a role that had suited him far better a few years earlier at the Old Vic, though this was when Edith Evans gave him one of the most useful backstage tips that he was ever to receive. "If you were to cry less on stage, dear John," Edith wrote, "you might find the audience cried rather more." "Oh yes," replied John, "I have always cried very easily, my Terry tears, you know; I cry for trumpets, I cry for Queens, oh dear, perhaps I should never have said that."

As the war drew toward its end, so did this season at the Haymarket. John, tiring of his wartime lodging with Binkie and John Perry in Park Lane, now bought himself the Queen Anne house on Cowley Street, close to his old boyhood haunts near Westminster School, and the last home he would make for himself in London before moving out to the country with Martin Hensler early in the 1960s. At the time, such London property was far from expensive.

Immediately after the war, Basil Dean's ENSA (the Entertainment National Services Association, but irreverently known as Every Night Something Awful) was still required to provide touring entertainment for the many British troops that now remained stationed abroad on some kind of garrison or peacekeeping duties. John was duly requested by Dean to take his *Hamlet* back on the road, but this time to alternate it with the role of Charles in Noël Coward's *Blithe Spirit,* for a little light relief. This tour, which occupied John all through the autumn and winter of 1945–1946, was again not one of Gielgud's finest hours. With John Perry now as the company manager, but the usual rather hit-and-miss touring cast, it opened in Cairo before moving on to Baghdad, Bombay, Madras, Colombo, Singapore, Saigon, Hong Kong, Rangoon, and Karachi, before closing back in Cairo early in February 1946. This was where John played his Hamlet for the very last time, and it was something of an anticlimax:

> It was a schools matinee, packed with children, and as we started the play, I thought, "Well, this is the last time I shall ever play this wonderful part. I'm over forty, and it is high time to give it up." Early on in the performance, the unfortunate actor playing Horatio fell into my arms in an epileptic fit on the line "My Lord, I think I saw him yesternight." The audience was somewhat bewildered as I shouted rather crossly to the prompt corner, "Drop the Curtain. Put something between his teeth, and fetch the understudy." The understudy, rescued from the bowels of the theatre, where he was making up for Guildenstern, did not know a line of the other part. When he pointed to the Ghost and said "Look, my Lord, it comes" I said "No, you bloody fool, the other side!" or words to that effect. Fortunately, the epileptic Horatio recovered the next day for *Blithe Spirit,* but I have never been able to forgive him for totally ruining my farewell appearance as Hamlet. I should probably have given up the role years earlier.

Nor had John been entirely thrilled, before leaving England, to receive a letter from a seventeen-year-old schoolboy, one Kenneth Tynan, suggesting that as Gielgud would doubtless need to do a shortened version of *Hamlet* on tour, he might like to use the cuts that Ken had recently devised for a production of his own in Birmingham. Gielgud, ever courteous, wrote back that he had already chosen the version he was going to use and did, in fact, already have a certain amount of experience with the play.

After giving up to eight performances a week in eighteen weeks around the Far East, John returned exhausted to London to start work on his first postwar project. This was to be his old friend Rodney Ackland's dramatization of *Crime and Punishment,* and the first plan was that John should merely direct, with Robert Helpmann in the leading role. But before rehearsals could even begin, Helpmann was taken ill; John therefore agreed to play Raskolnikoff (with Edith Evans as Madame Marmeladovna and Peter Ustinov as the chief of police), and the ever-reliable Anthony Quayle now stepped in as director. This production was Ustinov's first encounter with Gielgud:

John is so contorted with shyness at first meetings that he makes someone like me feel brash and even boorish . . . and yet, despite his gossamer delicacy, an ego, totally invisible at first, imperceptibly takes over at the approach of an audience. He had been the idol of the drama students of my generation, and his single-mindedness has been constant, even when superficially challenged by the meteoric energies of Laurence Olivier, but Raskolnikoff was not his greatest role. His tremulous voice, so exquisite an instrument in illuminating classical texts with clarity and passion, seemed to me a little highly-strung for the sly, down-to-earth subtleties of Dostoyevsky. . . . One night I noticed he had left his small pink and white suitcase at the stage door, so I told him I would deliver it to his hotel bedroom. Unfortunately I got waylaid by the celebrated Jewish comic Max Bacon, and it wasn't therefore until about three in the morning that I remembered about the suitcase. Despite the lateness of the hour, I determined to try and deliver it. When I reached John's room I knocked with the greatest discretion. A voice both clear and brilliant rang out. "Come In!" The door was on the latch. Because of the timbre of his voice, I did not so much enter the room as make an entrance into it. He was lying on his bed as though posing for a sacred picture by

El Greco, naked and immobile. He put an end to my confusion by another ringing phrase, this time with a dying cadence and a throb of bitterness. "My pyjamas," he cried, "are in that bag!" and immediately his eyes grew moist.

Playing a minor role in this *Crime and Punishment* was the actor Eric Holmes, currently Ackland's lover and the man with whom he would openly walk down the street hand in hand, hoping to shock conservative passersby. This they abruptly ceased doing one morning when they boarded a bus, still hand in hand, and an old lady fondly enquired of Rodney, "And how is your poor blind friend today?"

John now found it hard to join in the general celebrations for the ending of the war. He was in any case back in New York, having been invited there to do a double revival. Alan Webb, still living at that time with Noël Coward, was duly instructed to take over in London a production that John had started to rehearse and was amused to receive, within hours of Japan's surrender, the following cable from Gielgud: "All those entering upstage right, now enter down left, and vice versa. Wonderful news. Love John."

Always more concerned with his own life and problems than those of the world around him, Gielgud now, like many others at the end of hostilities, felt "pretty well tired out. I had fulfilled so many of my youthful ambitions that I really did not know where to go. I had a fairly bad patch for a few years, when I seemed very bad at choosing new plays and was left reviving old Shakespearean hits which I really should have left alone. But I was already too old even for Raskolnikoff, and when the Americans invited me to New York to play a double of *The Importance* and *Love for Love*, it seemed somehow a safe thing to do, at a time when I really couldn't think of anything else. I felt empty of ideas and much more apprehensive of choosing badly."

Predictably, the Americans took to *The Importance of Being Earnest* (with Margaret Rutherford now graduating from Miss Prism to Lady Bracknell), but had very little interest in *Love for Love*, which they boycotted during a heat wave, thereby ensuring that the season ended on *The Importance* alone. Rutherford had scored a considerable success as Lady

Bracknell, despite the fact that one night she managed to miss the last act altogether, having confused the second interval with the end of the play, only to rush back on set from the stage door in her street clothes when she discovered her mistake.

What really mattered during this Broadway time, however, was John's discovery of the new energy and excitement of the postwar American theater. Here and now, for the first time, he met Tennessee Williams and Gore Vidal and Elia Kazan and, away from the theater, even the great Garbo herself, "lovely, child-like expression and great sweetness—she never stopped talking, but to absolutely no purpose. She said her life was empty, aimless, and yet the time passed so quickly, one could never get anything done . . . I began to wonder whether her whole attitude was perhaps a terrific pose."

By the time he returned to England, there was yet more unwelcome news. Knighthoods had been announced for both Laurence Olivier and Ralph Richardson, and although they both wrote him letters of abject apology, indicating that they felt Gielgud should also have been so honored, this was undoubtedly a considerable blow to his pride. The precise reasoning has never been clearly established; either the honors committee was nervous of his private life (no admitted homosexual actor had ever yet received a knighthood), or, equally possibly, they felt that Olivier's war record as the director and star of the patriotic film *Henry V,* together with his albeit short-lived directorship with Richardson of the postwar Old Vic, somehow made them both better qualified for honors as player-kings who had performed notable public service in wartime. True, Gielgud had undertaken long overseas troop tours, but then again so had such other leading actors of the time as Noël Coward, and many of them were to remain similarly unknighted for many years to come.

As though drawing a line under his past, John now returned to London invigorated by American energy and enterprise. He had already committed to returning to Broadway in October to direct and costar, with Judith Anderson, in *Medea* and repeat his Raskolnikoff in *Crime and Punishment.* But now, realizing that he badly needed a major new project at home, he and Binkie bought from Alec Clunes the West End rights in a play called *The Lady's Not for Burning,* written by a young Christopher Fry. As Fry wrote: "Clunes had already produced and acted my play at the Arts The-atre, with some success, but generously he realised that only Binkie and Gielgud could now deliver a West End transfer. It was all very slow because we realised that we needed Pamela Brown to repeat her performance in the title role, but she was now filming and would not be free again for almost a year."

In the meantime, there was *Medea*. Ever since, at drama school, John had been directed in scenes from the play by Sybil Thorndike, he had been determined to return to it, and now, on Broadway, he was able to give Ju-dith Anderson a considerable success while failing in his own mind to do quite enough with the role of Jason. When it came to *Crime and Punish-ment*, rehearsals had once again been fraught, not least because John had insisted on bringing in his old mentor Komisarjevsky as director, now rather down on his luck and running a drama school in Manhattan. Komis was, however, his old confrontational self, and after several major rows with both Judith and John, climaxing in a twenty-hour first dress re-hearsal, he was persuaded to leave the theater, and John took over in the nick of time. On the first night, Komis returned to tell the assembled com-pany of actors that they were all rubbish, with the possible exception of Lil-lian Gish. Also in this cast was a young Marian Seldes, already fascinated with the history of Stanislavsky and so impressed by John that he had fi-nally to ask her not to stare at him quite so intently.

During the subsequent run, Vladimir Sokoloff became the first of many actors to write (for *The New Yorker*) a detailed account of what it was like to work with John: "We played *Crime and Punishment* for forty perfor-mances on Broadway, and each one was to me just like a first night. Giel-gud is so flexible, so hospitable to each nuance that you give him, that there was always something new to find in what you yourself did. . . . We were playing doubles with the audience, and we always won. It was such bliss to act with a man like that."

Gielgud had less happy memories, not only of having to go onto salary cuts when the box office rapidly collapsed, but also of being so exhausted, by having to pacify all the people Komis had insulted backstage, that he was aware of having given a rather lackluster first performance.

While he was in New York, Gielgud revived a prewar friendship with the dramatist Terence Rattigan, who now paid him the tremendous honor of writing him not one but two new plays. This was the double-bill of *Harlequinade* and *The Browning Version,* which would have allowed John to play not only a camp theatrical hysteric (in *Harlequinade*), but also the wonderful role of the old disillusioned schoolmaster, Andrew Crocker-Harris, in *The Browning Version.* Gielgud was the natural choice here, not least because the comedy of *Harlequinade* had in fact been based on Rattigan's own memory of his disastrous appearance as an undergraduate in Gielgud's *Romeo and Juliet.*

John did not take kindly to this, however, and although he recognized the brilliance of *The Browning Version,* he decided that such a double-bill might be risky, especially given his lack of faith in the first half. Unfortunately he chose to tell Rattigan the bad news while they were strolling one spring afternoon in Central Park. "You see," John said, by way of explanation, "I have to be very careful what I do next, and I can't afford to be seen in second-rate plays."

Rattigan, hurt and for years unforgiving, took his plays back to London where, under the joint title *Playbill,* they scored a tremendous success with Eric Portman and Mary Ellis in the leading roles. Years later still, Michael Redgrave was to star heartbreakingly in the film version, and John had to be content with playing Crocker-Harris only on radio in 1957, and then two years later in his American television debut for the director John Frankenheimer.

Soon after Gielgud's refusal, Rattigan had written to the producer Binkie Beaumont in some fury, "In future I am resolved to act firmly on the assumption that my plays will only be performed privately in the Colney Hatch mental home, whither the actor for whom they were written is plainly bound."

Having, for neither the first nor the last time in his career, proved so totally inept at judging new plays on the page that he carelessly threw away precisely the West End and Broadway hit that would have given him what he now most needed, a new and successful start to the postwar years, John was to drift unhappily back to London, with no real idea of what to do next. His two greatest classical and modern rivals had just been knighted, the Old Vic was moving into a postwar phase in which there apparently was no place for him, and in the West End, Binkie and John Perry had now reverted to a prewar policy of safe old stars in safe old shows. It looked as though John's frustrated dreams of another permanent company, his inability to find film fame, and his general despair would add up to a total collapse in his fortunes, not only onstage, but also in his private life, where he had still not found any real successor to John Perry. Having survived the war, he was now to find real trouble surviving the peace.

13. THE UNKINDNESS OF STRANGERS

(1948–1949)

The problem for any romantic actor, as his youth begins to evaporate behind him, is what to do next.

*W*hen *Crime and Punishment* closed on Broadway at the beginning of 1948, it was to be the start of almost an entire year in which John G. did not act at all. One of the longest-ever breaks in his acting career was brought about by his continuing uneasiness about his place in the postwar theater, as much as the ongoing delay in the transfer of *The Lady's Not for Burning*. But he was not exactly idle. He first took the chance to travel around America, exploring it in a way that he had never been able to do while on tour. Greatly impressed by a first meeting with Tennessee Williams, he went to have a look at New Orleans and the Deep South; equally impressed by the energy of postwar New York, he also went to the ballets of Martha Graham and began thinking about the possibility of using her stylized movement and abstract settings for Shakespeare, something he was first to achieve in 1955 with the controversial Japanese *King Lear*.

He also realized that even the success in London of his *Lady Windermere's Fan* had merely confirmed the feeling that he belonged to a prewar world, and that he was therefore going to have much more trouble than Olivier, Richardson, or Redgrave in rebuilding himself for a drastically different audience. Somehow, almost inchoately, he seemed to sense that the answer might well lie in America itself, as though that country's theater was the way ahead, and he must somehow separate himself—at least for a while—from Wilde, Shakespeare, and Chekhov, all representatives of the old Europe.

It was, curiously, Tennessee Williams who showed the way ahead. His first real success, *The Glass Menagerie,* had recently opened on Broadway, and Williams now suggested to John that he might like to direct it for London. John may have seemed an unlikely choice, but Helen Hayes, who had agreed to star in London as Amanda, was already an old friend; it was she who virtually bullied John into overcoming his doubts. A London deal was duly struck with Binkie; Williams had just won the Pulitzer Prize and was riding as high as he was ever to do. His arrival in London was celebrated by a lavish party, attended by the then young actress Maria Britneva, who as Lady St. Just was later to become Tennessee's guardian angel and the dragon who was to stand at the gates of his posthumous estate. As a young actress, Britneva had already become a friend of John's while playing small roles in Gielgud's last wartime tour of *Hamlet* and *Blithe Spirit.* John had then cast her as Edith Evans's daughter in *Crime and Punishment,* where they had confirmed their friendship in difficult conditions.

As Maria recalled,

Edith took an instant dislike to me on two counts, firstly, I was foreign and therefore unhealthy, secondly I was clearly becoming a close friend of John's. Every night, she used to give me a vicious slap before curtain up. As a Christian Scientist she took pains to point out that she had never had a cough in all her life; amazingly, however, she managed to cough loudly through all John's speeches in the play. John, as always too cowardly and too kind to say anything himself, asked me if I could do something about Edith's apparent choking fits. So I simply took a pillow and held it over her face on stage one night. The following morning I was sent for by Binkie Beaumont. "My dear," he said quietly, "if we wish to get on in the English theatre, we do not smother our leading ladies. We take them cups of tea."

At the party given by John were Laurence Olivier, Vivien Leigh, and Noël Coward. . . . I've no idea why I was invited. I'd borrowed a frock from somewhere. It was far too big for me, and I had to keep hiking the thing up. After a while, I noticed a little man sitting on a sofa. He was wearing a blue sock on one foot, and a red one on the other. He looked unassuming and vulnerable and no one was talking to him. I thought he must be an understudy so I went up to him and asked if he would like another drink.

But if this first meeting between Williams and Maria was to condition the rest of their lives, things were not going so well between the playwright and his new director. Williams started referring to John in rehearsal as "the old one" and was less than thrilled during the play's tryout in Brighton to have John refuse him a curtain call on the grounds that "I don't want the beautiful effect of this play diminished by a perspiring little author with a wrinkled shirt and a messy dinner jacket coming up on stage." The problem now was that despite earlier expectations, almost everything was to go wrong. Williams found London "stuffy and full of middle-aged fags" and complained that only Christopher Isherwood and Gore Vidal ever spoke to him at all. Nor was Brighton a natural home for a play steeped in the Williams's family neuroses of life in the Deep South. It was already becoming clear that Helen Hayes, despite her lifelong billing of "first lady of American theater," was not going to be able to live up to Laurette Taylor's searing creation of the role in New York. As Williams himself was to write in his memoirs, "The great Gielgud has never been, I'd say, much of a director, but even so Helen Hayes should not have happened to him. . . . At one of the last rehearsals she summoned John, me, and the entire supporting cast to her dressing room to announce that we were in for a tremendous disaster, as she could always feel that kind of thing in her bones."

British audiences, after a long war, were still looking to America for lighter and more escapist entertainment, on the level of *Oklahoma!*, and the all too realistic account of Williams's own brain-damaged sister was not something they were inclined to take to their hearts, even if they could find their way through the strong regional dialect on which John insisted. The first night at the Haymarket attracted a glittering audience, including Princess Margaret and Lady Colefax, but they again were not exactly Williams's natural constituency; unsurprisingly, *The Glass Menagerie* failed in London to live up to its original Broadway triumph. But the author himself was not among the first-night crowd. Depressed by the Brighton reaction, fearful of Helen Hayes's prediction, and now convinced that Gielgud was making a mess of his play and that he would therefore have a considerable disaster on his hands in the West End, Williams had fled to Paris, sending merely a telegram to his mother, Edwina, reading, "Take a bow for me."

A few days later, writing to an understandably outraged Helen Hayes, Williams explained that a condition of exhaustion, overwork, frayed nerves, emotional paralysis, and constant heart palpitations had led to his abrupt departure. He added, in a terrible echo of what was to become his life's pattern, that to quiet his nerves, he had taken an accidental overdose of the sedative Barbital, which had made him unconscious for six hours, thereby causing him to miss the London train. How much of this was genuine and how much caused by his unhappiness at what John was doing to his play remains unclear. About a week after the opening, Williams did overcome his unhappiness and took the young Gore Vidal, already a sexual interest, to a performance. "It was just as bad as I had expected from the Brighton try-out," he reported. "*Menagerie* cannot be tricked. It has to be honestly and more than competently performed and directed. There was no sign of this here, and to some extent that was all Gielgud's fault. He simply didn't understand the play."

The two men did achieve, in later life, a kind of wary friendship, and the reviews were, in fact, nowhere near as bad as Williams had feared. Nevertheless, there lingered the feeling that John had not really come to terms with the world of Tennessee Williams, and it was with a kind of relief that he immediately went back to work on yet another *Medea,* this one designed for the Edinburgh Festival, with Eileen Herlie in the title role and Ralph Michael as Jason. John was against bringing this production into London, but Binkie insisted, only to have Gielgud proved right by a barrage of hostile reviews; it was Audrey Williamson who noted, "This production fell well short of greatness, mainly because of the restrictions of an American translation of depressing colloquialism . . . John's direction could not overcome this handicap of prosaic flatness of speech, nor the limitations imposed by a weak and curiously stiff male cast; perhaps ours is not an age for tragedy."

And there was yet worse to come. At the very end of this difficult year, John was persuaded by Binkie to return to the stage as an actor in a curious play called *The Return of the Prodigal,* by St. John Hankin, who at the age of thirty-nine had drowned himself shortly after the original production in 1905. Lewis Casson had been an understudy in the play, and he and Sybil Thorndike now begged John to bring it back to the West End as a lost classic. John was still really marking time, waiting to get back to *The Lady's Not for Burning,* but always reluctant to be out of work, he agreed to join a starry cast under the direction of Peter Glenville, one which would include Sybil herself, Rachel Kempson, and three desperately overdecorated sets by Cecil Beaton.

The Times called the result "the best dressed and best acted bad play in London," and several other reviewers noted that in his knickerbockers and blond wig, John bore an unfortunate resemblance to the American comic Danny Kaye, then having a huge success at the London Palladium.

One of the advantages though, of John's reluctance ever to leave himself with even an offstage hour, was that he was able to put such disasters behind him while racing on to a new project, and he was always unable to reject pleas for help. No sooner had he opened in *Return of the Prodigal,* than Peggy Ashcroft and Ralph Richardson came to him in considerable despair. They were on the road with the British premiere of *The Heiress,* Ruth and Augustus Goetz's adaptation of Henry James's *Washington Square,* which had already triumphed on Broadway with Wendy Hiller and Basil Rathbone, but had both come to the reluctant conclusion that, with only five days to go before they were due to open at Brighton, they would have to fire John Burrell, a director of some standing, who had with Olivier and Richardson recently been one of the triumvirate running the Old Vic.

As a young member of the cast, Donald Sinden, recalls, "There was obviously a terrible problem with the production, which we lesser mortals never knew about. At the Old Vic, Ralph and Larry would usually direct each other, and Burrell's job was just to make sure that the extras didn't get in their way. Ralph was also famously chilly towards directors. 'I always say good morning to them, and ask if they have had a good breakfast.' Anyway, on the Friday before we opened in Brighton, Burrell limped onto the stage and said, 'Ladies and gentlemen, I am sorry to say that I am leaving the production, and John Gielgud will be taking over.'" Burrell abruptly left not just the theater, but England itself, to carve out a new career as a teacher and director in America.

The driving force behind the firing of Burrell by Binkie had come from Peggy Ashcroft, who felt that he was simply incapable of, as she put it, "un-knotting" the production; Richardson, uneasy about the insult to his Old Vic colleague, went around for days muttering, "We have assisted at the murder of Julius Caesar!" which didn't make John's life any easier.

As John remembered:

I arrived to find that the furniture on the set was all in the wrong places, and the characters seemed to be standing around as if waiting for a train. Burrell's blocking really was appalling—the cast were strung out from side to side like a football team, and Ralph kept going upstage to look out through the door, as if to see whether the police were coming. I started changing the moves, and luckily the whole thing suddenly came to life. At first everyone in the cast was at daggers drawn, the play was nowhere near ready to open at Brighton, and the only thing the cast seemed agreed on was that nobody except Peggy wanted me to take over the direction, fearing that as usual I would immediately try to change everything, and the result would be chaos. Even Ralph had grave doubts about accepting me because I have such a reputation for altering things at every rehearsal. I do it because I be-lieve actors have to try things, and then discard them and try others. I am very restless as a director and very apt to change my mind. I expect my actors to sift the wheat from the chaff, and to know when I suggest good ideas and more importantly how to discard my bad ones.

This last-minute rescue operation was a spectacular critical success, indeed the first that John had been able to enjoy in London since *Lady Windermere's Fan* four years earlier. The reviews were nothing short of ecstatic. Harold Hobson wrote of Ralph's "relentless figure whose cruelty and restlessness were due to a great grief within." As for Peggy, Hobson thought, "all superlatives are pale and feeble things. In her hands the exquisite tragedy of this unloved girl becomes one of the theatre's most moving experiences."

Things were definitely looking up. And now at last Pamela Brown was free of her other commitments, so that, after a year-long wait, John could get down to the production of Christopher Fry's *The Lady's Not for Burning*.

Fry was now in his early forties. He had made his name just after the war with two plays (*A Phoenix Too Frequent* and *Thor with Angels*); but these, like T. S. Eliot's prewar *Murder in the Cathedral*, had originally been designed for amateur players with a strong religious connection, and this was to be his West End debut, after the brief trial run of *The Lady's Not for Burning* at the Arts Theatre with Alec Clunes a year earlier.

Fry and Eliot were now to become the leaders (and virtually the only participants) in a movement of poetic drama that flourished in Britain very briefly at the end of the 1940s and early 1950s, only to disappear as rapidly as it had arrived, leaving remarkably little trace that it had ever existed. Nevertheless, for a few brief years it became the dominant and most discussed London theatrical form, hence John's determination to become associated with it at all costs.

Because of Fry's newfound fashionability, John was able to assemble an amazing company. He would play opposite Pamela Brown in ravishing sets by Oliver Messel, and the supporting cast was to be led by such veteran members of his prewar companies as Harcourt Williams and Esme Percy (who effectively also became John's assistant director), but more important by two hugely starry young players who had just begun to make their London names, Richard Burton and Claire Bloom.

Burton was an immensely good-looking Welsh actor who had already come to the notice of both Emlyn Williams and Peter Glenville while still an Oxford undergraduate; the two men, and Gielgud, now fell for his considerable charms. In the view of another contemporary, Frank Hauser, "He already had the essential selfishness of the star actor, and a very attractive self. There is no doubt that the gay mafia around H. M. Tennent all fell for him, and although Richard was always resolutely heterosexual, I think he already knew how to play that game."

The Lady's Not for Burning was set in the Middle Ages, and it told the story of a mercenary, back from seven years in the wars, and the young and beautiful witch who wants to be spared from death as eagerly as the soldier wishes to embrace it. Burton was hired at £10 a week to play the orphan clerk. John was always to retain a sharp impression of their first meeting: "Richard did an immensely impressive audition and was marvellous at rehearsals. There was a true theatrical instinct and you only had to indicate something for him to get it and never change it. There was a moment when he had to scrub the floor while Pamela Brown and I were having a long and involved discussion upstage, and Alec Guinness told me that the audience never took its eyes off Burton. That particular, immediately unmistakable talent comes along very rarely, and of course it can be dangerous because it is so very difficult to control. But at this time Richard was very sunny, no vanity but so confident. He boasted now and then, but in a rather Welsh, pub way. He was a real pub boy, had a great stable of ladies. He was always very respectful to me but incredibly careless. At the very first morning of rehearsal he began to yawn and look at his watch, already eager to get back to the pub for a drink." Characteristically, it was in these rehearsals that Burton started an affair with Claire Bloom that was to carry over well into the 1950s, when they were to be reunited on film in *Look Back in Anger,* and onstage at the Old Vic in *Hamlet.*

As usual, wherever Gielgud was concerned, rehearsals were less than easy, as Claire Bloom recalled:

John was anxious about this play, and desperately wanted it to be a success. He became more and more short-tempered with us all, until one actor playing a small part contracted jaundice as a consequence of the pressure, and disappeared from the cast. I came in for a nice share of his disapproval, and he kept telling me to try to emulate Richard, for whom everything seemed to come easily. Burton's eyes on stage were mesmeric, giving him even in repose absolute command over an audience. In time I became envious of that control; he seemed to achieve it by doing nothing. At 24 he was recognisably a star, a fact that strangely enough no one in rehearsal seemed to question, not John and least of all Richard himself. Eventually I too collapsed with a kind of nervous strain, and took to my bed, convinced that John would use the opportunity, which I had now so conveniently given him, to fire me. However, when I came back to work, I met him at the stage door, where he simply raised his hat to me and said, "I do hope you're feeling better. I am so glad you are back. We missed you."

The Lady's Not for Burning went on a twelve-week regional tour before coming in to London, throughout which John, unable to remember Claire's name, would simply refer to her as "That nice little girl upstairs," this being a reference to the distance from the stage to her dressing room. John, even though well aware of the importance to him of this production, and of the extreme difficulty of getting audiences around the country to tune themselves in to Fry's quirky, evanescent verse, nevertheless could not lose his old workaholic habits. Thus, with The Lady still on the road, he agreed to direct Diana Wynyard and Anthony Quayle in the new Stratford season's opening production of Much Ado About Nothing, to which he would commute from wherever he was playing in The Lady's Not for Burning. During this frantic period, John's father, who had been ailing for some months, died peacefully, leaving John all too little time to mourn him, recalling only that when he had made the film of Disraeli, Frank, who had frequently met the prime minister, was more than helpful. He died, as he had lived, the unobtrusive member of the family, leaving John's mother to press on indomitably for several years to come. Apart from Val, still at BBC Radio, and now using John whenever possible for broadcast drama, Gielgud's links with the rest of the family had become somewhat tenuous, although he was always to keep a careful eye on his mother, and within a few years his sister Eleanor had given up her career as a box-office manager to become, effectively, his secretary and personal assistant. At this time, John still had no regular partner, but his life in London and Stratford was now made considerably easier by a genial American manservant called Bernie whom John had hired as a combination cook and driver. He also now acquired a dresser, known only and always as Mac, who was to remain with him backstage for the next thirty years.

Perhaps because he had less time than usual to spend on the Stratford production, John's first *Much Ado* (for which Tony Quayle, already the resident director at Stratford, clearly took care of much of the staging) was a critical and public triumph. This was where John first fell in love with a play to which he would frequently return, both as actor and director. And his initial success with it meant that he could return to the tour of *The Lady's Not for Burning* in considerably higher spirits.

That production came in to the Globe Theatre on May 12, 1949, and although one or two critics thought that John lacked the masculinity for the bravura soldier Thomas Mendip, most others eagerly acclaimed the new verse drama, giving John the kind of social and professional success in London that he had not really enjoyed since his *Richard of Bordeaux* and *Hamlet* before the war. A junior member of that company was the actor and author Peter Bull, who remembered that from the very beginning there were considerable doubts about "a poetic drama about a witch who isn't a witch falling in love with a man who wants to be hanged, spending a night in jail, and being let off next morning."

"Is there," an understandably nervous Binkie Beaumont once asked the author, "anything more to it than that?" "Oh yes," he replied, "there's an old rag-and-bone man called Skips, who comes on at the end, trailing a lot of cans, dead drunk and it's all marvellous and ends happily."

It might even be possible to argue that in its own eccentric way *The Lady's Not for Burning* paved the audience's mood for the production of *Waiting for Godot* seven years later in which Bull was also to appear; though *The Lady* was somewhat more accessible, it, too, suggested to its audience a totally unfamiliar world to which they could only gain entrance by working rather harder than usual.

Bull recorded some bleakly funny moments on the tour, not least the night in Leeds when Esme Percy's glass eye fell onto the set, only to be followed by its owner hissing at the rest of the cast, "For God's sake don't step on it, it cost eight guineas!" In Northampton, they played a dour Holy Week to small audiences in total silence, not helped by the fact that the front-of-house advertising was for a variety show due the following week, starring "Real Frogmen in a Real Tank." Halfway through *The Lady's Not for Burning*, on a Monday night, several of the audience members stormed out, cursing that if real frogmen were advertised, they should at least have the grace to appear. Some nights even that would not have been surprising among the many confusions of the play. John was already tiring of the repetition, and one night he told Bull to try coming on from the other side of the stage, which resulted in Peter walking straight into a cupboard while Burton, already onstage, dissolved into a fit of hopeless giggles: "Sorry," said John after the show that night. "Better go back to doing it the other way."

It was John himself who finally summarized the joys and the problems of directing *The Lady:*

Since my return from America barely a year ago, I have directed five plays—*Medea, Much Ado About Nothing, The Heiress, The Glass Menagerie* and *The Lady's Not for Burning.* Each play needed, to some extent, imaginative treatment, but each was utterly dissimilar in style, period and approach. . . . *The Lady* was perhaps the most difficult task of the whole five. To begin with, I was to play the leading male part as well as direct, but the author gave me a very free hand, was entirely willing to make cuts, adjustments and a few additions to his already printed text, and I was fortunate to enlist Oliver Messel for the scenery and costumes. No play I have ever tackled demands more delicate handling; the lyric beauty of certain scenes and passages changes, almost violently from time to time, to modern idioms and phrases of wit and irony. The tone of the play is ironic but not bitter, tender yet never sentimental—the fantasy has something of *Alice in Wonderland,* the words have an Elizabethan boldness and splendour of imagery which must somehow be co-ordinated into an easy and fluent acting style. Comedy and movement must keep the stage alive without disturbing the concentration of the audience on the intricate pattern of the dialogue. I tried to get it played with the artless simplicity of children.

For Christopher Fry, the amazement of *The Lady* was the way in which it remained, for John, a kind of work in progress. "The spate of his directorial inventiveness was sometimes difficult to check. Ideas came not as single spies but in battalions. Changes of moves and emphasis went on all the time. . . . Pamela and John were always working to improve their performances and I was constantly struck by John's never-diminishing eagerness to learn his craft, as though he were always at the beginning of his career, and still seeing the fun of it all."

When they finally settled down to a triumphant London reception, John immediately occupied himself with new projects including a charity matinee revival of *Richard of Bordeaux*, for which he invited Bull to play the Archbishop of York. "You see," explained John to a somewhat crestfallen Bull, "you can wear your *Lady's Not for Burning* costume, and that will save us having to hire one." From there, Gielgud went back to Stratford on non-matinee days and Sundays to direct one of the few Shakespeares he had neither seen nor read, a *Love's Labour's Lost*, of which his only recollection was "a great lesson in how not to move actors around while they are speaking verse." Back in the West End, he also directed another play by his former lover John Perry and his Irish collaborator Molly Keane, called *Treasure Hunt*, in which Sybil Thorndike gave one of her greatest comic performances. At this moment, toward the end of 1949, John had no less than three productions running simultaneously in the West End—*Treasure Hunt, The Lady's Not for Burning,* and the still-surviving *The Heiress*. He thus ended the 1940s in much better professional shape than he could have imagined possible at any time since the end of the war.

14. SHAKESPEARE AT STRATFORD

(1950–1951)

In 1950, I had what amounted to a new beginning in a glorious season at
Stratford, playing four wonderful parts and meeting the young Peter Brook,
who really started me off on a totally new line of work.

*I*t was Anthony Quayle, the actor owing his own start to Gielgud in
his prewar companies at the Queen's Theatre and the Old Vic, who first
had the idea of bringing John (who had become available in the gap between the year-long London run of *The Lady's Not for Burning* and its
Broadway premiere) together with the young director Peter Brook, who
had then just made his name with Paul Scofield in some early seasons at
the Birmingham Rep.

On the face of it, this was not going to be a marriage made in heaven.
More than any other young director of his time, Brook, now twenty-five,
stood for everything that was hostile to John's lyrical, poetic way of working. John had first met him while he was an Oxford undergraduate and
had even lent him some old sets from *Love for Love* with which Peter had
made his first film, a version of *Sentimental Journey,* which he brought in
on a budget of £250.

Already, Gielgud knew that Brook was going to be one of those rare directors, like Komisarjevsky and Granville-Barker, from whom an old dog
could learn some new tricks. John was now nearly twice Brook's age and,

alongside Olivier, still the most famous Shakespearean in the land. But from the first rehearsal of *Measure for Measure* Brook set about deconstructing him, picking up on all his more facile vocal and emotional effects, and trying to remind a now somewhat mannered player king to go for the psychology of the man under the skin, rather than rely on a magnificent voice and some spectacular costumes.

Unlike some of his predecessors, however, Brook realized instantly that he was dealing with theatrical genius, and although their relationship was to disintegrate badly during a National Theatre *Oedipus* nearly twenty years later, at this point Brook was in no doubt that

John's highly developed sense of responsibility to an audience is greater than his responsibility to himself. . . . Unlike a number of actors he will sacrifice not only himself but the reality of his own work for the sake of not letting the audience down. The moment he hears a cough, he will sense that the house is restless and produce a brilliant but well-tried stage trick to catch the audience's attention. That's where his great professionalism and his enormous experience are both a virtue and a vice. . . . What you do as a director is gradually build a glass wall around him, with an intense spotlight in the middle of it. When this spotlight of his own creativity turns inward on his own work, it has a shedding effect . . . he abandons the unimportant to get closer to the essential. Submerged in each of John's performances is a core which is pure, clear, strong, simple and utterly realistic. . . . Where, historically, his Angelo in *Measure for Measure* seemed so striking was that there was more of the essential John in it than had been seen for a long time, and less of the superficial, extravagant and tricksy John that had been seen in plays where he had been concentrating on everything except his own inner work.

In other words, it was high time that John now found a director who was not himself, and in Peter Brook he was more than lucky. Brook went for the subtext of Angelo, having John play him not as the old evil sensualist whom Guthrie had found in Charles Laughton (the last famous Angelo in 1934), but instead a repressed Puritan, fervently trying to dampen his own lust.

Brook's recollections of working with John are, as one would expect, particularly illuminating. First, there was the inevitable dropping of Gielgud bricks, in this case at the beginning of the first read-through of *Measure for Measure*, when everyone was understandably nervous, not least because of the awe in which the younger actors held John G.

As Brook remembered: "To break the ice I made a short speech, then asked the actor playing the Duke to begin. He opened his text, waited for a moment, then boldly declaimed the first line: 'Escalus!' Gielgud listened attentively. 'My lord?' came the answer, and in those two words, hardly audible, one could hear the panic of a young actor, wishing for the ground to open and playing safe with a token murmur. 'Peter!' From John came an impulsive, agonized cry of alarm. 'He's not really going to say it like that, is he?' The words had flown out of John's mouth before he could stop them. But just as swiftly he sensed the dismay of his poor fellow actor, and immediately was contrite and confused. 'Oh, I'm so sorry, dear boy, do forgive me. I know, it'll be splendid. Sorry everybody, let's go on.'"

Brook sympathized with Gielgud's notorious changeability in rehearsal, seeing him as "an aircraft circling before it can land," and realizing that although his approach could be maddening, it could also, with the right caliber of actors, bring out the best possible performances from them: "His generosity toward them in performance comes from his need for quality, which has always been more important to him than his own personal success. When he directs, often he neglects his own performance and one has grown accustomed to seeing him in a leading role standing to the side, back turned to the audience, an observer, deeply involved in the work of others."

This constant traffic jam of ideas within Gielgud's mind, and the instant relay of his thoughts to his tongue, "the sensitive instrument that captures the most delicate shades of feeling in his acting, and just as readily produces gaffes, indiscretions and outrageous puns," meant that, in Brook's opinion, he required strong direction to remove the accumulated ideas of several weeks' rehearsals: "He has too many ideas: they pile in so fast, hour after hour, day after day, that in the end the variation on top of variation, the detail added to details, all overload and clog his original impulses. When we worked together [on *Measure for Measure*], I found that the most important time was just before the first performance, when I had to help him ruthlessly to scrap ninety percent of his over-rich material, and remind him of what he had himself discovered at the start."

Brook and Tony Quayle surrounded John with powerful support, including (as Isabella) a nineteen-year-old Barbara Jefford, along with Alan Badel and Harry Andrews. And it was the drama critic of *The New Statesman* who immediately recognized the importance of the change that was going on here: "Gielgud has continually been haunted by his own Hamlet; he has never before entirely shed the last vestiges of that part, though not for want of trying. Now, with this Angelo, he makes a complete break with his past. In his thin, spinsterish characterisation there are no traces of romantic gestures, no echoes of the youthful tones. His Angelo is a bloodless civil servant hiding an ambivalent itch, and he cuts a clean swathe of sense through the play such as has not often been given to it."

Apart from Laughton, Gielgud was the only star player until then who had ever agreed to take on Angelo, widely considered a character role. But his success gave him a new confidence with which he was easily able to go forward and become the leading actor and director of Tony Quayle's first five years at Stratford.

After *Measure for Measure*, he stayed to direct a revival of the *Much Ado About Nothing* that he had first staged there in the previous year, with Tony Quayle and Diana Wynyard. With Quayle's generous blessing, John himself now took over as Benedick and brought in his beloved Peggy Ashcroft to play Beatrice. This became another landmark production; John had not been on stage with Peggy for five years, and by the time they got together again both had acquired a new kind of maturity.

As if to give himself a treat after the somber psychiatric reality of Brook's *Measure for Measure*, this *Much Ado* was picturesque, opulent, formal, and redolent of the High Renaissance. As usual, John's notes in rehearsal were not always exactly helpful: "Come on with panache" was his chief instruction to a somewhat bewildered Ashcroft, and yet their partnership here was compared by one critic to the joy of listening to the finals in a verbal badminton championship. Peggy herself always said that her stage alliance with John was akin to ballroom dancing: "It was like following your partner, never knowing quite which steps were to come next, but always knowing that you could instantly respond, because you were so in tune with him."

But Peggy was determined to create her own Beatrice (a role that both Diana Wynyard and Margaret Leighton also played with John), and to secure her own contrast with the lavish sets all around her. As a result, John found her performance "a revelation—an impish, rather tactless girl with a curious resemblance to Beatrice Lillie," and a teenage Peter Hall here first observed in her "English containment and decency, contrasted with a wild passion." Richard Findlater wrote of "one of the most enjoyable evenings I have spent in any theatre, especially John's succession of remarkable hats: blacmange mould, florid cartwheel and even tarboosh, all worn with an air of amused disbelief."

"I have now realised," wrote Eleanor Farjeon to an old friend, "that Henry Irving is only the second-best Benedick I have ever seen."

John's third production this Stratford summer was to be a *Julius Caesar* codirected by Quayle and Michael Langham, in which John first played the Cassius that he was famously to film with Brando three years later. With Quayle himself as Mark Antony and Harry Andrews as Brutus, rehearsals started in the only pitched battle between Gielgud and his old friend Quayle. Earlier in the season, Tony had watched from the wings with delight at the changes Peter Brook had brought to bear on Gielgud's acting style, but to his horror John was now reverting to his old romantic ways, and Tony was determined to have Cassius as a tough and bitter soldier.

"Go down to Whitehall," he told John, "and look at the hard-bitten faces of men trained for action as they come out of the War Office. Cassius is a soldier, up against a better one in Caesar, and he is bitter like Iago because he too has been passed over. You should really be playing him with a clipped moustache."

John remained unconvinced, but the critics were on Quayle's side, noting that they had never seen John play with such sustained vehemence. For

J. C. Trewin, this was a production of "passionate intensity, memorable force, reproachful nobility and flashing indignation—in the quarrel in the tent with Brutus, Gielgud has a questing, restless, impulsive, opportunistic discontent which I have never seen in him before." For the second time this summer, John was learning the value of taking advice to heart from other directors, and in the view of *The Times*, "Gielgud's burning sincerity makes Brutus and even Mark Antony seem puny by comparison."

Gielgud had saved for last the production he most wanted to do at Stratford, and as soon as *Caesar* was up and running, he codirected with Quayle a *King Lear* in which for the third time he would be playing the title role.

This production, as John said in a curtain speech on the first night, was openly dedicated to the help that Harley Granville-Barker had given him when he had last played the role in 1940. Ten years later, this was to be for many critics and audiences the definitive Gielgud *Lear*. Around him he had gathered Peggy Ashcroft as Cordelia, Maxine Audley as Goneril, and Gwen Ffrangcon-Davies as Regan, with Harry Andrews as Edgar, and Alan Badel now playing the Fool as a young boy in the only performance of the evening that radically differed from the rules laid down for the play by Granville-Barker.

But to his credit Gielgud made no attempt to force Badel in other directions, once he realized that Alan was determined to go it alone. And John was especially thrilled by his mother, now eighty-two, who wrote after the first night: "I can only be thankful that I have lived to see John so wholly master of his art and of his public—a great actor and a great artist. To have heard his voice break in 'howl, howl, howl, howl' and die in infinite tenderness on a final 'never' of utter desolation is to hold a memory unspeakably exquisite. Earlier, he is the primitive man at bay, opposed, frustrated, battered alike by the world and by the elements, forsaken by Cordelia, hounded adrift by his other daughters and their faction. His fight for power, for light itself, rises and falls like the force of a great tide against breakwaters."

Critics, however, were not so sure; on the first night John had slightly lost his nerve and several reviews noted that his performance had not really developed since the Vic revival of 1940. But Tony Quayle cleverly invited several of them to come back and take another look, later in the season, by which time John had come into his own and collected some glowing headlines—many of them, to John G.'s delight, comparing him favorably with the last major *Lear,* the Olivier production at the New Theatre, four years earlier.

As the season came to an end, Richard Findlater summed up: "Gielgud has deepened and widened his acting range, ripening his fine sensibility, intelligence and skill; he seems to have renewed confidence in his powers, and a new awareness of his inner strengths and potential."

The one thing that John had learned by the Avon was that he wanted to work with Peter Brook again as soon as possible ("He is so awfully good at knowing when I am false or bad, and unlike many directors he knows how to tell me so without making me lose my confidence."), and the opportunity arose very quickly with Brook's Festival of Britain production of *The Winter's Tale* early in the following year. Meanwhile he was gratified to learn from Quayle that the 1950 Stratford season had broken all the theater's records, playing to a total of 350,000 people.

Before his reunion with Brook, however, there was still the Broadway transfer of *The Lady's Not for Burning* to be undertaken. This was not, by any standards, going to be easy. As one American seeing the play in London had remarked, "Not only can I not understand the accents, I can't understand the language that it is written in." Nevertheless the word of mouth spreading from London was to make this one of the first great postwar "snob hits" on Broadway—the kind of play you had to see, even if you weren't entirely sure what it was about.

Pamela Brown and Peter Bull did not get off to the best of starts when they arrived at immigration with trunks entirely full, in Pamela's case, of dead flowers, and in Peter's, his large collection of teddy bears, plus several strings of pearls that were always worn by Esme Percy, who had given them to him for safekeeping. The American customs officer decided he was dealing with lunatics, and they were sent immediately to Boston, where the play was opening, without being allowed to spread their chaos around New York.

But Boston went very well, and by the time they reached Broadway, Bull noticed a curious phenomenon. They played the whole of the first night to a totally silent audience; the following morning, however, both *The New York Times* and *The Herald Tribune* announced that Christopher Fry was a brilliant new comic dramatist, and by the matinee that afternoon the theater was entirely full of old ladies rolling about the aisles at every line. Gielgud gave his entire company tickets to a Christmas matinee of *Guys and Dolls,* and the play continued triumphantly at the Royale Theatre all through a bitter New York winter, even on the night when a confused front-of-house commissionaire got lost backstage and appeared in his full uniform in the middle of the set. The play simply went on around him until he wandered off, leaving the audience rolling about at what they assumed was yet another Christopher Fry joke. The company also managed during the day to rehearse a radio version of *Hamlet* not made any easier when John was told that in order to allow for the commercials, the running time could not be more than fifty-five minutes. This was by no means Gielgud's greatest radio *Hamlet,* but it was certainly his fastest.

After the Broadway run, John and his *Lady* company went on the road again, this time breaking all box-office records in Washington and Philadelphia. Then, after a short holiday, he returned to London and Peter Brook for the production of *The Winter's Tale* with which they were to mark the Festival of Britain.

Leontes, like Angelo in the earlier *Measure for Measure,* is one of the fundamentally unsympathetic Shakespearean heroes that star players traditionally had avoided, but Brook saw that here, too, was a chance for John to surprise his critics by going deeply into the psychology of the character. Opening first at Brighton, then playing the Edinburgh Festival and finishing up at the Phoenix, this *Winter's Tale* was to run for a record-breaking 166 performances, the longest ever in Britain. As Peter Brook was later to write: "Working with John Gielgud, first at Stratford in *Measure for Measure* and then a year later in London with *The Winter's Tale,* I was able to enter a unique and endlessly inventive mind, always open to change. As a director himself, John had acquired a notorious reputation for never knowing what he wanted, but I found this to be totally untrue. I felt very close to him and could easily follow his restless hesitations, as he had only one reference—his intuitive sense of quality. Everything that he questioned and discarded related to an impossible exacting standard that he could never reach. This indecision is far from the confusion that comes from weakness, for when John directed a company, the rejection of the mediocre, the constant demand to go further, to do better, and the sensitive awareness of every fine detail, always led to an impressive unity."

For the critics, T. C. Worsley summed it up in *The New Statesman:* "Until Gielgud played Angelo in *Measure for Measure* at Stratford last year, he seemed unable to liberate himself from a certain softness which derived, I suspect, from the romantic actor's besetting fault of feeling it is always essential to win the sympathy of an audience. Freed by Peter Brook from that restriction, he is now discovering in himself new depths of feeling and ranges of voice which did not seem to be there before."

As the run of *The Winter's Tale* came to its end, John decided to stay at the Phoenix and revive his *Much Ado About Nothing* from the previous season at Stratford. With Peggy Ashcroft now being otherwise engaged, his new Beatrice was to be Diana Wynyard, who had just been playing Hermione to his Leontes.

As Ronald Hayman has noted, there was no problem of rivalry here; Ashcroft and Wynyard had been at school together and remained best friends ever afterward, even often playing Brutus and Cassius in a celebrated party piece at which they were already trying to point out how much better were the roles Shakespeare wrote for men than for women.

This revival of *Much Ado* was also notable for the casting of a twenty-one-year-old Dorothy Tutin as Hero, an equally young Robert Hardy as Claudio, and the veteran Lewis Casson as Leonato. By now, thought *The Times* critic, Gielgud "has become adept at turning his minor failings as a tragedian, his natural hauteur and air of remoteness, into comic virtues."

For Gielgud himself, "Angelo and Leontes are both given wonderful scenes of repentance in which they are shamed, humiliated and at last forgiven. These later scenes give a fine opportunity for the actor to show both sides of the character."

John now felt a considerable commitment to Tony Quayle at Stratford, but this season, because of the long run of *The Winter's Tale*, his sole contribution was to be a somewhat disastrous production of *Macbeth*, starring Ralph Richardson. Relations between the two actors, so good before the war, had now become more than a little strained by what John saw as Richardson's rather threatening wartime alliance with Larry Olivier, which had led to their stunning success for the Old Vic at the New Theatre, at a time in the mid-1940s when John had felt at his most alone and unloved.

Moreover, even at this postwar moment, Richardson was still very uneasy about John's homosexuality; only a few seasons earlier, when Olivier had suggested that for their production of *Othello* it might be rather clever to play Iago gay, Richardson had simply and wordlessly left the theater for two entire days, thereby conveying the unmistakable message that he wasn't getting involved in anything like that, even onstage.

All the same, he now welcomed the chance to be again directed by John, albeit in a part at which John had himself spectacularly failed, and one that Richardson had never played. The critic Kenneth Tynan, already making his name as the brightest and most savage of the new generation, was to note that he had been "unmoved to the point of paralysis by this production," coming as it did when Richardson had already had one disaster at Stratford this season with *Volpone*.

The *Macbeth* was not a lot better, and for years afterward Ralph was to surprise young actors by going up to them in rehearsal and demanding five pounds with the threat, "If you don't give it to me, cocky, I shall put it about that you were in my *Macbeth*."

The real problem here was twofold: John had never been entirely happy with the play, and Ralph could never convey characters who were the victim of blind passions. In a curious way he was just too ordinary, and although it was unfair of Tynan to complain that Richardson was "sleepwalking through the role," there was no doubt that neither he nor Margaret Leighton was ever happy with a production for which John himself (with Michael Northern) had designed sets consisting largely of black velvet drapes and very little else.

15. CASSIUS AND CALIFORNIA

(1952)

Joseph Mankiewicz's Julius Caesar *was the first film I really enjoyed making, even though during the battle scenes, which we shot in a great hurry in the Hollywood Bowl, I was nearly killed by a horse leaping on top of me.*

*U*nlike all his Shakespearean star contemporaries from Redgrave to Richardson, who were now spending almost as much time in movies as plays, John was still seldom making more than £75 a week. Not only was that the going rate for leading players at Stratford, but in London Binkie was still keeping him on a very tight rein, having persuaded Gielgud that he never needed an agent, and that simply by joining a loose alliance run by himself and John Perry and termed The Company of Four (partly because they reckoned that their theatrical ideal would be four weeks in rehearsal, four on the road and then four in town, and partly because the original managerial quartet was to feature Binkie, Tony Guthrie of the Vic, Rudolph Bing of Glyndebourne, and the regional theater manager at Cambridge, Norman Higgins), he would simply continue to be paid at a minimal rate for whatever he did.

Binkie's best trick was to tell the ever innocent John that if he really wanted Peggy Ashcroft or Gwen Ffrangcon-Davies or lavish sets and costumes, there would alas be very little left to pay him at anything like the going rate. Whether John was really dumb enough to believe this or, more likely, whether he had just decided as usual to keep his head down and not make waves, the fact remains that only with an offer from Hollywood (his first since the one he had rejected long before the war, to play Romeo) did John even begin to think that it might be a good idea to have some sort of professional representation.

On his last visit to New York, he had also been somewhat flabbergasted to meet his beloved Vivien Leigh at a party. As their conversation turned to the costs of living in New York during a long run "on our kind of salaries," Vivien, in some amazement, told him she was having no trouble at all on her salary, since this was 10 percent of the gross. John, still on a "friendly nation" deal whereby he was taking home at most five hundred dollars as against Vivien's five thousand dollars a week, began for the very first time to realize that there was something a little wrong with Binkie's mathematics. But even so, he might well have done nothing about the situation, because he was so paralyzed with embarrassment and shyness at any mention of cash or contracts until much later in his long life.

But John, with the Hollywood offer in his pocket, now went at Vivien's recommendation to see Laurie Evans, who having been Olivier's production manager on *Henry V* had set up as an agent and managed immediately to negotiate for John a contract on a sliding scale, up to twenty thousand dollars depending on the length of the shooting. For 1952, and an actor who had no Hollywood profile of any kind, this was an amazingly good deal, as even John realized. Shortly afterward, he asked Laurie to become his permanent agent, with the proviso that Evans rather than Gielgud himself would have to break the news to an understandably irate Binkie, who took it as a gesture of deep disloyalty, despite the fact that he had cheerfully for almost fifteen years been paying everybody in and around Gielgud's companies, including himself and John Perry, vastly more money than was ever paid to John himself, without whom there would have been no such companies in the first place.

The Hollywood project—a film version of *Julius Caesar*—was one of considerable fascination. With Joe Mankiewicz as director, the producer was to be John Houseman, who had worked with Orson Welles on both

War of the Worlds and *Citizen Kane,* and who was now retained by MGM as its executive in charge of culture, since the studio moguls had recognized that there was still something to be said for appeasing the critics as well as the public, as long as it didn't cost them too much. Houseman had also been, before the war, the director of the short-lived Leslie Howard *Hamlet* on Broadway, so Gielgud had always been in his sights—indeed he had unsuccessfully begged Howard not to open in New York until Gielgud had safely returned to London and there was no immediate danger of comparison.

So now, more than fifteen years later, it was Houseman's idea to bring Gielgud into the film that he was about to make: "Against studio advice, I argued that the film should not be made in Europe, where at the time MGM did many of their pictures, but instead at their home base in Culver City, and with an even balance of actors from either side of the Atlantic. Our first casting was John Gielgud, in the role he had just played with success at Stratford-on-Avon, of Cassius. But to balance that, I wanted Louis Calhern for Caesar—an aging, tired, nervous dictator, rather than the more usually triumphant one. For Brutus, we chose James Mason, now widely regarded as a Hollywood star, who although he had not appeared on stage in many years, had a classical training and the right quality for an honest, serious man torn between his republican ideals and his moral reluctance to shed blood. To play the wives, we used two MGM contract stars, both English-born but now generally accepted in American roles— Deborah Kerr as the devoted, fanatically loyal Portia, and Greer Garson as Caesar's neurotic and apprehensive mate, Calpurnia. For the small but crucial role of Casca, I chose Edmond O'Brien who was only cast now for detectives and crooked lawyers, but who I remembered as a young Shakespearean."

On his way to California John stopped over briefly in New York, where he noted, in a letter to his mother, a change in the Broadway climate:

It is interesting how action has been stolen almost completely by the cinema nowadays and the American theatre is given over more and more to psychological exploitation with almost embarrassingly real-istic dialogue, and atmosphere and character taking the place of strong situations—not the long-winded perorations of Shaw and Ib-sen but nostalgia mixed with violence, which seems to be so charac-teristic of Tennessee Williams and other young writers . . . I am looking forward to getting out to Hollywood, especially as the plan we once had to do a *Julius Caesar* in London with Larry as Mark Antony and Ralph as Brutus seems to have disappeared. . . . New York seems to me now like a gigantic monster waiting to swallow one up . . . traffic seems to drive right through one's bedroom and the noise on the streets is unbelievable . . . I find New York immensely stimulating, both in people and climate. The shops and streets are an endless kaleidoscope of colour and I seem to have made lots of friends here who are always glad to see me back. I rather fear we are never as hospitable to Americans in London as they are to us over here. . . . I hope we manage to do *Julius Caesar* better than Orson's film of *Macbeth* which I have just seen—not uninteresting, but slow and dragged-out despite huge cuts and transpositions. The costumes are splendid, but the finer language is defeated by the limitations of the screen.

Houseman's careful casting still left him with one major gap: the actor who was to play the central role of Mark Antony. On a visit to London, he asked Gielgud for advice and John recommended the young Paul Scofield, who had just begun to make his name with Peter Brook at Stratford, and around whom John was soon to build his last resident company. But the Hollywood moguls weren't having any of that and went instead for House-man's second, and amazingly courageous, choice—Marlon Brando, who was just coming off his controversial triumph as Stanley Kowalski in the stage and screen versions of *A Streetcar Named Desire*. Houseman knew, as most did not, that Brando was in fact capable of much more, and he in-vited Brando privately to make a tape of the "Friends, Romans, Country-men" speech, which was in fact so impressive that Mankiewicz cast him right away, with the provision (then unknown, but later to become standard for "serious" movies) that the entire cast should assemble for a three-week rehearsal period before any filming actually began.

As Houseman recalled, "Gielgud, from the first moment, set the tone. Not only was he already of course word-perfect and totally secure in the role of Cassius, but he seemed to inspire everyone in the cast, down to the smallest bit-player, with his own high sense of professional dedication. His perfectionism was apparent not only to his fellow actors but to everyone even remotely connected with the production. Hollywood technicians (a notoriously sceptical and bigoted lot) are men of great technical expertise, capable of recognising and appreciating such skills in others. Whenever Gielgud was working, our 'closed' set was invaded by grips, carpenters, electricians and sound men who left their own stages and dubbing rooms to come and admire the amazing skill of this English master of the spoken word, and to debate how such fluent speech could be transferred to film without loss of quality."

Houseman's budget was a mere $1.5 million, compared to the $5 million that MGM had recently spent on *Quo Vadis*. Again going against advice from the moguls, he insisted on shooting in black and white, thereby preserving a grainy reality that brought back to audiences the wartime newsreels of the recent past, and even memories of *Citizen Kane*.

Gielgud at first kept his distance from Brando, determined not to seem the arrogant English classicist trying to teach the Hollywood natives correct styles of Shakespeare. His relationship with James Mason was of course much easier, in that John had given Mason one of his earliest breaks in the short-lived 1934 *Queen of Scots*. James had really been the idea of the director Joe Mankiewicz: "I knew he had once played Brutus in Ireland at a very early age, and he was precisely the one I wanted: very complex, and broody and unhappy, a man who looked as though he belonged on a lonely battlefield. I was very glad that Houseman had won the battle for black and white, because even though colour was then all the rage, I knew that the assassination scene would be nothing but a great bloody mess and the audience would be looking at the blood instead of the face of Brutus, which was really the heart of the film. There was always a romantic sadness about James, which was just perfect."

As for John, "James had much more to teach me on that film than I ever had to teach him. I used to observe his technique in the close-ups, and saw how brilliantly he expressed his character's thoughts without making faces or grimacing. I thought his Brutus was underrated by most critics, since it is certainly the most difficult part in the play. He was extremely kind and generous to me, especially as I was still afraid they would all think I was this star actor from London who had come over to teach them how to do it. But I was surprised how much of my performance I was able to keep from the stage. It was only a question of modifying the volume and I was able to play it much faster, which I had always wanted to do in the theatre."

Even so, the first read-through was not easy, as Houseman recalled: "Gielgud, justly celebrated as the finest reader of verse on the English-speaking stage, just sailed through the part of Cassius with terrifying bravura. Mason, both depressed and embarrassed by the brilliance of his compatriot, chose to read the entire role of Brutus with a pipe clenched firmly between his teeth."

Meanwhile, MGM was taking no chances at the box office. A STORY GREATER EVEN THAN IVANHOE, read the posters, and for John G. on this first Hollywood assignment, the entire project was rich in local eccentricities. "All right, kids," he once heard an assistant director exhorting a crowd of recalcitrant American extras, just before the filming of the forum scene, "It's hot, it's Rome and here comes Julius!" On another occasion, Gielgud recalled, "I was waiting to go onto the Rome street set with a whole menagerie of sheep, dogs and pigeons, which had been brought in to make the city look more lively . . . one of the pigeons left its perch and began walking around the floor of the studio, whereupon a hefty cowboy, who had evidently been hired to look after all the animals, dashed up and yelled at the bird, 'Get back! Get back to your place! Don't you want to work tomorrow?'"

Altogether, the filming took very nearly four months. At first, John stayed at the luxurious Bel Air Hotel, but soon he moved into a little house on North Kentner Drive, owned by a doctor friend of Merle Oberon's who

was away in Europe for the summer. He rented John the house complete
with a resident cook, and like so many English actors who had arrived and
often settled there before him, John now began to understand the joys of
the Californian life. Coming from a usually rain-soaked West End, where
he had hardly even bothered to see daylight, the sudden availability of all
that sunshine and sea and sand was not the only attraction. Around such
Anglophile directors as George Cukor, writers such as Christopher Isherwood, and actors such as Roddy McDowall, there was already a strongly
established gay community, one which was able to function in comparative freedom. The local press was still strictly controlled by the studios, and
as long as one did not actually attract the attention of the local police, a
discreet gay life was entirely possible. Moreover, if one went to the right
dinner parties, handsome young men were often invited to entertain the
male guests afterward, or later assignations could easily be arranged.

From the very beginning of the *Julius Caesar* shooting, John was much
taken by Brando: "A funny, intense, egocentric boy of twenty-seven with a
flat nose and bullet head, huge arms and shoulders and yet giving the effect
of a lean, Greenwich Village college student. He is very nervous indeed,
muttering his lines and rehearsing by himself all day long. Very deferential
to me, drags me off to record the speeches of Antony onto his tape machine where he also listens to his own voice, and studies recordings of
Olivier, Barrymore and Maurice Evans, to improve his diction. I think his
sincerity may bring him to an interesting performance; his English is not
all that bad, but I fear he lacks humour."

From the moment of his first arrival in Los Angeles, John wrote a series
of weekly letters home to his mother in London, which can be read as a diary of that long, hot summer:

> The sudden change is a bit bewildering, and I feel like a new boy at
> school. Luckily I have persuaded them not to make me wear a beard,
> but the general atmosphere of California is restless and ugly—like a
> poor copy of the worst of the South of France. Yet people are terribly
> kind to me; I had hardly unpacked before Danny Kaye rang up and

sent his car to take me to his house for dinner—a very rich crowd and very nasty food, but everyone frightfully welcoming, the men in sports clothes and the women in deep evening dress. Los Angeles is really too hot for comfort, and the town is a horror of ugliness, as flat as your hand and crawling with cars. Nobody dreams of walking anywhere, and all the shops and houses are miles apart . . .

James Mason seems rather nasal as Brutus, and is playing him like a modern army officer but certainly much more intelligent than Harry Andrews in the role. . . . Brando belongs to a student theatre in New York, but surprisingly the real star here at the moment is dear Richard Burton, having a huge success making Daphne du Maurier's *My Cousin Rachel*. Last night he drove me to Malibu Beach to dine with the Selznicks—she is Jennifer Jones. Chaplin was there, and I had a long and fascinating talk with him. He is prissy, weary and neat, with carefully waved white hair and wonderful little expressive hands. He alternates between rather pretentious philosophical generalities and sudden bursts of very natural sweetness and warmth. He has a funny, shy little young wife, the daughter of Eugene O'Neill, who obviously worships him. He talked to me with great nostalgia of his young days in London, and seeing from the gallery Beerbohm Tree and Eleonora Duse, of whom he can still do wonderful imitations, really brilliant.

Parties here are grand but clumsy—awful food, too much drink, too much noise and the weirdest mixture of clothes, but it is not difficult to pick out the people one really wants to talk to, and the other guests don't seem to trouble one, or expect one to trouble about them. I have hired a superb pale green Oldsmobile by the week, and drive to a little beach ten miles away, watching the enormous breakers. Conversations are always about local ambitions and disappointments, very like the West End, really, except for the fact that dining-room walls are hung with fabulous pictures by Matisse, Van Gogh, Daumier and Picasso. Sometimes one wall rises mysteriously into the air, complete with its paintings, and a film projector emerges to show us the latest films, all of which seem fairly terrible. Last night I went to the Ballet in the Hollywood Bowl, and again it was amazing to be able to sit in the open air until nearly midnight, without a coat. The local houses and gardens are very artificial and over-elegant, usually imitation Tudor or American Colonial, and everyone looks very healthy. There is an extraordinary abundance of everything—fruit and flowers and vegetables laid out under the sky in the open-air markets, but in some curious way the whole of Los Angeles looks like an Ideal Home Exhibition at Olympia, which will all be taken down in a month or two and rebuilt for next year.

My Cassius is looking rather like the thirteenth apostle, but everyone seems very happy with it, and Brando and Mason are really going to be very good, although I fear Calhern is very hammy as Caesar, and both Deborah Kerr and Greer Garson simper horribly as the wives. Every night I get taken to a party, but some people are really intelligent and nice, and they love to display their elaborate homes, which are all like the sets for a play. At the studio, I have a dressing room with a sofa, so that is lovely. . . . We don't seem to get much news from England, though everyone here has been terribly shocked by the sudden death of Gertie Lawrence; like Ivor [Novello, who had died in March 1951], she really did go much too young. . . . People seem delighted with the rushes, and Ethel Barrymore came regally to visit our set, wheezing heavily.

I spent Labour Day lying on the beach, and am hoping to visit San Francisco one week-end before I leave. The filming is getting rather dull, and I am now restless and eager to be home . . . I was taken to a dinner for Stravinsky, who seemed charming but rather vague, and I have begun already to make plans for a new season in London. I really have enjoyed being here, although the studio workers are really much more fun than the local high society, or all the English exiles who seem somehow vaguely disgruntled, trapped by the weather and the money but secretly yearning to be home. The last few days' shooting was the battle scene, which we had to do in the Hollywood Bowl un-

der scorching sunlight and as usual I hated being on horseback, especially in the heat and dust. I have seen some early footage and think I
am rather good in the tent scene, although I still blink and fidget far
too much in the close-ups.

I have just been to see Charles Laughton, Charles Boyer, Cedric
Hardwicke and Agnes Moorehead reading Shaw's *Don Juan in Hell.*
As you know, I am no Shaw addict and it seemed to me a perfectly
terrible exhibition of fake spontaneity and a terrific bore. As for the
film, Calhern is dreadful as Caesar, and some of the sets are terribly
over-decorated as regards furniture and accessories. Caesar's house is
so full of statues and gongs and elephant tusks that you can hardly
move, and at least one of the sets had been rebuilt from *Ben-Hur.* I
showed it to a knowledgeable friend, who pointed out quietly that all
the statues were of Emperors who had not yet been born, and one of
the things that amuses me most is that the extras are paid different
salaries, according to their looks—those closest to the camera are the
ones with the most striking faces and the best salaries, while the ones
at the back are allowed to keep their trousers on under their togas.
But I have to admit that the plot comes over very clearly, and the poetry not at all badly.

As for Brando, already on twice John's salary and earning forty thousand dollars for the film, he alone suggested that the word around the studio was that Gielgud was nervous at the possibility that his homosexuality
might come across on the big screen. According to Brando, Gielgud had
told the director that he was frightened of his mannerisms but as soon as
he got into the armor of Cassius, Brando began to take a shine to him, especially when Gielgud offered him the chance to play Hamlet in London,
which Brando, perhaps wisely, declined.

Quite late in the filming, Brando, unaccustomed to the vocal disciplines
of a long Shakespearean role, lost his voice completely, putting the production four days behind schedule. But when he returned, recalled John, "He
never once seemed to lose his energy or concentration, and when he did

falter he would stop, apologise gracefully, compose himself and start again."

As for Joe Mankiewicz, who was to return some ten years later to this Roman territory with the more epic and troublesome Burton/Taylor *Cleopatra,* the film was everything he hoped it would be, and when it opened a few months later Bosley Crowther for *The New York Times* wrote enthusiastically of the way in which "he brings us so close to the characters that the very warmth of their body heat, and the intensity of their passions in thoughtful or violent moods, seems to come right out of the frame and create the dynamic of the picture." Other critics, however, were less enthusiastic.

Mankiewicz memorably described the film as "a good, rip-snorting piece of blood and thunder, coupled with eternally new and up-to-date characters." As the years went by the rather cool initial critical reception began to change; although several critics still objected that the film lacked a central, organizing principle (in, for instance, the way that Olivier's film of *Hamlet* a few years earlier had opened with his celebrated voice-over, "This is the story of a man who could not make up his mind"), others began to feel that Hollywood could do no better with Shakespeare. Bennett Cerf called it "the most impressive and exciting movie I have ever seen." One or two other reviewers would have preferred Montgomery Clift as Cassius and again took the view that John was too stagey. However, the film never takes too many liberties with the original text, and John Houseman could proudly note that even though many studio moguls had originally wanted Richard Burton rather than Brando, Marlon's performance in the end justified the risk and even achieved heroic proportions.

During the last few weeks of the *Julius Caesar* filming, John had plenty of time to think, while sitting around on the set between shots, of what he would like to do when he got home to London in the autumn of 1952. He had decided, perhaps for the last time, to try yet again his luck as the star and director of a resident classical West End stage company. But this time, even his faithful Binkie was only prepared to finance him at the Lyric, Hammersmith, rather than, as previously, on Shaftesbury Avenue. Whether this could be considered an example of Binkie's usual economic caution, or more spitefully as revenge on Gielgud for having gone off to Hollywood and, far worse, acquired the services of an agent, remains unclear.

As 1952 ended, John took the train across America and sailed from New York for home, blissfully unaware of the tempest that was about to break over his head and threaten to finish his career.

16. ANNUS HORRIBILIS

(1953)

You will leave this courtroom and immediately seek the help of your doctor.

*T*he worst year in John G.'s life started harmlessly and happily enough; he was now home again, at the Lyric, Hammersmith, at the head of the first resident management he had achieved since the war. The disaster of the previous summer—his production of *Macbeth* at Stratford with Ralph Richardson—had already been forgotten, and the long stay in Hollywood, for the filming of *Julius Caesar,* had given him a certain amount of cash in the bank for the very first time in his life.

Writing at this time the first of his many Gielgud profiles, Kenneth Tynan noted, "Gielgud is not so much an actor as *the* actor . . . he is a theatrical possession, an inscription, a figurehead and a touchstone . . . he is the guarantee, rather than the product. The seal and signature rather than the proclamation . . . he lends dignity to the ramshackle business of stage pretence and he is always a tireless endorser—on a Broadway poster this season showing a gigantic, leggy picture of the coloured singer Eartha Kitt, there is the legend 'Just my cup of tea—John Gielgud' . . . his own style is eclectic—it is not wholly of its century but its stamp stays on the mind . . . it joins hands across epochs . . . his is a teacher's face, and the voice thrills like an arrow . . . even at his worst, Gielgud has a way of sanctifying everything that goes on in whatever theatre he occupies; he transforms playgoers into pilgrims."

Financially supported by H. M. Tennent's nonprofit division, John had taken a six-month lease on the Lyric, Hammersmith, with the promise of a classical management, in many ways the only postwar forerunner (since Olivier's near-contemporary management of the St. James's was always a much more commercial West End project) of what would become the National Theatre a decade later, given that Stratford and the Old Vic were then purely Shakespearean. His repertoire was to consist of *Richard II*, Congreve's *The Way of the World*, and Otway's then rarely revived *Venice Preserv'd*. The arts diarist of *Vogue* could barely contain her anticipation: "John Gielgud, the non-pareil, the cynosure of the theatre, is the flashing, sparkling mind behind this new season of infinite promise—he will direct all three plays and act himself in the second and third. Now his powers are at their greatest—sensibility, strength, imagination, wit, all combine to make him the true aristocrat of both tragedy and comedy."

While he was setting up this season, John was introduced by Cecil Beaton to a flamboyant new figure on the West End scene, Kenneth Tynan, who had in 1945 already been writing to John with suggestions as to how John might cut his *Hamlet*. Tynan's exotic theatricality and his extravagant reviewing style had already brought him considerable attention, and as he now wrote to Beaton was basking in the starlight: "John G., whom I had never met, suddenly asked me to supper and we talked until 3, I coaxed into silence by his beauty, he garrulous and fluttering as a dove. What a possession he is for any theatre! It is irrelevant to say that he was fair in this part, good in that, brilliant in the other; Gielgud is more important than the sum of his parts, and any theatre that has him securely lashed to its mast will not steer dreadfully wrongly."

Surprisingly, perhaps, the only leading role in this season that John was not playing was the one with which, Hamlet aside, the public still most identified him; but at forty-nine, he had reluctantly decided that his years as Richard of Bordeaux were at last over, and his casting of Paul Scofield, the young actor who in many ways most resembled him, was a torch being graciously passed on to the next generation. Scofield himself, then just thirty, found it somewhat uneasy being directed as Richard II by the man who above all others had made the role his own this century, especially as John was not above giving actual line readings in rehearsal, and vaguely expecting Paul to recall precisely how his director had played the role, and exactly where onstage he had always stood for any one scene.

Nevertheless, the reviews were ecstatic, though John was perhaps less than thrilled to read in at least one of them that Scofield was now "the true Richard" and less of a "butterfly artist" than his director. But no sooner had this opened than John was already in rehearsal for *The Way of the World* as both director and Mirabell, with Pamela Brown as his Millamant and Scofield rather less happy as the flashy Witwoud. This was the play that, with Edith Evans and Robert Loraine, had restored the always dodgy prewar fortunes of the Lyric, Hammersmith, and there was the feeling that the role of Millamant still essentially belonged to Dame Edith, whom John had seen play it when he was just twenty. But again, the general tenor of the reviews was ecstatic, not least perhaps because at a less than wonderful time for Stratford or the Vic, critics were delighted to have a third classical company at their disposal. John had initially described his new company, in a wondrous word of his own invention, as the "conglamouration of stars," and certainly this production, with not only himself and Scofield and Brown but also Margaret Rutherford in a rare classical appearance as Lady Wishfort, was glamorous and starry enough even for Tynan, who wrote in *The Observer* of Scofield's "beautifully gaudy performance, pitched somewhere between Stan Laurel and Hermione Gingold"; of Rutherford he added, "the soul of Cleopatra has become trapped in the corporate shape of an entire lacrosse team," and of the two principals, "Mr. Gielgud, an impeccable Mirabell in plum velvet, has Pamela Brown begging for mercy almost before their battle is even joined."

It was left, unusually, to Brooks Atkinson of *The New York Times* to enter a more chilly verdict: "As an exercise in stylization the acting is immaculate, satirically mannered and accomplished, but in perfecting the style Mr. Gielgud has omitted the life . . . both he and Miss Brown sacrifice the fun to the technique. His Mirabell is too scholarly, and her Millamant lacks force."

But there was better to come: For the last play in the Hammersmith season, well into the spring of 1953, Gielgud had chosen Otway's *Venice Preserv'd*, arguably the last great verse tragedy in the English language but at that time one that had only been seen once in the century, in a 1920 production at the Royalty Theatre with Cathleen Nesbitt, Ion Swinley, and Balliol Holloway. But Gielgud had always known the play and recognized its special virtue: like *Othello* but almost no other classic, it offered two virtually equal male roles, those in which he now, of course, cast himself and Scofield. Rather than direct the third play of the season himself, he brought in Peter Brook, then still two years away from his thirtieth birthday.

Brook now brought all of his beady, brooding intelligence to the major rediscovery of the Gielgud season and the London year: It was entirely because of this revival that *Venice Preserv'd* was brought back into the twentieth-century vision, and Brook's genius here lay, as one of the most reliable of all theater historians J. C. Trewin observed, "in neither forcing the tragedy, nor fussing nor pampering it as a fragile antique ... even now I can recreate scene after scene, from the conspirators' heavy-arched cellar to the Senate, enthroned against the darkly glowing depths, the lagoon's sombre calm, the Execution scene suggested without some dolorous parade."

This noble, romantic, morbid play gave Gielgud as Jaffeir, and Scofield as his friend and ally Pierre, the chance to play one of the great double-acts of the classical decade, one which was to be challenged only three years later by Richard Burton and John Neville alternating Othello and Iago at the Vic, though Tynan was now less impressed: "The play's major flaw is that Otway allows Jaffeir far too much self-pity, a mood of which John Gielgud as an actor is far too fond. The temptation sometimes proves too much for him: inhaling passionately through his nose, he administers to every line a tremendous parsonical quiver."

Before the worst, the best was yet to come. Both Ralph Richardson and

Laurence Olivier were still feeling uneasy about the omission of Gielgud from any subsequent honors list, their contemporary, rival, sometime friend and (vocally at least) their superior, could they but admit it. Both actor-knights put the case to Churchill, who in 1953 overcame whatever official doubts there may have been about Gielgud's reasonably well-known, if still never publicly acknowledged, homosexuality. The case for knighting great actors with "unusual" private lives was then always a difficult one, best acknowledged by Gielgud himself in a flash of instant wit when, five years later, a still edgy Buckingham Palace agreed to the next great classical knighthood, the one awarded to Michael Redgrave. He, too, had an "unusual" private life, which had already combined marriage to Rachel Kempson, and the fathering of Vanessa, Corin, and Lynn, with long gay friendships (notably the American producer Fred Sadoff) and a widely rumored love of homosexual bondage. "Ah," said Gielgud, meeting Redgrave in the street a day or two after he had returned jubilant from the palace, "Sir Michael Redgrave, I'll be bound!"

But for now, Gielgud's own knighthood was a cause of considerable celebration; he received it in the Coronation Honors list of 1953, announced just twenty-four hours before the queen came to be crowned, and a man stood on Everest for the first time in a summer of general rejoicing. Indeed when he came onstage in what the *Venice Preserv'd* cast irreverently referred to as their "gondola garage" of a Venetian set, to speak Jaffeir's opening line, "My lord, I am not that abject wretch you think me," the audience rose to cheer him as never before. As Paul Scofield recalls: "The audience exploded into wild cheering and applause. When, a long time later, I came on, John's face was streaming with tears and the whole theatre was charged with high, emotional excitement. It seemed as if the whole world was glad for him, and he was overwhelmed by this quite unexpected and clamorous revelation of public affection. And it was his own humility and vulnerability that was most moving; it was also quite funny, because it wasn't easy after that to get on with the play."

When, in July, the Hammersmith season had run its six-month course, John flew out to Africa, where his former lover John Perry was organizing a Rhodes Festival for Bulawayo. Gielgud had decided, after handing the mantle of *Richard II* to Scofield a few months earlier, that he would after all like to have one final crack at the role himself, a decision he rapidly came to regret: "On the verge of my fiftieth year I was simply too old for it, and all I really achieved was a rather poor imitation of the performance I had given in London sixteen years earlier."

He had other reasons to dislike the Rhodes Festival. On the way out, his Comet had lost its undercarriage at Rome, only then to have to land in the midst of a sandstorm in Khartoum. The considerable delays meant even less rehearsal time than had originally been allocated, and John now also had to deal with a supporting cast that was distinctly patchy, since Perry had been unable to attract to the new festival any other stars or leading character players. But driving through Victoria Falls, he wrote to his mother in England of "the most lovely light at every moment, two or three rainbows at a time spanning those great gorges where the vast heaps of water hurl themselves, while down below grey, heaving clouds of spray are like the bottom of a gigantic cauldron with rocks and slopes of trees that make the dramatic impact still finer." The Falls were clearly the highlight of the trip.

The theater in Bulawayo was cold and vast, and a production that had been acclaimed only a few months earlier, with Scofield in the lead, now looked suddenly tired and dispirited: "I was terribly disappointed to find that, contrary to all my expectations, it gave me no pleasure at all. I could only imitate the performance I gave when I was a young man, and the fact that I was older and wiser now didn't make me any better in the part; you can't imitate a young part with any kind of pleasure, and I realised I had done it so much better then. I should never have gone back to it."

It was therefore an unusually and unduly depressed Gielgud who returned to England in the late summer of 1953. The joy he had felt at the knighthood and the triumph of his Hammersmith season, both critically and commercially, had abruptly vanished to be replaced with a deep sense of mourning over the death that summer of his beloved elder brother Lewis, and a strong feeling that he had failed, and failed badly, at the Rhodes Festival.

Not that his career prospects appeared any less golden than they had been a few months earlier. His plans now included another season at Hammersmith (this one to feature Trevor Howard and Gwen Ffrangcon-Davies in *The Cherry Orchard,* a commercial revival of *Charley's Aunt* to star Johnnie Mills, and the choice of two major new plays, both of which required him as director and star). The first of these new efforts was John Whiting's *Marching Song,* a strange, poetic piece that had been written especially for him by a dramatist still sadly overlooked today but who, in a brief period of 1950s glory (*A Penny for a Song, Saints Day,* and later for the RSC, *The Devils*), was reckoned to be among the major white hopes of the postwar theater.

John announced to the theater press that he would do *Marching Song,* but then, and rather ashamedly, began to entertain serious doubts about its commercial chances in a West End then still deeply in love with elegant revivals. These doubts were amply justified when the play was eventually staged without Gielgud's participation a year later; but it is arguable that Whiting never fully recovered from what he saw as the actor's betrayal of a promise, and it was a somewhat sheepish Sir John who instead chose a vastly more commercial option.

This was to be N. C. Hunter's *A Day by the Sea,* reckoned by its admirers to be "English seaside Chekhov," and by Kenneth Tynan to be "an evening of unexampled triviality." But Hunter had already enjoyed a huge Haymarket success with *Waters of the Moon,* and the plan by Binkie Beaumont of H. M. Tennent was once again to bring together an all-star cast (this time Ralph Richardson, Sybil Thorndike, Lewis Casson, Irene Worth, and Megs Jenkins) in a production by Gielgud in which he would also star and which would safely and happily exemplify the Theatre Royal, Haymarket, at its most characteristically tea-matinee reassuring.

The play itself made few demands on John as either director or actor, since it was at best formulaic, and its merit can perhaps best be judged by the fact that it has never had a major London revival. But he himself was now deeply conflicted; on the one hand, the Hollywood filming of *Julius Caesar* and his first Hammersmith season, as well as the knighthood, all within the last twelve months, had represented new peaks in his career as actor and director, and his current dual engagement at the Haymarket was a reaffirmation of his standing in the commercial theater as well as the classics.

But on the other hand, the death of his brother, the failure (in his own eyes, at least) of his farewell *Richard II* in Africa, and perhaps above all the feeling of personal inadequacy and shame that he had taken the soft option of *A Day by the Sea* in lieu of Whiting's infinitely more risky but challenging *Marching Song*, all came together at a time of considerable personal and professional exhaustion to push him into the greatest tragedy of his life and one which to this day, some half a century later, still resonates throughout the sexual history of the British theater.

It is difficult, in a new century, after a Labor government has appointed an openly gay Minister for Arts and Heritage, and when its Tory predecessors knighted a crusading gay actor, Ian McKellen, in a deliberate attempt to allay accusations of sexual prejudice, to recall the precise social and sexual climate of Britain in coronation year. The early 1950s were a quite remarkably intolerant time; the Lord Chamberlain, still the theatrical censor, was reacting unfavorably to any but the most coded suggestions of homosexuality onstage, and in private, men were still committing suicide rather than live with any public knowledge of their homosexual lifestyles. In this summer of 1953, the most celebrated homosexual trial since that of Oscar Wilde in 1895 had started with two accusations by Boy Scouts that they had been sexually assaulted over a bank holiday weekend by Lord Montagu of Beaulieu and his friend, the assistant film director Kenneth Hume.

Montagu, who had just announced his engagement to Anne Gage, denied all charges and suggested that the Scouts had stolen a camera from him and were now trying to cloud the issue of theft with one of homosexual rape. Both Hume and Montagu (who had courageously returned from France when it was clear the case was not going to slide away) were sent for trial, and on the very last day, when at Winchester Crown Court it looked as though the police were easily going to lose their case because of the unreliability and conflict of the Scouts' testimony, they introduced an altogether different charge, that of indecent assault on two airmen. This resulted in Montagu being jailed for a year, while two other men, the author and *Daily Mail* diplomatic correspondent Peter Wildeblood and Montagu's cousin Michael Pitt-Rivers, got eighteen months each for sexual offenses. The magistrate, handing out what he called "these lenient sentences" (the critic Kenneth Tynan had stood bail for Wildeblood, and nobody was expecting him to suffer anything worse than a heavy fine), solemnly advised all three to "consult their doctors at the earliest opportunity."

The witch-hunt that Harold Nicolson, himself a closet homosexual virtually all his life, had first feared at the 1951 escape to Moscow of Burgess and Maclean (the most famous defectors to Moscow from Britain), had taken a little longer than he forecast, but there could be no doubt that by 1953 it was at full strength. For theater people, still accustomed to a more lenient wartime sexual climate, this shift in attitude presented special problems. Thousands believed that when, in 1944, Ivor Novello had been sentenced to two months in prison (a sentence that effectively led him to an early grave in 1951), his offense had to have been homosexuality. The fact that it was nothing of the kind, but instead a misdemeanor involving use of rationed petrol for private rather than wartime purposes, never somehow overcame the public perception, especially as it had been handed down by a notoriously antihomosexual judge. Not entirely surprisingly, there were soon to be a number of celebrated British theatrical figures who found that life might be safer and better rewarded in California and elsewhere, the further they got from the West End after the war.

One of these was, of course, Noël Coward who, while never settling in either movies or Hollywood except for the briefest of visits, now took up residence in, successively, Bermuda, Jamaica, and eventually Switzerland. The prime reason, as he never tried to disguise, was that the tax situations overseas were vastly more beneficial to a man who, like Gielgud, had never somehow been able to build up any reserves of cash. But when you read between the lines of Noël's diaries, as of so many other exiled artists of the period, it becomes clear that one of their primary reasons for abandoning little England was a rebellion against the sexual and social repression, which in the 1950s seemed somehow still to be worse at home than almost anywhere abroad. The spirit, which had moved Auden and Isherwood and

Benjamin Britten and Peter Pears to America at the beginning of World War II and was to move such later artists as David Hockney and Tony Richardson to Los Angeles in these postwar years, was at least partially inspired by the sexual intolerance of their homeland.

If there should be any lingering doubt about British theatrical homophobia at this time, you have only to consider the writings of such respectable names as those of John Osborne ("The first thing that struck me about the London stage was its domination at every level by poufs; I have been hag-ridden by these monsters ever since") and the longtime drama critic of *The Spectator* in the 1950s and early 1960s, Kenneth Hurren, who wrote, "At the home of Hugh 'Binkie' Beaumont in Lord North Street, conveniently only just around the corner from where John Gielgud then lived in Cowley Street, parties were given at which there were more fag-ends walking around the rooms than in the ashtrays . . . a great deal of wrist-flapping went on, and it certainly wasn't only the girls who called each other 'darling' . . . the majority of actors and directors employed by Beaumont were homosexuals, and as he was the most powerful manager in London, that inevitably affected the climate of the West End . . . if you weren't that way inclined, you always tried to hide the unfortunate fact from Binkie, whose iron fist was wrapped in fifteen pastel-shaded velvet gloves . . . he would hold his auditions in Lord North Street, reclining in pastel pyjamas on black silk bed sheets, while young men would hopefully camp it up around him in search of a role."

But John as usual failed to read the climate of the times. Much as he had enjoyed his recent stay in California for *Julius Caesar,* it had never for one moment occurred to him that he might find it safer to live there; for him, the only possible home had to be one within easy reach of the Old Vic, or the West End, or, in a pinch, Stratford. And it was not as though in the past his homosexuality had been a particular problem for him or for others; it had been a fact of his life since his very early twenties, when he was understudying Coward in *The Vortex* (1924) and came to the realization of how much in common they had both on- and offstage.

Like Noël, John was immensely discreet about his affairs, and happiest when in long-term relationships such as the one through the late 1930s with John Perry, or the one that he was to sustain for the last forty years of his life with Martin Hensler. Between these, he was certainly susceptible to more fleeting sexual affairs with other men, such as the interior decorator Paul Anstee, but (again as with Coward) these were very often with young actors or other theatrical workers who had more to lose than to gain by posing any kind of public or private threat. Moreover, soon after John's trial, his sister Eleanor virtually took up residence in Cowley Street, not only to deal with his correspondence, but also to keep a beady eye out for anyone who was likely to get John into further homosexual trouble. The affair with Anstee, therefore, had to be pursued in other places and at other times.

The London theater was still, in these long ago pre-AIDS days, a very tolerant and easygoing place to live and work, and there had seldom been any real sense of danger; indeed policemen around Shaftesbury Avenue were noted for their broadmindedness, and sometimes their complicity. Yet there would be the occasional sudden and sharp attacks on homosexuals, all the more frightening because they were unpredictable.

There had, of course, been arrests and frequent convictions in the past, but these had seldom received the press attention that was now granted to them in the aftermath of the Montagu affair. Before the war, Lady Astor's son was found guilty of gross indecency with another man and sentenced to prison in 1931, and four years later the louche Labor member of Parliament Tom Driberg was charged with homosexual offenses. Neither of these cases, however, was reported in the press, thanks to the power of the Fleet Street censorship then wielded by Lady Astor and Driberg's great protector, Lord Beaverbrook. If Britain could be kept in the dark about an affair between its king and a married American, it certainly didn't need to know about a few homosexuals in high places.

Rather less fortunate, however, was Sir Paul Latham, a member of Parliament and former chairman of the Labor Party, who was amid much publicity sentenced to two years imprisonment in 1941, having been found guilty of ten homosexual offenses. A year later, the leading theatrical photographer of his time and a close friend of Gielgud's, Angus McBean, was sentenced to two years in jail for similar offenses, but that, if we accept the confusion over the Novello petrol affair, was the limit of the arrests visited on theater people in Gielgud's circle prior to 1953. As a result, the "gay mafia" headed by Gielgud and Coward and Binkie Beaumont and John Perry took it that, so long as they were reasonably discreet and kept their liaisons well hidden within the theatrical community that they led, they would be unlikely to encounter any real public difficulty.

All that had abruptly changed, however, early in 1953, although John, as usual wildly unworldly in nontheatrical matters, could hardly be expected to have noticed any cases not involving his immediate circle. The Montagu affair was hotly followed by another widely publicized arrest, that of the prolific author and biographer of Wilde's friend Lord Alfred Douglas, Rupert Croft-Cooke. On October 4, 1953, he came up before a viciously homophobic magistrate, R. E. Seaton, at the East Sussex Quarter Sessions, where he was accused of having illicit gay sex with two adult sailors. Sir Compton Mackenzie and Lord Kinross both gave evidence for Croft-Cooke, being defended by one of the most able barristers of the day, G. D. "Khaki" Roberts, who managed to prove that both sailors had frequently changed their stories and almost certainly taken police immunity in return for telling their tales. In short, the police case here was thoroughly shaky, but that did not deter the jury from finding Croft-Cooke guilty, or Seaton from handing down a nine-month sentence. "Your house has been a den of iniquity," announced Seaton, "and you are a menace to young men." He added, however, just in case anyone might think him a shade prejudiced against homosexuals, that "I know a waiter at my club who is a flaming pansy . . . I do not dislike him. I do not watch him. It is all right until you are caught." In these pre-Wolfenden years, the issue was not one of age; two men could be "caught," to echo Seaton's words, in the privacy of their own home and still be found guilty of homosexuality, though in most of the cases that now came to trial there was usually some element of soliciting. Young men in any kind of uniform were for some obscure reason considered especially vulnerable to such solicitation.

Anyone with even fractionally more public awareness or general common sense than John G. would have realized that a pattern was being formed here, and an especially ugly one at that. In almost all the cases mentioned, house arrests were being made on Saturday mornings so that the police could obtain maximum coverage in such Sunday papers as the *News of the World,* famous for its front-page interest in sexual matters, preferably containing celebrities or vicars, or, if at all possible, a combination of the two. Social and sexual historians of the period still seem divided as to whether what was happening in 1953 was the result of a coordinated police crackdown, or whether it was just the last, vicious gasp of official puritanism before what was already seen as the inevitable reaction of the sixties.

Poet Philip Larkin may have blithely declared that sex may have started with the Beatles in 1963, but ten years earlier it was certainly stopping for a lot of people suddenly aware of a witch-hunt as potent as the one being contemporaneously waged on supposed Hollywood Communists by the McCarthy tribunals in the United States.

With the wisdom of almost fifty years' hindsight, it can be reckoned that although there was no organized antihomosexual British witch-hunt as such, a number of senior policemen and magistrates and even civil servants had decided that in this coronation year, at the start of a new Elizabethan Age, certain barriers did have to be repositioned if the country was not going to go to the dogs. As so often in England, this was not an especially organized or even sinister affair, merely the British in one of their periodic fits of hypocrisy.

Most high-ranking legal figures of the period had almost certainly gone to a public school of the 1920s and would have been lucky to have escaped some form of buggery in the dormitory. But what was still perfectly acceptable at Eton and Harrow, and Oxford and Cambridge, was reckoned "not a good thing" elsewhere, rather on the principle of Mrs. Patrick Campbell's celebrated dictum that she never cared what anyone did sexually "so long as they don't do it in the street and frighten the horses." Several people now seemed to think that altogether too many horses were being frightened for the public good, and that, in the celebrated English phrase, "Something must be done."

What, precisely, was to be done was never made clear, and certainly not in time to save Gielgud from the worst night of his life, and the greatest public and private humiliation of his career. On the evening of October 21, 1953, with rehearsals for *A Day by the Sea* coming to an end, and an opening on tour planned for the following week, John was arrested in a public rest room in Chelsea for soliciting.

The rest room had long been staked out by police as one much used for "cottaging" (casual homosexual pickups after dark involving strangers), and there is considerable evidence that Gielgud had been there several times in the last few weeks. Without a steady boyfriend, worried about the new play, and exhausted from the various ventures of the last few months, all of which had crowded in on him at an unhappy and insecure time in his life, he sought some form of physical relief among strangers in the night. It is even suggested, though without any solid proof, that charitable detectives, those who disliked the task of lurking around in plainclothes in underground gentlemen's lavatories hoping to secure an arrest, had actually warned Gielgud, telling him that now that he had the knighthood he really should be more circumspect, but that if he were ever to get caught he should be sure to give a false name. That way, it was said, the charge sheet could be effectively "doctored" overnight and there would be no danger of a public court appearance in the morning.

If that was the police plan or intention, it backfired badly. John, caught by a police decoy he had propositioned, remembered something about not giving his real name and therefore announced that he was Arthur rather than John Gielgud when questioned at the local Chelsea police station to which he had been immediately taken. In truth he had, of course, been christened Arthur John Gielgud, but as it was the surname that the friendly police were trying to avoid having to inscribe on the public register, the reversion to his first Christian name was of remarkably little advantage in the crisis. John had by now well and truly lost the plot.

His temporary loss of all common sense and any personal security could not have come at any worse time in the entire century. What Coward was to call "that deafening Kinsey Report" into sexuality had just been published in America, thereby giving an eager British press some legitimate excuse, however hazy, to put sex at the top of their headline agenda.

Added to that, 1953 had already seen the start of the debate over whether or not the newly crowned Queen's sister was to be allowed to marry "a divorced man" like Group Captain Peter Townsend, and the Church of England, as if aware of moral ground now fast slipping away beneath its feet, had just successfully demanded the imposition of a press council to control the greater sexual excesses and liberties of a newly liberated Fleet Street. The old Victorian order was at last ending, but there was no agreement as to what should take its place as the standard of public or even private morality.

None of this, of course, would have been noticed by John in any of his rare breaks from rehearsal, and when he was arrested his only words to the decoy policeman were, "I am so terribly sorry." An hour or two later, at Chelsea police station, he pleaded guilty to the charge of importuning, but rallied sufficiently to give what he thought was a suitably false name and to describe himself as "a clerk earning a thousand pounds a year."

He was bound over by an Inspector Puckey to reappear at Chelsea Magistrates' Court at 10:30 A.M. the following morning. The actor who had been a Knight Bachelor for barely three months then returned home to Cowley Street, to consider his options. Forty years later, I asked him what these had been. He replied:

Suicide, for a start; I thought about that a lot for an hour or two, and for the first and last time in my life. But even then, it seemed somehow ridiculously melodramatic even to me, and besides I hadn't the faintest idea how one would go about it. What I should have done, of course, was to telephone Binkie who was always said to be incredibly well-connected, and might well have known someone high enough up in Scotland Yard to help. He also had a wonderfully secretive press secretary called Vivienne Byerley; she was known in the business as "no news is good news," and ever afterwards Emlyn Williams always mischievously said that if I had simply told her, nobody would ever have found out.

So why didn't I call on Binkie's help? For all kinds of reasons, none of them perhaps good enough. I was thoroughly ashamed, not of what I had done but of being caught, and I couldn't bear to hear the anger or disappointment in Binkie's voice. Then again, I had some vague Westminster schoolboy idea that when you were in trouble you had to stand on your own two feet, and "take it like a man."

He stayed awake all night, and soon after eight next morning heard the phone ring. A desk sergeant, coming on duty at Chelsea police station, had been reading the overnight log and realized that the worst had now happened. Gielgud, drunk and confused, had given his real surname and nothing could be done to get his name off the arrest register, even by a policeman considerably more liberal than the one who had entrapped him.

But the desk sergeant had an idea that all might still not be totally lost. If he could get one of the duty magistrates to come in thirty or so minutes earlier than usual, before the official opening of the Chelsea police court at 10 A.M., then it was just about possible that Gielgud could be heard, fined, and gotten safely away before any members of the press arrived to report the business of the day.

A resident magistrate, E. R. Guest, proved grumpily willing to start his court's proceedings at 9:30 A.M., and Gielgud was now telephoned to attend. In the dock, he merely repeated his statement of the previous night, adding only, "I cannot imagine how I could have been so stupid; I was very tired, and had a few drinks. I was not responsible for my action."

Guest was, mercifully, not of the hanging or flogging persuasion and showed no sign that he had ever heard of the man who had been brought up before him. He merely fined John the standard ten pounds, solemnly adding the instruction, "You are to see your doctor the moment you leave this court, and tell him exactly what you have done. If he has any advice to offer, you are to take it, because this conduct is dangerous to other men, particularly young men, and it is a particular scourge in this neighbourhood." On the very same day, Douglas Byng, a notoriously camp cabaret star, was fined a mere seven pounds for driving without due care and attention.

Precisely what medical cure Guest had in mind is unclear, nor can one tell what evidence he had for the belief that Chelsea had suddenly and uniquely fallen victim to a "scourge" of homosexual, middle-aged actors importuning plainclothes policemen in public rest rooms.

But by now it was too late. A Fleet Street police reporter, on his way to some altogether different courtroom, had suddenly heard the most distinctive voice in British theater and had rapidly alerted his colleagues. As the press box filled up with hacks who could not believe their luck that morning, the magistrate rose to his theme: "I hear something like six hundred of these cases every year," he announced, more in sorrow than in anger, "and I begin to think that they ought to be sent to prison . . . I suppose on this occasion I can treat you as a bad case of drunk and disorderly, and fine you accordingly, but nobody will ever do that again."

Nor, of course, would John. He slunk back to rehearsal, only to find that the early edition of the *Evening Standard* already had him on its front page. His company, with the rather puritanical exception of one wardrobe mistress, was solidly behind him and yet deeply embarrassed, though no more so than John himself. After a terrible pause as he came on from the wings to start the afternoon rehearsal, it was left to the veteran Dame Sybil Thorndike, herself no stranger to police courts where she had frequently made personal appearances before and during World War I as a leading suffragette, to break the silence with the most brilliant phrase that had perhaps ever occurred to her. "Well, John," she murmured, "what a very silly bugger you have been." Her support for John, in this terrible time, was remarkable; she even arranged at the stage door to have the hate mail addressed to him redirected to her, whereupon she would write to all the correspondents, asking them "to extend Christian charity to somebody who was different."

By that evening the story was all over London. Kenneth Williams wrote in his diary the next day: "It appears from the papers that Sir John Gielgud has been arrested on a charge of homosexual importuning. He described himself on the charge sheet as 'a clerk of Cowley Street, with an income of £1000 a year.' Why tell these kinds of lies? Of course, this is clearly a case of persecution. Poor fellow."

During the afternoon John had been able to bury himself in the final re-hearsals of *A Day by the Sea*. But that night, in the private sanctuary of the house that Hugh Beaumont and John Perry shared in Lord North Street, just behind Westminster School, there was the inevitable crisis meeting. John, ever the man to do the right thing when his limited social skills enabled him to work out just what that might be, at once tendered his resignation as star and director of the production. This, however, was easier said than done, it now being late Wednesday night and the play due to open the following Monday at the Royal Court in Liverpool, at the start of its pre-London tour.

It was hardly likely that a leading actor/director could be found to replace him in less than four days, and the concept of simply not opening on Monday night was, in those days, totally unfamiliar. The show must indeed go on regardless. Besides, Hugh "Binkie" Beaumont, by now the most powerful theatrical manager in the whole postwar history of the British theater, was a treacherous and cunning bugger, to use an unusually literal expression. He had no choice but to play for time. John would have to open in Liverpool as planned, and it would then be up to the great British public. If they showed no sign of undue offense and, more important, still exhibited no tendency toward withdrawing support from Gielgud's box office on the road, then John could remain assured of his patronage and friendship. But if the tour had noticeably suffered through John's unfortunate indiscretion, then it would not perhaps be beyond the bounds of possibility to attract another actor and director to the project before the play eventually opened in town.

There is no doubt that John's career really did now hang in the balance. To the crisis meeting at Lord North Street, Binkie had summoned Glen Byam Shaw and his wife, Angela Baddeley; Larry and Vivien; and Ralph and his wife, Meriel Forbes. All but one of those present agreed that it would be fatal, not only to John's career, but possibly to John himself, if he were not to be allowed to open in Liverpool. The one dissenting voice was that of Olivier, never one of John's greatest supporters, who now saw the chance to do his old rival damage. He suggested that the production should be postponed for at least three months, whereupon Vivien Leigh turned on him in a savage outburst, pointing out that Larry had always been jealous of John and that his view should therefore be totally discounted by the meeting, which indeed it was.

And now, another voice was heard. John's brother Val was no longer especially close to him, and as a man who was to marry a total of five different wives, he had little or no understanding of John's homosexuality. He was, however, still his elder brother and felt now that as their mother was distinctly aged, he should stand in loco parentis for John. What Val now did had a kind of Machiavellian brilliance. He presented himself at Binkie's home with a direct threat. If, said Val, Binkie or his friends did anything to threaten John's position in the theater as a result of the arrest, Val would simply go public with the names of all of those actors, directors, designers, and playwrights who were within Binkie's gay circle of friends and employees, including Binkie and John Perry themselves.

Luckily for John, Binkie's resolve never had to be tested. What happened over the next weekend was that the company traveled to Liverpool and prepared for its opening night almost as if nothing untoward had happened to its director and star. "Almost," because Binkie had taken the precaution of hiring extra security men to make sure that no enraged antihomosexual Liverpudlians—and worse still, no journalists—could get past the stage door. Then came the Monday first night, as described by the theater historian Richard Huggett:

It is unlikely that there was ever a Tennent first night filled with such tension and gloomy foreboding. Gielgud's first entrance, as Julian Anson, the diplomat, was a quarter-hour into the first act, probably the longest and most crucifying fifteen minutes of his life. When the moment came, he could not enter: he was paralysed and shaking with fear. Once again, it was Sybil Thorndike who came to the rescue. She was on stage, having just completed a short scene with Irene Worth. When Gielgud failed to appear she could see him in the wings, knew what was the trouble and what had to be done. She walked off through the French windows, grabbed him and whispered fiercely, "Come on, John darling, they won't boo me," and led him firmly onto the stage. To everybody's astonishment, and indescribable relief, the audience gave him a standing ovation. They cheered, they applauded, they shouted. The message was quite clear. The English public had always been loyal to its favourites, and this was their chance to show that they didn't care about what he had done in his private life, he was still their adored leading actor, still a star, still their own, their very own John Gielgud, and that they loved and respected him dearly. It was a moment never to be forgotten by those who witnessed it, Sybil Thorndike hugging him and smiling with unmistakable defiance at the audience, as if to say, "I don't think it matters, do you?" and Gielgud, the famous Terry tears visibly running down his cheeks, unable to speak. It was a long time before he could stammer out his first line, one of delicious triviality: "Oh dear, I'd forgotten we had all those azaeleas," which, at a moment of such cosmic significance, was greeted by a roar of laughter and renewed applause.

There was a certain irony in the fact that John played his first post-trial performance at Liverpool, since it was there, before the war, that Alec Guinness, while a member of the local rep, was himself picked up for homosexual soliciting. This never came out in Alec Guinness's lifetime because, unlike John, he did remain alert enough to give the police a totally false name; the one he chose, Herbert Pocket, was of course from Dickens's *Great Expectations,* a role he had already played onstage and was soon to film. Luckily for him, Dickens appears not to have been required reading at the Liverpool Police headquarters and Pocket's name is still solemnly inscribed in the list of offenders.

In more ways than one, they were up and running and the tour continued in a triumph only to be repeated, albeit a little less vociferously, on the London first night at the Haymarket. Binkie, still nervous about some kind of counter-demonstration, had carefully arranged to have John exit through the front of the house after the show, thereby avoiding the stage-door crowds. "Nonsense," announced John, who had by now found his own voice again. "I shall leave through the stage door like any other actor." And he did, to renewed applause from the faithful.

Yet it would be wrong to suggest that all concerns for what had transpired disappeared entirely. The price John paid for his Chelsea indiscretion was considerable and very long-lasting—arguably, indeed, until the very end of his long life, nearly half a century later. In immediate terms, rumors that his knighthood could be withdrawn were immediately discounted; even when, thirty years later, Sir Anthony Blunt had his taken away, it was because of his pro-Soviet treachery rather than his homosexuality.

However, the Garrick Club, dominated then (as for so many years to come) by some extremely right-wing lawyers and judges with remarkably old-fashioned and intolerant views, seriously debated behind closed doors the removal of John's membership. By the time the club got round to honoring Sir John with a lunch to celebrate his Order of Merit in 1997, it was fervently hoped that if any of those who had threatened him in 1953 were still alive, they would at least have the grace to stay away from that celebration.

Feelings also ran high backstage, ranging from "There but for the grace of God" from many gay actors to a vicious whispering campaign, which climaxed in a petition sent anonymously to all stage doors demanding Gielgud's resignation from Equity. The organizer of this petition was the character actor Edward Chapman, who, ironically, a few years later, was to turn up as the mad Marquis of Queensbury in the Robert Morley film of *Oscar Wilde*. But so loved was John within the profession that Chapman found very few signatories, and when the petition appeared on the stage-door bulletin board of the Arts Theatre, the then director Alec Clunes commendably called his company together onstage to announce that anyone who signed it would be immediately fired. This was a gesture of special generosity considering that less than two years earlier John had effectively stolen *The Lady's Not for Burning* from Clunes, who had first produced the play and performed its leading role.

I also have here to admit, with some familial shame, that my grandfather Herbert Buckmaster, who had been married to two actresses (Gladys Cooper and Nellie Taylor), wrote to the *Evening Standard* at this time: "If the public refrained from going to theatres where actors with queer habits were employed, managements would not be so anxious to engage them. In older days, actor-managers like Sir Charles Hawtrey would never have one of them in his theatre." In Buck's defense, some forty years after his death, I can only add that he was a compulsive letters-to-the-editor writer on a vast range of topics, and that his opinions often changed sharply during a single day. He had many gay friends and even relatives, but conceivably felt that the predominantly military members of the Buck's Club he had founded just after World War I would expect some sort of harrumphing response from its leader.

There were, however, other, much more serious consequences. The United States, then still in the grip of its McCarthy intolerance, had a "moral turpitude" clause in its entry visas, which meant that in the following year, when Gielgud was invited to lead the Stratford Memorial Company to New York as Prospero in *The Tempest*, the British Embassy in Washington regretfully, if perhaps overcautiously, advised cancellation lest John's presence should prove to be "an embarrassment" in view of the local press comment that might occur. It was to be almost four years before he played the United States again.

But still that was not all; the after-effects of the Gielgud trial were being felt around the world. In Jamaica, Noël Coward wrote a diary entry that was virtually the only one of major significance that his editors (Graham Payn and I) decided, in deference to Gielgud's wishes, not to publish in his lifetime. Published now for the first time, it reads: "Poor, silly, idiotic, foolish, careless John. Of course I feel very sorry for him in what must be an agonising time, but did he not even for a moment think about what trouble his little indiscretion would cause the rest of us? England, my England, has always been full of intolerance and bigotry. Just when things might have started to improve for us all, John goes and does something so utterly careless that it will do us harm for years to come, at least among those who still think that our private sex lives are any of their bloody business. And to do this within months of a knighthood, which made it seem as though at long, long last things might have been beginning ever so slowly to change . . . how could he, how could he, have been stupid and so selfish?"

Coward did not get his own knighthood until 1970, fully seventeen years later, and it could well be argued that Gielgud was very largely to blame for his long wait. But Coward was concerned with more than just his own re-habilitation or return to English orthodoxy: always an astute social observer of the seismic shifts in the popular taste of his beloved countrymen, even when viewed through the long telescope of a Jamaican exile, he had realized that the issue here was still greater than the career of one man, however exalted.

That issue was also the concern of an Australian journalist, Donald Horne, writing in the *Sydney Sunday Telegraph* of October 25, 1953, four days after John had appeared in court. It was Horne who first formulated, at least in print, the still-contested notion that there was an official witch-hunt against celebrated gays in the years 1953–1954. This is a theory shared by such later biographers as Humphrey Carpenter on Benjamin Britten, Margaret Drabble on Angus Wilson, and Alan Hodges on Alan Turing, all of whom were in some form of homosexual troubles at the time, but it is equally strongly contested by the historian Patrick Higgins, who points out that there were in fact fewer gay arrests in these two years than during those immediately before.

Nevertheless, for Horne at least, the message was clear.

The sensational charges made this week against Lord Montagu of Beaulieu and actor Sir John Gielgud are the result of a Scotland Yard plan to smash homosexuality in London. The plan originated after strong United States advice to Britain to weed out homosexuals, as hopeless security risks, from important government jobs. One of the Yard's top rankers, Commander E. A. Cole, recently spent three months in America consulting with the FBI officials in putting finishing touches to the plan, one which was extended to a war on all vice when Sir John Nott-Bower took over as the new Commissioner at Scotland Yard in August 1953.

Sir John swore he would rip the cover off all London's filth spots. Montagu and Gielgud were the latest accused in his drive against the shocking crime of male vice which is now linked with drives on call-girl rackets, obscene postcards and the widespread vice trade. Until Sir John moved to the top job at the Yard as a man with a mission, Montagu and his film-director friend might never have been charged with grave offences with Boy Scouts. This week's conviction of Gielgud for persistently importuning also sprang from increased police vigilance.

The conspiracy theory is at first sight an attractive one, especially when linked to America in one of its periodic fits of social and sexual paranoia. But the evidence is seriously shaky here, and it even could be argued that the Gielgud arrest was, on the contrary, the start of a considerable liberalization of the laws governing homosexuality. Within a few days of the story breaking in the press, *The New Statesman* and *The Observer,* both publications of considerably more influence then than now, were calling for law reform to bring Britain into line with France and several other European countries where homosexual acts in private between consenting adults were considered in no way criminal. True, this would not have helped John's case since his act was not committed in private, nor could "soliciting" be considered in quite the same light as "consenting." Nevertheless, for the first time since the death of Oscar Wilde in 1900, the debate had now been formally reopened in print, and the Home Office was soon forced to include homosexuality within the remit of the report it had long promised on female prostitution, the two issues then being considered of a similarly scandalous nature.

But Gielgud still had ferocious enemies, not least one of Beaverbrook's leading editors, the deeply reactionary John Gordon of the *Sunday Express,* who wrote in his column on the Sunday following the court appearance:

Sir John Gielgud should consider himself a very lucky man to have met such a gentle magistrate. I am loath to make his punishment heavier by provoking a wider discussion of his delinquency, but the moral rot in the charge against him of "persistently importuning male persons" menaces the nation much more than most people realise. Because the offence to which Gielgud pleaded guilty, with the excuse that he had been drinking, is repulsive to all normal people, a hush-hush tends to be built up around it. Sensitive people shrink from discussing it. Newspapers are disinclined to switch on the searchlight of public exposure, regarding it as a peculiarly unsavory subject. What have been the consequences of that delicacy? The rot has flourished behind the protective veil until it is now a widespread disease. It has penetrated every phase of life. It infects politics, literature, the stage, the Church and youth movements, as the criminal courts regularly reveal to us. In the exotic world of international politics, it seems at times to be an occupational disease.

It is not purely a West End plague: it is often pleaded, on behalf of these human dregs, that they are artistic or ineffectual creatures, who because of their special qualities should have special freedoms. This is not so; the vice is as prominent among lowbrows as it is among highbrows, and the suggestion that peculiar people should be allowed peculiar privileges is arrant nonsense. The equally familiar plea that these pests are purely pathological cases, and should be pampered instead of punished, is almost as rubbishy. It is time our community decided to sanitise itself, for if we do not root out this moral rot it will bring us down, as inevitably it has brought down every nation in history that has become affected by it. There must be sharp and severe punishment; but more than that, we must get the social conscience of the nation so raised that such people are made into social lepers. Decent people should neither encourage them nor support them, and it is utterly wrong that men who corrupt and befoul other men should strut in the public eye, enjoying adulation and applause however great their genius. And I would suggest that in future the nation might suitably mark its abhorrence of this type of depravity by stripping from men involved in such cases any honours that have been bestowed upon them.

Gordon's hysterical, homophobic rant was, in fact, the only call in print for John to be stripped of his new knighthood. But before we dismiss it from the infinitely safer and more comfortable standpoint of a new century, it is worth recalling that Gordon was writing for some 12 million readers, at the height of the *Sunday Express*'s power and influence, and could have proved an extremely dangerous enemy, had he not been happy to set off the following Sunday on some equally manic tirade aimed elsewhere.

Other journalists were now inclined to leave the Gielgud case alone, not so much out of some newfound sense of probity or shame, but rather because the mass adulation that had swept across the footlights toward him onstage was a pretty fair indication of the way the public wind was blowing in his favor, and astute newsmen saw no good reason to challenge so open and vociferous a gesture of forgiveness, in Liverpool as in London.

Gordon was later to return to the fray, congratulating himself on having "taken the opportunity provided by the case of Sir John Gielgud to draw attention to this male perversion menace," and later still, in an increasingly desperate attempt to get him stripped of his knighthood, adding, "These men have earned social criticism and they should get it, whatever the nation may have conferred on them; for while they remain public idols, it demonstrates to all that fame not shame have been the fruits of their depravity, and they draw other men into the depths with them."

No barrister at the Wilde trials could have put the case for the prosecution more forcibly, but Gordon was immediately accused by such other Sunday editors as David Astor of *The Observer* of writing "in the most rabble-rousing tones of the witch-hunt," and already the word was coming over from America that on reflection, just possibly witch-hunts weren't such a good idea after all.

The debate ended up where such British debates almost always do, in the correspondence columns of *The Daily Telegraph*, where the row rumbled on for several weeks between liberals supporting continental tolerance, and irate colonels demanding that antihomosexuality laws should be printed as posters, akin to KEEP DEATH OFF THE ROADS.

For a while, the more liberal journalists demanded a relaxation of the laws, the more the judges hardened their view to the contrary, yet again all too eager to demonstrate that they weren't about to have their minds changed by columnists whom they dismissed as left-wing and suspected of harboring abnormal sexual desires into the bargain. The fact that large numbers of judges were only really happy when dressed in long robes and wigs was thought too sensitive to mention, even in *The New Statesman*. After one more sensational gay trial, the Liberace/Cassandra case of 1959, in which the columnist Bill Connor was fined a then-unprecedented eight thousand pounds for suggesting that a pianist eventually to die of AIDS was a "deadly, winking, sniggering, chromium-plated, scent-impregnated, luminous, quivering, giggling, fruit-flavoured, mincing, ice-covered heap of mother-love," matters were finally allowed to rest until the Wolfenden Report's recommendations, made in 1957, were finally passed into law in 1967, belatedly bringing Britain nearer its continental neighbors' tolerance of consenting homosexual relationships.

Peter Wildeblood, who had been charged with Lord Montagu, wrote a memoir called *Against the Law* soon after his release from prison, reminding readers that, "In most other countries, the behaviour of consenting adults in private is now considered a matter for themselves alone. Britain and America are almost the only countries left in which such behaviour constitutes an offence. . . . Most people, if they were asked to define the crime of Oscar Wilde, would still imagine that he was an effeminate poseur who lusted after small boys, whereas in fact he was a married man with two children who was found guilty of homosexual acts committed in private with male prostitutes whom he certainly did not corrupt, and who lied on oath to clear themselves of other charges . . . the Prosecution never attempted to prove that he had done any harm by his actions."

The Wildeblood case, and that of Gielgud, were the most famous gay trials since that of Wilde himself, who had, of course, given from beyond the grave one of John's greatest successes in *The Importance of Being Earnest* where, as Oscar's grandson Merlin Holland now suggests, the line about "all women take after their mothers, that is their tragedy; no man does, that is his" could be seen as yet another coded plea, this one for men in Victorian society to be allowed to exhibit more of the female side of their nature without fear of arrest.

Be that as it may, fully forty years after his own trial, Gielgud himself was still refusing to make public comment of any kind about his own sexuality. In this, of course, he was not alone: Alan Bennett once replied to Sir Ian McKellen (who was suggesting that he should "come out" with a precise declaration of his sexuality) that it was "like asking a man, crawling across the Sahara Desert, whether he would prefer Evian or Perrier." Sir Nigel Hawthorne was infamously "outed" by an American journalist at the time of his Oscar nomination, and there are still many actors for whom, as for John, the subject remains just too painful or too personal to allow of any public comment.

A few months after Gielgud's court case, he suffered a delayed nervous breakdown, which caused him to withdraw, temporarily and very uncharacteristically, from both *A Day by the Sea* and his rehearsals for the Trevor Howard/Ffrangcon-Davies *Cherry Orchard*. In the years that followed, John was ever careful about where and to whom he would give press or broadcast interviews, choosing wherever possible those he could trust not to enquire deeply, or at all, about his private life.

Perhaps the most enduring tragedy of the Gielgud trial is this: it contributed more than any other to a gradual shift in public attitude. Had John been able to come to any real terms with his own sexual identity, he could have taken some pride and pleasure in his nineties in the eventual outcome of his arrest, which was essentially to pave the way for a vastly more tolerant attitude toward homosexuality in England. But precisely because he himself came from the far side of the 1953 divide, he was never able to understand the change that he himself had wrought, and his terror of being outed was to reach such ludicrous proportions that, appearing at a celebrated literary festival some six months after his death, I was solemnly asked not to bring any of this up, as "there are those who still find the whole thing distasteful." Admittedly, it was Cheltenham.

But John was, in one way, very fortunate. The publicity surrounding the 1953 case meant that very few writers could be totally unaware that he had suffered and survived some kind of sexual scandal, and that it was more than likely to have been of a gay nature. In none of his own many volumes of stage and personal memoirs, nor in any biography published in his lifetime, nor in any of his numerous autobiographical radio and television broadcasts has the case ever been mentioned, and as John grew in distinction and fragility to his late-life status as our greatest living actor, it would somehow have been unusually churlish to bring it up. Somerset Maugham, Terence Rattigan, Noël Coward, Michael Redgrave, Emlyn Williams, and Binkie himself and even Dirk Bogarde had by then all managed to escape any "outing" in their lifetimes, not least because the laws of libel could have been invoked on their behalf, so professionally damaging was the suggestion of homosexuality still believed to be, even into the mid-1990s.

But the scars of John's court appearance never truly healed; until the very end of his long life, almost fifty years later, he was never openly to support any of his theatrical colleagues who felt it important for leading gay actors to declare themselves as such. Nor would he join the many hitherto silent gays who in 1991 signed a letter to the *Guardian* protesting Derek Jarman's vilification of McKellen for accepting a knighthood from what many then considered a virulently antigay Thatcher administration. Gielgud went to his grave believing, as Coward wrote in his last full-length play *A Song at Twilight* (1968), that "even when the actual law ceases to exist, there will still be a stigma attached to 'the love that dares not speak its name' in the minds of millions of people for generations to come. It takes more than a few outspoken books, and plays, and speeches in Parliament to uproot moral prejudice from the Anglo-Saxon mind."

And in 1953 the law did of course still exist; as a result, although in private he was to receive dozens of letters of support and love, in public ranks were now being closed, and the homosexual community decided that although it would do what it could for John behind closed doors, in public it would do nothing to support him that might endanger its own still precarious position. Typical of the private response was the letter that John received from the playwright Dodie Smith, for whom he had directed the triumphant *Dear Octopus* a few years earlier: "This damnable business will be forgotten in a few weeks, whereas the fact that you are the greatest figure in the present English theatre will remain unchanged . . . we think the world of you, and always shall."

Dodie also took the trouble to write to John's mother Kate: "Dear Mrs.

G., I find myself longing to send you our sympathy about John's misfortune. His magnificent achievements will never fade, and no one in the theatre is more loved and admired." Some indication of John's family's feeling about the crisis can be gathered from Mrs. Gielgud's brisk reply to Dodie: "Thank you for your kind letter. John has nothing to his discredit, save one drink too many at a Chelsea party."

Others concurred, although some with rather more reservations: "I do wish," as Christopher Isherwood wrote to Dodie from the comparative homosexual safety of California, "that we had a better issue to join battle on than Gielgud's stupid indiscretion."

And yet John's case, taken together with that of Lord Montagu, did begin to mark the shift in public opinion and the start of the long road to the reform that came about with the Sexual Offenses Act of 1957. For all those who still believed that homosexuals should be, if not actually hanged or flogged, nevertheless sent to prison, regardless of the fact that they would there find themselves in the kind of all-male community specifically designed to encourage precisely the kind of sexual behavior for which they were supposedly being punished, nevertheless there were faint signs of a new orthodoxy. *The Sunday Times* of March 28, 1954, less than six months after Gielgud's arrest, published an editorial that read, in part, "The case for the reform of the law as to acts committed in private between adults is very strong. The case for an authoritative enquiry into it is overwhelming."

At precisely this time, the Church of England's Moral Welfare Committee published a report concluding that such behavior, although sinful, should now no longer be treated as a crime, doubtless much to the relief of several hundred gay clergymen. In the House of Commons the member of Parliament Robert Boothby, now deeply in debt to the Kray brothers (the leading East End gangsters of the day) and himself a lifelong bisexual who had recently won £40,000 in damages from *The Daily Mirror* for suggesting (rightly) that he had criminal connections, now urged Parliament to set up a royal commission pointing out that the law as it stood led to many cases of blackmail and was being unfairly invoked around the country, depending on the sexual beliefs of the various magistrates concerned.

But still the government of the day hesitated. In the House of Lords, Earl

Winterton initiated the first ever debate there about homosexuality by announcing for the prosecution that it was a "filthy, disgusting and unnatural vice." Several younger peers pointed out that blackmail was surely the greater evil here, although the bishop of Southall memorably remarked "Once a people lets its ultimate convictions go, there can be no stopping halfway, and the moral bottom is in danger of falling out of Society."

Matters were rapidly becoming farcical; when at the end of 1954 Sir John Wolfenden, vice chancellor of Reading University, was finally charged by a reluctant Home Secretary (the reactionary David Maxwell-Fyffe) with leading a commission of enquiry, the first thing Wolfenden did was to write to his homosexual son Jeremy, "I have only two requests to make of you at the moment. One, that we stay out of each other's way for the time being, and two, that you wear rather less make-up."

Soon after the Committee on Homosexual Offenses and Prostitution (the title alone suggested what was then still public thinking on the issue) had begun to meet, a number of high-profile, nonhomosexual figures like the columnist Lord Arran (less formally known as Boofy Gore, and a Wodehousian figure around Fleet Street) came out in favor of reform, as did such gay members of Parliament as Tom Driberg and Robert Boothby. But that reform came very slowly: in 1955, as Norman Lebrecht notes in his critical history of Covent Garden:

> The People ran a headline "Music Chief leads big campaign against Vice," and the story that followed was as explicit as the times and libel laws permitted: "A campaign against homosexuality in British music is to be launched by Sir Steuart Wilson . . . Sir Steuart, 66, told The People last night "The influence of perverts in the world of music has grown beyond all measure. If it is not curbed soon, Covent Garden and other precious musical heritages could suffer irreparable harm. . . . Many people in the profession are worried. There is a kind of agreement among homosexuals which results in their keeping jobs for the boys." The People cast around for men of substance to authenticate its scoop. Mr Walford Haydn, "the famous composer and conductor" said "Homosexuals are damaging music and all the other

arts. I am sorry for those born that way, but many acquire it—and for them I have nothing but contempt. Singers who are perverted often get work simply because of this. And new works by composers are given preference by some people if the writer is perverted" . . . Wilson's target was unmistakable, and the report must have struck terror into (the general administrator) David Webster, coming as it did in the midst of a police crackdown on homosexual men. On a 1953 tour of Rhodesia, Webster was reportedly seen in the sauna with other white men and black boys "red all over and looking like a boiled lobster." According to rumor, he so injured an African boy in the act of love that the victim was rushed to the hospital, and Webster had to be hustled out on the next flight . . . most of his team at Covent Garden were lifelong bachelors. Christopher West was professedly gay; Morris Smith and John Sullivan were avowedly religious and hostile to women. "Nobody asked if they were gay," said stage manager Elizabeth Latham, "one was very careful what one said and did in those days."

In the next year or so, two Members of Parliament, William Field and Ian Harvey both had their careers ruined by prosecution for importuning, and it wasn't until 1958 that a first shift was detectable, in the Lord Chamberlain's decision no longer to ban overtly homosexual characters from the London stage. Three years later, in 1961, Dirk Bogarde (himself a lifelong but very closeted gay) courageously persuaded a very reluctant Rank Organization to make a film called *Victim*, entirely about the blackmailing of a married but homosexual barrister. In this same year, there were to be no less than two films about the Oscar Wilde trial (one starring Peter Finch, the other Robert Morley), and the actor Murray Melvin played the first overtly gay character on the West End stage in Shelagh Delaney's hit *A Taste of Honey*.

During the sixties the climate finally began to change forever; even the television hit *Z Cars* dealt with the blackmailing of homosexual couples, and on radio Barry Took and Marty Feldman for *Round the Horne* invented the outrageously camp couple "Julian and Sandy," immortally played for many years by Kenneth Williams and Hugh Paddick. Even so, the Sexual Offenses Act was not introduced into Parliament until 1967, more than ten years after the Wolfenden Committee had begun to meet. Under the new rules, gay male sex now became a noncriminal offense provided that it was committed in private by not more than two people, and that both of them were over twenty-one years of age. By 1975, a rally in Trafalgar Square brought together what the press described as the largest ever public gathering of homosexuals—2,500 in all. By the early 1990s, Gay Pride rallies attracted more than 300,000. Yet it wasn't until 1998 that the House of Commons voted on whether the age of consent should be lowered to seventeen or even sixteen, an argument that persists to this day, alongside the dispute over Clause 28 in a Local Authority Bill, forbidding the "promotion" of the homosexual lifestyle.

All the changes that were to come in both laws and attitudes toward homosexuality were too late for John. The events of 1953 were to leave him utterly unable to come to any real terms with the slow liberalization of British attitudes toward homosexuality, although toward the very end of his life some forty years later, he did grudgingly admit in a television interview, when asked why he went on working so very hard well into his nineties, "The man I live with has expensive tastes."

The Gielgud case was to find its way to a kind of immortality at the roots of the play that his old friend and sometime lover Terence Rattigan was now writing. Although in its final draft *Separate Tables* has no really gay theme at all, in the first version the protagonists of the first play were to have been two men, and the offense committed in the second play, by the Major, was to have been that of touching up young men rather than women in the local cinema. As Rattigan later explained, "John had enough courage to go and open his play only a few days after the trial, and that Liverpool audience had enough grace and sympathy to accept him purely as an actor . . . the acceptance by those very ordinary people of something about which they had very little understanding, I found very moving." In fact, as Geoffrey Wansell adds, "*Separate Tables* is really about the two themes that have always preoccupied Rattigan—the suppression of emotion, and the difficulty the English have always found in accepting sexual deviance. As another Rattigan character once said, 'You know what the real *vice anglais* is? Not flagellation, or pederasty, or whatever the French think it is, but the inability to express emotion.'"

Of course, it all could have been worse; when Lord Montagu was sent down, a few months after John's arrest, for a year in prison, one of the first letters of sympathy he received was from Gielgud: "There," wrote John, "but for the grace of God . . ."

17. King Lear Goes to Japan

(1954–1955)

I made one great mistake with the Japanese King Lear, *and it was purely technical. Noguchi, who is a sculptor, designed some brilliant sets, but no one had ever told me that he didn't also do costumes.*

*A*s 1954 began, John was still reeling from the shock of his arrest. Luckily, he had eight shows a week to play with a friendly and highly sympathetic cast in *A Day by the Sea*, but away from the theater he was now very reluctant to go to the parties he once loved. Embarrassed beyond belief by what had happened, his natural good manners also made sure that he would at no time give anybody else any cause for uneasiness.

At this time he was still living alone at 16 Cowley Street, and it is quite possible, of course, that if he had had a partner in residence, none of the events of the past October would have taken place. But Ben, the burly American he had originally hired in New York some years earlier as a kind of chauffeur and secretary, and who had joined him in London where their relationship became that of lovers, had now tired of the West End life, which he could never really fathom, and gone back home to New York, already suffering from the cancer that would soon kill him.

John's affair with the interior decorator Paul Anstee was still something less than a total commitment for either of them, and at this crucial time he was unable to look for too much support from Binkie or John Perry, as their relationship had now gone into a crisis of its own. Soon after the war, Binkie and John had taken into their Tennent management a young and very striking American, the producer and actor Toby Rowland, who was eventually to bring John G. together with playwright and actor Alan Bennett for one of Gielgud's greatest late-life hits in 1968, Bennett's *Forty Years On*. Although Rowland was already married, he had first come to England as a lover of Alan Webb's and was therefore soon to find himself at the heart of the H. M. Tennent gay coterie.

Within a few months Rowland was to leave Alan Webb for John Perry, an affair that came to Binkie's attention only when Noël Coward inadvertently let slip the news that Rowland was in Paris at precisely the same time that—as Binkie knew—John Perry was. The affair finally came to a head one weekend at Knots Fosse, when Binkie told John Perry that he was to decide there and then between him and Toby. Perry went to the phone and came back to announce to the somewhat startled dinner party that his affair with Toby was at an end. It was then Binkie's turn to leave the table; he phoned his manager Barney Gordon to instruct him to remove any trace of Toby from the London office and to fire him immediately as an associate producer of H. M. Tennent. It was, as Toby's widow Millie recalls, only to be in the very last months of Binkie's life, almost twenty years later, that he and Toby ever spoke again.

Back at the Haymarket Theatre, the continuing success of *A Day by the Sea* was a considerable relief. It was Milton Shulman who had perceptively noted in the *Evening Standard* that John's opening night performance was played "on a note of nervous tension that almost shrieked." But other critics seemed not to have noticed anything adrift, and the play ran for eighteen months on the strength of glowing reviews and its all-star cast, in which only Ralph Richardson still seemed to have difficulty coming to terms with the truth about John's private life.

John's high level of stress, however, his ongoing conviction that he had let down both friends and family (especially his now elderly mother) very badly indeed, and that he might well have done his future career considerable damage, led him toward a serious nervous breakdown five months into the run. By now he was not only still playing eight shows a week at the

Haymarket, but also directing the long-delayed *Cherry Orchard* with Trevor Howard and Gwen Ffrangcon-Davies, which he had been thinking about at the time of his arrest. The breakdown finally manifested itself as double vision, and John had to take to his bed for a couple of weeks.

Not everyone had been ecstatic about *A Day by the Sea;* for *The Guardian* Philip Hope-Wallace wrote that "with so many big guns on the stage, there is some wonder that the explosions are not louder," and Kenneth Tynan for *The Observer* thought the cast was wasting its time on "an evening of unexampled triviality . . . it was like watching a flock of eagles and macaws of magnificent plumage jammed for two hours into a suburban birdcage."

It was Irene Worth (another of the all-star cast) who alone noted that something special was now beginning to happen onstage between Gielgud and Richardson, something which, twenty years later, would lead to their remarkable late-life partnership in *Home* and *No Man's Land.* "They began," Irene recalled, "to spar with each other, trying to keep one another on his toes and under all this was the marvellous respect those two men had for each other. There seemed no rivalry or bitterness, but a sharpness with their ripostes; I had never seen anything like it in my life, and it was electric for the audience." Offstage, however, there was still some tension, especially when Richardson was sent a radical new play by Samuel Beckett called *Waiting for Godot,* which Beckett hoped Richardson would play with Alec Guinness under the direction of Peter Glenville. Richardson was totally bemused by it and gave it to other members of the company to read. Predictably, the intellectual Irene Worth told Richardson he would be mad not to do it; Gielgud, on the other hand, announced that it was all new-fangled rubbish and should not be touched with a barge pole, and when Beckett himself refused to answer any of Richardson's questions (a five-page list starting with, "Who is Pozzo?"), Richardson turned the job down, only then to regret it for the rest of his life.

Despite John's illness, the production of *The Cherry Orchard,* which he directed during the Haymarket run, was a considerable success, both for Trevor Howard and John's beloved Gwen Ffrangcon-Davies. As Noël Coward wrote in his diary, "a magical evening in the theatre, every part subtly and perfectly played, and a beautiful production by John, so integrated and timed that the heart melted. I came away prancing on my toes, and very proud that I belonged to the same theatre as John."

As for Trevor Howard, John himself wrote, "I loved working with him, and he gave a brilliant performance in the part of Lopakhin. But he was always really a film actor, and the discipline of playing eight times a week seemed to be too much for him. To my great regret, he only managed to last five weeks."

Toward the end of their time together at the Haymarket, both Ralph and John were asked by Olivier to join him in the film of *Richard III,* which he was now planning to direct and star in. But whereas Richardson got what was effectively the second lead, as the Duke of Buckingham, all that Olivier could bring himself to offer John was the Duke of Clarence, who is swiftly drowned in a butt of Malmsey within the first twenty minutes of the picture. This was to be John's first film since *Julius Caesar,* and although his recollections of the shooting were pleasant enough, he remained firmly convinced that Olivier, as well as the king he was playing, were both keen to see him dispatched as swiftly as possible.

Whatever the continuing unhappiness he experienced at this time, and several close friends acknowledged that he seemed to have grown older and wearier than usual as a result of the court case, John was still determined to keep working as hard as possible, as if only by doing so could he overcome a feeling of internal despair. Thus during the run of *A Day by the Sea* he also directed a brisk revival of *Charley's Aunt* with John Mills, before setting his sights on the forthcoming 1955 season at Stratford, where Anthony Quayle had once again offered him a summer home.

The plan was for two productions: John would open the season by directing Larry Olivier and Vivien Leigh in a starry *Twelfth Night* and then close it by playing and directing *King Lear* in a radical new setting with the scenery (and supposedly costumes) of the great Japanese designer Isamu Noguchi.

Rehearsals for *Twelfth Night* got off to a thoroughly uneasy start. Olivier was unusually exhausted from the strain of his *Richard III* movie;

Vivien Leigh had just emerged from one of her frequent nervous break-downs, this one so severe that she had been given electric-shock treat-ment; and Gielgud himself was still just getting over the trauma of his arrest. As if that were not enough, the Oliviers' marriage had barely recov-ered from Larry's unsuccessful attempt to drag Vivien away from Peter Finch during the Ceylon filming of *Elephant Walk,* where she had to be replaced by Elizabeth Taylor, and also from a disappointing Coronation staging of Rattigan's *The Sleeping Prince,* which Olivier had now decided (to Leigh's understandable jealousy and rage) that he would film with Marilyn Monroe.

In addition to all this, a new and major problem had arisen: Olivier, al-ways a master of disguise, had decided before rehearsals began that he would play Malvolio with a pointed nose, thick and crinkly hair, and the general demeanor of an outrageously camp, lisping hairdresser. Not sur-prisingly, Gielgud treated this as a personal insult. He and Olivier had not worked together (apart from the *Richard III* filming) for fully twenty years, not since they had alternated Romeo and Mercutio, and Olivier was not about to submit again to his direction without a fight. Nor was he exactly thrilled to discover that Peter Finch had moved into a nearby hotel to pur-sue his affair with Vivien, and the unhappiness of the Oliviers' marriage spread through rehearsals like a cancer. "The best you could say," recalled the American novelist Elaine Dundy, then married to Kenneth Tynan, "about Vivien and Peter's affair was also the worst thing you could say about it—they did nothing behind Olivier's back."

From the very first rehearsal, this *Twelfth Night* was clearly going to be more of a nightmare than a dream. On the very first morning, John G. an-nounced that he would like the cast to read through the play without any interruption from him. The Australian actor Keith Michell, cast as Orsino, duly began the opening speech, "If music be the food . . . " but got no fur-ther as John came racing down the aisle, screaming, "No, no, no, no, no! Not like that at all!"

At one point during rehearsals, relations between Olivier and John reached such a crisis that Olivier turned to his director saying, "Darling

John, please go for a long walk by the river and let us just get on with it."
John, brooding on the problem of Larry's Malvolio, and unable to sleep,
rang his old rival at two the next morning. As Olivier sleepily answered the
phone, John said, "I've got it, darling boy, just play him very, very Jewish."
Olivier uttered a stream of invective about the time of night and the general idiocy of the suggestion, at the end of which John just said, "Oh, alright then, play him very, very not Jewish," and put the phone down.
Olivier, whose nights and weekends at the nearby Notley Abbey were not
being made any easier by the presence of Finch, and who was also trying to
learn *Macbeth* for the next production of the season, eventually opened
Twelfth Night with no reference to Gielgud whatsoever.

"In rehearsal as in performance," John said later, "I thought Larry's
Malvolio terribly vulgar—he strongly resented my criticisms and although
I thought Vivien was delightful as Viola, I suspected that she was torn between my attempts at directing her and Larry's views of how she should
play the part, which were different from mine, but of course influenced her
strongly." This was, in fact, a very bad time for John; banned from rehearsals, torn between Larry and Vivien, and still bruised badly by the
court case of nearly two years ago, he became increasingly confused and
disheartened.

Critics in general soon echoed John's uncertainty. Olivier's performance
was generally thought to be vulgar and over-the-top, while Vivien, although as always described as "graceful and pretty," was reckoned to be
speaking so quickly that she lost all the poetry of the role. As W. A. Darlington wrote in *The Daily Telegraph*, "What might have been a great occasion became merely a fairly good one."

As Vivien's biographer, Alexander Walker has noted: "By temperament
as well as by technique, Vivien was always closer to Gielgud than to her
own husband. She enjoyed Gielgud's intellectual playfulness, his pouncing
on an apt word, his love of poetry, his wide reading, and his knowledge of
some of the most eminent players to whom he was related by blood. Both
of them were sprinters on the middle track, unshaped for the gruelling
marathons in which Olivier always entered himself. Vivien and John

shared a quizzical, well-mannered, amused social assuredness—polishing the apples on the applecart, not upsetting it."

Another problem here was pinpointed by John Barber, writing in *The Daily Express:* "I hate the phrase 'The Oliviers,' which kow-tows to the pair royally known as Larry-and-Viv. Look beyond the gloss. Olivier was a great actor. But since his gleaming, viperish Richard III and his fiery Hamlet he has lost his way. Now, at 48, he is an ageing matinee idol desperately fighting to win back his old reputation while she, at 42, is still a great beauty, but as an actress only good in a dainty, waspish way that seldom touches the heart." There was worse to come; when, a few weeks later, the Oliviers opened under Glen Byam Shaw's direction in *Macbeth,* Kenneth Tynan wrote, "Olivier shakes hands with greatness here, but Vivien Leigh's Lady Macbeth is more niminy-piminy than thundery-blundery . . . still quite competent in its small way."

Unsurprisingly, Vivien Leigh moved that summer toward one of her worst nervous breakdowns, one that John could do little to tranquilize in the face of the constantly savage onslaughts of Kenneth Tynan. Writing of her Lavinia in *Titus Andronicus* (the third of the Oliviers' Shakespeares that Stratford season), Tynan added, "Vivien Leigh receives the news that she is about to be ravished on her husband's corpse with little more than the mild annoyance of one who would have preferred foam rubber."

Another major problem with this *Twelfth Night* was a set by Malcolm Pride, which had very difficult sight lines, and a decision by John to play all the comedy upstage behind a box hedge. As for Vivien Leigh, John could not understand why she did not dissolve into tears as Viola—"all my leading ladies always cry," he told her after the first night. "Oh I do," she replied, "but only when I have to go home to Notley with Larry afterwards."

By now, the Oliviers' marital collapse was obvious to everyone who called in at their dressing rooms by the Avon. "Their life together is really hideous," wrote Coward at this time, "as they are trapped by their own public acclaim, and have to scrabble about in the cold ashes of a physical passion that burnt itself out years ago."

As for Olivier, he found himself one afternoon describing the plot of

Macbeth to Tynan in terms that clearly referred to his own marriage: "*Macbeth* is a domestic tragedy, the passage of two people; one going up and one going down. And there comes a moment in the play when he looks at her and realises that she can't take it any more. He goes on, and she stops." For John, this Stratford summer should have been a tranquil time for the preparation of his long-awaited *King Lear;* instead he found himself increasingly caught up in the still greater real-life drama of the Oliviers in meltdown.

What he had to do was, for the first time, to form an "away" Stratford company, which would tour abroad through the late summer and autumn of 1955, only returning to its Stratford base at the end of November. John's company was to be headed by himself, and such old Gielgud regulars as Peggy Ashcroft and George Devine. They were to present two plays, *Much Ado About Nothing* and *King Lear,* and the touring schedule (at a time when the Stratford company very rarely played away from home) was nothing if not ambitious. Opening in Brighton, they were to play Vienna, Zurich, the Hague, Amsterdam, and Rotterdam, before coming home to four weeks at the Palace Theatre in London and then going on to Berlin, Hanover, Bremen, Hamburg, Copenhagen, Oslo, Newcastle, Edinburgh, Glasgow, Manchester, and Liverpool before finishing up, exhausted, at Stratford, where they played most of December.

The two productions were wildly different. *Much Ado About Nothing,* which John again directed and played opposite Peggy Ashcroft, was the familiar old vehicle in which they had been totally at home for several seasons. *King Lear,* however, was to be designed by the Japanese-American sculptor Isamu Noguchi, who had done sets for ballets—Balanchine's *Orpheus* and Martha Graham's *Appalachian Spring*—but never yet for a play. In addition, the play had an equally radical score by the avant-garde composer Roberto Gerhard. The idea here was clearly to prove to audiences at home and abroad that Stratford was not just in the business of elegant museum pieces. As John's program note now explained: "Our object in this production has been to find a setting and costumes free of all historical and decorative associations, so that the timeless, universal and mythical quality of the story may be clear in a simple and basic manner; so the play comes to life through words and acting and nothing else."

That may well have been the intention, and a worthy one, but the production was not designed to appeal to the critics. J. C. Trewin, usually an admirer of Gielgud, reported that John now came on stage "with around his face a vast, drooping circlet of white horse-hair, on his head what seemed to be an inverted hatstand, and in his grasp a decorated lavatory brush." For *The Tatler*, Anthony Cookman found Goneril and Regan like "sinister geishas from *The Teahouse of the August Moon*," and the critic of *Punch* found "women hideously wrapped up, while the men wear cellular bath-mats over space-suits in heavy leather. No wonder Lear is eager to leave a palace in which he has to sit side-saddle on an abstract horse." As for his throne, noted the usually respectful Harold Hobson, this most closely resembled the seat of a golden metaphysical lavatory. Other critics were all too eager to quote Lear's "I do not like the fashion of your garments," and Gielgud's Lear was elsewhere more flatteringly described as a great oak struck by lightning.

John was given no credit at all for the courage of this experiment, and indeed many critics thought that the sets and costumes had simply "got him down."

Although Peter Brook was later to acknowledge this production as the starting point for his triumphant Paul Scofield *Lear* of eight years later, John himself was in no doubt about the scale of the disaster: "The great mistake I made in the Japanese *Lear* was a purely technical one. Noguchi, who is a sculptor, designed the sets and sent them to us and we thought them thrilling—and I still think they are, but I did not know at the time that he had never designed costumes. So he arrived with no costumes at all, designed them very hastily, and left again before he had even seen the fittings. Nor was he at the dress rehearsal, or even the first night. I remember suggesting then to the director George Devine that we simply abandon all the costumes, and play in non-descript black cloaks. This might just have worked, but we hadn't the courage to make such a drastic alteration at the last minute and we went through with it because I felt that Noguchi was too individual and brilliant a designer to throw overboard completely."

And for John, on the long pre-Stratford tour, there were one or two consolations, not least while in Berlin the chance to see Brecht's own production of *The Recruiting Officer*. "A strange propaganda version," he wrote to his mother, "with a rather indifferent company but very attractive décor . . . I found Brecht's presentation very interesting, though I resented his twisting of a light comedy into a savage attack on the British army." In Vienna, the army had to be called out to control a stage-door crowd of several hundred, and in Germany the applause every night was timed at thirty minutes. Obviously, Noguchi was rather more accessible to European audiences than he was to those at home, who still expected their Shakespeare at Stratford to be a more traditional and familiar affair.

This *Lear* was in fact to be George Devine's last production as a classical Stratford director. By now he and John had lost all the intimacy of their early years together at Oxford and the Old Vic; Devine had long since gone off to manage companies of his own, leaving John feeling vaguely bereft, and the *Lear* that brought them together again was so dominated by Noguchi that neither of them could really claim the production as his own.

Devine already regarded the Shakespeare Memorial Theatre as "a death trap—there it is, that great lump of masonry standing on the river bank, imposing itself on everyone who has to work there." Devine's hope had been that Noguchi would dynamite all that, but, in fact, they were simply out of the frying pan and into the fire. In later years Gielgud himself never flinched from calling the production "a disaster," and Devine was so horrified by it all that he increasingly retreated into his own performance as Gloucester. For Peggy Ashcroft, who was playing Cordelia while trying to sustain yet another tumultuous backstage affair—this one with Tony Britton—it was "a matter of awful despair. With those clothes I didn't see how anybody could act . . . the intention was that they should be totally negative, but they were in fact the most positive thing on the stage. You simply couldn't get over them."

Peggy was therefore not entirely sorry to give up her Cordelia to Claire Bloom when the production eventually returned to Stratford; she had not

been happy during the tour but, as so often happens in a Gielgud company, a kind of greatness was to be plucked from disaster. Waiting in the
wings one night in Berlin, George Devine happened to ask her if she might
be interested in playing Brecht's *The Good Woman of Setzuan* for a new
company he was thinking of forming in the following year at the Royal
Court Theatre. This was to be the English Stage Company, and within a
few months of *Setzuan* it was to have its first real hit—John Osborne's *Look
Back in Anger.*

18. BACK ON THE AVENUE

(1956–1957)

I act these plays—I never understand them.

*A*s the ill-fated Noguchi *Lear* ground to a halt at Stratford just before Christmas 1955, John decided once again that it was time to get back to Binkie and the commercial theater of the West End. What was on offer now was a new play by Enid Bagnold, a formidable novelist and dramatist of the period whose reputation also rested on her having once had an affair with Frank Harris (of Oscar Wilde fame), and a long marriage to one of the founders of Reuters.

The Chalk Garden was, depending on which critic you read, either an autumnal comedy or a Chekhovian thriller. It turned on an eccentric dowager hiring a governess for her wayward granddaughter, only to discover (over an uneasy lunch with a neighboring judge) that the woman has, in fact, recently completed a prison term for murder. The play had already opened with considerable success on Broadway, though rehearsals had not been easy. In addition to the presence of Bagnold, in the leading role was Gladys Cooper, and the producer was the equally formidable Irene Mayer Selznick, the daughter of Louis B. Mayer of MGM, and only recently divorced from David, the maker of *Gone With the Wind.*

These three determined dowagers were more than a match for any male director, and George Cukor indeed left the production during the pre-Broadway tryout, feeling distinctly henpecked. Nor were relations much better between the author and the star: "Before the first rehearsal," wrote Bagnold, "Gladys always called me Enid. After the first rehearsal she called me Miss Bagnold, and after the first night she called me Lady Jones. Gladys was an old hand; she had run her own theatre in management, and I think she regarded me as a rather silly society outsider. We were about the same age and very positive characters, and we both annoyed each other from the start."

Nevertheless, by the time it reached Broadway, *The Chalk Garden* was the hit of the season, and Binkie Beaumont (despite his initial doubts about the play) immediately decided on a London production. This would need an entirely new cast, under John's direction, and the two men decided to play safe; they would try to get Edith Evans for the dotty dowager, and Peggy Ashcroft for the sinister governess.

This they duly did, and it could be argued that in the year that was to see the creation of George Devine's English Stage Company and the ongoing success of Joan Littlewood's Theatre Royal, Stratford East, London, *The Chalk Garden* was the final flourish of the old guard at the Haymarket—the last truly all-star, elegant, country-house party onstage. It was Kenneth Tynan who noted, "at least the West End cavalry is going out with a flourish, its banners resplendent in the last rays of the dying sun."

In fact, there is a good deal more than comedy going on beneath the soil of *The Chalk Garden*. Reviewers at the time referred it to both Pirandello and Ronald Firbank, as well as to Chekhov, and the play's enduring power lies in its ability to counterweight an Agatha Christie kind of murder mystery with strange, surreal dialogue, affected certainly, but also curiously poetic.

During the Haymarket run, Peggy was awarded both her Dame of British Empire and a Best Actress award from the *Evening Standard*, although it was always largely Edith's evening, from her wondrous first off-stage line, "Where are my teeth?" Tynan went as far as to call *The Chalk Garden* "the finest artificial comedy to have flowed from an English pen since the death of Congreve," and Gielgud as director knew enough not to get in the way of any of that, but simply to give his two most beloved actresses their freedom onstage and arrange the rest of the cast tactfully upstage.

However, he had decided that the Broadway original was about twenty minutes too long, and therefore put in some useful cuts; these would not have been a problem, had it not been that about nine months into the run Dame Edith suddenly collapsed onstage with an intestinal complaint, which her fervent belief in Christian Science had led her to ignore for far too long. By apparent good fortune, the Saturday night on which she collapsed was also the closing night of *The Chalk Garden* on Broadway. Binkie rapidly telephoned Gladys, demanding that she spend Sunday on a plane and open at the Haymarket in place of Edith on the Monday night. This she duly did, unaware of the difference in the London production, so for the next few nights Gladys played the Broadway version while Peggy and the rest of the London cast persevered with the London text, only occasionally meeting somewhere mid-stage in a state of mutual confusion.

Gladys was subsequently heartbroken to lose the film of *The Chalk Garden* to Edith, but by any standards the play did nothing but good for all of those involved on either side of the Atlantic.

Meanwhile, as soon as the show was open, John picked up a role from Noël Coward, the first time the two men had worked together since *The Constant Nymph,* exactly thirty years earlier. Admittedly, this new play was not one of Coward's best, and John was by no means his first choice of either star or director. *Nude with Violin* was, not unlike Yasmina Reza's *Art* some forty years later, a satire about perceptions of modern art. Its central character was an all-knowing valet whom Coward had originally written for Rex Harrison and, on his refusal, rewritten as the role of a housekeeper for Yvonne Arnaud. When she, too, turned it down, Coward turned the character back into a man and would have played the role himself (as he did subsequently on Broadway) had it not been that he had just entered into a controversial and highly publicized tax exile, which meant that only in Dublin could he get to see the play, let alone appear in it.

From the very start John had his doubts; as he wrote to his mother, "It is very broad and a bit vulgar, but full of some surefire situations, and Noël's plays are usually quite successful, so I think I shall do it, while taking great care not to give just another imitation of him."

Coward was now at his most unpopular. The British press, headed by Beaverbrook's *Daily Express,* vilified him not only as one of Britain's very first tax exiles, but one who, in plays like *Cavalcade* and films like *In Which We Serve,* had set himself up as the kind of patriot who should not be residing abroad. But as Coward himself explained, "I am not a businessman; I have never made real money, my brain is my only fortune, and at fifty-six I have got to tread pretty carefully."

The plan was that although John would, of course, direct the play, Coward himself would supervise it during the Dublin tryout. He duly arrived in Ireland to a storm of tabloid indignation, and a full program's late-night discussion on television as to whether or not he had the right to live how and where he chose. This row completely overshadowed *Nude with Violin,* not a bad thing considering that Coward himself was by now having premonitions of disaster:

I do not think John is anything like ideal for the part, but he is such a wonderful man of the theatre that I am sure that it is all being done with taste and dignity . . . he really is rather better than I expected, looks fine, and although not yet comedically very sure he is neither embarrassing nor mannered in the role, both of which I dreaded. There are still a few ringing Terry tones in his voice, but I am hoping to eliminate those before London. The rest of the cast are fairly terrible, especially David Horne, hopelessly miscast and bellowing like a mad water-buffalo. . . . The set by Paul Anstee [John's current lover] is very good, but the lighting far too dim and John has directed everyone with so much fussy business that all my best lines are getting lost. The actors get up, sit down, carry trays, change places and move around so incessantly that I am nearly going out of my mind . . . it is extraordinary that so fine a director as Johnny, who has done *The Cherry Orchard* definitively, could have gone so very far wrong with me. I can only conclude that it is all about over-anxiety.

Coward's doubts were unfortunately all too accurate; although the Inland Revenue did grant him ten days in London to see the play at the Globe ("I am staying," he told the *Evening Standard,* "in the Oliver Messel suite at the Dorchester; all that luxury is not really me, but doubtless I shall be able to rise above it; thanks to the vilifications of *The Daily Express* I am now nearly as famous as Debbie Reynolds, which I find most gratifying"), he could not do very much to rescue a play that, said one critic, "started as a farce and ended as a corpse." Kenneth Tynan also put the boot in for *The Observer:* "Sir John never acts seriously in modern dress; it is the lounging attire in which he relaxes between classical bookings, and his present performance as a simpering valet is carried out with extreme elegance but the general aspect of a tight, smart, walking umbrella." Yet despite that very hostile press, it is some tribute to the enduring box-office power of Coward and Gielgud, fully thirty years after they had first worked together, that the play ran on Shaftesbury Avenue for more than twelve months, during which time Gielgud was replaced first by a wildly unhappy, stammering Michael Wilding, and then more successfully by Robert Helpmann. As for Gielgud, "I really only took it on because I was longing to do something frivolous, and I wanted to see if I could do a Coward play without giving an imitation of its author. I think I managed, but only just."

Indeed, when Coward himself came to play the role in America a year later, he had rather less success than John had enjoyed in London.

During the nine months that John played Sebastien in *Nude with Violin,* he was frenetically otherwise engaged on day jobs. There were two films: first a cameo appearance, again with Noël Coward, in Mike Todd's all-star *Around the World in Eighty Days* (in which he has one memorable scene as a tearful valet fired by David Niven as Phineas Fogg), and then a rather more serious role as the forbidding father in *The Barretts of Wimpole Street.*

This was, of course, the role that Cedric Hardwicke onstage and Charles Laughton on film had made their own well before the war, and the only possible alibi for the remake was the coming of CinemaScope and the need of MGM to complete a three-picture deal with Jennifer Jones. Bill Travers was cast as the young Robert Browning, and the result was predictably dire. Even CinemaScope didn't help, because, as Keith Baxter (then a drama school student, later to become a lifelong friend of John's) was to observe, the screen was now so wide that those like him in minor roles tended to disappear off the sides. John's role consisted mainly of appearing at inopportune moments to interrupt the romance, though there was a good giggle to be had when he comes in to find his cherished daughter helping the hated suitor on with his uniform: "Since when," he asks her, "has it been your custom to button on his accoutrements?"

Keith also recalled lunching with John and Maxine Audley in the studio canteen, and to his horror hearing John complain that as he had no other work offer, he would have to take up a not very strong new play (*Nude with Violin*) from Noël Coward. "At that moment John's eyes suddenly lit up as into the canteen strode Yul Brynner, dressed in his full glory for *Anastasia* which was being shot on a nearby soundstage. 'Isn't he gorgeous?' John whispered. Maxine asked if Gielgud would like to meet him. Thinking she knew him, John eagerly agreed. What Maxine then did was simply to stick out her leg so that Yul would fall, literally into John's lap. It was a splendid introduction, but I don't think it led to anything very much. All I can recall is the shocked realisation that if John in all his eminence was still scratching around for work, my own life in the theatre was unlikely to be any easier."

Apart from these two films, which did more for John's still shaky bank balance than for his reputation, his other project during the run of *Nude with Violin* was altogether more ambitious, and some might say even foolhardy. At the suggestion of his friend David Webster, he was invited to direct at Covent Garden the first uncut version ever performed anywhere of Berlioz's *The Trojans*. This opera had normally either been heavily cut or performed in two quite separate parts (*The Fall of Troy* and *The Trojans at Carthage*). Not only was this to be the first complete version, but it was also to be John's first-ever opera, one which would involve five Irish wolfhounds, a chorus of 180, forty extras, twenty-two principals, and two entire orchestras.

Faced with this vast multitude, John decided to borrow the system pioneered by Noël Coward while directing his equally epic *Cavalcade* at Drury

Lane back in 1930. The cast was therefore divided into teams bearing plac-
ards carrying their respective numbers, and John took to blowing a whistle
and shouting from the stalls when he wanted any of the groups to move
anywhere. His plan worked well enough at the early rehearsals, but once
the orchestra arrived it was inclined to drown out the sound of the Gielgud
whistle. By the final dress rehearsal he was more than frantic, and seen by
the surprised conductor Rafael Kubelik rushing down the aisle shouting at
the orchestra, "Do stop making that terrible noise and give me time to
think!"

The end result was somewhat catastrophic, not least because Amy
Shuard as Cassandra politely declined to make any of Gielgud's moves, on
the grounds that only if she stayed close to the prompter could she get any
assistance with the lines, should she dry up during an aria. One critic complained of the costumes that "the Trojans are all dressed as jesters, while
the Carthaginians all look like chefs." John himself was not greatly thrilled
when his now eighty-eight-year-old mother mistook the Trojan horse for a
ship in full sail, and all in all the experience was not inclined to endear him
to a life at Covent Garden.

All the same, when the production came back in 1960 he seemed a little
happier: "I was always totally bewildered by the volume of noise; I never
knew how to stop the chorus and if I ever succeeded, I could never get
them started again. They kept having half-hour breaks in which they
seemed to do a great deal of knitting, and I was also amazed by the way
that, unlike actors, singers never wait behind after a performance for production notes. We would have a dress rehearsal, and by the time I got up
onto the stage at the end they had all left the building. They seemed to expect my notes to come from my secretary, but the trouble was that I didn't
have one. And just when I got everybody finally in the right place, the chorus master would suddenly rearrange my moves because he had to have all
the tenors on the same side of the stage. None of the chorus seemed to
have the faintest interest in the scenes, and all I could do was try not to
treat them like cattle. I think I failed."

John's connection to Covent Garden was not only through the homosexual network that existed backstage. All through his career he had taken

a passionate interest in music, not only going to concerts, operas, and ballets at home and abroad whenever he had a rare evening off, but also, where possible, giving as much importance to background music as to sets and costumes. In productions such as *Much Ado About Nothing* and *The School for Scandal* he had insisted on very melodic scores: "It is a pity theatres no longer have live orchestras. In the old days if a play was rather thin, orchestral interludes brightened things up a little, even though all too often what you got was a little palm court orchestra sawing away at teashop music between the acts. During the war I managed to persuade William Walton to write a complete score for *Macbeth* which we recorded up at Maida Vale with a vast orchestra. It was immensely expensive, and at the end of the overtime session I found myself signing mad cheques like Ludwig of Bavaria, but the score was one of the best things about the production, and having had to pay for it, Binkie Beaumont was determined not to waste it, so it turned up rather surprisingly some years later as the score for Thornton Wilder's *The Skin of Our Teeth*."

Relieved to have escaped more or less intact from Covent Garden and the long run of *Nude with Violin,* John now planned to return to Stratford for the 1957 season, solely to play Prospero in Peter Brook's *Tempest,* but with the understanding that they would take it into Drury Lane for Christmas, as the theater was unexpectedly vacant, awaiting the arrival of Rex Harrison in *My Fair Lady.* This *Tempest* was to be entirely Peter Brook's, in that he not only directed and designed all the sets and costumes, but also composed a musique concrète (montage of natural sounds) score. With Alec Clunes as Caliban and Patrick Wymark as Stephano, the Ariel was to be a young newcomer from drama school, Brian Bedford, whose looks, charm, and passion for theater had already enabled him to move into Gielgud's backstage circle and had also much impressed Peter Brook. It was Brook, giving Bedford *The Tempest* to read, who invited him to choose himself a role; Bedford unerringly went for Ariel and managed in rehearsal and performance to stay closely by Gielgud's side, learning everything he could and noting with some surprise that the great actor was far more giggly and lighthearted than he had somehow expected:

John struck me at first as a nervous kind of thoroughbred, and there was one of his characteristic bricks when, leaving rehearsal one afternoon, he suddenly looked at me and said, "Tell me, is it difficult being so short?" As I was only four inches shorter than him, that seemed a little harsh, but all through my early career he was just wonderfully helpful. Once, when I was playing Hamlet in the regional theatre, he sent me fourteen pages of notes in his minute, extraordinary handwriting, advising me to look up Granville-Barker on the subject.

Another time, when he invited me to lunch, I asked him what I should wear, and his reply was, "Nothing beaded." But all through *The Tempest* I shadowed him, and perhaps the most important thing he taught me was that Shakespearean speeches are like trains—you have to run with them right to the end of the track, keeping up your energy for the whole journey. When Brook first cast me as Ariel I'd had hardly any experience at all of speaking Shakespearean verse, and so while John was in Noël's *Nude with Violin* I used to go along every Wednesday and Saturday to his dressing room after the matinee for master classes in verse speaking. As I got to know him better, John used to invite me to wonderfully theatrical dinners at his house in Cowley Street, where everywhere you looked, everything was absolutely exquisite, taste and beauty all over the place, and everything in the right place. All the same, I fear he was not terribly impressed by my Ariel. All he could bring himself to say at the end of the Drury Lane run was, "I met a man in the Burlington Arcade today, who thought you were really quite good!"

In fact, John had been rather more impressed, on- and offstage, by Bedford than he cared to admit, and it was because of him that Bedford soon got his first real West End break in modern dress, although even this came to him in a somewhat grudging way. "I have," John told him at dinner one night, "been reading this new play by someone called Peter Shaffer. I fear it is dreadfully suburban, but maybe it would suit you." The play was *Five Finger Exercise,* which Brian was to act for almost three years in London and then on Broadway, at the start of his long American and Canadian life.

John's Prospero was his third in thirty years, but at Brook's insistence he was determined to do away with the turbaned conjurer of 1931 and the angry old man of 1941. This Prospero was to be a kind of biblical hermit in a magnificent blue robe, black skull cap, and coronet. As John said, "I tried to play it this time with strength and passion, as a kind of Jacobean revenge drama. The whole action of the play is Prospero growing to the final understanding that hatred and revenge are useless—all he has left is agony."

Prospero now became the last great Shakespearean figure of John's life; he was to play the role once more onstage (at the National Theatre in 1974), and finally in his long-desired film, although as this was directed by Peter Greenaway in 1991, it was sadly not quite *The Tempest* on which he would have wanted to go out.

As for the Peter Brook production, *The Times* found that "Gielgud takes little joy in Prospero's magic powers. He is an angry and embittered aristocrat speaking his tortured thoughts as though they disgusted him. Cleanshaven with the grizzled hair of virile middle age, and half-bare to the waist, he looked like a workman about to strike the anvil . . . his speeches of harsh intemperance work better than those which give rein to parental and human tenderness."

Eileen Atkins was one of the childlike nymphs in this production, and Brook said that he had been trying for "a mescaline world of sound and light," but this hint of a drugged dream was not pursued far by Gielgud, who relied yet again on all the majesty of his magnificently poetic voice. As Ralph Richardson wrote in a backstage note, "magnificent, I felt I was back with giants, the best Shakespearean acting I have ever seen, and I am sure that WS would have been delighted." As Ronald Hayman has noted, this was more than generous, considering that when a few years earlier Gielgud had gone backstage after Richardson's Prospero, it was only to say, "I think I hated you more in the first half than I did in the second." Unwisely, Richardson asked why. "Because there is more of you in the first half."

When *The Tempest* reached the Theatre Royal, Drury Lane, in London, which had seen no Shakespeare since Ivor Novello in *Henry V* in 1938, the reviews improved considerably. This was where Tynan wrote of John G. as "the finest actor, from the neck up, in the world today," and he went on to add, "his face is all rigour and pain, his voice all cello and woodwind. The rest of him may be totem-pole but he speaks the great passages perfectly, and always looks full of thinking. Prospero demands no more." For Derek Granger in *The Financial Times,* "Gielgud, of course, has all the qualities for Prospero. He is, above all else, the speaking poet of our theatre and here, appearing in the handsome stamp of an Old Testament prophet in the wilderness, he speaks the poetry with an enthralling appreciation for its sense and music." For *The Sunday Times,* Harold Hobson wrote, "Gielgud comes to Drury Lane at one of the triumphant points of his career . . . his reading of Prospero is darker than that of most actors. He does not offer us a well-meaning old bore, ready with a few tricks like a conjuror at a Christmas party. The night hangs over his whole performance, a night that is lit by dazzling and magic stars. The sternness in it is inescapable, and so is its incredible and sinister beauty. By subduing all gentleness, Gielgud unites the twin aspects of Prospero and creates a nobly isolated figure whose resolution is taxed only by the inner battle caused by relinquishing his cherished magical powers."

It was toward the end of this *Tempest* that John, at the request of the British Council, was given two nights' leave to slip over to Paris and present a recital of Shakespearean verse, the kind of thing that he had been doing occasionally at troop concerts during the war, but which he was now (with the considerable help of his beloved Cambridge professor George Rylands) to reshape into what was soon to become his *Ages of Man,* the most successful solo Shakespeare show of the entire twentieth century in Britain, and all over the world as well.

While he was still playing Prospero at Drury Lane, John also agreed to take up the challenge of a new play by Graham Greene. This was *The Potting Shed,* which he had originally rejected as being altogether too poetic and difficult to understand. As a result, the play had first opened in New York with his old friends Robert Flemyng, Lewis Casson, and Sybil

Thorndike in the central roles. By now, the play had become the snob hit of the Broadway season, and its success encouraged John to think again about playing it in the West End.

Greene's play, as the critic Robert Tanitch has noted, is a spiritual detective story in which a Nottingham journalist, trying to discover the source of his own midlife crisis, discovers instead that at the age of fourteen he has, in fact, hanged himself in the garden shed of the title, only to have been raised from the dead by the Roman Catholic priest who is also the boy's uncle. In some ways the best part was that of the priest, who in order to get the boy back has to lose his own faith. But an immensely strong cast (Irene Worth, Gwen Ffrangcon-Davies, Lockwood West, and Redmond Phillips) got the play off to an impressive London start, although the run had to be curtailed because, characteristically not confident of a success here, John had already committed himself to playing Cardinal Wolsey in an Old Vic *Henry VIII*.

The reviews for *The Potting Shed* were bemused but generally respectful: Milton Shulman thought it was a spiritual whodunit, and the play soon acquired the fashionable status of something you had to see, even if you weren't very likely to enjoy or even fully comprehend it. For *The Observer* Kenneth Tynan wrote a brilliant parody of Greene's usual Catholic despair, noting that Gielgud always talked to other members of his company "as though he were about to tip them." He also decided that this was not so much a whodunit as a Goddunit and was amazed to find beside him in the audience row after row of rapt, attentive faces who were actually taking this play seriously "and there, suddenly, in a blaze of darkness, I knew that my faith in the theatre and the people who attend it had been withdrawn from me." Others were, however, more enthusiastic: "His playing," wrote Derek Granger, "suggested a convulsive inner struggle kept under rigid control; nothing he does is without a sense of tautness and strain." For the *Daily Mail*, Cecil Wilson wrote "Gielgud's ability to cry genuine tears as the hero's uncle, yet another of Graham Greene's shambling whisky priests, lays bare his whole dread childhood secret. He only has to make himself look as insignificant as possible to mesmerise his audience."

Harold Hobson, reflecting years later on *The Potting Shed*, wrote:

John played the part of a man who, without knowing it, had been raised from the dead. I found his performance of the resurrected boy masterly, especially as I knew that personally he did not believe in the resurrection of this boy, or of Christ, or of anyone else. If ever, I felt, there could be presented on the stage a good man from whom God has removed his presence, then in this play Sir John presented him, with cheekbones sharp under shaven flesh, looking like a man carrying within him a world of Polar ice. The poignancy of this performance lay in Gielgud's capacity to suggest ice which even at its thickest yearns for the sun. . . . This is why Gielgud, though an unbeliever, could always play expositions of belief. There are two things in the theatre which exalt me—faith, which Gielgud can always arouse, and love. . . . He has not the tremendous self-confidence of an Olivier, but always seeks guidance and advice. He found help chiefly in Granville-Barker and once described a rehearsal with him as like being at a masseuse's—you felt bruised and broken, but with muscles functioning that you never even suspected of being there.

All through his non-Shakespearean career, John was to make a habit of appearing in "difficult" modern work, from André Obey's *Noah* in the 1930s through Christopher Fry's *The Lady's Not for Burning* and Greene's *The Potting Shed,* all the way up to Edward Albee's 1960s' *Tiny Alice* and Harold Pinter's *No Man's Land.* But friends and fans alike had long since learned not to go backstage to John for any enlightenment. On one famous occasion Gielgud irritably retorted, "I merely act these plays; I am not supposed to understand them."

And his courage in going after new work still had certain strict limits; at this time, while his old friend and director George Devine was setting up his company at the Royal Court, it was mooted that John might like to open a season there as Hamm in Samuel Beckett's *Endgame.* But Gielgud, having already firmly discouraged Ralph Richardson from playing in Beckett's *Waiting for Godot,* was not about to change his mind now. "When I saw *Godot,* I felt there was no communal experience at all. The audience was glum, and miserable, while in *Endgame* there is nothing but loneliness and despair."

Even by his standards, John was again moving into a period of intense activity. While playing eight times a week in *The Potting Shed*, he was also now planning to direct the premiere of a new Terence Rattigan drama (*Variation on a Theme*), and continuing to work with his beloved professor George Rylands on the solo *Ages of Man* recital, which he would open in America and Canada toward the end of 1958. Meanwhile, there was still an Old Vic *Henry VIII* in which he was about to play Wolsey and, added to all of that, a few weeks' filming as the Earl of Warwick in Otto Preminger's screen version of Bernard Shaw's *Saint Joan*.

With a screenplay by Graham Greene, sets by Roger Furse, and a cast of stars (Richard Widmark, Richard Todd, Kenneth Haigh, Anton Walbrook, Felix Aylmer, and Harry Andrews), this should have been a success, but in the title role Preminger had cast an eighteen-year-old unknown girl from Iowa, Jean Seberg, who (as John noted) was sadly inexperienced for the role: "Having chosen her but then decided it was a mistake, Preminger was utterly horrible to her on the set and I desperately wanted to help in any way I could. There wasn't an unkind bone in her body, but she was desperately insecure about everything and when one day I gave her a cup and saucer that had belonged to my great-aunt Ellen Terry, she simply broke down in tears. She didn't know anything about phrasing or pacing or climax—all the things the part needed—but she was desperately eager to learn, and we became great friends. The next time she was in London she rang to say she was with Gary Cooper, and would I like to join them for dinner? I had never seen quite so many flash photographers and for once I felt terribly important. What was so lovely about Jean was that she learnt how to be a star long before she learnt how to be an actress."

When the film came out, it was to very tepid reviews, although John's Warwick was applauded for its chilly, icy, malevolence. As for Jean Seberg, after several suicide attempts, she was found dead in her car in the backstreets of Paris early in 1979; she was just forty-one.

19. THE AGES OF MAN

(1958–1960)

I toured The Ages of Man *for so many years that I began to fear I would be out of practice when it came to acting again with other people. Also, eight performances a week, all by myself, and sitting alone in a dressing-room during the interval, was a very lonely and sometimes depressing business.*

In the closing weeks of *The Potting Shed,* in which he had somehow failed to repeat the success that Robert Flemyng had in the play on Broadway, John agreed to direct for Binkie what must have seemed another of their really safe bets—a new play by Terence Rattigan, *Variation on a Theme.* However, this was Rattigan in a newly liberated form. In the past there had always been the suggestion that *Separate Tables* and even *The Deep Blue Sea* were coded homosexual dramas, in which the sex of the leading character had simply been changed from a man to a woman in order to satisfy the Lord Chamberlain. But now the Wolfenden Report (a government inquiry into prostitution and homosexuality, which advocated liberalization but was not put into action for several more years) had just been published, and *Variation on a Theme* was to some extent intended as Rattigan's response. Loosely derived from Dumas's *La Dame aux Camélias* (hence the *Variation*), it was to be the story of Rose Fish, a wealthy, much-married, middle-aged woman falling in love with a gay ballet dancer—an affair that ends (like *La Dame aux Camélias* and the subsequent Garbo *Camille*) with Rose coughing herself to death of consumption.

But as with Noël Coward's *Song at Twilight,* written a decade later, there was all manner of reality lurking just below the greasepaint of an apparently conventional Shaftesbury Avenue drama. Many saw the character of Rose as being Rattigan in disguise, with his current real-life lover Ron Vale as the young dancer. Then again, Margaret Leighton, a lifelong friend of Rattigan's for whom the play was written, had also just married a much younger man, the actor Laurence Harvey, a Lithuanian who (again like Ron Vale) had anglicized his name and, famously, had a long gay affair with the film producer James Woolf, who had recently committed suicide when Harvey left him for Leighton. So the coded messages here threatened to overbalance what was in truth far from one of Rattigan's best plays. Its moral was intended to be of the tragedy that lies in store when rich and older people fall in love with feckless opportunists, whose sexuality has always been their calling card to both men and women alike. Margaret Leighton and Vivien Leigh (soon to star in a film with a very similar script, Tennessee Williams's *The Roman Spring of Mrs. Stone*) were both famous for having built up networks of gay male friends to whom they could turn in their serial moments of marital despair. Rattigan had already had one gay lover (Kenneth Morgan) commit suicide at the end of their affair, the producer Hugh Beaumont was still living with John Perry, and Gielgud was far from totally able, even now, to banish the shadows of his court case five years earlier.

All in all, therefore, this was going to be a rough emotional ride for all of the principals concerned, and it failed to get off to the best of starts when Laurence Harvey (only recently married to Leighton, but already having second thoughts about her) turned down the role of the young dancer, which went first to the actor Tim Seely, to whom Binkie Beaumont had taken a considerable fancy when he had recently played the boy in *Tea and Sympathy.* It was, however, to prove an unhappy choice. As Seely recalled: "I was entirely heterosexual, which didn't help much in that company, and I was pitifully inexperienced and lacking in confidence. I also couldn't cope with all those famous people, or with Gielgud's habit of changing everything a dozen times in rehearsal. 'For Christ's Sake!' I shouted at John one afternoon, 'Can't you ever make up your fucking mind?'"

Not entirely surprisingly, Seely was fired at the end of the tour and replaced by a young Jeremy Brett, who was about to marry Anna Massey, the daughter of Adrianne Allen, and therefore to join, at least as an in-law, the charmed and often closed circle of the H. M. Tennent backstage family.

But the central problem with *Variation on a Theme* was that although it appeared to be topical, in allowing for an overtly gay leading character onstage, in truth it creaked along on the tracks laid down by Dumas a century earlier; critics who might have been charitable to Rattigan's apparently newfound courage of exposure were turned off by a pallid script. A number of them instantly realized the problem he had faced in keeping this modern Camille figure female rather than male. As Alan Brien wrote in *The Spectator,* "The subject of Rattigan's play should be a homosexual relationship between a bored and ageing 'rentier' and a sharp, oily male tart." Harold Hobson also thought he was being asked to review a play that was really about something that was not its ostensible subject, and Tynan put the boot in by accusing Rattigan of clumsily disguising a blatantly homosexual theme in a pathetic attempt to stay on the right side of his own traditional Aunt Edna audiences and, of course, of the Lord Chamberlain, who was still then in charge of censoring West End plays.

In Rattigan's defense, his old friend the critic T. C. Worsley in *The Financial Times* attacked any suggestion of a covert homosexual theme as "a seamy line of personal smear," but because he was known to be both gay and a close friend of the author, this defense did the play, author, and critic more harm than good.

Rattigan resented the critical attacks, maintaining that he had purposely tried to show the reality behind the apparently romantic characters in *La Dame aux Camélias.* Ultimately, the play achieved lasting fame only for what it inadvertently led to: a teenage schoolgirl called Shelagh Delaney had been in the audience at a matinee during the Manchester tryout of *Variation on a Theme* and went home convinced that, although she had never written anything in her life (apart from school essays), even she could do better than that. Within a few months she had written *A Taste of*

Honey, which ran in the West End and New York for two years, compared to the barely four months for which *Variation on a Theme* was to last.

In many ways the failure of *Variation on a Theme,* despite the involvement of Rattigan, Gielgud, Leighton, and Binkie Beaumont, was the wake-up call that John G. should have heard whenever he was tempted to go back to the West End of his earlier years. In fact, however, the call was not to be answered until the utter fiasco of Enid Bagnold's *The Last Joke,* two years later. As for Rattigan, his biographer Michael Darlow pinpoints the problem that now faced all gay writers in rapidly changing theatrical times: "Until the late 1950s, Rattigan's art as a dramatist depended upon the oblique, the implicit, the struggle of frightened, damaged people to find self-expression and fulfillment in a society whose strict moral codes had always inhibited them. But once those moral codes began to be relaxed, Rattigan was not only out of fashion, he was stranded. Not only his technique as a writer, but his background and lifetime's conditioning, meant that however passionately he resented the old hypocrisies, he was not equipped to make do without them. The result was that when he tried to confront sex, however frankly and sincerely, in the permissive atmosphere of the post-Osborne theatre he always seemed evasive, insincere and sometimes actually embarrassing."

No sooner had *Variation on a Theme* opened than John went back to the Old Vic, for his only postwar appearance there before it became the first home of the National Theatre. *Henry VIII* was also to mark the climax of the Vic's Five Year Plan for which, under the overall direction of Michael Benthall, all thirty-six Shakespearean First Folio plays had now been produced. To close that marathon project Harry Andrews was cast in the title role, with John as an unusually lean and unpadded Wolsey. Inevitably, during rehearsal, Gielgud felt occasionally obliged to make a few suggestions. When Harry Andrews objected to yet one more of these at the dress rehearsal, John merely murmured, "Oh, yes, of course, I always forget Harry that you really are very slow. Alright then, just do it your way."

In a starry cast, Edith Evans was playing Queen Katharine, but even so John remained unhappy, not so much with Benthall's production as with the play itself, which he found episodic and unsatisfactory: "I was not even now sufficiently confident to try and change the character to accord with my own style, although after the first night I did pad out my clothes and changed my make-up altogether."

Edith Evans's biographer Bryan Forbes was to recall this production for its quality of stillness: "There were moments that made me regret that Edith and Gielgud had never established a more permanent company together. Their partnerships were always made in heaven, whether Edith was acting alongside John or being directed by him. So different in temperament—John gregarious and volatile, working with a sentimental intensity of emotion to gain his ends; Edith withdrawn, feeling her way by instinct—they were yet ideally suited, and on those few occasions when they found the right vehicle, they complemented each other superbly."

The young John Mortimer, just beginning to turn from the law to the theater, found Gielgud's Wolsey "wearing an expression of pained disgust, rather like a clergyman who shrewdly suspects that someone is frying fish in the vestry . . . in his farewell, however, he produces a brilliant study of the bitter but noble resignation of a man who could never be likeable and will always be greater in failure than success—a performance the more to be respected, in that it never plays for sympathy or easy emotion."

The Vic's Five Year Plan went out on a note of triumph with *Henry VIII* playing a gala season in Paris, and the last London performance was marked by a mass visit from the actors of the Moscow Art Theatre, who were themselves on a gala season in London. As this short run was coming to its end, John at last found the time to focus on a project that had been at the back of his mind for all of ten years—a version of the solo Shakespearean recitals that he had tentatively and hesitantly started on some of his wartime troop tours. Although originally the critic Ivor Brown had been responsible for putting these together with Gielgud, the actor now stayed with his old friend from Cambridge, Professor George Rylands, who had just published a Shakespearean anthology under the title *The Ages of Man*. As John was to recall,

This was meant to be for people who had not seen me in my early days . . . it needed a totally different technique, the use of my voice which I had learnt from radio and early recordings, and then carefully planted moments of Leontes, Richard II and Lear full out . . . I kept changing the order every night, to get the contrasts and balances in the right spaces. That's where the sonnets were so useful; I used them to leaven the mixture, rather like a cheese sandwich.

Of all the times I played it over the next nine years, at home and abroad, the only time the *Ages of Man* recital was not a success was when Binkie Beaumont suggested that, as I'd had such a success touring Shakespeare around the provinces before the war, I should go back to Edinburgh, Liverpool, Cambridge and Brighton. At Liverpool no one would come near it, and Edinburgh was also very hard. When I got to Brighton, the houses were so terrible for the first three nights that Godfrey Winn and Alan Melville both wrote letters to the local paper saying it was an outrage that I was not a success. The theatre was packed for the rest of the week, but I found it somewhat humiliating having to write and thank them. Audiences outside London seemed to be suspicious of a one-man show, perhaps because they felt they were not getting their money's worth. I toured *Ages of Man* for so many years that I began to fear I would be out of practice when it came to acting again with other people. Also, eight performances a week, all by myself, and sitting alone in a dressing-room during the interval, was a very lonely and sometimes depressing business.

Here again, in fact, John was merely reverting to family type; Ellen Terry had toured a solo recital called *Shakespeare's Heroines* all through her later years, and as a boy John had seen it at the Haymarket, where she would link the excerpts together with a personal narrative spoken intimately to the audience. It was precisely this technique that John now adopted and adapted, having also seen his old friend Emlyn Williams in his solo Dickens recitals, which had brought this format back to popularity all around the world early in the 1950s. John, however, remained extremely wary of performing for any kind of a run a classical anthology that was still a work in progress, and although he played it for one night in Bath immediately after the Old Vic *Henry VIII,* he did not bring it into the West End until the following June.

Although the brief English tour of *Ages of Man* would not prove entirely triumphant, John was now tempted by an attractive amount of dollars to take his recital all over America, through the autumn and winter of 1958. Before that, however, he had to honor a promise to Binkie and Brian Bedford that he would direct Peter Shaffer's first play, *Five Finger Exercise,* for which he now also cast Roland Culver, Adrianne Allen, Johnnie Mills's eldest daughter Juliet, and an equally young and untried Michael Bryant.

The play itself was, in many respects, the most immediately contemporary that John had tackled since his prewar work with Rodney Ackland and Ronald Mackenzie. It told the relatively simple story of a young Austrian tutor (Bryant) coming to stay with a hidebound English family, and subtly changing all their lives, not always for the better.

In rehearsal, John was his usual indecisive self, on one occasion telling Michael Bryant, "Oh, it is so boring to have you just come down the staircase. Why not come in through the French windows?" Bryant politely explained that, as he had gone upstairs in a previous scene, this would look somewhat odd. "Or have I," Bryant inquired, "climbed down a drainpipe? And if so, why?" "Oh, Michael," was John's only reply, "do stop being so drearily practical."

On the road there was considerable doubt, shared by John and Binkie, as to whether this somewhat downbeat, domestic, psychological drama was really going to work in the West End, and although they had shored it up as far as possible for Shaftesbury Avenue with two well-established West End stars of the period, Roland Culver and Adrianne Allen, the rest of the cast members were as unknown and untried as their author. It was, therefore, with some surprise as well as relief that they opened to ecstatic reviews and played to packed houses for fourteen months. The story did not, though, have an altogether happy ending; there was the offer of Broadway and a long American tour to follow, but Binkie and John decided that to make this work, they would need at least one American star for the posters. Accordingly, Jessica Tandy (in fact English by birth, but by now long resident in America and married to Hume Cronyn) was hired, but neither Gielgud nor Beaumont could find the courage to tell their old friend Adrianne Allen that she alone would not be crossing the Atlantic with all the rest of the cast. When she did find out, largely by accident, Adrianne was so hurt by what she saw as a total betrayal that, on the last night of the London run, she abruptly gave up acting after a star thirty-year career, leaving not just the theater but England itself to spend the rest of her life in a Swiss exile, separated angrily not only from her children, Anna and Daniel Massey, but also from Binkie and John, to neither of whom she ever spoke again. "It all might," noted Anna later, "have been more tactfully managed."

This had only been Bryant's second London engagement after several years in regional repertory companies; John had seen him in *The Iceman Cometh* at the Arts and offered him the role of the tutor. As Bryant said of the experience,

> I remember having to audition with a young friend of John's, a young friend of Binkie's and a young friend of John Perry's, all of whom I was convinced were going to get the role instead of me, because this was still a very homosexual time in the West End, and I was already married. But to my amazement they all agreed they wanted me, and except for John's incredible indecisiveness in rehearsal it was a lovely engagement, nearly a year in London and then another year in New York, but of course without Adrianne. John handled all that very badly; he really wasn't good in a crisis, and this was at least for her a real crisis. She took it very badly.
>
> I realised, very quickly in rehearsal, that I had to be very careful about adopting John's suggestions; I'd already worked with some really terrible directors in the regions, and I knew how they could mess you up. I had to stand up for what I believed about the character, and John wasn't always very used to that. I remember he tried to make me cut a wonderful speech beginning "My father was a Nazi." John kept telling me how boring I was and to cut it, and finally I told him that he could cut it if he liked, but I certainly wasn't going to do any such thing; I think he suddenly realised he was dealing with a new genera-

tion of actors, who did a little thinking for themselves and guarded their own backs, and that seemed to unnerve him. Another speech he wanted me to cut was the one about the tutor having slept with a girl, and finding next morning at the wash-basin nothing had really changed. John was convinced the audience would think he was going to wash his private parts, and somehow found it all terribly embarrassing, but I stuck to it.

In all fairness, neither he nor Binkie nor anyone ever tried anything on with me, and at the first-night party all John said was that I had been right to reject his cuts. But then a very funny thing happened; I started getting letters from old Colonels and Admirals in the audience, saying that their wives were away for the weekend and would I like to come down for a little shooting or sailing? I realised at last what was going on, and insisted that in the programme the management should explain that I was married, whereupon all the letters stopped. I steered well clear of the H. M. Tennent world, though Brian Bedford was right in the middle of it and so was Keith Baxter; I was a jobbing, ambitious young actor, and I didn't want to get caught up in that very closeted little community. By now the Royal Court had started up, and I knew there was something out there beyond Shaftesbury Avenue and the Haymarket.

With *Five Finger Exercise* now safely installed in the West End, for the rest of 1958 and well into 1959 John toured *The Ages of Man* through no less than sixty American and Canadian cities, finally arriving at a unique format, of which his old friend and mentor Michel Saint-Denis noted, "John devised a programme in which he could present himself in three ways—as an actor, as a director indicating how these various roles ought to be played, and as a man talking directly to the audience between excerpts."

Just before the start of the coast-to-coast American tour, there had, however, been one great sadness. In August 1958, John's mother Kate died at eighty-nine. In all the letters that John wrote her it is eminently clear that, since Lewis's early death, John had replaced him as her favorite son, although she was to remain until the very end sharply critical of those occasions on which she felt he was failing to live up to Terry family standards. All through the aftermath of his 1953 trial she had remained rock-solid, maintaining that it had all been a drunken escapade, and refusing to allow herself to hear any of the malicious gossip that at that time surrounded her son. Her daughter, Eleanor, had been working as John's unofficial secretary until now, but with a deep dislike of flying, she opted to stay behind and sort out Kate's effects, leaving John on the road in America with an even greater than usual feeling of backstage isolation.

But this long tour, the start of what really could be considered John's greatest Shakespearean achievement, almost failed to happen at all. Because he had originally performed it under the auspices of the British Council, it still had a certain interest in the production, and this would, of course, be the first time that John had gone back to work in America since his trial for homosexuality. Although at home he had managed to overcome the negative episode with remarkable speed, at least on the surface, the case and its publicity had not been forgotten by an official of the British Council in Washington, who solemnly wrote a report back to headquarters in London suggesting that *The Ages of Man* tour should not be allowed to go ahead, in view of the very real danger that John might be refused a work permit for America, on the grounds that his police record made him "an undesirable alien."

How much of this ever got back to John is unclear; happily the official was overruled by the British Council's headquarters in London, and throughout a long and triumphant tour no reference was ever made in the American press to John's arrest.

This six-month North American tour of *The Ages of Man* was utterly triumphant, as John himself later recalled: "Beginning in Stratford, Ontario, and ending in Tallahassee, Florida, I travelled eighteen thousand miles, giving eighty-one performances in sixty different towns and cities. I motored and flew everywhere in small cars and aeroplanes, never knowing from one day to another whether I was going to appear in theatres, stadiums, chapels or schools, or if the audience would be two thousand or two hundred. I never had the chance of staying more than one or two days in each place, so I saw the whole of America, but have very little recollection of any of it. It was all motels and travelling. . . . Of course I enjoyed working on my performance, and although at first I had no real plan of doing it in London or New York, towards the end of the tour the recital began to be such a success that I felt at last I had found the way to present it in its best possible shape. I certainly owed the eventual success of the recital to that long tour."

The Ages of Man was divided into three sections, the first referring to youth, the second to manhood, and the third to old age. The stage was hung with red velvet curtains, but there were no other props or costumes save for a downstage lectern containing the script. John would occasionally move across to this and turn over a page or two, but it was obvious from the very first performance that he had in fact learned it all by heart—speeches from *Hamlet, Richard II, Macbeth, Julius Caesar, Romeo and Juliet,* and *King Lear,* all of which he had, of course, already played in context, and most of them more than once. But this recital format also allowed him speeches from plays he had never performed, among them *Othello* and *Henry VI.*

By the very end of the tour, John had agreed to play a limited six-week season at the 46th Street Theater on Broadway, although this almost failed to start on time. Having only a few days' holiday between the end of a grueling road tour and the Broadway opening, John, with uncharacteristic traveler's courage, had decided to explore Havana, Cuba. He arrived at his hotel to find the city unusually and ominously quiet. The following morning the Castro revolution broke out, and John spent several nervous hours trying to get an exit visa at the now rebel-occupied airport. In the end, he made it back to New York with only hours to spare before the first Broadway night, a gala affair with Marlene Dietrich, Lauren Bacall, and Lillian Gish among those in the audience.

The following morning, it was announced that the season would be extended by three more weeks; John's good fortune, which had threatened to run out on him in Cuba, now kicked back in with a vengeance. The day after his New York opening was the first in which newspapers were back on the streets after a six-week strike, so the reviews for *The Ages of Man,* all ecstatic, were the first to have been seen in print for over a month.

Immediately after the Broadway run of *The Ages of Man,* he was invited by CBS to make his television debut, ironically in a role that had been written for him but that he had declined to play onstage, that of the failed schoolmaster with the unfaithful wife in Rattigan's *The Browning Version.* The director was to be John Frankenheimer, later a celebrated Hollywood filmmaker, and his costar, as the chilly, resentful wife, was to be his old friend Margaret Leighton. Gielgud did not take easily to the new medium, however, and found the proximity of the camera more than a little offputting. But as always he was a quick study, and the broadcast was acclaimed not only by all the American television critics, many of whom described John's as the performance of the year, but also—and far more important to John—in a rare letter of praise from Larry Olivier who, filming in Hollywood, admitted somewhat ruefully that it had been a much greater success than his own recent American television debut as *John Gabriel Borkman:* "Your old friend was bursting with pride and admiration. Your performance was quite flawless and dreadfully moving, it haunts me still. Bravo, dearest Johnny, it's just fascinating and most inspiring, the way you seem still to find room for improvement all the time."

Having suddenly thus discovered that he could manage television, John was eager to try it again on home territory, and as soon as he got back to London in the spring of 1959, at the time of his fifty-fifth birthday, he agreed to star on ITV for "Binkievision" (a television offshoot of the H. M. Tennent management) in the play he had opened at the Haymarket during the term of his trial six years earlier, N. C. Hunter's *A Day by the Sea.* Gladys Cooper now flew home from California to play the Sybil Thorndike part, and although it went out to an audience of 22 million viewers, the result was not entirely successful, largely because this was an ensemble play that now had to be shot in a series of disconnected close-ups.

As soon as that play was televised, he went back to work in the theater for H. M. Tennent, this time directing rather than starring in another play by Graham Greene. If his previous venture into Greeneland, *The Potting Shed,* had been considered somewhat obscure, *The Complaisant Lover* was altogether more user-friendly. In it, Ralph Richardson played a suburban dentist whose wife (Phyllis Calvert) is having an affair with a local bookseller (Paul Scofield). All three decide, rather as though they were in Coward's *Design for Living*, that a triangular affair might be the best way forward. And Gielgud now understood that with Greene at least, less was more—he did not so much direct the play as arrange it neatly for an audience, allowing Richardson to do his own thing, and the other actors merely to settle down around him. During the run Richardson was also filming Graham Greene's *Our Man in Havana* by day, with Noël Coward now playing the role of the master spy, which John had rather unwisely rejected.

He was, however, now beginning to realize that if he was ever to make any real money he would have to cease turning his back on the world of film, and it was at this time that he instructed his agent Laurie Evans to pick up any movie offers within reason that were to come his way. Evans did not always find this easy, as John was perfectly capable of abandoning a film, even after he had signed a contract, if something theatrical were to come along. He still regarded the cinema as essentially a secondary medium and was not for several more years to bring to it or television any of the selfless dedication he brought to his work both onstage and backstage. The shadow of Alfred Hitchcock and John's unhappy time in *The Secret Agent* still seemed to hang over him more than a quarter of a century later.

Shortly after finishing work on the Greene play, Gielgud took his *Ages of Man* to the Spoleto Festival in Italy, the first of many such festive engagements, and then early in June he brought it for the first time to the West End, reopening the Queen's Theatre on Shaftesbury Avenue, which had lain in ruins since its 1940 bombing and was now the first new theater to open in the West End for twenty-eight years.

From the romantic youth of Romeo, through the tragedy of King Lear to Prospero's fond farewell to the magic of his art, this was, as Philip Hope-Wallace wrote, "one of the most memorable evenings I have ever spent in a theatre. I find it hard to think that any other living actor could so deliver Clarence's dream speech—this was like great singing, paradoxically not to be analysed in words . . . even after more than two hours of concentrated attention on an unusually hot night, there was not a stir in the house . . . without forcing his voice, Sir John managed to bring into it every kind of cadence. He was born, he grew up, he was even funny, and he died under our eyes. The anthology is sometimes a dangerous form, but I have seldom heard speaking which impelled us to listen so intently. Standing slim and erect in a dinner suit, he ranged in age and mood without any sense of strain—he appeared as fresh at the end of the recital as he was at its beginning."

Not everyone, however, was equally impressed: "Went to John G.'s opening in his solo Shakespeare show," records Noël Coward's diary, "he was superb in his quiet moments, but not so good when he wept and roared."

During the London run, John gave a very rare interview (to *The Times*) in which he analyzed, in some detail, his own development as an actor: "When I was young, I enjoyed colouring the words . . . now, I try to shut the phrases, so to speak, in rat traps. I try not to sing, not to elongate syllables or vowels . . . I try now to exert a rigid discipline, and above all not to indulge. As Leontes or Wolsey, I weep at the same point for exactly the same amount of time each night, and no longer. When I hold any mood or tone for too long, I am aware of the fact and try to change it. Poetry has a beginning, middle and end, held in a kind of arc which must not be broken, although inside it there can be many variations. Like a Gothic arch, within it there can be elaborations, but the arch remains intact."

As soon as *The Ages of Man* closed its first West End season, John returned to America, first to revive the recital at an alfresco summer festival in a huge tent outside Boston, and then to open his third *Much Ado About Nothing* there, at the start of an American tour. Among the cast was Barry Ingham, who remembers John G. as being "unkind in rehearsals, at one point saying, in exasperation, 'Barry! Why on earth did I bring you out here? You're terrible.'" Ingham also remembers a culture clash between Gielgud's approach to acting, and that of the local American Method school: "He told the young American actors, on for just a scene or two as extras, to 'Walk like Lords.' One young, cocky guy asked John what a Lord was. John replied, 'A great English gentleman. A powerful man. Walk like one, come on the stage, go to the altar, cross yourself then come back and stand with your hand on your hilt, as if you own the stage.' The boy swaggered across the stage to the altar, said, 'Hi, God!' then came back down to the front to await John's reaction. 'No! No!' said John, 'that's not it at all. Walk as if you're a Lord, a great English gentleman.' The boy continued to play up: 'But, Sir Gielgud, if I'm going to walk like this guy Lord, I need to know something about him. Who am I? Where do I come from?' John, having got the measure of him, shot back, 'Oh, you silly, silly boy! You come from off-stage, of course!' When we eventually reached New York my first-night present from John was a book, inscribed: 'To dear Barry, in remembrance of your New York debut and laboursome struggles with the elusive and difficult Claudio. John Gielgud.'"

After Peggy Ashcroft and Diana Wynyard, Margaret Leighton was now his third Beatrice, but their initial experience at the Cambridge summer festival tent near Boston was, as John later wrote, far from happy:

First of all a bulldozer broke through the pipe laid on for our water supply, so we could neither drink nor wash off our make-up. . . . Before the matinee, I was asked to sign autographs for a party of blind people, who were the only ones who had bothered to turn up in an otherwise empty house. For some reason they got to their seats late, helped or hindered by usherettes who then sank exhausted into the chairs nearest the stage, and, yawning heavily, started to buff their nails and chew gum directly beneath our feet. People whose seats were in the direct rays of the sun kept moving their canvas chairs to get into the shade, and in the interval some of the cast went outside to the river bank to gasp for air, thereby missing several entrances. One local actress outraged me by trying to photograph the production in all the scenes she wasn't actually in. During the last act a cloudburst meant that not a single word could be heard, because of the noise of the rain hitting the canvas roof. By now the aisles were running with water and the audience sat with their feet tucked under them, preparing to plunge out at the earliest possible opportunity, umbrellas at the ready.

After that unhappy start, things did not get much better when *Much Ado* reached Broadway, where a number of critics pointed out that, despite the arrival of Margaret Leighton, this was still essentially the production that John had opened at Stratford-upon-Avon ten years earlier and was now looking a little the worse for wear. But John also had the Broadway transfer of *Five Finger Exercise* to occupy him, and when that repeated its London success, he returned home for Christmas to consider the possibility of a new play by Enid Bagnold, which Glen Byam Shaw was to direct for Binkie Beaumont.

The Last Joke had an amazingly starry cast, including Ralph Richardson, Anna Massey, Ernest Thesiger, and Robert Flemyng: it was, however, to prove such a fiasco that John did not do another new play for five years (and even then he was to have not much better luck with Edward Albee's *Tiny Alice*), while for the Tennent management it was almost the final straw. If Richardson and Gielgud could survive only two weeks in a play written by the author of *The Chalk Garden* and directed by the recently retired head of the Shakespeare Memorial Theatre, then clearly the revolutionaries who had taken over the Royal Court in Chelsea four years earlier were now beginning to invade the commercial West End as well. After *The Last Joke,* the old Shaftesbury Avenue empire of Binkie Beaumont was really and truly finished. Bagnold, however, was more inclined to blame the two knights. Richardson had missed the first week of rehearsal because a film overran in Cyprus, and John, claiming he couldn't really understand any of it, allowed Glen Byam Shaw to change several speeches on the grounds that "I had to be saved from myself."

Gielgud was cast here as a Romanian prince, and Richardson appeared as a Levantine millionaire; both knew almost at once that they had made a terrible mistake. One reporter even rang Bagnold the morning after the first night to ask what total failure really felt like. The savagery of the reviews stunned both stars, who had not appeared onstage together since *A Day by the Sea,* and were still over ten years away from their triumphant late-life partnership as the brokers' men in David Storey's *Home* and Harold Pinter's *No Man's Land.* The critic for the *Daily Mail* found the play "A perfectly dreadful charade, both baffling and boring," and Milton Shulman for the *Evening Standard* wrote, "It is a long time since such a caravan of overblown nonsense has rolled into the West End, masquerading as a serious vehicle for some of our best actors." Harold Hobson, usually among Gielgud's and Richardson's greatest fans, added, "At the opening night everything came out of the top drawer. The dresses were by Balmain, the acting by Gielgud, Richardson, Flemyng and Massey, the guns by Bapti and the apathy and boredom by an audience of rank and beauty." Apparently the awfulness of *The Last Joke* defeated even both stars' usual supporters; the old actor Charles Doran, by now well over ninety, who had given Ralph his start, went backstage and was only able to mutter, "It's quite a good wig!"

The moment that they closed after only two deeply unhappy weeks, Richardson fled to America to film *Long Day's Journey into Night* while John stayed in London where, although his professional life had taken a considerable beating, his private life had suddenly begun to look up. A chance meeting in the Tate Gallery had brought him into contact with a very good-looking but somewhat mysterious Hungarian exile, Martin Hensler, with whom he tentatively began the affair that was, in fact, to last for the rest of both their lives.

Hensler was strikingly good-looking, and in many ways precisely what John had always wanted: someone to take care of him and his house, someone to love, but above all someone so discreet and private and low-maintenance that there was never any fear of another homosexual "outing."

There were those who believed that Martin had once had a wife and even possibly a child; others maintained that he had always been gay, and eventually there was some agreement that he had probably fled Hungary at the time of the 1956 uprising. He himself always divulged so little of his past, and so frequently changed his stories of it, that in the end he went to his grave keeping almost all of his pre-Gielgud secrets intact.

None of this is to suggest that Martin was always undemanding in his relationship with John. He had (perhaps because of an obscure but possibly somewhat aristocratic background) expensive tastes and very good taste. He, therefore, always encouraged John to work, so that their lifestyle on Cowley Street could be supported, and he made sure that, with the help of housekeepers, the place always looked immaculate. He had, however, unlike John, a certain taste for gardening and the countryside, and now began to work on his new partner in the hope that Gielgud might eventually be persuaded to quit his beloved London and settle somewhere more rural—a dream that could not be achieved for another ten years or so, by which time John's film profits were able to finance the wing of a large country house near Aylesbury, where both men were to spend the last thirty years of their lives in an autumnal partnership of great love and only intermittent irritability.

As Keith Baxter, the actor who perhaps was closest to John toward the end of his life, explains,

> Martin could be very cruel. I remember driving them both down to the country one night around this time and Martin screaming from the back seat, "John, you terrible actor. You always terrible." John amazingly seemed to take all this without complaint, but you have to understand the nature of their relationship, and John's sexuality. Like Noël Coward, he was not especially highly sexed, and took a rather schoolboyish view of the whole thing, forming crushes on often very unsuitable people. Ever since his arrest he had been traumatised by the possibility of it happening again. His sister Eleanor made sure that at Cowley Street young men were not encouraged to stay the night. So John's early meetings with Hensler were almost furtive— week-ends when John Perry was in the country with Binkie, they would take over his rather small flat in Pimlico, and I can still see them there sitting up in bed sharing a cup of tea.
>
> Some people had this fantasy of Binkie and John Perry running a kind of male brothel at Knots Fosse, the week-end cottage they had bought in Essex, but having stayed there a great deal, I know it wasn't like that at all. Binkie had an Italian couple looking after the house, the sheets on the beds were frequently darned, and Binkie could be seen in Viyella pyjamas. It was more old English village life than gay theatrical, and there were always women like Vivien Leigh and Margaret Leighton down for the weekend.

Speaking again of Hensler and John's home life, Keith Baxter recalls:

Martin always had three opening questions for any newcomer he met. Are you rich? Are you famous? Are you homosexual? And depending on the answers he got, he would then carry on the conversation. At first, he always seemed to be wearing the same clothes, so he must somehow have washed them every night, as he appeared tremendously chic but something of a trial for all John's other friends, who had to keep bringing him into conversations about the theatre, of which he seemed to know little and care less.

He was strikingly tall, and I would guess in his early or middle thirties when they had first met. But, as Orson Welles once said, if you have a Hungarian for a friend, you don't need enemies, and certainly there was something very uneasy, always, about Martin. His constant rudeness, his savage attacks on John's talent, and his refusal ever to join anyone for meals suggested that here must have been a very unhappy man, working out some of his Hungarian background by taking it out on others. On the other hand, John was absolutely devoted to him, came more and more to rely on him, and we eventually all came to realise that Martin was the price we had to pay for maintaining any kind of relationship with John.

Hungarians can be hell. If you are happy, they tell you you have no right to be, and if you are sad, they keep telling you to cheer up. His English was always heavily accented, as though he had never bothered to learn how to speak it properly. And there is always, in the theatre, something especially terrible about the civilian partner who wants to tell you what he or she thinks is wrong with what you are doing; the chances are you already know, and don't want to hear it— least of all from them. But Martin became especially tiresome at this, increasingly voicing his own uninformed, incoherent and often unintelligible suggestions, which John just accepted with a weary smile, so as not to provoke Hensler's terrible temper. There was also an appalling occasion when the two Johns [John Perry] and Martin were all in New York, and Martin was lecturing John G. as to how he was far too gentle and submissive with the management of *Ivanov,* and how John should lay in to the producer Alexander Cohen and threaten not to appear unless he was treated better by him. Finally Perry let rip at Martin, telling him that it was none of his business, and that he had not the faintest idea of the relationship between a star and a producer, least of all on Broadway. Martin simply left the room, but it was John Perry who was then banned from Gielgud's company, by Martin, for the next thirty years.

20. OTHELLO'S OCCUPATION GONE

(1961–1964)

I have neither the voice nor the power for Othello, and I should simply never have attempted it.

*W*hile John was thus reorganizing his private life, and still reeling from the shocking collapse of *The Last Joke,* he began to pick up whatever work he could, sometimes for his brother Val in BBC radio drama, but then most happily in a return to the world of opera. Early in 1961, again at Covent Garden, with Georg Solti conducting, and some brilliant designs by John Piper, Gielgud directed the first London performance of Benjamin Britten's *A Midsummer Night's Dream* to considerable acclaim. After the difficult time he'd had with *The Trojans* three years earlier, he was relieved to find that now, because he knew the play so well, he was on much more familiar territory with the opera. His success was more than welcome after *The Last Joke,* but it was to prove a false dawn. The year 1961 was to be yet another distinctly uneven year, though it concluded with John finally retrieving his reputation, in the nick of time, with a memorable Gaev for the newly formed Royal Shakespeare Company at its Aldwych Theatre home.

The first project for the new year was to be the Broadway premiere of a new play by one of John's many New York friends, the London-born

American dramatist Hugh Wheeler, who was to achieve considerable success in later years as Stephen Sondheim's librettist on *A Little Night Music, Pacific Overtures,* and *Sweeney Todd.* But *Big Fish, Little Fish* was, in fact, Wheeler's first play, and for it the Broadway management had assembled a starry cast led by Jason Robards, George Grizzard, and the actor now married to John's beloved Jessica Tandy, Hume Cronyn, whose diary of the production suggests that John's technique as a director had not changed much over the years:

FEBRUARY 7TH: Rehearsals begin. No introductions, no explanation, just "Shall we read it?" Everybody stiff and nervous, until halfway through Act 1 someone lets go with an uninhibited fart. Everyone seems relieved.

FEBRUARY 8TH: Johnny G. seems to have sixteen new ideas a minute. I write and erase, write and erase. Script now covered with lunatic markings.

FEBRUARY 28TH: John expects his actors to do a great deal of work for themselves, which is perhaps a reflection of his own superb powers as an actor. At the same time, he is better able to do those things for an actor that no actor can be expected to do for himself, and that lie purely within the realm of direction, than any other director I have ever worked for. John expects everyone to act as well as he does, which is of course an impossible order to fill, and his machine-gun delivery of instructions always makes me feel that I am going to bump into myself either coming or going: "Hume, cross left on that line . . . No, quite wrong. Go to the sofa . . . try it there . . . No, that's terrible, cross right . . . No! No! You just came from there, so try standing still." Despite my extravagant admiration for John as actor and director, I somehow feel I am never able to please him, and always I know that whatever he tells me to do, he could do so much better himself. I ask him if he always changes everything every day to make it better, or simply because he is bored of all of us, and in truth he never really replies.

Nevertheless, *Big Fish, Little Fish* opened to some rave reviews ("Mr. Cronyn is so good it hurts"—*The New York Times*) and John was soon to be the proud holder of two Broadway Tony awards, neither for his acting, but for the directing of first *Five Finger Exercise,* and then *Big Fish, Little Fish.*

John's good fortune, however, was to prove only Broadway bound; back home in London, amazingly enough, he still seemed to have not entirely learned the lesson of *The Last Joke,* which was basically that whatever had worked in the West End before 1956 was highly unlikely to work there after that date. Out of his extraordinary long-lasting loyalty to Binkie, and to John Perry, he now agreed to direct the last of Perry's collaborations with Molly Keane, yet another Irish country-house comedy, this one rather misleadingly entitled *Dazzling Prospect.* Despite a cast headed by Margaret Rutherford and the young Sarah Miles, with sets and costumes by the ever-faithful Motley, the play barely survived two weeks at the Globe, although it did allow John to bring the already eccentric Sarah into his circle of friends. As she remembers, "I always had a great deal of time for John— such dapper style and inborn good manners. Genuine humility, too, so rare among directors . . . each morning he would come into rehearsal at the Globe and say, 'Good morning, everyone, you are all going to have to be very patient with me today, I'm afraid. Because I really want to start again from scratch. I really am most terribly sorry.'"

John now decided, for what, in fact, was to be the last time, that he would like to go back to the Shakespeare Memorial Theatre in Stratford, the scene of so many of his classical successes. But the theater by the Avon to which he now returned was very different; both Anthony Quayle and Glen Byam Shaw had given up their management in the late 1950s, and Stratford was now being run by a hot, new twenty-five-year-old director, Peter Hall, whose ambition it was to establish a permanent company, not only by the Avon but also at the Aldwych Theatre in London, one which was about to become known as the Royal Shakespeare Company.

Hall knew that he would have to find something very tempting to bring John back to the home where he no longer felt himself to be so closely allied to the directorate, and in due course he found it. The Italian director Franco Zeffirelli had recently made his name in London, not only in opera but also with a stunning Old Vic *Romeo and Juliet*, and he was now keen to direct *Othello* at Stratford with an all-star cast including Peggy Ashcroft as Emilia, Dorothy Tutin as Desdemona, and the young Ian Bannen as Iago. Peter Hall himself takes up the story of the nightmare that was to come:

> Franco had designed realistic Italian sets, more suited to Verdi than to Shakespeare, which took forever to change. I sat with him in the auditorium all through one night until six the next morning, trying unsuccessfully to get him to cut some of the scenery. It was clear to me that if things were left as they were, the interval was going to last some 40 minutes. Franco took the view that audiences would not mind the wait if what they saw, finally, was beautiful. I told him nothing could be that beautiful. Also, I was desperately worried that the full sexuality Gielgud had found in previous years, in his tortured Angelo, his jealous Leontes, and his questing Hamlet, were eluding him as he came to the simple naivety of Othello. He was unhappy and uncertain, and appeared swamped in the enormous, misplaced splendour of the production. The setting was so dark that against it Gielgud's darkened face all but disappeared, added to which Zeffirelli made the fatal mistake of dressing John in Venetian robes—so he looked, as many critics said, like an Indian Civil Servant having a bad day.
>
> On the first night, monumental stone-like pillars swayed whenever John leant against them, and Ian Bannen, uncertain of his lines, pluckily improvised Iago to disastrous effect. It was one of those nightmare evenings when everything went wrong—a famous catastrophe, as much talked about as any of our successes. I felt very responsible for John's failure in the part. After all, I had listened when he and Franco had said they wanted to do the play. It had seemed to me, given the extraordinary sweetness and innocence of one side of Gielgud's personality, that he could create the trusting Moor, but he was never the soldier; the poetry was extraordinary, but the animal wasn't there.

Yet one more problem was John's apparent inability to register any kind of jealousy, as Peggy Ashcroft recalled, "In desperation one morning I said, 'Surely, John, you must have been jealous of something or somebody in your life.' John thought for a long time, then said, 'Well, I did cry once when Larry had his big success as Hamlet.'"

Hall's verdict was one with which the critics could only agree. The production probably had been doomed from the very beginning, not least because, as is indicated by a series of letters to Hall from John, the final casting bore almost no resemblance to the initial hopes. Having failed to interest Peter Brook, John had gone to Zeffirelli suggesting that Peter O'Toole should play his Iago. When he proved unavailable, John drew up an amazing list of alternatives, led by Rex Harrison, Peter Finch, John Mills, Robert Shaw, Alan Badel, Robert Stephens, Albert Finney, Jack Hawkins, Maurice Evans, and John Clements, all of whom proved otherwise engaged, leaving the comparatively inexperienced Ian Bannen to carry the ultimate catastrophe alongside John.

Zeffirelli himself, never given to understatement onstage or off, later said that the opening night was the most disastrous and ill-fated in the whole history of English, and possibly world theater. This was conceivably an exaggeration, but not a very great one; it ran for over four hours, at the end of which Ian Bannen as Iago was heard to announce, "Cassio is dead, er, I mean he must be almost dead." John's beard kept coming astray, thereby causing Michael Billington to note that if *Hamlet* was the tragedy of a man who could not make up his mind, *Othello* was here the tragedy of a man who could not make up his beard. Proceedings were not helped by a wall that mysteriously flew upward in Act Two, taking with it several surprised actors who happened to be sitting on it at the time.

After that, anything the critics had to say proved almost an anticlimax. Tynan merely noted that Bannen was "all warts and no face," and that Gielgud was simply "overparted." Intriguingly, during the endless search for an Iago, Zeffirelli said to Peter Hall, "I see him as very young, with a baby face, and always smiling. But behind that young, round, smiling face, is a heart of steel. By the way, Mr Hall, do you act at all?"

Peggy Ashcroft, whose memories of *Othello* went back thirty years to her own Desdemona opposite Paul Robeson, always maintained that John was on the verge of giving a great performance, which was then totally destroyed by Zeffirelli's scenery. But in fact Hall got closer to the truth—Gielgud was simply not now, or ever, going to be a plausible Othello, either vocally or physically. Like Richard III and Henry V, this was always going to be one of the great Olivier roles that John could never attempt to make his own.

Luckily, both John and Peggy were able, immediately afterward, to retrieve their reputations in John's own adaptation of his beloved *The Cherry Orchard,* which went into production at the Aldwych for Peter Hall's new company, with Michel Saint-Denis directing, immediately after the rapid withdrawal of *Othello* from the repertoire. For this they were allowed a full eight weeks of rehearsal, twice the usual length.

Even so, some critics had reservations about Saint-Denis's production, which featured not only Gielgud and Ashcroft but also Judi Dench, Dorothy Tutin, Ian Holm, and Patience Collier in the first great takeover of the Aldwych by the RSC. It was heavily—some thought perhaps too heavily—influenced by the recent visit to London of the Moscow Art Theatre players. John, given his Russian ancestry and the fact that they were using his own adaptation, was unusually at home from the very beginning, and the production generally caught what Michael Billington called "the essential point about Chekhov, which is that his plays are a collision of solitudes, in which people marooned in their own private worlds are brought into social contact to act out their inner lives, in a way that is both farcical and sad."

As for Michel Saint-Denis, "When one sees Gielgud, it does not take long to discover that he is restless, anxious, nervous and impressionable. He is not over-confident in himself. His restlessness goes with a tendency to be dissatisfied. Therefore he works out more and more plans, more and more ideas, rejecting one for another, working all the time from instinct rather than from careful study."

Robert Muller, for *The Daily Express,* noted, "Gielgud makes of the monumental bore, Gaev, a more endearing individual than I would ever have thought possible. His silences are pregnant with memories; time passes visibly behind his closed eyelids; there is no more use for the Gaevs of this world, and he knows it and suffers accordingly." Alan Brien found John "wearing an elaborate outfit of petty, potty mannerisms with the superb comical unself-consciousness of an ex-King receiving courtiers in his pyjamas. I have never seen that brief role count for so much." As for J. C. Trewin, John's Gaev was "the most extraordinary piece of creative acting I have ever seen. . . . He has, in his very bearing, the great poetry of the dying life of the aristocracy, and yet whatever is in his mind reaches us as the sentimental or the trivial . . . behind all is the wistfulness of a weak man who has betrayed his trust and can now only move himself by his own speeches." Kenneth Tynan found John simply "just right—elegant and gravely foolish, lost in thought, and leaning on a bookcase being solemnly dusted by Firs, the butler, as if he were a piece of furniture."

But sadly, having retrieved his classical reputation with this considerable Aldwych success, John was now to move into another two lean years, propped up only by revivals of his *Ages of Man,* and even they were beginning to suffer from the law of diminishing returns. The recital had simply been seen already by most of Gielgud's most faithful audiences.

His first project after *The Cherry Orchard* was to direct his old friend and partner Ralph Richardson in a glossily old-fashioned H. M. Tennent revival of *The School for Scandal,* with a cast that would also feature John Neville, Margaret Rutherford, and Anna and Daniel Massey. The initial reviews here were far from glorious, but the combination of Gielgud and Richardson and Richard Brinsley Sheridan was enough to carry a somewhat dull production through to a new box-office record at the Haymarket Theatre. During the run, there were considerable cast changes; John himself took over from John Neville as Joseph Surface, the role he had played triumphantly in 1937, Gwen Ffrangcon-Davies came in for Margaret Rutherford, and Geraldine McEwan replaced Anna Massey. The production, thus heavily recast, went on a long American tour and then to Broadway, where Walter Kerr for *The New York Times* thought "the staging has a convalescent air about it, as though the entire population of eighteenth-century London was just getting over bad colds and couldn't possibly think of going out for a couple of days."

Others, however, were more impressed; for *The New York World*, Norman Nadel noted, "By slightly raising a corner of his mouth, and distending the left nostril, Gielgud can express a cargo of contempt better than other actors can in fifty lines." But John had arrived at yet another dangerous corner; his choice of new plays was still almost unerringly terrible. At Stratford Peter Hall had effectively hijacked his scheme for a permanent company, at the Old Vic the rebirth brought about by the National Theatre was still several years off, and the prospect of returning to a freelance life as a jobbing actor and director was somehow not how Gielgud had hoped or expected to enter his fifth decade as an actor, nor indeed his sixth in real life.

Nevertheless, he did not have much choice. He lacked the financial resources to set up yet another company and was, therefore, effectively at the mercy of whatever projects were on offer. Unfortunately, the next of these was to be Jerome Kilty's dramatization of Thornton Wilder's *The Ides of March*, an imaginary correspondence between Caesar and Cleopatra, which required John to appear in modern dress as the Roman dictator. The reason that Gielgud took on what must have seemed even to him a dodgy project, something halfway between a recital and a drama, was that Kilty had recently enjoyed a major worldwide hit with *Dear Liar*, based on the letters of Bernard Shaw and Mrs. Patrick Campbell; the thinking here seems to have been that lightning might strike twice at the post office, but, in fact, it was to be another thirty years before A. R. Gurney's *Love Letters* was to breathe life into what so easily could be a deadly, static format.

Long before they opened at the Haymarket, John knew they were in trouble, not least because, wearing a laurel leaf and a toga over his lounge suit, he felt distinctly uneasy having to read out of an old paperback the account by Suetonius of Caesar's death at the Capitol. This considerable fiasco was best summed up for *Punch* by Gerald Barry: "Here is an SOS. Will Sir John Gielgud, now believed to be wasting his great talent at the Haymarket, kindly return at once to the theatre of Shakespeare where his admirers are getting dangerously restive?"

The only good thing to have emerged from *The Ides of March* was John's newfound fascination with presenting the classics in modern dress, which was to lead him a year later successfully back to Broadway with a Richard Burton *Hamlet* set entirely in a contemporary rehearsal room.

Before that, however, he managed to reactivate his long-dormant movie career with an appearance in the minor but flashy role of Louis VII of France in the film of Anouilh's *Becket,* which Richard Burton and Peter O'Toole were now shooting for Peter Glenville, the director whom John had first encountered as one of many good-looking gay undergraduates around the Oxford University quadrangles when he was there in 1932 directing *Romeo and Juliet.* The importance of this *Becket* was considerable and long-lasting; for the very first time it established John as a useful character player who could bring his unrivaled theatrical dignity to bear on roles and films that often did not deserve it, but were nevertheless greatly enhanced by it. On this occasion it was Richard Burton who wrote, from the set, "John is the only actor I've met who makes me feel slightly uncomfortable with awe. In truth, from my earliest years, I modelled my acting on Gielgud's, though, because of our vast differences in temperament, voice and body, nobody has ever remarked on it."

Glenville took considerable pride in what *Becket* was to achieve for John: "I think this was the first time in his later years that John realised films didn't have to be rubbish, and I was very careful in trying to show him how to tone down his staginess for the camera. I think it also helped that we had known each other for so long, and that as I had always been a stage director he trusted me much more than some of his other film people. You could actually see John, in the few short weeks we filmed his role, learning how best to do it for the camera, and I would go as far as to suggest that his whole late-life and very profitable career as a film actor really starts with *Becket.*"

It was also the filming of *Becket* that led to John's last Shakespearean production as a director. On the set, he had renewed the acquaintance with Burton that went back to *The Lady's Not for Burning* fifteen years earlier. Burton now was at the very height of his considerable fame, just coming off the filming of *Cleopatra* and about to embark on the marriage to Elizabeth Taylor, which would condition virtually the whole of the rest of their lives, whether married (as they twice were) or not.

In the breaks between camera set-ups, Burton noticed that his old mentor was unusually depressed. With Olivier already installed at Chichester and soon to form the first National Theatre company, Stratford Shakespeare having moved into an era of realism and youth, and the West End still shell-shocked by the Royal Court revolution, John seemed literally to have no home except of course the one made for him by Martin Hensler, who had now moved into Cowley Street as lover, friend, and housekeeper. True, John could go on slogging around the world playing his *Ages of Man* in ever smaller and remoter venues, but the prospect was not exactly cheering. Even the faithful Binkie had begun to abandon major classical revivals on the grounds of cost alone, and John's famous ineptitude at finding the right new plays for himself meant that Shaftesbury Avenue had also become a cul-de-sac.

The men who had always advised him, notably Binkie and John Perry, were now themselves beginning gently to wind down their management, having realized however reluctantly that the 1960s was a decade for much younger men and fresh theatrical visions, while the new directors and playwrights of this period were either nervous about approaching John, or else convinced, however wrongly, that his melodious Terry elegance could not possibly suit the modern British theater.

So back on the set of *Becket,* it was essentially in an effort to cheer up the man who had given him his first real break that Burton genially asked one morning what were John's plans for the forthcoming Shakespeare quartercentenary in 1964. Discovering to his amazement that Gielgud had none, and that nobody had approached the greatest Shakespearean of his time with even the suggestion of a celebration season, Burton wondered idly whether John might like to direct him in the modern-dress *Hamlet* he now wished to play on Broadway, if only to maintain his classical status at a time when he was chiefly known as the man who had just stolen Elizabeth Taylor from her husband Eddie Fisher.

Gielgud agreed with alacrity, even though he still had certain reservations about Richard's suggestion that they should work in modern dress. Gielgud had seen Burton's Old Vic *Hamlet* and knew that the talent was all there. What he had failed to take into account, however, was the hysteria surrounding the Welsh actor who actually married Taylor during the pre-Broadway tour, thereby ensuring that the production, for better or worse, would be totally overshadowed by the publicity surrounding what was then quite simply the most famous couple in the world.

During the winter, John carefully assembled a strong Broadway cast to support Burton; Eileen Herlie was to play Gertrude, Alfred Drake was Claudius, John himself would play the Ghost in sound only, and Hume Cronyn was to play Polonius. Two entire books have been written about this production, both by players of its minor roles; Richard Sterne, cast as "a gentleman," published one volume (*John Gielgud Directs Richard Burton in Hamlet*), and the other (*Letters from an Actor*) was written by William Redfield, who had been cast as Guildenstern. What emerges from them both is, once again, an account of John uncertain in rehearsal, frequently changing his mind and having considerable problems in dealing with Burton, who, having already triumphed in the role at the Vic in 1953, now had some equally strong ideas about how the role should be played. In order to achieve his book, Sterne actually hid a sizable tape recorder in his briefcase, which he then left in the rehearsal room to capture every one of Gielgud's comments—a breach of rehearsal confidentiality for which he was later castigated in the trade press.

Where Redfield's book focuses on the difference in temperament, ambition, and training between British and American actors, Sterne's is a blow-by-blow description of work in progress toward what was to be at best a theatrical curiosity. "The whole of the rehearsals," writes Sterne, "were a brilliant, butterfly-brained lecture by Gielgud on *Hamlet*, Shakespeare, Forbes-Robertson, John Barrymore, Alec Guinness, Paul Scofield, Laurence Olivier and an actor John had once seen play Hamlet in Inverness in 1928, but now alas could not recall by name. . . . What was chiefly fascinating here were the gymnastics and scattered scholarship of John's remarkable mind." As Burton himself later added, "We talked endlessly about how to make the impact of the play as modern as possible without destroying the essential beauty of its line. And we both agreed that very often the final run-through of a show, before the costumes start to entrammel the actors, seems more exciting than the final thing. . . . We wanted our production to look deliberately unfinished, so each actor was allowed to choose the clothes he felt most comfortable in, though we ruled out pyjamas and biki- nis. I wanted above all for people to feel that they were seeing the play for the first time, and if that meant that the verse had to be mauled and bru- talised a little, then mauling and brutalising should go on, although John, the most mellifluous verse speaker of our time, never approved of some of my more horrendous line readings."

As for Hume Cronyn, now more acclimatized to John's way of working;

The entire production was a replay of the hysteria which I had first encountered in Rome the previous year during the filming of *Cleopa- tra*. The world press was obsessed by the Burton-Taylor romance, es- pecially as they actually married in Montreal during the *Hamlet* tour. I have never in my life been frightened by a crowd, but I was every time I went out of the stage door with Richard. You had to make your way through a gauntlet of snatching hands, cheers, jeers, and waving autograph books . . . teenagers would risk their lives by climbing on to the roof of Richard's car, and what I remember best is Elizabeth, in- side the car, sweetly smiling and waving like royalty while silently mouthing "Fuck you—and you—and you over there—and you too, dear." Somewhere inside of all this madness there was a play to do, with rehearsals and opening nights and reviews, by no means all of them very good. Although this production of *Hamlet* was to break every known record in terms of its length of run and box office re- ceipts, I wish I could say this was Shakespeare's triumph, or the col- lective effort of a hard-working company, or even a discriminating audience starved for classical theatre and given by us a rare opportu- nity to see a production of one of the greatest plays of all time. Sadly, it was to be none of the above, but rather a triumph of publicity and curiosity. . . . Sometimes I felt I was the only member of the company reasonably content, although I cannot tell you how intimidating it is to rehearse a play when the director knows every word of it without reference to the text. That was perhaps our main problem—American actors in general do not have the classical background of the best of English actors, and the occasional gulf between our company and our director was largely attributable to our company's inexperience. . . . Of course, John had certain idiosyncrasies as a director that were easy to mock—he believed in trial and error, and moved so quickly that the actors sometimes felt they were caught in [a] blender. He also never hesitated to read a line for an actor, or to demonstrate a move he thought might be helpful—a practice some American actors find reprehensible and even downright insulting. . . . On one occasion, I remember sitting in my dressing room, hearing Phil Coolidge, a bony-faced New England actor of considerable experience, being directed as Voltemand by an increasingly frantic John—"No, no, no! You are absolutely terrible! Why not try wearing a hat?"

Reviews, on the road as in New York, were mixed to chilly. *The Toronto Star* wrote of "An unmitigated disaster," and even on Broadway several weeks later, there was the feeling that somehow this whole production had failed to come together. As Walter Kerr wrote for the *New York Herald Tribune,* "Richard Burton is one of the most magnificently equipped actors alive today. He places on open display not only all of his own reverberating resources, but also all the myriad qualities which the man Hamlet requires. All except one. Mr Burton is totally without feeling."

This *Hamlet* lives on for one of John's most celebrated slips of the tongue. Struggling backstage through the Broadway first-night crowds and what seemed like several thousand Burton-Taylor freaks, he finally reached Burton's dressing-room door, only to find his star still in costume. What John meant to say was that he would return when Burton was ready to go out to dinner; what he actually said, once again giving unfortunate voice to his current thinking, was, "I'll come back when you're better."

By now, the New York police were having to close off the whole of the street so that Burton and Taylor could reach the safety of their limousine after the show. Burton, still relatively inexperienced in these matters, once asked his wife the reason for such crowds. "Basically," explained Liz after years of Hollywood experience, "they are frustrated sex maniacs, and we are their favorite sinners and freaks."

During the run, John did himself get to star in one special performance, that of the opening of the John F. Kennedy Center for the Performing Arts in Washington, where during the inauguration ceremony led by President Lyndon Johnson, he read some Shakespearean sonnets, thereby becoming the first actor to work at the new arts palace by the Potomac.

This new *Hamlet* ran 138 Broadway performances, four more than John himself had achieved there back in 1936. During the run, as Daniel Rosenthal writes, Burton arranged for a unique record of this production to be made: "Three performances were recorded through a revolutionary process called Electronovision, which used five small electronic cameras that could deliver for the first time adequate picture quality using only the available stage lighting. The result, said *Variety,* was 'distressingly dark' . . . apart from Burton and Cronyn, the rest of the largely American cast seem terribly wooden. Alfred Drake's Claudius, unwisely kitted out in cosy slacks and cardigan, is more a self-satisfied Manhattan executive than a ruthless killer. . . . Burton insisted that this *Hamlet* could only be shown for two days in cinemas, but it was seen by an estimated five million people and netted Burton about $500,000. . . . The deal also required that all prints should then be destroyed, but in 1991 Burton's widow Sally discovered three rusty cans of film at their Swiss home, which, carefully restored, have enabled a whole new generation to discover Burton's *Hamlet* on video."

Watching it at the time, Gielgud was horrified by how much broader Burton's performance had become during the run. This was to be John's last-ever *Hamlet,* and he never managed to disguise the fact that it had always remained vaguely unsatisfactory, not least because Burton, despite a wonderful Welsh sense of the poetry, could never quite achieve the princely bearing that John thought the role demanded: "In directing Burton, I tried to show him how the more relaxed scenes were placed, so that for instance he need not tear himself to shreds in the ghost scene, or other passages between the big emotional climaxes. But he never seemed to want to work with me alone. And eventually I was reduced to writing long notes, which I would leave in his dressing room before the evening performance. He would then read them through very quickly, discard most of my suggestions, but use three or four of them during that same evening's performance, without even rehearsing them. All the same, he was very often instinctively right, and he was shrewd, generous, intelligent and co-operative. I grew very fond of him, but I felt he was, finally, something of a 'Shropshire Lad' as Hamlet, and I would rather have had the opportunity of working with him as either Macbeth or Coriolanus. It would have been much better for us both if we had come to *Hamlet* absolutely fresh."

21. All's Welles

(1964–1967)

I don't think any of us understood what the last act of Tiny Alice *was about, and as Edward Albee would never discuss the play with me, I never really could find any indication of what he wanted me to do with it.*

*W*hile he was still in New York, fighting his way nightly through the Burton-Taylor crowds to try to keep *Hamlet* roughly on the rails, John was asked by Tony Richardson if he would like to fly out to California to play Sir Francis Hinsley, in Evelyn Waugh's memorable Hollywood parody of the American way of death, *The Loved One.*

In the original novella, Hinsley is clearly modeled on Sir C. Aubrey Smith, the crusty doyen of the Hollywood Raj of veteran British actors in California, who suddenly finds himself fired by the studio where he has worked for forty years. It could have been a wonderful role, but Richardson was so intent on unnecessarily updating the story, and generally camping it up and messing around with it, that Gielgud, like so many others in the cast, including Robert Morley and Margaret Leighton, found his part cut to shreds. *The Loved One* had been through several hands before it reached those of Tony Richardson, himself now starting a long Hollywood exile. Evelyn Waugh had originally hoped for Alec Guinness and noted in his diary: "The film has now been sold to a mad Mexican, who will doubtless sell it on to Hollywood, where they will doubtless produce an elaborate and tasteless travesty—no redress." "The mad Mexican" turned out to be Luis Buñuel, but Waugh's gloomy prediction came all too true. By the time the film fell into Richardson's hands, he and Christopher Isherwood, another Hollywood exile who should have known better, made the fatal mistake of trying to update it to the 1960s, complete with bodies flying around in outer space.

What might have been a brilliant period gem became instead a neurotic travesty billed desperately as "The motion picture with something to offend everyone."

"A spineless farrago of collegiate gags," thought Pauline Kael for *The New Yorker*, "this sinking ship only makes it to port because everyone on board is too giddy and self-obsessed to panic." But for John, if for no one else, *The Loved One* was to have a happy outcome—four years later, as if by way of apology, Richardson gave him one of his finest movie roles as the benignly dotty Lord Raglan in *The Charge of the Light Brigade*.

By now, the two men had established a firm friendship, as Richardson recalled: "John is, quite simply, the nicest, most human actor I've ever worked with. And, together with Jack Nicholson, the most intelligent: John adores the theatre, theatre gossip, actors, actresses—he is steeped in them—but he equally adores books, poetry, music, films and travel. What he likes delights him, and he can delight you with his delight. And what he loathes, he can amuse you with. He is a constant responder, a constant enjoyer. That is what has kept him so perpetually young, and perhaps is why he has outlasted so many of his great contemporaries who have fallen by the wayside. To work with him for the first time (he based his performance on Cecil Beaton) was pure joy, as it always is."

After the filming, John packed his *Ages of Man* suitcase yet again, this time taking the recital to Ireland, Russia, Finland, Poland, Sweden, and Denmark and then set off for Spain on one of the greatest movie adventures of his life.

This was to be Orson Welles's long-planned filming of *Chimes at Midnight*, the Falstaff anthology from Shakespeare's *Henry IV* and *Henry V*, which he had already staged in Dublin and was now determined to commit to film.

Relations between John and Orson Welles had not been entirely tranquil since the occasion when the two of them, and Ralph Richardson, had been working for a day on an unintentionally hilarious recording of some *Sherlock Holmes* stories for long-playing records. In the early part of the recording, Welles makes a fine Moriarty, with John as Holmes and Richardson as the faithful Dr. Watson, but on the second side of the old LP Welles's performance seems to tail off somewhat abruptly. John, when asked if he knew why this was, replied, "Oh yes, I'm afraid it was all my fault. During the lunch break I asked Orson what he was planning to do next, and when he said, '*Othello*,' before I could stop myself I replied, 'Not in London, surely?' whereupon he sulked for the rest of the afternoon's recording."

But all that was now forgotten, as Welles begged John to come out to Spain and play the dying King Henry IV, a role that he had always longed to try at the Old Vic with Richardson as Falstaff. Now, of course, Welles himself was to be Falstaff, with an amazing supporting cast led by Margaret Rutherford as Mistress Quickly, Jeanne Moreau as Doll Tearsheet, and Keith Baxter as Prince Hal. As Gielgud himself later recalled:

Like most of Orson's films, it was full of very fascinating things, but did not work as a whole, though it did have a real Shakespearean feeling. Orson was splendid to work with, although he was always pressed for money and usually in rather poor health. Having engaged a very fine company, he could never afford to keep us all permanently employed, so we each did our parts in separate weeks and he only did his own scenes at the very end, by which time he was exhausted, and there was nobody left for him to act with. I never even saw him in character as Falstaff until the film was released. But he had found a marvellous setting, a great empty building in the hills above Barcelona, which had once been a prison, and had a huge hall with a stone floor. However, there was no glass in the windows, and the cold November air poured in. I was wearing tights and a dressing gown, but practically nothing else for my death scene. I would sit on my throne with a tiny electric fire to warm my feet, while Orson spent his last pesetas sending out for brandy to keep me going. . . . The organisation was chaotic, but I was lost in admiration for Orson's unfailing flair in choosing camera set-ups, encouraging me with an extremely perceptive appreciation of the Shakespearean text, and managing fifty or so Spanish extras who spoke no English and were always wandering about demanding money. There were no kind of sanitary facilities on the premises, so the results were apt to be unsightly and demoralising to say the least. Orson was suffering from eczema, and worrying about two other unfinished films, *Treasure Island* and *Don Quixote*, on which he had already started sporadic work in various other parts of Spain.

Because John was himself already committed to starring in a new Edward Albee play on Broadway, all his scenes had to be shot out of sequence, and usually in tight close-up, as Orson had yet again run out of money for any other actors. As with so much of his post–*Citizen Kane* work, the result was a mixture of major weaknesses combined with some brilliant moments. Jeanne Moreau was, to say the least, an implausible Doll Tearsheet, and much of the dubbing and post-synchronization proved incomprehensible; but as the Welles biographer Frank Brady notes, "aside from the temporary difficulties of understanding some of his lines, there was the sheer presence of the hippopotamic Orson looking like a figure from a Reubens painting, or an early Victorian Christmas card picture of Santa Claus. In the role of his life, Orson duels, dances, drinks, and revels through the night. A greatly articulated Falstaff, he was filled with relish and tenderness, first as the self-destructive roisterer and anti-king, and then with expert balance as the self-pitying exile poisoned by unendurable melancholy for the loss of his old friend Hal. In the last scene, of rejection, it is hard to tell where Falstaff begins and Welles ends."

When the film eventually reached art-house cinemas on a very limited release, several European critics realized that Welles and Falstaff had much in common—never the king, always the clown, and as Orson himself once told Kenneth Tynan, "I see Falstaff like a Christmas tree, decorated with vices." Sadly, however, the film initially reached such limited

With Edmond O'Brien in the 1953 film of *Julius Caesar*. *(Hulton Getty Images)*

Now Sir John Gielgud, with his mother as they left Buckingham
Palace after the ceremony at which he was knighted, 1953.
(Mander & Mitchenson Theatre Collection)

With Vivien Leigh and Diana Wynyard at a Stratford farewell party for Anthony Quayle, who was about to embark on a nine-month world tour, 1953. (*Blau/Camera Press Ltd./Retna*)

John and artist Isamu Noguchi checking makeup options for Noguchi's production of *King Lear*, 1955. (© *Larry Burrows Collection*)

Laurence Oliver (left), John Mills (center), and John camping it up as Noël Coward's "Three Juvenile Delinquents" for a midnight charity matinee at the London Palladium in 1953. (*Mander & Mitchenson Theatre Collection*)

With Noël Coward in the 1956 film *Around the World in 80 Days*. *(Archive/Getty Images)*

With Jean Seberg and Richard Widmark in Otto Preminger's film production of *Saint Joan*, 1957. *(The Kobal Collection)*

Performing in his one-man show, Shakespeare's *Ages of Man*, 1958. *(AP/Wide World Photos)*

In his American television debut, appearing with Margaret Leighton in *The Browning Version*, 1959. *(AP/Wide World Photos)*

With Richard Burton in the 1963 film *Becket*. *(The Kobal Collection)*

With Claire Bloom in a West End production of *Ivanov*, 1965. *(Ormond Gigli/TimePix)*

With Irene Worth in the New York production of Edward Albee's *Tiny Alice*, 1964. *(Mander & Mitchenson Theatre Collection)*

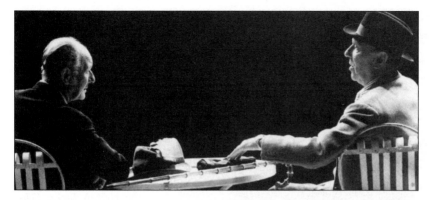

With Ralph Richardson in *Home* by David Storey, at the Royal Court Theatre in 1970. *(Mander & Mitchenson Theatre Collection)*

Appearing in an American television special with Carol Channing, 1970. *(MPTV)*

John in his ill-fated directorial stint during rehearsals for the Broadway-bound musical *Irene*. Here with (from left to right) Monte Markham, Debbie Reynolds, Billy DeWolfe, and Patsy Kelly, 1972. *(AP/Wide World Photos)*

With Ralph Richardson in London, 1979. *(Arnold Newman/Getty Images)*

On a London street, framed by pedestrians frozen in recognition, 1974. *(Joseph Schilling/TimePix)*

On the set of the film *Arthur,* 1980, for which John was awarded the Academy Award as Best Supporting Actor. *(New York Times Co./Fred R. Conrad/Archive Photos)*

With Lindsay Anderson in the award-winning film *Chariots of Fire,* 1981. *(The Kobal Collection)*

Being introduced to the press by Globe Theatre owner Janet Holmes à Court, as the Globe is renamed the Gielgud Theatre in honor of John's 90th birthday, 1994. *(AP/Wide World Photos)*

Reteamed with Dudley Moore in the *Arthur* sequel, *Arthur 2—On the Rocks*, 1988. *((c) 1988 Warner Bros./MPTV)*

In costume but out of character on the set of the CBS Television production of *The Master of Ballantrae*, 1984. *(Sven Arnstein/MPTV)*

Appearing in the television miniseries
of *Scarlett*, 1995. *(Sipa Press)*

At home in Wotton Underwood, 1991. *(AP/Wide World Photos)*

audiences that a couple of years later, a Hollywood studio chief wrote quite seriously to Welles, asking if he had ever thought of playing Falstaff on film. As Welles told Frank Brady, "what is a man to do but weep—you make the greatest film of your life, and nobody in your own country even bothers to go see it."

Years later, John was making similarly frustrated attempts to film *The Tempest* and suggested that Welles might be a perfect Caliban. Sadly, that idea never even reached any kind of studio. At the time they were shooting, Gielgud found Orson's hit-and-miss techniques rather unnerving and was not best pleased to find himself doing his final scenes in close proximity to a sound recordist with appalling flatulence. "I don't mind," John told Welles, "handing the crown over to Keith Baxter, and I don't even mind dying, but does it have to be in a gas chamber?" Welles eventually ran into such economic difficulties that when Norman Rodway came to film his Hotspur scenes, they couldn't even afford a horse for him to ride into battle, so he had to sit on the shoulders of two sturdy extras who jiggled him as he spoke. Keith Baxter found himself in long shots also standing in for Justice Silence, and Margaret Rutherford is often represented, again from a distance, by a male assistant director, wearing her clothes.

But as so often with the films of Orson Welles, distance has lent enchantment. The film, upwardly revalued these last ten years or so, regularly features in Welles's retrospectives and has gradually grown in stature, and now it is widely recognized as one of the best, albeit most eccentric, of all Shakespearean movies. Several critics have found traces here of both *Citizen Kane* and *The Magnificent Ambersons,* but as David Thomson, another Welles biographer, has noted, "*Chimes at Midnight* is an unlikely epiphany; it bespeaks an extraordinary act of will, not to mention the idealism that saw such a thing might be . . . if Welles had only ever made *Chimes at Midnight,* I suspect I would know it as a footprint of genius."

The play for which John had to leave *Chimes at Midnight* was Albee's *Tiny Alice.* Although at this time there were still those who seemed to find Albee's *Who's Afraid of Virginia Woolf?* hard to fathom, that apparent obscurity was nothing compared with *Tiny Alice.* Asked, in some desperation, by John and his costar, the faithful Irene Worth, what the play was about, Albee simply replied, "Forget about the meaning of the play, just play the meaning of the characters," which was not, perhaps, the answer they were looking for. The director Alan Schneider did his best to bridge the gap between author and star, writing afterward to John, "I have simply never met an actor like you—all I can do is thank you for your willingness, your trust and your understanding."

As Albee's biographer Mel Gussow has noted,

The first choice for the role of Brother Julian was Albert Finney . . . Albee never formally objected to the casting, but in retrospect he revealed his hesitation: "It wasn't my idea to have somebody whose sexual fires were dampened. I remember I wanted somebody younger and more sexual. But when John became available, I guess I was talked into it; what thirty-five-year-old playwright is going to turn down John Gielgud for a leading role?" . . . In contrast to Gielgud, Irene Worth [in fact John's idea] loved the play. That is not to say that she understood it much more than John or anyone else did, but from the beginning she seemed to have a greater feeling for its mystery and an enthusiasm for its subject matter. . . . Alan Schneider agreed to direct the play although he, too, had serious reservations about it and felt that it became 'murkier and murkier, ending in a scene I had difficulty in believing on any level' . . . He was also disturbed by the idea of Gielgud playing such a young innocent, a role he thought was better suited to Marlon Brando or Montgomery Clift.

As Schneider was to write in his autobiography: "Gielgud wanted to withdraw almost every day, and was sustained mainly by post-rehearsal brandy and Irene's good-natured joshing. Pleas to Edward to rewrite and clear up at least some of the confusion went unanswered. I don't think he knew what to do either." At one point somebody backstage asked John if he was embarrassed by the seduction scene. "Oh, no," he replied. "I just think to myself, thank God it's only dear old Irene."

So hot was Albee on the back of *Virginia Woolf* that despite very mixed reviews and audiences who booed virtually every night, the production in fact ran two hundred performances on Broadway with John as the lay priest who has lost his faith and Irene as the richest woman in the world, prepared to pay him for sexual favors. All three of the leading Broadway critics cheerfully admitted that they couldn't understand a word of it, though one did add how lucky it was that Gielgud could convey such religious belief: "He is the master of tensile wonder, uniquely equipped to skim delicately over surfaces while sinking slowly into the depths. His arms and legs never seem to know quite where his head is leading him, but he is a spirit vibrating in repose, sighing at the edge of the world." Others, however, were less impressed: John Chapman for the *Daily News* reckoned "there is even less to this than meets the eye," and the critic of the *Journal American* wrote of "a wildly abstruse and unfathomable three hours, impossible to explain but full of elaborate symbolism concerning mysticism, faith and worldliness in contemporary society."

Tiny Alice marked the start of Broadway's determination now to turn its back on Albee, sending him into a critical exile from which he was not totally to emerge until the coming of *Three Tall Women*, thirty years later. In the meantime, in conversation with Albee, John began to talk about his early thoughts on the play: "Of course I was very frightened, especially by the scene in which I am seduced onstage, because I really thought I had passed the age limit for all that, but I was enormously flattered by the idea that this play was actually written for me. None of the young English avant garde playwrights has dreamt of writing me a part, and I've always had the feeling that the 'kitchen sink' school in London despises me as being a part of the Establishment and a bit snooty. In fact, one longs to create a new part more than anything else in the theatre. And although to me it's often very depressing to go to a contemporary play and see completely gloomy and subhuman characters in despair, I think that is something to do with my generation and the war. Young people today don't seem to mind that so much. And as for the critics, it is very rare that you get the reviews you want. I don't think many interesting actors or good plays are ever really ignored or dismissed, but critics see too many bad plays and always have to write in a hurry. If they are proud of their craft, they get more interested in their own writing style than what they are supposed to be writing about.

That's why Shaw and Beerbohm were so wonderful—they only worked as full time critics for a year or two."

Ever since he had begun starring in the plays of André Obey and Christopher Fry, John had become well accustomed to playing leading roles in scripts that he never fully understood; as he always admitted, sometimes with pride, his secondary education had been minimal. And he was inclined entirely to trust his own theatrical instincts, rather than his intelligence. As Albee had virtually requested, he now played the part rather than the play. It was his costar Irene Worth, on one of the very rare occasions when she agreed to talk about John, who perhaps expressed this best:

> John practices and performs his roles by the rules of classical discipline, and these have made him a romantic actor of such unique spirit . . . once when we were doing a Shakespeare recital together, I asked him how he made poetry so accessible. "I just follow the beat," he said. "It may be obscure, but the rhythm makes it clear" . . . His mind works at lightning speed, his energy is positive, he relies on his strength. He is never idle, never ill. He is prompt. He replies to all letters, has time for everything and learns his roles by writing them out in his fine, nearly illegible longhand.
>
> John has an undiminished curiosity and interest in the theatre, in new actors, writers, directors; he searches them out like truffles, and remembers the names of all his colleagues from time immemorial. . . . He has reserves of commitment and fairness, patience and equilibrium and endurance. His agreeable nature and his humility give him resilience. He is a radiant man and a rare friend.

Their friendship survived *Tiny Alice* and became one of the most important of John's life, though the rehearsals had been somewhat nightmarish. Shortly before the first night, John told Albee that there would have to be some cuts in his closing ten-minute monologue, especially as he was supposed to be delivering it flat on his back, dying from a bullet in the belly. As Albee recalls, "This gave me a certain dilemma: I could fire John, which would have been unusually stupid; I could have him do the first half of the monologue, or the second half, or the monologue's greatest hits. In the end we did the greatest hits and got it down to about six minutes. Nobody except me missed the other four, and when, some years later, in another production, I put them back, it was only to realize how utterly right John had been—his instincts were always impeccable."

As Noël Coward wrote in his diary, "The first act of *Tiny Alice* was hopeful, but after that a chaotic mess of sex and symbolism. Beautifully directed and acted except for poor Johnny G, who was strained and unconvincing. Altogether a maddening evening in the theatre, so nearly good and yet so bloody pretentious."

For the critic Stanley Kauffmann, "throughout the evening, Gielgud and his colleagues had done their best with this spurious work, but had progressively lost the audience, some of whom started to boo. Then he was left alone (deserted one could say) to finish, in a torrent of fevered rhetoric, a play that had long ceased to matter. The audience continued to murmur and rustle their programmes as he kept on and on. The buzz swelled a bit, punctuated now by giggles. Toward the end, Gielgud seemed utterly isolated, separated by an invisible wall of protest. I was filled with admiration, not because of any 'show must go on' hokum, but at his powers of concentration, his inner ear. He had kept his own music going, against a hostile chorus."

Irene was to repeat her performance in the London premiere of *Tiny Alice* a few months later, with David Warner in the Gielgud role; it did not achieve much greater success, and perhaps the whole experience was best summarized by a *New Yorker* cartoon showing a middle-aged couple in bed, the husband sound asleep and the wife suddenly alert: "Hayden!" she says. "Wake up at once! The meaning of *Tiny Alice* just came to me!"

After struggling with the still-obscure symbolism of *Tiny Alice* for almost six months on Broadway, it was with some relief that John went back to his *Ages of Man,* taking it this time all over the Far East and Australia. When he got to Auckland, he was contending not against the hostile audiences of *Tiny Alice,* but—possibly still worse—the noise of a nearby nightclub belting out pop tunes for teenagers. "I just dread going on each night," said John, "those guitars can penetrate through any walls." The nightclub owner proved unrelenting: "Ask most New Zealanders whether they prefer the Top Twenty or Shakespeare, and I think you would get a swift answer."

By the summer of 1965, John was back home in England and still in a career crisis as he embarked on his sixties; Olivier had now established his National Theatre company at the Old Vic and was conspicuously failing to invite Gielgud anywhere near it, as either actor or director. At Stratford, Peter Hall, perhaps also remembering the fiasco of the Zeffirelli *Othello*, apparently had no other offers to send his way, and John's recent unhappiness on Broadway in *Tiny Alice* had not exactly encouraged him to go on seeking out new plays. As for the West End, H. M. Tennent was still being managed by Binkie Beaumont and John Perry, but they too had nothing to offer John, and all he could find for the time being was a rather unhappy television version of Anouilh's *The Rehearsal*, which again failed to convince him that his future lay in that new medium.

During this fallow period he began to work on his second Chekhovian adaptation, this one of *Ivanov*, which he himself now proposed to direct at the Phoenix Theatre, playing the title role opposite Claire Bloom as Sasha. Although this was (amazingly) to be the play's first full-scale commercial production in the West End, John had known it since 1925, when he had first seen the Komisarjevsky production at Barnes. The critics were divided, some taking the view that John had neglected his own performance in order to draw fine ones not only from Claire Bloom, but also from a starry supporting cast led by Roland Culver, Yvonne Mitchell, Angela Baddeley, and the young Richard Pasco.

On the other hand, writing for *The Sunday Times*, J. W. Lambert thought John's Ivanov ranked with his Hamlet and Richard II among his three best performances, and the run was extended by six weeks before going on a long American road tour (for which Yvonne Mitchell was replaced by Vivien Leigh) and then a rather brief Broadway run, at a time when most critics wished that Gielgud and Leigh could have come back to them in one of Chekhov's more familiar dramas.

At the time of the London opening of *Ivanov*, Ronald Bryden wrote for

The New Statesman an intriguing summary of Gielgud's stage status at this time:

> For a decade or more, new movements in British drama have driven Gielgud from the London stage . . . not that he is blameless in the matter, of course. His published statements on the post-war theatre have not shown a notably keen or receptive intellect. And it is partly his fault if he has not been offered the kind of opportunity that Olivier seized in *The Entertainer,* or become the kind of national figure that Jean-Louis Barrault cuts in France . . . Gielgud is the least showy actor in the world. He has always confined himself to a coinage of classically simple physical signs—the hands outstretched in gentle eagerness or clenched in pained nobility; the profile turning with a hint of slyness and vanity, or straining aside in wincing self-contempt. . . . The heart of his acting is vocal and internal. Its richness lies in the infinitely expressive range of his voice, the clarity with which it is sustained by every turn of thought and emotion. His style may seem glassy, but through that glass you read the darting of motives, watch the tick of the heart, and see the intelligence perform like a stripped-down motor. . . . He sees himself as the champion of old theatrical virtues (good speaking, graceful movement, style) against the anarchy of The Method . . . in consequence he has never become a character actor. He has never won the ability to impersonate like Olivier, building a characterisation up from the rich, coarse soil of mimicry. He has never learned the Brechtian trick of presenting someone other than himself—his Lear was the imagination of Gielgud old, his Leontes the imagination of Gielgud jealous. His is an art we have come to undervalue, associating the technical name of "romantic" acting with the fustian age of the actor-managers in the pre-war West End.

As if in response to Bryden, Gielgud now gave a fifty-minute BBC television interview to Derek Hart for the *Great Acting* series, in which he

atypically allowed himself considerable license to consider his own character in public: "I'm a terrible escapist in life, and it has always given me
great pleasure to go to a theatre, shut myself up in a dressing-room and
come out as somebody else. I have always tried to live in a fantasy
world. . . . Nowadays I think we have lost an enormous stage public to
television and the movies, but I hope that if you can retain vitality and
keep your balance between the old and the new, then you can still go on
being of some use to your art and your craft. If not I think you ought to
stop. Now I would be quite prepared to play smaller roles, provided that I
could find things that I really thought I could do, in my own way, better
than anyone else. I would love to direct a musical, as they seem to be so
profitable, and I would like to take my *Ages of Man* to the few countries I
have never visited, like Turkey and Greece. I don't really want to fling myself into violent action again, but nor do I want to retire or slacken off. I
would just like to be what Ellen Terry always called 'a useful actor' for the
rest of my life."

Before leaving *Ivanov,* John played the role in a rather unsatisfactory
television adaptation and then took on an altogether more intriguing
small-screen project which, although this was scarcely noticed at the time,
was, in fact, the role that first released him into a whole late-life career of
eccentric comedy. John had by now become painfully aware that he was
missing out on an entire generation of new young writers, who somehow
regarded him still as a poetically prewar dinosaur. As he wrote at this time
in a letter to Lillian Gish, "I have just met Harold Pinter for the first time,
and he really is surprisingly nice—not nearly as gloomy as his plays." Another group of newcomers of whom he had become an eager fan were the
four young Oxford and Cambridge postgraduates who had revolutionized
revue with *Beyond the Fringe* (Jonathan Miller, Dudley Moore, Peter Cook,
and Alan Bennett). In later years he was to work with both Moore and
Bennett, and it was Dudley who asked him for a letter of introduction
when *Beyond the Fringe* was going to New York in 1965, because as Dudley
remarked, unlike the other three, he knew absolutely nobody on the other
side of the Atlantic. John duly obliged, giving Moore an envelope addressed "To Whom It May Concern." John had, however, failed to seal it,

and Dudley, sitting on a long transatlantic plane journey without anything else to read, decided to find out what the great classical tragedian had said about him by way of introduction to America and Americans. "This," said the letter, "is to introduce my new friend, a brilliant comic pianist called Stanley Moon. Please be very nice to him." Dudley spent several of his early weeks on Broadway having to pretend, in order to get into parties, that Moore was only his stage name.

But now, it was another of the Fringe quartet who came into John's life. Jonathan Miller was about to make a television version of *Alice in Wonderland* and had the characteristically eccentric notion that the Mock Turtle (played by John G.) and the Gryphon (played by Malcom Muggeridge) should be seen as a couple of lackadaisical Victorian uncles, still clinging to private incomes, but having totally lost the meaning of their lives in late middle age, and having nothing left to do but reminisce about their schooldays.

John was thus to be found walking along a beach singing, "Will you walk a little faster?" and although it was only a brief appearance (in an all-star cast featuring Peter Sellers, Peter Cook, Leo McKern, Michael Redgrave, and Wilfrid Lawson), he collected the best of the reviews and suggested for the first time a late-life talent for eccentric comedy, which was to stand him in very good stead over the next thirty years.

John's next television appearance was, however, somewhat more classical; again for Jonathan Miller, he played Chekhov in an anthology of the great playwright's letters, which also starred Peggy Ashcroft, Wendy Hiller, and Dorothy Tutin.

22. INTO THE VALLEY OF DEATH

(1967–1969)

The physical discomforts of filming do not worry me unduly . . . I find I am rather good at quietly doing my crossword and watching other people's scenes. One does, after all, have plenty of spare time to think about one's part, gossip with one's colleagues, and have fun. . . . It is no good being hysterical or highly strung in movies; at the same time, you need to have all your energy ready, coiled up inside you, awaiting the next take.

*I*n the absence of any major project on stage after *Ivanov*, John now occupied himself in London and New York with a couple of new television plays (*The Love Song of Barney Kempinski* and *The Mayfly and the Frog*), neither of great distinction, before yet again touring his *Ages of Man* around America, finishing up this time back in Hollywood, only returning home to turn up in a minor thriller (*Assignment to Kill*), as well as narrating a couple of television documentaries, one about the Spanish Civil War (*To Die in Madrid*) and the other about the early days of Lenin (*October Revolution*).

He was really marking time now, waiting for something interesting to come along, which it did, in the summer of 1967. The offer was to spend almost three months in Turkey, playing Lord Raglan, commander in chief of the allied forces in the Crimea, for Tony Richardson's *The Charge of the Light Brigade*.

With a script by John Osborne, based on Cecil Woodham-Smith's *The Reason Why*, this had been a work in progress for several years. The playwright Charles Wood had also been working on the screenplay, but it looked for a while as though the film would never get made, not least because the actor Laurence Harvey, hoping to make a rival version, had tied the project up in several lawsuits. These complications were finally resolved, however, and all that Richardson had to deal with was a recalcitrant Turkish government and an all-star cast (Trevor Howard, David Hemmings, Vanessa Redgrave, Jill Bennett, Harry Andrews), none of whom was especially happy with the location conditions outside Ankara.

But for John, this was still a rare chance to make his mark on the screen and he delivered a wonderfully cynical, jokey performance as the gently eccentric Raglan, a forerunner to his notable headmaster in Alan Bennett's *Forty Years On.* By now, Gielgud was learning how to establish himself in relatively minor screen roles as a genuine eccentric, one who could give to often very minor, and often badly underwritten, roles a curiously distant theatrical dignity. He seemed to bring all of his past performances and memories on to the location like a suitcase, and indeed during this long summer's filming he happily performed his *Ages of Man* for the film unit at the local opera house in Ankara.

Like *Chimes at Midnight, The Charge of the Light Brigade* is another of those movies that, after initially somewhat hostile reviews, has grown considerably in stature over the last thirty years. John's performance as the sublimely vague Raglan, always unable to separate the enemy from his own allies, was hailed by *Variety* as "a gem of a performance—Gielgud's polite, foolish, foppish old gentleman with fading memory and vapid, outworn ideas might have sprung straight from Lewis Carroll." Given a screenplay credited to Charles Wood from the Osborne original, it was hardly surprising that, unlike the previous Errol Flynn 1936 Hollywood version, the remake would be considerably more subversive, intent on ridiculing the class attitudes and bigotry of the mid-nineteenth-century British army and the futility of the Crimean War as a whole.

Some years before Attenborough's film of *Oh! What a Lovely War* (in which Gielgud was also to feature), Richardson's *Light Brigade* also ends on a note of bitter irony, with the generals standing on a corpse-strewn battlefield, heatedly passing the buck as quickly from hand to hand as if it were a bomb about to explode. The film is a scathing indictment of war, but

Gielgud's performance has a lightness of touch and a wonderful kind of fey grandeur, which give his scenes an altogether different and sometimes almost surreal dimension.

The shooting did not, however, get off to a very good start. John, as ever, deeply afraid of having to ride a horse, was put on one that promptly bolted, throwing him to the ground only an hour or two into his first scene. Luckily, he was not badly hurt, and from then on Richardson made sure that John's reins were secured by extras standing just out of sight on either side of him, to keep his mount reasonably stationary.

When Tony Richardson died in 1991, much too young, John wrote, "He was one of the first directors who really managed to persuade me to overcome my former dislike of filming."

For David Hemmings, the memories of John on this long location were of "an immensely witty man, deeply talented of course but imbued with a natural sense of humour that forced one to smile when in his company. He was also, as always, an incorrigible gossip, spreading the rumour that Jill Bennett was having an affair with our director, although none of us ever really established the truth of that one. He amazed us all by having *The Times* sent out from England and then finishing the crossword in record time, folding up the paper with the long-suffering look of one who has been presented with a task too belittling to be contemplated. The rest of us, when we could get hold of the paper, would struggle on for hours, until finally it dawned on us that John was not completing it at all; he would merely answer the clues he could and then fill in all the remaining spaces with totally random letters, but appeared not at all put out when we remarked rather unkindly that anyone could do *The Times* crossword that swiftly if they cheated."

Unlike Guinness or Olivier, John never really disguised himself onscreen, and made no attempt to modify his golden voice with any kind of accent; he was simply there to add dignity and sometimes a wry, cynical humor to whatever film was currently on offer. In it unashamedly for the money rather than the glory, he found in film studios and exterior locations all over the world, a kind of clubby companionship, a clash of egos and gossip, of love and loyalty and betrayal, which to a certain extent made up for what he now most missed—the life of a resident theatrical company. Just as he had come inevitably to be an outsider at Peter Hall's Stratford or Olivier's National Theatre, he now found himself an insider in movies, which was just as well, because in his private life the partnership with Martin Hensler had now, in a curious way, begun to alienate many of John's best friends.

When he was not working, John and Martin began to search for a country house where Martin's passion for gardening and especially bonzai-tree-growing could be satisfied. The search was to take several years, during which time they remained at 16 Cowley Street and were not thrilled by a 1967 robbery in which thieves got away with a Sickert portrait of John himself, which was never recovered. Their desire to leave London eventually took them to an amazing country house at Wotton Underwood, just outside Aylesbury, which was now to become their home for the rest of their lives.

Here, John began to live in a kind of exile from the West End that had for so long been his personal fiefdom; even in the country Martin was both cranky and shy, unhappy with having to share John, and even such old friends as John Perry stayed out in the cold, only really able to see John on his increasingly rare visits to London when he was usually on his own.

Because of this, film and theater jobs became all-important to Gielgud, not merely to finance the very considerable cost of restoring the country house that he had bought from the historian Sir Arthur Bryant, but also because only when he was working could John sustain contact with all his old friends even while making new ones. Martin was by contrast always something of a recluse, and John, utterly devoted to his last life partner, went along with his increasing need for almost total privacy. As for John, he now solemnly explained that he only signed on for film roles that would not occupy more than a week or so: "It would be so awful if I died, you see, in the middle of a part, and they had to send for Michael Denison."

True, a few old friends like the Denisons (who lived nearby), and Laurie Evans's wife Mary, and Johnnie and Mary Mills usually managed to break through the Martin barrier, as did some younger players like Keith Baxter, journalist-interviewers like the faithful John Powell, and old friends like

Alec Guinness and his wife Merula, but only by taking care to befriend Martin and deal with his eccentricities, in much the same way that they had first dealt with those of John himself. Other visitors to Wotton Underwood were first vetted by Martin and subsequently often vetoed by him. There is no doubt that Martin took great and loving care of John's creature comforts, but unlike all his earlier lovers, Hensler had no real interest in John's work and very seldom traveled with him on location or tours.

John thus began now to lead a double life; when working, or on the telephone as he was for hours a day, he was still fascinated by the backstage sagas of the stars and their supporting casts. At home, however, he led a rather more solitary life, over which Martin hovered as lover and housekeeper. Visitors reported that Hensler would seldom if ever sit down for meals, remaining detached somewhere halfway between kitchen and dining room, as if always somehow uncertain of the precise role he was supposed to be playing in John's life.

Returning home from Turkey after *The Charge of the Light Brigade,* John was drawn back to the West End by the offer to direct what seemed like a surefire commercial hit—a new play by Peter Ustinov, *Half Way Up the Tree.* This was a brittle, quirky comedy of modern manners chiefly concerned with General Sir Mallalieu FitzButtress, who returns from military duties in Malaysia to find that his beatnik son has been sent down from the university, and that his daughter has become pregnant by an unknown lover. The general's reaction is to climb a walnut tree in his garden, from where he makes occasional descents in full hippy gear himself, to hold forth to his amazed family on the changing times.

With Robert Morley in the role to which Gielgud had originally hoped to attract his old friend Ralph Richardson, and a strong supporting cast led by Morley's frequent stage partner Ambrosine Phillpotts, and including Jonathan Cecil (as a manic scoutmaster), this should have been the dream ticket, but all did not go smoothly in rehearsals. "Trying to direct your father," as Sir John said to me later, "was about as useful as trying to change the sequence on a set of traffic lights. He knew what he wanted to do, and did it regardless of all other suggestions." Luckily, Ustinov himself was otherwise engaged, and on very strong reviews the play lasted a year at the

Queen's Theatre. Toward the end of its run Ustinov finally caught up with it, letting out, as he said, "Little whoops of joy when I occasionally heard one of my own original phrases, as so many others had long since disappeared from the script." Peter did, however, venture to suggest that John might have made one of the younger actresses in the cast somewhat more assertive. "You're absolutely right," mused Gielgud, "I should have had her wear a hat."

During the run, it was announced that John would at last be joining Olivier's now somewhat beleaguered National Theatre company at the Old Vic, for a sequence of three productions in the 1967–1968 season. The first of these was to have been Ibsen's *The Pretenders,* in which Olivier and John were scheduled to costar, until the sudden onset of Olivier's long and near-terminal illness meant that the project had to be abandoned. That left just two productions, Molière's *Tartuffe* (in which John was to play Orgon opposite Robert Stephens in the title role), and then an eagerly awaited Peter Brook *Oedipus,* in which John was to play the title role opposite Irene Worth as Jocasta, in a new translation of Seneca's play by the poet Ted Hughes.

But although John's arrival at the National Theatre should have been a joyous homecoming to the kind of resident company that could not have existed had it not been for his pioneering work on Shaftesbury Avenue in the 1930s, this, in fact, was to prove a curiously unhappy time for him. With Olivier ailing and already feeling too insecure to give John any proper support, both productions were something of a disappointment. Tyrone Guthrie's *Tartuffe* was characteristically eccentric, turning the title character into a shabby country boy, and thereby making it hard to believe that John's Orgon could ever have been taken in by him.

Just before the opening night, Gielgud gave an unusually open interview to *The Times* about the current state of his career:

I began the 1950s feeling rather disappointed that my production of *A Day by the Sea,* though very successful, was written off by the critics as a Chekhovian pastiche and not held to be a text of much importance. Later, I think I did myself a great deal of harm by giving interviews expressing lack of sympathy with all the new writers. Larry has been much wiser in doing *The Entertainer* and *Rhinoceros,* and has always remained in the vanguard, while I myself could not really do a play like *Endgame,* which I was once offered but had no feeling for. Even *Tiny Alice* I never really understood, and refused to do over here. Of course, I am now very lucky to have my *Ages of Man* recital to fall back on—when I was younger, I was appalled at the thought of having to recite at parties, and always felt very self-conscious about it, although now I find I enjoy it very much indeed . . . at this juncture, the problem for me is to find the right point at which to discard the things about my style that have become old-fashioned, while retaining the essential qualities that make me the particular actor I am.

Tartuffe had a very rocky first night at the Old Vic, and such good reviews as there were went almost entirely to Joan Plowright as the pert young maid. But if that had proved a disappointing experience, it was nothing compared with the Peter Brook *Oedipus,* on which John immediately went to work. Brook was no longer the amenable ally of their previous relationship on *Measure for Measure.* His status now as a world-class theatrical guru meant that he allowed very little interference in his working methods, which included three whole weeks of body movement and vocal exercise before even starting on the text.

This method had never been John's favorite, and some of the improvizations were going on right up to the week of dress rehearsals and previews. One morning, around this time, Brook asked each member of his *Oedipus* cast to come downstage in turn and state the most frightening thing they could possibly imagine; when it came to Gielgud's turn, he simply murmured, "We open on Thursday." Nor was he much helped by a set dominated by a vast golden phallus, which was greeted from the stalls on the first night by a piercing whisper from Coral Browne: "Nobody we know, ducky."

In a more serious vein, Irene Worth tells the story of those fraught *Oedi-*

pus rehearsals: "John was really at his humblest and deepest, breaking right away from his classical training of being totally in command of his material . . . the old technical skills and the old tricks were no use. There was one session when John and Peter and I were in that filthy Old Vic rehearsal room for six hours while Peter tried to help John to achieve a certain note of pain, to make a real spring of truth for the speech. John tried and tried and tried. I've never seen an actor go through so much breaking down. He was like a loaf of bread being broken into small pieces."

But however hard he tried, John never really came to terms with this production, not least perhaps because he was now playing a role in which Olivier had once made his name. The first night was not helped by a blazing row between Brook and Olivier, who had threatened to cancel the entire production, so horrified was Olivier by the golden phallus and the way in which Brook had roped several of his actors to pillars in the stalls. As Ronald Bryden noted for *The Observer*, "Brook has turned the Old Vic into a kind of cathedral laboratory of the twenty-first century, a wind-tunnel designed to contain a hurricane of human emotions." Other critical reaction was deeply divided between those who saw Brook as a genius who could do no wrong, those who wished that Gielgud had not been so totally deconstructed by the production, and those who wished they could put the clock back twenty years to the comparative simplicity of the Olivier version for the Old Vic in exile, albeit in the other text.

John's reaction was as usual twofold. On the one hand he was justifiably proud that he'd had the courage to throw himself into Brook's now rather alien rehearsal methods, and on the other he wanted, as soon as possible after the first night, to make his way back onto safer theatrical shores.

It had been those rehearsal methods, and Brook's general attitude to his actors, that John had found most disturbing. His recollection of the experience, and his defensive self-deprecation, suggests that he found Brook's methods autocratic and unpleasant:

Peter enjoys his authority: he would walk into the rehearsal room and say curtly "No Newspapers!" and every morning the whole cast had to do exercises. It was rather like being in the Army and I dreaded it; but at the same time, I wanted to be part of such an experiment. Peter battered me down to my lowest ebb during the rehearsals, saying "You can't do that, it's awfully false and theatrical," and giving me extraordinarily difficult things to do.

In the big scene [where Oedipus realises he has killed his father and married his mother], I had to deliver a highly emotional speech kneeling on the ground, then get up quietly and go to sit at the side of the stage . . . while the messenger came on and described me putting my eyes out. At the end of his ten-minute monologue, I then had to get up from my stool and go into the voice and manner of the blinded Oedipus, trying to produce my voice in a strange, strangled tone which Peter had invented at rehearsal with endless experiment. It was one of the most difficult things that I have ever done in my life—but very good, I suppose, for my ego.

Olivier had nothing else to offer him at the National, and once the relatively short season of *Oedipus* and *Tartuffe* was over, John went back with some relief to a range of random assignments, none of which had the distinction of Brook's *Oedipus*, in which Irving Wardle, for *The Times*, had found him "dispensing honeyed cadences amid the carnage, and registering blood-freezing discoveries with a testy frown, as though only marginally in contact with the show."

By now, the death first of Vivien Leigh and then of Olivier's best friend and manager Cecil Tennent, who had crashed his car on the way back from her funeral, coupled with Olivier's own increasing illness, had cast a long and dark shadow backstage at the National. Tynan alone, as literary manager, still wanted to keep Gielgud with them, and had been making all kinds of random suggestions, including the intriguing one that Olivier and John might now like to alternate as Lear and Gloucester, just as they had thirty years earlier as Romeo and Mercutio. Olivier, however, was not up for that one at all, and in July 1967 Tynan wrote to John suggesting that he might like to do either a revival of Anouilh's *The Rehearsal*, or the first stage production of Beckett's *All That Fall,* or still more intriguingly, three short farces by John Maddison Morton, a nineteenth-century comic dramatist whom Tynan was ever eager to promote, although with no success.

Instead, what came now, in quick succession, were well-paid cameo roles in two major movies, *The Shoes of the Fisherman,* in which John played his first of several popes, and then Richard Attenborough's first feature, *Oh! What a Lovely War,* in which he was cast as Count Leopold von Berchtold, the inept Austrian foreign minister at the outbreak of World War I, memorably described by one historian as being "outstanding for the vacuity of his mind, and the snobbishness of his character."

Having now acquired the taste for these brief screen cameos, he also played the Inquisitor (heavily cut) in a BBC television production of Shaw's *Saint Joan,* before going back to the world of opera for the last time. He had been invited to mark the arrival of Sadler's Wells Opera at its new base in the London Coliseum with a production of Mozart's *Don Giovanni,* which attracted lukewarm reviews ("Gielgud's handling of the singers is mainly conventional, safe but dull."—*The Times*). However, Gielgud was to establish yet one more career here: as his designer, he had courageously chosen a twenty-five-year-old artist who was soon to make his mark as one of the outstanding talents of his generation, Derek Jarman, whose décor combined pop techniques with eighteenth-century pyramids. The critic Rodney Milnes was less than impressed: "It is understandable for the management to seek out celebrity names for so auspicious an occasion, but surely an opera director and designer would have been a better idea."

Gielgud remained unrepentant about Jarman: "I was so glad to have chosen him—he taught me more things than I knew myself about the world of opera."

It wasn't until the autumn of 1968 that John got the offer of the play that was finally to establish his late-life career and introduce him into a whole new world of satirical comedy. *Forty Years On* had begun its life as a series of separate parodies of such disparate literary figures as Oscar Wilde, T. E. Lawrence, and Virginia Woolf.

Gradually, however, the dramatist Alan Bennett had come to realize that these could be combined into a script that traced the history of twentieth-century Britain through the frame of an end-of-term school play at a minor public school, Albion House, where the headmaster is about to give way to an unwelcome new world. Bennett, whose first play this was, had not thought of offering it to Gielgud, but Patrick Garland, who was to direct, insisted that he would be perfect casting, and despite considerable initial doubts, John finally came to see that in this very loose metaphor for England he would have a wonderful chance to display the line of eccentric comedy that he had recently begun to develop for Tony Richardson in the films of *The Loved One* and *The Charge of the Light Brigade.*

What makes *Forty Years On* so memorable and, in the view of some, so important is its mixture of snobbery with violence. The play is at the same time a savage attack on the class structure and general upper-class idiocy of a dying Britain (hence the school name, Albion House), as well as an achingly nostalgic attempt to get back to the world it is even now sending up as rotten.

Forty Years On came at an utterly perfect theatrical and historical moment. The office of the Lord Chamberlain, as theatrical censor, had just been abolished, thereby allowing all kinds of jokes to get by. The recently published diaries of Chips Channon and Harold Nicolson had rekindled public interest in the period just before World War II and, perhaps above all, as for some of Bennett's sketches in the recent *Beyond the Fringe*, there had suddenly arrived a new West End audience keen for mockery and parody of what had until now been untouchable monuments of the old Empire.

Bennett developed here a unique form of mangled memory: "They are rolling up the maps all over Europe, we shall not see them lit again in our lifetime." Gielgud, however, now found himself in something of a backstage quandary; in putting himself into the hands of Alan Bennett and Patrick Garland, he was working, unusually, in a contemporary play with a relatively untried director and dramatist. Much of his role consisted of long speeches to the audience, in most of which he was being asked to send up the Edwardian world of the Sitwells and the elegant country house parties where, like Noël Coward, he had found some of his first homes. To his still somewhat old-fashioned aesthetic, Bennett's waspish parodies of people he either did know, or easily might have actually known, seemed wildly tasteless, and yet from the very first weeks on tour, he realized that they were onto something, despite the fact that in Manchester and Brighton some older members of the audience had stormed out in disgust.

There was also the little matter of the schoolboys; since this was to be a school play, there had to be a good many of them, and on one occasion, during Garland's early staging, John found himself not only surrounded by them, but forced by their sheer numbers to the very back of the set. Finally, he could stand it no longer. "Patrick!" came a querulous voice from way upstage, "I am not terribly happy here." "No, no, Sir John," said Garland, ever eager to appease his star, "where would you like to be?" "Well," said John G. thoughtfully, "I think downstage, in the middle, under a light, and on something." Seldom has stardom been better defined.

Bennett's rehearsal diary indicates John's constant uneasiness about some of the liberties taken with people he once revered, but the script led him to remember other stories of the period. At one stage, Gielgud decided that all they were missing was a Noël Coward parody and commanded Bennett to write one instantly. When Alan demurred, saying that his talents were not quite up to this, John announced dismissively, "Nonsense! Noël Coward dialogue is perfectly easy to write. Noël does it all the time."

Alan's diary continues: "John treats the production as a kind of open dress-rehearsal, his theory being that any audiences coming this early deserve everything they get, or don't get. But gradually the show is being carved into a slimmer, simpler shape. Gielgud is a very humble man. He can be wayward, obstinate and maddeningly changeable, but one can forgive all this because he sets so little store by his own reputation. He is entirely without malice or *amour propre,* and in a succession of gruelling rehearsals, he never once loses his composure. Today I find myself telling him how to deliver a line in order to get a laugh, and I begin to apologise, but he pooh-poohs the apology and begs me to go on. He will not be shielded by his own reputation, or allow it to intrude between him and his fellow actors."

As John grew more comfortable in this kind of anti-*Cavalcade,* he began to dominate its complex structure much after the fashion of the leader of a seaside concert party, moving swiftly through the century until he reached the heartbreaking final speech:

"The hedges come down from the silent fields. The lease is out on the corner site. A butterfly is an event . . . Once we had a romantic and old-fashioned conception of honour, of patriotism, chivalry and duty. But it was a duty which didn't have much to do with justice, with social justice anyway, and in default of that justice, and in pursuit of it, that was how the great words came to be cancelled out. The crowd has found the door into the secret garden. Now they will tear up the flowers by the roots, strip the borders and strew them with paper and broken bottles."

During the run of *Forty Years On,* John gave one of the longest and most revealing interviews of his career thus far to Katharine Brisbane of the *Guardian:*

It's a funny thing, but suddenly I've become very much more recognised. I suppose because I've done television and films a bit, people seem to know me in the street, which never really happened to me when I was at Stratford or the Old Vic. Now, the most extraordinary people come up to me in St. James's Park, which is very sweet of them; I have lived in London all my life, and I am frightfully nostalgic about its past. I adored this city when I was young, and the thrill of playing on Shaftesbury Avenue for the first time, and going to the Vic, but now I'm about to start a new life in the country, and I feel I've done all those things and I had better not appear too often, or they'll get bored of me. A lot of us older actors are not working at the moment—Scofield, Redgrave, Dame Edith—and Peggy is only playing in those short Pinter plays, which really isn't very much. I think we all feel we are in some danger of being left behind; I often think I should have played the father in *Look Back in Anger,* because that was a rebellious kind of play, and it might have made me look as though I wasn't just part of a forgotten establishment. The British theatre has in the past ten years become a director's theatre, no longer ideal for people like me, and although I love Chekhov and Shakespeare, I really wonder if there's anything major left for me to do. At sixty-five it is quite hard to keep your ambition going. The last war really changed everything, and the craftsmen have all gone . . . having beautiful clothes and shoes specially made, beautiful food and a wonderful staff of servants. You just can't live like that any more. All you can do is try to reconcile yourself to a world which seems to me to have gone mad. Alan Bennett in this play has a very nostalgic feeling for the Edwardian era, but I know that he would have hated to live in it himself. I'm rather glad we are not taking it to New York because over there people are very sentimental about patriotism, and I think they would hate to see us sending it all up. . . . As for me, as I reach 65, life is less a mad adventure, more a matter for careful thought. I have given up reading my own scrapbooks, and I know I have been so lucky with all my Lears and Macbeths and Hamlets. That's why I would really like now to go on acting in new plays by new writers—I feel I've said what I have to say in the old plays, and I am no longer nearly so bossy. I really prefer to be directed, especially in films and television, where I never have the faintest idea what is going on technically. I just sit at the side of the set trying to complete my *Times* crossword and waiting to be told what to do next.

In fact, what prevented *Forty Years On* from crossing the Atlantic were not only John's misgivings but also a savage review in *The New York Times* from Clive Barnes on a visit to London. A few years later, Barnes was given a CBE (Commander of the Order of the British Empire) for being the only British critic to have sustained a long New York career. "Giving Barnes a CBE for services to the British Theatre," muttered Alan Bennett at the time, "is rather like giving Göring a CBE for services to the RAF."

In the thirty years since *Forty Years On* first opened at the Apollo Theatre, both Paul Eddington and Alan Bennett himself (who were playing junior masters in the original) have taken on from Gielgud the role of the headmaster. Good as both were, onstage (Eddington) and radio (Bennett), neither could remotely recapture the curiously haunting, evanescent quality of the Gielgud original. Here, quite simply, was a man who had lived through almost the entire period of the play and was looking back at it not so much in anger as in weary, mild amazement at the way the twentieth century had gone. I was lucky enough to see Gielgud in many technically greater plays than *Forty Years On;* but I never once saw him so funny, so moving or so totally wrapped up in the material.

As for the play itself, it remains an amazing mixture of postgraduate satire ("When society has to resort to the lavatory for its humour, the writing is on the wall") and insights into a state of the nation that have really never been overtaken or improved. Bennett's final vision, of an England at the crossroads of the world—"at present on offer to European clients, outlying portions of the estate already disposed of to sitting tenants. Of some historical and period interest. Some alterations and improvements necessary"—remains as topical today as it was in 1968.

It was Benedict Nightingale, for *The New Statesman,* who summed up: "Gielgud dominates all with an unexpected caricature of a fastidious, maudlin old spinster. He is at his most elegant, attenuated and mellow, like a Stradivarius playing Mozart. From the great Mandarin of the theatre, a delicious comic creation."

After a year in *Forty Years On,* having revitalized his career and played to capacity houses, John felt the need for a rare holiday and was briefly replaced by his old friend Emlyn Williams, whereupon the run came to an abrupt halt. John now had something still more exciting in prospect; it was formally announced in October 1969 that he would come together with the director Richard Attenborough (for whom he had recently filmed a cameo in *Oh! What a Lovely War*) and the composer Benjamin Britten for a film of *The Tempest,* which was to be made on the isle of Bali. As John now told a press conference, "Prospero is one of the very few interpretations of mine that I would like to leave behind. *The Tempest* is a romantic, mysterious, religious play about revenge and compassion, and we all think that Bali, with its mysterious terrain, would be very evocative. I want to try to reconstruct the play from my knowledge of the scaffolding, and make it more coherent for the screen. I wouldn't harm the text, but I would put in episodes that the play merely describes. The cinema has, in my opinion, with the possible exception of Larry's *Henry V,* missed out on a great opportunity in Shakespeare. Zeffirelli, whom I much admire, put a lot of extraneous business and pageantry into his film of *Romeo and Juliet,* and only succeeded in slowing it down by wasting vast amounts of screen time."

Sadly, the Shakespearean film techniques that John began here to advocate really only came into use in the very last year or two of his life, by which time he was too fragile to play any major roles in them. As for his long-projected film of *The Tempest,* both Attenborough and Britten fell by the wayside, and although John did finally get to make a film based on the play for Peter Greenaway, *Prospero's Books* was never really going to be the orthodox *Tempest* that he had always yearned to film.

23. HOME, SWEET HOME

(1970–1973)

To be fired, on the brink of my seventieth birthday, from directing a Debbie Reynolds musical in Philadelphia did not perhaps constitute the high point of my theatrical career thus far.

*A*s the 1970s began, John became increasingly inclined to take up any stage or screen project that came his way (in this decade alone he was to make fifteen films), largely because he and Martin now wanted to restore, to all its original architectural and interior finery, the dream house they had found in the country. Their South Pavilion of Wotton Underwood was ornate, baroque, and in need of considerable refurbishment, but one of its most important assets, as Irene Worth recalled, was the land surrounding it: "John always had a profound love of architecture and a piercing eye. His taste pervaded his personal life so that wherever he lived had great warmth and allure, as well as immaculate taste. The garden of Wotton Underwood was large, simple, classically drawn and surrounded by smaller charming gardens created by Martin Hensler. On autumn days there you could see John making huge bonfires and surrendering totally to the countryside, which until now he had totally ignored. Away from Shaftesbury Avenue, which as he always said now was no longer the street he knew, he became privately a completely different character—no longer in the heart of the West End, but still fervently eager to keep in touch with all the gossip."

The departure from 16 Cowley Street of John and Martin did not go un-noticed or unmourned by the gay show business community, which still regarded it as a safe haven and a good address for discreet parties. Derek Jarman wrote in his diary, "After Gielgud's parties in Cowley Street broke up, I was often propositioned by cab drivers hired to take me home to Is-lington . . . the queer cabbies stalked out us stately homos, saying as they dropped me off, 'Aren't you going to invite me in for a cup of coffee then?' "

The films that John made at the beginning of this decade included the rather nondescript *Eagle in a Cage,* in which he and Ralph Richardson both appeared in a somewhat somnolent account of Napoleon's last years on Saint Helena, and then an unwise remake of *Julius Caesar,* in which John now played the title role to the Mark Antony of Charlton Heston, the Brutus of Jason Robards, and the Cassius of Richard Johnson. As Heston recalled, "Sir John was the ultimate professional, always on time and word perfect, though he had of course had rather more experience of the play than the rest of us put together. When I had to do the great speech over his dead body in the Capitol, he volunteered to lie there immobile, if it would be of any help. But I persuaded him to go home. The idea of having to do that speech in the presence of the greatest Shakespearean actor in the world was just too much."

As *Variety* was to note when the film opened, to some mildly terrible re-views, "Gielgud in the significant but smallish title role gives the rest of the cast a lesson in making every word and phrase of Shakespeare count. Of all the performances here, this is the one that comes nearest to true."

John was now clearly marking time; he also took on the Ghost in an undistinguished BBC television *Hamlet* and, somewhat more exotically, the Caliph in another television version of the old *Hassan* potboiler. What he was really doing (apart from occasional stints in the garden at Wotton Underwood, frequently consigning to his beloved bonfires there what ap-peared to him to be weeds, and were only later discovered by Martin to have been miniature bonzai trees that he had spent several years nurtur-ing) was filling his days while awaiting the arrival of something new, preferably by a living writer. When this eventually came, in the early months of 1970, it proved to be a rather mixed blessing.

The playwright Peter Shaffer, whom Gielgud had, of course, launched with his production of *Five Finger Exercise*, was very hot indeed, having had triumphs at the National Theatre and elsewhere with the *Royal Hunt of the Sun*, and *Black Comedy*. But what he had written now was *The Battle of Shrivings*, an immensely dark and ambitious work about human perfectibility as expressed through the career of an elderly philosopher (not unlike the recently deceased Bertrand Russell) who has adopted the role of figurehead in anti-arms demonstrations and built an entire, miniature, perfectly enclosed world in which he now lives surrounded by acolytes and an embittered wife. Into this idyllic Cotswold setting erupts an old pupil, an earthy poet, back from a lifetime of Mediterranean sun and sin, now determined to prove his old mentor wrong in every possible way.

These two characters (to put it crudely, the head versus the heart) are, of course, variants on the central figures of almost all Shaffer's major plays— Pizarro and Atthuallpa in *Royal Hunt of the Sun*, Salieri and Mozart in *Amadeus*, the psychiatrist and the boy who blinds horses in *Equus*. This time, Shaffer had specifically written these parts for Gielgud and Richardson, but when Richardson turned the play down, the poet who comes back to Shrivings to taunt his tutor was played by Patrick Magee, with Wendy Hiller as the wife trying to hold the ring between them. Despite that starry cast and a production by Peter Hall, *The Battle of Shrivings* was a disaster— generally reckoned to be overlong, portentous, and ultimately somewhat pointless.

One good thing, however, did emerge from the *Battle of Shrivings*. During the last days of a very short run, the director Lindsay Anderson, recognizing John's newfound eagerness to work in new plays, and his desire to renew his old partnership with Ralph Richardson, came upon a script that was to be the answer to all of those prayers. *Home*, by the novelist and poet David Storey, had begun as a conversation between two increasingly eccentric old men in what seemed to be some kind of a resort hotel. Halfway through writing the first scene, Storey came to realize that they were in fact the inmates of a mental home, though Jocelyn Herbert's minimal set never suggested this, and as no nurses or doctors were ever seen to appear in uniform, the audience only gradually came to realize precisely where they all were.

As the critic Gavin Lambert was to write, "In a fine example of less as more, a bare stage frames an isolated world containing only one white table and two metalwork chairs. Harry (Gielgud) and Jack (Richardson), the central figures, are not obviously mad or dangerous, and, unusually for Storey, they clearly belong to the upper middle class. . . . They may not even be clinically insane, just too estranged from reality to be capable of looking after themselves. Rejected by their families, who don't want to be responsible for them, their only 'Home' is an asylum—which makes *Home* a doubly ironic title for a play about the metaphorically homeless."

In its first production, *Home* seemed to many as despairingly funny and human as any of Samuel Beckett's plays, and considerably more accessible. John was, in rehearsal, far more nervous than Richardson, and there was a wonderful exchange of Pinteresque dialogue as recorded by Lindsay Anderson:

> *Gielgud:* Lindsay, it just is not possible for me to sit here without moving for twenty-five minutes.
> *Lindsay:* Move, in that case, if you feel like it.
> *Gielgud:* It's strange, but once sitting here I don't feel I want to move.
> *Lindsay:* In that case, don't.
> *Gielgud:* I shan't.

Anderson, in his diary, also came up with a careful distinction between the two men who were now, in Richardson's own phrase, resembling "the broker's men" as they moved into this autumnal partnership: "John can produce the most sensitive, apparently deep vibrations with apparently only a minimum of thought. Likewise, he is weak at concretely imagining—creating for us the clouds, the church in the distance, the dust on the table—or rather not weak (since he can do it brilliantly, magnetically) but just negligent. Such is his relationship, I suppose, with the world outside him. Ralph is a brilliantly contrasting talent. He thinks a great deal, but often tortuously, creating and sticking to an idea which is eccentric and quite wrong. Together, their relationship still has an element of distance, friendly and touching, but somehow formal, with Richardson always amused by John's inability to talk about anything that doesn't impinge on acting. 'Sometimes,' Ralph told me, 'I talk about diesel engines, just to see the horrified look in John's eyes.'"

In rehearsal, John could still be surprisingly waspish, even about his oldest friends. "I was disappointed," he told Lindsay now, "in Peggy's Ranevskaya and her Arkadina. She seems to have lost her way. Of course, she always had a very active sex life, and now that's over I think she rather misses it. She's never been good at getting her hair done, or spending money on dresses."

Rehearsals for *Home* continued in this gossipy, sometimes tempestuous way, with Richardson walking out one afternoon when Anderson had been more than usually dictatorial. "I am not," said Richardson, "any longer a schoolboy, and I don't like your fucking headmaster act." Nevertheless, *Home* opened in utter triumph at the Royal Court, soon transferring to a long West End run, and then Broadway.

Even those critics who were less than totally happy with the play as drama could not fail to recognize the magic of the Gielgud-Richardson double-act: "*Home* may not be where my heart is," wrote one of them, "but there is no greater exponent of mannered eccentricity than Sir Ralph, no more moving actor alive today than Sir John."

Ralph, however, already felt that they could be nearing the end of the road: "Actors like us never retire, they merely get fewer and fewer parts until they are offered none."

But after the fiasco of their last joint appearance in *The Last Joke*, both men warmed and mellowed in this newfound success. David Storey once likened them to a couple of racehorses, hoping they would run out of steam before they reached the edge of the cliff. "One reason," John later explained, "why I so enjoy working with Ralph is that we are old friends and we laugh a lot, and seem to balance each other's style in a very happy way. It is wonderful to play with somebody who is so absolutely opposed to you in temperament. We are a tremendous contrast in personalities."

Unlike John, who still guarded his privacy and was willing to talk in public only about his work, as if terrified that somebody might still be tactless enough to bring up the events of 1953, Richardson now became a familiar figure on television talk shows, where, somewhere halfway between Merlin and Mephistopheles, he would drive his interviewing hosts mad by the apparent incoherence of his answers. Asked once about his work with John, he replied, "I once took him pillion on my motor bicycle, I fear he didn't care for it. He's not a car or bike man, really, although the finest speaker of verse in the world today. I always loved him as Richard II and, of course, Richard III." The interviewer never dared point out that John had never in fact played Richard III, because by that time Richardson was already into a detailed account of the problems of wheel-wobble at high speed.

Because they also televised *Home*, Richardson and Gielgud became more famous for these two roles than for anything they had recently done individually. As Keith Dewhurst wrote of the broadcast, "When we watch Gielgud and Richardson, there is something sad and majestic and frail about them, like the Indian summer of great athletes." And it was left to Harold Hobson to sum up for the stage version: "In the enormous roll of their past triumphs I can find nothing more memorable, more controlled or more affecting than Gielgud and Richardson in *Home*. Mr. Anderson's direction is soft as silk, durable as steel. . . . At the very end, they stand, staring out above the heads of the audience, cheeks wet with tears in memory of some unnamed misery, weeping soundlessly as the lights fade on them. It makes a tragic, unforgettable close."

Gielgud and Richardson were only now making their first crossover to the kind of experimental and underfinanced theater that flourished at the Royal Court, some twelve years after Arthur Miller had first convinced Olivier to do the same. Peggy Ashcroft, always in the vanguard of theatrical innovation, had also begun to work at the Royal Court years earlier, but it would still be wrong to underestimate the courage it took for Gielgud and Richardson, steeped in the ways of the West End and the traditional Shakespearean life of Stratford and the Old Vic, to put themselves in the hands of writers like David Storey and directors like Lindsay Anderson, who really did seem to them at first like creatures from another theatrical planet. And, of course, the feeling was probably mutual. Richardson later reflected: "At first, neither John nor I trusted ourselves at all with the idea of a play like *Home,* and it wasn't until we actually met Storey and Anderson, both of whom inspired us with some confidence, that we had the courage to take on the play. Even so, during the early rehearsals we were extremely baffled by it, and extremely reluctant to go ahead. We thought we had both made a grave mistake in taking the play on—we couldn't understand it ourselves and we feared, in that case, we would never be able to make anyone else understand it either."

As for John, this was, all in all, a kind of career rebirth as he later recalled:

When *Look Back in Anger* opened, Olivier was immediately converted to the kitchen-sink school, as it was then christened, and was to be one of the first of the so-called West End stars to undertake a quite new kind of work in his superb performance in *The Entertainer.* There was later some talk of my appearing with him at the Court in Anouilh's *The Rehearsal,* but I was not able to undertake it at the time he suggested it. Much as I admired *Look Back in Anger* myself, rather to my surprise, I did not imagine that the new writers would want me in any of their plays, and I gave some rather ill-advised interviews saying that I was out of sympathy with Brecht and Beckett. I also lost touch with George Devine, as I greatly now regret, since we had worked together a great deal through his early career. When I was asked by William Gaskill, Lindsay Anderson and David Storey to appear in *Home,* Devine was already dead.

The text of *Home* naturally intrigued me but also somewhat mystified me. Construction, situation, dialogue—all was quite unlike anything I had ever been asked to tackle, but, as I had greatly enjoyed Storey's earlier play *The Contractor,* I thought I would like to take the chance. I had not liked Lindsay Anderson when I had met him on two previous occasions, once in England and once in New York, and I had the impression that he did not like me either, but David Storey approached us both with much confidence and charm. And once I began to work, the atmosphere of the rehearsals began to become enormously sympathetic and exciting, especially as my old friend Ralph Richardson was in the play, as well as two brilliant actresses, Mona Washbourne and Dandy Nichols.

Lindsay's quiet and subtle method of handling the production appealed to me tremendously, though we were all dismayed by the difficulty of learning the text correctly and convincing ourselves and one another of the essential task of communicating the play's implications. Jocelyn Herbert [the designer and lifelong partner of the late George Devine] contributed a set with inimitable charm and purpose. And the theatre seemed to welcome us as friends and colleagues and did not, as we had feared, find us stuck-up West End Establishment figures, hidebound by tradition and a superior attitude towards experiment and innovation. I am intensely grateful for the experience of *Home*. It gave me the greatest pleasure and encouragement to persevere in a new field so late in my career, and I shall always remember the play and all connected with it with the greatest affection and satisfaction.

One of the many things Gielgud and Richardson now had to learn was that in this modern theater a pause was not necessarily (as they had always believed) a sign that one or the other of them had forgotten what to say next. John in particular had always dreaded any kind of silence onstage, ever since the night some years earlier when, during a very brief pause in his production of *The Importance of Being Earnest*, he heard a voice from the circle announcing, "Ooh look now, you've come all over my nice umbrella."

But in the end it was Lindsay Anderson who, shortly before his death, best summarized the entire experience of the two knights in *Home:*

Nothing in John's wonderful career is more wonderful, it seems to me, or more exemplary than his sanguine acceptance of the passing of time, and his coming to friendly terms with a whole new generation of writers and directors and fellow-artists ... I always thought of him as a remote, distinguished planet circling with a certain hauteur above the contemporary struggle. I think at first he regarded our Royal Court activities with suspicion, and he had never replied when I once invited him to play Caesar there ... but by the time we reached *Home,* he was by now completely transformed from the careful conservative who had advised Ralph not to do *Waiting for Godot.* In fact it was he who suggested Ralph for the other role, and then, with Dandy Nichols and Mona Washbourne as the women, we began one of those uniquely happy, harmonious and fulfilling theatre experiences that happen, if one is lucky, once in a lifetime—the kind that forge friendships that last the rest of one's life ... we had a marvellous time exploring the long duologue, apparently so inconsequential but profoundly revealing, comic yet suggestive, with which the play begins. ... It is hard to express the sheer and absolute acting genius of John Gielgud. Not his lyrical voice and perfection of phrasing, which became a trap of which he was very well aware. Not his great, inherited actor's intelligence. Not intellect—John himself was always amused at the thought that he was considered an intellectual actor, as they are almost always bad actors. John Gielgud is an actor of instinct, sensibility, and emotion. His rhetoric is impeccable; but his moments of pure, exposed emotion are inexpressibly touching. In this, for me, lies the unique poetry of his playing.

Unusually, but realizing that he had now moved into a late and golden summer, John stayed with *Home* (as did Richardson) right through the Royal Court, West End, and Broadway runs, only finally letting it go with some reluctance after the television recording in 1971. But in the absence of any other major offer in the immediate future, John fell back into his usual late-life pattern of accepting every odd job that came over the phone. Thus, as 1970 turned into 1971, he did a BBC television film of *In Good Charles' Golden Days,* of which the only moment of distinction was the penultimate scene, when John got to play, for the only time of his life, opposite one of his great idols, Elisabeth Bergner.

He also, in this period, did a considerable amount of radio drama—both ancient and modern, put several Shakespearean plays onto long-playing records, turned up as a guest star in television celebrations of Noël Coward and Carol Channing, guest-starred in two television thrillers, narrated a life of Leonardo da Vinci, and appeared in *QBVII*, the movie of the Leon Uris courtroom best-seller. None of this did him any actual harm, but it was not exactly what he might have hoped for after the brave new world of *Home*.

It was, therefore, with a certain relief that, in the summer, he accepted Patrick Garland's invitation to make his debut at the Chichester Festival in Robin Phillips's production of Shaw's *Caesar and Cleopatra*. Of course, John already had the experience of playing Caesar for Charlton Heston, and in earlier times he had played both Shakespeare's Brutus and Cassius; but the Shaw version was something else altogether.

For this Chichester revival of the original Shaw script, which had hardly ever been seen onstage since the then Oliviers had doubled it with *Antony and Cleopatra* at the old St. James's Theatre in 1950, Robin Phillips now decided to set the whole affair in a kind of children's nursery, complete with sandpits and rocking horses. Anna Calder-Marshall was Cleopatra here. Having now worked with Peter Brook on the National Theatre's *Oedipus*, and Lindsay Anderson on the Royal Court's *Home*, John could no longer be accused of being unwilling to experiment with the avant-garde.

Even so, the sight of John's new Caesar bouncing across the stage on a white beach ball was more than most critics could stand, and the production opened to some distinctly lackluster reviews, thereby preempting any thought of a West End transfer. John was later to note that his luck was never great when it came to Shaw.

> GBS originally wanted me for the film of *Caesar and Cleopatra*, but I took an instant dislike to the director, and in later years although I have played the Inquisitor in *Saint Joan* several times, most recently in a television version with Janet Suzman, I have never really been happy in Shaw. I played Marchbanks for a week once at Oxford, and took over as Dubedat in a wartime *Doctor's Dilemma*, and once at the

Vic I was the Emperor in *Androcles,* but I have never played his really good parts, except Shotover once in a rather bad television [version] of *Heartbreak House.* The truth is, I'm afraid, that I'm not enormously fond of Shaw's plays; I have always enjoyed reading them much more than watching them, and I find it maddening, the way he puts in rather feeble gags and comic nicknames to keep the audience awake in his longer passages. Now that he is dead, of course, one can cut the plays, and they are much better for it. He said *Heartbreak House* was inspired by Chekhov, but it has always seemed to me a curiously bloodless play, quite fun and with a lot of eccentric characters, but none of the subtlety that Chekhov always achieves.

With John, at Chichester that summer, was the actor, songwriter, and broadcaster Hubert Gregg: "Acting with John was a joy, especially as my memories of him went back to my schooldays in the 1920s when I was theatre-mad and haunted the Old Vic. We had dressing-rooms next door to each other and shared *The Times* crossword every night. John as always was obsessed by this and used to go bright red under his make up when he couldn't finish it. Years later I would find him at the Garrick, where he always seemed nervous and over-polite. 'Hubert!' he would shout across the table. 'What are you doing? Something terribly exciting, I'm sure I've read about it.' Quite often I wasn't doing anything at all. But on one occasion I had been asked to talk about Shakespeare on a QE2 cruise. 'Oh, that should be lovely!' said John with a beatific smile. 'Of course they asked me, and I turned it down.'"

John's next offer brought him back into the land of living dramatists, in the person of Charles Wood, whose father had by coincidence been the stage manager of the 1945 Gielgud tour of the Far East, on which John played his farewell Hamlet. He and the younger Wood had first gotten to know each other on the long Turkish location shooting of *The Charge of the Light Brigade,* where Wood had become the last of its several writers. On their return to England, Wood had written a play called *H* and sent it to John, who declined but did suggest a suitable alternative title—*Monologues in Front of Burning Cities. H* proved something of a disaster, and John was well out of it; undeterred by this, the author now sent him an altogether different script, *Veterans*, a play inspired by the shooting of *The Charge of the Light Brigade*, and, as Wood wrote, "that period in Turkey, the long waits in the sun, the week-end picnics, and distinguished old actors waiting about for hours to perform a few lines."

This play, not entirely surprisingly, John warmed to at once, even though the part he was being asked to play, a gossipy old actor-knight who nearly always gets his own way by using his lethal charm, was effectively a kindly parody of Gielgud himself. But his experience with Alan Bennett in *Forty Years On* had taught him the virtues of self-mockery onstage, and John now took an eager part in casting the rest of the production, only mildly irritating Wood when a particular actress was discussed and Gielgud was heard to murmur, "No, no, she's doing awfully well now, and wouldn't want to do anything that wasn't absolutely first class."

Nevertheless, a starry cast was duly assembled for the Royal Court, with John Mills and Bob Hoskins at the head of it. The problem with the play was the usual one of backstage, or rather off-screen, parody. Anybody who had anything to do with *The Charge of the Light Brigade*, and that included a good many people who were still around the Royal Court, found *Veterans* utterly hilarious; audiences who had not been on the location were apt to get a little confused. They weren't the only ones: Three weeks into rehearsal, horrified by what it saw, and Gielgud's apparent inability to learn a very long part, the Royal Court management had insisted on delaying the London opening while sending it out on the road for three or four weeks. It did not go well.

As John Mills recalled:

I'd known Johnnie for many years, and been directed by him in *Charley's Aunt*, but we had never acted together before. Even during that, we had never exactly been close; after a dress rehearsal I asked Gielgud as director for some notes on my performance, and all he could come up with was the single word, 'interminable.' The play was concerned with the private lives of the actors and the goings-on around the set, during the shooting of a film on a foreign location. It was obviously *Charge of the Light Brigade,* and Johnnie played Sir Geoffrey Kendall (obviously himself), and I played Laurence d'Orsay, who was obviously Trevor Howard. It was full of in-jokes about location filming, of which I too had done a good deal, and there were several scenes containing language that was definitely not for the ears of Auntie Mabel or the grandchildren. It was fine for the Royal Court, but the management insisted that we open first in Edinburgh, where we played it to total silence—they simply didn't laugh at all. Manchester was slightly different. The audience was restless, uneasy, and there was a nasty feeling in the house. The curtain came down to little or no applause. Later I found a note in my dressing room saying, "Dear Mr. Mills, you must be very hard up, I enclose a pound." They told us that Brighton would be different. They were wrong; one night there my wife Mary, standing at the back of the dress circle, saw a large man storming down the aisle shouting, "I have been coming to this theatre for years, and John Gielgud and John Mills should be ashamed of themselves. There are ladies in this audience, and I have never heard such disgusting, filthy language in my life. If you're not leaving, I am." As he pushed past Mary, purple with rage, she heard his last, furious line. "And," he said, as he charged towards the exit door, "I paid good money to see them two fuckers!"

Also in the Brighton audience was Alan Bennett:

The audience left in droves, something audiences in Brighton are very prone to do. Indeed, having toured there several times myself, I am convinced that one of the chief pleasures of going to the theatre in Brighton is leaving it. The sleek Sussex matrons sit poised in the stalls like greyhounds in the slips. The first "fuck" and they're a mile down the front, streaking for Hove. . . . Actors of Gielgud's generation had a strong sense of what an audience expected, and what it should be given. In the '50s and '60s, it was Gielgud's sense of "my public," as much as a shortage of opportunity that kept him trundling out *Ages of Man.* In the last ten years he has shed his public and found another;

so has everybody else, though not as painfully . . . audiences are now so Polyglot that they no longer constitute an entity . . . the actor is a spectacle, and someone from Taiwan goes to see Gielgud in the same spirit as he takes in the Changing of the Guard—which he marginally prefers, if only because he is allowed to film it . . . Gielgud continues to amaze and delight, his powers not to stale, because at his best nowadays he does not seem to be acting at all. The skill lies in letting it seem that there is no skill. He has broken his staff, but he has kept his magic.

Once they reached the Royal Court, *Veterans* improved drastically, as every actor in the business came to see a play very largely about themselves, but based on the experience of the tour it was decided not to risk playing it in front of a wider civilian audience, and it duly closed after only six weeks in Sloane Square. As Jeremy Kingston noted for *Punch,* "Mr. Wood's previous plays have all been set either among soldiers or among actors, and now he brings the two together with Gielgud as a much-loved and respected actor-knight who talks on and marvellously on, fussing, gossiping, courteously apologetic, pleading for cigarettes, thinking aloud, an expert in back-handed compliments. It is a beautifully realised portrait of a man whose mind is almost totally concentrated on his own self and work, and who can only with an effort involve himself in the affairs of others."

For J. C. Trewin, "This is Gielgud's night, whether he is sitting bemused on a wooden horse high above some incomprehensible battle, or just worrying about his own fading memory. At length, unable to concentrate on what he is supposed to be doing (whatever that may be), he simply removes his toupee and withdraws his labour. It is one of the most eloquently comic scenes on the London stage today . . . never has Gielgud's sense of ironic comedy worked more perfectly."

This was not, however, an opinion shared by the gay actor Kenneth Williams as his diary indicates: "*Veterans* is spiritless and depressing. Endless trivia delighting in bad taste, like a man exposing his penis, denigration of queers, laughing at queers, and the terrible, masochistic self-indulgence of Gielgud. One becomes so sick of those half-strangulated, elongated vowels and breathlessness, and he is so dreadfully unattractive . . . I knew all about this kind of rubbish within ten minutes of the first act."

After *Veterans* closed at the Court Theatre, it was to be another two years before John took to the stage again, although in the meantime he was, as usual, seldom idle. His films in this period included two more undistinguished thrillers (*Gold* and *11 Harrowhouse*), but his most memorable appearance at this time was as a wandering priest in a spectacularly and hilariously terrible musical remake of the classic *Lost Horizon,* which became a collector's piece of high Hollywood camp, not least for the moment when John G., attired in what appeared to be a kind of tea cosy, greets the lost time-travelers, among them Peter Finch, Liv Ullmann, Michael York, and Olivia Hussey, with the news that "I come from a nearby Llamasery." As the unforgiving film critic Pauline Kael noted in *The New Yorker,* "It is quite rare to see a 1937 movie remade into one from 1932; I doubt it will ever play again outside Shangri-La itself."

But Gielgud did manage to make a new friend of the actor Michael York, who recalled, "John called me 'the Juve,' and I basked in his affection . . . his mind and spirit were irrepressibly youthful. Besides his famous ability to complete *The Times* crossword with contemptuous ease, I discovered that he had also read all the latest books, seen all the newly released films and was au fait with all the current gossip. Wreathed in scented smoke from his distinctive oval cigarettes, the eyes set far behind the noble nose would beam with wicked delight when struck by an amusing thought, and the incomparable mechanics of his diction would then smoothly engage to deliver it. He had an instinctive ability to turn a phrase, the elegance of which was doubly enhanced by his own stylish dress and demeanour. Even his laughter was finely wrought."

When they weren't needed on the set, Michael and Patricia York took John on guided tours of the Grand Canyon which was nearby, over which John gazed "like an omniscient Prospero, reviewing his wild kingdom."

The two actors also ventured on to see Debbie Reynolds dance in a Las Vegas spectacular, since there was now talk that John might direct her in a Broadway revival of the 1920s musical *Irene.*

As far as the press was concerned, John had developed the useful technique of lending his name and his presence to, but then escaping unscathed from, an amazing number of rubbishy scripts. Somehow critics never blamed him for taking the money, and he alone was by now managing to create an almost Zen-like separation between himself and the Hollywood trash with which he was so often to be involved. Quite simply, he had no shame; nor, by this time, had Olivier or Richardson. They would turn up in movie after movie as if they were working in some foreign country—which often, on location, they were—and as if their performances, such as they were, would have absolutely no effect on their real careers in the theater. In this, of course, they were, amazingly, absolutely right.

Back in the theater, the *Irene* experience was to prove deeply unhappy. John had always longed to direct a musical and formed a happy rehearsal relationship with Debbie Reynolds, but his utter inexperience with the million-dollar genre, and some truly terrible touring reviews, led to his being ignominiously fired—for the first and last time in his career—while in Philadelphia, weeks before a deeply troubled revival ever reached Broadway. He was replaced by the expert Gower Champion. John's feelings, however, were at least partly assuaged by a payoff of £40,000: "I kept telling them all in rehearsal how very little I knew about musicals, and I suppose that was a mistake because eventually the producers concluded that I was right, and they had better bring in someone who did know a thing or two about how to stage them."

From this debacle John progressed, if that is the right word, to playing Joan Collins's butler in a television *Tales from the Unexpected,* and the mad vicar of a small Cornish community who locks up his parishioners to keep them from evil in a television horror (in more ways than one) film called *Deliver Us from Evil.* There were, however, one or two brief moments of distinction amid these minor cameo roles, not least when he appeared as the Old Cardinal in Joseph Losey's television movie of Brecht's *Galileo,* and then as the faithful manservant of the murder victim in the 1974 all-star film *Murder on the Orient Express,* which happily reunited him with such old and new friends as Michael York, Lauren Bacall, Ingrid Bergman, and Wendy Hiller.

In this period, he also found the time to direct two major West End productions. The first of these should have worked out very much better than it did. His old friend Noël Coward, now only a year or so away from his death, had come back into fashion and favor with the knighthood of 1970, and it seemed high time that there should be a major Shaftesbury Avenue revival of a play that is still considered his signature piece, the 1930 comedy of bad manners *Private Lives.* And who better to play this now than the couple at the height of their post–National Theatre fame and fortune, Maggie Smith and Robert Stephens?

Unbeknownst to Gielgud, however, that marriage had already begun to fall spectacularly apart, leaving neither of them in any condition to play a light comedy that crucially depended on the relationship of its stars. Onstage, the chemistry simply wasn't there, and backstage their relationship unraveled entirely; Binkie, John Perry, and Gielgud ganged up against Stephens and persuaded him to leave the cast for a summer season with Jonathan Miller at Chichester. He was replaced by the infinitely safer John Standing, who (with Maggie) took the play on to Broadway and a sold-out North American tour, which finished in Toronto, where Maggie was now to stay for several seasons, marrying her very first love, the playwright Beverly Cross, and playing for Robin Phillips a number of major Shakespearean and other roles that she had unaccountably never yet been offered in London.

This troubled revival of *Private Lives* was also effectively the end of John's old life. The world that he had known so well, the world of Binkie and John Perry and Terence Rattigan and Emlyn Williams, and the life centered around the neighboring houses behind Westminster Abbey where he and Binkie had lived for so many years, was now fragmenting and dying almost by the day. John and Martin had begun to establish a whole new life for themselves at Wotton Underwood, a life in which London no longer really played any major part. Most of John's work was now in film and television studios at home and abroad, and it wasn't until close to his death, when they renamed the Globe Theatre the Gielgud, that he said to me, with a mixture of sorrow and satisfaction, "At last now there is a name I actually recognise in the lights along Shaftesbury Avenue."

And yet, for at least a few months after Binkie and Noël Coward died in the spring of 1973, John was unable to sever his links with the old-fashioned Shaftesbury Avenue star theater in which they had all spent so much of their lives. Accordingly, a few months later, he agreed to direct Ingrid Bergman—"Poor darling Ingrid, speaks five languages and can't act in any of them"—in a minor Somerset Maugham drama, *The Constant Wife*. This was essentially Ibsen's *A Doll's House* turned into boulevard farce. Ingrid was her usual self—charismatic, uncertain of her lines, but radiant even when reducing her fellow actors to a kind of panic, as night after night she inadvertently cut several key moments and even entire scenes. But now, sadly, it was all too late. Even the combination of Bergman and Gielgud and Maugham was unable to get this creaky 1927 comedy back on its feet, and as for John there was now a strong critical feeling that he really ought to be finding better things to do on stage and screen in his old age. *The Constant Wife* was seen as at best whimsical, and at worse totally anachronistic to the London theater of 1973. Nevertheless, Ingrid still had enough followers to keep the play running through the winter. Tragically, it was also during this run that she found the lump in her breast, which alerted her to the cancer of which she was eventually to die in August of 1982.

24. BLEAK HOUSE

(1974–1977)

No Man's Land will not change, or grow old, or move—it remains forever icy.

*E*arly in 1974, John returned to one of his earliest film roles, that of Benjamin Disraeli, for an epic thirteen-episode television drama series, *Edward VII.* It was also now that he would rejoin the National Theatre company, from which his old rival Olivier had just been somewhat unceremoniously ousted, a changeover which meant that several actors who had declined to work under him there were now prepared to go to the South Bank for the first time. The new director, a role hotly contested by Michael Blakemore, Kenneth Tynan, and Jonathan Miller, was now to be Peter Hall, who for his first production at the Old Vic (where the company was still lodged while work continued amid myriad delays on the new building) announced that Gielgud would star as Prospero in a radical new *Tempest.*

Apart from *The Ages of Man,* this would be John's first return to Shakespeare since 1958, and it came just in time for the celebrations of his seventieth birthday in April while he was not only playing for Peter Hall, but also campaigning for the freedom of the Soviet dancer Valery Panov, and announcing that he was about to play Shakespeare himself in a new Edward Bond play for the Royal Court. To celebrate this birthday, a book signed by countless actors and the likes of Tennessee Williams and Arthur Rubinstein was solemnly presented to him. "He is," wrote Alan Bennett, "a gentleman in the old-fashioned sense of the word. He's an almost Russian character, he's saintly, but it requires no effort. He was just born good, there has been no struggle to get there, and when he speaks Shakespeare it is as though he had also written it. If we don't understand a line, we always know it is our fault rather than his."

John was not exactly wasting any time during these Prospero rehearsals; he was also filming "an unspeakable little thriller" on a boat moored by Tower Bridge, and commuting to Leeds to read extracts from the Bible for Yorkshire Television's hugely popular *Stars on Sunday*, a task for which he was delighted to find there would be a large check, having vaguely assumed that as it was to do with God, he would probably be working for nothing.

Now that John had at last become fully accustomed to film and television cameras, Mark Amory asked him if he regretted not having made the move into movies rather earlier, to which he responded:

Before the war, they used to send me all the scripts that Leslie Howard had turned down, just as Larry was always getting Ronald Colman cast-offs. Then there was the possibility of my playing Louis XVI in *Marie Antoinette*, but Robert Morley got that, and then one day when Charles Laughton was proving difficult they even suggested I should be *The Hunchback of Notre Dame*. During *Julius Caesar*, Marlon Brando asked me to direct him on film as *Hamlet*, but nothing came of that either, and I was so awful in *The Barretts of Wimpole Street* that when I eventually went to see it, at the Odeon, Leicester Square, whenever I appeared on screen a lady in the row behind me said to her friend, "Oh God, here comes Old Beastly again!"

I suppose that over the years I have tended to rely rather too much on the Terry charm and the Terry tears. But people do seem to like that. Although of course I have had my disasters. When I explained to Emlyn Williams what Noguchi wanted to achieve by way of a stripped-down production, all Emlyn said was, "I see, you're now going to play Gypsy Rose Lear at last!"

When *Look Back in Anger* opened at the Royal Court, the aims of the company seemed to me to be both alien and ugly. The novelist Peter De Vries said I was just guilty of Noël Cowardice. Since then, I've had my toe in the avant-garde, but just paddling around, not yet up to my knees. I still feel rather guilty about my *Ages of Man* because it's really just all the purple passages stuck together, but people do seem to like it. . . . I've always been eager to please an audience in my old-fashioned sort of way. I was terribly unhappy when lots of old fans from *Richard of Bordeaux* came to see me on the road in *Veterans* last year, and I could almost feel their loathing of the language. One woman sent me a postal order for 40p saying, "If you are really so hard up that you have to do all this filth . . . " but by the end of this summer, I will have appeared over the last five years in the work of five playwrights, each of whom is at least a generation younger than me. So my life now is really not all rhetoric and robes. . . . The theatre has given me all that I ever asked for, but perhaps rather too soon. I have never had any outside interests; politics and world affairs leave me totally cold, though I suppose I might have been a better actor if I had been rather more worldly.

The inaugural Peter Hall *Tempest* at the Old Vic should have been rather more enjoyable for John than it was. This, after all, was to be his fourth Prospero (he had played the role in 1930 and 1940 at the Old Vic, and for Peter Brook at Stratford in 1957), and there would still be one more to come (Peter Greenaway's *Prospero's Books*, 1991), as well as yet another on radio. This time, Hall was very keen to play it as a masque, with a great deal of flying, as John recalled: "I found it very hard to know whether to start again from scratch, or throw in all that I had learned about the role in earlier productions. Prospero is really very difficult; he is a very passionate man, but he doesn't have any real contact with the other characters, and he can easily become either priggish, or boring, or didactic. There is not a single grain of humour in him."

When *The Tempest* opened in March, reviews were rather better for Gielgud than they were for Peter Hall. Milton Shulman for the *Evening*

Standard complained of "too many styles jostling each other for domination, like too many spices in an exotic meat dish," and Irving Wardle for
The Times added "Gielgud stands outside the stylistic framework of the
production. The part is peculiarly his own property, in the sense that the
character of Prospero resides in its verse rhythms; and no other actor in
the world is so well-equipped to handle those huge metrical paragraphs,
with their abrupt contractions and extensions of imagery, almost beyond
the bounds of syntax."

Peter Hall himself felt "this production didn't come off at all well; I had
tried to interpret the play as a masque, using my experiences of Baroque
theatre at Glyndebourne, but the play's complexities sank under the heavy
effects."

Michael Billington, for the *Guardian*, called it one of the four worst
Shakespeare productions he had ever seen; Hall gently replied that he
couldn't be sure, as he had never seen the other three. In fact, Gielgud had
not been Hall's first choice here; he had originally offered the role to Alec
Guinness, and only when Alec refused did he turn to John, despite the fact
that, as he wrote in his diary:

> John is too gentle and too nice, but I hope I know him well enough to
> push him into a sharper area of reality . . . John runs around in circles,
> with huge charm and energy. He keeps making self-deprecating re-
> marks, then reminding us that we shouldn't listen to him, and that he
> is really just a romantic who loves the old-fashioned theatre. I think I
> have persuaded him not to sing or emote so much, but now he wor-
> ries about being boring. Larry, who is still hovering around back-
> stage, insisted on coming to some of the early rehearsals, and I think
> he knows how uneasy he makes John . . . later John talked to me with
> the kind of modesty and frankness which makes him a great man. He
> said he knew that in some sense he had become old-fashioned—all
> actors do . . . the stage, he said, always went to his head. He loved to
> wander around, swinging his cloak and dominating the audience. It
> was a romantic style of acting which had served him well all his life,
> and his public loved it but, added John, I now want to get rid of my

easy solutions . . . during the dress rehearsal, at one o'clock in the morning, we were trying out the trap-door when to my incredulous eyes Sir John fell through it, apparently in slow motion. There ensued a long silence. I ran, and looked down. John was smiling amiably as he picked himself up from the entangled limbs of Miranda and Ferdinand, who were waiting below to come up. Miraculously, nobody was hurt.

A few days later, Peter Hall had the chance to take John and Ralph Richardson on a tour of the still-incomplete new building. "It was very funny. John, who is about to be seventy, treated Ralph, who is seventy-one, as if he were an extremely aged and endearing relative up from the country, and unused to city ways. 'Mind those holes . . . don't trip over those wires.' Both wore long coats and large trilbys, Ralph sporting a stick. They could have been nothing but actors. And great ones too. Both sleek with success."

During the run, Hall organized a surprise seventieth birthday celebration for John: "I introduced Larry, who introduced Ralph, who said happy birthday to John. Ralph is like an old soldier scenting battle when the audience is there. Suddenly he came to life and stamped round the stage, joking and shouting. John cried, which is appropriate, and was genuinely surprised. We had a short party upstairs in the rehearsal room afterward. There was a cake, with seventy candles, and the presentation of a Doulton figure of Ellen Terry, which all the company had subscribed to."

As *The Tempest* ended its Old Vic run, with Hall's National company now beginning to move into its new premises despite the builders, and John rather sadly aware that he would never play at the Vic again, he took on two more brief movie roles—the headmaster in *Aces High,* an unsatisfactory, airborne adaptation of *Journey's End,* and then a television version of Wilde's *Picture of Dorian Gray,* in which he played the elderly Lord Wooton. But his attention was really focused now on his return to the Royal Court, where he had scored such a personal success playing a version of himself in Charles Wood's *Veterans* a couple of years earlier.

This time the role was that of Shakespeare himself in Edward Bond's

Bingo, a stage biography of the playwright, which eventually developed into an attack on his double-dealing as a Warwickshire landlord in the last years of his life. Bond's drama was effectively a series of duologues between Shakespeare and his relatives and neighbors, but its high point was a confrontation with Ben Jonson, intriguingly played by Arthur Lowe, who on his way to Scotland stops in at Stratford to tell Will that the Globe has burned down and to touch him for a loan. It was in this confrontation between Gielgud as the ascetic but now retired Shakespeare, and Lowe as the Rabelaisian Jonson, in and out of prison four times, but better educated than Shakespeare and determined never to let him forget it, that a somewhat sedentary drama suddenly kicked into life.

John, in a neat beard, had no alternative than to play Bond's Shakespeare low-key and on a note of sustained melancholy; this was a curiously unrewarding part, in that all Shakespeare really gets to do in *Bingo* is sit around listening to other people yell at him. As Milton Shulman summed up for the *Evening Standard,* "Gielgud measures almost exactly our preconceptions of Shakespearean facial features, and throughout the entire evening he bears a concentrated look of contemplative sorrow. This is not only a gentle bard, but a very woeful one. Was such a gloomy fellow really capable of inventing the glorious clowns and provoking the heavenly laughter that graces so many of his plays? The major weakness of *Bingo* is that it never gives us the whole Shakespeare, only a philosophical argument based on one tiny sliver of his complex, mysterious and diverse character."

But there was better, much better, to come. During the run of *Bingo,* Peter Hall came back to John with something vastly more intriguing than yet another Shakespearean revival. Harold Pinter, now an associate of Hall's National Theatre, had delivered a new play. As Hall's diary indicates: "It is called *No Man's Land.* I was amazed by it. It is not at all what I was expecting. There is an icy preoccupation with time; and the long, sustained speeches have a poetic validity which would have seemed incredible in the days of the brisk, hostile repartee of *The Birthday Party.* . . . It is extremely funny, and also extremely bleak. A play about the nature of the artist: the real artist harrassed by the phony artist."

Although building delays on the South Bank meant that the National

Theatre company was still trapped at the Old Vic, the 1975 season was, after a distinctly rocky start, the one during which Peter Hall finally hit his form, having seen off the last of the dissenters from the previous Olivier regime. This was the season of Bill Bryden's *Spring Awakening,* John Schlesinger's *Heartbreak House,* the Peggy Ashcroft *Happy Days,* and the Ashcroft/Richardson (and Wendy Hiller) *John Gabriel Borkman.* But even in an unusually good time, *No Man's Land* was still the crowning achievement. Hall and Pinter had given the script to John, thinking he would want to play the grander role of Hirst. In fact, John recommended Ralph for that part, seeing immediately the potential for himself as Spooner: "It was very exciting to find a part like nothing I had ever played before, and I quickly found a way that he should look and dress. I remember saying to Harold Pinter, 'I think Auden. Don't you? Do you think sandals and socks?' And Harold jumped at the idea. Then I said, 'What about spectacles?' And he liked that, too. After the first week's rehearsals I came on stage with the wig, the suit and the spectacles, and everybody said, 'It's exactly right, perfect,' and I said, 'Yes, all I have to do now is find the performance to go with it.'"

He did, largely because, as Hall noted, "In rehearsal John is as quick as a thoroughbred horse, speeding this way, then suddenly changing direction and speeding the other. He improvises, takes risks, lives dangerously and is perfectly prepared to play a seedy, unsympathetic character like Spooner. He has the quality of mercury, and his instincts and his diction are so incredibly swift that I am sure it is this, together with his timing, wit and infallible sense of rhythm, that breeds such excitement in an audience. He seems to live several points faster than ordinary human beings. He is also very easy to direct. He demands help, demands stimulation, and he leaves you exhausted. But he also leaves you feeling slightly cleverer than you know you are."

Pinter noted this mercurial nature during the first dress rehearsal, when suddenly John changed one of the moves:

Ralph stopped the play as if paralysed, and turned very slowly to stare at him. "Are you going to do that, Johnny?" John leapt up as if stung by a wasp and immediately began to apologise, retreating from Ralph as he did so, until he had almost entirely left the set. I suddenly realised that Ralph had absolute authority on stage over John, although he very seldom had to use it.

This was the first time that I had actually worked with John, though of course I had watched him on stage since his Raskolnikov in *Crime and Punishment* just after the war, when I was still a young actor myself. I was in Wolfit's company for a while, and I think if there was anyone Donald hated more than John G. it was probably me, because he had so little faith in my acting. Perhaps rightly.

As I watched John over the years, he never failed to impress me—although he always seemed terribly gaunt, his nervous system energy on stage was electrifying. I never agreed with those who said that all he had was the golden voice; John always seemed to me to be acting with every fibre of his presence. His precision and grace and intelligence, in such roles as Benedick, is something I shall never forget. In the 1980s, I was responsible for organising a benefit at the Royal Court to raise funds for imprisoned writers overseas. Ralph disapproved thoroughly, and refused to take any part; indeed, he sent me a sharp note, reading, "Got to have a bit of law and order, old boy." John, on the other hand, always the more liberal of the two, agreed to do a speech from *Richard II;* and my greatest recollection of that night is of every great actor in the business crowding into the wings to watch John doing a very brief reading from Shakespeare. It was as though they all knew that he was their master.

As soon as I had shown *No Man's Land* to Peter, and John had asked to play Spooner, I think we both knew that although he had never played a character in any way at all like that, he knew something more than we did of the Bohemian world from which Spooner came. I'm not suggesting, of course, that John also used to hang around Hampstead Heath at night, but he had certainly known people who did, and he had an instinctive understanding of Spooner which was simply wonderful to watch. The whole Auden connection came from John and I thought it was absolutely right for the character. He used elements of Auden and indeed of himself, but to build up a totally new character in a way that I certainly had almost never seen him do before; it was an act of creation rather than interpretation.

Early on, Peter and I had lunch with John to discuss who should be playing Hirst; we went through a long list of actors without mentioning Ralph, because we somehow thought that he might not now be up to learning it. John disagreed at once. "I think you should approach him; it's very important for the play that the actor playing Hirst should not have a weaker stage presence than me. And with Ralph, of course, you'd be getting a stronger one!"

They had of course already worked together in David Storey's *Home,* but I knew from the beginning that there was no danger of them repeating themselves, because the roles in *No Man's Land* are so totally different. I saw less of them in rehearsal than I would like to have done, because my home life was in total chaos—it was the time that I was leaving home and my wife Vivien Merchant to live with Antonia Fraser. Whenever I did look in, they seemed to be having a really good time, and I was just so pleased and honoured with what they were doing in my play.

They were both of course great world-wide stars with tremendous individual followings, and I'm sure that some of their fans couldn't make any sense at all of *No Man's Land;* but I'm used to that, and most of the audiences always seemed to be having a really good time as well. During the run in London and later on Broadway, Antonia and I used to take John and Ralph out to lunch sometimes, but they would hardly ever talk about themselves or their work. Instead, they both seemed fascinated by Antonia's history books, and by other times and other places. Between them, they really did have an extraordinary range of knowledge and interests. And they both read widely, all the time. They both had wonderful theatre stories, but I always knew not to go into politics, not because I thought they would necessarily disagree with me, but because they both seemed so bleakly uninterested in that whole territory.

Ralph was somehow always more suspicious than John, who had

an extraordinary kind of innocence. And although they had been friends and colleagues for almost half a century, they seemed to lead very separate daytime lives, only coming together on the stage at night, or at matinees. "When we do meet," Ralph once said to me, "it is always as other people."

What was remarkable about John, quite apart from his extraordinary intelligence, was that although he may not have been any greater as an actor than Olivier, Gielgud alone was at the centre of every development of the British theatre in the twentieth century. As an actor and a director he was just somehow always there.

"*No Man's Land* will not change or grow old or move—it remains forever icy" as Spooner says to Hirst, a line that is repeated at the end of the play and will also serve as its epitaph. As the play begins, an aging alcoholic man of letters, much prone to sudden physical collapse (Richardson), is being visited by a distinctly crumpled poet (Gielgud) whom he has encountered on Hampstead Heath, where the latter is wont to indulge in a little light voyeurism when not washing up the glasses at Jack Straw's Castle nearby. It later transpires that this is no mere chance encounter; the two men are known to each other, inextricably linked by an unseen wife whom one married and the other lived with, and their relationship is as ambiguous as that of the two sinister servants with whom the Richardson character shares his house—a house in which the conversation is apt to roam from high comedy ("Lord Lancer? One of the Bengal Lancers, is he?") to lengthy discussions of the utter impossibility of reaching Bolsover Street by any form of human transport.

What we have here are four characters in search of several answers ("Tell me about your wife—did she google?"), none of which is forthcoming; but along the way the sight and sound of Sir John and Sir Ralph in Pinter's spare, ritualistic drama was a sustained joy—the last high watermark of both their careers.

As Pinter's biographer Michael Billington has noted, "I took Hirst and Spooner to be projections of Pinter's own darkest fears. Hirst—wealthy, immured, isolated and increasingly cut off from the source of his original inspiration—seemed to me Pinter's nightmare vision of the kind of artist he might, unless he were careful, become. Spooner, the pub poetaster, haunted by memories of other men's lines—was a distant memory of the marginalised versifier Pinter might once have been . . . Like all his best plays, *No Man's Land* addresses universal issues while stemming from some deeply personal core of anxiety—Pinter's nightmares and fears become ours."

It was Antonia Fraser who pointed out that the play also stems from a very unhappy period in Pinter's personal life, when his first marriage was in terminal decline and when many of his natural political instincts were repressed; "*No Man's Land* is a very bleak play, which I only understood when I visited his house in Hanover Terrace, immaculate with terrible silence. This is not the work of someone who was going to take a banner and protest about the state of the world."

When reviews of the National Theatre production first appeared, they were ecstatic, strong enough to ensure a long West End and Broadway transfer. But in the last few rehearsals Hall had suddenly started to worry about what John was doing as Spooner: "At the moment, John is inclined to play what the audience should conclude about the character, rather than the character himself. . . . He is over-experimenting: playing it humble, playing it conceited, playing it creepy, playing it arrogant. He is searching for a simple key, whereas the truth is that Spooner is many things and changes his posture from second to second, so there is no simple key."

By opening night, however, Gielgud had solved this problem and came through so strongly in the reviews that Peter Hall felt constrained to reflect, "Richardson is being undervalued. John's performance is magnificent but there are other actors who could do it, whereas I do not think any other actor could fill Hirst with such a sense of loneliness and creativity as Ralph does."

Critics, ecstatic about the reunion of Gielgud and Richardson, had also begun to notice that they were now the best double-act since Laurel and Hardy. As Billington wrote for the *Guardian*, "Richardson's Hirst, contrasting a peppery, ramrod-backed power with chilling geriatric collapses and exits on all fours, has precisely that other-worldliness which makes this actor such a magician; and Gielgud's Spooner, based on a mixture of Auden, his brother Lewis, and the Bohemian semi-failures who run ballet book-shops off the Charing Cross Road comes as a shock; the baggy, grey pin-striped demob suit, the untidy, sandy hair, the beer belly, the sandals implying slightly odorous socks, the creased, tobacco-breathed quality of the kind of aging 1940s relic that you still meet in BBC pubs like The George, superbly sly, mellifluous and ingratiating."

As Irving Wardle wrote in *The Times,* "*No Man's Land* remains palpably the work of our best living playwright in its command of language and its power to erect a coherent structure in a twilight zone of confusion and dismay."

Final confirmation that Gielgud and Richardson had now become the most distinguished classical double-act in all theater history was confirmed by a two-page conversation in the *Observer* as transcribed by the critic John Heilpern:

Sir John Gielgud: Come on the motorbike?

Sir Ralph Richardson: Best way.

JG: The last time you took me pillion, I practically had a fit. I was a stretcher case.

RR: I have been killed several times myself. . . . Would you say we look alike, Johnny? I have several times been mistaken for you.

JG: I've been stopped twice in London for Kenneth Clark.

RR: I should be most flattered to be mistaken for him.

JG: I was so angry with myself at the Garrick the other day. I just couldn't remember the name of an actor I knew, and even now I can't think of it. Someone like Sybil Thorndike never forgets anybody.

RR: Never.

JG: She even remembers people she met in Australia.

RR: She remembers everyone.

JG: I have to look up names in *Spotlight* [the actors' casting directory]. Emlyn Williams used always to turn the pages, and whenever he saw a photograph of an actor wearing a hat, he would shout "Bald!" Emlyn could always spot that.

RR: What was that terrible production you did for Peter Brook?

JG: Oedipus?

RR: That's it. Awful.

JG: Oh, I thought it was extraordinary. I'll never regret doing it. I wasn't very good, I didn't know how to do what he wanted. But you know, there were some terrible rows between Brook and Olivier. When Olivier saw that great phallus on the stage, he thought the Old Vic would be closed down by the police. Brook wouldn't give in, though, and they were arguing in my dressing room. So I left them to fight it out between them. When I came back half an hour later, there was a huge mirror with a crack going right through it, just like *The Lady of Shalott.* I never did find out which of them did it.

RR: Here comes our photographer. It must be so difficult. Whenever I try to photograph anyone, they always look as if they've been hit over the head with a meat axe.

JG: I'd still rather be photographed than drawn. David Hockney did a drawing of me at seventy, and I thought if I really look like that, I must kill myself tomorrow. Richard Avedon once made me cry for two hours to get an unusual angle, so I thought of everyone I knew who had died, and the tears fairly flowed like mad, but he never used the shot. So that was a terrible waste of an afternoon.

From the Old Vic, *No Man's Land* moved to Wyndham's through the winter of 1975, and then back to the finally completed Lyttleton auditorium of the National Theatre on the South Bank. During this effectively year-long run, John took part in a moving farewell to the Old Vic and also found the time to direct Judi Dench and Daniel Massey in a rather disappointing West End revival of Pinero's *The Gay Lord Quex.* This, as Judi's biographer John Miller notes, was a play that Gielgud had yearned to direct for years; it had been a favorite of his mother's, and she had passed on her enthusiasm for a drawing-room drama that had not been seen in London for more than half a century. "Stupidly," said John, "I became obsessed with the idea that I must do it exactly as it was written in the 1890s. So we did it very elaborately, spent an awful lot of money, and I miscast several parts in it."

As Miller also relates, "The rehearsals had some memorable moments for Judi: 'We were rehearsing in the crypt at St James's Piccadilly one morning, when suddenly, out of the men's loo, ran a man carrying a pair of trousers, followed by another without any, and John laughed so much that he had to give us the day off, he simply couldn't go on rehearsing.'"

There was also a memorable moment at the costume parade, when Judi came on in her nightgown, only to be greeted by an anguished Gielgud voice from the stalls: "Oh, no, no, no, Judi! You look just like Richard III!" Things were not much better when Sian Phillips arrived in her long evening gown. "It's dreadful!" came the voice from the stalls. "The trouble is, Sian, when you're standing up, you are so terribly tall!"

Reviews for this hopelessly dated theatrical folly were generally terrible, and John was unable to find any real escape from the disaster, because *The Gay Lord Quex* was playing at the Albery Theatre, whose stage door backed on to that of Wyndham's, where he and Richardson were still playing *No Man's Land*. Judi Dench's last memory is of going into the Albery stage door one night with Massey, and hearing John call out, "Hello, Dan. I hear your show is coming off. No good? Oh, my God, I directed it!"

It was, therefore, with some relief that John took *No Man's Land* back to the National Theatre, and then on to Washington and New York where, late in 1976, he and Richardson scored the greatest hit of their late lives.

Gielgud and Richardson basked in the autumnal glow of a huge Broadway success; they were beyond doubt the snob hit of the season, and it was now that Kenneth Tynan wrote, for *The New Yorker*, his epic profile of Ralph Richardson, in which, of course, John inevitably costarred: "Since the two knights appeared together in *Home* seven years ago, they have been endlessly interviewed and photographed together, and are frequently mistaken for one another on the street. 'We are just like the broker's men in *Cinderella*,' said John. And for interview purposes he and Sir Ralph have evolved what amounts to a double act in which certain routines and catch phrases, including the one about the broker's men, ritually recur:

Sir Ralph: 'You're looking very well today, Johnny.'
Sir John: 'Thank you.'
Sir Ralph: 'I haven't seen much of you lately.'
Sir John: 'We only seem to meet in costume.'
Sir Ralph: 'We meet as other people.'"

As Tynan somehow fails to note, neither Pinter nor Beckett could have written that impromptu exchange better. In fact, their enduring friendship and partnership was based on an absolute understanding that they would separate their private from their public lives, only really meeting in rehearsal or performance, except on very special celebratory occasions. Richardson still took a wary view of John's now rather tranquil homosexuality, which consisted of little more than the occasional visit to gay movies, and Richardson had also been involved in a celebrated contretemps during the Peter Brook *Oedipus,* when he insisted on trying to purchase a program from one of the actors whom Brook had lashed to the pillars in the dress circle. In Richardson's view, John was rather over-eager to go with the prevailing theatrical fashions of the time, whatever time it happened to be.

While they were in New York, Gielgud noted rather sadly, "Ralph always insists on the best restaurants, whereas I seem to eat out of tins. He loves the craftsmanship of his art—he prepares his work and then exhibits it with utmost finesse, rather like Edith Evans, who would open a window to her heart and then slam it shut again, so that the audience would come back the next night to see more. My own tendency is always to show too much, too soon, whereas Ralph has acquired such control of movement, such majesty. Of course, he does have a violent side to his nature—a powerful sadistic streak, sudden outbursts of temper."

Profiling Gielgud some years earlier, Tynan had written, "His uniqueness lies in the fact that he is greater than the sum of his parts. But his style lacks heart and stomach. When Olivier enters, lions pounce into the ring and the stage becomes an arena. Gielgud, on the other hand, just appears. He does not make an entrance, and he looks like one who has an appointment with the brush of Gainsborough or Reynolds. . . . Gielgud's sheer technocratic art is transparent, and shows through his skin . . . like Irving, he is not really a tragedian, but a romantic—ductile and aloof. His inherited task is to preserve tradition, which has seldom had a more jealous custodian. Both as director and as actor he takes few risks and becomes in time predictable, as only the dedicated and single-minded can be. . . . He is still about the only English actor of any eminence who has consistently disregarded films—he believes that acting should always be an ephemeral business, passed on by word of mouth. . . . His energy is unwaning, and his hold on the reins of rhetorical acting is unchallenged in all the world. . . . In modern terms, John Gielgud is Kemble to Olivier's Kean—the aesthete as opposed to the animal. John is claret and Larry is burgundy."

Tynan later extended this comparison to make two lists: "Gielgud: Air. Poet. Mind. Spiritual. Feminine. Introvert. Jewel. Olivier: Earth. Peasant. Heart. Animal. Masculine. Extrovert. Metal."

While he was in New York, John also gave a long interview to the historian Toby Cole, about his life as an actor:

I still have extremely good eyesight, and I am very observant. From the stage, if I am not careful, I can recognise people I know, eight or ten rows back in the stalls. Even on a first night, when I am shaking with nervousness. Latecomers, people who whisper or rustle chocolates, or fall asleep, I have an eye for every one of them, and my performance suffers accordingly . . . to play the same part eight times a week for more than a year, as I have in *No Man's Land,* is a severe test for any actor. The routine is nerve-racking, and it is agonizing work trying to keep one's performance fresh, without either slackening or over-acting. I am usually guilty of the latter fault, and my tendency to exaggerate every effect becomes more and more marked as the weeks go by. . . . I have frequently envied painters, writers and critics. I have thought how happy they must be to do their work in private, at home, unkempt and unobserved, able to destroy or renew or improve their creations at will, to judge them in their unfinished state, to watch their gradual development and to admire the final achievements ranged round them on their bookshelves, or hung upon their walls. I have often wondered how these artists would face the routine of the actor, which demands not only that he shall create a fine piece of work, but that he shall repeat it with unfaltering love and care for perhaps 300 performances on end. In my envy, I have often wished that I were able to rise in the middle of the night, switch on the light, and examine some performance of mine, calmly and dispassionately, as I looked at it standing on the mantelpiece.

When *No Man's Land* eventually closed on Broadway, at the end of the 1976–1977 season, John G. returned to London to the welcome news that he had been awarded not only the Companion of Honour, one of the highest orders in the queen's gift, but also had been made a Chevalier of the French *Legion d'Honneur,* both of which he now added to honorary degrees from the universities of Oxford, London, and St. Andrews. Olivier may have beaten him to the peerage, but John now seemed to be collecting every other honor in reach.

In the absence of any stage offers, he soon made three more screen appearances: Captain Shotover in a rather unsatisfactory BBC television *Heartbreak House,* and the brief role of the preacher in Joseph Strick's arthouse movie of *A Portrait of the Artist as a Young Man;* he also turned up for BBC Open University television in the title role of Dostoyevsky's *The Grand Inquisitor.*

But then, in the summer of 1977, something much more intriguing came along. The film director Alain Resnais (who had made his name with *Last Year in Marienbad*) had decided to make his first English-speaking picture. *Providence* would have a complex, multilayered screenplay by David Mercer which, like Pinter's *No Man's Land,* was to take John into areas of acting altogether new to him. His role in the film was to be that of a roaring, drunken, foul-mouthed, randy seventy-eight-year-old novelist, determined not to go gently into any kind of night—"You won't get me, you fucking bastards."

The sight of John drinking bottle after bottle of Chablis while sticking pessaries up his backside came as something of a shock to his faithful audience, but then again, as Robert Tanitch has noted, "Gielgud seemed to relish all the scatological abuse, self-disgust and even the pain of one of his most challenging screen roles." Tom Hutchinson, for *The Sunday Telegraph*, reckoned, "This must be Gielgud's finest and most sustained film performance—an elegantly ferocious gauge against which others must be compared in the future. We have heard his rapier-swish before, but never his sledgehammer-smash—this is acting with the guts, as well as the mind."

The premise of *Providence* was that John, as the dying author, would be spending his last night on earth casting his own family as the characters in his latest novel. But a highly extravagant structure (the narrative is constantly interrupted by flashbacks and memories and nightmares) meant that the audience had a hard time working out what was real and what was merely fantasy. John said this was "by far the most exciting film I have ever made," and apart from him and Dirk Bogarde, there were only three other actors involved—Ellen Burstyn, David Warner, and Elaine Stritch.

"Here we all are together," as Dirk said one morning to John on the set, "in some extraordinary part of France. After all the time we have both spent on our various careers, we are now aging gentlemen [John was seventy-three, Dirk a mere fifty-six], both in a new script written specifically for us by David Mercer, both in a new form of an old craft. We are both going ahead, that's what's exciting. At least we are not doing a revival of *No, No, Nanette*."

When the reviews appeared, virtually all came out in favor of John, but proved much less enthusiastic for Bogarde and Resnais. The film never really came into its own, despite yet another of Gielgud's remarkable valedictories—"Just leave . . . now please . . . neither kiss nor touch . . . go with my blessing." As Anthony Lane wrote for the *Independent*, John's was "a camp and succulent portrait of decaying daydreams."

Originally, Bogarde himself had rather hoped to play the old man: "It was a brilliantly placed role, and I knew that with John Gielgud playing it, none of the rest of us would stand a chance. He'd pinch the picture. Which he did . . . shortly before we started work, Resnais suggested that I might like to give a little supper party for him in the small hotel where I was staying on location . . . Resnais really just wanted the chance to observe John closely; he talked and talked, happily aware that he was holding the table and that nobody would interrupt him. I don't know what Resnais knew before about Ellen Terry, Marie Tempest, Peggy Ashcroft, Edith Evans, Eleonora Duse or the third act of *King Lear,* but by the end of that supper he should have known all that he ever needed to know. John's fund of stories, funny and often gloriously irreverent, was limitless, and he was enjoying himself tremendously."

Later in the shooting, Bogarde had to persuade John to tape-record a birthday greeting to Resnais. As John demurred, Bogarde said desperately, "Please do this, you probably have one of the most beautiful English-speaking voices in the world." John looked up over the top of his glasses. "*The,*" he said sharply. Curiously, that was almost the beginning and the end of Bogarde's relationship with John. On the face of it, the two actors, though from very different generations and backgrounds, had a great deal in common. Both had remained closeted homosexuals throughout most of their careers; both had an aquiline, poetic quality, which made their performances even in minor screenplays unmissable. Both read and wrote far more widely than most actors and were blessed with considerable native intelligence. Both had partners (Martin Hensler and Anthony Forwood) who managed their lives with remarkable efficiency and discretion and exhibited a passion for gardening. Unlike Bogarde, John never exiled himself from the heartland of his trade; but precisely because they had so much else in common, the two men, while maintaining a warily distant respect for each other's work, never became close friends. They were perhaps just too alike.

There was, though, one great difference between them: while Bogarde, like Alec Guinness and James Mason but precious few other British actors of John's time, took filming very seriously indeed and turned down many screen roles for which he felt himself in some ways unsuited, Gielgud, like Olivier and Richardson and Redgrave, spent the last years of his long career effectively grabbing every offer that came over the phone. John's decision about whether or not to make a film depended almost entirely on the money, and whether the diary was clear that week. He made almost no real distinction between prestigious projects like *Providence* and another episode of a minor Hollywood miniseries. Filming, to him, was now a convenient way of living well, keeping in touch with old friends in the acting business, and going on location at the expense of others to see the comparatively few countries he had never yet visited. The idea, central to Bogarde's way of thinking, that cinema was somehow an art form, to be taken as seriously as theater, simply never crossed John's mind.

25. GORED BY VIDAL

(1977–1984)

Half my new cinema audience comes to see if I really am still alive; the other half think they had better catch me before I die.

*B*ack in England, after the shooting of *Providence*, John now rejoined Peter Hall's National Theatre for three farewell performances. In the first of these, he was yet again to play the title role in *Julius Caesar*, this time in a production by the film director John Schlesinger that, as Peter Hall recalled, was in trouble from the very first preview: "I don't think it's going to work. I believe we shall be slaughtered for the weaknesses in the young and inexperienced cast, for all the clarity of Schlesinger's direction." Of the first night, Hall simply added: "The audience were way ahead of the play, and that always spells death. I went backstage to find a great number of dispirited actors, all in shock." For the *Guardian*, Michael Billington merely noted of Gielgud, "a gratuitous attempt to kill off the best verse speaker on the English stage."

From that, Gielgud went on to work for Peter Hall himself in a reunion with Paul Scofield for *Volpone*, although despite a very strong supporting cast (Ben Kingsley, Paul Rogers, Elizabeth Spriggs) this too proved a disappointment, with Gielgud uneasily cast as Sir Politic Wouldbe. Both these productions were withdrawn from the National repertoire as early as could be arranged.

Luckily, however, John's third—and in fact farewell—appearance for Hall's National company, the last he would make in any classical surroundings, worked out considerably better. Opening next was Julian Mitchell's *Half-Life*, in which Gielgud played Sir Noel Cunliffe, a professor of archaeology who, discovering that his whole life has been built on a lie, determines to avenge himself by making sure that neither his university nor his so-called friends will profit in any way by his death.

As Milton Shulman for the *Evening Standard* noted, "Gielgud spits and hisses insults like a self-satisfied snake, enchanted with the sound of its own rattle. When, for a moment, his past looms up like an awful lie, his temporary loss of composure is deeply moving."

Early in 1978, John moved *Half-Life* to the West End, but somehow this was to prove a mistake; apparently, anybody who had wished to see Gielgud as the acid, old archaeology professor had done so at the National, and John, unusually, began to find himself playing to distinctly empty houses. The commercial run soon closed, and he threw himself back into the usual range of movies—good, bad, and indifferent. He played Gillenormand in an American television *Les Misérables*, though without the songs that have now made Hugo's novel such a musical triumph all around the world.

From that, John progressed to a BBC television version of *Romeo and Juliet*, for which he spoke the chorus, dressed like a doge of Venice, and another BBC classic Shakespeare, this one the Derek Jacobi *Richard II* in which he played John of Gaunt, looking, said the *Daily Telegraph*, "like a burst horse-hair sofa."

From those unexceptional but perfectly respectable appearances, Gielgud now moved on to what was quite clearly the single most embarrassing chapter of his entire film or stage career. The publisher of *Penthouse*, Bob Guccione, had developed a surprising taste for making movies. Undeterred by the fiasco of his Roman Polanski/Kenneth Tynan *Macbeth*, he now moved on to a Gore Vidal version of *Caligula*, for which John was originally offered the title role. Even he, seldom able to reject a few weeks on a rich movie, sensed trouble here, especially when he began to read a script that was clearly pornographic. He, therefore, politely had his agent reject the offer to play Emperor Tiberius, only to receive an outraged letter from Gore Vidal himself, saying how impertinent it was of John to refuse the role, and that if he only knew what Tennessee Williams and Edward Albee were saying about him behind his back, he would not be so grand. Somewhat chastened, John finally agreed to play the smaller, and at least theoretically more innocent, role of the old tutor to Tiberius, now being played by Peter O'Toole, with Malcolm McDowell in the title role.

Unfortunately, once a *Penthouse* film, always a *Penthouse* film. Although John's sequences had been shot in relative isolation, the finished film shows him in a pool full of very small boys and buxom blondes: "I played my whole scene in a bath of tepid water. It took three days to shoot, and every two hours some terrible hags dragged me out, rubbed me down, and put me back into the water again. It was all most extraordinary."

It was also a considerable tribute to John's now apparently impregnable critical standing that although the film eventually opened on a budget of $17 million to some of the worst reviews of the decade, nobody actually blamed John at all. Critics seemed to assume that in some vague way the film had been shot without his knowledge, and that his presence in the midst of these appallingly seedy, soft-porn surroundings just must have been some kind of mistake. It was now almost as though there were two Gielguds—the real one who would appear in scripts of some merit, and then a kind of virtual John, almost a hologram, who would be seen in rubbish for which he was never taken to task. Moviemakers specializing in the latter were assumed to have borrowed his image, much after the fashion of Madame Tussaud's, without ever directly involving the actor himself.

Ten years were to elapse between *Half-Life* in the West End and John's next—and last—stage appearance there or anywhere, in 1988; in these ten years, he made an astounding total of twenty-two films, not counting several television appearances. Of this collection, perhaps only six films (*The Elephant Man, Chariots of Fire, Gandhi, Arthur, The Shooting Party,* and *Plenty*) could be considered in any way notable, and in most of these he was to play relatively minor roles. Nevertheless, for a man now in his seventies and eighties, the output was prodigious, and even of the really bad movies it safely could be said that John did not make any of them actually worse, sometimes even lending moments of grace and charm and distinction to screenplays that little deserved them. All the same, this was the late-life movie career of a Redgrave or a Richardson or an Olivier; there was still no sign that he was going into the twilight, as was Alec Guinness, making only those films about which he truly cared.

After *Caligula,* his first guest-starring role was as Lord Salisbury, the prime minister, in *Murder by Decree,* in which Christopher Plummer and James Mason played Sherlock Holmes and Dr. Watson, respectively, hot on the trail of Jack the Ripper. Next came *The Human Factor,* another of those movies that started with distinction and ended in chaos. Graham Greene's novel, about an innocent man mistakenly believed to be a foreign office spy, had been adapted for the screen by Tom Stoppard, and the director Otto Preminger duly assembled a stunning cast, led by Nicol Williamson, Richard Attenborough, Derek Jacobi, Robert Morley, and John himself. Unfortunately, and this was truly a sign of the new Hollywood times, Preminger's money ran out halfway through the shooting, thereby resulting in a botched ending to the story, and lawsuits that dragged on for several years, as the actors desperately tried to collect their pay.

John was, however, to have better luck with his next movie. David Lynch, the leading avant-garde director of his generation, had decided to film the real-life story of the *Elephant Man,* a destitute vagrant in 1884 London, deformed by a rare illness, and finally turned, by a pioneering doctor, from a fairground freak to someone much-pitied and visited by fashionable society. With Anthony Hopkins as the doctor, Gielgud played a pillar of the Victorian medical establishment who is won over to the elephant man's case when he hears him reciting, by heart, one of the Psalms. John's performance, more central to the picture than was usually the case, won him another batch of enthusiastic notices and the rare friendship of Tony Hopkins, who from now on became one of his most devastatingly accurate mimics.

1979 was also, of course, the year of John's seventy-fifth birthday, an anniversary marked on a wide selection of fronts. Determined not to be thought of as in any way retired, he himself announced that he still had a

Prospero and a King Lear to play, quite possibly for Hall's National Theatre if the right casts and directors could be assembled. Sadly, they never were, but in the meantime John published revisions of two of his earliest books, *Early Stages* and a collection of essays about the great stars of his childhood. He also took part in a fascinating project for which the Radio 4 producer John Powell and the interviewer John Miller recorded more than twenty hours of Gielgud talking about every facet of his career, resulting in a memorable radio series and subsequently a book, which stands as the best hardcover documentary of his working life, though John was as ever determined to keep his private life well out of the public gaze.

This was also the time when most theater critics and historians began to consider Gielgud in a rather new light, as the grand old man of the British classical theater. As Michael Billington noted, "Gielgud has made the difficult transition from the world of Beerbohm Tree and Du Maurier to that of Harold Pinter and Peter Brook, partly because he is a restless workaholic, partly because he is totally without false pride, and partly because, for him, the theatre at its best is life raised to the pitch of ecstasy."

John himself, perhaps unaware that his working life had twenty more years to run, also began now to sum up:

Like all professions, acting has terrible drawbacks. It can be fearfully boring and fearfully unglamorous. But what is such fun about our profession is that we do get our prizes while we are still alive to enjoy them. We have the pleasure of audience reaction, we have the applause, we have the publicity, we have the tributes and the honours, many more than probably we really deserve.

I must admit that now, though, I have given up on London. All those hideous new buildings, you can't find a taxi, the buses and the underground are filthy, and even walking is painful—they don't let you cross the street, so you have to go down some smelly passageway. My life is now that of the Buckinghamshire countryside, and of course anywhere that a film is being made. For years, people only thought of me in costume parts, and then my older fans were rather disappointed when I started having to say four-letter words on stage and screen. But the truth is that they don't come to the theatre much any more, and I have found an entirely new public, which you need to strip your work of its affectations. We live in a much more realistic world now, and I hope I have managed to get rid of the romantic mannerisms of my youth—lately, three directors have been the making of me: Lindsay Anderson, Peter Brook, and Peter Hall.

Another cause for anniversary celebration was the television screening of *No Man's Land,* which worked much better than any of John's other attempts to transfer stage hits to the small screen. And it wasn't as though he was totally detached even now from the realities of Britain in the late 1970s. He, Olivier, and Richardson all campaigned for Peter Hall in his struggles against the backstage unions that were at this time frequently closing down the National Theatre in a series of sudden stoppages. John was now and always a fervent petition signatory, ranging over a wide area—he signed everything, from demands that the BBC World Service be allowed to retain autonomy, to the campaign for preserving wild minks from being turned into fur coats. He also crusaded for the right of Russian artists to defect from the totalitarian USSR and joined yet another campaign, this one rather more successful than most, to prevent the threatened demolition of the Old Vic.

For those few who wondered, at this golden time in his career, why he still picked up every unconsidered trifle that came his way on screen, the answer was very simple, albeit one which he never gave in public. First, the current rates of taxation under a socialist government were so prohibitive that he was actually keeping very little of the money he made; second, the close community of actors on a film set still provided a welcome and gossipy change from the seclusion of life with Martin at Wotton Underwood, which tended to seem desirable when he was working elsewhere, but to pall quite rapidly when he actually got home. John also now began to contribute an amazing number of book reviews and nostalgic articles to publications at home and abroad. He had always been a writer and a historian, but now the fact that almost he alone had total recall of the West End during and just after World War I made him much in demand for all kinds of historical, scholarly, and archival projects. John had suddenly become, faintly to his own surprise, the living history of the British theater in this century.

But despite all this late-life acclaim, John G. amazingly had still not resolved his financial headaches:

> After thirty years living in Westminster, I have quite taken to life in the country, but it is costing me a fortune. I live in quite an old house, and the other day one of the walls just fell down, but they said it was an Act of God, and so I couldn't claim any insurance. I would rather like to keep a flat in London for when I am working there, but I simply can't afford two addresses. I have never really had such financial difficulties. The more you earn nowadays, the more they tax you, and my accountant has told me I will never be solvent again until the day I die.
>
> Sometimes I think of moving to America because you really can live better there, and the money is wonderful. I have just been over to introduce 22 episodes of *The Pallisers* on American television and to do some documentary voice-overs, and they really pay you a very handsome sum. But I love England, and I could never really live anywhere else, although I am having to sell some family treasures to make ends meet. The expense of a chauffeur is the most awful drain, but I was such a menace on the roads that I gave up driving at the age of twenty. I find I depend more and more on the kindness of strangers, and usually they come from wealthy American television companies. It really worries me that I may be taken ill or lose my memory. What on earth would I live on? Savings are worth so much less now, and food has gone up five-fold, even though I am paid better now than I ever dreamt I would be.

And so saying, John went back into make-up, to get his face covered in warts for an unsatisfactory Tony Richardson film of *Joseph Andrews*—"Just my luck," said John later, "to have Tony offer me that one and not *Tom Jones.*"

"I am terrified," John told another interviewer at this time, "of becoming ridiculous in my old age. What I've always had is an athletic quality of voice and attitude, but I have only just begun to learn how to control it. One of the great things about growing old is that you suddenly dare to stand on stage and do nothing, and people start to listen and to understand."

One of John's more mournful duties now was to start writing lengthy obituaries for stars like Edith Evans and Sybil Thorndike, with whom virtually his entire stage career had been spent. His own strength of survival continued to stand him in good stead; although he had seemed in so many ways to be the leanest and sometimes weakest of the great Olivier-Richardson-Redgrave generation, he was in fact to outlive all of them, many by almost twenty years.

John also began ceaselessly to reflect on the changing times: "I've never forgotten my grandmother telling me when I started out as an actor—'Be on good terms with your colleagues, but be intimate with none of them'—and I suppose I have rather kept to her advice, although I have come to love walking around a film set chatting to everyone. When I started, stars never even spoke to minor players, but all that has changed, and I think acting is a lot more fun today. I have finally learnt not to be frightened of the camera, and I really can relax on a film and start to enjoy it, especially as time goes on. Nowadays the whole thing does not really depend on me. I am just hired to lend a bit of elderly grandeur."

His private life was still just that, though there was an unwelcome burst of sudden publicity when John's cousin, the actress Hazel Terry, took her own life and John had to explain to the coroner's court about her depression and alcoholism. Although he did now begin to take an interest in his niece Maina, who, in her career as a ballet dancer and choreographer, was the only one of his relatives to continue the Gielgud artistic line, he and Martin always took care to distance themselves from the rest of an extended family, as if terrified that some child or grandchild of Lewis or Val would invade the privacy of Wotton Underwood. The relatives, however distant, were still kept on the Christmas card list, but closer communication was never sought and sometimes actively discouraged by Martin, who took the view that when John was home between movies he should only be disturbed by a very small group of approved friends.

John's next three films were again somewhat patchy, although one by the great Polish director Andrzej Wajda (*The Conductor*) did achieve a brief art-house life. John's diary of this filming noted: "The Poles are infinitely courteous and considerate, and work with a dedicated enthusiasm. But the technical problems are considerable; I speak no Polish, they speak no English, there are no stand-ins, and because film stock is terribly expensive we only ever get to do a scene once. Wajda is a dynamic personality, utterly concentrated and direct, though once or twice when he is very tired I find him curled up on the floor, where he sleeps soundly between scenes. I have to appear to listen intelligently to Polish speeches spoken by the other actors and devise a way to warn them when it is my turn to speak."

It was on the location for *The Conductor* that John formed the last crucial partnership of his life. Mavis Walker had started her career as an actress and first worked with John as the understudy to Peggy Ashcroft during the London run of *The Chalk Garden* back in 1956. From there, she went on to become a director at RADA and to accompany Michael Redgrave on his American tour of *The Hollow Crown*. Mavis was thus an immediate and logical casting choice when John decided that, with more and more of his life now being taken up by foreign location shooting and Martin unwilling to leave Wotton Underwood empty, the time had come to hire a secretary and traveling companion.

Mavis herself explained the precise division of labor:

I was to take care of John while abroad, everything from unwrapping his plastic lunches on aeroplanes to making sure that his bedroom was roughly the right temperature at night. Martin meanwhile stays at home in Buckinghamshire where he cooks, shops, gardens and deals with John's fan mail and Christmas cards. He also redesigns, repairs and repaints bargains he picks up in salerooms, feeds the peacocks and cockatoos, walks the dog and talks to the tortoise. He is never seen eating in public, and apart from John of course, I think he far prefers animals to people. Wherever we go in the world from now on, he rings John every night to keep him in touch with the real world—floods, earthquakes, obituary notices and other interesting topics; John greatly looks forward to this.

In fact, as I discovered in Poland, in spite of his elegant home life, John is wonderfully adaptable, and perfectly happy with a small hotel bedroom and bath. When he is not working he sleeps a lot, reads other scripts and tries to work out how to communicate with Wajda. While we were in Warsaw the great event was the visit of Pope John Paul. We saw him on television kissing the ground of his native land, and John managed to get a window overlooking the motorcade: "Funny," he said, "His Holiness looks just like Harry Andrews!"

One night we went to see a production of *The Seagull* in Polish, and at the end John with extraordinary serenity listened while all the cast made incomprehensible speeches. The only time in filming that he ever seems unhappy is when they put him on a horse, whereupon he always says nervously, "When does it start?"

One night we were taken to a terribly depressed area of the city, where nothing happened for hours until John, boredom getting the better of him at last, suddenly rose to his feet, and in the stentorian tones of his uncle Fred Terry called out, "I am Sir Percy Blakeney. Lady Blakeney is my wife. And I am the Scarlet Pimpernel!" The Poles took all this in their polite but uncomprehending stride.

When we finally got the plane back to Heathrow, there were two Poles sitting across the gangway. "Gielgud?" said one. "Yes," replied John. Then the other Pole pointed at me. "And wife?" he asked. "No, no!" replied John. "Only on film!" This seemed to confuse them so much that we spent the rest of the flight in total silence. When we landed, John's faithful driver Peter met us with a parcel "from Mr Martin." It consisted of two large smoked salmon sandwiches, a reward for our travails.

The other two films he was making now, *Lion of the Desert* and *Sphinx*, were both deeply embarrassing. For *Sphinx*, John was cast as a Cairo black-market antiques dealer, who mercifully gets murdered early on, leaving only Margaret Hinxman in the *Daily Mail* to note that he looked "like an Egyptian Old Mother Riley."

On the Cairo location for *Sphinx,* talking to the *Evening Standard*'s arts editor Michael Owen, John gave a brisk insight into the kind of breathless life he was now leading as a film actor:

> I worked here in Cairo once before, you know, in 1945 when I played my very last Hamlet. It was a riot; Horatio had an epileptic fit halfway through the last matinee, and fell into my arms. We had to carry on with the understudy. He was Egyptian of course, but nobody seemed to notice.
>
> I keep myself busy in old age doing nice, small parts. I've been to three countries and now I'm off to do one scene with George C. Scott in a Marlon Brando film, though I don't think I ever get to meet him. I've also been to Poland for Wajda, to play a conductor, and they had to give me a crash course in how to conduct Beethoven's Fifth, which was all very strange as nobody but me seemed to speak any English. Next I go back home to do *Brideshead Revisited,* and then of course *The Elephant Man,* and I got my little part in *The Human Factor* all done in one day, which was lovely, though I'm still trying to get the money. It is so nice now being asked to do so many little things, only I have real difficulty in remembering the names of all the directors, but they are terribly patient with me and I find I can turn it on very quickly. I just try to be agreeable and never get temperamental or cross.
>
> Everybody keeps asking me about another *King Lear,* but Peter Hall can never decide if it should be in the Olivier or the Cottesloe theatre, and whether he or John Dexter or Peter Gill should direct, so I think I'm going to cancel the whole thing before people think I am just getting ga-ga or too nervous to do it at my advanced age.
>
> Unlike poor Larry and Michael Redgrave, who have had to fight the most terrible illnesses in their old age, I have really been very lucky with my health, but there's not a lot I really want to do. The

trouble with the National and the Royal Shakespeare nowadays is that they are so huge, and they keep doing far too many plays. People like Alan Howard and Judi Dench must be absolutely worn out, poor things.

Filming, for me, has come a surprising extension of my stage career. A new film is like a visit to another planet, with unknown territory to explore. It's also like being on tour, seeing new towns and lands and meeting a variety of people . . . working with young directors is always instructive. It gives one a glimpse of tomorrow.

When I'm not working, I'm amazed to find how little I miss the bright lights. You make a new life for yourself when you're old. I sleep in the afternoon, I play my records, do my crosswords, watch television for an hour after dinner and then go to bed early with a really trashy American novel. I find Harold Robbins is a great read, as is Judith Krantz, and I always wonder how many pages their publishers demand between sex scenes. Somehow I have never managed Barbara Cartland; she is altogether too pure, whereas I love all the filthy details.

For *Lion of the Desert*, he was cast as the treacherous Sheikh Gariani, a performance that John presumably gave in the comforting knowledge that he couldn't have been any worse than Olivier had been as the Mahdi in *Khartoum*.

This film finished up with a week in Rome, at a time when Alec Guinness was also working there. "Hello, Alec!" said John, meeting him in the street. "What are you doing here?" "Lying in state," replied Alec. "Ah," said John, "I've done that twice this year, usually as the Pope. How long have you been lying in state? Isn't this getting all rather sinister?"

To complete this mediocre run, John also turned up in two Agatha Christie whodunits for LWT: one was *The Mystery of Seven Dials* and the other was *Why Didn't They Ask Evans?* He also—reflecting his, or at any rate Martin's, obsession with flower beds—agreed to host and narrate a seven-part Thames Television series called *The English Garden*, and to make another *Tales from the Unexpected,* this one based on a Roald Dahl story about a crooked antique dealer, masquerading as a clergyman.

Mercifully, 1981 was to find him in two crucial new movies, one of which was to prove the key to his late-life fortune. In the first of these he played the provost of Trinity College Cambridge in Hugh Hudson's *Chariots of Fire,* the film about the 1924 Olympic running champions Harold Abrahams and Eric Liddell. This was the film that, more than any other, put the British cinema back on the Hollywood map; it won Oscars for best picture, score, costume design, and the scripting of Colin Welland, and in it, John and his old *Home* director Lindsay Anderson were cast as the two reactionary masters of Cambridge colleges, both racially and socially bigoted, who do their best to hinder Abrahams right down to the winning stretch.

The other film was to involve John for his longest Hollywood stay since the making of *Julius Caesar,* almost thirty years earlier, and this again was to be an unexpected but total triumph.

Dudley Moore, the actor and pianist whom John had solemnly introduced to America as Stanley Moon, was now at the height of his Hollywood fame and about to embark on *Arthur,* the story of a playboy millionaire who refuses to grow up, despite the attempts of his butler, a Jeeves figure, but one with a much more vicious and scatological vocabulary. This was where John won his only Oscar, not least for the scene where Arthur announces that he is going to take a bath and John replies, "I'll alert the media," followed by, "And I suppose you want me to wash your dick for you, you little shit!"

But as so often where John and movies were concerned, he had totally failed to see the potential of this one, and indeed twice turned down the role because of its foul language. Eventually, however, he was persuaded by his agent, Laurie Evans, that this could well be something more than just another Jeeves, and for Dudley the experience was to prove one of the happiest of his California career: "I had seen John in Alan's *Forty Years On,* and I thought his aptitude for comedy was delicious. . . . He brought to comic situations the same kind of passion that he had for the classics, and I loved his no-nonsense approach during the filming. Neither of us believed in too much discussion, so we just did it, and he brought a sense of humanity to the part of Hobson which, coupled with his wonderful sense of the acerbic and the priggish in that character, made for a marvellously rounded performance. Above all, I love the scene when I am looking after him in hospital and he says, 'Arthur, you're a good son.' That moment expresses all the longings we all have for approval from a gentle father . . . the poetry in John always sustains him and nurtures his spirit . . . we all need to find what John has."

Liza Minnelli, who had also turned the film down twice, came (like Moore) to realize the joy of having John on the set: "He hated being called Sir John, so I called him Uncle Johnny, and he seemed to like that, but he never quite knew just how funny he was; some of his lines were very raunchy, and to hear them spoken in his brilliant accent was magic. We used to improvise a lot, throwing in jokes and gags, and John was never at a loss. He just caught everything we threw at him."

For once, John was actually sorry when the filming came to an end. "Both Dudley and Liza were very sweet to me, and enormously professional and proficient. It was really their film, but they must have seen what a good part I had, and yet they made me feel totally at ease. I am only sorry that I didn't see more of them off the set, but we were all working very hard and somehow there didn't seem time for anything else." The following year he won the Oscar for his role, and the statuette was to remain on his bathroom shelf for the rest of his life. It was not exactly lonely—*Arthur*, John's most honored film performance ever, also won him a Golden Globe and awards from both the New York and the Los Angeles Film Critics' Circle(s).

Despite the awards, however, he was still not getting much more than $100,000, for a movie that paid Moore and Minnelli millions. But just as he was winding up his role, he got an offer that really would make him, for the first time, very rich indeed. He was invited to repeat his new butler role in a series of television commercials for Paul Masson California wines, and over the next few months, entirely because of these, he was finally able to pay off all the costs of Wotton Underwood, and put money in the bank. Ironically, the previous star of these commercials had been John's old nemesis, Orson Welles, now considered rather too chubby to sell a light Californian wine. "I'm very fond of Orson," said John at this time, "and I don't like doing him out of a job." All the same, he did so with remarkable alacrity.

Back home in England, the best was yet to come. Charles Sturridge now approached him with the offer of the role of Edward Ryder in the Granada Television series, *Brideshead Revisited*. In fact, it had been Olivier whom Sturridge first approached with the offer of either this role, or that of the old, dying Lord Marchmain. Olivier, never one to refuse a good death scene, plumped for Marchmain, only later to realize that the senior, cranky, irritable Ryder was far and away the better part. In this whole series, the scenes between Jeremy Irons as Charles and John as his craggy, unrelenting, petulant, malicious father are as good as it gets. As Peter Ackroyd wrote in *The Times*, "Gielgud plays Mr. Ryder as if he has been doing it all his life, and perhaps he has—aloof and yet alert, calculating but dismissive, he seems to have sprung onto the screen from the pages of Evelyn Waugh without pausing to alter that wry, malevolent expression."

In *Brideshead*, as in *Chariots of Fire*, John had now somehow managed to plug himself into the heart of the whole new "heritage" industry of Britain in the early 1980s. Although he was never actually to appear in one of the Merchant-Ivory carpets-and-curtains extravaganzas, they were to some extent made possible by the success of *Brideshead* and *Chariots of Fire*, which opened up for cinema and television audiences alike a whole new world of nostalgia and snobbery with violence.

But sadly, that was also where, for John, it almost came to an end. Of the thirty more movies he still had to make, only *The Shooting Party* and *Plenty* and *Prospero's Books* could really be considered distinguished additions to his long career, though he was also able to make very fleeting appearances in three other hits—*Gandhi*, *Elizabeth*, and *Shine*. But these were the exceptions to the rule under which John still lived his film career, that rule being to accept everything on offer, so long as the money and the dates were roughly suitable.

In this mood he went straight from *Arthur* to play Albert Speer, Sr., the father of Hitler's architect, in a Third Reich movie and followed that with a deeply embarrassing black comedy called *Scandalous,* which required him to dress as a Hell's Angel, complete with ear studs and studded leather jacket. As if hoping to be forgiven, he then hastened on to Rome to play another pope, this one Pius XII, who failed so conspicuously to speak out against the wartime persecution of the Jews. By now, there was virtually nothing that he would not do on camera, and to prove it he went into a Michael Winner remake of *The Wicked Lady,* with Faye Dunaway now in the role made infamous by Margaret Lockwood forty years earlier. Asked to explain what on earth he thought he had been doing in this film, John merely noted that it reminded him of the kind of silent-movie rubbish that he had been taken to see as a child.

After that came an extraordinary reunion. For the first and last time, Gielgud, Olivier, and Richardson all came together on screen—as three ministers at the court of the mad Ludwig II, for Tony Palmer's epic (ten-hour) television series about the life of *Wagner,* shot on location in Vienna. It was, however, not an entirely happy experience. Richard Burton—playing Wagner—was still drinking heavily, Olivier was in the midst of a television *King Lear,* which John had always wanted to do himself, and Richardson as usual appeared to be dotty.

The three surviving knights had, of course, all been in Olivier's *Richard III* thirty years earlier, but not in the same scene, and the only saving grace now was to watch them discreetly and sometimes not so discreetly trying to upstage each other. The rivalry continued offscreen as well; each of them decided to give a celebration Viennese dinner for the other two, plus Burton. Richardson's party was ruined by waiters, John's by an ugly scene with the chef, and Olivier gave his guests the wrong arrival time and spent an hour or two sitting at an otherwise totally empty table. On the set, Burton found Olivier "a grotesque exaggeration of an actor—all technique and no emotion," and Richardson had to have his lines written out on idiot boards. John, as usual, just did the work and left as soon as possible, once his scene was safely in the can.

This was to be yet another of those end-of-an-era moments. Although Richardson now only had a few more months to live, John kept in close touch. His relationship with Olivier, however, had grown distinctly chilly.

They had really only been kept together in private by John's devotion to Vivien Leigh, and so, following her divorce and death, they had once again gone their separate ways, with John later never quite able to forgive Olivier for publishing in his own memoirs so much of the truth (at least as he saw it) about her.

Professionally, in film and television, John simply went on doing what he had always done best—in Hazlitt's definition of a great actor, "showing us all that we are, all that we wish to be, and all that we dread to be."

John's sheer survival now seemed to give him an extraordinary kind of late-life courage. When he wasn't working, he would stay quietly in the country, often writing learned theater articles for specialist magazines, reviewing biographies for the Sunday papers (among actors, only Dirk Bogarde now seemed to do even more of this), and re-editing yet another series of reprints of his early autobiographies and collections of theatrical essays. At the other end of the spectrum, he was perfectly prepared to turn up as the Goose King in a one-night charity pantomime also starring Elton John and, more sadly, to read the lesson at countless memorial services for actors and actresses who had often led far briefer lives than John himself.

Something better did now come along; the minor role of an eccentric animal-rights campaigner sharing one rather good scene with James Mason in the film version of Isabel Colegate's *The Shooting Party*. This, like *Brideshead Revisited* and *Chariots of Fire,* was another of the heritage movies at which John now excelled. As the title suggests, it told the story of an aristocratic house party on the very verge of World War I, and in his last film Mason gave one of his very best performances, reunited for the only time since *Julius Caesar* with Gielgud himself. In fact, this might have been a still more intriguing reunion; Paul Scofield was to have played the Mason role, and only lost it by being severely injured in a carriage accident on the first day of shooting, whereupon he had to be replaced by James. But in this account of an aristocratic, Edwardian prewar society on the verge of being as surely blasted away as the birds they have gathered to shoot, John was cast for once totally against type as an impoverished outsider, yet again reminding audiences of his newfound versatility on camera.

As John approached his eightieth birthday in April 1984, his workload continued to be prodigious. When he wasn't actually filming, he would spend long hours still reading the Bible for Yorkshire Television, or taking part in a marathon sixteen-part series called *Six Centuries of Verse,* in which he read everything from Chaucer to Ted Hughes, sharing the readings with his old friend Peggy Ashcroft. Asked why it had now been five years since he last worked onstage, John replied, "I suppose I have failed to find the right part. I'm very lucky in that, at eighty, I have hardly ever had a day of illness in my life, but I am still not sure that I want to go back to touring, or playing eight shows a week."

His actual eightieth was celebrated at a press conference on the stage of his beloved Old Vic, where he had first appeared at the age of eighteen. The celebration ended with actor Christopher Reeve producing a birthday cake, but John was always deeply uneasy about parties like this. Quite simply, he believed that if he went around advertising his age, he would lose work. And since, apart from Martin, work was really all he had to live for, he remained determined to do nothing that could in any way endanger his employability. It was also in this mood, and at this time, that he (like Emlyn Williams and Alec Guinness) wrote the will that came as such a surprise to many on his death in 2000, ordaining a totally private funeral and that there should be no memorial service of any kind. They had perhaps attended all too many of these already and feared for the casting and audience make-up of a production over which they would, inevitably, have no control at all.

There was also another birthday book, this one called *The Ages of Gielgud,* in which Derek Granger attempted, as had Tynan so many years earlier, to work out what distinguished the great actor: "If Olivier is fire, thunder, animal magnetism and danger, and Richardson is bemused wonder, slyness and compassion, then John is poetic sensibility, philosophical introspection, detachment, reason, quicksilver wit and everything that is expressive of an intense inner life."

John himself had now taken very occasionally to commenting on Olivier. He never said in public how sad he felt that Olivier's intense, neurotic jealousy had always made him unable to be his friend, or how he had on several occasions done his best to keep John well away from whatever theater or movie Olivier was currently organizing. But John did allow himself to note, "Larry seems to spend ages preparing for parts, doing gymnastics and things. I fear I am too lazy for all that. I just turn up on the set nowadays, and hope that inspiration will strike."

In the old days, John had often joked that when his friends tired of his intense round-the-clock theatricality, they would simply stick a crown on his head and send him onstage. Now, even that option seemed closed to him. Awards were still coming his way from all over the world, and *Time* magazine jokingly described him as the hottest young actor around, one without whom it was all but impossible to make an English film. Several of his surviving colleagues and critics contributed essays to Ronald Harwood's birthday celebration volume, though John himself remained oddly uneasy:

I fear I no longer really enjoy my birthdays; in fact I no longer like public occasions of any kind. They tend to remind me how quickly time is passing, and regular events like Ascot or the Trooping of the Colour all seem to come around again much too fast. Also, I worry more and more about illness, and the death of so many of my friends. In my early days I used to have great ambitions, but I think I am much less impatient, and more philosophical now.

Away from the theatre, I have always been a very timid, shy, cowardly man, and I was only ever able to show my emotions through acting. I still find that true, but although I sometimes miss the rehearsals and the planning of productions nowadays, if I were to come back to the theatre I would also have to move back to London, and I really don't want that. . . .

I am really in two minds about doing all the cameo roles I now get offered. Financially, they have been a godsend, because when my accountant died last year, I suddenly found I owed seventy thousand pounds in back tax, and I could never have paid that off, had it not been for the films and the Californian wine commercials. On the other hand, I've only really been proud of two things I've done in the last ten years or so—the Alain Resnais *Providence,* and the television of *Brideshead*. I rather like being paid to go and perform on wonderful locations all over the world, and it means I never have to pay for a holiday, but I think there is a danger that if one keeps turning up in everything, the audience will get tired of me. I seem to have an enormous range of acquaintances, but maybe only a dozen real friends. I shun parties, gatherings, public dinners—all the stuff I used to enjoy so much. I can't drive a car. I can't shoot, or fish, or play cards. I have no inclination to go riding. I am not remotely capable of doing anything really, except acting, and I rather thank God I never had a family, as I don't think I would be very good, even with grandchildren.

Perhaps the most surprising of the essays was one by the drama critic Harold Hobson who, amazingly unaware, it would seem, of John's homosexuality, wrote, "I remember on one occasion asking him if he had ever thought of marriage . . . he said no, because he could not bear taking the responsibility for someone else's life, or of children. . . . In all the sixty years that I have known Gielgud, I have never seen him otherwise than poised and happy, buoyed up by his irrepressible enthusiasm . . . and yet I have always felt that there is something in him which life has not satisfied, and for which he is still constantly searching. Of all the people I have known in the theatre, he is the man who goes about most constantly questioning. He gives me the impression of someone who, deep down in himself, knows that there are fundamental things which he does not comprehend, and who is determined to find them out . . . Gielgud has a capacity to suggest ice which even at its thickest yearns for the sun."

Invited, around this time, to a local dinner party, he was amazed to find John Mortimer and his second wife Penny bringing their newborn baby with them. Peering nervously into the carry-cot, John inquired, "Why on earth would you bring it with you? Are you afraid of burglars at home?"

When he wasn't actually working, or following Martin around the garden with a wheelbarrow, John found himself becoming passionately attached to such American television series as *Dynasty* and *Dallas*. Ever since his earliest silent-film-going days he had acquired a devotion to serials, one which only the small screen could now satisfy. When he did come to London, it was only for the occasional meeting with his agent, or lunch at the Garrick. "I walk down Shaftesbury Avenue, so close to where I spent most of my early life, and find I can no longer recognise any of the names in lights."

Although *Arthur* had brought John to a whole new and younger audience around the world, his movie career could still be subject to strange humiliations. He was, for instance, at this time paid very well by Woody Allen to record the commentary for *Zelig*, only to be cut out later because the director had found his voice "altogether too grand." But there were also moments of such rare delight as a reunion after more than forty years with the veteran Lillian Gish, who brought, for his birthday, a pocket watch that had once belonged to D. W. Griffith. It was still in working order, and John was to carry it for many more years.

His affection for radio drama, which dated back to his relationship with his brother Val, who had only recently died, meant that he continued to be a familiar figure around the corridors of Broadcasting House, where he had by now recorded virtually all the major plays in the Shakespeare canon, but was also perfectly happy to turn up in such brand new work as (in 1984) Rhys Adrian's wonderfully aptly titled *Passing Time*.

He also continued to write articles and essays about his now all-too-rapidly vanishing generation: "How sadly I now miss Ralph's cheerful voice on the telephone, telling me of a new book he had just finished reading (a copy would arrive by the next post), and his patience with my chattering tongue—I have lost a most dear friend, and that loss is only equalled by the loss of one of the greatest men of the English theatre." Apart from Peggy Ashcroft, there were really only two actors now who could be said to share Gielgud's greatness and many of his more reclusive characteristics, but precisely because both Alec Guinness and Paul Scofield shared John's distaste for any kind of social life, they too were now somewhat distanced by geography and inclination from John's daily life.

His eightieth birthday had prompted the *Evening Standard* to give him a Life Achievement Award for sixty years in the theater—only Olivier, Ashcroft, and Richardson had ever been so honored.

A few weeks later, John went back to work as a Texan missionary in

Invitation to a Wedding, all the while campaigning for a Theatre Museum in Covent Garden, and preparing for his next important role as Major Sir Louis Cavagnari in M. M. Kaye's *The Far Pavilions*. This was a six-hour television miniseries, in which John was seen in shirtsleeves with a pistol defending the British Mission at Kabul against the Afghan rebels.

Occasionally now, as much out of boredom as anything else, John would invite the kind of journalist who could be trusted not to rake up his past, or make any mention of his life with Martin, to Wotton Underwood. One wrote in open-mouthed amazement of "a vast drawing-room which might have been part of a palace, with its blue silk sofa, priceless vases and chandeliers, and the floor hand-painted with an intricate gold-feather design . . . three gardeners are required to toil outside on half-completed gazebos, flower-beds and patios." Waving at the thirty-foot-high ceiling and the ornate carved gilt mouldings, John said, "There's a certain kind of cosiness here, don't you think?" apparently wonderfully oblivious to the way that a bronze bust of himself, and candelabras in the downstairs lavatory, might strike less theatrical mortals.

He also, at this time, gave a long and thoughtful interview to Michiko Kakutani of *The New York Times*.

I have just begun to realise how very hermetic my life has been. What first attracted me to a life in the theatre were the gilt boxes and big curtains of the old London playhouses, their sentimental melodramas with noble heroes and evil villains, and the old-time stars with their fur coats and their grand gestures; but now I find there is not much in the West End that I want to see anymore, so I stay in the country, keeping up with all the new actors and actresses by watching television, which spares me the embarrassment of having to go backstage and tell them what I thought of the play. The only thing I'm ashamed of is that the whole drama of life has totally passed me by. It wasn't until quite lately, when I started watching television, that I suddenly became aware of all the troubles and horrors of the world. I honestly had never noticed them before. . . . I'm very helpless as a person. I've never understood politics, and I was never any good at games or sports. . . . I love to have everything done for me, except of course in the theatre, where I do everything myself . . . except for reading and doing puzzles and going to art galleries, I have never had any hobbies at all. . . . I still have a sort of dream of playing King Lear again, but now that Larry has done it on television, I think perhaps I won't. Acting is half shame and half glory. The shame of exhibiting yourself, the glory of forgetting yourself, but there is something about being eighty that seems to appeal to the public. Survival fascinates them—half the audience is amazed that I have lasted so long, and the other half think I am some sort of sacred monster and that they had better catch a final look at me before, as Noël once said, my death places that somewhat macabre pleasure beyond their reach.

And there was yet another birthday honor still to come, this one perhaps the least likely of all: His recording of *The Ages of Man* won him the Grammy for best spoken-word disc of the year, the first non-American ever to receive this award.

26. The Best of Friends

(1984–1994)

The Angel of Death seems quite to have passed me by.

*J*ohn continued making films almost as if they were going out of fash-ion. A minor role in *Gandhi* for Richard Attenborough was followed by a television appearance as Lord Durrisdeer in Robert Louis Stevenson's *The Master of Ballantrae*, this one provoking Daniel Farson in the *Daily Mail* to comment, "If Gielgud is going to prostitute his talent by accepting such ab-surd parts as this one, he really should not give the impression that he is slumming in a smelly neighbourhood, or has just swallowed the juice of eleven lemons." Fortunately, there was better to come.

Early in the following year, he turned up in the film of David Hare's *Plenty* as the old-school diplomat who resigns at the time of Suez, putting honor before patriotism, a performance that drew a rave from Pauline Kael in *The New Yorker:* "Gielgud can make you laugh by an almost imper-ceptible straightening of his hand or neck; there was an audibly happy stir from the audience each time he appeared, and when he makes an exit speech, you pity the poor actors who are left behind, because he invariably takes all the energy of the scene out the door with him."

After *Plenty,* came *Romance on the Orient Express,* an American television drama starring Cheryl Ladd, in which John played an aging executive and, also for television, a nostalgic appearance as the patriarch of an eccentric Anglo-Irish family living in a derelict house in County Wicklow. John's reason for doing this latter film was simply that it derived from a novel, *Time after Time*, by his beloved Molly Keane, now enjoying an autumnal kind of fame. The filming, for BBC 2, brought back charmed memories of a world that John and Molly Keane had once shared, when indeed he had become godfather to her daughter Sally.

"All of us who were brought up in the Edwardian era can't help but regret the passing of the big house. We were all at ease with our circumstances there, servant and master. We were fearfully arrogant, but I do miss that mixture of privacy and ostentation. I miss the extravagance of those times: the black-tie dressing in the evenings, and the placement at dinner."

From Ireland, John and the faithful Mavis Walker went straight to Paris, where John had now located some useful European employers who specialized in what he memorably called "potted classics." The first of these had been *The Hunchback of Notre Dame*, and now came *Camille* in which John once again had just a couple of scenes as the Duc de Charles, protector of Marguerite Gauthier as played by the young Greta Scacchi. As so often, the fun here was entirely the chance for John to catch up with such old friends as Denholm Elliot, Billie Whitelaw, and Rachel Kempson.

Next came an appearance as the writer John Middleton Murry, in a film about his life with Katherine Mansfield (*Leave All Fair*), and then, for BBC schools television, a classical double, playing Tiresias in Sophocles' *Antigone* and *Oedipus the King*.

John also found the time now to round up three surviving members of the *Hamlet* company, which forty-six years earlier had closed the Lyceum theatre. He, Harry Andrews, Andrew Cruickshank, and Marius Goring wrote to the *Times*:

"We members of that *Hamlet* company bade a sad farewell to the Lyceum; however the threatened demolition and translation into a traffic roundabout were mercifully averted by the outbreak of war. But today, the same owner, now the GLC, is deliberating whether to perpetuate the 200-

year-old Lyceum's temporary post-war service as a ballroom, or rather to encourage its restoration to full theatrical use. . . . We now welcome another generation's rediscovery of this great theatre, and we echo the last words spoken from that stage in 1939: 'Long live the Lyceum! Long live Henry Irving! Long live Ellen Terry!' A theatre with such resonance of the past and such promise for the future cannot be allowed to perish."

And, amazingly, it wasn't; unlike so many other campaigns for doomed theatres, such as Vivien Leigh's memorably manic crusade for the St. James's, this one actually worked, and after another few years of uncertainty the Lyceum was handsomely refurbished and restored to become the home for such major musicals as a revival of *Jesus Christ Superstar* and *The Lion King*.

John also now took on a long and punishing role in *War and Remembrance*, an epic twelve-hour American television series for which he played a victim of the Nazis in concentration-camp sequences that were truly horrific, both to shoot and to watch. This entire series was, in fact, a sequel to *The Winds of War*, also by Herman Wouk. In that, Gielgud's character had first been played by John Houseman, who had produced him in *Julius Caesar*. "The sequel," Houseman said, "takes place all over Europe, in gas chambers and crematoria. I think Gielgud's figure will be more convincing in a state of emaciation than mine could ever be."

As Mavis Walker recalled, *War and Remembrance* was incredibly punishing for Gielgud. One week they filmed in three different countries, and although John felt enormous sympathy for the character, he was keen not to make it sentimental. "We finished up in Yugoslavia where John had to be filmed being thrown naked onto a pit of dead bodies. He never admitted to being tired, although he did once say how awkward it would be if he were to die in real life. The six-month shooting schedule was really punishing; long tramps through the snow, or through the blazing heat, according to the season. Standing about in the rain, real and artificial, waiting to board the death trains to Auschwitz. An interminable walk at night to the gas chamber. Sitting there stark naked, and enduring the overheated atmosphere and the smell of humanity. Finally, lying on a stretcher and pretending to be put into a red hot burning furnace. At the end of it all, I told John how terribly moving I had found it. 'Yes,' he said. 'And what's more, I even managed to finish the crossword.'

"John's attitude to these tragic scenes is always professional. As he says, 'I try not to be too aware of the horror of it all. I don't allow the setting to interfere any more than in the theatre I ever allow the scenery to overwhelm me. I suppose I am slightly dismayed to be making money out of the sort of horrors that people suffered—still, it's all a part of acting.'"

During the shooting in Cracow several weeks later, John was able to introduce Herman Wouk to some young and distant cousins whom he had managed to track down—almost the only occasion in his long life when John was to have any contact at all with his father's side of the family.

With some relief, through the end of 1985 and well into 1986, he then took on three infinitely easier roles: as the headmaster of the language school in a television version of Simon Gray's *Quartermaine's Terms* (a role he had rejected onstage); also for television, he turned up in a ludicrous updating of Oscar Wilde's *The Canterville Ghost;* then on the wide screen as a KGB mole in Michael Caine's *The Whistleblower.* He also, on a brief but luxurious location in Venice, celebrated his eighty-third birthday while making a real curiosity, a film called *Barbalu, Barbalu,* in which he played an aged Bluebeard, onto his third marriage. John, the only English speaker in the film, was dubbed into Italian, from a soundtrack that never reverted to English.

The four other films that John completed in these still workaholic 1980s were of little merit. One was yet another glossy but soft-centered Agatha Christie thriller (*Appointment with Death*), with Peter Ustinov now replacing Albert Finney as Hercule Poirot. Another, unfortunately, was a catastrophic sequel to *Arthur* (*Arthur 2: On the Rocks*), which started Dudley Moore's precipitate Hollywood decline. For John, the role merely involved a few lovely days just before Christmas, filming in New York, and organizing reunion dinners with Irene Worth and Lillian Gish, who, he told a rather surprised Mavis Walker, was the only woman he might ever have married, if only he could have found the courage to ask her. The day after the filming finished, Mavis with some difficulty obtained two tickets for

Peter Brook's sold-out, nine-hour *Mahabarata*. John considered the prospect for a moment, then said to Mavis, "I think you had better go, and tell me all about it. I shall be at the matinee of *Anything Goes*."

The other two films he made at this time were a dire comedy loosely based on a novel by Elizabeth Jane Howard about a hairdresser in the London of the Swinging Sixties (*Getting It Right*), and a pointless remake of Graham Greene's *Loser Takes All* with John in the role of the sinister millionaire (one that had been turned down by both Alec Guinness and Max Wall), based on Alexander Korda and played in the 1956 original by Robert Morley. This new version, starring Robert Lindsay and Molly Ringwald, proved uneventful for John, except for one sequence on a yacht, when a sudden swell threw the ship broadside, landing him in a heap of lighting apparatus with very sharp edges. To the relief of the crew, he picked himself up unhurt and sat down to light a cigarette. From his earliest days in pictures with Alfred Hitchcock, he said, he had always been taught how to fall.

At the end of these few days' filming in Nice and Cannes, John drove up into the hills above Eze, to meet his former sister-in-law, Zita Gordon, once married to Lewis but now living in considerable luxury and eager to tell John about her daughter Maina, who was already making a name for herself in the Australian Ballet.

As these 1980s came to an end, John had the chance to make a farewell appearance in the West End, as well as the film he had always yearned for—Shakespeare's *The Tempest*, as now drastically revised by Peter Greenaway.

Coming in to the Apollo, Hugh Whitemore's *The Best of Friends* was an epistolary play in the tradition of *Dear Liar* and *84 Charing Cross Road*, but built this time around three people (the playwright Bernard Shaw, the Fitzwilliam Museum director Sydney Cockerell, and the Stanbrook abbess Laurentia McLochlan), who for most of their long lives wrote a marathon series of letters to each other. Those letters made up the whole of this evening, Whitemore wisely did not attempt to dramatize anything that was not already in the correspondence, and so what the audience got is what they wrote about—distant memories of Cockerell's lunch with Tolstoy, Shaw's thoughts on being offered the Nobel Prize ("I can forgive that man for inventing dynamite, but only a fiend incarnate could have invented the prize"), ideas about travel, sex, friendship, careers, and of course religion—in which last area the formidable abbess was dominant, never more so than when banishing Shaw from her friendship for several years for having dared to write *The Black Girl in Search of God.*

The Best of Friends was admittedly not a major play, but its overriding importance was that it brought John back to the London theater after an absence of ten years, for what he well knew would be his farewell stage performance, not least because, despite an almost sold-out run of four months, he never entirely managed to learn it. Though he never announced this as a farewell performance, audiences seemed somehow to sense that they were never going to see him again in the flesh, except possibly at an increasing number of other actors' memorial services for which he was still much in demand.

But as final characters go, Cockerell was a little gem; by his own admission, he was a collector of the famous, a man so cautious that he had bought his engagement ring on sale or return, and eventually a museum curator aging happily in the knowledge that he could still afford an egg with his tea. While Ray McAnally as a jovial Shaw and Rosemary Harris as the abbess were allowed occasional bursts of irritation and anger, John's Cockerell moved sublimely and gracefully if forgetfully through their triangular friendship, the orchestrator of a rich and rare conversation piece that concluded with him alone in the spotlight, the sole survivor of the trio, noticing that the Angel of Death seemed quite to have passed him by. It was a solo moment of breathtaking theatrical poetry at the end of an evening of whimsical and wayward charm, and few who saw it could have failed to realize that here, too, was John's very own farewell to the West End where he had now been working for all of sixty-six years.

During the run at the Apollo, the new British Theatre Museum in Covent Garden was finally opened, after much political and financial wrangling and several campaigns in which John had always played his part. Now he was delighted to find that the museum contained its very own Gielgud Gallery, and walking around the exhibits he was able to find memories of Ellen Terry, Lilian Baylis, and all the theatrical figures of his own past. He also found, somewhat to his surprise, a portrait of himself as Hamlet: "Amazing, I can't ever remember selling that to anyone, but I suppose I might have given it away. The artist was Nigel Newton, brother of the actor Bobbie who was a legendary drunk. Did you know that when he died they found 200 empty bottles of whisky at the bottom of a lake in his garden? I love seeing all this, but I really don't think I want to be immortalised any more. I really must stop living in the past, although I do find it absolutely fascinating."

While he was playing in the West End, several magazines took the opportunity for what were effectively to be the last profiles of John as a working West End star. "Here he comes," wrote Nicholas de Jongh for the *Illustrated London News,* "striding with that quick, young man's walk into his eighty-fourth autumn; broad-shouldered, back as straight as a schoolboy's ruler, memory clear as a bell, eyes a little hooded, but not missing a trick. He looks like a Harley Street physician in his early sixties, or a recently retired Permanent Under-Secretary. For Gielgud is still in a lucky and long Indian summer, at a time when the best of his acting generation have mostly shuffled from the limelight or been laid to rest. He has dodged the sly, persistent ambushes of old age—apart from twinges of lumbago— as if to ensure that he could go on working at full stretch; the need to act still courses through his blood. It is his adrenaline and his addiction, and he could never voluntarily retire.

"And yet, although he has been all his life the most extrovert of performers, tearing passions to a tatter of tears and grief, he is himself a natural introvert. There are in him traces of unease, and that air of studied aloofness, a sense of mountain-high remoteness. But such *froideurs* are compensated for by the fantastic fizz, dazzle and exhilarating comedy of Gielgud caught in conversation. His mind is like a butterfly. It skims, darts and settles in a helter-skelter of insight, opinion, revelation and analysis, not to mention gossip."

"After the last matinee of *Best of Friends*," recalled the director James Roose-Evans, "and before the final performance at the Apollo, John said to Ray McAnally, 'Tonight is the last night,' meaning that he would not return to the stage again . . . he had returned in triumph, and that was enough. The audience that night must have sensed this, even though they did not know it, for at the curtain call, as Rosemary Harris and Ray McAnally deliberately stepped away from Gielgud, leaving him alone at the centre of the stage (something they had never done before because, in the nature of the play, they had always shared the curtain call) the entire audience rose to its feet, stalls to circle, circle to upper circle and gallery, cheering, pouring out its gratitude for the greatness and gentleness and wit . . . and for his lifetime of work in the theatre."

Honors were now raining down on him from all sides. The Theatre Museum staged its largest-ever celebration of his career, and RADA, of which he had so long been president, made him its first-ever Honorary Fellow, thereby allowing the new Princess of Wales to succeed him as president.

John was now beginning to allow himself, in occasional interviews, to speak his mind in a way that he never had before. Talking to me during the run of *The Best of Friends*, he said,

I really hate the new National Theatre. It looks like an aircraft hangar, and the dressing rooms are all so uncomfortable. The only decent theatre is the Cottesloe, and even that is like a coffin. I tried to persuade them to put a nice big sign on the roof to brighten it up, but they said the architect would never allow it. As for the Barbican, it looks like a hospital, and there really is no point any longer in coming up to London. Most of my friends now seem to be either dead, extremely deaf, or living in the wrong part of Kent, and when I go backstage after a play, the cast all regard me as some terrible old Dalai Lama come to give them advice. Which I never do, as it always leads to trouble.

"The truth is that I also hate a lot of what is happening in the modern theatre, especially the idea some directors have that they must impose their own ideas on a classic text. In my time we knew the audience had enough trouble just dealing with the verse, let alone a lot of "relevance" rubbish as well. I find I still yearn, though, for a theatrical routine, the night after night of improving or changing a performance rather than sitting around in some caravan abroad, waiting for a film crew to get themselves organised. I fill up the time, when I can't find a crossword, by listing to myself the names of all my school-friends at Westminster three-quarters of a century ago, or the names of all the assistant stage managers when I started at the Old Vic in the 1920s. Rather embarrassingly, I find I can recall all of those accurately, but almost never the name of the film director I am currently working for.

I'm not altogether sure I like this sudden burst of interest in me. It's probably because journalists and producers all think I'm about to die. Most of the scripts I get sent nowadays are about men at death's door, and the television people keep saying they want to film a celebration of my life, when I know very well that what they really want is to have the obituary ready in the can in case I suddenly pop off.

I've reached an age now where I really dread talking to people unless they are very old friends . . . I do miss Ralph terribly, although I was never really nearly as close to Larry. We had a kind of love-hate thing, and I think he thought me basically rather frivolous. Whenever I went to stay for the week-end it was always at Vivien's invitation, and Larry seemed to be disguising himself for the next role, always keeping a beady eye on what I was doing. A few years ago he suddenly said, "Not thinking of another *Lear* by any chance are you, old boy?" and I knew that he had probably got one in mind. . . . As for Ralph, he always said that it was disgraceful of me to appear in those California wine commercials and that a classical actor should never dirty his hands with work like that. Months later I discovered that he had slyly gone off and done one himself for Concorde. My real ambition was to do one for underwear which would start with me saying, "At my time of life, all is quiet on the Y-front."

At the time of this interview, Gielgud and Olivier had been appearing together regularly for some years in front of a television audience, on the satirical program *Spitting Image,* whose caricature puppets were matched by some remarkable vocal impressions. They were portrayed as a couple of old luvvies constantly mourning the passing of colleagues or commenting on current ones, always using the preface, "Dear, dear" before the name of the thespian in question. Olivier's puppet was given an expression of pinched malice, which matched his usually caustic comments, and Gielgud's was a gentle, other-worldly creature with an elegiac approach to life.

That life was now increasingly spent in retrospection; John Miller, the interviewer for whom he had recorded his epic series of radio interviews, put together a television program in which John was again able to reflect on the changes in the British theater through which he had lived, from Pinter all the way back to Pinero. At the same time Gielgud published yet another slender volume of memoirs, this one largely made up of the reprinted *Distinguished Company*, and a further selection of profiles of the leading characters of his past.

As another actor, Paul Daneman, who had been with Gielgud at the Old Vic in *Richard II* and on a television version of *Antigone*, once noted, "Gielgud's gossip should never be mistaken for mere actor's tattle . . . he illuminates a whole lost world of theatre in the first half of this century, a theatre dominated by commercial interests and imperious personalities and still undisturbed by the inroads of cinema and radio and television. When he describes walking down Shaftesbury Avenue, seeing an open taxi slowly driving along, and Elisabeth Bergner sitting on the hood with flowers in her lap, waving to a mass of shouting fans, it seems hard to believe that it's the same sleazy old traffic jam we struggle through today. . . . Gielgud recaptures the excitement of going to the theatre, as opposed to just being there."

John G.'s next assignment was to rejoin Charlton Heston, for whom he had played Julius Caesar, in yet another pointless television remake, this one of Robert Bolt's *A Man for All Seasons*, which had already been definitively filmed by Paul Scofield for Fred Zinnemann. But Heston had long been giving stage appearances as Sir Thomas More, and now he was determined to commit it to film, with Vanessa Redgrave as his wife, and John Gielgud as a rather thinner Cardinal Wolsey than the original Orson Welles. Heston and Redgrave had already played *Macbeth* onstage in Los

Angeles, a production mainly notable for the efforts of the redoubtable Australian actress Coral Browne to get tickets for the first night. Having tried with no success in both her own name and that of her husband Vincent Price, she decides to dial the box office one more time. "Hello," she says, to a surprised box-office manager. "I'd like two tickets for just after the interval of the first night Charlton Heston *Macbeth*." By that time of the evening, she could have had several dozen.

On the set of *A Man for All Seasons*, John now reflected that what you really got paid for as a screen actor was the time you sat around waiting for something to happen. The acting, he did for nothing; it was the waiting he charged for, and he was no longer sure that he approved of all the attention he was getting in an old age now sustained by a nourishing diet of wine and cigarettes and no exercise of any kind: "Now I have people calling me Sir John, and opening doors for me, but I've never demanded, or even wanted, all this red-carpet treatment. I like it when the technicians just shove past me, calling me John. The one thing about being eighty-four is that you must never risk being ill, because everyone then thinks you are done for, and I am really terrified of that."

John was, therefore, still determined to keep his screen career in overdrive. Pausing only to appear as Virgil in several episodes of a quirky television version of Dante's *Inferno* for Peter Greenaway, who would eventually film his last Prospero, John now went to work in Italy on what was to be his last sustained television serial.

John Mortimer, who had already given John one of his best television roles in *Brideshead Revisited*, had now adapted his own bestselling *Summer's Lease* for the small screen. This was essentially an elegantly comic look at the British in Tuscany, and for it Mortimer had created one of his best comic roles, that of Haverford Downs, a spry, elderly, would-be roué living on memories both real and imagined, and the precarious proceeds of his weekly column "Jottings from Chiantishire."

In the novel Downs was a rather subsidiary character, but by the time John had taken him over for the screen, there was no doubt about who was going to run away with the series, much as he had with *Brideshead*.

This, John's last major television series, was not to be an easy shoot. The plan was to spend two months living outside Siena, but halfway through the filming John was shocked to hear over the phone of the death of his lifelong opposite number, Laurence Olivier. The two men had never exactly been best friends, yet John now found himself feeling suddenly bereft: "Now that Larry is gone, I cannot help feeling sad, and somewhat ashamed too, that I did not strive to know him better, as our careers and ambition spanned so many of the same years. Of course, we acted many of the same classical parts, and the press hinted of rivalry between us, which was not the truth . . . to me, he seemed personally rather secretive, and knowing my frivolous and often indiscreet nature, he never confided to me his fears or deepest thoughts. I was happy to feel sure that in his last marriage to Joan Plowright he achieved so much private joy, and lived to delight in the children he had always longed for. He was certainly the proud successor to the very great ones—Kean and Irving—and he respected tradition, while delighting in breaking it. . . . I shall always think of him as one of the most brilliant, gifted, indefatigable and controversial figures of our time, and I am very proud to have been lucky enough to be his contemporary and colleague over these long, eventful years."

A few months later, John was to read Donne's sonnet "Death Be Not Proud" at Olivier's epic, majestic, wildly over-the-top memorial service in Westminster Abbey. John, Peggy Ashcroft, Alec Guinness, and Johnny Mills were now the surviving quartet of the greatest generation of actors the world had ever known, but for John G. at least, the Olivier memorial was a bridge too far. He found it inexpressibly vulgar and curiously impertinent to the memory of the statesmen and monarchs who were also buried, in his view rather more rightfully, within the abbey. As for Kean's sword, which John had handed over to Olivier as part of an ongoing custom in the British theater whereby one great Shakespearean thereby saluted the next, it all stopped with Olivier, who let it be known to general amazement that he now regarded the sword as his in perpetuity, whatever the historical precedent.

Back in Siena, on the *Summer's Lease* location, there was worse to come. A few weeks after hearing of Olivier's death, John himself collapsed with a blood clot in his legs and had to be flown home to a hospital near Aylesbury. Determined not to acquire a reputation for being ill and, therefore, uninsurable and so unemployable, John struggled back to the location and completed the filming only a week behind schedule, later collecting yet another clean sweep of glowing reviews.

Back home at Wotton Underwood, John's health continued to be fragile. He'd been forced to miss a gala lunch for his eighty-fifth birthday earlier in 1989, and a good deal of his time was now taken up with writing obituaries or regretful letters to the papers about the death of yet another friend— Tony Quayle was the one who died toward the end of this year.

To keep working now became a kind of urgency. The money was no longer really essential, although Martin was still perfectly capable of going through it at more than reasonable speed. Rather, for John the next assignment was really the only indication that he was still desirable. Having taken on a new agent, Paul Lyon Maris, he could now command fifty thousand pounds for a day's work on film or television, though for this rate he would usually throw in the second or third day for free. His time was also now taken up increasingly in paying tribute to deceased contemporaries in a vast range of television documentaries. In one week of 1989 alone, he paid eloquent and elegant tributes to Vivien Leigh, Coral Browne, and Michael Redgrave. For all of these, he was filmed sitting on one of the magnificent sofas in Wotton Underwood, telling stories both touching and irreverent, as he delved back into his own shared heritage with the dramatic deceased.

At this time he also did a long interview on the stage of the Playhouse with David Frost for American television, and began to work on a massive two-part *Omnibus*, which was to go out a year later, as well as to narrate a *South Bank Show* on Hindemith.

It was not, however, until the beginning of 1991, by which time he had also published a new collection of Shakespearean essays, that he finally got the offer to make what was not only to be his last major film appearance, but also the one that he had most desired. A film of *The Tempest* had been on his wish list since he had first played Prospero more than half a century earlier. Many previous attempts had failed for lack of financing, and at eighty-seven he was now at last being offered the role by Peter Greenaway

who (with *The Draughtsman's Contract* and the television *Dante* in which John had appeared as Virgil) was making his name as an eccentrically individualist film director. As John recalled:

> I had always wanted to make this film, more than any other. Prospero has always been a favourite part, and I felt that the magical aspects of the play would work very well on screen. The problem has always been to find the right director. I wrote a synopsis myself years ago, which I passed around a few friends, and I remember having long conversations with Benjamin Britten about the soundtrack—he wanted to use real sounds like crashing seas, cries, shouts and footsteps on flagstones for the early part of the film.
>
> I then had wild ideas about Kurosawa and setting it as a Japanese fairy tale, but I could never find anyone who knew where he lived. I wrote to Ingmar Bergman, who sent me a telegram explaining that his English wasn't up to it, and eventually I talked to Alain Resnais and Giorgio Strehler, and Derek Jarman asked me to be in his television version, as did the BBC, but I turned them both down—somehow I must have had a feeling that this film was just around the corner, and quite soon Peter Greenaway rang me with the offer not only of Prospero, but of reading the whole of the rest of the text on the soundtrack.
>
> We filmed for four months in Amsterdam, and I had to wear the most extraordinarily heavy cloak, which took four people to put it on me. Back in 1934 I said that Shakespeare was not a good idea for the screen, but since then we have had Larry's *Henry V* and Orson Welles' *Chimes at Midnight*, and I have had to reconsider my opinion.

When *Prospero's Books* first opened at the New York Film Festival in November 1991, Vincent Canby of *The New York Times* reviewed "a movie which is a kind of obsessed collector's inventory of the Renaissance—its thought, art, architecture, religion, superstition, music and painting ... this tumultuously over-packed movie is less a screen adaptation of Shakespeare's haunting and elegiac last play than a grand jumping-off spot for a work that will make some people run for the exits, and others more than angry at the liberties taken . . . Gielgud holds his own against all of the magnificent technical effects, but only just."

Inevitably, this was to be Greenaway's rather than Gielgud's vision of *The Tempest*. It had such brilliant conceits as the opening storm sequence beginning with a single drop of water in immense close-up, splashing into Prospero's outstretched palm. But as the film went on, the decision by Greenaway to load whole layers of other meanings onto the Shakespearean original meant that John was somehow out of his depth. Greenaway himself agreed with Donald Sinden that Gielgud alone could speak Shakespeare as though he had written it: "We got on very well, though as usual the studio in Amsterdam meant 90% waiting and 10% frenetic activity. John never seemed to tire and eventually I thought of him as Prospero/Gielgud, the puppetmaster who writes and speaks the words so that he in his double role and Shakespeare are really all one and the same. We also had a great choreographer, Michael Clark, and although as usual the English critical reaction was rearguard and shocked, around the rest of the world the film has done a great deal better and I think that Gielgud really trusted me."

As for John, "I wanted to leave something behind as a record of my Shakespearean work, and it's the only part that I was the right age for. I do hope that it's all right. I was so frightened that I would come out very hammy and old-fashioned and declamatory, having played it so often on stage. It was an extraordinary appearance; one morning Peter told me to take off all my clothes and be naked in the bath, and there were all these girls and fat women in the nude, but after a day or two one had completely forgotten. I don't think it offends in the least, except in Japan, where they have had to cut out all the genitals."

Greenaway was to recall John "thoroughly amused by the entourage, naked except for their body paint; he made a lot of unrepeatable jokes." For *Prospero's Books,* as for *Caligula,* John seemed to be giving over a surprising amount of his late-life screen time to frolicking in pools surrounded by naked people.

While John was in Amsterdam, news came of the death of both Peggy

Ashcroft and Ralph Richardson, and he was somewhat unnerved to hear a reporter murmuring audibly, "I suppose this one will be the next to go."

Prospero's Books duly opened a few months later, to surprisingly mixed reviews. Greenaway himself wrote of John as "the still, calm figure in the midst of all my pyrotechnical extravagance—whatever else is going on in the film, it is always Gielgud you watch." John himself, however, was sharply aware of the problems here: "I think the film is original and fascinating, but very over-elaborate. I liked Greenaway very much; he assembled a strong cast, with Mark Rylance as Ferdinand, and because Greenaway is a painter himself, strongly influenced by Tintoretto and Titian, he organises and choreographs all his scenes with remarkable taste and feeling for depth and colour. With him, I had the same feeling I'd had with Peter Brook and Granville-Barker, and Lindsay Anderson and Peter Hall and Alain Resnais, but no other directors in my entire career, that I could really trust his judgement and criticism, and put myself entirely in his hands . . . Above all, I was greatly impressed by Greenaway's control. A very quiet man who never raises his voice, he walked about the studio all day long, never sat down, and seemed to work equally easily with the sound man who was British, the lighting man who was French, and a mixed crew, many of whom were Dutch . . . there was no hammering or tantrums or bad behaviour, and for once the whole thing was wonderfully organised.

"True, there did seem to be an awful lot of people sitting around without clothes, and I wasn't always quite sure what Greenaway really wanted, but I did my best to go along with it."

For the *Independent*, Anthony Lane had severe reservations: "It is all very well asking us to imagine the whole of *The Tempest* being played out on the stage of Prospero's capacious brain . . . he can wheedle his enemies into the storm as he splashes about in his bath, or freeze them as if they were celluloid and he the divine projectionist. Gielgud's Prospero is sadist, conjuror and scribe . . . he bosses everyone else around and speaks almost all the lines, rolling the pentameters around like an archbishop tasting burgundy . . . the trouble is that Greenaway, unlike Shakespeare, never bothers to make it clear who anybody is—the men all wear ruffs the size of dustbin lids and the kind of platform clogs that you would hire from Elton John . . . Oh, wow, you think, isn't that Tom Bell, imagine him dressed up like that, what a plonker he must feel . . . and isn't that the baldie from *Monsieur Hire?* And look, that's the guy from all the Bergman films. Hang on, you must be Gonzalo, so which is Antonio, and where the hell is Sebastian? Michael Nyman's music still parps on in its dreary Rolf Harris stylophone way, and finally the players break off and sidle past the camera, looking really embarrassed. Our revels now are ended, and thank God."

And, as Douglas Brode added, "whereas Shakespeare, in his own theatrical endgame provides answers in *The Tempest* that more or less explain the meaning of life (which is that the secret to happiness is maintaining a perpetual, if guarded sense of optimism despite endless disappointments) Greenaway only wants to transform the play into another of his cinematic conundrums, which are puzzles without any answers, less truly complex than simply confusing."

On his return to England, John went to work, suitably enough, as God, in a BBC radio dramatization of the Book of Genesis, and then put together, with his faithful chronicler John Miller, a collection of his thoughts on the acting of Shakespeare. He also began to get back at those whom he thought had treated him harshly, notably the recently deceased Kenneth Tynan: "He said I only had two gestures, the left hand up, or the right hand up. What did he want me to do, get out my prick?" Looking back at his 1950s *King Lear,* he also noted:

> I should have remembered that you have to have a light Cordelia. Peggy Ashcroft was wonderful, but lifting her in the last act every night made me wish I had never taken up the bloody classics. . . . I suppose the irony is that now I feel just about ready to play anything. I am either too old or I simply don't feel like doing it. I also don't approve of all the modern invasions into people's privacy—it must be so embarrassing for the family. One of the great difficulties of the modern world is that people want to intrude now into the private life

of celebrities. After *Arthur* they set up five separate fan clubs for me in Germany, and when I was filming in Berlin people laid in wait for me outside my hotel. It was all most extraordinary.

Nor am I really any good at television chat shows—I am sick of becoming a club bore, and trotting out all the old stories. We know that Nell Gwyn sold oranges outside the Drury Lane theatre, but once she became the mistress of the King, she no longer had to go on selling. But look at me . . . I'm also now getting very embarrassed by Ian McKellen, who keeps on asking me to join him in all sorts of gay demonstrations. I always refuse—they exploit the exhibitionist side of one's nature, which should be kept for one's acting. If I have any regrets, it is that I have led a very narrow life. Looking back, I wish I had been called up into the war, because however bad a soldier I would have been, I would at least have met all kinds of different people.

Peter Conrad, writing of John for *The New York Times*, noted that "he is now undergoing something perilously like an apotheosis . . . his Prospero is also a revelation of Sir John himself—simultaneously noble and naughty, a high priest and a joker, contemplating at the end of a long life the value of the art he practises . . . what other voice can be an orchestra of special effects—as mellifluous as a violin, as plaintive as a clarinet, and occasionally as ominous as a kettle drum.

"In private, he seems to have no Prospero-like regrets, although he does consider Greenaway's film to be both a summary of his career, and a formal farewell to it . . . he now resembles a cross between a rural colonel, with his thin white moustache and a corduroy smoking jacket, and an impish, worldly, ruddy Abbot . . . Sir John's character remains complex and contradictory: his English gentility always vies with his Slavic melancholy."

In another interview around this time, John was as usual asked to explain the longevity of his stage career: "Perhaps it is that I never think about a part too much in advance. I always go into it like a game of charades, I always have, and that seems to keep it reasonably fresh. But years ago I watched the actress Ethel Barrymore doing a death scene three times in three different plays during one year, and I thought how awful it must be, having dress-rehearsals for your own death; but now I, too, seem to be dying rather too much. I always used to think that when I got very old, I would end up in Hollywood as a grand old character man, rather like Sir C. Aubrey Smith, playing ambassadors. But it hasn't happened like that and I am glad, I really should prefer to die in England. The graveyards seem so much friendlier over here."

But even now, John's publicity was not always favorable; there was an embarrassing row when he failed to turn up at Cambridge to receive an honorary doctorate from the university, and there was worse to come when a new history of World War II revealed that in March 1940, John had joined Sybil Thorndike and George Bernard Shaw in signing a secret letter to the then Prime Minister Neville Chamberlain, urging him to make peace with Hitler. But John, as always bleakly uninterested in politics, was doubtless merely trying to get the lights back on in the West End, and it was reckoned unlikely that Chamberlain had even received the letter. Certainly, it was never answered.

John's visits to London were becoming increasingly rare, and nearly always only in order to speak at the memorial service of yet another beloved theatrical friend. His routine was now very simple. He and Martin had taken on an assistant gardener, Vincent, and a driver, Peter, both of whom were to stay with John until the end of his life. In the meantime, with Peter driving, John would travel down the M40 to the Actor's Church, St. Paul's in Covent Garden, where, usually late because of the traffic, he would simply walk firmly up into the pulpit and deliver "Fear no more the heat of the sun" from *Cymbeline*. This was always fine, and often followed by lunch at the Garrick Club across the road, unless of course the service happened to be taking place in some altogether other church. On those occasions, while Donald Sinden or Michael Denison were having to fill in for the absent Gielgud, a totally strange family that happened to be using the Covent Garden church for its funeral would stand around afterward in some amazement wondering how it was that their own dear deceased had known Sir John so well, without ever telling them.

And now, another of the classical players with whom he started was to leave the stage; in January 1992 Gwen Ffrangcon-Davies died at 101, and a few months later Lillian Gish, his Broadway Ophelia, was also to go, in her middle nineties.

For John, however, it was work as usual. Soon after *Prospero's Books,* he returned to BBC Radio to play a more traditional *Tempest* for the World Service, and then to television for the filming of his last stage role in *The Best of Friends.* Once that was completed, he went to Germany to play the role of a resistance worker in a dire Michael Douglas/Melanie Griffith wartime thriller called *Shining Through.*

In 1992 he also played briefly in a French movie (*Puissance de L'Ange*) and, with Richard Briers (and Kenneth Branagh as director), made a heartbreaking appearance in *Swan Song,* the brief Chekhov script about an old actor, Svet Lovidov, trying to recall his days of glory. But now, the major movies no longer seemed to need him, even as a character player. Undeterred and still determined to get out of the house whenever possible, he began to make frequent appearances in such television dramas or miniseries as could still afford him. Accordingly, between 1993 and 1999 he was to be found to greater or lesser advantage in episodes of *Inspector Morse, Under the Hammer, Summer's Daydream, Scarlett, Lovejoy, Inspector Alleyn, Gulliver's Travels, Dance to the Music of Time,* and *Merlin.* Additionally he also made a fleeting appearance in Al Pacino's documentary, *Looking for Richard,* in which he somewhat patronizingly explained that Europeans were usually better than Americans at Shakespeare because they read more widely and had often been rather better educated.

In this same period, effectively the last five years of his working life, he also appeared briefly on the wide screen in *First Knight, Haunted, Portrait of a Lady, Shine,* the Kenneth Branagh *Hamlet, Dragonheart, Elizabeth,* and *The Tichborne Claimant,* not to mention further documentary appearances in programs about Noël Coward, Edmund Kean, and Sergei Rachmaninoff.

For an actor now in his nineties, this was a remarkable achievement; even allowing for the fact that he would not usually put in more than two or three days on any one production, and that in one or two of his last appearances he can clearly be seen reading lines off a prompter, it would still be impossible to find any other actor of his age working at anything like

John's rate, and in some of these performances, notably the doctrinaire piano teacher in *Shine*, and the wily Pope in *Elizabeth*, there were still strong traces of the Gielgud magic.

By happy chance, two of these late-life projects, the episode of *Inspector Morse* and the film of *The Tichborne Claimant*, reunited John for the first time in almost half a century with one of the actors he most liked and admired, Robert Hardy:

John was in a way the great good fortune of my working life. I remember exactly when and where I first saw him; in Oxford, just at the end of the war. It was a time when we were all half in uniform and half in student gowns, and I suddenly saw John on the pavement talking to Nevill Coghill and M. R. Ridley, who was also of course the thriller writer Michael Innes. Then, in my first Stratford season, 1949, when he was directing *Much Ado* for the first time, I was in a group of young actors auditioning for very minor roles. Gossip had it that I was about to meet a monster of homosexual vice who would only cast us if he fancied us; instead, here was this immensely swift, gentle, courteous man already giving us master classes in verse-speaking, even if we were only about to speak two lines.

A year or two later, he gave me my first West End role, Claudio in the West End *Much Ado* which I believe still holds the record for the longest nightly run of any non-*Hamlet* Shakespearean play in the commercial London theatre. Then again, I was a sort of composite of the Knights in his 1950 *Lear:* I'd started out as an Olivier man, all for realism and slightly doubtful of John's poetic qualities, so I decided to give the Knight a stammer and John never once pointed out what a daft idea that was. His patience with all of us was remarkable; well, nearly all of us. Alan Badel, whom he later came to love, was driving him mad telling him how *Lear* should be directed. One night I came offstage, and to my horror John wasn't in his usual place in the wings. I thought, unbelievably, he was going to be off, but then through the darkness I heard that unmistakeable voice from further upstage: "It's all right, I'm over here, just hiding from Alan Badel."

John was always subtle, always gentle, and just when I had decided that being gay he couldn't play love scenes with women, he would break your heart in one. There's a moment in *Much Ado* when Claudio has to pretend to be Benedick in a mask, and some nights I used to do a real Gielgud imitation to amuse myself and the cast, and any friends out front. One night I had just done, I thought, a really expert bit of mimicry, and we were lining up for the next scene when I heard John say to one of the other actors, "It's a funny thing, but I have always found that very good mimics are seldom any good at anything else." That was the last time I tried that.

The filming of *Inspector Morse* led to a wonderful reunion, as we had several days on location in Oxford, where of course we had first met; his energy and his memory were still remarkable, and he would recall in fantastic detail anecdotes and characters from his own student days. He even began talking to me about Larry, who had only recently died. He wondered why I had always been so keen to play Henry V and other Shakespearean Kings in plays that seem to me to teach us the history of our nation: "I never cared for any of that, crashing and clanking about in armour. They always seemed to me rough and rather boring plays, compared to the romantic comedies of Shakespeare, but then of course Larry too was frightfully keen on all of that. Not my scene, I fear."

By the time we got to *The Tichborne Claimant*, age did seem at last to be catching up with him; the studio was fearfully hot, and his wig and robes as the Lord Chief Justice must have been agony, though he never complained. I was still struck by the speed of his thought; he was older, calmer, but there was still that certain waspishness, not to be confused with malice. John was never malicious, and if in rehearsal he was sharp, you weren't supposed to bleed. He never bore a grudge, though his tact was questionable. Once he told me that the world was too much with me, that I should appear on stage "looking better bred, like me. Oh but I forgot, you are quite well bred, aren't you?" I loved him very much, and my life as an actor was always made better when he was there.

Kenneth Branagh now became one of John's last great heroes, not surprisingly considering that Branagh, too, had formed his own company at a very early age and was gradually working through the Shakespearean canon. For him, Gielgud played the Ghost in a radio *Hamlet*, Priam in the film, the Chorus in *Romeo and Juliet*, and, to celebrate his ninetieth birthday in 1994, his very last *King Lear* in a BBC Radio Three production, which was also issued on tape and disc, and for which Branagh assembled an amazing cast, all eager to work with John on this quietly festive occasion—Judi Dench (Goneril), Eileen Atkins (Regan), Emma Thompson (Cordelia), Michael Williams (Fool), and Richard Briers (Gloucester). In smaller roles could also be heard Bob Hoskins, Derek Jacobi, and Simon Russell Beale, who found himself so paralyzed with nerves at meeting the great man that when John asked him for the way to the exit, Simon could only stand aghast and silent.

It was the critic Michael Billington who made the point of this broadcast, that "it is not something wistful, embalmed or elegiac, but a compelling and urgent study of an imperious tyrant splintering into madness."

John was still determined, wherever possible, to avoid advertising his age, lest it cause prospective producers to think he was now really past it. Accordingly, he spent his ninetieth birthday at home with Martin and firmly vetoed plans mooted by the impresario Duncan Weldon for some kind of stage gala: it would, he wrote to Duncan, "look just like my obituary, and I would so much rather just stay in work, proving I can still do a bit, than standing around receiving congratulations on my longevity." He did, however, consent to be given lunch at the House of Commons by the M.P.s Glenda Jackson and Gyles Brandreth: "I should be delighted to join you both, especially as, you see, all my real friends are dead."

John was also still publishing with amazing regularity: not only the inevitable obituaries and tributes (which he also had to broadcast regularly for radio and television), but also a magical little volume called *Notes from the Gods*, which consisted of his own 1920s collection of West End theatre programs, complete with the notes he had made on them at the time.

And there were still certain ceremonies for which he had to make an appearance. In 1993 he was given the first annual Shakespeare's Globe Trust

Award, and a year later the Gielgud Award for Excellence in Dramatic Arts was established in New York. He also, in 1994, won the Imperial Prize of the Japan Arts Association, one to be taken very seriously in that it came with a cash sum of $100,000. There was, however, just one slight drawback: The rules stated that in order to collect this award, the recipient actually had to fly to Tokyo, a journey that John's doctor utterly forbade him to take. As I had recently taken on the role of John's biographer, he summoned me to sort this out, demanding only that I ensured he would not lose the money. After several difficult conversations with the Japanese ambassador in London, and the production of several medical certificates, it was agreed that the Crown Prince of Japan would himself fly to London to present John with this notable honor, one which had previously gone only to Edward Heath. I sat next to John during a long and sometimes incomprehensible ceremony at the Japanese Embassy, during which he kept audibly hissing at me, "When do we get the check?" Luckily, and to my great relief, it arrived a couple of days later, tax free.

John was much in demand also for the new medium of audio books and happily lent his still unmatched tones to recording work by Dickens, Oscar Wilde, Alan Bennett, and Evelyn Waugh. In 1998 he made his last major radio broadcast in a characteristically courageous choice of role—one he had never previously played, Gower in *Pericles.* He also made a video for Brigitte Bardot expressing his horror of the force-feeding of ducks for pâté and was amused to find, on reaching ninety-five, that reports of his death were now being widely circulated: "I think people now see death as an indecent race between myself, the Pope, and Boris Yeltsin."

Inevitably, such conversations as could still be had with his few surviving old friends were usually conducted on the telephone. A kind of sadness and even loneliness was now creeping into life at Wotton Underwood. John Perry had finally been forgiven by Martin for telling him all those years earlier to stay out of John's theatrical business, but even he found a weekend at South Pavilion almost impossible to endure, as he told Keith Baxter: "I had no way of knowing that Martin had already been diagnosed with cancer, simply because he never told anyone, not even John. Martin would get up at some ungodly hour like five in the morning to deal with all the birds and peacocks and other weird animals which he had collected into a sort of menagerie, and would not come back indoors until lunchtime. I even thought of offering to help with the gardening, but I realised that while I was into simply digging and weeding, Martin's flowerbeds required far more delicate expertise. John would not come downstairs until almost lunchtime, which we ate alone, with Martin hovering somewhere in the kitchen chewing an apple. Then he would disappear outside again. John would fall asleep by the fire, and there was nothing to do until dinner, which again Martin would ignore, having apparently eaten by himself at about six. Then, at about nine, he would start looking at his watch and saying 'bedtime' to John, and that was it for another day."

Another account of Gielgud around the time of his ninety-fifth birthday comes from the writer Julie Kavanagh, who was living nearby and had become a late-life friend of John's while she was working on a biography of Frederick Ashton. From this it became clear that the great ballet master and John had once been very close, as Ashton had, of course, collaborated on the Nevill Coghill *Midsummer Night's Dream* of 1945, starring, as Ashton wrote, "Old Ma Gielgud." Ashton was also among those appalled by John's arrest in 1953, noting at the time, "He's ruined it for all of us."

As Kavanagh wrote of an invitation to lunch at Wotton Underwood in 1998, "We sit at a long Regency table laden with crystal and silver. Martin Hensler, John's partner of thirty years, sits at a slight distance in his usual place, his chair against the wall. He does not eat or drink—he cannot stomach much besides bread and black coffee, a legacy he says of his impoverished Hungarian past, but he talks animatedly in a guttural accent, his long Rothman's Royal spilling ash onto his knees. . . . Looking like a retired accountant, with heavy spectacles and thick, toupee-textured black hair, Martin was tolerated rather than liked by Gielgud's friends, most of whom resented his emphatic opinions, unremitting nagging or worse . . . Martin was a mystery to everyone, Gielgud included.

"He won't speak about his early life at all. I do know that he had a terrible time in Hungary. Obviously they had great estates and palaces and parks and things. I'm fascinated, but I know he hates talking about it, so I never urge him to do so. If people speak Hungarian to him he won't answer."

In fact, there was a very good reason for Martin to be reticent about his Hungarian past, although John remained too innocent, too much in love, or simply too nervous of him ever to work it out. The evidence now suggests that although Martin may well have been Hungarian, the rest of it—the palaces and parks, perhaps even the wife and children—were all total inventions. When in the 1980s it became easily possible to revisit Hungary and track down relatives there, Martin made no effort of any kind to do so; nor, since his death, has anyone emerged to claim his estate, or establish any connection with him.

In these middle 1990s there were still two great tributes to be paid to John. In 1996 the queen gave him the Order of Merit, the highest honor in her personal gift, and one which (apart from Olivier) had very seldom ever been awarded to an actor. John may have failed to join Olivier and Bernard Miles in the ranks of the peerage, but in holding both the O.M. and the C.H. he established perhaps an even greater distinction.

The other honor came with the strong feeling that his name should now be given to a major Shaftesbury Avenue theater, just as Olivier's was to be found at the National. At first, the obvious choice seemed to be the Queen's, which he had so memorably reopened with his *Ages of Man* forty years earlier. It was the Australian owner (at that time) of the Stoll Moss chain, the redoubtable Janet Holmes à Court, who remarked in her no-nonsense way that having a theater known as the old Queen's was not perhaps the most tactful of tributes to Sir John. Besides, she had a still better idea. Shakespeare's Globe had recently been opened, thanks to the tireless work of the late Sam Wanamaker, and London theater listings could clearly not support two Globes, so it was the one on Shaftesbury Avenue that duly became the Gielgud. "At last," John G. said to me on that splendid morning in 1995, "there is again a name in lights along Shaftesbury Avenue that I can actually recognise."

Robert Hardy talked of the great Gielgud paradox, "his beguiling humility, mixed with his marvellous arrogance." And talking to yet another admiring interviewer at this time, John was still full of plans for the future:

> For years I've been looking for the financial backing to make a television series about the father of Osbert and Edith Sitwell, old Sir George, an eccentric millionaire who allowed his wife to go to prison for minor debts, but nobody seems interested in that world any more. Bryan Forbes wants to direct, and Maggie Smith has agreed to play the wife, and two or three times in the past year it has almost come to the boil, but then the money falls through, usually because the television people say the public is no longer interested in aristocratic families, which I think is absolute rubbish. So many things now infuriate me—people taking their jackets off in restaurants, or not dressing properly for the theatre. All the pleasant rituals of life have gone, and people now speak so badly; I often can't understand a word they say on television. And Vanessa Redgrave actually went cockney for a period, although I could never understand why. I don't even turn out my old stories any more because nowadays all I can see is my mother's face when father started up a story she had heard a thousand times before.
>
> I used to adore parties—showing off, giving a performance, being thought very funny and tactless, but I rarely go out nowadays. I dread going back to London where the streets are so full for me of people who are no longer there.

He did, however, turn up for the unveiling of a plaque to Oscar Wilde in Westminster Abbey in 1995, on the centenary of Wilde's imprisonment. Benedict Nightingale, saluting another rare appearance by John in the great ballroom at Buckingham Palace to celebrate Prince Charles's patronage of the Royal Shakespeare Company, remembered what Lee Strasberg, the director of New York's Actors' studio, had once said: "When Gielgud speaks a line, you can hear Shakespeare thinking."

At this time, Clive Francis, the actor and caricaturist, published a collection of drawings with, inevitably, some more of John's sayings. Ralph

Michael recalled asking John during World War II whether he thought that Turkey should join the hostilities: "John put down his crossword for a moment. 'Well,' he inquired, 'are they very keen?'" On another occasion, he was directing the chorus in his epic Covent Garden *Trojans*, and was trying to persuade them to show feelings of violent passion, curiosity, and fear. After they tried this a few times without notable success, John ran down the aisle screaming, "This won't do at all! Not at all! You all look as if you are seeing not very good friends off from Waterloo Station!"

27. Goodnight, Sweet Prince

(1995–2000)

We are such stuff as dreams are made on; and our little life
Is rounded with a sleep.

THE TEMPEST, WILLIAM SHAKESPEARE

*A*s if aware that, as he had so often said, his life had been altogether too bound up in acting at the expense of everything else, John now became a fervent campaigner, crusading for the survival of the old Home Service values on Radio 4—something still especially close to his heart because of his brother Val—and also that of the British Theatre Museum and theatrical subsidy. He even, at this late stage, edged onto the political arena, signing with the novelist William Golding and the filmmaker David Puttnam an appeal on behalf of the Cambodia Trust, a charity established to alleviate the suffering of Cambodians by providing artificial limbs.

However, politics were still not his strongest suit; he had explained several years earlier that he seldom voted on account of being unable to distinguish between the Whigs and the Tories, and at a meeting with Mrs. Thatcher during her premiership he solemnly inquired where she was now living.

He was also playing a favorite game on the telephone, of casting unlikely projects. When, in all seriousness, a stage musical was announced based on the life of Sarah Bernhardt, John could hardly contain himself. "It'll be

Barbra Streisand for the first two acts, and then for the third Dame Judith Anderson will take over with a wooden leg." A caustic sense of backstage humor had clearly been with him since the very earliest days; his recent collection of program notes from the early 1920s included some vitriolic comments on Barrymore's 1925 *Hamlet* ("Romantic in appearance and good in period clothes, but fails terribly in the graveyard scenes"), and of Somerset Maugham's *East of Suez* ("Badly written, scenes loosely strung together and much too long"), and of the robot play *RUR* ("Edith Evans gives her usual brilliant performance but looks even uglier than usual, and the rest of the cast is abominable").

He also now recalled an occasion several years earlier, when on one of the many *Ages of Man* tours, which had developed into quasi-ambassadorial progress through distant lands, he had, at the invitation of some local British consul, had to sit through an entire circus night consisting very largely of men throwing other men around the stage or else forming themselves into endless human pyramids. "I suppose, Gielgud," said the consul by way of making intermission conversation, "you had to start like that, too?"

Some indication of the way in which various strands in John's long life were now coming together occurred when the newly refurbished Criterion Theatre on Piccadilly Circus reopened with a screening of his latest film, the Chekhov *Swan Song*, the story of the backstage encounter between a drunken old actor and his admiring prompter, played by Richard Briers. This gave John the chance, on-screen, to look back on his performances as Lear, Romeo, and Othello. The gala premiere was held in a theater Gielgud had first played sixty years earlier (in Ronald Mackenzie's *Musical Chairs*), and all proceeds were going to Sir Ian McKellen's Stonewall group. But John himself was still curiously traumatized by the idea of giving any public support to gay campaigns; only after his death did it emerge that he had frequently sent gay charity checks to McKellen, with the absolute proviso that there should be no publicity of any kind. The shadows of 1953 still hung over him, almost half a century later, and John was to go to his grave still unable to take any consolation from the way in which his trial had begun to alter public perception of the need for homosexual tolerance where minors were not involved.

Privately, however, John had now found a new fan. The Queen Mother, four years older than he, would now regularly send a car to Wotton Underwood to have John driven over to Royal Lodge at Windsor, where he would entertain Her Majesty and a few select guests with readings of favorite Shakespearean and other verse. By now, actors were using his tapes of *The Ages of Man* as a master class, as Ian McKellen explained: "I play that recording every time I'm about to do Shakespeare, because there is still so much to learn from it. The rapidity with which he delivers the lines, and the agility with which the poet's mind and the character's mind are both revealed. There is no need for pauses while John gets himself into the emotion, which, in turn, is absolutely in accord with the words. Those words are the cello, and John just plays it better than any actor alive or dead."

Although John went on through 1998 doing two or three days' work on such major movies as *Elizabeth* and *Shine,* he was now almost on automatic pilot, as if he had somehow realized that his Prospero for Peter Greenaway really was the farewell to all his magic. But there were still television commercials to make; although the Paul Masson campaign had now died a natural death, John was gainfully employed, along with Alan Bates and Ben Kingsley, to read poems for a very classy series of ads made for the Union Bank of Switzerland, though these were not shown in Britain, where the bank did not have a sufficiently high profile. And then, around Christmas of that year, there was a double disaster in his private life at Wotton Underwood. Martin, although characteristically he never admitted it even to John (who must have known, but also refused to face the truth), was now suffering terminally from cancer and was reluctantly taken into the local hospital at Aylesbury. Almost immediately afterward, alone in the house, John fell down some stairs, breaking a small bone in his foot, and had to be taken into the same local hospital.

As Keith Baxter recalls, "There was a kind of Gothic horror about what happened next. Martin was refusing to be seen by any visitors at all, but just down the corridor John could hear him screaming in pain, but was himself unable even to get out of bed. Eventually his foot was well enough to allow him to return home, and Martin also insisted on going home to die; so over that Christmas the two men were in their own bedrooms, well looked after, of course, by the faithful staff of Peter and Vincent, but still in a kind of agony. One night John shuffled down to the doorway of Martin's room and just stood there, tears pouring down his face, watching his partner. A few hours later, Martin was dead."

Hensler had insisted on a virtually anonymous cremation and left a will of considerable horror, demanding that all his beloved animals be killed. This was not, of course, what happened. But now, increasingly, it was Peter and Vincent who had to make all kinds of difficult decisions, since John had not even been well enough to attend Martin's cremation.

He himself now had fifteen months to live, and they were months of sad decline. Dulcie Gray, living nearby and herself now mourning the recent death of her husband Michael Denison, became John's most regular visitor, as she explained to Gyles Brandreth: "Johnny was heartbroken when Martin died. They had, after all, been together for all of thirty years and he missed him dreadfully. Some people had reservations about Martin but I always liked him, and John was never the same after his death. He suddenly became terribly frail, walking on sticks, which he hated. He had always been so erect, so proud of his wonderful posture, so full of style. And when he came to see me for the last time, he was on crutches, and his driver had to help move him from chair to chair. It was sad to see him like that, and he hated it, but the real blow had been losing Martin—his death broke John's spirit, broke John's heart."

His niece, the ballerina and now choreographer Maina, also noticed a terrible change in John: "He had always been so cheerful, but now, whenever we spoke on the telephone, he would say to me, 'I just wish there could be some work. They have all forgotten me. All I do is wait for the phone to ring, and it never does. . . . I can't get over Martin's death; I never thought he would die before me.'"

But this, too, was of course a somewhat theatrical exaggeration. Mary Evans and Dulcie Gray would ring him virtually every day, and such old friends as Keith Baxter drove down to Wotton Underwood as often as they could. As Keith recalls, "I had been working abroad for a few months, but I was very touched to hear that when Martin died John kept asking people to find me, and have me come see him as soon as I could. So I drove down as soon as I was back in England. By now, I was one of the very few male friends still around who went back a long way with John. He had never had many close women friends, and it was interesting that now, with Mary and Dulcie, he suddenly seemed to realise, at the end of his life, all that he had been missing with them. Before that, only really Peggy Ashcroft and Molly Keane had been close to him. And I think just as he regretted not spending more time in the real world, he also somehow sensed that he had missed out on the company of women."

And now, there was another one, a splendid New Zealand male nurse called Alex, who moved in to take care of Gielgud in these last few months. He seemed for a while to rally, and by the summer of 1999, at least on the telephone, was sounding almost like his old self, always enquiring after the latest theatrical gossip. But the very few people he would allow to visit him were now tremendously aware of his mortality; he was moving very badly and beginning to lose the drift of conversation, seeming suddenly to Dulcie as though he was no longer entirely sure where, or even perhaps who, he was.

On the other hand, Keith found him still sometimes incredibly alert, at least about the past. "One afternoon he described to me in perfect detail a *Hamlet* he had seen Ernest Milton play more than seventy years earlier. He never talked about death, never talked about Martin, seemed to be living in a kind of theatrical museum, constantly re-examining all the people he found there, as if determined to keep his own memories intact, because they were now really all that he had left."

In the autumn of 1999, unadvertised and unannounced in advance, John turned up in one last television studio, being interviewed by Jeremy Paxman for BBC2's *Newsnight* on the stage of the Old Vic. Despite his age and infirmities, John was superbly well-groomed—nothing of the wispiness or untidiness of extreme old age—in a beautifully cut suit, and in a voice that was clear yet subdued. Yet Paxman chose to focus this brief encounter not on John's remarkable career, or even on his memories, but largely on his feelings about old age and even death. John's strength of feeling on the subject was apparent: "I hate being old, and I find it humiliating now to have to rely on help from other people. . . . I never thought I should be at a loss for someone to phone and say I'm coming to see you . . . " Picking up this theme, Paxman asked whether he feared death himself, to which John replied that he was more concerned with being in pain (Martin's experience had shown him how unpleasant the approach to death can be) and added that he also disliked not being able to enjoy food or parties anymore. "I've had wonderful innings, I knew all the great people of my time, and I do resent that I can't have some of them back."

Paxman then asked him about the nature of fame, and John pointed out the dangers that it had caused to a career like that of Richard Burton. He also regretted, he said, that his life had been so very cut off from the realities of the world. Clearly he had been too young to fight in World War I, but he had only recently discovered, to his horror, that Binkie Beaumont had quite untruthfully told the authorities that he was totally unfit to fight World War II, merely so as to keep him on or near Shaftesbury Avenue. Finally, Paxman asked him if he had any regrets: "Only perhaps that in radio and television now there is never the same companionship that I so loved in the theatre. . . . Would I have done anything differently? No, I don't think so."

John's last Christmas treat, in December 1999, was being taken by Nanette Newman to a matinee of *The Lion King,* which predictably he loved, recognizing—as always—something new and vital in theatrical fashion. Amazingly, he was still writing, albeit in a very fragile hand; for the biographer Gordon McVay he penned a tribute to Peggy Ashcroft, listing her virtues in precisely those terms that could have been applied to him:

Generous, eager, forthright

No taste for luxury

Extraordinary range of enthusiasm for playwrights—Shakespeare, Ibsen, Chekhov, Brecht, Rattigan, Pinter

Exquisite reader of poetry

Champion of team companies and good causes, but never pressing them on others

No spite or jealousy

Unfailing professional attitude to directors and colleagues—punctual, diligent, humorous, cheerful

Never pompous or unapproachable

Unaffected, wonderful company; warm-hearted

Great control of emotion, and brilliantly selective reserves of power

Unselfish, loyal, affectionate appreciation of fellow artists

Around this time the critic Michael Billington made Gielgud the subject of a *Guardian* lecture: "I was recently invited by Sir John to have lunch at his club where I sense, not for the first time, how cruelly inaccurate is the *Spitting Image* caricature of Gielgud as a nostalgic old party forever dwelling on the past. He lives very much in the present, works incessantly, and talks as enthusiastically about a new role as an actor just out of drama school . . . he is very much more than the Establishment figurehead and violoncello melodist he is often assumed to be. It is true that he has done more than anyone living to keep the classic tradition alive in the British theatre, but he is also a pioneer . . . at a time when the West End was full of fluff and trivia (when was it not?) he swam against the tide by setting up at the New Theatre from 1934–36 and at the Queen's in 1937–38 seasons of classics for which he engaged progressive directors and surrounded himself with the best actors of his day. Gielgud, long before subsidy became part of our common vocabulary, proved that the best results in theatre only come from permanence . . . under the stylish, patrician-seeming surface there lurks a man and an actor fascinated by new currents in the arts . . . Of all the tributes to Sir John, one in particular has stuck in my mind. It came from the playwright, David Hare, who said, 'Acting is a judgment of character' and that as actors grow older it is who and what they were as human beings that sustains their art. Gielgud's innate dignity, nobility and generosity of temper shine through all his recent work, and today we love and admire Gielgud for what he has achieved, but even more for what he is—an uncommon man who brings to acting a life-enhancing zest, energy and elan."

And this was still a time for introspection; as John had written in an epilogue to his collection of Shakespearean essays (*Shakespeare Hit or Miss?*):

> I was always as absorbed throughout my years in the theatre as a director as well as an actor, though when I combined the two occupations, as I did many times, I sometimes became too divided to maintain the necessary concentration required. When I was directed by others, I learned a great deal from them. I did not make many enemies, though I was fairly autocratic in the theatre. I never had to be concerned with money matters, always worked for sympathetic managers, was given a free hand in casting and choice of colleagues and designers, and very seldom had to work in plays I did not like. I always found rehearsals fascinatingly lively, matinee days extremely arduous, and long runs as difficult to sustain as they were valuable for practice and selectivity. Often I failed to intimidate, and was apt to listen to too many people, to appear unduly impulsive towards my colleagues, and to change my mind too often. I have always been too fond of popularity, and wanted everyone to like me. I have often been too timid and cowardly in my behaviour, dreading crises and quarrels, because I was always so happy in the theatre. I should perhaps have been a better mixer, and also a more formidable character. Olivier was not always an easy man; like Irving, he was feared as well as deeply respected, but both men inspired enormous devotion and enthusiasm in their companies, and I have always hoped to do the same—"and thus the whirligig of time brings in his revenges."

Introspection was mingled with an irritation at what he felt was a falling away of the offers to work. Brian Bedford, on a brief return to England at this time, remembers a somewhat despairing John complaining about how terrible it was to be out of work. "And how long has this been going on?" asked Bedford. "Oh," replied John, "since Friday."

And, for John, almost unbelievably, there was still one more role to play;

he spent his ninety-sixth birthday, April 14, 2000, filming for the play-wright and director David Mamet a very brief Samuel Beckett play entitled *Catastrophe*, in which the only other player was another world-class play-wright, Harold Pinter. That night I rang John to wish him a happy birth-day, see if he had received my ritual bottle of champagne, and ask him how it felt to be back in front of a camera. "Very surprising, but I wish they had told me that it was a non-speaking role. I really am rather too old to appear as an extra!"

And there was yet one more television interview still to record: Richard Eyre, formerly director of the National Theatre, was now filming a six-part BBC series called *Changing Stages*, and it was for the opening Shake-spearean survey that, for the very last time, Gielgud recalled his tales of Lil-ian Baylis and Harley Granville-Barker, of Olivier and their perceived enmity over Romeo and Mercutio more than sixty years earlier.

John then made his last public appearance on April 18, four days after his birthday, at the funeral of one of his last surviving intimates, Ralph Richardson's widow Meriel Forbes, at the church of Our Lady of the As-sumption, just off Regent Street. By now he was on two sticks, and the end came barely a month later. On Sunday, May 21, he had finished lunch, and his driver, Peter, helped him through to the drawing room at Wotton Un-derwood to enjoy the thin spring sunshine. As he reached his chair, John collapsed onto it. His death, unlike his life, was achieved with a minimum of theatricality.

The following day, in newspapers and radio and television broadcasts all over the world, the passing of the greatest classical actor in the whole of the twentieth century was marked with due observance; that night lights were dimmed all over the West End, and many leading players paid tribute in their curtain speeches to the actor who was now generally recognized as the head of their profession. Corin Redgrave, recalling how much Gielgud had influenced his father, said, "The odds is gone, and there is nothing left remarkable beneath the visiting moon," and John's agent Laurie Evans, who had also represented Olivier and Richardson, noted, "Of the three, Gielgud was by far the greatest actor."

In contrast to this public praise, however, John had left strict instructions that his funeral was to be intensely private, and so on June 1, at the little parish church of Wotton Underwood, a very few friends and relatives gathered. Alec Guinness, himself to die barely six months later, was of course there, as were John Mills, Donald Sinden, Paul Scofield, Maggie Smith, and Irene Worth.

Sir Donald Sinden read "No Man Is an Island" by John Donne; John Mills recited the poem "Do Not Despair for Johnny Head in Air," which he had first spoken in the film *The Way to the Stars;* and Paul Scofield read Shakespeare's Sonnet 71, the one starting, "No longer mourn for me when I am dead."

Of the multitude of tributes, it is perhaps worth recalling just two, from either end of the journalistic spectrum. For *The Sunday Times,* Paul Scofield wrote

For the vast majority of actors and actresses since the late 1930s, John has been the consummate epitome of style in the theatre . . . his sense of style, together with the extreme beauty and musicality of his speaking (notably of verse) has been the most dominant component of his art, but he was also a deeply emotional actor, and if there could be said to be any conflict in his work, it was to be found in the confrontation of style and feeling . . . his criticism of himself, often shot through with humour, would have been annihilating had it been directed at others; his discipline came from within and was compounded of self-appraisal and care for others, perhaps a rare combination of trust and mistrust . . . he directed other actors with both autocratic authority and a nervous awareness of points of views other than his own, which created an atmosphere sometime uncomfortable, and always stimulating . . . sometimes he seemed too vulnerable to random suggestions, often to the despair of actors who felt their performances threatened by apparently arbitrary changes in physical staging or relationships, but which might in hindsight be seen as anticipation of present improvisational techniques . . . it is a curious fact that the actor most renowned for poetic and aesthetic sensibility should also have been the toughest; that his fastidiousness should have been fortified by nerves and muscles of steel.

At the lower end of the scale of journalism, I think even John himself might have been delighted by a headline in the *Daily Sport*, which read, simply but in bold capital letters, BUTLER IN DUDLEY MOORE FILM DIES.

In a curious and oblique way, which he would never, of course, himself have acknowledged in public, perhaps one of the greatest tributes to John came just two months after his death, with a Home Office report proposing, at last, a change in the sex laws, which would finally abolish the crimes for which both Oscar Wilde and Gielgud were prosecuted—those of buggery and gross indecency involving consenting adults. The review finally advocated that public homosexual activity should be dealt with in precisely the same way as public heterosexual sex.

John's will was published some six months after his death. It listed specific cash legacies to friends and organizations such as RADA, the Actors' Charitable Trust, and the King George V Fund for Actors and Actresses. He also left the Theatre Museum in London a number of personal items, including a snuff box, which had once belonged to Charles Kean. To the National Portrait Gallery he left a painting of his great-aunt, Ellen Terry. Beyond that, the bulk of his fortune was to be given over to charitable causes chosen at the discretion of his executors, who were also charged with disposing of his papers and archives.

John's name lives on, not only in the theater that bears his name, but also in countless awards at drama schools around the world.

John's estate was eventually valued at £1,468,451, though this did not include his last car, a Volvo that he had cannily sold to his own driver for £2,000 a few weeks before his death; the man who had once described himself as "a silly emotional gubbins" had at the last learned the value of his possessions.

These were duly auctioned at Sotheby's in March 2001. "Don't open a drawer," someone had warned the valuers, "or Ellen Terry's teeth are sure to fall out." The auction (followed a few weeks later by that of Sir Ralph

Richardson) featured such treasures as twenty of John's own pencil drawings of actors and actresses, his Panama hat, gloves, and a brown leather Dunhill cigarette case. Then there were playbills, scrapbooks, a writing table, ornate Venetian mirrors, classical busts. It was the showbiz garage sale of all time, and a day of countless memories for all of us lucky enough to have known John at home.

That was, however, as he recalled in his 2000 diary for the *London Review of Books*, an experience narrowly missed by Alan Bennett:

21 MAY. Gielgud dies. Asked to appear on various programmes, including the Nine O'Clock News but say no. Reluctant to jump on the bandwagon, particularly when the bandwagon is a hearse. Some notes:

Despite the umpteen programmes of reminiscence Gielgud did both on radio and television there was always more and I never felt he had been sufficiently debriefed. Anyone of any distinction at all should, on reaching a certain age, be taken away for a weekend at the state's expense, formally interviewed and stripped of all their recollections.

It was hard to tell if he liked someone, only that he didn't dislike them. I think I came in the latter category. I went round to see him after *Home* and he said how much he liked David Storey. "He's the ideal author . . . never says a word!"

In *Chariots of Fire* he shared a scene with Lindsay Anderson, both of them playing Cambridge dons. Lindsay was uncharacteristically nervous but having directed John G. in *Home* felt able to ask his help, saying that if he felt Lindsay was doing too much or had any other tips he was to tell him. Gielgud was appalled: "Oh no, no. I can't do that, I shall be far too busy thinking about myself!"

The last time I saw him was when we were filming an episode of the TV adaptation of *A Dance to the Music of Time*. We were supposedly talking to one another but the speeches were separately recorded and intercut. His speech was haltingly delivered (but then so had mine been) and we did several takes. At the end he was given a round of applause by cast and crew, which I felt had not much to do with the quality of the speech itself so much as his having stayed alive long enough to deliver it. I imagine this kind of thing happened on most of the jobs he did (and he did a good many) in his nineties, and it was probably one of the things he hated about being old as there was inevitably some condescension to the applause. But he would just smile, do his funny snuffle and say that people were awfully kind.

23 MAY. Watch the *Omnibus* tribute to John G. in which *Oedipus* and *Forty Years On,* which came after it, both go unmentioned, though much is made of *Prospero's Books* largely because he took his clothes off in it (not, incidentally, for the first time, as he did so in Bob Guccione's *Caligula;* this too goes unmentioned, though more out of kindness, I would have thought). To some extent the omissions simply reflect the material that is available—the programme is archiveled. The BBC did have film of *Forty Years On* but lost it or wiped it or certainly made no effort to preserve it, though I would have thought that even in 1968 it was plain that any film or tape of Gielgud needed to be set aside. Thirty years and more later, I doubt the situation has improved much and it remains a scandal that a public corporation should still have no foolproof archive system.

Letters from Gielgud were always unmistakable because of the one-in-five slope of his handwriting, the text sliding off the page. I always felt it was slightly unfriendly that I'd never been invited down to Buckinghamshire but then I reread a letter he wrote me after I'd reviewed one of his books and in it I find an open invitation to lunch any time, with telephone number, directions, and how to get from the station. So now, of course, I feel mortified.

It would be tempting to end this authorized biography with the obvious Shakespearean farewells of either Hamlet or Prospero, both of which Gielgud had spoken so many times, onstage and in the pulpit, with an unrivaled sense of the verse and the valedictory emotion; but I am inclined instead to go back to the Chekhov *Swan Song,* which John had first played in the war and later filmed for Kenneth Branagh only a few years before his death:

> Old age? No such thing. Stuff and nonsense . . . Where you've got art, where you've got talent, there's no room for old age, no room for loneliness or being ill. Even death is only half itself . . . Our song is sung, our race is run. What talent do I have? I'm a squeezed lemon, a melting icicle, a rusty nail . . . an old theatre rat . . . off we go, then.

John Gielgud, actor and director, 1904–2000

CHRONOLOGY

In the following list, "director"'is indicated as "(d)".

THEATRE

Year	Theatre	Production	Role
1915			
Dec	Mathilde Verne Piano-forte School	HMS Pinafore	Sailor
1920			
Jul	Battle Abbey	As You Like It	Orlando
1921			
Jan	Old Court Studio	Romeo and Juliet	Mercutio
	Old Court Studio	Belinda	German Officer
Nov	Old Vic	Henry V	Walk-on
1922			
Jan	YMCA Hall, Tottenham Ct. Rd.	The Importance of Being Earnest	John Worthing (d)
Feb	Church Hall, Barnet	I'll Leave It to You	Bobbie
	Training Ship Stork	I'll Leave It to You	Bobbie
Mar	Old Vic	Peer Gynt	Walk-on
	Old Vic	King Lear	Walk-on
Apr	Old Vic	Peer Gynt	Walk-on
	Old Vic	As You Like It	Walk-on
	Old Vic	Wat Tyler	Walk-on
Apr	Old Vic	Love Is the Best Doctor	Walk-on
	Old Vic	The Comedy of Errors	Walk-on
Sept	New, Oxford and touring	The Wheel	Lt. Manners
Dec	Eton College	The Masque of Comus	Younger Brother

483

1923

Jan	Apollo	A Roof and Four Walls	Designer
Mar	Inner Temple	The Masque of Comus	Younger Brother
	RADA	The School for Scandal	Peter Teazle
May	Regent	The Insect Play	Poet Butterfly
Jun	RADA	Twelfth Night	Sir Toby
	RADA	The Young Person in Pink	Lord Stevenage
	Regent	Robert E. Lee	Aide-de-camp
Jul	RADA	Hamlet (scenes from)	Hamlet
Aug	Regent	Robert E. Lee	David Peel
Dec	RADA	Les Caprices de Marianne	Celio
	RADA	L'Aiglon	Hartmann
	RADA	Arms and the Man	Sergius
	RADA	Reparation (scenes)	Fedya
	RADA	Joan of Arc	Paul
	Comedy	Charley's Aunt	Charles

1924

Jan	Oxford Playhouse	Captain Brassbound's Conversion	Johnson
Feb	Oxford Playhouse	Mr. Pim Passes By	Brian Strange
Feb	Oxford Playhouse	Love for Love	Valentine
Feb	Oxford Playhouse	She Stoops to Conquer	Young Marlowe
Feb	Oxford Playhouse	Monna Vanna	Prinzevalle
Apr	RADA	Romeo and Juliet	Paris
May	Regent	Romeo and Juliet	Romeo
Oct	RADA Players	The Return Half	John Sherry
Oct	Oxford Playhouse	Candida	Marchbanks
Oct	Oxford Playhouse	Deirdre of the Sorrows	Naisi
Nov	Oxford Playhouse	A Collection Will Be Made	Paul Roget
Nov	Oxford Playhouse	Everybody's Husband	A Domino
Nov	Oxford Playhouse	The Cradle Song	Antonio
Nov	Oxford Playhouse	John Gabriel Borkman	Erhart
Nov	Oxford Playhouse	His Widow's Husband	Zurita

Dec	Oxford Playhouse	Madame Pepita	Augusto
Dec	Charterhouse	French Leave	Lt. George Graham
1925			
Jan	Oxford Playhouse	A Collection Will Be Made	Paul Roget
Jan	Oxford Playhouse	Smith	Algernon
Jan	Oxford Playhouse	The Cherry Orchard	Trofimov
Feb	Royalty	The Vortex	Understudy
Mar	Comedy	The Vortex	Understudy & Nicky
Apr	RADA Players	The Nature of the Evidence	Ted Hewitt
May	Aldwych	The Orphan	Castalio
May	Little	The Vortex	Understudy & Nicky
May	Lyric, Hammersmith	The Cherry Orchard	Trofimov
Jun	Garden	The High Constable's Wife	J. de Boys-Bourredon
Jun	Royalty	The Cherry Orchard	Trofimov
Aug	Oxford Playhouse	The Lady from the Sea	A Stranger
Aug	Oxford Playhouse	The Man With the Flower in His Mouth	Title Role
Sept	Apollo	Two Gentlemen of Verona	Valentine
Oct	Little	The Seagull	Konstantin
Oct	New Oxford	Dr. Faustus	Good Angel
Dec	Little	Gloriana	Sir John Harringdon
Dec	Prince's	L'Ecole des Cocottes	Robert
Dec	Daly's	Nativity Play	Second Shepherd
1926			
Jan	Savoy (matinée)	The Tempest	Ferdinand
Jan	RADA Players	Sons and Fathers	Richard Southern
Feb	Barnes	Three Sisters	Tusenbach
Mar	Barnes	Katerina	Georg
May	Royal Court	Hamlet	Rosencrantz
Jun	Coliseum	Romeo and Juliet (excerpt)	Romeo
Jun	Lyric, Hammersmith	Henry VI (dramatized reading)	Richard

Jul	Garrick	The Lady of the Camelias	Armand
Jul	Court (300 Club)	Confession	Wilfred Marlay
Oct	New	The Constant Nymph	Lewis Dodd
1927			
Apr	Apollo	Othello	Cassio
Apr	New	The Good Old Days	Boulter
Apr	New	The Hectic Present	Guest
Jun	Strand	The Great God Brown	Dion Anthony
Nov	King's, Hammersmith	The Constant Nymph	Lewis Dodd
1928			
Jan	Majestic, New York	The Patriot	csarevitch
Mar	Wyndham's (matinées)	Ghosts	Oswald
Apr	Arts	Ghosts	Oswald
Jun	Globe	Holding Out the Apple	Gerald Marlowe
Jun	Arts	Prejudice	Jacob Slovak
Aug	Shaftesbury	The Skull	Capt. Allenby
Oct	Court	The Lady from Alfaqueque	Felipe Rivas
Oct	Court	Fortunato	Alberto
Nov	Strand	Out of the Sea	John Martin
1929			
Jan	Arts	The Seagull	Konstantin
Feb	Little	Red Rust	Fedor
Mar	Prince of Wales	Hunters Moon	De Tressailles
Apr	Garrick	The Lady With a Lamp	Tremayne
Apr	Palace (matinée)	Shall We Join the Ladies?	Capt. Jennings
Jun	Arts	Red Sunday	Bronstein
Sept	Old Vic	Romeo and Juliet	Romeo
Oct	Old Vic	The Merchant of Venice	Antonio
Oct	Old Vic	The Imaginary Invalid	Cléante
Oct	Old Vic (special perf.)	Romeo and Juliet	Romeo
Nov	Old Vic	Richard II	Richard II
Dec	Prince of Wales	Douaumont	The Prologue

Dec	Old Vic	A Midsummer Night's Dream	Oberon

1930

Jan	Old Vic	Julius Caesar	Mark Antony
Jan	Haymarket (matinée)	Romeo and Juliet	Romeo
Feb	Old Vic	As You Like It	Orlando
Feb	Old Vic	Androcles and the Lion	Emperor
Mar	Old Vic	Macbeth	Macbeth
Apr	Old Vic	The Man With the Flower in His Mouth	Title Role
Apr	Old Vic	Hamlet	Hamlet
Jun	Queen's	Hamlet	Hamlet
Jul	Lyric, Hammersmith	The Importance of Being Earnest	John Worthing
Jul	Smallhythe	Hamlet (scene)	Hamlet
Sept	Old Vic	Henry IV, Part I	Hotspur
Oct	Old Vic	The Tempest	Prospero
Oct	Old Vic	The Jealous Wife	Lord Trinket
Nov	Old Vic	Richard II	Richard II
Nov	Old Vic	Antony and Cleopatra	Antony

1931

Jan	Sadler's Wells	Twelfth Night	Malvolio
Feb	Sadler's Wells	The Tempest	Prospero
Feb	Old Vic	Arms and the Man	Sergius
Mar	Old Vic	Much Ado About Nothing	Benedick
Apr	Old Vic	King Lear	Lear
Apr	Old Vic	Shakespeare Birthday Festival (scenes)	Hamlet
May	His Majesty's	The Good Companions	Jollifant
Jul	Smallhythe	Much Ado About Nothing (scenes)	Benedick
Nov	Arts	Musical Chairs	Schindler
Nov	Tour	The Good Companions	Jollifant

1932

Feb	New, Oxford	Romeo and Juliet	Director

Mar	New	Romeo and Juliet	Director
Apr	Criterion	Musical Chairs	Schindler
Apr	Old Vic	Shakespeare Birthday Festival (scenes)	Richard II
Jun	New	Richard of Bordeaux	Richard II (co-d)
Jul	Smallhythe	Twelfth Night (scenes)	Orsino
Sept	St. Martin's	Strange Orchestra	Director
Dec	Old Vic	The Merchant of Venice	Director
Dec	Golders Green	Musical Chairs	Schindler
1933			
Feb	New	Richard of Bordeaux	Richard II
Feb	Sadler's Wells (matinée)	The Merchant of Venice	Director/Designer
Jul	New	Richard II (scenes)	Richard II
Jul	Ambassadors	La Voix Humaine	Director
Aug	King's, Hammersmith	Musical Chairs	Director
Sept	Wyndham's	Sheppey	Director
Dec	New (matinée)	A Kiss for Cinderella	The Censor
1934			
Jan	Shaftesbury	Spring 1600	Director
Apr	Tour	Richard of Bordeaux	Richard II
Jun	New	Queen of Scots	Director
Jul	Wyndham's	The Maitlands	Roger Maitland
Jul	Smallhythe	Shakespeare Sonnets	Speaker
Nov	New	Hamlet	Hamlet (d)
1935			
Apr	New	The Old Ladies	Director
Apr	Tour	Richard of Bordeaux	Richard II
May	Drury Lane (jubilee perf.)	The Player's Masque	Mercury
Jul	New	Noah	Noah
Jul	Smallhythe	Hamlet (scenes)	Hamlet
Oct	New	Romeo and Juliet	Mercutio/Romeo (d)
Nov	His Majesty's	Punch Cartoons	Director
1936			
Feb	OUDS	Richard II	Director
Apr	Tour	Romeo and Juliet	Romeo (d)

May	Tour	Romeo and Juliet	Romeo (d)
May	New	The Seagull	Trigorin
Sept	Alexandra, Toronto	Hamlet	Hamlet
Oct	Empire, New York	Hamlet	Hamlet
Oct	St. James, New York	Hamlet	Hamlet
1937			
Feb	Schubert, Boston	Hamlet	Hamlet
Apr	Tour	He Was Born Gay	Mason (d)
May	Queen's	He Was Born Gay	Mason (d)
May	His Majesty's	Nijinsky Matinée	Speaker
Sept	Queen's	Richard II	Richard II
Nov	Golders Green	Richard II	Richard II
Nov	Queen's	The School for Scandal	Joseph Surface
Dec	Winter Garden	King George's Pension Fund Matinée	Speaker
1938			
Jan	Queen's	Three Sisters	Vershinin
Apr	Queen's	The Merchant of Venice	Shylock (d)
May	Ambassadors	Spring Meeting	Director
Jul	Piccadilly	Spring Meeting	Director
Sept	Manchester	Dear Octopus	Nicholas
Sept	Queen's	Dear Octopus	Nicholas
1939			
Jan	Globe	The Importance of Being Earnest	John Worthing (d)
Apr	Old Vic	Shakespeare Birthday Festival	Hamlet
Apr	Globe	Scandal in Assyria	Director
May	Brighton	Spring Meeting	Director
May	Globe	Rhondda Roundabout	Co-producer
Jun	Lyceum	Hamlet	Hamlet (d)
Jul	Elsinore	Hamlet	Hamlet (d)
Aug	Globe	The Importance of Being Earnest	John Worthing (d)
Sept	Tour	The Importance of Being Earnest	John Worthing (d)

Oct	Tour	Shakespeare in Peace and War	Speaker
1940			
Mar	Haymarket	The Beggar's Opera	Director
Apr	Haymarket	The Beggar's Opera	Macheath
Apr	Old Vic	King Lear	Lear
May	Old Vic	The Tempest	Prospero
Jul	Globe/ENSA Tour	Fumed Oak	Henry Crow (d)
		Hands Across the Sea	Peter Gilpin
		Hard Luck Story	Old Actor
Aug	Edinburgh (ENSA)	The Dark Lady of the Sonnets	Shakespeare (d)
1941			
Jan	Globe	Dear Brutus	Will Dearth (d)
Jun	Tour	Dear Brutus	Will Dearth (d)
Nov	Apollo	Ducks and Drakes	Director
Dec	Royal Albert Hall	All-Star Concert	Speaker
1942			
Jan	Tour	Macbeth	Macbeth (d)
Oct	Phoenix	The Importance of Being Earnest	John Worthing (d)
Nov	New	Special Matinée, Way of the World	Mirabell
Dec	Gibraltar	ENSA Tour Revue	Various
1943			
Jan	Haymarket	The Doctor's Dilemma	Louis Dubedat
Mar	Tour	Love for Love	Valentine (d)
Apr	Phoenix	Love for Love	Valentine (d)
Jul	Tour	Nursery Slopes	Director
Oct	Westminster	Landslide (Nursery Slopes)	Director
1944			
Jan	Apollo	The Cradle Song	Director
Mar	Tour	Crisis in Heaven	Director
Jun	Lyric	The Last of Summer	Director
Jul	Tour	Hamlet	Hamlet

Aug	Tour	Love for Love	Valentine (d)
Sept	Tour	The Circle	A. Champion-Cheney
Oct	Haymarket	The Circle	A. Champion-Cheney
Oct	Haymarket	Love for Love	Valentine (d)
Oct	Haymarket	Hamlet	Hamlet
1945			
Jan	Haymarket	A Midsummer Night's Dream	Oberon
Apr	Tour	The Duchess of Malfi	Ferdinand
Apr	Haymarket	The Duchess of Malfi	Ferdinand
Aug	Haymarket	Lady Windermere's Fan	Director
Oct	Far East Tour (ENSA)	Hamlet	Hamlet (d)
		Blithe Spirit	C. Condomine (d)
		Shakespeare in Peace and War	Speaker
1946			
Jun	Tour	Crime and Punishment	Raskolnikoff
Jun	New	Crime and Punishment	Raskolnikoff
Jul	Smallhythe	Macbeth (Reading)	Reader
Sept	Globe	Crime and Punishment	Raskolnikoff
1947			
Jan	USA/Canada Tour	The Importance of Being Earnest	John Worthing (d)
Apr	King's, Hammersmith	Lady Windermere's Fan	Director
May	USA Tour	Love for Love	Valentine (d)
Oct	Royale, New York	Medea	Jason (d)
Dec	Royale, New York	Crime and Punishment	Raskolnikoff
1948			
Jul	Haymarket	The Glass Menagerie	Director
Aug	Tour	Medea	Director
Sept	Globe	Medea	Director
Dec	Globe	The Return of the Prodigal	Eustace Jackson
1949			
Feb	Haymarket	The Heiress	Director
Apr	Memorial, Stratford	Much Ado About Nothing	Director

May	Globe	The Lady's Not for Burning	Thomas Mendip (d)
Jul	Smallhythe	Henry IV (Scene)	Hotspur
Sept	Apollo	Treasure Hunt	Director
Nov	Coliseum	Gala: Richard of Bordeaux (Scene)	Richard II
1950			
Jan	Lyric, Hammersmith	The Boy With a Cart	Director
Jan	Lyric, Hammersmith	Shall We Join the Ladies?	Director
Mar	Memorial, Stratford	Measure for Measure	Angelo
May	Memorial, Stratford	Julius Caesar	Cassius
Jun	Memorial, Stratford	Much Ado About Nothing	Benedick (d)
Jul	Memorial, Stratford	King Lear	Lear (co-d)
Oct	Schubert, Boston	The Lady's Not for Burning	Thomas Mendip (d)
Nov	Royale, New York	The Lady's Not for Burning	Thomas Mendip (d)
1951			
Jun	Phoenix	The Winter's Tale	Leontes
Jul	Smallhythe	Ellen Terry Anniversary Performance	Speaker
Aug	Tour	The Winter's Tale	Leontes
Oct	Coliseum	Salute to Ivor Novello	Speaker
Dec	Criterion	Indian Summer	Director
1952			
Jan	Phoenix	Much Ado About Nothing	Benedick (d)
Mar	Memorial, Stratford	Macbeth	Director
Dec	Lyric, Hammersmith	Richard II	Director
1953			
Feb	Lyric, Hammersmith	The Way of the World	Mirabell (d)
May	Lyric, Hammersmith	Venice Preserv'd	Jaffier
Jul	Bulawayo	Richard II	Richard II (d)
Nov	Haymarket	A Day by the Sea	Julian Anson (d)

Dec	Tour	Charley's Aunt	Director
1954			
Feb	New	Charley's Aunt	Director
May	Lyric, Hammersmith	The Cherry Orchard	Director
1955			
Apr	Memorial, Stratford	Twelfth Night	Director
Jun	Tour	King Lear	Lear
Jul	Palace	Much Ado About Nothing	Benedick (d)
Jul	Palace	King Lear	Lear
Jul	European Tour	Much Ado About Nothing & King Lear	Benedick (d), Lear
Nov	Memorial, Stratford	King Lear	Lear
Dec	Memorial, Stratford	Much Ado About Nothing	Benedick (d)
1956			
Apr	Haymarket	The Chalk Garden	Director
Jul	Smallhythe	Much Ado About Nothing (Scene)	Benedick
Oct	Tour	Nude with Violin	Sebastian (co-d)
Nov	Globe	Nude with Violin	Sebastian (co-d)
Dec	Royal Festival Hall	The Ages of Man	Speaker
1957			
Jun	Covent Garden	The Trojans	Director
Aug	Memorial, Stratford	The Tempest	Prospero
Aug	Tour	The Ages of Man	Speaker
Dec	Drury Lane	The Tempest	Prospero
1958			
Feb	Globe	The Potting Shed	James Callifer
Mar	Tour	Variation on a Theme	Director
Apr	Globe	Variation on a Theme	Director
May	Old Vic, then Tour	Henry VIII	Cardinal Wolsey
Jul	Comedy	Five Finger Exercise	Director
Sep	Tour (America/Europe)	The Ages of Man	Speaker
1959			
Jun	Globe	The Complaisant Lover	Director

Jun	Queen's	The Ages of Man	Speaker
Sept	Boston/New York	Much Ado About Nothing	Director
Dec	Music Box, New York	Five Finger Exercise	Director
1960			
Apr	Haymarket	The Ages of Man	Speaker
Sept	Phoenix	The Last Joke	Prince Cavanati
1961			
Feb	Covent Garden	A Midsummer Night's Dream	Director
Mar	ANTA Theatre, New York	Big Fish, Little Fish	Director
Jun	Globe	Dazzling Prospect	Director
Sept	Memorial, Stratford	The Ages of Man	Speaker
Oct	Memorial, Stratford	Othello	Othello
Dec	Memorial, Stratford	The Cherry Orchard	Gaev
	Aldwych	The Cherry Orchard	Gaev
1962			
Apr	Haymarket	The School for Scandal	Director
Apr	Tour	The Ages of Man	Speaker
Oct	Haymarket	The School for Scandal	Joseph Surface (d)
Nov	USA Tour	The School for Scandal	Joseph Surface (d)
1963			
Jan	Majestic, New York	The Ages of Man	Speaker
Apr	Lyceum, New York	The Ages of Man	Speaker
Jul	Tour	The Ides of March	Caesar (co-d)
Aug	Haymarket	The Ides of March	Caesar (co-d)
Dec	Australia/NZ Tour	The Ages of Man	Speaker
1964			
Feb	O'Keefe Centre	Hamlet	Voice of Ghost (d)
Mar	New York/Princeton	Homage to Shakespeare	Speaker
Mar	Shubert, New York	Hamlet	Voice of Ghost (d)
Apr	Tour (UK/Europe)	The Ages of Man	Speaker
Jul	Lunt-Fontanne, New York	Hamlet	Voice of Ghost (d)
Dec	Billy Rose, New York	Tiny Alice	Julian

1965

Mar	The White House	The Ages of Man	Speaker
Aug	Tour	Ivanov	Ivanov (d)
Sept	Phoenix	Ivanov	Ivanov (d)

1966

Mar	Shubert, New York	Ivanov	Ivanov (d)
Oct	Norway	The Ages of Man	Speaker
Nov	International Tour	Men, Women, and Shakespeare	Speaker

1967

Jan	Festival Hall	Oedipus Rex	Narrator
Jun	Ankara, Turkey	The Ages of Man	Speaker
Nov	Old Vic	Tartuffe	Orgon
Nov	Queen's	Halfway Up the Tree	Director

1968

Mar	Old Vic	Oedipus	Oedipus
Aug	Coliseum	Don Giovanni	Director
Oct	Apollo	Forty Years On	Headmaster
Dec	Phoenix	A Talent to Amuse	Speaker

1970

Feb	Lyric	The Battle of Shrivings	Sir Gideon Petrie
Jun	Royal Court	Home	Harry
Jul	Apollo	Home	Harry
Nov	Morosco, New York	Home	Harry

1971

Mar	Martin Beck, New York	All Over	Director
Jul	Chichester	Caesar and Cleopatra	Caesar

1972

Mar	Royal Court	Veterans	Sir Geoffrey Kendle
Sept	Queen's	Private Lives	Director
Oct	Shubert, New York	Irene	Director

1973

Sept	Albery	The Constant Wife	Director

1974

Mar	Old Vic	The Tempest	Prospero
May	Old Vic	Tribute to the Lady	Hamlet

Aug	Royal Court	Bingo	Shakespeare
Sept	46th St. Theatre, New York	Private Lives	Director
Dec	Shubert, New York	The Constant Wife	Director
1975			
Apr	Old Vic	No Man's Land	Spooner
Jun	Albery	The Gay Lord Quex	Director
Jul	Wyndham's	No Man's Land	Spooner
1976			
Feb	Old Vic	Tribute to the Lady	Hamlet
Apr	Lyttleton, National	No Man's Land	Spooner
Nov	Longacre, New York	No Man's Land	Spooner
1977			
Mar	Olivier, National	Julius Caesar	Caesar
Apr	Olivier, National	Volpone	Sir Politick Would-Be
Nov	Cottesloe, National	Half-Life	Sir Noël Cunliffe
1978			
Mar	Duke of York's	Half-Life	Sir Noël Cunliffe
1979			
Jan	Tour	Half-Life	Sir Noël Cunliffe
1984			
Feb	Duke of York's	Gala Performance	Speaker
May	Marriott Hotel	Old Vic Tribute Dinner	Speaker
1988			
Jan	Apollo	The Best of Friends	Sir Sydney Cockerell
Mar	Royalty	A Tale of Two Cities	Voice Only
1990			
Jul	Palladium	Royal Birthday Gala	Compère

FILM AND TELEVISION

Year	Production	Role	Film or television
1924	Who Is the Man?	Daniel	Film
1929	The Clue of the New Pin	Rex Trasmere	Film

1932	Insult	Henri Dubois	Film
1933	The Good Companions	Inigo Jollifant	Film
1936	The Secret Agent	Ashenden/Brodie	Film
1941	The Prime Minister	Benjamin Disraeli	Film
	Airman's Letter to his Mother	Narrator	Film
1944	Unfinished Journey	Commentator	Film
1953	Julius Caesar	Cassius	Film
1955	Richard III	Clarence	Film
1956	Around the World in 80 Days	Foster	Film
	The Barretts of Wimpole Street	Edward Moulton-Barrett	Film
1957	Saint Joan	Warwick	Film
1959	A Day by the Sea	Julian Anson	Television
	The Browning Version	Andrew Crocker-Harris	Television
1963	The Rehearsal	The Count	Television
1964	Becket	Louis VII	Film
1964	Hamlet	Voice of the Ghost	Film
1965	The Loved One	Sir Francis Hinsley	Film
1966	Chimes at Midnight	Henry IV	Film
	Alice in Wonderland	Mock Turtle	Television
	The Mayfly and the Frog	Gabriel Kantara	Television
1967	From Chekhov with Love	Chekhov	Television
	Sebastian	Secret Services Chief	Film
	Assignment to Kill	Kurt Valayan	Film
	Revolution D'Octobre	Narrator	Film
1968	The Charge of the Light Brigade	Lord Raglan	Film
	The Shoes of the Fisherman	Pope	Film
	Saint Joan	The Inquisitor	Television
	From Chekhov with Love	Cast Member	Television
1969	Oh! What a Lovely War	Count Berchtold	Film

1970	Julius Caesar	Caesar	Film
	Eagle in a Cage	Lord Sissal	Film
	Hassan	The Caliph	Television
	Hamlet	The Ghost	Television
1972	Lost Horizon	Chang	Film
	Home	Harry	Television
1973	Frankenstein	Chief Constable	Television
	Menace	F. W. Densham	Television
1974	11 Harrowhouse	Meecham	Film
	Gold	Farrell	Film
	Murder on the Orient Express	Beddoes	Film
	Galileo	Cardinal	Film
1975	Shades of Greene: Special Duties	Mr. Ferraro	Television
1976	Edward VII	Disraeli	Television
	The Picture of Dorian Gray	Lord Wotton	Television
	Aces High	Headmaster	Film
	Caesar and Cleopatra	Caesar	Film
	Joseph Andrews	Doctor	Film
1977	Providence	Clive Langham	Film
	Heartbreak House	Captain Shotover	Television
	A Portrait of the Artist . . .	Preacher	Film
	The Grand Inquisitor	Title Role	Television
1978	No Man's Land	Spooner	Television
	Richard II	John of Gaunt	Film
	The Cherry Orchard	Gaev	Television
	Les Misérables	Valjean's father	Film
	Murder by Decree	Lord Salisbury	Film
	Romeo and Juliet	Chorus	Television
1979	The Conductor	Title Role	Film
	The Human Factor	Brigadier Tomlinson	Film
	Caligula	Nerva	Film
	Tales of the Unexpected	Jelks	Television
1980	The Elephant Man	Carr Gomm	Film

	Tales of the Unexpected	Cyril Boggis	Television
	Sphinx	Abdu	Film
	Seven Dials of Mystery	Marquis of Caterham	Television
	The English Garden	Presenter	Television
	Soul of a Nation	Narrator	Television
	The Lion of the Desert	Sharif El Gariani	Film
1981	Arthur	Hobson	Film
	Chariots of Fire	Master of Trinity	Film
1981	The Formula	Dr. Esau	Film
	Priest of Love	Herbert G. Muskett	Film
	Brideshead Revisited	Edward Ryder	Television
1982	Marco Polo	Doge	Film
	The Critic	Lord Burleigh	Television
	The Hunchback of Notre Dame	Torturer	Television
	Inside the Third Reich	Speer's father	Television
	Buddenbrooks	Narrator	Film
1983	Wagner	Pfistermeister	Film
	Gandhi	Lord Irwin	Film
	Scandalous	Uncle Willie	Film
	The Wicked Lady	Hogarth	Film
	The Vatican Story	Pope Pius VII	Film
	Invitation to the Wedding	Clyde Ormiston	Film
	The Master of Ballantrae	Lord Dunsdeer	Television
1984	The Far Pavilions	Cavagnari	Television
	The Shooting Party	Cornelius Cardew	Film
	Frankenstein	De Lacey	Television
	Camille	The Duke	Television
	Plenty	Sir Leonard Darwin	Film
	Romance on the Orient Express	Charles Woodward	Film
1985	Leave or Fare	John M. Murray	Film
	Time After Time	Jasper Swift	Television
	The Theban Plays: Oedipus	Teiresias	Television

1986	The Theban Plays: Antigone	Teiresias	Television
	The Whistle Blower	Sir Adrian Chapple	Film
	The Canterville Ghost	Sir Simon de Canterville	Film
	War and Remembrance	Dr. Aaron Jastrow	Television
1987	Bluebeard	Title Role	Film
	Arthur 2: On the Rocks	Hobson	Film
	Quartermaine's Terms	Loomis	Television
1988	Getting It Right	Sir Gordon Munday	Film
	A Man for All Seasons	Cardinal Wolsey	Television
	Appointment with Death	Colonel Carbury	Film
1989	Summer's Lease	Haverford Downs	Television
1990	Prospero's Books	Prospero	Film
	Shining Through	Konrad Friedrichs	Film
	A TV Dante	Virgil	Television
	Hindemith: A Pilgrim's Progress	Narrator	Television
1991	The Best of Friends	Sir Sydney Cockerell	Television
	The Power of One	Headmaster St. John	Film
1992	Swan Song	Vasily Svetlovidov	Film
1993	Inspector Morse	Lord Hincksey	Television
1994	Scarlett	Scarlett's grandfather	Television
	Inspector Alleyn Mysteries	Percival Pyke Period	Television
	Summer Day's Dream	Stephen Dawlish	Television
1995	First Knight	Oswald	Film
	Words from Jerusalem	Narrator	Television
	Haunted	Dr. Doyle	Television
1996	Shine	Cecil Parkes	Film
	A Dance to the Music of Time	St. John Clarke	Television
	Looking for Richard	Interviewee	Film
	Gulliver's Travels	Professor of Sunlight	Television
	Dragonheart	Voice of King Arthur	Film
	Portrait of a Lady	Mr.. Touchett	Film

	Quest for Camelot	Voice of Merlin	Film
1998	Merlin	King Constant	Television
	The Tichbourne Claimant	Lord Chief Justice	Television
1999	Elizabeth	The Pope	Film
	Sergei Rachmaninov: Memories	Narrator	Film
2000	Beckett on Film	Protagonist	Film

BIBLIOGRAPHY

Allen, David, *Performing Chekhov* (Routledge, 2000)

Alpert, Hollis, *Burton* (G. P. Putnam's Sons, 1986)

Annan, Noël, *The Dons* (HarperCollins, 1999)

Bagnold, Enid, *Enid Bagnold's Autobiography* (Heinemann, 1969)

Baxter, Keith, *My Sentiments Exactly* (Oberon, 1999)

Beaton, Cecil, *Self Portrait With Friends* (Weidenfeld & Nicolson, 1979)

Billington, Michael, *Peggy Ashcroft* (John Murray, 1988)

Black, Kitty, *Upper Circle* (Methuen, 1984)

Blakelock, Denys, *Round the Next Corner* (Victor Gollancz, 1967)

Boose, Lynda E., *Shakespeare, The Movie* (with R. Burt) (Routledge, 1997)

Brady, Frank, *Citizen Welles* (Hodder & Stoughton, 1990)

Brandreth, Gyles, *John Gielgud, A Celebration* (Pavilion, 1994)

Brine, Adrian, *A Shakespearean Actor Prepares* (Smith & Kraus, 2000)

Brode, Douglas, *Shakespeare in the Movies* (OUP, 2000)

Brook, Donald, *The Romance of English Theatre* (Rockliff, 1945)

Brook, Peter, *The Shifting Point* (Methuen, 1987)

———. *Threads of Time* (Methuen, 1999)

Brown, Dennis, *Actors Talk* (Limelight Editions, 1999)

Brown, Ivor, *Theatre* (Max Reinhardt, 1955)

———. *Theatre 1955–6* (Max Reinhardt, 1956)

Bull, Peter, *I Know the Face, But . . .* (Peter Davies, 1959)

———. *Bull's Eyes* (Robin Clark, 1985)

Burnett, Mark, *Shakespeare, Film, Fin de Siècle* (Macmillan, 2000)

Burton, Hal, *Great Acting* (BBC, 1967)

Carpenter, Humphrey, *OUDS* (OUP, 1985)

Cheshire, David F., *Portrait of Ellen Terry* (Amber Lane, 1989)

Cockin, Katharine, *Edith Craig* (Cassell, 1998)

Cottrell, John, *Richard Burton* (with Fergus Cashin) (Arthur Baker, 1971)

Coward, Noël, *The Noël Coward Diaries* (Macmillan, 1982)

Craig, Edith, *Ellen Terry's Memoirs* (with Christopher St. John) (Victor Gollancz, 1933)

Craig, Edward, *Gordon Craig* (Victor Gollancz, 1968)

Craig, Edward G., *Ellen Terry and Her Secret Self* (Sampson Low, Marston)

Conrad, Peter, *Feasting With Panthers* (Thames & Hudson, 1994)

Croall, Jonathan, *Gielgud, A Theatrical Life* (Methuen, 2000)

Cronyn, Hume, *A Terrible Liar* (William Morrow, 1991)

Culver, Roland, *Not Quite a Gentleman* (William Kimber, 1979)

Darlow, Michael, *Terence Rattigan, The Man and his Work* (Quartet, 2000)

Davies, Anthony, *Shakespeare and the Moving Image* (CUP, 1997)

Dean, Basil, *The Theatre at War* (Harrap, 1956)

Denison, Michael, *Double Act* (Michael Joseph, 1985)

Drummond, John, *Tainted by Experience* (Faber & Faber, 2000)

Duff, Charles, *The Lost Summer* (Nick Hern, 1995)

Epstein, Edward, *Portrait of Jennifer* (Simon & Schuster, 1995)

Esslin, Martin, *Pinter: The Playwright* (Methuen, 2000)

Fay, Stephen, *Power Play* (Hodder & Stoughton, 1995)

Findlater, Richard, *The Player Kings* (Weidenfeld & Nicolson, 1971)

Forbes, Bryan, *Ned's Girl: The Life of Edith Evans* (Elm Tree, 1977)

Geist, Kenneth, *Pictures Will Talk* (Charles Scribner's Sons, 1978)

Gielgud, John, *Early Stages* (Falco Press, 1939)

———. *An Actor and his Time* (Sidgwick & Jackson, 1989)

———. *Shakespeare–Hit or Miss?* (Sidgwick & Jackson, 1991)

———. *Notes From the Gods* (Nick Hern, 1994)

———. *Acting Shakespeare* (Pan, 1997)

Gielgud, Kate, *Kate Terry Gielgud* (Max Reinhardt, 1953)

Gilder, Rosamond, *John Gielgud's Hamlet* (OUP, 1937)

Gish, Lillian, *The Movies, Mr. Griffith, and Me* (W. H. Allen, 1969)

Gottlieb, Sidney, *Hitchcock on Hitchcock* (Faber & Faber, 1995)

Grove, Valerie, *Dear Dodie: The Life of Dodie Smith* (Chatto & Windus, 1996)

Guinness, Alec, *My Name Escapes Me* (Penguin, 1996)

———. *Blessings in Disguise* (Penguin, 1997)

———. *A Positively Final Appearance* (Penguin, 2000)

Gussow, Mel, *Edward Albee: A Singular Journey* (Oberon, 1999)

Guthrie, Tyrone, *A Life in the Theatre* (Columbus, 1987)

Hall, Peter, *Making an Exhibition of Myself* (Sinclair-Stevenson, 1993)

Harding, James, *Emlyn Williams: A Life* (Weidenfeld & Nicolson, 1993)

Harwood, Ronald, *Sir Donald Wolfit* (Secker & Warburg, 1971)

———. *The Ages of Gielgud* (Hodder & Stoughton, 1984)

Hawkins, Jack, *Anything For a Quiet Life* (Coronet, 1973)

Hayman, Ronald, *Gielgud* (Heinemann, 1971)

Heston, Charlton, *In the Arena* (Simon & Schuster, 1995)

Hoare, Philip, *Noël Coward* (Mandarin, 1996)

Hobson, Harold, *Theatre 2* (Longmans, 1950)

———. *Verdict at Midnight* (Longmans, 1952)

Houseman, John, *Unfinished Business* (Columbus, 1986)

Howard, Ronald, *In Search of my Father* (St. Martin's Press, 1981)

Hugget, Richard, *Binkie Beaumont* (Hodder & Stoughton, 1989)

Hurren, Kenneth, *Theatre Inside Out* (W. H. Allen, 1977)

Isherwood, Christopher, *Diaries, 1939–1960* (Methuen, 1996)

Jackson, Russell, *Shakespeare on Film* (CUP, 2000)

Jarvis, Martin, *Acting Strangely* (Methuen, 2000)

Jenkins, Graham, *Richard Burton, My Brother* (Michael Joseph, 1988)

Kavanagh, Julie, *Secret Muses* (Faber & Faber, 1986)

Keown, Eric, *Peggy Ashcroft* (Rockliff, 1955)

Laffey, Bruce, *Beatrice Lillie* (Robson, 1989)

Lambert, Gavin, *Lindsay Anderson* (Faber & Faber, 2000)

Lebrecht, Norman, *Covent Garden: The Untold Story* (Simon & Schuster, 2000)

Lewenstein, Oscar, *Kicking Against the Pricks* (Nick Hern, 1994)

Lewis, Roger, *Stage People* (Weidenfeld & Nicolson, 1989)

———. *The Real Life of Laurence Olivier* (Arrow, 1996)

Little, Stuart W., *The Playmakers* (Max Reinhardt, 1970)

McBean, Angus, *Shakespeare Memorial Theatre* (Max Reinhardt, 1956)

MacCarthy, Desmond, *Theatre* (MacGibbon & Kee, 1954)

McIntyre, Ian, *The Expense of Glory* (HarperCollins, 1993)

Manthorpe, Victoria, *Children of the Empire* (Victor Gollancz, 1996)

Manvell, Roger, *Ellen Terry* (Heinemann, 1968)

Massey, Raymond, *When I Was Young* (Little, Brown & Company, 1976)

Masters, Brian, *Thunder in the Air* (Oberon, 2000)

Miles, Sarah, *Serves Me Right* (Macmillan, 1994)

Miller, John, *Ralph Richardson* (Sidgwick & Jackson, 1995)

———. *Judi Dench* (Orion, 2000)

Mills, John, *Still Memories* (Hutchinson, 2000)

Morley, Sheridan, *Gladys Cooper* (Book Club Associates, 1979)

———. *James Mason: Odd Man Out* (Weidenfeld & Nicolson, 1989)

———. *Our Theatre in the Eighties* (Hodder & Stoughton, 1990)

———. *Rank Outsider* (Bloomsbury, 1996)

Nesbitt, Cathleen, *A Little Love and Good Company (Stemmer House, 1977)*

Nicolson, Harold, *Diaries and Letters, 1945–1962* (Atheneum Books, 1968)

O'Connor, Garry, *Ralph Richardson: An Actor's Life* (Hodder & Stoughton, 1986)

———. *Alec Guinness, Master of Disguise* (Sceptre, 1994)

———. *The Secret Woman* (Weidenfeld & Nicolson, 1997)

Paskin, Barbra, *Dudley Moore* (Sidgwick & Jackson, 1997)

Peake, Tony, *Derek Jarman* (Little, Brown & Company, 1999)

Perry, George, *Hitchcock* (Macmillan, 1975)

Quayle, Anthony, *A Time to Speak* (Barrie & Jenkins, 1990)

Redfield, William, *Letters From An Actor* (Viking Press, 1967)

Reynolds, Debbie, *My Life* (Sidgwick & Jackson, 1989)

Richards, David, *Played Out: The Jean Seberg Story* (Random House, 1981)

Richardson, Tony, *Long Distance Runner* (Faber & Faber, 1993)

Rossi, Alfred, *Astonish Us in the Morning* (Hutchinson, 1977)

Schneider, Alan, *Entrances* (Limelight Editions, 1987)

Shellard, Dominic, *British Theatre in the 1950s* (Sheffield Academic, 2000)

Sinden, Donald, *A Touch of the Memoirs* (Hodder & Stoughton, 1982)

———. *Laughter in the Second Act* (Hodder & Stoughton, 1985)

Speaight, Robert, *The Property Basket* (Collins & Harvill, 1970)

Spoto, Donald, *Alfred Hitchcock: The Dark Side of Genius* (Little, Brown & Company, 1983)

———. *The Kindness of Strangers* (Bodley Head, 1985)

———. *Laurence Olivier* (HarperCollins, 1991)

Sprigge, Elizabeth, *Sybil Thorndike Casson* (Victor Gollancz, 1971)

Steen, Marguerite, *A Pride of Terrys* (Longmans, 1962)

Stephens, Robert, *Knight Errant* (Hodder & Stoughton, 1995)

Sterne, Richard L., *John Gielgud Directs Richard Burton in Hamlet* (Random House, 1967)

Swaffer, Hannen, *Hannen Swaffer's Who's Who* (Hutchinson,)

Taylor, John R., *The Life and Work of Alfred Hitchcock* (Faber & Faber, 1978)

———. *Alec Guinness: A Celebration* (Pavilion, 1985)

Terry, Ellen, *The Story of My Life* (Hutchinson, 1908)

Thomson, David, *Rosebud: The Story of Orson Welles* (Little, Brown & Company, 1996)

Trewin, J. C., *A Play Tonight* (Elek Books, 1952)

———. *Edith Evans* (Rockliff, 1954)

————. *Peter Brook* (Macdonald, 1971)

————. *Five & Eighty Hamlets* (Hutchinson, 1987)

Tynan, Kenneth, *He That Plays the King* (Longmans, Green, 1950)

————. *Alec Guinness* (Rockliff, 1953)

————. *Persona Grata* (illus. Cecil Beaton) (Wingate, 1953)

————. *Curtains* (Longmans, 1961)

————. *Letters* (Weidenfeld & Nicolson, 1994)

Vickers, Hugo, *Cecil Beaton* (Weidenfeld & Nicolson, 1985)

Walker, Alexander, *Vivien: The Life of Vivien Leigh* (Weidenfeld & Nicolson, 1987)

Wansell, Geoffrey, *Terence Rattigan* (Fourth Estate, 1995)

Wardle, Irving, *The Theatres of George Devine* (Jonathan Cape, 1978)

————. *Theatre Criticism* (Routledge, 1992)

Warwick, Christopher, *The Universal Ustinov* (Sidgwick & Jackson, 1990)

Wells, Stanley, *The Actors' Choosing* (Long Barn, 1997)

————. *Shakespeare in the Theatre* (Oxford, 2000)

Welsh, James M., *The Cinema of Tony Richardson* (State University of New York, 1999)

Williams, Dakin, *Tennessee Williams, An Intimate Biography* (Arbor House, 1983)

Williams, Emlyn, *George* (Hamish Hamilton, 1961)

Williams, Harcourt, *Old Vic Saga* (Winchester Publications, 1949)

Williams, Kenneth, *Diaries* (HarperCollins, 1993)

Williams, Tennessee, *Five O'Clock Angel, Letters to Maria St. Just* (André Deutsch, 1991)

Williamson, Audrey, *Old Vic Drama* (Rockliff, 1948)

Wolfit, Donald, *First Interval* (Odhams, 1954)

York, Michael, *Travelling Player* (Headline, 1991)

INDEX

Ackland, Rodney, 109–10, 128, 137, 213, 214, 319

Ackroyd, Peter, 431

à Court, Janet Holmes, 466

Adrian, Rhys, 437

Against the Law (Wildeblood), 279

Agate, James, 60, 61, 70, 80, 88, 94, 104, 108–9, 126, 129, 176, 202

Ages of Man, 312, 313, 339, 342, 364, 369, 391

  Broadway and West End runs of, 319, 323, 324, 325–26, 466

  recording of, 257, 471

  reviews of, 323, 325–26

  selections and delivery of, 190, 309, 317–18, 321, 323, 399

  tours of, 7, 50, 318, 319, 321–23, 350, 357–58, 360, 363, 470

Ainley, Henry, 38, 89, 116, 150

Albee, Edward, 311, 328, 349, 352, 353–55, 356–57, 419

Albery, Sir Bronson, 131, 153

Alexander, George, 38, 173

Alice in Wonderland, 35, 361

Allen, Adrianne, 315, 319–20

Allen, Woody, 437

Amory, Mark, 398

Anderson, Judith, 151, 155–57, 159, 160, 163, 167, 215, 216, 470

Anderson, Lindsay, 381–83, 384–85, 386–87, 388, 422, 429, 456, 480

Anderson, Maxwell, 161

Andrews, Harry, 127, 139, 155, 156, 161, 174, 175, 181, 234–35, 236, 248, 312, 316, 364, 426, 442

Anouilh, Jean, 341, 358, 371, 385

Anstee, Paul, 199, 263, 287, 302

Arnaud, Yvonne, 205, 211, 301

Arran, "Boofy" Gore, Lord, 283

Arthur, 419, 429–31, 437, 444, 458

Ashcroft, Peggy, 32, 105, 125, 147, 150, 161–62, 177, 211, 301, 361, 425, 434, 452, 455–56, 473, 474–75

  in Chekhov plays, 152, 153, 154, 178–79, 383

  in contemporary antiestablishment theater, 297, 375, 384, 403

  honors received by, 300, 437

  JG as director of, 223, 224, 225, 300

  on JG's performances, 99, 138–39, 235, 337–38

  in JG's repertory company, 174, 175, 178–79, 180, 181

  romantic affairs of, 62, 99, 113–14, 126, 154, 162, 296, 383

  Shakespearean roles of, 103, 106, 112, 113, 140, 142, 144, 145, 146, 152, 175, 180, 234–35, 236, 239, 294, 296–97, 327, 336, 457

Ashton, Frederick, 465

Astor, David, 278

Astor, Nancy, 206, 263

Atkins, Eileen, 308, 463

Atkins, Robert, 47, 83–84, 85

Atkinson, Brooks, 79, 255–56

Attenborough, Richard, 364, 372, 377, 378, 420, 441

Auden, W. H., 261–62, 403, 404–5, 408

Audley, Maxine, 236, 304

Avedon, Richard, 409

Aylmer, Felix, 51, 312

Ayrton, Michael, 200, 203

Bacall, Lauren, 323, 395

Baddeley, Angela, 122, 174, 188, 205, 270, 358

Badel, Alan, 200, 234, 236, 337, 461

Bagnold, Enid, 299, 300, 316, 328

Bakst, Leon, 41, 53

Baldwin, Stanley, 117

Ballets Russes, 41–42

Banbury, Frith, 133

Banks, Leslie, 205, 207

Bannen, Ian, 336, 337

Barber, John, 293

Bardot, Brigitte, 464

Barnes, Clive, 376

Barretts of Wimpole Street, The, 303–4, 398

Barrie, J. M., 27, 38, 50, 82, 197

Barron, Marcus, 202

Barry, Gerald, 340

Barrymore, Ethel, 145, 249, 458

Barrymore, John, 99, 161, 166, 247
    Hamlet portrayed by, 52, 71–72, 155, 156, 157, 164, 165, 470

Bates, Alan, 471

Battle of Shrivings, The (Shaffer), 381

Baxter, Keith, 182–83, 304, 321, 330–32, 351, 353, 366, 464–65, 471–72, 473

Baylis, Lilian, 83–87, 93, 94, 96, 98, 99, 112, 162, 177, 447, 477

BBC Radio Drama, 61, 205, 227, 333, 457, 460, 463

Beale, Simon Russell, 463

Beaton, Cecil, 29, 209, 210–11, 223, 254, 350

Beaumont, Hugh "Binkie," 134, 204, 210, 396
    homosexuality of, 262, 264, 271, 281, 321
    and JG's arrest, 267–68, 270–272
    as JG's manager, 182, 200, 241–42, 318, 474
    Perry's affair with, 102, 182–83, 206, 211, 287–88, 314, 330
    as producer, 102, 181–86, 188, 189, 200, 205, 206–7, 209, 215–18, 220, 222, 223, 224, 228, 241, 251–52, 259, 262, 270–71, 299, 300, 301, 306, 313, 314, 319–20, 328, 335, 342, 358, 395

Beaverbrook, William Maxwell Aitken, Lord, 263, 276, 302

Becket (film), 341–42

Beckett, Samuel, 23, 25, 289, 311, 372, 382, 385, 411, 477

Bedford, Brian, 306–8, 319, 321, 476

Beerbohm, Max, 153, 356

Beggar's Opera, The (Gay), 191

Bennett, Alan, 23, 280, 288, 360, 364, 373–77, 390, 391–92, 398, 429, 464, 480–81

Bennett, Jill, 364, 365

Benson, Lady, 44–49, 127, 145

Benthall, Michael, 316

Bergman, Ingmar, 454, 457

Bergman, Ingrid, 395, 396

Bergner, Elisabeth, 111, 387, 450

Bernhardt, Sarah, 31, 43, 61, 101, 118, 158, 165, 469–70

Best, Edna, 73, 110, 117

Best of Friends, The (Whitemore), 445–46,
    447–48, 460
Beyond the Fringe, 360–61, 373
Big Fish, Little Fish (Wheeler), 334–35
Billington, Michael, 106, 337, 338, 400,
    406–8, 417, 421, 463, 475–76
Bing, Rudolph, 191, 241
Bingo (Bond), 402
Blakemore, Michael, 397
Blixen, Baroness (Isak Dinesen), 187
Bloom, Claire, 225, 226–27, 296, 358
Blunt, Anthony, 273
Bogarde, Dirk, 281, 284, 414–16, 433
Bond, Edward, 397, 401–2
Booth, Edwin, 165
Boothby, Robert, 282, 283
Brady, Frank, 352, 353
Branagh, Kenneth, 460, 463, 482
Brando, Marlon, 160, 235, 244–45, 247,
    248–51, 354, 398, 427
Brandreth, Gyles, 472
Brecht, Bertolt, 296, 297, 385, 394
Brett, Jeremy, 315
Brideshead Revisited, 427, 431, 433, 436,
    451
Brien, Alan, 315, 339
Briers, Richard, 463, 470
Brisbane, Katharine, 375
British Council, 322
British Theatre Museum, 71, 438, 446–47,
    448, 469
Britneva, Maria (Lady St. Just), 220–21
Britten, Benjamin, 262, 275, 333, 377, 378,
    454
Brode, Douglas, 457
Brook, Peter, 231–34, 238–39, 244, 256, 295,
    306–8, 337, 399, 445

JG's acting style influenced by, 232–34,
    235, 237, 239, 422, 456
Oedipus directed by, 232, 368, 369,
    370–71, 388, 409, 411
Brown, Ivor, 59, 126, 129, 139, 190, 201, 317
Brown, John Mason, 160
Brown, Pamela, 216, 225, 226, 230, 237,
    255–56
Browne, Coral, 369, 451, 453
Browning Version, The (Rattigan), 217, 324
Bryant, Michael, 319, 320–21
Bryant, Sir Arthur, 24, 366
Bryden, Bill, 186, 403
Bryden, Ronald, 358–59, 370
Brynner, Yul, 304
Buckmaster, Herbert, 273–74
Bull, Peter, 228, 229, 230, 237–38
Burrell, John, 223–24
Burstyn, Ellen, 414
Burton, Richard, 208, 225–27, 229, 248, 251,
    256, 341, 432, 474
    in *Hamlet* directed by JG, 164, 341,
    342–47, 349
Burton, Sally, 346
Byerley, Vivienne, 267
Byrne, Dawson, 164–65

Cadell, Jean, 137
Caesar and Cleopatra (Shaw), 206, 388
Calder-Marshall, Anna, 388
Calhern, Louis, 243, 249, 250
Caligula, 418–19, 420, 455, 481
Campbell, Mrs. Patrick, 73, 80, 109, 110,
    160, 161, 165–66, 168, 265, 340
Canby, Vincent, 454–55
Carpenter, Humphrey, 104, 275
Carroll, Madeleine, 148, 151

Carus-Wilson, Mary, 126

Casson, Lewis, 191, 192, 207, 223, 239, 259, 309

Cavalcade (Coward), 302, 304–5, 374

Cecil, Lord David, 107

Cerf, Bennett, 251

Chalk Garden, The (Bagnold), 299–301, 328, 425

Chamberlain, Neville, 459

Champion, Gower, 394

Changing Stages, 477

Chaplin, Charles, 248

Chapman, Edward, 273

Chapman, John, 355

Charge of the Light Brigade, The, 350, 363–65, 373, 389, 390, 391

Chariots of Fire, 419, 429, 431, 433, 480

Charley's Aunt (Thomas), 56, 259, 290

Chekhov, Anton, 29, 60–63, 66, 69–71, 109, 153–55, 179, 195, 300, 338, 358, 361, 389

Cherry Orchard, The (Chekhov), 29, 60–61, 62, 69–70, 138, 259, 280, 289–90, 302, 338–39

Chester, Elsie, 49

Chimes at Midnight, 350–53, 364, 454

Christie, Agatha, 300, 428, 444

Christie, John, 191

Churchill, Winston, 257

Church of England, 267, 282

Clark, Michael, 455

Clue of the New Pin, The, 82, 101

Clunes, Alec, 215, 216, 225, 273, 306

Cockerell, Sydney, 445–46

Coghill, Nevill, 208, 461, 465

Cohen, Alexander, 332

Cole, E. A., 275

Cole, Toby, 412

Collier, Patience, 338

Complaisant Lover, The (Greene), 324–25

Compton, Fay, 186, 191, 192, 195

Congreve, William, 205, 254, 301

Connor, Bill, 279

Conrad, Peter, 458

Constant Nymph, The (Kennedy), 72–74, 77–78, 301

Constant Wife, The (Maugham), 396

Cook, Peter, 360, 361

Cookman, Anthony, 295

Coolidge, Philip, 345

Cooper, Gladys, 7, 71, 77, 109, 173, 188, 273, 299, 300, 301, 324

Coward, Noël, 7, 45, 78–79, 152, 167, 266, 288, 293, 304–5, 314, 325, 374, 388, 395, 396, 439

  acting career of, 40, 53, 64–65, 72–73, 74, 303

  as expatriate, 261, 275, 301, 302

  homosexuality of, 65, 75, 76, 90, 214, 262, 263, 264, 281, 330

  JG in plays of, 47, 63, 65, 66, 194, 195, 212, 301–3, 304

  on JG's arrest, 274–75

  on JG's work, 108, 159–60, 289–90, 302, 326, 357

  social circles of, 63–64, 66, 373

  success of, 65, 66, 67, 111, 188

  wartime service of, 189, 190, 215

Cowie, Laura, 109, 132, 186

Craig, Edward Gordon, 21, 23, 31, 32, 41, 42, 85, 96, 131, 155, 165, 172

Crime and Punishment (Ackland's dramatization), 155, 213–15, 216, 219, 220, 404

Croft-Cooke, Rupert, 264

Cronyn, Hume, 320, 334, 335, 343, 344–45, 346
Crowther, Bosley, 251
Cruickshank, Andrew, 442
Cukor, George, 247, 300
Cusack, Cyril, 204, 205

Daneman, Paul, 450
Dare, Zena, 198
Darlington, W. A., 106, 119, 202, 208, 292
Darlow, Michael, 316
Daviot, Gordon, *see* Mackintosh, Elizabeth
Day by the Sea, A (Hunter), 133, 259–60, 266, 270, 280, 287, 288, 289, 290, 324, 328, 368–69
Dazzling Prospect (Perry and Keane), 335
Dean, Basil, 72–74, 77, 78, 211–12
Dear Brutus (Barrie), 197–98
Dear Octopus (Smith), 181, 183–84, 185, 186, 281
de Jongh, Nicholas, 447
Delaney, Shelagh, 284, 315–16
Dench, Judi, 338, 409, 410, 428, 463
Denison, Michael, 24, 152–53, 188, 366, 459, 472
Dent, Alan, 201
Devine, George, 125, 181, 386
    as actor, 103, 139, 154, 174, 178, 294, 296
    innovative theater company of, 297, 300, 311, 385
    JG directed by, 103, 194, 295, 296
    on JG's Hamlet, 135
    at OUDS, 103, 104, 105, 106–7, 152
Devlin, William, 103
De Vries, Peter, 399
Dewhurst, Keith, 384
Diaghilev, Sergey Pavlovich, 42

Dickens, Charles, 139–40, 272, 464
Dickinson, Thorold, 195
Dinesen, Isak (Baroness Blixen), 187
Disraeli, Benjamin, 151, 195–96, 227, 397
Distinguished Company (Gielgud)), 450
Dixon, Adele, 85, 87, 88, 110
Doctor's Dilemma, The (Shaw), 204–5, 206, 388
Donat, Robert, 112, 140, 147, 195
Don Giovanni (Mozart), 372
Doran, Charles, 329
Douglas, Lord Alfred, 188, 264
Drabble, Margaret, 275
Drake, Alfred, 343, 346
Driberg, Tom, 263, 283
du Maurier, Daphne, 189, 248
du Maurier, Gerald, 38, 52, 66, 173, 197, 198
Dundy, Elaine, 291
Duse, Eleonora, 31, 43, 53, 118, 248

Early Stages (Gielgud), 28, 421
Eddington, Paul, 376
Edward VIII, King of England, 166
Elephant Man, The, 419, 420, 427
Eliot, T. S., 185, 225
Elizabeth, 23, 431, 460, 461, 471
Elizabeth, Queen Mother, 13, 471
Elliot, Denholm, 442
Endgame (Beckett), 311, 369
English Stage Company, 103, 297, 300
Enthoven, Gabrielle, 71
Ervine, St. John, 142
Evans, Edith, 67, 82, 105, 144, 153–54, 213, 375, 411, 424, 470
    classical roles of, 84, 103, 106, 140, 142, 146, 152, 255, 316, 317
    JG as director of, 137, 300, 301

on JG's tearfulness, 211

as Lady Bracknell, 188–89, 203

romantic affairs of, 113, 191

on troop tours, 203, 204

upstaging tactics of, 220

Evans, Laurence, 24, 143, 242, 325, 366, 429, 477

Evans, Mary, 366, 472, 473

Evans, Maurice, 112, 120, 165, 166, 247, 337

Eyre, Richard, 477

Faber, Leslie, 77, 78, 88

Fagan, J. B., 56, 57, 60, 61, 63, 66, 70, 79, 127

Farjeon, Eleanor, 235

Farjeon, Herbert, 144, 178, 193

Farrell, M. J., *see* Keane, Molly

Farson, Daniel, 441

Feldman, Marty, 284

Ffrangcon-Davies, Gwen, 26, 110, 126, 280, 289, 459

    JG's roles opposite, 59, 82, 127–28, 116, 174, 178, 179, 200, 202, 203, 236, 310, 339

Fielden-Kay, Beatrix, 202

Finch, Peter, 284, 291, 292, 337, 393

Findlater, Richard, 7–8, 10, 235, 237

Finney, Albert, 337, 354, 444

Five Finger Exercise (Shaffer), 308, 319–21, 328, 335, 381

Fleming, Peter, 98–99, 176

Flemyng, Robert, 104, 309, 313, 328, 329

Forbes, Bryan, 183, 317, 467

Forbes, Meriel, 270, 477

Forster, E. M., 76

Forty Years On (Bennett), 288, 364, 372–75,

376–77, 390, 429, 481

Forwood, Anthony, 415

Francis, Clive, 467

Frankenheimer, John, 217, 324

Fraser, Antonia, 405, 407

French, Leslie, 85, 90, 100

Frost, David, 453

Fry, Christopher, 215–16, 225, 227, 230, 238, 311, 356

Furse, Roger, 194, 312

Gandhi, 419, 431, 441

Garbo, Greta, 215, 314

Garland, Patrick, 373, 374, 388

Garnett, Constance, 179

Garrick Club, 179, 273, 459

Garson, Greer, 243, 249

Gay Lord Quex, The (Pinero), 409–10

Gerhard, Roberto, 294

Ghosts (Ibsen), 53, 80, 84

Gielgud, Eleanor (JG's sister), 26–27, 206, 228, 263, 322, 330

Gielgud, Frank (JG's father), 25–27, 33–34, 37, 49, 90, 205–6, 227

Gielgud, John:

    on acting styles, 38, 62, 63, 71, 74, 78, 97, 100, 118, 326, 411, 458

    agents for, 24, 58, 241–42, 252, 325, 453

    on aging, 424, 427, 428, 435, 439, 449, 451, 458–59, 474

    artistic talents and interests of, 29, 35–36, 40, 166, 248, 480

    author's family's links to, 7, 77

    biographies of, 7–10, 22, 280

    birthday celebrations of, 397–98, 401, 434, 435, 437, 463

birth of, 25

celebrity of, 99, 115, 120–21, 146, 161, 164, 375, 392, 426, 458

childhood of, 26–44, 107, 211, 268, 356, 432

conversational gaffes of, 10, 100, 106, 121, 157, 175, 217, 253, 307, 345, 351, 390, 410, 462

death of, 8, 9, 10, 23, 24, 434, 464, 477–80

family background of, 21, 22, 25–29, 30–34, 41, 45, 48, 55–56, 79, 96, 110, 190, 210, 338, 444

on films of Shakespeare plays, 149–50, 377–78, 454

finances of, 22, 57, 74, 77, 84, 97, 120, 149, 166, 174, 181, 182, 241–42, 253, 330, 340, 366, 422–23, 430, 435, 453, 464, 479

gossip enjoyed by, 211, 365, 367, 380, 447

health problems of, 25, 28, 280, 288–89, 452–53, 464, 471, 472

homes of, 24, 74, 76, 104, 123–25, 134, 146, 183, 206, 211, 307, 366, 379, 380, 395, 423, 438

homosexuality of, 65, 74, 75, 94, 110, 117, 126–27, 143–44, 199, 215, 240, 250, 257, 262–63, 280–81, 330, 411, 436, 458

honors received by, 23, 179, 215, 257, 273, 335, 396, 413, 429–30, 437, 439, 448, 459, 463–64, 466

knighthood of, 23, 257, 266, 267, 273, 274, 277, 278

long-term romantic involvements of, 262–63, 287; *see also* Hensler, Martin; Perry, John

music enjoyed by, 34, 124, 306

on New York, 79, 156, 167, 219, 244

1953 soliciting arrest of, 8–9, 22, 117, 265–82, 285, 286, 287, 291, 314, 322, 330, 465, 470–71

operas directed by, 191, 304–5, 333, 372, 468

personal assistants of, 228, 287, 322, 425–26, 459, 472, 473

physical appearance of, 57, 76, 77, 94, 111, 112, 118, 151, 210, 253, 393, 408, 447, 458, 473–74

politics of, 77, 120, 166, 199, 399, 405, 422, 438, 442–43, 459, 468, 469

as portrait subject, 101, 203, 366, 409, 447, 450

privacy guarded by, 76, 121, 280, 366, 384, 421, 424–25, 457–58, 470

professional commitment of, 29, 34, 42–43, 44, 48, 76–77, 325

in radio, 22, 61, 205, 227, 388, 399, 437, 457, 460, 463, 464

recordings of, 189–90, 351, 388, 439, 463, 464

religion and, 40, 41, 311

on Shaw's plays, 388–89

shyness of, 55, 121, 213, 242, 435, 447

social circles of, 63–64, 76, 77, 124, 125, 134, 167, 247–49, 335, 365–67, 373–74, 380, 395–96, 424–25, 436, 437, 464, 472–73

tearfulness of, 211, 214, 257, 272, 310, 401, 409

voice of, 9, 23, 35, 51, 57, 98–99, 112, 133, 136, 145, 176, 202–3, 210, 213,

Gielgud, John: *(cont.)*
   253–54, 302, 308, 317–18, 325–26, 333, 359,
      387, 393, 415, 437, 458
   work as main focus of, 65, 75–77, 123,
      138, 182, 199, 211, 227, 290, 383, 399,
      434, 463, 476
   writings of, 8, 280, 421, 423–24, 433, 450,
      453, 463, 474–75, 476
Gielgud, John—film and television career:
   in Bible series, 398, 434
   in Chekhov and Shaw, 360, 372, 389, 413,
      470
   in commercials, 430–31, 449, 471
   on daily work schedule, 111, 151, 363, 451
   directors of, 150, 151, 325, 341, 350, 351–53,
      365, 454, 455, 456
   on dissatisfaction with film work, 111,
      137, 150, 169, 365
   in documentaries, 363, 453
   earnings of, 166, 182, 242, 250, 325, 330,
      365, 394, 398, 416, 430
   eccentric comic characters of, 361, 364,
      373, 413–14, 429–30
   film acting style of, 101, 102, 149, 151, 196,
      246, 250, 341, 365, 398, 424, 433
   final performances of, 471, 477
   first roles of, 61, 101–2
   historical figures played by, 195–96, 227,
      341, 363, 364, 372, 397, 442, 467
   Hollywood shooting of, 241, 242–43,
      245, 246, 249–51
   indiscriminate choices in later years of,
      387, 394, 415–16, 418–20, 422,
      426–27, 428–29, 431–32, 441–42,
      444, 445, 450–51, 460
   in interviews, 359–60, 473–74, 477
   location shootings of, 351–52, 363, 364,

      365, 393, 425, 426, 427, 436, 443,
         445, 449
   in miniseries, 397, 431, 436, 438, 443–44,
      451–52, 480–81
   in modern plays, 324, 358, 363, 384, 422
   reviews of, 150, 251, 364, 380, 383, 384,
      394, 414, 431, 441, 455, 458
   roles rejected by, 206, 242, 325, 418–19,
      429
   Shakespearean roles of, 243, 245, 246,
      251, 290, 351–52, 353, 377, 380, 418,
      445, 453–57, 458, 463
Gielgud, John—theater career:
   acting style honed by, 232, 234, 235–37,
      239, 326, 392, 424
   actors' appreciation of, 216, 235, 356,
      461–62
   Chekhovian roles of, 60–61, 62, 69–71,
      153–55, 178, 333, 338–39, 358, 360,
      362
   classical repertory companies run by,
      22, 83, 127, 171–81, 207, 251–57,
      259–60, 340, 463, 475
   classics presented in modern dress by,
      340–41, 342, 344
   costume and set designers hired by, 105,
      112, 116, 125, 200–201, 203, 225, 287,
      290, 294–96, 372
   design interests of, 35, 40–41, 42, 46, 141,
      155, 219, 240
   on difficult audiences, 327, 357–58, 412
   as director, 71, 103–7, 109, 112–14, 116,
      121–22, 125–27, 131, 132–33, 137, 140,
      180, 183, 191, 209–10, 221–27,
      229–30, 238–39, 240, 255, 289–92,
      302, 314–15, 319, 320–21, 325,
      326–27, 334–35, 341, 343, 345–47,

367, 390, 394, 395, 409–10, 461, 468,
476, 478
as drama student, 44–52, 69, 216
early professional appearances of,
47–49, 50, 51, 56–57, 69
fencing deficiencies of, 158
film and television seen as secondary
arts by, 325, 412, 416
final appearances of, 419, 445–47
on "impenetrable" modern plays, 311,
349, 356
memorization method of, 356
Method actors and, 326–27, 359
modern playwrights' tensions with, 217,
221–22, 356–57
musical scores used by, 306
in Old Vic company, 84–91, 93, 94–100,
112, 125, 171
on performance repetition, 412–13,
448–49
physical mannerisms of, 46, 47, 51, 69,
339, 355, 359
plays written for, 217, 259, 355
playwriting efforts of, 139–40
in postwar contemporary theater, 103,
121, 225, 228, 229–30, 309–11,
328–29, 340, 354–57, 372–77,
381–87, 388, 399, 401–8
as producer, 121, 125, 174, 175, 176
rehearsal-process and JG's frequent second thoughts, 233–34, 238–39, 374,
382, 403, 407
reviews of, 48, 57, 59, 60, 67, 79, 80, 86,
88–89, 94, 98–99, 119, 129, 133–34,
139, 144, 154–55, 160, 162–63, 176,
180, 193–94, 198, 202–3, 208,
234–37, 239, 255–56, 303, 308–9,

310–11, 323, 325–26, 338–39, 355,
357, 358, 370, 371, 377, 392,
399–400, 402, 407, 418
on role choices, 214, 217, 258, 259, 260,
301–3, 333, 336, 338, 340, 342, 354,
355, 385–86, 434
romantic style of, 117, 118, 120, 129, 234,
235, 239, 336, 359, 400, 412, 422,
478–79
in school plays, 35, 46, 48, 50–52
Shakespearean roles of, 46, 47, 58–60,
71–72, 84–91, 95–100, 103, 115,
118, 131–37, 140–47, 149, 150,
155–60, 164–65, 175–76, 180,
191–94, 197, 200, 202–3, 207–9, 211,
232–39, 255, 258, 290, 294–95, 306,
308–9, 316–17, 323, 326, 333,
336–38, 343, 384, 388, 397–401, 417,
427, 462
solo Shakespeare program performed
by, see Ages of Man, The
U.S. appearances of, 78–79, 147, 151,
155–69, 214–15, 216, 237–38, 274,
326, 327–28, 339–40, 355, 358, 410
verse-speaking of, 98, 106, 144, 187, 203,
208, 307, 326, 344, 356, 398, 400,
417, 434, 467, 471, 478
on wartime tours, 194–95, 203–4, 211–12,
213, 215, 220, 309, 317
Gielgud, Kate Terry Lewis (JG's mother),
25–26, 28, 32, 33, 37, 39, 44, 49, 205–6,
227, 305
death of, 321–22
on JG's acting, 90, 236
on JG's arrest, 281–82, 322
Gielgud, Lewis (JG's brother), 26, 28, 37,
39, 43, 206, 258, 321, 408, 445

Gielgud, Maina (JG's niece), 24–25, 424, 445, 472

Gielgud, Val (JG's brother), 43–44, 70, 77, 78, 82, 206

   childhood of, 26, 28–30, 39

   on JG's arrest, 271

   radio drama career of, 22, 61, 205, 227, 333, 437, 469

Gilder, Rosamund, 158, 161

Gish, Lillian, 151–52, 159, 168, 199, 216, 323, 360, 437, 444, 460

Glass Menagerie, The (T. Williams), 220, 221–22

Glenville, Peter, 104, 204–5, 223, 225, 289, 341

Good Companions, The (Knoblock), 100, 101, 102, 104, 105, 107, 110, 112, 120

Gordon, John, 276–78

Gordon, Zita, 445

Goring, Marius, 139, 186, 187, 191, 194, 442

Graham, Martha, 219, 294

Granger, Derek, 309, 310, 434

Granville-Barker, Harley, 27, 79, 85, 86, 172–73, 176, 186–87, 231, 307, 311, 456, 477

   King Lear directed by, 191–92, 193, 194, 236

Gray, Dulcie, 24, 472, 473

Greenaway, Peter, 96, 308, 378, 399, 445, 451, 453–57, 458, 471

Greene, Graham, 29, 61, 309, 310, 311, 312, 324, 325, 420, 445

Gregg, Hubert, 389

Grizzard, George, 334

Guccione, Robert, 418, 481

Guest, E. R., 268–69

Guinness, Alec, 125, 272, 367, 434, 437, 452, 478

   in films, 349, 365, 415, 420, 428, 445

   on JG's acting, 23, 142, 201–2, 226

   in plays with JG, 132–33, 135–36, 139, 154

   stage career of, 127, 132–33, 136, 174, 177, 181, 208, 289

   in wartime, 189, 190, 198–99

Gussow, Mel, 354

Guthrie, Tyrone, 56–60, 113, 114, 125, 146, 188, 191, 192, 241

   as director, 175, 177–78, 179, 186, 232, 368

   on JG's performances, 139, 179, 201–2, 208–9

Haggard, Stephen, 128, 153, 194

Half-Life (Mitchell), 418, 419

Half Way Up the Tree (Ustinov), 7, 367–68

Hall, Peter, 235, 335–38, 340, 358, 366, 381, 397, 399–405, 407, 417, 418, 421, 422, 427, 456

Hamlet (Shakespeare), 71–72, 150, 186–87, 205, 251, 337, 427, 442, 463, 470

   Burton directed by JG in, 164, 341, 342–47, 349

   JG in title role of, 22, 87, 88, 89–91, 93, 131–37, 155–60, 162–65, 168, 175, 186–88, 207–9, 212–13, 234, 238, 346, 389, 447

   JG/Leslie Howard rivalry, 157, 159, 160, 162, 163–64, 243

Hankin, St. John, 223

Hardwicke, Cedric, 138, 166, 250, 303

Hardy, Robert, 7, 239, 461–62, 466–67

Hardy, Sally, 7

Hare, David, 441, 475

Harlequinade (Rattigan), 104, 217

Harris, Margaret, 23, 105, 181

Harris, Rosemary, 446, 448

Harris, Sophia, 23, 105

Harrison, Rex, 192, 209, 301, 306, 337

Hart, Derek, 359

Hart-Davis, Rupert, 99–100

Harvey, Ian, 284

Harvey, Laurence, 314, 364

Harwood, Ronald, 116–17, 435

Haskell, Arnold, 41

Hassall, Christopher, 103

Hastings, Basil MacDonald, 61, 70

Hauser, Frank, 226

Hawkins, Jack, 110, 112, 128, 132, 133, 139, 186, 187, 337

Hawthorne, Nigel, 280

Hawtrey, Charles, 38, 274

Haxton, Gerald, 122

Haydn, Walford, 283–84

Hayes, Helen, 160, 161, 168, 220, 221, 222

Hayman, Ronald, 94, 108, 180, 200, 239, 308

Hazlitt, William, 433

Heartbreak House (Shaw), 52, 206, 389, 403, 413

Heilpern, John, 408

Heiress, The (Goetz and Goetz), 223–25, 230

Helpmann, Robert, 152, 208, 213, 303

Hemmings, David, 364, 365

Henry V (film), 143, 207, 215, 377, 454

Henry VIII (Shakespeare), 310, 312, 316–17

Hensler, Martin:

    background of, 329, 331, 465–66

    death of, 23, 24, 25, 471–72, 474

    on JG's career, 330, 331–32, 367

    JG's homes with, 183, 211, 329–30, 342, 366, 379, 380, 425, 459

    JG's relationship with, 23, 24, 263, 329, 331, 366, 367, 415, 425–26, 434, 453, 464–65, 472

    Perry banished by, 183, 331–32, 366, 464

    social relationships of, 331, 366–67, 397, 424–25, 465

    temperament of, 24, 330, 331, 366

Herbert, Jocelyn, 381–82, 386

Herlie, Eileen, 222, 343

Heston, Charlton, 380, 388, 450–51

He Was Born Gay (Williams), 169, 171–72

Higgins, Norman, 241

Hiller, Wendy, 205, 223, 361, 381, 395, 403

Hinxman, Margaret, 427

Hitchcock, Alfred, 101, 140, 144, 147–48, 150, 151, 169, 176, 195, 325, 445

H. M. Tennent, 181, 183, 189, 206, 226, 254, 259, 288, 315, 321, 324, 358

Hobson, Harold, 175, 178, 199, 225, 295, 309–11, 315, 329, 384, 436

Hockney, David, 262, 409

Holland, Merlin, 279

Holland, Vyvyan, 210

Holm, Ian, 338

Home (Storey), 289, 328, 381–87, 388, 405, 429, 480

homosexuality:

    British emigration and, 261–62

    heterosexual actors' discomfort with, 117, 143–44, 240, 273

    knighthoods and, 215, 257, 273, 275, 281

    legal prohibition of, 51, 75, 76, 122, 124

    prosecutions on charges of, 260–61, 263–84

    reform of laws against, 279, 282–85, 313, 479

homosexuality: *(cont.)*
    as subject in dramas, 63, 76, 115, 284–85,
        315–16
Hope-Wallace, Philip, 210, 289, 325–26
Hopkins, Anthony, 420
Hopkins, Justine, 200
Horne, David, 302
Horne, Donald, 275–76
Hoskins, Bob, 390, 463
Houseman, John, 242–46, 251, 443
Houston, Renee, 60
Howard, Alan, 428
Howard, Leslie, 71, 84, 157, 159, 160, 162,
        163–64, 204, 243, 398
Howard, Trevor, 259, 280, 289, 290, 364, 391
Howe, George, 49, 132, 174, 186
Hudson, Hugh, 429
Huggett, Richard, 209, 271–72
Hughes, Ted, 368
Human Factor, The, 420, 427
Hume, Kenneth, 260
Hunt, Hugh, 103
Hunt, Martita, 85, 88, 132, 154, 185
Hunter, N. C., 110, 133, 259, 324
Hurren, Kenneth, 262
Hutchinson, Tom, 414
Huxley, Aldous, 35, 37, 46

Ibsen, Henrik, 66, 70, 80, 244, 368, 396
Ides of March, The (Wilder), 161, 340–41
Importance of Being Earnest, The (Wilde),
        47, 93–94, 186, 188–89, 190, 203,
        214–15, 279, 386
Ingham, Barry, 326–27
Insect Play, The (Kapek), 50, 59
Insult, 101–2
Irene, 394

Irons, Jeremy, 431
Irving, Henry, 21, 27, 31, 32, 48, 81, 91, 99,
        118, 135, 145, 158, 164, 165, 173, 235, 412,
        443, 476
Isham, Gyles, 58, 59, 87
Isherwood, Christopher, 29, 221, 247,
        261–62, 282, 350
Ivanov (Chekhov), 332, 358, 360

Jacobi, Derek, 418, 420, 463
Jarman, Derek, 281, 372, 380, 454
Jeans, Isabel, 125
Jeans, Ursula, 198, 209
Jefford, Barbara, 234
Jerrold, Mary, 137, 198
John Paul II, Pope, 426
Johnson, Celia, 113–14
Johnson, Richard, 380
Jones, Jennifer, 248, 303
Julius Caesar (films), 160, 241–47, 249–51,
        290, 380, 429, 433, 443
Julius Caesar (Shakespeare), 36, 235–36, 417

Kael, Pauline, 350, 393, 441
Kahn, Florence, 153
Kakutani, Michiko, 438
Kapek, Karel, 50
Kauffmann, Stanley, 357
Kavanagh, Julie, 465–66
Kaye, Danny, 143, 223, 247–48
Kean, Edmund, 21, 412, 452
Keane, Molly (M. J. Farrell), 75, 181, 198,
        230, 335, 442, 473
Keen, Malcolm, 112, 113, 155, 156, 159
Kempson, Rachel, 223, 257, 442
Kennedy, Margaret, 72
Kerr, Deborah, 243, 249

Kerr, Walter, 339, 345

Kilty, Jerome, 340

King Lear (Shakespeare), 98–100, 103, 191,
192–94, 219, 236–37, 287, 290,
294–96, 299, 421, 427, 439, 457, 461,
463

Kingsley, Ben, 417, 471

Kingston, Jeremy, 392

King-Wood, David, 152

Knoblock, Edward, 100

Komisarjevsky, Theodore, 23, 62–63, 71, 82,
107–8, 110, 113, 128, 131, 152–55, 162,
165, 172, 216, 231, 358

Korda, Alexander, 101, 172, 206, 445

Krantz, Judith, 428

Kubelik, Rafael, 305

Lady's Not for Burning, The (Fry), 215, 219,
223, 225–27, 228–30, 231, 237–38, 273,
311, 341

Lady Windermere's Fan (Wilde), 209–10,
211, 219, 225

Lambert, Gavin, 382

Lambert, J. W., 358

Lane, Anthony, 414, 456–47

Langham, Michael, 235

Larkin, Philip, 265

Last Joke, The (Bagnold), 316, 328–29, 333,
335, 383

Latham, Elizabeth, 284

Latham, Sir Paul, 263

Lathom, Earl of, 63–64

Laughton, Charles, 111, 138, 166, 177, 232–33,
250, 303, 398

Lawrence, Gertrude, 167, 249

Lawson, Wilfrid, 361

Lebrecht, Norman, 283–84

Lees-Milne, James, 104

Lehmann, Beatrix, 49, 134–35

Lehmann, Rosamund, 134–35

Leigh, Vivien, 8, 242, 330, 371, 443, 453
in films, 195, 206, 314
JG's arrest and, 270, 271
JG's friendship with, 143, 144, 152,
292–93, 433, 449
Olivier's marriage to, 143, 152, 291,
293–94, 433
stage roles of, 152, 153, 186, 204, 290, 292,
293, 358

Leighton, Margaret, 235, 240, 314, 316, 324,
327, 328, 330, 349

Lejeune, C. A., 111

Liberace, 279

Lillie, Beatrice, 162, 195, 203, 204, 235

Lion King, The, 474

Lion of the Desert, 426, 428

Littlewood, Joan, 300

Loewe, Frederick, 198

Look Back in Anger (Osborne), 226, 297,
375, 385, 399

Loraine, Robert, 38, 255

Lorre, Peter, 148, 149

Loser Takes All, 445

Losey, Joseph, 394

Lost Horizon, 393

Loved One, The, 7, 349–50, 373

Love for Love (Congreve), 57, 205, 206, 207,
209, 214

Lowe, Arthur, 402

Lyceum Theatre, 186, 442–43

Lynch, David, 420

McAnally, Ray, 446, 447, 448

McBean, Angus, 263

Macbeth (Shakespeare), 61, 88–89, 97, 197, 200–203, 240, 244, 253, 293, 294, 306

MacCarthy, Desmond, 67, 119, 193, 198

McClintic, Guthrie, 151, 154–56, 157, 159, 160, 162, 164, 165

McDowall, Roddy, 247

McDowell, Malcolm, 419

McEwan, Geraldine, 339

McKellen, Ian, 260, 280, 281, 458, 470, 471

Mackenzie, Ronald, 35, 101, 107, 109, 110, 128–29, 319, 470

Mackenzie, Sir Compton, 264

McKern, Leo, 361

Mackintosh, Elizabeth (Josephine Tey), also (Gordon Daviot), 101, 115, 118–19, 120, 127–28, 140, 175

McPhail, Angus, 148

McVay, Gordon, 474

Magee, Patrick, 381

Maitlands, The (Mackenzie), 128–29, 131, 136

Mamet, David, 23, 477

Man for All Seasons, A (Bolt), 450–51

Mankiewicz, Joseph, 241, 242, 244–45, 251

Marching Song (Whiting), 259, 260

Maris, Paul Lyon, 24, 453

Marquess, Don, 80

Marshall, Herbert, 117

Martin-Harvey, Sir John, 140

Mason, James, 160, 243, 245–46, 248, 249, 415, 420, 433

Massey, Anna, 315, 320, 328, 329, 339

Massey, Daniel, 320, 339, 409, 410

Massey, Raymond, 56, 57, 158

Matthews, Jessie, 100, 110

Maugham, W. Somerset, 79, 122, 147, 148, 207, 209, 281, 396, 470

Maxwell, Elsa, 161, 167

Maxwell-Fyffe, David, 283

May, Akerman, 58

Measure for Measure (Shakespeare), 98, 232–34, 238, 239, 369

Medea (Euripides), 215, 216, 222–23

Melvin, Murray, 284

Mercer, David, 413, 414

Merchant, Vivien, 405

Merchant of Venice, The (Shakespeare), 35, 84, 86, 112–13, 114, 180, 181

Meredith, Burgess, 160, 162

Messel, Oliver, 25, 61, 194, 225, 229, 303

Michael, Ralph, 222, 468

Michell, Keith, 291

Midsummer Night's Dream, A (Britten), 333

Midsummer Night's Dream, A (Shakespeare), 88, 197, 207, 209, 211, 465

Mielziner, Jo, 155

Mildmay, Audrey, 191

Miles, Bernard, 23, 466

Miles, Sarah, 335

Miller, Arthur, 384

Miller, John, 9, 409–10, 421, 450

Miller, Jonathan, 360, 361, 395, 397

Mills, John, 259, 290, 319, 337, 366, 390–91, 452, 478

Mills, Juliet, 319

Mills, Mary, 366, 391

Milnes, Rodney, 372

Milton, Ernest, 48, 60, 88, 473

Minnelli, Liza, 430

Minton, John, 200

Mitchell, Julian, 418

Mitchell, Yvonne, 205, 358

Moissi, Alexander, 89

Molière, 84, 368

Montagu, Ivor, 148

Montagu of Beaulieu, Lord, 260–61, 263, 264, 275, 276, 279, 282, 286

Montgomery, Elizabeth, 104–5

Moore, Dudley, 360–61, 429–30, 444, 479

Moreau, Jeanne, 351, 352

Morgan, Charles, 94, 171

Morley, Joan, 7

Morley, Robert, 7, 205, 273, 284, 349, 367, 398, 420, 445

Mortimer, John, 116, 317, 436, 451

Mortimer, Penny, 436

Morton, John Maddison, 372

Moscow Art Theatre, 155, 317, 338

Motley, 23, 105, 110, 112, 113, 116, 125, 131, 133, 137, 141, 152, 176, 186, 188, 335

Mozart, Wolfgang Amadeus, 372

Much Ado About Nothing (Shakespeare) 98, 227, 228, 234–35, 239, 294, 306, 326–28, 461, 462

Muggeridge, Malcolm, 361

Muller, Robert, 338–39

Musical Chairs (Mackenzie), 101, 107–9, 114, 128, 470

Nadel, Norman, 340

National Theatre, 83, 366, 401, 409, 422, 428, 448
    establishment of, 173–74, 254, 342, 358
    JG's roles at, 308, 368–72, 397, 417–18
    at Old Vic, 368–71, 397, 402–3

Neilson, Julia, 206

Neilson-Terry, Phyllis, 21, 34, 48, 49

Nesbitt, Cathleen, 192, 193, 256

Neville, John, 256, 339

Newman, Nanette, 474

Newton, Bobbie, 447

Newton, Nigel, 447

Nichols, Beverly, 104, 188

Nichols, Dandy, 386, 387

Nicholson, Jack, 350

Nicolson, Harold, 97–98, 261, 373

Nightingale, Benedict, 377, 467

Niven, David, 7, 303

Noah (Obey), 138–39, 172, 311

Noguchi, Isamu, 103, 287, 290, 294, 295–96, 299, 398

No Man's Land (Pinter), 289, 311, 328, 402, 403–10, 412, 413, 422

Northern, Michael, 240

Notes from the Gods (Gielgud), 463

Nott-Bower, John, 275–76

Novello, Ivor, 72, 103, 111, 118, 249, 261, 264, 309

Nude with Violin (Coward), 65, 301–3, 304, 306

Nyman, Michael, 457

Obey, André, 138, 311, 356

O'Brien, Edmond, 243

Oedipus (Seneca), 232, 368, 369–71, 388, 409, 411, 481

Oh! What a Lovely War, 364, 372, 377

Old Ladies, The (Ackland), 137–38, 141, 172

Old Vic, 47, 83–85, 91, 93, 112, 121, 177, 191–94, 316, 317, 422
    National Theatre established at, 358, 368–61, 397, 401, 402–3
    Olivier-Richardson directorship of, 207, 215, 223, 224, 240

Olivier, Laurence, 23, 45, 177–78, 181, 247, 254, 290–94, 388, 422, 427, 431, 437, 449–50, 466, 476

Olivier, Laurence, *(cont.)*
acting style of, 22, 51, 131, 142, 146, 292, 293, 311, 338, 359, 411–12, 434, 461, 462
death of, 8, 452
film career of, 101, 172, 182, 190, 195, 207, 242, 251, 290, 291, 365, 377, 394, 398, 415, 428
as Hamlet, 158, 164, 186, 208, 251, 293, 337
ill health of, 368, 371, 427
JG as rival to, 22, 131, 141–43, 145–46, 164, 202, 207, 213, 232, 237, 270, 290, 337, 406, 411–12, 413, 432–35, 449, 452, 477
JG's alternate Romeo-Mercutio with, 131, 140–46, 147, 477
on JG's arrest, 270–71
JG's knighthood and, 215, 257
marriages of, 140, 143, 152, 204, 291, 293–94, 433, 452
in modern roles, 359, 369, 384, 385
National Theatre run by, 174, 342, 358, 366, 368, 371, 378, 397, 400, 403, 409
Old Vic company run by, 207, 208, 215, 223, 224, 240
on television, 324, 431, 432, 439
in war effort, 190, 215
Osborne, John, 262, 297, 316, 363, 364
Othello (Shakespeare), 150, 240, 256, 333, 336–38, 358
O'Toole, Peter, 337, 341, 419
Otway, Thomas, 67, 254, 256
Ouspenskaya, Maria, 163
Owen, Michael, 427
Oxford Playhouse Company, 56–57, 58, 60, 61, 67, 69, 70, 122, 205

Oxford University Dramatic Society (OUDS), 103–5, 106, 152

Pacino, Al, 460
Palmer, Lilli, 148
Palmer, Tony, 432
Panov, Valery, 397
Pascal, Gabriel, 206
Pasco, Richard, 358
Pavlow, Muriel, 198
Paxman, Jeremy, 473, 474
Payn, Graham, 76, 274
Percy, Esme, 67, 118, 225, 229, 237
Pericles (Shakespeare), 464
Perry, John, 78, 79, 109, 123, 124, 134, 155, 264, 271, 320
Beaumont's romantic relationship with, 182–83, 206, 211, 270, 287–88, 314, 330
Hensler's banishment of, 183, 331–32, 366, 464
on JG's career, 76–77, 140, 174, 186, 212, 241, 358
JG's relationship with, 7, 74, 76–77, 102, 104, 161, 172, 182, 183, 218, 263
as playwright, 75, 181, 183, 230, 335
as theater producer, 183, 185, 189, 218, 242, 257–58, 342, 358, 395
wartime service of, 189, 204, 206
Peter Pan (Barrie), 27, 29, 32–33
Phillips, Eric, 87
Phillips, Robin, 388, 395
Phillips, Sian, 410
Phillpotts, Ambrosine, 367
Pinter, Harold, 23, 25, 121, 311, 328, 360, 375, 382, 402, 403–7, 411, 413, 477
Piper, John, 333

Pitt-Rivers, Michael, 261

Playfair, Giles, 76

Playfair, Nigel, 50, 51, 55, 60, 61, 69–70, 93,
    94, 127, 191

Plenty, 419, 431, 441

Plowright, Joan, 369, 452

Plummer, Christopher, 420

Portman, Eric, 122, 217

Potting Shed, The (Greene), 309–11, 312,
    313, 324

Powell, John, 9, 366, 421, 457

Preminger, Otto, 312, 420

Price, Dennis, 174, 209

Prime Minister, The, 195–96

Prospero's Books, 378, 399, 431, 453–55,
    456–57, 460, 481

Providence, 413–17, 435

Quartermaine, Leon, 174, 205

Quayle, Anthony, 112, 127, 175, 181, 187, 227,
    453
    as director, 213, 228, 235, 236
    in Stratford management, 231, 234,
        236–37, 239, 290, 335
    wartime service of, 189, 190

Queen of Scots (Daviot), 127–28, 141, 245

Queen's Theatre, classical repertory at,
    174–81, 182

RADA (Royal Academy of Dramatic Art),
    27, 49–50, 51–52, 448

Rains, Claude, 49, 50, 51–52, 55, 206

Rattigan, Terence, 76, 104, 109, 124, 134, 281,
    324
    as playwright, 140, 217, 285–86, 291, 312,
        313–16, 324

Rawlings, Margaret, 198

Redfield, William, 343

Redgrave, Corin, 257, 477

Redgrave, Michael, 8, 22, 217, 257, 281, 361,
    427, 453
    film career of, 101, 151, 172, 176, 178, 181,
        182, 188, 241, 415
    stage career of, 174, 175–76, 177, 178–79,
        191, 375, 425

Redgrave, Vanessa, 257, 364, 450–51, 467

Reeve, Christopher, 434

Rehearsal, The (Anouilh), 358, 371, 385

Resnais, Alain, 413, 414, 415, 435, 454, 456

Return of the Prodigal, The (Hankin),
    223

Reynolds, Debbie, 303, 379, 394

Reza, Yasmina, 301

Richard II (Shakespeare), 84, 87–88, 115,
    118, 152–53, 165, 175–76, 180, 254–55,
    258, 260, 418

Richard III (film), 290, 291, 432

Richard of Bordeaux (Daviot), 87, 101,
    114–22, 125, 127, 134, 136, 228, 230,
    399

Richardson, Ralph, 108, 112, 146, 172, 182,
    190, 259, 270, 401, 422, 437, 449, 456,
    477, 480
    classical theater career of, 94–97, 99,
        100, 240, 253, 308
    contemporary postwar roles played by,
        23, 223–25, 311, 324–25, 328, 329,
        381–87, 403–8, 410
    directors' relationships with, 223–24,
        240, 383
    in film, 101, 172, 241, 290, 325, 328, 329,
        380, 394, 415, 432
    homophobia of, 143–44, 240, 288
    on JG's knighthood, 215, 256–57

Richardson, Ralph, *(cont.)*
  JG's stage partnership with, 94, 95,
      96–97, 289, 328, 339, 351, 381–85,
      387, 403–8, 411
  Old Vic company run by, 207, 208, 215,
      223, 224, 240
  in plays directed by JG, 122, 223–24, 240,
      253, 324–25, 339, 367
  publicity on, 384, 408–9, 410–11
Richardson, Tony, 7, 262, 349, 350, 363, 364,
      365, 373, 423
Ridgeway, Philip, 61–62, 63
Robards, Jason, 334, 380
Robbins, Harold, 428
Roberts, G. D. "Khaki," 264
Rodway, Norman, 353
Rogers, Paul, 417
Romeo and Juliet (Shakespeare), 58–60, 84,
      85–86, 103–7, 140–46, 150–52, 157, 217,
      378, 418, 463
Roose-Evans, James, 447
Roosevelt, Eleanor, 164
Rosenthal, Daniel, 346
Rosmer, Milton, 202
Rowland, Millie, 288
Rowland, Toby, 288
Royal Academy of Dramatic Art (RADA),
      27, 49–50, 51–52, 448
Royal Court Theatre, 297, 311, 384, 387, 390,
      401
Royal Shakespeare Company, 83, 333, 335,
      338, 428, 467
Rubinstein, Arthur, 398
Russell, Bertrand, 381
Rutherford, Margaret, 183, 190, 214–15, 255,
      335, 339, 351, 353
Rylance, Mark, 456

Rylands, George "Dadie," 190, 208, 309,
      312, 317

Sadoff, Fred, 257
Saint-Denis, Michael, 138, 139, 148, 165, 175,
      178–79, 189, 321, 338
Saint Joan (film), 111, 312
Saint Joan (Shaw), 116, 118, 206, 372, 388
St. Just, Maria Britneva, Lady, 220–21
St. Lawrence, Ayot, 206
Salaman, Merula, 139, 367
Sarner, Alexander, 49
Saville, Victor, 120
Scacchi, Greta, 442
Schlesinger, John, 403, 417
Schneider, Alan, 354
School for Scandal, The (Sheridan), 176–78,
      179, 181, 306, 339–40
Scofield, Paul, 231, 244, 254–55, 256, 257,
      258, 295, 325, 375, 417, 433, 450, 478–79
Scott, George C., 427
Seagull, The (Chekhov), 70–71, 81, 152,
      153–55
Seaton, R. E., 264
Seberg, Jean, 111, 312
Secret Agent, The, 141, 148, 150–51, 166, 325
Seely, Tim, 314–15
Seldes, Marian, 216
Sellers, Peter, 361
Selznick, Irene Mayer, 299
Seneca, 368
Separate Tables (Rattigan), 109, 285–86, 313
Seyler, Athene, 209, 210
Shaffer, Peter, 307–8, 319, 381
Shakespeare, William, 38, 342, 401–2,
      478
Shakespeare, William, plays of:

British wartime presentations of, 190, 191–94, 197, 200–203, 207–9

commercial theater vs. 66

fencing required in, 158

film versions of, 144, 149–50, 242–47, 350, 351–53, 377–78, 453–57

in modern dress, 342, 344, 346

modern plays based on characters of, 115, 118

Old Vic presentations of entire canon of, 83–84, 316

performance pace in, 84, 85, 86, 135

psychological complexity in, 22–23, 232–33, 235–36, 238

stylized settings for, 219, 294–96

verse delivery in, 98, 142, 144, 146, 202–3, 307, 344, 356, 467, 471

Victorian style vs. modern presenta- tions of, 22, 84

see also specific Shakespearean plays

Shakespeare Hit or Miss? (Gielgud), 476

Shaw, George Bernard, 27, 31, 81, 96, 116, 118, 154, 172, 244, 250, 312, 340, 356, 445, 446, 459

JG in works of, 206, 372, 388–89, 413

Shaw, Glen Byam, 270

acting career of, 56, 127, 132, 144, 158, 174, 186, 187

as director, 152, 181, 183, 293, 328, 335

Sheldon, Edward, 168

Sheppey (Maugham), 122

Sheridan, Richard Brinsley, 339

Shine, 23, 431, 460, 461, 471

Shooting Party, The, 419, 431, 433

Shuard, Amy, 305

Shulman, Milton, 288, 310, 328–29, 399–400, 402, 418

Sinden, Donald, 223–24, 455, 459, 478

Smith, C. Aubrey, 349, 459

Smith, Dodie, 181, 184, 281–82

Smith, Maggie, 395, 467, 478

Smith, Morris, 284

Sokoloff, Vladimir, 216

Solti, Georg, 333

Sondheim, Stephen, 334

Song at Twilight, A (Coward), 281, 314

Sothern, E. H., 164, 165

Spender, Stephen, 193

Sphinx, 426–27

Spitting Image, 449–50, 473

Spriggs, Elizabeth, 417

Spring Meeting (Farrell and Perry), 181, 183, 198

Spring 1600 (E. Williams), 122–23, 125–26

Standing, John, 395

Stanislavsky, Constantine, 62, 165, 173, 216

Steen, Marguerite, 30

Stephens, Robert, 337, 368, 395

Sterne, Richard, 343

Stoppard, Tom, 123, 420

Storey, David, 23, 121, 328, 381–82, 383, 384, 385–86, 405, 480

Strange Orchestra (Ackland), 109–10, 137

Strasberg, Lee, 63, 467

Stravinsky, Igor, 161, 249

Strick, Joseph, 413

Stritch, Elaine, 414

Sturridge, Charles, 431

Sullivan, John, 284

Summer's Lease, 116, 451–52

Sunday night play societies, 66–67

Suzman, Janet, 388

Swan Song (Chekhov), 195, 460, 470, 482

Swinley, Ion, 60, 81–82, 256

Tale of Two Cities, A (Dickens), 139–40, 141

Tandy, Jessica, 132, 139, 191, 193, 319–20, 334

Tanitch, Robert, 310, 414

Tartuffe (Molière), 368, 369

Taylor, Elizabeth, 251, 291, 341, 342, 343,
   344, 345–46, 349

Taylor, Laurette, 221

Taylor, Nellie, 273

Taylor, Valerie, 71, 81

Tearle, Sir Godfrey, 56, 135

Tempest, Marie, 93, 155, 181, 184

Tempest, The (Shakespeare), 71, 96, 194,
   274, 306–9, 397, 399–401, 460, 469

   film version of, 308, 353, 377, 378, 445,
      453–55, 456–57

Tennent, Cecil, 371

Tennent, Harry M., 102

Terhune, Albert Payson, 165

Terry, Ellen, 21, 30–32, 38, 41, 43, 80, 81, 85,
   96, 133, 164, 312, 318, 360, 401, 443, 479

Terry, Fred, 21, 34, 38, 48, 79, 89–90, 119, 426

Terry, Hazel, 424

Terry, Kate Lewis, 39, 46–47

Terry, Marion, 30, 38, 80

Terry-Lewis, Mabel, 38, 93, 188, 206,
   209–10

Tey, Josephine, *see* Mackintosh, Elizabeth

Thatcher, Margaret, 281, 469

theater:
   actor-managers in, 137, 173, 359
   celebrity in, 74–75, 120–21
   censorship in, 50, 76, 260, 284, 315, 373
   classical vs. antiestablishment, 375–76,
      384–87
   commercial vs. classical/experimental
      venues of, 66–67
   in epistolary format, 340, 445–46

   knighthoods in, 215, 257
   modern poetic dramas in, 185, 225, 228
   postwar vitality of, 215, 220
   psychological realism in, 243–44
   repertory companies in, 22, 127, 172–81
   solo recitals in, 318; *see also Ages of
      Man*
   in U.S. vs. England, 156, 220, 244–45,
      460

Thesiger, Ernest, 328

Thomas, Amy, 56

Thomas, Brandon, 56

Thompson, Emma, 463

Thomson, David, 353

Thorndike, Russell, 48, 84, 85

Thorndike, Sybil, 7, 8, 45, 48, 185, 408, 424,
   459
   on JG's acting, 52, 90, 216
   on JG's arrest, 269, 271–72
   stage career of, 27, 84, 223, 230, 259, 310,
      324

Three Sisters, The (Chekhov), 62, 70,
   178–79, 180

Tiny Alice (Albee), 311, 328, 349, 353–57, 358,
   369

Todd, Mike, 65, 303

Took, Barry, 284

Toone, Geoffrey, 158

Townsend, Peter, 267

Toye, Wendy, 88

Travers, Bill, 303–4

Tree, Sir Herbert Beerbohm, 38, 127, 135,
   164, 165, 173, 248

Trewin, Ion, 8

Trewin, J. C., 133, 142, 236, 256, 295, 339, 392

Trojans, The (Berlioz), 304–5, 333, 468

Tutin, Dorothy, 239, 336, 338, 361

Twelfth Night (Shakespeare), 123, 290–92, 293

Tynan, Kenneth, 212–13, 259, 261, 289, 291, 300–301, 315, 352, 418

   on JG's acting, 22, 253–56, 303, 309, 310, 337, 339, 411–12, 434, 457

   at National Theatre, 371–72, 397

   on Olivier's acting, 293, 411–12

   on R. Richardson, 240, 410–11

Ullmann, Liv, 393

Ustinov, Peter, 49–50, 213–14, 367–68, 444

Vale, Ron, 314

Vanbrugh, Irene, 93

Variation on a Theme (Rattigan), 312, 313–16

Venice Preserv'd (Otway), 254, 256, 257

Verneuil, Louis, 61

Veterans (Wood), 390–93, 399, 401

Vidal, Gore, 215, 221, 222, 418, 419

Volpone (Jonson), 417–18

Vortex, The (Coward), 63, 64, 66, 67, 69, 72, 73, 262

Vosper, Frank, 74, 108, 132, 134

Wagner, 432

Waiting for Godot (Beckett), 228, 289, 311, 387

Wajda, Andrzej, 425, 427

Walker, Alexander, 292–93

Walker, Mavis, 425–26, 442, 443–45

Walpole, Hugh, 117–18, 137, 138, 193

Walton, William, 200, 201, 306

Wanamaker, Sam, 466

Wansell, Geoffrey, 124, 285–86

War and Remembrance, 443–44

Ward, Genevieve, 32, 38

Wardle, Irving, 103, 139, 371, 400, 408

Warlock, Peter, 112

Warner, David, 357, 414

Washbourne, Mona, 386, 387

Waugh, Evelyn, 61, 349–50, 431

Way of the World, The (Congreve), 203, 254, 255–56

Webb, Alan, 90–91, 214, 288

Webster, David, 284, 304

Webster, Margaret, 85, 155

Welch, Elisabeth, 203

Weldon, Duncan, 463

Welland, Colin, 429

Welles, Orson, 242–43, 244, 331, 350–53, 431, 450, 454

West, Christopher, 284

Whale, James, 80

Wheeler, Hugh, 334

Whistler, Rex, 205

Whitelaw, Billie, 442

Whitemore, Hugh, 445

Whiting, John, 128, 259, 260

Whitty, May, 128, 185

Who Is the Man?, 61, 82, 101

Wicked Lady, The, 432

Wilde, Oscar, 25, 58, 264, 299, 372

   bisexuality of, 76, 94, 279

   prosecution of, 260, 276, 278, 279, 284, 467, 479

   works of, 47, 93, 94, 188, 209, 210, 279, 401, 464

Wildeblood, Peter, 261, 279

Wilder, Thornton, 160–61, 306, 340

Wilding, Michael, 203, 303

Williams, Emlyn, 24, 122–24, 131, 267, 408–9, 434

Williams, Emlyn, *(cont.)*
  as actor, 123, 161, 318, 377
  bisexuality of, 123, 126, 225–26, 281
  on JG's work, 57, 135, 160, 398
  as playwright, 123, 125–26, 169, 171
Williams, Harcourt, 83–87, 89, 94, 96, 98,
  99, 112, 113, 114, 174, 191, 225
Williams, Kenneth, 269, 285, 392–93
Williams, Mary Carus-Wilson, 126
Williams, Michael, 463
Williams, Tennessee, 215, 219, 220, 221–22,
  244, 314, 398, 419
Williamson, Audrey, 118, 134, 154–55, 187,
  189, 193–94, 202, 222–23
Williamson, Nicol, 420
Wilson, A. E., 133–34
Wilson, Cecil, 310
Wilson, Effingham, 173
Wilson, Sir Steuart, 283
Winner, Michael, 432
Winter's Tale, The (Shakespeare), 237,
  238–39
Winterton, Lord, 283
Wolfenden, Sir John, 283
Wolfenden Report (1957), 279, 313
Wolfit, Donald, 85, 86, 88, 89, 116–17, 197,
  198, 404
Wood, Charles, 363, 364, 389–90, 392, 401

Woodham-Smith, Cecil, 363
Woolf, James, 314
Woollcott, Alexander, 79, 144–45, 160,
  165–66
World War II, 185, 208, 459
  British theater in, 189–90, 191, 194–95,
  197–203, 205, 209
  end of, 209, 214
  films in, 195–96, 205, 207, 215
  onset of, 178–79, 183–84, 187–88
  shows for military in, 194–95, 203–4,
  211–12, 215
Worsley, T. C., 239, 315
Worth, Irene, 357, 379–80, 444, 478
  on JG's acting, 356, 369–70
  in plays with JG, 259, 271, 289, 310,
  353–54, 355, 356, 368
  on Richardson-JG stage rapport, 289
Wouk, Herman, 443, 444
Wymark, Patrick, 306
Wynyard, Diana, 90, 195, 227, 234, 235, 239,
  327

York, Michael, 393, 395
York, Patricia, 393
Young, Robert, 148, 150

Zeffirelli, Franco, 336, 337, 338, 358, 378

AMONG THE DEAD CITIES

AMONG THE DEAD CITIES

The History and Moral Legacy of the WWII
Bombing of Civilians in Germany and Japan

A. C. Grayling

WALKER & COMPANY
NEW YORK

Copyright © 2006 by A. C. Grayling

Maps by Reginald Piggot

All rights reserved. No part of this book may be used or reproduced in any manner
whatsoever without written permission from the publisher except in the case of brief
quotations embodied in critical articles or reviews. For information address
Walker & Company, 104 Fifth Avenue, New York, New York 10011.

Published by Walker Publishing Company Inc.
Distributed to the trade by Holtzbrinck Publishers

All papers used by Walker & Company are natural,
recyclable products made from wood grown in well-managed
forests. The manufacturing processes conform to the
environmental regulations of the country of origin.

Library of Congress Cataloging-in-Publication Data has been applied for.

ISBN-10: 0-8027-1471-4
ISBN-13: 978-0-8027-1471-8

First U.S. edition 2006

Visit Walker & Company's Web site at www.walkerbooks.com

Typeset by Hewer Text UK Ltd, Edinburgh
Printed in the United States of America by Quebecor World Fairfield

2 4 6 8 10 9 7 5 3 1

For
Madeleine Grayling,
Luke Owen Edmunds,
Sebastian, Thomas, Nicholas and Benjamin Hickman
and Flora Zeman
who are our future
and need us to do justice in all things.

'The term "war crimes" . . . includes . . . murder, extermination, enslavement, deportation and other inhumane acts committed against any civilian population before or during the war.'

US State Department to the British Ambassador in Washington, 18 October 1945

CONTENTS

Acknowledgements   x

Picture credits   xi

Maps   xiii

1   Introduction: Was it a Crime?   1

2   The Bomber War   15

3   The Experience of the Bombed   81

4   The Mind of the Bomber   117

5   Voices of Conscience   179

6   The Case Against the Bombing   209

7   The Defence of Area Bombing   247

8   Judgement   271

Appendix   283

Notes   329

Bibliography   345

Index   349

Acknowledgements

My warm thanks go to Naomi Goulder, Bill Swainson, George Gibson, Jo Foster and Catherine Clarke for various but always invaluable help in the preparation of this book. It could not have been written without the existence of the British Library, the London Library, the Imperial War Museum Duxford, and the Royal Air Force Museum Hendon, and certainly not without the many fine historians of the Second World War, and particularly the historians of its air war aspects, to all of whom my indebtedness is gratefully manifested in the notes and bibliography.

Picture Credits

Lancasters on a bombing run. (*Dpa Bilderdienste, Frankfurt/M*)

Air Marshall Sir Arthur Harris. (*Hulton Archive/Getty Images*)
Air Marshall Sir Charles Portal. (*Time & Life/Getty Images*)
Crew of a Lancaster bomber. (*Fox Photos/Getty Images*)

An Allied bomber above its target. (*Imperial War Museum*)
B-17 Flying Fortresses in 'box' formation. (*Bildarchiv Preussicher Kulturbesitz*)

Aachen in 1900. (*Ullstein Bild*)
Würzburg in 1938. (*Ullstein Bild*)
The rooftops of old Hamburg. (*Ullstein Bild*)
Lübeck before 1900. (*Ullstein Bild*)

Berlin under attack in July 1944. (*Bildarchiv Preussicher Kulturbesitz*)
Hamburg burning during Operation Gomorrah, July 1943. (*Chronos-Media*)
The Hamburg University bookshop after Operation Gomorrah. (*Denkmalschutzamt Hamburg Bildarchiv*)

Nuremberg, 1945. (*Bildarchiv Preussicher Kulturbesitz*)
Hannover, 1945. (*Stadtarchiv Hannover*)

Berlin, 1944. (*Bildarchiv Preussicher Kulturbesitz*)
Cologne, 1945. (*Bettman/Corbis*)

Victims of the Dresden bombing, 14 February 1945. (*Hulton Archive/Getty Images*)
Victims of the firebombing of Hamburg, Operation Gomorrah, July 1943. (*Archiv Michael Födrowitz*)

Survivors of Operation Gomorrah, Hamburg, July 1943. (*Ullstein Bild*)

General Curtis Le May, 3 August 1945. (*Bettman/Corbis*)

A B-29 'bombing up', 24 November 1944. (*Hulton Archive/Getty Images*)

A B-29 on a bombing run over Osaka, Japan. (*Imperial War Museum*)
Osaka under attack by 500 B-29 Superfortresses on 1 June 1945. (*Imperial War Museum*)
Osaka as it looked to aerial reconnaissance on 9 June 1945. (*Imperial War Museum*)

Tokyo's Ginza Street before being bombed in 1945. (*Imperial War Museum*)
Bombs falling on Kobe, 4 June 1945. (*Imperial War Museum*)
Kamamatsu destroyed by bombing, 9 June 1945. (*Imperial War Museum*)

The atom bomb exploding over Nagasaki. (*Corbis*)

Hiroshima after the explosion of the atom bomb, 1945. (*Corbis*)
Survivor, Nagasaki. (*Corbis*)

Maps

Extent of the destruction of German cities and towns, 1945
Principal bombing targets in Germany
Principal Japanese cities targeted by US Air Force, 1944–45

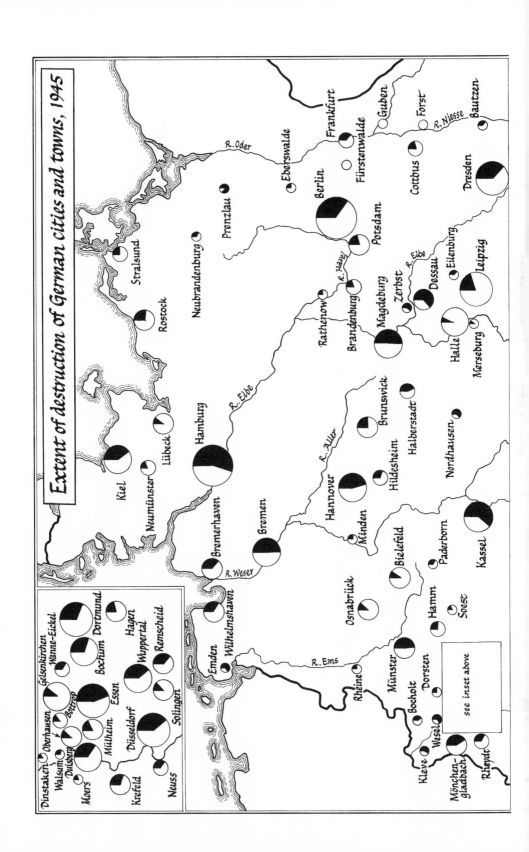

Extent of destruction of German cities and towns, 1945

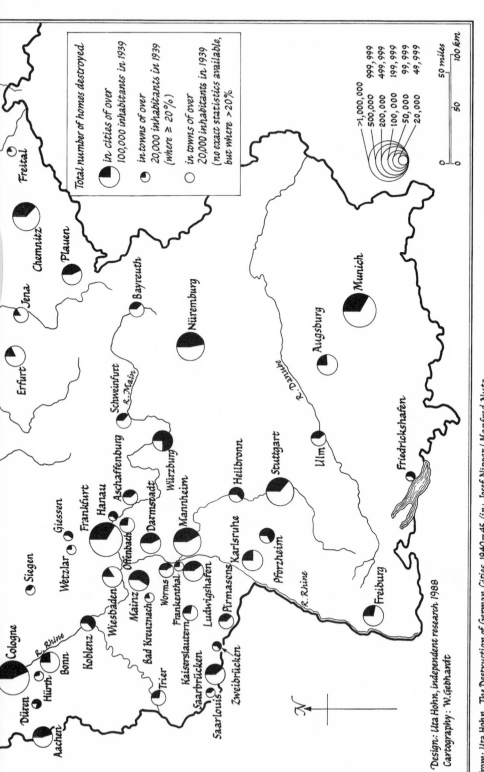

Total number of homes destroyed

in cities of over 100,000 inhabitants in 1939

in towns of over 20,000 inhabitants in 1939 (where ≥ 20%)

in towns of over 20,000 inhabitants in 1939 (no exact statistics available, but where >20%)

>1,000,000
500,000   999,999
200,000   499,999
100,000   199,999
50,000   99,999
20,000   49,999

0   50 miles

0   50   100 km

Aachen
Düren
Hürth
Cologne
R. Rhine
Bonn
Koblenz
Siegen
Wetzlar
Giessen
Frankfurt
Hanau
Aschaffenburg
Offenbach
Darmstadt
Würzburg
Schweinfurt
R. Main
Wiesbaden
Mainz
Bad Kreuznach
Trier
Worms
Frankenthal
Ludwigshafen
Mannheim
Kaiserslautern
Saarbrücken
Zweibrücken
Pirmasens
Karlsruhe
Pforzheim
Heilbronn
Stuttgart
Freiburg
R. Rhine
Saarlouis
Erfurt
Jena
Chemnitz
Plauen
Freital
Bayreuth
Nüremburg
Augsburg
Munich
R. Danube
Ulm
Friedrickshafen

N

Design: Uta Hohn, independent research 1988
Cartography: W.Gebhardt

From: Uta Hohn, The Destruction of German Cities 1940–45 (in: Josef Nipper / Manfred Nutz (Eds), Wartime Destruction and Rebuilding of German Cities, Cologne 1993, pp. 3–23)

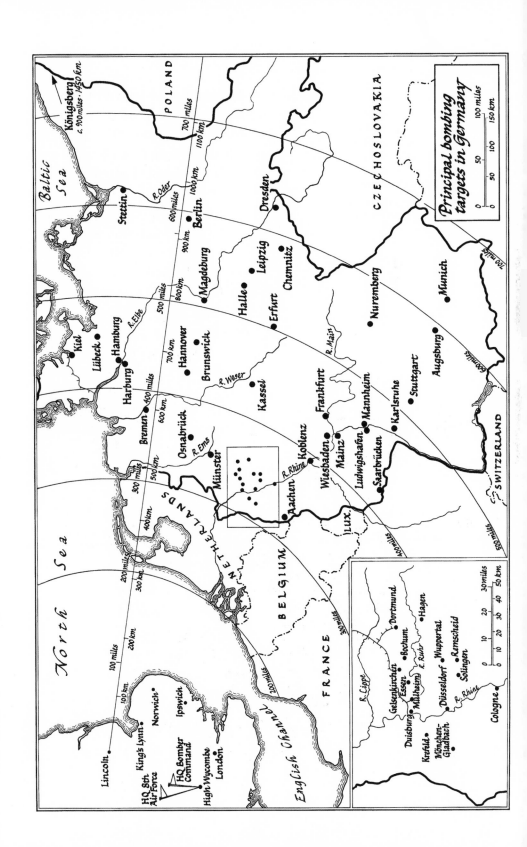

Principal bombing targets in Germany

Baltic Sea

POLAND

Königsberg
c. 900 miles = 1450 km.

700 miles
1100 km.

Stettin

R. Oder

600 miles
1000 km.

Berlin
CZECHOSLOVAKIA

Dresden

900 km.

Magdeburg

Leipzig

500 miles
800 km.

Hamburg
Halle
Chemnitz

R. Elbe
Kiel
Lübeck

700 km.
Hannover
Erfurt

Harburg
Brunswick
Nuremberg

400 miles
600 km.
R. Weser

Bremen
Kassel
R. Main

Augsburg

500 miles
500 km.
Osnabrück

Munich

R. Ems
Frankfurt

Stuttgart

Münster
Koblenz

Wiesbaden
Mannheim

300 miles
500 km.
Aachen
Mainz
Karlsruhe

400 km.
R. Rhine
Ludwigshafen

NETHERLANDS
Lux.
Saarbrücken

200 miles
300 km.
BELGIUM

SWITZERLAND

North Sea

FRANCE

100 miles
200 km.

200 miles

English Channel

100 km.

Lincoln

Norwich

King's Lynn.
Ipswich.

HQ 8th Air Force

High Wycombe
HQ Bomber Command
London.

0   50   100 miles
0   50   100   150 km.

R. Lippe

Dortmund

Gelsenkirchen
Bochum
Hagen

Duisburg
Essen
Mülheim
R. Ruhr
Wuppertal
Remscheid

Krefeld
Düsseldorf
Solingen

München-
Gladbach
R. Rhine

Cologne

0   10   20   30 miles
0   10   20   30   40   50 km.

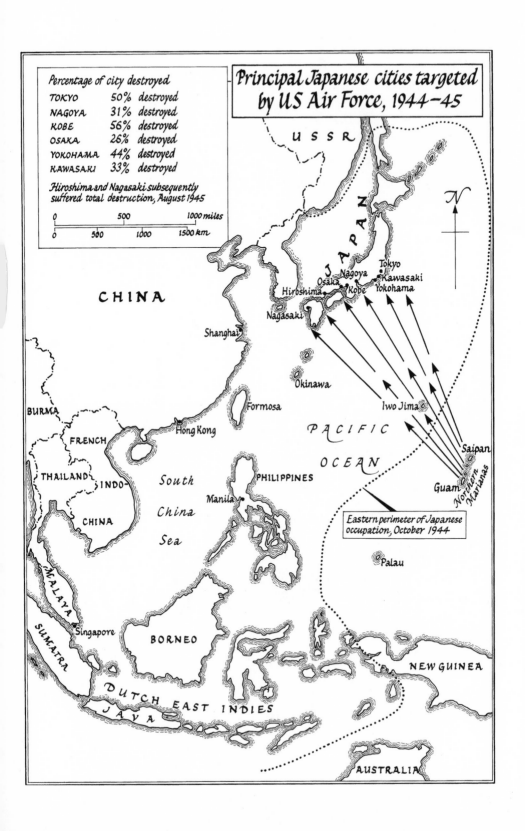

Principal Japanese cities targeted
by US Air Force, 1944–45

Percentage of city destroyed

TOKYO	50%	destroyed
NAGOYA	31%	destroyed
KOBE	56%	destroyed
OSAKA	26%	destroyed
YOKOHAMA	44%	destroyed
KAWASAKI	33%	destroyed

Hiroshima and Nagasaki subsequently
suffered total destruction, August 1945

0   500   1000 miles
0   500   1000   1500 km

N

USSR

JAPAN

CHINA

Tokyo
Nagoya Kawasaki
Osaka Yokohama
Kobe
Hiroshima

Nagasaki

Shanghai

Okinawa

Formosa

BURMA

FRENCH

Hong Kong

THAILAND

INDO-

South

PACIFIC

Iwo Jima

Saipan

OCEAN

Guam   Northern Marianas

CHINA

China

PHILIPPINES

Manila

Sea

Eastern perimeter of Japanese
occupation, October 1944

Palau

MALAYA

SUMATRA

Singapore

BORNEO

NEW GUINEA

DUTCH EAST INDIES

JAVA

AUSTRALIA

1

Introduction: Was it a Crime?

IN THE COURSE of the Second World War the air forces of Britain and the United States of America carried out a massive bombing offensive against the cities of Germany and Japan, ending with the destruction of Dresden and Tokyo, Hiroshima and Nagasaki. Was this bombing offensive a crime against humanity? Or was it justified by the necessities of war?

These questions mark one of the great remaining controversies of the Second World War. It is a controversy which has grown during the decades since the war ended, as the benefit of hindsight has prompted fresh examination of the 'area bombing' strategy – the strategy of treating whole cities and their civilian populations as targets for attack by high explosive and incendiary bombs, and in the end by atom bombs.

Part of the reason why the area-bombing controversy continues to grow is that in today's Germany and Japan people are beginning to speak about what their parents and grandparents endured in the bomber attack, and to see them as victims too, to be counted among the many who suffered during that immense global conflict. What should we, the descendants of the Allies who won the victory in the Second World War, reply to the moral challenge of the descendants of those whose cities were targeted by Allied bombers?

This fact – that the descendants of the bombed have begun to raise

their voices and ask questions about the experience of their parents and grandparents – provides one powerful reason why it matters today to try to reach a definitive settlement of the controversy.

Another and connected reason is that history has to be got right before it distorts into legend and diminishes into over-simplification, which is what always happens when events slip into a too-distant past. At time of writing there are still survivors of those bombing campaigns, both among those who flew the bombers and those who were bombed by them. Historians of the future will in part be guided by judgements we make now. With our proximity to the war, its survivors still in our midst or close to our personal memories, but with the hindsight of a generation's length from the events, what we say will help shape the future's understanding of this aspect of the Second World War.

A third and even more contemporary reason for revisiting Allied area bombing is to get a proper understanding of its implications for how peoples and states can and should behave in times of conflict. We live in an age of tensions and moral confusion, of terrorism and deeply bitter rivalries, of violence and atrocity. What are the moral lessons for today that we can learn from the vast example of how, when bombing brought civilians into the front line of the conflict in the Second World War, the Allies acted?

In the decades after 1945 these implications were obscured by the fact that a much larger and more important moral matter occupied the mental horizon of the post-war world, and quite rightly so – the Holocaust. This egregious crime against humanity was a central fact of Nazi aggression and the racist ideology driving it, and in comparison to it other controversies seemed minor. Other controversies do not fade through lack of attention, but grow unnoticed, until – as we have seen in recent years with neo-Nazi efforts to exploit the victimhood of the bombed for their own political purposes – they become a worse problem than if they were addressed with clarity, frankness and fairness.

In all these ways a new urgency attaches to the question: did the

Allies commit a moral crime in their area bombing of German and Japanese cities? This is the question I seek to answer definitively in this book.

To explain my personal motivation for trying to answer this question, I need only describe what I can see from where I sit writing these words. There is a small park across the road from my house in south London, completely grassed over, with a scattering of chestnut and linden trees standing in it. The trees have been growing there for half a century, and are close to maturity. As always, the chestnuts are first to break into leaf in spring; in the height of summer the lindens' tassels of yellow flowers make a fine show against the dark green of their heart-shaped leaves. It is easy to judge the age of these trees, because the open space in which they stand became a park just a little over fifty years ago, so the trees and their park began life together. Before then, for a few years, that open space was filled with ruins, a bare scar of bricks and rubble cleared to ground level. Before then again it was a row of houses; a dozen of them, three-storeyed semi-detached Victorian villas identical to the others still standing near by – one of them being the house where I live, and from whose windows I look out.

The green and tranquil appearance of this little London park belies the reason for its existence. It is in fact a Second World War bombsite. The houses that stood there were blown up in the Blitz of 1940–1. It is possible to follow the line of bombs that destroyed them as they fell in this street, to be succeeded by more falling in the next street – there is a little park there too, also with fifty-year-old linden trees – and on to the very big park just beyond. Until 29 December 1940 this big park was not an open stretch of grass and playing fields, but a tangle of crowded built-up streets on either side of the Surrey Canal. It is now, as a result of one of the worst nights of the Blitz on London, an expanse of 120 acres containing football and cricket pitches, a lake, cycling paths, shrubberies, and avenues of trees. Here and there stubborn protuberances of broken brick and

concrete remain, half buried beneath ivy, with some ruined adjoining walls standing beside them. One street is left intact in the park, with houses along one side and a stoutly constructed Victorian school on the other, still alive with children each day in term time (my youngest child began her education there).

The street and its school protrude into the park's open spaces as a reminder of what had been a densely crowded urban scene, and therefore as a memorial to the nights when bombs rained down on London, killing and destroying. Contemplating the street where I live and the surrounding area, I am daily reminded of the horrors of that time, and the memory drives home a point too often forgotten once wars end and memories dim: that in discussions of war and its effects on humanity, there is an argument that says that deliberately mounting military attacks on civilian populations, in order to cause terror and indiscriminate death among them, is a moral crime.

Is this assertion – 'deliberately mounting military attacks on civilian populations is a moral crime' – an unqualified truth? If it is, people in today's Western democracies must revisit the recent past of their countries to ask some hard questions about their behaviour in the great wars of the twentieth century, so that the historical record can be put straight. Attacks on civilian populations have often happened in wars throughout history, but this fact does not amount to a justification of the practice. If ever such a practice could be justified or at least excused, it will be because the following questions have received satisfactory answers. Are there ever circumstances in which killing civilians in wartime is morally acceptable? Are there ever circumstances – desperate ones, necessities, circumstances of danger to which such actions are taken as a defensive measure – that would justify or at least exonerate turning civilians into military targets? Can there be mitigating factors that would compel us to withhold the harshest judgement from those who planned and ordered such attacks? If one committed a crime in preventing or responding to a worse crime, would that mitigate or – more – even excuse the former?

We need to know the answers to these questions, because they are crucial to resolving the controversy about Allied area bombing in the Second World War. It cannot be right to hold that the mere fact of being a victor in a conflict sanitises one's actions; if questions arise about the morality of what one's own side did in winning a war, they should be squarely addressed and honestly answered.

Because moral questions about Allied area bombing (otherwise called 'carpet bombing', 'saturation bombing', 'obliteration bombing' and 'mass bombing') are deeply controversial, they arouse strong feelings. In discussion of these questions – discussion that began during the war itself – there have been outright defences of the Allied bombing campaigns (on various grounds but mainly that of military necessity) and outright condemnations, the former by far in the majority. Alternatively writers have said, 'this question is too difficult, and must be left to philosophers to debate'. This last is the challenge taken up here.

Two things must be made emphatically clear at the outset. First, it is unquestionably true that if Allied bombing in the Second World War was in whole or part morally wrong, it is nowhere near equivalent in scale of moral atrocity to the Holocaust of European Jewry, or the death and destruction all over the world for which Nazi and Japanese aggression was collectively responsible: a total of some twenty-five million dead, according to responsible estimates. Allied bombing in which German and Japanese civilian populations were deliberately targeted claimed the lives of about 800,000 civilian women, children and men. The bombing of the aggressor Axis states was aimed at weakening their ability and will to make war; the murder of six million Jews was an act of racist genocide. There are very big differences here.

But if the Allied bombing campaigns did in fact involve the commission of wrongs, then even if these wrongs do not compare in scale with the wrongs committed by the Axis powers, they do not

thereby cease to be wrongs. The figure of 800,000 civilians killed by Allied bombing, almost all of them in the course of deliberately indiscriminate attacks on urban areas, is staggeringly high in its own right, and even so says nothing about the injured, traumatised and homeless, who in many respects suffered worse.

The debate about the question has often been clouded by comparing what the Allies did with what the Axis did in the way of immoral actions, always (and rightly) to the credit of the Allies – only to leave the matter there, as if drawing the comparison by itself resolves matters. It does not; which is the reason for revisiting the question and trying to settle it.

But nothing in this book should be taken as any form of revisionist apology for Nazism and its frightful atrocities, or Japanese militarism and its aggressions, even if the conclusion is that German and Japanese civilians suffered wrongs. A mature perspective on the Second World War should by now enable us to distinguish between these two quite different points. Revisionist excuses for Nazism are unacceptable, and it has to be acknowledged that large numbers of people in Germany in the Nazi era, quite possibly the majority of them, supported Hitler in much of what he did. This has made many think that the civilian populations of the Axis countries deserved what they got, and that therefore it is a waste of time wringing one's hands over the question whether the Allies committed wrongs. But – again – such an attitude will not do. An SS trooper who machine-gunned unarmed Jews in an open pit might merit a death sentence for the crime; but a civilian who had given Hitler a stiff-arm salute and approved of his policies, and who otherwise worked as (say) an accountant, scarcely merits being executed (by bombing) for doing so. And whereas an SS trooper would be identified and prosecuted before punishment, the Nazi-supporting accountant might die in a civilian bomb shelter alongside someone who disliked Hitler and did not support the Nazis' war. Thus even if the first person's death were merited by the mere fact of his Nazism – which it is not – his companion's death would be too high a price for it.

In any case, these thoughts do not address the main point, which remains that if the Allies countered great Axis wrongs with lesser wrongs, the latter remain wrongs.

Still – and here the need for nuance enters – justice requires that one ask, Was it the case that these wrongs – if such they were – committed in countering greater wrongs, were unavoidable or necessary? Is there a plea of justification or mitigation that can be entered in their behalf, if they need either? For one must remember this: killing a man is wrong; but if one man kills another in self-defence, or in defending his family from murderous attack, the wrong in question at least becomes subject to qualification. So this too has to be taken into account, once the full picture has been considered.

The second thing that must be emphatically clear is that this examination of the moral status of Allied area bombing is not intended to impugn the courage and sacrifice of the men who flew RAF and USAAF bombing missions over Nazi-dominated Europe. Criticism – or even merely discussion – of the morality of the Allied bombing campaigns has often been read as tantamount to impugning the contributions made by those aircrews, and as devaluing their sacrifices in fighting what was after all a just war, and a necessary one, against wicked and dangerous aggressors.

Nothing in this book should be taken as detracting from the bravery of those men. It does not take much to imagine what it was like to fly into hostile skies, to face attacks by fighters and anti-aircraft guns, to see burning aeroplanes falling from the sky with one's comrades in them, and to know that the odds are against surviving the dozens of missions over enemy territory that one's duty made obligatory.

Nevertheless, if the actions that required such courage amounted to the commission of wrongs, the courage with which they were carried out does not alter the fact that they were wrongs. This has been an argument often implicitly offered, as when historians of the bombing war in 1939–45 refuse to address the moral question by saying that to do so is unjust to the pilots and gunners, navigators and bomb-aimers

who risked their lives to carry the war to those who had started it and who threatened the world with oppression.

This defence is often given the support of an added justification. In the circumstances of the time, the number of those who thought that bombing civilians was wrong was not large. Many, and almost certainly a majority, of the civilian populations of Britain and America were in favour of it, regarding it as both revenge and punishment well deserved by the Axis powers. In doing what they did, Allied aircrews therefore had popular support as well as their explicit orders from government and high command. In 1945, as concentration camps were liberated inside Germany (the British and American people first saw shocking newsreel footage from Belsen and Buchenwald in the spring of 1945; Auschwitz had been reached by Russian troops some months earlier but it was empty, having already been evacuated) popular anger against Germans waxed even greater. In consequence, accompanying newsreels showing devastated cities had the effect of making the Allied home populations think that Germany's punishment – as the country which had inflicted war on the rest of the world, and whose people had behaved with appalling inhumanity – was fitting.

All this means that the airmen who clambered aboard their bombers and flew into the dangerous skies of Nazi-controlled Europe, were buoyed by the belief that they were fighting a just war – which was true – and doing so acceptably to their own, which was also true. To be told after the war, and moreover by people who never had to face the dangers they faced, that they had been party to the commission of a moral crime, and in the retrospective light of subsequent international law a legal crime also, must understandably feel like a bitter insult.

No such insult is here intended to the men who flew into peril over Europe in the Second World War.

To explain just how far from this is the intention in what follows, a fragment of autobiography might help. When I was a small boy in the decade after the war's end, one of my fantasies was of being a Spitfire

pilot in the Battle of Britain. I spread my arms and rushed about the garden making machine-gun noises as I swooped on imaginary Dorniers and Heinkels, Ju-88s and Messerschmitts. But my interest in the history of the 1940s air war was not limited to fighter battles. I read everything I could about all the air war's aspects, and built scale models of most types of aircraft flown in it, from the biplane Gloucester Gladiators still in service when the war began, to the ME 262 jet fighters in service with the Luftwaffe when the war ended – including not only minority types like Lysanders and Swordfish and modified versions like clipped-wing Spitfires for desert warfare, but every one of the bomber types from Whitleys and Hampdens to the magnificent Avro Lancaster.

The RAF was of course the home team, but I was keen to know about the other air forces and their equipment, and to read about the experience of their flyers. And I took what opportunities offered to attend air shows and museums of flight. In the Imperial War Museum, not far from my home in London, one can peer into the cockpit of a Lancaster, and muse on what it was like to see the searchlights and the bursts of flak rising about one, seeking one's death. The only time I ever suffered chilblains was on a spring day at Duxford in Cambridgeshire, where a score of Spitfires had been assembled to perform fly-pasts, the sound of their Merlin Rolls-Royce engines – that amazingly beautiful and utterly distinctive sound – flowing as music to the ears of the watching crowds. The chilblains came because I could not let go of the railing all day long as I watched those famous aircraft fly with exquisite grace, and land and take off like eagles.

This absorbing passion led me to take some flying instruction, and to welcome any opportunity (quite a few offered while I was living in central Africa) to take the controls of a Piper Cub, a twin-engined Cessna, or a war-remaindered DC-3 Dakota, for part of a flight among the thermals above the African savannah. This interest and its practical expression fed into the vivid curiosity I felt about the air war of the 1940s. And part of it was – and remains – the profoundest respect for anyone who went to war in the air in those fraught times.

This included the bombing war; for to sit at the controls of an aeroplane that requires attention to keep straight and level on a steady compass setting – as was the case with the old crab-walking DC-3, perhaps not greatly dissimilar to a Wellington or Halifax bomber in handling qualities – is to learn to wonder at how those brave men could repeatedly venture into the violent nights over the Ruhr or Berlin.

But although I have the greatest admiration for these individuals and their courage in fighting a just war, they are not the subject of this enquiry. Their story has been often and stirringly told, as befits those who as young men saw themselves as serving their country, and the cause of right, to their best ability. Nothing I say here is intended to reduce by one iota what is owed to them and especially to the 55,000 of their comrades who died in RAF Bomber Command, and the 40,000 who died in the USAAF bomber forces in Europe and the Pacific, during World War II.

My aim in this book lies quite elsewhere. It is the specific one of examining the Allied bombing of Germany and Japan in order to settle the question whether it was in whole or in part immoral. The task is in effect a judicial one – a passing of judgement – and to do that one has to take fully into account the circumstances of the time, the intentions and the state of knowledge of the principal decision-makers, and the effects of the practical application of their decisions.

Earlier in this chapter I reported the assertion that 'deliberately mounting military attacks on civilian populations, in order to cause terror and indiscriminate death among them, is a moral crime'. I then asked: Are there ever circumstances in which killing civilians in wartime is not a moral crime? Are there ever circumstances – desperate ones, circumstances of danger to which such actions constitute a defence – that would justify or at least exonerate them?' I take the assertion and these questions as my terms of reference.

I begin by telling the story of the bomber war as conducted by the Allies (chapter 2), and describing its effects on Germany and Japan

(chapter 3). This provides the factual background to the investigations in the chapters that follow. It is hard not to mention, as this story unfolds, the many difficult questions it raises, but in general I leave discussion of them to appropriate places in the later chapters.

I then discuss the sources of Allied thinking about bombing, what intentions the Allied leaders formed on this basis, and how those intentions translated into strategy (chapter 4). Key questions arise here, because if there is culpability in the case, it is going to lie with the intentions formed, and the decisions deliberately taken and implemented, by the Allied leaders.

Then I look at the arguments put forward during the war against the strategy of area bombing, and the efforts made to stop it (chapter 5). This is important as showing that the campaigns were not uncontroversial even as they took place, and that everyone involved was acutely aware of the questions that could be asked about them, and the moral dilemmas they posed.

At the war's end the Allies put Nazi and Japanese leaders on trial as war criminals. I look at the principles used in the trial of the Nazi leaders – the Nuremberg Principles – to see how the Allied conduct of the air war would stand up in the light of those same principles if the roles at Nuremberg had been reversed. Relevant aspects of subsequent international law took account of what happened on all sides in the Second World War as its empirical basis; it is significant to see what this post-war judgement implies for the Allied bombing campaigns (chapter 6). And I look at the defences offered – often eloquent, and containing important points and arguments that must be taken seriously – of the area-bombing strategies of the Allies; defences that include, among other things, the military justification for, or even the military necessity of, the bombing strategies pursued (chapter 7).

With all these considerations to hand, I then and finally offer a judgement about the morality of the Allied bombing campaigns in the Second World War, and the reasons for my judgement (chapter 8). Among these latter are, I believe, some points that have not

previously figured in discussion of the Allies' air attack on Germany and Japan, and they might be particularly significant ones.

It is important to note that although surveying the history of area bombing in the Second World War is necessary for deciding the moral question asked by this book, I do not attempt a history of the bombing war as a whole. Area bombing was only part of the bombing war, though a very large part for Britain's RAF Bomber Command in Europe, and a very large part for the United States Army Air Force in the Pacific theatre. In Europe the USAAF did not, as a matter of chosen policy, engage in area bombing, although in a dramatic change of tactics it did so over Japan in the last months of the war. Because the USAAF became fully engaged in the bombing war in Europe only in late 1943, and because it devoted its endeavours there to precision bombing of specific industrial and military targets rather than 'saturation' bombing of civilian populations, if figures most prominently in the following pages when the air attacks on Japan become central to the story.

As a final preliminary, I must mention a coincidence of mainly personal interest. The phrase adopted as the title of this book, *Among the Dead Cities*, occurs in a report prepared by an Allied group assigned to find a suitable venue for holding criminal trials of Nazi leaders at the war's end. Nuremberg was chosen not only because it had been the scene of spectacular Nazi rallies before the war, but also because it had been 90 per cent destroyed by bombing, and seemed therefore to be an object lesson in itself, graphically illustrating the punishment brought upon Germany by the Nazis' criminal liability for instigating world war and committing unspeakable atrocities during its course. The report, in allusion to Nuremberg's ruin by bombing, described it as being 'among the dead cities of Germany'.

Imagine my surprise when, late in the process of writing this book, I came across the code-name for the last bombing raid carried out against Nuremberg by the RAF, on the night of 16–17 March 1945. The code-name was my own name – 'Grayling'. The city had already

been heavily damaged by numerous earlier raids, and the *Altstadt*, Nuremberg's historic centre, by then existed only as rubble. But the 277 Lancasters and 16 Mosquitoes of 'Grayling' pounded its rubble even further into dust, leaving 529 people dead and among other things burning down the Steinbuhl district, almost the only part of the city then still standing.

It was a costly raid from Bomber Command's point of view. Luftwaffe night-fighters shot down 24 Lancasters, 8.7 per cent of the night's force, nearly double what Bomber Command regarded as an 'acceptable' loss rate during the height of the bombing war; and this despite the fact that by March 1945 the Luftwaffe had been almost entirely swept from the skies. It was effectively the last gasp of the Luftwaffe air defence; in the remaining month of Bomber Command operations, which ended on 25 April 1945, losses were nothing like so high, and almost always light.

The coincidence of the raid's name – for that is all it is – extends to the fact that this final bombing of Nuremberg should so painfully illustrate the cost to both sides in the titanic struggle whose morality is here under discussion. Nuremberg also reminds us that as the cases for and against the bombing war's moral status are put, there looms in the background a decision already taken: one that concerns the moral status of Nazism and its crimes, which the menacingly triumphalist rallies of Nuremberg prefigured, and which the ruin of Nuremberg and the Third Reich unequivocally proves was unacceptable to the rest of mankind.

2

The Bomber War

ON THE NIGHT of 24 July 1943, in the hour before midnight, a
fleet of 791 heavily laden Royal Air Force bombers took off
from bases in the flat and relatively unpopulated counties of eastern
England, and aimed their noses across the North Sea. In their bases at
Wangerooge and Heligoland the Luftwaffe's radar operators could see
the stream of aircraft beginning to approach, and they put their night-
fighter and anti-aircraft defences on alert. The stream moved steadily
eastwards above latitude 54 degrees, and the watching Germans
judged that if it turned south before the coast of Schleswig-Holstein,
its likely target would be Bremen; but if it crossed the neck of the
Danish peninsula before turning south, it would most likely be
aiming for Berlin.

At fifteen minutes after midnight, just as the Luftwaffe ground
controllers were beginning to plot interception points for their night-
fighters, the orderly cluster of traces on their radar screens suddenly
and startlingly dissolved into a snowstorm of writhing streaks and
dashes. It looked as if the bomber stream, already large, had suddenly
multiplied hundreds of times over, and begun to move in all
directions at once. The Luftwaffe night-fighter pilots were equally
thrown into confusion, for their airborne radar – mounted cumber-
somely on their aircraft's noses like old-fashioned television aerials –
had likewise gone haywire.

The cause was a simple technical innovation employed for the first time by RAF Bomber Command: a device called 'Window', consisting of strips of tinfoil cut to correspond to the wavelength of German radar frequencies. Dropped in clusters from the bombers at one-minute intervals, 'Window' disrupted the defenders' radar, effectively blinding its operators and the crews of the night-fighters patrolling above them.

Still, the night-fighter pilots had their eyes, and observers on the ground their ears. The former saw yellow marker flares appear in the sky over the mouth of the Elbe river, and then the latter heard the sound of many aircraft swinging south above them, like the distant humming of a huge swarm of bees. At last it was clear that the night's target was neither Bremen nor Berlin, but Hamburg.

What no one could guess, either among the Luftwaffe defenders or Hamburg's citizens as they heard the air-raid warnings begin, was that the assault about to be unleashed on the city – a series of bombing raids lasting a week and a half – would be something new and terrible even by the standards of industrialised violence so far experienced in the Second World War. This was Operation Gomorrah, mounted by RAF Bomber Command with the aim of wiping Hamburg from the map of Europe.

The choice of name for the operation was apt. The Book of Genesis tells how the 'cities of the plain', Sodom and Gomorrah – the latter means 'submersion' – were destroyed by a rain of fire and sulphur from the sky. When Abraham (not Lot, who had been forbidden to look) rose from sleep the morning after the event, and stood on a peak in his mountain fastness, he 'looked toward Sodom and Gomorrah, and toward all the land of the plain, and beheld, and lo, the smoke of the country went up as the smoke of a furnace'; the cities were no more.

Operation Gomorrah consisted of five major and several minor attacks on Hamburg on the nights of 24–5, 27–8, 29–30 July and 2–3 August, and in the daylight hours of 25 and 26 July. Small forces of Mosquitoes followed on days subsequent to the main raids to cause

annoyance and take photographs. The two daylight raids were carried out by the United States Eighth Army Air Force, which sent fleets of 230 bombers on each occasion to attack Hamburg's shipyards and engineering plants. The American raids did not much affect the citizens of Hamburg in their residential areas and city centre, whereas the raids by the RAF most certainly did; these latter had as their aiming point Hamburg's most central point, the *Altstadt* – the old city. But it was the Americans who suffered most among the attackers, because angry German fighters were waiting for them in force on each of their daylight raids, and gave the American formations a severe mauling. Nineteen B-17 Flying Fortresses were shot down over Hamburg on 25 July alone.

On the first night of bombing the RAF's Lancasters, Halifaxes, Stirlings and Wellingtons dropped 2,396 tons of bombs on the city, the majority of them incendiaries. These latter were small bombs filled with highly flammable chemicals, among them magnesium, phosphorus and petroleum jelly. The phosphorus could not be doused with water, and it clung to whatever it splashed over, burning fiercely. Large clusters of incendiaries were dropped to scatter fires across the target area, simultaneously broken apart by high explosive (HE) bombs and thereby made readier for combustion. A proportion of the HE bombs were time-delayed, armed to go off in the hours and sometimes days after the beginning of a raid in order to disrupt efforts by emergency workers to put out fires, rescue the injured, mend water and gas pipes, and shore up unstable buildings.

Bomber Command had quickly grasped the value of incendiaries. During the Blitz on London and other British cities in 1940–1, civil-defence authorities issued warnings about the Luftwaffe's 2-lb. thermite and magnesium incendiaries. Cigarette cards bore the legend,

The 2lb magnesium bomb does not explode, its only object being to start a fire. It will probably penetrate no further than an attic or an upper floor, setting light to anything within a few feet. Vast

numbers of these light bombs can be carried by a single aeroplane, and many more fires started than could be dealt with by fire brigades.

The Blitz lesson had been well learned in retaliation. On the second major attack by the RAF during Operation Gomorrah, during the night of 27–8 July, Hamburg's fire-fighters were overwhelmed by the torrents of incendiaries that fell on to the city, so many and in such concentration that they initiated a terrifying phenomenon: a fire-storm. Fires in different streets progressively joined together, forming into vast pyres of flame that grew rapidly hotter and eventually roared upwards to a height of 7,000 feet, sucking in air from the outlying suburbs at over a hundred miles an hour to fuel their oxygen hunger, creating artificial hurricanes 'resonating like mighty organs' as W. G. Sebald put it, which intensified the fires further.[1] It was the first ever firestorm created by bombing, and it caused terrible destruction and loss of life. Its greatest intensity lasted for three hours, snatching up roofs, trees and burning human bodies and sending them whirling into the air. The fires leaped up behind collapsing façades of buildings, roared through the streets, and rolled across squares and open areas 'in strange rhythms like rolling cylinders'.[2] The glass windows of tramcars melted, bags of sugar boiled, people trying to flee the oven-like heat of air-raid shelters sank, petrified into gro-tesque gestures, into the boiling asphalt of the streets.

The bomber crews reported that they could feel the heat of the city's fires in their aircraft as they made their bombing runs. The next day smoke from the destroyed city rose 25,000 feet into the sky. Little bluish flames still flickered around some of the disfigured corpses. The victims of the first attack were either blown up, suffocated in their air-raid shelters from which the air had been sucked away, or cremated instantly in the raging fires outside. Many bodies were found so shrivelled by the heat that adult corpses had shrunk to the size of infants.[3]

On this second night raid, 787 bombers had crossed the Denmark

peninsula as if intent on Berlin, only to swing back and attack Hamburg from the north-east. This attack was much more accurate than the first, and its high degree of concentration was one of the principal factors in the creation of the devastating firestorm. Some commentators cite also the hot dry July weather as a contributory factor, and the fact that bomb and fire damage from the earlier raids, and strain on the city's emergency services, made the city more vulnerable.

By the third night attack on 29–30 July the effectiveness of 'Window' had diminished because the German defences had worked out ways to take countermeasures, and as a result RAF losses were higher and the bombing less accurate. More night-fighters were allocated to Hamburg's defence, and with them day-fighters whose pilots adapted themselves to their nocturnal task by taking advantage of the raging fires in the city, flying very high and watching for the bombers underneath them to become silhouettes against the glow.

The fourth and final night raid, on 2–3 August, was the least effective of all because Hamburg lay under thickly piled clouds, the rain from which helped the fire-fighters on the ground while obscuring the target from attackers in the air. Only half the bomber stream could locate the city despite the fact that it was still burning, and none of the marker flares could be seen in the murk. Nevertheless the series of attacks had already done their worst. In over 3,000 sorties above the city in four separate raids, the RAF had dropped more than 9,000 tons of bombs, the majority of them incendiaries. Only eighty-six of its bombers had been lost, a remarkably low rate for which the novelty of Window takes the credit. Bomber Command felt that it had scored an outstanding success; its official historians wrote, 'the victory was complete. In the earlier months and years of the war it was without precedent, and in those that were still to come it was never excelled'.[4] This was a sentiment shared at the time by the bomber crews themselves; one said,

The first two raids on Hamburg were so *obviously* successful to those of us who took part in them. And this was, in itself, unusual. Forgetting the standard line-shooting, one returned from most trips in what I would call a neutral frame of mind. Relief to be back and glad that one more was under your belt – and that was about all. But, with those two to Hamburg, there was an added exhilaration which came from the absolute conviction – actually on the night – that we had pulled off something special.[5]

In Hamburg itself, sentiment was of course very different. No one knows exactly how many died, but at least 45,000 corpses lay among the smoking ruins, with many more injured and traumatised. Half the city had been reduced to rubble – a total of 30,480 buildings according to official contemporary German figures. The shock of the devastating attack was felt across Germany. A tidal wave of one and a quarter million refugees from the city flowed to the very borders of the country during the following months, carrying with them first-hand news of the city's sufferings.[6]

The Official History remark just quoted – 'the victory was complete' – implies that Operation Gomorrah was a high point in RAF Bomber Command's endeavours in the Second World War. In one sense it was, because the ratio of damage inflicted to losses incurred was so favourable to the bombers. But it was not a high point in terms of tonnages of bombs dropped or devastation caused. Rather, it marked a beginning; the real beginning of the kind of bombing campaign that the British government and its Air Force commanders in the bomber force had been planning since early in the war, but had until then only been able to deliver occasionally and with great effort – as in the first 1,000-bomber raids on Cologne, Essen and Bremen on 30 May, 1 June and 25 June 1942 respectively. That month of effort had effectively been a one-off; such raids could not be repeated for some time afterwards, for the numbers involved had been plumped up considerably by aircraft and crews borrowed from Training Com-

mand and (less hazardously) Coastal Command, and as a result losses were unacceptably high – in the Bremen raid forty-nine bombers were lost. It was only in 1943, the fourth year of the war, that the RAF began to have the resources and equipment to bomb on a scale and in a manner required by the philosophy of 'area bombing', the official term for attacks aimed at civilian populations.

Those resources continued to mount as the war progressed, and alongside them, from 1943 onwards, the United States Army Air Force likewise grew in strength, contributing greatly to winning control of the European skies. The USAAF did this not by area bombing after the manner of the RAF, but by tactical bombing of key industrial resources for Germany's defence against air attack, and by fighting the Luftwaffe out of the sky partly by means of its formidably many-gunned Flying Fortress bombers, but more especially its Lightning and Mustang long-range fighter escorts. It was constant policy that, in the European theatre of war the USAAF did not follow the RAF's example of deliberate targeting of civilians, but concentrated almost wholly on military and industrial targets. In the Japanese theatre matters were otherwise; there the USAAF adopted exactly the RAF technique of incendiary area attacks upon cities.

Allied domination of the European skies was at last so complete that in the final months of bombing, from the autumn of 1944 to the official stand-down of the bombing campaign in April 1945, the Allies were able to fly over enemy territory in greater safety. The same was true in the Pacific theatre; as the US forces came close enough to Japan to mount bombing raids from captured islands, the air defence of the Japanese homeland was almost non-existent. This is a key fact in explaining how it is that the greatest percentage of bombs dropped in the entire war, and therefore the greatest destruction of German and Japanese cities, occurred in the war's final months – when the war, in the opinion of most qualified commentators, was already won.[7]

This controversial point plays a significant part in the moral assessment of the Allied bombing campaigns, for in addition to

the main question about whether deliberate targeting of civilian populations was morally acceptable, the remorseless and continued destruction of German and Japanese cities when victory was near forces one to raise the further question: was there a half-spoken intent on the part of the Allies, and most particularly among those closely associated with the planning and prosecution of the bombing campaigns, to effect what might be called 'culturecide' upon the two main Axis powers? Destroying cities meant – in addition to killing and traumatising many tens of thousands of people – destroying monuments, libraries, schools and universities, art galleries, architectural heritage, the cultural precipitate and the organs of corporate life that make an identifiable society.

In 1942 a decision was taken by the War Cabinet and the Air Staff to destroy all of Germany's cities with populations over 100,000, and among the plans made for post-war Germany – a plan partially implemented by events – was one that saw a territorially divided and diminished Germany turned into a solely agricultural region, with neither the industries nor the economic structure (including the educational and cultural institutions required to service it) to permit the resurrection, as had happened after the First World War, of another powerful and warlike Germany intent upon a European imperium. In the event, Cold War realities – whose imminence was already apparent before the war's official end in Europe in May 1945 – would have made the victorious Allies anyway quick to abandon this notion, and to see the point of helping Germany to rebuild as an industrial power. But even if the punitive conception of making Germany a farm inhabited by bucolics was one only among a number of suggestions being canvassed on the subject of what to do with post-war Germany, it cannot be allowed the comfortable status of 'just one of those ideas'. It is diffusely linked with the massive obliterating endeavour of the Allied bombers, and therefore is an idea that must not be left to slip into the shadows of history without an examination of its implications for the great moral question that the Allied bombing raises.[8] Apart from anything else, ignoring such matters

only hands them on a platter to neo-Nazis and right-wing extremists who use them for unsavoury political ends, not for frank inspection of the past and the precepts it offers.

No understanding of questions about the morality of Allied area bombing in the Second World War can be attempted without having before us the following three matters: what actually happened in the bombing war; what was known, thought, intended and hoped by those who carried it out; and what effect it had. These last two points are dealt with in subsequent chapters. Here I now turn, as a necessary preliminary, to give a brief history of the bomber war, as the background of fact for those discussions.

On 3 September 1939, only minutes after Prime Minister Neville Chamberlain announced the British government's declaration of war on Germany, air-raid sirens sounded over London. Sixty thousand beds had been prepared in the capital's hospitals for what was expected to be immediate massive air attack, and the apprehensive citizenry might have feared, when they heard that first siren, that 60,000 extra beds would not be sufficient. In the event, it transpired that the air-raid warning was the result of a lone French aviator's forgetfulness about filing a flight plan.

The assumption behind the provision of thousands of extra hospital beds in London was that Germany would bomb civilian areas indiscriminately, as it had done in the First World War, and as all theorists of air war since 1918 had predicted would be an inevitable feature of future wars. By contrast, RAF Bomber Command was under strict instructions not to attack targets on the mainland of Europe, in order to avoid the risk of civilian casualties. One of the chief reasons for this was that Chamberlain did not want to provoke retaliatory attacks on British cities. And at first both Germany and Britain were restrained towards each other in the matter of bombing, which on the British side anyway started immediately: on 3 September itself, within hours of Chamberlain's declaration of war on Germany, a group of Hampden and Whitley bombers attempted to

find and attack a fleet of German warships reportedly at sea near Wilhelmshaven.[9] They failed; but even as they returned unblooded from the hunt, a flight of ten Whitley bombers was setting course for the Ruhr – to drop not bombs but leaflets on the civilian population, inviting them to surrender.

Chamberlain's reluctance to allow bombing that might harm civilians had as its ostensible reason an assurance he had given, two days before the outbreak of war, that Britain would not bomb civilians. The assurance came in response to an appeal by President Roosevelt of the United States that the European nations would not permit 'bombardment from the air of civilian populations or un-fortified cities'. Another – more pragmatic – reason was that Britain was weaker than Germany in the air, and needed time to build strength.

This self-denying ordinance lasted until May 1940; but RAF's Bomber Command was not fully in a position to deliver major attacks on Germany until 1942, and even then it was 1943 before its campaign was able to reach levels – still not fully sustainable – of the kind desired by its planners and prosecutors. It was only in 1944 that the numbers of bomber crews, bomber aircraft and bombs began to reach those levels.

The weakness of Bomber Command at the beginning of the war was the result of several co-operating causes. At the close of hostilities in 1918 Britain possessed the mightiest air force in the world, but within two years its strength had been reduced by a massive nine-tenths. The reasons were a combination of peacetime expenditure savings, a general revulsion against the idea of war, and the opposition of the Army and Navy to the existence of a separate air force. The nascent air force might have vanished altogether had it not been for the redoubtable independence struggle fought by the RAF's chief, Sir Hugh Trenchard, and the sudden revival of military anxieties in 1923, induced by France's occupation of the Ruhr over Germany's default on reparations. By then the RAF was down to a mere three squadrons from the 382 squadrons of 1918.[10] The Ruhr crisis

prompted Parliament to vote a substantial increase in RAF funding, aimed at building within five years a 'Home Defence Air Force' of 52 squadrons, two-thirds of them bombers.[11]

In the event, when Hitler came to power in 1933 the Home Defence Air Force had risen only to 42 squadrons. The Nazi aim of rapidly building an air force was limited by none of the dithering and penny-pinching of British and French attitudes. Germany had a strong civil-aviation sector, dozens of amateur flying clubs, a growing aircraft-manufacturing industry, and secret cadres of pilots trained during the Weimar years. And because the Luftwaffe was starting from scratch it could arm itself with the latest metal monoplanes with retractable undercarriage, very different from the wooden fixed-wheel biplanes still being flown by the British and French air forces.

The RAF had a secret weapon of its own, however: excellent training. This was the legacy of Air Marshal Sir Hugh Trenchard, forged during his time as Chief of the Air Staff from 1919 to 1929. Despite the paucity of resources available to his command, Trenchard built an infrastructure that outstripped anything elsewhere in the world: the cadet college for officer pilots at Cranwell, the Staff College for senior personnel at Andover, and a number of other research and training establishments for all aspects of the force's work. The system of short-service commissions – four years full-time service followed by five years in the reserve – ensured a pool of highly trained pilots who could instantly be called upon in an emergency. When war broke out in September 1939 the RAF could summon more than 700 pilots from among former members of the Oxford University Air Squadron alone.[12]

The destabilising presence of the Nazi regime on the world stage from 1933 onwards, together with the increasingly dangerous situation in the Far East following Japan's invasion of Manchuria and China, prompted the British government to reconsider its defence policies. In 1934 it announced an enlargement of the RAF to 75 squadrons by 1939. In March 1935 Hermann Goering officially announced the birth of the Luftwaffe, and shortly afterwards Hitler

told the British ambassador in Berlin that his new air force was already as large as the RAF. Whether the information was correct or not did not matter; it galvanised London into boosting RAF targets yet again, to 112 squadrons – and not by 1939 but 1937. The aim was to ensure equality of strength with the Luftwaffe by that date, but German rearmament was proceeding much more quickly than London realised, so even with its revamped target RAF strength still lagged behind.

These plans were premised on the old concept of the 'balance of power'. In October 1935 Italy invaded Abyssinia. This was the last straw for the balance-of-power argument, which rested on arrangements invented long beforehand, at the Congress of Vienna in 1815. By the 1930s that structure was fragmenting fast, and the international situation appeared more menacing by the month. By the end of 1935 British policy-makers had at last accepted that war was a greater likelihood than peace, and they began to address themselves seriously to the task of preparing for it. The game of squadron numbers did not meet the situation by itself; new types of aircraft, manufacturing capacity to produce them, and an adequate depth of reserves were all required. The result was a plan called 'Scheme F', the first of a series of detailed arrangements to meet all aspects of air-defence needs.[13]

An immediate consequence of Scheme F was that designs of heavy bombers began to appear on drawing-boards. In some of the successor plans, notably Scheme J, priority was given to fighter-aircraft design and production because the need for defence of British air space was recognised as more urgent.[14] In fact it was already the case – luckily, from the point of view of Britain's solitary survival in the face of German aggression in 1940 – that matters were well advanced in the design of new fighters. Chief among them was the elegant and highly effective Supermarine Spitfire, evolved from the design of a beautiful seaplane which had won the Schneider Trophy (an air-speed prize), and the Hawker Hurricane, the robust gun-platform that so ably played its part in defending the English skies in the fateful summer of 1940.[15] Britain also, and every bit as importantly, had the life-saving

technological advantage of radar, without which the Battle of Britain might well have been lost.

Because of Scheme J the heavy bomber designs were left in a much less advanced state, and what RAF Bomber Command had available when war began was nowhere near suited to the task it faced.[16] It consisted of 53 front-line squadrons, each notionally – but only notionally – of 16 aircraft. There was no reserve, which meant that a third of these squadrons had to be withdrawn into non-operational status for training and reinforcement purposes. And the aircraft available – Blenheims, Whitleys, Hampdens, Wellingtons and Battles – were in their different ways too slow, light, under-armed and outdated for the war that broke upon them.[17]

To understand how the concept of 'area bombing' – targeting civilian populations in urban areas – evolved out of Britain's clear initial policy of avoiding harm to civilians, one has to know something of how the bomber war itself evolved. This is because in the perilous years 1940–2 Britain had only one resource for carrying the war to Germany, and that was Bomber Command; but, as just remarked, Bomber Command was a largely ineffective instrument while it had only Whitleys, Hampdens and the others at its disposal. The policy of area bombing was a response to a set of problems and a need: problems of navigation and bomb-aiming which made the task of finding and hitting precise targets exceedingly difficult, and the need for a forceful way of delivering blows at Nazi Germany which would hurt it and therefore its will and capacity to make war.

These facts were made plain very early in the war, in the intermittent series of attacks mounted by Bomber Command against German warships in Wilhelmshaven, the Schillig Roads, and the Heligoland Bight, and in reconnaissance flights over northern Germany. Bad weather made these efforts sporadic in the autumn of 1939 and the winter of 1939–40, but they were enough to teach some bitter lessons about the inadequacies of the types of aircraft at Bomber Command's disposal.

At very first, though, the auguries seemed good; a daylight raid on elements of the German fleet in the Heligoland Bight on 3 December 1939 saw all twenty-four of the attacking Wellingtons survive flak and assaults by ME 109 and 110 fighters. One of the German planes was damaged by return fire from a Wellington, adding to the sense that a tight formation of bombers could defend itself well, given that each Wellington had four machine guns in its rear turret.

But the optimism was premature. Ten days later a Royal Navy submarine damaged two German cruisers in torpedo attacks, and as the cruisers struggled back into the Jade Estuary leading to Wilhelmshaven, a dozen Wellingtons were sent to deliver the *coup de grâce*. Low clouds covered the sky over the target area, forcing the bombers to fly beneath them, at less than 600 feet. Anti-aircraft fire from warships and armed merchantmen in the estuary did the Wellingtons much damage, but then the barrage suddenly stopped, signifying the arrival of a flock of Messerschmitt 109s. Within minutes five Wellingtons had been shot down, and a sixth was so badly damaged that it crashed on landing when, with great difficulty, it managed to reach its home base in eastern England.

Four days later, on 18 December 1939, twelve out of twenty-four Wellingtons were shot down, again over Wilhelmshaven. It was another daylight attack, this time conducted in brilliant sunshine under a clear blue sky. Indeed the weather was so good that operators of the Luftwaffe's experimental Freya radar stations at Heligoland and Wangerooge could not believe how suicidally the RAF offered itself to the Messerschmitts stationed near by.

The attrition rate of 50 per cent on this and the earlier raid was disastrous, not least because Bomber Command was under orders to conserve its forces while reserves were built up and new crews trained. The reasons for the heavy losses were quickly identified. One was that the Wellingtons had fuel tanks in their port wings which were neither self-sealing nor protected by armour plating. Enemy fire directed there either set the Wellington ablaze, or at best drained it of fuel. The Wellington was a rather inflammable aircraft anyway, and hits any-

where could be disastrous. Another reason was that although the Wellington had four rear-mounted machine guns, it was vulnerable to beam attack, a weakness made worse – and this is a third reason – by its low air speed relative to the Messerschmitt fighters, which could easily catch and overtake it, then swing round and mount another assault, with no hope of the Wellington outrunning its attacker.

The Air Officer Commanding No. 3 Group in Bomber Command from which this mauled squadron came, Air Vice-Marshal John Baldwin, was convinced that bombers would be safe if they stayed in tight formation, using their combined fire-power to fend off attackers. It was a doctrine that, later, the United States Army Air Force vigorously adhered to, but with an aeroplane much more likely to make it work: the Flying Fortress B-17, bristling with guns at every angle. Baldwin was sure that inexperience had led his men to break formation during the 18 December débâcle, thus making themselves vulnerable. But Lieutenant-Colonel Carl Schumacher of the Luftwaffe, who had led the attacking Messerschmitts that day, later wrote that although the damage inflicted on some of his fighters was the result of the 'tight formation and excellent rear-gunners of the Wellington bombers', it was their discipline that had actually been their undoing; 'their maintenance of formation and rigid adherence to course,' Schumacher said, 'made them easy targets to follow.'[18]

The disaster of 18 December showed the Air Staff that they needed to change their thinking, not least about the wisdom of daylight raids. But even as they debated how best to use their limited forces – and their limitations were becoming daily more obvious in every sense – the pace of war forced them up an even steeper learning curve. In April 1940 Germany invaded Norway, and the British and French responded by landing an expeditionary force. The venture was a failure; the Allied force was driven back into the sea within two weeks of arriving. Sorties by Wellingtons and Hampdens against German ships crossing the Skagerrak were brutally repulsed; on 12 April eight out of twelve Hampdens were shot down trying to find the famous

German warships *Scharnhorst* and *Gneisenau*. The method of their destruction spoke volumes about their capacity as machines of war. ME 110s simply flew up and took a position parallel to them and a little ahead, a mere hundred or so yards away, thus sitting comfortably out of the Hampdens' limited line of fire; and then the German rear gunners aimed at the Hampden pilots in their cockpits, and killed them.[19] Following the 12 April débâcle Hampdens were reserved to night operations only.

On the night of 16–17 April a solitary Whitely was despatched to Oslo to bomb the airfield there in the hope of denying it to German squadrons. Only Whitleys among the aircraft at Bomber Command's disposal had the range to fly that far. The crew had a hard time; navigation was made difficult by cloud cover obscuring vital landmarks, and although the city itself was found under a gap in the cover, its outlying airport was still obscured, and moreover under fog. The crew could see nothing. At that point in the war standing orders were that bombing was to occur only on definite visual identification of a target, to avoid accidental harm to civilians; so the Whitley had to turn for home without attacking.

Although Oslo's airport was bombed in the next few days by small formations of Whitleys, the range limitation and the navigational difficulties involved were ominous signs. How could deep-penetration attacks on Germany itself be contemplated in the light of these problems? The month of operations over Norway between 9 April and 10 May had seen thirty-three bombers lost, with scarcely anything to show by way of return in damage to the enemy.

But the worst section of the learning curve had yet to be climbed.

During the 'phoney war' – the period between September 1939 and May 1940 during which there was no actual ground fighting in western Europe – the squadrons sent to France as part of the British Expeditionary Force provided the Air Staff at home with greatly more matter to ponder. The aircraft in question were all Fairey Battles, classed as 'light bombers' or 'fighter-bombers' to distinguish them

from the Wellingtons, Whitleys and Hampdens which then counted as 'heavy bombers'. The Battle squadrons formed what was called the Advanced Air Striking Force. Events proved that they were, by a considerable margin, the least effective elements in Britain's air fleet. On 30 September 1939 five of them flying an 'armed reconnaissance' over the Siegfried Line were attacked by ME 109s, and only one got home. Thereafter they flew almost always at night only, and even then kept as much as possible out of harm's way. Their most adventurous endeavour of the 'phoney war' was to drop leaflets over the Rhineland in February 1940. Efforts were vigorously made to replace the Battles with Blenheim light bombers, but by the time the 'phoney war' became suddenly real on 10 May 1940 – the day on which the German blitzkrieg in the west began – only two of the Battle squadrons had been replaced by Blenheims.

It was the ferocious defensive fighting between 10 May and the end of the Dunkirk evacuation of the British army on 3 June 1940 that revealed the inadequacies of the Battles, for all that they were flown with extraordinary courage. In the very first day of serious fighting, thirty-two Battles were sent against the German advance through Luxembourg, and thirteen were shot down by anti-aircraft fire. All the rest were damaged. Three hours later a second attack, also of thirty-two Battles, was launched against this dangerous target, and this time Messerschmitts appeared and helped the anti-aircraft batteries to shoot down ten more of them. These were completely unsustainable rates of loss, and yet what the Battles were achieving in return was practically nothing. The image of Polish cavalry galloping at German Panzers comes to mind. The next day, as a result of a Luftwaffe attack, one of the two new Blenheim squadrons was destroyed in its entirety as it stood on the grass of the Vaux airfield near Soissons, its crews drinking tea while they waited for flying orders. That afternoon eight Battles returned to the fray over Luxembourg; only one came back.

A significant consequence of the Wehrmacht thrust into the Low Countries was that on 10 May 1940 Neville Chamberlain resigned, and Winston Churchill took his place in Downing Street. The

change-over immediately led to a more assertive use of British air resources. Bomber Command's first large attack on German soil occurred on the night of 11–12 May, when thirty-six Whitleys and Hampdens set off to bomb the transport links around Mönchengladbach. About half reached the target; of these, three were shot down.

Efforts to halt the German advance necessitated bombing the bridges over the Albert Canal at Maastricht, and repeated and costly efforts were made both by French and British bombers to do so. On 11 May four out of twelve Blenheims, flying from bases in England, were shot down and all the rest damaged, with no effect on the bridges. The next day seven out of nine Blenheims were destroyed in a repeat attack, still without success.

And so the attrition went on, proving beyond any doubt the drastic inadequacies of Britain's bomber force. The effective end of the Advanced Air Striking Force came on 14 May, the day a major German attack in the Sedan sector surprised the French 2nd Army and rendered the entire circumstance of the war critical for the Allies. In a desperate effort to gain time, the French high command asked for every available French and British bomber to be thrown at the German advance. By the end of that day the French air force had ceased to exist, and Britain's Advanced Air Striking Force was in tatters, having lost twenty-six out of forty-two aircraft committed to the fray.

The French implored the new British government to send ten more Hurricane squadrons to France, but Air Marshal Sir Hugh Dowding, C-in-C Fighter Command, bluntly told the War Cabinet that Britain could not be saved from invasion unless every available fighter were kept back to maintain air superiority over the Channel. Losses among fighter planes in France had been very high; between the beginning of the invasion on 10 May and the last day of the Dunkirk withdrawal, seventy-one Hurricanes and Gladiators had been lost. But even as early as 14 May Dowding felt that the situation in France was irrecoverable, and was thinking grimly ahead. Church-

ill, however, had to do something to help not only the French but his own reeling forces; and all he had available was Bomber Command. He ordered it to do what it could from its bases in England.

Bomber Command had already begun to make night attacks on the transport links in the rear of the German advance, in an effort to slow it down and disrupt its supplies. The embargo on attacking other targets near civilian centres still held. But then an event occurred that shocked everyone, and began to loosen the no-civilian-attacks ethos prevailing in most of London's political and military minds. This crucial event was the Luftwaffe's bombing of Rotterdam on the same fateful 14 May 1940.

In the days since 10 May the Dutch had been giving their German attackers a difficult time, though outnumbered and outgunned. German landings on the beaches north of The Hague were almost annihilated by extraordinarily courageous Dutch pilots flying out-moded Fokker biplanes. It took three days for the Panzers under General Rudolf Schmidt's command to arrive at the outskirts of Rotterdam, where exhausted advance units of German paratroops had been pinned down since their initial attack.

Schmidt sent a message to the commander of the Dutch defenders of Rotterdam, Colonel Pieter Willem Scharroo, saying that if the Dutch did not surrender he would summon the Luftwaffe to mount a devastating attack on the city. The German high command was pressing Schmidt urgently to take Rotterdam so that the forces being delayed there could press on towards France through Belgium, thus pre-empting the British landing that was imminently expected on the Dutch coast. Time was of the essence for blitzkrieg, and the Dutch were making the Wehrmacht lose too much of it.

Scharroo had to relay the surrender demand to his government in The Hague, whose ministers replied that they would send a delega-tion to Rotterdam. The clock was ticking ominously, but Schmidt was prepared to wait; at last he was told that the Dutch delegation would reach the city at 2 p.m. At 1.30 p.m. he sent a signal to

Luftflotte 2, one hundred of whose Heinkel 111 bombers had been waiting on standby, to cancel their attack. Alas, five minutes before his message reached Luftflotte 2 HQ the last of those Heinkels had already taken off from their bases near Bremen. By the time Schmidt's signal was relayed from HQ to the bombers' controllers at the bases, the bombers were over Dutch territory, and had entered radio silence preparatory to their attack.

Frantic efforts to contact the bombers were repeatedly made by the base controllers, but unavailingly. Schmidt was told of the problem, and alerted his troops to fire red flares the moment they saw the bombers, to make them abort the mission. When the first wave of Heinkels appeared over the city from the south the flares duly went up, but the Heinkel pilots did not notice them; they were too busy searching for their aiming-point in the centre of the old city through the hazy glare of the afternoon sun and the smoke from flak bursts, and too distracted by concentrating on the line of the shining Maas river which was directing them to their target. Fifty-seven aircraft dropped their loads of 250-lb and 500-lb bombs into the city centre, shattering it and setting it on fire; then they climbed away towards the south-east and home.

The leader of the second wave, approaching from the south-west after a long detour, was also concentrating hard on the target area, now marked by fires and pillars of smoke; but perhaps because of the different angle of approach and the better play of light, out of the corner of his eye he saw a red flare, and instantly swung away, radioing 'Abort! Abort!' to the following aircraft. He was the only pilot to see a flare, and until his group of Heinkels had returned to base the other crews were astonished by the abrupt cancellation of their attack.

It was, however, too late. The first wave of attackers had dropped one hundred tons of explosives and incendiaries on Rotterdam, killing 900 civilians and reducing the heart of the old city to rubble. Two hours later Rotterdam's defenders surrendered. In London the next morning, and indeed in every city in the world outside the Axis

countries, newspapers blazoned the horror of the attack, claiming 30,000 dead and characterising the German demolition of the old city as an act of unmitigated barbarism.[20]

As far as the British War Cabinet was concerned, the fact that the Luftwaffe had mounted an area-bombing attack on a city changed the stakes. It was irrelevant that the city was garrisoned and defended; it was crowded with civilians, and the early high casualty estimates made it appear to be an atrocity. Everyone had learned to fear just such an atrocity as a result of bombings in earlier wars, chief among them the Zeppelin and Gotha raids on Britain in the First World War, and the attack on Guernica in the Spanish Civil War.[21] And it was irrelevant that the bombing of Rotterdam had in one sense been a terrible mistake; the Germans had contemplated, then planned, then actually put into execution, the deliberate and indiscriminate bombing of a city, and the efforts made to abort its execution could not change that.

In fact, German aircraft had already bombed civilian targets in the war. Warsaw in September 1939 was the notable example, but the alchemy of distance made it a different case. In those days the world was a much larger place, and distances were felt to be so great – not just in spatial and temporal terms, but more importantly in psychological ones – that the significance of events was almost always inversely related to them. For that reason the bombing of Warsaw, far away in the east of Europe, did not have the same impact on British sensibilities as the bombing of Rotterdam just across the Channel. As a result of the Rotterdam bombing, indeed on the very day after it – 15 May 1940 – Churchill's War Cabinet authorised bombing raids east of the Rhine for the first time. That same night ninety-nine bombers took off for the Ruhr, their official targets the oil plants, steel foundries and transport links in the region. There was a tacit understanding that there could be no guarantee of avoiding civilian casualties, but still the Air Staff insisted in their directive to Bomber Command that targets should be identified positively before they were attacked, and added, 'In no circumstances should night bombing be allowed to degenerate into mere indiscriminate action,

which is contrary to the policy of His Majesty's Government.' Rotterdam had brought Germany's home territory under the bomb-sights of the Royal Air Force, but despite it the British still maintained the official appearance of restraint so far as the explicit targeting of civilians was concerned.[22]

The limited and largely ineffectual nature of Britain's bombing efforts in the early stages of the war not only lasted until early 1942, but in fact got worse. The exception was Bomber Command's work in attacking the ships and barges being gathered for Operation Sealion, Germany's projected invasion of Britain in the summer of 1940. Here something of a victory could be claimed. The Command's bombers repeatedly attacked assemblages of German shipping in the Atlantic ports of occupied Europe, and achieved significant results in the process, making a vital contribution to the failure of Hitler's invasion plans.

Operation Sealion was scheduled to begin on 15 September; on 12 September Germany's Navy Group West HQ signalled to Berlin: 'Interruptions caused by the enemy's air forces, long-range artillery and light naval forces have become a major problem. The harbours of Ostend, Dunkirk, Calais and Boulogne cannot be used as night anchorages because of the danger of English bombing and shelling.' The next line of text doubtless warned Hitler that his invasion plans were very seriously at risk, for it underlined Goering's failure to conquer the English skies – 'Units of the British Fleet are now able to operate almost unmolested in the Channel' – and this was the achievement of RAF Fighter Command in the Battle of Britain. But the contribution of the bombers was clear. 'Owing to these difficulties,' Navy Group West HQ continued, 'further delays are expected in the assembly of the invasion fleet.' The clear implication was that an invasion could not take place until October at the earliest; by which time the tides and weather would be against it.

Hitler postponed the invasion to 17 September. On the morning of the preceding day Navy Group West HQ sent another signal about

the effects of RAF bombing: 'Considerable casualties have been inflicted on transports in Antwerp. Five transport steamers have been badly damaged, one barge sunk, two cranes destroyed, and an ammunition train blown up. Several sheds are still burning.' That night bombers sank a flotilla of invasion barges and two transport ships at sea off Boulogne, while all the ports along the coast between Antwerp and Le Havre were subjected to heavy attacks. On the day scheduled for the invasion Navy Group West HQ again signalled Berlin, 'The very severe bombing together with naval bombardment from across the Channel makes it necessary to disperse the naval and transport vessels already concentrated in the Channel, and to stop further movement of shipping to the invasion ports.'

Hitler had urged Goering to a last all-out endeavour to capture the skies over the Channel and southern England, and the hardest and most famous efforts of RAF Fighter Command's 'Few' followed during the course of that week. When it was at last clear that the Luftwaffe had failed, Hitler ordered the invasion fleet to be dismantled and dispersed, well away from Bomber Command's attentions.

As this shows, although most glory rightly belongs to the RAF's hard-pressed fighter pilots – it does not put matters too high to say that for a few critical weeks in the summer of 1940, world history rested in the hands of a few hundred young Britons – nevertheless the bomber crews also played an important role in combating the invasion menace. It was perhaps one of the best moments of the RAF's bomber war, though it has never been characterised as such.

But Bomber Command's efforts to hurt Germany by disrupting its communications and industry were greatly less successful. Attacks on canals (which transported a third of German production) and railway marshalling yards were persistent, costly and mainly ineffective. The huge marshalling yards at Hamm, the nerve centre of the German railway system, were attacked eighty-five times in the year June 1940 to June 1941 – that is an average of three times a fortnight – with scarcely any impact on movement of trains.[23] A scheme to drop

incendiary bombs on German forests and crops was also tried, but soon abandoned; the surplus numbers of incendiaries manufactured for this endeavour were kept in stock, and later dropped on cities when 'area bombing' began in earnest.

The next step towards the all-out war of area bombing occurred on the night of 24–5 August 1940. On that night a group of Luftwaffe bombers accidentally dropped their loads on London. They had been aiming for the Short aircraft factory at Rochester and the nearby oil-storage tanks on the banks of the Thames, but they were off course. The next morning a furious signal from Goering to the headquarters of the luckless bomber group announced that the aircrews responsible were to be transferred to infantry duties straight away.

In London, however, no one knew that the bombing was a mistake. The War Cabinet ordered an immediate retaliation in the interests of boosting home morale, overriding the protests of Bomber Command, which did not feel that it had enough time to prepare. A force of eighty-one bombers was mustered and sent to Berlin the very next night, 25–6 August. Only a third of them claimed to have got there and dropped their bombs on the designated targets; a further third said that they had found Berlin but in the difficult weather could not see well enough to identify their targets; and the rest – save for three aircraft that were lost – either bombed alternative targets or aborted and returned home early.

The material effect of the raid was that a few bombs fell on the outskirts of Berlin, doing scarcely any harm to anything other than Goering's reputation, for he had been adamant beforehand that the RAF would never be able to bomb the city. Its residents were shocked by the attack, and more so by others that followed in the ensuing weeks. Morale plummeted, a fact reported to London by independent observers. (Later, when Berlin became the subject of a major area-bombing campaign, morale did the exact opposite, rising not falling; proving the paradoxical nature of civilian responses to crisis conditions.) News of the effect on morale encouraged the Air Staff in

London to continue attacking Berlin whenever weather and other circumstances permitted, with its electricity and gas supplies as the official targets. 'The primary aim of these attacks,' said the relevant Air Staff Directive to Sir Charles Portal, then chief of Bomber Command, 'will be to cause the greatest possible disturbance and dislocation both to the industrial activities and to the civil population generally in the area.' Among Bomber Command's other duties, which during late 1940 and the whole of 1941 involved attempts to bomb the German navy and its dockyards, Berlin was therefore a recurrent target, and with it other industrial and transportation targets in Germany.

The restriction to visually identified targets remained, and with it the official avoidance of deliberate bombing of civilians, though the words 'the greatest possible disturbance and dislocation . . . to the civil population' suggest that thought on the matter was evolving. And indeed, as events proved, the days of both restrictions were numbered, because the most significant event in the bombing war during this early period now happened: the promotion on 25 October 1940 of Sir Charles Portal to the position of Chief of the Air Staff, his place as head of Bomber Command being taken by Sir Richard Peirse. With hindsight one can see that Portal's appointment was a crucial factor in the changes soon to come in Bomber Command strategy; for it was he who, more than anyone else – though enthusiastically supported by Sir Arthur Harris, who succeeded Peirse in early 1942 – led the way to deliberate targeting of civilian populations in Germany's cities.

The first indication of Portal's influence in this respect came five days after his appointment as Chief. On that day he sent Peirse his first directive. The directive told Peirse that Bomber Command's priorities were to be Germany's oil supplies and its aluminium and component factories. But it also ominously said that regular large-scale attacks were to be carried out on major urban areas and industrial centres, 'with the primary aim of causing very heavy material destruction which will demonstrate to the enemy the power

and severity of air bombardment and the hardship and dislocation which will result from it'.

When Portal's first directive was issued, no one could have guessed what its words would soon come to mean in real terms; but they had cast a die.

Thus was Portal's presence announced, less than a week into his new responsibilities. By itself it was not intended to herald a change towards an area-bombing strategy, and it did not amount to a repudiation of the hitherto official policy of eschewing indiscriminate bombing of targets where civilian casualties were likely. This was to come some months later, on 9 July 1941. But between Portal's first directive and the July 1941 directive, RAF bomber crews gradually became less observant of the restrictions that had hitherto hampered it. Its efforts to bomb industrial and port targets in Germany increasingly, and without censure, caused 'collateral damage' to housing and civilian facilities near the factories, marshalling yards, oil installations and harbour-works that it attacked.

The thoughts forming in Portal's mind were much influenced by the London Blitz, which was already in full swing, having started on 7 September with a large-scale raid on the Docklands area of the city.[24] According to one version of events, the Luftwaffe's switch from bombing Fighter Command airfields to bombing London – thereby easing the pressure on Fighter Command, no small factor in its ability to hold on to English skies, and hence a fatal error by Germany – was part of the tit-for-tat begun by the accidental Luftwaffe bombing of London on 24–5 August, and the RAF's retaliatory bombing of Berlin on the next and subsequent nights. Hitler had been at his retreat at the Berghof during August, but when Berlin was bombed he returned to the city and summoned to his office Field Marshal Erhard Milch, Inspector-General of the Luftwaffe and Goering's deputy. Hitler ordered Milch to increase the manufacture of heavy bombs, evidently with a change of bombing tactics in mind. A few days later Hitler addressed a mass rally at the Sportpalast in Berlin, in the course

of which he spoke about the RAF bombing raids, saying that since he had driven the British into the channel he had deliberately not responded to the provocation of their bombing raids, but that now, lest they take this as a sign of weakness, he was going to teach them a lesson. In his familiar and carefully rehearsed mounting style of rhetoric, he said to wild acclaim,

> If the British air force drops two thousand or three thousand or four thousand kilograms of bombs, then we shall drop a hundred and fifty thousand, two hundred and thirty thousand, three hundred thousand, four hundred thousand, one million kilograms . . . When they say that they will attack our cities, then we will wipe out their cities . . . The hour will come when one of us will break, but it will not be National Socialist Germany![25]

No doubt this is part of the explanation for the change of Luftwaffe tactics, but there were other factors too. According to Paul Deichmann, a former Luftwaffe general and author of a post-war study of the Luftwaffe, military reasons were chief among them.[26] These were that Luftwaffe intelligence had overestimated the losses of RAF fighters in 11 Group, based to the south and south-east of London, and now wished to draw the fighter reserves of 12 Group into the fray from north of London. Attacking the capital would be the perfect way to do this. Deichmann claimed that he had been personally told as much by Field Marshal Albert von Kesselring, who with his other commanders had been assessing the balance of forces preparatory to launching Operation Sealion.

But the reliability of this account is thrown into doubt by the fact that when the Luftwaffe switched its attack to London, it did so primarily at night, when not only its own fighter escorts were unable to fly, but the RAF fighters found it difficult to fly also. The night-bombing tactic was therefore irrelevant to the object of defeating the British fighter force in the sky, and since it involved no attacks on 12 Group airfields, neither would it destroy it on the ground.

The switch to night bombing is in fact much more plausibly explained by the Luftwaffe's high losses during the Battle of Britain. In the six weeks between 15 July and 31 August 1940 the Luftwaffe had 621 bombers destroyed, with 344 damaged, a casualty rate of 69 per cent. Add this to the 724 lost or damaged aircraft in the period between 10 May and mid-July – that is, between the invasion of the Low Countries and the beginning of the Battle of Britain – and it becomes evident that the Luftwaffe's attrition rate was too high to be sustainable. Speaking in 1945, the commander of the German fighters in Luftflotte III, which fought in the Battle of Britain, said that he had urged a change to night attacks early in the battle because of the Luftwaffe's high losses; he described the battle as 'a sort of air-Verdun, in which the Germans were at a disadvantage'.[27]

It is clear enough that the new aim premised by the change to bombing London and other cities – for London was not alone in receiving the visitations of the Luftwaffe from September 1940 onwards – was the hope that it would disrupt British war production and affect 'morale'. General Jodl had said as early as 30 June 1940 that 'occasional terror raids announced as "reprisals", and the depletion of Britain's food stocks, will paralyse the people's will to resist, and eventually break it altogether, forcing their government to surrender'.[28] Hitler made it clear that he alone would decide if and when bombing should explicitly target civilians, though it was obviously a live option for him; 'if eight million go mad, it would be a catastrophe; after that even a little invasion would go a long way,' he remarked.[29] But the ostensible target of Luftwaffe bombing was the economic and industrial capacity of Britain, and its governmental institutions. Thus the full force of German bombing was felt by London's docks, the City, Whitehall, and the dense residential districts of the East End and south London where the capital's factories were mainly located. When British civilian casualties mounted, Berlin could claim both that they were (to use more recent terminology) 'collateral damage', and also revenge for RAF bombing of German civilians.

The Luftwaffe's effort to disrupt Britain's economy and pound its population into submission lasted from 7 September 1940 until the German invasion of Russia in May 1941. The result was considerable destruction – one raid alone, on 29 December 1940, almost obliterated the City of London – and by the end of that period there were 30,000 British dead and 50,000 injured. But civilian morale did not break, and the British economy did not falter; war production increased quickly and steadily throughout the period, and continued to do so for the rest of the war.

But no one in Britain took these facts to be any indication of the inadequacy of bombing to bring about the submission of an enemy. As both the British and the Germans knew, the Luftwaffe lacked the means to do worse, because it had no true heavy bomber. One was planned – the Heinkel 177 – and if it had come into existence in large numbers and had been used to assault Britain, the result might have been more like the devastation caused to Germany by the genuinely big heavy bombers that entered Allied service as the war progressed.

Even so, the Blitz was a horrific event, which did much to make the idea of severe retaliation against German cities more acceptable – even, indeed, welcome – to many in the British (and later, when the United States entered the war in December 1941, the American) public at large – though not, as we shall see, to all.

If any one event in the Blitz was especially significant in preparing the ground for the strategy hinted by Portal in his first directive, it was not any of the raids on London, but the devastating attack on Coventry on the night of 14–15 November 1940. The psychological effect of this attack, the largest and most intense air raid of the war to that point, was enormous; but not in shaking British will: rather the contrary. And it turned American and world opinion against Germany even more.

It has been claimed that the War Cabinet knew there was going to be a massive attack on Coventry, but took no action in order to protect its intelligence sources.[30] Whether or not this claim is true,

the fact is that Bomber Command attempted pre-emptive attacks on Luftwaffe bomber airfields in France and Belgium that night, having at least been told that a major raid was expected on an unnamed British city.[31] German propaganda after the Coventry attack said that it was a retaliation for RAF bombing of Munich. The Bomber Command War Diaries record a number of raids on unspecified German cities in the preceding two months, and one of them might well have been Munich, but the city is not mentioned by name. When one sets the cultural and (to the Nazis) political importance of Munich alongside the severity of the Coventry raid, the claim comes to have a ring of truth.

The raid on Coventry lasted ten hours, starting at twenty minutes past seven in the evening of 14 November 1940, and ending at a quarter past six the following morning. The German communiqué which described the raid as a retaliation for Munich went on to say that the bombing was targeted at the many military-related engineering works in the city, but contemporary British reports pointed out that because of the heavy anti-aircraft fire that greeted them, the Luftwaffe aircraft had to maintain very high altitudes from which accurate bombing was impossible. The result was that HE and incendiary bombs fell everywhere on the city indiscriminately. Night-fighting skills and technical capacities were still very rudimentary in RAF Fighter Command, which was therefore unable to do much to mitigate the attack.

The German communiqué went on to claim that the raid was the heaviest of the war, with over 500 bombers involved. The damage they did to Coventry was extensive: its fourteenth-century cathedral was destroyed, its tram system smashed, its gas and water supplies put out of action, four and a half thousand of its houses demolished, three-quarters of its factories damaged, and 600 of its citizens killed, with over 800 more injured.

This was not the first attack on Coventry – there had been several minor ones in preceding weeks – and it was not the last; the city was bombed forty-one more times in the course of the war, and had to put

up with hundreds of air-raid alarms when Luftwaffe bombers were on their way to other cities. But this was the biggest attack Coventry suffered, and the psychological effect on the nation and its government was profound.

Given that London had been suffering under a nightly blitz since September, the special significance attached to the attack on Coventry in the moonlit middle of November 1940 might seem odd. But as the Official Narrative observes, the Coventry bombing was 'an occasion of singular importance in the history of air warfare', because for the first time in history, air power 'was massively applied against a city of small proportions with the object of ensuring its obliteration'.[32]

In the winter of 1940–1 Bomber Command was no bigger than it had been a year before in numbers of front-line aircraft, but it was nevertheless gaining strength as a consequence of the inflow of newly trained aircrews, many of them from the Dominions and colonies (together with several squadrons of French and Polish fliers who had escaped to Britain), and the gearing-up of aircraft and munitions production. The first new heavy four-engined bombers did not begin to arrive in service until later in 1941, bringing teething-troubles with them, but the existing bombers were by now somewhat improved, with self-sealing fuel tanks and armour-plating fitted over vulnerable points.

During this winter and the following spring and summer of 1941, Peirse's bombers made fitful efforts to find and bomb oil plants, and made many sorties against industrial cities and ports, among them Essen, Cologne, Dusseldorf, Duisberg, Kiel, Hamburg and Bremen. Berlin remained a target whenever opportunity offered, and frequently Bomber Command had to take a part in the vital Battle of the Atlantic, a war of tonnages between German U-boats and merchant convoys crossing from America with vital supplies. So far as results were concerned, Bomber Command's main thrust against industrial and port targets remained largely ineffectual, and sometimes quite nugatory, as when photographs taken during an air raid

supposedly on the giant Krupp armament works in Essen showed that the bombers had flattened a forest instead.

As this incident showed, the worst problems affecting Bomber Command related to navigation and bombing accuracy. Aircrews were wont to claim that they had reached targets and bombed them, though some of them realised that their endeavours were often extremely approximate. In the summer of 1941 Lord Cherwell, Churchill's scientific adviser, persuaded the latter to have bombing efficiency investigated by a member of the War Cabinet Secretariat, Daniel M. Butt. Butt studied hundreds of photographs taken during and after bombing operations, and compared them with aircrew reports and target orders. His devastating conclusions were published in August 1941. They were that many bomber aircraft never found their targets at all; even in good weather on moonlit nights, only two-fifths of bombers found their targets, but in hazy or rainy weather only one in ten did so. On moonless nights the proportion fell to a hopeless one in fifteen. In all circumstances, of those that reached their designated target only a third of them placed their bombs within five miles of it.[33]

On these results, the bombing campaign was a massively wasteful and futile effort. In September 1941 Portal sent Churchill a plan for 'Coventry-style' attacks on Germany's forty-five largest cities, claiming that if a force of 4,000 bombers could be built up and unleashed in this fashion, the war would come to an end in six months. But Churchill, still fuming in response to the Butt Report, replied, 'It is very debatable whether bombing by itself will be a decisive factor in the present war . . . the most we can say is that it will be a heavy and I trust seriously increasing annoyance.'[34] The reasons he gave were that Luftwaffe defences would quite likely overwhelm the bomber attack, that only a quarter of bombs were falling anywhere near their targets, and that anyway the British population had shown that being bombed merely 'stimulated and strengthened' civilian resistance.

Portal knew that despite the Butt Report and Churchill's irritation, Bomber Command was all that Britain had in the way of an offensive

arm, so he responded quietly by reminding Churchill that new navigation and bomb-aiming technologies were being devised, and that new heavy bombers were being built to benefit from them. He received in reply a less cantankerous letter assuring him that Bomber Command would continue to receive full support from the War Cabinet for its role.

And by this time its role had come 180 degrees round from the one to which it had been restricted in the war's opening months. For on 9 July 1941 Portal's Air Staff – with the sanction of course of the War Cabinet – had issued a new directive to Bomber Command, switching its primary attention from oil and naval targets to 'dislocating the German transportation system' and '*destroying the morale of the civil population as a whole and of the industrial workers in particular*'.[35] With these fateful words the area bombing campaign became explicit and deliberate policy.[36]

There was one final step before the area-bombing policy began to take major effect. Sir Richard Peirse was still in charge of Bomber Command, and his Command was still doing its best with inadequate aircraft and navigation aids all through 1941, until a disastrous raid on Berlin on the night of 7–8 November ended his career, and caused a temporary retrenchment in the bombing campaign.

Portal's second-in-command on the Air Staff, Wilfrid Freeman, had throughout 1941 been urging Portal to discontinue raids on Berlin on the grounds that they were futile and costly, a view that he felt inclined to apply to much of the Command's efforts, as indeed the Butt Report confirmed. But Portal's response was to say that taking a few tens of tons of bombs away from other targets to 'get four million people out of bed and into the shelters' in Berlin was worth it. In fact the cost was not merely one of tonnages: loss rates of 16 per cent of aircraft sent to bomb Berlin were experienced in the summer months of 1941, with very little damage to show in return, for on every occasion less than half of the bombers sent found the city.

But on the night of 7–8 November things got even worse. It has

been supposed that Peirse wished to rebut Butt by mounting an impressive attack on the German capital, and for that reason mustered the biggest force of the war so far – 392 aircraft, 169 of them detailed to bomb Berlin, the rest to attack a variety of targets between the Atlantic coast and the Ruhr. In the event the weather was worse than expected, and less than half the Berlin force reached the city. Because it was at the extreme end of the range for Wellingtons and Whitleys, and because the poor weather made them suffer heavy icing which caused their straining engines to use up more fuel, most had virtually empty tanks on reaching home. But 12.5 per cent of them did not reach home. Given that the upper limit for a bearable loss rate was 5 per cent this represented not just a failure but a major disaster for Bomber Command.

Portal investigated the failure thoroughly, and in early January 1942 concluded that Peirse had displayed poor judgement in authorising the attacks to go ahead when the weather reports showed that they should be aborted. Within days of Portal's discussing his findings with Churchill, Peirse was sent to command the nascent air forces in the Far East, and a man of quite different character and talents was summoned to take his place: Sir Arthur Harris.

When Harris took up his post at Bomber Command HQ in High Wycombe on 22 February 1942 he was forty-nine years of age, and looked like a portly and not very friendly bank manager of the old-fashioned type. His appearance completely belied his colourful past. He had left school at the age of seventeen to go to Rhodesia, with the aim of learning how to farm. By the age of twenty-one he was a farm manager, but in the interim had also engaged in gold-mining, cattle-ranching, game-hunting, and driving teams of oxen. At the outbreak of the 1914–18 war he joined the Royal Rhodesian Regiment and walked hundreds of miles through the veld of South-West Africa, hunting Germans. Determined henceforth to 'go to war sitting down' he returned to England, mastered the rudiments of flying in a half-hour lesson at Brooklands airfield, and was commissioned into the

Royal Flying Corps. He had experience both as a night-fighter shooting down Zeppelins over England, and as a squadron commander on the Western Front. Daily from his cockpit he saw the miles of trenches and mud and struggling men central to that epic struggle, and the sight engendered in him an emphatic belief: that wars should be won from the air. That opinion was unchanged when he took the helm of Bomber Command twenty-five years later.

During the 1920s Harris commanded squadrons in the Middle East and India, and developed techniques of night-bombing with the already obsolescent aircraft then in service, among them the Vickers Virginia two-engined 'heavy bomber' biplane. He made the standard ascent of all senior officers through staff college, and served in the Air Ministry and in procurement in the United States, from which he wrote acerbic memoranda about the taste displayed by American military personnel for hot dogs (Harris was a gourmet – indeed perhaps, as his figure suggests, a gourmand). But in between he was Air Officer Commanding Bomber Command's No. 5 Group, then equipped with the difficult and inadequate Hampdens. His handling of this command, evidenced by his lower than average loss rate despite at the same time showing an appetite for attack, had demonstrated his qualities to Portal before the latter asked him to serve as his deputy on the Air Staff. It was here, evidently, when the two men were in daily contact, that Portal saw in Harris the man he wanted for Bomber Command HQ at High Wycombe, for it cannot be doubted that their thinking about bombing strategy was very close, that Portal's belief in area bombing as the way to win the war exactly chimed with Harris's view, and that the policies which issued from the Air Staff under Portal's leadership indubitably had input from Harris. One night during the Blitz – the night of 29 December 1940 – Harris and Portal went up on the Air Ministry roof to watch the City of London burning under Luftwaffe attack, and saw the dome of St Paul's 'standing out in the midst of an ocean of fire'.[37] After watching in silence for a time, Harris said to Portal, 'Well, they are sowing the wind.'[38]

*   *   *

The bombing force that Harris took over was still weak, but beginning to grow in strength and capability. It had recently been equipped with a new navigational device called GEE, and with increasing numbers of the new four-engined heavy bombers that first appeared on drawing-boards in 1936. Chief among them was the Avro Lancaster, a remarkably successful aircraft which became the mainstay of the bomber force, and which flew its first operational sorties in March 1942 within weeks of Harris taking office.

Much more pertinent, though, was a new directive from the Air Staff, which had been issued on 14 February 1942 in preparation for Harris's assumption of command at High Wycombe. It stated in unequivocal terms, 'The *primary object* of your operations should now be focused on *the morale of the enemy civil population*, and in particular on the industrial workers.'[39] In the summer of that year a pamphlet was dropped on Germany, purporting to be the text of a broadcast given (in German) by Harris, warning its population of the dire threat it faced:

> We are bombing Germany, city by city, and ever more terribly, in order to make it impossible for you to go on with the war. That is our object. We shall pursue it remorselessly. City by city; Lubeck, Rostock, Cologne, Emden, Bremen, Wilhelmshaven, Duisberg, Hamburg – and the list will grow longer and longer. Let the Nazis drag you down to disaster with them if you will. That is for you to decide . . . We are coming by day and by night. No part of the Reich is safe . . . people who work in [factories] live close to them. Therefore we hit your houses, and you.[40]

In fact Harris himself made no such broadcast; it was a propaganda exercise by 'enthusiastic amateurs', as Harris called them, in the Political Warfare Department, seeking to profit from the alarm in Germany caused by the first series of raids organised by Harris. The sanguinary tones of the supposed broadcast attracted criticism from those opposed to the idea of 'saturation' or 'carpet' bombing (terms

more accurately descriptive than 'area bombing'), which annoyed Harris, who took himself to be doing his best to win the war. As it happens, Harris had agreed to the use of his name on the pamphlet without reading it; but nothing in his views would have led him to disagree with its contents anyway.[41]

Because Bomber Command's primary focus was now the 'enemy civil population', the Air Staff was eager to experiment with a bombing technique using a high proportion of incendiaries. For this purpose the old Hanseatic city of Lubeck on the Baltic coast was chosen, because it contained many timbered buildings dating from medieval times. As justification for the attack it is always said that Lubeck was the main port for iron ore entering Germany from neutral Sweden, and moreover was home to a U-boat training station. But the timbered medieval buildings were a temptation for incendiary experiments, and therefore on the night of 28–9 March 1942 a force of 234 RAF bombers took off, of which 191 claimed to reach the target. 'The result,' writes Denis Richards, 'was devastation on a scale never before inflicted by Bomber Command; the later raiders could see the conflagration a hundred miles ahead.'[42] Harris himself wrote, 'On the night of 28–9 March, the first German city went up in flames.' A thousand people died in Lubeck; within a month another of the wooden Hanseatic cities was in ashes, this time Rostock, 70 per cent destroyed in three raids between 23 and 26 April. Here the ostensible justification was a persuasive one – there was a Heinkel factory in the city's southern suburbs.

The outrage in the German leadership at the destruction of these medieval towns inspired the retaliatory 'Baedeker' raids on Norwich, Bath, Exeter, York and (later, as a reprisal for the massive Cologne attack of 30–1 May) Canterbury. In fact the Baedeker raids began even before the Rostock bombing; Exeter was attacked on 23 April as a reprisal for the attack on Lubeck, but the fact that Rostock was attacked on the same night angered the Germans more. On 24 April Baron Gustav Braun von Sturm said, 'We shall go out and bomb every building in Britain marked with three stars in the Baedeker Guide', thus giving the series of raids their name. The Luftwaffe's

reprisals killed 1,637 people, injured 1,760, and destroyed 50,000 buildings, including York's ancient Guildhall and Bath's beautiful Assembly Rooms.[43] At this stage of the war it might have seemed as if it was not only the Luftwaffe that was sowing the wind; but the balance of power was altering inexorably against Germany in the bombing war, as Harris's ambitions very soon showed. For Lubeck and Rostock had whetted his appetite for an even greater spectacular: a 1,000-bomber raid to wipe out a city and prove his contention that bombing can win a war by terrifying and pounding a population into surrender. It was also part of his and Portal's motivation to erase the impression of ineffectiveness left by Peirse on the minds of the War Cabinet. Thus was 'Operation Millennium' – the 1,000-bomber raid on Cologne – set in motion.

The effective front-line force that Harris inherited when he first stepped through the doors at Bomber Command HQ in High Wycombe was 600 aircraft. To launch 1,000 aircraft into the sky all at the same time meant that he had to get the support of Training Command, Coastal Command, and Army Co-operation Command. He wrote to their respective chiefs to say that he, with the backing of Portal and the Air Staff, 'proposed at about the full moon to put over the maximum force of bombers on a single and extremely important town in Germany, with a view to wiping it out in one night, or at least two'.[44] The city chosen was Hamburg, with Cologne as second choice. Preparations involved ground crews working long hours to make all the aircraft ready, among other things fitting a number of them with GEE equipment, necessitating special training for the navigators who were to use them.

The idea was that by massing 1,000 bombers over a city in the space of an hour and a half, the defences of the city – its fire-fighters and medical services as well as its anti-aircraft batteries – would be overwhelmed, and the concentration of explosive and incendiary power would lay it waste. The fear of collisions among so many aircraft was abated by organising the fleet into three separate bomber streams issued with careful timing instructions; the bombing was to

be carried out from 8,000 feet, and the aircraft were loaded with a maximum capacity of incendiaries, among them a seeding of delayed-fuse 4-lb. 'X' bombs designed to kill or scare away fire-fighters after they had arrived at the scene of a blaze.

Despite the last-minute withdrawal of Coastal Command aircraft because of Admiralty fears about the effect of their absence on the Atlantic battle, and despite several days of delays occasioned by adverse weather, Harris at last made his choice of which target to attack. It was Cologne. At 9 p.m. on the evening of 30 May his mighty air fleet took off, carrying with it Harris's hope of persuading his political masters to continue building the air armada he believed could win the war. Interestingly, at this point the available armada was still technically far below what Harris knew would be required for the devastation of Germany by bombs; his first 1,000-bomber fleet contained over 600 Wellingtons, and only seventy-three Lancasters.

Nevertheless the 900 bombers that reached the target between them dropped 915 tons of incendiaries and 840 tons of high explosives. More damage was done to the city on this one night than all previous air raids on it put together. Over 600 acres of the city were flattened, and its gas, water, electricity and transport amenities badly disrupted. Some 13,000 buildings were destroyed, making 45,000 people homeless; but amazingly for an attack of such magnitude, only 469 people were killed – a mark of the level of preparedness of German cities, whose air-raid precautions and shelters were extremely well organised.

British public morale was greatly boosted by the raid, and Harris's gamble – he had committed his entire front line and all his reserves in one throw of the dice – was vindicated. He had wanted to show what a really big air raid could do, and it was from his point of view an unqualified success. In his memoirs he wrote, 'My own opinion is that we should never have had a real bomber offensive if it had not been for the 1000 bomber attack on Cologne, an irrefutable demonstration of the power of what was to all intents and purposes a new and untried weapon.'[45]

But what also convinced Churchill and the War Cabinet to continue building Bomber Command's strength was the fact Harris did not have the resources to repeat such a large attack more than two more times that summer. The second 1,000-bomber attack was against Essen, and was largely unsuccessful because the bomber streams became spread out in time and space, and scattered their loads to little real effect over a wide area of the Ruhr. The third, against Bremen, was less successful still, proving expensive in lost aircraft because the weather was adverse and the inexperienced crews sent to make up numbers suffered badly at the German defenders' hands.

Harris was experimenting against the day when he had the right bombers in the right numbers to prove his theory that very big bomber formations would overwhelm defences by delivering their loads in a concentrated manner over a short period of time, the aim being to cause destruction, shock and casualties on a scale that would bring about logistical paralysis and the failure of the German will to fight. But in the summer of 1942 his Command was still in the process of re-equipping with the new big bombers, and although the pace of production and training was rising all the time, it had not yet reached the levels he and Portal required. And of course problems remained. The need for better navigation and bomb-aiming was only fitfully being met, with GEE sometimes proving effective and sometimes not, and bomb-sights and aiming effectiveness still far from satisfactory. The War Diaries suggest that between half and three-quarters of bombs dropped in this period were still well off target.[46] Moreover the German defences were improving all the time; Bomber Command's average loss rate in the first half of 1942 was 4.3 per cent of sorties, and the percentage kept rising over the rest of the year.

Nevertheless there could be no remission of the bombing war; one of the chief factors in necessitating its continuation at the highest possible intensity was that Russia was in desperate straits, and needed its Western allies to do everything they could to distract as much of Germany's attention from the Eastern Front as they could.[47]

The first task was to make Bomber Command's efforts count for more by addressing the deficiencies in navigation. Against Harris's initial resistance the Air Staff formed a special group, the Pathfinder Force, to achieve excellence in navigation and to lead bombing raids to their targets, there to mark them with flares and to drop incendiaries so that following bombers could use the resulting fires as aiming-points.[48]

The Pathfinders had a sticky start, the first raids they led going badly astray. Indeed on the very first of them the force they led ended by bombing a village in Denmark instead of their proper target, which was a submarine yard in Flensburg on the Baltic coast. To make matters worse, German scientists had now worked out how to jam GEE. Even when the Pathfinders began to find their targets with a higher degree of accuracy, as in the attack on Nuremberg on the night of 28–9 August 1942, ill luck still seemed to dog Bomber Command's efforts; 14 per cent of the bombers on this raid were lost, a disastrous number. The main victims were the now-ageing Wellingtons, still forming one-third of the bomber force, but failing badly in their contest with German air defences. Their replacements – the Halifaxes, Lancasters and Stirlings (these latter, with their inability to make good altitude, a rather unsuccessful aircraft) – were still feeling their way into service.

Bomber Command might have welcomed some relief in this transitional period, as new aircraft and techniques were coming on stream, but events in the wider war would not permit them to have it. The fighting in North Africa was intensifying, and the Command had to include Italy in its work. Genoa, Milan, Turin and other targets took up the bulk of its efforts in the autumn months of 1942; 1,646 sorties were flown against Italy, with a loss rate of only 3.7 per cent. The Italian raids were understandably popular with aircrews, who found the defences they encountered there much weaker than German ones.

By the end of 1942 keen-eyed spectators could see that the tide was turning in the war in almost all its aspects, and Bomber Command

was not excepted. In Russia the Germans were suffering major setbacks, prefiguring the terrible nemesis of Hitler's aggressions. While Allied arms were beginning to enjoy success in North Africa – Montgomery's offensive at El Alamein began on 23 October, and the Anglo-American landings in French North Africa took place in November – Bomber Command was beginning to feel the effect of new technologies designed to solve its navigation and bomb-aiming problems. These were OBOE, a long-distance wireless navigational aid directing aircraft to their targets, and H2S, a radar system for recognising what lay below an aircraft, so that it could locate its target from above and aim more accurately. OBOE could only direct a few aircraft at a time, but with the Pathfinder Force finding its feet this was not too great a restriction. H2S promised greater effectiveness all round, but especially in bad weather. Gadgets were becoming available for countering German defence technology too, among them a means of jamming German radar.

These advances came not a moment too soon. Bomber Command's loss rate had crept up to 6.7 per cent by the autumn of 1942 (recall that the maximum acceptable rate was 5 percent, and even that was too high: it meant lives as well as aircraft lost), and most of the increase was owed to the growing effectiveness of the Luftwaffe's night-fighters. But things were changing. What Harris in his memoirs called 'the preliminary phase' was over; he could now contemplate mounting a proper offensive. The new heavy bombers were entering Bomber Command's squadrons in real force as 1943 dawned. During the preceding year, leaving aside the artificially concocted 1,000-bomber raids, the average maximum force that could be sent against a target was 250 aircraft, with a large admixture of the increasingly obsolescent types. In the first months of 1943 the average was 450 aircraft, almost all of the new large four-engined type.[49] Two-thirds of the squadrons in Bomber Command were equipped with Lancasters and Halifaxes by the spring of 1943, and by that year's end there were sixty-five operational bomber squadrons, four of them equipped with the fast, high-flying wooden Mosquitoes, which were superbly

adapted for the tasks of reconnaissance, pathfinding, target marking, and photography after the event. This was a major boost in offensive power; the new heavy aircraft carried more than double the bomb load of the old – two and a half tons as against one ton. Accompanied by improved Pathfinder performance and the new technological aids, this increase in striking capability represented a sea-change.[50]

And this was just part of a continuing increase in strength; the curve was reaching upwards on an ever steeper slope. By March 1944 an average of 1,000 aircraft was available each day to Harris, by then all of the heavy type.[51]

In all, Portal and Harris could hope for a much more effective year in 1943. Harris was especially keen to prove his theory, long since abandoned by Churchill and the War Cabinet, and by now perhaps only half held by Portal, that intense bombing could win the war by itself. Although Churchill no longer agreed with Harris on this point, he nevertheless remained convinced that bombing was an important element of the war effort. At the Casablanca Conference held at the beginning of that year (14–23 January 1943), he and President Roosevelt of the United States decided that round-the-clock bombing of Germany was an important adjunct of their aim to invade Europe, first through Sicily in 1943, and then through France in 1944.

As this last point shows, a highly important added factor was by then in the picture. This was that the United States Army Air Force had entered the bombing war against Germany too, its contributions increasing during 1943. Its efforts were tentative at first, and attended by heavy losses because its aircraft bombed by day and did not yet have long-range fighter-plane protection. But by the beginning of 1944 the American bomber force was having a powerful effect.

In fact, units of the US Eighth Army Air Force had first arrived in Britain in 1942 under the command of General Ira Eaker, but they needed time to prepare, and their first bombing raid was not carried out until 17 August 1942, a modest affair comprising eighteen B-17s under Spitfire escort, which bombed a factory near Rouen in France. By the end of the air war in April 1945 the presence of the USAAF

was a decisive factor; the 'Mighty Eighth', as its England-based bomber force came to be called, was then deploying 200,000 personnel in the European theatre, and could put 2,000 aircraft into the air at any one time, its raids defended by the exceptionally effective Mustang and Lightning long-range fighters. But all this was yet to come.

Harris could not embark on an all-out bombing war on Germany straight away, though, because his Command was called upon to help in the Battle of the Atlantic by attacking Germany's submarine bases. Harris believed in advance that these attacks would be a futile distraction – and so indeed they proved; the submarine pens lay under impenetrable masses of concrete, and were unaffected by bombing, though the French coastal towns and populations around them were not. Harris fumed, eager to use his new resources to pound Germany itself.

At last, in March, he was able to return his attention to this task. Between 5 March and the end of July 1943 Harris waged what he called 'the Battle of the Ruhr', aimed at causing maximum damage and disruption to the industrial cities of the Ruhr valley, and the workers who lived in them. It began with an attack on Essen, where the huge Krupps armament factories were situated, and continued with repeated visits to Essen, Duisberg and Bochum. In the longer nights of the early part of the battle, Harris sent his bombers elsewhere in Germany also – to Berlin, Kiel, Frankfurt, Stuttgart and Mannheim among other targets – but as the days shortened, making the longer flights into Germany more hazardous, he concentrated more intensively on the Ruhr, and caused great material damage to its towns: Dortmund and Mulheim were devastated, as were Wuppertal and Elbefeld, and Bochum and Oberhausen were not much less severely handled. In the attack on Elbefeld on 24–5 June, in which 630 bombers took part, more than 1,800 people were killed.

If anything showed the increasing power of Bomber Command's attacks, it was the fact that when 600 of its aircraft bombed Cologne

on the night of 3–4 July, they did more damage than the previous year's 1,000-bomber raid, in the process killing 4,400 people. A repeat attack five nights later added greatly to the process of 'dehousing' the city's population; the two raids destroyed the homes of 350,000 people in all. One of the express aims of the campaign was to create paralysing logistical difficulties for the Nazi authorities in having to deal with so many people dead, injured, bereft of homes and domestic resources – and of course to reduce the effectiveness of the survivors in their factory work.[52]

It seems impossible to believe that these attacks could not have had an effect on industrial output and therefore the German capacity to wage war. Yet – in ways and for reasons to be discussed later – whatever the disruption and inconvenience, until close to the end of the war German industrial production continued to rise. Bomb damage to factories was repaired within days or at most weeks, and output resumed.

Even the most spectacular of the bombing achievements of 1943 – the Dam Buster raid – did not have the desired effect of crippling German industrial activity. The raid was an amazing feat of technology coupled with great flying skill and courage. Its heroes were Barnes Wallis, the eccentric genius who invented many unusual and sometimes effective devices of war, in this instance the celebrated 'bouncing bomb', and Guy Gibson – who won the VC for the feat – and his crews, who had to fly very low into the teeth of anti-aircraft fire to drop their bouncing bombs accurately. Eight of the nineteen aircraft that carried out the attack were lost; 52 out of their 133 aircrew were killed, and three captured.

In the event, the breaches in the Mohne and Eder dams (the Soper dam could not be breached) did not shut off the electricity supply to the Ruhr industries, and although 1,294 people died in the rush of water from the breached dams, the figure is tiny in comparison to the hope that many towns would be drowned by flooding. The Official History states that 'the total effect was small'; its chief result was to raise morale mightily at home among the war-benighted British.[53]

If the Dam Buster raid was spectacular, the already described Hamburg attacks known as 'Operation Gomorrah' were equally so from Bomber Command's point of view. What placed their measure of destructiveness and death above that of such badly hit Ruhr towns as Wuppertal and Elbefeld was the firestorm caused by the intense concentration of bombs dropped. The Hamburg experience reinforced Harris's conviction that bombing was *par excellence* the war-winning weapon, and he was determined to continue his efforts to prove it.

But events elsewhere in the war prevented Harris from mounting any more 'Hamburgs' for the time being. The situation in Italy was poised on a knife-edge, and the War Cabinet wanted Bomber Command to turn its attention to Milan, Turin and Genoa. This was no hardship to Bomber Command's crews; they greatly preferred north Italy to Germany. The loss rate on raids there was very low, in large part because when bombing started the defenders' searchlights became stationary and the anti-aircraft guns stopped firing, suggesting that their crews knew where the better part of valour lay. Fighter defences in the Italian skies, likewise, were effectively non-existent.

Harris claimed that Bomber Command's activities in Italy were the reason for Mussolini's fall. Doubtless they were part of the reason; but there were many factors at play, and it is not clear that bombing in north Italy was individually more significant than any of those others. Allied air forces were operating over southern and central Italy with great intensity, and British and American troops were fighting their way up the peninsula. Moreover, the Italian population at large did not have, and perhaps throughout the war had never had, an appetite for Mussolini's war. Most of the fighting done in their country was by Germans.

But when the effects of Bomber Command's work over Milan and the other cities were surveyed soon afterwards, the extent of the damage it had caused was painfully clear. In Milan the factories of Alfa Romeo, Pirelli, Breda and Isotto-Fraschini among others had all been badly damaged; so had the city itself, and within it some of its

treasures. La Scala opera house was damaged, and at the church of Santa Maria della Grazie just one wall remained standing – the wall bearing Leonardo's mural of the Last Supper.[54]

The Ruhr attacks, 'Operation Gomorrah', and the success of endeavours in Italy to which Bomber Command had contributed, led Churchill to write to Harris on 11 October, 'The War Cabinet have asked me to convey to you their compliments on the recent successes of Bomber Command . . . Your Command, with the day-bomber formations of the 8th Air Force fighting alongside it, is playing a foremost part in the converging attack on Germany now being conducted by the forces of the United Nations on a prodigious scale.' Churchill also had in mind the fact that Harris's bombers had also achieved success in a precision-bombing raid on Peenemunde, where Hitler's secret weapons were being developed, and had continued to inflict damage on German cities, among them Nuremberg, several times attacked and badly damaged during 1943. Harris circulated Churchill's letter to the whole of Bomber Command, together with his reply, in which he said, 'It is an unfailing sense of strength to us to realise that every bomb which leaves the racks makes smoother the path of the armies of the United Nations as they close in to the kill.'[55]

Heartened by this exchange, Harris decided that the time had come to put his theory about the war-winning capacity of bombing to a yet fuller test. The obvious target for a 'Hamburg' was Berlin, which until then had not been as hard hit as the cities of western and northern Germany because of its great distance from the bomber airfields of eastern England – it was nearly twice as far away as the cities of the Ruhr. Distance meant opportunity for the German defences, especially its night-fighters, and of course it also posed greater difficulties of navigation and greater strain on the nerves of RAF crews. But as the longer nights of the autumn of 1943 approached, Harris made his plans for an assault on Berlin, and on the night of 18–19 November he launched it, calling it 'the Battle

of Berlin'. By this time he had a regular daily average of 800 bombers at his disposal, and the navigational technologies that had become available at the beginning of the year were now operating with efficiency and effectiveness. He felt that he had a real chance to show what a powerful bomber force could do. He wrote in optimistic and excited vein to Churchill saying, 'We can wreck Berlin from end to end . . . It will cost us between 400–500 aircraft. It will cost Germany the war.'

In the four months November 1943–March 1944 repeated heavy attacks were made on Germany's capital. Much damage was done, and in just two nights of raids early on – those of 22–3 and 23–4 November – 9,000 Berliners were killed or injured. Increasing use of H2S meant that the bomber stream did not have to fly along a corridor of marker flares to their target, thus showing Luftwaffe night-fighters where to find them. And Harris's increased resources meant that he could send decoy raids of several hundred aircraft against other cities, and also use a special force of fighters on 'Intruder' missions to distract the Luftwaffe night-fighters, and to jam its radar with a variety of electronic countermeasure devices which the RAF's scientists were at constant pains to invent.

Enthused by the early promise of the Berlin campaign, Harris wrote to the Air Staff, iterating his claim that his bombers could win the war by themselves provided that Lancaster production and maintenance was given the highest priority, that the successful navigational aids now available were produced more rapidly so that all – or as many as possible – of his bombers could individually have them; and that he be allowed so to organise missions that the rate of loss be kept below 5 per cent. In effect the letter was a repeat of Harris's consistently held view that if Bomber Command's needs were given priority, and if he were given operational latitude, there would be no need for a land invasion of the European continent, which meant a bloody infantry war to conquer Germany. Bombing would, he insisted, do it by itself.

Churchill's War Cabinet, and the Chiefs of Staff committee which

advised it, did not stint Harris, but equally its members – Churchill included – still did not believe that bombing alone would win the war. The most they thought it would do would be to weaken Germany. And despite all the advantages accruing to Harris in aircraft numbers and technical advances, the Berlin campaign was nowhere near the success he had hoped. One reason was that Bomber Command could not even then manage to 'wreck Berlin' by itself. The words Harris had actually written to Churchill before the campaign were, 'We can wreck Berlin from end to end if the USAAF will come in on it.' This was unrealistic. One problem was that the USAAF was still not in a position to manage so deep a penetration of Germany. This, remember, was November 1943, and the long-range fighter planes needed by the American bombers for protection during their daylight attacks were only just becoming available in operational terms. At that point the Flying Fortress echelons, for all their formidable armament, were still finding their war a too costly one. Moreover, American bombers attacked by day because US policy in the European theatre remained strictly focused on precision attacks upon vital military and industrial targets, so General Ira Eaker would anyway not have been permitted to join Harris's attempt to obliterate Berlin.

All these factors meant in practical terms that the periods elapsing between each of Harris's attacks, even when they took place on successive nights, gave Berlin's population time to recover, despite the great material damage to the city's fabric. To add to the problems for Bomber Command, weather conditions were consistently against its Berlin forays, and after the promising early attacks there were a number that became diffused over target, with a rising percentage of bombs falling harmlessly in the Brandenburg countryside. On the raid of 16–17 December a disaster overtook the bombers when they returned to their bases, finding the weather there so bad that twenty-nine Lancasters crashed. Some of the crews parachuted to safety, but 140 crewmen died.

Harris's big campaign against Berlin lasted until March 1944, and took place amidst continued heavy bombing of many other cities in

Germany. It did not destroy German morale or bring the Nazi regime to its knees. Its cost to Bomber Command was high in numbers of aircraft and air crews lost; and as a result most commentators, and the Official History, conclude that 'the Battle of Berlin' was a failure. 'The Luftwaffe hurt Bomber Command more than Bomber Command hurt Berlin' was how one commentator summarised matters,[56] and the Official History's judgement was painfully brusque in going further: 'The Battle of Berlin was more than a failure, it was a defeat'.[57] One of the primary reasons was that the Luftwaffe's night-fighter and ground-defence forces had proved too effective. If circumstances elsewhere were not changing, the outcome of the 'Battle of Berlin' would have been major grounds for rethinking by everyone involved in the RAF's bomber campaign.[58]

By February 1944 the USAAF was ready to contribute greatly more to the bomber war over Germany than had hitherto been possible. In 1943 it had made a courageous and hazardous start on its daylight mission, suffering terrible casualties during its ill-fated attacks on a crucial industrial bottle-neck in the German war economy, the ball-bearing factory in Schweinfurt. The attacks took place on 17 August and 14 October 1943, and the Eighth Army Air Force lost 120 bombers in the process. The October débâcle in effect amounted to a great victory for the Luftwaffe, which by this means forced the Eighth to suspend its daylight operations over Germany. During the course of 1943 the Eighth's bombers increasingly received protection from P-38 Lightning and P-47 Thunderbolt fighters, fine aircraft but still not able to accompany the bombers far enough into Germany to make daylight raids less than potentially suicidal. But in the first months of 1944 the Eighth began to have at its disposal the out-standing Mustang fighter, powered by Rolls-Royce Merlin engines and capable of flying with the bombers all the way to Berlin and back. This meant that it could start making a really major contribution.

With this resource the picture changed. At the Casablanca Conference a year before, in January 1943, the Allied leaders had called for

round-the-clock bombing of Germany. Harris had without success asked for it in his Berlin campaign; now at last it was going to be possible, and in a co-ordinated and cohesive way known as the 'Combined Bomber Offensive'. Between February 1944 and the stand-down of the air campaign in April 1945 – with the important exception of the summer of 1944, when the American and British bomber forces switched to tactical (that is, battlefield) bombing in the weeks before D-Day and the summer months following it – their joint forces could together pound the German homeland, and they did so with constantly increasing ferocity.

One main target of the co-ordinated assault was the Luftwaffe, by means of attacks on the factories that produced its aircraft and spare parts. The first manifestation of the new arrangement was 'Big Week', commencing 19 February 1944 with an 800-aircraft night raid by RAF Bomber Command on Leipzig, home to four Messerschmitt factories and a ball-bearing plant. The Americans followed next day with 200 aircraft, a further 800 of its bombers raiding a variety of other cities at the same time. The RAF bombed the city, the USAAF bombed the factories. The pattern thus set continued for the remainder of the week, with hundreds of aircraft from Bomber Command attacking at night, and hundreds of aircraft from the Eighth Army Air Force attacking by day, unleashing an almost incessant rain of bombs on Germany. Stuttgart, Brunswick, Halberstadt, Regensburg, Schweinfurt and Augsburg were just some among the aiming-points of major raids. Augsburg's ancient city centre – to take just one example of the effects – was obliterated in the Bomber Command attack of 25–6 February 1944.

'Big Week' was just the start. The combined offensive might as well be called 'big year', given that it continued, on either side of the D-Day period of tactical bombing, as it started – only more so. In fact when the period of tactical bombing ended and the attacks on the German homeland resumed in full force in the autumn of 1944, the effect was massively greater, because by then the Allied air forces had virtual control of the skies, and their aircraft and munitions factories

had kept on producing *matériel* in ever greater quantities. What had happened at Augsburg at the end of February, and what happened to Frankfurt at the beginning of March – 'a blow,' as Frankfurt's own municipal report put it, 'which simply ended the existence of the Frankfurt which had been built up since the Middle Ages'[59] – was to be the fate of many German towns, bombed and so far unbombed, before the order came to stop the bombing in April 1945.

Harris did not want to switch from the area bombing of cities to tactical bombing in support of 'Operation Overlord', the Allied invasion of Normandy. He had consistently believed and argued that bombing would make a land invasion unnecessary; but even when, in January 1944, he recognised that Overlord was an inevitability, he protested in writing that his force was not adapted to tactical bombing and must be allowed to continue to weaken the German heartland. 'It can be stated without fear of contradiction that the heavy bomber is a first-class strategic weapon and one of the least effective tactical weapons,' he said in a lecture as late as 15 May 1944, given to the headquarters of 21 Army Group at which Field Marshal Sir Bernard Montgomery was present.[60]

Portal in the end had to order Harris to collaborate with the planning for Operation Overlord. At a meeting on 25 March attended by the RAF's highest command and the scientific adviser Professor Zuckermann, a plan was drawn up for presentation to Churchill, based on the idea of bombing key rail centres in France and Belgium. The advantage was that it promised paralysis of German battlefield logistics; the disadvantage was that it risked French and Belgian civilian casualties. Portal estimated that the acceptable upper limit of such casualties would be 10,000 people. Legend has it that one of those present – Air Chief Marshal Sir Trafford Leigh-Mallory – remarked that he did not want to go down to posterity as a man who had killed thousands of Frenchman, to which Harris growled in reply, 'What makes you think you're going down to posterity?'[61]

Harris reserved his greatest scorn for what he called 'panacea' plans

– plans premised on the idea that a single factor would win the war: attacks on oil facilities, attacks on ball-bearing factories, and – as in this plan – attacks on railway communications. He wrote to a personal friend,

> Our worst headache has been a panacea plan devised by a civilian professor whose peacetime forte is the study of the sexual aberrations of the higher apes. Starting from this sound military basis he devised a scheme to employ almost the entire British and US bomber forces for three months or more in the destruction of targets mainly in France and Belgium.[62]

But Harris was a military man, and once he had been given an order and had lost the argument against it, he obeyed it to his best ability. His bombers went to war on the railway network of France and Belgium on 18 April 1944, mounting sixty such attacks between then and D-Day, and earning Portal's plaudits and Churchill's gratitude that 'care had been taken to avoid heavy civilian casualties'. This showed that RAF Bomber Command could conduct precision attacks avoiding civilian deaths as much as possible: a point much to be borne in mind.

In fact the tactical work of the two bomber forces was a major success overall, and in its way greatly more effective as a contribution to winning the war than the years of urban area bombing beforehand. In addition to railway centres, the bombers attacked airfields, munitions dumps and military encampments. Harris was still able to mount area attacks against a variety of German cities on moonless nights, arguing (plausibly enough) that it stopped the Germans from sending anti-aircraft defences to France. But the main thrust of the air attack was tailored to the needs of the impending invasion, including – in the immediate run-up to it – bombing of coastal batteries and defences. On the night of 4–5 June, Bomber Command dropped its greatest load of the war to date, battering the coastal defences – over 5,000 tons of bombs. The navy was shelling the same target at the

same time, and between the two forces nine out of the Germans' ten Normandy batteries were rendered incapable of sustained fire.[63]

In the weeks after D-Day, Bomber Command flew over 3,500 sorties to interdict German communications, scoring notable successes – just one example of which, early in the invasion, was its delaying a shipment of Panzers travelling to the front by train, by precision bombing of a railway tunnel. All this work was undertaken at a very low loss rate. It included close tactical support of troops on the ground, and attacks on German naval units attempting to disrupt supplies across the Channel. Rather like its successes against the German invasion fleet of 1940, Bomber Command's part in the invasion of 1944 might be one of its chief glories of the war.

At the time, though, Harris was itching to resume area bombing, and another panacea – a return to the idea of hurting German oil supplies – served only to irritate him. But it too was an order, and Bomber Command duly joined the Eighth in attempting to limit the flow of fuel to Germany's tanks and aircraft. Losses were brutally high on these raids – on one of them, to Wesseling, nearly a third of the attacking aircraft were lost – and it was almost a relief to both air forces that the needs of the tactical situation recalled them from oil targets deep in Germany to military and transport targets in France.

The success of Allied air power in this period was in part a matter of sheer numbers. Between them the two air forces mustered 14,000 aircraft of all types, and the Luftwaffe faced them with 1,000. In a telling remark on this disparity in strength, Denis Richards in his history of the bombing war says, 'So overwhelming was the air superiority of the Allies . . . that once substantial ground forces and their supplies had been successfully landed and positioned for battle, the issue could hardly be in doubt.'[64] The circumstances, remember, were that Soviet forces were making headway in the east too. The Germans were capable – and proved it – of prolonging the battle by means of their formidable abilities and determination, especially in the east where fighting to the death seemed vastly preferable to submitting to a vengeful and brutal enemy.

But the inevitability of an Allied victory was by this time – the autumn of 1944 – plain to all who could count and add. For even though at this stage of the war German military production was still increasing, it had no chance of competing with the overwhelming productive power of the Allies, chief among them the United States; nor did it have the manpower reserves to last much longer, whereas the manpower of America and the British Empire, then still just intact, was far from being exhausted. So the war was effectively won by the end of summer 1944; no one on the Allied side believed anything other than that victory was a matter of time. The Allied determination to have nothing but unconditional surrender was one factor in ensuring that seven more months of bitter fighting remained; demanding unconditional surrender leaves defenders with a sense of nothing to lose, though in fact the loss Germany thereby incurred was tremendous. It was in this period that Bomber Command dropped more than a third of the total tonnage of bombs it unleashed on Germany in the entire war; and it was in this period that it turned its attention to towns and cities until then unscathed, in search of targets where enough was still standing to make it worth while to knock them down.

In mid-September 1944, Bomber Command returned to the control of the Air Staff in its new combined Allied guise, having been under General Dwight D. Eisenhower's orders for the main period of the invasion. The nights were beginning to draw in; long nights meant safer conditions for flying into Germany to bomb. Harris wrote to Churchill to say that because of the tactical support given to the ground war following D-Day, Germany itself had been given a 'considerable breather' and must now be attacked again, using the Allies' vast air superiority to 'knock Germany finally flat'. Churchill replied that although he continued to disagree that bombing could do it all alone, he liked Harris's spirit, and encouraged him in his intent: 'I am all for cracking everything in now on to Germany that can be spared from the battlefields.'[65]

These words were music to Harris's ears, and gave him what he needed to ignore the thrust of a new directive issued to him on 25 September, expressly requiring him to regard oil installations and communications as his *primary* objective, and only *secondarily* the 'general industrial capacity' of Germany, which in effect meant cities. These latter raids were meant to be carried out whenever weather or other conditions made attacks on the primary oil targets difficult. In the light of Churchill's encouragement, however, Harris took his 'secondary' target orders to be in effect a *carte blanche* to resume area attacks. It was operationally up to him to decide whether conditions were right for precision bombing of oil installations, or whether it would be better to attack cities. He now had a mighty force; it gave him, on an average day, 1,400 bombers almost all of the best type: Lancasters and Halifaxes, supported by Mosquitoes. (By April 1945 this figure rose to 1,600 operational bombers per day.) Technology had continued to develop too, making navigation and bombing accuracy ever better. And the Luftwaffe had been defeated during the invasion months, and was now a rump of its former self.

This all meant that, from Harris's point of view, conditions were perfect for the demolition of Germany's cities. He did not hesitate to take advantage of them. Nothing better reveals his intentions than the fact that only 6 per cent of the bombs his Command dropped in the war's final months were on oil targets. Harris's superiors kept pressing him to attack oil, and he kept attacking cities: already devastated Cologne was visited by 733 bombers in the daylight hours of 28 October, by 905 bombers on 30–1 October, and by 493 bombers on 31 October–1 November. This was a bombing of rubble into powder. Losses to the attacking force were 0.4 per cent; the cities were all but defenceless.

Portal's efforts to keep Harris's mind on oil targets resulted in a strengthened restatement of the oil directive, issued on 1 November. Intelligence assessments then, and evaluation after the war aided by Albert Speer's own accounts of the situation in Germany, showed that oil was absolutely the crucial consideration. Yet Harris could not be

budged from his disdain for 'panaceas'. After receiving Portal's reissued directive he replied that weather and circumstances were the decisive factors in choosing targets, so that when weather was against precision raids on refineries and the like, 'bombing anything in Germany was better than bombing nothing'. Moreover, he continued, although he disagreed with the 'panacea merchants' he was doing his best to attack oil – though there were fifteen major German cities not yet attacked, and he was convinced that completing the 'city programme' would be a greater factor in hastening the war's end than anything the Allied ground forces could do. The fifteen unscathed major German cities on his destruction list included Dresden.[66]

Portal replied, 'I have at times wondered whether the magnetism of the remaining German cities has not in the past tended as much to deflect our bombers from their primary objectives as the tactical and weather difficulties you describe.' Evidently Portal, from his more senior position, had learned to see a wider war. In response Harris had a trump card, apart from Churchill's support; it was the claim that in the interests of his crews' safety, he had to keep the German defences guessing about where the next attack would be; if they were all on oil installations, the defence could be concentrated, and Bomber Command losses – now very low – would rise dramatically. Portal attempted yet again to get Harris to focus on oil, and the quarrel between them escalated – until Harris forced Portal's hand by hinting that Portal should dismiss him if he, Portal, disagreed with the way he, Harris, was running his war. Portal replied soothingly, saying that he could of course continue to 'flatten some at least of the cities Harris had been naming'[67] but (rather forlornly) trusting that Harris would do his best on oil.

Thus the cities scheduled for demolition on Harris's list met their fate. Attacks on oil did indeed increase in January 1945, but an intervention by no less than Churchill boosted Harris's city-demolition plan. The Prime Minister wanted Bomber Command to do something to interfere with the German retreat from Breslau in the

face of the Soviet advance. Portal sought the agreement of the Allied Chiefs of Staff for a big attack on Berlin, Dresden, Leipzig and Chemnitz, where 'a severe blitz will not only cause confusion in the evacuation from the East but also hamper the movement of troops from the West'.[68] On 3 February the US Eighth Air Force attacked Berlin as part of this endeavour, mounting one of their biggest raids: 1,000 bombers, with railway and administrative sites as their primary targets. The devastation was enormous and the German authorities said that 25,000 Berliners were killed. After ten days of bad weather the next major effort took place – this time against Dresden.

Eight hundred RAF bombers attacked on the night of 13–14 February 1944; and the next day and the day after, the Americans followed with 300 and 200 aircraft respectively. The Americans aimed at the railway marshalling yards, but the RAF night attack of the 13–14 used a stadium in the city centre as its aiming-point. The majority of bombs dropped in Bomber Command's night attack were incendiaries, 650,000 of them. The firestorm that resulted wiped out the Baroque city, and killed somewhere in the region of 25,000 people.[69]

The destruction of Dresden was an epochal moment. Suddenly and markedly, attitudes to the whole strategy of area bombing changed among those who had supported or at least tolerated it throughout its employment. An outcry went up in Germany of course, but the first effect was the shock felt in the United States when the words of an RAF intelligence officer were quoted by an American war correspondent covering Allied HQ. The RAF officer told a press briefing that the Allied Air Chiefs were employing a strategy of 'deliberate terror-bombing of German population centres as a ruthless expedient of hastening Hitler's doom'.[70] The words reached front pages in the United States, but were censored in England.

But the risk that public concern over the destruction of Dresden would escalate into a major problem for the Allied governments was defused by something even more horrifying: the news of what was

found when Belsen, Buchenwald and other camps were liberated by Allied troops. Newsreel footage from the concentration camps hugely revived anger and hostility towards Germany. For many in this mood, the area bombing in general and the destruction of Dresden in particular seemed no more than just punishment.

Churchill, however, had for some time been pondering the possibility that Germany and its army might be needed in a forthcoming struggle against the Soviet Union, and news of the destruction of Dresden gave him disturbing second thoughts. In the weeks that followed Dresden, other historical cities found themselves subjected to seemingly arbitrary attack, their residents bemusedly convinced that they were bombed for the simple reason that they had not already been bombed, and that the huge number of RAF bombers needed something to do (the USAAF bombers were still mainly attacking oil and transport targets – and helping to win the war thereby). Such cities as Worms, Mainz, Würzburg, Hildesheim, Gladbeck, Hanau and Dulmen were among them.[71] These facts seemed cumulatively to weigh on Churchill's mind. No doubt too Sir Anthony Eden, his Foreign Secretary, and others had been making him think more carefully about the post-war world, and about the problems of reconstruction and social order in post-war Germany in particular. At last he wrote to Portal and the other Chiefs of Staff on 28 March, in a minute quoted by the Official Historians: 'It seems to me that the moment has come when the question of bombing German cities for the sake of increasing the terror, though under other pretexts, should be reviewed. Otherwise we shall come into control of an utterly ruined land. The destruction of Dresden remains a serious query against the conduct of Allied bombing.'[72]

The effect of this minute has been a source of controversy ever since, and will be discussed again in the course of these chapters. But area bombing virtually ceased after Churchill sent it, and the last raid by RAF heavy bombers took place just over three weeks later, on 25–6 April.

As soon as Bomber Command's war was over, it began the much more agreeable humanitarian task of ferrying relief supplies to the devastated regions of Europe, and bringing prisoners of war back home to Britain.

The main thrust of this story has so far been about RAF Bomber Command for the good reason that until early 1944 it carried the bulk of the air war to Germany. In 1943, but especially from early 1944, the US Eighth Air Force joined it as a major player, and to the American intervention is owed the destruction of the Luftwaffe in the air by combat, and its disablement on the ground by choking its fuel supplies.

As noted already, the attitudes and strategies of the Eighth Army Air Force differed both officially and in practice from that of Bomber Command. Where most of the latter's campaign consisted of area bombing of population centres, the Americans attempted more precise targeting, flying by day so that they could see the marshalling yards, bridges, oil plants and factories they were aiming to hit. They did not eschew area bombing entirely in the European theatre of war, but officially it was not their way.

When elements of the US Army Air Force began arriving in Britain in 1942 the USAAF overall commander, Lieutenant-General 'Hap' Arnold, the commander of its forces in Britain, Major-General Carl 'Tooey' Spaatz, and the commander of the bomber groups in those forces, Brigadier-General Ira Eaker, were all of one mind, both with each other and with Portal and Harris, about the war-winning potential of bombing. But the Americans differed greatly from their British counterparts in their view of how that was to be done. For them the right way was the destruction of key aspects of the enemy's industrial capacity. For the British, after the failures of the early years of the war, it was by attacking enemy 'morale'.

The American strategy of bombing in daylight was justified by their belief that the massive firepower of their aircraft, flying in tight 'boxed' formations, would keep enemy fighters away. The Flying

Fortresses carried heavier-calibre guns than did British aircraft – .5 as opposed to .33 – and more of them, providing overlapping fields of fire from the tail, the upper, lower and beam waist positions, and the nose. The power of the .5 machine gun was formidable, and much respected by Luftwaffe fighter pilots. But the latter quickly got the measure of the way American bomber formations sought to defend themselves, and the Americans as quickly therefore learned the shortcomings of their tactics. This was the main reason why the Eighth's attack on Germany itself, apart from the catastrophic Schweinfurt raids of 1943, had in effect to wait until Mustang escorts were available to protect their raids from January 1944 onwards.

Because their greater protective plating and armament added weight and reduced space, the American aircraft carried at most only half the bombing load of the RAF's heavies. This was true when the mainstay of Bomber Command was the Wellington, when the Eighth Air Force was arriving and making its tentative start in 1942; and the disparity was greater still when Bomber Command's superlative Lancasters were the mainstay of the British attack, with the Eighth continuing to operate B-17 and B-24 Fortresses. (American air forces in Europe and North Africa did not receive the B-29 'Superfortress', which operated only in the Pacific theatre.) But great bomb weight was not necessarily a decisive factor in precision bombing, and nor was exceptionally large numbers of aircraft. Because of the demands on the USAAF in North Africa and the Pacific, its concentration of aircraft in the European theatre did not reach high levels until 1944.

For all these reasons, therefore, it was RAF Bomber Command that did the main work in pounding Germany for most of the war, and that is why histories tend to devote more pages to its activities. But in doing so, they overlook the crucial role of the US Eighth Army Air Force in defeating the Luftwaffe. It is worth repeating that the Eighth did this by attacking the factories that produced it, by fighting it out of the air, and – crucially – by bombing the sources of the fuel it

needed to fly, which was the single most significant factor in grounding the Luftwaffe in the closing phase of the war.

But they also overlook the astonishing contrast between the strategy of the American bombing campaign in Europe and the strategy of the American bombing campaign over Japan. Hereby hangs a tale. For whereas American bombers in Europe concentrated on precision attacks, over Japan they resorted to wholly indiscriminate area raids.

A bombing campaign over the home islands of Japan was not an option for US forces until the Mariana Islands were in their possession. From the autumn of 1943 efforts were made to attack Japanese factories in Manchuria and Kyushu from bases in China, but the effort was a limited one, partly because the B-29s had to compete with Chinese forces for supplies of fuel and bombs being brought laboriously from India. That meant they could only mount a couple of strikes each month, and the overall effect of these efforts was minor. When in November 1944 long-range attacks could be launched against the Japanese islands from Tinian, Saipan and Guam, the China-based B-29s were transferred to join the campaign.

But it was in March 1945 that the main thrust of sustained American heavy air attacks against Japan really began. They were seen as subserving both the primary objective of forcing Japan to surrender without an invasion, and reducing the Japanese 'will to resist' as a preliminary to invasion should one prove necessary. The remit given to the USAAF was 'disruption of railroad and transportation system by daylight attacks, coupled with destruction of cities by night and bad-weather attacks'[73] In the event, the city attacks came first; the 'urban area attacks were initiated in force in March 1945, the railroad attack was just getting under way when the war ended [in August 1945]'.[74]

The reason for the delay between November 1944, when the airfields on the captured Marianas became operational, and March 1945, when the area bombing of Japanese cities began, was one of

logistics: at first the bombers available in the Marianas were few, and the Japanese fighter resistance was still significant enough to limit their activities. The small forces of bombers dropped their loads in daylight from very high altitudes – 30,000 feet – in an effort to disrupt Japanese aircraft production, but at best they managed to get only 10 per cent of their bombs near their targets.

In March 1945 the strategy changed. The remit described above was issued, and more aircraft had become available for its realisation. It was also by now recognised that Japanese fighters were far less effective at night; so the area-bombing campaign started with night-time incendiary attacks on the four principal Japanese cities of Tokyo, Nagoya, Osaka, and Kobe, all of them made of wood. The bombers flew in at low altitude – 7,000 feet – which allowed them to carry heavier loads of incendiaries, and to bomb more accurately. The commander of XXI Bomber Command was General Curtis E. LeMay, to whom the credit is given for devising the strategy of low-level night attacks. He ordered his B-29 Superfortresses to be stripped of some of their guns so that they could carry even more incendiaries.

The first attack took place on the night of 9–10 March 1945. It was against Tokyo, which received 1,667 tons of incendiary bombs on fifteen square miles of its most densely populated districts. They were burned to the ground in a ferocious firestorm that killed more than 85,000 people.[75] The death and destruction here was greater than that caused by either of the atom bombs dropped in August that year on Hiroshima and Nagasaki. It was the most destructive of the area attacks apart from the atom bombings, but the others that followed – in which over 9,000 tons of incendiaries fell on the remaining three principal cities, destroying thirty-one square miles of them – were devastating enough.

Over the next five months General LeMay extended the area-bombing campaign across Japan. In all, according to the US Strategic Bombing Survey for the Pacific theatre, nearly half of the built-up areas of sixty-six Japanese cities was destroyed. Adding the casualties

from the atom-bomb attacks, a total of 330,000 people were killed and a further 460,000 injured. 'The principal cause of civilian deaths,' says the US Survey, 'was burns.'[76]

The consummation of the area bombing of Japan was of course the dropping, on 6 and 9 August 1945 respectively, of single atom bombs on each of Hiroshima and Nagasaki. Between them the two atomic blasts killed 100,000 people and destroyed half the buildings in each city. The US Strategic Bombing Survey paid particular attention to the effects of these attacks, given the immense curiosity of the US government about the capacities of its new weapon – a curiosity for which there were significant reasons, some obvious and some controversial. The Survey Report descends to detailed scrutiny of such things as the effect (for example) of the difference made to radiation burns by whether the victim was wearing clothes or not. Authorities in Washington were especially interested in the Survey's conclusion that 'the damage and casualties caused at Hiroshima by the one atomic bomb dropped from a single plane would have required 220 B-29s carrying 1,200 tons of incendiary bombs, 400 tons of high explosives, and 500 tons of anti-personnel fragmentation bombs, if conventional weapons, rather than an atomic bomb, had been used'.[77]

The atom-bomb attacks cause grave concern for many about the morality of United States area bombing over Japan, just as the firebombing of Dresden does for RAF Bomber Command and the US Eight Air Force, which accompanied it. These attacks stand out because of special circumstances – the beauty and cultural importance of Dresden; the first use of the stupendous power of the atom as a weapon. But they do not differ in principle from the firebombings of Tokyo and Hamburg, or any other area-bomb attacks on German and Japanese cities. Except, perhaps in one respect: that if area bombing is a moral crime, then the bombings in the last six months of the war in both the European and Japanese theatres of war have what lawyers call an aggravated character – an intensified moral

questionability, partly because victory was no longer genuinely doubtful, and partly because the motives for dropping the atom bombs might have been additional to realisation of the Allied war aims regarding Japan.[78]

Such is the story of the bombing war. The next task is to see what effect it had on those beneath the bombers and their bombs in Germany and Japan.

3

The Experience of the Bombed

ON THE EVENING of 27 July 1943 the western districts of Hamburg were still dotted with fires from the first RAF attack three nights earlier. Stocks of coal and coke heaped in the open air were smouldering fiercely, and at night made a vivid glow that could be seen for scores of miles in every direction. This posed an air-raid danger, so the authorities ordered a maximum effort to extinguish the fires. When the bombers returned for the great firestorm attack of 27–8 July, their bombs fell chiefly in the east of the city; the municipal fire-fighting appliances were still struggling with the coal fires in the western districts.

Most of the civilians 'dehoused' in the first attack had been evacuated, and although many others had also been trying to leave they were discouraged by the authorities because of strain on transport facilities. Reinforcements were arriving in the city in the form of extra flak batteries, and in the warm summer nights their crews slept on the ground next to their guns.

Many of the city's residents did likewise, finding patches of grass outside the public air-raid shelters and resting their heads on their bundles, ready to hurry into the shelters as soon as bombing started. When the air-raid warming sounded on 27 July everyone readied themselves to take shelter, but for more than an hour nothing happened: no bombing, no bombers, no flak; so they hesitated at

the entrances of the shelters, and after a time returned to their patches of grass. The citizens of Hamburg did not know it, but the bomber stream was passing to the north of the city, ready to swing round and attack from the east. Bomber Command planners hoped that an approach from this unexpected quarter of the sky would disorganise the defences. And so it did. The attackers' bombs fell on the most densely populated districts east of the Elbe – Billwarder Ausschlag, crammed with eight-storey workers' apartment blocks, St Georg, Barmbek, Wandsbek, and the three areas of Hamm – Hamm-Nord, Hamm-Süd and Hammerbrook.

Gunners manning flak batteries could not take shelter as others could, and for that reason had a perilous grandstand view of what happened as the bombers arrived over their target. Leutnant Hermann Bock – who had been born in Hamburg, and was now commander of a flak battery which had been sent hastily from Mönchengladbach to strengthen the defences of his native city – wrote:

> Hamburg's night sky became in minutes, even seconds, a sky so absolutely hellish that it is impossible even to try to describe it in words. There were aeroplanes held in the probing arms of the searchlights, fires breaking out, billowing smoke everywhere, loud, roaring waves of explosions, all broken up by great cathedrals of light as the blast bombs exploded, cascades of marker bombs slowly drifting down, stick incendiary bombs coming down with a rushing noise. No noise heard by humans – no outcry – could be heard. It was like the end of the world. One could think, feel, see and speak of nothing more.[1]

Hamburg's citizens had to take turns as fire wardens in their places of work. They had uniforms and steel helmets, some rudimentary training, and instructions to watch for fires and put them out as quickly as possible. In some cases the 'fire wardens' were, despite the appearance of authority and expertise bestowed by the uniforms, just

young teenagers (as also were the gunners on flak batteries). One, a sixteen-year-old girl, described how she cowered in a cellar as the walls around her shook and cracked, while she and her companions prayed silently. One of their number, another young girl, became hysterical – as if presciently so: the girl's mother and grandmother were killed at her home that night.[2] Another fire warden, older and more experienced, described trying to remain on watch on the steps of his shelter, ready with his comrades to hasten out at the first sign of flames, when the firestorm struck without warning:

> Suddenly there came a rain of fire from heaven. We tried to get out to pump but it was impossible. The air was actually filled with fire. It would have meant certain death to leave the shelter . . . Smoke seeped into the shelter through every crack. Every time you opened the steel doors you could see fire all around . . . Then a storm started, a shrill howling in the street. It grew into a hurricane . . . The whole yard, the canal, in fact as far as we could see, was just a whole, great, massive sea of fire.

Another survivor described the howling of the firestorm as 'the devil laughing'.[3]

The firestorm started in Hammerbrook at about 1.20 a.m., the ferocious heat of the inferno sucking in air at hurricane speeds and reaching temperatures of 800 degrees centigrade or more. The bombing was still in progress, and lasted for another half an hour, spreading the area of the firestorm beyond its original core to the outer suburbs and into the city centre. In all, an area of about four square miles (ten square kilometres) was effectively incinerated.[4] The firestorm raged until 3.30 a.m., more than an hour after the last bombs had been dropped.

During the firestorm its victims were confronted with a terrible choice: to stay in their cellars, where the temperatures were rising to impossible heights, the air was filling thickly with smoke, and the buildings above them were crashing down; or risk running outside

where the air itself seemed to be aflame. Survivors from the margins of the firestorm – few people within its perimeters survived – described the scene in apocalyptic terms.

> They spoke of the tremendous force of hot, dry winds against which even strong men were unable to struggle, and which forced open doors of houses and broke the glass in their windows. Anything light was immediately whipped away, bursting into flames as it went . . . what appeared to be 'bundles of flames' or 'towers or walls of fire' sometimes shot out of a burning building and along a street. There were 'fiery whirlwinds' which could snatch people in the street and immediately turn them into human torches while other people, only a few yards away, were untouched. The wind was always accompanied by clouds of sparks which looked like 'a blizzard of red snowflakes' and all survivors remember the shrieking, howling of the storm as it raced through the streets.[5]

In the 'pan of a gigantic oven' that Hamburg had become, the searing winds changed direction violently and unpredictably, sweeping the walls of fire along with them. Women found their light summer frocks bursting into flame, and tore them off to run naked from the inferno.[6] In the cellars, otherwise unscathed people suffocated to death. Police reports and eyewitness accounts later confirmed many of the horror stories told 'of demented Hamburgers carrying bodies of deceased relatives in their suitcases – a man with the corpse of his wife and daughter, a woman with the mummified body of her daughter, or other women with the heads of their dead children'[7]. One of these shocking details is to be found in an account, quoted by W. G. Sebald, given by someone who saw refugees from Hamburg trying to board a train in Bavaria, in the struggle dropping a suitcase which 'falls on the platform, bursts open and spills its contents. Toys, a manicure case, singed underwear. And last of all, the roasted corpse of a child, shrunk like a mummy, which its half-deranged mother has

been carrying about with her, the relic of a past that was still intact a few days ago'.[8]

Some families survived together: 'Mother wrapped me in wet sheets, kissed me, and said, Run!' reported Traute Koch, aged fifteen at the time of the attack, and living in Hamm.

> I hesitated at the door. In front of me I could see only fire – everything red like the door of a furnace. An intense heat struck me. A burning beam fell in front of my feet. I shied back, but then when I was ready to jump over it, it was whipped away by a ghostly hand. I reached . . . the building in front of which we had arranged to meet again . . . Someone came out, grabbed me in their arms, and pulled me into the doorway. I screamed for my mother and somebody gave me a drink – wine or schnapps – I still screamed and then my mother and my little sister were there. About twenty people had gathered in the cellar. We sat, holding tightly to each other and waited. My mother wept bitterly and I was terrified.[9]

Others were not so lucky. Rolf Witt, who lived in Borgfelde, close to the epicentre of the firestorm, made a dash for freedom from the chokingly smoke-filled cellar where he was sheltering with his parents and others. He thought his parents were following close behind, but when he looked back they were not there, and he saw that their apartment block had collapsed. 'I never found my parents and it was never sure where or how they died. I have always felt guilty that I abandoned them. Later, when their shelter was cleared, they found fifty-five bodies – at least they found fifty-five skulls . . . I never met another survivor from my home or the houses at the back.'[10]

A greengrocer who lived near the canal in the Loschplatz told the compiler of a police report following the raid:

> Many people started burning and jumping into the canal. Horrible scenes took place at the quay. People burned to death with horrible suffering; some became insane. Many dead bodies were all around

us and I became convinced that we too would perish here. I crouched with my family behind a large stack of roofing material. Here we lost our daughter. Later on, it transpired that she had jumped into the canal and almost drowned but was saved by an army officer and she returned to us early next morning. Please spare me from having to describe further details.[11]

When the firestorm was over, a stream of refugees began to leave the city, first in a trickle, then in a mighty flood. Traute Koch and her mother and sister at first went home, only to find the house a pile of rubble. They could not stand staring at it for long because the ground beneath their feet was too hot.

We came to the junction of the Hammer Landstrasse and Louisen-weg. I carried my little sister and also helped my mother climb over the ruins. Suddenly, I saw tailors' dummies lying around. I said, 'Mummy, no tailors lived here and, yet, so many dummies lying around.' My mother grabbed my arm and said, 'Go on. Don't look too closely. On. On. We have to get out of here. Those are dead bodies.'[12]

A fireman searched for his war-disabled brother.

I only got to the Heidenkampsweg. In the entrance to the Maizena Haus [a large office building] I saw a lot of dead, naked people on the steps. I thought that they had been killed by a blast bomb and been blown out of the basement air raid shelter. What surprised me was that the people were all lying face downwards. Only later did we find out that these people had died there through lack of oxygen. I climbed over the ruins further into the damaged area. There were no people alive at all. The houses were all destroyed and still burning. In the Süderstrasse I saw a burnt out tramcar in which naked bodies were lying on top of each other. The glass of the windows had melted. Probably these people had sought refuge from the storm in the tram. I eventually reached my brother's

home on the Grevenweg; it was just a heap of smoking bricks. I helped to clear their shelter five weeks later. There was only charred bones and ash. I found a few objects that belonged to my relatives – their house keys and some coins that my nephew was always playing with.[13]

A woman who hurried to Hamburg the day after the firestorm to find her parents, had to fight with sentries posted to keep people from entering the worst-affected areas. Anne-Lies Schmidt said,

My uncle and I went on foot into this terror. No one was allowed into the devastated district but I believe that one's stubbornness becomes stronger at the sight of such sacrifice. We fought bodily with the sentries on duty and we got in. My uncle was arrested.

Four-storey-high blocks of flats were like glowing mounds of stone right down to the basement. Everything seemed to have melted . . . Women and children were so charred as to be unrecognisable; those that had died through lack of oxygen were half charred and recognisable. Their brains tumbled from their burst temples and their insides from the soft parts under the ribs. How terribly must these people have died. The smallest children lay like fried eels on the pavement. Even in death they showed signs of how they must have suffered – their hands and arms stretched out as if to protect themselves from that pitiless heat.

I found the bodies of my parents but it was forbidden to take them because of the danger of epidemic. Nothing to remember them by. No photographs. Nothing! All their precious little possessions they had taken to the basement were stolen. I had no tears. The eyes became bigger but the mouth remained closed tight.[14]

When the bombers left Hamburg that night they could see it burning from 120 miles away. Two nights later they were back; and they were back yet again a further three nights after that.

*　　*　　*

The distinguished Australian statesman Richard Casey, later Lord Casey of Berwick, kept a diary while serving in Churchill's War Cabinet. He recorded watching with Churchill a film showing RAF bombers in action over the Ruhr. 'All of a sudden Churchill gives a start,' Casey wrote, 'and he says to me "Are we animals? Are we taking this too far?" I tell him it wasn't us who had started all this and that this was what it was about: us or them.'[15] Casey's robust reply forms part of the standard justification given for the bomber war, but the Prime Ministerial pang of conscience thus recorded was by far not the only one Churchill had – though at other times, especially earlier in the war, he made uncompromising pronouncements about the necessity of unleashing an 'exterminating attack' on the Nazi home-land[16] – nor does it represent more than a hint of the reason why he had it. This was that Churchill knew what relatively few others did: exactly what was being dropped from the bombers as they passed high over the flashes of explosions and the pulsing regions of fire below them.

To say that the bomb loads consisted of a mixture high explosive and incendiary weapons does little to convey what that meant in practice. Those sheltering in cellars during a Bomber Command raid felt the mighty thud and tremor of high explosives falling about them, and the accompanying alternation of suction–pressure–suction–pressure they caused.[17] They learned to distinguish by sound the different kinds of incendiaries that showered down among the big bombs. A rustle like a flock of birds suddenly taking off represented a stick of incendiaries breaking apart as it neared the ground, sending indivi-dual incendiaries in all directions. An explosion like a sudden crack was a 12-kilogram fire bomb, shooting out flames to a distance of eighty metres. A big splash was a 14-kilogram fire bomb, which spread liquid rubber and benzene over a radius of fifty metres. The sound of a wet sack flopping heavily down was a canister containing twenty litres of benzol. A sharp explosion heralded a 106-kilogram bomb that hurled out rags soaked in benzene or heavy oil, or it was a 112-kilogram bomb that ejected a thousand patties of benzol and

rubber over the surrounding area.[18] Phosphorus, magnesium and thickened or gelled petroleum (the best example of which is 'napalm', invented at Harvard University in 1942 and used by the USAAF in Japan later in the war) were almost impossible to extinguish, splashing viscously and adhesively over buildings and people like lava, and burning at ferocious temperatures. People who leaped into canals when splashed with burning phosphorus found to their horror that it would spontaneously reignite when they got out of the water.

Among the incendiaries were scattered 2-kilogram 'X' bombs with a delayed fuse, designed to explode later when fire-fighters and other emergency workers had arrived on the scene.

The firestorm of Hamburg on the night of 27–8 July 1943, heralded as one of RAF Bomber Command's greatest successes in its area-bombing campaign, does not have the historical status of the fire-bombing of Dresden on the night of 13–14 February 1945, nor of the firebombing of Tokyo on 9–10 March 1945, nor of the atom bomb attacks on Hiroshima and Nagasaki on 6 and 9 August 1945 respectively. The reasons are obvious ones. Dresden was a city of great beauty, one of the cultural treasures of Europe, and its immolation occurred at a time and in circumstances which many have found hard to justify. (I return to the Dresden bombing later.) The firebombing of Tokyo caused even greater immediate loss of life than the devastation of Hiroshima. The atom-bomb attacks were different again; they were *sui generis*, involving the use of a new weapon of unprecedented destructive power, the manner of whose effects on the cities and the people – especially, as regards the latter, the lingering effects of radiation sickness, and the still longer-term effects of illness and trauma – had no parallel even in the worst episodes of bombing in that or any other war. (I return to the Japanese bombings later, too.)

But there are other questions about Dresden, Tokyo, Hiroshima and Nagasaki. They fall into a category made special not just by their character but by their timing. The bombing of Hamburg in Opera-

tion Gomorrah took place at the height of the war, when the outcome of the struggle was not yet certain, even though the Allied powers knew that they had industrial and manpower advantages that so far outstripped those of the Axis states that the balance of likelihood already lay well on their side.[19] These other, later, bombings occurred when almost everyone involved could see that the war's end was approaching. One can seriously ask for their justification even if one is already persuaded that such area attacks as Operation Gomorrah, conducted at the height of the war, were necessary or at least warranted by the circumstances at the time.

This is not intended to beg a question about any part of the Allies' area-bombing campaigns. If Operation Gomorrah cannot be justified on moral grounds, then the massive deposit of explosive and incendiary power unleashed by the Allies between September 1944 and August 1945 has less chance of being so. Of this, more later.

In any case, the experience of those subjected to bombing in Hamburg can serve as an example of what it was like for those subjected to bombing anywhere, whether in Coventry early in the war or Tokyo close to its end. For each individual who experienced the terrifying ordeal of being on the receiving end of tons of high explosives and incendiaries, there can be no fine distinctions between occasions. There is scarcely need for a competition in ghastliness here. In recalling details of the aftermath of the firebombing of Dresden, the writer Kurt Vonnegut – a prisoner of war in Dresden at the time – described how the asphyxiated but otherwise unscathed bodies of victims in cellars were cremated by flame-throwers directed down the cellar stairs from the street.[20] In recounting the experiences of individuals in Hiroshima, John Hersey described how a Jesuit priest found a group of about twenty soldiers who had been looking up at the *Enola Gay* as it flew above them high over the city, and whose eyes had in consequence been liquefied by the flash of the bomb, so that the jellies ran down their cheeks like tears.[21]

In the latter case the frisson of dread created by the thought of what atomic weaponry can do affects those who contemplate it more than

those who actually suffer from it; for whether it is an atom bomb rather than tons of high explosives and incendiaries that does the damage, not a jot of suffering is added to its victims that the burned and buried, the dismembered and blinded, the dying and bereaved of Dresden or Hamburg did not feel.

This remark applies to the immediate trauma, of course: the real difference came afterwards, for to their blast deaths and injuries the atom bombs added years of illness and later premature deaths from cancer and other diseases. But from the point of view of those who dropped the bombs, these latter longer-term consequences were at best matters of speculation. What they knew when they planned to drop the atom bombs is what they knew when they planned to drop tons of high explosive and incendiaries on urban areas: that they would kill many, among them the elderly and children, and would destroy much in the way of buildings, facilities, schools, clinics, shops, houses, libraries, bus stations, vehicles, and an uncountable number of valuable things, even if only sentimentally so. That was the certainty on which the attacks were premised. And that is what they made happen. This is a bare statement of fact, on which all can agree, whether or not area bombing was right or wrong, necessary or otherwise.

Even before the war in Europe was over, the US authorities instituted a survey of the effects of strategic bombing on Nazi Germany. The resulting Summary Report of the United States Strategic Bombing Survey (European War) was published on 30 September 1945. One of its principal aims was to provide information for use by the high command in the Pacific theatre as it pondered the application of air power to the war against Japan.

After the surrender of Japan a Strategic Bombing Survey was instituted for the Pacific theatre too. It resulted in a much longer Summary Report, which was published on 1 July 1946. The reason for the greater length of the Pacific report was its detailed focus on the results of the atom-bomb attacks, and the fact that the survey team had longer to collect and digest its data.

Both reports are models of their kind, and make absorbing and instructive reading for anyone wishing to understand the reasons for, and the value of, the strategic bombing carried out in the Second World War, and the difference made by the advent of atomic weapons.

As one would expect, to a great extent the effects of the bombing campaigns depended upon how well prepared Germany and Japan respectively were for aerial attack, and how their populations responded to it. In the Pacific report the US survey team stated that 'Japan's will and capacity for reconstruction, dispersal, and passive defence were less than Germany's'.[22] This might have been a function of the fact that whereas Germany sustained five years of bombing attacks – in three of these years very heavy attacks – Japan experienced nine months of bombing, and in that time suffered nearly the same number of civilian casualties as did Germany. The survey gives the figures as follows:

> Total civilian casualties in Japan, as a result of 9 months of air attack, including those from the atomic bombs, were approximately 806,000. Of these, approximately 330,000 were fatalities. These casualties probably exceeded Japan's combat casualties [that is, soldiers, sailors and airmen] which the Japanese estimate as having totalled approximately 780,000 during the entire war. The principal cause of civilian death or injury was burns. Of the total casualties approximately 185,000 were suffered in the initial attack on Tokyo of 9 March 1945. Casualties in many extremely destructive attacks were comparatively low. Yokahoma, a city of 900,000 population, was 47 percent destroyed in a single attack lasting less than an hour. The fatalities suffered were less than 5000.[23]

One reason for the high casualty rate in Tokyo was the relative unpreparedness of the population, and the firestorm that raged through the wooden city. As a result of the Tokyo bombing, other

cities made fire breaks by tearing down whole streets of buildings. In some cities the fear of an attack grew proportionally with the length of time that the city remained unscathed. 'The day before the bomb was dropped on Hiroshima,' writes John Hersey, 'the city, in fear of incendiary raids, had put hundreds of schoolgirls to work helping to tear down houses and clear fire lanes. They were out in the open when the bomb exploded. Few survived.'[24]

This, though, was five months after the Tokyo attack, which suggests that organisation of defence against air attack was not optimal. The main precaution taken by Japanese civilians was to flee the towns; an estimated eight and a half million urban dwellers sought shelter in rural districts. Everywhere in Japan civilians could see American aircraft flying overhead, on their way to or from bombing raids, unchallenged because the Japanese air force had ceased to resist. The demoralising effect of this was as great as that caused by actually being a victim of an air raid.

> A striking aspect of the air attack was the pervasiveness with which its impact on morale blanketed Japan. Roughly one-quarter of all people in cities fled or were evacuated, and these evacuees, who themselves were of singularly low morale, helped spread discouragement and disaffection for the war throughout the islands. This mass migration from the cities included an estimated 8,500,000 persons. Throughout the Japanese islands, whose people had always thought themselves remote from attack, United States planes criss-crossed the skies with no effective Japanese air or anti-aircraft opposition. That this was an indication of impending defeat became as obvious to the rural as to the urban population.[25]

Matters were considerably different in Germany. Its Nazi rulers – the Party and the State were one and the same – anticipated war because they knew they were going to start one, and as early as 1935 had begin to plan air-raid alarm systems and shelters, first-aid services, and methods for dealing with gas attacks. Large underground shelters and

massive above-ground shelters were built, and the entire programme of defence against bombing was intensified in 1940 when an emergency decree from the Führer's office nominated eighty-two cities as key sites for special air-raid defence.

One of them was Cologne. By the time of the 1,000-bomber raid on 30–1 May 1942 the city had public shelters for 75,000 people, with twenty-five special deep bunkers for a further 7,500 (and twenty-nine additional such bunkers in process of being built). A total of 42,000 small air-raid shelters had been provided under or next to houses and apartment buildings for residents. Fourteen auxiliary hospitals had been constructed, giving an extra 1,760 emergency beds. The total cost of air-raid defences in Cologne prior to the 1,000-bomber raid was thirty-nine million marks. It was money well spent. The 1,000 bombers dropped 2,500 tons of high explosives and incendiaries, and destroyed centuries of history; the German dead numbered 469.[26]

Very soon after the drone of bombers had receded westwards in the early hours of 31 May 1943, the roads to Cologne started to fill with lorries bringing relief supplies – 34,000 items of clothing for adults, 50,000 items of clothing for children, 61,000 sheets, 90,000 boxes of soap powder, 100,000 metres of curtain material, 700,000 cakes of soap, 10,000,000 cigarettes. Bonn and Dusseldorf sent clerks to help local officials in Cologne deal with claims for war damage, and within a month 140,000 claims had been processed. When all claims had been processed (370,000 of them) a total of 126 million marks was paid out in damages to citizens. A small army of helpers arrived to assist the 5,200 workmen in Cologne detailed to clean up the city: 2,500 soldiers, 3,400 glaziers, and 10,000 building workers.[27]

The pattern was repeated whenever and wherever severe bombing occurred, at least up until the later part of 1944. When Frankfurt was repeatedly bombed in February and March 1944, losing the whole of its old city centre and large tracts of its suburbs, relief trains arrived after the raids bringing kettles of noodle soup with meat, bread and butter, and sausages.[28]

The efficiency and energy of the German people comes as no surprise, and prompts two immediate and contrary questions. The first is: how could Bomber Command hope to defeat a people capable of such swift and robust responses to what it could drop on them in the way of bomb loads? And the second is: what would Germany have been capable of as a military power, if it had not had to repair homes and water supplies, and supply sheets and soap to bombed cities?

Hamburg is an example of Bomber Command's efforts to answer the first question. If a German city could bounce back so quickly from a massive bombing attack, as Cologne had done after the 1,000-bomber raid of the previous year, then the bombing attack needed to be even more massive. The target needed to be attacked again and again, both before recovery could start, and afterwards to hamper its efforts. The weight and frequency of attack was the crucial factor; early in the war Bomber Command could not mount anything like the scale of assault required to demoralise Germany's populace and paralyse it logistically. In mid-1943 it was able to manage an Operation Gomorrah. By the last year of the war, and certainly in its last six months, Bomber Command and the Eighth Air Force between them were close to the required scale, and their effect on the urban landscape of Germany was clear for all to see.

The answer to the second question is one that plays a significant part in defences of the Allied bombing campaign. It is related to a larger fact about the effects of bombing on Germany: which is that it did not halt the growth of productivity in German industry, whose output grew throughout the war until its last months, and was at a markedly higher level at the end of 1944 than it had been in 1940. The question: what might Germany have done if it had not been bombed almost daily for all those years? takes on extra weight in the light of this consideration.

The facts and figures of Germany's war production are themselves a matter of record, but controversy surrounds their significance. Until 1942 the Germany economy was far from being on a 'total war'

footing, partly because the Nazi leadership believed that its wars would be quick and successful, and partly because it wished to keep economic activity as normal as possible in order not to burden the populace, wishing to avoid a repeat of the situation that followed the First World War when economic dislocation stirred popular unrest. This is not to say that Germany's economy was functioning exactly as normal; to pay for their military adventures in the war's opening years the Nazi government increased taxes sharply between 1938 and 1941, and limits on consumer activity raised levels of saving fivefold in the same period.

But when by the beginning of 1942 Germany found itself facing a longer and more demanding struggle than it had anticipated – by then it was fighting on several fronts simultaneously and suffering serious reverses on two of them (Russia and North Africa) – it accepted the need to move the economy on to a more dedicated war footing. On 8 February 1942 Hitler appointed Albert Speer as Minister of Armaments and Munitions, a post made vacant that same day by the death of Fritz Todt in a somewhat mysterious air crash. Todt was convinced that the difficulties being experienced on the Eastern Front portended the defeat of the Reich, and he ill-advisedly told Hitler so. A few hours later he was dead, and a few hours after that, Speer was given his job. Speer had until then been Hitler's architect, and because architecture and grandiose schemes for magnificent Thousand-Year Reich cities stood high among Hitler's hobbies, Speer was a favourite. He had designed and in a remarkably short time built Hitler's splendid new Chancellery in Berlin, and had even designed the furniture for the Führer's office in it. Hitler thought him the man for the job; and he was abundantly proved right.

Speer's standing with Hitler meant that it was easy for him to take responsibility for war production away from Hermann Goering's Reichswerke and Four-Year Plan, and from the Wehrmacht's Arma- ment Office, which had made itself unpopular with industry because of its continual interfering. By centralising and streamlining the

organisation of procurement, thereby improving the co-ordination of industrial efforts to meet both military and domestic demand, Speer rapidly increased output. This was not achieved by converting more German industry to military production – a fuller war mobilisation of the economy came later, after Speer had with great difficulty persuaded Hitler to allow him to do it – but by making better use of what was already being done.[29] The US Strategic Bombing Survey for Europe points out that the German economy's ability to keep increasing production year on year to the end of 1944 showed that it was very under-utilised in the war's early years. 'Germany's early commitment to the doctrine of the short war was a continuing handicap,' the Survey team wrote:

> Neither plans nor state of mind were adjusted to the idea of a long war. Nearly all German sources agree that the hope for a quick victory lasted long after the short war became a long one . . . The increase [in production] cannot be considered a testament to the efficiency of dictatorship. Rather it suggests the degree of industrial under-mobilisation in the earlier years. An excellent case can be made that throughout the war top government management in Germany was not efficient.[30]

However inefficient government management was, the result of Speer's appointment was that between 1942 and the autumn of 1944 the production of rifles doubled, the production of hand grenades trebled, and the production of artillery pieces increased sevenfold. Three times as many aircraft were built in 1944 as in 1941. At the war's end Nazi Germany had ten million men between the ages of 18 and 38 in uniform (this ignores the additional numbers, effectively useless, of the 'Volkssturm' home guard, in which boys from the age of 16 and men up to the age of 60 served). Despite the stories of bootless troops wearing summer uniforms on the Russian front in winter, which happened not because of production failures but because of military failures, the soldiers fighting in the streets of

Berlin in May 1945 still had boots, rifles, artillery pieces, ammunition and hand grenades.[31]

How did the German economy sustain this prodigious effort? One factor was that Germany had conquered almost all of Europe, and had its resources to use at will. The industrial and agricultural capacity of occupied and client states was available for the Reich's purposes, for example the bread-basket of the Ukraine, the coal and iron reserves of Silesia, the Romanian oil fields of Ploesti, and the sophisticated automotive, aircraft, electronics and armament factories of France, Czechoslovakia and Holland.[32]

Another factor is the immense labour resource that fell into Germany's hands by the same means. Contract labour from conquered and client states, slave labour and prisoners of war, added vastly to Germany's productive capacity. By the end of 1941 there were 3.5 million foreign labourers in Germany, including prisoners of war; a year later there were 4.6 million, most of the new influx from the Soviet Union; and by the autumn of 1944 there were 7.65 million, of whom 1.9 million were prisoners of war. These foreign workers accounted for more than a quarter of all those employed in the German economy. They made up half of the agricultural labour force, and a third each of the mining and construction industries. The largest contingents consisted of Russians and Poles, numbering respectively 2.12 million and 1.68 million. When not actually prisoners – who were paid nothing, and were effectively worked to death if they were Jewish or from the East – the foreign workers were paid relatively little, and not very well fed.[33]

It is no exaggeration to say that prisoners in the SS concentration camps were worked to death. One of the most notorious of the work camps was Mittelbau-Dora, which existed to serve armaments production – most notoriously, of the V2 'wonder weapon' – in a vast network of underground tunnels near Nordhausen. The eleven-mile tunnel system had been built before the war to store Germany's strategic oil reserves. In the damp chilly air where the prisoners both lived and, for long arduous hours, worked, fed on minuscule rations,

the death rate was very high. Not many lasted more than a matter of weeks even if they arrived in good health.[34]

The presence of foreign labourers, under whatever guise, meant that although the Wehrmacht made heavy demands on home-grown German manpower, the supply of labour was always sufficient for large numbers to be diverted to repair bomb damage in cities, factories and railway marshalling yards, to clear rubble, and to collect and cremate the dead, without compromising industrial and agricultural production.

A third factor is that Germany plundered a vast amount of wealth from the conquered territories, and from its own and conquered Jewish populations. Jewish banks were taken over by German ones, shops and factories, homes and their contents, indeed fixed and liquid assets of all kinds, together amounting to the wealth of an advanced country, were taken costlessly into German hands; and supplemented yet further the Nazi state's productive capacity.

With these advantages it is not surprising that German production quickly recovered from any industrial damage that occurred as a result of bombing attacks, even those as devastating as Operation Gomorrah. Of the 574 large factories in Hamburg, 186 were completely destroyed in Operation Gomorrah, and with them 4,118 of the 9,068 small factories. Half the workers in war-related industrial production in Hamburg were laid off for up to two months.[35] The precision daylight bombing of the harbour and submarine works by Flying Fortresses of the US Eighth Army Air Force sank or damaged 180,000 tons of shipping and, according to post-war calculations, diminished total wartime U-boat production by 26 or 27 vessels. But the net loss of production in Hamburg's big factories amounted to a mere 1.8 months' output only; 'Patriotism, the German character and the SS were enough to ensure that in the absence for many months of further heavy raids, Hamburg made a remarkable recovery.'[36]

Speer was very anxious when he first received news of the damage caused by Operation Gomorrah. He said that another half-dozen such raids would cripple Germany's war production and force it to

surrender. When he saw how quickly Hamburg recovered, however, he revised his opinion. Moreover, the expense of effort by Bomber Command was such that it could not mount any more Operation Gomorrahs for a while, not least because the cities Speer was worried about – Berlin, Munich, Stuttgart, Frankfurt, Leipzig and Augsburg – required such long flights over enemy territory that to attack them would invite high losses. Indeed, the 'Battle of Berlin' waged by Harris in the winter of 1943–4 in his effort to prove that bombing alone could win the war, proved this very point. The 'Battle of Berlin' was a costly defeat for Bomber Command, and it was not until Germany was on its knees in the winter of 1944–5 that Bomber Command could begin to 'knock Germany flat' as Harris phrased it: which in effect meant that Harris could achieve his aim only when Germany was already all but defeated.[37]

The second question, What would German industry have succeeded in doing if there had been no area-bombing campaign? has in fact received quantified answers. According to the US Strategic Bombing Survey for Europe, German industry lost 9 per cent of production in 1943 and 17 per cent in 1944 because of area bombing. The figures were based on a small sample, so the British figures might be more indicative, though they are even less flattering: they have it that in the second half of 1943 German industrial production was down 8.2 per cent, in the second half of 1944 it was down 7.2 per cent, and in the first four months of 1945 it was down 9.7 per cent. The figures for specific areas of war production are the significant ones: the British survey estimated that armament output was down by about 3 per cent in 1943 and less than 1 per cent overall for 1944. 'Considering that urban bombing had taken up about 45% of Bomber Command's efforts in terms of tonnage dropped,' writes Denis Richards, 'these estimates seemed to show that the area offensive had profoundly disappointing results.'[38]

The principal target of Bomber Command's area-bombing endeavours, remember, was 'morale' – the 'will of the people' of Germany

to continue making war. On this point the man responsible for keeping up German morale was, to begin with, even more worried than Speer about the ability of Germany to survive, although in this case the anxiety concerned the psychological survival of its people. The man in question was Joseph Goebbels, Minister of Propaganda.

After Lübeck was bombed on 28–9 March 1942 as an experiment in incendiary attack, Goebbels wrote in his diary, 'The damage is really enormous. I have been shown a newsreel of the destruction. It is horrible. One can well imagine how such a bombardment affects the population.'[39] During the Battle of the Ruhr in the following spring and summer he visited some of the target cities, in Dortmund exclaiming that the raid of 23–4 May 1943 had 'virtually totally destroyed' the city.[40] He was, however, surprised and pleased when, going on a walkabout in Berlin during the 1943–4 winter blitz of the city, crowds cheered him and patted him on the back: the Berliners were angered by the bombing, and welcomed the speeches in which he spoke of revenge.[41] This was so despite the ferocity of the attacks. 'The picture that greeted my eye in the Wilhelmplatz was one of utter desolation,' he wrote in his diary. 'Hell itself seems to have broken loose over us.'[42] And he had no illusions about the extent or importance of the damage that was being done. After the bombing of Leipzig on 2–3 December 1943 he wrote, 'The centre of the city was especially hard hit. Almost all public buildings, theatres, the University, the Supreme Court, the Exhibition Halls etc have been completely destroyed or seriously damaged. About 150,000–200,000 people are without shelter.' (He did not mention that the Exhibition Halls had been commandeered for the production of Junkers aircraft.)[43]

But until the closing months of the war, morale did not break. Even those actively opposed to Nazism were made grimly determined by the bombing, if only to weather the storm: 'We repair because we must repair,' wrote Ruth Andreas-Friederich, an anti-Nazi activist,

because we couldn't live another day longer if one forbade us the repairing. If they destroy our living room, we move into the kitchen. If they knock the kitchen apart, we move over into the hallway. If only we can stay 'at home'. The smallest corner of 'at home' is better than any palace in some strange place. For this reason all who have been driven out of the city by the bombs return home someday. They work with shovel and broom, with hammer, pliers and pick-axes. Until one day over the bombed-out foundations a new 'at home' exists. A Robinson-Crusoe lodge perhaps. But it is still 'at home'. The last thing one saves from a burning house is a pillow because it is the last piece of 'at home'.[44]

Goebbels sought to counter the morale challenge of bombing with an incessant stream of speeches and articles. He was still doing so even in the last devastating weeks of the war, with an article entitled 'Life Goes On' in *Das Reich* for 16 April 1944. In it, in a vein by then far too falsely optimistic, he spoke of the spirit with which the German people had survived under bombing – helping each other, pooling their resources, rebuilding their homes and factories, getting to work even if they had to walk miles over rubble-strewn streets, bearing hardships patiently and with humour. This picture was true of Germany at least into the autumn of 1944. Survivors of Operation Gomorrah reminisced that bombed-out families lived communally together in cellars, sharing everything and encouraging one another.[45] The *Berlin Diaries* of Marie Vassiltchikov describe the mutual help that was commonplace during the winter of the Berlin blitz.[46] It was even possible to say that the frequency of the bombing raids 'began to convert the experience of living under the bombs almost into a routine'.[47]

But as the bombing and the ground fighting intensified hugely in the final months of the war, turning Germany into a horrendous killing-ground and displacing millions of its people, the spirit cracked; Goebbels' 'Life Goes On' was published as the exact opposite was happening.

But the collapse of German morale at the very end of the war was not the result of bombing alone, nor was it even largely because of it. What finally unnerved a population that had borne so much during the final three years of the war, were two things. One was the newly severe hardships of the last months under the inexorable and palpable inevitability of defeat. The other was panic fear of the Russians – a fear exacerbated by the Nazi leadership's years of hysterical anti-Soviet propaganda, which proved self-fulfillingly true as a result of the cruel treatment to which the Germans had subjected the Russians, who now in their own turn, as the Red Army fought its way to Berlin, unleashed a season of terror on their defeated enemies, in the form of a revenge orgy of brutality and rape.[48]

But until those final months the effect of years of bombing on German civilian morale was very limited, even indeed counter-productive. So also – and this might well be part of the reason why – was the effect on the material conditions of German civilian life, despite the huge amount of attrition to the country's housing stock, 20 per cent of which was destroyed or damaged (485,000 dwellings were totally destroyed, and 415,000 heavily damaged).[49] The US Strategic Bombing Survey for Europe is unequivocal on this score:

A word should perhaps be added on the effect of the air war on the German civilian and on the civilian economy. Germany began the war after several years of full employment and after the civilian standard of living had reached its highest level in German history. In the early years of the war – the soft war period for Germany – civilian consumption remained high. Germans continued to try for guns and butter. The German people entered the period of the air war well stocked with clothing and other consumer goods. Although most consumer goods became increasingly difficult to obtain, Survey studies show that fairly adequate supplies of clothing were available for those who had been bombed out until the last stages of disorganisation. Food, though strictly rationed, was in

nutritionally adequate supply throughout the war. The Germans' diet had about the same calories as the British.[50]

What, then, did the bombing achieve in quantifiable terms? In the war as a whole, according to the US Strategic Bombing Survey, bombs killed 305,000 German civilians and injured 780,000. Other estimates give an upper limit on the number of German bombing dead as close to 500,000. Some of these deaths were caused by the Eighth Army Air Force, but by far the greater part was the result of RAF area bombing.

In return for this number of civilian deaths in Germany, Bomber Command suffered the deaths of 55,000 of its own members. Taking the highest figure for German civilian deaths, this makes a ratio of one Bomber Command airman killed for every 9 German civilians killed. Taking the lower estimate, it is a ratio of one British airman for every 5.5 German civilians.

In 1940 Bomber Command dropped 5,000 tons of bombs on Germany. In 1941 it dropped 23,000 tons. In 1942 it dropped 37,000 tons. In 1943 it dropped 180,000 tons. In 1944 it dropped 474,000 tons. And in the four months January–April 1945 inclusive, when the war was already palpably won, it dropped a mammoth 181,000 tons (an annual rate of 724,000, just for comparison). This last figure is nearly one fifth of the total for the whole war put together, and it represents a bombing inundation. These totals exclude US Eighth Army Air Force tonnages.

At a rough estimate, these figures suggest that it took 2.25 tons of bombs to kill one German civilian. It also means that it took one ton of bombs to destroy or damage one German flat or house. The number of Bomber Command aircraft lost in the process was 7,700.

Just in material terms, therefore, Bomber Command's war on Germany represents a very expensive campaign indeed.

The fact that it took so many tons of bombs to kill people and destroy buildings is partly a function of the fact that a high proportion of the bombs were dropped well away from their intended targets,

many of them in open fields, because of problems with navigation and bomb-aiming. This was diminishingly so as the war went on, but optimal conditions for bombing – in clear daylight without interference from defences – were only achieved very late in the war in Germany, and in the nine months of the US bombing of Japan. In fact, the 'good bombing conditions' of the USAAF campaign over Japan explain why the casualty and destruction figures in Japan exceed those of Germany, despite the fact that the latter was bombed continuously for five years and the former for less than one year.

What the figures just given for Germany do not yet show is the military cost to Germany of defending against air attack – specifically, in terms of the number of anti-aircraft guns and fighter planes required for home defence, therefore keeping them away from the Eastern and later Western front lines. Justifiers of the RAF area-bombing campaign keenly strees this point. Historians of the air war point out that some 10,000 of the Germans' excellent 88-mm. artillery pieces had to be deployed as anti-aircraft guns in the homeland when they could have been used in their other chief role on the Eastern Front as anti-tank guns. They also point out that the necessities of air defence meant that aircraft production had to be focused on fighters rather than bombers, which further weakened German capacity to wage war effectively. (They have in mind the tactical use of bombers over battlefields.) Moreover, of the bombers Germany produced, none were heavy bombers, and its light bombers were in no position to compete with the tonnages that the RAF's Lancasters and Halifaxes could carry.

And finally, the historians point out that a million men were required to man the homeland defences, and a further million to serve as emergency workers in the cities, representing a significant drain on manpower resources – all directly attributable to the bombing campaign.[51]

These are good points, though not quite as good as they look. Those who manned the anti-aircraft guns were not suitable as front-

line troops, and had much more the character of 'Volkssturm' recruits than fully trained soldiers. They included boys as young as sixteen and men over thirty-eight years of age. The majority of the men and women who manned emergency services were not additional to factory and business workers, but the self-same people detailed to take their turn on air-raid precaution and fire-watch duties. The lack of bombers, heavy or light, was not regarded as a problem by the German leadership because throughout the war they were busy devising missiles to take the place of bombers – the V1 and V2 rockets were merely the beginnings of what was planned to be an arsenal of such. It is true that Hitler personally delayed the ME 262 jet fighter's appearance in the war because he mistakenly demanded that it should be converted into a bomber for tactical use, suggesting a belated awareness of a deficit in this aspect of Germany's air capabilities. But it is likely that he thought of this as a stop-gap while the missile programme was under development.

Taken all in all, the argument that the bombing campaign diverted a slice of Germany's war effort to home defence is correct, but as these remarks show, the diversion was not as significant as an unqualified statement of it suggests.

Almost every authority on the subject of Bomber Command's area-bombing campaign agrees that it was a failure – a failure in military terms, that is; answers to the question of its ethics come later. It sought to undermine the morale and weaken the will of the German people, and it signally failed to do either. It has been pointed out that it represented the war's single longest continuous battle, in which its front line was engaged with the enemy on most days of the war. This extraordinary fact is a testament to the fortitude and endurance of air crews and ground crews, the energy of the force's high command, the dedication of factory workers who produced the bombers and the bombs, and the ingenuity of scientists who waged a war of ideas against an equally clever and inventive enemy. But for the mighty endeavour thus represented, the result of its effort to

break the enemy's heart was not just null but actually contrary to hopes.

The question whether the area-bombing effort to some extent slowed the pace of increase of German war production remains open. It certainly did not halt it, or prevent it from growing. And when, close to the end of the war, German production did at last falter and finally halt, other and more compelling factors had became operative in causing that to happen – among them precision bombing of the kind to which most of the US Eighth Army Air Force's effort had been dedicated.

This last point leads to something else that almost every authority is in agreement about, namely what the successes of the bombing campaigns in Europe actually were. There were two. One was the precision bombing carried out throughout their presence in the European theatre by the US Eighth Army Air Force and later the Fifteenth Army Air Force operating from Italy, and (with a few honourable exceptions such as the Dam Busters raid) late in the war by Bomber Command too. The other was the contribution made by tactical bombing to the success of the invasion on and after D-Day in 1944.

An examination of the details of this latter show that in post-D-Day operations in the invasion area, ground-attack fighters and fighter-bombers were the major air factor in assisting the Allied struggle.[52] Nevertheless before the invasion, and in the two months immediately following it, bombing forces of the RAF and the US Eighth Army Air Force played a major role in reducing defences on the invasion coasts, and disrupting communications behind the German lines. The bombers were far from perfect tactical weapons – a point on which Sir Arthur Harris always vigorously insisted – but they proved much more effective in the role than he expected or, presumably, wanted.[53] They attacked harbours, fuel and ammunition dumps, and at times enemy forces in strongholds preventing the advance of the Allied ground forces. One such was Caen, which (with great loss of French civilian life) Bomber Command reduced to

rubble on 7 July 1944 after Montgomery had requested that it be softened up before an infantry advance upon it. As it happened, this speciality of Bomber Command was not quite what the troops on the ground needed, for the rubble blocked their way, and if it did not make capture of Caen more difficult, it certainly introduced new difficulties in place of the old.[54]

Harris laid on a spectacular 1,000-bomber raid to clear the way for the Canadian First Army in its advance towards Falaise on 7–8 August 1944. A War Office observer was deeply impressed by the sight, as were the Canadian troops themselves: the noise, flame and smoke were tremendous. A week later in the same combat zone some of Harris's bombers strayed off target and killed sixty-five Canadians in a 'friendly fire' incident that took the shine off the previous week's efforts. But when in September 1944 Bomber Command was released from its obligations to the ground war, Harris received fulsome thanks from Eisenhower for what the Command had done, and Harris himself was awarded the US Order of Merit by President Roosevelt.

Much more important still, however, was the success of what many, and especially the American bomber leaders, regarded as the true strategic value of the bomber: the attack on crucial sectors of Germany's war production, and, most crucially of all, its oil supplies. If there is a single thing that bombing can be said to have contributed to Allied victory over Nazi Germany, it is precisely this: its success in severely limiting the fuel supplies needed by the Wehrmacht and Luftwaffe. Harris, it will be remembered, was strongly against the 'panacea' of singling out oil or anything else – ball-bearings, or railway marshalling yards – that the economic warfare experts had identified at their desks as a bottle-neck in German production, and which, if pinched, would strangle the German war effort. But Harris was wrong, and the experts and the Americans were right.

Repeated bombing attacks on the oil fields of Romania and Hungary, on synthetic oil plants in Germany, and on oil refineries near Vienna, Bleckhammer and Odenthal, in the end proved fatal to

Germany. The oil campaign started in earnest in the spring of 1944 when attacks were mounted – and sustained – on the synthetic oil plants at Leuna, Brux, Bohlen, Zeitz, Lutzendorf, Magdeburg and a number of other sites. Speer sought an emergency meeting with Hitler to press him to take emergency measures in response. As a result, Hitler appointed Edmund Geilenberg to the post of Reich commissioner with special responsibility for oil supplies, and gave him priority to requisition 350,000 workers for repair of oil plants and for the task of moving production to new underground sites. But the effort had come too late; as fuel supplies dwindled during the rest of 1944 and into the final months of the war, aircraft were grounded, tanks halted, training for replacement pilots could not be maintained, and most of the new and highly effective Messerschmitt 262 jet-fighter aircraft, of which over 1,200 had been produced by the end of 1944 and which might have considerably prolonged the war, had neither fuel to fly nor trained pilots to fly them.[55] The ME 262s were anyway extremely fuel-hungry aircraft, and those that went into action had to be towed to the end of their runways to conserve fuel – by cows, so Adolf Galland reports, to further save the fuel of tractors and lorries.[56]

Speer's acute anxieties over fuel were fully justified. Before bombing attacks on the oil infrastructure began in May 1944, Germany was producing an average of 316,000 tons a month. Bombing caused production to fall to 107,000 tons in June 1944, and 17,000 tons in the following September. Aviation fuel from the synthetic-oil plants fell from 175,000 tons in April 1944 to 30,000 in June and then to 5,000 tons in September. In his letter to Hitler of 30 June 1944 Speer wrote, 'The enemy has succeeded in increasing our losses of aviation gasoline up to 90 percent by 22 June. Only through speedy recovery of damaged plants has it been possible to regain partly some of the terrible losses.'[57]

Despite his wholly misplaced scepticism about the oil 'panacea', Harris came to recognise the value of the attack on oil – after the war's end. In his memoirs he wrote,

In the weeks before the end of the war all the German armed forces were immobilised by lack of fuel. The amount of oil produced by the synthetic oil plants and other factories was so little that it would not have paid the enemy to use up fuel in conveying it to the armed forces. The triumph of the offensive against oil was complete and indisputable.[58]

One cannot help feeling that Harris, now wise after the event, was exploiting what turned out to be one of the few unequivocal successes that could be claimed for bombing. He had not been merely sceptical, he had been scathing about the oil 'panacea', and – worse – had bitterly resisted the efforts of Portal and the Air Staff to make him concentrate upon it. As an officer he had of course eventually obeyed, grudgingly and a little belatedly, and during the course of the four combat months of 1945 Bomber Command carried out seventy-four operations against oil targets, half of them by day and half by night, dropping 43,636 tons of bombs in the process. The RAF effort against oil was however far less than that of the USAAF; between them the lion's share of the work was done by the US Eighth Army Air Force from its bases in England and the US Fifteenth Army Air Force from its bases in Italy, profiting from their greater experience of accurate daylight bombing.

An example of the effort made is the series of attacks on Leuna, the Germans' largest synthetic-oil plant. It was strongly defended by effective smoke-screen machines and a massive anti-aircraft-gun concentration. It was one of the least popular assignments for air crews in the war, because it was one of the most dangerous. Leuna was attacked twenty-two times between May and December 1944, twenty times by the US Eighth Army Air Force and twice by the RAF. Every time it was attacked it was repaired, but always at a lower level of output, averaging a mere 9 per cent of full capacity over the period.[59] The US Strategic Bombing Survey reported:

Consumption of oil exceeded production from May 1944 on. Accumulated stocks were rapidly used up, and in six months were

practically exhausted. The loss of oil production was felt acutely by the armed forces. In August the final run-in time for aircraft engines was cut from two hours to one-half hour. For lack of fuel, pilot training, previously cut down, was further curtailed. Through the summer, the movement of German Panzer Divisions in the field was hampered . . . By December, according to Speer, the fuel shortage had reached catastrophic proportions. When the Germans launched their counter-offensive on December 16, 1944 [the Ardennes offensive], their reserves of fuel were insufficient to support the operation. They counted on capturing Allied stocks . . . In February and March of 1945 the Germans massed 1200 tanks on the Baranov bridgehead at the Vistula to check the Russians. They were immobilised for lack of fuel, and overrun.[60]

It is right to add that although attacks on oil plants proved far more than the 'panacea' Harris believed it to be, major war production declined in almost all sectors from the autumn of 1944. On 27 January 1945, in a letter to General Heinz Guderian, Speer reported that coal and steel output were sharply down, as was aircraft production. Speer had planned to manufacture 12,000 fighter planes in the last three months of 1944, but only 8,600 were actually built. (One might, in the circumstances, write 'only'.)[61] The fact that output was at these levels so late in the war is itself a function of the bombing campaign, which had caused aircraft factories to be dispersed and hidden.

It is also right to add that the historians disagree among themselves as to whether the laurel should be given to attacks on oil supplies or on transportation in the final year of the war. The US Strategic Bombing Survey for Europe was definite in its opinion that oil mattered most, whereas others focus on the disruption of railway links within the Reich. In a detailed study of the German war economy Alfred Mierjewski concluded that the transportation crisis caused by bombing of railways in the autumn of 1944 meant that coal supplies from the Ruhr and Silesia to factories everywhere in Germany were

interrupted, and were responsible for their downturn in output. Speer organised a rapid transfer of labour to railway-repair work, and supplies moved again; but when the transport links were attacked again in the first months of 1945, the progress of Allied ground forces from both east and west meant that the problem had become irremediable.[62]

But now a new question has to be asked, suggested by the contrast between the bombing of Germany and the bombing of Japan. In the case of Japan, a relatively short and catastrophic air attack was quickly followed by Japanese surrender. It is too easy to conclude a causal connection between the facts here; 'this follows that so that caused this' is a logical fallacy. At the same time it seems highly relevant to ask whether there is a causal connection, especially given that the devastating bombing campaign was concluded by the atom bomb attacks, followed within mere days by the unprecedented appearance of Emperor Hirohito on national radio to announce his country's surrender.

If it turns out that American bombing of Japan is the key factor in ending the Pacific war, then it has to be concluded that Sir Arthur Harris and all the theoreticians of bomber power (see the next chapter) were right in holding that a sufficient weight of aerial attack will bring an enemy to his knees and thus end a war. And then the explanation of why this did not happen in the case of Germany would be that, until the closing stages of the war, the Allies simply did not have enough bomb weight – as for example would have been provided by the atom bomb – with which to achieve this effect.

One can imagine someone arguing that too little weight of attack would indeed have effects contrary to the desired one; the effects, that is, of strengthening an enemy's morale, and – worse – the enemy's capacity to survive and resist bombing. For if a bombing attack was incremental from a low starting level, as happened with Bomber Command's activities from 1940 onwards, enemy defences and preparedness would increasingly learn how to deal with it, so that

even as the weight of attack increased, its effect would be negated by the equally increasing capacity of the enemy to absorb it.

But if enough – so this argument continues – in the way of aircraft and bombs had been available to deliver a massive and sustained assault right from the beginning, the war would have ended in months rather than years, as happened when at last Japan came under just such bombing.

Are these arguments right? It all turns on whether there are factors other than bombing involved in Japan's surrender, and on their relative degree of significance. The answer to this in turn depends upon whether the reason for Japan's surrender was civilian or military. If civilian vulnerability was what impelled surrender, then bombing probably played a large part in it. Civilian vulnerability could be a function of hunger or other privations, but in the circumstances it would be plausible to see it as arising either from the shock of bombing, or fear of further devastation of the kind wrought by atomic bombs, or both.

If, however, the reason for Japan's surrender was military – that is, based on a realisation that the war could not be won – then bombing was not the decisive factor, even if it was a contributory one. In this latter case, Sir Arthur Harris and the theoreticians of bombing as a war-winning strategy could not appeal to the Japanese example as a vindication.

The question of why Japan surrendered in August 1945 is a complex one, and this is not the place for a full analysis of it. The conclusion reached by Robert Pape in his detailed and masterly dissection of the matter is however unequivocal:

> The principal cause of Japan's surrender was the ability of the United States to increase the military vulnerability of the home islands sufficiently to persuade Japanese leaders that their defence was highly unlikely to succeed. The key military factor causing this effect was the sea blockade, which crippled Japan's ability to produce and equip forces necessary to execute its strategy. The

most important factor accounting for the timing of the surrender was the Soviet attack against Manchuria [9 August 1945, the same day as the Nagasaki bomb], largely because it convinced recalcitrant Army leaders that the homeland could not be defended.

Contrary to the assertion of the Strategic Bombing Survey that bombing was so effective that even if there had been no atomic bomb, Soviet attack, or planned American invasion, surrender would have occurred at exactly the same time, in actuality the naval blockade, invasion threat, and Soviet attack ensured that surrender would have occurred at *precisely* the same time even if there had been no strategic bombing campaign.[63]

Pape's view is based on an examination of Japan's military and civilian leadership decisions in the final year of the Pacific war. As he states, he expressly dissents from the conclusion of the US Strategic Bombing Survey for the Pacific war, which was that even without the atom bombs the strategic-bombing effort was the decisive factor. This conclusion might appear odd to some, for whom the atom-bomb attacks appear to be precisely what adds the final weight of force that the area-bombing campaign over Germany lacked. If anything could be supposed to render the USAAF campaign against Japan decisive, therefore, the atom bombs would be it. Yet the Survey concluded that they were inessential to the outcome.

That surprising view, and the fact that Pape's analysis, careful and convincing though it is, no doubt remains controversial among some historians of the Pacific war, can be left as open matters here, for the present concern is tangential to them. The present concern requires only that we note that the claim that area-bombing was a *major* factor in victory is hotly disputed for Japan and denied for Germany. This matters because defenders of the campaigns draw heavily on their supposed military efficacy or even necessity.

More important still is how these considerations bear on the question of the morality of area bombing. If area bombing was unavoidable as a means of defeating the Axis powers – especially given

the moral status of the Axis powers themselves – a claim of justification, or at very least mitigation, must be entertained. If area bombing was not an essential component in the defeat of the Axis powers, the degree of their exposure to moral questioning rises. To this matter, of course, I return in detail later.

The longer-term effects of area bombing on Germany and Japan – not just on the physical fabric of their countries, but more importantly on the psychological fabric of their societies – constitutes an entirely different story, and a very complex one. It figures as part of the much larger story of post-war German and Japanese attitudes to the war as a whole, and it takes contrastingly different forms in the two nations. (An excellent place to begin exploring these matters is Ian Buruma's *The Wages of Guilt*[64]). The guilt felt about the Holocaust by most individual Germans of the immediate post-war generations, and by German society as a required collective stance, for long made it impossible for them to see the catastrophe they experienced in 1945 as anything other than deserved punishment. Japanese attitudes to the war as a whole lie behind a characteristically equivocal mask of demurral; but when one talks to individuals about the atom bombings of Nagasaki and Hiroshima, one learns that Japan sees them as war crimes.[65]

This makes some Japanese intellectuals angry with their own. Buruma reports an occasion on which the writer Kenzaburo Oe castigated his country as racist and as never having faced up to its crimes in the Second World War.[66] Oe was in conversation with Günter Grass at a book fair just at the time that the separated parts of Germany were reuniting, an event that Grass deprecated: 'Auschwitz should have made reunification impossible; a unified Germany was a danger to itself and the world,' he said.[67] Whereas Grass's assertion was characteristic of a standard German attitude, Oe's was uncharacteristic of Japanese attitudes. But as Buruma points out, even though Japan had to answer for atrocities in China and against prisoners of war, the sexual slavery of Korean women, the notorious

'Unit 731' in Manchuria, where appalling medical experiments were conducted on live human guinea pigs referred to by the Japanese staff as 'logs', and the acts of aggression in precipitating war first against China and then against the United States, it nevertheless had no Holocaust to answer for, and Nazi Germany had all these things or their equivalents to answer for *and* the Holocaust.[68]

The Holocaust throws such a deep and jagged shadow over the Second World War that the sum total of harm done by all other non-Holocaust-related means is diminished by it; which is one reason why there has been so little said about culpabilities on the Allied side of the struggle – culpabilities which pale in comparison to Nazi atrocity, and which the victor nations have therefore allowed themselves to neglect. Dresden makes periodic appearances on public consciousness, but very few people (apart from apologists for ultra-right-wing interests; but they are not interested in truth or historical proportion; they have other fish to fry) see that the Allied area bombing campaigns over Germany and Japan merit inspection and evaluation. For if they constitute a wrong, even though it is dwarfed by the Holocaust and other Axis-committed aggressions and atrocities, they would still be a wrong. And that, to repeat, is what is being examined here.

4

The Mind of the Bomber

AFTER THE OPERATION Gomorrah attacks on Hamburg, Bomber Command's chief, Air Marshal Sir Arthur Harris, said 'I had always wanted to have a real dead set at Hamburg. It was the second biggest city in Germany and I wanted to make a tremendous show.'[1] Hamburg's size was one reason why it was chosen for a major display of bombing power. A big city could be hurt even if bombing was not especially accurate. Another reason was that it is relatively easy to find, because it lies on the River Elbe near a coast with a shape easily recognisable from high in the air even at night. A third reason was that it is relatively easy to get to, not involving too long a trip for the bomber stream, which meant less time exposed to Luftwaffe night-fighters; and moreover much of the trip there and back could be carried out over the North Sea, empty of flak, searchlights and Luftwaffe airfields.

Harris's remark is interesting as giving a glimpse into the mind of a man who, on an almost daily basis, planned bombing raids – 'area bombing', 'carpet bombing', indiscriminate raids – upon densely inhabited cities, and sent hundreds of aircraft, carrying tons of explosives and incendiaries, to carry them out. The remark has an impersonal air, which does not quite represent the man who made it; for it is false to say that Harris was merely a callous and unimaginative man for whom mass killing by bombing was a matter of indifference.

He was indefatigably concerned with the welfare of his Bomber Command personnel, he was fully conscious that he was sending young men in his charge to their deaths almost every day – and having lived in London during the Blitz, and watched the City burning around St Paul's Cathedral, he had a clear idea of what he was unleashing on German civilians.[2] He was not a man of culture, and he was certainly capable of the kind of toughness required to carry out a policy of mass killings on a regular basis; but balance requires that one remember that (in the phrase much then employed) 'there was a war on', and he took himself to be in command of a campaign that would not only defend his own country from a dangerous aggressor, but would win the war to boot, and thereby destroy the regime which had plunged the world into catastrophe.[3] And like other proponents of area bombing as a war-winning strategy, he could claim to believe that it would shorten the war and therefore save lives overall – especially on his own side, by rescuing tens of thousands of young soldiers from the hazards of invasion. This, certainly, is what Americans claimed after the war in defence of their bombing of Japan, and especially the atom-bomb attacks.

Some might say, regarding the point about Harris's personal experience of watching London burn after the Luftwaffe's big fire raid of 29 December 1940, that his knowledge of what he was inflicting on Germany was not only clear but vengefully so. An anecdote is often repeated to illustrate this. Harris, driving himself at high speed back to his HQ in High Wycombe after an Air Ministry meeting in London, was stopped by two police motor-cyclists. One of them said, 'Sir, you are travelling much too fast; you might kill someone.' Harris replied, 'I'm on important business. Now that you mention it, it is my business to kill people: Germans.' Allegedly the policeman replied, 'Are you Air Marshal Harris, sir?' and when Harris confirmed that he was, the policeman said, 'That's different, sir; sorry I stopped you. Follow us,' and the two acted as outriders to speed Harris home. Harris told an aide afterwards, 'It was the quickest trip I ever made – they must have liked me.'[4]

Harris's assertion about the nature of his business was not merely flippant. In a discussion with the Air Ministry about the types of bombs to be used in attacks on German cities, Harris maintained that the proportions should be two-thirds incendiaries to one-third high explosives. This was in response to the Air Ministry's view that the blitz on Britain, and the RAF's experimental incendiary bombing of the wooden city of Lübeck, suggested that bomb loads should consist wholly of incendiaries. 'I am always being pressed to concentrate entirely on incendiaries,' he wrote to the Ministry,

> but I do not agree with this policy. The moral [that is, psychological] effect of HE is vast. People can escape from fires, and the casualties on a solely fire-raising raid would be as nothing. What we want to do in addition to the horrors of fire is to bring the masonry crashing down on top of the Boche, to kill Boche, and to terrify Boche; hence the proportion of HE.'[5]

Had Harris known of the horrific effects of firestorms rather than just City of London-type fires, he might have been as sanguine and sanguinary about incendiaries as high explosives. At any rate, his attitude to the purpose of area bombing was unequivocal, and thus on record: 'we want . . . to bring the masonry crashing down on top of the Boche, to kill Boche, and to terrify Boche.'

Nor did he think that this purpose should be disguised. In November 1943, effectively announcing the launching of his 'Battle of Berlin', he stated publicly that Berlin, the heart of Nazi Germany, would be attacked repeatedly 'until it ceased to beat'. Lord Salisbury, a vocal critic of the area-bombing policy, wrote to the Minister for Air, Sir Archibald Sinclair, complaining that Harris's statement was contrary to official government policy, which was that bombs were aimed only at industrial and military targets, not at civilian areas. Since the government was loath to acknowledge the area-bombing policy publicly, Sinclair gave a prevaricating reply. Harris was annoyed by this on two counts. First, he thought that his air crews

would not get proper recognition for their endeavours if the endeavours themselves were not officially recognised. And second and relatedly, since area bombing at night was a largely inaccurate proceeding, any suggestion that Bomber Command was trying to hit precise targets would inevitably invite criticism, because by that criterion Bomber Command would always appear to fail.[6]

Harris's attitudes to area bombing, which he said required that people with 'sensitive minds' should not seek leadership positions in the bombing force,[7] rested on his unshakeable belief that war was to be won by attacking the morale of an enemy population until its will to resist was broken. He had seen the trenches of the First World War from his biplane, and he thought that the pain and expense of ground fighting could be made unnecessary by the right application of enough power from the air. This fixed belief governed his thinking to such an extent that, as noted in the preceding chapter, he could not accept the logic of precision bombing – in the case of his virtual insubordination to the Air Staff, of oil targets – except as a minor ancillary to the main task.

But in thinking this way, Harris was merely following the precepts of earlier theorists of air power, and they in turn had extrapolated their views from the experience of bombing in the first three decades of flight (that is, from 1910 to 1939) in the First World War, colonial wars, and the Spanish Civil War. Understanding the development of this thinking explains the beliefs and intentions in the minds of those responsible for bombing policy in both the British and American militaries (and as we have already seen, British and American thinking about bombing diverged significantly for a time). This is crucial, for in seeking to judge the morality of the Allied bombing campaign, one has to have a clear picture of what was known, what was believed, and what was hoped by those who carried it out.

One also has to know the circumstances that influenced their thinking in carrying it out – specifically, the state of the war at the time they committed themselves to one or another policy. This chapter concerns the first of these two crucial matters; the second I

defer to chapter 7 where arguments in defence of area bombing are considered.

In 1899 an international peace conference was held at The Hague. It had been suggested by an adviser to Russia's Czar Nicholas II, the outstanding Russian international-law theorist Fedor Fedorovich Martens, as an appropriate sequel to a series of conferences held in The Hague earlier in the 1890s, all aimed at building a regime of international law.

Queen Wilhelmina of the Netherlands served as the 1899 conference's host, so that with its two royal sponsors it had the highest official sanction. Its purpose was not to settle a current war (though one was just then beginning in South Africa between the British and the Afrikaaners of the Boer Republics, and a short but highly consequential one had just ended between the United States and Spain, extending American influence from the Caribbean to the Pacific). The conference's aim, rather, was to frame the conditions for lasting international peace. The principal behind it is summarised in the celebrated 'Martens clause', named for the conference's prime mover, which gave preliminary encapsulation to the idea of a legal framework governing conflict between nations:

> Until a more complete code of the laws of war is issued, the High Contracting Parties think it right to declare that in cases not included in the Regulations adopted by them, populations and belligerents remain under the protection and empire of the principles of international law, as they result from the usages established between civilised nations, from the laws of humanity and the requirements of the public conscience.[8]

The eloquence of the last thirty-seven words of this passage well suits the ideal they express: *populations and belligerents remain under the protection and empire of the principles of international law, as they result from the usages established between civilised nations, from the laws of humanity and the requirements of the public conscience.*

With remarkable prescience the conference gave consideration to the matter of aerial bombing, in the form of 'projectiles or explosives' launched from balloons (heavier-than-air manned flight was still four years away). The preamble to the Declaration accordingly drawn up, known as Hague IV, quoted the St Petersburg Declaration of 1868, in which an International Military Commission hosted by Russia's Imperial Cabinet agreed to forbid the use of specified projectiles, among them exploding or incendiary bullets. The St Petersburg Declaration reads:

> On the proposition of the Imperial Cabinet of Russia, an International Military Commission having assembled at St. Petersburg in order to examine the expediency of forbidding the use of certain projectiles in time of war between civilised nations, and that Commission having by common agreement fixed the technical limits at which the necessities of war ought to yield to the requirements of humanity, the Undersigned are authorised by the orders of their Governments to declare as follows:
>
> Considering:
>
> That the progress of civilisation should have the effect of alleviating as much as possible the calamities of war;
>
> That the only legitimate object which States should endeavour to accomplish during war is to weaken the military forces of the enemy;
>
> That for this purpose it is sufficient to disable the greatest possible number of men;
>
> That this object would be exceeded by the employment of arms which uselessly aggravate the sufferings of disabled men, or render their death inevitable;
>
> That the employment of such arms would, therefore, be contrary to the laws of humanity;
>
> The Contracting Parties engage mutually to renounce, in case of war among themselves, the employment by their military or naval troops of any projectile of a weight below 400 grams, which is

either explosive or charged with fulminating or inflammable substances . . .

The Contracting or Acceding Parties reserve to themselves to come hereafter to an understanding whenever a precise proposition shall be drawn up in view of future improvements which science may effect in the armament of troops, in order to maintain the principles which they have established, and to conciliate the necessities of war with the laws of humanity.

Were we discussing these matters *viva voce*, it might be appropriate to pause for a minute's silence to ponder the good sense and humanitarian impulse animating these words, written down now so long ago, in their effort to restrain the murderous uses to which misapplications of burgeoning science were even then tending. The men gathered in St Petersburg could not see what science would produce by 1945, as proved on two August mornings in Japan that year; but they felt the onrush of dangers, and were men of good faith. The key words are unequivocal: 'The Contracting or Acceding Parties reserve to themselves to come hereafter to an understanding whenever a precise proposition shall be drawn up *in view of future improvements which science may effect in the armament of troops*, in order *to maintain the principles which they have established, and to conciliate the necessities of war with the laws of humanity.*'

Inspired by this example, and looking ahead, those gathered at The Hague in 1899 agreed to 'prohibit, for a term of five years, the launching of projectiles and explosives from balloons, or by other new methods of a similar nature'. As the time restriction to five years implies, the Declaration was meant to be a stop-gap until a formal Law of War could be agreed by the international community. The absence of agreement on a Law of War – wars, such as the Boer War and the Sino-Japanese war, among other things, put talk of such a thing far on to the back burner – made it necessary for the stop-gap to remain in force, so Hague IV was renewed by another Hague conference in 1907, and in the same terms. By this time the phrase

or by 'new methods of a similar nature' had taken on added meaning; the air was already filling with aeroplanes. This gave the irony that attends human endeavours full play, for it meant that the declaration was still in force when – inevitably, and in defiance of Hague IV – the first bombs were dropped from the air on 1 November 1911, by a pilot in the Italian forces fighting the Ottoman Turks in Libya.

As we know too well, agreements and declarations, however full of good sense and humanity, have no hold on mankind when fighting starts; but they provide a benchmark for thinking about the rights and wrongs of what happens once it does; and they seldom leave much room for excuses. The principles, and even more the spirit, of both the St Petersburg Declaration of 1868 and the Hague IV Declaration of 1899 and 1907, are crystal clear; and the first act of bombing in the Libyan desert blew a hole right through them both.

That first bombing was carried out by Lieutenant Giulio Gavotti, an artillery spotter in the Italian army. Entirely on his own initiative he took four grenades with him on a flight over the Ottoman army encampment at Ain Zara, and threw them from his Taube monoplane on to the angry Turks below. No one was hurt. News of the escapade was greeted with disgust and disdain by civilised opinion, which chiefly thought it unsporting. But military men thought otherwise, and immediately began to research ways of making it an effective resource of war.

All the major nations of Europe designed and produced bomber aircraft during the First World War, and some of them began before the war started. Both France and Germany did so, the former developing its Voisin bomber and the latter adapting the Zeppelin dirigible for the purpose. Appropriately therefore, one of the earliest air actions of the First World War was the bombing of the Zeppelin base at Metz-Frascaty by Voisin aircraft on 14 August 1914. The Voisin was a durable steel-framed pusher biplane which, as the war went on, was equipped with increasingly more powerful engines, in the end allowing it to carry 300 kilograms of bombs (660 lb.). France

had a force of about 600 Voisins which it used to attack the German lines of the Western Front. It did not have the range to penetrate Germany itself, and the French were loath to use it against occupied areas where French citizens lived; so its use remained purely tactical. The Zeppelin, as we shall see, was by contrast the first truly strategic bomber, being used in raids against towns in England.

Russia and Italy were not far behind France in acquiring bomber aircraft. The Imperial Russian Air Service provided itself with the giant 'Ilya Mourometz' designed by Igor Sikorsky, the first-ever four-engined aeroplane. It was a prodigy for its time; able to stay in the air for over five hours at a stretch, with a speed of 85 miles an hour and a 'ceiling' of 9,000 feet, it bristled with machine guns and was capable of carrying a maximum bomb load of 700 kilograms (1,540 lb). The Imperial Russian Air Service trained its bomb-aimers well, and the Ilya Mourometz had an excellent record for bombing accuracy. Under the command of Major-General M. V. Shidlovski the Russian bomber fleet was one of the successes of that country's generally unsuccessful endeavours on the Eastern Front.

Italy entered the war relatively late, in May 1915, and although otherwise ill-prepared for taking part in a major conflict, it by that time had a force of three-engined Caproni bombers in service. The Caproni was capable of crossing the Alps at 95 miles per hour, carrying 540 kilograms of bombs (1,190 lb), and accordingly did so, seeking targets in Austro-Hungarian territory.

The United States was neither a major producer of aircraft nor a major air power in the First World War. It had the Curtiss 'Jenny' biplane on which its pilots trained (and which after the war became the staple of the 'barnstormer' fliers), but when US army aviators entered the war in the spring of 1918 they were equipped with the French-made Nieuport and Spad fighter planes, and took no part in bombing activities.

In August 1914 Britain had no bomber aircraft, though soon after hostilities began, the Royal Navy indented for some, offering a design specification for an aircraft of modest capacity compared to those in

service elsewhere among the belligerents: a twin-engined two-seater which could fly at 75 miles per hour and carry 50 kilograms of bombs (110 lb). The result was the Handley Page 0/100, which entered service in November 1916. Although at first reserved to navy-related operations, it soon saw service on the Western Front and as a night bomber.

It was the Germans who proved the most adventurous bombers in the Great War, beginning with Zeppelins and later the feared Gotha C-V bomber, whose enormous 24-metre wingspan made it a terrifying sight when it swept over civilian targets, dropping explosives. Between them, Zeppelins and Gothas mounted 103 raids over Great Britain, ostensibly attacking industrial and military targets but in fact bombing towns and cities. Between January 1915 and November 1916 Zeppelins conducted 208 sorties, and from May 1917 to May 1918 Gothas conducted 435 sorties, between them dropping approximately 300 tons of bombs on Britain in what was a curtain-raiser for the practice of area bombing. In the process they killed 1,400 Britons and injured 3,400 more, and did about three million pounds' worth of damage to property at 1914 values.

But most of all the Zeppelins and Gothas created great panic, and gave rise to the belief – the false belief, as it too late proved – that bombing civilian populations is a weapon of peculiar psychological potency. For by one of the more terrible of history's ironies, hindsight shows that a little bombing or even the mere sight of bombers swooping overhead, terrifies populations that are not used to them; but a bit more bombing than Britain received in the First World War has a rebound effect on morale, as witnessed in both Britain and Germany in the Second World War. If Germany had mounted a more sustained and weighty area-bombing attack on British towns and cities in 1916–18, intelligent observers would have seen that it was in fact counter-productive – and therefore, although murderous and destructive, uselessly so.

Indeed, intelligent observers might have recognised this truth anyway. At first there was great panic in towns struck by Gothas.

Their first attack fell on Folkestone in May 1917, killing 95 people and injuring 195, the largest single blow of any bombing raid to that date. A wave of horror ran through the country. But it quickly subsided; no mass hysteria followed, nor any uprisings against the government, making popular demands to end the war. Instead the Gotha raids provoked a strong military reaction. A home-defence fighter group came into existence (Arthur Harris among its pilots) to defend against bomber raids, which it did with such success that, first, Zeppelins had to be withdrawn from the attack, and then Gothas had to switch to night bombing. Moreover a ring of barrage balloons went up to protect London, tethered so high that Gothas had difficulty overflying them; and searchlights and anti-aircraft guns entered service. These formidable defences proved effective. Between September 1917 and May 1918, sixty-one Gothas were shot down over the British Isles, an attrition rate too great for the Germans to sustain. After May 1918 the bombers were limited to attacking along the Western Front; they had been seen off.[9]

But although the Gotha bombings did not cause a collapse in civilian morale, it was understandable enough why observers concluded the contrary. They played the game of extrapolation. The citizens of Folkestone were shocked by the Gotha raid. In other towns workers had to quit their benches to take shelter when an attack occurred, or if the attack came at night they were tired the next day as a result of the sleeplessness caused. Imagine – so the observers told themselves and one another – bomber fleets tenfold, a hundredfold, larger, coming over every day and dropping many more bombs. Of course it was easy for them to conclude that the result would be devastating to civilian ability to function. Here was the seed of subsequent theory about bombing.

In the first years of manned heavier-than-air flight it was noted that biplanes flew better than monoplanes. It was predicted that the aeroplanes of the future would therefore have twelve wings. This is an example of the game of extrapolation and its too frequent result. The game of bombing extrapolation followed this pattern. However, it did

so only for the natural extension of Gotha and Ilya Mourometz bombers to Lancasters. With their heavy bomb loads the Lancasters multiplied the quantum of death and destruction in area bombing, but this not only diminished the effect on morale, it reversed it.

But what if the extrapolation were carried on, beyond the bombing capacity of a thousand Lancasters, all the way to the nuclear weapons of the post-Second World War period? Perhaps here at last the doctrine about morale comes into its own; for the very thought of the area-bombing effect of nuclear weapons has, at time of writing, been enough to stop anyone actually using them, and has kept wars 'local' (not that this is any consolation to those involved in them). To stop a war starting has to be the desirable logical limit of a bombing policy which sees bombs as a way of stopping wars once started. Does this mean that the strategic-bombing theory is, after all, right – provided that the bombing capacity is such that a single attack could wipe out entire cities in a blow, killing millions rather than 'merely' tens of thousands?

One thought in response might be to say that the aptly named 'MAD' thesis applied to nuclear weapons – 'mutually assured destruction' – is such that if it advanced beyond its deterrent purpose and a major nuclear exchange occurred between two or more nations, the area bombing thus carried out would end the war not because of effect on morale (although such an effect would certainly exist) but because the combatant nations would be physically incapable of continuing after the first assaults. To have a war-winning effect on morale, nuclear weapons would best be deployed by one country against another which could not retaliate in kind.

But this, again, would quite likely be self-defeating in another way, for the victor country would not be able to exploit any advantages over the defeated country, tracts of which would be uninhabitable as a result of radioactive fall-out, and the citizens of which would likely be in a highly dependent state, placing great and costly long-term demands on medical services and other aid, which the putative victor would have to provide.

These considerations suggest that if the theory of the effect on morale of area bombing is thought to come into its own at last in the nuclear age, it continues to do so self-defeatingly. Were Sir Arthur Harris still alive, he would see that even the 'right' weight of bombing power would still not be much use as a war-winning weapon, even if, as in this last scenario, it indeed won a war – with the hollowest of victories.

The rapid evolution of aircraft and their impact on warfare had an electric effect in the years 1914–18. In Britain the air forces of the British army and navy – respectively, the Royal Flying Corps and the Royal Naval Air Service – were reorganised jointly into the Royal Air Force, and in 1918 a dedicated bomber command was set up within it, led by the redoubtable Sir Hugh Trenchard. Remarkably, the British air force had leaped from practically nothing in 1914 to a force of 300,000 men by the war's end, and in that same four-year period Britain manufactured 50,000 aircraft of all military types. These prodigious facts in part explain why it is that in the decade and more after the war, even though air forces in most countries (and not least the United Kingdom) were rapidly reduced in size, military theoreticians should dwell on the possibilities of air warfare, and why some diplomatic initiatives among the major powers should try – futilely as it proved – to bring about international agreement on limiting or even banning the military use of aircraft, especially for bombing.

The theoreticians were quickly off the mark. In fact the first of them, in order both of time and significance for the area-bombing theory, had arrived at his views well before the outbreak of the First World War, after he had seen just three aircraft and before he had himself flown in one. This was Giulio Douhet, an extraordinary individual from the Savoy region of north Italy, who wrote books about military theory (and plays and poems besides) before enlisting in the Italian military in 1909. He was put in command of the fleet of nine aircraft sent to Libya for the war there with the Turks, and was therefore in charge when three aerial firsts were scored: the first

aeroplane reconnaissance in combat conditions, which occurred on 23 October 1911, the first bombing (see p. 124) on 1 November 1911, and the first aircraft shot down (by Turkish rifle fire).

As a result of his Libyan activities Douhet was given command of the Italian army's newly formed aviation battalion. He had ideas about how an Italian air capacity should evolve, and lobbied tirelessly but fruitlessly for purpose-built bombers for his force. In the end he commissioned a bomber aircraft on his own initiative from the aero designer Gianni Caproni, who as a result produced the eponymous three-engined bomber described above. But since Douhet had done this without official sanction he was stripped of his aviation command and sent to an infantry regiment instead. His military career came to an end when he was court-martialled and imprisoned for a year after writing an article predicting disaster for the Italian army on account of its many deficiencies. (He was all too soon proved right; the disaster duly occurred at Caparetto in 1917 where, in their worst-ever defeat, Italy's forces suffered over half a million casualties.[10])

Released from military duties and obligations, Douhet devoted himself to writing about the future of war. He produced a book that has become a classic of its kind: *The Command of the Air*, published in 1921. In it is set out the theory adopted, in all fundamentals, by RAF Bomber Command in the Second World War.[11] It was also highly influential on American air-power thinking, as we shall see.

The nub of Douhet's thesis is by now familiar, since it is exactly the thesis premised by Bomber Command from February 1942 onwards, and constituted Sir Arthur Harris's article of faith. It is that bombing should be targeted at the civilian population of an enemy state in order to break its morale and make it force its government to sue for peace. Terror, material destruction and privation caused by shortages of food and other necessities are the key elements.

Take the centre of a large city and imagine what would happen among the civilian population during a single attack by a single bombing unit [Douhet wrote]. I have no doubt that its impact on

the people would be terrible . . . What civil or military authority could keep order, public services functioning, and production going under such a threat? . . . A complete breakdown of the social structure cannot but take place in a country subjected to this kind of merciless pounding from the air. The time would soon come when, to put an end to horror and suffering, the people themselves, driven by the instinct for self-preservation, would rise up and demand an end to the war.[12]

This thesis might as well be called the Douhet–Trenchard thesis, for when Sir Hugh Trenchard was placed in charge of the newly formed RAF's bombers in 1918, he set about building a force that would put exactly this view into effect. The British members of a group set up in 1917 to co-ordinate British, French and American air policy, the Inter-Allied Aviation Committee, expressed Trenchard's view in words that might have directly inspired Douhet: '[the effect of bombing civilian targets] would be that the German government would be forced to face very considerable and constantly increasing civil pressure which might result in political disintegration.'[13] The war ended before Trenchard could carry out the policy to any great extent, but he adhered vigorously to it in thinking about how to prosecute a war against Britain's natural enemy – the French: 'I feel that although there would be an outcry,' he wrote in 1925 after asserting that the French population should be bombed if hostilities resumed between the neighbours, 'the French in a bombing duel would probably squeal before we did.'[14] Believing that wars would be very short if civilian bombing were central to them, Trenchard argued that there would be no point in attacking industrial targets. Like Douhet his entire focus was on the 'moral [i.e. morale] effect': 'The nation that would stand being bombed longest would win in the end . . . The end of war is usually attained when one nation has been able to bring such pressure to bear on another that public opinion obliges the government to sue for peace.'[15] This has the further implication that it is vital to get in

the earliest blows, before the enemy can mount an attack on the morale of one's own civilians.

For reasons that no one has been able to fathom, and on no known empirical basis, Trenchard asserted that the ratio of moral to material effect created by bombing is 20:1. But together with his general view it gave rise to the belief that what would win a war consisting of a bombing duel is national character; and naturally Trenchard and most of his fellow officers felt that this gave the British a long head start over possible Continental adversaries, especially the French.[16] Pape quotes one senior British officer remarking that during the First World War 'casualties affected the French more than they did the British. That would have to be taken into consideration too, but the policy of hitting the French nation and making them squeal before we did is a vital one – more vital than anything else'. The underlying assumption here appears to be, to put it bluntly, racist. It was, for example, claimed by J. F. C. Fuller that the people who most had panicked during Gotha raids on London in 1917 were 'East End Jews'. In the 1920s, British forces used bombing to keep order among Iraqi and Afghanistani tribesmen, and the ease with which bombing pacified them was taken as confirmation not only of the general efficacy of bombing but its peculiar efficacy in cases where people 'lacked moral fibre' – a failing universally attributed by British colonisers to those they colonised. Not coincidentally, Arthur Harris served in the Middle East in command of a bomber force at that time, and doubtless his Douhet–Trenchard outlook was much boosted by the experience.[17]

As mentioned in chapter 2, during the 1920s the RAF was fighting for its separate existence against the encroachments of the Royal Navy and the Army, and Trenchard, now chief of the RAF, needed arguments to persuade the government to keep in being what had become a rump force. The bombing arguments played a crucial part. It was not only Trenchard who advanced them; he had compelling support from the distinguished military historian Basil Liddell Hart, who in a book published in 1925 made an eloquent case for the idea

that bombing would make wars shorter and cheaper, and would save lives overall.[18] 'When it is realised that [strategic bombing would inflict] a total of injury far less than when [a war is] spread over a number of years, the common sense of mankind will show that the ethical objection to this form of war is at least not greater than to the cannon-fodder wars of the past.'[19] He went so far as to add that the war would end even more quickly and cheaply (in lives lost) if gas were used: 'gas may well prove the salvation of civilisation from the otherwise inevitable collapse in the case of another world war.'[20] An implication of Liddell Hart's view was that the deterrent effect of gas attacks from the air might prevent war altogether – an argument standardly deployed by those in favour of nuclear weapons.

Trenchard was so taken with these views that he had copies of Liddell Hart's book sent to his senior colleagues and to the new RAF staff college at Andover. He was not to know then that Liddell Hart would later dramatically change his mind; in 1942, when the true effects of area bombing were plain to see, Liddell Hart wrote, 'It will be ironical if the defenders of civilisation depend for victory upon the most barbaric, and unskilled, way of winning a war that the modern world has seen . . . We are now counting for victory on success in the way of degrading war to a new level – as represented by indiscriminate (night) bombing and indiscriminate starvation.'[21]

By 1928 Trenchard found it necessary to qualify the expression of his views, if not the views themselves, no doubt because the nagging voice of moral conscience was intruding from directions outside RAF staff-college seminars. In a memo to other service chiefs in the Army and Navy – the source of these doubts – he now conceded that it is 'contrary to the dictates of humanity [to carry out] the indiscriminate bombing of a city for the sole purpose of terrorising the civilian population'. But he maintained that it was wholly legitimate to demoralise munitions workers and stevedores loading military supplies. Why should the person who made the gun be less a target than he who fired it? 'Moral effect is created by bombing in such circumstances but it is the inevitable result of a lawful operation

of war – the bombing of a military objective.'[22] Thus was developed the official fig leaf used throughout the Second World War to justify the area-bombing campaigns. But it does at least raise a legitimate question: what is a 'military objective'? Where is the front line in modern war – surely the armaments factory is on it too?

So far did the British believe their own theoreticians on the subject of the effect of bombing that in 1939 the government made the following preparations for London: it estimated 250,000 dead in the first three weeks of suffering attack by bombers, with 3–4 million refugees flooding into the surrounding countryside. It predicted three million psychiatric cases from terror and confusion. It estimated that 50 per cent of London would be destroyed in that same first three weeks. Even before then the mathematicians had been at work, calculating the number of deaths and injuries per ton of bombs dropped, on which basis they estimated a monthly need for 2.8 million hospital beds and twenty million square feet of coffin timber. As part of the preparation for this horrendous disaster, the Ministry of Health – in one of those gestures that amaze by their sheer futility – issued an extra million death certificates to local authorities.[23]

It was not just the words of the theoreticians that convinced the British government to think in these terms; it was the continued trickle of apparent empirical confirmation from sites of conflict. The Italians bombed Addis Ababa in 1936, the Japanese bombed Nanking in 1937, and in that same year the German Condor legion in Spain carried out the Guernica bombing, killing a thousand people and destroying 70 per cent of the town. Because Spain was close to home in Europe, extreme shock was caused by reports of the screaming Stuka dive-bombers and what they did to the town and its people, whom they strafed as they fled into the surrounding fields. The atrocities in Nanking, immensely greater but on the other side of the world and anyway a matter between orientals, had nothing like the same impact. Even so, the mere report of yet another demonstration of the horrors of air power fed into the fear everywhere felt. That these attacks took place in 'ideal bombing conditions' – there was no

air defence, and the attacks took place in daylight – did not then make a difference to calculations. The corpses and the smoking ruins seemed to speak far too eloquently even for mildly sceptical voices to be heard.

All through the 1930s the British, and not them alone, were repeatedly told of the horrors of bombing and the immense threat it posed. Liddell Hart, not yet converted from his views, wrote a graphic account of terrified civilians fleeing bombed cities in the *Daily Telegraph* in November 1933.[24] In London the government decided to build up fighter defences against bomber attack. Bomber Command, so named, had come into official existence in 1936, but as described in chapter 2, although plans were simultaneously laid for a bomber force (including the large four-engined heavy bombers that eventually came into service when Sir Arthur Harris was chief of the Command) it now took second place to the urgent need for fighter defence. Moreover Bomber Command's first directive unequivocally stated that its role was not to enact the Trenchard–Douhet–Liddell Hart thesis, but to provide army support and to attack enemy airfields only. It was explicitly told 'to do nothing that might be construed as an attack on civilians and so to give the enemy an excuse to do likewise'.[25]

In fact so great was the desire not to provoke an enemy – now recognised to be Germany – into applying the Trenchard–Douhet thesis to British cities, that a special subcommittee of the Committee on Imperial Defence, assigned to examine the whole question of bombing, suggested that the government should publicly offer to refrain from bombing Germany's industrial Ruhr region, and also not to impose a naval blockade given that it would impose privations on German civilians, in the hope that Germany would reciprocate with restraint in the matter of bombing cities.

American air-power theory was wholly different. It was also aimed at causing an enemy collapse, but not by attacking civilians directly. Instead it focused on the idea of destroying key industrial links in the

enemy economy, which would have the effect of disrupting supplies required to sustain the enemy population, and therefore its willingness to continue supporting a war. The doctrine was devised by a group of officers at the Air Corps Tactical School, the top American air-officer academy, during the 1930s. Four of the officers from this academy, Harold L. George, Haywood Hansell, Kenneth Walker and Laurence S. Kuter, wrote the first United States air-strategy plan in 1941, the 'Air War Plans Division Plan 1' (AWPD-1 for short).

The premise on which the theory underlying AWPD-1 turned was that the stresses imposed on an economy by war would be such that a relatively small number of bomber aircraft, dropping a relatively small quantity of bombs on carefully selected targets, would snap vital threads in the enemy's 'industrial web', and as a result secure a quick victory. The primary objectives specified by AWPD-1 were electricity, transport, and oil. Failure of these economic essentials, so the plan's authors claimed, would soon cause civilian discomfiture; indeed, they believed that the enemy would surrender within six months if fifty-four nominated targets in these sectors were hit. The plan recognised that accurate bombing required control of the air, and so as supplementary objectives it specified attacks on enemy air bases, on aircraft factories, and on sources of indispensable raw materials for aircraft production, such as aluminium and magnesium.

The credo at work in this view is expressed with commendable clarity in lectures given at the Air Corps Tactical School in 1939, quoted by Robert Pape in his study of the coercive use of air power. 'The ultimate object of all military operations . . . is to destroy the will of the people at home, for that is the real source of the enemy's national policy,' says a lecture entitled 'The Aim of War'; 'the loss of morale in the civilian population is far more conclusive than the defeat of the soldier on the battlefield . . . Air forces are capable of immediate employment towards accomplishing the ultimate aim. They can be used directly to break down the will of the mass of the enemy people.'[26]

Another lecture sets out the 'industrial web' thesis: 'Modern

warfare places an enormous load upon the economic system of a nation, which increases its sensitivity to attack many-fold. Certainly a breakdown in any part of this complex interlocked organisation must seriously influence the conduct of war by that nation, and greatly interfere with the social welfare and morale of its nationals.' The lecture goes on to invite the audience to consider what would happen in the United States if 'section after section of our great industrial system [ceased] to produce all those numberless articles which are essential to life as we know it'.[27] A third lecture applies these tenets to a practical example: if New York City's water supplies were stopped, the city would soon have to be evacuated because of thirst, the danger of fire, and the undermining of sanitation. If railway bridges were wrecked by bombs, shortages in supplies of foodstuffs would quickly become apparent and make the city 'untenable' – so once again the population would have to be evacuated. This applies also to bombing of electric power stations: lack of electricity 'would cause refrigerated food to spoil'.[28]

In the light of what people can put up with in real rather than imagined war, it is obvious that the unwitting premise of these last remarks is that what would quickly end a war is a population's effeteness or softness, its inability to do without refrigerators or WCs. The lecturer had evidently forgotten that the majority of his contemporaries in the world lived reasonably happily without refrigerators and WCs. As the bombed civilians of the Second World War all over the world proved beyond a shadow of doubt, human beings are – short of devastating atomic bomb attack – much hardier than the Air Corps Tactical School lecturer seemed to realise.[29]

These remarks show a marked parallel, noticed by Pape, with the views of a Russian-born American theorist of air power called Alexander de Seversky, who argued in a book on the subject that the civilian will to support war would surely be broken by 'destroying effectively the essentials of their lives – the supply of food, shelter, light, water, sanitation, and the rest'.[30] Evidently there was a wide consensus among those in the United States applying their minds to

the use of air power. On its merits the thesis seemed plausible, and the empirical evidence until then available appeared to support it.

But as always, the merits and evidence were not the only factors in play. Inter-service politics had their part in shaping the debate. Just as the Royal Air Force managed to maintain a separate identity after the First World War by appeal to the risks and promises of bombing – the risks implying a need for a separate fighter defence force against enemy bombers, the promise implying quicker and cheaper victories over enemies by bombing them first – so in America military fliers were able to compete for resources by emphasising the risks and promises of their craft likewise. They had long since been helped in this by their first and most enthusiastic prophet of bomber war, General William 'Billy' Mitchell, who in 1921 had given an apparently irrefutable demonstration of his thesis by sinking six surplus-to-requirement warships in a bombing demonstration that radically changed United States thinking about air power.[31] Mitchell later appeared to have hindered rather than helped the air-power cause by outspoken criticism of colleagues in the US Army and Navy who were sceptical about his views; indeed he succeeded in getting himself court-martialled and cashiered because of the heated and intemperate remarks he made about them. But by the time the Air Corps Tactical School was producing a cadre of air theoreticians of its own, they had arguments to bring to bear that the War Department in Washington could no long ignore.

Received wisdom in the US was that America was so far from potential major enemies, whether to the east or the west, that it was in no danger of aerial bombing. The risk, if it faced any, was from an enemy navy. To trump the US Navy's card on this score, the new theoreticians of air power pointed out – with Billy Mitchell's ringing lesson in mind – that bombers were the surest defence against naval attack. This of course meant precision bombing. One of the immediate effects of this tack was that the US Army Air Force therefore developed one of the first accurate bomb-sights, the famous Norden sight, and was so jealous of it that it refused to share it even with its

British friends. Happily for the air theoreticians, enemy warships and 'industrial web' targets both made the same demand for a precision-bombing capacity, so its proponents could offer Washington a compelling twin-track argument that offered both.[32]

In Pape's view there was an additional motivation for the precision-bombing strategy adopted by the US Army Air Force. This was that the constrained economic conditions in America in the 1930s made it necessary to devise strategies that would be relatively cheap.

> Attacking the enemy's will through the more humane and eco-nomic method of selective attack made sense in the 1930s [he writes], because the total budgets of the Army, of which the Air Corps was part, were in decline. Accordingly the Air Corps required a doctrine that promised victory not only at less cost relative to the Army and Navy but cheaply in absolute terms.[33]

Added to this was the thought that liberal sentiment in the United States would not readily tolerate 'the mass slaughter of civilians'. In an interestingly temporising remark, two men who were to have re-sponsibility for carrying out American air strategy in the coming war, General H. H. 'Hap' Arnold and General Ira Eaker, wrote in their jointly authored book *Winged Warfare* – published mere months before America entered the war – 'Human beings are not priority targets except in special situations. Bombers in far larger numbers than are available today will be required for wiping out people in sufficient numbers by aerial bombardment to break the will of a whole nation.'[34]

When AWPD-1 was presented to the War Department in Wa-shington in 1941, the Department's joint Army-Navy Board re-sponded with scepticism to its claim that air power could by itself bring victory, asserting that 'only land armies can finally win wars'. The Board therefore allocated to the Army air corps a lesser role, that of supporting the other forces by gaining air superiority, weakening the effectiveness of the enemy forces, reducing the capacity of the

enemy economy, and (the last item on its list) undermining civilian morale. This response meant that American air units were to remain under the control of land-force commanders, something that the American fliers had hoped AWPD-1 would free them from. It was not until mid-1943 that the US air arm gained operational independence, as the result of the issue of a new Field Manual for the US Army, which gave much greater autonomy and flexibility to air commanders – a first major step to the ultimate independence of the American air arm as the United States Air Force (no longer the United States *Army* Air Force) after the end of the war.[35]

Because the new Field Manual's directions on the use of air power incorporated pre-war Air Corps Tactical School thinking, it can be regarded as a partial triumph for AWPD-1, and so it was. But the precision-bombing versus area-bombing argument had long been won by the draughtsmen of AWPD-1; in theory that had never been in question. This was so even though AWPD-1 had officially been abandoned in favour of a second air-war plan, called AWPD-42, as the result of AWPD-1 being leaked to the press soon after it was submitted to the War Department.[36] In most essentials the two plans were similar, the differences being mostly of emphasis in their respective lists of crucial targets. Whereas AWPD-1 had been drafted by fliers, AWPD-42 was drafted by a committee of economic experts and industrialists. In revising AWPD-1 the committee revisited the question of which bottle-necks in Germany's economy would be the right ones to target in order to strangle the German war effort. But as this implies, the official air strategy of US bomber forces remained – indeed, was reinforced in the direction of – precision bombing.

When the USAAF arrived in Britain to take its part in the attack on Nazi Germany, reality proved a harsh spoiler of hopes. Europe's weather – low cloud, rain, patchy mist, dense fog, hazy days, abrupt and unreliable changes from sun to showers – would by itself have made the ideal of precision daylight bombing a hard enough thing to achieve, if it were not for the added and infinitely worse disruptions of the Germans' anti-aircraft guns and Messerschmitt fighters. The

fabled Norden bomb-sight required a straight and steady run of many miles with the bomb-aimer in clear visual command of the approaching target, no problem in training conditions in the United States but very hard to achieve in actual war conditions in European weather. In a deeply sceptical account of what really happened when the B-17s came to Europe, Stewart Ross – an academic historian with experience of analysing bombing-accuracy tests on behalf of the US Army Ordance Corps – claims that there was vastly more myth than fact in the accounts given of USAAF endeavours.[37] One of his conclusions is that although US bombers were officially required to attack only military or industrial targets and to avoid deliberate bombing of civilians, in practice any city with a population over 50,000 was regarded as likely to contain military or industrial assets and accordingly to be a legitimate target, and that therefore the USAAF not only conducted area bombing by default when 'blind bombing' (through cloud, at targets picked out by H2S radar), but when area bombing as such. He traces the Americans' increasing acceptance of area bombing in the European theatre to its logical conclusion in the explicit and open area bombing conducted by Curtis LeMay's XXI Bomber Command in its war over Japan.[38]

This suggests that the difference between RAF Bomber Command practice and USAAF practice in the European theatre was less than might be implied by the express rhetoric of USAAF bombing principles. But two points merit mention. The first is that the RAF always attempted to give the impression officially – as noted, to Harris's annoyance – that it was not indiscriminately bombing civilians, but attacking the enemy industrial capacity. The fact that it was doing so by bombing the workers (and everyone else around them) rather than their factories, and trying to undermine the German economy's effectiveness by demoralising, 'dehousing' and causing privations to those who survived bombing attacks, was cloaked in rhetoric similar to that used by the Americans. But whereas the Americans wanted to conduct precision bombing and were forced by circumstances to engage in area bombing, RAF Bomber Command wanted to engage

in area bombing and used the rhetoric of attacking industrial and military targets as a conscious cover for what they were really doing.

The second point is that when the USAAF Eighth and Fifteenth Army Air Forces were able to engage in precision bombing, they did so; this happened principally in the closing months of the war when the Allies had greater command of the skies, and the Flying Fortresses had better 'bombing conditions' for their attacks on vital sectors of German war production, especially oil – with, as we have also seen, decisive effect. In that same period Bomber Command continued to carry out area bombing – in fact, Harris positively insisted on bombing those cities on his list which remained unbombed; and so his aircraft destroyed cities like Würzburg and Hildesheim, noted far more for their historical beauty than for their military importance.[39]

This fact, however, only increases the contrast between the American efforts in the European theatre and the area attacks carried out by XXI Bomber Command under Curtis LeMay in the Pacific theatre. Even here an effort, though not an especially great one, was made to disguise area bombing as directed at war production. Claiming that the Japanese produced military equipment on a cottage-industry basis, in which parts were manufactured in the little wooden houses of the civilians, LeMay said after the firebombing of Tokyo on 9–10 March 1945, 'There are no innocent civilians . . . The entire population got into the act and worked to make those aeroplanes or munitions . . . men, women, and children.'

The Mind of the Bomber II: The Fate of Gomorrah

All the theory and practice described in the last chapter had not been taking place in a vacuum. The efforts made at the Hague conferences of 1899 and 1907 to prevent the sky becoming another scene of war did not end there. It was the opinion of Sir Edward Grey, British Foreign Secretary from 1905 to 1916 and therefore one of those involved in – some say, one of those responsible for – the outbreak of the First World War, that the accumulation of armaments in the years

Lancasters on a bombing run: notice the anti-aircraft shell-burst ('flak') on the right of the picture.

Air Marshall Sir Arthur Harris.

Air Marshall Sir Charles Portal.

Crew of a Lancaster bomber walk away from their plane after a flight
while ground crew check it over, April 1943.

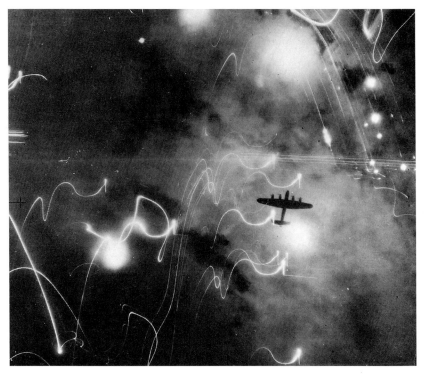

An Allied bomber above its target.

USAAF B-17 Flying Fortresses in 'box' formation, with fighter aircraft above.

Aachen in 1900.

Würzburg in 1938.

The rooftops of old Hamburg before the
Second World War.

Lübeck before 1900.

Berlin under attack in July 1944.

Hamburg burning during Operation Gomorrah, July 1943.

The Hamburg University bookshop after Operation Gomorrah.

Nuremberg, 1945.

Hannover, 1943.

Berlin, 1944.

Cologne, 1945.

Victims of the Dresden bombing, 14 February 1945.

Victims of the firebombing of Hamburg, Operation Gomorrah, July 1943.

Survivors of Operation Gomorrah, Hamburg, July 1943.

General Curtis Le May, Commander of USAAF XXI Bomb Group,
giving a press briefing, 3 August 1945.

A B-29 'bombing up', 24 November 1944.

A B-29 on a bombing
run over Osaka, Japan.

Osaka under attack by 500 B-29
Superfortresses on 1 June 1945.
Between them they dropped
3,000 tons of incendiary bombs.

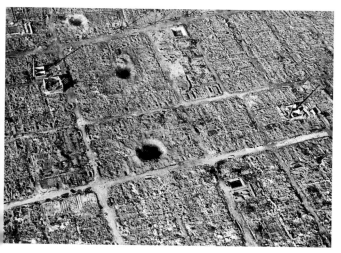

Osaka as it looked to aerial
reconnaissance on 9 June 1945.

Tokyo's Ginza Street before being bombed in 1945.

Bombs falling on Kobe, 4 June 1945.

Kamamatsu destroyed by bombing, 9 June 1945.

The atom bomb exploding over Nagasaki.

Hiroshima after the explosion of the atom bomb, 1945.

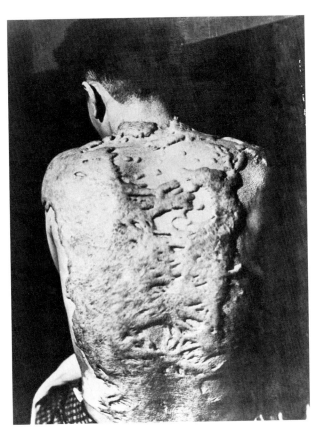

Survivor, Nagasaki.

prior to 1914 was a major factor in the war's occurrence.[40] The fourth of Woodrow Wilson's famous Fourteen Points iterated the need for limitation of armaments: 'Adequate guarantees [must be] given and taken that national armaments will be reduced to the lowest point consistent with domestic safety.' Throughout the inter-war years efforts were made to limit the size of armies and navies, and to place constraints on the kinds of weapons that might be used; and this included air power. This was an obligation to which all participating members of the League of Nations and signatories to the Treaty of Versailles committed themselves after the First World War.

Some success in limiting naval forces was reached in 1922, and an important rhetorical moment occurred when the Kellogg–Briand Pact was signed in 1928, this being the international treaty signed by many members of the League of Nations – chief among them the United States, Britain, France and Germany – renouncing war as an instrument of policy.[41] But the question of air power proved greatly more difficult to resolve. The fullest and most thoughtful attempt to provide rules for air warfare was made at a conference held at The Hague between December 1922 and February 1923. The then five major powers of Britain, France, the United States, Italy and Japan took part, neither Germany nor Russia then being in a position to count as such. The articles drawn up by the conference were never signed by the participating governments, so no Rules of Air Warfare came into existence; but the draft rules arrived at by the participants are fascinating, showing as they do how clearly the dangers of air power were foreseen. What happened in conflicts after the powers considered these rules, and especially what happened in the Second World War, has to be measured against the principles they embody.

ARTICLE XXII

Aerial bombardment for the purpose of terrorising the civilian population, of destroying or damaging private property not of a military character, or of injuring non-combatants, is prohibited. [. . .]

ARTICLE XXIV

1) Aerial bombardment is legitimate only when directed at a military objective, that is to say, an object of which the destruction or injury would constitute a distinct military advantage to the belligerent.

2) Such bombardment is legitimate only when directed exclusively at the following objectives: military forces; military works; military establishments or depots; factories constituting important and well-known centres engaged in the manufacture of arms, ammunition, or distinctively military supplies; lines of communication or transportation used for military purposes.

3) The bombardment of cities, towns, villages, dwellings, or buildings not in the immediate neighbourhood of the operations of land forces is prohibited. In cases where the objectives specified in paragraph 2 are so situated, that they cannot be bombarded without the indiscriminate bombardment of the civilian population, the aircraft must abstain from bombardment.

4) In the immediate neighbourhood of the operations of land forces, the bombardment of cities, towns, villages, dwellings, or buildings is legitimate provided that there exists a reasonable presumption that the military concentration is sufficiently important to justify such bombardment, having regard to the danger thus caused to the civilian population.

ARTICLE XXV

In bombardment by aircraft all necessary steps must be taken by the commander to spare as far as possible buildings dedicated to public worship, art, science, or charitable purposes, historic monuments, hospital ships, hospitals, and other places where the sick and wounded are collected, provided such buildings, objects or places are not at the time used for military purposes. Such buildings, objects and places must by day be indicated by marks visible to aircraft. The use of marks to indicate other buildings, objects or places than those specified above is to be deemed an act of perfidy.

The marks used as aforesaid shall be in the case of buildings protected under the Geneva Convention the red cross on a white ground, and in the case of other protected buildings a large rectangular panel divided diagonally into two pointed triangular portions, one black and the other white.

A belligerent who desires to secure by night the protection for the hospitals and other privileged buildings above mentioned must take the necessary measures to render the special signs referred to sufficiently visible.

ARTICLE XXVI

The following special rules are adopted for the purpose of enabling States to obtain more efficient protection for important historic monuments situated within their territory, provided that they are willing to refrain from the use of such monuments and a surrounding zone for military purposes, and to accept a special regime for their inspection.

1) A State shall be entitled, if it sees fit, to establish a zone of protection round such monuments situated in its territory. Such zones shall in time of war enjoy immunity from bombardment.

2) The monuments round which a zone is established shall be notified to other Powers in peace time through the diplomatic channel; the notification shall also indicate the limits of the zones. The notification may not be withdrawn in time of war.

3) The zone of protection may include, in addition to the area actually occupied by the monument or group of monuments, an outer zone, not exceeding 500 meters in width, measured from the circumference of the said area . . .

The failure of this effort, and slow progress on other fronts, prompted the League of Nations to convene a full conference of all members in order to achieve disarmament – or more accurately, arms control, which is a different thing. A preliminary commission sat between 1925 and 1932, trying to establish a basis for discussion on which

arms would be limited, and how.[42] When the Geneva Disarmament Conference officially began in February 1932, most of the attending powers were in agreement that air attacks on civilians were in violation of fundamental principles; but the conference as a whole quickly stalled on the political realities of the time. France did not wish to limit its forces, fearing hostilities from Germany. Germany stated that unless the rest of the world disarmed to its own level as specified by the terms of the Treaty of Versailles, it would regard itself as entitled to rearm to the point where it achieved equality with the other powers. During one of the adjournments of the deadlocked conference Hitler came to power, and not long afterwards withdrew Germany from the conference. Although officially the conference remained in (mainly adjourned) session until 1937, the hope of preventing war by limiting the means for making it had long since vanished.

When the conference began, with calls from various countries about abolishing submarines and limiting the armaments of battle-ships, Italy and Japan called for the outlawing of aerial bombardment. France wanted bombing to be forbidden beyond a radius of a given number of miles from the front lines – which assumed that there would be front lines, as in 1914–18; but the British were determined that there should be no repeat of such a thing. Both Britain and to a lesser extent France had far-flung empires, parts of which occasionally needed to be bombed in the interests of good order, so neither was keen on an outright bombing ban. The conference contemplated banning offensive weaponry but permitting defensive weapons, only to find that what counted as either was a matter of perspective: submarines for Germany were defensive weapons against British naval blockade, while for the British they were offensive weapons against Britain's sea trade routes. The same difficulty affected the question of bombs.

At one point it was (in the crazed way understandable among the impasses of a major international conference) mooted that flight itself should be banned, since while it existed – even for civilian purposes –

it was a certainty that someone would assuredly use it to bomb someone else. Stanley Baldwin, former British Prime Minister but at the time of the conference serving as President of the Board of Trade, was profoundly concerned about the threat of bombing. He told the US delegate that 'the course we are now following is straight toward the destruction of our civilisation and something radical has to be done unless we are all going down together'. His proposal, slightly less swingeing than the ban on flight as such, was the 'total abolition of all military aviation'.[43] When Sir Anthony Eden took over as representative at the conference he suggested instead severe limitations on when bombing would be permissible, but in any event he suggested a prohibition against air attacks on civilian populations. The RAF suspected that Eden was moving in the direction of a complete ban on bombing, and were very unhappy about it. The then chief of the RAF, Sir John Salmond, wrote to Eden with his 'deep misgivings' about the tendency of the British proposals, saying that in circumstances where a country is fighting for its very life it would be 'inconceivable' that it would not use bombing to defend itself; the idea 'has nothing in logic or common-sense to recommend it'.[44] Although he was opposed to the bombing of civilians – 'no military advantage is likely to accrue to a country which employs its bombing aircraft to terrorise rather than to disarm its opponent', Salmond wrote – he was adamant that bombing was a necessary weapon of war, and that therefore the main thrust of British efforts should go to defining what a 'military target' is, for in the absence of a definition belligerents would simply resort to indiscriminate bombing.[45]

At one point discussion at Geneva really did seem to be tending towards an outright ban on aerial bombing, and both the US and British governments, the latter in the teeth of RAF opposition, were in favour. But difficulties of detail kept arising, chief among them the position of civil aviation in the light of such a ban – for, again, it is easy to convert an airliner to a bomber, and no country, especially not the United States, was prepared to retrench on civil aviation. Disillusioned by the lack of progress, on 10 November 1932 Stanley

Baldwin made a famous speech. 'The bomber,' he said, 'will always get through . . . The only defence is offence. You have to kill more women and children more quickly than the enemy if you want to save yourselves.'[46] It is interesting to note that these remarks were then found highly offensive by the RAF, thus in effect accused of wishing to make war on women and children, whereas – so its leaders then passionately believed – bombing would shorten war and make it less costly in life overall, and perhaps even have the deterrent effect of preventing war altogether.

As usual, of course, RAF objections to banning bombers were intimately linked to the very survival of the RAF, for in the event of a ban the non-bombing remnants of the force would be returned to the Army and Navy for adjunctival roles. From the RAF point of view, therefore, it was as well that the conference collapsed in 1934; from the point of view of humanity it was not.

The failure of efforts to secure international agreement limiting bombers and restraining bombing meant that when a widening of hostilities threatened in 1939, Britain's then Prime Minister, Neville Chamberlain, was very anxious. The country was still under-strength in its air defences and its ability to retaliate if a bombing war started, and the government was alarmed by the propaganda that the British had themselves been promoting about the horrors of air war, horrors repeatedly insisted upon by the RAF in seeking to preserve not just its independence but its existence, and by politicians like Stanley Baldwin who saw all too clearly what unrestrained air war would be like. So when on 1 September 1939, two days before Britain declared war on Germany, President Roosevelt made his radio broadcast calling upon the European powers to promise not to bomb civilians, Chamberlain was eager to respond in the affirmative, as much out of conviction – he was by instinct a pacific man – as canniness, hoping to stave off devastating aerial bombardment of Britain at least until Britain was ready to counter such an attack. In his broadcast Roosevelt said that he was afraid 'hundreds of thousands of

innocent human beings who have no responsibility for, and who are not even remotely participating in, the hostilities' would be killed. He asked the world's nations 'to affirm [a] determination that [their] armed forces shall in no event, and under no circumstances, undertake the bombardment from the air of civilian populations or of unfortified cities'.

Chamberlain was not alone in responding positively to the President's appeal; so did the French – and so did Hitler, at the very moment that the Luftwaffe's Stukas were bombing Warsaw. Even if there was a measure of calculation in Chamberlain's public pronouncements about abjuring the bombing of civilians, the frequency with which he made them and their emphatic character suggest an at least equal measure of genuine sentiment. In the House of Commons on 14 September 1939 he made his commitment in the clearest terms: 'His Majesty's Government will never resort to the deliberate attack on women and children and other civilians for the purpose of mere terrorism.'[47]

There was a greater victim of the failure of international efforts during the 1920s and 1930s to limit armaments and to outlaw bombing attacks on civilians. This victim, without overmuch drama, might be described as the future of mankind itself. For in the absence of agreements to restrict the development of new and more dangerous weapons, the race to produce atom bombs was by default allowed to go ahead. Not only were they used against the civilians of Hiroshima and Nagasaki, but they have held the world to ransom since, and it is only a matter of time before such a weapon is used – experts on conflict say: at the minimum either by terrorists, or in a regional war in (for example) south or east Asia.

From the outset the meaning of atomic weapons was clearly understood by those engaged in researching their production, and to many of these, in turn, their moral repugnance was equally clear. The Hungarian physicist Leo Szilard, who had fled his homeland in 1933, was so concerned by the possibilities that he urged his

colleagues in the field of atomic research to keep their findings secret. When he discovered in March 1939 that a uranium nucleus would emit two neutrons if penetrated by one neutron, which meant that chain reactions are possible, he was filled with terrible foreboding. 'That night there was very little doubt in my mind that the world was headed for grief,' he said.[48] He and a colleague persuaded Einstein to write to Roosevelt to explain the dangers – and the possibilities; for Szilard and others thought that in the parlous international situation it was advisable for the democracies to develop atomic weapons before the dictatorships did. In one respect they were right; in Germany, despite the fact that its scientific community had been depleted by expulsion of 'non-Aryans' in the Civil Service Restoration Law of 1933, which removed Jewish scientists from the country's leading universities and laboratories (almost all went to Britain or America), work was under way on atomic weapons in a research project headed by Werner Heisenberg. (To a much lesser extent similar research programmes had also begun in Russia and Japan.) Some of the German scientists were as worried by the moral implications of atomic weapons as their colleagues elsewhere. But once the promise and dangers had been grasped by the politicians on both sides of a rapidly impending war, the production of atomic bombs had ceased to be a matter for moral anxiety, and had become an inevitability.

Before this, though, development of atomic weapons by the United States and Britain was almost stalled – not by moral scruples, but by bureaucracy; for in both countries committees were set up to evaluate the claims that scientists were making about atomic potential, and to consider the costs and benefits of experimental application of their theories. The US committee was especially sceptical; at its first meeting its members scornfully told the scientists presenting the possibilities of atomic weapons (Szilard among them) that it was the morale of troops, not the power of bombs, that eventually won wars. In Britain in 1940 a crucial breakthrough in the study of chain reactions in uranium-235 brought the reality of a bomb much closer, thereby prompting the setting-up of a British committee headed by

the physicist G. P. Thomson. Although it agreed with its American counterpart in initially thinking that research into the possibility of a bomb was a 'wild goose chase', Thomson's committee changed its mind in the summer of 1941, and reported to Churchill that atom bombs were a genuine possibility and could have a decisive influence on the war. When this was communicated to Roosevelt in the early autumn of 1941 he immediately ordered a full-scale development effort. Thus the Manhattan Project came into existence; the rest is history.

The men who made the breakthrough in research into chain reactions in U-235 were Otto Frisch and Rudolph Peierls at the University of Birmingham in England. When they had made their calculations on the size of the critical mass required to produce reactions reaching temperatures equivalent to those in the centre of the sun, they were staggered: the required quantity was only two or three pounds of material rather than the tons they had expected. 'We stared at each other and realised that an atomic bomb might after all be possible,' Frisch said. Their figures told them that 2–3 lb of U-235 would cause an explosion equivalent to several thousand tons of TNT, and that the radiation released would be 'fatal to living beings even a long time after the explosion'. They further saw that nothing could resist the power of such an explosion, that wind would spread radiation far beyond the blast area and that therefore an atom bomb 'could not be used without killing large numbers of civilians' – which they therefore thought meant that 'this may make [atom bombs] unsuitable as a weapon for use by [Britain]'; and finally they concluded that if 'Germany is, or will be, in possession of this weapon [the] most effective reply would be a counter-threat with a similar weapon'.[49]

This memorandum by Frisch and Peierls succinctly and effectively covers the ground as regards atomic weapons: their immense danger, their moral repugnance, their inevitability, and the need to counter their threat with a threat of the same: a prefiguring of the doctrine of deterrence.

Whereas scientists were mainly thinking in terms of a deterrent, Roosevelt and his military advisers, and with them Churchill, thought explicitly in terms of a weapon for deployment when ready. Roosevelt's Secretary of War, Henry Stimson, said after the war that he never heard Roosevelt say that atomic bombs should not be used; rather, their role as a decisive war-winning instrument was alone what justified the effort and cost involved in developing them. Churchill concurred: 'the decision whether or not to use the atomic bomb,' he later wrote, '. . . was never an issue. There was unanimous, automatic, unquestioned agreement.'[50]

There was no 'unquestioned agreement' among those who really understood the implications. Niels Bohr managed to secure a personal meeting with Churchill on 16 May 1944 to press upon him how awful an atomic bomb attack would be, and to urge him not to allow one to be made. Churchill impatiently replied, 'I cannot see what you are talking about. After all this new bomb is just going to be bigger than our present bombs. It involves no difference in the principles of war. And as for any post-war problems there are none that cannot be amicably settled between me and my friend President Roosevelt.'[51] Bohr had no more luck with Roosevelt, whom he saw on 26 August 1944, and whom he urged to arrange for international controls on atomic weaponry and for the Russians to be included in knowledge about them. Roosevelt's friendly manner gave Bohr the impression that he had succeeded with the President where he had failed with the Prime Minister. But at a meeting between the two Allied leaders the following month it was Churchill's attitude that prevailed: the atom bomb was going to be kept secret, so no steps would be taken to institute international control of its use; the bomb would be used against Japan if 'after mature consideration' it was deemed necessary; and Professor Bohr was to be watched to ensure that he did not pass information about the atom bomb to the Russians. Churchill indeed thought he ought to be imprisoned as a security measure.[52]

Bohr was far from alone among scientists in campaigning to stop Washington's political and military leaders actually using the bomb,

rather than brandishing it as a threat. In June 1944 a group of Chicago scientists lobbied Washington not just on the moral question, but on the pragmatic grounds that use of the atom bombs would trigger a disastrous arms race. They argued that the US government should announce to the world that it had the bomb but would not use it, and would indeed renounce it if everyone else would join them in forswearing the military use of atomic power.

In July 1944 Leo Szilard also renewed his efforts by submitting a petition, signed by himself and sixty-nine fellow physicists, insisting that the government had an 'obligation of restraint'. But the government had already resolved to use the atom bomb; its committee overseeing deployment of the new weapon noted the scientists' concerns in its minutes, but without further comment simply iterated its decision that the bomb should be deployed 'at the earliest opportunity . . . without warning'.[53]

There was one senior member of the Washington government who was not in favour of the bomb, and who used his position and influence first to try to stop its use, and when this failed, to try to mitigate its use. This was Henry Stimson, the Secretary of War to President Roosevelt and then to President Truman. One thing Stimson managed to do was to strike Kyoto off the list of possible targets. It had been selected as such along with Hiroshima, Kokura and Nigata, all of which were left unbombed by conventional means after the decision to use the atomic weapon had been taken, so that its effects on them could be measured more clearly. Kyoto was the capital of Japan from 794 until the seat of imperial government was moved to Edo, later called Tokyo, in 1868. A city of nearly 2,000 temples, monasteries and gardens, it was then as it is now the chief repository of Japan's culture and traditions, and Stimson was very much alive to its significance. General Leslie Groves, the military head of the Manhattan Project, was annoyed that Stimson had removed Kyoto from the list, but Stimson told him that 'such a wanton act' as dropping an atom bomb on Kyoto would make the post-war task of managing a conquered Japan vastly more difficult.

Stimson was also worried by the targeting policy adopted for the atom-bomb attack. The group of White House advisers considering this aspect of the matter, the Interim Committee, concluded that the bomb should be dropped over a city centre, not on the outskirts where industrial or military targets would usually be located, because there its effects would be diminished by the proximity of sparsely inhabited countryside. In any case, said the committee, industrial targets in large cities would be too small and insignificant as targets *per se*. Stimson objected to targeting city centres, arguing that it would give the United States a 'reputation for outdoing Hitler in atrocities'. He argued that the Japanese should be warned in advance of an attack so that the US could avoid 'the opprobrium which might follow from an ill-considered employment of such force'.[54] His efforts, together with those of several junior members of the government who agreed with him, were of course unavailing. President Truman was more inclined to listen to the man he had appointed as his Secretary of State, James Byrnes. In the Roosevelt administration Byrnes served as Director of the Office of War Mobilization, and as such had worked hard to ensure that the Manhattan Project received priority in money and manpower. Now he was determined that the effort should be seen to bear fruit. At a meeting of the Interim Committee on 1 June 1945 Byrnes strongly recommended that the atomic bomb should be used on an urban area, and very soon; and his principal reason was that the United States should demonstrate to Russia the considerable edge that possession of atomic weapons gave it, in order (as Leo Szilard observed) to 'make Russia more manageable in Europe'.

This motivation has been much discussed, and figures as part of the defence of the use of the atom bombs on Hiroshima and Nagasaki. The point therefore comes back into focus in chapter 7 below.

In a discussion of the 'mind of the bomber' – which is to say: the attitudes of those who planned and ordered bombing, especially of civilian targets – it is not possible to leave the story of the atom bomb without noting the effect of its dropping. One of the witnesses in the

B-29 that accompanied the *Enola Gay* on 6 August 1945 was Luis Alvarez, a Manhattan Project scientist. On the return flight from the sky above Hiroshima where the mushroom cloud still stood, he felt he had to write to his four-year-old son. 'What regrets I have about being party to killing and maiming thousands of Japanese civilians this morning,' he wrote, in stricken mood, 'are tempered with the hope that this terrible weapon we have created may bring the countries of the world together and prevent future wars.' Robert Lewis, a member of *Enola Gay*'s crew, shouted as he watched the effects of the explosion, 'Look at that! Look at that! Look at that! . . . My God! Look at that son-of-a-bitch go!' In his mission log shortly afterwards, when reflection had replaced excitement, he wrote, 'My God, what have we done?'[55]

Popular sentiment in America was one of exhilaration and triumph; polls showed 85 per cent of people in favour. But on both wings of the political spectrum there were grave regrets. A liberal commentator, Dwight McDonald, wrote sadly of America's 'decline to barbarism', while the conservative David Lawrence said, '[appeals to] military necessity . . . will never erase from our minds the simple truth that we, of all civilized nations . . . did not hesitate to employ the most destructive weapon of all times indiscriminately against men, women and children'.[56]

Of great interest is what President Truman thought and said at the time. In response to urging from a US Senator to use the toughest means possible to force Japan to surrender, Truman replied in a letter dated 9 August 1945 – that is, three days after the Hiroshima bomb and on the same day as the Nagasaki bomb – in the following terms:

I know that Japan is a terribly cruel and uncivilized nation in warfare but I can't bring myself to believe that, because they are beasts, we should ourselves act in the same manner. For myself, I certainly regret the necessity of wiping out whole populations because of the 'pigheadedness' of the leaders of a nation and, for your information, I am not going to do it unless absolutely

necessary . . . my object is to save as many American lives as possible but I also have a humane feeling for the women and children in Japan.[57]

Next to this passage must be placed one from a speech broadcast by Truman on the radio that same day:

> The world will note that the first atomic bomb was dropped on Hiroshima, a military base. That was because we wished in this first attack to avoid, insofar as possible, the killing of civilians. But that attack is only a warning of things to come. If Japan does not surrender, bombs will have to be dropped on her war industries and, unfortunately, thousands of civilian lives will be lost. I urge Japanese civilians to leave industrial cities immediately, and save themselves from destruction.[58]

As these passages show, the same official line was adopted by the United States for the atom-bomb attacks as by the British government for RAF area bombing of Germany: that the targets were industrial and military. It is significant to note that in *public* statements of this line, no effort was made to redefine civilians as legitimate military targets in circumstances of total war; that thought was reserved for discussions within government and high-command circles, and later among defenders of the bombing strategies adopted by the Allies in the Second World War.

A thorny problem now faces this examination of the attitudes of those who planned and directed Allied bombing campaigns. Why was it taken by Air Marshals Portal and Harris to be acceptable that, as a means of beating Germany, its cities should be destroyed? It cannot be that they saw nothing beyond the goal of victory in itself; they must have thought about how things would be in Germany after victory was secured. In the months following the D-Day landings they had direct knowledge of difficulties caused to Allied troops who were obliged to

move – and more to the point, fight – across areas of France and the Low Countries which had been severely damaged by Allied bombing. Caen was a striking instance. Its streets were so piled with rubble that vehicles could not move through them until they had been cleared, and it was obvious that a part-demolished urban environment was excellent territory for defenders, who could only be defeated building by broken building. The Air Force chiefs, and their political masters, must assuredly have realised that a pulverised Germany was going to present an even more difficult task for troops on the ground.

But what about their forward planning for the situation when Allied forces would be in possession of Germany? Did it not occur to the Air Force chiefs and their political superiors that a defeated population would need to be governed and policed, and in the process at very least fed, watered, housed, and given medical attention? Portal and Harris themselves might have thought that this would be the responsibility of others, and that their task was solely to beat Germany into surrender, after which they could wash their hands of the affair. This would have involved taking a very limited view of matters. Suppose they did so; did not higher authority have a view on the matter? What was government on both sides of the Atlantic thinking about post-war affairs? What plans were being made, and why did they not take into account the potential difficulties represented by the immense material damage daily being made worse in Germany's main cities even as the war drew to a close?

Or were these considerations indeed being taken into account, and welcomed?

At the end of *The Natural History of Destruction* W. G. Sebald reports receiving a letter from one Dr H, a citizen of Darmstadt. 'I had to read it several times, because at first I could not believe my eyes,' Sebald tells us.

It propounds the theory that the Allies waged war in the air with the aim of cutting off the Germans from their origins and inheritance by destroying their cities, thus paving the way for

the cultural invasion and general Americanisation that ensued in the post-war period. This deliberate strategy, continues the letter from Darmstadt, was devised by Jews living abroad, exploiting the special knowledge of the human psyche, foreign cultures and foreign mentalities that they are known to have acquired in their wanderings.[59]

Sebald was rightly disturbed by this letter, the anti-Semitism of which betrays its affinities with German neo-Nazism. Had Sebald consulted the internet he might have seen there that neo-Nazis everywhere, and not least their North American 'white supremacist' subset, make common cause in racism and conspiracy theories of the kind suggested by Dr H. Unhappily, some of the thinking put forward during the course of the Second World War about what to do with post-war Germany plays directly into their hands – just as it played into Goebbels' hands during the war, giving him a propaganda coup and the Nazi regime an excuse for encouraging Germany as a whole to fight to the very last ounce of its strength in 1945. For alas, responsible individuals in Roosevelt's government did indeed put forward a plan for post-war Germany that, if not quite Dr H's fantasy, was uncomfortably close to it. The area bombing of Germany's cities meant destroying its libraries, schools, universities, theatres, museums, art galleries, shops, monuments, architectural treasures, clinics, hotels, workshops, studios, concert halls – in short: its cultural fabric, its embodied memory and character. And this was in addition to the destruction of its houses and factories, municipal offices and waterworks, roads and bridges, to say nothing of its people – in short: its capacity to function. This pulverisation of the physical, cultural and human fabric of Germany was allowed to continue on a massive scale until the very last month of the war, not just unabated but with increasing intensity; which makes it natural to wonder whether it represented an intention to so cripple Germany that it could not revive to become yet again, as it had twice been in the preceding thirty years, a dangerous and oppressive destroyer of world peace.

For material destruction is merely instrumental to a more profound kind of destruction – the destruction of what has since come to be called 'social capital', in the form of the institutions and culture on the basis of which a society functions. No one wished Nazism and its institutions to survive, for very good reasons; but the question is, was the area-bombing campaign in any way an adjunct to a desire to put an end to Germany as such? Was it an attempt at what might be called 'culturecide'?

The controversial plan for post-war Germany briefly accepted by Roosevelt and Churchill is known as the Morgenthau Plan after the man who devised it, Henry Morgenthau Jr, Secretary of the Treasury to President Roosevelt for eleven years from 1934 to 1945, and therefore a key figure in Roosevelt's New Deal. As the war in Europe was reaching a climax Morgenthau put forward a plan to de-industrialise the Ruhr, reassigning parts of Germany to France and Poland, and divide the remainder of Germany into two purely agricultural states. The aim of weakening and 'pastoralising' Germany was of course to ensure that it could not again become powerful; and as Morgenthau's book *Germany Is Our Problem* (1945) argued, it was necessary to ensure this by institutional means, since the Germans were in his view by nature 'militaristic'.[60] After initial acceptance by both Roosevelt and Churchill at the second Quebec conference in 1944 it was abandoned by both, partly through the efforts of the indefatigable Henry Stimson, and partly because Churchill recognised that a restored Germany would be needed in the coming stand-off with the Soviet Union in Europe. At one point, indeed, he contemplated quickly allying the Allies with a post-Nazi Germany so that the Wehrmacht could be used in fighting back a Soviet advance which – so Churchill for a time feared – might go all the way to the Atlantic coast.

But the rejection of the Morgenthau Plan did not happen quickly enough to escape the notice of Goebbels, who made good use of it to stiffen German fighting resolve. Any Germans contemplating sur-render to the Allies in the West, in order to forestall too great a

conquest by the Soviets in the East, were discouraged by the 'apocalyptic vision' that Goebbels could now paint of life under Allied occupation, given the terms of the Plan.[61] Alluding also to suggestions put forward by others who thought that radical steps should be taken to prevent Germans from again being a threat to peace, he wrote:

> [Our enemies say] that Germany had been treated too mildly by the Treaty of Versailles, and that it must be entirely beaten down after this war . . . A few days ago, the official English news agency Reuters carried a cable from an overseas émigré newspaper supported by the British government. It proposed that all German children between two and six years of age should be taken from their mothers and sent abroad for 25 years. This would lead the Germans, it said, to forget their nationality. A mixed ethnic brew would result that could no longer be called German. Had Reuters not carried this nonsense, one might have done the English government the favour of assuming that this outrageous proposal was the result of a deranged mind . . . Our women know what their sons are fighting for, and our women know what their husbands are fighting for. Each worker and each farmer is more certain than ever before of why he is swinging his hammer or standing behind his plough. Millions of children look to us. The enemy sees our future in them, and wants to destroy them. So let us get to work! The enemy has told us what is at stake.[62]

The Morgenthau Plan's negative effects seem to have been felt after the war, at least in an indirect and temporary way. They did this by influencing Roosevelt's attitude to the concessive plans drawn up by his State and War Departments for post-war Germany. These plans jointly envisaged a self-supporting Germany in which a reasonably high standard of living would be maintained, and for this to happen (so the State Department plan required) there should be 'no large-scale and permanent impairment of . . . German industry'. Roosevelt,

apparently at Morgenthau's insistence, sent a highly critical memorandum to Stimson and Secretary of State Cordell Hull, saying that these plans were unacceptable because they would bring Germany too rapidly back to its pre-war state.[63]

Roosevelt and Churchill agreed to the Morgenthau Plan on 15 September 1944 at the second Quebec conference, initialling a draft of it which provided for 'eliminating the war-making industries in the Ruhr and the Saar' and 'looking forward to converting Germany into a country primarily agricultural and pastoral in character'. Anthony Eden, Churchill's Foreign Secretary, and Cordell Hull, his equivalent in the Roosevelt administration, were both horrified when they found this out. In his memoirs Eden wrote, 'I did not like the plan, nor was I convinced that it was to our national advantage.' Hull called it 'a plan of blind vengeance', and Stimson said it was 'just fighting brutality with brutality'.[64]

It seems that Churchill had at first been hostile to the idea, telling Morgenthau that it meant Britain would be 'chained to a dead body'; but he was then temporarily induced into accepting it by two considerations. One was that Britain was in desperate need of funds, and Morgenthau had given him to understand that 6.5 billion dollars' worth of post-war Lend-Lease arrangements were on offer. Since Roosevelt was in favour of the Plan, and since Churchill was the beggar not the chooser at the conference table, he felt that it would be politic to go along with it.

The other consideration was that his adviser Lord Cherwell (Professor Frederick Lindemann) persuaded him that the Morgenthau Plan would be to Britain's economic advantage in another way too. Cherwell claimed (in a communication to Churchill's physician Lord Moran) that Churchill began by saying that the plan was 'a cruel threat to the German people' – as indeed the Germans themselves did not need Goebbels' help to see – but that Cherwell had 'explained to Winston that the plan would save Britain from bankruptcy by eliminating a dangerous competitor . . . Winston had not thought of it in that way'.[65]

In the event Eden was able to dissuade Churchill, and more importantly Hull and Stimson were able to dissuade Roosevelt, and the plan was dropped.[66] In Churchill's case it did not take long to restore him to his first instinctive distrust of the idea of an economically inert Germany which could not be a trading partner for Britain and a market for British goods – to say nothing of needing profitable British input in the reconstruction process. But he had also quickly come to see the point earlier made, that a restored and viable Germany was needed for what would prove to be the coming Cold War, which Churchill foresaw with greater clarity than most, as his celebrated 'Iron Curtain' speech soon showed.

If the Morgenthau Plan had been a single instance of punitive thinking about Germany's post-war future, it might not be such fruitful terrain for far-right-wing apologists for Germany's Nazi past. But there were other advocates of a reduction of Germany, not a few of them calling for further and sometimes more extreme measures.[67] One was Bernadotte Schmitt, the Professor of Modern History at Chicago University, who specialised in Germany. He had first visited that country in 1906 while a Rhodes Scholar at Oxford, and had taken a profound dislike to it because of its militaristic character. 'I have never trusted Germany since', he wrote. In a speech to the National Council for Social Studies at Indianapolis in late November 1941, just over a week before the Japanese attack on Pearl Harbor, he called for a reduction of Germany's population from eighty million to thirty million, so that it would be less of a cuckoo in the European nest. He did not say how this was to be done.[68]

More extreme was Theodore Kaufman's *Germany Must Perish!*, self-published in 1940. It is an egregious example of the genre; it called for the systematic sterilisation of the German people so that once the existing German population died out there would no longer be an aggressive militaristic nation in the world to threaten its peace. 'Today's war is not a war against Adolf Hitler', the book begins.

Nor is it a war against Nazis. It is a war of peoples against peoples, of civilised peoples envisioning Light, against uncivilised barbarians who cherish Darkness . . . [Hitler, the Kaiser, Bismarck are] merely mirrors reflecting centuries-old inbred lust of the German nation for conquest and mass murder . . . This time Germany has forced TOTAL WAR upon the world. As a result, she must be prepared to pay a TOTAL PENALTY. And there is one, only one, such Total Penalty: Germany must perish forever! In fact – not fancy![69]

And so on. It is noteworthy that although this book was published by its own author, it was widely and on the whole positively reviewed; and this was before the United States entered the war, and before the mass murder of European Jewry in the Holocaust had fully begun.[70]

In 1944 a lawyer called Louis Nizer published (with a reputable publishing house, unlike Kaufman) *What to Do with Germany*, calling for the Nazi leadership, Gestapo and SS, army officers about the rank of colonel, officials of the German People's Courts (the kangaroo courts used for summary despatch of Nazism's opponents, 'defeatists', and others), and members of the Reichstag, to be put on trial for murder; and arguing that Germany should be de-industrialised, or at least that German industry be placed under foreign control. His indictment of the German character is uncompromising:

[N]o people can be innocent who have twice in one generation burst forth in aggression against all their neighbours, near and far. How is it that one spot on the surface of the earth, no larger than Texas, should so persistently explode and ravage the world?

And what were the toasts, the slogans, the anthems, the battle cries of this people? 'Der Tag' – when Germany will rule the world. 'Deutschland über Alles'. 'Tomorrow we will rule the world.' Rule the world! Rule the world! No people who can thrill to such a mission are innocent victims of wicked leaders.[71]

Worse, Nizer accused the Germans nation of being psychiatrically ill, suffering from a variety of sexually based disorders, principally sadism, homosexuality and bestiality. In a flight of rhetoric not entirely consistent with this thesis he asks, 'Is it possible that German cruelty and blood lust is traceable to sexual inhibitions? Is there significance in the pornographic tendencies of the German fed by such official documents as Streicher's *Stuermer*?'[72]

And so on again. But one refrain in Nizer's book, for all its mixture of intemperance and legalism – which no doubt struck a chord with many, given the degree of animosity against 'the Boche' during the war years – was the idea that the German people, not just its leaders but the people as a whole, bore a common responsibility for the engulfment of the world in war. This was because as a people – the generalisation comes all too naturally in such arguments – Germans are possessed of excessive characteristics that have always made them a menace to peace and stability. 'Under [Hitler, the Kaiser, Bismarck, Charlemagne] millions of Germans fought fanatically, heroically, sacrificially. Theirs was not conduct induced by compulsion,' Nizer argued, 'theirs was a will to execute a program and a readiness to die for it. The vaunted efficiency of German aggression depends on millions of little cogs acting in perfect co-ordination which involuntary compliance could not possibly produce.'[73]

The chorus of anti-German sentiment in the United States was a large one. Norman Cousins, editor of the *Saturday Review of Literature*, argued for the necessity of 'deep burning hatred' of Germans to potentiate the struggle against them.[74] The level of rhetoric rose when Rex Stout and Clifton Fadiman joined sixteen other literary figures on America's War Writers Board, a department of the Office of War Information responsible for propaganda. The Board provided the Office of War Information with supportive pens when skilful writing tasks needed to be done. According to James Martin, 'Fadiman was regarded by some as the most towering Germanophobe throughout the war, while others had as their outstanding figure in the field of action such as Lord Vansittart of

England, and such Americans as Shirer, Kaufman, Quentin Reynolds, Walter Winchell, Ben Hecht, Stout, Louis Nizer, and Henry Morgenthau, though a full roll-call would number in the hundreds.'[75]

The term 'collective guilt' as applied to the German people was coined by Robert, Lord Vansittart, who had been secretary to Stanley Baldwin and Ramsay MacDonald, and then Permanent Under-Secretary of State in the Foreign Office until his outspoken Germanophobia and his hostility to 'appeasers' led him to be sidelined in 1937 in a notional promotion to 'Foreign Office adviser'. (There is some suggestion that either then or during the course of the war he had a role in the intelligence services; he was described in the Canadian press in 1945 as 'a spokesman for British intelligence'.) In the mid-1930s British opinion about Hitler and Germany was deeply divided, and much acerbity infected the opposition between the two views. The *Times* newspaper was the flagship for pro-German and indeed pro-Hitler sentiment, while Churchill, Vansittart and others maintained a robust anti-German line, warning of the dangers posed by Hitler and the prospect of revived German military adventurism. In the event they were proved right, but in Vansittart's case the argument went beyond the need to defeat Nazi Germany; he wanted to see measures that would decisively and permanently prevent Germany from a second resurrection as a military menace.

Vansittart was raised to the peerage in 1940, and used the House of Lords as a platform for proposing harsh measures against Germany once the war was over. So uncompromising were his views that extremer versions of Germanophobia came to be called 'vansittartism'. In his book *Bones of Contention* (published just before the war's end, in March 1945) he wrote 'The Germans are savage to a degree almost inconceivable to anyone who has not had actual experience of them, and are a people born to deceit.' These were not his own words; he was quoting the first-century Roman historian Paterculus, and he went on to quote Tacitus, Seneca, Claudian, Nazarius, Ammianus, Marcellinus, Ennodius, Quintilian and Josephus to the same effect.[76]

In the House of Lords on 10 March 1943, during the course of a debate on the question of post-war Germany, he said,

> I am not wishing to destroy Germany. I desire only . . . to destroy Germany utterly and for ever as a military power; and I further desire . . . to make an end for ever of all German pretensions, intrigues and efforts to gain economical hegemony of Europe . . . Subject to those trifling reservations, I welcome the survival of Germany with one proviso only, and that is that it shall be a totally different Germany.[77]

Akin to the ideas of 'collective guilt' and 'flawed national character' is the premise for Daniel Goldhagen's *Hitler's Willing Executioners: Ordinary Germans and the Holocaust*, published in 1996, which imputes to the entire German people a practically genetic anti-Semitism and therefore capacity for genocide, in which any 'ordinary German' is by his nature capable of participating, and for which the character of the German people as a whole is responsible. Goldhagen's book was controversial not only for reviving this view, but for the questionable character of its scholarship, which is a separate matter.[78] The point of interest for present purposes is that if in 1996 such indictments of the German people *as a whole* were still possible, attitudes during the war itself to the question of post-war Germany were, obviously and at least, as likely to be coloured by generalised thinking of just that kind. The examples cited of extreme views such as Kaufman's and Nizer's, and views that almost translated into policy such as Morgenthau's, accordingly provide a background to understanding the thinking of those directly engaged in the struggle with Germany. Army men had the opposing army to fight; the Navy had the opposing navy to fight; the RAF alone had the towns, cities and people of Germany deliberately and literally in its sights, and therefore the question of what might be done during the course of the war to influence matters after it, was much more present for them than for

those in the army and navy. (Given the precision-bombing aspirations of the USAAF in the European theatre, consideration of its leaders' attitudes are more relevant to the question of post-war Japan.)

A way of viewing this point from another perspective helps to clarify it further. In the Bosnian war of 1992–5, ultra-nationalist Serbs targeted Sarajevo's library in order to destroy the thousands of Ottoman, Persian and Arabic manuscripts held there. The Spanish writer Juan Goytisolo described this as an attempt to kill Bosnian Muslim memories and to make way for a new Serbian mythology of conquest. He called it 'memoricide'. In fact and legend alike the examples of memoricide, or what I suggest more generally and accurately might be called *culturecide*, are legion; history runs over with stories of the sack and destruction of cities, the extinction of cultures (think of native cultures in North and Central America, the ancient Celts of Western Europe, the aboriginals of India), iconoclasm (the Puritan destruction of murals, statuary and devotional objects), the burning of books and those who wrote them (by Qin Shi, the First Emperor of China; by the Inquisition) – examples are legion.

For some – and this does not include latter-day neo-Nazis and their like, for whom such questions are not matters of serious speculation but rabid certainty – it matters to ask how different was the attempt to raze Germany's major cities to the ground. Such an attempt was made: so much is fact. What was the intention? A city does not consist just of houses and factories (we are leaving aside for the moment the question of the people living there). To repeat and re-emphasise: it has libraries, schools, hospitals, universities, theatres, museums, monuments, churches, meeting halls, laboratories, concert halls with violins and pianos in them, art galleries with paintings and sculpture in them, craft workshops, antique shops, bookshops, newspaper offices, buildings of architectural importance, in fact the whole array and panoply of culture, education, literacy, artistic endeavour and civilised life. In the immediate aftermath of a bombing attack the survivors need victuals and shelter. But in the longer term, water, food

and a place out of the rain are not enough for permanency, still less for revival and growth. And once the inheritance of a community has gone, it takes time to build a new one. Many of Germany's cities were places of beauty and charm before the Nazi period; when it was over, 40 per cent of the seventy largest cities had been demolished, mainly by bombing. Tracts of them are functional and visually rather sterile places now. Is it possible to believe that this programme of destruction was carried out without any thought of its effect on the post-war situation, and even the longer-term future of the country and its population?

As shown by how Eden, Cordell Hull, Stimson and eventually Churchill reacted to the Morgenthau Plan, there was in the end no serious possibility that a Morgenthau-style policy would be implemented in full for post-war Germany – although in the event Germany was indeed divided, a result that was accepted with a degree of satisfaction in some quarters, despite the Cold War implications. Correlatively, given the need seen by the Allied leadership for the eventual reconstruction of at least West Germany and its post-Nazi rehabilitation into the international order, there can also have been no intention to so pulverise Germany that recovery would be impossible. Yet the bombing of Germany gives every appearance to hindsight of a concerted smashing of as much of Germany, its people and its cultural heritage as possible. The same can be said of the USAAF's area bombing of Japan. If the war in either the European or the Pacific theatre had lasted months more, or another year, with the area-bombing campaigns continuing their intensifying curve, the impression given would be one of an attempt at annihilation. Harris, famously or notoriously, had a list of cities to be bombed, and which he insisted on bombing. In February and March of 1945 his bombers systematically sought them out and bombed them – which meant that they destroyed ancient and beautiful German towns with little or no military significance, as the destruction of Würzburg and Hildesheim shows.[79]

What explains the large and apparent discrepancy between the

continued campaign of destruction and the fact that the thrust of official Allied policy on post-war Germany was that it would be de-Nazified, reconstructed, and returned to the international fold?

The answer I offer has to be tentative because it is speculative. In the case of RAF bombing in the European theatre, two factors were jointly operative. One was the relative autonomy of Bomber Command, and the other was the dynamic of its constantly growing number of bombers and bombs, all needing to be used, and in the closing period of the war in skies far less dangerous than in the early years. This gave an impetus to its campaign like the gathering speed of a lorry without brakes rolling down a hill. Until April 1945 the Wehrmacht was resisting on the Western Front with tenacity, and Allied progress was painfully slow. So the continued use of every available means of battering the enemy – even the bombing of unmilitary towns behind the front – continued to be permitted, though the strategic (as opposed to tactical, i.e. battlefield) bombing was not regarded by army commanders on the ground as having much relevance to their immediate task.

In the case of the USAAF in the Pacific theatre, the ferocity and destructiveness of its area-bombing campaign there is also explainable by two factors. One was the belief and hope that a bombing campaign could win the war against Japan without an invasion. The other was – to use blunt terms – racism towards and anger against the Japanese. There were at least four main reasons for this. One was the perfidy of the Pearl Harbor attack. Another was Japanese cruelty to American prisoners of war as testified by those liberated during the American advance along the Pacific islands. A third was the ferocity of the Japanese as fighters in contesting those advances. The fourth was the tactic of Kamikaze attacks, displaying what the Americans took to be a repugnant degree of weird oriental fanaticism. All these factors made the Japanese seem subhuman. American propaganda at the time portrayed them as such, in words and pictures, and the attitude was not merely rhetorical.

Ronald Schaffer remarks that American attitudes to the Japanese

had begun to harden well before Pearl Harbor, not least because of stories about the atrocities they committed in China. They knew about the infamous Bataan Death March before their bombers had bases within range of the Japanese home islands, and they knew that captured American airmen had been executed by Japanese troops. All this made American military attitudes to the Japanese deeply hostile. General 'Tooey' Spaatz reported after the war that there was a widespread feeling in the US Army Air Force of repugnance for the Japanese; General Haywood Hansell said it was a 'universal feeling' among American airmen and troops that the Japanese were 'subhuman'.[80]

The USAAF's chief, General 'Hap' Arnold, shared this view. He wrote in his diary for 16 June 1945 after visiting Manila, lately liberated from the Japanese:

> Apparently the atrocities by the Japs have never been told in the US – babies thrown up in the air and caught on bayonets – autopsies on living people – burning prisoners to death by sprinkling them with gasoline and throwing in a hand grenade to start a fire. If any tried to escape they were killed by machine guns as they came out of the door. More and more of the stories which can apparently be substantiated.[81]

He heard stories about rape and murder, and found that those who had suffered at the Japanese troops' hands had no thought of 'sparing any Japs, [whether] men, women or children', but instead a desire 'to use gas, fire, anything to exterminate the race'.[82]

The next entry in Arnold's diary is the sketch of a plan for the air attack on Japan, 'to completely destroy Jap industries and major cities' and 'complete destruction of Japan proper'. This was very different from the 'Hap' Arnold of the European theatre, one of the architects of precision bombing. Schaffer records a telling anecdote about a meeting after the Hiroshima bomb was dropped, at which Leslie Groves, the director of the Manhattan Project, was told by

General George Marshall not to rejoice too much about what had happened, because of the civilian deaths caused. Groves replied that his thoughts were not on the Japanese dead but the men of the Bataan March. Outside Marshall's office Arnold slapped Groves on the back and said, 'I'm glad you said that – that's just the way I feel.'[83]

General Curtis LeMay, in charge of the area bombing of Japan, felt the same way as his comrades did. He described the firebombing of Tokyo in uncompromising terms: 'We scorched and boiled and baked to death more people in Tokyo on that night of March 9–10 than went up in vapour in Hiroshima and Nagasaki combined.'[84] He is famous for saying, 'Killing Japanese didn't bother me very much at the time . . . I suppose if I had lost the war, I would have been tried as a war criminal . . . every soldier thinks something of the moral aspects of what he is doing. But all war is immoral and if you let that bother you, you're not a good soldier.' And he is equally famous for saying, when Chief of Staff of the US Air Force during the early years of the Vietnam War, that he planned to bomb the North Vietnamese 'back to the Stone Age'.[85]

It might seem odd to invoke the autonomy of RAF Bomber Command as an explanation for the unremitting character of its area bombing of Germany as the war approached an end. Two facts explain it. One is an examination of the diaries of Lord Alanbrooke, who as Field Marshal Sir Alan Brooke was Chief of the Imperial General Staff during the Second World War, and therefore chairman of the Chiefs of Staff (COS) committee comprising the heads of the British army, navy and air force. His diaries show – and they give one a frisson of surprise in doing so – how very little importance was attached by COS and the British government to the area-bombing campaign carried out by Bomber Command.[86] That is to say: COS and Churchill's war cabinet were content to let the entire apparatus of bombing continue to function, from aircraft and bomb production to Harris's almost independent direction of efforts at the sharp end, partly because they thought it kept general pressure on the enemy,

and partly because it would have been more complicated to stop it than to leave it running.

In Alanbrooke's diary every COS meeting is mentioned, and its topic; these meetings were held on an almost daily basis. Air Marshal Sir Arthur Harris is mentioned just twice in the whole diary, both times disparagingly. On 13 October 1943, as Bomber Command's endeavours were gearing up towards the Battle of Berlin, Alanbrooke wrote (with his characteristic plethora of exclamation marks):

> Bert Harris came to see us this morning during the COS meeting. According to him the only reason why the Russian Army has succeeded in advancing is due to the results of the bomber offensive!! According to him I am certain that we are all preventing him from winning the war. If Bomber Command was left to itself it would make much shorter work of it all![87]

On 15 May 1944 Alanbrooke recorded the meeting at which General Eisenhower, King George VI, all the British and American Chiefs of Staff, and commanding officers in positions like Harris's, were present to review the D-Day plans. He writes, 'Bert Harris told us how well he might have won this war if it had not been for the handicap imposed by the existence of the other two services!'[88]

Sir Charles Portal figures much more in Alanbrooke's diaries, because the two were colleagues on the COS committee and therefore in continual contact. As shown in chapter 2 above, Portal began as an eager advocate of area bombing's war-winning potential, but in the later stages of the war he also saw the point of precision attacks on vital industries such as oil. As already noted, he conducted a long-running tussle with Harris to try to get the latter to redirect Bomber Command's energies towards this task. The very fact of this tussle is proof of the high degree of independence Harris enjoyed as a result of the relative irrelevance of his area-bombing campaign to the rest of the war effort. 'Spent afternoon in the office battling with Portal's latest ideas for the policy of conduct of this war. Needless to say it is based

on bombing Germany at the expense of everything else,' Alanbrooke wrote on 29 September 1942.[89] Portal's commitment to the idea that bombing wins wars never diminished. Alanbrooke reports that at a 'long and difficult' COS meeting on 1 May 1945, devoted to discussion of the war in the East, Portal tabled a proposal 'to establish long range bomber groups on an island near Formosa'.[90]

It is clear that Alanbrooke and Churchill were in agreement about what could be expected from bombing, namely, that at most and best it was an 'annoyance' to Germany. Churchill, it will be remembered, said as much after receiving the Butt report on bombing accuracy (or more correctly, inaccuracy): 'It is very debatable whether bombing by itself will be a decisive factor in the present war . . . the most we can say is that it will be a heavy and I trust seriously increasing annoyance.'[91]

Bomber Command did have two other uses, though. One was its utility as a morale-booster on the home front, as shown by the excitement generated in the press by the 1,000-bomber attack on Cologne, the Dam Busters raid, the firebombing of Hamburg, and stories about the pounding given to Berlin in the winter before the invasion. There was nothing adventitious about the improvement in civilian morale thus generated. In a long war whose first years had been gloomy and fraught with danger, the knowledge that Britain was hitting back was a powerful psychological support. It released other feelings too, at least for some, of satisfaction that the Germans were being paid in kind, and more, for what they had done to British cities and towns in the Blitz of 1940–1.

The other major use of the area-bombing campaign was as a means of pacifying Stalin – at least to some extent – who was desperate for the western Allies to take action in their region of the war to ease the pressure on the Eastern Front. What he most wanted was a Second Front – an invasion of the European continent from the west – and he wanted it in 1942, long before it was possible for the western Allies to contemplate such a thing. Temporising, they made vague promises to the effect that a Second Front would be opened in that year, but what

happened instead was that Rommel captured Tobruk, and Germany seemed poised for victory. The Russians by sheer blood and guts turned the balance of the war by themselves in the closing weeks of 1942. In the preceding summer of that year relations between Russia and the western Allies were strained by Stalin's accusations against them of bad faith, weakness and cowardice. Provoked by this, at the end of July Churchill suggested to Stalin that they meet face to face, and Stalin invited Churchill to the Kremlin. Churchill arrived in Moscow on 12 August 1942, and set about explaining to Stalin why nothing could be done about a Second Front in the remainder of that year.[92] It began as a bad-tempered meeting, with Stalin accusing the Allies of being afraid of the Germans and reluctant to take risks, without which, he said, wars cannot be won. But Churchill had two trump cards to play; one was the plan for Operation Torch, the Anglo-American landings in North Africa in the rear of Rommel's army; and the other was the plan for a massive assault on Germany by Bomber Command. Richard Overy describes what happened when Churchill told Stalin of these prospects:

> The mood of the meeting lightened. Stalin liked Torch. He saw straight away that it would secure the defeat of Rommel, and speed up the withdrawal of Italy from the war. But what he liked most was the bombing. The American envoy, Averill Harriman, who was present throughout the meeting, wired Roosevelt the next day that the mention of bombing elicited 'the first agreement between the two men'. Stalin came to life for the first time in the conference. He told Churchill to bomb homes as well as factories; he suggested the best urban targets. 'Between the two of them,' Harriman continued, 'they had soon destroyed most of the important industrial cities of Germany.' The tension eased. Stalin accepted that the British could, as Churchill put it, only 'pay our way by bombing Germany'. [Churchill] promised a 'ruthless' bombardment to shatter the morale of the German people.[93]

And so Bomber Command was set on its course, interrupted only by the temporary needs of the invasion in 1944, but able to return to the path Harris regarded as its destiny in the autumn of that year. It had already been given its area-bombing remit in the directive of 14 February 1942, and that remit was reinforced by the 'Pointblank' directive agreed between Britain and the United States at the Casablanca conference of January 1943, which outlined the direction of the combined offensive to be undertaken by the RAF and USAAF bomber forces: the former to continue its night attacks, the latter to seek its targets by day.[94]

Apart from the efforts made by Portal to engage Harris in attacks on oil late in the war, the only move made to redirect or limit area bombing thereafter came when Churchill issued his famous minute of 28 March 1945, at last questioning the area-bombing strategy.[95] A point not often stressed in connection with this minute relates to its concluding paragraph: 'The Foreign Secretary has spoken to me on this subject, and I feel the need for more precise concentration upon military objectives, such as oil and communications behind the immediate battle-zone, rather than on mere acts of terror and wanton destruction, however impressive.'[96] This minute was withdrawn after protests from Portal and the Air Ministry, but it had let a cat out of the bag. Sir Anthony Eden, the Foreign Secretary, had evidently become anxious about post-war reflection on the nature of the area-bombing campaign, perhaps as a result of discussions with Stimson, whose views on the subject were clear. Eden evidently therefore decided to urge Churchill to the same thoughts, and the 28 March minute was the result. Just before the Dresden bombing six weeks earlier, Churchill had been enthusiastic for a blow to show support for the Russian advance; and perhaps, in the same spirit as American use of atomic bombing to educate Russian sensibilities, he also wished to show the Russians what British bombing could do.[97] At the Yalta conference Stalin had asked for communications behind Germany's Eastern Front to be attacked, to interdict the movement of reinforce-ments. Berlin and Leipzig were mentioned as targets, but not

Dresden, one important reason being that the Russians 'clearly preferred to keep the RAF and USAAF away from territory they might soon be occupying'.[98] Whatever the logic, by the time Churchill came to write the 28 March minute, his attitude to the area-bombing campaign had changed. If beforehand it had been an alternating mixture of interest and relative indifference, it was now negative. In his victory broadcast on BBC radio on 13 May 1945 he did not mention Bomber Command. No campaign medal was struck for those who took part in Bomber Command's work, and Arthur Harris was not allowed to publish his final Despatch summarising his command's activities in the war.

The speculative conclusion that might be reached, in the light of all this, is that although there was no Allied policy to cripple Germany so badly that after the war it would be fit for nothing but 'pastoralisation', nevertheless the quasi-autonomy of Bomber Command meant that right until the last weeks of the war it continued to act in ways that gave every impression of trying to bring about just such a result. In the minds of Harris especially and of Portal too, a perhaps unspoken assumption seems to have operated: that a bombing strategy aimed at *destroying the will and capacity of the German people to wage war* easily translates into the thought that such bombing also ensures *the destruction of the will and capacity to be in a position to wage war again* or at least *later*, once the present war was over.

It would I think be too much to claim that RAF Bomber Command in a semi-autonomous way consciously attempted a kind of Morgenthau Plan of its own. But by default that is exactly what the tendency of massive urban destruction was. Note that this is a point still independent of the question whether the area-bombing campaign was morally right or wrong. After all, there were voices, among them Morgenthau's, arguing that this was the right thing to do. But Harris and Portal cannot themselves be blamed or praised alone – depending on point of view – for the Morgenthau-like tendency of the bombing campaign. The top level of Allied, and especially British, military and political leadership have to accept the major share of responsibility for

initiating it and for letting it continue. Whether that responsibility is culpable is the chief point at issue in this book.

One very important point remains to be discussed to complete an understanding of the mind of the bombers, which is to comment on the war circumstances in which their thinking unfolded. These circumstances explain the reasons for the change in British and American thinking about air strategy, which in turn led to changes in practice from attempts at precision bombing to area bombing. For the British this change occurred in February 1942, and for the Americans it occurred in the Pacific theatre in late 1944. In the case of both countries the policy followed the facts rather than the other way round. Bomber Command's navigational and bomb-aiming difficulties meant that it had in practice been bombing civilian areas already, although trying to hit more specific targets, before the area-bombing directive of 14 February 1942. The same applies to the endeavours of the Eighth and Fifteenth Army Air Forces over Europe. But the practical difficulty of hitting precision targets was only one factor in forcing that change. More significant were the war situations in both Europe and the Pacific. It is these that are standardly invoked as part of the justification for area bombing in both theatres. A discussion of these factors is given in chapter 7 below.

5

Voices of Conscience

THERE WERE MORE conscientious objectors in the First than in the Second World War for the good reason that the latter was, from the Allied point of view, a justified war, and widely understood to be so. It was justified because it consisted in resistance to the unarguable fact of military aggression by jack-booted Fascism. But there were people for whom it mattered that the war should be not only a justified one, but a justly fought one, and to whom therefore some of the Allies' actions were unacceptable. One thing such people were concerned about was the blockade of continental Europe, in light of the suffering it caused to those in occupied countries such as Greece where, for a time, famine threatened.

But a much greater concern was the area-bombing campaign. In the summer of 1941 a Committee for the Abolition of Night Bombing was set up by the British Quaker pacifist Corder Catchpool, who had been a volunteer ambulance driver in the First World War until conscription was introduced. Then, because he refused to take part in any alternative to military duties which might aid the war effort, he was sent to prison for two years' hard labour. After the outbreak of the Second World War he was impelled by two things to set up his committee against night bombing: the experience of the Blitz, and a letter to *The Times* newspaper on 17 April 1941 from George Bell, Bishop of Chichester, who asked, 'if Europe is civilised at

all, what can excuse the bombing of towns by night and terrorising of non-combatants?' In his letter Bell called on both Germany and Britain to forswear the tactic, and Catchpool decided to lobby to try to get at least his own country to comply.

Catchpool's commitment to the cause of peace was a deep and active one. While still in prison in 1918 he published an account of his experiences as both pacifist and prisoner.[1] After his release he went to Germany to work for the Friends War Victims Relief Committee, set up to further the task of reconciliation between the combatant nations. He remained in Germany for a time after the Nazi regime came to power, but his help for Jews attracted the attentions of the Gestapo, and he was arrested and interrogated by them. He returned to England soon afterwards. He had no illusions about Nazi Germany, but he adhered to his Quaker pacifist principles despite that.

Among those Catchpool invited to join his committee were Professor Stanley Jevons, T. C. Foley, Stuart Morris, and the novelist and eloquently vocal pacifist Vera Brittain. Not all of its members were pacifists like Vera Brittain and Catchpool himself, but they were all deeply opposed to bombing civilians. The committee's first endeavour was to organise a petition asking the British government to give up bombing by night; surprisingly for the time and circumstances, the petition gathered 15,000 names, among them those of three bishops, six Members of Parliament, and a mixture of pacifists and non-pacifists.

When it became clear in the spring of 1942 that the RAF was stepping up its bombing efforts – this was at the time of Arthur Harris's appointment – the Committee for the Abolition of Night Bombing reconfigured itself as the Bombing Restriction Committee, and redoubled its efforts. In her fortnightly *Letter* written and published for the peace movement, Vera Brittain wrote: '[We] must decide whether we want the government to continue to carry out through its Bomber Command a policy of murder and massacre in our name. Has any nation the right to make its young men the instruments of such a policy?'[2]

The committee's aim was to gather information about the status of area bombing in international law, to support the International Red Cross's efforts to designate 'sanctuary areas' free from bombing, and to provide data for Bishop Bell to use in his attacks on area bombing in the House of Lords. In the matter of data-gathering it was singularly successful.

George Bell's attitude to the conduct of the war was not a function of other-worldly innocence. He knew rather better than many what was at stake in Nazi Germany. Before the outbreak of hostilities in 1939 he was active in helping people of Jewish origin gain asylum in Britain, and he had maintained contact with people engaged in the opposition to Hitler, among them Dietrich Bonhoeffer and Martin Niemöller. In 1942 Bell and Bonhoeffer met in neutral Stockholm, and Bonhoeffer asked Bell to convey a message to the British government, asking for its support in a plot to overthrow Hitler. The German underground required that Britain would recognise a successor government to the Nazi regime, and agree to a truce. Bell told Anthony Eden and Stafford Cripps about the request when he returned home, and they in turn told Churchill. But the British government did not respond; it gave no assurances, and instead soon afterwards adopted the policy, devised in discussions with Roosevelt at the Casablanca Conference, of 'unconditional surrender'.

The disappointment of these endeavours did not stop Bell from trying to moderate Britain's bombing campaign, to which he gave the frank name of 'obliteration bombing'. He was almost a lone voice in the Church, which disapproved of his stance; it is commonly agreed that because of his repeated and outspoken criticism of the bombing he was not chosen to succeed William Temple as Archbishop of Canterbury when the latter died in October 1944.[3] He did however have one church ally in the House of Lords, in the form of Cosmo Lang, a former Archbishop of Canterbury. More representative of the Church's official line was the Archbishop of York, Cyril Foster Garbett, who went so far as to state his support for area bombing in print.

But Bell was not alone in Parliament as a whole. In the upper House his views were shared by Lord Addison and the Marquis of Salisbury as well as Lord Lang, and in the House of Commons by Richard Stokes, Reginald Sorensen and Rhys Davies.

In addition to providing parliamentarians with ammunition for their efforts, the Bombing Restriction Committee was concerned to keep the public informed of what was being done on its behalf and in its name, and to challenge the obfuscations and untruths in government statements about the aims and nature of the bombing offensive. The committee published posters and leaflets, and Vera Brittain began work on what was to be a pamphlet but turned into a short book which had an explosive impact on the debate about bombing: her *Seed of Chaos: What Mass Bombing Really Means*, published in the spring of 1944.

The immediate impulse for this remarkable little book was Operation Gomorrah – the firebombing of Hamburg in July 1943 – and the opening of the 'Battle of Berlin' in November 1943, together with the triumphalist tone of reports about these attacks in the British press. Angered and disgusted by this, and filled with a sense of urgency, Brittain set to work to digest the information amassed by the Bombing Restriction Committee so that the public could have a full picture of what was happening. She chose her title from Alexander Pope's *Dunciad* Book IV: 'Then rose the seed of Chaos, and of Night/ To blot out order and extinguish light', and her epigraph from the Book of Jeremiah 6: 15: 'Were they ashamed when they had committed abomination?'[4]

Despite both the fame of its author and the rage of controversy it caused, *Seed of Chaos* did not remain in print long because, no doubt, it was regarded merely as a book of its moment, and its polemical and exhortatory purpose is tied to that moment. But any discussion of the morality of war and the place of civilians in war is in fact its moment too, which is one good reason for summarising it here.[5] But a yet more compelling reason is that it is a truly invaluable resource for showing the nature and degree of contemporary understanding of the

bombing campaign as it unfolded, for it wonderfully preserves a record of the intellectual battle Britain had with itself about the bombing campaign's justification and moral status, even at a period when the war's outcome – though looking more optimistic every day – was still uncertain, and when the comparative question of the heinousness of Nazi atrocities, not least against European Jewry, had not yet made it easier for people on the Allied side to forgo inspection of their own moral linen.

What is further remarkable about Brittain's little book is that its insights, judgements, and factual grasp would be commendable enough had it been written a decade after the war, and yet it was written in the winter of 1943–4, even as the bombing campaign it criticised was increasing in volume and power, though still a year away from its crescendo in the war's final months. The book's very existence, then, shows that there can have been no illusions in informed minds, at least, about the nature of the bombing campaign and its effects; which makes questions about the intentions and knowledge of those who conducted the campaign easy to answer.

Brittain's book begins by suggesting that the British public did not fully comprehend what was happening in the bombed cities of Germany and elsewhere in Europe. Because of a national lack of imagination, she says, 'Throughout our history wrongs have been committed, or evils gone too long unremedied, simply because we did not perceive the real meaning of the suffering which we had caused or failed to mitigate.' By telling the public what the true facts are, she is confident that they will 'rise and demand a change of policy on the part of our rulers'.[6]

The government, she continues, have been skilful in concealing from the public the true nature of 'obliteration bombing'. They use such phrases as 'softening-up an area', 'neutralising the target', 'area bombing', 'saturating the defences', and 'blanketing an industrial district'. Until the summer of 1943 reports of air attacks on Germany and German-occupied Europe received small notices on the back

pages of newspapers; but then a change occurred, led by the *Daily Telegraph.* Full front-page coverage started to be given to bombing raids, and expert articles by pilots appeared on the inside pages. The first attacks of the Battle of Berlin in November 1943 'were apparently treated as gala occasions on which the whole Press was permitted to let itself go'. But when the facts are known, said Brittain, we realise the terrible sum of suffering this represents.[7]

People try to hide from the discomfort of this by using two main arguments. The first is that the bombing will shorten the war, 'a contention much favoured by Ministers, officials, Members of Parliament, and some leading Churchmen'. The second argument is that 'we too have suffered from obliteration bombing attacks', and are entitled to pay back in kind.

To the first argument Brittain gave four replies. First, there can be no certainty that bombing will shorten the war. But only absolute certainty could be invoked as a justification for what one commentator described as 'British boys being burnt to death in aeroplanes while they are roasting to death the population down below'. 'Mr Churchill himself has called the mass bombing an "experiment",' Brittain continued, thus showing that neither was he certain that it would shorten the war; but 'what does appear certain is the downward spiral in moral values, ending in the deepest abysses of the human spirit, to which this argument leads'. The Germans had argued in the First World War that their submarine blockade of Britain would shorten the war, but no one in Britain then thought this justified the policy.[8]

Churchill's 'experiment' remark had been reported in an article in *Time* magazine on 7 June 1943, which said that the commanders of the British and American bomber forces (Arthur Harris and Ira Eaker) had 'assured their military superiors that Germany can be bombed out of the war this year' but that Churchill had (as *Time* put it) 'stated the reaction of global strategists when he said, "The experiment is well worth trying so long as other measures are not excluded"'. The editor of *Time* had put Churchill's words in italics.

Brittain's second reply to the claim that bombing would shorten the war was that 'shorten' is a misleading concept in the circumstances. It implies the limiting or reduction of the total quantity of destruction and suffering that the war might cause, but 'in a vast, concentrated raid, lasting a few minutes, more persons may be killed or injured than in a modern major battle lasting two or three weeks'. And she added, this happens 'in addition to the destruction of an irreplaceable cultural heritage of monuments, art treasures and documents, representing centuries of man's creative endeavour. In fact, a mass bombing of great centres of population means *a speed-up of human slaughter, misery and material destruction imposed on that of the military fighting fronts*'.[9]

The third reply is that mass bombing does not cause revolt or the collapse of morale. The victims are too stunned and exhausted, too absorbed in the immediate tasks of survival, to start a revolution against their rulers. 'But when they recover, who can doubt that there will be, among the majority at any rate, the desire for revenge . . . thus we are steadily creating in Europe the psychological foundations for a third World War.'[10]

And fourth, the systematic demolition of German industry constitutes an injury to ourselves in the long term, given that the prosperity of the Continent has largely depended on it, and that Germany is one of Britain's best markets.[11] This argument, although doubtless from other sources, eventually weighed with Churchill a year later, after his Morgenthau lapse at the Quebec conference.

Brittain rebutteds the second argument – that the Germans had tried obliteration bombing on Britain first, and deserved to be repaid in kind – by quoting a characteristically sharp riposte to the idea from George Bernard Shaw: 'The blitzing of the cities has carried war this time to such a climax of infernal atrocity that all recriminations on that score are ridiculous. The Germans will have as big a bill of atrocities against us as we against them if we take them into an impartial international court.'[12] Here is one respect in which Shaw and Brittain were insufficiently informed, situated as they were in

1943: so far as a 'bill of atrocities' was concerned, Nazi Germany was going to outstrip all others by a very long way; so far as bombing was concerned, the Germans were already well behind the Allies.

But Brittain's book has other answers to the justified-reprisal argument. One is that the question of who started bombing civilians in areas far from the front lines of military conflict is not easy to answer. Bombs intended for industrial targets might be dropped by mistake on civilian areas; a reprisal raid is organised in kind; it provokes a further such reprisal – until eventually full-scale carpet bombing of cities is happening: 'the grim competition goes on, until the mass murder of civilians becomes part of our policy – a descent into barbarism which we should have contemplated with horror in 1939.'[13]

Moreover, although Britain suffered cruelly in the Blitz, the methods and weapons available to the RAF by the end of 1943 made mass bombing vastly worse. 'My own experience is relatively small, but as a Londoner who has been through about 600 raid periods and has spent 18 months as a volunteer fireguard, I have seen and heard enough to know that I at least must vehemently protest when this obscenity of terror is inflicted upon the helpless civilians of another country.' And she added, 'Nor do I believe that the majority of our airmen who are persuaded that mass bombing reduces the period of their peril really want to preserve their own lives by sacrificing German women and babies, any more than our soldiers would go into action using "enemy" mothers and children as a screen.'[14]

And third, retaliation 'in kind' simply reduces one to the level of one's enemies, and it is the perverted values of our enemies that made us fight them in the first place. Those in Britain who understood this most clearly were those who had most suffered from bombing. This was made plain by an opinion poll conducted in April 1941, when the Blitz was still happening, on the question: 'Would you approve or disapprove if the RAF adopted a policy of bombing the civilian population of Germany?' In heavily bombed areas such as inner London, 47 per cent disapproved of reprisals, 45 per cent approved,

and the rest were undecided, whereas in the northernmost counties of England where there had been no bombing, 76 per cent approved.[15]

As Brittain then points out, this poll showed the inaccuracy of a claim made by Churchill just two months afterwards: 'If tonight,' he said in a speech at London's County Hall, 'the people of London were asked to cast their vote whether a convention should be entered into to stop the bombing of all cities, the overwhelming majority would cry, "No, we will mete out to the Germans the measure, and more than the measure, that they have meted out to us".'[16]

Brittain was anxious to show how the progress of the war had effected a regress in the moral standards of its conduct. She therefore contrasted Churchill's County Hall speech with one he made on 27 January 1940, before he became Prime Minister, condemning the German bombing of urban targets in Poland as 'a new and odious form of attack', and stating the government's refusal to follow its example when people called for the RAF's bombers to be loaded with bombs instead of leaflets.[17] Eighteen months later Churchill told the House of Commons, 'As the year advances, German cities, harbours and centres of war production will be subjected to an ordeal the like of which has never been experienced by any country in continuity, severity or magnitude.'[18] A year later again, in a speech to the US Congress in Washington, he said, 'It is the duty of those who are charged with the direction of the War to . . . begin the process so necessary and desirable of laying the cities and the other military centres of Japan in ashes, for in ashes they must surely lie before peace comes to the world.'[19] Press reports in London the following day said that members of Congress were so enthusiastic that they did not applaud but 'shouted their approval'; which, as Brittain dryly pointed out, was not entirely consistent with the speech made to the same august body by Roosevelt just four months later, on 8 September 1943, when he assured Congress that 'we [Americans] are not bombing tenements for the sadistic pleasure of killing as the Nazis did, but blowing to bits carefully selected targets – factories, ship-yards, munition dumps'.[20]

In the same month, on 21 September, Churchill told the House of Commons,

> The almost total systematic destruction of many of the centres of German war effort continues on a greater scale and at a greater pace. The havoc wrought is indescribable and the effect upon the German war production in all its forms . . . is matched by that wrought on the life and economy of the whole of that guilty organisation . . . There are no sacrifices we will not make, no lengths in violence to which we will not go, to destroy Nazi tyranny and Prussian militarism.

Shortly afterwards he sent a message of commendation to Bomber Command for its endeavours in 'beating the life out of Germany'.[21] As the record shows, he was quite wrong about the effect on German war production, which was still increasing year on year.

The rhetoric in play was an agreed one. Brendan Bracken, the Minister for Information, told the press in August 1943 while on a visit to Canada, 'Our plans are to bomb, burn, and ruthlessly destroy in every way available to us the people responsible for creating this war.' Sir Archibald Sinclair, the Minister for Air, told a public meeting in Cheltenham on 5 November 1943, 'We shall continue to hammer the enemy from the skies until we have paralysed their war industries, disrupted their transport system, and broken their will to war.'[22]

Most striking of all, perhaps, are the unwitting contradictions and ironies revealed by Brittain in the pro-bombing rhetoric of the British press. An editorial by John Gordon in the *Sunday Express* on 20 April 1942, written to comment on the content of the Bomber Command directive of 14 February once it had been made public, reads: 'Germany, the originator of war by air terror, is now finding that terror recoiling on herself with an intensity that even Hitler in his most sadistic dreams never thought possible.' On the next day the *News Chronicle* asserted that

the German people must be made to feel in their own brick and bones the mad meaning of their rulers' creed of cruelty and destruction . . . if by the ferocity of our retribution we can convince them at last that violence does not pay and induce them to become good citizens of the world – then the loss of their monuments will be as nothing compared to the contribution to our common inheritance which their conversion to civilised conduct will make.[23]

And Brittain adds, after commenting on the contradictions in both editorials – British war by air terror will outstrip Hitler's most sadistic dreams; 'ferocious retribution' will convert Germans to civilised behaviour – 'A people who have been beaten into apathy and defeatism by their conquerors are hardly likely to conclude that violence does not pay.'

In August 1943, in the weeks following Operation Gomorrah, the British press publicised a government statement saying that 'at least 50 of Germany's main cities will meet the fate of Hamburg by Christmas'. The RAF employed some of its heroes in publicity roles to maintain public support and morale. One such was the Australian pilot Group Captain (later Air Commodore Sir) Hugh Edwards, VC DSO DFC, who won his VC for leading an intrepid bombing raid on Bremen in which, to his own great danger, he stayed over the target from first to last to direct his squadron's efforts, himself flying so low to place his bombs that telegraph wires were dangling from his bullet-riddled Blenheim when he returned to base. He made various radio broadcasts explaining the bombing campaign's aims, and on 13 October 1943 published an article in the *Daily Mail* in which he said, 'Bomber Command is obliterating vast areas of industrial Germany.'[24]

The official position of the government remained that the primary objects of Bomber Commands attentions were 'military'. In the House of Commons on 31 March 1943 the Minister for Air, Sir Archibald Sinclair, said 'The targets of Bomber Command are always

military', thus implying that industrial and communication targets are military too, and with them workers, and with them again anyone living near the workers; for Sir Archibald continued, '. . . but night bombing of military objectives necessarily involves bombing the area in which they are situated.' This method of explaining why cities were being carpet-bombed gave the supporters of the bombing campaign ammunition of their own to attack those who were against area bombing of civilians; an editorial in the *Sunday Dispatch* for 21 March 1943 said, 'Bomber personnel, often in miserable weather, and under attack by vicious fighters, try to hit their targets. Any attempt to persuade them to worry unduly about civilians is an attempt to impair their military value.'[25] Not just truth but temperance is a victim of war; the fighters defending German cities were 'vicious', in contrast to the heroic Few who fought the Battle of Britain. The reference to weather is of great interest in this respect. In his autobiography Harris wrote that in the first four years of the war 'weather . . . had absolute power to make or mar an operation', which is why the navigational aid GEE was so important to Bomber Command hopes when first introduced, though in small numbers, in 1942. Harris wrote:

> [C]ould GEE be used for blind bombing, that is, would it give the bomb-aimer so accurate a fix that he could release the bombs on this alone, without sight of the target? Opinion at the Air Ministry was that GEE could definitely be used for the blind bombing of large industrial towns, though not of individual factories. It was believed that a large town could therefore be attacked through ten-tenths cloud; the estimate was that if Essen was attacked through cloud, nearly half of all the bombs dropped would fall on the city.[26]

These remarks sit very awkwardly next to Sir Archibald Sinclair's claim that 'all of Bomber Command's targets are military'.

Critics of the bombing campaign were aware, as Brittain showed, not just of the obvious point that Bomber Command's tactics and weapons were designed to maximise damage to targets, but of what

some of those tactics and weapons were. Thus 'cascade bombing' or 'saturation bombing' – dropping as large a number as possible of high explosives and incendiaries in the shortest possible time over a wide urban area – was designed to overwhelm the emergency services on the ground. Part of the tactic involved bombing a ring around the main target area in order to prevent air-raid personnel and fire-fighters entering it.[27]

Describing the second, firebombing, raid of Operation Gomorrah on the night of 27–8 July 1943, the British press called it 'the heaviest air raid of all time'. One newspaper report said: 'A million fire-bombs and hundreds of huge two-ton "block-busters" were dropped in 45 minutes, five minutes quicker than in the 2,300 ton raid on the same target on Saturday. Every such cut in the bombing period means greater destruction and greater safety for men and aircraft. Defences are swamped.'[28]

What this meant on the ground was as clear to people in Britain as it had been to survivors in Hamburg itself. Less than two weeks after Operation Gomorrah was over, the *Daily Telegraph* helpfully described for its readers the firestorm and its effects:

> The terrific heat [of the fires started by the bombing] causes a vacuum of air in the bombed districts, and air rushes from other parts of the town. In this way regular tornadoes arise. They are so strong that people were thrown flat on the ground, and the fire brigades cannot get to the blitzed area with their equipment. These violent currents of air help to spread the fire to surrounding districts . . . A number of people there died through lack of oxygen caused by the terrible heat . . . it was found on opening some [air raid shelters] that though [the shelters] were undamaged, many people had died from suffocation.[29]

The air correspondent of the *News Chronicle*, Ronald Walker, quoted Harris after Operation Gomorrah:

The six attacks on the city, port and U-boat yards of Hamburg during four nights and three days probably came nearer than any other series of attacks on Germany to the Harris aim of blotting out a target . . . Air Chief Marshal Sir Arthur Harris, RAF Bomber Command Chief, has made his bombing plan quite plain – the complete destruction of the German industrial cities and ports, one by one. His ideal is to pound them with blows of devastating weight and to keep up that pounding until there is no question of salvage or repair.[30]

The press portrayed Arthur Harris in commendatory terms as 'a tiger with no mercy in his heart'. They attributed to him the credit for forging Bomber Command as a weapon of formidable destructive power, and described his policy as 'the destruction of Germany's cities section by section'.[31] This portrait of Harris, together with the aggressive rhetoric of the press coverage given to the bombing campaign, was of course encouraged by everyone from Churchill down as part of the propaganda effort which, it was hoped, would frighten the German civilian population into surrendering, while at the same time persuading the Nazi leadership of their cause's hopelessness. But fearsome threats of total destruction of cities have to be carried out if surrender does not come, so the rhetoric created a self-imposed necessity to make it come true. And the less successful it proved, the harder became the efforts to make it succeed. Even before Operation Gomorrah – and long before the immense onslaught of the last six months of the war – *Time* magazine was therefore able to say: 'The air offensive against Germany and Axis Europe is suffering from understatement. The objective is not merely to destroy cities, industries, human beings and the human spirit on a scale never before attempted by air action. The objective is to defeat Hitler with bombs, and to do it in 1943.'[32]

To show the British public what this meant in practical terms, the air correspondent of the *Daily Telegraph* wrote in late October 1943 that 'Hamburg has had the equivalent of at least 60 "Coventries",

Cologne 17, Dusseldorf 12, and Essen 10 . . . from July 9th to October 17th no less than 74,000 tons of bombs were dropped on Germany and German-occupied Europe'.[33]

The response was not one of universal rejoicing. The *New States-man* published a letter from six residents of Coventry on 30 November 1943 which read as follows:

> Sir – Many citizens of Coventry who have endured the full horror of intense aerial bombardment would wish to dispute statements made in the *Daily Express* to the effect that all the people of Coventry expressed the opinion that they wished to bomb, and bomb harder, the peoples of Germany. This is certainly not the view of *all* or even the majority of the people of Coventry. The general feeling is, we think, that of horror, and a desire that no other peoples shall suffer as they have done. Our impression is that most people feel the hopelessness of bombing the working classes of Germany and very little satisfaction is attained by hearing that Hamburg is suffering in the same way as Coventry has suffered.'[34]

The citizens of Coventry who wrote in these terms were not alone. A letter from a resident of Southwark in London, one of the capital's most heavily bombed areas, appeared in the *Spectator* for 24 September 1943, asking, 'Why is it that so many religious leaders, politicians and journalists, who denounced German barbarism during the heavy raids on this country, now either applaud such methods when they are adopted in intensified form by the Allies, or acquiesce by their silence?'[35] From another heavily bombed city, Hull, came this:

> When Hull was mercilessly blitzed and civilians were the chief sufferers, we condemned out of hand such barbarous methods of warfare; and what was wrong for Germany to do then does not become right for us to do now, merely by the passage of time and the fact that we seem to be 'on top'. You can't maintain that it is

right for Britain to bomb whole areas indiscriminately without justifying the equally inhuman blitzing of Hull.[36]

What these expressions of dissent represented in general terms was a minority of public opinion. Rose Macaulay, dismayed by the 'lamentable lapse in the moral outlook of the British people', thought she was accurately reporting the national mood when she wrote to her sister about public reaction to George Bell's attack on the bombing campaign:

I wonder what it is about any pleas for greater humanity or civilised care in war that makes so many people see red. I have heard the most passionate references to 'these old bishops' in shops; one woman said it was lovely to think of the way we 'gave Berlin a doing' on Tuesday night; and she'd like to 'throw old Chichester on the top of the bonfire'. It is nonsense of Lord Latham [leader of the London Country Council] to say 'there is no gloating or exaltation' among the English; he can't listen much.[37]

But although the dissenters were in a minority, it was a sizeable one. The Mass Observation Unit published a report in the *New Statesman* on 12 February 1944, describing what it found when canvassing opinion about bombing at various stages during the war. The report began with an account of opinion in 1940 at the height of the Blitz: 'It was regularly found that, after a blitz, people in bus, street and pub seldom talked of getting their own back.' Now, at the beginning of 1944, 'nearly one person in four expresses feelings of uneasiness or revulsion' about British methods of bombing the enemy.[38]

The opposition to the bombing campaign came from ordinary people with experience of being bombed, as the foregoing quotations show; and it came from those with military knowledge, and from leading cultural figures:

In the last war it was the artillery battle [wrote Major-General J. F. C. Fuller]; in this war it is air bombardment. By means of the one

he obliterated entire battlefields, and by doing so denied to himself all possibility of exploiting the initial success gained by becoming bogged down in the slough he created. By means of the other he has annihilated great cities and vast industrial areas and in consequence has pulverised the very foundations upon which eventual peace must be made.[39]

'As to atrocities,' wrote George Bernard Shaw in January 1944,

> we have rained 200,000 tons of bombs on German cities; and some of the biggest of them have no doubt fallen into infants' schools or lying-in hospitals. When it was proposed to rule this method of warfare out, it was we who objected and refused. Can we contend that the worst acts of the Nazis whom our Russian allies have just hanged were more horrible than the bursting of a bomb as big as a London pillar-box in a nursery in Berlin or Bremen . . . German papers, please copy. Our enemies had better know that we have not all lost our heads, and that some of us will know how to clean our slate before we face an impartial international court.[40]

Opposition to Bomber Command's methods was not restricted to reflective minorities in the public at large. In Parliament the war-coalition government faced repeated questioning on the matter. On 14 March 1943 the *Sunday Times* reported debates in the Commons during the preceding week in terms calculated to give heart to the Bombing Restriction Committee:

> Our power continues to grow, and, to the lasting credit of the House of Commons, Members made it plain that they wanted a reassurance that the original clear distinction between military industrial objectives and the indiscriminate dropping of as much high explosive as possible on congested areas, was not being progressively abandoned, just as our superiority should remove any temptation to lower standards. Captain Balfour gave the

reassurance, but the Air Ministry can hardly make it too plain that
we do not take our standards in these matters from the enemy; for
we are fighting for the preservation of civilisation and he is not.[41]

Two months after this report, Clement Attlee was asked in the House
of Commons whether the government had been approached by any
of the Christian churches on the subject of bombing. He replied in
the negative. Corder Catchpool called this 'a direct challenge, almost
an invitation' from the government to the churches to say what they
thought.[42] Apart from individual clergymen such as George Bell and
a few others, the churches remained silent. William Temple, Archbishop of Canterbury, declined a request from an anti-bombing
group to see him. One Canon Hannay wrote scornfully to the *Sunday
Express* about German 'squealing' over Cologne. The churches might
have been expected to show more interest when, in answer to a
question in the House of Commons 'whether the same principles of
discrimination that are applied to Rome are being and will be applied
to other cities', Sir Archibald Sinclair replied, 'The same principles are
applied to all centres. We must bomb important military objectives.
We must not be prevented from bombing important military
objectives because beautiful or ancient buildings are near them.'[43]

A good sense of the House of Commons atmosphere during
discussions of bombing can be gathered from the *Evening Standard*
report, on 1 December 1943, of the debate following Sir Archibald's
announcement that, in the preceding month of November 1943,
13,000 tons of bombs had been dropped on Germany:

> When Mr Stokes asked for the area, in square miles, in Berlin
> within which it was estimated that 100 per cent of the 350 block-
> buster bombs recently dropped in a single raid would fall, Sir
> Archibald said he could not reply without giving useful informa-
> tion to the enemy. Mr Stokes: Would not the proper answer be
> that the Government dare not give this information? Sir Archibald:
> No. Berlin is the centre of twelve strategic railways, it is the second

largest inland port in Europe. In that city are AEG, the Rhein
Metall, Siemens, Focke Wulf, Heinkel and Dornier factories.
(Cheers). Mr Stokes: Do you not admit that the Government
are now approving the indiscriminate bombing of Germany? Sir
Archibald: You are incorrigible. I have mentioned a series of vitally
important military targets. Mr Shinwell: Will you appreciate that
much as we deplore the loss of civilian life we wish to encourage
and applaud the efforts of your Ministry in trying to bring the war
to a speedy conclusion? (Cheers). Mr Simmonds: Are not these
bombings likely to reduce, vastly, our military casualties when we
invade Europe? Sir Archibald: Yes. Mr Stokes also asked whether
the policy of limiting objectives of Bomber Command to targets of
military importance had or had not been changed to the bombing
of towns and wide areas in which military targets are not situated.
Sir Archibald: There has been no change of policy.

Hansard continues where the *Standard* leaves off:

Mr Stokes: May I say that the reply of my Right Hon. Friend does
not answer this question. Am I to understand that the policy has
changed, and that new objectives of Bomber Command are not
specific military targets but large areas, and would it not be true to
say that probably the minimum area of a target now is 16 square
miles? Sir Archibald Sinclair: My Hon. Friend cannot have listened
to my answer. I said there had been no change of policy.[44]

Debate in the House of Lords, both in fact and by tradition, is
seemlier and more modestly phrased. George Bell's efforts to press
questions about the bombing campaign there conform themselves to
that model. *The Times* gave a full report of his speech to that House
on 9 February 1944:

He [the Lord Bishop of Chichester] was not forgetting the
Luftwaffe or its tremendous bombing of Belgrade, Warsaw, Rot-

terdam, London, Portsmouth, Coventry, Plymouth, Canterbury, and many other places of military, industrial, and cultural importance. Hitler was a barbarian. There was not a decent person on the allied side who was likely to suggest we should make him our pattern . . . The question with which he was concerned was this: Did the Government understand the full force of what our aerial bombardment was doing and what it was now destroying? Was it alive not only to the vastness of the material damage, much of which is irreparable, but also to the harvest it was laying up for the future relationships of the peoples of Europe? He recognised the legitimacy of concentrated attack on industrial and military objectives . . . He fully realised that any attacks on centres of war industry and transport inevitably carried with it the killing of civilians. But there must be a fair balance between the means employed and the purpose achieved. To obliterate a whole town because certain portions contained military and industrial objectives was to reject the balance.

He would instance Hamburg, with a population of between one and two millions. It contained targets of first-class military importance. It also happened to be the most democratic town in Germany, where the anti-Nazi opposition was strongest . . .

Berlin, the capital of the Reich, was four times the size of Hamburg. The military, industrial, and war-making establishments in Berlin were a fair target, but up to date half the city had been destroyed and it was said that 74,000 persons had been killed and 3,000,000 were already homeless. The policy was obliteration, openly acknowledged, and that was not a justifiable act of war. Berlin was one of the greatest centres of art galleries in the world. It had one of the best picture galleries in Europe, comparable to the National Gallery, and had one of Europe's finest libraries. All these non-industrial, non-military buildings were grouped together, and the whole of the area is reported to have been demolished. These works of art and libraries would be wanted for the re-education of the Germans after the war . . .

There were old German towns away from the great centres which almost certainly would be subjected to the raids of Bomber Command. In these places the historic and beautiful centres were well preserved and the industrial and military establishments were on the outskirts. We had destroyed much; we ought to think once, twice, three times, before we destroyed the rest . . .

He emphasised particularly the danger outside Germany, to Rome. The principle was the same . . . The history of Rome was our own history. Its destruction would rankle in the memory of every good European as the destruction of Rome by the Goths or the sack of Rome. The blame must not fall on those who were professing to create a better world. It would be the sort of crime which even in the political field would turn against the perpetrator.

It had been said that area bombing was definitely designed to diminish the sacrifice of British lives and to shorten the war. Everybody wishes with all his heart that these two objects could be achieved, but to justify methods inhumane in this way smacked of the Nazi philosophy of 'might is right'.[45]

The reply Bishop Bell received from the Government spokesman, Lord Cranborne, was brief and unconcessive. He said, 'These great war industries can only be paralysed by bringing the whole life of the cities in which they are situated to a standstill.'[46]

After setting out the facts and arguments, Brittain stated what the Bombing Restriction Committee proposed, which was that the belligerents should recognise 'sanctuary areas' to which women, children and the elderly could be evacuated, in advance of bombing, from towns containing military objectives. The Committee listed examples of towns without military significance which could be centres for sanctuary zones – among them Bonn, Heidelberg, Baden and Homburg. A corps of observers could be instituted, drawn from neutral countries and placed under Red Cross supervision, to ensure that no military or industrial assets were hidden in the sanctuary zones.

Independently of the Bombing Restriction Committee but with its full support, a group of notables led by the popular science-fiction writer J. D. Beresford presented a letter to the War Cabinet, asking for a moratorium on 'obliteration bombing', and for a debate to take place in Parliament and the country 'in order that this policy, by which the British nation will be judged in years to come, may have the free and considered verdict of the British people pronounced upon it'.[47]

In the closing pages of *Seed of Chaos*, as if wearied by all that she had to report in it, Vera Brittain wrote, 'From the story of our bombing during the past eighteen months only a mental or moral lunatic could fail to draw the conclusion that modern war and modern civilisation are utterly incompatible, and that one or the other must go.'[48]

As this extraordinary document shows, in the winter of 1943–4 the facts and the arguments about area bombing were as plain to anyone who then seriously enquired as they are to us now, even with today's added perspective, which includes Dresden, the massive tonnage of bombs dropped in the war's final months, the discovery of just how truly wicked Nazism was, and the analyses made after the war of the degree of significance that bombing had for the war effort. In the case assembled by the Bombing Restriction Committee and those who voiced its concerns, whether in letters to the press or in speeches in Parliament, are to be found some of the elements of an indictment that an accuser could lay against the bombing campaigns. In the answers given by ministers, airmen and the pro-area-bombing press, and in the aims of those who conducted the bombing campaigns, lie some of the elements of the defence. I return to each in the chapters to come.

An early draft of *Seed of Chaos* was taken to America before Christmas 1943 by one of the Bombing Restriction Committee's supporters, to show campaigners in America the facts and arguments that the

Committee had gathered in Britain. Without Vera Brittain's knowledge or permission the draft was published under the title 'Massacre by Bombing' in *Fellowship*, the magazine of an American peace organisation called the 'Fellowship of Reconciliation'. What drew public attention to Brittain's essay was the twenty-eight signatures of writers and – mainly – clergymen,[49] who endorsed the article and added to it a declaration that 'Christian people should be moved to examine themselves concerning their participation in this carnival of death, even though they be thousands of miles away'.[50]

The response to her pamphlet was a surprise and a shock to Vera Brittain. It is graphically described by the historian James Martin:

> Attacks on Miss Brittain occurred from coast to coast by the hundreds in every imaginable medium of communication; the printed condemnations alone would have filled a number of volumes. *The New York Times* reported its mail running fifty to one against it, and notables entered the arena repeatedly. Because so many of the signers of the preface of 'Massacre by Bombing' were renowned Protestant clergy, it appeared as though there were a compulsion on the part of those clergy of similar faith supporting the obliteration bombing to come out immediately in rejection of Miss Brittain and her small company of supporters. Famed Episcopal Bishop William T. Manning denounced Miss Brittain in a letter to *The New York Herald Tribune*, and the Rev. Daniel A. Poling, editor of the quarter-of-a-million circulation *Christian Herald*, a major in the Army Chaplain Corps and president of the International Christian Endeavour Society, was especially bitter, charging the entire group involved in the protest against bombing with 'giving comfort to the enemy,' which turned out to be a common, expectable, and widespread charge.[51]

A choice item of invective was provided by a Catholic priest in Connecticut, the Reverend Paul Koslowksi, who in the process of denouncing Brittain wrote, 'There is no other way but to attack

these beasts in the lairs – that is, in the German cities – where they plan further mass murders of innocent people. Christ's saying, "if one smite thee on one cheek, give him the other" is a beautiful theory, but not with human beasts, drunk with vengeance and conquest.'[52] One of the few who supported Brittain among the American clergy was the editor of the *Catholic World*, Father Gillis, who pointed out that the logic of her critics' arguments came down to saying that 'missionaries should eat cannibals because cannibals eat missionaries'.[53]

Even the thoughtful journals in America, such as the *New Republic* and *Nation*, were against Brittain's stance, though phrasing their opposition more moderately. The *New Republic* said that 'those who take up arms to end aggression by others against humanity must do what is necessary to win', and it added that in contemporary war there were no longer any non-combatants. (James Martin, in a pertinent aside, remarks that this opinion was formed in the safety of a New York office block.)[54] The *Nation* claimed that Brittain's book (by now circulating as a self-standing reprint) was 'hardly objective or reliably documented' – its editors' grounds for this judgement being that they wondered whether 'obliteration bombing' was actually taking place at all – but they concluded that if it was indeed taking place, then although it was 'a revolting necessity' it was nevertheless a necessity.[55]

The celebrated American journalist Dorothy Thompson had a column in London's *Sunday Chronicle*, and she used it to tell the British public that 'British Woman Pacifist Rouses U.S. Fury'. Far from rousing opposition to the bombing campaign, Thompson wrote, Brittain had 'actually released a more furious defence of air warfare than any single political action to date'.[56]

Vera Brittain responded to only one of the US attacks on her, and even then only in private. It was by William Shirer, the foremost American journalist of his day, famous for his *Berlin Diary*, based on observations of Hitler and the Nazis during his time as a correspondent in Germany before the war. In the *New York Herald Tribune* on

12 March 1944, under the headline 'Rebuttal to the Protest Against Bombing', Shirer accused Brittain of being a mouth-piece for Nazi propaganda. To her husband George she wrote that Shirer had virtually accused her and the Bombing Restriction Committee of being not just 'Nazi dupes' but 'Nazi agents', and suggesting that all the information in the book came from Nazi sources. '[He] omits to mention that most of these sources were British newspaper correspondents and British papers – to say nothing of repatriated prisoners of war!' she wrote.[57]

The outcry in America went all the way up to the White House. The Under-Secretary of State for War, Robert Patterson, accused the Bombing Restriction Committee of 'giving encouragement to the enemy'; Eleanor Roosevelt, the President's wife, called Brittain's arguments 'sentimental nonsense'; and the President himself 'delivered a stinging rebuke' to the twenty-eight signatories to the original *Fellowship* appearance of Brittain's essay. On the President's behalf a letter had been sent to *Fellowship*, stating that although the President was 'disturbed and horrified' by the 'destruction of life' involved, the only way to save more lives was to compel the enemy to change their ways.[58]

When *Seed of Chaos* appeared in Britain in the spring of 1944, a few weeks after its controversial publication in America, it caused hardly a stir. Vera Brittain surmised that this was because Americans had not actually experienced bombing, and were therefore more ready to be bloodthirsty. As C. E. Montague once wrote, 'Hell hath no fury like a non-combatant.'[59] The only substantial response aroused by the book came from what might seem an unexpected quarter: George Orwell, who attacked it in *Tribune* on 19 May 1944.

Miss Vera Brittain's pamphlet, *Seed of Chaos*, is an eloquent attack on indiscriminate or 'obliteration' bombing [Orwell wrote] [She is] not, however, taking the pacifist standpoint. She is willing and anxious to win the war, apparently. She merely wishes us to stick to

'legitimate' methods of war and abandon civilian bombing, which she fears will blacken our reputation in the eyes of posterity . . .

Now, no one in his senses regards bombing, or any other operation of war, with anything but disgust. On the other hand, no decent person cares tuppence for the opinion of posterity. And there is something very distasteful in accepting war as an instrument and at the same time wanting to dodge responsibility for its more obviously barbarous features. Pacifism is a tenable position; provided that you are willing to take the consequences. But all talk of 'limiting' or 'humanising' war is sheer humbug, based on the fact that the average human being never bothers to examine catchwords.[60]

The catchwords Orwell picks out for scrutiny are 'killing civilians', 'massacre of women and children' and 'destruction of our cultural heritage', and he challenges the assumptions they contain: that air bombing does more of these things than ground warfare, and that it is worse to kill civilians than soldiers.

Obviously one must not kill children if it is in any way avoidable [he says], but it is only in propaganda pamphlets that every bomb drops on a school or an orphanage. A bomb kills a cross-section of the population; but not quite a representative selection, because the children and expectant mothers are usually the first to be evacuated, and some of the young men will be away in the army. Probably a disproportionately large number of bomb victims will be middle-aged. (Up to date, German bombs have killed between six and seven thousand children in this country. This is, I believe, less than the number killed in road accidents in the same period.)[61]

A key to Orwell's attitude was his belief that the immunity of civilian populations in past wars is what made them possible – rather as with the bloodthirsty American enthusiasm, enjoyed at a safe distance, for area bombing. In 1937 he had written, 'Sometimes it is a comfort to

me to think that the aeroplane is altering the conditions of war. Perhaps when the next great war comes we may see that sight unprecedented in all history, a jingo with a bullet hole in him.' But now the burden of war was being more equally shared by everyone in the combatant nations. 'The immunity of the civilian, one of the things that have made war possible, has been shattered. Unlike Miss Brittain, I don't regret that. I can't feel that war is "humanised" by being confined to the slaughter of the young and becomes "barbarous" when the old get killed as well.'[62]

Brittain sent a letter to *Tribune* in response, remarking that Orwell 'seems to assume that if pacifists do not succeed in preventing war, they just throw up the sponge and acquiesce in any excesses which war-makers choose to initiate'.[63] She might have added that air bombing does indeed kill more civilians, massacre women and children, and destroy more cultural heritage than ground war does; and that the reason why it is worse to kill civilians than soldiers is that the latter are contracted and trained to kill us and ours, and are armed for the purpose, whereas civilians are not. The point becomes moot when the civilian stands at a lathe, producing the weapons that the soldier will use against us; but then no one in the debate, then or now, who accepted the necessity for the war, ever said that the war industries and the workers in them should be immune, as George Bell's House of Lords speech illustrates.

Orwell went to Germany as a war correspondent in the spring of 1945 for the *Observer*. He was appalled by what he saw, and in what looks like a change of mind wrote, 'To walk through the ruined cities of Germany is to feel an actual doubt about the continuity of civilisation.'[64] Vera Brittain, meanwhile, had been receiving through her letter-box hate mail from all over North America and Britain, among it an envelope filled with dog faeces. She was relatively unconcerned about the opposition and vituperation she had aroused; she pointed out that when arguing for an unpopular cause, the worst thing is to be ignored, for if one gets a strong reaction it shows that one has managed to get under the opponent's skin.[65]

In any case, in such circumstances what matters is the opinion of those whose opinion is worth having. In July 1944 she received a letter from Basil Liddell Hart, many years before an eloquent proponent of air bombardment, now emphatically against it. His letter expressed 'profound respect for your courage in upholding the claims of human decency in a time when war fever is raging', and he added that his particular reason for writing was that 'since you are likely to have abundant evidence of the resentment you create, you may like to have some evidence of the respect you inspire'.[66]

Events stifled the controversy. In the summer of 1944 the V1 flying-bombs or 'doodlebugs' began to appear over London, at first not in sufficient numbers or with sufficient explosive power to be a serious menace to others than those they fell upon, but apt to cause anxiety, because people knew that when their engines cut out they were about to crash down on to the city, and it was very disconcerting to hear a V1 droning towards one and then suddenly going quiet. In June the D-Day landings occurred, and together with the flood of news from the invasion front, the fact that Bomber Command and the Eighth Army Air Force were busy on tactical duties meant that the area-bombing campaign left the news. When area bombing resumed with even greater intensity in the autumn, the land battles were still dominating the newspapers and radio broadcasts; and moreover London was suffering a serious area-bombing threat of its own again, with the arrival of the V2 rockets, which flew at faster than the speed of sound and therefore were not heard until they exploded. The V-weapons attack on London was not an insignificant one; it killed nearly 9,000 people in the final fourteen months of the war, with up to a hundred rockets a day falling on London at the peak of the attack in June and July 1944. This was Hitler's 'wonder weapon' riposte to the invasion, and one of the triumphs of Allied bombing was the July 1944 attack on V-weapon launch sites that reduced the intensity of attacks on London.[67]

And then there came the devastating footage of the concentration camps liberated by Allied troops in April 1945 – Bergen-Belsen,

Neuengamme, Ohrdruf, Buchenwald and Dachau – which produced such a feeling of revulsion against Germany that further discussion of moral duties owed to its civilians became impossible. British troops liberated Neuengamme and Bergen-Belsen, American troops the others. At Bergen-Belsen there were 60,000 prisoners, almost all in critical conditions of disease and starvation; 10,000 of them died in the weeks immediately following the liberation. Pictures of British Tommies using bulldozers to push piles of emaciated corpses into mass graves made discussion of morality in any other connection a nullity.

At the war's end the vast problems of a devastated Germany and Europe, and the need to arrest and put on trial as many of the Nazi leadership as could be found, consumed what attention was possible in the exhaustion and relief of the time. It is plausible to argue that the area bombing of Japan, and the dropping of the atom bombs, raised scarcely a flicker of negative public concern in either the United States or Europe for this very reason. Everyone wishes to move on as quickly as possible after such immense trauma; the immediate post-war years were not a time for self-examination and a clear-eyed adjustment of accounts. Even in the much larger and more significant matter of the Holocaust, time had to pass before survivors and witnesses were able to recover enough, after a time of forgetting and silence, to address the experience and its profound meanings. The right time for thinking about other aspects of the war's harms and wrongs, if such they were, was not yet, either for those who suffered under the terrific onslaught of area bombing in Germany and Japan, or for those in the victor nations whose air forces had executed it, week in and week out, for years.

The point of importance to be carried forward from this chapter is that the bombing campaigns were controversial even as they took place, and that anyone who was prepared to think about them and to look at what was said and known about them at the time could have been nearly as well informed about the facts, and as fully apprised of

the arguments pro and con, as anyone today. This was certainly true of those charged with the conduct of the war in general and the bombing campaigns in particular; the relevant information crossed their desks daily, and the aims and intentions are on record, as quoted throughout here. From the point of view of the intentions and knowledge of those who planned and carried out area bombing on behalf of the Allied nations, there was therefore what the lawyers called *mens rea* in full and without qualification. At very least this means that no one can say, 'forgive them, for they knew not what they did.'

6

The Case Against the Bombing

To MAKE OUT the claim that the Allied practice of area bombing in the Second World War was wrong, two things are needful. One is to clarify the sense of 'wrong' at stake, and the other is to measure the facts of the bombing, and the knowledge and intentions of those who planned and directed the area-bombing campaigns, against the relevant principles of ethics and law. Previous chapters have sketched the area-bombing campaigns, their effects, and the background of knowledge and intentions on the part of those who devised and supervised them. Here I set out a case for saying that area bombing was wrong, and that its conductors committed wrong; and I do it by setting out the humanitarian and ethical considerations against which the facts of the preceding chapters are to be judged.

As this last point shows, by 'wrong' here I mean a moral wrong, a violation of humanitarian attitudes and civilised standards of treatment of human beings. In the seminars of philosophers it is easier to find objections, refutations and counter-examples to any proposed definition of morality – and of such associated concepts as 'the good' and 'right conduct' – than it is to secure general agreement about what any of these fundamentally important notions mean. This is not to claim that we do not know what 'right' and 'wrong' mean, it is instead an indictment of contemporary philosophy, which has

allowed the term 'academic' in the phrase 'it's only academic' to mean 'empty and futile'. Once outside the seminar room and confronted with (say) a gang of thugs attacking an old lady, problems of definition evaporate. There are of course major disagreements within any society, and between societies, about fundamental matters of ethics, but there are also fundamental agreements; and it is easy to forget that the major ethical theories of the philosophical tradition, and the major world religions, have more in common on the question of what is good, than otherwise. Suffice it to say that if someone finds nothing wrong *per se* with dropping a bomb on a house in which unarmed and non-combatant women, children and elderly people are trying to shelter from harm – and leaving aside relevant complexities such as, for example, the possibility that all of the women, children and elderly huddled there are workers in an armaments factory – then that person is not going to get the point of efforts to devise humanitarian rules which protect civilians in wartime, and which thereby embody ethical principles of the kind that this chapter premises.

To anyone of humane and pacific instincts, the phrase 'a just war' looks like a contradiction. But a moment's thought shows otherwise. The idea that war, however ugly in itself, is sometimes unqualifiedly just is amply demonstrated by the example of Allied opposition to militaristic Fascism in the Second World War, a struggle which provides the focal case of a legitimate use of armed force to defend against aggression and to put an end to oppression and genocide. In this case the just war was the one waged by the Allies, not of course by the Axis, whose instigation and prosecution of war constituted aggression of an egregious kind, which few apart from the lunatic fringe of neo-Nazi apologists would regard as anything other than criminal and immoral.

But the fact that a war is just does not automatically make right every act committed during the fighting of it. Acts of injustice can be perpetrated in the course of a just war, and if the injustices committed

are themselves very great, their commission can threaten the overall justice of the war in which they took place.

The theory of just war finds its first clear articulation in the writings of St Augustine and St Thomas Aquinas. In Part Two of his *Summa Theologica* Aquinas examined the proposition 'that it is always sinful to wage war', and argued to the contrary that, on three conditions, war can be justified. The conditions are, first, that there is a just cause of war, second, that it is begun on proper authority, and third, that it is waged with the right intention, meaning that it aims at 'the advancement of good, or the avoidance of evil'. The first two conditions constitute the *justum ad bellum*, the just cause for war, which Augustine centuries earlier had invoked to argue that having a just cause for going to war makes anything done in the course of it justified: 'When we do a thing for a good and lawful purpose, if thereby we unintentionally cause harm to anyone, it should by no means be imputed to us.'[1] But this leaves aside what later theorists regarded as a second kind of requirement for the *justum bellum*, namely, just conduct in the course of the war: *jus in bello*.

Aquinas's three conditions are clear and persuasive in themselves, offering what is from the point of view of ethics the unusual gift of an unambiguous set of principles. Difficulty enters when a case has to be made for whether the circumstances of a given prospective war are such that the principles apply to it, especially as regards the first and third, for the first always prompts the question: does such-and-such really count as a just cause for going to war? And the third always prompts the question, Are the aims for the intended war good ones?

There are clear examples of a just cause for going to war. Defence against aggression is one, as is going to the rescue of people being subjected to aggression. Is it equally just to engage in pre-emptive military action against a potential aggressor? The lesson of history teaches that appeasement and inaction are dangerous tactics; but how can one be sure that an unfulfilled threat is genuinely dangerous, and can one be sure that alleging a threat is not a mask for one's own aggression? On the other hand, a people has a right to defend itself,

and the best form of defence is to prevent attack in the first place – by diplomacy if possible, but by force if necessary. A leadership fails its people if it does not do its best to prevent them from being harmed by aggressors, consistently with other values such as the liberty and privacy of its people.

What might count as just war aims? Aquinas said: promoting the good or avoiding evil. By this is meant that a war waged for such reasons as self-interest, *Lebensraum*, other people's oil fields, or pure aggrandisement, is not justified. 'Avoiding evil' can be invoked by those seeking to defend themselves preventatively, and – if they are right about the threat posed by a delinquent regime which is a danger to its neighbours – with justification. The positive aim, that of promoting good, which in the standard current view of the dominant Western world at least involves bringing about peace, stability, democracy, prosperity, and a situation in which both victor and defeated can cease to be enemies, is equally easy to identify. Too many wars, whether just in their inception or not, fail to achieve this outcome, because the harder struggle of 'winning the peace' is too often fudged or dodged.

Although the Aquinas conditions are clear and compelling, they can never, by themselves alone, count as sufficient conditions for going to war. Other considerations apply. Have all diplomatic means failed? Is there consensus over the 'just cause' and 'right intentions' requirements among all parties implicated on the side of the intending belligerent? Are there no means other than military action to bring about the desired aims? In practice, diplomacy and various forms of pressure, including sanctions, are the standard means for adjusting international disagreements (and those within a state that threaten civil war), and in most cases actual military conflict is a last resort, whether just or not. Certainly it seems hard to describe a war as just if it is not a last resort, that is, if further efforts could still be made to find other routes away from conflict.

To Aquinas's three conditions modern theorists have added two others: that to be just a war must have a reasonable chance of success,

and that the means used to conduct it must be proportional to the ends sought. The first addition is a pragmatic one; it can be glossed as saying that a leadership commits an injustice against its own people if it leads them into a war they are sure to lose, in the process also causing harm and loss to those who, having been provoked into war, bring about their defeat. A problem with transforming this prudential consideration into a moral one is that it seems, by contrast, rather immoral, not to say spineless, to avoid engaging in an otherwise just war because it threatens to be too costly. When the Polish cavalry galloped towards Hitler's Panzers in defence of their homeland in the late summer of 1939, they were going futilely to war, but their courage gave them a moral victory, and was an inspiration to others.

The second addition – that the means used to conduct the war must be proportional to the ends sought – is one that matters centrally to my argument in this book. It is a controversial one; for as war leaders otherwise as different in outlook as Churchill and Mao Zedong both emphatically believed, it seems prudent to hold that, once involved in a war, there is no point in fighting with one hand tied behind one's back. As Mao succinctly put it, 'War is not crochet.' Whether this justifies using nuclear weapons, poison gas, or 'conventional' area bombing against civilian centres of population, is the very moot point at issue here. There is a view that if victory is the aim, and 'overwhelming force' is a sure means to attain it, then the use of overwhelming force is justified. But this in turn ignores a plethora of questions about the effects of its use, and especially about those on whom its effects fall.

So the question before us is not what makes a war a just war, nor whether the Allies' reasons for going to war in 1939 and 1941 respectively were such that their war was just or not; we can take that point as settled in the affirmative. In a different book questions might arise about a later matter – the Allied determination to settle for nothing less than unconditional surrender, thereby prolonging the war considerably, with consequent great destruction and loss of life. That topic might itself raise problems about the *justum ad bellum*. But

in this book area bombing – a *jus in bello* point – is the focus, and the question being asked about it is whether the Allies, in carrying out area bombing, acted justly once engaged in their just war. Does British and American area bombing in the Second World War, in other words, constitute a failure of *jus in bello* in the midst of a *justum bellum*?

And what if it does constitute such a failure? Consider again the thought that it is not only the ends but the means which settle whether or not a war is just. Reflection suggests that questions of ends and means can and sometimes should be considered apart, as when for example one argues that ends do not justify certain means – as we are here considering in the case of area bombing. But even if we take it that means and ends must always be considered together, are we are bound to say that if the area-bombing campaign turns out on examination to be unjust, that detracts from the justice of the Allied cause?

I think not. It would be hard to conclude that opposing Nazism in particular and Axis aggression in general was anything but just in principle. And this is not a matter of hindsight only, to which the full extent of the Holocaust and other atrocities is clear: the nature of the Nazi regime was clear before the outbreak of war – and the outbreak of war itself made manifest its aggressions.[2]

One standard view offered in philosophical discussions about war is that if the practice of war is governed by rules, then whatever the rules are they must at least dictate what can be attacked and how it can be attacked (unless the rules are so permissive that they say 'anything' and 'anyhow' respectively, thus not really being rules at all). A straightforward principle might apply both to what counts as a legitimate target and what counts as a legitimate weapon or method of attack, namely, that whatever damage or loss of life is caused by military activities, it should be necessary to the attainment of the war's aims, and it should be proportionate to them. Thus, the definition of a just military action is any action *necessary and proportionate* to winning the war. By the same token, any unnecessary or disproportionate act is wrong.

An alternative view is that there are some things that should never be attacked or harmed even if doing so brings about or helps to bring about victory. The main such things are innocent persons and their property. The concept of 'innocence' is very important here: *nocens* is the Latin for 'engaged in harmful activity'; the prefix *in-*means 'not' or 'un'; thus *in-nocens* means 'not engaged in harmful activity'. This idea imposes an obligation on anyone engaged in fighting a war to distinguish between combatants and non-combatants, and they must not intend to cause harm to the latter either as a means to their ends, or as an end in itself, in their conduct of the war.

This formulation – 'they must not intend to harm the innocent' – accepts that innocents might be harmed in the course of military activity, as a by-product of it; the current euphemism for this is 'collateral damage'. No wrong is committed by the belligerent if the harm he does to innocents is an unavoidable ancillary to military operations – even if such harm can be foreseen. This is because the 'doctrine of double effect' applies here. This doctrine says that it is legitimate to do harm if the harm is the unintended side-effect of an effort to achieve a legitimate goal. Consider doctors who, by increasing morphine doses to control the pain of terminally ill patients, thereby shorten the lives of those patients. They foresee what effect the drug will have in this second respect, but their intention is not to kill but to palliate suffering. The 'double effect' is the palliation of suffering and the shortening of life; only the former is intended; and since it is a good and legitimate goal, the second effect, though foreseen, is accordingly not wrong.

The principle of double effect is controversial for various reasons, one being that it provides a ready mask for hypocrisy or dishonesty. It is easy to claim, hide or disavow intentions; we often recognise that whereas others may seem to have an identifiable intention, 'ulterior motives' can be in play. One control on the doctrine's applicability is the requirement that the foreseen but unintended effect should not only be a necessary concomitant of achieving the main and desired effect, but must just be sufficient – which is another way of saying,

should be proportional. For example, if someone sought to cure another person's toothache by cutting off his head, the second effect, namely, the death of the toothache sufferer, is out of all proportion to achieving the intended effect, namely, ending the toothache.

A key question is this: suppose the threat posed by an adversary is mortal; is it not legitimate to use any means whatever of fighting him? Cannot one say that ordinary moral rules do not apply in extreme situations? If this is so, then we can say that in such situations even acts normally regarded as evil are permissible.

Some moral philosophers, chief among them Immanuel Kant, emphatically disagree with this view. They hold fast to the principle that it is never right to do evil in pursuit of a good, even if the good is one's own survival, or the defeat of a dangerous enemy. In its contrast to this absolute line, the thought that extreme situations license extreme remedies is part of an outlook which says that moral rules are instrumental – that is, are merely tools for realising such desiderata as the good ordering of relationships within a community. Accordingly they can be adjusted to circumstances, including being abandoned for the duration of an extremity such as war.

Both views have their obvious drawbacks. Strict rules easily prove ineffective by their rigidity; flexible rules might be made to bend before any glib tongue able to make a situation seem extreme enough for the purpose.

The foregoing remarks raise a few of the general moral considerations that need to be brought to bear. Ideas about 'laws of war' try to be more specific, bringing questions about just war down from the level of ethical abstraction to an attempt at stating concrete and definite principles.

The first systematic attempt to think about what is right and wrong in war is owed to the seventeenth-century Dutch philosopher Hugo Grotius, the effective founder of international law. His *De Jure Belli ac Pacis* (On the Law of War and Peace), published in 1625, is a major source for thinking about the difficult questions that war raises, not

least because of his motivation in trying to bring some order, clarity, and moral principle to the problem. 'I saw in the whole Christian world a license of fighting at which even barbarous nations might blush,' he wrote. 'Wars were begun on trifling pretexts or none at all, and carried on without any reference to law, divine or human.' Moreover he took it that 'conscience [has] a judicial power to be the sovereign guide of human actions, by despising whose admonitions the mind is stupefied into brutal hardness'. Putting these two thoughts together explains his motivation for trying to systematise thinking about just war and just conduct of war. The first two books of his great work are devoted to the question of when a war is just; the third book addresses the question of what counts as just acts in the fighting of a war.

When Grotius wrote, the phrase 'laws of war' did not denote a body of agreed and binding rules dictating when wars are legitimate and what is permissible and impermissible in the course of them. Rather, it denoted an assemblage of assumptions and beliefs that had grown up by custom and usage, which generally permitted almost any treatment of prisoners, hostages, non-combatants, and property. As Grotius thought about the rights and wrongs of war he was presented with constant examples of the latter, for the terrible and bloody Thirty Years War was in progress, having begun in 1618. That war was about religion and power; the Holy Roman Emperor, a Habsburg prince, was trying to win back for Catholicism the small Protestant states, mainly of northern Europe, which had abandoned the Roman version of Christianity after the Reformation in the preceding century.

As too well illustrated by that war, which was by far the worst Europe had known to that date, the 'laws of war' were understood to mean something tough and uncompromising. They said such things as that if you put non-combatants to the sword during the course of sacking their town, you are not committing murder, for this is no less than their soldiers would do if matters were the other way round and they were sacking your town instead. In Grotius's lifetime there were

some egregious examples of this view in practice; the most notorious was the sack of Magdeburg, which happened just five years after *De Jure Belli ac Pacis* was published. A famous account of it was given by Magdeburg's Bürgermeister, one of the few survivors of the atrocity:

> Thus it came about that the city and all its inhabitants fell into the hands of the enemy . . . Then was there naught but beating and burning, plundering, torture, and murder. Most especially was every one of the enemy bent on securing much booty . . . In this frenzied rage, the great and splendid city that had stood like a fair princess in the land was now, in its hour of direst need and unutterable distress and woe, given over to the flames, and thousands of innocent men, women, and children, in the midst of a horrible din of heartrending shrieks and cries, were tortured and put to death in so cruel and shameful a manner that no words would suffice to describe, nor no tears to bewail it.[3]

Eighty-five per cent of the citizens were slaughtered, and ashes from the fire that destroyed the town flew on the wind to neighbouring cities miles away.

Grotius accepted that 'an individual or belligerent power may, in the prosecution of a lawful object, do many things, which . . . in themselves it would not be lawful to do'; but that 'what is conformable to right taken in its strictest sense is not always lawful in a moral point of view. For there are many instances, in which the law of charity will not allow us to insist upon our right with the utmost rigour'. He quotes with approval Cicero's point that people are apt to call lawful what they can do with impunity – that is, what they can get away with – and and moreover that what one should consider is not what the utmost rigour of the law allows one to do, but what is 'becoming to one's character'.[4]

But the key question for Grotius is 'how far the power of lawfully destroying an enemy, and all that belongs to him, extends'. The answer is not a comforting one; the uses and customs of war

throughout history suggest that combatants have always given themselves what license they choose, of whose extent, he writes,

> we may form some conception from the very circumstance, that
> even women and children are frequently subject to the calamities
> and disasters of war . . . The Psalmist's expression of the Bab-
> ylonian children being dashed against the stones is a much stronger
> proof of the custom commonly prevailing among nations, in the
> use of victory, to which the language of Homer bears a close
> resemblance, where the poet says, that 'in the cruel rage of war,
> even the bodies of infant children were dashed against the ground'.
> Thucydides relates, that when Mycalessus was captured by the
> Thracians, they put all, even women and children to the sword.
> Arrian relates the same of the Macedonians, when they took the
> city of Thebes. And Germanicus Caesar, according to the account
> of Tacitus, laid waste whole cantons of the Marsians, a people of
> Germany, with fire and sword, to which the historian adds,
> 'without sparing either age or sex.' The Jewish women and children
> too were exposed by Titus, to be torn to pieces by wild beasts at a
> public spectacle. Yet neither of those generals were thought
> deficient in humanity, so much had custom reconciled the minds
> of men to this barbarous usage. So that the massacre of the aged,
> like that of Priam by Pyrrhus, is no way surprising.[5]

And to add to the discomfort, Grotius quotes Cicero as saying in the
third book of his *Offices* 'that there is nothing repugnant to the law of
nature in spoiling the effects of an enemy whom by the same law we
are authorised to kill' – that is, to destroy or take possession of the
enemy's property. Since that is so, it is not surprising that the laws of
nations permit the same:

> Polybius, for this reason, in the fifth book of his history, maintains,
> that the laws of war authorise the destruction of an enemy's forts,
> harbours, and fleets, the seizure of his men, or carrying off the

produce of his country, and every thing of that description And we find from Livy that there are certain rights of war, by which an enemy must expect to suffer the calamities, which he is allowed to inflict, such as the burning of corn, the destruction of houses, and the plunder of men and cattle. Almost every page of history abounds in examples of entire cities being destroyed, walls levelled to the ground, and even whole countries wasted by fire and sword.[6]

To these despairing points Grotius opposes the answer of humanity, which Cicero likewise gave: 'some duties are to be observed even towards those, from whom you have received an injury. For even vengeance and punishment have their due bounds.' And Cicero praises those palmy periods of Rome's Republic when 'the events of war were mild, and marked with no unnecessary cruelty'. If this reads as milksop in the face of the acknowledged harshness that the right of might affords, Grotius has a slightly firmer answer. It is that

> No one can justly be killed by design, except by way of legal punishment, or to defend our lives, and preserve our property, when it cannot be effected without his destruction . . . But to justify a punishment of that kind, the person put to death must have committed a crime, and such a crime too, as every equitable judge would deem worthy of death.

This is not a law of war but of morality as applied to law, a forbearance which is 'not only a tribute to justice, it is a tribute to humanity, to moderation, to greatness of soul. It was in this moderation, says Sallust, that the foundation of Roman greatness was laid'.[7]

The nobility of Grotius's endeavour to infuse considerations of humanity into the iron laws of war does him credit, but it is insufficient as a means of opposing the inhumanity which those iron laws represent. What people continued to mean by 'laws of war' was the custom and attitude that attended whatever sense of honour

or humanity happened to subsist in individual commanders, officers and soldiers, and in regimental or national traditions about what counted as acceptable practice towards enemies, prisoners, non-combatants, and appropriate behaviour in occupied territories. There was often a lot of both honour and humanity in times of war; and as often – one suspects, more often – there was none of either. The description of what Voltaire's Candide saw as he decamped from the army of the 'Bulgarian King' is as true of the realities as if it were a despatch from the field, even in Enlightenment times:

> At length, while the two kings were causing Te Deums to be sung in their camps, Candide took a resolution to go and reason somewhere else upon causes and effects. After passing over heaps of dead or dying men, the first place he came to was a neighbouring village, in the Abarian territories, which had been burned to the ground by the Bulgarians, agreeably to the laws of war. Here lay a number of old men covered with wounds, who beheld their wives dying with their throats cut, and hugging their children to their breasts, all stained with blood. There several young virgins, whose bodies had been ripped open, after they had satisfied the natural necessities of the Bulgarian heroes, breathed their last; while others, half-burned in the flames, begged to be dispatched out of the world. The ground about them was covered with the brains, arms, and legs of dead men.
>
> Candide made all the haste he could to another village, which belonged to the Bulgarians, and there he found the heroic Abares had enacted the same tragedy.[8]

Actually the very first effort to say anything about restraint in war predates Grotius by a long way – in a classic Chinese text of the sixth century BC, Sun Tzu's *The Art of War*. In its second chapter, which cautions the would-be maker of war on its likely expense and the risks of a long campaign, Sun Tzu advises maintaining the morale of troops by allowing them booty, including the weapons and chariots of those

they have defeated. But he adds, 'captured soldiers must be kindly treated and kept'.[9] In circumstances where war consisted almost exclusively in combat between armies, the first humanitarian restraint to come to mind naturally concerns defeated troops; and in most thinking about war from then until the nineteenth century the focus was on the idea that war is conducted by the armies of states, not by the whole peoples of states. It is doubtless for this reason that the first fully international agreement of a humanitarian kind relating to war is the 1864 Geneva Convention protecting sick and wounded soldiers. The person responsible for getting this convention accepted was Henri Dunant, founder of the Red Cross. His organisation has ever since played a major role as a neutral agency seeking to mitigate the harms of war, often in the very midst of it being waged.

Evidently the idea of controls by law or treaty on certain practices in circumstances of war had found its time. In 1865 an officer on the Confederate side of the American Civil War, Captain Henry Wirz, was tried and executed by the victorious Union government for the death of Union army soldiers at a prisoner-of-war camp at Andersonville in Georgia, of which he had been commandant.[10] He was the only person tried for war crimes in that bloody conflict. Summary accounts of the significance of his conviction usually point out that it set a precedent for war-crimes trials in the twentieth century, by establishing that a defence of 'I was only following orders' is not acceptable against a charge of acting in ways that violate the laws of war and humanity. From Wirz onwards it has been accepted that military personnel can be held personally liable for crimes committed as a result of following orders.

In the way of these things, Henry Wirz is a hero to some of a pro-Confederate persuasion, and books and articles in plenty have been written to refute allegations of cruelty at Andersonville stockade, at the same time defending Wirz as an upstanding officer.[11] The testimony in his trial is however conclusive, at least as regards the extremely bad conditions in the camp; of the 45,000 prisoners held at Andersonville in the fourteen months between February 1864 and

May 1865, nearly a third died of starvation and disease. Allegations of murder and such cruel practices as setting dogs on prisoners are controversial, and the testimony more ambiguous. Wirz claimed that everything he had done had been ordered by his superior, General John H. Winder. Winder died in February 1865 and so escaped trial, but Wirz's defence was rejected, thus establishing the key precedent in question.

The Wirz case was just one expression of the unprecedented degree of thinking in this period about laws of war. When the American Civil War broke out, the government of the North asked the jurist Franz Lieber to write a code-book for its army on the rules of war. One reason was that most of the pre-war professional officer corps were engaged on the Confederate side of the conflict, while the Union army was led by relatively inexperienced officers 'who would need all the instruction they could get about how to fight *comme il faut* . . . in a contest with Southern gentlemen'.[12] This was followed by the Brussels Project for an International Declaration on the Laws and Customs of War (1874) and the manual produced by the Institute of International Law at its Oxford meeting in 1880, *The Laws of War on Land*. Both sets of suggestions expressly included protections for non-combatants and – most importantly for our purposes – the outlawing of bombardment of towns other than fortified military places.

These efforts contributed significantly to the thinking of those engaged in the International Peace Conference at The Hague in 1899 (see chapter 4 above) as involving the first-ever effort to restrict aerial bombing. Both the Brussels Project and the Oxford manual provided much of the actual wording for the resulting convention relevant to present purposes, known as 'Hague IV'. The Hague Conference was a response to the obvious fact that war in the industrial age was a vastly more threatening prospect than at any previous point in history. Cynical comment then and now has it that one of the sponsors of the conference, Tsar Nicholas II, knew that Russia was so far behind the other major powers in military strength that he saw an arms-limitation agreement as a strategy of self-protection while Russia caught up.

Whatever the motive for the conference, the sentiments on which it was publicly premised were unimpeachable; its intention, as the then Russian Foreign Minister, Count Mikhail Nikolaevich Muraviev, expressed it, was 'a possible reduction of the excessive armaments which weigh upon all nations', and a revision of the existing principles, such as they were, governing war on land and sea.

After ten weeks of discussion the twenty-five participating governments adopted a number of conventions and agreed to a number of declarations. Among the former were the Convention for the Peaceful Adjustment of International Differences; the Convention Regarding the Laws and Customs of War on Land; and the Convention for the Adaptation to Maritime Warfare of the Principles of the Geneva Convention of the 22nd August, 1864.

The document that counts most for present purposes is the Convention Regarding the Laws and Customs of War on Land (Hague IV). It contains the following explicit provisions:

> Seeing that while seeking means to preserve peace and prevent armed conflicts between nations, it is likewise necessary to bear in mind the case where the appeal to arms has been brought about by events which their care was unable to avert;
>
> Animated by the desire to serve, even in this extreme case, the interests of humanity and the ever progressive needs of civilisation;
>
> Thinking it important, with this object, to revise the general laws and customs of war, either with a view to defining them with greater precision or to confining them within such limits as would mitigate their severity as far as possible [and] until a more complete code of the laws of war has been issued, the High Contracting Parties deem it expedient to declare that, in cases not included in the Regulations adopted by them, the inhabitants and the belligerents remain under the protection and the rule of the principles of the law of nations, as they result from the usages established among civilised peoples, from the laws of humanity, and the dictates of the public conscience . . .

The High Contracting Parties . . . have agreed upon the following . . .

SECTION II: HOSTILITIES

CHAPTER I: Means of injuring the enemy, sieges, and bombardments.

Article 22. The right of belligerents to adopt means of injuring the enemy is not unlimited.

Article 23. In addition to the prohibitions provided by special Conventions, it is especially forbidden:

(a) To employ poison or poisoned weapons;

(b) To kill or wound treacherously individuals belonging to the hostile nation or army . . .

(d) To declare that no quarter will be given . . .

(e) To employ arms, projectiles, or material calculated to cause unnecessary suffering . . .

(g) To destroy or seize the enemy's property, unless such destruction or seizure be imperatively demanded by the necessities of war . . .

Article 25. The attack or bombardment, by whatever means, of towns, villages, dwellings, or buildings which are undefended is prohibited.

Article 26. The officer in command of an attacking force must, before commencing a bombardment, except in cases of assault, do all in his power to warn the authorities.

Article 27. In sieges and bombardments all necessary steps must be taken to spare, as far as possible, buildings dedicated to religion, art, science, or charitable purposes, historic monuments, hospitals, and places where the sick and wounded are collected, provided they are not being used at the time for military purposes.

It is the duty of the besieged to indicate the presence of such buildings or places by distinctive and visible signs, which shall be notified to the enemy beforehand.

Article 28. The pillage of a town or place, even when taken by assault, is prohibited.[13]

If this document had been regarded as binding on the United Kingdom during the Second World War, any competent lawyer could easily defend the area-bombing campaign against imputations of having violated its provisions. Germany's cities were not undefended; their populations had been amply warned, both explicitly by leaflets and broadcasts, and by example; the destruction of enemy property was – so defenders of area bombing say – necessary to defeating him; and so on for all the provisions, even perhaps the one in Article 27, on the grounds that the enemy had not marked its culturally and morally important buildings clearly enough, and that anyway no bomb-aimer flying high above marker flares in the night would be deliberately seeking a church or hospital to bomb.

But of course such a defence is beside the main point; for the convention conveys a moral attitude towards the conduct of war which, however legalistically one might claim that its provisions were not violated in the letter, seems quite clearly and emphatically violated in spirit by area bombing.

The 1899 conventions and declarations sought to ban not only aerial bombardment but the use of asphyxiating gases and (iterating the provision of the 1864 conference) expanding bullets and other inhuman projectiles. These efforts reflected the ages-old anxiety felt about new weapons which conferred a disproportionate and, in the light of their efficacy, savage advantage on their first possessors. For example, in 1139 Pope Innocent II sought to ban the cross-bow as a weapon 'too murderous for Christian warfare'. This by implication contains the idea of proportionality, and of restriction to means minimally necessary for victory, that Aquinas made central to the idea of just war.

In 1907 most of the First International Peace Conference agreements were reasserted, and in 1925 they were followed by the Geneva Gas Protocol, which reconsidered the gas question in the light of First World War experience, and prohibited the use of poison gas and the practice of bacteriological warfare. This was one agreement that the combatant nations observed in the Second World War with respect to

each other, though the Germans did not observe it with respect to Jews and others they sought to exterminate. Britain contemplated using gas in defending its coast in the event of a German invasion in 1940.[14]

As noted in chapter 4, at the General Conference for the Limitation and Reduction of Armaments held in Geneva between 1932 and 1934 efforts were made to restrict bombing from aircraft, and failed. In the opinion of some, this was because the British had found its twin-engined Vickers Virginia biplane bombers too useful in colonial policing. The relevant points discussed earlier concerned the question whether a bomber is an offensive or defensive aircraft; on this unresolvable question the conference failed. In the climate of the times a disarmament conference was never likely to get far anyway. Such good as had been done by earlier conferences attempting to introduce humanitarian restraint into war was, if anything, undone by the collapse of those discussions at Geneva in the 1930s, remembering that it was from this conference that both Germany and Japan withdrew, the latter for good measure resigning from the treaty reached in 1922 to limit naval armaments. A 1934 observer of the situation regarding humanitarian restraint in war would have had reason to think that scarcely any progress had been made since a sagacious Roman 2,000 years beforehand commented that *inter arma silent leges*: in time of war the laws are silent.

As this sketch shows, from Grotius's day until the outbreak of war in 1939 there was little success for those trying to establish binding international agreement on the laws of war, except in certain restricted respects such as the treatment of prisoners. In particular, these efforts were unavailing as regards the protection of civilians. In acknowledging that 'International law was not at that time copiously explicit about the protection of civilians', Geoffrey Best has argued that this was 'partly because . . . it was well understood that the conduct of some legitimate war operations precluded the separation of civilians from their country's posture of belligerence, and partly for

the reason that the "standard of civilisation" so far accepted by the lawmaking States had made it seem unnecessary to elaborate legal instruments around so self-evident a principle'.[15] As this suggests, from the mid-nineteenth century onwards war had been changing in a way that implicitly called into question the assumption that 'civilians' – meaning, people not in the armed forces – were by definition 'non-combatants' or 'innocents' (recall the root in *innocens*), for in the industrial age the contribution made to the war effort by people in factories and railway depots, on farms and down mineshafts, in newspaper offices and even hospitals, was becoming more and more difficult to separate from that of the actual soldiery. In Britain part of the propaganda effort was directed at extolling the great contribution made by coal miners and 'Land Army' girls to winning the war. As this therefore implied, everyone was in fact or potentially on the front line of a war that had no traditional front lines. A term had come into menacing use to describe war in the mid-twentieth century, one part of whose definition embraced civilians in its scope. This term was 'total war'.[16]

But what these points do not acknowledge is that the efforts made at defining 'laws of war' assumed the principle that civilian populations should be treated as non-combatant, even if some of their members were engaged in producing weapons or food for troops, because others of their members, perhaps – and probably – the majority of them, would be innocent in the exact meaning of this term: namely, children, the elderly, the lame and ill, and at least many of the women. It was to these that the idea of 'standards of civilised treatment' were supposed to apply.

In the light of this, one can say that humane thinking wished to see civilians unharmed as far as possible in war, and (*pace* the implication of Best's remarks, which suggest that no great effort was being made to introduce protections for civilians) in fact a considerable effort was devoted to this aim before 1939. Anyone alert to civilised and informed opinion knew as much at the time, as is for example shown by the Geneva conference of 1932–4, and by the debate about

the dangers anticipated from aerial bombing. Therefore to engage in activities which went deliberately against the principle at stake is a central point for the indictment sheet.

But even sharper points for the indictment sheet come from the laws of war and humanitarian declarations that followed the war, starting in the three years immediately after the war's end (1945–8). For these were framed expressly to address the atrocities that the war had seen, chief among them genocide. But they sought to address a number of other things besides: protection of the rights of the individual, outlawing of military aggression, outlawing of destruction of cultural heritage – and in the Geneva Convention of 1949 and its protocols, protection for civilians in time of war.

This thinking bears directly on the experience of the war and what, in its immediate aftermath, was thought about its moral character. So the protection of civilians against bombing included in these immediate post-war declarations and conventions constitutes a retrospective indictment of the practices they outlaw.

In late June 1945 delegates from the victorious powers – the United States, Britain, Russia and France – met in London to discuss the prosecution of Nazi leaders for what, from the outset, was described as 'war crimes', even before the Charter of the International Military Tribunal (IMT) was agreed. The chief problem facing the delegates was the unprecedented nature of their task. The Nazis had unquestionably done terrible things, from causing a worldwide war to committing genocide of European Jewry. The question was, under what laws were these atrocities to be prosecuted? In the absence of a clear pre-existing code of laws relevant to the circumstances, the IMT was open to the criticism that it was creating *ex post facto* law, laws devised after the commission of the crimes they themselves defined, thus breaching principles of natural justice.

In fact it was possible to argue that Germany's aggression brought it into breach of a number of conventions and treaties to which it was a signatory – the Hague rules of 1907, the Treaty of Versailles, the

Kellogg–Briand Pact of 1928 outlawing war, and the Locarno Pact.
Its invasions of Poland, Norway, the Low Countries and France,
Greece, Yugoslavia and Russia, multiply violated the terms and spirit
of these agreements.[17]

Moreover, all civilised nations had laws against murder, torture and
enslavement, and the drafters of the IMT's charter recognised that
they would simply be applying them to the activities of the Nazi
regime within the boundaries of its home and conquered territories.
The IMT was not creating laws *ex post facto* – so it was therefore
claimed – but bringing established law to bear in the special
circumstances it faced. The IMT was in effect an instrument of
enforcement, not of legislation.[18]

In the discussion that preceded the drafting of the IMT's charter it
was agreed that the Wirz defence of 'following orders' would not be
acceptable even in a regime where the *Führerprinzip* reigned, this
being the principle that the leader has absolute authority and that
subordinates must unhesitatingly and unquestioningly obey. It happened in any case that in the paybook of every German soldier was a
clause stating that he was not required to obey an illegal order. And it
transpired too that in cases where the Wehrmacht carried out
executions or mass killings, for example on and behind the lines
of the Eastern Front, individual soldiers could and did exempt
themselves from involvement. These two facts undermined appeal
to the *Führerprinzip* as an excuse.[19]

A further difficulty foreseen by the delegates to the London
meeting was that the work of the IMT would appear to be 'victor's
justice', given that atrocities had been committed by all sides in the
conflict. Doubtless these were not specified in the meetings; the
matter seems to have been discussed under the heading of an
attempted defence of 'tu quoque' ('you also') by those indicted.
But the truth was that in addition to the terrible crimes committed by
Soviet troops as they fought their way westwards to and past Berlin –
hundreds of thousands of acts of rape, to say nothing of other acts of
brutality, murder and rapine – there was the unspoken fact of five

years of increasingly heavy civilian-targeted bombing by the western Allies' air forces – most of it in Europe by the RAF, with the USAAF following suit in Japan. In the event it was decided that although there were arguments that could be adduced to counter a 'tu quoque' defence, the simplest and surest means was to make it impermissible in the terms of the charter.[20]

By the end of the first week in August 1945 the Charter of the International Military Tribunal was drafted, agreed and signed, and it specified four crimes for which Nazi leaders would be tried: conspiracy to carry out aggressive war, the launching of aggression, killing and destroying beyond the justification of military necessity, and 'crimes against humanity'.

The concept of crimes against humanity addressed the attempted extermination of the Jews, together with other crimes against civilians, and it was a novel concept, no older than the war just ended. In the Nuremberg Indictment 'crimes against humanity' was defined with precision to denote 'murder, extermination, enslavement, deportation, and other inhumane acts committed against any civilian population, before or during the war, or persecutions on political, racial or religious grounds in execution of or in connection with any crime within the jurisdiction of the Tribunal'.[21] These last fifteen words tie crimes against humanity to the war crimes being prosecuted by the IMT, and they have ambiguous scope: do they apply only to 'persecutions on political [etc.] grounds', or do they apply to all the crimes against humanity listed? The standard reading given by students of international law seems to be the latter; which restricts the concept's application. These same students of international law say that the concept now has little independent meaning given that its content is covered by the laws on war crimes, genocide and human rights that have since come into existence.[22] For present purposes, the inclusion of a specific indictment of 'inhumane acts committed against any civilian population' embodies an ethical spirit which is relevant to considering the moral status of area bombing.

The provisions of the Charter of the IMT that especially matter for present purposes are as follows:

ARTICLE 6 The following acts, or any of them, are crimes coming within the jurisdiction of the Tribunal for which there shall be individual responsibility:

(a) Crimes against Peace . . .

(b) War Crimes: namely, violations of the laws or customs of war. Such violations shall include, but not be limited to, murder, ill-treatment or deportation to slave labour or for any other purpose of civilian population of or in occupied territory, murder or ill-treatment of prisoners of war or persons on the seas, killing of hostages, plunder of public or private property, wanton destruction of cities, towns, or villages, or devastation not justified by military necessity;

(c) Crimes against Humanity: namely, murder, extermination, enslavement, deportation, and other inhumane acts committed against any civilian population, before or during the war, or persecutions on political, racial, or religious grounds in execution of or in connection with any crime within the jurisdiction of the Tribunal, whether or not in violation of domestic law of the country where perpetrated.

Leaders, organisers, instigators, and accomplices participating in the formulation or execution of a Common Plan or Conspiracy to commit any of the foregoing crimes are responsible for all acts performed by any persons in execution of such plan.

ARTICLE 7 The official position of defendants, whether as Heads of State or responsible officials in Government departments, shall not be considered as freeing them from responsibility or mitigating punishment.

ARTICLE 8 The fact that the defendant acted pursuant to order of his Government or of a superior shall not free him from responsibility, but may be considered in mitigation of punishment if the Tribunal determine that justice so requires.

The passages especially relevant here are *wanton destruction of cities, towns, or villages, or devastation not justified by military necessity*, and *inhumane acts committed against any civilian population*. The last two quoted articles unequivocally assign responsibility for the crimes identified by the charter to those who required and authorised them as well as those who, thus authorised, planned and executed them.

If the Allies were put on trial by the lights of their own Nuremberg Charter, how would they fare? Taken out of the specific context of Nazi-perpetrated aggression and its associated crimes, and considered purely as embodying ethical requirements to measure Allied area bombing against, the following immediately suggests itself. The second – *inhumane acts committed against any civilian population* applies to Allied area bombing without qualification. The first – *wanton destruction of cities, towns, or villages, or devastation not justified by military necessity* – invites defence on the grounds that area bombing was not 'wanton' but 'justified by military necessity', as we shall see in the next chapter. But among the answers this invites, the following is immediately pertinent: one does not have to appeal only to the smaller German towns and cities destroyed in the war's final months to contest this defence – the little Dresden of Würzburg among them. Massive bombing of civilian targets by any standard is disproportionate, which is what this indictment in effect charges. Take the atomic bombings of Hiroshima and Nagasaki: if these were claimed to be attacks on targets of military value, assuming there to have been industrial units or military barracks in these cities which 'military necessity' demanded should be destroyed, dropping an atom bomb on them is equivalent to chopping off a man's head to cure his toothache, such is the degree of disproportion involved. The same applies to the firebombing of Tokyo, Operation Gomorrah, the bombing of Berlin, Dresden, and indeed all aspects of the bomber war to which the description 'area bombing' applies. It is not a defence to say that there was no other way of destroying the militarily necessary target contained within the urban area, and that therefore the civilians killed and the collateral destruction caused is protected

by the doctrine of double effect. Even if we did not have on record the public avowals – as we do – of the conductors of area bombing to the effect that they were specifically aiming at civilian morale, the degree of indifference to human life and suffering that would be involved in bombing a whole city in order to hit a barracks or factory within it, would remain culpable. But as it is, those avowals are indeed on record.

The moral culpability of area bombing was so well recognised during and immediately after the war that when at last an effort was made to arrive at a firm and binding statement of the laws of war, it was explicitly outlawed by them. This happened in the Fourth Geneva Convention of 1949 and the protocols subjoined to it afterwards. Its aim is to detail what counts as acceptable treatment of civilians during time of war, including hostages, diplomats, spies, bystanders, and populations under military occupation. The convention outlaws torture, collective punishment, and the introduction and settlement by occupying powers of their own civilians in the territories occupied. From the time of its adoption in 1949 until the time of writing these words, the Fourth Geneva Convention has never been invoked, though there have been a number of cases to which it clearly applies, such as Tibet, Bosnia, Rwanda, Kosovo and the Palestinian territories.

As with many of the earlier efforts at introducing humanitarian constraints into war, the mover of this Geneva Convention was the International Red Cross. And as with the contemporary endeavour to have the newly created United Nations commit itself to a declaration of universal human rights, the great powers of the United States, Britain, Russia and France were at first reluctant to sign up to it. In the case of human rights it was small countries, colonies and non-governmental organisations that insisted on the United Nations making an explicit commitment to the protection of human rights, against the reluctance of the great powers who saw it as posing obstacles to their international and imperial activities.

The same happened with the proposed new Geneva Convention. When the Red Cross invited the great powers to participate in a review of the laws of war and a discussion of how to protect civilians in future wars if any, the British government responded with impatience, saying that it was too busy to bother with such a thing for at least the next five years. The Soviet Union to begin with did not wish to participate at all.[23] What followed was a complicated and protracted story which, despite the convolutions of international diplomacy and internal Red Cross politics, eventually issued in 1949 in the Fourth Geneva Convention, and in 1977 in two Additional Protocols. Parts of the Convention and the first Additional Protocol are central to present purposes:

Geneva Convention relative to the Protection of Civilian Persons in Time of War. Adopted on 12 August 1949 by the Diplomatic Conference for the Establishment of International Conventions for the Protection of Victims of War, held in Geneva from 21 April to 12 August, 1949.

PART I GENERAL PROVISIONS

Article 3 Persons taking no active part in the hostilities, including members of armed forces who have laid down their arms and those placed hors de combat by sickness, wounds, detention, or any other cause, shall in all circumstances be treated humanely, without any adverse distinction founded on race, colour, religion or faith, sex, birth or wealth, or any other similar criteria.

To this end, the following acts are and shall remain prohibited at any time and in any place whatsoever with respect to the above-mentioned persons:

(a) Violence to life and person, in particular murder of all kinds, mutilation, cruel treatment and torture . . .

PART II GENERAL PROTECTION OF POPULATIONS AGAINST CERTAIN CONSEQUENCES OF WAR . . .

Article 14 In time of peace, the High Contracting Parties and, after the outbreak of hostilities, the Parties thereto, may establish in their

own territory and, if the need arises, in occupied areas, hospital and safety zones and localities so organised as to protect from the effects of war, wounded, sick and aged persons, children under fifteen, expectant mothers and mothers of children under seven . . .

Article 15 Any Party to the conflict may, either directly or through a neutral State or some humanitarian organisation, propose to the adverse Party to establish, in the regions where fighting is taking place, neutralised zones intended to shelter from the effects of war the following persons, without distinction:

(a) Wounded and sick combatants or non-combatants;

(b) Civilian persons who take no part in hostilities, and who, while they reside in the zones, perform no work of a military character . . .

Article 16 The wounded and sick, as well as the infirm, and expectant mothers, shall be the object of particular protection and respect . . .

Article 18 Civilian hospitals organised to give care to the wounded and sick, the infirm and maternity cases, may in no circumstances be the object of attack, but shall at all times be respected and protected by the Parties to the conflict . . .

PART III STATUS AND TREATMENT OF PROTECTED PERSONS

SECTION I

Article 33 Reprisals against protected persons and their property are prohibited . . .

SECTION 111

Article 53 Any destruction by the Occupying Power of real or personal property belonging individually or collectively to private persons, or to the State, or to other public authorities, or to social or co-operative organisations, is prohibited, except where such destruction is rendered absolutely necessary by military operations . . .

The circumspect language of these provisions, which identify aerial bombing of civilian targets by what they do *not* say in providing

protection for children, women, the wounded and the infirm, and for safe places for such individuals to be housed away from attack, is explainable by immediate post-war sensitivities and politics. The two countries that had most experience to offer in drafting provisions to protect civilians from aerial attack, namely Germany and Japan, were not at the conference table because they were the defeated parties to the war; while the two countries who had most to gain from not mentioning aerial bombing of civilians as something so wrong as to require being outlawed, namely the victor nations of Britain and the United States, were very much present. So it took until 1977, a further quarter of a century, for the required explicit wording to appear, in the form of the first Additional Protocol to the 1949 Convention. This document at long last clearly and unequivocally states that area bombing is unacceptable, and outlaws it. It is a retrospective condemnation of area bombing, a passing of judgement by history on the area-bombing campaigns of the Second World War. It merits full quotation therefore. It reads as follows:

Protocol Additional to the Geneva Conventions of 12 August 1949, and relating to the Protection of Victims of International Armed Conflicts (Protocol 1). Adopted on 8 June 1977 by the Diplomatic Conference on the Reaffirmation and Development of International Humanitarian Law applicable in Armed Conflicts.
PART III METHODS AND MEANS OF WARFARE
SECTION I. Article 35. Basic rules
1. In any armed conflict, the right of the Parties to the conflict to choose methods or means of warfare is not unlimited.
2. It is prohibited to employ weapons, projectiles and material and methods of warfare of a nature to cause superfluous injury or unnecessary suffering.
3. It is prohibited to employ methods or means of warfare which are intended, or may be expected, to cause widespread, long-term and severe damage to the natural environment.
Article 36. New weapons

In the study, development, acquisition or adoption of a new weapon, means or method of warfare, a High Contracting Party is under an obligation to determine whether its employment would, in some or all circumstances, be prohibited by this Protocol or by any other rule of international law applicable to the High Contracting Party.

Article 40. Quarter

It is prohibited to order that there shall be no survivors, to threaten an adversary therewith or to conduct hostilities on this basis.

PART IV CIVILIAN POPULATION

SECTION I.-GENERAL PROTECTION AGAINST EFFECTS OF HOSTILITIES

CHAPTER 1. Article 48. Basic rule

In order to ensure respect for and protection of the civilian population and civilian objects, the Parties to the conflict shall at all times distinguish between the civilian population and combatants and between civilian objects and military objectives and accordingly shall direct their operations only against military objectives.

CHAPTER 11.-CIVILIANS AND CIVILIAN POPULATION

Article 50. Definition of civilians and civilian population

1. A civilian is any person who does not belong to one of the categories of persons referred to in Article 4 A (1), (2), (3) and (6) of the Third Convention and in Article 43 of this Protocol. In case of doubt whether a person is a civilian, that person shall be considered to be a civilian.

2. The civilian population comprises all persons who are civilians.

3. The presence within the civilian population of individuals who do not come within the definition of civilians does not deprive the population of its civilian character.

Article 51.-Protection of the civilian population

1. The civilian population and individual civilians shall enjoy general protection against dangers arising from military operations. To give effect to this protection, the following rules, which are

additional to other applicable rules of international law, shall be observed in all circumstances.

2. The civilian population as such, as well as individual civilians, shall not be the object of attack. Acts or threats of violence the primary purpose of which is to spread terror among the civilian population are prohibited . . .

4. Indiscriminate attacks are prohibited. Indiscriminate attacks are:

(a) Those which are not directed at a specific military objective;

(b) Those which employ a method or means of combat which cannot be directed at a specific military objective; or

(c) Those which employ a method or means of combat the effects of which cannot be limited as required by this Protocol; and consequently, in each such case, are of a nature to strike military objectives and civilians or civilian objects without distinction.

5. Among others, the following types of attacks are to be considered as indiscriminate:

(a) An attack by bombardment by any methods or means which treats as a single military objective a number of clearly separated and distinct military objectives located in a city, town, village or other area containing a similar concentration of civilians or civilian objects; and

(b) An attack which may be expected to cause incidental loss of civilian life, injury to civilians, damage to civilian objects, or a combination thereof, which would be excessive in relation to the concrete and direct military advantage anticipated.

6. Attacks against the civilian population or civilians by way of reprisals are prohibited.

CHAPTER III.-CIVILIAN OBJECTS

Article 52.-General protection of civilian objects

1. Civilian objects shall not be the object of attack or of reprisals. Civilian objects are all objects which are not military objectives as defined in paragraph 2.

2. Attacks shall be limited strictly to military objectives. In so far as objects are concerned, military objectives are limited to those

objects which by their nature, location, purpose or use make an effective contribution to military action and whose total or partial destruction, capture or neutralisation, in the circumstances ruling at the time, offers a definite military advantage.

3. In case of doubt whether an object which is normally dedicated to civilian purposes, such as a place of worship, a house or other dwelling or a school, is being used to make an effective contribution to military action, it shall be presumed not to be so used.

Article 53.-Protection of cultural objects and of places of worship

[I]t is prohibited:

(a) To commit any acts of hostility directed against the historic monuments, works of art or places of worship which constitute the cultural or spiritual heritage of peoples . . .

(c) To make such objects the object of reprisals.

Article 54.-Protection of objects indispensable to the survival of the civilian population

2. It is prohibited to attack, destroy, remove or render useless objects indispensable to the survival of the civilian population, such as foodstuffs, agricultural areas for the production of foodstuffs, crops, livestock, drinking water installations and supplies and irrigation works, for the specific purpose of denying them for their sustenance value to the civilian population or to the adverse Party, whatever the motive, whether in order to starve out civilians, to cause them to move away, or for any other motive . . .

4. These objects shall not be made the object of reprisals.

CHAPTER IV.-PRECAUTIONARY MEASURES

Article 57.-Precautions in attack

1. In the conduct of military operations, constant care shall be taken to spare the civilian population, civilians and civilian objects.

2. With respect to attacks, the following precautions shall be taken:

(a) Those who plan or decide upon an attack shall:

(i) Do everything feasible to verify that the objectives to be attacked are neither civilians nor civilian objects and are not subject to special protection but are military objectives within the meaning of

paragraph 2 of Article 52 and that it is not prohibited by the provisions of this Protocol to attack them;

(ii) Take all feasible precautions in the choice of means and methods of attack with a view to avoiding, and in any event to minimising, incidental loss of civilian life, injury to civilians and damage to civilian objects;

(iii) Refrain from deciding to launch any attack which may be expected to cause incidental loss of civilian life, injury to civilians, damage to civilian objects, or a combination thereof, which would be excessive in relation to the concrete and direct military advantage anticipated;

(b) An attack shall be cancelled or suspended if it becomes apparent that the objective is not a military one or is subject to special protection or that the attack may be expected to cause incidental loss of civilian life, injury to civilians, damage to civilian objects, or a combination thereof, which would be excessive in relation to the concrete and direct military advantage anticipated . . .

3. When a choice is possible between several military objectives for obtaining a similar military advantage, the objective to be selected shall be that attack which may be expected to cause the least danger to civilian lives and to civilian objects.

4. In the conduct of military operations at sea or in the air, each Party to the conflict shall, in conformity with its rights and duties under the rules of international law applicable in armed conflict, take all reasonable precautions to avoid losses of civilian lives and damage to civilian objects.

5. No provision of this Article may be construed as authorising any attacks against the civilian population, civilians or civilian objects.

This protocol now has the force of law. Britain is a party to it, as it is to the main convention itself. The United States is party to the main convention, but not to its additional protocols, having refused to sign them. But this does not exempt the United States from the requirements of the convention and its additional protocols, because they are

considered part of customary international law, and therefore as binding on all countries whether signatories or not.

In practice, if a country fails in its obligations under the convention, the High Contracting parties to it can be called on to 'take action to ensure respect for international humanitarian law', a phrase vague enough to encompass everything from diplomatic notes of protest to armed intervention. Enforcement of international humanitarian law has been the Achilles heel of efforts to introduce a global regime of such law since the end of the Second World War; but one aspect of it has been the institution of special tribunals to try those who have violated human rights, as with those for Nuremberg and the former Yugoslavia, and the International Criminal Court.

The basic demands of the fourth Geneva Convention and its protocols come down to requiring that states must give unequivocal instructions to their armed forces not to mount direct attacks against civilians or civilian targets; not to mount indiscriminate attacks, that is, they must first seek to distinguish between military targets and civilians or civilian objects; not to mount attacks which, though aimed at legitimate military objectives, have a disproportionate impact on civilians in the vicinity; not to use weapons that are inherently indiscriminate in their effects; and otherwise to take all necessary measures to protect civilian populations from the effect of military operations.

As each and every one of these provisions shows, if this Geneva Convention had been in force during the Second World War, the British and American conductors of area bombing would have been straightforwardly liable for prosecution under its terms. It was not of course then in force, so this is not the point of quoting it here; and no suggestion is being offered that it should be made to apply *ex post facto* – apart from anything else, none of the individuals responsible are alive to be indicted. Rather, the point of quoting it, as with the other instruments and efforts made to protect civilians in war, is to reveal the ethical thrust that underlies it, and to measure area bombing against it. The claim that area bombing manifestly fails when

measured against it is strengthened by noting, also once again, that the principles enunciated in the first protocol were clearly present to the minds of British leaders before the outbreak of the Second World War, and to some of them indeed those principles already seemed to have the force of customary international law. 'In the first place,' said Prime Minister Neville Chamberlain in the House of Commons on 21 June 1938,

> it is against international law of bomb civilians as such and to make deliberate attacks upon civilian populations. That is undoubtedly a violation of international law. In the second place, targets which are aimed at from the air must be legitimate military objectives and must be capable of identification. In the third place, reasonable care must be taken in attacking these military objectives so that by carelessness a civilian population in the neighbourhood is not bombed.[24]

That the British government then took this seriously is attested by the restrictions on bombing applied throughout the opening phase of the war, as shown in the account of the bombing war given in chapter 2. And as that chapter shows, this was a policy which, in part through sheer ineffectiveness, was explicitly abandoned in February 1942, with the consequences we all know. When Sir Arthur Harris came to write his memoirs immediately after the war, he felt able to say,

> Whenever the fact that our aircraft occasionally [sic] killed women and children is cast in my teeth I always produce this example of the blockade, although there are endless others to be got from the wars of the past. I never forget, as so many do, that in all normal warfare of the past, and of the not distant past, it was the common practice to besiege cities and, if they refused to surrender when called upon with due formality to do so, every living thing in them was in the end put to the sword . . . And as to bombardment, what city in what war has ever failed to receive the maximum bombard-

ment from all enemy artillery within range so long as it has
continued resistance? International law can always be argued
pro and con, but in this matter of the use of aircraft in war there
is, it so happens, no international law at all.[25]

In the opinion of Geoffrey Best, Harris's claim that there was 'no
international law at all' applicable to aerial bombing goes too far; 'but
he would not have gone too far if he had restricted himself to saying
that there was not much of it, and that what there was lay mostly in
the realm of principles' – after which Best immediately adds the point
that will be central, as we shall see in the next chapter, to the defence
of area bombing: 'as to whose practical application in circumstances
of desperate total war against an exceptionally nasty enemy there was
bound to be much controversy'.[26]

   For present purposes it is enough that there is a recognised ethical
principle at stake. If there was in addition a principle of customary
international law present to the minds of competent persons before
and during the Second World War, then there is indeed a debate to be
had about the use that should have been made of it during the
lifetimes of Presidents Roosevelt and Truman, Winston Churchill,
their war cabinets, and the senior officers commanding their bombing
forces – General Hap Arnold, General Curtis LeMay, Lord Portal and
Sir Arthur Harris not least among them.

Much of the discussion here has been about 'laws of war', conventions, treaties, declarations, all straining towards the status of binding
laws that could be invoked to indict, try, and if they are found guilty
punish, those who violate them. The question whether there was
anything in force having the status of law in this sense, at the time that
Allied area bombing was carried out, was, as we see, moot; but that is
not the point here. The effort made from the time of Grotius onwards
to outlaw unnecessary and disproportionate conduct in war, and to
avoid harm to non-combatants and their cultural treasures, their
schools and their hospitals, embodies an ethical spirit whose character

and intention is crystal clear. In the light of it, the question being asked here is whether Allied area bombing was contrary to that ethical spirit; and the indictment is, that it was.

The point about strict legality matters in one respect. If all those efforts from Grotius onwards had translated into actual law, then as we see there would be a proper question about whether Allied area bombing broke that law. From a juridical point of view this matters because in the absence of such law, no crime as such was committed: as an ancient principle of Roman law states, *nullum crimen et nulla poene sine lege*, there is no crime and no punishment without a law. So if there was no law in existence which Allied area bombing broke, then it is not strictly correct to describe area bombing as a 'war crime', and those who planned and conducted it as 'war criminals'.

One way of viewing the Nuremberg procedure is to say that it involved taking certain acts not previously proscribed by laws, and saying of them that their egregious nature required that they be regarded as crimes, and those charged with perpetrating them tried and, if found guilty, punished accordingly. On this view, because of the particular nature of the offence done to humanitarian instincts and ideals of natural right and justice, the offence itself was seen as creating the law it breaks; it taught observers that there is an implicit law in the case, and that in these special circumstances it accords with natural justice that that implicit law should be made explicit, and applied.

If this was indeed the idea at work at Nuremberg, then – as mentioned already – it risks contravening the fundamental principle whose shadow hung over the International Military Tribunal at Nuremberg: the principle that laws should not be created retrospectively. Hereby hangs an opportunity for much debate. But here the crucial point is different: it concerns the fundamental *ethical* thrust that lay behind Nuremberg as behind all the efforts to infuse humanitarian considerations into the conduct of war. This ethical point includes saying, among other things, that deliberately bombing cities and towns to kill and terrorise civilians, not all of whom were

engaged in manufacturing arms or aiding their country's military, and many of whom were children and elderly folk – and at the same time, destroying much that belongs to the culture and necessities of those people, including schools and hospitals – contravenes every moral and humanitarian principle debated in connection with the just conduct of war.

This, then, is the indictment of British and United States area-bombing activities in Europe and Japan in the Second World War: that it was a moral crime. The next task is to see if this accusation survives the defence now to be offered to it.

7

The Defence of Area Bombing

I N H I S M E M O I R of the bombing war Sir Arthur Harris
wrote,

> In spite of all that happened at Hamburg, bombing proved a
> comparatively humane method. For one thing, it saved the flower
> of the youth of this country and of our allies from being mown
> down by the military in the field, as it was in Flanders . . . But the
> point is often made that bombing is specially wicked because it
> causes casualties among civilians. This is true, but then all wars
> have caused casualties among civilians. For instance, [in] the last
> war . . . our blockade of Germany . . . caused nearly 800,000
> deaths – naturally these were mainly of women and children and
> old people because at all costs the enemy had had to keep his
> fighting men adequately fed.[1]

There is a double defence of Bomber Command's war in this
paragraph, though both parts are aimed at supporting the conclusion
that bombing is 'relatively humane' as a weapon of war. Harris's claim
that bombing saved Allied military lives is the same justification given
by the United States for its area bombing of Japanese cities, and
constitutes the main defence of its atom-bomb attacks. Harris's
second claim, that civilians have always been targeted in war, has

the merit of being true; the figure he cites for civilian deaths by blockade-induced starvation in Germany during the First World War is likewise correct.

These are just two of the arguments deployed by defenders of the Allied area-bombing campaigns. They offer at least five others. They say that area bombing undermined enemy civilian morale; that it reduced the capacity and efficiency of enemy war industries; that it created logistical difficulties for the German economy and administration by obliging them to deal constantly with repairs and refugees; that it kept soldiers, guns and fighter planes away from the battlefronts to protect the cities instead; and that it distracted enemy soldiers at the front by making them worry about what was happening to their families at home.

Officially it was easy to claim that area bombing's main aim was the enemy's war industry, and that civilian casualties were an unavoidable side-effect. When challenged on the disproportion of this side-effect, defenders of the strategy were apt to say that the enemy started it first, that the enemy's crimes deserved punishment, that it was 'them or us', and that war is not a place for sentiment but requires resolution and tough choices in the effort to survive and win. This, after all, was a war against a formidable and dangerous enemy, and – for the British – well into 1942 the outcome was not merely uncertain, but threatening, for although the United States had entered the war in December 1941 – which meant that in the longer term victory was more likely than not – in 1942 the forces of the United States were not yet mustered in sufficient strength in the European theatre to help protect against, for example, another attempt by Germany to invade the British Isles. At that point practically the only means available to Britain for fighting back against Germany was bombing. Thus a strongly urged argument was that the resort to area bombing was the result of the necessities of war, implying that it was crucial that enemy morale and industry should be attacked, and that civilian casualties were an unavoidable outcome of doing so.

Among these arguments the four that are especially relied upon by

post-war defenders of the area-bombing campaigns are: the effect on enemy war industry, the logistical difficulties created for the economy and administration, the holding-back of military resources from the battle-fronts, and the fact that area bombing was a major means, and for a time the only means, of 'carrying the war to Germany'.

Before turning to these, let us consider Harris's two arguments first, since evidently they were the ones that sustained him, as Bomber Command's chief, during the arduous years of sending bombers over Germany on every night that the weather allowed.

The answer to the first point he offers – that bombing civilians saved soldiers' lives – was given by Vera Brittain in her *Seed of Chaos*. It is that saving military lives by substituting civilian deaths for them is no different morally from a soldier on the battlefield using a civilian as a shield. Soldiers are contracted, trained and armed for battle, and although they are placed in danger, their commanders usually try to keep as many of them unharmed as possible, by appropriate tactics. Civilians are in a very different situation from soldiers. Many, whether or not in a minority, will not be willing parties to the war that affects them. Civilians also have efforts made on their behalf to protect them, but the conditions of modern war – especially in respect of bombs and missiles from the air – place them in great hazard despite all that defence measures can do.

The defender of bombing can reply to this, in turn, that an army is equipped, fed, and otherwise supported by the civilian population at home, and there is in principle no difference between the civilian factory worker who makes a gun and the soldier who fires it. Therefore the civilian armaments worker is a legitimate target. And if he is a legitimate target in his factory, why is he not a legitimate target in his home?

This answer is in part right. War industries are certainly a legitimate target for military action. But it is obviously better to destroy the factory than to kill the people who work in it; and if their deaths are covered by the principle of double effect – as the 'collateral damage' done in the process of the factory being destroyed – killing their families and neighbours is not. Killing their families and neighbours instead violates

the principle established by Aquinas and Grotius that a just action in war is a proportionate one. To stop guns being made by killing an armaments worker *and* his family and neighbours is disproportionate.

Sometimes the argument about the relation of civilians to war is extended to the limit, by saying that in modern war there are no non-combatants: 'everyone is in the front line'. This assertion is alas true, but not because infants and the elderly are somehow indistinguishable from armed and trained infantrymen or bomber crews in their aeroplanes. Rather it is because civilians are placed on the front line by having military attacks launched at them. If any civilians are involved in working to support the military efforts of their country, it is because they are specifically the workers and technicians in the industries crucial to the military effort; they and they alone are legitimate targets for attack therefore; and they are certain to be a minority of the civilian population as a whole.

The question of proportion is a major one for the area-bombing war. Bomber Command sought to demoralise the German population by killing as many of its members as possible, and by 'dehousing', terrorising, and causing hardship to the survivors. That was a direct assault on non-combatants, unacceptable on moral grounds even allowing that living among them they had that minority directly engaged in war-supporting activities. But in claiming that this was not only damaging the will but the ability to continue the war – that is, that it was reducing the capacity of Germany's war industries – the means was obviously disproportionate to this latter end. This is not a point about the fact – though fact it is – that area bombing did not reduce German war production; it is a point about the fact that there were other ways of aiming to hurt war production that greatly lessened impact on civilians, for example precision bombing, as with the American endeavour in the European theatre, which in the end – in its attack on oil – proved highly effective. The American oil attack was proportionate and pertinent; it could also legitimately claim to be a necessary part of the effort to defeat Germany. The area bombing of civilian populations was not necessary.

Harris's attempt to defend the area-bombing strategy by saying that civilians always die in war – his second argument – is no defence, nor is the game of numbers he adds to it. He says in effect that his killing civilians was licensed by the fact that civilians have always been killed in war; and anyway he killed fewer than were killed by the First World War blockade. To see what is wrong with this argument, imagine someone who has done something wrong and who asks to be let off on the grounds that wrongs have always been done, and that some of them were greater wrongs. For a robust example: imagine a murderer defending himself by saying that there have always been murders, and that anyway he only murdered two people when someone else had murdered five. Would this argument exonerate him? It would not. But this is exactly the form of Harris's 'blockade' argument; and these analogies dispose of it. A shorter way of putting the point is to recall that a greater wrong does not excuse a lesser; and that two such do not make a right.

Harris also claimed, in connection with his blockade example, that the means by which civilians died in previous wars was sometimes crueller than death by bombing. But it is debatable whether starvation is a crueller form of death than being blown up, burned, crushed under a fallen building, or asphyxiated in a cellar.[2]

One point that Harris mentions by implication rather than directly, and which post-war defenders of area bombing no longer mention much if at all, is the once-vaunted bombing aim of 'undermining civilian morale'. This was thought to be a key part of the aim of shortening the war, and that is what Harris meant in talking of saving young soldiers' lives. As we saw, it turned out that heavy bombing did not undermine civilian morale – where it did not buoy it, it numbed it – nor therefore did it cause a collapse in the will to fight or work, nor did it precipitate a revolution. But a thought canvassed earlier was that this perhaps was because the weight of bombing was still insufficient, even by the measure of the closing months of the war in Europe. By contrast, the claim is often made that the atom-bomb

attacks on Hiroshima and Nagasaki were the last straw for Japanese morale, and that it was these particular instances of area bombing that won the war in the East.

If civilian morale were a decisive factor, was it necessary to kill so many residents of Hiroshima and Nagasaki? Could not the same result have been attained by means of dropping a demonstration bomb, either within sight of a major Japanese population centre, or showing this on film to the Japanese? It might well have been enough to give a demonstration of the atom bomb to the Japanese forces.

In his account of the American bombing war over Japan, Ronald Schaffer notes that at first this was precisely the intention. Truman at one point instructed his Secretary of War, Henry Stimson, to arrange matters so that 'military objectives and soldiers and sailors are the target and not women and children . . . The target will be a purely military one and we will issue a warning statement asking the Japs to surrender and save lives'.[3] There was quite a wide consensus among scientists working on the bomb, and among some of the military high command, that this was the appropriate way to proceed.

And indeed half of this way of proceeding was to some extent implemented. At the Potsdam Conference on 26 July 1945 a warning was issued to Japan that if they continued with the war they would meet with the 'utter destruction of their homeland'.[4] Nothing was said about a new kind of weapon being used, and by this time the decision to opt for a demonstration explosion rather than an attack on a city had been changed – in favour of the latter. The Japanese had for some time already been making tentative approaches to end the war, not directly but through the Russians (who were then not yet at war with Japan); but some commentators allege that Russian designs on Japanese-controlled territory in the East meant that they delayed passing on to the western Allies details of Japan's approaches, and misrepresented them when they did.

In the event, when the order reached General Carl 'Tooey' Spaatz, now in command of the USAAF strategic bombing in the Pacific, to drop an atom bomb on Hiroshima, he requested the order in writing,

not wanting an imputation of responsibility on his own head. He did not believe that dropping an atom bomb was necessary; like his colleagues in RAF Bomber Command, although as a late and surprising convert, he believed that massive conventional bombing was enough. Still, he carried out his orders. He then suggested that the second bomb be dropped on an unpopulated area 'so that it would not be so devastating to the city and the people'.[5] His orders were otherwise, and the Nagasaki bomb was duly dropped.

It is very hard now to see what possible *justification* can be given for the atom-bomb attacks, though *explanations* abound: among them the desire to make a demonstration to the Russians of the new access to American power, and the frank desire to wreak retribution on Japan, perceived as an evil and brutal aggressor which had given America a humiliating surprise at Pearl Harbor, threatened to dominate America's Pacific back-yard, and needed to be taught a severe lesson. The atom bombings were intended to be that lesson – though many would judge the Tokyo firebombing, the devastation of other Japanese cities, and the imminence of total defeat, as more than enough punishment already.

Harris's conception of a bombing war, as we have seen, was to have forces so overwhelming that every night they could reproduce an Operation Gomorrah, or more than an Operation Gomorrah, destroying one major city after another until the population of Germany could take it no longer. He fervently believed that bombing was a war-winning weapon, and he did everything possible – to the point of near-insubordination – to prove the point right.

And some, to repeat, might argue that he was indeed right. They might point at Hiroshima and Nagasaki to show that he was right, and that the reason why people thought he was mistaken was that even at the war's end he still did not have enough pulverising power available. If he had possessed atom bombs, and had dropped them on Berlin, Hamburg, Munich, Cologne, the Ruhr cities, one per night, night after night, the war would have ended very quickly. In the big

attacks he mounted, the 1,000-bomber raids and the repeated attacks on Berlin, he was seeking to bring about the crushing effect that was only achieved when atomic bombs were available.

The biggest problem with the idea of winning a war by city bombing, however, is that it involves the mass killing of civilians to do so. And if winning by the means just described – a series of atom-bomb attacks until either the enemy surrenders or there is no enemy left – is the logical extension of the belief that bombing can win war, then it offers an appalling prospect of what such bombing would have to be like to make this belief true. As argued in chapter 4, this technique at least would be self-defeating: the saying 'to make a wasteland and call it peace', with 'victory' substituted for or added to 'peace', applies here.

Let us now examine the other main arguments offered by area bombing's defenders, returning to the European theatre in search of justifications because that is where the area-bombing campaign was carried out if not more comprehensively, then for longer.

One of the arguments is that area bombing prevented Germany's 88-mm. anti-aircraft guns and Messerschmitt fighters from being used on the battle-fronts. This is a significant matter, for the 88-mm. guns could have been used as highly effective anti-tank guns against the Russians on the Eastern Front, and 70 per cent of the Luftwaffe's fighter force was detained in the home arena to defend against the bombers. Because it was recognised by the Eighth Army Air Force that the key to the success of their precision-bombing efforts was control of the skies – a mirror-image of the situation in 1940 and the Battle of Britain – a major effort was made to achieve exactly that. In the closing months of 1943 the long-range Mustangs, Lightnings and Thunderbolts quadrupled in number; the Luftwaffe losses grew alarmingly, and began to outstrip production. The Eighth Army Air Force attacked the Luftwaffe on the ground too – its factories and airfields, its fuel, the aircraft factories' component suppliers – and the result was that by the time D-Day arrived, the Luftwaffe had 300

operational aircraft to pit against 12,000 Allied aircraft.[6] On the Eastern Front 500 Luftwaffe fighters faced 13,000 Soviet aircraft. This is one good reason why an observer in the summer of 1944 could see that the war was won.

It is therefore true to say that the bomber campaign kept the 88-mm. guns and the Messerschmitts in Germany instead of the battle-fronts. But note that what kept the Luftwaffe at home was the presence of bombers in the German sky, whether they were bombing precision targets as the Eighth Army Air Force attempted to do, or whether they were bombing urban areas as the RAF did. It was not necessary that the bombers were seeking to attack cities; it was sufficient that they were there at all. If a principal aim of the bombing campaigns was to anchor defensive resources to Germany, then however inaccurate the attempts to bomb factories, power stations, railway lines and marshalling yards, airfields, canals, bridges, har-bours, dams and coal mines, the mere effort would have been enough to achieve this aim.

Moreover, the troops who manned searchlights and anti-aircraft batteries in Germany were not front-line troops. Many of them were youths and older men. The airmen in the fighter-defence force were certainly front-line material; and doubtless their absence from the Eastern Front made a difference. But they were not absent from the Western Front during the crucial invasion period, because Bomber Command and the Eighth Army Air Force were busy at the Western Front too. So the argument that the bombing campaign kept military resources confined in Germany is, though true up to a point, not quite the truth defenders of bombing wish it to be, and anyway – as just noted – would have happened whether or not the bombing attempted to be precise.

Mention of the anti-aircraft guns and Luftwaffe fighters reminds one that Bomber Command turned to area bombing because it found precision bombing too dangerous by day and too difficult by night. Is this fact a moral defence against the charge that deliberately targeting civilians is wrong? It is not. Consider an analogy: politicians have

sometimes failed to persuade their publics by argument, and have therefore resorted to coercing them instead, by imprisoning and even shooting them, as in Stalin's Russia and Pinochet's Chile. This in effect is what Bomber Command did, and with the same degree of moral justification. Arguably, its action in this respect was worse, because its early precision-bombing efforts were expressly premised on the attempt to avoid or at least limit civilian casualties; so the switch to area bombing was a complete reversal of policy and an abandonment of avowed principle. The discovery of its inability to achieve its ends without performing a moral volte-face as to means comes nowhere near a defence of those means.

The argument that area bombing put logistical pressure on German resources because of the need for burying the dead, caring for the injured, housing those whose homes had been demolished, dealing with refugees, clearing rubble, restoring electricity, water and sewerage services, and getting food and clothing to those who had been bombed out, is not a strong one. As shown in connection with the efficient management of affairs after the 1,000-bomber raid on Cologne, Germany was well able to deal with the problems caused by bombing until the last months of the war, when the overall degree of social disorganisation swiftly reached critical levels. This was in large part a result of the remorseless bombing of the last months, but also because of the approach of hostile armies and the final breakdown of supplies.

Germany had an abundance of slave and prisoner labour available for the disagreeable task of clearing corpses and shovelling rubble, and an army of foreign workers for repair and restoration work. The capacity of its economy (as discussion of the next point shows) was such that it could absorb and deal with bomb damage without major distraction from either the military or the industrial tasks it faced; in the latter sense it had surplus capacity.

This leads directly to the argument that area bombing affected German industry in general and its war industry in particular. The argument was discussed and dismissed in chapter 3. As there shown,

the rate of output of German industry increased until the last months of the war, and it was precision bombing not area bombing that then had an impact – on oil certainly, and on the movement of coal from the mines to the industrial plants that needed them. When Albert Speer was in prison in Nuremberg, awaiting trial, he was invited to give a lecture to an Allied group interested in German industrial activity during the war. What he told them about the way industry in the Third Reich continued to increase output despite years of bombing should not have surprised them; with the possible exception of the Soviet Union, all the major combatants had spare industrial capacity – and in the United States, spare manpower – throughout the war, which if necessary could have been adapted to meet military demand. 'Throughout the war,' writes Richard Overy, 'the German economy produced fewer weapons than its raw resources of materials, manpower, scientific skill and factory floor space could have made possible.'[7]

This point is cited by Roger Chickering and Stig Forster in questioning the concept of 'total war' as applied to the Second World War, a pertinent challenge given that area bombing is sometimes exempted from moral critique on the grounds that it was one element in a 'total war' with all the implications of this for seeing every individual member of a society as pitched in battle against every member of the enemy society. The phrase 'total war' implies just that: that everyone was in fact or potentially on the front line of a war that had no traditional front lines.[8]

The shocking figures bear out the fact that the Second World War was certainly a war of peoples even more than of armies: an estimated 15 million soldiers, sailors and airmen were killed in all theatres of the war between 1939 and 1945, whereas in excess of 45 million civilians were killed. 'The preponderance of civilians was no accidental or peripheral feature of this war; it reflected the central significance of civilians in the conflict, the indispensable roles that they played in the war's outcome, as well as the vulnerabilities that they shared, as a direct consequence, with the soldiers.'[9]

But there is of course an elision of ideas here. Even if 'total war' means that everyone in a society is affected or involved in some way by the fact of their country's being at war – and this was certainly so in the belligerent nations of Europe, far less so in the United States, and only so in the last six months of the war in Japan itself – it does not make every individual himself or herself a combatant. But the fact is that the Second World War was not a 'total war' in this or indeed any sense, as Chickering and Forster argue. Most of the land surface of the world was unaffected, many nations were bystanders merely, and the engaged nations (other possibly than Russia) had not put their every last tooth-pick and shoe-horn to the struggle.[10]

Industry was a legitimate target, yes. The move from this to seeing the workers as legitimate targets too, given the difficulty of hitting their factories, meant a slide to accepting that their families and neighbours were legitimate targets. This was the point at which moral trespass occurred, because it is where disproportion enters. It is sometimes said that we make virtues of our necessities; in this case we allowed what we mistakenly supposed was a necessity to make our vices.

A defender of area bombing might be prepared to concede that bombing the whole city where an industry was located, rather than trying to hit the industry itself, is questionable; but he might then say: what if the city was full of troops on the move towards a front line, contained many refugees who if caught up in bombing attacks might create serious difficulties for military movement and for logistics, and also had several crucial war-industry plants, and was an equally crucial transport hub? Would not such a target be a legitimate and indeed important one, if it was located close to an important stretch of the front?

Just this argument has been offered in defence of the bombing of Dresden on 14 February 1944, in the outstanding book by Frederick Taylor which examines the attack in detail, and offers the fullest picture of the circumstances yet given.[11] Taylor points out that the

degree of devastation suffered by Dresden was partly the result of unfortunate weather conditions – the prevailing wind helped create the firestorm that did much of the damage and caused many of the deaths, so this aspect of the raid's consequences was not intended by the attackers, who, at the request of the advancing Russian forces, had seen Dresden as an important choke-point for supplies and troops moving east, and refugees streaming west. Moreover, says Taylor, the air-raid precautions were inadequate, and the city's residents were inexperienced at being bombed; and the absence of fighter defences, and the presence of good luck for the attackers, for whom everything went smoothly, made this 'the raid which went horribly right'.[12]

Taylor agrees with the conclusion reached by the distinguished historian Richard Overy in his *Why the Allies Won*, that Allied bombing was a decisive factor in the victory over Germany and Japan (Overy says that 'bombing mattered most' in the victory over Germany). It is interesting therefore to note that Overy's analysis of how this was so focuses on the two points that, first, the bombing campaign kept guns and fighter aircraft away from the fronts to defend the homeland, and second, that by January 1945 bombing had at last so depleted Germany's industrial capacity that Speer was moved to write to Hitler saying that 'realistically, the war is over in this area of heavy industry and armaments'.[13]

This however is not a vindication of area bombing. For once again one has to point out that precision-bombing efforts against industry, transport, power and military targets would have kept those guns and fighter planes in Germany; and once again one has to point out that it was precision-bombing endeavours against oil and transport, not area bombing, that forced German war production to diminish and at last falter in the closing months of the war.

In this sense bombing was decisive; but not area bombing. And it is area bombing which is the moral issue at stake here.

Among the questions that might be asked about the bombing of Dresden are these. Given that the chief point of bombing Dresden was its importance as a transport hub close to a region where crucial

military events were unfolding, why was the bombing effort not directed at the railways and roads in the environs of the city, or leading to and from the city along the crucial west–east axis? The aiming-point issued to Bomber Command crews was not the railway yards, but a stadium close to the city centre.

The city was known to be full of tens of thousands of refugees fleeing the approach of the Soviet troops. Was this a reason to bomb the city? Why was it not, on humanitarian grounds, a reason not to bomb the city?

Indeed, instead of asking what the reasons were for bombing the city (rather than others near by also involved in the movement of troops and refugees), one might ask for the reasons not to bomb it, and the answer might have been the same that America's Secretary of State Henry Stimson gave when he struck Kyoto off the list of possible targets for atom-bomb attack.

It is recognised that one of the main motives for the atom-bomb attacks on Hiroshima and Nagasaki was to demonstrate to the Russians the superiority in weaponry that the United States had attained. In the case of Dresden something similar is regrettably true. Max Hastings, a trenchant critic of the area-bombing campaigns carried out by the Allies, quotes a briefing note sent out to Bomber Command squadrons detailed for the attack on Dresden. Its final paragraph reads: 'The intention of the attack is to hit the enemy where he will feel it most, behind an already partially collapsed front, to prevent the use of the city in the way of further advance, and incidentally to show the Russians when they arrive what Bomber Command can do.'[14] Considered in hindsight, the degree of moral set-aside obvious here in the idea of 'hitting the enemy where he will feel it most' – that is, a civilian population in an iconic city – and the calculation involved in using civilian lives and the precipitates of history to make a gesture in a game of diplomatic politics, is breathtaking.

*   *   *

Another argument offered in defence of area bombing is that for the first half of the war at least it was the only means Britain had of 'carrying the war to Germany', and since precision bombing was impracticable, area bombing had to be the means employed.

The phrase 'carrying the war to the enemy' is not a very clear one, though at the least it means 'reminding the enemy that there is a war on', and perhaps also reminding the enemy 'that we are still here and in pugnacious mood', which is certainly the message Britain wished to convey in the perilous period between the summer of 1940 and the turn of the tide in late 1942. Because this aim was not being realised by precision attacks, in February 1942 the fateful decision was taken to switch to area attacks. Was area bombing the only way to 'carry the war to the enemy' in this sense? Obviously not. Almost any belligerent act, such as attacking the enemy's navy and harbours, and harassing its military dispositions in the occupied territories of France and the Low Countries, as well as attempting precision attacks on important industrial and transport targets, would have constituted 'carrying the war to the enemy'. Area bombing was not exclusively the right way to do it, though it perhaps carried the satisfaction that it was causing pain, grief and damage to part of the enemy's corporate being, however little real impact it was having on the course of the war.

The war situation was a factor in the bombing campaign in a number of ways. From the summer of 1940, when the British army was rescued without its equipment from the beaches of Dunkirk, until the tide of war began to turn strongly and permanently against Germany in late 1942, Britain was in a perilous state. It had seen off the invasion threat of 1940, and Germany's attack on Russia in 1941 meant that there was unlikely to be a repeat of that threat at least for a year or two. But the 'Battle of the Atlantic' was a serious worry; throughout the period between Dunkirk and the crisis of this battle on the high seas in early 1943, the threat to Britain's lifeline across the ocean to America was very real. In reminiscing about the war once it was safely over, Churchill said 'the only thing that ever really frightened me was the U-boat peril'. A combination of factors

won the Battle of the Atlantic for the Allies, after a terrible struggle in which millions of tons of shipping were sent by U-boats to the sea-bed. The principal ones were British decipherment of the Enigma code, the development of long-range aircraft for anti-submarine operations, and the fact that the Americans built ships (the famous 'Liberty' ships) faster than Germany's U-boats could sink them. In the end this last factor was by far the most important; once again, the war was a matter of numbers: industrial output, shipping tonnages, personnel, resources in general.

In this period Britain carried the struggle against Germany alone. The United States presence in the European theatre began in a small way with advance units of its Army Air Force in 1942, but it was well into 1943 before the American bomber force began to have the numbers and the right methods to make an impact on the aerial campaign over Germany. By this time the Allies were fighting their way up Italy, albeit slowly and painfully; Germany was in retreat from Russia; and the build-up had begun towards the continental invasion that took place on D-Day. Harris himself nominated 5 March 1943 as the moment that Bomber Command was at last ready to get down to the kind of work he wanted from it; that was the date on which the navigational aid OBOE was at last fully operational, and when Harris was beginning to have the kind of aircraft in the kind of numbers he saw as desirable.[15]

But it is an interesting fact that Bomber Command's readiness for its major area-bombing campaign coincided with the turn of the tide in the Allies' favour. The argument that says that Bomber Command was the only means of 'carrying the war to Germany' during Britain's time of greatest weakness, when it was alone in the struggle and woefully undermanned and under-equipped for the task, overlooks the fact that during that fragile time Bomber Command was itself very limited in both respects, meagre in capacity and range, and ineffective as an instrument of war.[16] And for a large part of that period anyway – from the outbreak of hostilities until February 1942 at the earliest – Bomber Command was still 'hamstrung' (as Portal

and Harris saw it) by not having *carte blanche* to conduct area bombing of German towns and cities by night.

When that *carte blanche* was given in February 1942, Harris began preparing the three 1,000-bomber raids of the coming summer. The raids effectively shot Bomber Command's bolt for that year, and were propaganda successes merely; Cologne was badly damaged, but its civilian casualties were low, and the two succeeding big raids did little harm because they were so off-target. As far as 1942 was concerned, on a few occasions Bomber Command's activities managed a certain amount of sound and fury, but with disappointing results in concrete terms.

So the anomaly is that area bombing began in full earnestness only when the tide of the war had already begun to run against Germany, and it reached its most devastating proportions when Germany's defeat was recognised to be a matter of time only – in the last six months of the war.

As the discussion of America's air war over Japan has already shown, the same applies. The defeat of Japan was not in question when the Tokyo firebombing happened in March 1945, and it was certainly not in question when the atom bombs were dropped in August of that year. Victory in the war as a whole was a matter of numbers – of industrial capacity and manpower reserves – and once America was in the war, the Allies were in effect guaranteed victory. The Axis powers' only hope was to induce a favourable early ending to hostilities by some decisive or lucky stroke that would make the Allied powers decide that the process of gaining victory would be too long or costly, even though inevitable in the long run. That eventuality was made unlikely by the Allied decision at the Casablanca Conference in early 1943 to seek nothing less than unconditional surrender from the Axis powers; but the combination of hope for a lucky break, and having nothing to lose given the unconditional terms, kept the Axis powers going until the last drop of fuel – in Germany's case – and in Japan's case, the last drop of hope. Japan's military command had come to recognise, by the spring of 1945, that the defence of the

home islands was a lost cause, and from then on – four months before the atom-bomb attacks – they began to send out feelers to discover what the prospects were for an end to the war.

These points – that the defeat of Germany and Japan were seen to be inevitable, months if not indeed years before they actually happened – is vigorously contested by some, who say that the outcome of the war was in doubt in both theatres until close to the end, and that continued assault from all quarters on all aspects of the military, civil and administrative organisation of the Axis powers was required to realise the overwhelming necessity of the war, which was to defeat them.

Does this objection have weight? On the question whether it was unclear that the Allies had won until close to the end, one need only quote the agreement of the historians. Robin Neillands says that by September 1944 'Germany was going to lose the war, and quite soon – that much was clear'.[17] John Terraine agrees; 'By the end of August, 1944, Germany was palpably defeated.'[18] One could quote the same from many sources, and for Japan too.

The point about the 'overwhelming necessity of the war was to win' is a good one. In light of it, it is often argued that the greatest immorality would have been to lose the war, and that since this is so, anything and everything done to win it was legitimated by this overriding aim.

It can certainly be granted that the overwhelming aim was to defeat the Axis powers, and it is surely right that it would have been an act of immorality not to strive fully and effectively to achieve that goal. But it is wrong to use this to justify indiscriminate bombing of towns and cities, for the familiar reason that ends do not automatically justify means. Suppose that the Axis powers had won the war: would that fact justify everything they did in the course of it? Obviously not. In practice victory tends to provide absolution for all wrongs, since the victor is the judge and jury in his own behalf – and history is written by victors. In the same way, the victor nations of the Second World War have allowed their

victory to excuse them from self-examination over some aspects of their behaviour. But that is a wrong in itself.

Let us for a moment suppose that all the arguments of the defenders of area bombing are correct, namely, that it damaged enemy morale, reduced enemy industrial capacity, kept enemy military resources away from battle-fronts, reduced military deaths, and 'carried the war' to the enemy. We have seen that these arguments do not persuade; but let us for a moment accept them. Do they make area bombing morally acceptable? One thing would be needed to make an affirmative answer more likely, namely, the claim that there was no other way to survive against the Axis powers than by carrying out area bombing. Is this true? Manifestly not. For one thing, Britain survived its greatest threat from Nazi Germany in the two years before area bombing became its policy. For another, the effects claimed by defenders of area bombing, and which we are temporarily granting, could have been gained, as we have seen, by efforts at precision-bombing – and may indeed have been more successfully gained by it. This too shows that area bombing was not necessary.

Remember the criteria for *jus in bello*: that the means employed be necessary, and proportional. Area bombing was neither necessary nor proportional, and it was neither of these things by quite a long way.

It is striking to notice the judgements made by historians, even those sympathetic to the endeavours and sufferings of Bomber Command, about the merits of its campaigns in the Second World War. In his excellent history of Bomber Command's war, Denis Richards lists its outstanding achievements as follows. First, there were its mine-laying activities, which interrupted the movement of merchant ships supplying Germany, kept U-boats in their bases at the time of critical operations such as Operation Torch in North Africa in 1942, and Operation Overlord on 6 June 1944. Moreover, the mine-laying interfered with U-boat training in the Bay of Danzig when Admiral Dönitz was trying to bring his new large submarines into service for

the Atlantic struggle.[19] Bomber Command also sank or put out of action six of Germany's twelve major warships; its epic sinking of the *Tirpitz* involved three raids, one from temporary bases in Russia which the attacking Lancasters had to use as a staging post before trying to bomb the battleship in its hiding place in Kaafiord. The same Lancasters eventually sank the *Tirpitz* on 12 November 1944 at moorings near Tromsø. Finally, Bomber Command delayed and reduced V-weapon production by its attacks of Peenemunde and rocket-launch sites, making a valuable impact on the missile attacks on London in the summer and autumn of 1944.[20]

Note that these are all precision attacks. To them can be added Bomber Command's help in preventing the threatened invasion of 1940, and its contribution to the strangulation of Germany's fuel supplies in the last months of the war – though this was chiefly an American success. These again were precision attacks. The only recognition given by Richards to area bombing is its role in helping to persuade the Italian populace to change sides in the war. Almost any of the military actions of the Allies in the Italian theatre could be praised for this, but it is only fair to include Bomber Command, whose crews found that attacks on Milan, Genoa and Turin were relatively safe in comparison to the danger posed by fighter planes and anti-aircraft defences in Germany. It is easy to be dismayed by the thought of the indifference thus displayed to the centuries of cultural treasures cavalierly subjected to bombing, though the indifference to the possibility of civilian deaths – children, women and the elderly almost certainly the majority among them – is infinitely worse.

Naturally, and rightly enough, the defender of bombing will respond to all the foregoing criticisms of the area-bombing campaign by asking: what should the Allies have done instead? The answer is given in the mere process of making the question itself more precise: what should the Allies have done *instead of area bombing*? The answer is: Bomber Command should have continued its efforts at precision bombing, and devoted its energies to making this tactic safer for its

bombers and more effective. The fact that precision bombing proved highly dangerous in the early years of the war was the practical reason for switching to area bombing, but there was an alternative which, if the principle of limiting harm to civilians had been maintained, could and doubtless would have been taken: namely, seeking remedies to the danger – as the Eighth Army Air Force did, finding their answer in long-range fighter escorts. The RAF made no efforts in this direction, because it chose to concentrate on night area bombing. But the same quantum of effort could have been devoted to making daylight precision bombing practicable, exactly as the Americans did.

All four of the desiderata specified by the main defence of the bombing campaign would have been realised by a precision bombing effort. Anti-aircraft guns and fighter planes would have had to remain in Germany. The war would have been 'carried to' Germany. A concentrated effort at precision bombing of crucial industrial and economic targets might have reduced the capacity of Germany's war industries far earlier than the actual precision-bombing efforts by the Eighth Army Air Force did – and as area bombing did not – thus perhaps genuinely shortening the war. And this in turn might have had an impact on morale too, and where it mattered most: not so much the morale of the civilian population, but of the troops kept short of equipment and fuel and thus made more vulnerable to their enemies.

And all this would have been achieved without the deliberate targeting of civilians, and therefore with lower civilian casualties. The Allies could accordingly have maintained moral standards through-out, consistently with their professions before and at the beginning of the war that they would never stoop to deliberate bombing of civilians.

A point that defenders of area bombing might make at this juncture is to say that it was not obvious, at the time that the bombing campaign was actually going on, that it was having little effect on Germany's war industry or on the population's morale. The hope that it would

shorten the war by making German civilians demand that their leaders end it, was a real hope, and if it does not justify area bombing at the very least it excuses it, or allows a plea of mitigation to be entered on its behalf.

To this the answer is that the conductors of area bombing knew, from pre-war discussions and widely advertised fears, and from the pre-war efforts to limit civilian bombing by international agreement, that the very act of targeting civilians was wrong. Indeed at the outset of war the British government had repeatedly and pointedly forsworn the idea of targeting civilians as a barbarous and uncivilised technique of war. So not being aware of its ineffectiveness, yet hoping that it was effective enough that it might shorten the war, cannot be invoked as a justification nor even as an excuse. The combination of ignorance and hope might be an *explanation* of why the conductors of area bombing chose it as a strategy and allowed it to continue; but an explanation is not an excuse.

For a perspective on the standards Roosevelt, Chamberlain and others sought to uphold in respect of bombing at the outbreak of the Second World War – in Chamberlain's case, as earlier chapters showed, partly out of conviction and partly out of a pragmatic desire to dissuade Germany from area-bombing Britain – a much more recent example might be given. Writing in the spring of 2005 on the subject of US treatment of prisoners in Afghanistan and Iraq, the American commentator Thomas Friedman said:

> Yes I know war is hell and ugliness abounds in every corner. I also understand that in places like Iraq and Afghanistan, America is up against a vicious enemy, which, if it had the power, would do great harm to the United States. You do not deal with such people with kid gloves. But killing prisoners of war, presumably in the act of torture, is an inexcusable outrage. The fact that Congress has just shrugged this off, and no senior official or officer has been fired, is a travesty.[21]

The comment can be applied retrospectively to the Second World War, with a few changes of names and nouns, and exactly the same principle holds: civilised standards have to be made to apply even in severe situations, both for intrinsic reasons and because there is, properly, a reckoning always to come.

There is one final throw of the dice for defenders of area bombing, and that, with respect to the points just made, is to ask, 'Has morality any place in war at all?' If it does not, then anything goes, and with it area bombing of civilian targets. This would be the ultimate defence of anything done under the cloak of war – and alas, it often is, given the frightful facts of war, from terrible battles like Stalingrad, to the atrocities, bombing victims, Japanese prisoner-of-war camps, men dying in submarines at the bottom of the sea or burning in the cockpits of aeroplanes – and so on and on – the list is ghastly and endless, and as one contemplates it, the refined nuances of ethical debate seem wholly out of place.

Robin Neillands, whose question 'Has morality any place in war at all?' I quote, cites both Clausewitz and Macaulay in support of the idea that once war has broken out the only aim is to win it 'at any cost, and especially if that cost can be met by the enemy'.[22] Clausewitz says that the will of the enemy is a legitimate target: 'the destruction of his capacity to resist, the killing of his courage rather than his men' is what warfare is about. For Macaulay, writing in 1831, 'The essence of war is violence; moderation in war is imbecility'.[23] For Neillands, the idea that war is something to be won at any cost, preferably to be paid by the enemy, is 'a point that can be endlessly debated by moral philosophers, who tend to find so blunt a point unacceptable; but wars are not usually fought by moral philosophers'.[24] Interestingly, the convergence between the views of moral philosophers, on the one hand, and on the other hand soldiers who have seen the battlefield, tends to be greater than between the latter and the historians of their doings. Hereby hangs a tale. But Neillands continues, '[Wars] are fought by ordinary people . . . once they are in it they find moral

questions largely academic; their main aim is to stay alive, and to win.'
This is doubtless true. But the high command in wars, both military
and political – the people who make the choices and take the
decisions – are not the ordinary soldiers who find themselves
reluctantly at war. This implies an important difference. Greater
responsibility demands a more encompassing view not just of the
strategic but of the political, diplomatic, and finally human implications of what is involved in going to war, and in the conduct of war.

Yet even the ordinary people who get caught up in war might find
themselves doing some moral philosophy after all, as Neillands now
changes tack to acknowledge:

> To win, these people may be obliged to do dreadful things to their
> fellow men, often in the interests of personal survival, but most of
> these ordinary people would agree that even in war some actions are
> beyond the pale. The killing of prisoners or women and children is
> certainly among them. In short, there has to be morality in war; to
> suppose otherwise is to condone barbarism.[25]

This last remark, I think, says it all. It is of course infinitely easier to
say than to apply in times of dreadful emergency. But it is the mark of
a truly civilised arrangement that in even such emergency, the effort is
made, not abandoned.

I conclude that the defences offered for area bombing are un-
persuasive, and that therefore the indictment stands.

8

Judgement

THROUGHOUT THIS BOOK the principal example I have cited of a bombing assault on civilians is Operation Gomorrah, the Hamburg raids of July–August 1943. I could have cited Dresden and the atom-bomb attacks on Hiroshima and Nagasaki as my central examples; but I chose Hamburg. Why?

Readers will note that with one exception all my sources for this discussion have been works in English. I could have given attention to the recent spate of publications in German about the experience of German civilians under bombing in the Second World War, but I chose to approach the question of the morality of Allied area bombing from the point of view of the literature on the subject in the language of the victor nations. Why?

My reasons for both these things are conscious and deliberate, and they are as follows.

The bombing of Dresden and the atom-bomb attacks on Hiroshima and Nagasaki are, for very good reason, obvious targets for moral disapprobation when area bombing is criticised. Earlier I offered reasons why they are special. They took place when the war was effectively over, and each has a particular claim to notice. Dresden's claim is the terrible casualties suffered by its residents, and the horror of the way they were crushed, asphyxiated and burned to death by the attack, so at odds with the great beauty and cultural

significance of their city. The atom-bombed cities' claim is that they were destroyed by a horrific new weapon, and remain unique – at time of writing – in being so; and that the attacks left a poison in the survivors, which killed them over the months, years and decades following, a hellish legacy that seems unjustifiable on any grounds.

However, I choose Operation Gomorrah as the principal example of an area-bombing atrocity because it took place when the war was, although running in the Allies' favour, by no means securely won. It was conducted by means that were 'conventional' for the Second World War, at least until August 1945; that is, a mixture of incendiary and high-explosive bombs. It clearly and unequivocally targeted the civilian population of a large city, which was carpet-bombed at night to fulfil the aim, graphically described in Sir Arthur Harris's own words, quoted earlier, of 'crushing Boche, killing Boche, terrorising Boche'.

If Operation Gomorrah was an immoral act, then how much more so were Dresden, Hiroshima and Nagasaki. If Operation Gomorrah was *unnecessary* and *disproportionate*, to use the language of just-war theory, then how much more so were the attacks on Dresden, Hiroshima and Nagasaki – and indeed the firebombing of Tokyo and other Japanese cities, the bombing of Berlin, and the destruction of Würzburg and so many other German towns indiscriminately bombed in the very last months of the war for no better reason than that they were unbombed, and that there were many bombers and bombs waiting to be used.

If Operation Gomorrah was a moral crime, then the area-bombing campaigns of the Second World War were as a whole morally criminal. Bombing attacks that were genuine attempts at precision bombing – targeting oil, V-weapon launch sites, railway lines, U-boat pens – killed people too; but here the defence applies that there was a war on, and that these things happen in war. It cannot be said that deliberately targeting civilians and dropping thousands of tons of bombs on them remorselessly over many years is a side-effect of war.

The second point is that I have used only English-language sources

in compiling this account. Most of these, it is true, themselves rely partly on German sources in their turn, and facts, figures and anecdotal material culled from German sources therefore finds its way into these pages by their means. And a couple of my sources are books by Germans either written in English or translated into English. But I have deliberately avoided drawing on such recent publications as Jorg Friedrich's *Der Brand* and *Brandstatten*, or the collection edited by Volker Hage, *Hamburg 1943: Literarische Zeugnisse zum Feuersturm*, or Christoph Kucklick's *Feuersturm: Der Bombenkrieg gegen Deutschland*. These books invite their German readers to set alongside the national sense of guilt for the Nazi era a second thought, which is that hundreds of thousands of Germans suffered in the war years from the area-bombing attacks, which not only killed over 300,000 people but did immense damage to the built fabric and cultural heritage of Germany. Two of these books, Friedrich's *Brandstatten* and Kucklick's *Feuersturm*, provide photographic evidence of the devastation and the torment of the casualties, some of it never seen before; and the first of them constitutes a photographic essay on the architectural treasures that were lost under the bombs, and by implication what they contain – for in *Der Brand* Friederich gives an account of the cultural losses too, in the form of the contents of historic buildings, churches, palaces, museums, and libraries.

These books seem to me to be legitimate and now timely contributions to the process of discussion required for putting the Second World War into proper proportion. I neither expect nor wish that this will change anything on the question of Nazi war crimes and crimes against humanity, which so weigh against the Germany of the time that nothing can excuse or abate what happened in it, or in its name. The point is not to make up a balance sheet, and by entering into it the sufferings of Germans under area bombing, thereby to diminish the culpability of Nazism. This is what neo-Nazis try illegitimately to do. I do not think that Germany's responsible historians are seeking to do this. But at any rate, what I have written here, and what I judge

on the basis of it, is independent of their view of the matter, however closely in many points their conclusions and mine converge. In writing this book I wished to view the matter solely from the standpoint of someone in one of the victor nations, who inherited the benefits of that victory, but hopes that by now there is enough perspective available for a frank acknowledgement of the wrongs done in the course of how it was won.

There are two major reasons why it matters to recognise and accept that the Allied bomber forces' area-bombing campaigns constitute moral crimes. One is so that we in the victor nations can face up to our part in committing crimes in the course of that terrible war; crimes by a long way far less in magnitude than those committed by Nazism, though in the matter of comparisons the culpability of Allied area bombing should prompt uncomfortable reflections about the moral company it keeps, given that it is more akin to Japanese actions in their infamous attack on Nanking than it is to, say, Henry Stimson's withdrawal of Kyoto from the list of atom-bomb targets. It is an obvious enough comment that only if a civilisation looks at itself frankly and accepts what it sees, can it hope to learn from the exercise, and progress in the right way and direction thereafter. The cliché, no less true and pertinent for being one, that applies here is that we owe it to our future to get matters straight about the past.

The second reason is that we are at risk of repeating mistakes if we do not face up to their commission in the past. There is a very particular reason for being anxious about this. Look at what the United States military forces recently have to say in their interpretation of those aspects of International Humanitarian Law (the Geneva 1949 conventions and their two protocols) which protect civilians. The Geneva Convention Protocol 1 of 1977 forbids military attacks upon civilians and civilian targets, and these latter are defined in Protocol I, Article 52 (1) as follows: 'Civilian objects are all objects which are not military objectives.' Article 52 (2) defines military objectives as 'those objects which by their nature,

location, purpose or use make an effective contribution to military action and whose total or partial destruction, capture or neutralisation, in the circumstances ruling at the time, offers a definite military advantage'. Now observe the very wide latitude that US military manuals apply here: 'Military advantage may involve a variety of considerations, including the security of the attacking force . . . Economic targets of the enemy that indirectly but effectively support and sustain the enemy's war-fighting capability may also be attacked' (Annotated Supplement to the Commander's Handbook on the Law of Naval Operations, 8.1.1.); 'The official US Air Force doctrine suggests that the morale of the civilian population may, in itself, legitimately be targeted since weakening of the will to fight would offer a military advantage' (Air Force Doctrine Document 1: Air Force Basic Doctrine, AFDD-1 (1997)). In other words, the US Navy and Air Force still think in Second World War terms about 'civilian morale' and the legitimacy of attacking what can be described as 'economic' targets – not, note, 'war industries' or some more closely defined economic target such as oil, electricity, transport or water. 'Economic targets' covers far too much.

Such interpretations of the Geneva Convention and protocols are not permissible in the light of an acceptance that Allied area bombing in the Second World War was a moral crime. This acceptance places much sharper constraints on such interpretations. It therefore matters.

To see the hard truth about the morality of Allied area bombing, we need only ask the relevant questions. Was it necessary? Was it proportionate? Is it really true that all civilians without exception belong in the front line of war? Why do Western militaries try so hard now – even if only in theory; even if it is only a matter of lip-service or propaganda – to avoid 'collateral damage'? Why did we come up with the Geneva Convention provisions in 1949 to protect civilians in time of war, and more explicitly so in the protocols to that convention? Does the Allies' Second World War area bombing pass the test

of the Nuremberg principles drawn up by the Allies themselves? How does Allied area bombing square with the sentiment behind the United Nations' Universal Declaration of Human Rights?

Talk of declarations and conventions on rights and on lawful practice in war in the wake of 1945 was the result of a determination to try to avoid the gross human-rights violations that had taken place during the war. They came in the immediate wake of the war's horrors as a judgement on them, and as a statement of what was unacceptable in what had happened. The Holocaust properly occupied centre stage in thinking about these matters; but that thinking also embraced other atrocities of the war, and as the evolution of the fourth Geneva Convention shows, area bombing was a part of that, though its chief perpetrators – the British and Americans – did not permit a specific reference to it. The history behind the provisions of the 1977 first protocol to the Geneva Convention of 1949 is left in silence by it. But its meaning is crystal clear: as a retrospective judgement on area bombing, it nominates it as a crime.

The questions can go on, adding to the discomfiture they cause. What is the moral difference between bombing women and children and shooting them with a pistol? Is it that when you bomb them you cannot see them – you did not intend *that* particular woman and *that* particular child to die – and anyway they might escape the bombing, perhaps by reaching a shelter? But if they are here against a wall just feet away from the muzzle of your pistol they cannot escape: it is more personal; you can see their eyes. Is that the difference – the anonymity of the act of killing from 20,000 feet?

On the basis of the foregoing chapters the answer I give to the following questions are these:

Was area bombing necessary? No.

Was it proportionate? No.

Was it against the humanitarian principles that people have been striving to enunciate as a way of controlling and limiting war? Yes.

Was it against general moral standards of the kind recognised and agreed in Western civilisation in the last five centuries, or even 2,000 years? Yes.

Was it against what mature national laws provide in the way of outlawing murder, bodily harm, and destruction of property? Yes.

In short and in sum: was area bombing wrong? Yes.

Very wrong? Yes.

And now there come some very hard questions for us to ask ourselves about our own airmen – our own kinsmen.

Should airmen have refused to carry out area-bombing raids? Yes. In the hypothetical ideal world which does not exist and certainly not in wartime, they should have insisted on being sent against genuine industrial and military targets, and unavoidable 'collateral damage' should have been the worst they accepted as regards the effects of their actions on civilians. Doubtless many thought or made themselves think that this was what they were doing anyway; and standardly they were told as much, and doubtless some chose to believe the line in psychological self-defence. But many also knew full well what they were doing, and accepted it, or suffered silently because of it, or regretted it. But in wartime people are taught to hate their enemy, and in the Second World War the Allied fliers had good reason to believe that the enemy regime was a bad lot. Bomber Command crews, and in the Pacific theatre USAAF crews, had the backing of most of the public and their seniors for their area bombing of civilian populations, and they needed both, together with the conviction that they were fighting a just war – which was true – to give them the courage to go and do a job which, whatever else might be said about it with this comfort of hindsight, was a very dangerous one.

In warfare, the 'element of surprise' is regarded as a valuable tactic, and all military planning is kept secret unless the threat of an attack has propaganda value or is aimed at distracting enemy resources. When Japan attacked Pearl Harbor in 1941 the Unites States forces

were wholly unprepared, and suffered major losses. A student of Japanese military strategy would have known that the sudden surprise attack was a Japanese speciality – in 1905 the Russian fleet in Port Arthur was surprised by Japanese forces in a manner closely pre-figuring Pearl Harbor. Naturally, the United States represented the Japanese attack as 'perfidy'. This is not a rhetorical notion only; perfidy is forbidden by the laws of war, though rather futilely so, given what war is. By a superb act of historical management, and by its resounding victory in the war, the United States has changed perceptions of Pearl Harbor from an ignominious defeat into a noble national tragedy.

But at least the Pearl Harbor attack was aimed at military assets. On the second night raid of Operation Gomorrah, the one that created the horrific firestorm, Bomber Command created the equiva-lent of the element of surprise by flying past Hamburg to its north, as if proceeding to targets deeper into Germany; only to swing round and unexpectedly attack the city from the east. Here the target was the civilian population. Similarly, the lone aircraft droning above Hiro-shima on 6 August 1945 gave no cause for alarm to the hundreds of thousands of people below, who accordingly went about their normal business, taking no precautions. When the first atom bomb exploded in the sky above the city's centre, not one individual in the purlieus of the blast expected it.

A surprise attack on a civilian population aimed at causing maximum hurt, shock, disruption, and terror: there comes to seem very little difference in principle between the RAF's Operation Gomorrah, or the USAAF's atom bomb attacks on Hiroshima and Nagasaki, and the destruction of the World Trade Center in New York by terrorists on 11 September 2001. And this latter, prescinding from differences in scale and the drama of the target, is no different in turn from terrorist bombings carried out in Madrid by Basque separatists or in London by the IRA. All these terrorist attacks are atrocities, consisting in deliberate mass murder of civilians to hurt and coerce the society they belong to. To say that the principle underlying

'9/11', Hamburg and Hiroshima is the same is to say that the same moral judgement applies to all three.

No doubt these will seem unduly provocative comparisons. It can be pointed out that the Allied bombings were carried out in time of declared war, in which offensive operations are in effect a form of defensive operation, given that the enemy will seek to do the same if given an opportunity; whereas Pearl Harbor and 9/11 were perfidious attacks on unprepared targets, the first military and the second civilian.

This point is a good one, for there is indeed a difference here, though some will attempt to make it a debating point whether those who carry out terrorist attacks believe that they are at war and that their offence is in the same way a form of pre-emptive defence. Very well: grant the difference; yet focus on the net effect. In all these cases the centre-piece is an attack on a civilian population aimed at causing maximum hurt, shock, disruption and terror. This is what these events have in common, whether in the midst of declared war or not, and so far as this core point is concerned, adjustments of fine moral calibration are at best irrelevant. All such attacks are moral atrocities.

Recognising this ought to bring home with full force the degree of moral concern raised by Allied area bombing in the Second World War. It should by now be time for a mature and dispassionate acceptance of this point. The benefit of accepting it is that it secures the importance of the 1977 first protocol to the fourth Geneva Convention protecting civilians, one day perhaps enforceable in an international court; and explains why it is genuinely important that so much attention is paid to avoiding 'collateral damage' in wartime – again: no doubt too often as lip service merely; but the aspiration is what matters as a start.

Above all it will help to infuse a more honest appreciation of the character of the war fought by the Allies against the Axis between 1939 and 1945: a just war against morally criminal enemies, in which in some important respects the eventual victors allowed themselves to join their enemies in the moral depths, a fact which should be profoundly and frankly regretted.

Getting the record straight is all that can be done now. But it is far from little. Speaking from the point of view of an inheritor of the triumph of morally better forces over worse in the epic conflict of 1939–45, I think it places on even firmer footing our just condemnation of the atrocities of Nazism in particular and Axis aggression in general, because we do not pretend to have clean hands ourselves. What we can claim is that they were far cleaner than those of the people who plunged the world into war and carried out gross crimes under its cover, and that the explanation – not the excuse – for why we allowed our own hands to get dirty at all is because of what we had to clean up.

A fitting conclusion to the debate is provided by someone who was a participating witness to the Second World War, and whose judgement about the use of area bombing was made in an interesting context. This was a navy airman, Admiral Ralph Ofstie of the United States Navy, who contributed to the post-Second World War debate in his country about the role of atomic weapons in its future military arrangements. Part of his qualification for doing so – and it was an excellent one – was that he had served on the US Strategic Bombing Survey. He told a hearing of the House Armed Services Committee that as the Allied bombing campaigns of the war had shown, strategic bombing was 'inherently inaccurate' and no matter how its objectives were defined it inevitably involved 'mass slaughter of men, women and children in the enemy country'. It was not only militarily ineffective but with its 'ruthless, barbaric methods' it lowered the moral standards of the society whose forces carried it out. 'Must we,' asked Admiral Ofstie, 'translate the historical mistake of World War II into a permanent concept merely to avoid clouding the prestige of those who led us down the wrong road in the past?'[1]

And a fitting *envoi* is provided by the closing words of Vera Brittain's *Seed of Chaos*. From the very midst of war she prophesied with 'complete confidence that the callous cruelty which has caused us to

destroy innocent human life in Europe's most crowded cities, and the vandalism which has obliterated historic treasures in some of her loveliest, will appear to future civilisation as an extreme form of criminal lunacy with which our political and military leaders deliberately allowed themselves to become afflicted'.

Appendix

Schedule of RAF bombing attacks on Germany, with civilian casualties caused and RAF loses sustained.

1940

11/12 May
Mönchengladbach
19 Hampdens, 18 Whitleys (2
Hampdens, 1 Whitley lost)

15/16 May
Ruhrgebiet
(first strategic bombing of German
industry)
39 Wellingtons, 36 Hampdens, 24
Whitleys (1 Wellington crashed in France)

17/18 May
Hamburg, Bremen, Cologne
48 Hampdens to Hamburg, 24 Whitleys
to Bremen, 6 Wellingtons to Cologne (no
losses)

21/22 May
between Mönchengladbach and
Euskirchen, Münster
52 Whitleys, 47 Wellingtons, 25
Hampdens (3 Wellingtons, 1 Hampden, 1
Whitley lost)

22/23 May
Merseberg
35 Hampdens (all but one recalled)

5/6 June
Hamburg
36 Hampdens, 34 Wellingtons, 22
Whitleys, some to the Somme (1
Hampden, 1 Wellington lost)

6/7 June
Hamburg
24 Hampdens (no losses)

14/15 June
Ruhrgebiet, Süddeutschland, Konstanz
24 Wellingtons, 5 Hampdens

17/18 June
Cologne, Ruhrgebiet, Norddeutschland
51 Whitleys, 49 Wellingtons, 39
Hampdens (2 Whitleys lost)

18/19 June
Ruhrgebiet, Mannheim, Bremen,
Hamburg
38 Whitleys, 26 Wellingtons, 5
Hampdens 2 Whitleys, 1 Wellington lost)

19/20 June
between Hamburg and Mannheim
53 Hampdens, 37 Wellingtons, 22
Whitleys (1 Wellington, 1 Whitley lost)

20/21 June
Rheinland
39 Whitleys, 17 Hampdens (1 Hampden,
1 Whitley lost)

21/22 June
Ruhrgebiet, Nord-/Mittel-deutschland
42 Hampdens, 33 Wellingtons, 30
Whitleys (1 Hampden, 1 Wellington lost)

23 June
Osnabrück, Soest, Hamm
26 Blenheims (3 lost)

23/24 June
Bremen, Ruhrgebiet, Rheinland
53 Hampdens, 26 Whitleys (no losses)

30 June/1 July
Darmstadt, Hamburg, Hamm, Hanau
88 aircraft (no losses)

1/2 July
Osnabrück, Kiel
73 aircraft (1 Hampden and 1 Whitley
lost)

3 July
Hamburg
33 Blenheims

5/6 July
Kiel
51 aircraft despatched, did not all bomb
Kiel (1 Wellington lost)

15/16 July
Hamborn, Hannover, Osnabrück,
Paderborn
33 Hampdens (no losses)

17/18 July
Gelsenkirchen
7 Wellingtons to Gelsenkirchen, 3
Hampdens (mine-laying)

26/27 July
Hamm, Ludwigshafen
18 Wellingtons, 9 Whitleys (1 lost)

27/28 July
Hamburg, Bremen, Willhelmshaven,
Borkum
24 Wellingtons, 19 Hampdens (no losses)

29/30 July
Homburg, Cologne, Hamm
76 Hampdens, Wellingtons and Whitleys
(no losses)

5/6 August
Hamburg, Kiel, Willhelmshaven, Wismar
85 Hampdens, Wellingtons and Whitleys
(no losses)

6/7 August
Homburg, Reisholz
26 Wellingtons, also to Holland

7/8 August
Emmerich, Hamm, Soest, Kiel
50 Hampdens and Wellingtons (no losses)

9/10 August
Cologne, Ludwigshafen
38 Wellingtons and Whitleys, also to
Dutch airfields (no losses)

10/11 August
Hamburg
57 Hampdens, Wellingtons and Whitleys
to 9 targets (1 Hampden lost)

11/12 August
Ruhrgebiet
59 Hampdens, Wellingtons and Whitleys
to 6 targets (1 Whitley lost)

16/17 August
Ruhrgebiet, Frankfurt, Augsburg, Jena,
Leuna
150 Blenheims, Hampdens, Wellingtons
and Whitleys, also to Dutch airfields (4
Whitleys, 2 Hampdens, 1 Wellington lost)

17/18 August
Brunswick
102 Blenheims, Hampdens and
Wellingtons to 5 targets, also to Holland,
Belgium and France (no losses)

18/19 August
Rheinfelden, Freiburg
20 Whitleys (no losses)

24/25 August
Stuttgart
68 Wellingtons and Whitleys to 5 targets
(2 Whitleys lost)

25/26 August
Berlin, Bremen, Cologne, Hamm
103 aircraft despatched, with about half
going to Berlin (6 Hampdens, 3
Blenheims lost)

26/27 August
Hannover, Leipzig, Leuna, Nordhausen
99 Blenheims, Hampdens and
Wellingtons (1 Hampden lost)

28/29 August
Berlin
79 Blenheims, Hampdens, Wellingtons and Whitleys to 6 targets in Germany and French airfields (1 Blenheim, 1 Hampden lost)

29/30 August
Bottrop, Essen, Mannheim, Soest
81 Blenheims, Hampdens, Wellingtons and Whitleys, also to Dutch and French airfields (1 Blenheim, 1 Hampden lost)

31 August
Berlin, Cologne
77 Blenheims, Hampdens, Wellingtons and Whitleys, also to Belgian airfields (1 Hampden lost)

3/4 September
Berlin, Magdeburg, Ruhrgebiet
90 Blenheims, Hampdens, Wellingtons and Whitleys, also to French airfields (no losses)

4/5 September
Stettin, Magdeburg, Berlin
86 Blenheims, Hampdens, Wellingtons and Whitleys, also to French airfields (1 Hampden, 1 Whitley lost)

8/9 September
Hamburg, Bremen, Emden
133 Blenheims, Hampdens, Wellingtons and Whitleys, also to Holland (1 Hampden lost)

10/11 September
Berlin, Bremen
17 Whitleys (2 lost)

23/24 September
Berlin
129 Hampdens, Wellingtons and Whitleys (1 Hampden, 1 Wellington, 1 Whitley lost)

26/27 September
Dortmund, Kiel
77 Blenheims, Hampdens, Wellingtons and Whitleys, also to Channel ports (1 Blenheim, 1 Hampden lost)

5/6 October
Cologne, Gelsenkirchen, Hamm, Osnabrück, Soest
20 Hampdens (1 lost)

7/8 October
Berlin
140 Blenheims, Hampdens, Wellingtons and Whitleys (1 Wellington lost)

13/14 October
Ruhrgebiet, Willhelmshaven, Kiel
125 Battles, Blenheims, Hampdens and Wellingtons (1 Wellington lost)

14/15 October
Berlin, Stettin, Magdeburg, Böhlen
78 Hampdens, Wellingtons and Whitleys, also to France (2 Hampdens, 1 Wellington lost, 1 Whitley crashed in England)

16/17 October
Bremen, Kiel, Merseburg
73 Hampdens and Wellingtons, also to France (2 Hampdens, 1 Wellington lost. 10 Hampdens and 4 Wellingtons crashed on return)

18/19 October
Hamburg, Lünen
28 Blenheims, Hampdens and Whitleys (no losses)

19/20 October
Osnabrück
2 Whitleys, 1 Hampden (no losses, 1 Whitley crashed in England)

20/21 October
Berlin
139 Blenheims, Hampdens, Wellingtons and Whitleys to various targets in Germany, Italy and occupied countries (1 Hampden and 3 Whitleys lost)

21/22 October
Cologne, Hamburg, Stuttgart, Reisholz
31 Wellingtons, 11 Whitleys (1 Whitley lost)

28/29 October
Hamburg
97 aircraft to various targets, with 20 Hampdens going to Hamburg (1 Blenheim, 1 Whitley lost)

30/31 October
Duisburg, Emden
28 Blenheims and Wellingtons, also to
Belgium and Holland (no losses)

1/2 November
Berlin, Gelsenkirchen, Magdeburg
81 Blenheims, Hampdens, Wellingtons
and Whitleys, also to Belgian, Dutch and
French airfields (2 Hampdens lost)

6/7 November
Berlin
64 Hampdens, Wellingtons and Whitleys
to various targets, with 18 Wellingtons
going to Berlin (1 Wellington and 1
Whitley lost)

7/8 November
Essen, Cologne
91 Blenheims, Hampdens, Wellingtons
and Whitleys, also to occupied countries
(no losses)

12/13 November
Gelsenkirchen
77 Blenheims, Hampdens, Wellingtons
and Whitleys to various targets, with 24
Wellingtons to Gelsenkirchen (1 Whitley
lost)

14/15 November
Berlin, Hamburg
82 Hampdens, Wellingtons and Whitleys
(4 Hampdens, 4 Whitleys, 2 Wellingtons
lost)

15/16 November
Hamburg
67 Hampdens, Wellingtons and Whitleys
(no losses)

16/17 November
Hamburg, Kiel
130 Blenheims, Hampdens, Wellingtons
and Whitleys (2 Wellingtons, 1 Blenheim
lost)

17/18 November
Gelsenkirchen, Hamm
49 Wellingtons and Whitleys (no losses)

18/19 November
Merseburg
11 Whitleys (no losses)

20/21 November
Duisburg
68 Blenheims, Hampdens, Wellingtons
and Whitleys, with 43 going to Duisburg
(1 Whitley lost)

22/23 November
Dortmund, Duisburg, Wanne-Eickel
95 Blenheims, Hampdens, Wellingtons and
Whitleys, also to Bordeaux (1 Hampden lost)

24/25 November
Hamburg
42 Blenheims, Hampdens and Wellingtons
(1 Blenheim, 1 Hampden lost)

25/26 November
Wilhelmshaven
36 Hampdens, Whitleys and Wellingtons
(1 Wellington lost)

27/28 November
Cologne
62 Blenheims, Hampdens, Wellingtons
and Whitleys (1 Whitley lost)

28/29 November
Düsseldorf
24 Blenheims (1 lost)

29/30 November
Bremen, Cologne
42 Blenheims, Hampdens, Wellingtons
and Whitleys, also to Channel ports (1
Blenheim lost)

3/4 December
Duisburg, Essen, Mannheim
20 Blenheims and Whitleys (1 Blenheim
lost, 4 aircraft crashed in England)

4/5 December
Düsseldorf
83 Blenheims, Hampdens, Wellingtons
and Whitleys, also to Turin (1 Blenheim
and 1 Wellington lost)

5/6 December
Gelsenkirchen
5 Whitleys (no losses)

7/8 December
Düsseldorf
69 Blenheims, Hampdens, Wellingtons and
Whitleys, mostly to Düsseldorf (3
Wellingtons, 1 Hampden and 1 Whitley lost)

8/9 December
Düsseldorf
90 Blenheims, Hampdens, Wellingtons
and Whitleys, also to France and airfields
(1 Hampden and 1 Wellington lost)

9/10 December
Bremen
39 Blenheims and Wellingtons, also to
Holland and France (1 Blenheim lost)

11/12 December
Mannheim
42 Blenheims, Wellingtons and Whitleys,
also to France (1 Blenheim and 1
Wellington lost)

13/14 December
Bremen, Kiel
33 Wellingtons and Whitleys (1 Whitley lost)

15/16 December
Berlin, Frankfurt, Kiel
71 Hampdens, Wellingtons and Whitleys
(3 Whitleys lost)

16/17 December
Mannheim (first RAF area bombing)
61 Wellingtons, 35 Whitleys, 29
Hampdens and 9 Blenheims (2
Hampdens and 1 Blenheim lost, 4 aircraft
crashed in England)

17/18 December
Mannheim
9 Whitleys (no losses)

18/19 December
Mannheim
17 Wellingtons and 9 Whitleys (1
Wellington lost)

19/20 December
Cologne, Duisberg, Gelsenkirchen
85 Blenheims, Hampdens, Wellingtons
and Whitleys, also to France (1 Blenheim
lost)

20/21 December
Berlin, Gelsenkirchen
125 Blenheims, Hampdens, Wellingtons
and Whitleys, also to Channel ports (no
losses)

23/24 December
Mannheim, Ludwigshafen
43 Blenheims, Hampdens and
Wellingtons, also to Holland and France
(1 Wellington lost)

29/30 December
Frankfurt/M., Hamm
27 Blenheims, Wellingtons and Whitleys,
also to Boulogne and French airfields (2
Wellingtons lost)

1941

1/2 January
Bremen
141 Blenheims, Hampdens, Wellingtons
and Whitleys, also to Belgian, Dutch and
French ports (no losses, 4 aircraft crashed
in England)

2/3 January
Bremen, Emden
47 Hampdens, Wellingtons and Whitleys,
also to Amsterdam (1 Whitley lost)

3/4 January
Bremen
71 Blenheims, Hampdens, Wellingtons
and Whitleys (1 Whitley lost)

8/9 January
Wilhelmshaven, Emden
48 Hampdens, Wellingtons and Whitleys
(no losses)

9/10 January
Gelsenkirchen
60 Wellingtons, 36 Blenheims, 20
Hampdens, 19 Whitleys (1 Whitley lost)

11/12 January
Wilhelmshaven
35 Hampdens and Wellingtons (no losses)

13/14 January
Wilhelmshaven
24 Wellingtons and Whitleys, also to
French ports (no losses)

15/16 January
Wilhelmshaven
96 Blenheims, Hampdens, Wellingtons
and Whitleys (1 Whitley lost)

16/17 January
Wilhelmshaven
81 Blenheims, Hampdens, Wellingtons
and Whitleys (2 Wellingtons, 2 Whitleys,
1 Hampden lost)

22/23 January
Düsseldorf
28 Wellingtons, 12 Blenheims (no losses)

26/27 January
Hannover
10 Whitleys, 7 Wellingtons (no losses)

29/30 January
Wilhelmshaven
25 Wellingtons, 9 Hampdens (no losses)

4/5 February
Düsseldorf
30 Hampdens (1 lost)

10/11 February
Hannover
112 Wellingtons, 46 Hampdens, 34
Blenheims, 30 Whitleys (2 Wellingtons, 1
Blenheim, 1 Hampden lost, 3 aircraft shot
down in England by German intruders)

11/12 February
Bremen
79 Hampdens, Wellingtons and Whitleys
(no losses, 11 Wellingtons, 7 Whitleys, 4
Hampdens crashed in England)

14/15 February
Gelsenkirchen, Homburg
44 Wellingtons to Gelsenkirchen, 22
Blenheims and 22 Wellingtons to
Homburg (no losses)

15/16 February
Homburg
37 Blenheims and 33 Hampdens (no
losses)

21/22 February
Wilhelmshaven
34 Wellingtons (1 lost), 7 Whitleys to
Düsseldorf

25/26 February
Düsseldorf
43 Wellingtons, 22 Hampdens, 15
Whitleys (1 Wellington lost)

26/27 February
Cologne
126 aircraft

28 February
Wilhelmshaven
116 Blenheims, Hampdens, Wellingtons
and Whitleys (1 Blenheim lost)

1/2 March
Cologne
131 Blenheims, Hampdens, Wellingtons
and Whitleys (5 Whitleys and 1
Wellington lost, 14 aircraft crashed in
England)

3/4 March
Cologne
71 Hampdens, Wellingtons and Whitleys
(1 Hampden lost)

10/11 March
Cologne
19 Hampdens (1 lost)

11/12 March
Kiel
27 Wellingtons (no losses)

12/13 March
Hamburg, Bremen, Berlin
Hamburg: 40 Hampdens, 25 Whitleys, 16
Wellingtons, 4 Manchesters, 3 Halifaxes
(no losses)
Bremen: 54 Wellingtons, 32 Blenheims (1
Blenheim lost)
Berlin: 30 Hampdens, 28 Wellingtons, 14
Whitleys (1 of each lost)

13/14 March
Hamburg
53 Wellingtons, 34 Hampdens, 24
Whitleys, 21 Blenheims, 5 Manchesters, 2
Halifaxes (2 Wellingtons, 2 Whitleys, 1
Blenheim, 1 Hampden lost. 1 Manchester
shot down by intruder in England)

14/15 March
Gelsenkirchen, Düsseldorf
Gelsenkirchen: 61 Wellingtons, 21
Hampdens, 19 Whitleys (1 Wellington
lost)
Düsseldorf: 24 Blenheims (no losses)

15/16 March
Düsseldorf
21 Hampdens (no losses)

17/18 March
Bremen, Wilhelmshaven
57 Hampdens, Wellingtons, Whitleys and
1 Stirling to Bremen, 21 Blenheims to
Wilhelmshaven (no losses, 1 Wellington
shot down by intruder)

18/19 March
Kiel, Wilhelmshaven
Kiel: 40 Hampdens, 34 Wellingtons, 23
Whitleys, 2
Manchesters (no losses)
Wilhelmshaven: 44 Blenheims (1 lost)

19/20 March
Cologne
36 Wellingtons (no losses)

23/24 March
Berlin, Kiel, Hannover
Berlin: 35 Wellingtons and 28 Whitleys
(no losses)
Kiel: 31 Hampdens (no losses)
Hannover: 26 Blenheims (1 lost)
5 Hampdens mine-laying off Kiel

27/28 March
Cologne, Düsseldorf
Cologne: 38 Wellingtons and 1 Stirling (1
Wellington lost)
Düsseldorf: 22 Hampdens. 13 Whitleys, 4
Manchesters (1 Manchester and 1 Whitley
lost)

31 March/1 April
Bremen
28 Wellingtons (1 lost)

7/8 April
Kiel, Bremerhaven
Kiel: 117 Wellingtons, 61 Hampdens, 49
Whitleys, 2 Stirlings (2 Wellingtons, 2
Whitleys lost)
Bremerhaven: 24 Blenheims (no losses)
9 aircraft to Emden

8/9 April
Kiel, Bremerhaven
Kiel: 74 Wellingtons, 44 Whitleys, 29
Hampdens, 12 Manchesters, 1 Stirling (2
Wellingtons, 1 Hampden, 1 Manchester

lost, 9 aircraft crashed in England)
Bremerhaven: 22 Blenheims (no losses)
2 Blenheims to Emden

9/10 April
Berlin
36 Wellingtons, 24 Hampdens, 17
Whitleys, 3 Stirlings (3 Wellingtons, 1
Stirling, 1 Whitley lost)
7 aircraft to Emden

10/11 April
Düsseldorf
29 Hampdens and 24 Whitleys (5
Hampdens lost)

15/16 April
Kiel
49 Wellingtons, 21 Whitleys, 19
Hampdens, 5 Halifaxes, 2 Stirlings (1
Wellington lost)

16/17 April
Bremen
62 Wellingtons, 24 Whitleys, 21
Hampdens (1 Whitley lost)

17/18 April
Berlin
50 Wellingtons, 39 Hampdens, 28
Whitleys, 1 Stirling (5 Whitleys, 2
Hampdens, 1 Wellington lost)

20/21 April
Cologne
37 Wellingtons, 12 Whitleys, 11
Hampdens, 1 Stirling (2 Hampdens, 1
Wellington lost)

24/25 April
Kiel
39 Wellingtons, 19 Whitleys, 10
Hampdens, 1 Stirling (1 Whitley lost)
9 aircraft to Wilhelmshaven

25/26 April
Kiel
38 Wellingtons, 14 Whitleys, 10
Hampdens (1 Wellington lost)
5 aircraft to Bremerhaven, 4 to Emden, 3
to Berlin (no losses)

26/27 April
Hamburg
28 Hampdens and 22 Wellingtons (1
Hampden lost)
4 Wellingtons to Emden (no losses)

29/30 April
Mannheim
42 Wellingtons, 15 Whitleys, 14
Hampdens (1 Wellington lost)

30 April/1 May
Kiel
43 Wellingtons, 25 Whitleys, 13
Hampdens (no losses)

2/3 May
Hamburg
49 Wellingtons, 21 Whitleys, 19
Hampdens, 3 Manchesters, 3 Stirlings (1
Hampden, 1 Manchester, 1 Whitley lost)
17 Wellingtons and 6 Whitleys to Emden
(1 Wellington lost)

3/4 May
Cologne
37 Wellingtons, 35 Whitleys, 27
Hampdens, 2 Manchesters (no losses)

5/6 May
Mannheim
70 Wellingtons, 33 Hampdens, 30 Whitleys,
4 Manchesters, 4 Stirlings (no losses)

6/7 May
Hamburg
50 Wellingtons, 31 Whitleys, 27
Hampdens, 4 Manchesters, 3 Stirlings (no
losses)

8/9 May
Hamburg, Bremen, Bremerhaven, Kiel
Hamburg: 100 Wellingtons, 78
Hampdens, 9 Manchesters, 1Stirling (3
Wellingtons, 1 Hampden lost)
Bremen: 78 Whitleys, 55 Wellingtons (3
Wellingtons, 2 Whitleys lost)
Kiel: 23 Blenheims (no losses)
Bremerhaven: 4 Blenheims (no losses)

9/10 May
Mannheim, Ludwigshafen
69 Wellingtons, 42 Whitleys, 24
Hampdens, 11 Manchesters (1
Wellington, 1 Whitley lost)

10/11 May
Hamburg, Berlin
Hamburg: 60 Wellingtons, 35 Hampdens,
23 Whitleys, 1 Manchester (3
Wellingtons, 1 Whitley lost)
Berlin: 23 aircraft (2 Stirlings, 1
Manchesters lost) 6 Wellingtons to
Emden (no losses)

11/12 May
Hamburg, Bremen
Hamburg: 91 Wellingtons, 1 Stirling (3
Wellingtons lost)
Bremen: 48 Whitleys, 31 Hampdens, 2
Manchesters (1 Hampden lost)

12/13 May
Mannheim, Ludwigshafen, Cologne
42 Wellingtons, 41 Hampdens, 18
Whitleys, 4 Manchesters, with 65 going
to Mannheim and 40 to Ludwigshafen.
16 aircraft reported bombing Cologne (no
losses)

15/16 May
Hannover
55 Wellingtons, 27 Hampdens, 18
Whitleys, 1 Stirling (2 Wellingtons, 1
Hampden lost)
14 Manchesters to Berlin (1 lost)

16/17 May
Cologne
48 Wellingtons, 24 Hampdens, 20
Whitleys, 1 Stirling (1 Whitley lost)

17/18 May
Cologne, Kiel
Cologne: 44 Wellingtons, 28 Whitleys, 23
Hampdens (1 Hampden, 1 Whitley lost)
Kiel: 33 Wellingtons, 19 Whitleys, 18
Hampdens (no losses)

23/24 May
Cologne
24 Hampdens, 22 Wellingtons, 5 Stirlings
(no losses)

27/28 May
Cologne
46 Whitleys, 18 Wellingtons (no losses)

28/29 May
Kiel
14 Whitleys (1 lost)

2/3 June
Düsseldorf, Duisburg, Berlin
Düsseldorf: 68 Wellingtons, 43
Hampdens, 39 Whitleys (2 Hampdens, 1
Whitley lost)
Duisburg: 25 Wellingtons (no losses)
Berlin: 8 Stirlings, 3 Wellingtons (1
Stirling lost)

11 June
Bremerhaven
25 Blenheims (1 lost, 19 turned back)

11/12 June
Düsseldorf, Duisburg
Düsseldorf: 92 Wellingtons, 6 Stirlings (6
Wellingtons lost)
Duisburg: 36 Whitleys, 35 Hampdens, 9
Halifaxes (1 Whitley lost)
20 Hampdens mine-laying in Kiel Bay (1
lost)

12/13 June
Soest, Schwerte, Hamm, Osnabrück, Hüls
Soest: 91 Hampdens (2 lost)
Schwerte: 80 Whitleys, 4 Wellingtons (3
Whitleys lost)
Hamm: 82 Wellingtons (no losses)
Osnabrück: 61 Wellingtons (1 lost)
Hüls: 11 Halifaxes, 7 Stirlings (no losses)

14/15 June
Cologne
29 Hampdens (no losses)

15/16 June
Cologne, Düsseldorf, Hannover
Cologne: 49 Wellingtons, 42 Hampdens
(1 Hampden lost)
Düsseldorf: 31 Whitleys, 28 Wellingtons
(no losses)
Hannover: 16 aircraft (no losses)

16/17 June
Cologne, Düsseldorf, Duisburg
Cologne: 47 Hampdens, 39 Whitleys, 16
Wellingtons, 3 Halifaxes (1 Whitley, 1
Wellington lost)
Düsseldorf: 65 Wellingtons, 7 Stirlings
(no losses)
Duisburg: 39 Wellingtons (1 lost)

17/18 June
Cologne, Düsseldorf, Duisburg
Cologne: 43 Hampdens, 33 Whitleys (1
Whitley lost)
Düsseldorf: 57 Wellingtons (no losses)
Duisburg: 26 Wellingtons (no losses)
11 aircraft to Hannover (no losses)

19/20 June
Cologne, Düsseldorf
Cologne: 28 Wellingtons (1 lost)
Düsseldorf: 20 Whitleys (1 lost)

20/21 June
Kiel
47 Wellingtons, 24 Hampdens, 20
Whitleys, 13 Stirlings, 11 Halifaxes (2
Wellingtons lost)

21/22 June
Cologne, Düsseldorf
Cologne: 68 Wellingtons (no losses)
Düsseldorf: 28 Hampdens, 28 Whitleys
(no losses)

22/23 June
Bremen, Wilhelmshaven
Bremen: 45 Wellingtons, 25 Hampdens
(1 of each lost)
Wilhelmshaven: 16 Wellingtons, 11
Whitleys
3 Wellingtons to Emden, 1 Hampden to
Düsseldorf (no losses)

23/24 June
Cologne, Kiel, Düsseldorf
Cologne: 44 Wellingtons, 18 Whitleys (1
Wellington lost)
Düsseldorf: 30 Hampdens, 11
Manchesters (no losses)
Kiel: 13 Stirlings, 10 Halifaxes, 3
Wellingtons (1 Halifax lost)
1 aircraft to each of Bremen, Emden and
Hannover (no losses)

24/25 June
Cologne, Kiel, Düsseldorf
Cologne: 32 Whitleys, 22 Wellingtons (no
losses)
Kiel: 25 Hampdens, 23 Wellingtons (1
Wellington lost)
Düsseldorf: 23 Wellingtons, 8
Manchesters (no losses)

25/26 June
Bremen, Kiel
Bremen: 56 Wellingtons, 8 Whitleys (1
Wellington lost)
Kiel: 30 Hampdens, 17 Wellingtons (1
Hampden lost)
1 aircraft each to Cologne and Düsseldorf
(no losses)

26/27 June
Cologne, Düsseldorf, Kiel
Cologne: 32 Wellingtons, 19 Whitleys (1
Wellington lost)
Düsseldorf: 30 Hampdens, 14
Wellingtons (1 Wellington lost)
Kiel: 18 Manchesters, 15 Stirlings, 8
Halifaxes (2 Manchesters lost)

27/28 June
Bremen
73 Wellingtons, 35 Whitleys (11
Whitleys, 3 Wellingtons lost)
3 aircraft to Emden, 1 to Cologne, 1 to
Düsseldorf (no losses)

29/30 June
Bremen, Hamburg
Bremen: 52 Wellingtons, 30 Hampdens,
24 Whitleys (4 Wellingtons, 2 Hampdens,
1 Whitley lost)
Hamburg: 13 Stirlings, 7 Wellingtons, 6
Manchesters, 2 Halifaxes (4 Stirlings, 2
Wellingtons lost)

30 June/1 July
Ruhrgebiet
32 Wellingtons, 18 Whitleys, 14
Hampdens (2 Hampdens, 2 Whitleys lost)

2/3 July
Bremen, Cologne, Duisburg
Bremen: 57 Wellingtons, 6 Stirlings, 4
Halifaxes (1 Wellington lost)
Cologne: 33 Whitleys, 9 Wellingtons (1
Wellington lost)
Duisburg: 39 Hampdens (2 lost)

3/4 July
Essen, Bremen
Essen: 61 Wellingtons, 29 Whitleys (2 of
each lost)
Bremen: 39 Hampdens, 29 Wellingtons
(2 Wellingtons, 1 Hampden lost)

5/6 July
Münster, Osnabrück, Bielfeld
Münster: 65 Wellingtons, 29 Whitleys (1
Whitley lost)
Osnabrück: 39 Hampdens (3 lost)
Bielfeld: 33 Wellingtons (no losses)
13 Halifaxes, 3 Stirlings to Magdeburg
(no losses)

6/7 July
Münster, Dortmund
Münster: 47 Wellingtons (2 lost)
Dortmund: 31 Whitleys, 15 Wellingtons
(2 Whitleys lost)
2 Wellingtons to Emden

7/8 July
Cologne, Osnabrück, Münster
Cologne: 114 Wellingtons (3 lost)
Osnabrück: 54 Whitleys, 18 Wellingtons
(3 Whitleys lost)
Münster: 49 Wellingtons (3 lost)
40 Hampdens to Mönchengladbach (2
lost)
14 Halifaxes, 3 Stirlings to Frankfurt

8/9 July
Hamm, Münster, Bielefeld, Merseburg
Hamm: 45 Hampdens, 28 Whitleys (4
Whitleys, 3 Hampdens lost)
Münster: 51 Wellingtons (1 lost)
Bielefeld: 33 Wellingtons (no losses)
Merseburg: 13 Halifaxes, 1 Stirling (1
Halifax lost)

9/10 July
Aachen, Osnabrück
Aachen: 39 Hampdens, 27 Whitleys, 16
Wellingtons (1 Hampden, 1 Whitley lost)
Osnabrück: 57 Wellingtons (2 lost)

10/11 July
Cologne
98 Wellingtons, 32 Hampdens (2
Wellingtons lost)

11/12 July
Wilhelmshaven
36 Hampdens (no losses)

12/13 July
Bremen
33 Hampdens, 28 Wellingtons (no losses)

14/15 July
Bremen, Hannover
Bremen: 78 Wellingtons, 19 Whitleys (4
Wellingtons lost)
Hannover: 44 Hampdens, 21
Wellingtons, 14 Halifaxes, 6 Stirlings (2
Wellingtons lost)

16/17 July
Hamburg
51 Wellingtons, 32 Hampdens, 24
Whitleys (3 Wellingtons, 1 Hampden
lost)

17/18 July
Cologne
50 Wellingtons, 25 Hampdens (no losses)

19/20 July
Hannover
20 Whitleys, 17 Wellingtons, 12
Hampdens (1 Wellington, 1 Whitley lost)

20/21 July
Cologne
46 Wellingtons, 39 Hampdens, 25
Whitleys, 3 Stirlings (no losses)

21/22 July
Frankfurt, Mannheim
Frankfurt: 37 Wellingtons, 34 Hampdens
(no losses)
Mannheim: 36 Wellingtons, 8 Halifaxes
(1 Wellington lost)

22/23 July
Frankfurt, Mannheim
Frankfurt: 34 Hampdens, 16 Whitleys, 13
Wellingtons (no losses)
Mannheim: 29 Wellingtons (no losses)

23/24 July
Mannheim, Frankfurt
Mannheim: 51 Wellingtons (no losses)
Frankfurt: 33 Hampdens (1 lost)

24/25 July
Kiel, Emden
Kiel: 34 Wellingtons, 30 Hampdens (1 of
each lost)
Emden: 31 Whitleys, 16 Wellingtons (2
Wellingtons lost)

25/26 July
Hannover, Hamburg
Hannover: 30 Hampdens, 25 Whitleys (4
Whitleys, 1 Hampden lost)
Hamburg: 43 Wellingtons (2 lost)

30/31 July
Cologne
62 Wellingtons, 42 Hampdens, 7
Halifaxes, 5 Stirlings (2 Hampdens, 1
Wellington lost, 6 aircraft crashed in
England)

2/3 August
Hamburg, Berlin, Kiel
Hamburg: 58 Wellingtons, 21 Whitleys, 1
Stirling (2 Wellingtons lost)
Berlin: 40 Wellingtons, 8 Halifaxes, 5
Stirlings (3 Wellingtons, 1 Stirling lost)
Kiel: 50 Hampdens (5 lost)
5 Hampdens mine-laying off Kiel (no
losses)

5/6 August
Mannheim, Karlsruhe, Frankfurt
Mannheim: 65 Wellingtons, 33
Hampdens (2 Wellingtons, 1 Hampden
lost)
Karlsruhe: 50 Hampdens, 28 Wellingtons,
11 Halifaxes, 8
Stirlings (1 Halifax, 1 Hampden, 1
Wellington lost)
Frankfurt: 46 Whitleys, 22 Wellingtons (2
Whitleys, 1 Wellington lost)
13 Wellingtons to Aachen (2 lost)

6/7 August
Frankfurt, Mannheim, Karlsruhe
Frankfurt: 34 Whitleys, 19 Wellingtons (2
of each lost)
Mannheim: 38 Wellingtons (no losses)
Karlsruhe: 38 Hampdens (1 lost)

7/8 August
Essen, Hamm, Dortmund
Essen: 54 Hampdens, 32 Wellingtons, 9
Halifaxes, 8 Stirlings, 3 Manchesters (2
Hampdens, 1 Stirling lost)
Hamm: 45 Welingtons, 1 Stirling (no
losses)
Dortmund: 20 Wellingtons, 20 Whitleys
(no losses)

8/9 August
Kiel, Hamburg
Kiel: 50 Hampdens, 4 Whitleys (2 Hampdens, 1 Whitley lost)
Hamburg: 44 Wellingtons (1 lost)

11/12 August
Krefeld, Mönchengladbach
Krefeld: 20 Hampdens, 9 Whitleys (no losses)
Mönchengladbach: 29 Wellingtons (no losses)

12/13 August
Berlin, Hannover, Magdeburg, Essen
Berlin: 40 Wellingtons, 12 Halifaxes, 9 Stirlings, 9 Manchesters (3 Manchesters, 3 Wellingtons, 2 Halifaxes, 1 Stirling lost)
Hannover: 65 Wellingtons, 13 Hampdens (4 Wellingtons lost)
Magdeburg: 36 Hampdens (no losses)
Essen: 30 Wellingtons, 3 Stirlings, 2 Halifaxes (1 Wellington shot down in England by an intruder)

14/15 August
Hannover, Brunswick, Magdeburg
Hannover: 96 Wellingtons, 55 Whitleys, 1 Stirling (5 Wellingtons, 4 Whitleys lost)
Brunswick: 81 Hampdens (1 lost)
Magdeburg: 27 Wellingtons, 9 Halifaxes, 9 Stirlings, 7 Manchesters (2 Wellingtons, 1 Halifax, 1 Stirling lost)

16/17 August
Cologne, Düsseldorf, Duisburg
Cologne: 37 Wellingtons, 29 Whitleys, 6 Halifaxes (7 Whitleys, 1 Wellington lost)
Düsseldorf: 52 Hampdens, 6 Manchesters (3 Hampdens, 2 Manchesters lost)
Duisburg: 54 Wellingtons (1 lost)

17/18 August
Bremen, Duisburg
Bremen: 39 Hampdens, 20 Whitleys (2 Hampdens lost)
Duisburg: 41 Wellingtons (no losses)

18/19 August
Cologne, Duisburg
Cologne: 42 Hampdens, 17 Whitleys, 3 Wellingtons (5 Whitleys, 1 Wellington lost)
Duisburg: 41 Wellingtons (2 lost)

19/20 August
Kiel
54 Wellingtons, 41 Hampdens, 7 Stirlings, 6 Halifaxes (3 Wellingtons, 1 Hampden lost)

22/23 August
Mannheim
51 Wellingtons, 41 Hampdens (1 Hampden lost)

24/25 August
Düsseldorf
25 Whitleys, 12 Hampdens, 7 Halifaxes (2 Whitleys, 1 Halifax lost)

25/26 August
Karlsruhe, Mannheim
Karlsruhe: 37 Wellingtons, 12 Stirlings (2 Wellingtons, 1 Stirling lost)
Mannheim: 38 Hampdens, 7 Manchesters (3 Hampdens lost)

26/27 August
Cologne
47 Wellingtons, 29 Hampdens. 22 Whitleys, 1 Manchester (1 Wellington, 1 Whitley lost)

27/28 August
Mannheim
35 Hampdens, 41 Wellingtons, 15 Whitleys (no losses. 7 Wellingtons, 1 Whitley crashed in England)

28/29 August
Duisburg
60 Wellingtons, 30 Hampdens, 13 Stirlings, 9 Halifaxes, 6 Manchesters (3 Wellingtons, 1 Halifax, 1 Hampden, 1 Stirling lost)
6 Hampdens on searchlight-suppression duty (2 lost)

29/30 August
Frankfurt, Mannheim
Frankfurt: 73 Hampdens. 62 Whitleys, 5 Halifaxes, 3 Manchesters (2 Hampdens, 1 Whitey lost)
Mannheim: 94 Wellingtons (2 lost)

31 August
Cologne, Essen
Cologne: 45 Wellingtons, 39 Hampdens, 7 Halifaxes, 6 Manchesters, 6 Stirlings (3 Hampdens, 1 Manchester, 1 Wellington lost. 1 Wellington shot down by an intruder in England)
Essen: 43 Whitleys, 28 Wellingtons (1 Whitley lost)

2/3 September
Frankfurt, Berlin
Frankfurt: 71 Wellingtons, 44 Whitleys, 11 Hampdens (3 Wellingtons, 1 Hampden lost)
Berlin: 32 Hampdens. 7 Halifaxes, 6 Stirlings, 4 Manchesters (2 Halifaxes, 2 Hampdens, 1 Manchester lost)

6/7 September
Hüls
41 Whitleys, 27 Wellingtons, 18 Hampdens (5 Whitleys, 2 Wellingtons lost)

7/8 September
Berlin, Kiel
Berlin: 103 Wellingtons, 43 Hampdens, 31 Whitleys, 10 Stirlings, 6 Halifaxes, 4 Manchesters (8 Wellingtons, 2 Hampdens, 2 Whitleys, 2 Stirlings, 1 Manchester lost)
Kiel: 30 Wellingtons, 18 Hampdens, 3 Stirlings (2 Hampdens, 1 Wellington lost)

8/9 September
Kassel
52 Wellingtons, 27 Hampdens, 16 Whitleys (no losses)

11/12 September
Rostock, Kiel, Warnemünde
Rostock: 39 Hampdens, 12 Wellingtons, 5 Manchesters (2 Hampdens lost)
Kiel: 55 Wellingtons (2 lost)
Warnemünde: 32 Whitleys (1 lost)

12/13 September
Frankfurt
71 Wellingtons, 31 Hampdens, 18 Whitleys, 9 Stirlings (2 Wellingtons lost)

15/16 September
Hamburg
169 aircraft (3 Wellingtons, 2 Hampdens, 1 Halifax, 1 Stirling, 1 Whitley lost)

16/17 September
Karlsruhe
55 Wellingtons (no losses)

17/18 September
Karlsruhe
38 Wellingtons (1 lost)

19/20 September
Stettin
72 aircraft, mostly Wellingtons (1 Wellington, 1 Whitley lost)

20/21 September
Berlin, Frankfurt
Berlin: 74 aircraft, all recalled due to weather. 10 did not receive signal and carried on, none reached Berlin. (3 Wellingtons, 1 Whitley lost. 12 aircraft crashed in England)

26/27 September
Cologne, Emden, Mannheim
104 aircraft, all recalled due to fog. 23 aircraft carried on. (1 Wellington lost. 4 Wellingtons crashed in England)

28/29 September
Frankfurt
30 Hampdens, 14 Wellingtons (1 Hampden, 1 Wellington lost. 5 aircraft crashed in England)
6 Wellingtons, 1 Stirling to Emden (no losses)

29/30 September
Stettin, Hamburg
Stettin: 67 Wellingtons, 56 Whitleys, 10 Stirlings, 6 Halifaxes (4 Whitleys, 2 Wellingtons, 2 Stirlings lost)
Hamburg: 93 aircraft, most Hampdens and Wellingtons (2 Wellingtons lost, 2 Hampdens crashed in England)

30 September/1 October
Hamburg, Stettin
Hamburg: 48 Hampdens, 24 Wellingtons, 10 Whitleys (1 Wellington lost)
Stettin: 40 Wellingtons (no losses)

1/2 October
Karlsruhe, Stuttgart
Karlsruhe: 44 Hampdens, 1 Wellington, all recalled due to fog. 3 flew on to Karlsruhe, 23 bombed alternative targets (1 Wellington lost)
Stuttgart: 27 Whitleys, 4 Wellingtons (no losses)

10/11 October
Essen, Cologne
Essen: 78 aircraft (2 Hampdens, 2 Whitleys lost)
Cologne: 69 aircraft (5 Wellingtons lost)
5 Hampdens on searchlight-suppression raids in Essen and Cologne

12/13 October
Nuremberg, Bremen, Hüls
Nuremberg: 82 Wellingtons, 54 Whitleys, 9 Halifaxes, 7 Stirlings (5 Wellingtons, 1 Halifax, 1 Stirling, 1 Whitley lost. 5 aircraft crashed in England)
Bremen: 99 aircraft, mostly Wellingtons and Hampdens (2 Wellingtons, 1 Hampden lost)
Hüls: 79 Hampdens, 11 Manchesters (1 of each lost)

13/14 October
Düsseldorf, Cologne
Düsseldorf: 53 Wellingtons, 7 Stirlings (1 Wellington lost)
Cologne: 30 Hampdens, 9 Manchesters

14/15 October
Nuremberg
58 Wellingtons, 13 Whitleys, 5 Halifaxes, 4 Stirlings (4 Wellingtons lost)

15/16 October
Cologne
27 Wellingtons, 7 Stirlings (3 Wellingtons lost)

16/17 October
Duisburg
47 Wellingtons, 26 Hampdens, 14 Whitleys (1 Wellington lost)
8 Hampdens on searchlight-suppression flights

20/21 October
Bremen, Wilhelmshaven, Emden
Bremen: 82 Hampdens, 48 Wellingtons, 15 Stirlings, 8b Manchesters (2 Hampdens, 2 Wellingtons, 1 Manchester lost)
Wilhelmshaven: 40 Whitleys, 4 Wellingtons, 3 Hampdens (no losses)
Emden: 35 Wellingtons, 1 Halifax (1 Wellington lost)

21/22 October
Bremen
136 aircraft (2 Wellingtons, 1 Hampden lost)
4 Manchesters to Kiel Bay

22/23 October
Mannheim
50 Wellingtons, 45 Hampdens, 22 Whitleys, 6 Halifaxes (3 Wellingtons, 1 Hampden lost)

23/24 October
Kiel
43 Wellingtons, 38 Hampdens, 27 Whitleys, 6 Manchesters (1 Hampden lost)

24/25 October
Frankfurt
70 aircraft (2 Wellingtons, 1 Hampden, 1 Whitley lost)

26/27 October
Hamburg
115 aircraft (3 Wellingtons, 1 Hampden lost)
5 Hampdens mine-laying at Kiel Bay

31 October
Hamburg, Bremen
Hamburg: 123 aircraft (4 Whitleys lost)
Bremen: 40 Wellingtons, 8 Stirlings (1 Wellington lost)

1/2 November
Kiel
72 Wellingtons, 32 Hampdens, 30 Whitleys (2 Whitleys, 1 Hampden lost)
5 Hampdens, 2 Manchesters mine-laying in Kiel Bay

4/5 November
Essen
28 Wellingtons (no losses)

7/8 November
Berlin, Cologne, Mannheim
Berlin: 101 Wellingtons, 42 Whitleys, 17
Stirlings, 9 Halifaxes (10 Wellingtons, 9
Whitleys, 2 Stirlings lost)
Cologne: 61 Hampdens, 14 Manchesters
(no losses)
Mannheim: 53 Wellingtons, 2 Stirlings (7
Wellingtons lost)
30 Halifaxes, Hampdens, Wellingtons,
Whitleys on rover patrols in Essen and
other areas (6 aircraft lost)

8/9 November
Essen
54 aircraft (3 Wellingtons, 2 Whitleys, 1
Hampden lost)
8 Hampdens on searchlight-suppression
flights (1 lost)

9/10 November
Hamburg
103 aircraft (1 Wellington lost)

15/16 November
Emden, Kiel
Emden: 49 aircraft (4 Wellingtons lost)
Kiel: 47 aircraft (4 Wellingtons lost)

26/27 November
Emden
80 Wellingtons, 20 Hampdens (2
Wellingtons, 1 Hampden lost)

27/28 November
Düsseldorf
41 Wellingtons, 34 Hampdens, 6
Manchesters, 5 Stirlings (1 Hampden, 1
Wellington lost)

30 November/1 December
Hamburg, Emden
Hamburg: 92 Wellingtons, 48 Hampdens,
24 Whitleys, 11 Halifaxes, 4 Manchesters,
2 Stirlings (6 Wellingtons, 4 Whitleys, 2
Hampdens, 1 Halifax lost)

7/8 December
Aachen
130 aircraft (1 Halifax, 1 Hampden lost)

11/12 December
Cologne
60 aircraft (1 Halifax lost)

16/17 December
Wilhelmshaven
57 Wellingtons, 14 Hampdens, 12
Whitleys (no losses)

22/23 December
Wilhelmshaven
12 Whitleys, 10 Wellingtons (no losses)

23/24 December
Cologne
33 Wellingtons, 20 Hampdens, 15
Whitleys (no losses)

27/28 December
Düsseldorf
66 Wellingtons, 30 Hampdens, 29
Whitleys, 7 Manchesters (5 Whitleys, 2
Wellingtons lost)

28/29 December
Wilhelmshaven, Hüls, Emden
Wilhelmshaven: 86 Wellingtons (1 lost)
Hüls: 81 Hampdens (4 lost)
Emden: 25 Wellingtons, 14 Whitleys, 1
Stirling (1 Whitley lost)

1942

10/11 January
Wilhelmshaven
124 aircraft (3 Wellingtons, 2 Hampdens
lost)

14/15 January
Hamburg
95 aircraft (2 Hampdens, 2 Wellingtons lost)

15/16 January
Hamburg, Bremen
Hamburg: 96 aircraft (3 Wellingtons, 1

Hampden lost, 8 aircraft crashed in
England)
Emden: 50 aircraft (1 Wellington, 1
Whitley lost)

17/18 January
Bremen
83 aircraft (3 Wellingtons lost, 1 Stirling
crashed in England after being fired on)
24 aircraft to Emden

20/21 January
Emden
20 Wellingtons, 5 Hampdens (3 Wellingtons, 1 Hampden lost)

21/22 January
Emden, Bremen
Bremen: 54 aircraft (2 Hampdens, 1 Wellington lost)
Emden: 38 aircraft (3 Hampdens, 1 Whitley lost)

22/23 January
Münster
47 aircraft (1 Wellington lost)

26/27 January
Hannover, Emden
Hannover: 71 aircraft (no losses)
Emden: 31 aircraft (2 Whitleys lost)
2 Whitleys to Germany on leaflet flights

28/29 January
Münster
55 Wellingtons, 29 Hampdens (4 Hampdens, 1 Wellington lost)

11/12 February
Mannheim
49 aircraft (no losses)

14/15 February
Mannheim
98 aircraft (1 Hampden, 1 Whitley lost)

22/23 February
Wilhelmshaven
31 Wellingtons, 19 Hampdens (no losses)
7 aircraft to Emden, 5 Manchesters mine-laying off Wilhelmshaven (no losses)

25/26 February
Kiel
43 Wellingtons, 12 Manchesters, 6 Stirlings (3 Wellingtons lost)

8/9 March
Essen
115 Wellingtons, 37 Hampdens, 27 Stirlings, 22 Manchesters, 10 Halifaxes (5 Wellingtons, 2 Manchesters, 1 Stirling lost)

9/10 March
Duisburg, Essen
Essen: 136 Wellingtons, 21 Stirlings, 15 Hampdens, 10 Manchesters, 5 Halifaxes (2 Wellingtons, 1 Halifax lost)

10/11 March
Essen
56 Wellingtons, 43 Hampdens, 13 Manchesters, 12 Stirlings, 2 Lancasters (2 Hampdens, 1 Stirling, 1 Wellington lost)

12/13 March
Kiel
68 Wellingtons (5 lost)
Emden: 20 Wellingtons, 20 Whitleys (3 Whitleys lost)

13/14 March
Cologne
135 aircraft, 6 types (1 Manchester lost)

25/26 March
Essen
192 Wellingtons, 26 Stirlings, 20 Manchesters, 9 Hampdens, 7 Lancasters (5 Manchesters, 3 Wellingtons, 1 Hampden lost)

26/27 March
Essen
104 Wellingtons, 11 Stirlings (10 Wellingtons, 1 Stirling lost)
36 aircraft mine-laying off Wilhelmshaven

28/29 March
Lübeck
320 dead
39,000 bombed out
146 Wellingtons, 41 Hampdens, 26 Stirlings, 21 Manchesters (7 Wellingtons, 3 Stirlings, 1 Hampden, 1 Manchester lost)

1/2 April
Hanau
35 Wellingtons, 14 Hampdens (12 Wellingtons, 1 Hampden lost)

5/6 April
Cologne
179 Wellingtons, 44 Hampdens, 29 Stirlings, 11 Manchesters (4 Wellingtons, 1 Hampden lost)

6/7 April
Essen
110 Wellingtons, 19 Stirlings, 18 Hampdens, 10 Manchesters (2 Hampdens, 1 Manchester, 1 Stirling, 1 Wellington lost)

8/9 April
Hamburg
177 Wellingtons, 41 Hampdens, 22 Stirlings, 13 Manchesters, 12 Halifaxes, 7 Lancasters (4 Wellingtons, 1 Manchester lost)

10/11 April
Essen
167 Wellingtons, 43 Hampdens, 18 Stirlings, 10 Manchesters, 8 Halifaxes, 8 Lancasters (7 Wellingtons, 5 Hampdens, 1 Halifax, 1 Manchester lost)

12/13 April
Essen
171 Wellingtons, 31 Hampdens, 27 Stirlings, 13 Halifaxes, 9 Manchesters (7 Wellingtons, 2 Hampdens, 1 Halifax lost)

14/15 April
Dortmund
142 Wellingtons, 34 Hampdens, 20 Stirlings, 8 Halifaxes, 4 Manchesters (5 Wellingtons, 4 Hampdens lost)

15/16 April
Dortmund
111 Wellingtons, 19 Hampdens, 15 Stirlings, 7 Manchesters (3 Wellingtons, 1 Stirling lost)

17/18 April
Hamburg
134 Wellingtons, 23 Stirlings, 11 Halifaxes, 5 Manchesters (7 Wellingtons, 1 Manchester lost)

22/23 April
Cologne
64 Wellingtons, 5 Stirlings (2 Wellingtons lost)

23/24 April
Rostock
93 Wellingtons, 31 Stirlings, 19 Whitleys, 11 Hampdens. 6 Manchesters, 1 Lancaster (2 Wellingtons, 1 Manchester, 1 Whitley lost)

24/25 April
Rostock
125 aircraft, 6 types (1 Hampden lost)

25/26 April
Rostock
128 aircraft, 6 types (no losses)

26/27 April
Rostock
200 dead
30,000 bombed out
106 or 109 aircraft, 7 types (1 Stirling, 1 Wellington, 1 Whitley lost)

27/28 April
Cologne
76 Wellingtons, 19 Stirlings. 2 Halifaxes (6 Wellingtons, 1 Halifax lost)

28/29 April
Kiel
62 Wellingtons, 15 Stirlings, 10 Hampdens, 1 Halifax (5 Wellingtons, 1 Hampden lost)

3/4 May
Hamburg
43 Wellingtons, 20 Halifaxes, 13 Stirlings, 5 Hampdens (3 Halifaxes, 2 Wellingtons lost)

4/5 May
Stuttgart
69 Wellingtons, 19 Hampdens, 14 Lancasters, 12 Stirlings, 7 Halifaxes (1 Stirling lost)

5/6 May
Stuttgart
49 Wellingtons, 13 Stirlings, 11 Halifaxes, 4 Lancasters (3 Wellingtons, 1 Stirling lost)

6/7 May
Stuttgart
55 Wellingtons, 15 Stirlings, 10 Hampdens, 10 Lancasters, 7 Halifaxes (5 Wellingtons, 1 Halifax lost)

8/9 May
Warnemünde
98 Wellingtons, 27 Stirlings, 21 Lancasters, 19 Halifaxes, 19 Hampdens, 9 Manchesters (8 Wellingtons, 4 Lancasters, 3 Hampdens, 2 Halifaxes, 1 Manchester, 1 Stirling lost)

19/20 May
Mannheim
105 Wellingtons, 31 Stirlings, 29
Halifaxes, 15 Hampdens, 13 Lancasters, 4
Manchesters (4 Halifaxes, 4 Stirlings, 3
Wellingtons lost)

30/31 May
Cologne
486 dead
45,000 bombed out
602 Wellingtons, 131 Halifaxes, 88
Stirlings. 79 Hampdens, 73 Lancasters, 46
Manchesters, 28 Whitleys (29
Wellingtons, 4 Manchesters, 3 Halifaxes,
2 Stirlings, 1 Hampden, 1 Lancaster, 1
Whitley lost)

1/2 June
Essen
545 Wellingtons, 127 Halifaxes, 77
Stirlings, 74 Lancasters, 71 Hampdens, 33
Manchesters, 29 Whitleys (15
Wellingtons, 8 Halifaxes, 4 Lancasters, 1
Hampden, 1 Manchester, 1 Stirling, 1
Whitley lost)

2/3 June
Essen
97 Wellingtons, 38 Halifaxes, 27
Lancasters, 21 Stirlings, 12 Hampdens (7
Wellingtons, 2 Halifaxes, 2 Lancasters, 2
Stirlings, 1 Hampden lost)

3/4 June
Bremen
170 aircraft, all types (4 Wellingtons, 2
Halifaxes, 2 Lancasters, 2 Stirlings, 1
Manchester lost)

5/6 June
Essen
98 Wellingtons, 33 Halifaxes, 25 Stirlings,
13 Lancasters, 11 Hampdens (8
Wellingtons, 2 Stirlings, 1 Halifax, 1
Lancaster lost)

6/7 June
Emden
124 Wellingtons, 40 Stirlings, 27
Halifaxes, 20 Lancasters, 15 Hampdens, 7
Manchesters (3 Manchesters, 3
Wellingtons, 2 Stirlings, 1 Halifax lost)

8/9 June
Essen
92 Wellingtons, 42 Halifaxes, 14 Stirlings,
13 Lancasters, 9 Hampdens (7
Wellingtons, 7 Halifaxes, 3 Lancasters, 1
Hampden, 1 Stirling lost)

16/17 June
Essen
40 Wellingtons, 39 Halifaxes, 15
Lancasters, 12 Stirlings (4 Halifaxes, 3
Wellingtons, 1 Stirling lost)

19/20 June
Emden
112 Wellingtons, 37 Halifaxes, 25
Stirlings, 11 Hampdens, 9 Lancasters (6
Wellingtons, 2 Stirlings, 1 Halifax lost)

20/21 June
Emden
185 aircraft, 5 types (3 Wellingtons, 2
Stirlings, 1 Halifax, 1 Lancaster lost)

22/23 June
Emden
144 Wellingtons, 38 Stirlings, 26
Halifaxes, 11 Lancasters, 8 Hampdens (4
Wellingtons, 1 Lancaster, 1 Stirling lost)

25/26 June
Bremen
472 Wellingtons, 124 Halifaxes, 96
Lancasters, 69 Stirlings, 51 Blenheims, 50
Hampdens, 50 Whitleys, 24 Bostons, 20
Manchesters, 4 Mosquitoes
(also 102 Hudsons and Wellingtons from
Coastal Command and 5 aircraft from
Army Co-operation Command) (48
aircraft lost)

27/28 June
Bremen
55 Wellingtons, 39 Halifaxes, 26 Stirlings,
24 Lancasters (4 Wellingtons, 2 Halifaxes,
1 Stirling lost)

29/30 June
Bremen
108 Wellingtons, 64 Lancasters, 47
Stirlings, 34 Halifaxes (4 Stirlings, 4
Wellingtons, 3 Halifaxes lost)

2/3 July
Bremen
175 Wellingtons, 53 Lancasters, 35
Halifaxes, 34 Stirlings, 28 Hampdens (8
Wellingtons, 2 Hampdens, 2 Stirlings, 1
Halifax lost)

8/9 July
Wilhelmshaven
137 Wellingtons, 52 Lancasters, 38
Halifaxes, 34 Stirlings, 24 Hampdens (3
Wellingtons, 1 Halifax, 1 Lancaster lost)

11 July
Danzig
44 Lancasters (2 lost)

13/14 July
Duisburg
139 Wellingtons, 33 Halifaxes, 13
Lancasters, 9 Stirlings (3 Wellingtons, 2
Stirlings, 1 Lancaster lost)

19/20 July
Bremen
40 Halifaxes, 31 Stirlings, 28 Lancasters,
also to Vegesack (3 Halifaxes lost)

21/22 July
Duisburg
170 Wellingtons, 39 Halifaxes, 36
Stirlings, 29 Lancasters, 17 Hampdens (10
Wellingtons, 1 Halifax, 1 Hampden lost)

23/24 July
Duisburg
93 Wellingtons, 45 Lancasters, 39
Stirlings, 38 Halifaxes (3 Wellingtons, 2
Lancasters, 2 Stirlings lost)

25/26 July
Duisburg
177 Wellingtons, 48 Stirlings, 41
Halifaxes, 33 Lancasters, 14 Hampdens (7
Wellingtons, 2 Halifaxes, 2 Lancasters, 1
Stirling lost)

26/27 July
Hamburg
337 dead
14,000 bombed out
181 Wellingtons, 77 Lancasters, 73
Halifaxes, 39 Stirlings, 33 Hampdens (15
Wellingtons, 8 Halifaxes, 2 Hampdens, 2
Lancasters, 2 Stirlings lost)

28/29 July
Hamburg
161 Wellingtons, 71 Stirlings, 24
Whitleys (20 Wellingtons, 9 Stirlings, 4
Whitleys lost. 1 Whitley crashed in the
sea)

29/30 July
Saarbrücken
291 aircraft, 5 types (3 Wellingtons, 2
Halifaxes, 2 Lancasters, 2 Stirlings lost)

31 July/1 August
Neuss
279 dead
12,000 bombed out
Düsseldorf
308 Wellingtons, 113 Lancasters, 70
Halifaxes, 61 Stirlings, 54 Hampdens, 24
Whitleys (16 Wellingtons, 5 Hampdens, 4
Halifaxes, 2 Lancasters, 2 Whitleys lost)

6/7 August
Duisburg
216 aircraft, 5 types (2 Halifaxes, 2
Stirlings, 1 Wellington lost)

9/10 August
Osnabrück
91 Wellingtons, 42 Lancasters, 40
Stirlings, 19 Halifaxes (3 Halifaxes, 3
Wellingtons lost)

11/12 August
Mainz
68 Wellingtons, 33 Lancasters, 28
Stirlings, 25 Halifaxes (3 Wellingtons, 2
Halifaxes, 1 Lancaster lost)

12/13 August
Mainz
138 aircraft, 4 types (2 Lancasters, 1
Hampden, 1 Stirling, 1 Wellington lost)

15/16 August
Düsseldorf
131 aircraft, 5 types (2 Lancasters, 1
Hampden, 1 Wellington lost)

17/18 August
Osnabrück
139 aircraft, 5 types (3 Wellingtons, 1
Lancaster, 1 Stirling lost)

18/19 August
Flensburg
118 aircraft, including 31 Pathfinders (2 Wellingtons, 1 Halifax, 1 Stirling lost)

24/25 August
Frankfurt/M.
104 Wellingtons, 61 Lancasters, 53 Stirlings, 8 Halifaxes (6 Lancasters, 5 Wellingtons, 4 Stirlings, 1 Halifax lost)

27/28 August
Kassel
306 aircraft, 5 types (21 Wellingtons, 5 Stirlings, 3 Lancasters, 1 Halifax, 1 Hampden lost)

28/29 August
Nuremberg, Saarbrücken
Nuremberg: 71 Lancasters, 41 Wellingtons, 34 Stirlings, 13 Halifaxes (14 Wellingtons, 4 Lancasters, 3 Stirlings, 2 Halifaxes lost) Saarbrücken: 71 Wellingtons, 24 Halifaxes, 17 Hampdens, 1 Stirling (4 Hampdens, 2 Halifaxes, 1 Wellington lost)

1/2 September
Saarbrücken
231 aircraft, 5 types (1 Halifax, 1 Lancaster, 1 Stirling, 1 Wellington lost)

2/3 September
Karlsruhe
200 aircraft, 5 types (4 Wellingtons, 2 Lancasters, 1 halifax, 1 Stirling lost)

4/5 September
Bremen
98 Wellingtons, 76 Lancasters, 41 Halifaxes, 36 Stirlings (7 Wellingtons, 3 Lancasters, 1 Halifax, 1 Stirling lost)

6/7 September
Duisburg
207 aircraft, 6 types (5 Wellingtons, 2 Halifaxes, 1 Stirling lost)

8/9 September
Frankfurt M., Rüsselsheim
249 aircraft, 5 types (5 Wellingtons, 2 Halifaxes lost)

10/11 September
Düsseldorf
242 Wellingtons, 89 Lancasters, 59 Halifaxes, 47 Stirlings, 28 Hampdens, 14 Whitleys (20 Wellingtons, 5 Lancasters, 4 Stirlings, 3 Halifaxes, 1 Hampden lost)

13/14 September
Bremen
446 aircraft (15 Wellingtons, 2 Lancasters, 1 Halifax, 1 Hampden, 1 Stirling, 1 Whitley lost)

14/15 September
Wilhelmshaven
202 aircraft, 5 types (2 Wellingtons lost)

16/17 September
Essen
369 aircraft (21 Wellingtons, 9 Lancasters, 5 Stirlings, 3 Halifaxes, 1 Whitley lost)

19/20 September
Saarbrücken, Munich
Saarbrücken: 72 Wellingtons, 41 Halifaxes, 5 Stirlings (3 Wellingtons, 2 Halifaxes lost)
Munich: 68 Lancasters, 21 Stirlings (3 of each lost)

23/24 September
Wismar
83 Lancasters (4 lost)
24 Stirlings to Vegesack (1 lost)

1/2 October
Wismar
78 Lancasters (2 lost)
25 Stirlings to Lübeck (3 lost)

2/3 October
Krefeld
95 Wellingtons, 39 Halifaxes, 31 Lancasters, 23 Stirlings (3 Halifaxes, 2 Wellingtons, 1 Lancaster, 1 Stirling lost)

5/6 October
Aachen
101 Wellingtons, 74 Lancasters, 59 Halifaxes, 23 Stirlings (5 Halifaxes, 2 Stirlings, 2 Wellingtons, 1 Lancaster lost)

6/7 October
Osnabrück
101 Wellingtons, 68 Lancasters, 38 Stirlings, 30 Halifaxes (2 Halifaxes, 2 Lancasters, 2 Stirlings lost)

13/14 October
Kiel
100 Wellingtons, 82 Lancasters, 78 Halifaxes, 28 Stirlings (5 Wellingtons, 1 each of the others lost)

15/16 October
Cologne
109 Wellingtons, 74 Halifaxes, 62 Lancasters, 44 Stirlings (6 Wellingtons, 5 Halifaxes, 5 Lancasters, 2 Stirlings lost)

9/10 November
Hamburg
74 Wellingtons, 72 Lancasters, 48 Halifaxes, 19 Stirlings (5 Lancasters, 4 Stirlings, 4 Wellingtons, 2 Halifaxes lost)

22/23 November
Stuttgart
97 Lancasters, 59 Wellingtons, 39 Halifaxes, 27 Stirlings (5 Lancasters, 3 Wellingtons, 2 Halifaxes lost)

2/3 December
Frankfurt/M.
48 Halifaxes, 27 Lancasters, 22 Stirlings, 15 Wellingtons (3 Halifaxes, 1 each of the others lost)

6/7 December
Mannheim
101 Lancasters, 65 Halifaxes, 57 Wellingtons, 49 Stirlings (5 Wellingtons, 3 Halifaxes, 1 Lancaster, 1 Stirling lost)

20/21 December
Duisburg
111 Lancasters, 56 Halifaxes, 39 Wellingtons, 26 Stirlings (6 Lancasters, 4 Wellingtons, 2 Halifaxes lost)

21/22 December
Munich
119 Lancasters, 9 Stirlings, 9 Wellingtons (8 Lancasters, 3 Stirlings, 1 Wellington lost)

1943

3/4 January
Essen
3 Pathfinder Mosquitoes, 19 Lancasters (3 Lancasters lost)

4/5 January
Essen
4 Pathfinder Mosquitoes, 29 Lancasters (2 Lancasters lost)

7/8 January
Essen
3 Pathfinder Mosquitoes, 19 Lancasters (no losses)

8/9 January
Duisburg
3 Pathfinder Mosquitoes, 38 Lancasters (3 Lancasters lost)

9/10 January
Essen
2 Pathfinder Mosquitoes, 50 Lancasters (3 Lancaster lost)

11/12 January
Essen
4 Pathfinder Mosquitoes, 72 Lancasters (1 Lancaster lost)

12/13 January
Essen, Remscheid, Solingen, Wuppertal
4 Pathfinder Mosquitoes, 55 Lancasters (1 Lancaster lost)

13/14 January
Essen
3 Mosquitoes, 66 Lancasters (4 Lancasters lost)

16/17 January
Berlin
190 Lancasters, 11 Halifaxes (1 Lancaster lost)

17/18 January
Berlin
170 Lancasters, 17 Halifaxes (19 Lancasters, 3 Halifaxes lost)

27/28 January
Düsseldorf
124 Lancasters, 33 Halifaxes, 5 Mosquitoes (3 Halifaxes, 3 Lancasters lost)

30/31 January
Hamburg
135 Lancasters, 7 Stirlings, 6 Halifaxes (5 Lancasters lost)

2/3 February
Cologne
116 Lancasters, 35 Halifaxes, 8 Stirlings,
2 Mosquitoes (3 Lancasters, 1 Halifax, 1
Stirling lost)

4 February
Emden, Hamm
No aircraft data

3/4 February
Hamburg
84 Halifaxes, 66 Stirlings, 62 Lancasters,
51 Wellingtons (8 Stirlings, 4 Halifaxes, 3
Wellingtons, 1 Lancaster lost)

11/12 February
Wilhelmshaven
129 Lancasters, 40 Halifaxes, 8 Stirlings (3
Lancasters lost)

14 February
Hamm
No aircraft data

14/15 February
Cologne
90 Halifaxes, 85 Wellingtons, 68 Stirlings
(3 of each lost)

18/19 February
Wilhelmshaven
127 Lancasters, 59 Halifaxes, 9 Stirlings
(4 Lancasters lost)

19/20 February
Wilhelmshaven
120 Wellingtons, 110 Halifaxes, 56
Stirlings, 52 Lancasters (5 Stirlings, 4
Lancasters, 3 Wellingtons lost)

21/22 February
Bremen
130 Lancasters, 7 Stirlings, 6 Halifaxes
(no losses)

24/25 February
Wilhelmshaven
71 Wellingtons, 27 Halifaxes, 9 Stirlings,
8 Lancasters (no losses)

25/26 February
Nuremberg, Fürth
169 Lancasters, 104 Halifaxes, 64 Stirlings
(6 Lancasters, 2 Stirlings, 1 Halifax lost)

26/27 February
Cologne
145 Lancasters, 126 Wellingtons, 106
Halifaxes, 46 Stirlings, 4 Mosquitoes (4
Wellingtons, 3 Lancasters, 2 Halifaxes, 1
Stirling lost)

1/2 March
Berlin
709 dead
64, 909 bombed out
156 Lancasters, 86 Halifaxes, 60 Stirlings
(7 Lancasters, 6 Halifaxes, 4 Stirlings lost)

3/4 March
Hamburg, Duisburg
Hamburg: 149 Lancasters, 123
Wellingtons, 83 Halifaxes, 62 Stirlings,
also bombed Wedel (4 Lancasters, 2
Wellingtons, 2 Halifaxes, 2 Stirlings lost)

4 March
Hamm
No aircraft data

5/6 March
Essen
461 dead
30,000 bombed out

8/9 March
Nuremberg
170 Lancasters, 103 Halifaxes, 62 Stirlings
(4 Stirlings, 2 Halifaxes, 2 Lancasters lost)

9/10 March
Munich
142 Lancasters, 81 Halifaxes, 41 Stirlings
(5 Lancasters, 2 Halifaxes, 1 Stirling lost)

11/12 March
Stuttgart
152 Lancasters, 109 Halifaxes, 53 Stirlings
(6 Halifaxes, 3 Stirlings, 2 Lancasters lost)

12/13 March
Essen
158 Wellingtons, 156 Lancasters, 91
Halifaxes, 42 Stirlings, 10 Mosquitoes (8
Lancasters, 7 Halifaxes, 6 Wellingtons, 2
Stirlings lost)

18 March
Bremen
No aircraft data

22 March
Wilhelmshaven
No aircraft data

26/27 March
Duisburg
173 Wellingtons, 157 Lancasters, 114
Halifaxes, 9 Mosquitoes, 2 Stirlings (3
Wellingtons, 1 Halifax, 1 Lancaster, 1
Mosquito lost)

27/28 March
Berlin
191 Lancasters, 124 Halifaxes, 81 Stirlings
(4 Halifaxes, 3 Lancasters, 2 Stirlings lost)

29/30 March
Berlin, Bochum
Berlin: 162 Lancasters, 103 Halifaxes, 64
Stirlings (11 Lancasters, 7 Halifaxes, 3
Stirlings lost)
Bochum: 8 *Oboe* Mosquitoes, 149
Wellingtons (12 Wellingtons lost)

3/4 April
Essen
225 Lancasters, 113 Halifaxes, 10
Mosquitoes (12 Halifaxes, 9 Lancasters
lost, 2 Halifaxes crashed in England)

4/5 April
Kiel
203 Lancasters, 168 Wellingtons, 116
Halifaxes, 90 Stirlings (5 Lancasters, 4
Halifaxes, 2 Stirlings, 1 Wellington lost)

8/9 April
Duisburg
156 Lancasters, 97 Wellingtons, 73
Halifaxes, 56 Stirlings, 10 Mosquitoes (7
Wellingtons, 6 Lancasters, 3 Halifaxes, 3
Stirlings lost)

9/10 April
Duisburg
5 Mosquitoes, 104 Lancasters (8
Lancasters lost)

10/11 April
Frankfurt
144 Wellingtons, 136 Lancasters, 124
Halifaxes, 98 Stirlings (8 Wellingtons, 5
Lancasters, 5 Stirlings, 3 Halifaxes lost)

14/15 April
Stuttgart
619 dead
146 Wellingtons, 135 Halifaxes, 98
Lancasters, 83 Stirlings (8 Stirlings, 8
Wellingtons, 4 Halifaxes, 3 Lancasters
lost)

16/17 April
Mannheim
159 Wellingtons, 95 Stirlings, 17
Halifaxes (9 Wellingtons, 7 Stirlings, 2
Halifaxes lost)

17 April
Bremen
No aircraft data

20/21 April
Stettin
586 dead
Rostock
194 Lancasters, 134 Halifaxes, 11 Stirlings
(13 Lancasters, 7 Halifaxes, 1 Stirling lost)

26/27 April
Duisburg
215 Lancasters, 135 Wellingtons, 119
Halifaxes, 78 Stirlings, 14 Mosquitoes (7
Halifaxes, 5 Wellingtons, 3 Lancasters, 2
Stirlings lost)

30 April/1 May
Essen
190 Lancasters, 105 Halifaxes, 10
Mosquitoes (6 Halifaxes, 6 Lancasters lost)

4/5 May
Dortmund
693 dead
40,000 bombed out
255 Lancasters, 141 Halifaxes, 110
Wellingtons, 80 Stirlings, 10 Mosquitoes
(12 Halifaxes, 7 Stirlings, 6 Lancasters, 6
Wellingtons lost)

12/13 May
Duisburg
238 Lancasters, 142 Halifaxes, 112
Wellingtons, 70 Stirlings, 10 Mosquitoes
(10 Lancasters, 10 Wellingtons, 9
Halifaxes, 5 Stirlings lost)

13/14 May
Bochum
302 dead
135 Halifaxes, 104 Wellingtons, 98
Lancasters, 95 Stirlings, 10 Mosquitoes
(13 Halifaxes, 6 Wellingtons, 4 Stirlings,
1 Lancaster lost)

14 May
Kiel
No aircraft data

16/17 May
Möhnetalsperre
1,294 dead
The Dams Raid: 19 Lancasters

19 May
Kiel
No aircraft data

23/24 May
Dortmund
599 dead
343 Lancasters, 199 Halifaxes, 151
Wellingtons, 120 Stirlings, 13 Mosquitoes
(18 Halifaxes, 8 Lancasters, 6 Stirlings, 6
Wellingtons lost)

25/26 May
Düsseldorf
323 Lancasters, 169 Halifaxes, 142
Wellingtons, 113 Stirlings, 12 Mosquitoes
(9 Lancasters, 8 Stirlings, 6 Wellingtons, 4
Halifaxes lost)

27/28 May
Essen
274 Lancasters, 151 Halifaxes, 81
Wellingtons, 12 Mosquitoes (11 Halifaxes,
6 Lancasters, 5 Wellingtons, 1 Mosquito
lost)

29/30 May
Wuppertal
3,400 dead
130,000 bombed out

11 June
Wilhelmshaven, Cuxhaven
No aircraft data

11/12 June
Düsseldorf
1,292 dead

140,000 bombed out
326 Lancasters, 202 Halifaxes, 143
Wellingtons, 99 Stirlings, 13 Mosquitoes
(14 Lancasters, 12 Halifaxes, 10
Wellingtons, 2 Stirlings lost)
Münster
29 Lancasters, 22 Halifaxes, 21 Stirlings
(2 Halifaxes, 2
Lancasters, 1 Stirling lost)

12/13 June
Bochum
312 dead
323 Lancasters, 167 Halifaxes, 11
Mosquitoes (14 Lancasters, 10 Halifaxes
lost)

13 June
Bremen
No aircraft data

14/15 June
Oberhausen
197 Lancasters, 6 Mosquitoes (17
Lancasters lost)

16/17 June
Cologne
202 Lancasters, 10 Halifaxes (14
Lancasters lost)

20/21 June
Friedrichshafen
60 Lancasters (no losses)

21/22 June
Krefeld
1,056 dead
72,600 bombed out
262 Lancasters, 209 Halifaxes, 117
Stirlings, 105 Wellingtons, 12 Mosquitoes
(17 Halifaxes, 9 Lancasters, 9
Wellingtons, 9 Stirlings lost)

22 June
Hüls
No aircraft data

22/23 June
Mülheim
578 dead
242 Lancasters, 155 Halifaxes, 93
Stirlings, 55 Wellingtons, 12 Mosquitoes
(12 Halifaxes, 11 Stirlings, 8 Lancasters, 4
Wellingtons lost)

24/25 June
Wuppertal
1,800 dead
112,000 bombed out
251 Lancasters, 171 Halifaxes, 101
Wellingtons, 98 Stirlings, 9 Mosquitoes
(10 Halifaxes, 10 Stirlings, 8 Lancasters, 6
Wellingtons lost)

25 June
Wangerooge
No aircraft data

25/26 June
Gelsenkirchen, Solingen, Düsseldorf
214 Lancasters, 134 Halifaxes, 73
Stirlings, 40 Wellingtons, 12 Mosquitoes
(13 Lancasters, 7 Halifaxes, 6 Stirlings, 4
Wellingtons lost)

28/29 June
Cologne
4,377 dead
230,000 bombed out
267 Lancasters, 169 Halifaxes, 85
Wellingtons, 72 Stirlings, 12 Mosquitoes
(10 Halifaxes, 8 Lancasters, 5 Stirlings, 2
Wellingtons lost)

3/4 July
Cologne
588 dead
72,000 bombed out
293 Lancasters, 182 Halifaxes, 89
Wellingtons, 76 Stirlings, 13 Mosquitoes
(9 Halifaxes, 8 Lancasters, 8 Wellingtons,
5 Stirlings lost)

8/9 July
Cologne
502 dead
48,000 bombed out
282 Lancasters, 6 Mosquitoes (7
Lancasters lost)

9/10 July
Gelsenkirchen
218 Lancasters, 190 Halifaxes, 10
Mosquitoes (7 Halifaxes, 5 Lancasters lost)

13/14 July
Aachen
294 dead
40,000 bombed out

214 Halifaxes, 76 Wellingtons, 55
Stirlings, 18 Lancasters, 11 Mosquitoes
(15 Halifaxes, 2 Lancasters, 2
Wellingtons, 1 Stirling lost)

24/25 July
Hamburg
1,500 dead
380,000 bombed out
347 Lancasters, 246 Halifaxes, 125
Stirlings, 73 Wellingtons (4 Halifaxes, 4
Lancasters, 3 Stirlings, 1 Wellington lost)

25 July
Hamburg, Kiel
No aircraft data

25/26 July
Essen
More than 500 dead
100,000 bombed out
294 Lancasters, 221 Halifaxes, 104
Stirlings, 67 Wellingtons, 19 Mosquitoes
(10 Halifaxes, 7 Stirlings, 5 Lancasters, 4
Wellingtons lost)

26 July
Hannover
No aircraft data

27/28 July
Hamburg
35,000 dead
800,000 bombed out
353 Lancasters, 244 Halifaxes, 116
Stirlings, 74 Wellingtons (11 Lancasters, 4
Halifaxes, 1 Stirling, 1 Wellington lost)

29 July
Kiel
No aircraft data

29/30 July
Hamburg
1,000 dead
150,000 bombed out
340 Lancasters, 244 Halifaxes, 119
Stirlings, 70 Wellingtons, 4 Mosquitoes
(11 Halifaxes, 11 Lancasters, 4 Stirlings, 2
Wellingtons lost)

30 July
Kassel
No aircraft data

30/31 July
Remscheid
1,120 dead
40,000 bombed out
95 Halifaxes, 87 Stirlings, 82 Lancasters,
9 Mosquitoes (8 Stirlings, 5 Halifaxes, 2
Lancasters lost)

2/3 August
Hamburg
329 Lancasters, 235 Halifaxes, 105
Stirlings, 66 Wellingtons, 5 Mosquitoes
(13 Lancasters, 10 Halifaxes, 4
Wellingtons, 3 Stirlings lost)

9/10 August
Mannheim
269 dead
286 Lancasters, 171 Halifaxes (6
Halifaxes, 3 Lancasters lost)

10/11 August
Nuremberg
585 dead
28,000 bombed out
318 Lancasters, 216 Halifaxes, 119
Stirlings (7 Halifaxes, 6 Lancasters, 3
Stirlings lost)

12 August
Bochum, Recklinghausen, Gelsenkirchen
No aircraft data

17 August
Regensburg
No aircraft data

17/18 August
Peenemünde
780 dead
324 Lancasters, 218 Halifaxes, 54 Stirlings
(2 aircraft lost)

22/23 August
Leverkusen, Düsseldorf, Solingen
257 Lancasters, 192 Halifaxes, 13
Mosquitoes (3 Lancasters, 2 Halifaxes lost)

23/24 August
Berlin
899 dead
103,558 bombed out
335 Lancasters, 251 Halifaxes, 124
Stirlings, 17 Mosquitoes (23 Halifaxes, 17
Lancasters, 16 Stirlings lost)

27/28 August
Nuremberg
349 Lancasters, 221 Halifaxes, 104
Stirlings (11 of each lost)

30/31 August
Mönchengladbach
297 Lancasters, 185 Halifaxes, 107
Stirlings, 57 Wellingtons, 14 Mosquitoes
(8 Halifaxes, 7 Lancasters, 6 Stirlings, 4
Wellingtons lost)

31 August/1 September
Berlin
331 Lancasters, 176 Halifaxes, 106
Stirlings, 9 Mosquitoes (20 Halifaxes, 17
Stirlings, 10 Lancasters lost)

3/4 September
Berlin
623 dead
39,844 bombed out
316 Lancasters, 4 Mosquitoes (22
Lancasters lost)

5/6 September
Ludwigshafen
127 dead
20,000 bombed out
299 Lancasters, 195 Halifaxes, 111
Stirlings (13 Halifaxes, 13 Lancasters, 8
Stirlings lost)

6 September
Stuttgart
No aircraft data

6/7 September
Munich
257 Lancasters, 147 Halifaxes (13
Halifaxes, 3 Lancasters lost)

22/23 September
Hannover
322 Lancasters, 226 Halifaxes, 137
Stirlings, 26 Wellingtons, also 5 American
B-17s (12 Halifaxes, 7 Lancasters, 5
Stirlings,
2 Wellingtons lost)

23/24 September
Mannheim, Ludwigshafen, Darmstadt
Mannheim: 312 Lancasters, 193 Halifaxes,
115 Stirlings, 8 Mosquitoes (18
Lancasters, 7 Halifaxes, 7 Wellingtons lost)
Darmstadt: 21 Lancasters, 8 Mosquitoes
(no losses)

27 September
Emden
No aircraft data

27/28 September
Hannover, Brunswick
Hannover: 312 Lancasters, 231 Halifaxes,
111 Stirlings, 24 Wellingtons, also 5
American B-17s (17 Halifaxes, 10
Lancasters, 10 Stirlings, 1 Wellington lost)
Brunswick: 21 Lancasters, 6 Mosquitoes
(1 Lancaster lost)

29/30 September
Bochum
213 Lancasters, 130 Halifaxes, 9
Mosquitoes (5 Halifaxes, 4 Lancasters lost)

1/2 October
Hagen
266 dead
30,000 bombed out
243 Lancasters, 8 Mosquitoes (1 Lancaster
lost)

2 October
Emden
No aircraft data

2/3 October
Munich
294 Lancasters (8 lost)

3/4 October
Kassel
223 Halifaxes, 204 Lancasters, 113
Stirlings, 7 Mosquitoes (14 Halifaxes, 6
Stirlings, 4 Lancasters lost)

4 October
Frankfurt/M., Wiesbaden, Saarbrücken
No aircraft data

4/5 October
Frankfurt/M.
529 dead
162 Lancasters, 170 Halifaxes, 70

Stirlings, 4 Mosquitoes (5 Halifaxes, 3
Lancasters, 2 Stirlings lost)
Ludwigshafen
66 Lancasters (no losses)

7/8 October
Stuttgart, Böblingen
343 Lancasters (4 lost)
16 Lancasters to Friedrichshafen (no
losses)

8 October
Bremen
No aircraft data

8/9 October
Hannover
1,200 dead
282 Lancasters, 188 Halifaxes, 26
Wellingtons, 8 Mosquitoes (14 Lancasters,
13 Halifaxes lost)
Bremen
95 Stirlings, 17 Halifaxes, 7 Lancasters (3
Stirlings lost)

9 October
Anklam, Marienburg, Danzig
No aircraft data

10 October
Münster
473 dead
20,000 bombed out
No aircraft data
Coesfeld
No aircraft data

14 October
Schweinfurt
No aircraft data

18/19 October
Hannover
360 Lancasters (18 lost)

20 October
Düren
No aircraft data

20/21 October
Leipzig
358 Lancasters (16 lost)

22/23 October
Kassel
7,000 dead
53,800 bombed out
322 Lancasters, 247 Halifaxes (25 Halifaxes, 18 Lancasters lost)

3 November
Wilhelmshaven
No aircraft data

3/4 November
Düsseldorf
622 dead
344 Lancasters, 233 Halifaxes, 12 Mosquitoes (11 Lancasters, 7 Halifaxes lost)
Cologne
52 Lancasters, 10 Mosquitoes (no losses)

5 November
Gelsenkirchen, Münster
No aircraft data

11 November
Münster
No aircraft data

13 November
Bremen
No aircraft data

17/18 November
Ludwigshafen
66 Lancasters, 17 Halifaxes (1 Lancaster lost)

18/19 November
Berlin, Mannheim, Ludwigshafen
Berlin: 440 Lancasters, 4 Mosquitoes (9 Lancasters lost)
Mannheim/Ludwigshafen: 248 Halifaxes, 114 Stirlings, 33 Lancasters (12 Halifaxes, 9 Stirlings, 2 Lancasters lost)

19/20 November
Leverkusen
170 Halifaxes, 86 Stirlings, 10 Mosquitoes (4 Halifaxes, 1 Stirling lost)

22/23 November
Berlin
2,000 dead
175,000 bombed out
469 Lancasters, 234 Halifaxes, 50 Stirlings, 11 Mosquitoes (11 Lancasters, 10 Halifaxes, 5 Stirlings lost)

23/24 November
Berlin
1,000 dead
100,000 bombed out
365 Lancasters, 10 Halifaxes, 8 Mosquitoes (20 Lancasters lost)

25/26 November
Frankfurt/M.
236 Halifaxes, 26 Lancasters (11 Halifaxes, 1 Lancaster lost)

26 November
Bremen
No aircraft data

26/27 November
Berlin, Stuttgart
Berlin: 443 Lancasters, 3 Mosquitoes (28 Lancasters lost)
Stuttgart: 157 Halifaxes, 21 Lancasters (6 Halifaxes lost)

29 November
Bremen
No aircraft data

30 November
Solingen
No aircraft data

1 December
Leverkusen
No aircraft data

2/3 December
Berlin
425 Lancasters, 18 Mosquitoes, 15 Halifaxes (37 Lancasters, 2 Halifaxes, 1 Mosquito lost)

3/4 December
Leipzig
1,717 dead
114,000 bombed out
307 Lancasters, 220 Halifaxes (15 Halifaxes, 9 Lancasters lost)

11 December
Emden
No aircraft data

13 December
Kiel, Hamburg
No aircraft data

16 December
Bremen
No aircraft data

16/17 December
Berlin
628 dead
30,063 bombed out
483 Lancasters, 10 Mosquitoes (25 Lancasters lost)

20 December
Bremen
No aircraft data

1/2 January
Berlin
421 Lancasters (28 lost)

2/3 January
Berlin
362 Lancasters, 12 Mosquitoes, 9 Halifaxes (27 Lancasters lost)

4 January
Kiel, Neuss, Düsseldorf
No aircraft data

5/6 January
Stettin
348 Lancasters, 10 Halifaxes (14 Lancasters, 2 Halifaxes left)

7 January
Ludwigshafen
No aircraft data

11 January
Oschersleben, Halberstadt, Brunswick, Osnabrück, Meppen
No aircraft data

14/15 January
Brunswick
496 Lancasters, 2 Halifaxes (38 Lancasters lost)

20/21 January
Berlin
306 dead

20/21 December
Frankfurt/M.
390 Lancasters, 257 Halifaxes, 3 Mosquitoes (27 Halifaxes, 14 Lancasters lost)

23/24 December
Berlin
364 Lancasters, 8 Mosquitoes, 7 Halifaxes (16 Lancasters lost)

29/30 December
Berlin
457 Lancasters, 252 Halifaxes, 2 Mosquitoes (11 Lancasters, 9 Halifaxes lost)

30 December
Ludwigshafen
No aircraft data

1944

20/21 January
Berlin
306 dead
20,938 bombed out
495 Lancasters, 264 Halifaxes, 10 Mosquitoes (22 Halifaxes, 13 Lancasters lost)

21/22 January
Magdeburg
421 Lancasters, 224 Halifaxes, 3 Mosquitoes (35 Halifaxes, 22 Lancasters lost)

24 January
Eschweiler
No aircraft data

27/28 January
Berlin
426 dead
19,945 bombed out
515 Lancasters, 15 Mosquitoes (33 Lancasters lost)

28/29 January
Berlin
531 dead
69,466 bombed out
432 Lancasters, 241 Halifaxes, 4 Mosquitoes (26 Halifaxes, 20 Lancasters lost)

29 January
Frankfurt/M.
903 dead
No aircraft data

30 January
Brunswick, Hannover
No aircraft data

30/31 January
Berlin
582 dead
82,980 bombed out
440 Lancasters, 82 Halifaxes, 12
Mosquitoes (32 Lancasters, 1 Halifax lost)

3 February
Wilhelmshaven
No aircraft data

4 February
Frankfurt/M.
No aircraft data

8 February
Frankfurt/M.
No aircraft data

10 February
Brunswick
No aircraft data

11 February
Frankfurt/M.
No aircraft data

15/16 February
Berlin
302 dead
561 Lancasters, 314 Halifaxes, 16
Mosquitoes (26 Lancasters, 17 Halifaxes
lost)

19/20 February
Leipzig
817 dead
30,000 bombed out
561 Lancasters, 255 Halifaxes, 7
Mosquitoes (44 Lancasters, 34 Halifaxes
lost)

20 February
Rostock, Leipzig, Gotha, Helmstedt
No aircraft data

20/21 February
Stuttgart
460 Lancasters, 126 Halifaxes, 12
Mosquitoes (7 Lancasters, 2 Halifaxes lost)

21 February
Diepholz, Verden, Brunswick, Lingen,
Rheine
No aircraft data

22 February
Aschersleben, Bernburg, Halberstadt,
Magdeburg
No aircraft data

24 February
Rostock, Schweinfurt, Gotha
No aircraft data

24/25 February
Schweinfurt
554 Lancasters, 169 Halifaxes, 11
Mosquitoes (26 Lancasters, 7 Halifaxes
lost)

25 February
Regensburg, Augsburg, Fürth
No aircraft data

25/26 February
Augsburg
720 dead
85,000 bombed out
461 Lancasters, 123 Halifaxes, 10
Mosquitoes (16 Lancasters, 5 Halifaxes
lost)

29 February
Brunswick
No aircraft data

1/2 March
Stuttgart
415 Lancasters, 129 Halifaxes, 13
Mosquitoes (3 Lancasters, 1 Halifax lost)

2 March
Frankfurt/M., Offenbach
No aircraft data

3 March
Wilhelmshaven
No aircraft data

4 March
Bonn, Cologne
No aircraft data

6 March
Berlin, Potsdam, Wittenberg
No aircraft data

8 March
Berlin
No aircraft data

9 March
Berlin, Hannover, Brunswick, Nienburg/
Weser
No aircraft data

10 March
Münster
No aircraft data

15 March
Brunswick
No aircraft data

15/16 March
Stuttgart
617 Lancasters, 230 Halifaxes, 16
Mosquitoes (27 Lancasters, 10 Halifaxes
lost)

16 March
Augsburg, Ulm, Friedrichshafen
No aircraft data

18 March
Oberpfaffenhofen, Landsberg, Munich,
Memmingen, Friedrichshafen
No aircraft data

18/19 March
Frankfurt/M.
421 dead
55,000 bombed out
620 Lancasters, 209 Halifaxes, 17
Mosquitoes (12 Halifaxes, 10 Lancasters
lost)

20 March
Frankfurt/M., Mannheim, Bingen
No aircraft data

22/23 March
Frankfurt/M.
1,001 dead
120,000 bombed out

620 Lancasters, 184 Halifaxes, 12
Mosquitoes (26 Lancasters, 7 Halifaxes
lost)

23 March
Brunswick, Münster, Osnabrück
No aircraft data

24 March
Schweinfurt, Frankfurt/M.
No aircraft data

24/25 March
Berlin
577 Lancasters, 216 Halifaxes, 18
Mosquitoes (44 Lancasters, 28 Halifaxes lost)

26/27 March
Essen
550 dead
476 Lancasters, 207 Halifaxes, 22
Mosquitoes (6 Lancasters, 3 Halifaxes lost)

29 March
Brunswick
No aircraft data

30/31 March
Nuremberg, Schweinfurt
572 Lancasters, 214 Halifaxes, 9 Mosquitoes
(64 Lancasters, 31 Halifaxes lost)

1 April
Pforzheim
No aircraft data

6/7 April
Hamburg
35 Mosquitoes (1 lost)

8 April
Brunswick, Oldenburg, Rheine
No aircraft data

9 April
Marienburg, Warnemünde, Parchim
No aircraft data

11 April
Oschersleben, Bernburg, Sorau, Stettin,
Rostock
No aircraft data

11/12 April
Aachen
1,525 dead

13 April
Schweinfurt, Lechfeld, Augsburg
No aircraft data

18 April
Oranienburg, Perleberg, Wittenberg,
Brandenburg, Rathenow
No aircraft data

19 April
Kassel, Lippstadt, Werl, Paderborn,
Gütersloh
No aircraft data

20/21 April
Cologne
664 dead
20,000 bombed out
357 Lancasters, 22 Mosquitoes (4
Lancasters lost)
Stettin

22 April
Hamm, Koblenz, Bonn
No aircraft data

22/23 April
Düsseldorf
1,200 dead
20,500 bombed out
323 Lancasters, 254 Halifaxes, 19
Mosquitoes (16 Halifaxes, 13 Lancasters
lost)
Brunswick
238 Lancasters, 17 Mosquitoes (4
Lancasters lost)

24 April
Friedrichshafen
No aircraft data

24/25 April
Munich
136 dead
70,000 bombed out
234 Lancasters, 16 Mosquitoes (9
Lancasters lost)
Karlsruhe
269 Lancasters, 259 Halifaxes, 9 Mosquitoes
(11 Lancasters, 8 Halifaxes lost)

26 April
Brunswick, Hildesheim
No aircraft data

26/27 April
Essen
313 dead
342 Lancasters, 133 Halifaxes, 18
Mosquitoes (6 Lancasters, 1 Halifax lost)
Schweinfurt
206 Lancasters, 11 Mosquitoes (21
Lancasters lost)

27/28 April
Friedrichshafen
322 Lancasters, 1 Mosquito (18
Lancasters lost)

29 April
Berlin
No aircraft data

7 May
Berlin, Münster, Osnabrück
No aircraft data

8 May
Berlin, Brunswick
No aircraft data

11 May
Saarbrücken, Völklingen
No aircraft data

12 May
Merseburg, Zwickau, Chemitz, Gera, Hof,
Zeitz, Böhlen
No aircraft data

13 May
Stettin, Stralsund, Tutow, Osnabrück
No aircraft data

19 May
Berlin, Brunswick
No aircraft data

20/21 May
Düsseldorf
30 Mosquitoes (no losses)

21/22 May
Duisburg
510 Lancasters, 22 Mosquitoes (29
Lancasters lost)

22 May
Kiel
No aircraft data

22/23 May
Dortmund
361 dead
361 Lancasters, 14 Mosquitoes (18
Lancasters lost)
Brunswick
225 Lancasters, 10 Mosquitoes (13
Lancasters lost)

24 May
Berlin
No aircraft data

24/25 May
Aachen
264 Lancasters, 162 Halifaxes, 16
Mosquitoes (18 Halifaxes, 7 Lancasters lost)

27 May
Ludwigshafen, Mannheim, Karlsruhe,
Saarbrücken, Neunkirchen
No aircraft data

27/28 May
Aachen
162 Lancasters, 8 Mosquitoes (12
Lancasters lost)

28 May
Dessau, Zwickau, Meißen, Leipzig,
Magdeburg
No aircraft data

29 May
Pölitz, Tutow, Leipzig, Schneidmühl,
Posen, Sorau, Cottbus
No aircraft data

30 May
Dessau, Halberstadt, Oldenburg,
Rotenburg/Wümme, Bad Zwischenahn
No aircraft data

31 May
Osnabrück, Schwerte, Gütersloh
No aircraft data

12/13 June
Gelsenkirchen
293 dead
286 Lancasters, 17 Mosquitoes (17
Lancasters lost)

18 June
Hamburg, Bremerhaven, Hannover,
Bremen, Stade, Brunsbüttel
No aircraft data

20 June
Magdeburg, Fallersleben, Hamburg, Pölitz
No aircraft data

21 June
Ruhland, Berlin
No aircraft data

29 June
Böhlen, Leipzig, Wittenberg, Bernburg,
Magdeburg
No aircraft data

7 July
Merseburg, Leipzig
No aircraft data

11/13/16 July
Munich
1,471 dead
200,000 bombed out
No aircraft data

13 July
Saarbrücken
No aircraft data

16 July
Stuttgart, Augsburg, Saarbrücken
No aircraft data

18 July
Kiel, Cuxhaven, Peenemünde
No aircraft data

18/19 July
Wesseling
No aircraft data

19 July
Augsburg, Kempten, Böblingen,
Schweinfurt, Saarbrücken, Koblenz
No aircraft data

20 July
Dessau, Merseburg, Leipzig, Erfurt,
Schmalkalden, Gotha
No aircraft data

21 July
Munich, Saarbrücken, Regensburg,
Schweinfurt
No aircraft data

23/24 July
Kiel
315 dead
20,000 bombed out
519 Lancasters, 100 Halifaxes, 10 Mosquitoes (4 Lancasters lost)

24/25 July
Stuttgart
461 Lancasters, 153 Halifaxes (17 Lancasters, 4 Halifaxes lost)

25/26 July
Stuttgart, Wanne-Eickel
Stuttgart: 412 Lancasters, 138 Halifaxes (8 Lancasters, 4 Halifaxes lost)
Wanne-Eickel: 114 Halifaxes, 11 Lancasters, 10 Mosquitoes (no losses)

28/29 July
Hamburg
265 dead
187 Halifaxes, 106 Lancasters, 14 Mosquitoes (18 Halifaxes, 4 Lancasters lost)
Stuttgart
494 Lancasters, 2 Mosquitoes (39 Lancasters lost)

29 July
Merseburg, Bremen
No aircraft data

31 July
Munich, Ludwigshafen
No aircraft data

4 August
Hamburg, Bremen, Peenemünde, Anklam, Kiel, Wismar, Rostock, Schwerin
No aircraft data

5 August
Magdeburg, Halberstadt, Brunswick, Hannover
No aircraft data

6 August
Brandenburg, Berlin, Hamburg
No aircraft data

9 August
Ulm, Pirmasens, Karlsruhe, Saarbrücken
No aircraft data

12/13 August
Brunswick, Rüsselsheim
Brunswick: 242 Lancasters, 137 Halifaxes (17 Lancasters, 10 Halifaxes lost)
Rüsselsheim: 191 Lancasters, 96 Halifaxes, 10 Mosquitoes (13 Lancasters, 7 Halifaxes lost)

14 August
Mannheim, Ludwigshafen
No aircraft data

15 August
Wiesbaden, Frankfurt, Cologne
No aircraft data

16 August
Delitzsch, Schkeuditz, Halle/S., Zeitz, Rositz, Dessau, Köthen, Magdeburg
No aircraft data

16/17 August
Stettin
1,117 dead
461 Lancasters (5 lost)

16/17 August
Kiel
195 Lancasters, 144 Halifaxes, 9 Mosquitoes (3 Halifaxes, 2 Lancasters lost)

18/19 August
Bremen
1,300 dead
30,000 bombed out
216 Lancasters, 65 Halifaxes, 7 Mosquitoes (1 Lancaster lost)

23/24 August
Cologne
46 Mosquitoes (no losses)

24 August
Brunswick, Weimar, Merseburg
No aircraft data

25 August
Rostock, Schwerin, Wismar, Rechlin, Pölitz, Peenemünde, Anklam, Neubrandenburg
No aircraft data

25/26 August
Rüsselsheim, Darmstadt
Rüsselsheim: 412 Lancasters (15 lost)
Darmstadt: 190 Lancasters, 6 Mosquitoes (7 Lancasters lost)

26 August
Gelsenkirchen
No aircraft data

26/27 August
Kiel, Königsberg
Kiel: 371 Lancasters, 10 Mosquitoes (17
Lancasters lost)
Königsberg: 174 Lancasters (4 lost)

29/30 August
Königsberg
500 dead
189 Lancasters (15 lost)
Stettin
1,033 dead
402 Lancasters, 1 Mosquito (23
Lancasters lost)

30 August
Kiel, Bremen
No aircraft data

3 September
Ludwigshafen
No aircraft data

5 September
Stuttgart, Karlsruhe
No aircraft data

6 September
Emden
No aircraft data

8 September
Ludwigshafen, Kassel, Karlsruhe
No aircraft data

9 September
Mannheim, Mainz, Düsseldorf
No aircraft data

9/10 September
Mönchengladbach
113 Lancasters, 24 Mosquitoes (no losses)

10 September
Ulm, Heilbronn, Nürnberg, Fürth,
Gaggenau, Sindelfingen, Zuffenhausen
No aircraft data

11 September
Fulda, Merseburg, Eisenach, Magdeburg
No aircraft data

11/12 September
Darmstadt
10,550 dead
49,000 bombed out
226 Lancasters, 14 Mosquitoes (12
Lancasters lost)

12 September
Münster, Magdeburg
No aircraft data

12/13 September
Frankfurt/M.
957 dead
50,000 bombed out
378 Lancasters, 9 Mosquitoes (17
Lancasters lost)
Stuttgart
469 dead
204 Lancasters, 13 Mosquitoes (4
Lancasters lost)

13 September
Osnabrück, Gelsenkirchen, Stuttgart,
Schwäbisch Hall, Ulm, Merseburg
No aircraft data

14 September
Wilhelmshaven
No aircraft data

15/16 September
Kiel
310 Lancasters, 173 Halifaxes, 7
Mosquitoes (4 Halifaxes, 2 Lancasters lost)

18/19 September
Bremerhaven
618 dead
30,000 bombed out
206 Lancasters, 7 Mosquitoes (1
Lancaster, 1 Mosquito lost)

19 September
Koblenz, Limburg, Hamm, Dortmund,
Unna
No aircraft data

19/20 September
Mönchengladbach, Rheydt
227 Lancasters, 10 Mosquitoes (4
Lancasters, 1 Mosquito lost)

21 September
Ludwigshafen, Mainz, Koblenz
No aircraft data

22 September
Kassel
No aircraft data

23/24 September
Neuss, Dortmund, Münster
Neuss: 378 Lancasters, 154 Halifaxes, 17
Mosquitoes (5 Lancasters, 2 Halifaxes lost)
Dortmund: 136 Lancasters, 5 Mosquitoes
(14 Lancasters lost)
Münster: 107 Lancasters, 5 Mosquitoes, 1
Lightning (1 Lancaster lost)

25 September
Ludwigshafen, Frankfurt, Koblenz
No aircraft data

26 September
Osnabrück, Hamm, Bremen
No aircraft data

26/27 September
Karlsruhe
226 Lancasters, 11 Mosquitoes (2
Lancasters lost)

27 September
Cologne, Ludwigshafen, Kassel
No aircraft data

27/28 September
Kaiserslautern
144 dead
30,000 bombed out
217 Lancasters, 10 Mosquitoes (1 of each
lost)

28 September
Magdeburg, Merseburg, Kassel
No aircraft data

30 September
Bielefeld, Münster, Hamm
No aircraft data

30 September
Bottrop
No aircraft data

2 October
Kassel, Cologne, Hamm
No aircraft data

3 October
Nuremberg, Gaggenau
No aircraft data

5 October
Wilhelmshaven, Cologne, Lippstadt,
Münster
No aircraft data

5/6 October
Saarbrücken
344 dead
25,000 bombed out
531 Lancasters, 20 Mosquitoes (3
Lancasters lost)

6 October
Stargard, Neubrandenburg, Stralsund,
Hamburg
No aircraft data

6/7 October
Dortmund
258 dead
100,000 bombed out
248 Halifaxes, 46 Lancasters, 20
Mosquitoes (4 Halifaxes, 2 Lancasters lost)
Bremen
65 dead
37,700 bombed out
246 Lancasters, 7 Mosquitoes (5
Lancasters lost)

7 October
Emmerich
641 dead
Kleve, Zwichau, Merseburg, Kassel,
Clausthal
No aircraft data

9 October
Bochum, Schweinfurt, Mainz, Koblenz
Bochum: 375 Halifaxes, 40 Lancasters, 20
Mosquitoes (4 Halifaxes, 1 Lancaster lost)

12 October
Wanne-Eickel, Osnabrück
Wanne-Eickel: 11 Halifaxes, 26 Lancasters

14 October
Duisburg
519 Lancasters, 474 Halifaxes, 20
Mosquitoes (13 Lancasters, 1 Halifax lost)

14/15 October
Brunswick
561 dead
80,000 bombed out
233 Lancasters, 7 Mosquitoes (1 Lancaster lost)
Duisburg
2,541 dead
498 Lancasters, 468 Halifaxes, 39 Mosquitoes (5 Lancasters, 2 Halifaxes lost)

15/16 October
Wilhelmshaven
257 Halifaxes, 241 Lancasters, 8 Mosquitoes

16/17 October
Cologne
39 Mosquitoes (no losses)

18 October
Bonn
313 dead
20,000 bombed out
128 Lancasters (1 lost)

19/20 October
Stuttgart
338 dead
565 Lancasters, 18 Mosquitoes (6 Lancasters lost)
Nuremberg, Karlsruhe
Nuremberg: 263 Lancasters, 7 Mosquitoes (2 Lancasters lost)

21/22 October
Hannover
242 Halifaxes, 21 Pathfinder Lancasters, all recalled

22 October
Neuss, Brunswick, Hannover, Hamm, Münster
Neuss: 100 Lancasters (no losses)

23/24 October
Essen
662 dead
561 Lancasters, 463 Halifaxes, 31 Mosquitoes (5 Lancasters, 3 Halifaxes lost)

25 October
Essen
820 dead
508 Lancasters, 251 Halifaxes, 12 Mosquitoes (2 Halifaxes, 2 Lancasters lost)
Homburg, Neumünster
Homburg: 199 Halifaxes, 32 Lancasters, 12 Mosquitoes (no losses)

26 October
Leverkusen, Bielefeld, Münster, Hannover
Leverkusen: 105 Lancasters (no losses)

28 October
Cologne
630 dead
20,000 bombed out
428 Lancasters, 286 Halifaxes, 19 Mosquitoes (4 Halifaxes, 3 Lancasters lost)
Münster, Hamm

30 October
Hamm, Münster
No aircraft data

30/31 October
Cologne
550 dead
438 Halifaxes, 435 Lancasters, 32 Mosquitoes (no losses)

31 October/1 November
Cologne
331 Lancasters, 144 Halifaxes, 18 Mosquitoes (2 Lancasters lost)

1 November
Gelsenkirchen
No aircraft data

1/2 November
Oberhausen
202 Halifaxes, 74 Lancasters, 12 Mosquitoes (3 Halifaxes, 1 Lancaster lost)

2 November
Merseburg, Bielefeld, Castrop-Rauxel
No aircraft data

2/3 November
Düsseldorf
748 dead
15,000 bombed out
561 Lancasters, 400 Halifaxes, 31 Mosquitoes (11 Halifaxes, 8 Lancasters lost)

4 November
Neunkirchen, Saarbrücken, Hannover, Hamburg, Gelsenkirchen
No aircraft data

4/5 November
Bochum
984 dead
10,000 bombed out
384 Halifaxes, 336 Lancasters, 29
Mosquitoes (23 Halifaxes, 5 Lancasters lost)

5 November
Solingen
1,882 dead
20,000 bombed out
173 Lancasters (1 lost)
Frankfurt/M., Ludwigshafen, Karlsruhe

6 November
Gelsenkirchen
518 dead
383 Halifaxes, 324 Lancasters, 31
Mosquitoes (3 Lancasters, 2 Halifaxes lost)
Hamburg, Miden, Bottrop, NeuMünster

6/7 November
Koblenz
104 dead
25,000 bombed out
128 Lancasters (2 lost)
Merseburg

8 November
Merseburg, Homburg
Homburg: 136 Lancasters (1 lost)

9 November
Wanne-Eickel
256 Lancasters, 21 Mosquitoes (2
Lancasters lost)

10 November
Saarbrücken, Hanau, Wiesbaden, Cologne
No aircraft data

11 November
Oberlahnstein, Gelsenkirchen, Bottrop
No aircraft data

11 November
Castrop-Rauxel
122 Lancasters (no losses)

11/12 November
Harburg, Dortmund
Harburg: 237 Lancasters, 8 Mosquitoes (7
Lancasters lost)
Dortmund: 209 Lancasters, 19
Mosquitoes (no losses)

16 November
Düren
2,900 dead
485 Lancasters, 13 Mosquitoes (3
Lancasters lost)
Eschweiler
No aircraft data

18 November
Münster
367 Halifaxes, 94 Lancasters, 18
Mosquitoes (1 Halifax crashed in Holland)

18/19 November
Wanne-Eickel
285 Lancasters, 24 Mosquitoes (1
Lancaster lost)

20/21 November
Koblenz
43 Lancasters (no losses)

21 November
Merseburg, Gießen, Westlar, Osnabrück,
Hamburg
No aircraft data

21/22 November
Aschaffenburg
344 dead
274 Lancasters, 9 Mosquitoes (2
Lancasters lost)
Castrop-Rauxel
176 Halifaxes, 79 Lancasters, 18
Mosquitoes (4 Halifaxes lost)

23 November
Gelsenkirchen
168 Lancasters (lost)

25 November
Merseburg, Bingen
No aircraft data

26 November
Fulda, Bielefeld, Hamm, Misburg
Fulda: 75 Lancasters (no losses)

26/27 November
Munich
270 Lancasters, 8 Mosquitoes (1 Lancaster
crashed in France)

27 November
Bingen, Offenburg
No aircraft data

27/28 November
Freiburg i. Br.
2,700 dead
40,000 bombed out
341 Lancasters, 10 Mosquitoes (1
Lancaster lost)
Neuss
173 Halifaxes, 102 Lancasters, 15
Mosquitoes (1 Mosquito lost)

28/29 November
Essen, Neuss
Essen: 270 Halifaxes, 32 Lancasters, 14
Mosquitoes (no losses)
Neuss: 153 Lancasters (no losses)

29 November
Dortmund, Duisburg
Dortmund: 294 Lancasters, 17
Mosquitoes (6 Lancasters lost)
Duisburg: 30 Mosquitoes (no losses)

30 November
Zeitz, Merseburg, Neunkirchen, Homburg
No aircraft data

30 November/1 December
Duisburg
425 Halifaxes, 126 Lancasters, 25
Mosquitoes (3 Halifaxes lost)

2 December
Bingen
No aircraft data

2/3 December
Hagen
583 dead
20,000 bombed out
394 Halifaxes, 87 Lancasters, 23
Mosquitoes (1 Halifax and 1 Lancaster
crashed in France)

4 December
Oberhausen, Kassel, Mainz
Oberhausen: 160 Lancasters (1 lost)

4/5 December
Karlsruhe
357 dead
20,000 bombed out
369 Lancasters, 154 Halifaxes, 12
Mosquitoes (1 Lancaster, 1 Mosquito lost)
Heilbronn
7,000 dead

50,000 bombed out
282 Lancasters, 10 Mosquitoes (12
Lancasters lost)

5 December
Berlin, Münster
No aircraft data

5 December
Hamm
1,000 dead
20,000 bombed out
94 Lancasters (no losses)

5/6 December
Soest
385 Halifaxes, 100 Lancasters, 12
Mosquitoes (2 Halifaxes lost)

6 December
Merseburg, Bielefeld
No aircraft data

6/7 December
Gießen
813 dead
30,000 bombed out
255 Lancasters, 10 Mosquitoes (8
Lancasters lost)
Osnabrück
363 Halifaxes, 72 Lancasters, 18
Mosquitoes (7 Halifaxes, 1 Lancaster lost)

9 December
Stuttgart
No aircraft data

10 December
Bingen, Koblenz
Koblenz: 8 Mosquitoes (no losses)

11 December
Frankfurt/M., Mannheim, Hanau, Gießen
No aircraft data

12 December
Witten
409 dead
20,000 bombed out
140 Lancasters (8 lost)
Merseburg, Hanau, Darmstadt
No aircraft data

12/13 December
Essen
349 Lancasters, 163 Halifaxes, 28
Mosquitoes (6 Lancasters lost)

15 December
Kassel, Hannover
Hannover: 62 Mosquitoes

15/16 December
Ludwigshafen
327 Lancasters, 14 Mosquitoes (1 Lancaster lost)

16 December
Siegen
348 dead
108 Lancasters (1 lost)

17/18 December
Ulm
606 dead
50,000 bombed out
317 Lancasters, 13 Mosquitoes (2 Lancasters lost)
Duisburg, Munich
Duisburg: 418 Halifaxes, 81 Lancasters, 24 Mosquitoes (8 Halifaxes lost)
Munich: 280 Lancasters, 8 Mosquitoes (4 Lancasters lost)

18 December
Mainz, Koblenz, Kaiserslautern
No aircraft data

19 December
Trier
32 Lancasters (no losses)

21 December
Trier
113 Lancasters (no losses)

21/22 December
Cologne, Pölitz, Bonn
Cologne: 67 Lancasters, 54 Halifaxes, 15 Mosquitoes (no losses)
Pölitz: 207 Lancasters, 1 Mosquito (3 Lancasters lost. 5 Lancasters crashed in England)
Bonn: 97 Lancasters, 17 Mosquitoes (no losses)

22/23 December
Bingen, Koblenz
Bingen: 90 Halifaxes, 14 Lancasters, 2 Mosquitoes (2 Halifaxes, 1 Lancaster lost)
Koblenz: 166 Lancasters, 2 Mosquitoes (no losses)

24 December
Babenhausen, Groß Ostheim, Zellhausen, Biblis, Darmstadt, Frankfurt/M., Merzhausen
No aircraft data

27 December
Fulda
No aircraft data

27/28 December
Opladen
227 Halifaxes, 66 Lancasters, 35 Mosquitoes (2 Lancasters lost)

28 December
Kaiserslautern, Koblenz
No aircraft data

28/29 December
Bonn
486 dead
162 Lancasters, 16 Mosquitoes (1 Lancaster lost)
Mönchengladbach
129 Lancasters, 46 Halifaxes, 11 Mosquitoes (no losses)

29 December
Koblenz
162 Halifaxes, 107 Lancasters, 8 Mosquitoes (no losses)

30/31 December
Cologne
356 Halifaxes, 93 Lancasters, 21 Mosquitoes (1 Halifax, 1 Lancaster lost)

31 December
Hamburg, Neuss, Krefeld, Mönchengladbach, Remagen, Koblenz
No aircraft data

31 December
Vohwinkel
155 Lancasters (2 lost)

1945

1 January
Kassel, Göttingen, Koblenz, Andernach
No aircraft data

2 January
Gerolstein, Mayen, Daun, Bitburg, Koblenz,
Bad Kreuznach, Kaiserslautern, Lebach
No aircraft data

2/3 January
Nürnberg
1794 dead
100,000 bombed out
514 Lancasters, 7 Mosquitoes (4
Lancasters lost. 2 Lancasters crashed in
France)
Ludwigshafen
351 Halifaxes, 22 Lancasters, 16
Mosquitoes (1 Halifax crashed in France)

3 January
Fulda, Aschaffenburg, Gemünd, Schleiden,
Koblenz, Pforzheim, Homburg,
Zweibrücken, Neunkirchen, Landau,
Pimasens, St Vith, Cologne
No aircraft data

5 January
Neustadt/W., Sobernheim, Pirmasens,
Hanau, Neunkirchen, Frankfurt/M.,
Kaiserslautern, Heilbronn, Niederbreisig,
Niedermendig, Koblenz
No aircraft data

5 January
Ludwigshafen
160 Lancasters (2 lost)

5/6 January
Hannover
340 Halifaxes, 310 Lancasters, 14
Mosquitoes (23 Halifaxes, 8 Lancasters lost)

6 January
Worms, Kaiserslautern, Ludwigshafen,
Cologne, Bonn, Koblenz
No aircraft data

6/7 January
Hanau
90 dead
20,000 bombed out
314 Halifaxes, 154 Lancasters, 14
Mosquitoes (4 Halifaxes, 2 Lancasters lost)

7 January
Hamm, Paderborn, Bielefeld, Cologne,
Landau, Kaiserslautern, Zweibrücken,
Rastatt
No aircraft data

7/8 January
Munich
505 dead
70,000 bombed out
645 Lancasters, 9 Mosquitoes (11
Lancasters lost. 4 Lancasters crashed in
France)

8 January
Speyer, Frankfurt/M.
No aircraft data

10 January
Cologne, Düsseldorf, Bonn, Euskirchen
No aircraft data

11 January
Krefeld
152 Lancasters (no losses)

13 January
Mainz, Worms, Kaiserslautern,
Rüdesheim, Germersheim, Mannheim
No aircraft data

14 January
Derben, Magdeburg, Cologne
No aircraft data

15 January
Ingolstadt, Freiburg/Br., Reutlingen,
Augsburg
No aircraft data

16/17 January
Magdeburg
16,000 dead
190,000 bombed out
320 Halifaxes, 44 Lancasters, 7
Mosquitoes (17 Halifaxes lost)
Zeitz
328 Lancasters (10 lost)

17 January
Hamburg, Paderborn
No aircraft data

18 January
Kaiserslautern
No aircraft data

20 January
Rheine, Heilbronn, Mannheim
No aircraft data

21 January
Aschaffenburg, Mannheim, Heilbronn
No aircraft data

22/23 January
Duisburg
286 Lancasters, 16 Mosquitoes (2 Lancasters lost)

23 January
Neuss
No aircraft data

28 January
Cologne, Duisburg
Cologne: 153 Lancasters (3 lost. 1 crashed in France)

28/29 January
Stuttgart
316 Halifaxes, 258 Lancasters, 28 Mosquitoes (6 Lancasters, 4 Halifaxes, 1 Mosquito lost)

29 January
Siegen, Koblenz, Bad Kreuznach, Kassel, Bielefeld, Hamm, Münster
No aircraft data

1 February
Mannheim, Ludwigshafen, Wesel
No aircraft data

1/2 February
Mainz, Ludwigshafen, Siegen
Mainz: 293 Halifaxes, 40 Lancasters, 8 Mosquitoes (no losses)
Ludwigshafen: 382 Lancasters, 14 Mosquitoes (6 Lancasters lost)
Siegen: 271 Lancasters, 11 Mosquitoes (3 Lancasters, 1 Mosquito lost)

2/3 February
Wiesbaden
1,000 dead
20,000 bombed out
495 Lancasters, 12 Mosquitoes (3 Lancasters crashed in France)
Wanne-Eickel, Karlsruhe
Wanne-Eickel: 277 Halifaxes, 27 Lancasters, 19 Mosquitoes (4 Halifaxes lost)

Karlsruhe: 250 Lancasters, 11 Mosquitoes (14 Lancasters lost)

3 February
Berlin
2,541 dead
119,057 bombed out
Magdeburg
No aircraft data

3/4 February
Bottrop, Dortmund
Bottrop: 192 Lancasters, 18 Mosquitoes (8 Lancasters lost)
Dortmund: 149 Lancasters (4 lost)

6 February
Chemnitz, Gotha, Gießen, Magdeburg
No aircraft data

9 February
Magdeburg, Weimar, Gießen, Fulda, Bielefeld, Paderborn, Dülmen
No aircraft data

13/14 February
Dresden
More than 30,000 dead
250,000 bombed out
796 Lancasters, 9 Mosquitoes (6 Lancasters lost. 2 Lancasters crashed in France, 1 in England)
Böhlen
326 Halifaxes, 34 Lancasters, 8 Mosquitoes (1 Halifax lost)

14 February
Dresden, Chemnitz, Bamberg, Magdeburg, Wesel, Dülmen
No aircraft data

14/15 February
Chemnitz
499 Lancasters, 218 Halifaxes (8 Lancasters, 5 Halifaxes lost)

15 February
Cottbus, Dresden, Magdeburg, Rheine
No aircraft data

16 February
Hamm, Dortmund, Münster, Osnabrück, Rheine, Wesel
Wesel: 100 Lancasters, 1 Mosquito (no losses)

16/17 February
Wesel
562 dead
No aircraft data

17 February
Frankfurt/M., Gießen
No aircraft data

19 February
Osnabrück, Meschede, Siegen, Dortmund,
Bochum, Gelsenkirchen, Münster, Rheine,
Wesel
Wesel: 168 Lancasters (1 lost)

20 February
Nürnberg
No aircraft data

20/21 February
Dortmund, Düsseldorf
Dortmund: 514 Lancasters, 14
Mosquitoes (14 Lancasters lost)
Düsseldorf: 156 Halifaxes, 11 Mosquitoes,
6 Lancasters (4 Halifaxes, 1 Lancaster lost)

21 February
Nürnberg
1,356 dead
69,385 bombed out
No aircraft data

21/22 February
Worms
239 dead
35,000 bombed out
288 Halifaxes, 36 Lancasters, 25
Mosquitoes (10 Halifaxes, 1 Lancaster lost)

22 February
Bamberg, Ansbach, Ulm, Halberstadt,
Nordhausen, Peine, Hildesheim,
Wittenberg, Stendal, Uelzen, Ludwigslust
No aircraft data

23 February
Treuchtlingen, Crailsheim, Plauen,
Meiningen, Kitzingen, Weimar, Gera,
Osnabrück, Paderborn
No aircraft data

23 February
Essen
1,555 dead
297 Halifaxes, 27 Lancasters, 18

Mosquitoes (1 Halifax crashed in
Holland)
Gelsenkirchen
133 Lancasters (no losses)

23/24 February
Pforzheim
Up to 20,000 dead
50,000 bombed out
367 Lancasters, 13 Mosquitoes (10
Lancasters lost. 2 crashed in France)

24 February
Kamen
290 Halifaxes, 26 Lancasters, 24
Mosquitoes (1 Halifax lost)

24 February
Hamburg, Lehrte, Bielesfeld, Bremen,
Wesel
No aircraft data

25 February
Friedrichshafen, Munich, Ulm,
Aschaffenburg, Schwäbisch
Hall
No aircraft data

26 February
Berlin
636 dead
71,283 bombed out
No aircraft data

27 February
Leipzig
677 dead
Halle
No aircraft data

27 February
Mainz
311 Halifaxes, 131 Lancasters, 16
Mosquitoes (1 Halifax, 1 Mosquito lost)

28 February
Soest, Hagen, Siegen, Meschede,
Arnsberg, Bielefeld, Kassel
No aircraft data

1 March
Mannheim
372 Lancasters, 90 Halifaxes, 16
Mosquitoes (3 Lancasters lost)

1 March
Bruschal
1,000 dead
30,000 bombed out
Reutlingen, Neckarsulm, Ulm, Heilbronn,
Ingolstadt, Augsburg
No aircraft data

2 March
Chemnitz, Magdeburg
No aircraft data

2 March
Cologne
500 dead
531 Lancasters, 303 Halifaxes, 24
Mosquitoes (6 Lancasters, 2 Halifaxes lost.
1 Halifax crashed in Belgium)

3 March
Hannover, Chemnitz, Bielefeld, Herford,
Magdeburg, Brunswick
No aircraft data

3/4 March
Kamen, Dortmund
Kamen: 201 Halifaxes, 21 Lancasters, 12
Mosquitoes (no losses)
Dortmund: 212 Lancasters, 10
Mosquitoes (7 Lancasters lost)

4 March
Ulm, Ingolstadt
No aircraft data

5 March
Chemnitz, Hamburg
No aircraft data

5/6 March
Chemnitz
498 Lancasters, 256 Halifaxes, 6
Mosquitoes (14 Lancasters, 8 Halifaxes
lost, 9 aircraft crashed in England)

7 March
Soest, Bielefeld, Dortmund, Siegen,
Gießen, Datteln
No aircraft data

7/8 March
Dessau
600 dead
20,000 bombed out
526 Lancasters, 5 Mosquitoes (18
Lancasters lost)

Harburg
422 dead
234 Lancasters, 7 Mosquitoes (14
Lancasters lost)

8 March
Siegen, Dortmund, Gießen, Essen, Hüls
No aircraft data

8/9 March
Hamburg
241 Halifaxes, 62 Lancasters, 9
Mosquitoes (1 Halifax lost)

9 March
Frankfurt/M., Kassel, Münster, Rheine,
Osnabrück
No aircraft data

10 March
Arnsberg, Paderborn, Bielefeld, Soest,
Dortmund, Schwerte
No aircraft data

11 March
Essen
897 dead
750 Lancasters, 293 Halifaxes, 36
Mosquitoes (3 Lancasters lost)

11 March
Kiel, Hamburg, Bremen
No aircraft data

12 March
Dortmund
895 dead
748 Lancasters, 292 Halifaxes, 68
Mosquitoes (2 Lancasters lost)

12 March
Swinemünde
Up to 23,000 dead
Wetzlar, Friedberg, Marburg, Siegen,
Betzdorf, Dillenburg
No aircraft data

13 March
Wuppertal
562 dead
310 Halifaxes, 24 Lancasters, 20
Mosquitoes (no losses)

14 March
Hannover, Hildesheim, Gütersloh, Gießen
No aircraft data

15 March
Zossen, Oranienburg
No aircraft data

15/16 March
Hagen
505 dead
32,500 bombed out
134 Lancasters, 122 Halifaxes, 11
Mosquitoes (6 Lancasters, 4 Halifaxes lost)

16/17 March
Nuremberg
517 dead
35,000 bombed out
277 Lancasters, 16 Mosquitoes (24
Lancasters lost)
Würzburg
225 Lancasters, 11 Mosquitoes (6
Lancasters lost)

17 March
Ruhland, Bitterfeld, Plauen, Böhlen,
Mölbis, Jena, Erfurt,
Münster, Hannover
No aircraft data

18 March
Berlin
336 dead
79,785 bombed out
No aircraft data

18/19 March
Witten
500 dead
20,000 bombed out
259 Halifaxes, 45 Lancasters, 20
Mosquitoes (6 Halifaxes, 1 Lancaster, 1
Mosquito lost)
Hanau
2,000 dead
30,000 bombed out
277 Lancasters, 8 Mosquitoes (1 Lancaster
lost)

19 March
Zwickau, Jena, Plauen, Neuburg,
Leipheim, Bäumenheim
No aircraft data

20 March
Hamburg
No aircraft data

22 March
Hildesheim
1,645 dead
40,000 bombed out
227 Lancasters, 8 Mosquitoes (4
Lancasters lost)

23/24 March
Wesel
195 Lancasters, 23 Mosquitoes (no losses)

24 March
Gladbeck
3,095 dead
40,000 bombed out
153 Halifaxes, 16 Halifaxes (1 Halifax
lost)

25 March
Osnabrück
143 dead
20,000 bombed out
132 Halifaxes, 14 Lancasters, 10
Mosquitoes (no losses)
Hannover, Münster
Hannover: 267 Lancasters, 8 Mosquitoes
(1 Lancaster lost)
Münster: 151 Halifaxes, 14 Lancasters, 10
Mosquitoes (3 Halifaxes lost)

27 March
Paderborn
330 dead
30,000 bombed out
268 Lancasters, 8 Mosquitoes (no losses)

31 March
Hamburg
361 Lancasters, 100 Halifaxes, 8
Mosquitoes (8 Lancasters, 3 Halifaxes lost)

3 April
Kiel
624 dead
No aircraft data

3/4 April
Nordhausen
8,800 dead
20,000 bombed out
3 April: 247 Lancasters, 8 Mosquitoes (2
Lancasters lost)
4 April: 243 Lancasters, 1 Mosquito (1
Lancaster lost)

4/5 April
Leuna, Harburg, Lützkendorf
Leuna: 327 Lancasters, 14 Mosquitoes (2
Lancasters lost)
Harburg: 277 Halifaxes, 36 Lancasters, 14
Mosquitoes (2 Lancasters, 1 Halifax lost)
Lützkendorf: 258 Lancasters, 14
Mosquitoes (6 Lancasters lost)

6 April
Leipzig
733 dead
No aircraft data

8 April
Halberstadt
1,866 dead
25,000 bombed out
No aircraft data

8/9 April
Hamburg
263 Halifaxes, 160 Lancasters, 17
Mosquitoes (3 Lancasters lost)

9/10 April
Kiel
591 Lancasters, 8 Mosquitoes (3
Lancasters lost)

10 April
Leipzig
134 Lancasters, 90 Halifaxes, 6
Mosquitoes (1 Halifax, 1 Lancaster lost)

10/11 April
Plauen
20,000 bombed out
307 Lancasters, 8 Mosquitoes (no losses)

11 April
Bayreuth, Nuremberg
Nuremberg: 129 Halifaxes, 14 Lancasters
(no losses)
Bayreuth: 100 Halifaxes, 14 Lancasters, 8
Mosquitoes (no losses)

13/14 April
Kiel
377 Lancasters, 105 Halifaxes (2
Lancasters lost)

14/15 April
Potsdam
5,000 dead
40,000 bombed out
500 Lancasters, 12 Mosquitoes (1
Lancaster lost)
Zerbst
No aircraft data

18 April
Helgoland
617 Lancasters, 332 Halifaxes, 20
Mosquitoes (3 Halifaxes lost)

20 April
Regensburg
100 Lancasters (1 lost)

20/21 April
Berlin
76 Mosquitoes (no losses)

21/22 April
Kiel
107 Mosquitoes (2 lost)

22 April
Bremen
651 Lancasters, 100 Halifaxes, 16
Mosquitoes (2 Lancasters lost)

24 April
Bad Oldesloe
700 dead
110 Lancasters (no losses)

25 April
Wangerooge, Berchtesgaden
Wangerooge: 308 Halifaxes, 158
Lancasters, 16 Mosquitoes (5 Halifaxes, 2
Lancasters lost)
359 Lancasters, 16 Mosquitoes (2
Lancasters lost)

2/3 May
Kiel
126 Mosquitoes (no losses)

Notes

Abbreviations Used in the Notes

BCWD Bomber Command War Diaries
OH   Official History, from Charles Webster and Noble Frankland, *The Strategic Air Offensive Against Germany 1939–45*, HMSO, 1961
USSBS United States Strategic Bombing Survey AHB
AHB   Air Historical Branch

2 The Bomber War

1 W. G. Sebald, *The Natural History of Destruction*, London, 2003, pp. 27–29.
2 Ibid.
3 The story of Operation Gomorrah is told in detail by Martin Middlebrook in his *The Battle of Hamburg*, London, 1980, one in his excellent series of volumes on aspects of the bomber war.
4 *The Firestorm Raid*, OH, vol. II, pp. 154–5. For casualty figures and Bomber Command losses see Henry Probert, *Bomber Harris His Life and Times*, London, 2001, p. 261.
5 Quoted by Middlebrook, *Battle of Hamburg*, p. 251.
6 See chapter 3 below for a discussion of the significance of the post-Hamburg panic in Germany, and the degree to which it confirmed Sir Arthur Harris's belief about the 'moral effect' of large-scale targeting of civilian populations by bombers.
7 Chapter and verse for this claim occurs in the appropriate places below, where the effects of the bombing campaigns are discussed. See especially chapters 3 and 8.
8 The idea that Allied thinking canvassed the idea of an effective 'culturecide' of Germany by means of bombing all its major cities and turning the country into a farm must not be taken as an excuse for forgetting that the Nazi regime in Germany, with the active support of many among its population, not only contemplated but enacted an actual genocide against European Jewry, and had plans to do the same for East Europe's Slavic population too, except in so far as it could be useful as slave labour. I repeat the point, however, that the fact that a wrong is less than a competing wrong does not make it a

right; and the fact that the Allies seriously contemplated permanently crippling German
– and Japanese – culture, and set about doing so by means of the area-bombing
campaigns, is one that must be looked squarely in the face.

9 This shows how much emphasis was placed on naval considerations in war planning
before the outbreak of hostilities. Some argue that over-concentration on naval planning
was typical of British thinking, given the country's splendid naval history and the great
power of its fleets, but was not tailored to the realities, as they proved, of the Second
World War. This is so even when one considers the importance of the war at sea; if
Britain had lost the Battle of the Atlantic it would have lost the war as surely as if it had
lost the Battle of Britain. But the war at sea was only marginally about great battleships
and cruisers – it was much more about long-distance aircraft hunts for submarines, the
technique of convoy sailings, the courage and endurance of merchant crews, and the
weather.

10 In 1918 the newly formed RAF consisted of 188 operational and 194 training squadrons.

11 Denis Richards, *The Hardest Victory: RAF Bomber Command in the Second World War*,
London, 1994, chapter 1 *passim.*

12 Ibid., p. 4.

13 It was followed by further schemes, not all accepted; for example, Scheme H was put
before the British Cabinet in 1937, calling for 2,500 front-line aircraft of which 1,659
were to be bombers. The figures were arrived at by looking at what the Luftwaffe had
available, and aimed at parity. The scheme was rejected, because the British government,
on the basis more of wishful thinking than clarity of vision, believed German assurances
that Luftwaffe strength would not be so great that such an expansion of British air power
would be needed.

14 The new bomber specifications that eventuated in the Halifaxes and Lancasters that
became the mainstay of Bomber Command – this especially true of the latter, a
magnificent aircraft ideally suited to the task and the conditions of the time – were
laid down in 1936.

15 The fighter specifications had been laid down in 1934.

16 See Robert Jackson, *Before the Storm: The Story of Bomber Command 1939–42*, London,
1972, chapter 2 *passim.*

17 In the period of expansion before the war the RAF also had, among other quickly
obsolescent types, the Handley Page Harrow and the Wellesley long-range bomber. The
latter saw some service in the early part of the war in the Middle East, and because of its
geodetic design (one of its designers was the remarkable Barnes Wallis) it was 40 per cent
lighter than it would have been if conventionally constructed. This is what helped to give
it an enormous range. Both types would have been a terrible liability in the air war as it
evolved from 1940 onwards.

18 Quoted in Jackson, *Before the Storm*, p. 76. The preceding account is based on *Before the
Storm*, pp. 70–5.

19 Ibid., p. 89.

20 Robert Jackson, *Bomber! Famous Bomber Missions of World War II*, London, 1980, pp.
21–8.

21 Of these bombing episodes and their effect on modern consciousness, more below.

22 In the first five days of Germany's invasion of the Low Countries and France, the
Luftwaffe lost over 539 aircraft, while the RAF lost 205 of all types. At that point in the
war, however, the relative rates of attrition were not the concern; that was a consideration
for the longer term. Rather, as Dowding's worries showed, it was the absolute rate of the
RAF's own losses that mattered for the immediate future: the days, weeks, and at most
months ahead in 1940.

23 Admittedly, sometimes by single aircraft.

24 See Denis Richards, *Portal of Hungerford*, London, 1977, p. x.

25 T. Taylor, *The Breaking Wave*, London, 1957, p. 157–8; newsreel footage.

26 General Paul Deichmann (ex-Luftwaffe), The Karlsruhe Studies; 'Reasons of the Luftwaffe for changing over to mass attacks on London' 1953–8; reprint of USAF Historical Studies.

27 USSBS interviews with Werner Junck, 20–4 April 1945.

28 T. Taylor, *Breaking Wave*, p. 44. See the excellent account given by John Ray in *The Night Blitz 1940–41*, London, 1996, which has been a helpful guide here.

29 Quoted in Ray, *Night Blitz*, p. 103.

30 This much-rehearsed accusation is discussed at length in (e.g.) Group Captain F. W. Winterbotham, *The Ultra Secret*, New York, 1974; Cave Brown, *Bodyguard of Lies* (2 vols) New York, 1974; William Stevenson, *A Man Called Intrepid*, New York, 1976; etc. An apparently definitive statement of the case is given by one who was intimately in the know: John Colville, who worked in Downing Street in the war years. In his *The Churchillians* (London, 1981, p. 62) he writes: 'All concerned with the information gleaned from the intercepted German signals were conscious that German suspicions must not be aroused for the sake of ephemeral advantages. In the case of the Coventry raid no dilemma arose, for until the German directional beam was turned on the doomed city nobody knew where the great raid would be. Certainly the Prime Minister did not. The German signals referred to a major operation with the code name "Moonlight Sonata". The usual "Boniface" secrecy in the Private Office had been lifted on this occasion and during the afternoon before the raid I wrote in my diary (kept under lock and key at 10 Downing Street), "It is obviously some major air operation, but its exact destination the Air Ministry find it difficult to determine".'

31 BCWD, p. 103.

32 Official Narrative.

33 As an indication of the relative inefficacy of aerial bombing at this juncture of the war, the figures scrupulously kept by the city of Cologne – subject of the devastating 1,000-bomber attack in July 1942 – showed that in the period June 1941 to February 1942 the city was bombed 33 times, but that only 17 per cent of the tonnage dropped fell within the city limits. Although houses and factories had been damaged, and over 13,000 people temporarily dehoused, only 138 people had died in all those raids.

34 Quoted Richards, *The Hardest Victory*, p. 97.

35 OH, vol. IV, pp. 135–40.

36 On the night of 16–17 December 1940, as a retaliation for the Coventry raid, an area-bombing attack was carried out on Mannheim. The largest assembly of RAF bombers so far gathered for a single mission – 134 aircraft – took part in the attack, which killed forty-seven people and demolished nearly 500 buildings. But this raid, although 'Coventry-style', did not by itself herald the onset of area bombing, though of course it made the later acceptance of the policy easier.

37 Edmund Fawcett drew my attention to the fact that the striking photograph showing the dome of St Paul's floating in a sea of fire was in fact concocted for propaganda purposes; it was by Harry Morgan, as reported in *St Paul's: The Cathedral Church of London 604–2004* edited by Derek Keene, Arthur Burns and Andrew Saint, New Haven, CT, 2004.

38 Sir Arthur Harris, *Bomber Offensive*, London, 1947, pp. 51–2.

39 OH, vol. IV, pp 143–8.

40 Harris, *Bomber Offensive*, pp. 115–17.

41 Ibid., p. 115.

42 Richards, *The Hardest Victory*, p. 120.

43 Other towns are sometimes included in the Baedeker raid story: Ipswich, Cambridge, Bury

St Edmunds and Great Yarmouth; but these were small raids and did nowhere near as much damage as the principal Baedeker attacks.

44 Quoted Richards, *The Hardest Victory*, p. 127.

45 Harris, *Bomber Offensive*, p. 113.

46 BCWD, p. 297.

47 This crucial point is discussed along with others in the next chapter.

48 Harris believed that the formation of an élite corps would damage Bomber Command morale, and in this he was supported by all of his Group commanders. In the event a force was constituted by having the best crews nominated by Groups themselves, and it was placed under the charge of an extremely able Australian airman, Donald Bennett, an expert in navigation as in other aspects of the air arts. Harris devised the name 'Pathfinder Force' (abbreviated to 'PFF') and invented a badge for it: an eagle.

49 The superb Mosquito was also in service with Bomber Command by now too, flying with the Pathfinder Force and also able to bomb and photograph by day, because its speed and altitude were able to keep it for the most part away from fighters.

50 Probert, *Bomber Harris*, pp. 252–3.

51 Ibid., p. 253.

52 Richards, *The Hardest Victory*, pp. 172–3.

53 OH, vol. II, p. 291.

54 Richards, *The Hardest Victory*, p. 196.

55 Quoted in Probert, *Bomber Harris*, p. 263.

56 Ibid., p. 266.

57 OH, vol. II, p. 193.

58 The statistics are these: the sixteen major raids between mid-November and the end of March involved 8,700 sorties, from which about 500 bombers failed to return. This is a loss rate of 5.8 per cent, above the 'acceptable' upper limit of 5 per cent. In the view of commentators favourable to Harris, he did not call off the 'Battle of Berlin' because he felt, as the official historians did, that it was a defeat, but because preparations for Operation Overlord – the D-Day landings – and the Combined Offensive required the attention of Bomber Command elsewhere. One possibility is that if Overlord had not been imminent, and if the USAAF had not still been having doubts about deep-penetration attacks into Germany, Harris might have continued – with yet worsening results. The German defences were at this stage more than equal to the challenge, though very soon they were to suffer defeats, and continuing attrition, as the Allied offensives on all fronts wore with increasing effectiveness on their capacity.

   In a detailed account of the bomber war, there would appear at this juncture an account of a catastrophically unsuccessful raid on Nuremberg at the end of March 1944 which cost Bomber Command many aircraft and air crews for scarcely any return, most of the bomber force being blown far off target by unexpectedly strong winds, and finding navigation difficult because of adverse weather generally. Harris never spoke of this débâcle, but it is likely that if the Combined Offensive had not begun at about the same time, with some major successes to show for itself, this single disaster might well have cost Harris his job.

59 Quoted Richards, *The Hardest Victory*, p. 217.

60 Probert, *Bomber Harris*, p. 293.

61 Ibid., p. 291.

62 Ibid., pp. 291–2.

63 Richards, *The Hardest Victory*, p. 233.

64 Ibid., p. 239.

65 Quoted Probert, *Bomber Harris*, p. 305.

66 Ibid., p. 308.

67 Ibid., p. 311.

68 Richards, *The Hardest Victory*, p. 270.

69 Widely divergent figures are given for the dead in the Dresden raid, from 25,000 to 150,000. I give the most conservative figure, though the number of unrecognisable bodies, and the number of refugees, probably means that the figure should be higher. See Frederick Taylor, *Dresden*, London, 2004, pp. 370–1.

70 AHB Narrative, vol. IV, p. 203.

71 See Hermann Knell, *To Destroy a City: Strategic Bombing and its Human Consequences in World War II*, Cambridge, MA, 2003, p. 17 *et. seq.* Knell was a boy in Würzburg when it was destroyed in air raids in February and March 1945. The main reason for its being a target seems to be that its population was just over 100,000, and hence 'on the list' of cities to be destroyed.

72 OH, vol. III, p. 112.

73 US Strategic Bombing Survey Summary Report (USSBS) (Pacific War), Washington DC, 1 July 1946, p. 16.

74 Ibid.

75 The USSBS said 185,000 dead; see ibid., p. 20; subsequent reports lower the figure to 100,000. The exact number will of course never be known, but it is likely to be somewhere between these figures, perhaps in the region of the lower of them.

76 Ibid., p. 20.

77 Ibid., p. 24.

78 I return to all these points in later chapters.

3 The Experience of the Bombed

1 Quoted Middlebrook, *Battle of Hamburg*, p. 257.

2 Ibid., p. 258.

3 Ibid., pp. 258–9.

4 In London such an area lies between King's Cross, Hyde Park, the Thames and the Tower of London; in New York it would be all of Lower Manhattan from Madison Square Park to Battery Park. See ibid., p. 263.

5 Ibid., p. 265.

6 Earl R. Beck *Under the Bombs: The German Home Front 1943–45*, Lexington, KY, 1986, p. 69.

7 Ibid., p. 70.

8 W. G. Sebald, *Natural History of Destruction*, p. 29.

9 Middlebrook, *Battle of Hamburg*, pp. 264–5.

10 Ibid., p. 266.

11 Ibid., p. 268.

12 Ibid., p. 274.

13 Ibid., p. 275.

14 Ibid., p. 276.

15 Quoted in Christoph Kucklick, *Feuersturm: Der Bombenkrieg gegen Deutschland*, Hamburg, 2003, p. 32.

16 See Churchill's 'exterminating attack' remark.

17 Beck, *Under the Bombs*, p. 60.

18 Ibid., p. 62; Beck is here describing the experiences reported by Josef Fischer, a citizen of Cologne who made a record of his experience under bombing.

19 See chapter 7 below, where I discuss the question of when the Allies knew that victory, even if it still had to be fought for, was inevitable given their industrial and manpower superiority over the Axis.

20 Kurt Vonnegut, *Slaughterhouse 5*, New York, 1969, p. 157.

21 John Hersey, *Hiroshima*, London, 1946, p. 68.

22 USSBS Pacific, p. 17.

23 Ibid., p. 20.

24 Hersey, *Hiroshima*, p. 182.

25 USSBS Pacific, p. 21.

26 The figures are quoted in Beck, *Under the Bombs*, pp. 8–9.

27 Ibid., p. 9.

28 Ibid., p. 111.

29 Richard Overy, *War and the Economy in the Third Reich*, Oxford, 1994, p. 312. Overy's book is an excellent study of the German war economy, and provides correctives to what had hitherto been a number of misconceptions about it. See also Gitta Sereny, *Albert Speer: His Battle with Truth*, New York, 1995; Joachim Fest, *Speer: The Final Verdict*, London, 2001.

30 USSBS Europe, p. 2.

31 The photographs in Antony Beevor's marvellous *Berlin – The Downfall 1945*, London, 2002, reveal as much; the text testifies to the ferocity of the German resistance, impossible without at least the basic equipment.

32 It is a fact forgotten by many that the giant Skoda armaments works in Czechoslovakia, and the separate Skoda automative works, were leaders in their fields in central Europe, for the country had been the industrial powerhouse of the Austro-Hungarian empire, and its genius for design was second to none.

33 In Britain the labour shortfall occasioned by men going into the armed forces was made up by women entering the workforce. In Germany this did not happen; the percentage of women in work in Germany was the same before and after 1939. Contract and prisoner labour in wartime Germany included women, but the proportions of them depended on the status of the group from which they came. Thus, Jewish and Slav women were allowed, or made, to work, whereas French and Dutch women were not.

34 Richard Bessel, *Nazism and War*, London, 2004, pp. 132–3. The prisoners of Mittelbau-Dora remind one of the Earthmen in C. S. Lewis's *The Silver Chair*, slaves of the Lady of the Green Kirtle.

35 Richards, *The Hardest Victory*, p. 194.

36 Ibid., p. 195.

37 Robin Neillands, *The Bomber War: The Allied Air offensive Against Germany*, New York, 2001, p. 343.

38 Richards, *The Hardest Victory*, p. 301.

39 *The Goebbels Diaries*, London, 1948, p. 113.

40 Ibid., p. 393.

41 Ibid., pp. 496–8.

42 Ibid., pp. 425–7.

43 Ibid., p. 485, and Richards p. 212.

44 Quoted Beck, *Under the Bombs*, pp. 87–8.

45 Middlebrook, *Battle of Hamburg*, p. 360.

46 Princess Marie Vassiltchikov, *The Berlin Diaries*, London, 1985. Admittedly, 'Missie' Vassiltchikov had aristocratic and well-placed friends, and after being bombed out could resort to the commodious hospitality in Potsdam of Count Gottfried Bismarck-Schonhausen. But the contrast between this and families sharing a cellar is one of degree not kind: the point was that everyone pulled together, even those who – like

Count Bismarck-Schonhausen, shortly afterwards put on trial for anti-Hitler activities – had no interest in a German victory in the war.

47 Beck, *Under the Bombs*, p. 108.

48 The horrific story of the Russian advance at the end of the war is told by Antony Beevor in his excellent and excoriating *Berlin*, London, 2002.

49 USSBS Europe, p. 15.

50 Ibid., p. 14.

51 Richards, *The Hardest Victory*, p. 303.

52 John Terraine gives a graphic account of the Typhoon attacks on Panzer divisions in the attempted counter-thrust by the Wehrmacht on 7 August 1944 westward from Mortain. As the rocket-firing Typhoons of the Second Tactical Air Force defeated the tanks, fighters from the Ninth Air Force kept the Luftwaffe fighters away. Terraine quotes Sir A. M. Coningham: 'This was to date one of the best demonstrations of the tactical use of air power which had been given in this war. It showed that a Tactical Air Force may be a decisive battle winning factor, and it showed the smooth co-ordination of air effort which could be achieved at short notice by the team work which had been perfected between the Ninth Air Force and the second Tactical Air Force.' John Terraine, *The Right of the Line: The Royal Air Force in the European War 1939–1945*, London, 1985, p. 661.

53 Probert, *Bomber Harris*, p. 293. In May 1944 Harris told a meeting at Montgomery's HQ: 'it can be stated without fear of contradiction that the heavy bomber is a first-class strategic weapon and one of the least effective tactical weapons.'

54 Ibid., p. 297.

55 Beck, *Under the Bombs*, pp. 130–1.

56 Neillands, *The Bomber War*, p. 336.

57 USSBS Europe, p. 8.

58 Harris, *Bomber Offensive*, p. 233.

59 USSBS Europe, p. 9.

60 Ibid.

61 Figures quoted in Richards, *The Hardest Victory*, pp. 301–2.

62 Alfred Mierzejewski, *Collapse of the German War Economy 1944–1945: Allied Air Power and the German National Railway* Chapel Hill, NC, 1988, p. 192.

63 Robert A. Pape, *Bombing to Win: Air Power and Coercion in War*, Ithaca, NY, 1996.

64 Ian Buruma *The Wages of Guilt Memories of War in Germany and Japan*, London, 1994.

65 During a spell as Visiting Professor at Tokyo University I had the opportunity to visit Nagasaki and Hiroshima, and heard this view at first hand in conversations in both cities. What is said in the course of such conversations might be demurred in more public contexts, but the sense that at least some Japanese have of Japanese victims of area bombing being *victims* is not equally the default attitude among Germans of the war and immediately post-war generations, at least in anything like the same straightforward way. That attitude is now changing.

66 Buruma, *Wages of Guilt*, p. 12.

67 Ibid., p. 11.

68 Ibid., p. 162.

4 *The Mind of the Bomber*

1 Beck, *Under the Bombs*, p. 64.

2 Henry Probert's *Bomber Harris* is a sympathetic portrayal, intended – and with a good measure of success – to redress the balance of hostile opinion that Harris attracted

whenever the ethics of Bomber Command's activities in the war was at issue. Whatever else might be said about Harris, he was clearly an outstanding leader, and his concern for the welfare and proper reward of those under his command does him credit. He had his callous and uncompromising side, he was arguably wrong-headed in his larger theories, and he was not an easy subordinate for the Air Staff to manage, to the point of reducing the effectiveness of the air contribution to the war. But most men are of mixed alloy, and Probert does a masterly job in leaving one with a sense of Harris's large qualities while not masking his warts and failings.

3   No doubt some would say that being cultured and yet still able to carry out such policies is worse; the thought has weight – for this must have been true of many German SS personnel.

4   Probert, *Bomber Harris*, pp 154–5.

5   Ibid., p. 223.

6   Ibid., pp. 193–4, 227.

7   Ibid., p. 208.

8   See A. Nussbaum, 'Frédéric de Martens, Representative Tsarist Writer on International Law', XXII *Acta Scandinavica juris gentium* (in: *Nordisk Tidsskrift for International Law*), 1952, pp. 51–66.

9   Information about the effects of the German bombing assault on the British Isles in the First World War can be found in Colin McInnes and G. D. Sheffield, (eds.) *Warfare in the Twentieth Century*, London, 1988. See the article by J. Pimlott 'The Theory and Practice of Strategic Bombing' in McInnes and Sheffield, p 121.

10 Caparetto is now Kobarid in Slovenia. Its battle is the setting of Hemingway's, *A Farewell to Arms*.

11 Douhet's book appeared in English twenty years later, translated by Dino Ferrari (New York, 1942; all references here are to this edition) but its tenets were widely known and discussed long before this.

12 Douhet *The Command of the Air*, pp 28, 47–8, 57–8, 309.

13 Quoted Pape, *Bombing to Win*, pp. 60–1.

14 Quoted ibid., p. 61.

15 Ibid.

16 Ibid.

17 Ibid., pp. 61–2.

18 Basil Liddell Hart, *Paris, or the Future of War*, London, 1925.

19 Ibid., p. 50.

20 Ibid., p. 45.

21 Quoted in Brian Bond, *Liddell Hart*, London, 1979, p. 145.

22 Memo of May 1928 to fellow service chiefs, quoted in OH, vol. IV, p. 74.

23 A. D. Harvey, ref p. 665.

24 Ibid., p. 663.

25 Ibid., vol. 1, p. 99.

26 Pape, *Bombing to Win*, p. 63.

27 Ibid., p. 63–4.

28 Ibid., p. 64.

29 The lecturer quoted by Pape is M. S. Fairchild, an instructor at the Air Corps Tactical School. These lectures were given in 1939, and are to be found in the archives of the US Air Force Historical Research Agency at Maxwell Air Force Base in Alabama. Ibid., p. 63.

30 Quoted ibid.

31 Like Douhet, Mitchell's passionate enthusiasm for air power got him into trouble. He had shown brilliant imagination in using massed air power in support of ground operations in the reduction of the St Mihiel salient in the last year of the First World

War, while in charge of the US combat aircraft in France; but his outspokenness in criticising US Army and Navy foot-dragging over air-power matters resulted in a court martial in 1925, and the end of his military career. At the time of the court martial he held the rank of brigadier-general. He wrote several books on air strategy, and a bomber aircraft was posthumously named after him, a tribute after the dust of old political rivalries had settled down.

32 Pape, *Bombing to Win*, p. 65.
33 Ibid., p. 66.
34 Quoted ibid.
35 The field manual in question was the War Department Field Manual 100–20 (FM 100–20, *Command and Employment of Air Power*), the 'Declaration of Independence' of the US air force. It embodied a good deal of Air Corps Tactical School pre-war thinking, not least in asserting that 'concentrated use of the air striking force is a battle winning factor of the first importance. Control of available air power must be exercised through the air force commander if this inherent flexibility and ability to deliver a decisive blow are to be fully exploited'.
36 This is said to have been the work of a pro-German US Senator called Burton Wheeler, who gave copies of AWPD-1 to the *Chicago Tribune* and the *Washington Times-Herald* in the autumn of 1941.
37 Stewart Halsey Ross, *Strategic Bombing by the United States in World War II: The Myths and the Facts*, Jefferson, NC, 2003. He points out that trying to hit a target smaller than a football field from five miles up in the air with an ordinary (that is, unguided or 'unsmart') 'iron bomb' would be extremely difficult in the best circumstances, let alone in combat conditions. The point is well made.
38 Ibid., chapter 5, *passim.*
39 Almost any town in Germany during the war could be claimed to have some military importance; German war production had been widely dispersed, rail links were always a target, refugees were everywhere, and of course the premise of area bombing is that civilians support their country's military effort. Frederick Taylor in his *Dresden* shows how much can be nominated as having military and strategic value in that city and its environs. Two observations are relevant: Dresden doubtless had some military value to an attacker, but its cultural value might have been a better reason for not bombing it; and in the case of Wurzberg and other historical towns, the same definitely applies.
40 Presciently Grey said when hostilities began, 'The lamps are going out all over Europe; we shall not see them lit again in our lifetime.' Given that the events of 1914 ushered in hot and cold war for the next seventy-five years, until the Berlin Wall came down in 1989, he was right.
41 The relatively successful naval conferences were held in 1921, 1927 and 1930. Frank B. Kellogg and Aristide Briand were respectively the US Secretary of State and the French Foreign Secretary who originally brokered the treaty.
42 This commission was established following the agreement reached in the Locarno Pact, establishing the borders of Germany. It seemed, but did not prove to be, an auspicious moment for continuing the peace process with a discussion about limiting the means to war.
43 Philip S. Meilinger (US Naval War College), 'Clipping the Bomber's Wings: The Geneva Disarmament Conference and the Royal Air Force 1932–34', *War in History* 1999 6 (3).
44 Ibid.
45 Ibid.
46 Quoted in F. Emme (ed.), *The Impact of Air Power*, Princeton, NJ, 1959, pp. 51–2.
47 Hansard, House of Commons, 14 September 1939.
48 Spencer Weart and Gertrude Szilard, *Leo Szilard: His Version of the Facts*, Boston, MA, 1979 pp. 54–5.

49 Quoted by Gerard DeGroot in his excellent history of the development of the atom
   bomb, *The Bomb*, London, 2004, p. 24.
50 Ibid., p. 28.
51 Ibid., p. 69.
52 The meeting took place on 19 September 1944 at Roosevelt's country retreat of Hyde
   Park. Ibid., p. 70.
53 Ibid., p. 74.
54 Ibid., p. 77.
55 Ibid., p. 85.
56 Ibid., p. 103.
57 Quoted ibid., p. 96.
58 Quoted ibid.
59 Sebald, *Natural History of Destruction*, p. 99.
60 Revisionist and neo-Nazi historians alike claim that the true architect of the Morgenthau
   Plan was Harry Dexter White, Morgenthau's influential aide in the Treasury Department, who in the McCarthy era was accused of being a Soviet spy, and who is (therefore)
   said by revisionists and neo-Nazis to have invented the idea of the 'pastoralisation' of
   Germany so that it would fall all the more readily into Communist hands. This is among
   the more moderate of the conspiracy theories that all too fruitfully spring up in this
   connection. The theorists' speculations are fuelled by the fact that the McCarthy witch-
   hunts embroiled a number of Treasury Department officials, and that White himself,
   after his appearance before the Un-American Activities Committee, died of a heart attack
   just a few days later – suspected by the conspiracy theorists, of course, of having
   committed suicide. His two daughters have consistently defended their father's probity,
   as recently as 2003 writing to the *Washington Times* to protest against a repeat of the
   McCarthy accusations in a new book.
61 Ralf Georg Reuth, *Goebbels: The Life of Joseph Goebbels*, translated by Krishna Winston,
   London, 1993, p. 339.
62 Joseph Goebbels, 'What Is At Stake', *Das Reich*, 27 September 1944. Source: 'Was auf
   dem Spiele steht', *Der steile Aufstieg*, Munich: Zentralverlag der NSDAP, 1944, pp. 3–9.
   One wonders, if those who proposed bringing up German children away from the
   influences that made Nazism possible were 'deranged' to propose this, what description is
   to be given to people who gassed children to death in Auschwitz and elsewhere.
   Interestingly, in the earlier part of this article Goebbels wrote: 'Those who bear no
   responsibility have the prerogative to think about life and the world however they wish.
   Those in government are different. They must represent the whole interest of their
   people, not only the interests of the present, but even more importantly those of the
   future. Their wishes and actions must follow rules that take account of the most varied
   factors affecting the life of their nation, as well of the nations in their sphere of influence
   . . . One cannot accuse the German government of ever violating this principle in the
   course of the war. It has carefully avoided laying out broad theoretical war goals, always
   limiting itself to fighting for the freedom, independence, and vital living space of its
   people. Most of its military actions were forced upon it. Its offensives always had their
   origins in a desire to defend the nation. After defeating an enemy, it made reasonable
   demands that were both practical and absolutely necessary.' Ibid.
63 The source for these putative facts is the Morgenthau Diaries, held at Hyde Park, the
   Roosevelt house in New York State, and this interpretation of their contents is owed to a
   paper by Anthony Kubek, 'The Morgenthau Plan and the Problem of Policy Perversion', in
   a revisionist publication called *The Journal for Historical Review* (vol 9 no 3 Summer 1989)
   pp. 287 *et. seq.* Because of this provenance the report to this point here is tentatively given.
   Morgenthau's book is however in the public domain, and responsible historians have

acknowledged its degree of influence on Roosevelt and Churchill independently; for example, Martin Gilbert, *The Second World War*, 2nd edn, London, 2000, p. 592.

64 Gilbert, ibid.

65 Lord Moran, Diary (unpublished) 13 September 1944; see Lord Moran, *Churchill at War 1940–1945*, London, 2002, pp. 177–8.

66 In his Memoirs Cordell Hull was unequivocal in his condemnation of Morgenthau's interference in what was mainly State Department business: 'Emotionally upset by Hitler's rise and his persecution of the Jews, Morgenthau often sought to induce the President to anticipate the State Department or act contrary to our better judgment. We sometimes found him conducting negotiations with foreign governments which were the function of the State Department. His work in drawing up a catastrophic plan for the post-war treatment of Germany and inducing the President to accept it without consultation with the State Department, was an outstanding instance of this interference.'

67 One of the very first calls for Germany to be diminished in size and/or broken up into smaller states, de-industrialised or not, came from France in the earliest part of the war. The proposals were not taken seriously by those, among them H. G. Wells in *What Are We Fighting For* (London, 1940), who were thinking instead of what kind of international regime should come into existence after the war to prevent future wars – the failed promise of the 'war to end all wars' that had not quite succeeded in ending war twenty years before.

68 B. E. Schmitt's speech was reported in *Time* magazine for 1 December 1941, pp. 57–8, under the title 'History Lesson'. See also Bernadotte Schmitt, *What Shall We Do with Germany?*, Public Policy Pamphlets no 38, University of Chicago Press, 1943.

69 The entire text of this extraordinary book has been reprinted by the revisionist Institute for Historical Review and placed by it, with other documents conducing to its view of the past, on the internet, where it is easy to find. For its bona fides as not being a forgery, it has Library of Congress call number DD222.K3; and it can be purchased through Amazon.com.

70 Kaufman's book was reviewed in, among other places, *Time* (24 March 1941, pp. 95–6).

71 Louis Nizer, *What to Do with Germany*, Chicago and New York, 1944, p. 13.

72 Ibid., p. 17.

73 Ibid., pp. 18–19.

74 Norman Cousins, 'The Time for Hate Is Now', *The Saturday Review of Literature*, 4 July 1942, pp. 14–18, quoted in James Martin, 'The Bombing and Negotiated Peace Questions – in 1944', *Rampart Journal*, vol. IV, no. 1, Spring 1968, p. 78.

75 Martin, ibid., p. 79. Clifton Fadiman was the host for many years of a popular radio show called 'Information Please', and he is otherwise best known for the anthologies of children's literature he edited. He condensed the *Encyclopaedia Britannica*, chaired the selection process for the Book of the Month Club and died in 1999 at the age of ninety-five. From such genial material could come 'the fury of the non-combatant', in C. E. Montague's pungent phrase. To him is owed the remark that 'The German mind has a talent for making no mistakes but the very greatest'.

76 Robert Lord Vansittart, *Bones of Contention*, London, 1945. See the review in *Time*, 16 July 1945. According to Anthony Eden, Vansittart was 'a sincere, almost fanatical, crusader' rather than 'an official giving cool and disinterested advice'.

77 Hansard, House of Lords, 10 March 1943. For the whole question at issue here see also: Steven Casey, 'The Campaign to Sell a Harsh Peace for Germany to the American Public 1944–48, *History*, 2005, vol. 90, no. 297, pp. 62–92.

78 I reviewed this book on its first appearance, in the *Financial Times* in 1996. For a longer and more detailed criticism of the book see Richard Neuhaus in *First Things* 65 (August–September 1996), pp. 36–41.

79 See Knell, *To Destroy a City*, chapter 1 *passim*.

80 Ronald Schaffer *Wings of Judgment*, New York, 1985, p. 153.

81 Quoted ibid.

82 Ibid.

83 Ibid., p. 154.

84 Curtis LeMay, *Mission with LeMay: My Story*, New York, 1965, p. 387.

85 See Thomas M. Coffey, *Iron Eagle: The Turbulent Life of General Curtis LeMay*, New York, 1986.

86 Field Marshal Lord Alanbrooke, *War Diaries 1939–45*, edited by Alex Danchev and Daniel Todman, London, 2001. The diary is littered with exclamation marks, sometimes two or three at a time, and reports of bird-watching excitements, making the book read like a boy-scout memoir at times. Alanbrooke had a reputation for imperturbability and sang-froid to which the diary gives the lie.

87 Ibid., p. 460.

88 Ibid., p. 547.

89 Ibid., p. 325.

90 Ibid., p. 586.

91 Quoted Richards, p. 97; see chapter 2 above.

92 An account of this meeting is given in Richard Overy's powerful and absorbing analysis of the Allied victory in World War Two, *Why The Allies Won*, London, 1995, p. 102.

93 Ibid.

94 The phrase 'combined offensive' is not exactly descriptive; in fact the two air forces continued more or less separate campaigns, occasionally bombing the same targets on alternating nights and days, but generally speaking each following a different drum.

95 OH, p. 112.

96 Quoted ibid.

97 This has been suggested a number of times as part of the reason for the Dresden attack.

98 Richards, *The Hardest Victory*, p. 270.

5 *Voices of Conscience*

1   Corder Catchpool, *On Two Fronts: Letters of a Conscientious Objector*, London, 1918.

2   Quoted in Paul Berry and Mark Bostridge, *Vera Brittain: A Life*, Boston, MA, 2002, p. 431.

3   Given that the appointment to Canterbury effectively lay in Churchill's gift, and that Bell was regarded as the natural successor to Temple, it is clear that Bell's opposition to the bombing aspect of the war effort was an irritant to the government.

4   Vera Brittain, *Seed of Chaos*, London, 1944. Published for the Bombing Restriction Committee by New Vision Press.

5   *Seed of Chaos* was republished just as this book was going to press, by Continuum in London. It is included in Vera Brittain, *One Voice: Pacifist Writings from the Second World War*.

6   Ibid., p. 7.

7   Ibid., pp. 7–8.

8   Ibid., pp. 8–9. The comment quoted occurred in the *New Statesman*, 18 December 1943; Churchill's remark about an 'experiment' is from an interview in *Time* magazine, 7 June 1943.

9   Ibid., p. 9, italics in the original.

10 Ibid., p. 10.

11 Ibid.

12 Ibid. The Shaw remark comes from a letter by him to the *Sunday Express*, 28 November 1943. As the highly contemporary nature of Brittain's quotations show, the debate about the bombing was a lively one in the pages of the national press.

13 Ibid., p. 11.

14 Ibid., p. 12.

15 The results of this poll were published in the *News Chronicle*, 2 May 1941.

16 The speech was given on 15 July 1941. Ibid., p. 13.

17 Churchill, then First Lord of the Admiralty, made this speech on 27 January 1940.

18 Brittain, *Seed of Chaos*, p. 16.

19 Ibid. The speech was made on 19 May 1943.

20 Ibid.

21 Ibid., p. 17.

22 Ibid., p. 18.

23 Ibid., pp. 19–20.

24 Ibid., p. 20.

25 Ibid., p. 21.

26 Harris, *Bomber offensive*, p. 92.

27 Brittain, *Seed of Chaos*, p. 25, quoting the *Daily Telegraph* of 12 August 1943, itself in turn quoting German claims about how RAF Bomber Command was operating. Given the difficulties of accuracy in night area bombing, the claim might relate to an aspiration rather than a standardly successful practice on Bomber Command's part.

28 Ibid., p. 24.

29 Quoted ibid., p. 25.

30 Quoted ibid.

31 Ibid., p. 26.

32 *Time* magazine, 7 July 1943, quoted ibid., p. 27.

33 Ibid., p. 34.

34 Quoted – and with names of the signatories appended – ibid., p. 37.

35 Quoted ibid., p. 97.

36 Letter to the Hull *Daily Mail*, 26 November 1943, quoted ibid., p. 98.

37 Quoted in Paul Berry and Mark Bostridge, *Vera Brittain: A Life*, Boston, MA, 1995, p. 438.

38 Brittain, *Seed of Chaos*, p. 97.

39 Article in *Evening Standard*, 4 January 1944, quoted ibid., p. 100.

40 Article in the *Daily Mail*, 6 January 1944, quoted ibid.

41 Quoted ibid., p. 102.

42 Corder Catchpool in the *Friend*, 25 June 1943.

43 Hansard, House of Commons, 28 July 1943 – in the midst of Operation Gomorrah.

44 Quoted ibid., pp. 104–5.

45 Quoted ibid., pp. 106–7.

46 Ibid., p. 108.

47 Ibid., p. 114.

48 Ibid., p. 115.

49 The signatories were George A. Buttrick, J. Henry Carpenter, Allan Knight Chalmers, Henry H. Crane, Albert E. Day, Phillips P. Elliott, Harry Emerson Fosdick, Georgia Harkness, John Hayes Holmes, Allan A. Hunter, Josephine Johnson, E. Stanley Jones, John Paul Jones, Rufus Jones, John H. Lathrop, Kenneth Scott Latourette, W. Appleton Lawrence, Elmore M. McKee, Walter Mitchell, Kirby Page, Clarence Pickett, Edwin McNeill Poteat, Richard Roberts, Paul Scherer, Ralph Sockman, Earnest F. Tittle, Oswald Garrison Villard, and Winifred Wygal. Most of these were widely known in their own day.

The US did not have an anti-area-bombing campaign as such, apart from the support given to Brittain's pamphlet, but it had a small and courageous pacifist movement, much vilified and often physically attacked by members of the public and armed forces on leave.

50 Berry and Bostridge, *Vera Brittain*, p. 439.
51 James Martin, 'The Bombing and Negotiated Peace Questions – in 1944', *Rampart Journal*, vol. IV, no. 1, Spring 1968, p. 112.
52 Quoted ibid., p. 113.
53 Ibid., p. 114.
54 Ibid.
55 Ibid.
56 Berry and Bostridge, *Vera Brittain*, p. 440.
57 Ibid.
58 Ibid.
59 Charles E. Montague, *Disenchantment*, London, 1922, p. 220.
60 George Orwell, 'As I Please,' *Tribune*, 19 May 1944.
61 Ibid.
62 Ibid.
63 Berry and Bostridge, *Vera Brittain*, p. 441.
64 Quoted ibid.
65 Ibid.
66 Ibid., p. 442.
67 See Benjamin King and Timothy Kutta, *Impact: The History of Germany's V-Weapons in World War II*, Cambridge, MA, 1998.

6 *The Case Against the Bombing*

1 Augustine ref.
2 For completeness it is worth pointing out that the *justum bellum* is one that has both *justum ad bellum* – just causes for war and aims in them – and *jus in bello* – just practice in the conduct of war. On this definition if either *justum ad* or *jus in* fails, there is no *justum bellum*. In my remarks here I am implicitly arguing that a war can remain just given its causes and the aims of the (so to say) aggrieved combatant, even if some aspect of *jus in bello* fails. But too much of the latter must threaten to impugn the justice of the whole; there is a question of proportions. The thought here is that even if World War II Allied area bombing turns out on examination to be unjust, it does not make the war as a whole so from the Allied point of view.
3 Otto von Gericke, 'The Sack of Magdeburg,' *Readings in European History*, ed. J. H. Robinson, New York, 1906.
4 Hugo Grotius, *De Jure Belli ac Pacis*, Book III, chapter 1, section iv; chapter 4, section ii.
5 Ibid., chapter 4, section ix.
6 Ibid., chapter 5, section i.
7 Ibid., chapter 5, section ii.
8 Voltaire, *Candide*, chapter 3, 'How Candide Escaped from the Bulgarians and What Befell Him Afterwards'.
9 Sun Tzu, *The Art of War*, translated by Lionel Giles, London, 1910, chapter II.
10 See US Congress, House, *The Trial of Henry Wirz*, 40th Cong., 2nd sess, 1867–8. H. Doc. 1331.
11 One of the earliest of these was published in 1908 by a man who had himself been a Union prisoner of the Confederate forces; James Madison Page, *The True Story of*

Andersonville Prison: A Defence of Major Henry Wirz, New York, 1908. Wirz was a captain at the time of the atrocities, a major by the time of his trial.

12 Geoffrey Best, *War and Law Since 1945*, Oxford, 1994, p. 41.

13 This is the text of the relevant part of Convention IV 'respecting the Laws and Customs of War on Land and its annex: Regulations concerning the Laws and Customs of War on Land'. This version was deposited at The Hague on 18 October 1907.

14 Self-denying ordinances like the Gas Protocol of 1925 would doubtless not be observed in war if the advantage of violating the protocol outweighed the disadvantage. But the combatant nations had learned in 1914–18 that the vagaries of the wind made gas an unreliable friend; considerations of prudence probably had a greater part to play than principle in the 'restraint' shown by the Allied and Axis forces in this regard.

15 Best, *War and Law*, p. 185.

16 In this connection one must see a book of quite exceptional interest, *A World at Total War*, edited by Roger Chickering, Stig Forster and Bernd Greiner, Cambridge, 2005. The Introduction is a brilliant survey of the questions prompted by the idea of 'total war'. Some of the points raised by the papers in this volume come into focus in the next chapter.

17 Joseph E. Persico, *Nuremberg: Infamy on Trial*, New York, 1994, pp. 33–4.

18 Ibid., p. 33.

19 Ibid., p. 35.

20 See Antony Beevor's excoriating account of the atrocities involved in Soviet–German fighting in the last months of the war in *Berlin – The Downfall 1945*. As regards the 'tu quoque' problem, Persico, *Nuremberg: Infamy on Trial*.

21 See Best, *War and Law*, pp. 180–1.

22 Ibid., p. 181.

23 Ibid., p. 81.

24 Hansard, House of Commons, 5th Series, 1937–8, vol. 337, col. 937.

25 Harris, *Bomber Offensive*, p. 177.

26 Best, *War and Law*, p. 201.

7 The Defence of Area Bombing

1 Harris, *Bomber Offensive*, p. 176.

2 Perhaps his claim becomes understandable when we remember that Harris was a gourmand.

3 Quoted Schaffer, *Wings of Judgment*, p. 146.

4 Ibid.

5 Ibid., p. 148.

6 Overy, *Why the Allies Won*, p. 124.

7 Ibid., p. 198.

8 See Chickering, Forster and Greiner, *A World at Total War: Global Conflict and the Politics of Destruction 1937–1945*, Cambridge, 2005.

9 Ibid., p. 3.

10 Ibid., p. 7.

11 Taylor, *Dresden*.

12 Ibid., p. 406.

13 Overy, *Why the Allies Won*, pp. 128–30.

14 Quoted Taylor, *Dresden*, p. 406.

15 Harris, *Bomber Offensive*, p. 144.

16 But one should add: with the honourable and important exception of its contribution to staving off the invasion threat of 1940.

17 Neillands, *The Bomber War*, p. 343.

18 Terraine, *The Right of the Line*, p. 663.

19 Richards, *The Hardest Victory*, pp. 298–9.

20 Ibid., p. 289.

21 Thomas L. Friedman, *International Herald Tribune*, 25 March 2005.

22 Neillands, *The Bomber War*, p. 386.

23 Clausewitz and Macaulay, quoted ibid.

24 Ibid.

25 Ibid.

8 *Judgement*

1 Schaffer, *Wings of Judgement*, p. 196.

Bibliography

Anderson, Christopher, *The Men of the Mighty Eighth: The US Eighth Army Air Force 1942–45*, London, 2001

Astor, Gerald, *The Mighty Eighth*, New York, 1997

Beck, Earl R., *Under the Bombs: The German Home Front 1943–45*, Lexington, KY, 1986

Beevor, Anthony, *Berlin – The Downfall 1945*, London, 2002

Bennett, Donald, *Pathfinder*, London, 1958

Bergerud, Eric, *Fire in the Sky: The Air War in the South Pacific*, Colorado, 2001

Berry, Paul, and Mark Bostridge, *Vera Brittain: A Life*, Boston, MA, 1995

Bessel, Richard, *Nazism and War*, London, 2004

Best, Geoffrey, *War and Law Since 1945*, Oxford, 1994.

Boiten, Theo, and Martin Bowman, *Battles with the Luftwaffe: The Bomber Campaign Against Germany 1942–1945*, New York, 2001

Bond, Brian, *Liddell Hart*, London, 1979

Boog, Horst (ed.), *The Conduct of the Air War in the Second World War*, New York, 1992

Bowman, Martin W., *The USAF at War*, New York, 1995

Bradley, James, *Flyboys: The Final Secret of the Air War in the Pacific*, New York, 2003

Brittain, Vera, *Seed of Chaos*, London, 1944

Brittain, Vera, *One Voice: Pacifist Writings from the Second World War*, London, 2005

Brown, Cave, *Bodyguard of Lies*, 2 vols, New York, 1974

Buckley, John, *Air Power in the Age of Total War*, Bloomington, IN, 1999

Budiansky, Stephen, *Air Power: From Kitty Hawk to Gulf War II*, London, 2003

Buruma, Ian, *The Wages of Guilt: Memories of War in Germany and Japan*, London, 1994

Calder, Angus, *The Myth of the Blitz*, London, 1991

Catchpool, Corder, *On Two Fronts: Letters of a Conscientious Objector*, London, 1918

Chickering, Roger, Stig Forster and Bernd Greiner, *A World at Total War: Global Conflict and the Politics of Destruction 1937–1945*, Cambridge, 2005

Churchill, Winston, *The Second World War*, London, 1948

Coffrey, Thomas M., *Iron Eagle: The Turbulent Life of General Curtis LeMay*, New York, 1986

Colville, John, *The Churchillians*, London, 1981

Cook, Ronald, and Roy Conyers Nesbit, *Target: Hitler's Oil – Allied Attacks on German Oil Supplies 1939–45*, London, 1985

Craven, Wesley, and James Cate (ed.), *The Army Air Forces in World War II*, 3 vols, Washington, D.C., 1983

Danchev, Alex, and Daniel Todman, *Lord Alanbrooke War Diaries 1939–45*, London, 2001

Davis, Richard, *Carl G. Spaatz and the Air War in Europe*, Washington, D.C., 1993

DeGroot, Gerard, *The Bomb: A Life*, London, 2004

Douhet, Giuhon, *The Command of the Air*, trans by Dino Ferrari, New York, 1942

Emme, F. (ed.), *The Impact of Air Power*, Princeton, NJ, 1959

Ethell, Jeffrey L., *Bomber Command: American Bombers in World War II*, Osceola, WI, 1994

Falconer, Jonathan, *Bomber Command Handbook 1939–1945*, London, 1998

Fest, Joachim, *Hitler*, New York, 1974

Fest, Joachim, *Speer: The Final Verdict*, London, 2001

Fischer, Klaus, *Nazi Germany; A New History*, London, 1995

Frankland, Noble, *History at War*, London, 1998

Freeman, Roger, *The Mighty Eighth: A History of the Units, Men and Machines of the US 8th Army Air Force*, London, 1970

Friedrich, Jorg, *Brandstatten: Der Anblick des Bombenkriegs*, Berlin, 2003

Friedrich, Jorg, *Der Brand: Deutschland im Bombenkrieg 1940–1945*, Berlin, 2003

Garbett, Mike, and Brian Goulding, *Lancaster at War: 5: Fifty Years On*, London, 1995

Garrett, Stephen A., *Ethics and Airpower in World War II: The British Bombing of German Cities*, New York, 1993

Gibson, Guy, *Enemy Coast Ahead*, London, 1946

Gilbert, Martin, *The Second World War*, London, 1989; new edition, 2000

Giovannitti, Len, and Fred Freed, *The Decision to Drop the Bomb*, London, 1967

Groehier, Olaf, *Der Bombenkrieg gegen Deutschland*, Berlin, 1990

Grotius, Hugo, *De Jure Belli ac Pacis* (On the Law of War and Peace), Amsterdam, 1625

Hage, Volker (ed.), *Hamburg 1943*, Frankfurt am Main, 2003

Harris, Sir Arthur, *Bomber Offensive*, London, 1947

Hart, Basil Liddell, *Paris or the Future of War*, London, 1925

Hastings, Max, *Bomber Command*, revised edition, London, 1999

Hastings, Max, *Armageddon: The Battle for Germany 1944–45*, London, 2004

Hersey, John, *Hiroshima*, London, 1946

Jackson, Robert, *Before the Storm: The Story of Bomber Command 1939–42*, London, 1972

Jackson, Robert, *Bomber! Famous Bomber Missions of World War II*, London, 1980

Kaplan, Philip, *Bombers: The Aircrew Experience*, London, 2000

Kaufman, Theodore, *Germany Must Perish!* (self-published), 1940

King, Benjamin, and Timothy Kutta, *Impact: The History of Germany's V-weapons in World War II*, Cambridge, MA, 1998

Knell, Hermann, *To Destroy a City: Strategic Bombing and its Human Consequences in World War II*, Cambridge, MA, 2003

Kucklick, Christoph, *Feuersturm: Der Bombenkrieg gegen Deutschland*, Hamburg, 2003

Kurzman, Dan, *Day of the Bomb: Hiroshima 1945*, New York, 1986

LeMay, Curtis, *Mission with LeMay: My Story*, New York, 1965

Lindqvist, Sven, *A History of Bombing*, London, 2001

Longmate, Norman, *The Bombers*, London, 1983

Magenheimer, Heinz, *Hitler's War: Germany's Key Strategic Decisions 1940–1945*, London, 1998

McKee, Alexander, *The Devil's Tinderbox: Dresden 1945*, London, 1982

McInnes, Colin, and G. D. Sheffield, *Warfare in the Twentieth Century*, London, 1988

Middlebrook, Martin, *The Battle of Hamburg: The Firestorm Raid*, London, 1980

Middlebrook, Martin, *The Berlin Raids: RAF Bomber Command Winter 1943–44*, London, 1988

Middlebrook, Martin, and Chris Everitt, *The Bomber Command War Diaries: An Operational Reference Book 1939–1945*, London, 1985

Mierzejewski, Alfred, *Collapse of the German War Economy 1944–1955: Allied Air Power and the German National Railway*, Chapel Hill, NC, 1988

Montagne, Charles, E., *Disenchantment*, London, 1922

Neillands, Robin, *The Bomber War: The Allied Air Offensive Against Germany*, New York, 2001

Nichol, John, and Tony Rennell, *Tail End Charlies: The Last Battles of the Bomber War 1944–45*, London, 2004

Nizer, Louis, *What to do with Germany*, Chicago and New York, 1944

Overy, Richard, *War and the Economy in the Third Reich*, Oxford, 1990

Overy, Richard, *Why the Allies Won*, London, 1995

Page, James Madison, *The True Story of Andersonville Prison: A Defence of Major Henry Wirz*, New York, 1908

Pape, Robert A., *Bombing to Win: Air Power and Coercion in War*, Ithaca, NY, 1996

Peniston-Baird, Corinna, *Blitz: A Pictorial History of Britain Under Attack*, London, 2001

Persico, Joseph E., *Nuremberg: Infamy on Trial*, London, 1994

Probert, Henry, *Bomber Harris: His Life and Times*, London, 2001

Ratner, Steven, and John Abrams, *Accountability for Human Rights Atrocities in International Law*, 2nd edition, Oxford, 2001

Ray, John, *The Night Blitz 1940–41*, London, 1996

Read, Anthony, and David Fisher, *The Fall of Berlin*, London, 1992

Reuth, Ralf Georg, *Goebbels: The Life of Joseph Goebbels*, London, 1993

Richards, Denis, *Portal of Hungerford*, London, 1977

Richards, Denis, *The Hardest Victory: RAF Bomber Command in the Second World War*, London, 1994

Robertson, Geoffrey, *Crimes Against Humanity*, London, 1999

Ross, Stewart Halsey, *Strategic Bombing by the United States in in World War II: The Myths and the Facts*, Jefferson, NC, 2003

Russell, Alan (ed.), *Why Dresden?*, Arundel, 1998

Saward, Dudley, *'Bomber' Harris*, London, 1984

Schaffer, Ronald, *Wings of Judgment: American Bombing in World War II*, New York, 1985

Schmitt, Bernadotte, *What Shall We Do with Germany?*, Public Policy Pamphlets no. 38, Chicago, 1943

Sebald, W. G., *The Natural History of Destruction*, London, 2003

Sereny, Gita, *Albert Speer: His Battle with Truth*, New York, 1995

Sloan, John, *The Route as Briefed: The History of the 92nd Bombardment Group, USAAF 1942–1945*, New York, 1976

Speer, Albert, *Inside the Third Reich*, London, 1970

Stevenson, William, *A Man Called Intrepid*, New York, 1976

Taylor, Frederick, *Dresden: Tuesday, 13 February, 1945*, London, 2004

Taylor, James, and Martin Davidson, *Bomber Crew*, London, 2004

Taylor, T., *The Breaking Wave*, London, 1957

Terraine, John, *The Right of the Line: The Royal Air Force in the European War 1939–1945*, London, 1985

Thorne, Alex, *Lancaster at War: 4: Pathfinder Squadron*, London, 1990

Tzu, Sun, *The Art of War*, London, 1910

Vaccaro, Tony, *Entering Germany 1944–1949*, Cologne, 2001

Vansittart, Lord Robert, *Bones of Contention*, London, 1945

Vassiltchikov, Princess Marie, *The Berlin Diaries*, London, 1985

Vonnegut, Kurt, *Slaughterhouse 5*, New York, 1969

Weart, Spencer, and Gertrude Szilard, *Leo Szilard: His Version of the Facts*, Boston, MA, 1979

Webster, Charles and Frankland, Noble, *The Strategic Air Offensive Against Germany, 1939–1945*, London, 1961

Winterbotham, Group Captain F. W., *The Ultra Secret*, New York, 1974

Wragg, David, *Bombers: From the First World War to Kosovo*, London, 1999

Index

Abyssinia, 26
Addis Ababa, 134
Addison, Lord, 182
Admiralty, 53
Advanced Air Striking Force, 31–2
Afghanistan, 132, 268
Ain Zara, 124
Air Corps Tactical School, 136–8,
    140, 337
Air Staff, 55, 69; bombing directives,
    22, 35, 47, 50; and bombing
    tactics, 29–30, 38, 51, 110, 120
aircraft: biplanes, 25, 33, 49, 120,
    124–5, 127, 227; design and
    production, 26–7, 45, 124–8;
    navigation, 27, 46–7, 50, 54–5,
    62, 70, 105, 177; bomb-aiming
    capabilities, 27, 46–7, 54, 56, 70,
    105, 125, 138, 141, 177; bomb
    capacity, 57, 75; numbers, 68; total
    losses, 104; German, 105–6, 111;
    First World War, 124–8; first shot
    down, 130; anti-submarine, 262
aircraft types: Battle, 27, 30–1;
    Blenheim, 27, 31–2, 189; Caproni,
    125, 130; Curtiss 'Jenny', 125;
    Dornier, 9; Flying Fortress B-17,
    17, 21, 29, 57, 63, 74–5, 99,
    141–2; Flying Fortress B-24, 75;
    Flying Fortress B-29 'Superfortress',
75–7, 155; Fokker, 33; Gladiator,
    9, 32; Gotha C-V, 35, 126–8,
    132; Halifax, 17, 55–6, 70, 105;
    Hampden, 9, 23, 27, 29–32, 49;
    Harrow, 330; Heinkel, 9; Heinkel
    111, 34; Heinkel 177, 43;
    Hurricane, 26, 32; Ilya
    Mourometz, 125, 128; Ju-88, 9;
    Lancaster, 9, 13,17, 50, 53, 55–6,
    62–3, 70, 75, 105, 266; Lightning,
    21, 58, 64, 254; Lysander, 9;
    Messerschmitt, 9, 29, 31, 140,
    254–5; ME 109, 28, 31; ME 110,
    28, 30; ME 262 jet fighter, 9, 106,
    109; Mosquito, 13, 16, 56, 70;
    Mustang, 21, 58, 64, 75, 254;
    Nieuport, 125; Spad, 125; Spitfire,
    9, 26, 57; Stirling, 17, 55; Stuka,
    134, 149; Swordfish, 9; Taube,
    124; Thunderbolt, 64, 254;
    Typhoon, 335; Virginia, 49, 227;
    Voisin, 124–5; Wellesley, 330;
    Wellington, 17, 27–9, 31, 48, 53,
    55, 75; Whitley, 9, 23–4, 27, 30–
    2, 48
aircrews, 45–6, 61, 71, 106, 118–20,
    186; moral position, 7–8, 277;
    casualties, 10, 64, 104; German,
    38; preference for Italy, 55;
    unpopularity of oil targets, 110

Alanbrooke, Lord, 171–3, 340
Albert Canal, 32
Alvarez, Luis, 155
American Civil War, 222–3
Ammianus, 165
Andersonville, 222
Andover, 25, 133
Andreas-Friedrich, Ruth, 101
Antwerp, 37
Ardennes offensive, 111
area bombing: civilian attitudes
    towards, 8, 43, 139, 183, 186–7,
    193–4, 200–3, 207, 277; policy
    develops, 20–1, 47, 50, 177;
    opposition to, 50–1, 119, 179–
    206; change in attitudes after
    Dresden raid, 72–3; cessation of,
    73; of Japan, 76–9, 105, 141–2,
    168, 207, 247; timing of, 89–90,
    261–4, 272; statistics, 104–5;
    judged a failure, 106–7, 114–15;
    contrast between Germany and
    Japan, 112–15; development of
    theory, 126–35; press reports on,
    182–4, 188–92; clerical responses
    to, 196, 201–2; 'sanctuary areas'
    proposal, 199; and mens rea
    knowledge, 208; case against, 233–
    46; outlawed by Geneva
    Conventions, 237; defence of,
    247–70; judgement on, 271–81
Army (British), 132–3, 148, 166–7
Army Co-operation Command, 52
Arnold, Lieutenant-General 'Hap', 74,
    139, 170–1, 244
Arrian, 219
Asia, 149
atomic bombs, 77–8, 112, 114, 251–
    4, 271; decision to use, 79, 152,
    252–3, 260, 263; as sui generis, 89–
    91, 272; as war crimes, 115, 233,
    335; defence of, 118, 154–6, 247;
    development of, 149–54; public
    response to, 155–6, 207; element of
    surprise, 278; see also Hiroshima;
    Nagasaki; nuclear weapons

Attlee, Clement, 196
Augsburg, 65–6, 100
Auschwitz, 8, 115, 338
AWPD-1, 136, 139–40, 337
Axis powers, 5–8, 22, 90, 114–15,
    210, 214, 263–5, 279–80

Baden, 199
Baedeker raids, 51–2, 331–2
Baldwin, Air Vice-Marshal John, 29
Baldwin, Stanley, 147–8, 165
Baranov bridgehead, 111
Bataan Death March, 170–1
Bath, 51–2
Battle of Britain, 9, 27, 36–7, 42,
    190, 330
Battle of the Atlantic, 45, 53, 58,
    261–2, 266, 330
Bavaria, 84
Bay of Danzig, 165
Belgium, 33, 44, 66–7
Belgrade, 197
Bell, Bishop George, 179–82, 194,
    196–9, 205, 340
Belsen, see Bergen-Belsen
Bennett, Donald, 332
Beresford, J. D., 200
Bergen-Belsen, 8, 73, 206–7
Berghof, 40
Berlin, 15, 19, 64, 98, 100, 175,
    253; bombing of, 38–40, 45, 47–
    8, 58, 72, 173, 194–5, 233, 254,
    272; 'Battle of Berlin', 61–5, 100,
    119, 172, 182, 184, 332; casualty
    figures, 62, 72, 198; Chancellery,
    96; response to bombing, 101–2;
    falls to Soviets, 103, 230
Best, Geoffrey, 227–8, 244
'Big Week', 65
Bismarck, Otto von, 163–4
Bismarck-Schonhausen, Count
    Gottfried, 334–5
Bleckhammer, 108
Blitz, 17–18, 42–3, 119, 173, 179,
    186, 194; see also London
Bochum, 58

Bock, Leutnant Hermann, 82

Boer War, 121, 123

Bohlen, 109

Bohr, Niels, 152

Bomber Command: area-bombing policy, 12, 20–1, 130, 141; loss rates, 13, 19, 21, 28, 49, 54–6, 60, 68, 70–1; Official History, 19–20, 45, 59, 64, 73; early resources and tactics, 21, 24, 27–33, 262; early policy, 23, 30, 33, 35–6; early successes and failures, 36–8; change in policy, 39–40, 50–1, 175, 177, 188, 197, 256, 267; War Diaries, 44, 54; increasing strength, 45, 50, 52, 54, 56–7, 62, 112, 262; Harris joins, 48–50; activities in Italy, 55, 60–1; role in Battle of the Atlantic, 58; defeated in 'Battle of Berlin', 61–5, 100, 172, 332; role in support of D-Day invasion, 65–9, 107–8, 175, 206, 255; aircraft numbers, 68; Dresden raid, 72–3, 78; post-war role, 74; casualty figures and aircraft losses, 104; established, 129, 131, 135; autonomy, 169, 171, 176; role in supporting Russians, 174–5; denied campaign medal, 176; commended by Churchill, 188; achievements, 265–6

bombing: estimated moral to material effect, 132; draft rules on, 143–5; 'cascade' or 'saturation', 191; see also area bombing; precision bombing; tactical bombing

Bombing Restriction Committee, 180–2, 195, 199–203

bombs: incendiary, 17–19, 21, 38, 44, 51, 53, 72, 77, 88, 91, 119, 272; high explosive, 17, 44, 53, 88, 91, 119, 272; heavy, 40; 'X' bombs, 53, 89; fire, 88; tonnages, 104, 193, 196; first dropped, 124, 130; 'block-buster', 191, 196; see also atomic bombs

Bonhoeffer, Dietrich, 181

Bonn, 94, 199

Bosnia, 167, 234

Boulogne, 36–7

Bracken, Brendan, 188

Braun von Sturm, Baron Gustav, 51

Bremen, 15, 20–1, 34, 45, 50, 54, 189, 195

Breslau, 71

Britain: bombing policy, 23–4, 35–6, 119–20, 135, 156, 177, 243, 268; Zeppelin and Gotha raids, 35, 126–7; threatened German invasion, 36, 261, 266; economy and industry, 42–3; civilian casualties, 42–3, 204; public morale, 53, 59, 126; national character, 131–2; preparations for bombing, 134–5; arms control negotiations, 143, 146–8, 227; atomic weapons development, 150–1; opinion about Germany, 165; propaganda effort, 228; and war crimes trials, 229; and Geneva conventions, 234–5, 237, 241, 276

British Empire, 69

British Expeditionary Force, 29–30

Brittain, Vera, 180, 182–7, 189–90, 199–203, 205, 249, 280

Brunswick, 65

Brussels Project for an International Declaration on the Laws and Customs of War, 223

Brux, 109

Buchenwald, 8, 73, 207

Buruma, Ian, 115

Bury St Edmunds, 331–2

Butt, Daniel M., 46–8, 173

Byrnes, James, 154

Caen, 107–8, 157

Calais, 36

Cambridge, 331

Canada, 188

Canadian First Army, 108

Canterbury, 51, 198

Caparetto, 130
Caproni, Gianni, 130
Casablanca Conference, 57, 64, 175,
    181, 263
Casey, Richard, 88
Catchpool, Corder, 179–80, 196
Celts, 167
Chamberlain, Neville, 23–4, 31, 148–
    9, 243, 268
Charlemagne, 164
Chemnitz, 72
Cherwell, Lord, 46, 161
Chickering, Roger, 257–8
Chiefs of Staff (COS) committee,
    171–3
Chile, 256
China, 25, 76, 115–16, 170
Churchill, Winston, 31–3, 48, 62,
    66, 213; response to Butt Report,
    46–7, 173; attitudes to bombing
    policy, 54, 57, 61–3, 69–71, 73,
    88, 173, 175–6, 184–5, 192;
    attitude to civilian casualties, 67;
    and atomic bomb, 151–2; and
    post-war Germany, 158–9, 161–2,
    168; 'Iron Curtain' speech, 162;
    pre-war opposition to Germany,
    165; meets Stalin, 174; and plot
    against Hitler, 181; speeches on
    bombing, 187–8; and international
    law, 244; and Battle of the
    Atlantic, 261
Cicero, 218–20
civilians: casualties, 5–6, 78, 92, 104,
    171, 204–5, 247–8, 257, 266–7;
    targeting of, 23–4, 27, 30, 33–6,
    39–40, 42–3, 47, 186–7, 231–3,
    268–9, 272, 277, 279; morale, 38,
    46–7, 126–33, 136–7, 140, 173,
    185, 248, 251–2, 275; British
    casualties, 42–3; French and
    Belgian casualties, 66–7, 107;
    resilience, 137; definition of, 142,
    156, 227–8, 250–1; German
    experiences, 271, 273
Claudian, 165

Clausewitz, Karl Marie von, 269
Coastal Command, 21, 52–3
Cold War, 22, 162, 168
collateral damage, 215, 249, 275, 279
Cologne, 45, 50, 58–9, 70, 193, 196,
    253; first 1,000 bomber raid, 20,
    51–3, 59, 94–5, 173, 256, 263,
    331; casualty figures, 53, 59, 94,
    263, 331; air-raid preparations, 94
Combined Bomber Offensive, 65,
    67–8, 175, 332
Committee for the Abolition of
    Night-Bombing, 179–80
Committee on Imperial Defence, 135
concentration camps, 8, 73, 98, 206–
    7
Condor legion, 134
conscientious objectors, 179
corpses, 18, 84, 86–7, 90
Cousins, Norman, 164
Coventry, 43–5, 90, 192–3, 198, 331
Cranborne, Lord, 199
Cranwell, Staff College, 25
crimes against humanity, 231–2, 273
Cripps, Stafford, 181
'culturecide', 22, 158–9, 167–8, 329–
    30
Czechoslovakia, 98, 334

Dachau, 207
Dam Buster raid, 59–60, 107, 173
Darmstadt, 157–8
Davies, Rhys, 182
D-Day, 65, 67–9, 107, 156, 172,
    206, 254, 262, 332
de Seversky, Alexander, 137
Deichmann, Paul, 41
Denmark, 15, 18–19, 55
deterrence, doctrine of, 151–2
Dönitz, Admiral, 265
Dortmund, 58, 101
double effect, doctrine of, 215–16,
    234, 249
Douhet, Giulio, 129–32, 135
Dowding, Air Marshal Sir Hugh, 32,
    330

Dresden, 71–3, 78, 89–91, 116, 175–6, 200, 233, 272; casualty figures, 72, 333; responses to bombing, 72–3; defence of and reasons for bombing, 258–60
Duisberg, 45, 50, 58
Dulmen, 73
Dunant, Henri, 222
Dunkirk, 31–2, 36, 261
Dusseldorf, 45, 94, 193
Duxford, 9

Eaker, General Ira, 57, 63, 74, 139, 184
Eden, Sir Anthony, 73, 147, 161–2, 168, 175, 181
Eder dam, 59
Edwards, Group Captain, Hugh, 189
Einstein, Albert, 150
Eisenhower, General Dwight D., 69, 108, 172
El Alamein, 56
Elbe, River, 16, 82, 117
Elbefeld, 58, 60
Emden, 50
English Channel, 32, 35–7, 68
Enlightenment, 221
Ennodius, 165
Enola Gay, 90, 155
Essen, 20, 45–6, 58, 190, 193
Exeter, 51

Fadiman, Clifton, 164, 339
Fairchild, M. S., 336
Falaise, 108
Far East, 48
Fascism, 179, 210
Fighter Command, 36–7, 40, 44
firestorms, 18–19, 60, 72, 77, 83–5, 89, 92, 119, 259
First World War, 22–4, 35, 96, 129, 138, 184; Harris's experience of, 48–9, 120; aircraft in, 124–8, 336–7; presumed effect of casualties, 132; causes of, 142–3; conscientious objectors, 179;

blockades, 184, 243, 247–8, 251; use of gas, 226
Flanders, 247
Flensburg, 55
Foley, T. C., 180
Folkestone, 127
Forster, Stig, 257–8
France, 32–3, 44, 57, 98, 230, 261; occupation of the Ruhr, 24; in First World War, 30; bombing in, 66–8, 107–8, 157; bomber production, 124–5; national character, 131–2; arms control negotiations, 143, 146, 149; and post-war Germany, 159, 339; and war crimes trials, 229; and Geneva conventions, 234
Frankfurt, 58, 66, 94, 100
Freeman, Wilfrid, 47
Friedman, Thomas, 268
Friedrich, Jorg, 273
friendly fire, 108
Friends War Victims Relief Committee, 180
Frisch, Otto, 151
Führerprinzip, 230
Fuller, Major-General J. F. C., 132, 194

Galland, Adolf, 109
Garbett, Cyril Foster, 181
gas, 133, 213, 226–7, 343
Gavotti, Lieutenant Giulio, 124
GEE equipment, 50, 52, 54–5, 190
Geilenberg, Edmund, 109
Geneva Conventions: (1864), 222; (1949 and protocols), 229, 234– 43, 274–6, 279
Geneva Disarmament Conference, 146–8, 227–8
Geneva Gas Protocol, 226
Genoa, 55, 60, 266
George VI, King, 172
George, Harold L., 136
Germany: post-war, 22, 73, 115, 157–69, 205, 207; bombing policy,

23–4, 268; reparations, 24; civil
aviation, 25; invasion of Norway,
29, 230; projected invasion of
Britain, 36, 261, 266; economy
and industry, 37, 39–40, 59, 64,
69–70, 74, 95–100, 103–4, 107,
111–12, 140, 185, 188, 250, 256–
7, 259, 267; oil supplies, 39, 45,
68, 70–1, 73, 98, 108–11, 120,
142, 172, 175, 250, 257, 259,
266, 272; invasion of Russia, 43,
54, 56, 96–7, 230, 261–2; public
morale, 47, 50, 64, 74, 100–3,
106–7, 112, 126, 174, 176, 250,
267; losing war, 52, 55–6, 69,
100, 103, 263–4; response to
Dresden bombing, 72; preparedness
for war, 92–5, 112–13, 256; effects
of area bombing, 95–100; foreign
labour in, 98–9, 256, 334;
homeland defences, 105–6;
reunification, 115; First World
War bomber production, 124; arms
control negotiations, 143, 146,
227; atomic weapons development,
150–1; 'collective guilt' and 'flawed
national character', 164–6; anti-
Semitism, 166; and Geneva
Conventions, 237; First World
War blockade, 243, 247–8, 251;
records of civilian experience, 271,
273
Gibson, Guy, 59
Gillis, Father, 202
Gladbeck, 73
Gneisenau, 30
Goebbels, Joseph, 101–2, 158–61,
338
Goering, Hermann, 25, 36–8, 96
Goldhagen, Daniel, 166
Gordon, John, 188
Goytisolo, Juan, 167
Grass, Günter, 115
Great Yarmouth, 332
Greece, 179, 230
Grey, Sir Edward, 142

Grotius, Hugo, 216–21, 227, 244–5,
250
Groves, General Leslie, 153, 170–1
Guam, 76
Guderian, General Heinz, 111
Guernica, 35, 134

H2S radar, 56, 62, 141
Hage, Volker, 273
Hague IV Declaration, 122–4, 223–5,
229
Halberstadt, 65
Hamburg, 45, 50, 52, 78, 193, 198,
247, 253; Operation Gomorrah
attacks, 16–20, 60–1, 81–7, 89–
91, 95, 99, 117, 173, 182, 189,
191–2, 233, 271–2, 278; casualty
figures, 20; recovery from
bombing, 99–100, 102; element of
surprise, 278–9
Hamm, 37, 73
Hannay, Canon, 196
Hansell, General Haywood, 136, 170
Harriman, Averill, 174
Harris, Sir Arthur, 129, 135, 272;
commitment to area bombing, 39,
60, 62, 66, 68–9, 74, 112–13,
117–20, 130, 141, 156–7, 176,
184, 253–4; takes over Bomber
Command, 48–50, 180;
background, 48–9, 120, 127, 132;
endorses bombing pamphlet, 50–1;
list of cities to be bombed, 50, 71,
142, 168, 333; plans first 1,000
bomber raid, 52–3, 263;
'preliminary phase', 54–7; launches
'Battle of the Ruhr', 58; receives
Churchill's support, 61, 69–71;
and 'Battle of Berlin', 61–5, 100,
119, 172, 332; and tactical and
precision bombing, 66–71, 107–
10, 120, 172, 175; disdain for
'panaceas', 66–8, 71, 108–11;
confrontations with Portal, 66–7,
70–1, 110, 172, 175; receives US
Order of Merit, 108; character,

117–19; reasons for area bombing
policy, 156–7; autonomy, 171–2;
final despatch suppressed, 176; on
role of weather, 190; defence of
area bombing, 243–4, 247–9, 251;
press coverage, 191–2; and dating
of bombing campaign, 262
Hastings, Max, 260
Hecht, Ben, 165
Heidelberg, 199
Heisenberg, Werner, 150
Heligoland, 15, 27–8
Hersey, John, 90, 93
High Wycombe, 48–50, 52, 118
Hildesheim, 73, 142, 168
Hirohito, Emperor, 112
Hiroshima, 89, 93, 149, 153–6, 170,
252–3, 260, 271–2; casualty
figures, 77–8, 171; individuals'
experiences, 90; as war crime, 115,
233, 335; element of surprise,
278–9
Hitler, Adolf, 56, 72, 154, 162–4;
popular support for, 6; and
establishment of Luftwaffe, 25–6;
invasion plans, 36–7; decides
bombing policy, 40, 42; and Speer,
96–7, 109, 259; delays ME 262 jet
fighter, 106; and arms control
negotiations, 146, 149; British
opinions about, 165; plot against,
181; cited in debate over bombing
campaign, 188–9, 192, 198, 202;
launches 'wonder weapon', 206
Holland, 98; see also Rotterdam
Holocaust, 2, 5, 115–16, 163, 207,
214, 276
Homburg, 199
Home Defence Air Force, 25
Homer, 219
Hull, 193–4
Hull, Cordell, 161, 168, 339
Hungary, 108

iconoclasm, 167
Imperial Russian Air Service, 125

Imperial War Museum, 9
India, 49, 76
'innocence', 215, 228
Innocent II, Pope, 226
Inquisition, 167
Institute of International Law, 223
Inter-Allied Aviation Committee, 131
International Criminal Court, 242
International Military Tribunal
(IMT), 229–32, 245
International Red Cross, 181, 199,
222, 234–5
Ipswich, 331
Iraq, 132, 268
Italy, 26, 55, 60–1, 107, 110, 262;
military aircraft, 125, 130; war in
Ethiopia, 134; arms control
negotiations, 143, 146; changes
sides, 266

Japan: militarism, 6; area bombing of,
12, 21, 76–9, 105, 112–15, 118,
141–2, 168, 187, 247; invasion of
China, 25, 115–16; casualty figures,
78; and decision to use atom
bombs, 79, 152, 252–3, 260, 263;
napalm used in, 89; surrender, 91,
112–14, 155–6, 252; preparedness
for war, 92–3; air force, 93; public
morale, 93, 112, 252; naval
blockade, 113–14; post-war, 115,
153, 167; atrocities, 115–16, 169–
70; bombing of Nanking, 134, 274;
arms control negotiations, 143, 146,
227; atomic weapons development,
150; and Geneva Conventions, 237;
facing certain defeat, 252, 263–4;
and total war, 258; military strategy,
278
Jeremiah, Book of, 182
Jevons, Professor Stanley, 180
Jews, 6, 98–9, 150, 158, 180–1, 339;
genocide against, 5, 163, 183, 227,
229, 231, 329; East End, 132
Jodl, General, 42
Josephus, 165

Kaafiord, 266
Kamikaze attacks, 169
Kant, Immanuel, 216
Kaufman, Theodore, 162–3, 165–6
Kellogg–Briand Pact, 143, 230, 337
Kesselring, Field Marshal Albert von, 41
Kiel, 45, 58
Kobe, 77
Koch, Traute, 85–6
Kokura, 153
Koslowski, Revd Paul, 201
Kosovo, 234
Kucklick, Christoph, 273
Kuter, Laurence S., 136
Kyoto, 153, 260, 274
Kyushu, 76

Land Army, 228
Lang, Cosmo, 181–2
Latham, Lord, 194
Lawrence, David, 155
laws: international, 8, 11, 121–4, 181, 227, 231, 242–4, 275; of war, 216–29, 234–5, 244–5; *ex post facto*, 229–30, 242, 245; Roman, 245; implicit, 245; *see also* Geneva Conventions
Le Havre, 37
League of Nations, 143, 145
Leigh-Mallory, Air Chief Marshal Sir Trafford, 66
Leipzig, 65, 72, 100–1, 175
LeMay, General Curtis E., 77, 141–2, 171, 244
Lend-Lease, 161
Leuna, 109–10
Lewis, Robert, 155
Liberty ships, 262
Libya, 124, 129–30
Liddell Hart, Basil, 132–3, 135, 206
Lieber, Franz, 223
Livy, 220
Locarno Pact, 230, 337
London, 23, 198, 333; Blitz, 3–4, 17–18, 40–3, 45, 49, 118, 186;

accidentally bombed, 38, 40; City of, 42–3, 49, 118–19; East End, 42, 132; in First World War, 127, 132; preparations for bombing, 134–5; V-weapon attacks, 206, 266; meeting to establish IMT, 229–30; IRA attacks, 278
Low Countries, 31, 42, 157, 230, 261
Lübeck, 50–2, 101, 119
Luftwaffe: established, 25–6; bombing of Rotterdam, 33–6, 197–8; bombing of Warsaw, 35, 149, 198; accidental bombing of London, 38, 40; changes tactics and launches Blitz, 40–3; Battle of Britain losses, 42; Baedeker raids, 51–2; night-fighter defences, 56, 62, 64, 117; destruction of, 65, 70, 74–5; aircraft numbers, 68, 254–5; fuel supplies, 75–6, 108–9, 111, 254
Lutzendorf, 109
Luxembourg, 31

Maas, River, 34
Maastricht, 32
Macaulay, Rose, 194
Macaulay, Thomas Babington, 269
McCarthy, Senator Joe, 338
McDonald, Dwight, 155
MacDonald, Ramsay, 165
Madrid, 278
Magdeburg, 109; sack of, 218
Mainz, 73
Manchuria, 25, 76, 114, 116
Manhattan Project, 151, 153–5, 170
Manila, 170
Mannheim, 58, 331
Manning, Bishop William T., 201
Mao Zedong, 213
Marcellinus, 165
Mariana Islands, 76–7
Marshall, General George, 171
Martens, Fedor Fedorovich, 121
Martin, James, 164, 201–2
Mass Observation, 194

'memoricide', 167
Messerschmitt, 65
Metz-Frascaty, 124
Middle East, 49, 132
Mierjewski, Alfred, 111
Milan, 55, 60–1, 266
Milch, Field Marshal Erhard, 40
Mitchell, General William 'Billy', 138, 336–7
Mittelbau-Dora, 98, 334
Mohne dam, 59
Mönchengladbach, 32, 82
Montague, C. E., 203
Montgomery, Field Marshal Sir Bernard, 56, 66, 108
Moran, Lord, 161
Morgenthau, Henry, Jr, 159, 161, 165–6, 168, 176, 338–9
Morgenthau Plan, 159–62, 168, 176, 185, 338
Morris, Stuart, 180
Moscow, 174
Mulheim, 58
Munich, 44, 100, 253
Muraviev, Count Mikhail Nikolaevich, 224
Mussolini, Benito, 60
mutually assured destruction (MAD), 128

Nagasaki, 89, 114, 149, 154–5, 252–3, 260, 271–2; casualty figures, 77–8, 171; as war crime, 115, 233, 335
Nagoya, 77
Nanking, 134, 274
napalm, 89
Nazarius, 165
Nazi leadership, 11, 207, 229, 231
Nazism, 6, 13, 101, 159, 162, 200, 214, 273–4, 280, 338
Neillands, Robin, 264, 269–70
neo-Nazism, 2, 23, 158, 167, 210, 273, 338
Neuengamme, 207
New York City, 137, 333; World Trade Center, 278

Nicholas II, Czar, 121, 223
Niemöller, Martin, 181
Nigata, 153
Nizer, Louis, 163–6
Norden bomb sight, 138–9, 141
Nordhausen, 98
Normandy invasion, 66, 68
North Africa, 55–6, 75, 96, 174, 265
North Sea, 117
Norway, 29–30, 230
Norwich, 51
nuclear weapons, 128–9, 133, 213, 280; see also atomic bombs
Nuremberg, 12–13, 55, 61, 257, 332
Nuremberg trials, 11, 231, 233, 245, 276; see also International Military Tribunal

Oberhausen, 58
OBOE navigational aid, 56, 262
Odenthal, 108
Oe, Kenzaburo, 115
Ofstie, Admiral Ralph, 280
Ohrdruf, 207
Operation Gomorrah, 16–20, 60–1, 95, 99–100, 102, 117, 182, 233, 253; timing of, 89–90, 272; press treatment, 189, 191–2; as moral touchstone, 271–2; element of surprise, 278
Operation Grayling, 12–13
Operation Millennium, 52
Operation Overlord, 66, 265, 332
Operation Sealion, 36, 40
Operation Torch, 174, 265
Orwell, George, 203–5
Osaka, 77
Ostend, 36
Overy, Richard, 174, 257, 259
Oxford University Air Squadron, 25

Palestinian territories, 234
Pape, Robert, 113–14, 132, 136–7, 139
Paterculus, 165
Pathfinder Force, 55–7, 332

Patterson, Robert, 203
Pearl Harbor, 162, 169–70, 253, 277–9
Peenemunde, 61, 266
Peierls, Rudolph, 151
Peirse, Sir Richard, 39, 45, 47–8, 52
perfidy, 278–9
Pinochet, General Augusto, 256
Ploesti, 98
Plymouth, 198
Pointblank directive, 175
Poland, 159, 187, 230
Poles, 98, 213
Poling, Revd Daniel A., 201
Political Warfare Department, 50
Polybius, 219
Pope, Alexander, 182
Port Arthur, 278
Portal, Sir Charles, 39–40, 244, 262; commitment to area bombing, 46–7, 52, 54, 57, 72–4, 156–7, 172–3, 176; recruits Harris, 48–9; confrontations with Harris, 66–7, 70–1, 110, 172, 175
Portsmouth, 198
Potsdam Conference, 252
precision bombing, 12, 67, 138–41, 167, 170, 172, 257, 259, 261; by Americans, 63, 74–6, 107, 142, 177, 250, 254–6, 267; moral preference for, 265–7, 272
prisoners of war, 74, 90, 98, 115, 169–70, 203, 222, 227, 268–9

Qin Shi, 167
Quakers, 179–80
Quebec Conference, 159, 161, 185
Quintilian, 165

racism, 2, 5, 115, 132, 158, 169
radar, 15–16, 27–8, 56, 62, 141
RAF: early history, 24–6, 129, 131–2, 138; and bombing negotiations, 147–8; and post-war policy, 166–7; *see also* Army Co-operation Command; Bomber Command;
Coastal Command; Fighter Command; Training Command
Red Army, 103
Reformation, 217
refugees, 20, 258–60
Regensburg, 65
Reynolds, Quentin, 165
Rhine, River, 35
Rhineland, 31
Rhodesia, 48
Richards, Denis, 51, 68, 100, 265–6
Rochester, 38
Rolls-Royce, 64
Roman Catholicism, 217
Romania, 98, 108
Rome, 196, 199; Republican, 220
Rommel, Field Marshal Erwin, 174
Roosevelt, Eleanor, 203
Roosevelt, Franklin D., 24, 108, 148–9, 174, 268; at Casablanca Conference, 57, 181; and atomic bomb, 150–3; and post-war Germany, 158–62; Congress speech on bombing, 187; rebukes opposition to area bombing, 203; and customary international law, 244
Ross, Stewart, 141
Rostock, 50–2
Rotterdam, 33–6
Rouen, 57
Royal Flying Corps, 49, 129
Royal Naval Air Service, 129
Royal Navy, 28, 67, 125–6, 132–3, 148, 166–7
Ruhr crisis, 24
Ruhr valley, 35, 48, 54, 59, 58–61, 88, 111, 135, 253; 'Battle of the Ruhr', 58, 61, 101; in Morgenthau Plan, 159, 161
Russia: German invasion, 43, 54, 56, 96–7, 230, 261–2; arms control negotiations, 122, 143, 223; military aircraft, 125; atomic weapons development, 150, 152, 154; and use of atom bombs, 152,

252–3, 260; Allied support for, 174–5; and war crimes trials, 229; and Geneva conventions, 234; and Japanese surrender, 252, under Stalin, 256; and total war, 258; fleet attacked in Port Arthur, 278; *see also* Soviet Union
Russians, 98
Rwanda, 234

Saar valley, 161
St Augustine, 211
St Paul's Cathedral, 49, 331
St Petersburg Declaration, 122–4
St Thomas Aquinas, 211–12, 226, 250
Saipan, 76
Salisbury, Lord, 119, 182
Sallust, 220
Salmond, Sir John, 147
Sarajevo, 167
Savoy, 129
Schaffer, Ronald, 169–70, 252
Scharnhorst, 30
Scharroo, Colonel Pieter Willem, 33
Schellig roads, 27
Schmidt, Anne-Lies, 87
Schmidt, General Rudolf, 33–4
Schmitt, Bernadotte, 162
Schneider Trophy, 26
Schumacher, Lieutenant-Colonel Carl, 29
Schweinfurt, 64–5, 75
Sebald, W. G., 18, 84, 157–8
Second World War: survivors, 2; casualty figures, 5–6, 257; relative situation, 21–2, 89–90, 261–4, 272; 'phoney war', 30–1; relative crimes, 115–16; as just war, 179, 210; and Hague IV, 226; retrospective judgements on, 237, 242, 269, 271–81; as total war, 257–8; victor nations, 264–5
Sedan, 32
Seneca, 165
Shaw, George Bernard, 185, 195

Shidlovski, Major-General M. V., 125
Shinwell, Emmanuel, 197
Shirer, William, 165, 202–3
Sicily, 57
Siegfried Line, 31
Sikorsky, Igor, 125
Silesia, 98, 111
Sinclair, Sir Archibald, 119, 188–90, 196–7
Sino-Japanese War, 123
Skagerrak, 29
Soper dam, 59
Sorensen, Reginald, 182
South Africa, 121
Southwark, 193
Soviet Union, 73, 98, 103, 159, 257; forces, 68, 72, 111, 160, 230, 260; attack on Manchuria, 114; and Geneva conventions, 235
Spaatz, Major-General Carl 'Tooey', 74, 170, 252
Spain, 121, 134
Spanish Civil War, 35, 120
Spanish-American War, 121
Speer, Albert, 70, 96–7, 99–101, 109, 111–12, 257, 259
Stalin, Joseph, 173–4, 256
Stalingrad, 269
Stimson, Henry, 152–4, 159, 161–2, 168, 175, 252, 260, 274
Stockholm, 181
Stokes, Richard, 182, 196
Stout, Rex, 164–5
Streicher, Julius, 164
Stuttgart, 58, 65, 100
Sun Tzu, 221
Sweden, 51
Szilard, Leo, 149–50, 153–4

Tacitus, 165, 219
tactical bombing, 65–9, 105–8, 169
Taylor, Frederick, 258–9
Temple, William, 181, 196, 340
Terraine, John, 264, 335
terrorism, 2, 149, 278–9
Thames, River, 38

The Hague, 33, 121, 123, 142–3, 223

Thirty Years War, 217

Thompson, Dorothy, 202

Thomson, G. P., 151

Thucydides, 219

Tibet, 234

Tinian, 76

Tirpitz, 266

Tobruk, 174

Todt, Fritz, 96

Tokyo, 77–8, 90, 93, 142, 171, 233, 253, 263, 272; casualty figures, 77, 92, 333; as seat of government, 153

Training Command, 20–1, 52

Trenchard, Sir Hugh, 24–5, 129, 131–3, 135

Tromsø, 266

Truman, Harry S., 153–6, 244, 252

'tu quoque' defence, 230–1

Turin, 55, 60, 266

Turks, 124, 129

U-boats, 45, 51, 99, 261–2, 265, 272

Ukraine, 98

unconditional surrender, 69, 181, 213, 263

United Nations, 234; Universal Declaration of Human Rights, 276

United States Air Force, 140, 171, 275

United States Army Air Force (USAAF): bombing policy, 12, 21, 63, 73–4, 76, 120, 138–42, 167–70, 177; formation tactics, 29, 74–5; decisiveness of Japanese campaign, 114; repugnance for Japanese, 170; arrives in Europe, 262

United States Eighth Army Air Force, 61, 72, 95, 99, 206; losses, 17, 57, 63–4; precision bombing, 63, 74–6, 107, 142, 177, 250, 254–5, 267; role in Combined Bomber

Offensive, 65, 68; aircraft numbers, 68; and Dresden bombing, 78; civilian casualty figures, 104; efforts against oil targets, 110

United States Fifteenth Army Air Force, 107, 110, 142, 177

United States of America, 45, 49, 69, 113, 116, 257–8, 260–1; enters war, 43, 248, 262; shock at Dresden bombing, 72; and Spanish-American War, 121; in First World War, 125, 131; air-power theory, 130, 135–42; economy in 1930s, 139; attitudes to area bombing, 139, 200–3, 207; arms control negotiations, 143, 147; atomic weapons development, 150–4; responses to atom bombs, 155–6, 207; anti-German sentiment, 164; and war crimes trials, 229; and Geneva conventions, 234, 237, 241, 274–6; defence of bombing policy, 247; response to Pearl Harbor, 253, 277–8; treatment of prisoners, 268

US Army, 138–40; Ordnance Corps, 141

US Navy, 138–9, 275, 280

US Strategic Bombing Survey (European War), 91–2, 97, 100, 103–4, 110–11

US Strategic Bombing Survey (Pacific theatre), 77–8, 91–2, 114, 280

Vansittart, Lord, 164–5, 339

Vassiltchkov, Marie, 102, 334

Vaux airfield, 31

Versailles, Treaty of, 143, 146, 160, 229

Vienna, 108; Congress of, 26

Vietnam War, 171

Vistula, River, 111

Volkssturm, 97, 106

Voltaire, 221

Vonnegut, Kurt, 90

V-weapons, 98, 106, 206, 266, 272

Walker, Kenneth, 136
Walker, Ronald, 191
Wallis, Barnes, 59, 330
Wangerooge, 15, 28
war: just war theory, 7–8, 179, 210–
    14, 217, 265, 272, 279, 342; laws
    of, 216–29, 234–5, 244–5;
    restraint in, 221–2, 227; total, 228,
    244, 257–8, 343; morality in,
    269–70
War Cabinet, 32, 88; and bombing
    policy, 22, 57, 60, 62–3, 171, 200;
    response to Rotterdam bombing,
    35; response to accidental London
    bombing, 38; and Coventry raid,
    43; support for Bomber Command,
    47
war crimes, 222, 229, 231–2, 245,
    273; atom bomb attacks as, 115,
    233, 335; see also crimes against
    humanity
War Writers Board, 164
Warsaw, 35, 149
Wehrmacht, 31, 33, 96, 99, 108,
    159, 169
Wells, H. G., 339
Wesseling, 68

West Germany, 168
Wheeler, Senator Burton, 337
White, Harry Dexter, 338
Wilhelm II, Kaiser, 163–4
Wilhelmina, Queen, 121
Wilhelmshaven, 24, 27–8, 50
Wilson, Woodrow, 143
Winchell, Walter, 165
Winder, General John H., 223
Window, 16, 19
Wirz, Captain Henry, 222–3, 230
Witt, Rolf, 85
Worms, 73
Wuppertal, 58, 60
Würzburg, 73, 142, 168, 233, 272,
    333, 337

XXI Bomber Command, 141–2

Yalta Conference, 175
Yokohama, 92
York, 51–2
Yugoslavia, 230, 242

Zeitz, 109
Zeppelins, 35, 49, 124–7
Zuckermann, Professor Solly, 66

A NOTE ON THE TYPE

The text of this book is set Adobe Garamond. It is one of several versions of Garamond based on the designs of Claude Garamond. It is thought that Garamond based his font on Bembo, cut in 1495 by Francesco Griffo in collaboration with the Italian printer Aldus Manutius. Garamond types were first used in books printed in Paris around 1532. Many of the present-day versions of this type are based on the *Typi Academiae* of Jean Jannon cut in Sedan in 1615.

Claude Garamond was born in Paris in 1480. He learned how to cut type from his father and by the age of fifteen he was able to fashion steel punches the size of a pica with great precision. At the age of sixty he was commissioned by King Francis I to design a Greek alphabet, for this he was given the honourable title of royal type founder. He died in 1561.

- Updated discussion of organizational use of competency information
- Discussion of employee preferences for job rewards based on new surveys
- Updated discussion of job relatedness based on recent court cases

Chapter Five: External Recruitment

- New learning objectives and introduction
- Increased discussion of the role of applicant tracking systems as a means of gathering staffing metrics
- Updated discussion regarding social networks like Twitter and Facebook in recruiting
- Revised coverage of several recruiting sources
- Enhanced discussion of the advantages of increasing age-related diversity
- New section covering word of mouth as a source of information about job openings
- Enhanced coverage of richness and credibility in persuasive messages
- Discussion of the legal implications of electronic recruitment

Chapter Six: Internal Recruitment

- New learning objectives and introduction
- Increased discussion of the organizational justice implications of mobility policies
- Increased coverage of talent management systems
- Updated discussion of the use of formal requisitions in the internal staffing process
- New example of an organization's use of talent management systems
- New exhibit covering the advantages of open vs. closed systems for internal recruitment
- Updated discussion of the use of information technology in communicating with employees

Chapter Seven: Measurement

- New learning objectives and introduction
- Updated discussion of validity generalization and its meaning in the staffing process
- Updated discussion of web-based selection methods
- New discussion of computer adaptive testing

Chapter Eight: External Selection I

- New learning objectives and introduction
- Updated discussion of educational requirements in selection
- Revised section on biodata
- Enhanced discussion of applicant reactions to selection procedures
- Updated coverage of background checks, including their limitations, and discussion of credit checks in the selection process
- New section on video and computer interviews

Chapter Nine: External Selection II

- New learning objectives and introduction
- Substantially revised material on personality tests, including updated material on social desirability and faking and new coverage of facets of personality
- Revised section on ability tests, including new material on their limitations and an updated example of cognitive ability testing in the NFL
- New section on emotional intelligence tests
- New exhibit on emotional intelligence test items
- Revised and updated material on situational judgment tests
- Revised material on interest inventories
- New coverage of self-presentation issues in interviews
- New material related to the selection and training of interviewers

Chapter Ten: Internal Selection

- New learning objectives and introduction
- Enhanced discussion of talent management and succession systems
- New discussion of the importance of experience
- Updated discussion of assessment centers

Chapter Eleven: Decision Making

- New learning objectives and introduction
- New coverage of applicant reactions in the decision-making process
- Enhanced exhibit describing how to determine assessment scores
- New discussion of companies that are in perpetual hiring cycles
- Examples of organizations using computer-based decision aids for staffing
- Updated discussion of the use of multiple-hurdle selection systems
- New material related to employee reactions to perceived overqualification

Chapter Twelve: Final Match

- New learning objectives and introduction
- Updated references on employment contracts
- New discussion of e-mail in contracts
- New material on job offer content
- Updated examples of formulating and presenting the job offer
- Review of the research on how to negotiate effectively
- Revised material on timing of job offers
- New example of reneging on job offers
- New example of organizational socialization practices
- New material on immigration E-Verify requirements

Chapter Thirteen: Staffing System Management

- New learning objectives and introduction
- New examples of organizational arrangements
- Updated discussion of the role of information technology
- Discussion of the use of social network applications for information sharing
- Updated discussion of outsourcing staffing systems
- New examples of organizational learning from HRISs
- New information on record keeping with Internet and mobile device applicants

Chapter Fourteen: Retention Management

- New learning objectives and introduction
- New research references related to voluntary turnover
- Updated data related to job openings and labor turnover covering the "great recession"
- Updated discussion of exit interviews
- New discussion of employee engagement
- New material on the organization-level research on turnover
- New material covering individual dispositions in the turnover process
- Updated charts reflecting organizational practices to cut staffing costs and avoid layoffs
- Expanded coverage of layoffs and downsizing

In preparing this edition, we have benefited greatly from the critiques and suggestions of numerous people whose assistance was invaluable. They helped us identify new topics, as well as clarify, rearrange, and delete material. We extend our many thanks to the following individuals:

- Amy Banta, Franklin University
- Fred Dorn, University of Mississippi
- Hank Findley, Troy University
- Diane Hagan, Ohio Business College
- Mark Lengnick-Hall, University of Texas–San Antonio

We wish to extend a special note of thanks to the McGraw-Hill/Irwin publishing team—in particular, John Weimeister, Laura Spell, and Susanne Riedell—for their hard work and continued support of the number one staffing textbook in the market. Thanks also to the staff at Kinetic Publishing Services, LLC, for their dedicated work in this collaborative undertaking. Finally, we wish to thank you—the students and faculty who use the book. If there is anything we can do to improve your experience with *Staffing Organizations*, please contact us. We would be happy to hear from you.

CONTENTS

PART ONE

The Nature of Staffing   3

CHAPTER ONE
Staffing Models and Strategy   5
Learning Objectives and Introduction   6
  Learning Objectives   6
  Introduction   6
The Nature of Staffing   7
  The Big Picture   7
  Definition of Staffing   8
  Implications of Definition   8
  Staffing System Examples   12
Staffing Models   14
  Staffing Quantity: Levels   14
  Staffing Quality: Person/Job Match   15
  *Staffing Quality: Person/Organization
    Match   17*
  Staffing System Components   19
  Staffing Organizations   21
Staffing Strategy   25
  Staffing Levels   25
  Staffing Quality   30
Staffing Ethics   31
Plan for the Book   34
Summary   35
Discussion Questions   36
Ethical Issues   37

Applications   37
  Staffing for Your Own Job   37
  Staffing Strategy for a New Plant   38
Tanglewood Stores Case   40
  The Situation   40
  Your Tasks   40
Endnotes   40

PART TWO

Support Activities   43

CHAPTER TWO
Legal Compliance   45
Learning Objectives and Introduction   47
  Learning Objectives   47
  Introduction   47
The Employment Relationship   48
  Employer–Employee   48
  Independent Contractors   50
  Temporary Employees   50
Laws and Regulations   51
  Need for Laws and Regulations   52
  Sources of Laws and Regulations   53
EEO/AA Laws: General Provisions and
    Enforcement   54
  General Provisions   55

Enforcement: EEOC   57
Enforcement: OFCCP   64
EEO/AA Laws: Specific Staffing
    Provisions   64
Civil Rights Acts (1964, 1991)   64
*Age Discrimination in Employment Act
    (1967)   67*
*Americans With Disabilities Act (1990,
    2008)   68*
*Genetic Information Nondiscrimination Act
    (2008)   72*
Rehabilitation Act (1973)   72
Executive Order 11246 (1965)   73
Other Staffing Laws   73
Federal Laws   73
State and Local Laws   76
Civil Service Laws and Regulations   77
Legal Issues in Remainder of Book   78
Summary   80
Discussion Questions   80
Ethical Issues   81
Applications   81
Age Discrimination in a Promotion?   81
*Disparate Impact: What Do the Statistics
    Mean?   83*
Endnotes   83

CHAPTER THREE
Planning   85
Learning Objectives and Introduction   87
Learning Objectives   87
Introduction   87
External Influences   88
Economic Conditions   88
Labor Markets   89
Technology   94
Labor Unions   95
Human Resource Planning   95
Process and Example   95
Initial Decisions   98
Forecasting HR Requirements   100

Forecasting HR Availabilities   103
Reconciliation and Gaps   112
Staffing Planning   114
Staffing Planning Process   114
Core Workforce   117
Flexible Workforce   120
Outsourcing   123
Diversity Planning   125
*Demography of the American
    Workforce   125*
Business Case for Diversity   126
Planning for Diversity   127
Legal Issues   128
Affirmative Action Plans   128
*Legality of AAPs and Diversity
    Programs   133*
EEO and Temporary Workers   136
Summary   136
Discussion Questions   137
Ethical Issues   138
Applications   138
Markov Analysis and Forecasting   138
*Deciding Whether to Use Flexible
    Staffing   139*
Tanglewood Stores Case   141
The Situation   141
Your Tasks   141
Endnotes   141

CHAPTER FOUR
Job Analysis and Rewards   145
Learning Objectives and Introduction   146
Learning Objectives   146
Introduction   146
Changing Nature of Jobs   147
Job Requirements Job Analysis   149
Overview   149
Job Requirements Matrix   150
*Job Descriptions and Job
    Specifications   162*
*Collecting Job Requirements
    Information   164*

Competency-Based Job Analysis   174
   Nature of Competencies   174
   Collecting Competency Information   178
Job Rewards   179
   Types of Rewards   180
   Employee Value Proposition   180
   Collecting Job Rewards Information   181
Job Analysis for Teams   187
Legal Issues   188
   Job Relatedness and Court Cases   188
   Essential Job Functions   189
Summary   193
Discussion Questions   194
Ethical Issues   194
Applications   194
   Conducting a Job Requirements or Job
     Rewards Job Analysis   194
   Maintaining Job Descriptions   195
Endnotes   196

PART THREE

Staffing Activities: Recruitment   201

CHAPTER FIVE
External Recruitment   203
Learning Objectives and Introduction   205
   Learning Objectives   205
   Introduction   205
Recruitment Planning   206
   Organizational Issues   206
   Administrative Issues   207
   Recruiters   214
Strategy Development   215
   Open Versus Targeted Recruitment   215
   Recruitment Sources   217
   Recruiting Metrics   233
Searching   237
   Communication Message   237
   Communication Medium   242
Applicant Reactions   248

   Reactions to Recruiters   249
   Reactions to the Recruitment Process   249
   Reactions to Diversity Issues   250
Transition to Selection   251
Legal Issues   252
   Definition of a Job Applicant   252
   Affirmative Action Programs   254
   Electronic Recruitment   255
   Job Advertisements   257
   Fraud and Misrepresentation   257
Summary   258
Discussion Questions   259
Ethical Issues   259
Applications   260
   Improving a College Recruitment
     Program   260
   Internet Recruiting   262
Tanglewood Stores Case   263
   The Situation   263
   Your Tasks   263
Endnotes   264

CHAPTER SIX
Internal Recruitment   271
Learning Objectives and Introduction   272
   Learning Objectives   272
   Introduction   272
Recruitment Planning   273
   Organizational Issues   273
   Administrative Issues   278
   Timing   279
Strategy Development   281
   Closed, Open, and Hybrid
     Recruitment   281
   Recruitment Sources   285
   Recruiting Metrics   292
Communication Message and Medium   294
   Communication Message   294
   Communication Medium   295
Applicant Reactions   296
Transition to Selection   296

Legal Issues   297
  *Affirmative Action Programs
    Regulations   297*
  Bona Fide Seniority Systems   298
  The Glass Ceiling   299
Summary   303
Discussion Questions   304
Ethical Issues   305
Applications   305
  *Recruitment in a Changing Internal Labor
    Market   305*
  Succession Planning for a CEO   306
Endnotes   307

PART FOUR

Staffing Activities: Selection   311

CHAPTER SEVEN
Measurement   313
Learning Objectives and Introduction   315
  Learning Objectives   315
  Introduction   315
Importance and Use of Measures   316
Key Concepts   316
  Measurement   317
  Scores   320
  Correlation Between Scores   323
Quality of Measures   327
  Reliability of Measures   328
  Validity of Measures   335
  Validation of Measures in Staffing   337
  Validity Generalization   346
  Staffing Metrics and Benchmarks   348
Collection of Assessment Data   349
  Testing Procedures   350
  Acquisition of Tests and Test Manuals   351
  Professional Standards   352
Legal Issues   353
  Determining Adverse Impact   353

  Standardization   355
  Best Practices   356
Summary   357
Discussion Questions   358
Ethical Issues   358
Applications   359
  *Evaluation of Two New Assessment
    Methods for Selecting Telephone
      Customer Service Representatives   359*
  *Conducting Empirical Validation and
    Adverse Impact Analysis   361*
Tanglewood Stores Case I   364
  The Situation   364
  Your Tasks   364
Tanglewood Stores Case II   365
  Adverse Impact   365
Endnotes   365

CHAPTER EIGHT
External Selection I   369
Learning Objectives and Introduction   370
  Learning Objectives   370
  Introduction   370
Preliminary Issues   370
  The Logic of Prediction   371
  The Nature of Predictors   373
  Development of the Selection Plan   374
  Selection Sequence   376
Initial Assessment Methods   377
  Résumés and Cover Letters   377
  Application Blanks   381
  Biographical Information   388
  Reference and Background Checks   392
  Initial Interview   398
  Choice of Initial Assessment Methods   400
Legal Issues   405
  Disclaimers   405
  Reference Checks   406
  *Background Checks: Credit and
    Criminal   406*
  Preemployment Inquiries   408

Bona Fide Occupational
   Qualifications   410
Summary   416
Discussion Questions   417
Ethical Issues   417
Applications   417
   Reference Reports and Initial Assessment in
      a Start-Up Company   417
   Developing a Lawful Application
      Blank   419
Endnotes   421

CHAPTER NINE
External Selection II   425
Learning Objectives and Introduction   426
   Learning Objectives   426
   Introduction   426
Substantive Assessment Methods   427
   Personality Tests   427
   Ability Tests   434
   Emotional Intelligence Tests   443
   Performance Tests and Work Samples   445
   Situational Judgment Tests   449
   Integrity Tests   452
   Interest, Values, and Preference
      Inventories   455
   Structured Interview   457
   Choice of Substantive Assessment
      Methods   468
Discretionary Assessment Methods   471
Contingent Assessment Methods   472
   Drug Testing   472
   Medical Exams   478
Legal Issues   479
   Uniform Guidelines on Employee Selection
      Procedures   479
   Selection Under the Americans With
      Disabilities Act   481
   Drug Testing   485
Summary   486
Discussion Questions   487

Ethical Issues   487
Applications   487
   Assessment Methods for the Job of Human
      Resources Director   487
   Choosing Among Finalists for the Job of
      Human Resources Director   490
Tanglewood Stores Case   491
   The Situation   491
   Your Tasks   491
Endnotes   492

CHAPTER TEN
Internal Selection   503
Learning Objectives and Introduction   505
   Learning Objectives   505
   Introduction   505
Preliminary Issues   506
   The Logic of Prediction   506
   Types of Predictors   507
   Selection Plan   507
Initial Assessment Methods   508
   Talent Management/Succession
      Systems   508
   Peer Assessments   509
   Self-Assessments   511
   Managerial Sponsorship   512
   Informal Discussions and
      Recommendations   513
   Choice of Initial Assessment Methods   513
Substantive Assessment Methods   515
   Seniority and Experience   515
   Job Knowledge Tests   517
   Performance Appraisal   518
   Promotability Ratings   519
   Assessment Centers   520
   Interview Simulations   526
   Promotion Panels and Review Boards   527
   Choice of Substantive Assessment
      Methods   527
Discretionary Assessment Methods   529

Legal Issues   529
   Uniform Guidelines on Employee Selection
      Procedures   529
   The Glass Ceiling   530
Summary   531
Discussion Questions   532
Ethical Issues   532
Applications   532
   Changing a Promotion System   532
   Promotion From Within at Citrus
      Glen   533
Endnotes   535

PART FIVE

Staffing Activities: Employment   539

CHAPTER ELEVEN
Decision Making   541
Learning Objectives and Introduction   543
   Learning Objectives   543
   Introduction   543
Choice of Assessment Method   544
   Validity Coefficient   544
   Face Validity   545
   Correlation With Other Predictors   545
   Adverse Impact   546
   Utility   546
Determining Assessment Scores   551
   Single Predictor   551
   Multiple Predictors   551
Hiring Standards and Cut Scores   557
   Description of the Process   557
   Consequences of Cut Scores   558
   Methods to Determine Cut Scores   559
   Professional Guidelines   564
Methods of Final Choice   564
   Random Selection   564
   Ranking   565
   Grouping   566
   Ongoing Hiring   566

Decision Makers   566
   Human Resource Professionals   566
   Managers   567
   Employees   568
Legal Issues   568
   Uniform Guidelines on Employee Selection
      Procedures   568
   Diversity and Hiring Decisions   569
Summary   571
Discussion Questions   572
Ethical Issues   572
Applications   572
   Utility Concerns in Choosing an
      Assessment Method   572
   Choosing Entrants Into a Management
      Training Program   573
Tanglewood Stores Case   574
   The Situation   576
   Your Tasks   576
Endnotes   576

CHAPTER TWELVE
Final Match   579
Learning Objectives and Introduction   581
   Learning Objectives   581
   Introduction   581
Employment Contracts   582
   Requirements for an Enforceable
      Contract   582
   Parties to the Contract   583
   Form of the Contract   584
   Disclaimers   586
   Contingencies   587
   Other Employment Contract Sources   588
   Unfulfilled Promises   588
Job Offers   589
   Strategic Approach to Job Offers   589
   Job Offer Content   592
Job Offer Process   602
   Formulation of the Job Offer   604
   Presentation of the Job Offer   609

Timing of the Offer   610
Job Offer Acceptance and Rejection   611
Reneging   612
New Employee Orientation and
 Socialization   613
Orientation   614
Socialization   617
Examples of Programs   619
Legal Issues   620
Employment Eligibility Verification   620
Negligent Hiring   621
Employment-at-Will   622
Summary   622
Discussion Questions   623
Ethical Issues   624
Applications   624
Making a Job Offer   624
*Evaluating a Hiring and Variable Pay
 Plan   626*
Endnotes   627

PART SIX

**Staffing System and Retention
Management   633**

CHAPTER THIRTEEN
Staffing System Management   635
Learning Objectives and Introduction   636
Learning Objectives   636
Introduction   636
Administration of Staffing Systems   637
Organizational Arrangements   637
Jobs in Staffing   641
Policies and Procedures   644
*Human Resource Information
 Systems   648*
Outsourcing   651
Evaluation of Staffing Systems   655
Staffing Process   655
Staffing Process Results   658

Calculating Staffing Metrics   663
Customer Satisfaction   664
Legal Issues   665
Record Keeping and Privacy   665
EEO Report   670
Legal Audits   670
*Training for Managers and
 Employees   670*
Dispute Resolution   672
Summary   674
Discussion Questions   675
Ethical Issues   675
Applications   676
Learning About Jobs in Staffing   676
Evaluating Staffing Process Results   676
Endnotes   678

CHAPTER FOURTEEN
Retention Management   681
Learning Objectives and Introduction   683
Learning Objectives   683
Introduction   683
Turnover and Its Causes   684
Nature of the Problem   684
Types of Turnover   685
Causes of Turnover   687
Analysis of Turnover   689
Measurement   690
Reasons for Leaving   691
Costs and Benefits   694
Retention Initiatives: Voluntary Turnover   702
*Current Practices and Deciding to
 Act   702*
Desirability of Leaving   709
Ease of Leaving   715
Alternatives   716
Retention Initiatives: Discharge   717
Performance Management   717
Progressive Discipline   721
Retention Initiatives: Downsizing   723
*Weighing Advantages and
 Disadvantages   723*

Staffing Levels and Quality   724
Alternatives to Downsizing   725
Employees Who Remain   725
Legal Issues   727
Separation Laws and Regulations   727
Performance Appraisal   728
Summary   728
Discussion Questions   730
Ethical Issues   730

Applications   731
Managerial Turnover: A Problem?   731
Retention: Deciding to Act   732
Tanglewood Stores Case   734
The Situation   734
Your Tasks   735
Endnotes   735

INDEX   741

STAFFING ORGANIZATIONS
Seventh Edition

The Staffing Organizations Model

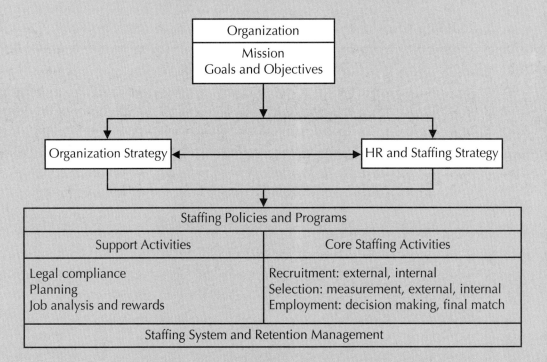

PART ONE

The Nature of Staffing

CHAPTER ONE
Staffing Models and Strategy

CHAPTER ONE

Staffing Models and Strategy

Learning Objectives and Introduction
   Learning Objectives
   Introduction

The Nature of Staffing
   The Big Picture
   Definition of Staffing
   Implications of Definition
   Staffing System Examples

Staffing Models
   Staffing Quantity: Levels
   Staffing Quality: Person/Job Match
   Staffing Quality: Person/Organization Match
   Staffing System Components
   Staffing Organizations

Staffing Strategy
   Staffing Levels
   Staffing Quality

Staffing Ethics

Plan for the Book

Summary

Discussion Questions

Ethical Issues

Applications

Tanglewood Stores Case

LEARNING OBJECTIVES AND INTRODUCTION

Learning Objectives

- Define staffing and consider how, in the big picture, staffing decisions matter
- Review the five staffing models presented, and consider the advantages and disadvantages of each
- Consider the staffing system components and how they fit into the plan for the book
- Understand the staffing organizations model and how its various components fit into the plan for the book
- Appreciate the importance of staffing strategy, and review the 13 decisions that staffing strategy requires
- Realize the importance of ethics in staffing, and learn how ethical staffing practice is established

Introduction

Staffing is a critical organizational function concerned with the acquisition, deployment, and retention of the organization's workforce. As we note in this chapter and throughout the book, staffing is arguably the most critical function underlying organizational effectiveness, because "the people make the place," because labor costs are often the highest organizational cost, and because poor hiring decisions are not easily undone.

This chapter begins with a look at the nature of staffing. This includes a view of the "big picture" of staffing, followed by a formal definition of staffing and the implications of that definition. Examples of staffing systems are given.

Five models are then presented to elaborate on and illustrate various facets of staffing. The first model shows how projected workforce head-count requirements and availabilities are compared to determine the appropriate staffing level for the organization. The next two models illustrate staffing quality, which refers to matching a person's qualifications with the requirements of the job or organization. The person/job match model is the foundation of all staffing activities; the person/organization match model shows how person/job matching could extend to how well the person will also fit with the organization. The core staffing components model identifies recruitment, selection, and employment as the three key staffing activities, and it shows that both the organization and the job applicant interact in these activities. The final model, staffing organizations, provides the entire framework for staffing and the structure of this book. It shows that organizations, human resources (HR), and staffing strategy interact to guide the conduct of staffing support activities (legal compliance, planning, and job analysis) and core staffing activities (recruitment, selection, and employment); employee retention and staffing system management are shown to cut across both types of activities.

Staffing strategy is then explored in detail by identifying and describing a set of 13 strategic staffing decisions that confront any organization. Several of the decisions pertain to staffing levels, and the remainder to staffing quality.

Staffing ethics—the moral principles and guidelines for acceptable practice—is discussed next. Several pointers that help guide ethical staffing conduct are indicated, as are some of the common pressures to ignore these pointers and compromise one's ethical standards. Suggestions for how to handle these pressures are also made.

Finally, the plan for the remainder of the book is presented. The overall structure of the book is shown, along with key features of each chapter.

THE NATURE OF STAFFING

The Big Picture

Organizations are combinations of physical, financial, and human capital. Human capital refers to the knowledge, skill, and ability of people and their motivation to use them successfully on the job. The term "workforce quality" refers to an organization's human capital. The organization's workforce is thus a stock of human capital that it acquires, deploys, and retains in pursuit of organizational outcomes such as profitability, market share, customer satisfaction, and environmental sustainability. Staffing is the organizational function used to build this workforce through such systems as staffing strategy, HR planning, recruitment, selection, employment, and retention.

At the national level, the collective workforces of US organizations total over 115 million (down from a peak of nearly 140 million in 2005), with employees spread across almost 8 million work sites. The work sites vary considerably in size, with 55% of employees in work sites of fewer than 100 employees, 37% in work sites between 100 and 1,000 employees, and 12% in work sites over 1,000 employees.[1] Each of these work sites used some form of a staffing process to acquire its employees. Even during the great recession that began in 2008 and its slow recovery, there were more than 4 million new hire transactions nationally each month, or over 50 million annually. This figure does not include internal transfers, promotions, or the hiring of temporary employees, so the total number of staffing transactions was much greater than the 50 million figure.[2] Volumewise, even in difficult economic times, staffing is big business for both organizations and job seekers.

For most organizations, a workforce is an expensive proposition and cost of doing business. It is estimated that an average organization's employee cost (wages or salaries and benefits) is over 22% of its total revenue (and generally a higher percentage of total costs).[3] The percentage is much greater for organizations in labor-intensive industries—the service-providing as opposed to goods-producing industries—such as retail trade, information, financial services, professional and business services, education, health care, and leisure and hospitality. Since service-providing industries now dominate our economy, matters of employee cost and whether the organization is acquiring a high-quality workforce loom large.

A shift is gradually occurring from viewing employees as just a cost of doing business to valuing employees as human capital that creates competitive advantage for the organization. Organizations that deliver superior customer service, much of which is driven by highly knowledgeable employees with fine-tuned customer service skills, have a definite and hopefully long-term leg up on their competitors. The competitive advantage derived from such human capital has important financial implications.

Organizations are increasingly recognizing the value creation that can occur through staffing. Quotes from several organization leaders attest to this, as shown in Exhibit 1.1.

Definition of Staffing

The following definition of staffing is offered and will be used throughout this book:

> Staffing is the process of acquiring, deploying, and retaining a workforce of sufficient quantity and quality to create positive impacts on the organization's effectiveness.

This straightforward definition contains several implications, which are identified and explained next.

Implications of Definition

Acquire, Deploy, Retain

An organization's staffing system must guide the acquisition, deployment, and retention of its workforce. Acquisition activities involve external staffing systems that govern the initial intake of applicants into the organization. It involves planning for the numbers and types of people needed, establishing job requirements in the form of the qualifications or KSAOs (knowledge, skill, ability, and other characteristics) needed to perform the job effectively, establishing the types of rewards the job will provide, conducting external recruitment campaigns, using selection tools to evaluate the KSAOs that applicants possess, deciding which applicants are the most qualified and will receive job offers, and putting together job offers that applicants will hopefully accept.

Deployment refers to the placement of new hires in the actual jobs they will hold, something that may not be entirely clear at the time of hire, such as the

EXHIBIT 1.1   The Importance of Staffing to Organizational Leaders

"Staffing is absolutely critical to the success of every company. To be competitive in today's economy, companies need the best people to create ideas and execute them for the organization. Without a competent and talented workforce, organizations will stagnate and eventually perish. The right employees are the most important resources of companies today."[4]

Gail Hyland-Savage, chief operating officer
Michaelson, Connor & Bowl—real estate and marketing

"The new economy, very much the Internet and the entrepreneurial opportunities it created, intensified the competition for outstanding people. And we started to grow to a size and scope where it was important for us not only to get outstanding people but also to get them in significant numbers. So the emphasis shifted towards making to people value propositions that were the absolute best they could be."[5]

Rajat Gupta, managing director
McKinsey & Company—consulting

"I think about this in hiring, because our business all comes down to people. . . . In fact, when I'm interviewing a senior job candidate, my biggest worry is how good they are at hiring. I spend at least half the interview on that."[6]

Jeff Bezos, chief executive officer
Amazon.com—Internet merchandising

"We missed a really nice nursing rebound . . . because we just didn't do a good job hiring in front of it. Nothing has cost the business as much as failing to intersect the right people at the right time."[7]

David Alexander, CEO
Soliant Health—health care

"GE's 100-year-plus track record is simply about having the very best people at every single position. That is its No. 1 core competency. No one has better people. No one else's bench strength comes even close. It's that obsession with people that requires all GE leaders to spend a huge amount of their time on human resources processes—recruiting, reviewing, tracking, training, mentoring, succession planning. When I was at GE, I spent over half of my time on people-related issues. When you get the best people, you don't have to worry as much about execution, because they make it happen."[8]

Larry Johnston, chief executive officer
Albertson's—retail grocery

specific work unit or geographic location. Deployment also encompasses guiding the movement of current employees throughout the organization through internal staffing systems that handle promotions, transfers, and new project assignments. Internal staffing systems mimic external staffing systems in many respects, such as planning for promotion and transfer vacancies, establishing job requirements and job rewards, recruiting employees for promotion or transfer opportunities, evaluating employees' qualifications, and making job offers to employees for new positions.

Retention systems seek to manage the inevitable flow of employees out of the organization. Sometimes these outflows are involuntary on the part of the employee, such as through layoffs or the sale of a business unit to another organization. Other outflows are voluntary in that they are initiated by the employee, such as leaving the organization to take another job (a potentially avoidable turnover by the organization) or leaving to follow one's spouse or partner to a new geographic location (a potentially unavoidable turnover). Of course, no organization can or should seek to completely eliminate employee outflows, but it should try to minimize the types of turnover in which valued employees leave for "greener pastures" elsewhere—namely, voluntary-avoidable turnover. Such turnover can be very costly to the organization, as can turnover due to employee discharges and downsizing. Through various retention strategies and tactics, the organization can combat these types of turnover, seeking to retain those employees it thinks it cannot afford to lose.

Staffing as a Process or System

Staffing is not an event, as in, "We hired two people today." Rather, staffing is a process that establishes and governs the flow of people into the organization, within the organization, and out of the organization. Organizations use multiple interconnected systems to manage the people flows. These include planning, recruitment, selection, decision making, job offer, and retention systems. Occurrences or actions in one system inevitably affect other systems. If planning activities show a forecasted increase in vacancies relative to historical standards, for example, the recruitment system will need to gear up for generating more applicants than previously, the selection system will have to handle the increased volume of applicants needing to be evaluated in terms of their KSAOs, decisions about job offer receivers may have to be speeded up, and the job offer packages may have to be sweetened to entice the necessary numbers of needed new hires. Further, steps will have to be taken to retain the new hires and thus avoid having to repeat the above experiences in the next staffing cycle.

Quantity and Quality

Staffing the organization requires attention to both the numbers (quantity) and the types (quality) of people brought into, moved within, and retained by the organization. The quantity element refers to having enough people to conduct business, and the quality element refers to having people with the requisite KSAOs so that jobs are performed effectively. It is important to recognize that it is the combination of sufficient quantity and quality of labor that creates a maximally effective staffing system.

Organization Effectiveness

Staffing systems exist and should be used to contribute to the attainment of organizational goals such as survival, profitability, and growth. A macro view of staffing like this is often lost or ignored because most of the day-to-day operations of staffing systems involve micro activities that are procedural, transactional, and routine in nature. While these micro activities are essential for staffing systems, they must be viewed within the broader macro context of the positive impacts staffing can have on organization effectiveness. There are many indications of this critical role of staffing.

Leadership talent is at a premium, with very large stakes associated with the new leader acquisition. Sometimes new leadership talent is bought and brought from the outside to hopefully execute a reversal of fortune for the organization or a business unit within it. Other organizations acquire new leaders to start new business units or ventures that will feed organization growth. The flip side of leadership acquisition is leadership retention. A looming fear for organizations is the unexpected loss of a key leader, particularly to a competitor. The exiting leader carries a wealth of knowledge and skill out of the organization and leaves a hole that may be hard to fill, especially with someone of equal or higher leadership stature. The leader may also take other key employees along, thus increasing the exit impact.

Organizations recognize that talent hunts and loading up on talent are ways to expand organization value and provide protection from competitors. Such a strategy is particularly effective if the talent is unique and rare in the marketplace, valuable in the anticipated contributions to be made (such as new product creations or design innovations), and difficult for competitors to imitate (such as through training current employees). Talent of this sort can serve as a source of competitive advantage for the organization, hopefully for an extended time period.[9]

Talent acquisition is essential for growth even when it does not have such competitive advantage characteristics. Information technology companies, for example, cannot thrive without talent infusions via staffing. An Internet start-up called edocs, inc., sold Internet bill presentment and payment software. It doubled its employee ranks to over 100 in five months and sought to double that number in another five months. The CEO said this was necessary, or "we won't have the resources we need to keep up the growth and go public. You grow fast or you die."[10] Shortages in the quantity or quality of labor can mean lost business opportunities, scaled-back expansion plans, the inability to provide critical consumer goods and services, and even threats to the organization's survival.

Finally, for individual managers, having sufficient numbers and types of employees on board is necessary for the smooth, efficient operation of their work unit. Employee shortages often require disruptive adjustments, such as job reassignments or overtime for current employees. Underqualified employees present special challenges to the manager, as they need to be trained and closely supervised. Failure of the underqualified to achieve acceptable performance may require termination, a difficult decision to make and implement.

In short, organizations experience and respond to staffing forces and recognize how critical these forces can be to organizational effectiveness. The forces manifest themselves in numerous ways: acquisition of new leaders to change the organization's direction and effectiveness, prevention of key leader losses, use of talent as a source of growth and competitive advantage, shortages of labor—both quantity and quality—that threaten growth and even survival, and the ability of individual managers to effectively run their work units.

Staffing System Examples

Staffing Jobs Without Titles

W. L. Gore & Associates is a Delaware-based organization that specializes in making products derived from fluoropolymers. Gore produces fibers (including dental floss and sewing threads), tubes (used, for example, in heart stents and oil exploration), tapes (including those used in space exploration), and membranes (used in Gore-Tex waterproof clothing).

In its more-than-half-century history, Gore has never lost money. Gore employs over 9,000 workers and appears on nearly every "best place to work" list. What makes Gore so special? Gore associates argue that it's the culture, and the culture starts with the hiring.

Gore has a strong culture, as seen in its structure: a team-based, flat lattice structure that fosters personal initiative. At Gore, no employee can ever command another employee—all commitments are voluntary, and any employee can say no to any request. The employees are called "associates" and managers are called "sponsors." How do people become leaders at Gore? "You get to be a leader if your team asks you to lead them."

Gore extends this egalitarian, entrepreneurial approach to its staffing process. The focal point of Gore's recruiting process is the careers section of its website, *www.gore.com*, which describes its core values and its unique culture. It also provides position descriptions and employee perspectives on working at Gore, complete with pictures of the associates and videos. Three Gore associates—Ron, Henri, and Dave—proudly discuss the protective barrier fabrics that Gore employees developed for firefighters. Sarah, Hannah, and Nitin discuss the work of their team to invent a minimally invasive device to help people born with a serious heart condition known as atrial septal defect, or "hole in the heart."

Gore finds that its employee-focused recruitment efforts don't work for everyone, which is exactly what it intends. "Some of these candidates, or prospects in the fields we were recruiting for, told us 'this company probably isn't for me'," says Steve Shuster, who helped develop the recruitment strategy. Shuster says that this self-selection is another benefit of its recruitment message. Potential recruits who prefer a more traditional culture quickly see that Gore isn't for them. Shuster says, "Rather than have them go through the interview process and invest their time and our time, we wanted to weed that out."

Of course, Gore is a culture that fits many. Says Gore associate Hannah, who works on the heart device team, "I feel like Gore is not just a job, that it's more of a lifestyle and a huge part of my life."[11]

Pharmaceutical Industry Managers

Though Pfizer has been recognized by other pharmaceutical companies as a leader in selecting and developing its employees, it recently realized it needed to dramatically overhaul its approach to staffing. Despite the previous success of its selection efforts, "Pfizer was not focused on managing the external environment," said Pfizer executive Chris Altizer. In the past, according to Altizer, Pfizer would project what kind of talent it would need in the next 10 years and then select employees whose skills matched the talent needs. Pfizer now believes that that plan no longer works, because there is increased global competition, especially from smaller start-up pharmaceutical firms that can rush products to market. That puts a premium on adaptability.

To address changing market conditions, Pfizer now looks at hiring employees who can jump from one position to another. This means that Pfizer focuses less on job descriptions (i.e., hiring for skills that fit a specific job) and more on general competencies that will translate from job to job. According to Altizer, Pfizer needs "a person who can switch from working on a heart disease product to one that helps people stop smoking"—in other words, rather than relying on past experience with one product (say, heart disease medications), Pfizer is looking for competencies that will allow the employee to quickly and proficiently move from one venture to the next.[12]

Direct Sales Representatives

Avon Products, Inc., uses multilevel direct selling of its many cosmetic products to its customers. Avon has 25,000 sales representatives who are part of a sales force Avon calls Leadership. The Leadership program was undertaken to reenergize the sales force and boost sales. The sales representatives are independent contractors, not employees. During the selling process and customer exchanges, the representatives use the opportunity to recruit the customers themselves to become sales representatives. The sales representative receives two biweekly checks: one is for sales commissions, and the other is a commission for recruiting and training new sales representatives. The program has helped increase the number of sales representatives by 3%, sales have grown by 4%, and profits have increased by 20%. Because the sales representatives are increasing the number of recruits they train and manage, Avon has been able to reduce the number of district managers. A remaining problem is turnover among the sales representatives, which runs more than 50% annually. To improve retention, Avon invested $20 million in a series of programs (e.g., training) to help sales representatives increase their sales and thus their desire to remain with Avon.[13]

STAFFING MODELS

Several models depict various elements of staffing. Each of these is presented and described to more fully convey the nature and richness of staffing the organization.

Staffing Quantity: Levels

The quantity or head-count portion of the staffing definition means organizations must be concerned about staffing levels and their adequacy. Exhibit 1.2 shows the basic model. The organization as a whole, as well as each of its units, forecasts workforce quantity requirements (the needed head count) and then compares these with forecasted workforce availabilities (the likely employee head count) to determine its likely staffing level position. If head-count requirements match availabilities, the organization will be fully staffed. If requirements exceed availabilities, the organization will be understaffed, and if availabilities exceed requirements, the organization will be overstaffed.

Making such forecasts to determine appropriate staffing levels and then developing specific plans for coping with them are the essence of planning. Being understaffed means the organization will have to gear up its staffing efforts, starting with accelerated recruitment and carrying on through the rest of the staffing system. It may also require developing retention programs that will slow the outflow of people, thus avoiding costly "turnstile" or "revolving door" staffing. Overstaffing projections signal the need to slow down or even halt recruitment, as well as to take steps to reduce head count, such as shortened workweeks, early retirement plans, or layoffs.

EXHIBIT 1.2   Staffing Quantity

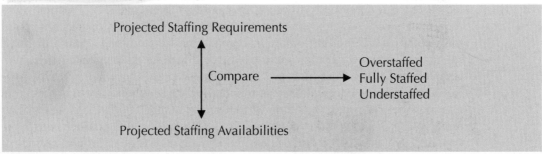

Staffing Quality: Person/Job Match

The person/job match seeks to align characteristics of individuals and jobs in ways that will result in desired HR outcomes. Casual comments made about applicants often reflect awareness of the importance of the person/job match: "Clark just doesn't have the interpersonal skills that it takes to be a good customer service representative." "Mary has exactly the kinds of budgeting experience this job calls for; if we hire her, there won't be any downtime while she learns our systems." "Gary says he was attracted to apply for this job because of its sales commission plan; he says he likes jobs where his pay depends on how well he performs." "Diane was impressed by the amount of challenge and autonomy she will have." "Jack turned down our offer; we gave him our best shot, but he just didn't feel he could handle the long hours and amount of travel the job calls for."

Comments like these raise four important points about the person/job match. First, jobs are characterized by their requirements (e.g., interpersonal skills, previous budgeting experience) and embedded rewards (e.g., commission sales plan, challenge and autonomy). Second, individuals are characterized by their level of qualification (e.g., few interpersonal skills, extensive budgeting experience) and motivation (e.g., need for pay to depend on performance, need for challenge and autonomy). Third, in each of the previous examples the issue was the likely degree of fit or match between the characteristics of the job and the person. Fourth, there are implied consequences for every match. For example, Clark may not perform very well in his interactions with customers; retention might quickly become an issue with Jack.

These points and concepts are shown more formally through the person/job match model in Exhibit 1.3. In this model, the job has certain requirements and rewards associated with it. The person has certain qualifications, referred to as KSAOs, and motivations. There is a need for a match between the person and the job. To the extent that the match is good, it will likely have a positive impact on HR outcomes, particularly attraction of job applicants, job performance, retention, attendance, and satisfaction.

There is actually a need for a dual match to occur: job requirements to KSAOs, and job rewards to individual motivation. In and through staffing activities, there are attempts to ensure both of these. Such attempts collectively involve what will be referred to throughout this book as the matching process.

Several points pertaining to staffing need to be made about the person/job match model. First, the concepts shown in the model are not new.[14] They have been used for decades as the dominant way of thinking about how individuals successfully adapt to their work environments. The view is that the positive interaction of individual and job characteristics creates the most successful match. Thus, a person with a given package of KSAOs is not equally suited to all jobs, because jobs vary in the KSAOs required. Likewise, an individual with a given set of needs or motivations will not be satisfied with all jobs, because jobs differ in the rewards they

EXHIBIT 1.3   Person/Job Match

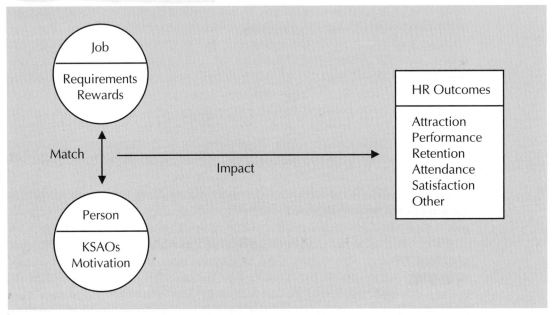

offer. Thus, in staffing, each individual must be assessed relative to the requirements and rewards of the job being filled.

Second, the model emphasizes a dual match of KSAOs to requirements and motivation to rewards. Both matches require attention in staffing. For example, a staffing system may be designed to focus on the KSAOs/requirements match by carefully identifying job requirements and then thoroughly assessing applicants relative to these requirements. While such a staffing system may accurately identify the probable high performers, problems could arise. By ignoring or downplaying the motivation/rewards portion of the match, the organization may have difficulty getting people to accept job offers (an attraction outcome) or having new hires remain with the organization for any length of time (a retention outcome). It does little good to identify the likely high performers if they cannot be induced to accept job offers or to remain with the organization.

Third, job requirements should be expressed in terms of both the tasks involved and the KSAOs needed to perform those tasks. Most of the time, it is difficult to establish meaningful KSAOs for a job without having first identified the job's tasks. KSAOs usually must be derived or inferred from knowledge of the tasks. An exception to this involves very basic or generic KSAOs that are reasonably deemed necessary for most jobs, such as literacy and oral communication skills.

Fourth, job requirements often extend beyond task and KSAO requirements. For example, the job may require punctuality, good attendance, safety toward fellow

employees and customers, and travel. Matching an individual to these requirements must also be considered when staffing the organization. Travel requirements
of the job, for example, may involve assessing applicants' availability for, and
willingness to accept, travel assignments.

Finally, the matching process can yield only so much by way of impacts on the
HR outcomes. The reason for this is that these outcomes are influenced by factors
outside the realm of the person/job match. Retention, for example, depends not
only on how close a match there is between job rewards and individual motivation
but also on the availability of suitable job opportunities in other organizations and
labor markets.

Staffing Quality: Person/Organization Match

Often the organization seeks to determine how well the person matches not only
the job but also the organization. Likewise, applicants often assess how well they
think they will fit into the organization, in addition to how well they match the specific job's requirements and rewards. For both the organization and the applicant,
therefore, there may be a concern with a person/organization match.[15]

Exhibit 1.4 shows this expanded view of the match. The focal point of staffing
is the person/job match, and the job is the bull's-eye of the matching target. Four
other matching concerns involving the broader organization also arise in staffing:
organizational values, new job duties, multiple jobs, and future jobs.

Organizational values are norms of desirable attitudes and behaviors for the
organization's employees. Examples include honesty and integrity, achievement
and hard work, and concern for fellow employees and customers. Though such
values may never appear in writing, such as in a job description, the likely match
of the applicant to them is judged during staffing.

New job duties are tasks that may be added to the target job over time. Organizations desire new hires who will be able to successfully perform these new duties
as they are added. In recognition of this, job descriptions often contain the catchall
phrase "and other duties as assigned." These other duties are usually vague at the
time of hire, and they may never materialize. Nonetheless, the organization would
like to hire people it thinks could perform these new duties. Having such people
will provide the organization the flexibility to complete the new tasks without having to hire additional employees.

Flexibility concerns also enter into the staffing picture in terms of hiring people
who can perform multiple jobs. Small businesses, for example, often desire new
hires who can wear multiple hats, functioning as jacks-of-all-trades. Organizations
experiencing rapid growth may require new employees who can handle several job
assignments, splitting their time among them on an as-needed basis. Such expectations obviously require assessments of person/organization fit.

Future jobs represent forward thinking by the organization and the person as to
which job assignments the person might assume beyond the initial job. Here the

EXHIBIT 1.4   Person/Organization Match

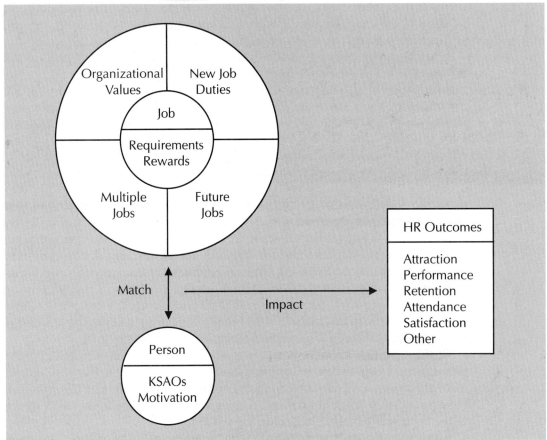

applicant and the organization are thinking of long-term matches over the course of transfers and promotions as the employee becomes increasingly seasoned for the long run. As technology and globalization cause jobs to change at a rapid pace, more organizations are engaging in "opportunistic hiring," where an individual is hired into a newly created job or a job that is an amalgamation of previously distributed tasks. In such cases, person/organization match is more important than person/job match.[16]

In each of the four concerns, the matching process is expanded to consider the requirements and rewards beyond those of the target job as it currently exists. Though the dividing line between person/job and person/organization matching is fuzzy, both types of matches are frequently of concern in staffing. Ideally, the organization's staffing systems focus first and foremost on the person/job match. This will allow the nature of the employment relationship to be specified and agreed to in concrete terms. Once these terms have been established, person/organization match possibilities can be explored during the staffing process. In this book, for simplicity's sake, we will use the term "person/job match" broadly to encompass both types of matches, though most of the time we will be referring to the actual person/job match.

Staffing System Components

As noted, staffing encompasses managing the flows of people into and within the organization, as well as retaining them. The core staffing process has several components that represent steps and activities that occur over the course of these flows. Exhibit 1.5 shows these components and the general sequence in which they occur.

As shown in the exhibit, staffing begins with a joint interaction between the applicant and the organization. The applicant seeks the organization and job opportunities within it, and the organization seeks applicants for job vacancies it has or anticipates having. Both the applicant and the organization are thus "players" in the staffing process from the very beginning, and they remain joint participants throughout the process.

EXHIBIT 1.5   Staffing System Components

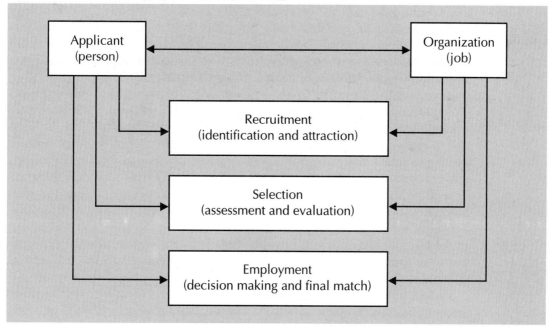

At times, the organization may be the dominant player, such as in aggressive and targeted recruiting for certain types of applicants. At other times, the applicant may be the aggressor, such as when he or she desperately seeks employment with a particular organization and will go to almost any length to land a job with it. Most of the time, the staffing process involves a more balanced and natural interplay between the applicant and the organization.

The initial stage in staffing is recruitment, which involves identification and attraction activities by both the organization and the applicant. The organization seeks to identify and attract individuals so that they become job applicants. Activities such as advertising, job fairs, use of recruiters, preparation and distribution of informational brochures, and "putting out the word" about vacancies among its own employees are undertaken. The applicant identifies organizations with job opportunities by reading advertisements, contacting an employment agency, mass mailing résumés to employers, and so forth. These activities are accompanied by attempts to make one's qualifications (KSAOs and motivation) attractive to organizations, such as by applying in person for a job or preparing a carefully constructed résumé that highlights significant skills and experiences.

Gradually, recruitment activities phase into the selection stage and its accompanying activities. Now, the emphasis is on assessment and evaluation. For the organization, this means the use of various selection techniques (interviews, application blanks, and so on) to assess applicant KSAOs and motivation. Data from these assessments are then evaluated against job requirements to determine the likely degree of person/job match. At the same time, the applicant is assessing and evaluating the job and organization on the bases of the information gathered from organizational representatives (e.g., recruiter, manager with the vacancy, and other employees), written information (e.g., brochures, employee handbook), informal sources (e.g., friends and relatives who are current employees), and visual inspection (e.g., a video presentation, a work site tour). This information, along with a self-assessment of KSAOs and motivation, is evaluated against the applicant's understanding of job requirements and rewards to determine whether a good person/job match is likely.

The last core component of staffing is employment, which involves decision making and final match activities by the organization and the applicant. The organization must decide which applicants to allow to continue in the process and which to reject. This may involve multiple decisions over successive selection steps or hurdles. Some applicants ultimately become finalists for the job. At that point, the organization must decide to whom it will make the job offer, what the content of the offer will be, and how it will be drawn up and presented to the applicant. Upon the applicant's acceptance of the offer, the final match is complete, and the employment relationship is formally established.

For the applicant, the employment stage involves self-selection, a term that refers to deciding whether to continue in the staffing process or drop out. This decision may occur anywhere along the selection process, up to and including the moment of the job offer. If the applicant continues as part of the process through the final match, the applicant has decided to be a finalist. His or her attention now turns to a possible job offer, possible input and negotiation on its content, and making a final decision about the offer. The applicant's final decision is based on overall judgment about the likely suitability of the person/job match.

Note that the above staffing components apply to both external and internal staffing. Though this may seem obvious in the case of external staffing, a brief elaboration may be necessary for internal staffing, where the applicant is a current employee and the organization is the current employer. Job opportunities (vacancies) exist within the organization and are filled through the activities of the internal labor market. Those activities involve recruitment, selection, and employment, with the employer and the employee as joint participants. For example, at the investment banking firm Goldman Sachs, candidates for promotion to partner are identified through a multistep process.[17] They are "recruited" by division heads identifying prospective candidates for promotion (as in many internal staffing decisions, it is assumed that all employees are interested in promotion). Candidates are then vetted on the basis of input from senior managers in the firm and are evaluated from a dossier that contains the candidate's photograph, credentials, and accomplishments. After this six-month process, candidates are recommended for partner to the CEO, who then makes the final decision and offers partnership to those lucky enough to be selected (partners average $7 million a year, plus perks). When candidates accept the offer of partnership, the final match has occurred, and a new employment relationship has been established.

Staffing Organizations

The overall staffing organizations model, which forms the framework for this book, is shown in Exhibit 1.6. It depicts that the organization's mission and its goals and objectives drive both organization strategy and HR and staffing strategy, which interact with each other when they are being formulated. Staffing policies and programs result from such interaction and serve as an overlay to both support activities and core staffing activities. Employee retention and staffing system management concerns cut across these support and core staffing activities. Finally, though not shown in the model, it should be remembered that staffing levels and staffing quality are the key focal points of staffing strategy, policy, and programs. A more thorough examination of the model follows next.

Organization, HR, and Staffing Strategy

Organizations formulate strategy to express an overall purpose or mission and to establish broad goals and objectives that will help the organization fulfill its mission. For example, a newly formed software development organization may have

EXHIBIT 1.6   Staffing Organizations Model

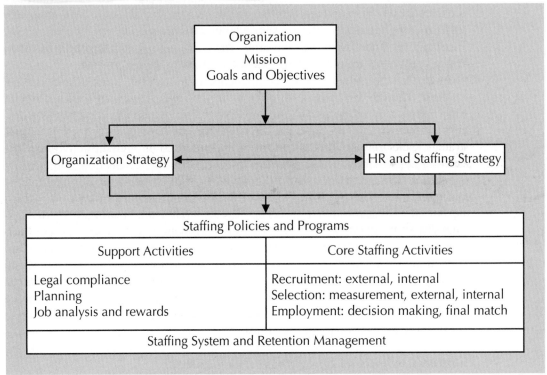

a mission to "help individuals and families manage all of their personal finances and records through electronic means." With this mission statement, the organization might develop goals and objectives pertaining to product development, sales growth, and competitive differentiation through superior product quality and customer service.

Underlying these objectives are certain assumptions about the size and types of workforces that will need to be acquired, trained, managed, rewarded, and retained. HR strategy represents the key decisions about how these workforce assumptions will be handled. Such HR strategy may not only flow from the organization strategy but also may actually contribute directly to the formulation of the organization's strategy.

Consider again the software development organization and its objective pertaining to new product development. Being able to develop new products assumes that sufficient qualified product-development team members are available internally and externally, and that assurances from the HR department about availability may have been critical in helping the organization decide on its product development goals. From this general assumption, HR strategy may suggest (1) obtaining new, experienced employees from other software companies rather than going after newly minted college and graduate school graduates, (2) building a new facility for software development employees in a geographic area that is an attractive place to work, raise families, and pursue leisure activities, (3) developing relocation assistance packages and family-friendly benefits, (4) offering wages and salaries above the market average, plus using hiring bonuses to help lure new employees away from their current employers, (5) creating special training budgets for each employee to use at his or her own discretion for skills enhancement, and (6) putting in place a fast-track promotion system that allows employees to rise upward in either their professional specialty or the managerial ranks. In all these ways, HR strategy seeks to align acquisition and management of the workforce with organization strategy.

Staffing strategy is an outgrowth of the interplay between organization strategy and HR strategy, described above. It deals directly with key decisions regarding the acquisition, deployment, and retention of the organization's workforces. Such decisions guide the development of recruitment, selection, and employment programs. In the software development example, the strategic decision to acquire new employees from the ranks at other organizations may lead the organization to develop very active, personalized, and secret recruiting activities for luring these experienced people away. It may also lead to the development of special selection techniques for assessing job experiences and accomplishments. In such ways, strategic staffing decisions shape the staffing process.

Support Activities

Support activities serve as the foundation and necessary ingredients for the conduct of core staffing activities. Legal compliance represents knowledge of the myriad laws and regulations, especially equal employment opportunity and affirmative action (EEO/AA), and incorporation of their requirements into all phases of the core staffing activities. Planning serves as a tool for first becoming aware of key external influences on staffing, particularly economic conditions, labor markets, and labor unions. Such awareness shapes the formulation of staffing levels—both requirements and availabilities—the results of which drive staffing planning for the core staffing activities. Job analysis represents the key mechanism by which the organization identifies and establishes the KSAO requirements for jobs, as well as the rewards that the jobs will provide, both first steps toward filling projected vacancies through core staffing activities.

Returning to the software development organization, if it meets various size thresholds for coverage (usually 15 or more employees), it must ensure that the staffing systems to be developed comply with all applicable federal, state, and local laws and regulations. Planning activities will revolve around first determining the major types of jobs that will be necessary for the new product development venture, such as computer programmers, Internet specialists, and project managers. For each job, a forecast must be made about the number of employees needed and the likely availability of individuals both externally and internally for the job. Results of such forecasts serve as the key input for developing detailed staffing plans for the core staffing activities. Finally, job analysis will be needed to specify for each job exactly which KSAOs and rewards will be necessary for these sought-after new employees. Once all these support activities are in place, the core staffing activities can begin.

Core Staffing Activities

Core staffing activities focus on recruitment, selection, and employment of the workforce. Since staffing levels have already been established as part of staffing planning, the emphasis shifts to staffing quality to ensure that successful person/ job and person/organization matches will be made. Accomplishment of this end result will require multiple plans, decisions, and activities, ranging from recruitment methods to use, communication with potential applicants with a special recruitment message, recruitment media, types of selection tools, deciding which applicants will receive job offers, and job offer packages. Staffing experts and the hiring manager will be involved in these core staffing activities. Moreover, it is likely that the activities will have to be developed and tailor-made for each type of job.

Consider the job of computer programmer in our software development example. It will be necessary to develop specific plans for such issues as, Will we recruit only online, or will we use other methods such as newspaper ads or job fairs (recruitment methods)? What exactly will we tell applicants about the job and our organization (recruitment message), and how will we deliver the message, such as on our website or in a brochure (recruitment media)? What specific selection tools, such as interviews, assessments of experience, work samples, and background checks, will we use to assess and evaluate the applicants' KSAOs (selection techniques)? How will we combine and evaluate all the information we gather on applicants with these selection tools and then decide which applicants will receive job offers (decision making)? What exactly will we put in the job offer, and what will we be willing to negotiate (employment)?

Staffing and Retention System Management

The various support and core staffing activities are quite complex, and they must be guided, coordinated, controlled, and evaluated. Such is the role of staffing system management. In our new product development example, what will be the role of the HR department, and what types of people will be needed to develop and manage the new staffing systems (administration of staffing systems)? How will we evaluate the results of these systems—will we collect and look at cost-per-hire and time-to-hire data (evaluation of staffing systems)? Data such as these are key effective indicators that both general and staffing managers are attuned to.

Finally, voluntary employee departure from the organization is usually costly and disruptive, and it can involve the loss of critical talent that is difficult to replace. Discharges can also be disruptive. Unless the organization is downsizing, replacements must be found in order to maintain desired staffing levels. The burden for such replacement staffing can be substantial, particularly if the turnover is unanticipated and unplanned. Other things being equal, greater employee retention means less staffing, and thus effective retention programs complement staffing programs.

In our software development organization example, the primary focus will likely be on "staffing up" in order to keep producing existing products and developing new ones. Unless attention is also paid to employee retention, however, maintaining adequate staffing levels and quality may become problematic. Hence, the organization will need to monitor the amount and quality of employees who are leaving, and the reasons they are leaving, in order to learn how much of the turnover is voluntary and avoidable; monitoring discharges will also be necessary. With these data, tailor-made retention strategies and programs to better meet employees' needs can be developed. If these are effective, strains on the staffing system will be lessened.

The remainder of the book is structured around and built on the staffing organizations model shown in Exhibit 1.6.

STAFFING STRATEGY

As noted, staffing strategy requires making key decisions about the acquisition, deployment, and retention of the organization's workforce. Thirteen such decisions are identified and discussed below. Some decisions pertain primarily to staffing levels and others primarily to staffing quality. A summary of the decisions is shown in Exhibit 1.7. While each decision is shown as an either-or, each is more appropriately thought of as lying on a continuum anchored at the ends by these either-or extremes. When discussing the decisions, continued reference is made to the software development organization involved in developing personal finances software.

Staffing Levels

Acquire or Develop Talent

A pure acquisition staffing strategy would have an organization concentrate on acquiring new employees who can "hit the ground running" and be at peak performance the moment they arrive. These employees would bring their talents with them to the job, with little or no need for training or development. A pure development strategy would lead to acquisition of just about anyone who is willing and able to learn the KSAOs required by the job. Staffing strategy must position the organization appropriately along this "buy or make your talent" continuum. For

---

EXHIBIT 1.7   Strategic Staffing Decisions

Staffing Levels
- Acquire or Develop Talent
- Hire Yourself or Outsource
- External or Internal Hiring
- Core or Flexible Workforce
- Hire or Retain
- National or Global
- Attract or Relocate
- Overstaff or Understaff
- Short- or Long-Term Focus

Staffing Quality
- Person/Job or Person/Organization Match
- Specific or General KSAOs
- Exceptional or Acceptable Workforce Quality
- Active or Passive Diversity

---

critical and newly created positions, such as might occur in the software organization example, the emphasis would likely be on acquiring talent because of the urgency of developing new products. There may be no time to train, and qualified internal candidates may not be available.

Hire Yourself or Outsource

Increasingly, organizations are outsourcing their hiring activities, meaning they use outside organizations to recruit and select employees. Although there are variations of staffing outsourcing (we'll have more to say about it in Chapter 3), in some cases, an organization wholly cedes decision-making authority to the vendor. Why might an organization do this? First, it may believe that the vendor can do a better job of identifying candidates than the organization itself can do. This is particularly true for small and midsized companies that lack a professional HR function. Second, in labor shortages, an organization may not be able to recruit enough employees on its own, so it may supplement its recruiting or selection efforts with those of a vendor that specializes in staffing. Finally, outsourcing may also have advantages for legal compliance, as many vendors maintain their own procedures for tracking compliance with equal-opportunity laws.

External or Internal Hiring

When job vacancies occur or new jobs are created, should the organization seek to fill them from the external or internal labor market? While some mixture of external and internal hiring will be necessary in most situations, the relative blend could vary substantially. To the extent that the organization wants to cultivate a stable, committed workforce, it will probably need to emphasize internal hiring. This will allow employees to use the internal labor market as a springboard for launching long-term careers within the organization. External hiring might then be restricted to specific entry-level jobs, as well as newly created ones for which there are no acceptable internal applicants. External hiring might also be necessary when there is rapid organization growth, such that the number of new jobs created outstrips internal supply.

Core or Flexible Workforce

The organization's core workforce is made up of individuals who are viewed (and view themselves) as regular full-time or part-time employees of the organization. They are central to the core goods and services delivered by the organization.

The flexible workforce is composed of more peripheral workers who are used on an as-needed, just-in-time basis. They are not viewed (nor do they view themselves) as regular employees, and legally, most of them are not even employees of the organization. Rather, they are employees of an alternative organization such as a staffing firm (temporary help agency) or independent contractor that provides these workers to the organization. Strategically, the organization must decide whether to use both core and flexible workforces, what the mixture of core versus flexible workers will be, and in what jobs and units of the organization these mixtures will be deployed. Within the software development organization, programmers might be considered part of the core workforce, but ancillary workers (e.g., clerical) may be part of the flexible workforce, particularly since the need for them will depend on the speed and success of new product development.

Hire or Retain

There are trade-offs between hiring strategies and retention strategies for staffing. At one extreme the organization can accept whatever level of turnover occurs and simply hire replacements to fill the vacancies. Alternatively, the organization can seek to minimize turnover so that the need for replacement staffing is held to a minimum. Since both strategies have costs and benefits associated with them, the organization could conduct an analysis to determine these and then strive for an optimal mix of hiring and retention. In this way the organization can control its inflow needs (replacement staffing) by controlling its outflow (retention).

National or Global

As we noted earlier, one form of outsourcing is when organizations outsource staffing activities. Of course, many organizations outsource more than staffing activities—technical support, database management, customer service, and manufacturing are common examples. A growing number of computer-chip makers, such as IBM, Intel, and Motorola, contract with outside vendors to manufacture their chips; often these companies are overseas. Offshoring is related to, but distinct from, outsourcing. Whereas outsourcing is moving a business process (service or manufacturing) to another vendor (whether that vendor is inside or outside the organization's home country), offshoring is the organization setting up its own operations in another country (the organization is not contracting with an outside vendor; rather, it is establishing its own operations in another country). In the computer-chip example, outsourcing would be if the organization, say, IBM, contracted with an outside vendor to manufacture the chips. Offshoring would be if IBM set up its own plant in another country to manufacture the chips.

Increasingly, US organizations are engaged in both overseas outsourcing and offshoring, a trend spurred by three forces. First, most nations have lowered trading and immigration barriers, which has facilitated offshoring and overseas outsourcing. Second, particularly in the United States and Western Europe, organizations find that by outsourcing or offshoring, they can manufacture goods or provide services more cheaply than they can in their own country. Third, some organizations cannot find sufficient talent in their host countries, so they have to look elsewhere. Many high-tech companies in the United States and Western Europe are facing severe talent shortages. Siemens, the German engineering giant, has 2,500 positions for engineers open in Germany alone. These shortages have required many companies like Siemens to outsource overseas, to offshore, or to do both.[18]

Attract or Relocate

Typical staffing strategy is based on the premise that the organization can induce sufficient numbers of qualified people to come to it for employment. Another version of this premise is that it is better (and cheaper) to bring the labor to the organization than to bring the organization to the labor. Some organizations, both established and new ones, challenge this premise and choose locations where there are ample labor supplies. The shift of lumber mills and automobile manufacturing plants to the southern United States reflects such a strategy. Likewise, the growth of high technology pockets such as Silicon Valley reflects the establishment or movement of organizations to geographic areas where there is ready access to highly skilled labor and where employees would like to live, usually locations with research universities nearby to provide the needed graduates for jobs. The software development organization might find locating in such an area very desirable.

Overstaff or Understaff

While most organizations seek to be reasonably fully staffed, some opt for being over- or understaffed. Overstaffing may occur when there are dips in demand for the organization's products or services that the organization chooses to ride out. Organizations may also overstaff in order to stockpile talent, recognizing that the staffing spigot cannot be easily turned on or off. Understaffing may occur when the organization is confronted with chronic labor shortages, such as is the case for nurses in health care facilities. Also, prediction of an economic downturn may lead the organization to understaff in order to avoid future layoffs. Finally, the organization may decide to understaff and adjust staffing level demand spikes by increasing employee overtime or using flexible staffing arrangements such as temporary employees. The software development organization might choose to overstaff in order to retain key employees and to be poised to meet the hopeful surges in demand as its new products are released.

Short- or Long-Term Focus

Although any organization would want to have its staffing needs fully anticipated for both the short term and the long term, optimizing both goals is difficult, so trade-offs are often required. In this case, it often means balancing addressing short-term labor shortages with identifying and developing talent for the long term. When forced to choose, organizations focus on their short-term needs. This is understandable because labor shortages can be debilitating. Even when the overall economy is sluggish, the pool of qualified applicants may be thin. One recruiting expert noted, "The weak labor market has really increased the noise level as more unqualified candidates apply for a decreasing number of job openings."[19] So, even in periods of economic duress, a labor shortage can happen in any industry. When business leaders in the trucking industry were asked to identify their top business concerns, 86% of executives listed the unavailability of drivers as one of their top three concerns.[20]

Balanced against this short-term "crisis management" focus are long-term concerns. Organizations with a long-term view of their staffing needs have put in place talent management programs. In some cases, this means thinking about the strategic talent, or future skill, needs for the entire organization. Bringing to mind John Maynard Keynes's comment, "In the long run we are all dead," the problem with a long-term focus is that long-term needs (demand) and availability (supply) are often unclear. Often, it seems as if calls for an upcoming labor shortage due to baby boomer retirements never end. As Peter Cappelli concludes, "They've been predicting a labor shortage since the mid-1990's and guess what, it's not happening." The Bureau of Labor Statistics (BLS) estimates that by 2018, the total labor force will shrink markedly, causing future labor shortages. However, BLS economist Ian Wyatt admits that whereas population and labor force growth can be forecasted fairly accurately, labor demand estimates are far less reliable. The future demand for workers "is a very tough question to answer," Wyatt said. "Perhaps because of this, while most organizations are aware of projected labor shortages, many fewer have any concrete plans to do anything about it."[21]

These long-term forecasting difficulties notwithstanding, growth *will* occur in some skill areas, while others will decrease in demand. Employers who make no efforts to project future supply and demand risk having their strategies derailed by lack of available labor. As a result of a lack of planning, some companies are facing unanticipated skilled labor shortages. For example, Linda Fillingham cannot find skilled laborers to work in her family's Bloomington, Illinois, steel plant. Fillingham expresses puzzlement as to her labor shortage, given the alleged lack of job growth in manufacturing: "It's there if you want to do it," she says. Perhaps long-term planning would have avoided or ameliorated Fillingham's dilemma.[22]

Staffing Quality

Person/Job or Person/Organization Match

When acquiring and deploying people, should the organization opt for a person/job or person/organization match? This is a complex decision. In part, a person/job match will have to be assessed any time a person is being hired to perform a finite set of tasks. In our software development example, programmers might be hired to do programming in a specific language such as Java, and most certainly the organization would want to assess whether applicants meet this specific job requirement. On the other hand, jobs may be poorly defined and fluid, making a person/job match infeasible and requiring a person/organization match instead. Such jobs are often found in technology and software development organizations.

Specific or General KSAOs

Should the organization acquire people with specific KSAOs or more general ones? The former means focusing on job-specific competencies, often of the job knowledge and technical skill variety. The latter requires a focus on KSAOs that will be applicable across a variety of jobs, both current and future. Examples of such KSAOs include flexibility and adaptability, ability to learn, written and oral communication skills, and algebra/statistics skills. An organization expecting rapid changes in job content and new job creation, such as in the software development example, might position itself closer to the general competencies end of the continuum.

Exceptional or Acceptable Workforce Quality

Strategically, the organization could seek to acquire a workforce that is preeminent KSAO-wise (exceptional quality) or that is more "ballpark" variety KSAO-wise (acceptable quality). Pursuit of the exceptional strategy would allow the organization to stock up on the "best and the brightest" with the hope that this exceptional talent pool would deliver truly superior performance. The acceptable strategy means pursuit of a less high-powered workforce and probably a less expensive one as well. If the software development organization is trying to create clearly innovative and superior products, it will likely opt for the exceptional workforce quality end of the continuum.

Active or Passive Diversity

The labor force is becoming increasingly diverse in terms of demographics, values, and languages. Does the organization want to actively pursue this diversity in the labor market so that its own workforce mirrors it, or does the organization want to more passively let diversity of its workforce happen? Advocates of an active diversity strategy argue that it is legally and morally appropriate and that a diverse workforce allows the organization to be more attuned to the diverse needs of the customers it serves. Those favoring a more passive strategy suggest that diversification of the workforce takes time because it requires substantial planning and assimilation activity. In the software development illustration, an active diversity strategy might be pursued as a way of acquiring workers who can help identify a diverse array of software products that might be received favorably by various segments of the marketplace.

STAFFING ETHICS

Staffing the organization involves a multitude of individuals—hiring managers, staffing professionals, potential coworkers, legal advisors, and job applicants. During the staffing process, all of these individuals may be involved in recruitment, selection, and employment activities, as well as decision making. Are there, or should there be, boundaries on these individuals' actions and decisions? The answer is yes, for without boundaries, potentially negative outcomes and harmful effects may occur. For example, many times staffing is a hurried process, driven by tight deadlines and calls for expediency (e.g., the hiring manager who says to the staffing professional, "Just get me someone now—I'll worry about how good they are later on"). Such calls may lead to negative consequences, including hiring someone without proper assessment and subsequently having him or her perform poorly, ignoring the many applicants who would have been successful performers, failing to advance the organization's workforce diversity initiatives and possible legal obligations, and making an exceedingly generous job offer that provides the highest salary in the work unit, causing dissatisfaction and possible turnover among other work unit members. Such actions and outcomes raise staffing ethics issues.

Ethics involves determining moral principles and guidelines for acceptable practice. Within the realm of the workplace, ethics emphasizes "knowing organizational codes and guidelines and behaving within these boundaries when faced with dilemmas in business or professional work."[23] More specifically, organizational ethics seeks to do the following:

- Raise ethical expectations
- Legitimize dialogue about ethical issues

- Encourage ethical decision making
- Prevent misconduct and provide a basis for enforcement

While organizations are increasingly developing general codes of conduct, it is unknown whether these codes contain specific staffing provisions. Even the general code will likely have some pertinence to staffing through provisions on such issues as legal compliance, confidentiality and disclosure of information, and use of organizational property and assets. Individuals involved in staffing should know and follow their organization's code of ethics. As pertains to staffing specifically, there are several points that can guide a person's ethical conduct. These points are shown in Exhibit 1.8 and elaborated on below.

The first point is that the person is serving as an agent of the organization and is duty bound to represent the organization first and foremost. That duty is to bring into being effective person/job and person/organization matches. The second point indicates that the agent must avoid placing his or her own interest, or that of a third party (such as an applicant or friend), above that of the organization. Point three suggests that even though the HR professional represents the organization, he or she should remember that the applicant is a participant in the staffing process. How the HR professional treats applicants may well lead to reactions by them that are favorable to the organization and further its interests, let alone those of applicants. Point four reminds the HR professional to know the organization's staffing policies and procedures and adhere to them. The fifth point indicates a need to be knowledgeable of the myriad laws and regulations governing staffing, to follow them, and to seek needed assistance in their interpretation and application. Point six guides the HR professional toward professional codes of conduct pertaining to staffing and HR. The Society for Human Resource Management (SHRM) has a formal code of ethics (*www.shrm.org/ethics*). The Society for Industrial and Organizational Psychology (SIOP) follows the ethics code of the American Psychological Association

---

EXHIBIT 1.8   Suggestions for Ethical Staffing Practice

1. Represent the organization's interests.
2. Beware of conflicts of interest.
3. Remember the job applicant.
4. Follow staffing policies and procedures.
5. Know and follow the law.
6. Consult professional codes of conduct.
7. Shape effective practice with research results.
8. Seek ethics advice.
9. Be aware of an organization's ethical climate/culture.

(APA) and has issued a set of professional principles to guide appropriate use of employee selection procedures (*www.siop.org*). The seventh point states that there is considerable useful research-based knowledge about the design and effectiveness of staffing systems and techniques that should guide staffing practice. Much of that research is summarized in usable formats in this book. The eighth point suggests that when confronted with ethical issues, it is appropriate to seek ethical advice from others. Handling troubling ethical issues alone is unwise.

The final point is that one must be aware of an organization's climate and culture for ethical behavior. Organizations differ in their ethical climate/culture,[24] and this has two implications for staffing. First, an organization may have expectations for *how* staffing decisions are made. How an organization communicates with recruits (including those who are rejected) and whether selection decisions are made hierarchically or collaboratively are two examples of ethical staffing issues that may well vary from organization to organization. Second, an organization's ethics climate may well affect *which* staffing decisions are made. An organization that has high expectations for ethics may weight selection information differently (placing more weight on, say, background checks) than an organization with more typical expectations.

In both of these ways, one needs to realize that while some ethics considerations are universal, in other cases, what is considered ethical in one climate may be seen as a breach of ethics in another.

It should be recognized that many pressure points on HR professionals may cause them to compromise the ethical standards discussed above. Research suggests that the principal causes of this pressure are the felt need to follow a boss's directive, meet overly aggressive business objectives, help the organization survive, meet scheduling pressures, be a team player, save jobs, and advance the boss's career.[25]

The suggestions for ethical staffing practice in Exhibit 1.8 are a guide to one's own behavior. Being aware of and consciously attempting to follow these constitute a professional and ethical responsibility. But what about situations in which ethical lapses are suspected or observed in others?

One response to the situation is to do nothing—not report or attempt to change the misconduct. Research suggests a small proportion (about 20%) chooses to ignore and not report misconduct.[26] Major reasons for this response include a belief that no action would be taken, a fear of retaliation from one's boss or senior management, not trusting promises of confidentiality, and a fear of not being seen as a team player. Against such reasons for inaction must be weighed the harm that has, or could, come to the employer, the employee, or the job applicant. Moreover, failure to report the misconduct may well increase the chances that it will be repeated, with continuing harmful consequences. Not reporting misconduct may also conflict with one's personal values and create remorse for not having done the right thing. Finally, a failure to report misconduct may bring penalties to oneself if that failure subsequently becomes known to one's boss or senior management.

In short, "looking the other way" should not be viewed as a safe, wise, or ethical choice.

A different way to handle unethical staffing practices by others is to seek advice from one's boss, senior management, coworkers, legal counsel, ethics officer or ombudsperson, or an outside friend or family member. The guidelines in Exhibit 1.8 can serve as a helpful starting point to frame the discussion and make a decision about what to do.

At times, the appropriate response to others' misconduct is to step in directly to try to prevent or rectify the misconduct. This would be especially appropriate with employees that one supervises or with coworkers. Before taking such an action, it would be wise to consider whether one has the authority and resources to do so, along with the likely support of those other employees or coworkers.

PLAN FOR THE BOOK

The book is divided into six parts:

1. The Nature of Staffing
2. Support Activities
3. Staffing Activities: Recruitment
4. Staffing Activities: Selection
5. Staffing Activities: Employment
6. Staffing System and Retention Management

Each chapter in these six parts begins with a brief topical outline to help the reader quickly discern its general contents. The "meat" of the chapter comes next. A chapter summary then reviews and highlights points from the chapter. A set of discussion questions, ethical issues to discuss, applications (cases and exercises), the Tanglewood Stores case (in some chapters), and detailed endnotes complete the chapter.

The importance of laws and regulations is such that they are considered first in Chapter 2 (Legal Compliance). The laws and regulations, in particular, have become so pervasive that they require special treatment. Therefore, Chapter 2 reviews the basic laws affecting staffing, with an emphasis on the major federal laws and regulations pertaining to EEO/AA matters generally. Specific provisions relevant to staffing are covered in depth. Each subsequent chapter has a separate section labeled "Legal Issues" in which specific legal topics relevant to the chapter's content are discussed. This allows for a more focused discussion of legal issues while not diverting attention from the major thrust of the book.

The endnotes at the end of each chapter are quite extensive. They are drawn from academic, practitioner, and legal sources with the goal of providing a balanced selection of references from each of these sources. Emphasis is on inclusion of recent references of high quality and easy accessibility. Too lengthy a list of references to each specific topic is avoided; instead, a sampling of only the best available is included.

The applications at the end of each chapter are of two varieties. First are cases that describe a particular situation and require analysis and response. The response may be written or oral (such as in class discussion or a group presentation). Second are exercises that entail small projects and require active practice of a particular task. Through these cases and exercises the reader becomes an active participant in the learning process and is able to apply the concepts provided in each chapter.

At the end of some chapters are instructions for completing assignments for the Tanglewood Stores case. The full case and assignments are located at *www. mhhe.com/heneman7e.* Tanglewood Stores is an up-and-coming retailing organization in the Pacific Northwest. Tanglewood is in an expansion mode, seeking to aggressively grow beyond its current 243 stores. As Tanglewood pursues expansion, numerous staffing issues arise that require analysis, decisions, and recommendations from you. You will receive assignments in the areas of staffing strategy (Chapter 1), planning (Chapter 3), external recruitment (Chapter 5), measurement (Chapter 7), external selection (Chapter 9), decision making (Chapter 11), and retention (Chapter 14).

SUMMARY

At the national level, staffing involves a huge number of hiring transactions each year, is a major cost of doing business (especially for service-providing industries), and can lead to substantial revenue and market value growth for the organization. Staffing is defined as "the process of acquiring, deploying, and retaining a workforce of sufficient quantity and quality to create positive impacts on the organization's effectiveness." The definition emphasizes that both staffing levels and labor quality contribute to an organization's effectiveness, and that a concerted set of labor acquisition, deployment, and retention actions guides the flow of people into, within, and out of the organization. Descriptions of three staffing systems help highlight the definition of staffing.

Several models illustrate various elements of staffing. The staffing level model shows how projected labor requirements and availabilities are compared to derive staffing levels that represent being overstaffed, fully staffed, or understaffed. The next two models illustrate staffing quality via the person/job and person/organization match. The former indicates there is a need to match (1) the person's KSAOs to job requirements and (2) the person's motivation to the job's rewards. In the person/organization match, the person's characteristics are matched to additional factors beyond the target job, namely, organizational values, new job duties for the target job, multiple jobs, and future jobs. Effectively managing the matching process results in positive impacts on HR outcomes such as attraction, performance, and retention. The core staffing components model shows that there are three basic activities in staffing: recruitment (identification and attraction of applicants), selection (assessment and evaluation of applicants), and employment (decision making and final match). The staffing organizations model shows that organization, HR, and staffing strategies are formulated and shape staffing policies and programs. In turn, these meld into a set of staffing support activities (legal compliance, planning, and job analysis), as well as the core activities (recruitment, selection, and employment). Retention and staffing system management activities cut across both support and core activities.

Staffing strategy is both an outgrowth of and a contributor to HR and organization strategy. Thirteen important strategic staffing decisions loom for any organization. Some pertain to staffing level choices, and others deal with staffing quality choices.

Staffing ethics involves determining moral principles and guidelines for practice. Numerous suggestions were made for ethical conduct in staffing, and many pressure points for sidestepping such conduct are in operation. There are appropriate ways to handle such pressures.

The staffing organizations model serves as the structural framework for the book. The first part treats staffing models and strategy. The second part treats the support activities of legal compliance, planning, and job analysis. The next three parts treat the core staffing activities of recruitment, selection, and employment. The last section addresses staffing systems and employee retention management. Each chapter has a section labeled "Legal Issues," as well as discussion questions, ethical issues questions, applications, the Tanglewood Stores case (in some chapters), and endnotes.

DISCUSSION QUESTIONS

1. What are potential problems with having a staffing process in which vacancies are filled (1) on a lottery basis from among job applicants, or (2) on a first come–first hired basis among job applicants?

2. Why is it important for the organization to view all components of staffing (recruitment, selection, and employment) from the perspective of the job applicant?

3. Would it be desirable to hire people only according to the person/organization match, ignoring the person/job match?

4. What are examples of how staffing activities are influenced by training activities? Compensation activities?

5. Are some of the 13 strategic staffing decisions more important than others? If so, which ones? Why?

ETHICAL ISSUES

1. As either the staffing professional in the department or the hiring manager of a work unit, explain why it is so important to represent the organization's interests (see Exhibit 1.8). What are some possible consequences of not doing so?

2. One of the strategic staffing choices is whether to pursue workforce diversity actively or passively. First suggest some ethical reasons for active pursuit of diversity, and then suggest some ethical reasons for a more passive approach. Assume that the type of diversity in question is increasing workforce representation of women and ethnic minorities.

APPLICATIONS

Staffing for Your Own Job

Instructions

Consider a job you previously held or your current job. Use the staffing components model to help you think through and describe the staffing process that led to your getting hired for the job. Trace and describe the process (1) from your own perspective as a job applicant and (2) from the organization's perspective. Listed below are some questions to jog your memory. Write your responses to these questions and be prepared to discuss them.

Applicant Perspective

Recruitment:

1. Why did you identify and seek out the job with this organization?
2. How did you try to make yourself attractive to the organization?

Selection:

1. How did you gather information about the job's requirements and rewards?
2. How did you judge your own KSAOs and needs relative to these requirements and rewards?

Employment:

1. Why did you decide to continue on in the staffing process, rather than drop out of it?
2. Why did you decide to accept the job offer? What were the pluses and minuses of the job?

Organization Perspective

Even if you are unsure of the answers to the following questions, try to answer them or guess at them.

Recruitment:

1. How did the organization identify you as a job applicant?
2. How did the organization make the job attractive to you?

Selection:

1. What techniques (application blank, interview, etc.) did the organization use to gather KSAO information about you?
2. How did the organization evaluate this information? What did it see as your strong and weak points, KSAO-wise?

Employment:

1. Why did the organization continue to pursue you as an applicant, rather than reject you from further consideration?
2. What was the job offer process like? Did you receive a verbal or written offer (or both)? Who made the offer? What was the content of the offer?

Reactions to the Staffing Process

Now that you have described the staffing process, what are your reactions to it?

1. What were the strong points or positive features of the process?
2. What were the weak points or negative features of the process?
3. What changes would you like to see made in the process, and why?

Staffing Strategy for a New Plant

Household Consumer Enterprises, Inc. (HCE) has its corporate headquarters in downtown Chicago, with manufacturing and warehouse/distribution facilities throughout the north-central region of the United States. It specializes in the design and production of household products such as brooms, brushes, rakes, kitchen utensils, and garden tools. The organization recently changed its mission from "providing households with safe and sturdy utensils" to "providing households with visually appealing utensils that are safe and sturdy." The new emphasis on "visually appealing" will necessitate new strategies for designing and producing new products that have design flair and imagination built into them. One strategy under consideration is to target various demographic groups with different utensil designs. One group is 25- to 40-year-old professional and managerial people, who it is thought would want such utensils for both their visual and conversation-piece appeal.

A tentative strategy is to build and staff a new plant that will have free rein in the design and production of utensils for this 25–40 age group. To start, the plant will focus on producing a set of closely related (designwise) plastic products: dishwashing pans, outdoor wastebaskets, outdoor plant holders, and watering cans. These items can be produced without too large a capital and facilities investment, can be marketed as a group, and can be on stores' shelves and on HCE's store website in time for Christmas sales.

The facility's design and engineering team has initially decided that each of the four products will be produced on a separate assembly line, though the lines will share common technology and require roughly similar assembly jobs. Following the advice from the HR vice president, Jarimir Zwitski, the key jobs in the plant for staffing purposes will be plant manager, product designer (computer-assisted design), assemblers, and packers/warehouse workers. The initial staffing level for the plant will be 150 employees. Because of the riskiness of the venture and the low margins that are planned initially on the four products due to high start-up costs, the plant will run continuously six days per week (i.e., a 24/6 schedule), with the remaining day reserved for cleaning and maintenance. Pay levels will be at the low end of the market, except for product designers, who will be paid above market. Employees will have limited benefits, namely, health insurance with a 30% employee copay after one year of continuous employment and an earned time-off bank (for holidays, sickness, and vacation) of 160 hours per year. They will not receive a pension plan.

The head of the design team, Maria Dos Santos, and Mr. Zwitski wish to come to you, the corporate manager of staffing, to share their preliminary thinking and ask you some questions, knowing that staffing issues loom large for this new venture. They ask you to discuss the following questions with them, which they have sent to you in advance so you can prepare for the meeting:

1. What geographic location might be best for the plant in terms of attracting sufficient quantity and quality of labor, especially for the key jobs?
2. Should the plant manager come from inside the current managerial ranks or be sought from the outside?
3. Should staffing be based on just the person/job match or also on the person/ organization match?
4. Would it make sense to initially staff the plant with a flexible workforce by using temporary employees and then shift over to a core workforce if it looks like the plant will be successful?
5. In the early stages, should the plant be fully staffed, understaffed, or overstaffed?
6. Will employee retention likely be a problem, and if so, how will this affect the viability of the new plant?

Your task is to write out a tentative response to each question that will be the basis for your discussion at the meeting.

TANGLEWOOD STORES CASE

In this chapter you read about the relationship between organizational strategy and organizational staffing practices. The introductory section of the casebook gives you an opportunity to see how these principles are put into practice. The goal of this section is to help you learn more about how competition, strategy, and culture jointly inform the effective development of staffing strategy.

The Situation

The case involves a series of staffing exercises related to the Tanglewood Department Stores. You will act as an external consultant for the organization's staffing services department. Tanglewood Department Stores is a chain of general retail stores with an "outdoors" theme, including a large camping and outdoor living section in every store. The organization's culture is based on a set of core values that includes employee participation and a commitment to being a positive place to work. The context section provides additional details regarding Tanglewood's industry, core jobs, market niche, and other strategic concerns.

Your Tasks

For each of the issues related to strategic staffing levels and staffing quality in Exhibit 1.7, state where Tanglewood should position itself. For example, the first decision is to either develop or acquire talent. To what extent should Tanglewood follow either strategy and why? Repeat this process for each of the staffing level and staffing quality dimensions. The background information for this case, and your specific assignment, can be found at *www.mhhe.com/heneman7e*.

ENDNOTES

1. A. Sadeghi, J. R. Spletzer, and D. M. Talan, "Business Employment Dynamics: Annual Tabulations," *Monthly Labor Review*, May 2009, pp. 45–56.
2. M. deWolf and K. Klemmer, "Job Openings, Hires, and Separations Fall During the Recession," *Monthly Labor Review*, May 2010, pp. 36–44.
3. Saratoga Institute, *The Saratoga Review* (Santa Clara, CA: author, 2009), p. 10.
4. G. Hyland-Savage, "General Management Perspective on Staffing; The Staffing Commandments," in N. C. Burkholder, P. J. Edwards, Jr., and L. Sartain (eds.), *On Staffing* (Hoboken, NJ: Wiley, 2004), p. 280.
5. J. V. Singh, "McKinsey's Managing Director Rajat Gupta on Leading a Knowledge-Based Global Consulting Organization," *Academy of Management Executive*, 2001, 15(2), p. 35.
6. G. Anders, "Taming the Out-of-Control In-Box," *Wall Street Journal*, Feb. 4, 2000, p. 81.
7. J. McCoy, "Executives' Worst Mistakes in Staffing," *Staffing Industry Review*, Sept. 2010, pp. 1–2.
8. "America's Most Admired: GE," *Fortune*, Mar. 6, 2006, p. 104.
9. J. B. Barney and P. M. Wright, "On Becoming a Strategic Partner: The Role of Human Resources in Gaining Competitive Advantage," *Human Resource Management*, 1998, 37(1), pp. 31–46;

C. G. Brush, P. G. Greene, and M. M. Hart, "From Initial Idea to Unique Advantage: The Entrepreneurial Challenge of Constructing a Resource Base," *Academy of Management Executive*, 2001, 15(1), pp. 64–80.

10. J. S. Lublin, "An E-Company CEO Is Also Recruiter-in-Chief," *Wall Street Journal*, Nov. 9, 1999, p. B1.

11. C. Fleck, "'Not Just a Job,'" *Staffing Management*, 2010, 6(1), (*www.shrm.org*); G. Hamel, "Inventing the Future of Management," Oct. 25, 2010, Ross School of Business, University of Michigan (*www.bus.umich.edu*); "Our Culture," W. L. Gore & Associates, Inc., 2010 (*www.gore.com*).

12. J. Marquez, "A Talent Strategy Overhaul at Pfizer," *Workforce Management*, Feb. 12, 2007, pp. 1, 3.

13. N. Byrnes, "Avon Calling—Lots of Reps," *Business Week*, June 2, 2003, pp. 53–54.

14. D. F. Caldwell and C. A. O'Reilly III, "Measuring Person-Job Fit With a Profile-Comparison Process," *Journal of Applied Psychology*, 1990, 75, pp. 648–657; R. V. Dawis, "Person-Environment Fit and Job Satisfaction," in C. J. Cranny, P. C. Smith, and E. F. Stone (eds.), *Job Satisfaction* (New York: Lexington, 1992), pp. 69–88; R. V. Dawis, L. H. Lofquist, and D. J. Weiss, *A Theory of Work Adjustment (A Revision)* (Minneapolis: Industrial Relations Center, University of Minnesota, 1968).

15. D. E. Bowen, G. E. Ledford, Jr., and B. R. Nathan, "Hiring for the Organization and Not the Job," *Academy of Management Executive*, 1991, 5(4), pp. 35–51; T. A. Judge and R. D. Bretz, Jr., "Effects of Work Values on Job Choice Decisions," *Journal of Applied Psychology*, 1992, 77, pp. 1–11; C. A. O'Reilly III, J. Chatman, and D. F. Caldwell, "People and Organizational Culture: A Profile Comparison Approach to Assessing Person-Organization Fit," *Academy of Management Journal*, 1991, 34, pp. 487–516; A. L. Kristof, "Person-Organization Fit: An Intergrative Review of Its Conceptualizations, Measurement, and Implications," *Personnel Psychology*, 1996, 49, pp. 1–50.

16. L. L. Levesque, "Opportunistic Hiring and Employee Fit," *Human Resource Management*, 2005, 44, pp. 301–317.

17. S. Craig, "Inside Goldman's Secret Rite: The Race to Become Partner," *Wall Street Journal*, Oct. 13, 2006, pp. A1, A11.

18. M. Kessler, "More Chipmakers Outsource Manufacturing," *USA Today*, Nov. 16, 2006, p. B1; C. Dougherty, "Labor Shortage Becoming Acute in Technology," *New York Times*, Mar. 10, 2007, pp. 1, 4.

19. B. Leonard, "Economic Climate Provides Chance to Refine Recruiting Practices," *Staffing Management*, July 14, 2009, (*www.shrm.org*).

20. S. Wisnefski, "Truckers' Worries: Fuel, Driver Short-fall," *Wall Street Journal*, Oct. 25, 2006, p. B3A.

21. K. R. Lewis, "Recession Aside, Are We Headed for a Labor Shortage?" *The Fiscal Times*, Aug. 26, 2010, (*www.thefiscaltimes.com*); K. Gurchiek, "Few Organizations Planning for Talent Shortage as Boomers Retire," *SHRM News*, Nov. 17, 2010, (*www.shrm.org*).

22. C. Bowers, "Skilled Labor Shortage Frustrates Employers," *CBS Evening News*, Aug. 11, 2010, (*www.cbsnews.com/stories/2010/ 08/11/eveningnews/main6764731.shtml?tag=mncol;lst;1*).

23. *www.shrm.org/kc*.

24. A. Ardichvili and D. Jondle, "Ethical Business Cultures: A Literature Review and Implications for HRD," *Human Resource Development Review*, 2009, 8(2), pp. 223–244.

25. J. Joseph and E. Esen, *2003 Business Ethics Survey* (Alexandria, VA: Society for Human Resource Management, 2003), pp. 1–10.

26. Joseph and Esen, *2003 Business Ethics Survey*, pp. 10–11.

The Staffing Organizations Model

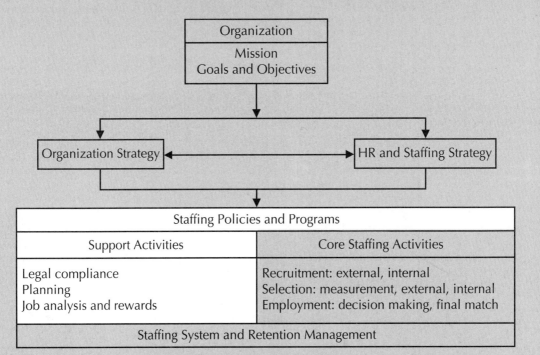

PART TWO

Support Activities

CHAPTER TWO
Legal Compliance

CHAPTER THREE
Planning

CHAPTER FOUR
Job Analysis and Rewards

CHAPTER TWO

Legal Compliance

Learning Objectives and Introduction
    Learning Objectives
    Introduction

The Employment Relationship
    Employer–Employee
    Independent Contractors
    Temporary Employees

Laws and Regulations
    Need for Laws and Regulations
    Sources of Laws and Regulations

EEO/AA Laws: General Provisions and Enforcement
    General Provisions
    Enforcement: EEOC
    Enforcement: OFCCP

EEO/AA Laws: Specific Staffing Provisions
    Civil Rights Acts (1964, 1991)
    Age Discrimination in Employment Act (1967)
    Americans With Disabilities Act (1990, 2008)
    Genetic Information Nondiscrimination Act (2008)
    Rehabilitation Act (1973)
    Executive Order 11246 (1965)

Other Staffing Laws
    Federal Laws
    State and Local Laws
    Civil Service Laws and Regulations

Legal Issues in Remainder of Book

Summary

Discussion Questions

Ethical Issues

Applications

LEARNING OBJECTIVES AND INTRODUCTION

Learning Objectives

- Contrast legal differences among employees, independent contractors, and temporary employees
- Appreciate why staffing laws are necessary, and their sources
- Review six major federal equal employment opportunity and affirmative action laws
- Distinguish between disparate treatment and adverse (disparate) impact approaches to enforcement
- Examine specific staffing provisions of the six major laws
- Look at other important staffing laws and regulations
- Gain an overview of legal issues covered in Chapters 3–14

Introduction

When the organization acquires people to do work for it, a legal employment relationship is established. The acquired people may be employees, independent contractors, or temporary employees. Laws are needed to define how the employer may use each type, as well as the rights of each type. In addition, laws have been developed to create fairness and nondiscrimination in staffing. The laws and accompanying regulations prohibit discrimination on the basis of many protected characteristics, such as race, sex, and disability. Actions based on these characteristics must be removed from staffing practices and decisions. Instead, employers must focus on job-related KSAOs (knowledge, skill, ability, and other characteristics) as the bases for those practices and decisions. Employers that ignore or side-step these laws and regulations could potentially face stiff penalties.

This chapter begins by discussing the formation of the employment relationship from a legal perspective. It first defines what an employer is, along with the rights and obligations of being an employer. The employer may acquire people to work for it in the form of employees, independent contractors, and temporary employees. Legal meanings and implications for each of these terms are provided.

The employment relationship has become increasingly regulated, and reasons for the myriad laws and regulations affecting the employment relationship are suggested. Next, the major sources of the laws and regulations controlling the employment relationship are indicated.

Equal employment opportunity and affirmative action (EEO/AA) laws and regulations have become paramount in the eyes of many who are concerned with staffing organizations. The general provisions of six major EEO/AA laws are summarized, along with indications of how these laws are administered and enforced. While voluntary compliance is preferred by the enforcement agencies, if it fails, litigation may follow. Litigation is based on the key concepts of disparate treatment and disparate impact.

For these same six laws, their specific (and numerous) provisions regarding staffing are then presented in detail. Within this presentation the true scope, complexity, and impact of the laws regarding staffing become known.

Attention then turns to other staffing laws and regulations. These include myriad federal laws, state and local laws, and civil service laws and regulations. These laws, like federal EEO/AA laws, have major impacts on staffing activities.

Finally, the chapter concludes with a discussion of the "Legal Issues" section that appears at the end of each of the remaining chapters. In these sections, specific topics and applications of the law are presented. Their intent is to provide guidance and examples (not legal advice, per se) regarding staffing practices that are permissible, impermissible, and required.

THE EMPLOYMENT RELATIONSHIP

From a legal perspective, the term "staffing" refers to formation of the employment relationship. That relationship involves several types of arrangements between the organization and those who provide work for it. These arrangements have special and reasonably separate legal meanings. This section explores those arrangements: employer–employee, independent contractor, and temporary employee.[1]

Employer–Employee

By far the most prevalent form of the employment relationship is that of employer–employee. This arrangement is the result of the organization's usual staffing activities—a culmination of the person/job matching process. As shown in Exhibit 2.1, the employer and employee negotiate and agree on the terms and conditions that will define and govern their relationship. The formal agreement represents an employment contract, the terms and conditions of which represent the promises and expectations of the parties (job requirements and rewards, and KSAOs and motivation). Over time, the initial contract may be modified due to changes in requirements or rewards of the current job, or employee transfer or promotion. Either party may terminate the contract, thus ending the employment relationship.

Employment contracts come in a variety of styles. They may be written or oral (both types are legally enforceable), and their specificity varies from extensive to bare bones. In some instances where the contract is written, terms and conditions are described in great detail. Examples of such contracts are collective bargaining agreements and contracts for professional athletes, entertainers, and upper-level executives. At the other extreme, the contract may be little more than some simple oral promises about the job, such as certain wages and hours, agreed to with a handshake.

EXHIBIT 2.1   Matching Process, Employment Contract, and Employment Relationship

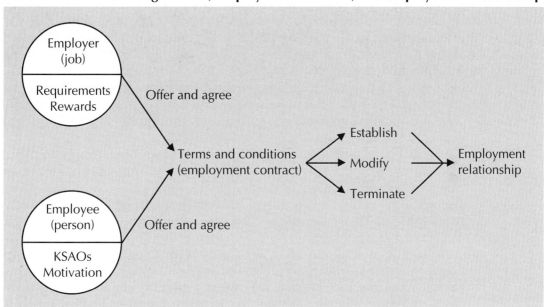

From a legal perspective, an employer is an entity that employs others (employees or independent contractors) to do its work or work in its behalf. When these "others" are employees, the employer has the right to specify both the work output (results) expected and the work methods to be followed. In exchange for this right to control employees, the employer incurs certain legal responsibilities and liabilities. Specifically, the employer is (1) required to withhold employee payroll taxes (income, Social Security), (2) required to pay taxes (unemployment compensation, employer's share of Social Security and Medicare), (3) covered under the myriad laws and regulations governing the employment relationship, and (4) liable for the acts of its employees during employment.

When and how the employment relationship ends is very important to the employer and the employee. For the employer, it bears on the degree of staffing flexibility possible to quickly terminate employees without constraint. For employees, the issue is the degree of continued employment and job security that will be expected. Under the common-law principle of employment-at-will, in the absence of any contract language to the contrary, the employment relationship is strictly an at-will one, meaning that either the employer or the employee may terminate the employment relationship at any time, for any reason, without prior notification. Restrictions on the employment-at-will right are usually established as part of the employment contract (such as termination for "just cause" only); other restrictions come from federal, state, and local laws (such as nondiscrimination in termination).[2]

Independent Contractors

As part of its staffing plan, the employer may hire independent contractors.[3] An independent contractor is not legally considered an employee, however. Therefore, the rights and responsibilities the employer has toward the independent contractor are different from those for its employees. Classifying and using a person as an independent contractor frees the employer of the tax withholding, tax payment, and benefits obligations it has for employees. It may also reduce employer exposure under laws and regulations governing the employment relationship, such as nondiscrimination (e.g., Civil Rights Act) and wage and hour laws.

In exchange for these advantages of using independent contractors, the employer substantially loses the right to control the contractor. In particular, while the employer can still control expected results, the employer cannot dictate where, when, or how work is to be done. Thus, the employer loses control over the means (work processes, tools, equipment, work schedules, and so forth) by which the work is performed.

Beyond this crucial distinction, the line of demarcation between what constitutes an employee and what constitutes an independent contractor is often fuzzy. Numerous other factors come into play. For example, a person is more likely to be considered an independent contractor than an employee in the following situations:

- Working in a distinct occupation or business
- Working without supervision or oversight from the employer
- Paying one's own business and travel expenses
- Setting one's own work hours
- Possessing a high degree of skill
- Using one's own tools, materials, and office
- Working on a project with a definite completion date
- Working on relatively short projects
- Being paid by the project or commission rather than by the time spent

These examples are based on common-law interpretations and on a list of 11 criteria used by the Internal Revenue Service (IRS) to classify people as employees or independent contractors. Misclassifying people as independent contractors can result in substantial tax liabilities and fines for the employer. The IRS has stepped up its audit of employers to combat a trend of classifying people as independent contractors in order to gain staffing flexibility and save on labor costs.[4]

Temporary Employees

Temporary employees do not have special legal stature. They are considered employees of the temporary help agency (staffing firm) that obtained them through its own staffing process. Temporary employees are given job assignments with other employers (clients) by the staffing firm. During these assignments the temporary employee remains on the payroll of the staffing firm, and the client employer simply reimburses the staffing firm for its wage and other costs. The client employer has a severely limited right to control temporary employees that it utilizes, because they are not its employees but employees of the staffing firm.

Use of temporary employees often raises issues of coemployment, in which the client employer and the staffing firm share the traditional role of employer.[5] Because both function as employers to an extent, their obligations and liabilities under various laws need to be sorted out. The Equal Employment Opportunity Commission (EEOC) provides guidance on coverage and responsibility requirements for staffing firms and their client organizations.[6] When both the firm and the client exercise control over the temporary employee and both have the requisite number of employees, they are considered employers and jointly liable under the Civil Rights Act, the Age Discrimination in Employment Act (ADEA), and the Equal Pay Act. The firm must make referrals and job assignments in a nondiscriminating manner, and the client may not set discriminatory job referral and job assignment criteria. The client must treat the temporary employees in a nondiscriminatory manner; if the firm knows this is not happening, it must take any corrective actions within its control. There are substantial penalties for noncompliance. There is a special guidance for issues related to the Americans With Disabilities Act (ADA).

The demarcation between an employee and a temporary employee becomes increasingly blurred when an employer uses a set of temporary employees from a staffing firm on a long-term basis, resulting in so-called permatemps. Nationally, 29% of such employees work for the same client employer for a year or more, so they appear more like employees of the client than of the staffing firm. Which are they? Court cases suggest that these individuals are in fact employees of the client employer rather than of the staffing firm, particularly because of the strong degree of control the client employer typically exercises over those people. Hence, to help ensure that permatemps will not be legally considered the client's employees, the client must give up, or never exercise, direct control over these people and treat them as truly separate from regular employees. This may require, for example, not training or supervising them, not listing them in the phone directory, and not allowing them to use the organization's stationery. In practice, this is difficult to do.[7]

LAWS AND REGULATIONS

Establishing and maintaining the employment relationship involve exercising discretion by both the employer and the employee. Employment laws affecting that relationship spring from a need to define the scope of permissible discretion and place limits on it. The need for laws and regulations and the sources of them are explored below.

Need for Laws and Regulations

Balance of Power

Entering into and maintaining the employment relationship involve negotiating issues of power. The employer has something desirable to offer the employee (a job with certain requirements and rewards), and the employee has something to offer the employer (KSAOs and motivation). Usually, the employer has the upper hand in this power relationship since it controls the creation of jobs, the definition of jobs in terms of requirements and rewards, access to those jobs via staffing systems, movement of employees among jobs over time, and the retention or termination of employees. While employees participate in these processes and decisions, it is seldom as an equal or a partner of the employer. Employment laws and regulations exist, in part, to reduce or limit such employer power in the employment relationship.

Protection of Employees

Laws and regulations seek to provide specific protections to employees that they are unlikely to get for themselves in an employment contract. These protections pertain to employment standards, individual workplace rights, and consistency of treatment. Employment standards represent the minimum acceptable terms and conditions of employment. Examples include minimum wage, nondiscrimination, overtime pay, and safety and health standards. Individual rights examples include organizing and collective bargaining, privacy protections, and constraints on unilateral termination. Finally, laws and regulations, in effect, guarantee consistency of treatment among employees. Hiring and promotion decisions, for example, cannot be made on the basis of protected employee characteristics (e.g., race, sex).

Protection of Employers

Employers also gain protections from laws and regulations. First, they provide guidance to employers as to what are permissible practices and what are impermissible practices. The Civil Rights Act, for example, not only forbids certain types of discrimination on the basis of race, color, religion, sex, and national origin but also specifically mentions employment practices that are permitted. One of those practices is the use of professionally developed ability tests, a practice that has major implications for external and internal selection. Second, questions about the meaning of the law are clarified through many avenues—court decisions, policy statements from government agencies, informal guidance from enforcement officials, and networking with other employers. The result is increasing convergence on what is required to comply with the laws. This allows the employer to implement needed changes, which then become standard operating procedure in staffing systems. In this manner, for example, affirmative action programs (AAPs) have been developed and incorporated into the staffing mainstream for many employers.

Sources of Laws and Regulations

Numerous sources of laws and regulations govern the employment relationship. Exhibit 2.2 provides examples of these as they pertain to staffing. Each of these is commented on next.

Common Law

Common law, which has its origins in England, is court-made law, as opposed to law from other sources, such as the state. It consists of the case-by-case decisions of the court, which determine over time permissible and impermissible practices, as well as their remedies. There is a heavy reliance on common law in the precedence established in previous court decisions. Each state develops and administers its own common law. Employment-at-will and workplace tort cases, for example,

---

EXHIBIT 2.2   Sources of Laws and Regulations

Source	Examples
Common law	Employment-at-will Workplace torts
Constitutional law	Fifth Amendment Fourteenth Amendment
Statutory law	Civil Rights Act Genetic Information Nondiscrimination Act Age Discrimination in Employment Act Americans With Disabilities Act Rehabilitation Act Immigration Reform and Control Act Fair Credit Reporting Act Employee Polygraph Protection Act Uniformed Services Employment and Reemployment Rights Act State and local laws Civil service laws
Executive order Agencies	11246 (nondiscrimination under federal contracts) Equal Employment Opportunity Commission (EEOC) Department of Labor (DOL) Office of Federal Contract Compliance Programs (OFCCP) Department of Homeland Security State fair employment practice (FEP) agencies

are treated at the state level. As noted, employment-at-will involves the rights of the employer and the employee to terminate the employment relationship at will. A tort is a civil wrong that occurs when the employer violates a duty owed to its employees or customers that leads to harm or damages suffered by them. Staffing tort examples include negligent hiring of unsafe or dangerous employees, fraud and misrepresentation regarding employment terms and conditions, defamation of former employees, and invasion of privacy.[8]

Constitutional Law

Constitutional law is derived from the US Constitution and its amendments. It supersedes any other source of law or regulation. Its major application is in the area of the rights of public employees, particularly their due process rights.

Statutory Law

Statutory law is derived from written statutes passed by legislative bodies. These bodies are federal (Congress), state (legislatures and assemblies), and local (municipal boards and councils). Legislative bodies may create, amend, and eliminate laws and regulations. They may also create agencies to administer and enforce the law.

Agencies

Agencies exist at the federal, state, and local levels. Their basic charge is to interpret, administer, and enforce the law. At the federal level, the two major agencies of concern to staffing are the Department of Labor (DOL) and the EEOC. Housed within the DOL are several separate units for administration of employment law, notably the Office of Federal Contract Compliance Programs (OFCCP). The Department of Homeland Security handles issues regarding foreign workers and immigration in its agency, the US Citizenship and Immigration Services.

Agencies rely heavily on written documents in performing their functions. These documents are variously referred to as rules, regulations, guidelines, and policy statements. Rules, regulations, and guidelines are published in the *Federal Register*, as well as incorporated into the Code of Federal Regulations (CFR), and they have the weight of law. Policy statements are somewhat more benign in that they do not have the force of law. They do, however, represent the agency's official position on a point or question.

EEO/AA LAWS: GENERAL PROVISIONS AND ENFORCEMENT

In this section, the major federal EEO/AA laws are summarized in terms of their general provisions. Mechanisms for enforcement of the laws are also discussed.[9] More details may be found online (*www.eeoc.gov*; *www.dol.gov*).

General Provisions

The major federal EEO/AA laws are the following:

1. Title VII of the Civil Rights Acts (1964, 1991)
2. Age Discrimination in Employment Act (1967)
3. Americans With Disabilities Act (1990, 2008)
4. Genetic Information Nondiscrimination Act (2008)
5. Rehabilitation Act (1973)
6. Executive Order 11246 (1965)

Exhibit 2.3 contains a summary of the basic provisions of these laws, pertaining to coverage, prohibited discrimination, enforcement agency, and important rules, regulations, and guidelines. These laws are appropriately labeled "major" for several reasons. First, the laws are very broad in their coverage of employers. Second, they specifically prohibit discrimination on the basis of several individual characteristics (race, color, religion, sex, national origin, age, genetic information, disability, and handicap). Third, separate agencies have been created for administration and enforcement of these laws. Finally, these agencies have issued numerous rules, regulations, and guidelines to assist in interpreting, implementing, and enforcing the law. Three sets of regulations that are of particular importance to staffing are the Uniform Guidelines on Employee Selection Procedures (*www.eeoc.gov*), Affirmative Action Programs Regulations (*www.dol.gov/ofccp*), and the Employment Regulations for the Americans With Disabilities Act (*www.eeoc.gov*). The specifics of these regulations will be discussed in subsequent chapters.

Exhibit 2.3 shows that for some laws, the number of employees in the organization determines whether the organization is covered. To count employees, the EEOC has issued guidance indicating that the organization should include any employee with whom the organization had an employment relationship in each of 20 or more calendar weeks during the current or preceding year. In essence, this means that full-time and part-time employees—and possibly temporary employees if there is true coemployment—should be included in the employee count.[10]

Individuals who oppose unlawful practices, participate in proceedings, or request accommodations are protected from retaliation under the laws shown in Exhibit 2.3. The term "retaliation" is broadly interpreted by the courts and the EEOC to include refusal to hire, denial of promotion, termination, other actions affecting employment (e.g., threats, unjustified negative evaluations), and actions that deter reasonable people from pursuing their rights (e.g., assault, unfounded civil or criminal charges). The EEOC has issued specific guidance on what constitutes evidence of retaliation, as well as special remedies for retaliatory actions by the employer.[11]

Three other general features of the EEO laws, as interpreted by the EEOC and the courts, should be noted.[12] First, state (but not local) government employers are immune from lawsuits by employees who allege violation of the ADA or the ADEA. State employees must thus pursue age and disability discrimination claims

EXHIBIT 2.3 Major Federal EEO/AA Laws: General Provisions

Law or Executive Order	Coverage	Prohibited Discrimination	Enforcement Agency	Important Rules, Regulations, and Guidelines
Civil Rights Act (1964, 1991)	Private employers with 15 or more employees Federal, state, and local governments Educational institutions Employment agencies Labor unions	Race, color, religion, national origin, sex	EEOC	Uniform Guidelines on Employee Selection Procedures Sex Discrimination Guidelines Religious Discrimination Guidelines National Origin Discrimination Guidelines
Age Discrimination in Employment Act (1967)	Private employers with 20 or more employees Federal, state, and local governments Employment agencies Labor unions	Age (40 and over)	EEOC	Interpretations of the Age Discrimination in Employment Act
Americans With Disabilities Act (1990, 2008)	Private employers with 15 or more employees Federal, state, and local governments	Qualified individual with a disability	EEOC	ADA–Employment Regulations Pre-Employment Disability-Related Questions and Medical Examinations
Genetic Information Nondiscrimination Act (2008)	Private employers with 15 or more employees Federal, state, and local governments Educational institutions Employment agencies Labor unions	Genetic information	EEOC	Final Regulations
Rehabilitation Act (1973)	Federal contractors with contracts in excess of $2,500	Individual with a handicap	DOL (OFCCP)	Affirmative Action Regulations on Handicapped Workers
Executive Order 11246 (1965)	Federal contractors with contracts in excess of $10,000	Race, color, religion, national origin, sex	DOL (OFCCP)	Sex Discrimination Guidelines Affirmative Action Programs Regulations

under applicable state laws. Second, organization officials and individual managers cannot be held personally liable for discrimination under the Civil Rights Act, the ADA, or the ADEA. They might be liable, however, under state law. Third, the ADA, the Civil Rights Act, and the ADEA extend to US citizens employed overseas by American employers. Also, a foreign company that is owned or controlled by an American employer and is doing business overseas generally must also comply with the Civil Rights Act, the ADA, and the ADEA.

An overview of the broadsweeping nature of the specific employment practices affected by the federal EEO/AA laws is shown in Exhibit 2.4.

EXHIBIT 2.4   Prohibited Employment Policies/Practices Under Federal Law

Under the laws enforced by the EEOC, it is illegal to discriminate against someone (applicant or employee) because of that person's race, color, religion, sex (including pregnancy), national origin, age (40 or older), disability, or genetic information. It is also illegal to retaliate against a person because he or she complained about discrimination, filed a charge of discrimination, or participated in an employment discrimination investigation or lawsuit.

The law forbids discrimination in every aspect of employment.

The laws enforced by the EEOC prohibit an employer or other covered entity from using neutral employment policies and practices that have a disproportionately negative effect on applicants or employees of a particular race, color, religion, sex (including pregnancy), or national origin, or on an individual with a disability or class of individuals with disabilities, if the policies or practices at issue are not job related and necessary to the operation of the business. The laws enforced by the EEOC also prohibit an employer from using neutral employment policies and practices that have a disproportionately negative impact on applicants or employees age 40 or older, if the policies or practices at issue are not based on a reasonable factor other than age.

Covered practices:
- Job advertisements, recruitment, and job referrals
- Application and hiring
- Job assignments and promotion
- Employment references
- Pre-employment inquiries
- Discipline and discharge
- Pay and benefits
- Reasonable accommodation and disability, religion
- Training and apprenticeship programs
- Harassment
- Terms and conditions of employment, dress code
- Constructive discharge/forced to resign

SOURCE: Equal Employment Opportunity Commission, 2010.

Enforcement: EEOC

As shown in Exhibit 2.3, the EEOC is responsible for enforcing the Civil Rights Act, the ADEA, and the ADA. Though each law requires separate enforcement mechanisms, some generalizations about their collective enforcement are possible.[13]

Disparate Treatment and Disparate Impact

Claims of discrimination in staffing ultimately require evidence and proof, particularly as these charges pertain to the staffing system itself and its specific characteristics as it has operated in practice. Toward this end, there are two avenues or paths to follow—disparate treatment and disparate impact.[14] Both paths may be followed for Title VII of the Civil Rights Act, ADA, and ADEA claims.

Disparate Treatment.   Claims of disparate treatment involve allegations of intentional discrimination in which the employer knowingly and deliberately discriminated against people on the basis of specific characteristics such as race or sex. Evidence for such claims may be of several sorts.

First, the evidence may be direct. It might, for example, refer to an explicit written policy of the organization, such as one stating that "women are not to be hired for the following jobs."

The situation may not involve such blatant action but may consist of what is referred to as a mixed motive. Here, both a prohibited characteristic (e.g., sex) and a legitimate reason (e.g., job qualifications) are mixed together to contribute to a negative decision about a person, such as a failure to hire or promote. If an unlawful motive such as sex plays any part in the decision, it is illegal, despite the presence of a lawful motive as well.

Finally, the discrimination may be such that evidence of a failure to hire or promote because of a protected characteristic must be inferred from several situational factors. Here, the evidence involves four factors:

1. The person belongs to a protected class.
2. The person applied for, and was qualified for, a job the employer was trying to fill.
3. The person was rejected despite being qualified.
4. The position remained open and the employer continued to seek applicants as qualified as the person rejected.

Most disparate treatment cases involve and require the use of these four factors to initially prove a charge of discrimination.

Disparate Impact.   Disparate impact, also known as adverse impact, focuses on the effect of employment practices, rather than on the motive or intent underlying them. Accordingly, the emphasis here is on the need for direct evidence that, as a result of a protected characteristic, people are being adversely affected by a practice. Statistical evidence must be presented to support a claim of adverse impact.[15] Three types of statistical evidence may be used, and these are shown in Exhibit 2.5. Refer to "Legal Issues" in Chapters 3 and 7 for elaboration.

Shown first in the exhibit are applicant flow statistics, which look at differences in selection rates (proportion of applicants hired) among different groups for a particular job. If the differences are large enough, this suggests that the effect of the selection system is discriminatory. In the example, the selection rate for men is .50 (or 50%) and for women it is .11 (or 11%), suggesting the possibility of discrimination.

A second type of statistical evidence involves the use of stock statistics. Here, the percentage of women or minorities actually employed in a job category is compared with their availability in the relevant population. Relevant is defined in terms of such things as "qualified," "interested," or "geographic." In the example shown,

---

EXHIBIT 2.5   Types of Disparate Impact Statistics

A. FLOW STATISTICS

Definition:

Significant differences in selection rates between groups

Example

Job Category: Customer Service Representative

No. of Applicants		No. Hired		Selection Rate (%)	
Men	Women	Men	Women	Men	Women
50	45	25	5	50%	11%

B. STOCK STATISTICS

Definition:

Underutilization of women or minorities relative to their availability in the relevant population

Example

Job Category: Management Trainee

Current Trainees (%)		Availability (%)	
Nonminority	Minority	Nonminority	Minority
90%	10%	70%	30%

C. CONCENTRATION STATISTICS

Definition:

Concentration of women or minorities in certain job categories

Example

	Job Category			
	Clerical	Production	Sales	Managers
% Men	3%	85%	45%	95%
% Women	97%	15%	55%	5%

there is a disparity in the percentage of minorities employed (10%) compared with their availability (30%), which suggests their underutilization.

The third type of evidence involves the use of concentration statistics. Here, the percentages of women or minorities in various job categories are compared to see if they are concentrated in certain workforce categories. In the example shown, women are concentrated in clerical jobs (97%), men are concentrated in production (85%) and managerial (95%) jobs, and men and women are roughly equally concentrated in sales jobs (45% and 55%, respectively).

Initial Charge and Conciliation

Enforcement proceedings begin when an employee or job applicant files a charge (the EEOC itself may also file a charge). In states where there is an EEOC-approved fair enforcement practice (FEP) law, the charge is initially deferred to the state. An investigation of the charge occurs to determine if there is reasonable cause to assume discrimination has occurred. If reasonable cause is not found, the charge is dropped. If reasonable cause is found, however, the EEOC attempts conciliation of the charge. Conciliation is a voluntary settlement process that seeks agreement by the employer to stop the practice(s) in question and abide by proposed remedies. This is the EEOC's preferred method of settlement. Whenever the EEOC decides not to pursue a claim further, it will issue a "right to sue" letter to the complaining party, allowing a private suit to be started against the employer.

Complementing conciliation is the use of mediation. With mediation, a neutral third party mediates the dispute between the employer and the EEOC and obtains an agreement between them that resolves the dispute. Participation in mediation is voluntary, and either party may opt out of it for any reason. Mediation proceedings are confidential. Any agreement reached between the parties is legally enforceable. More than 70% of complaints that go to mediation are resolved, and 96% of employers that use the EEOC mediation program say they would do so again.[16] In short, the EEOC prefers settlement to litigation. An example of a settlement is shown in Exhibit 2.6.

Litigation and Remedies

Should conciliation fail, suit is filed in federal court. The ensuing litigation process under Title VII is shown in Exhibit 2.7. As can be seen, the charge of the plaintiff (charging party) will follow either a disparate treatment or a disparate impact route.[17] In either event, the plaintiff has the initial burden of proof. Such a burden requires the plaintiff to establish a prima facie case that demonstrates reasonable cause to assume discrimination has occurred. Assuming this case is successfully presented, the defendant must rebut the charge and accompanying evidence.

In disparate treatment cases, the defendant must provide nondiscriminatory reasons during rebuttal for the practice(s) in question. In disparate impact cases, the

EXHIBIT 2.6   Example of a Settlement Agreement With the EEOC

DENVER—The U.S. Equal Employment Opportunity Commission (EEOC) announced today that it has reached agreement with Seattle-based window manufacturer, Milgard Manufacturing, Inc. (Milgard) to resolve a lawsuit alleging that Milgard engaged in racially discriminatory hiring practices at its Colorado facility and retaliated against a human resource assistant, Leigh Ann Ornelas (Ornelas), who complained about the unlawful practices. Ms. Ornelas, who was also named plaintiff in the lawsuit, was represented by Tom Arckey of the law firm Arckey & Reha, LLC.

While Milgard has denied engaging in any wrongful conduct, the company has agreed to pay a total of $3.1 million to resolve the lawsuit, plus up to $270,000 in expenses for administering the costs of the settlement. From the settlement, a fund will be established to provide payments to African Americans or other black individuals who have applied for work at Milgard since 1997 and were not offered jobs. The EEOC anticipates that the settlement fund will be ready to accept claims by July 1, 2004. In the meantime, individuals who believe they are entitled to receive payment from the settlement fund may contact the EEOC at (303) 866-1346.

In addition to the monetary settlement, Milgard has agreed to undertake a comprehensive review of its policies and procedures to ensure compliance with federal antidiscrimination laws; to provide increased training to its Colorado employees and managers regarding workplace discrimination issues; and to engage in recruitment and outreach programs to increase the proportion of African Americans and blacks in its applicant pool. Milgard has also agreed that its current operation in Colorado, and any future operations that might be opened in Colorado, will be under continued monitoring by the EEOC for a period of three years.

The lawsuit arose out of events in 1998, when Leigh Ann Ornelas was the person responsible for conducting initial interviews of job applicants at Milgard Windows' plant, then located in the Montebello area of Denver. The EEOC and Ms. Ornelas maintained that the then–plant manager of the Montebello facility told Ms. Ornelas not to hire or refer black applicants for certain positions in the plant. Ms. Ornelas and the EEOC also have alleged that when Ms. Ornelas complained to various managers concerning these instructions, no action was taken against the plant manager and Ms. Ornelas was subjected to retaliatory harassment and eventually forced to resign. The EEOC also asserted that a statistical analysis of the job applications submitted to Milgard's Colorado facility since 1997 shows that Milgard hired significantly fewer African Americans and blacks than would be predicted based on the demographics of the areas where applicants lived.

Joseph H. Mitchell, regional attorney for the EEOC's Denver District Office, said, "We are pleased to resolve this case and commend Milgard for acknowledging the importance of preventing discriminatory hiring practices and the importance of not retaliating against employees like Leigh Ann Ornelas, who risked her job to champion the rights of the black applicants who were being denied jobs."

SOURCE: Equal Employment Opportunity Commission, May 26, 2004 (*www.eeoc.gov*).

EXHIBIT 2.7 **Basic Litigation Process Under Title VII: EEOC**

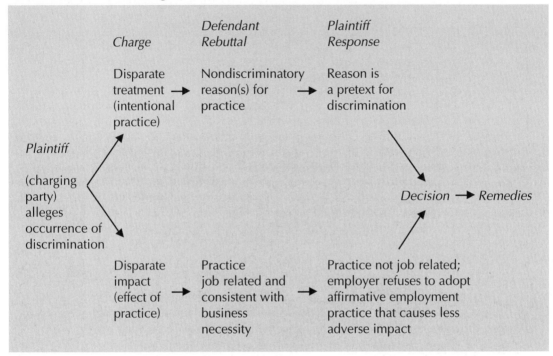

employer must demonstrate that the practices in question are job related and consistent with business necessity.

Following rebuttal, the plaintiff may respond to the defense provided by the defendant. In disparate treatment cases, that response hinges on a demonstration that the defendant's reasons for a practice are a pretext, or smoke screen, for the practice. In disparate impact cases, the plaintiff's response will focus on showing that the defendant has not shown its practices to be job related and/or that the employer refuses to adopt a practice that causes less adverse impact.

Disparate impact litigation involving age discrimination charges is somewhat different. After the disparate impact claim (supported by disparate impact statistics) is made, the defendant rebuttal will involve an attempt to prove that the challenged practice is supported by a reasonable factor other than age, and the plaintiff response will attempt to prove that the factor cited is unreasonable and not the true reason for the practice.

Who bears the final, or ultimate, burden of proof? In disparate treatment cases, the plaintiff must ultimately prove that the defendant's practices are discriminatory. For disparate impact cases, on the other hand, the burden is on the defendant. That is, it is the defendant who must prove that its practices are not discriminatory.

The plaintiff and the defendant have an opportunity to end their dispute through a consent decree. This is a voluntary, court-approved agreement between the two parties. The consent decree may contain an agreement to not only halt certain practices but also implement certain remedies, such as various forms of monetary relief and AAPs. An example of a consent decree is shown in Exhibit 2.8.

EXHIBIT 2.8   Example of a Consent Decree

LOS ANGELES—The U.S. Equal Employment Opportunity Commission (EEOC) and private plaintiffs today announced their mutual resolution of the lawsuit entitled *EEOC v. Abercrombie & Fitch Stores, Inc.*, Case No. CV-04-4731 SI, which was filed on November 10, 2004, in the United States District Court for the Northern District of California in San Francisco. The lawsuit alleged that Abercrombie & Fitch, which operates a nationwide chain of retail stores, violated Title VII of the Civil Rights Act of 1964 by maintaining recruiting and hiring practices that excluded minorities and women and adopting a restrictive marketing image, and other policies, which limited minority and female employment.

The lawsuit was amicably resolved by entry of a Consent Decree in the U.S. District Court, which provides that Abercrombie & Fitch will pay $50 million to resolve the EEOC lawsuit along with two private class actions filed against Abercrombie & Fitch: *Gonzalez et al. v. Abercrombie et al.* and *West v. Abercrombie et al.*

The Consent Decree enjoins Abercrombie & Fitch from:
a. Discriminating against applicants based upon race, color, national origin which includes African Americans, Asian Americans, and Latinos;
b. Discriminating against women due to their sex, and,
c. Denying promotional opportunities to women and minorities

Abercrombie & Fitch has also agreed to develop and implement hiring and recruiting procedures to ensure compliance under the Decree. Abercrombie & Fitch agreed to ensure that minorities and women are promoted into manager-in-training and manager positions without discrimination. A Monitor will be hired to ensure Abercrombie's compliance with the terms of the Consent Decree, including reporting. Abercrombie & Fitch will hire a vice president of diversity and employ up to 25 diversity recruiters. Abercrombie & Fitch will devise new protocols for each of these areas. Abercrombie & Fitch will post a notice on an internal Web site and at all stores which will be periodically distributed to employees. Additionally, Abercrombie & Fitch will provide training to all of its managers. Most importantly, Abercrombie & Fitch also agreed to ensure that its marketing materials will reflect diversity.

EEOC's General Counsel Eric Dreiband stated, "The retail industry and other industries need to know that businesses cannot discriminate against individuals under the auspice of a marketing strategy or a particular 'look.' Race and sex discrimination in employment are unlawful, and the EEOC will continue to aggressively pursue employers who choose to engage in such practices."

SOURCE: Equal Employment Opportunity Commission, Nov. 18, 2004 (*www.eeoc.gov*).

In the absence of a consent decree, the court will fashion its own remedies from those permitted under the law, of which several are available. First, the court may enjoin certain practices, which means requiring the defendant to halt the practices. Second, the court may order the hiring or reinstatement of individuals. Third, the court may fashion various forms of monetary relief, such as back pay, front pay, attorney's fees, and compensatory and punitive damages. Compensatory and punitive damages, which are capped at $300,000, may be applied only in cases involving disparate treatment; front pay and back pay are excluded from the cap. Finally, under the Civil Rights Act and the ADA, the court may order "such affirmative action as may be appropriate," as well as "any other equitable relief" that the court deems appropriate. Through these provisions, the court has considerable latitude in the remedies it imposes, including the imposition of AAPs.

Enforcement: OFCCP

Enforcement mechanisms used by the OFCCP are very different from those used by the EEOC. Most covered employers are required to develop and implement written AAPs for women and minorities. Specific AAP requirements for employers under Executive Order 11246 are spelled out in Affirmative Action Programs Regulations, discussed in "Legal Issues" in Chapter 3.

To enforce these requirements, the OFCCP conducts off-site desk audits and reviews of employers' records and AAPs, and on-site visits and compliance reviews of employers' AAPs. It also investigates complaints charging noncompliance. Employers found to be in noncompliance are urged to change their practices through a conciliation process. Should conciliation be unsuccessful, employers are subject to various penalties that affect their status as a federal contractor. These include cancellation of contracts and debarment from bidding on future contracts.

EEO/AA LAWS: SPECIFIC STAFFING PROVISIONS

Each of the major laws covered in the previous section contains specific provisions pertaining to staffing practices by organizations. This section summarizes those specific provisions, including agencies' and courts' interpretations of them. Phrases in quotation marks are from the laws themselves. Applications of these provisions to staffing policies, practices, and actions occur throughout the remainder of the book.

Civil Rights Acts (1964, 1991)

The provisions of the Civil Rights Acts of 1964 and 1991 are combined for discussion purposes here. The 1991 law is basically a series of amendments to the 1964 law, though it does contain some provisions unique to it.

Unlawful Employment Practices

This section of the law contains a comprehensive statement regarding unlawful employment practices. Specifically, it is unlawful for an employer

1. "to fail or refuse to hire or to discharge any individual, or otherwise discriminate against any individual with respect to his compensation, terms, conditions, or privileges of employment, because of such individual's race, color, religion, sex, or national origin"; or
2. "to limit, segregate, or classify his employees or applicants for employment in any way which would deprive or tend to deprive any individual of employment opportunities or otherwise adversely affect his status as an employee because of such individual's race, color, religion, sex, or national origin."

These two statements are the foundation of civil rights law. They are very broad and inclusive, applying to virtually all staffing practices of an organization. There are also separate statements for employment agencies and labor unions.

Establishment of Disparate Impact

As discussed previously, a claim of discrimination may be pursued via a disparate impact or disparate treatment approach. The law makes several points regarding the former approach.

First, staffing practices that may seem unfair, outrageous, or of dubious value to the employer but do not cause adverse impact are not illegal (assuming, of course, that no intention to discriminate underlies them). Thus, they are a matter of legal concern only if their usage causes disparate impact.

Second, staffing practices that the plaintiff initially alleges to have caused adverse impact are unlawful unless the employer can successfully rebut the charges. To do this, the employer must show that the practices are "job related for the position in question and consistent with business necessity." Practices that fail to meet this standard are unlawful.

Third, the plaintiff must show adverse impact for each specific staffing practice or component. For example, if an employer has a simple selection system in which applicants first take a written test and those who pass it are interviewed, the plaintiff must show adverse impact separately for the test and the interview, rather than for the two components combined.

Disparate Treatment

Intentional discrimination with staffing practices is prohibited, and the employer may not use a claim of business necessity to justify intentional use of a discriminatory practice.

Mixed Motives

An employer may not defend an action by claiming that while a prohibited factor, such as sex, entered into a staffing decision, other factors, such as job qualifications, did also. Such "mixed motive" defenses are not permitted. A plaintiff may pursue a mixed motive claim with either circumstantial or direct evidence of discrimination.

Bona Fide Occupational Qualification

An employer may attempt to justify use of a protected characteristic, such as national origin, as being a bona fide occupational qualification (BFOQ). The law permits such claims, but only for sex, religion, and national origin—not race or color. The employer must be able to demonstrate that such discrimination is "a bona fide occupational qualification reasonably necessary to the normal operation of that particular business or enterprise." Thus, a maximum security prison with mostly male inmates might hire only male prison guards on the grounds that by doing so it ensures the safety, security, and privacy of inmates. However, it must be able to show that doing so is a business necessity.

Testing

The law explicitly permits the use of tests in staffing. The employer may "give and act upon the results of any professionally developed ability test, provided that such test, its administration, or action upon the basis of results is not designed, intended, or used to discriminate because of race, color, religion, sex, or national origin."

Interpretation of this provision has been difficult. What exactly is a "professionally developed ability test"? How does an employer use a test to discriminate? Not discriminate? The need for answers to such questions gave rise to the Uniform Guidelines on Employee Selection Procedures (UGESP).

Test Score Adjustments

Test scores are not to be altered or changed to make them more fair; test scores should speak for themselves. Specifically, it is an unlawful employment practice "to adjust the scores of, use different cutoff scores for, or otherwise alter the results of employment-related tests on the basis of race, color, religion, sex, or national origin." This provision bans so-called race norming, in which people's scores are compared only with those of members of their own racial group and separate cutoff or passing scores are set for each group.

Seniority or Merit Systems

The law explicitly permits the use of seniority and merit systems as a basis for applying different terms and conditions to employees. However, the seniority or merit system must be "bona fide," and it may not be the result of an intention to discriminate.

This provision is particularly relevant to internal staffing systems. It in essence allows the employer to take into account seniority (experience) and merit (e.g., KSAOs, promotion potential assessments) when making internal staffing decisions.

Employment Advertising

Discrimination in employment advertising is prohibited. Specifically, the employer may not indicate "any preference, limitation, specification, or discrimination based on race, color, religion, sex, or national origin." An exception to this is if sex, religion, or national origin is a BFOQ.

Pregnancy

The Pregnancy Discrimination Act (PDA) is an amendment to Title VII. Under the PDA, an employer cannot refuse to hire a pregnant woman because of her pregnancy, because of a pregnancy-related condition, or because of the prejudices of coworkers, clients, or customers. There are also many provisions regarding pregnancy and maternity leave.

Preferential Treatment and Quotas

The law does not require preferential treatment or quotas. Thus, the employer is not required to have a balanced workforce, meaning one whose demographic composition matches or mirrors the demographic makeup of the surrounding population from which the employer draws its employees.

Note that the law does not prohibit preferential treatment, AA, and quotas. It merely says they are not required. Thus, they may be used in certain instances, such as a voluntary AAP or a court-imposed remedy.

Age Discrimination in Employment Act (1967)

Prohibited Age Discrimination

The law explicitly and inclusively prohibits discrimination against those aged 40 and older. It is unlawful for an employer

1. "to fail or refuse to hire or to discharge any individual or otherwise discriminate against any individual with respect to his compensation, terms, conditions or privileges of employment, because of such individual's age"; and
2. "to limit, segregate, or classify his employees in any way which would deprive or tend to deprive any individual of employment opportunities or otherwise adversely affect his status as an employee, because of such individual's age."

These provisions are interpreted to mean that it is not unlawful to favor an older worker over a younger worker, even if both workers are aged 40 or older (*www. eeoc.gov*).

Bona Fide Occupational Qualification

Like the Civil Rights Act, the ADEA contains a BFOQ provision. Thus, it is not unlawful for an employer to differentiate among applicants or employees on the basis of their age "where age is a bona fide occupational qualification reasonably necessary to the normal operation of the particular business."

Reasonable Factors Other Than Age

The employer may use reasonable factors other than age (RFOA) in making employment decisions. Such factors must be applied equally to all applicants, cannot include age in any way, must be job related, and cannot result in discrimination on the basis of age. Factors correlated with age, such as job experience, may be used. The EEOC is developing new rules to further clarify RFOA (*www.eeoc.gov*).

Seniority Systems

The law permits the use of seniority systems (merit systems are not mentioned). Thus, the employer is permitted "to observe the terms of a bona fide seniority system that is not intended to evade the purposes" of the act.

Employment Advertising

Employment advertising may not contain terms that limit or deter the employment of older individuals. It is permissible, however, to use terms or phrases that express a preference for older workers, such as "over age 60," "retirees," or "supplement your pension."

Americans With Disabilities Act (1990, 2008)

The ADA's basic purpose is to prohibit discrimination against qualified individuals with disabilities and to require the employer to make reasonable accommodation for such individuals unless that would cause undue hardship for the employer.

Prohibited Discrimination

The law contains a broad prohibition against disability discrimination. It specifically says that an employer may not "discriminate against an individual on the basis of disability in regard to job application procedures, the hiring, advancement or discharge of employees, employee compensation, job training, and other terms, conditions, and privileges of employment." Also prohibited is discrimination based on an applicant's or employee's association with a person with a disability.

The law does not apply to all people with disabilities, only those who are "otherwise qualified." To determine if a person is covered under the ADA, it must be determined if the person has a disability, and if so, is otherwise qualified for the job.

Definition of Disability

Under the amended ADA, the definition of a disability is to be interpreted in favor of broad coverage of individuals. The term "disability" means the following:

a. a physical or mental impairment that substantially limits one or more major life activities of the individual;

b. a record of such an impairment; or

c. being regarded as having such an impairment.

In more detail, this general definition of "disability" means the following. Both physical and mental impairments are covered; these can be current or past impairments, or even ones the individual is regarded as having. The impairment must be considered without corrective measures (e.g., medication, hearing aid, and learned modifications), except for ordinary eyeglasses or contact lenses. Current users of illegal drugs are not covered; recovering drug users and both practicing and recovering alcoholics are covered. An impairment that is episodic or in remission is covered if it would substantially limit a major life activity when active (e.g., epilepsy, major depression).

There are numerous major life activities that an impairment might substantially limit. These include (but are not limited to) caring for oneself, performing manual tasks, seeing, hearing, eating, sleeping, walking, standing, lifting, bending, speaking, breathing, learning, reading, concentrating, thinking, communicating, and working. Major bodily functions are also major life activities. These include functions of the immune system; normal cell growth; and digestive, bowel, bladder, neurological, brain, respiratory, circulatory, endocrine, and reproductive functions. New EEOC regulations will likely add other major life activities.

EEOC guidance on the definition of "substantially limits" is currently being developed. It will involve a commonsense assessment based on comparing an individual's ability to perform a specific major life activity with that of most people in the general population. Temporary, non-chronic impairments of short duration with little or no residual effects usually will not be considered disabilities (e.g., common cold, sprained joint, broken bone, and seasonal allergies). For an impairment to substantially limit the major life activity of working, it is proposed that it must substantially limit a person's ability to perform, or meet the qualifications for, a type of work.

In short, the definition of a disability is quite expansive, and it will undergo development and change by the courts and the EEOC over time.

Additional guidance from the EEOC pertains to persons with psychiatric disabilities as mental impairments (*www.eeoc.gov*). A mental impairment includes mental or emotional illness, examples of which are major depression, bipolar disorder, anxiety disorders (including panic disorder, obsessive-compulsive disorder, and post-traumatic stress disorder), schizophrenia, and personality disorders. To count as a disability, the mental impairment must substantially limit one or more of the major life activities as defined above.

The EEOC provides additional guidance in question-and-answer documents targeted to specific disabilities: deafness and hearing impairments, blindness and vision impairments, diabetes, epilepsy, intellectual disabilities, and cancer. The documents explain when each of these will count as a disability, address which questions may (or may not) be asked of job applicants, provide reasonable accommodation examples, and tell how to handle safety and harassment concerns (*www.eeoc.gov*). Finally, the EEOC and the courts are exploring if, and when, individuals who are obese might be considered disabled under the ADA.[18]

Qualified Individual With a Disability

A qualified individual with a disability is "an individual with a disability who, with or without reasonable accommodation, can perform the essential functions of the employment position that such individual holds or desires."

Essential Job Functions

The law provides little guidance as to what are essential job functions. It would seem that they are the major, nontrivial tasks required of an employee. The employer has great discretion in such a determination. Specifically, "consideration shall be given to the employer's judgment as to what functions of a job are essential, and if an employer has prepared a written description before advertising or interviewing applicants for the job, this description shall be considered evidence of the essential functions of the job." Subsequent regulations amplify on what are essential job functions; these are explored in Chapter 4.

Reasonable Accommodation and Undue Hardship

Unless it would pose an "undue hardship" on the employer, the employer must make "reasonable accommodation" to the "known physical or mental impairments of an otherwise qualified, disabled job applicant or employee." The law provides actual examples of such accommodation. They include changes in facilities (e.g., installing wheelchair ramps), job restructuring, telework, changes in work schedules, employee reassignment to a vacant position, purchase of adaptive devices, provision of qualified readers and interpreters, and adjustments in testing and training material. For mental impairment and psychiatric disabilities, EEOC guidance indicates several types of reasonable accommodations: leaves of absence and other work schedule changes, physical changes in the workplace, modifications to company policy, adjustment of supervisory methods, medication monitoring, and reassignment to a vacant position (*www.eeoc.gov*). In general, only accommodations that would be difficult to make or that would require significant expense are considered to create an undue hardship.

A suggested four-step problem-solving approach for handling a reasonable accommodation request from an applicant or employee is as follows.[19] First, conduct job analysis to determine the job's essential functions. Second, identify performance barriers that would hinder the person from doing the job. Third, work with the person to identify potential accommodations. Fourth, assess each accommodation and choose the most reasonable one that would not be an undue hardship.

Selection of Employees

The law deals directly with discrimination in the selection of employees. Prohibited discrimination includes

1. "using qualification standards, employment tests or other selection criteria that screen out or tend to screen out an individual with a disability or a class of individuals with disabilities unless the standard, test, or other selection criteria, as used by the covered entity, is shown to be job related for the position in question and is consistent with business necessity"; and
2. "failing to select and administer tests concerning employment in the most effective manner to ensure that, when such a test is administered to a job applicant or employee who has a disability that impairs sensory, manual, or speaking skills, such results accurately reflect the skills, aptitude or whatever other factor of such applicant or employee that such test purports to measure, rather than reflecting the impaired sensory, manual, or speaking skills of such employee or applicant (except where such skills are the factors that the test purports to measure)."

These provisions seem to make two basic requirements of staffing systems. First, if selection procedures cause disparate impact against people with disabilities, the employer must show that the procedures are job related and consistent with business necessity. The requirement is similar to that for selection procedures under the Civil Rights Act. Second, the employer must ensure that employment tests are accurate indicators of the KSAOs they attempt to measure.

Medical Exams for Job Applicants and Employees

Prior to making a job offer, the employer may not conduct medical exams of job applicants, inquire whether or how severely a person is disabled, or inquire whether the applicant has received treatment for a mental or emotional condition. Specific inquiries about a person's ability to perform essential job functions, however, are permitted.

After a job offer has been made, the employer may require the applicant to take a medical exam, including a psychiatric exam. The job offer may be contingent on the applicant successfully passing the exam. Care should be taken to ensure that all applicants are required to take and pass the same exam. Medical records should be confidential and maintained in a separate file.

For employees, medical exams must be job related and consistent with business necessity. Exam results are confidential.

Direct Threat

The employer may refuse to hire an individual who poses a direct threat to himself or herself or to the health and safety of others.

Affirmative Action

There are no affirmative action requirements for employers.

Genetic Information Nondiscrimination Act (2008)

The Genetic Information Nondiscrimination Act (GINA) prohibits the use of genetic information in employment, as well as its acquisition; confidentiality of genetic information is required.

Genetic Information

Genetic information includes an individual's genetic tests, genetic tests of family members, and the manifestation of a disease or disorder in family members (i.e., the family's medical history). Age and sex are not included as genetic information.

Prohibited Practices

It is an unlawful employment practice for the employer to fail or refuse to hire; discharge; discriminate regarding terms and conditions of employment; and limit, segregate, or classify employees because of genetic information. There are no exceptions to this ban on usage.

It is also an unlawful employment practice to acquire (require, request, or purchase) genetic information about the employee or family members. There are several specific exceptions to this.

Confidentiality of Information

Any genetic information is to be maintained in a separate file, but it is okay to use this same file for ADA purposes. There are strict limits on the disclosure of genetic information.

Rehabilitation Act (1973)

The Rehabilitation Act applies to federal contractors and subcontractors, and most of them are also covered by the ADA. The Rehabilitation Act has many similarities to the ADA, including that the 2008 ADA amendments apply to the Rehabilitation Act. Hence, the Rehabilitation Act provisions are only briefly mentioned.

Prohibited Discrimination

It is illegal to discriminate against a qualified individual with a disability. The definition of disability under the ADA applies here. Reasonable accommodation for a qualified individual with a disability must also be made.

Affirmative Action

Employers are required to develop and implement written AAPs for employing and promoting qualified individuals with disabilities. The OFCCP monitors the plans and conducts employer compliance reviews.

Executive Order 11246 (1965)

Prohibited Discrimination

The federal contractor is prohibited from discriminating on the basis of race, color, religion, sex, and national origin. (A similar prohibition against age discrimination by federal contractors is contained in Executive Order 11141.)

Affirmative Action

The order plainly requires affirmative action. It says specifically that "the contractor will take affirmative action to ensure that applicants are employed, and that employees are treated during employment, without regard to their race, color, religion, sex, or national origin. Such actions shall include, but not be limited to the following: employment, upgrading, demotion, or transfer; recruitment or recruitment advertising; layoff or termination; rates of pay or other forms of compensation; and selection for training, including apprenticeship." (Executive Order 11141 does not require affirmative action.) Regulations for these affirmative action requirements are discussed in Chapter 3.

OTHER STAFFING LAWS

In addition to the EEO/AA laws, a variety of other laws and regulations affect staffing. At the federal level are the Immigration Reform and Control Act (IRCA), the Employee Polygraph Protection Act, and the Fair Credit Reporting Act. At the state and local levels are a wide array of laws pertaining to EEO, as well as a host of other areas. Finally, there are civil service laws and regulations that pertain to staffing practices for federal, state, and local government employers.

Federal Laws

Immigration Reform and Control Act (1986)

The purpose of the IRCA and its amendments is to prohibit the employment of unauthorized aliens and to provide civil and criminal penalties for violations of this law. The law covers all employers regardless of size.

Prohibited Practices.   The law prohibits the initial or continuing employment of unauthorized aliens. Specifically,

1. "it is unlawful for a person or other entity to have, or to recruit or refer for a fee, for employment in the United States an alien knowing the alien is an unauthorized alien with respect to such employment"; and

2. "it is unlawful for a person or other entity, after hiring an alien for employment . . . to continue to employ the alien in the United States knowing the alien is (or has become) an unauthorized alien with respect to such employment." (This does not apply to the continuing employment of aliens hired before November 6, 1986.)

The law also prohibits employment discrimination on the basis of national origin or citizenship status. The purpose of this provision is to discourage employers from attempting to comply with the prohibition against hiring unauthorized aliens by simply refusing to hire applicants who are foreign-looking in appearance or have foreign-sounding accents.

Employment Eligibility Verification System.   The employer must verify that the individual is not an unauthorized alien and is legally eligible for employment by obtaining proof of identity and eligibility for work. The employer uses the I-9 form to gather documents from the new employee that establish both proof of identity and eligibility (authorization) for work. Documents that will establish proof are shown on the back of the I-9 form. Documents should not be obtained until the person is actually hired, and they must be acquired within three business days of the date of employment. To verify eligibility information, federal contractors and subcontractors must use E-Verify, which conducts electronic verification checks against federal databases. Other employers may voluntarily participate in E-Verify. There are detailed record-keeping requirements. More information on verification is in the "Legal Issues" section of Chapter 12.

Temporary Visas.   The employer may apply for temporary visas for up to six years for foreign workers under two major visa categories (there are other, minor categories not covered here). The first category is H-1B visa. An H-1B nonimmigrant must have a bachelor's degree (or equivalent) or higher in a specific specialty. These workers are typically employed in occupations such as architect, engineer, computer programmer, accountant, doctor, or professor. The employer must pay the person the prevailing wage for employees working in a similar position for the employer and attest that the employee will not displace any other US employee. Congress sets an annual cap of 65,000 for the number of visas issued. H-1B nonimmigrants employed by universities and nonprofit (including government) organizations are exempt from the annual cap. There is also an exception (with a 20,000 annual cap) for workers with a master's degree or higher from a US university. H-1B visa holders may change jobs as soon as their employer files an approval petition, and they are not restricted to their current geographic area.

The H-2B visa category applies to nonagricultural temporary workers. It is for employers with peak load, seasonal, or intermittent needs to augment their regular workforce. Examples of such employers are construction, health care, resort/hospitality services, lumber, and manufacturing. There is an annual cap of 65,000 workers.

Enforcement.   The law is enforced by the US Citizenship and Immigration Services (*www.uscis.gov*) within the Department of Homeland Security. Noncompliance may result in fines of up to $10,000 for each unauthorized alien employed, as well as imprisonment for up to six months for a pattern or practice of violations. Federal contractors may be barred from federal contracts for one year.

Employee Polygraph Protection Act (1988)

The purpose of the Employee Polygraph Protection Act is to prevent most private employers from using the polygraph or lie detector on job applicants or employees. The law does not apply to other types of "honesty tests," such as paper-and-pencil ones.

Prohibited Practices.   The law prohibits most private employers (public employers are exempted) from (1) requiring applicants or employees to take a polygraph test, (2) using the results of a polygraph test for employment decisions, and (3) discharging or disciplining individuals for refusing to take a polygraph test.

   The polygraph may be used in three explicit instances. First, employers that manufacture, distribute, or dispense controlled substances, such as drugs, may use the polygraph. Second, private security firms that provide services to businesses affecting public safety or security, such as nuclear power plants or armored vehicles, may use the polygraph. Third, an employer that experiences economic loss due to theft, embezzlement, or sabotage may use the polygraph in an investigation of the loss.

Enforcement.   The law is enforced by the DOL. Noncompliance may result in fines of up to $10,000 per individual violation. Also, individuals may sue the employer, seeking employment, reinstatement, promotion, and back pay.

Fair Credit Reporting Act (1970)

The Fair Credit Reporting Act, as amended, regulates the organization's acquisition and use of consumer reports on job applicants. A consumer report is virtually any information on an applicant that is compiled from a database by a consumer reporting agency and provided to the organization. The information may be not only credit characteristics but also employment history, income, driving record, arrests and convictions, and lifestyle; medical information may not be sought or provided without prior approval of the applicant. Specific requirements for gathering and using the information are provided in Chapter 8.

   A second type of consumer report is investigative. It is prepared from personal interviews with other individuals, rather than a search through a database. There are separate compliance steps for this type of report.

Enforcement.   The law is enforced by the Federal Trade Commission (*www.ftc.gov*). Penalties for willful or negligent noncompliance go up to $1,000.

Uniformed Services Employment and Reemployment Rights Act (1994)

The purpose of the Uniformed Services Employment and Reemployment Rights Act (USERRA) is to prohibit discrimination against members of the uniformed services and to extend reinstatement, benefit, and job security rights to returning service members.

Coverage. Both private and public employers, regardless of size, are covered. All people who perform or have performed service in the uniformed services have USERRA rights, but only a person who was employed, is an applicant, or who is currently employed can invoke these rights.

Requirements. Employers may not take negative job actions (e.g., firing, demoting, transferring, or refusing to hire) against members (and applicants for membership) in the uniformed services. The employer must reinstate (within two weeks of application for reinstatement) employees who have taken up to five total years of leave from their position in order to serve. These employees are entitled to be returned to the position they would have held if they had been continuously employed (this is called an "escalator" position). If the employee is not qualified for the escalator position, the employer must make a reasonable effort to help the employee qualify. Those employees are also entitled to promotions, raises, and other seniority-based benefits they would have received. There are many exceptions to both the five-year service limit and the reinstatement rights. Certain benefits must be made available to those who take leave for service, and benefits must be restored to those who return. An employee may not be fired, except for cause, for up to one year after returning from service.

Enforcement. The law is enforced by the Veterans Employment and Training Service (VETS) within the DOL (*www.dol.gov/vets*). There are also regulations for employer compliance.

State and Local Laws

The emphasis in this book is on federal laws and regulations. It should be remembered, however, that an organization is subject to law at the state and local levels as well. This greatly increases the array of applicable laws to which the organization must attend.

EEO/AA Laws

EEO/AA laws are often patterned after federal law. Their basic provisions, however, vary substantially from state to state. Compliance with federal EEO/AA law does not ensure compliance with state and local EEO/AA laws, and vice versa. Thus, it is the responsibility of the organization to be explicitly knowledgeable of the laws and regulations that apply to it.

Of special note is that state and local EEO/AA laws and regulations often provide protections beyond those contained in the federal laws and regulations. State laws, for example, may apply to employers with fewer than 15 employees, which is the cutoff for coverage under the Civil Rights Act. State laws may also prohibit certain kinds of discrimination not prohibited under federal law, for example, sexual orientation and gender identity or expression. The law for the District of Columbia prohibits 13 kinds of discrimination, including sexual orientation, physical appearance, matriculation, and political affiliation. Finally, state law may deviate from federal law with regard to enforcement mechanisms and penalties for noncompliance.

Other State Laws

Earlier, reference was made to employment-at-will and workplace torts as matters of common law, which, in turn, are governed at the state law level. Statutory state laws applicable to staffing, in addition to EEO/AA laws, are also plentiful. Examples of areas covered in addition to EEO/AA include criminal record inquiries by the employer, polygraph and "honesty testing," drug testing, AIDS testing, and employee access to personnel records.

Civil Service Laws and Regulations

Federal, state, and local government employers are governed by special statutory laws and regulations collectively referred to as civil service. Civil service is guided by so-called merit principles that serve as the guide to staffing practices. Following these merit principles results in notable differences between public and private employers in their staffing practices.

Merit Principles and Staffing Practices

The essence of merit principles relevant to staffing is fourfold:

1. To recruit, select, and promote employees on the basis of their KSAOs
2. To provide for fair treatment of applicants and employees without regard to political affiliation, race, color, national origin, sex, religion, age, or handicap
3. To protect the privacy and constitutional rights of applicants and employees as citizens
4. To protect employees against coercion for partisan political purposes[20]

Merit principles are codified in civil service laws and regulations.

Comparisons With Private Sector

Merit principles and civil service laws and regulations combine to shape the nature of staffing practices in the public sector. This leads to some notable differences between the public and private sectors. Examples of public sector staffing practices are the following:

1. Open announcement of all vacancies, along with the content of the selection process that will be followed
2. Very large numbers of applicants due to applications being open to all persons
3. Legal mandate to test applicants only for KSAOs that are directly job related
4. Limits on discretion in the final hiring process, such as number of finalists, ordering of finalists, and affirmative action considerations
5. Rights of applicants to appeal the hiring decision, testing process, or actual test content and method[21]

These examples are unlikely to be encountered in the private sector. Moreover, they are only illustrative of the many differences in staffing practices and context between the private and public sectors.

LEGAL ISSUES IN REMAINDER OF BOOK

The laws and regulations applicable to staffing practices by organizations are multiple in number and complexity. This chapter emphasized an understanding of the need for law, the sources of law, and general provisions of the law and presented in detail the specific provisions that pertain to staffing activities. Little has been said about practical implications and applications.

In the remaining chapters of the book, the focus shifts to the practical, with guidance and suggestions on how to align staffing practices with legal requirements. The "Legal Issues" sections in the remaining chapters discuss major issues from a compliance perspective. The issues so addressed, and the chapter in which they occur, are shown in Exhibit 2.9. Inspection of the exhibit should reinforce the importance accorded laws and regulations as an external influence on staffing activities.

It should be emphasized that there is a selective presentation of the issues in Exhibit 2.9. Only certain issues have been chosen for inclusion, and only a summary of their compliance implications is presented. It should also be emphasized that the discussion of these issues does not constitute professional legal advice.

EXHIBIT 2.9   Legal Issues Covered in Other Chapters

Chapter Title and Number	Topic
Planning (3)	Affirmative action plans and diversity programs
	Legality of affirmative action plans (AAPs) and diversity programs
Job Analysis (4)	Job-relatedness and court cases
	Job analysis and selection
	Essential job functions
External Recruitment (5)	Definition of job applicant
	Affirmative action programs
	Electronic recruitment
	Job advertisements
	Fraud and misrepresentation
Internal Recruitment (6)	Affirmative Action Programs Regulations
	Bona fide seniority system
	Glass ceiling
Measurement (7)	Disparate impact statistics
	Standardization and validation
External Selection I (8)	Disclaimers
	Reference checks
	Background checks
	Preemployment inquiries
	Bona fide occupational qualifications (BFOQs)
External Selection II (9)	Uniform Guidelines on Employee Selection Procedures (UGESP)
	Selection under the ADA
	Drug testing
Internal Selection (10)	UGESP
	Glass ceiling
Decision Making (11)	UGESP
	Diversity and hiring decisions
Final Match (12)	Employment eligibility verification
	Negligent hiring
	Employment-at-will
Staffing System Management (13)	Record keeping and privacy
	EEO-1 report
	Legal audits
	Training for managers and employees
	Alternative dispute resolution
Retention Management (14)	Separation laws and regulations
	Performance appraisal

SUMMARY

Staffing involves the formation of the employment relationship. That relationship involves the employer acquiring individuals to perform work for it as employees, independent contractors, and temporary employees. The specific legal meanings and obligations associated with these various arrangements were provided.

Myriad laws and regulations have come forth from several sources to place constraints on the contractual relationship between employer and employee. These constraints seek to ensure a balance of power in the relationship, as well as provide protections to both the employee and the employer.

Statutory federal laws pertaining to EEO/AA prohibit discrimination on the basis of race, color, religion, sex, national origin, age, genetic information, and disability. This prohibition applies to staffing practices intentionally used to discriminate (disparate treatment), as well as to staffing practices that have a discriminatory effect (disparate or adverse impact). The EEO/AA laws also contain specific provisions pertaining to staffing, which specify both prohibited and permissible practices. In both instances, the emphasis is on use of staffing practices that are job related and focus on the person/job match.

Other laws and regulations also affect staffing practices. At the federal level, there is a prohibition on the employment of unauthorized aliens and on the use of the polygraph (lie detector), constraints on the use of credit reports on job applicants, and specification of the employment rights of those in the uniformed services. State and local EEO/AA laws supplement those found at the federal level. Civil service laws and regulations apply to government employees. Many other staffing practices are also addressed by state and local laws. Finally, civil service laws and regulations govern staffing practices in the public sector. Their provisions create marked differences in certain staffing practices between public and private employers.

Legal issues will continue to be addressed throughout the remainder of this book. The emphasis will be on explanation and application of the laws' provisions to staffing practices. The issues will be discussed at the end of each chapter, beginning with the next one.

DISCUSSION QUESTIONS

1. Do you agree that the employer usually has the upper hand when it comes to establishing the employment relationship? When might the employee have maximum power over the employer?

2. What are the limitations of disparate impact statistics as indicators of potential staffing discrimination?

3. Why is each of the four situational factors necessary for establishing a claim of disparate treatment?

4. What factors would lead an organization to enter into a consent agreement rather than continue pursuing a suit in court?

5. What are the differences between staffing in the private sector and staffing in the public sector? Why would private employers probably resist adopting many of the characteristics of public staffing systems?

ETHICAL ISSUES

1. Assume that you're the staffing manager in an organization that informally, but strongly, discourages you and other managers from hiring people with disabilities. The organization's rationale is that people with disabilities are unlikely to be high performers or long-term employees, and are costly to train, insure, and integrate into the work unit. What is your ethical assessment of the organization's stance? Do you have any ethical obligations to try to change the stance, and if so, how might you go about that?

2. Assume the organization you work for strictly adheres to the law in its relationships with employees and job applicants. The organization calls it "staffing by the book." But beyond that it seems anything goes in terms of tolerated staffing practices. What is your assessment of this approach?

APPLICATIONS

Age Discrimination in a Promotion?

The Best Protection Insurance Company (BPIC) handles a massive volume of claims each year in the corporate claims function, as well as in its four regional claims centers. Corporate claims is headed by the senior vice president of corporate claims (SVPCC); reporting to the SVPCC are two managers of corporate claims (MCC-Life and MCC-Residential) and a highly skilled corporate claims specialist (CCS). Each regional office is headed by a regional center manager (RCM); the RCM is responsible for both supervisors and claims specialists within the regional office. The RCMs report to the vice president of regional claims (VPRC). Here is the structure of the organization:

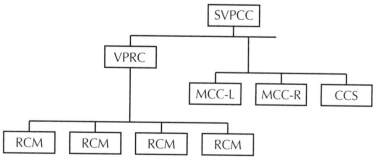

BPIC decided to reorganize its claims function by eliminating the four regional offices (and the RCM position) and establishing numerous small field offices throughout the country. The other part of the reorganization involved creating five new CCS positions. The CCS job itself was to be redesigned and upgraded in terms of knowledge and skill requirements. These new CCS positions would be staffed through internal promotions from within the claims function.

The SVPCC asked Gus Tavus, a 52-year-old RCM, to apply for one of the new CCS positions since his job was being eliminated. The other RCMs, all of whom were over 40 years of age, were also asked to apply. Neither Gus nor the other RCMs were promoted to the CCS positions. Other candidates, some of whom were also over age 40, were also bypassed. The promotions went to five claims specialists and supervisors from within the former regional offices, all of whom were under age 40. Two of these newly promoted employees had worked for, and reported to, Gus as RCM.

Upon learning of his failure to be promoted, Gus sought to find out why. What he learned led him to believe that he had been discriminated against because of his age. He then retained legal counsel, attorney Bruce Davis. Bruce met informally with the SVPCC to try to determine what had happened in the promotion process and why his client had not been promoted. He was told that there were a large number of candidates who were better qualified than Gus and that Gus lacked adequate technical and communication skills for the new job of CCS. The SVPCC refused to reconsider Gus for the job and said that all decisions were etched in stone. Gus and Bruce then filed suit in federal district court, claiming a violation of the Age Discrimination in Employment Act. They also subpoenaed numerous BPIC documents, including the personnel files of all applicants for the CCS positions.

After reviewing the documents and discussing things with Gus, Bruce learned more about the promotion process actually used by BPIC. The SVPCC and the two MCCs conducted the total process; they received no input from the VPRC or the HR department. There was no formal, written job description for the new CCS position, nor was there a formal internal job posting as required by company policy. The SVPCC and the MCCs developed a list of employees they thought might be interested in the job, including Gus, and then met to consider the list of candidates. At that meeting, the personnel files and previous performance appraisals of the candidates were not consulted. After deciding on the five candidates who would be offered the promotion (all five accepted), the SVPCC and MCCs scanned the personnel files and appraisals of these five (only) to check for any disconfirming information. None was found. Bruce's inspection of the files revealed no written comments suggesting age bias in past performance appraisals for any of the candidates, including Gus. Also, there was no indication that Gus lacked technical and communication skills. All of Gus's previous appraisal ratings were above average, and there was no evidence of decline in the favorability of the ratings. Finally, an interview with the VPRC (Gus's boss) revealed that he had not been consulted at all during the promotion process, that he was "shocked beyond belief" that Gus had not been promoted, and that there was "no question" but that Gus was qualified in all respects for the CCS job.

1. Prepare a written report that presents a convincing disparate treatment claim that Gus had been intentionally discriminated against on the basis of his age. Do not address the claim as one of disparate impact.
2. Present a convincing rebuttal, from the viewpoint of BPIC, to this disparate treatment claim.

Disparate Impact: What Do the Statistics Mean?

Claims of discrimination can be pursued under an allegation of disparate impact. According to this approach, the effect or impact of staffing practices can be discriminatory and thus in violation of the Civil Rights Act. Such an impact could occur even though there may be no underlying intention to discriminate against members of a protected group or class (e.g., women or minorities). Pursuit of a disparate impact claim requires the use of various statistics to show that, in effect, women or minorities are being treated differently than men or nonminorities under the law.

Exhibit 2.5 shows three types of disparate impact statistics: flow statistics, stock statistics, and concentration statistics. Also shown is a statistical example of disparate impact for each type. For each of these three types of statistics, prepare a report in which you discuss the following:

1. How can an organization collect and report these statistics in the form shown in Exhibit 2.5?
2. What rule of thumb or guidelines would you recommend for deciding whether statistical differences between men and women, or nonminorities and minorities, reflect discrimination occurring throughout an organization's staffing system?
3. What types of staffing activities (recruitment, selection, and employment) might be causing the statistical differences? For example, in Exhibit 2.5 the selection rate for men is 50% and for women is 11%. How would the organization collect the data necessary to compute these selection rates, how would you decide if the difference in selection rates (50% vs. 11%) is big enough to indicate possible discrimination, and what sorts of practices might be causing the difference in selection rates?

ENDNOTES

1. M. W. Bennett, D. J. Polden, and H. J. Rubin, *Employment Relationships: Law and Practice* (Frederick, MD: Aspen, 2004), pp. 1-1 to 3-50; D. J. Walsh, *Employment Law for Human Resource Practice*, second ed. (Mason, OH: Thompson Higher Education, 2007), pp. 33–60.

2. C. J. Muhl, "The Employment-at-Will Doctrine: Three Major Exceptions," *Monthly Labor Review*, Jan. 2001, pp. 3–11.

3. S. Bates, "A Tough Target: Employee or Independent Contractor?" *HR Magazine*, July 2001, pp. 69–74; Bennett, Polden, and Rubin, *Employment Relationships: Law and Practice,* pp. 1-4 to 1-7; K. D. Meade, J. W. Pegano, I. M. Saxe, and J. A. Moskowitz, "Revisit Independent Contractor Classifications," *Legal Report*, Society for Human Resource Management, Oct./Nov. 2007, pp. 7–8.

4. A. R. Midence, "A Risky New Trend: Replacing Employees With Independent Contractors," *Workforce Management Online*, Nov. 2009, accessed 5/18/2010.

5. D. C. Feldman and B. S. Klaas, "Temporary Workers: Employee Rights and Employer Responsibilities," *Employee Rights and Responsibilities Journal*, 1996, 9(1), pp. 1–21; B. Lanza and M. R. Maryn, "Legal Status of Contingent Workers," *Compensation and Benefits Review*, July/Aug. 2003, pp. 47–60.

6. Equal Employment Opportunity Commission, *EEOC Policy Guidance on Temporary Workers* (Washington, DC: author, 1997); Equal Employment Opportunity Commission, *Enforcement Guidance: Application of the ADA to Contingent Workers Placed by Temporary Agencies and Other Staffing Firms* (Washington, DC: author, 2000); N. Greenwald, "Use of Temporary Workers Also Invites Exposure to Lawsuits," *Workforce Management Online*, March 2010, accessed 3/25/2010.

7. R. J. Bohner, Jr., and E. R. Salasko, "Beware the Legal Risks of Hiring Temps," *Workforce*, Oct. 2003, pp. 50–57; Walsh, *Employment Law for Human Resource Practice,* pp. 42–43.

8. P. Salvatore and A. M. Gutterman, "The Risk of Intentional Torts," *HR Magazine*, Aug. 2003, pp. 109–114.

9. L. Guerin and A. DelPo, *The Essential Guide to Federal Employment Laws*, second ed. (Berkeley, CA: Nolo, 2009); D. D. Bennett-Alexander and L. P. Hartman, *Employment Law for Business*, sixth ed. (New York: McGraw-Hill Irwin, 2009).

10. Equal Employment Opportunity Commission, *EEOC Enforcement Guidance on How to Count Employees When Determining Coverage Under Title VII, the ADA, and the ADEA* (Washington, DC: author, 1997).

11. Equal Employment Opportunity Commission, *EEOC Guidance on Investigating, Analyzing Retaliation Claims* (*www.eeoc.gov*).

12. W. Bliss, "The Wheel of Misfortune," *HR Magazine*, May 2000, pp. 207–218; W. A. Carmell, "Application of U.S. Antidiscrimination Laws to Multinational Employers," *Legal Report*, Society for Human Resource Management, May/June 2001; S. Lash, "Supreme Court Disables State Employees," *HR News*, Apr. 2001, p. 6.

13. Bennett, Polden, and Rubin, *Employment Relationships: Law and Practice*, pp. 4-75 to 4-82.

14. Bennett, Polden, and Rubin, *Employment Relationships: Law and Practice*, pp. 4-75 to 4-82.

15. R. K. Robinson, G. M. Franklin, and R. F. Wayland, *Employment Regulation in the Workplace* (Armonk, NY: M. E. Sharpe, 2010), pp. 84–103.

16. K. Tyler, "Mediating a Better Outcome," *HR Magazine*, Nov. 2007, pp. 63–66.

17. Bennett, Polden, and Rubin, *Employment Relationships: Law and Practice*, pp. 4-75 to 4-82; T. S. Bland, "Anatomy of an Employment Lawsuit," *HR Magazine*, Mar. 2001, pp. 145–151.

18. J. Staman, "Obesity Discrimination and the Americans With Disabilities Act," Congressional Research Service, Library of Congress, 2007.

19. J. R. Mook, "Accommodation Paradigm Shifts," *HR Magazine*, Jan. 2007, pp. 115–120.

20. J. P. Wiesen, N. Abrams, and S. A. McAttee, *Employment Testing: A Public Sector Viewpoint* (Alexandria, VA: International Personnel Management Association Assessment Council, 1990), pp. 2–3.

21. Wiesen, Abrams, and McAttee, *Employment Testing: A Public Sector Viewpoint*, pp. 3–7.

CHAPTER THREE

Planning

Learning Objectives and Introduction
Learning Objectives
Introduction

External Influences
Economic Conditions
Labor Markets
Technology
Labor Unions

Human Resource Planning
Process and Example
Initial Decisions
Forecasting HR Requirements
Forecasting HR Availabilities
Reconciliation and Gaps

Staffing Planning
Staffing Planning Process
Core Workforce
Flexible Workforce
Outsourcing

Diversity Planning
Demography of the American Workforce
Business Case for Diversity
Planning for Diversity

Legal Issues
Affirmative Action Plans
Legality of AAPs and Diversity Programs
EEO and Temporary Workers

Summary

Discussion Questions

Ethical Issues

Applications

Tanglewood Stores Case

LEARNING OBJECTIVES AND INTRODUCTION

Learning Objectives

- Recognize external influences that will shape the planning process
- Understand how strategic plans integrate with staffing plans
- Become familiar with statistical and judgmental techniques for forecasting HR requirements and availabilities
- Know the similarities and differences between replacement and succession planning
- Understand the advantages and disadvantages of core workforce, flexible workforce, and outsourcing strategies for different groups of employees
- Learn how to incorporate diversity into the planning process
- Recognize the fundamental components of an affirmative action plan

Introduction

Human resource (HR) planning is the process of forecasting the organization's future employment needs and then developing action plans and programs for fulfilling these needs in ways that align with the staffing strategy. HR plans form the basis of all other activities conducted during staffing. An organization that thoroughly considers its staffing needs and how these needs fit with the external environment will find it much easier to recruit the right number and type of candidates, develop methods for selecting the right candidates, and evaluate whether its programs are successful.

In a nutshell, HR planning involves learning about the employment environment, determining how many employees an organization will need in the future, and assessing the availability of employees in both the internal and external markets. The HR planning process involves several specific components that we cover in this chapter, including making initial planning decisions, forecasting HR requirements and availabilities, determining employee shortages and surpluses, and developing action plans.

The chapter begins with an overview of external influences on the HR planning process, like labor markets, technology, and unions. Next, we provide an overview of the process of HR planning, including a review of methods for forecasting HR requirements and availability. The staffing planning process includes distinguishing between the core and flexible workforces, as well as understanding the environment for outsourcing. Diversity programs have become an increasingly important part of the staffing planning process, so they are also discussed. The major legal issue for HR staffing planning is that of affirmative action plans (AAPs). A different legal issue, that of equal employment opportunity (EEO) coverage for temporary employees and their agencies, is also discussed.

EXTERNAL INFLUENCES

There are four major sources of external influence on HR and staffing planning, namely, economic conditions, labor markets, technology, and labor unions. Exhibit 3.1 provides specific examples of these influences, which are discussed next.

Economic Conditions

Numerous macro forces operate to determine the overall economic climate in which the organization functions. These include product and labor market competition (both national and global), inflation, interest rates, currency exchange rates, and government fiscal and monetary policy. Resulting from such forces is the degree of overall economic expansion or contraction.

A direct derivative of expansion and contraction forces is the amount of job creation and growth, both positive and negative. Positive job growth means expanding job opportunities for individuals, while slowdowns or contractions in job growth yield dwindling job opportunities. Organizations move people into (new hires), within (internal labor markets), and out of (turnover) the organization at varying

---

EXHIBIT 3.1   Examples of External Influences on Staffing

ECONOMIC CONDITIONS
- Economic expansion and contraction
- Job growth and job opportunities
- Internal labor market mobility
- Turnover rates

LABOR MARKETS
- Labor demand: employment patterns, KSAOs sought
- Labor supply: labor force, demographic trends, KSAOs available
- Labor shortages and surpluses
- Employment arrangements

TECHNOLOGY
- Elimination of jobs
- Creation of jobs
- Changes in skill requirements

LABOR UNIONS
- Negotiations
- Labor contracts: staffing levels, staffing quality, internal movement
- Grievance systems

rates, depending on the amount of job growth. Job growth thus functions like a spigot governing the movement of people.

Consider the case of job expansion. When new jobs are created, new hire rates increase for both entry-level and higher-level jobs. These new hires are either new entrants into the labor force (e.g., recent college graduates) or current members of the labor force, both unemployed and employed. There will also be increased movement within organizations' internal labor markets through the operation of their promotion and transfer systems. This movement will be necessitated by a combination of new jobs being created that will be filled internally and the exit of current employees from the organization. Most likely, the departure of employees will be due to their taking new jobs at other organizations. Some, however, may be temporarily unemployed (while they look for new job opportunities), and others may leave the labor force entirely.

With lesser rates of job growth or actual job contraction, the movement flows are lessened. Organizations will hire fewer people, and job seekers will have longer searches and fewer opportunities to choose from. Promotion and transfer opportunities for current employees will dry up, voluntary turnover rates will decrease, and many employees may even be terminated through involuntary layoff or a voluntary early retirement program. The "great recession" of 2008 resulted in a massive decrease in job openings and employment levels that will continue to plague the economy for years to come.[1]

Labor Markets

In and through labor markets, organizations express specific labor preferences and requirements (labor demand), and persons express their own job preferences and requirements (labor supply). Ultimately, person/job matches occur from the interaction of the demand and supply forces. Both labor demand and supply contain quantity and quality components, as described below. Labor shortages and surpluses, and a variety of possible employment arrangements are also discussed.

Labor Demand: Employment Patterns

Labor demand is a derived demand, meaning it is a result of consumer demands for the organization's products and services. The organization acquires and deploys its workforce in ways that allow it to respond to consumer demand in a competitive manner.

To learn about labor demand, national employment statistics are collected and analyzed. They provide data about employment patterns and projections for industries, occupations, and organization size.

Projections to year 2018 indicate that most job growth will occur in the services sector, led by the education and health services industries, followed by business and professional services. Manufacturing and federal government employment will remain steady, and declines will occur in mining and agriculture.[2]

Employment growth to 2018 will vary across occupations, with most of the growth concentrated in health care and information technology, and most of the losses concentrated in clerical and manufacturing. Examples of growth "winners" include veterinarians (33%), medical assistants (34%), computer software engineers (34%), home health aides (49%), and personal financial advisors (41%). Examples of growth "losers" include file clerks (−23%), sewing machine operators (−34%), machine feeders and offbearers (−22%), and computer operators (−19%).

Labor Demand: KSAOs Sought

Knowledge, skill, ability, and other characteristics (KSAO) requirements or preferences of employers are not widely measured, except for education requirements. Data collected by the Bureau of Labor Statistics suggest a continued increase in demand for individuals with college degrees or more. The number of jobs requiring a bachelor's degree is expected to increase 17%, the number requiring a master's degree is expected to increase 19%, and the number requiring a doctoral degree is expected to increase 22%. By contrast, the number of jobs requiring only short-term on-the-job training is expected to increase by only 9%.[3] The increasing demand for education most likely reflects advances in technology that have made many jobs more complex and technically demanding.[4]

A very thorough and systematic source of information about KSAOs needed for jobs is the Occupational Outlook Handbook (available at *www.bls.gov*). It does not indicate KSAO deficiencies; rather, it provides detailed information about the nature of work and the training and KSAOs required for the entire spectrum of occupations in the United States. A survey of HR professionals and employees revealed that critical thinking skills, creativity, diversity, ethics, and lifelong learning were seen as especially relevant skills for today's employees.[5]

Survey results show that employers have multiple general KSAO requirements that accompany their quantitative labor requirements. Naturally, the more specific requirements vary according to type of employer and type of job. It also appears that employers have identified general future KSAO needs for their workforces from the skill gaps in their current workforces and, in the case of managers, what their projected critical KSAO requirements will be.

Labor Supply: The Labor Force and Its Trends

Quantity of labor supplied is measured and reported periodically by the Bureau of Labor Statistics in the US Department of Labor. An example of basic results for July 2005 through 2010 is given in Exhibit 3.2. It shows that the labor force, including both full- and part-time employees, reached about 154 million individuals (employed and unemployed) and that unemployment ranged from 4.4% to 9.7%. The data for 2009 to 2010 clearly show the effects of a major economic slowdown.

Data reveal several labor force trends that have particular relevance for staffing organizations. Labor force growth is slowing, going from an annual growth rate of

EXHIBIT 3.2   **Labor Force Statistics**

	2005	2006	2007	2008	2009	2010
Civilian noninstitutional population (in millions)	227	229	232	234	236	238
Civilian labor force (in millions)	150	152	153	155	154	154
Employed (in millions)	143	145	146	147	140	139
Unemployed (in millions)	7.3	6.7	7.0	9.4	14.5	14.6
Not in labor force (in millions)	77	78	79	78	82	84
Labor force participation rate (%)	66	66	66	63	65	65
Unemployment rate (%)	4.9	4.4	4.6	6.0	9.4	9.7

SOURCE: US Department of Labor, "The Employment Situation," July 2005, July 2006, July 2007, July 2008, July 2009, July 2010.

around 2% in the early 1990s to a projected rate of 1.0% by the year 2018. There are increasingly fewer new entrants to the labor force. This trend, coupled with the severe KSAO deficiencies that many of the new entrants will have, creates major adaptation problems for organizations.

Demographically, the labor force has become more diverse, and this trend will continue. Data starting in the 1980s and projected through 2018 show a slow trend toward nearly equal labor force participation for men and women, a slight decrease in the proportion of whites in the workforce, and large proportional growth in the representation of Hispanics and Asians. There will also be a dramatic shift toward fewer younger workers and more workers over the age of 55.

Other, more subtle labor force trends are also under way. There has been a slight upward movement overall in the average number of hours that people work and a strong rise in the proportion of employees who work very long hours in certain occupations, such as managers and professionals. Relatedly, there is an increase in multiple job holding, with 6.2% of employed people holding more than one job. The number of immigrants in the population is growing; nearly 1 in 10 people is foreign born, the highest rate in more than 50 years. New federal and state policies are increasingly pushing welfare recipients into the labor force, and they are mostly employed in low-wage jobs with low educational requirements. People historically out of the labor force mainstream—such as those with disabilities and the growing number of retirees—may assume a greater presence in the labor force.[6]

Labor Supply: KSAOs Available

A survey of 431 HR professionals found that 40% of employers indicated that high school graduates lack basic skills in reading comprehension, writing, and math required for entry-level jobs, and that 70% of employers said high school graduates are deficient in work habits such as professionalism, critical thinking, personal accountability, and time management.[7] Most respondents believed that college graduates were somewhat better prepared for work, but 44% of applicants with college degrees were still rated as having poor writing skills. There are also shortages of employees with the high skill levels required in contemporary manufacturing environments.[8] Economists and sociologists are quick to note that these skills shortages are being reported despite consistent gains in standardized test scores and educational attainment in the labor force since the 1960s.[9] Thus, it appears that the problem is that demand for advanced skills is increasing, as we noted earlier, and not that the supply of skilled workers is decreasing. This idea is reinforced by another survey of 726 HR professionals that found 98% of respondents reported that the competition for talented workers has increased in recent years.[10] Data such as these reinforce the serious KSAO deficiencies reported by employers in at least some portions of the labor force.

Labor Shortages and Surpluses

When labor demand exceeds labor supply for a given pay rate, the labor market is said to be "tight" and the organization experiences labor shortages. Shortages tend to be job or occupation specific. Low unemployment rates, surges in labor demand in certain occupations, and skill deficiencies all fuel both labor quantity and labor quality shortages for many organizations. The shortages cause numerous responses:

- Increased pay and benefit packages
- Hiring bonuses and stock options
- Alternative work arrangements to attract and retain older workers
- Use of temporary employees
- Recruitment of immigrants
- Lower hiring standards
- Partnerships with high schools, technical schools, and colleges
- Increased mandatory overtime work
- Increased hours of operation

These types of responses are lessened or reversed when the labor market is "loose," meaning there are labor surpluses relative to labor demand.

Employment Arrangements

Though labor market forces bring organizations and job seekers together, the specific nature of the employment arrangement can assume many forms. One form is whether the person will be employed on a full-time or part-time basis. Data show that about 83% of people work full time and 17% work part time.[11] Although many people prefer part-time work, approximately 23% of part-time workers are seeking full-time employment.

A second arrangement involves the issue of flexible scheduling and shift work. The proportion of the workforce covered by flexible shifts has steadily grown from 12.4% in 1985 to 27.5% in 2004. Many of these workers are covered by formal flextime programs. Work hours are often put into shifts, and about 15% of full-time employed adults work evening, night, or rotating shifts.[12]

Two other types of arrangements, often considered in combination, are (1) various alternative arrangements to the traditional employer–employee relationship, and (2) the use of contingent employees. Alternative arrangements include the organization filling its staffing needs through the use of independent contractors, on-call workers and day laborers, temporary help agency employees, and employees provided by a contract firm that provides a specific service (e.g., accounting). Contingent employees do not have an explicit or implicit contract for long-term employment; they expect their employment to be temporary rather than long term.

National data on the use of alternative employment arrangements and contingent employees are shown in Exhibit 3.3. It can be seen that 89.3% of surveyed individuals worked in a traditional employer–employee arrangement, and the vast majority of these (97.1%) considered themselves noncontingent. The most prevalent alternative was to work as an independent contractor (7.5%), followed by on-call employees and day laborers (1.7%), temporary help agency employees (.9%), and employees provided by a contract firm (.6%). The percentage of contingent employees in these alternative arrangements ranged from 3.4% (independent contractors) to 60.7% (temporary help employees).

EXHIBIT 3.3   **Usage of Alternative Employment Arrangements and Contingent Workers**

Arrangement	Total (millions)	Percent	Percent Contingent	Percent Noncontingent
Alternative Arrangements				
Independent contractor	10.3	7.5	3.4	96.6
On-call workers and day laborers	2.4	1.7	24.6	75.4
Temporary help agency workers	1.2	.9	60.7	39.3
Workers provided by contract firm	.8	.6	19.5	80.5
Traditional Arrangements	122.8	89.3	2.9	97.1
	137.5	100		

SOURCE: US Department of Labor, Bureau of Labor Statistics, *Contingent and Alternative Employment Arrangements,* Feb. 2005.

EXHIBIT 3.4 **Major Workforce Trends**

- Increasing number of workers over the age of 55 will mean higher health care costs for employers, threatening economic competitiveness
- Continued threat of recession or poor economic conditions globally
- Changing attitudes toward retirement, especially an increased tendency for retirees to remain in the workforce to some extent
- Changes in technology will lead to changes in skills demanded by employers
- Federal health care legislation
- Increased costs of health care for employers due to increased employee demand for insurance programs and increased premiums from insurance companies
- Demographic shifts will lead to a shortage of skills, especially for jobs requiring high skill levels

SOURCE: J. Schramm, *Workplace Forecast, 2008* (Alexandria, VA: Society for Human Resource Management, 2008).

Exhibit 3.4 shows several other workforce trends identified in a survey of 1,232 HR professionals.

Technology

Changes in technology can influence the staffing planning process significantly. In some cases, technology can serve as a substitute for labor by either eliminating or dramatically reducing the need for certain types of workers. As we noted earlier, the economy as a whole has shown decreased demand for positions like clerical workers, telephone operators, and many manufacturing operators as technology has replaced labor as an input to production. Ironically, changes in software that have made computers easier for nonspecialists to use have eliminated many jobs in computer programming.

At the same time, technology can serve to create new jobs as new business opportunities emerge. In place of the jobs that are eliminated, demand for technical occupations like robotics engineers, systems and database analysts, and software engineers has increased. The expansion of e-commerce and other Internet-based services has increased demand for those who design and manage websites. Increasing productivity as a result of technological change can also spur increased firm performance, and this will, in turn, create more jobs. Often these new jobs will require a completely different set of KSAOs than previous jobs, meaning that increased staffing resources will have to be devoted to either retraining or replacing the current workforce. Research conducted in both the United States and Germany shows that computerization has led to an increase in the demand for highly educated specialists, leading to an overall increased market demand for skills in science and mathematics, which in turn has led to dramatic increases in wages for individuals with these skills.[13] Employers that adopt new technology for any aspect of their operations will also have to consider how to tap into labor markets that have these new skills.

Labor Unions

Labor unions are legally protected entities that organize employees and bargain with management to establish terms and conditions of employment via a labor contract. About 12% of the labor force is unionized, with 7.4% unionization in the private sector and 36% in the public sector.[14] Trends suggest a continued decline in private sector unionization as well as an increasing level of public sector unionization.[15]

Labor and management are required to bargain in good faith to try to reach agreement on the contract. Many staffing issues may be bargained, including staffing levels, location of facilities, overtime and work schedules, job descriptions and classifications, seniority provisions, promotions and transfers, layoffs and terminations, hiring pools, KSAO requirements, grievance procedures, alternative dispute resolution procedures, employment discrimination protection, and, very important, pay and benefits. Virtually all aspects of the staffing process are thus affected by negotiations and the resultant labor agreement.

Labor unions thus have direct and powerful impacts on staffing and other HR systems. Even in nonunion situations the union influence can be felt through "spillover effects" in which management tries to emulate the pay and benefits, as well as staffing practices, found in unionized settings.

HUMAN RESOURCE PLANNING

Human resource planning (HRP) is a process and set of activities undertaken to forecast an organization's labor demand (requirements) and internal labor supply (availabilities), to compare these projections to determine employment gaps, and to develop action plans for addressing these gaps. Action plans include staffing planning to arrive at desired staffing levels and staffing quality.

A general model depicting the process of HRP is presented first, followed by an operational example of HRP. Detailed discussions of the major components of HRP are then given.[16]

Process and Example

The basic elements of virtually any organization's HRP are shown in Exhibit 3.5. As can be seen, the HRP process involves four sequential steps:

1. Determine future HR requirements
2. Determine future HR availabilities

EXHIBIT 3.5   The Basic Elements of Human Resource Planning

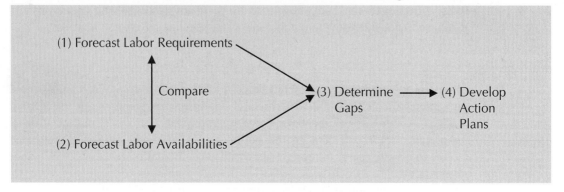

3. Reconcile requirements and availabilities—that is, determine gaps (shortages and surpluses) between the two

4. Develop action plans to close the projected gaps

An example of HRP, including results from forecasting requirements and availabilities, is shown in Exhibit 3.6. The exhibit shows a partial HRP being conducted by an organization for a specific unit (sales and customer service). It involves only two job categories (A, sales, and B, customer service) and two hierarchical levels for each category (1, entry level, and 2, manager level). All of the HRP steps are confined to this particular organizational unit and its job categories/levels, as shown.

The current workforce size (number of employees) is given for each job category/level. Requirements and availabilities are forecast for one year, and the results are shown in the relevant columns. After the reconciliation process, final gap figures are agreed on and entered into the gap column. It can be seen that there is an overall estimated shortage of 145 employees and that the shortage is very unevenly distributed across the four job categories/levels. Three areas show projected shortages of 39, 110, and 3, and the fourth area shows a projected surplus of 7.

These gap data serve as the basic input to action planning. Because the gaps show both shortages and a surplus, and because the gaps vary in severity relative to the current workforce, a specific action plan will probably have to be developed and implemented for each job category/level. The resultant four staffing (and other) plans hopefully will bring staffing into an orderly balance of requirements and availabilities over the course of the planning period.

The above process and example identify and illustrate the rudiments of HRP. Within them are several distinct components that require elaboration. We turn now to these components, emphasizing that each one represents a factor that must be considered in HRP and that specific choices must be made regarding the operational details for each component.

EXHIBIT 3.6 Operational Format and Example of Human Resource Planning

Organizational Unit: Sales and Customer Service

Job Category and Level	Current Workforce	Forecast for Workforce— One Year		Reconciliation and Gaps	Action Planning
		Requirements	Availabilities		
A1 (Sales)	100	110	71	−39 (shortage)	Recruitment
A2 (Sales manager)	20	15	22	+7 (surplus)	Selection
B1 (Customer service representative)	200	250	140	−110 (shortage)	Employment
B2 (Customer service manager)	15	25	22	−3 (shortage)	Retention
	335	400	255	−145 (shortage)	Compensation
					Training and development

Initial Decisions

Before HRP per se can be undertaken, several critical decisions must be made. These decisions will shape the nature of the resultant HRP process, and they will influence the output of the process, namely, the gap estimates. The quality and potential effectiveness of the action plans developed from the gap estimates are thus at stake when these initial decisions are confronted and made.

Strategic Planning

It is always a good idea to have a close, reciprocal linkage between business strategy and HR plans.[17] Managers engaged in HRP should be aware of environmental contingencies and strategic goals that will affect the size of various business units. Changes in technology and strategy will also impact the KSAOs that will be needed in the future. When HRP takes place as an integral part of an organization's strategic planning process, it is referred to as plan-based HRP. This is a wise approach because it helps integrate the organization's strategic planning process with HR implications.

However, not all important business developments are captured in formal business plans, particularly if they occur rapidly or unexpectedly. Sudden changes in consumer preferences or legal requirements, for example, can wreak havoc on business plans. Organizational responses to these changes often occur in the form of special projects, rather than in changes to the total business plan. Part of each response requires consideration of HR implications, however, resulting in what is called project-based HRP. This type of planning helps ensure that the necessary creation of new jobs, changes in requirements and rewards for existing jobs, and employee job changes are undertaken systematically and without undue interruption.

In addition, many organizations do HRP outside the formal planning cycle for critical groups of employees on a regular basis. This often occurs for jobs in which there are perennial shortages of employees, both externally and internally. Examples here include nurses in health care organizations, faculty in certain specialized areas at colleges and universities, and teachers in elementary and secondary schools. Planning focused on a specific employee group is referred to as population-based HRP.

A firm grasp of an organization's internal environment is also important. Thus, planners must be out and about in their organizations, taking advantage of opportunities to learn what is going on. Informal discussions with key managers can help, as can employee attitude surveys and the monitoring of key indicators such as employee performance, absenteeism, turnover, and accident rates. Special interest should be paid to recurring difficulties that threaten to interfere with the attainment of future business plans or other important organizational goals. High turnover in a sales organization, for example, is likely to threaten the viability of a business plan that calls for increased sales quotas or the rapid introduction of several new products.

The values and attitudes of managers, especially top managers, toward HR are also important to HRP. Trouble brews when these are inconsistent with the organization's business plans. For example, a midsized accounting firm may have formulated a business plan calling for very rapid growth through aggressive marketing and selected acquisitions of smaller firms, but existing management talent may be inadequate to the task of operating a larger, more complex organization. Moreover, there may be a prevailing attitude among the top management against investing much money in management development and against bringing in talent from outside the firm. This attitude conflicts with the business plan, requiring a change in either the business plan or attitudes.

Planning Time Frame

Since planning involves looking into the future, the logical question for an organization to ask is, How far into the future should our planning extend? Typically, plans are divided into long term (three years and more), intermediate (one to three years), and short term (one year or less). Organizations vary in their planning time frame, often depending on which of the three types of HRP is being undertaken.

For plan-based HRP, the time frame will be the same as that of the business plan. In most organizations, this is between three and five years for so-called strategic planning and something less than three years for operational planning. Planning horizons for project-based HRP vary depending on the nature of the projects involved. Solving a temporary shortage of, say, salespeople for the introduction of a new product might involve planning for only a few months, whereas planning for the start-up of a new facility could involve a lead time of two or more years. Population-based HRP will have varying time frames, depending on the time necessary for labor supply (internal as well as external) to become available. As an example, for top-level executives in an organization, the planning time frame will be lengthy.

Job Categories and Levels

The unit of HRP and analysis is composed of job categories and hierarchical levels among jobs. These job category/level combinations, and the types and paths of employee movement among them, form the structure of an internal labor market. Management must choose which job categories and which hierarchical levels to use for HRP. In Exhibit 3.6, for example, the choice involves two jobs (sales and customer service) and two levels (entry and manager) for a particular organizational unit.

Job categories are created and used on the basis of the unit of analysis for which projected shortages and surpluses are being investigated. Hierarchical levels should be chosen so that they are consistent with or identical to the formal organizational hierarchy. The reason for this is that these formal levels define employee promotions (up levels), transfers (across levels), and demotions (down levels). Having gap information by level facilitates planning of internal movement programs within the internal labor market. For example, it is difficult to have a systematic promotion-from-within program without knowing probable numbers of vacancies and gaps at various organizational levels.

Head Count (Current Workforce)

Exactly how does an organization count the number of people in its current workforce for forecasting and planning purposes? Sometimes it makes sense to simply count the number of employees on payroll at the start of the planning period. However, there are times when other methods of assessing head count might be preferable.

To account for the amount of scheduled time worked by each employee, an employee head count may be made and stated in terms of full-time equivalents, or FTEs. To do this, simply define what constitutes full-time work in terms of hours per week (or other time unit), and count each employee in terms of scheduled hours worked relative to a full workweek. If full time is defined as 40 hours per week, a person who normally works 20 hours per week is counted as a .50 FTE, a person normally working 30 hours per week is a .75 FTE, and so on. It is also often advisable to take current authorized vacancies into account when assessing head count.

Roles and Responsibilities

Both line managers and staff specialists (usually from the HR department) become involved in HRP, so the roles and responsibilities of each must be determined as part of HRP. Most organizations take the position that line managers are ultimately responsible for the completion and quality of HRP, but the usual practice is to have HR staff assist with the process.

Initially, the HR staff takes the lead in proposing which types of HRP will be undertaken and when, and in making suggestions with regard to comprehensiveness, planning time frame, job categories and levels, and head counts. Final decisions on these matters are usually the prerogative of line management. Once an approach has been decided on, task forces of both line managers and HR staff people are assembled to design an appropriate forecasting and action planning process and to do any other preliminary work.

Once these processes are in place, the HR staff typically assumes responsibility for collecting, manipulating, and presenting the necessary data to line management and for laying out alternative action plans (including staffing plans). Action planning usually becomes a joint venture between line managers and HR staff, particularly as they gain experience with, and trust for, one another.

Forecasting HR Requirements

Forecasting HR requirements is a direct derivative of business and organizational planning. As such, it becomes a reflection of projections about a variety of factors, such as sales, production, technological change, productivity improvement, and the regulatory environment. Many specific techniques may be used to forecast HR requirements; these are either statistical or judgmental in nature, and they are usually tailor-made by the organization.

Statistical Techniques

A wide array of statistical techniques are available for use in HR forecasting. Prominent among these are regression analysis, ratio analysis, trend analysis, time series analysis, and stochastic analysis. Brief descriptions of three of these techniques are given in Exhibit 3.7.

The use of integrated workforce planning software, which can be combined with data from other organizational databases, makes it easier to use these statistical techniques than it was in the past. As we noted earlier, HR practitioners are also increasingly expected to back up their proposals and plans with hard data. The three techniques shown in Exhibit 3.7 have different strengths and weaknesses. Ratio analysis, which uses data from prior sales figures or other operational data to predict expected head count, is useful for integrating HR plans with other departments. However, this model cannot directly account for any changes in technology or skill sets that might change these ratios. The regression analysis technique can be used with historical predictors and can make more statistically precise estimates of future expectations by taking several factors into account simultaneously; however, collecting enough data to make good estimates can be time-consuming and requires judgment calls. Trend analysis is useful when organizations have data mostly on historical staffing levels with less detailed information on specific predictors. The decomposition of data into specific time periods of demand is also often used in health care and retail settings, where staffing levels vary greatly over the course of a year or even at different times of the day. Unfortunately, trend analysis does not directly take into account external factors that might change trends. In light of the problems with each of these methods, managers should use these statistical estimates only as a starting point and modify them as needed due to ongoing strategic and environmental changes.

Judgmental Techniques

Judgmental techniques represent human decision-making models that are used for forecasting HR requirements. Unlike statistical techniques, judgmental techniques use a decision maker who collects and weighs the information subjectively and then turns it into forecasts of HR requirements. The decision maker's forecasts may or may not agree very closely with those derived from statistical techniques.

Implementation of judgmental forecasting can proceed from either a top-down or bottom-up approach. In the former, top managers of the organization, organizational units, or functions rely on their knowledge of business and organizational plans to predict what future head counts will be. At times, these projections may,

---

EXHIBIT 3.7   Examples of Statistical Techniques to Forecast HR Requirements

(A)   Ratio Analysis

1. Examine historical ratios involving workforce size.

$$\text{Example:} \quad \frac{\$ \text{ sales}}{1.0 \text{ FTE}} = ? \qquad \frac{\text{No. of new customers}}{1.0 \text{ FTE}} = ?$$

2. Assume ratio will be true in future.
3. Use ratio to predict future HR requirements.

$$\text{Example:} \quad \text{(a)} \frac{\$40{,}000 \text{ sales}}{1.0 \text{ FTE}} \text{ is past ratio}$$

   (b) Sales forecast is $4,000,000
   (c) HR requirements = 100 FTEs

(B)   Regression Analysis

1. Statistically identify historical predictors of workforce size.

   Example: $\text{FTEs} = a + b_1 \text{ sales} + b_2 \text{ new customers}$

2. Only use equations with predictors found to be statistically significant.
3. Predict future HR requirements, using equation.

   Example: (a) $\text{FTEs} = 7 + .0004 \text{ sales} + .02 \text{ new customers}$
   (b) Projected sales = $1,000,000
       Projected new customers = 300
   (c) HR requirements = 7 + 400 + 6 = 413

(C)   Trend Analysis

1. Gather data on staffing levels over time and arrange in a spreadsheet with one column for employment levels and another column for time.
2. Predict trend in employee demand by fitting a line to trends in historical staffing levels over time (this can be done by using regression or graphical methods in most spreadsheet programs).
3. Calculate period demand index by dividing each period's demand by the average annual demand.

   Example: January demand index = Avg. January FTE/Avg. annual FTE

4. Multiply the previous year's FTEs by the trend figure, then multiply this figure by the period's demand index.

   Example: A retail store finds that the average number of employees over the past five years has been 142, 146, 150, 155, and 160. This represents a consistent 3% increase per year; to predict the next year's average demand, multiply 160 by 1.03 to show a 3% expected increase. Over this same time period, it averaged 150 FTEs per month, with an average of 200 FTEs in December. This means the December demand index is 200/150 = 1.33, so its estimate for next year's December FTE demand will be $(160 \times 1.03) \times 1.3 = 219$ FTEs.

in fact, be dictates rather than estimates, necessitated by strict adherence to the business plan. Such dictates are common in organizations undergoing significant change, such as restructuring, mergers, and cost-cutting actions.

In the bottom-up approach, lower-level managers make initial estimates for their unit (e.g., department, office, or plant) on the basis of what they have been told or presume are the business and organizational plans. These estimates are then consolidated and aggregated upward through successively higher levels of management. Then, top management establishes the HR requirements in terms of numbers.

Forecasting HR Availabilities

In Exhibit 3.6 head-count data are given for the current workforce and their availability as forecast in each job category/level. These forecast figures take into account movement into and out of each job category/level and exit from the organizational unit or the organization. Described below are three approaches for forecasting availabilities: manager judgment, Markov Analysis, and replacement and succession planning.

Manager Judgment

Individual managers may use their judgment to make availability forecasts for their work units. This is especially appropriate in smaller organizations or in ones that lack centralized workforce internal mobility data and statistical forecasting capabilities. Continuing the example from Exhibit 3.6, assume the manager is asked to make an availability forecast for the entry sales job category A1. The template to follow for making the forecast and the results of the forecast are shown in Exhibit 3.8. To the current staffing level in A1 (100) is added likely inflows to A1 (10), and then likely outflows from A1 (37) are subtracted to yield the forecasted staffing

---

EXHIBIT 3.8 Manager Forecast of Future HR Availabilities

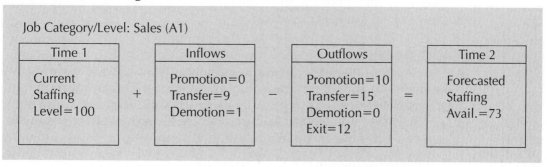

Job Category/Level: Sales (A1)

Time 1		Inflows		Outflows		Time 2
Current Staffing Level=100	+	Promotion=0 Transfer=9 Demotion=1	−	Promotion=10 Transfer=15 Demotion=0 Exit=12	=	Forecasted Staffing Avail.=73

NOTE: Promotion is A1 to A2, A1 to B2, B1 to B2, or B1 to A2; transfer is A1 to B1, A2 to B2, B1 to A1, or B2 to A2; demotion is A2 to A1, A2 to B1, B2 to B1, or B2 to A1.

availability (73). Determining the inflow and outflow numbers requires judgmental estimates as to the numbers of promotions, transfers, demotions, and exits. As shown at the bottom of Exhibit 3.8, promotions involve an upward change of job level within or between job categories, transfers are lateral moves at the same job level across job categories, and demotions are downward changes of job level within or between job categories. Separate forecasts may be done for the other job category/levels (A2, B1, and B2).

To provide reliable estimates, the manager must be very knowledgeable about both organizational business plans and individual employee plans or preferences for staying in their current job versus moving to another job. Knowledge of business plans will be helpful in judging the likely internal mobility opportunities for employees. Business expansion, for example, will likely mean expanding internal mobility opportunities. Knowledge of employee plans or preferences will help pinpoint which employees are likely to change jobs or leave the work unit or organization.

The estimated staffing availability (n = 73) in Exhibit 3.8 coincides closely with the availability estimate (n = 71) derived from forecasting based on Markov Analysis results, discussed below. This is intentional. Markov Analysis uses historical mobility data and probabilities to forecast future availabilities, while managers' judgment uses current knowledge of business and employees' plans to forecast employee movements person by person. Results from these two approaches to availability forecasts will not necessarily coincide, but they can be quite close if the manager is knowledgeable about past mobility patterns, employee mobility intentions, and mobility opportunities.

A major problem with using manager judgment to forecast availabilities is that the manager may lack the necessary business plan and employee intention information to provide solid estimates, as opposed to casual guesstimates. In addition, if there are large numbers of employees and job category/levels in the work unit, the sheer complexity of the forecasting task may overwhelm the manager. Markov Analysis presents a way out of this dilemma, since it substitutes historical data about internal mobility and exit rates for the manager's judgment as a basis for making availability forecasts, and it simultaneously considers all types of possible employee movement in the forecasts.

Markov Analysis

Markov Analysis is used to predict availabilities on the basis of historical patterns of job stability and movement among employees. Consider again the four job category/levels (A1, A2, B1, and B2) in the sales and customer service unit in Exhibit 3.6. Note that between any two time periods, the following possibilities exist for each employee in the internal labor market:

1. Job stability (remain in A1, A2, B1, or B2)
2. Promotion (move to a higher level: A1 to A2, A1 to B2, B1 to B2, or B1 to A2)

3. Transfer (move at the same level: A1 to B1, B1 to A1, A2 to B2, or B2 to A2)
4. Demotion (move to a lower level: A2 to A1, A2 to B1, B2 to B1, or B2 to A1)
5. Exit (move to another organizational unit or leave the organization)

These possibilities may be thought of in terms of flows and rates of flow or movement rates. Past flows and rates may be measured and then used to forecast the future availability of current employees, based on assumptions about the extent to which past rates will continue unchanged in the future. For example, if it is known that the historical promotion rate from A1 to A2 is .10 (10% of A1 employees are promoted to A2), we might predict that A1 will experience a 10% loss of employees due to promotion to A2 over the relevant time period. To conduct Markov Analysis we must know all of the job stability, promotion, transfer, demotion, and exit rates for an internal labor market before we can forecast future availabilities.

The elements of Markov Analysis are shown in Exhibit 3.9 for the organizational unit originally presented in Exhibit 3.6. Refer first to part A of Exhibit 3.9, where movement rates between two time periods (T and T+1) are calculated for four job category/level combinations. This is accomplished as follows. For each job category/level, take the number of employees who were in it at T, and use that number as the denominator for calculating job stability and movement rates. Next, for each of those employees, determine which job category/level they were employed in at T+1. Then, sum up the number of employees in each job category/level at

---

EXHIBIT 3.9 Use of Markov Analysis to Forecast Availabilities

	A. Transition Probability Matrix Job Category and Level	T + 1				
		A1	A2	B1	B2	Exit
	A1	.60	.10	.20	.00	.10
T	A2	.05	.60	.00	.00	.35
	B1	.05	.00	.60	.05	.30
	B2	.00	.00	.00	.80	.20

	B. Forecast of Availabilities	Current Workforce				
	A1	100	60	10	20	0
	A2	20	1	12	0	0
	B1	200	10	0	120	10
	B2	15	0	0	0	12
			71	22	140	22

T+1, and use these as the numerators for calculating stability and movement rates. Finally, divide each numerator separately by the denominator. The result is the stability and movement rates expressed as proportions, also known as transition probabilities. The rates for any row (job category/level) must add up to 1.0.

For example, consider job category/level A1. Assume that at time T in the past, A1 had 400 people. Further assume that at T+1, 240 of these employees were still in A1, 40 had been promoted to A2, 80 had been transferred to B1, 0 had been promoted to B2, and 40 had exited the organizational unit or the organization. The resulting transition probabilities, shown in the row for A1, are .60, .10, .20, .00, and .10. Note that these rates sum to 1.00.

By referring to these figures, and the remainder of the transition probabilities in the matrix, an organization can begin to understand the workings of the unit's internal labor market. For example, it becomes clear that 60%–80% of employees experienced job stability and that exit rates varied considerably, ranging from 10% to 35%. Promotions occurred only within job categories (A1 to A2, B1 to B2), not between job categories (A1 to B2, B1 to A2). Transfers were confined to the lower of the two levels (A1 to B1, B1 to A1). Only occasionally did demotions occur, and only within a job category (A2 to A1). Presumably, these stability and movement rates reflect specific staffing policies and procedures that were in place between T and T+1.

With these historical transitional probabilities, it becomes possible to forecast the future availability of the current workforce over the same time interval, T and T+1, assuming that the historical rates will be repeated over the time interval and that staffing policies and procedures will not change. Refer now to part B of Exhibit 3.9. To forecast availabilities, simply take the current workforce column and multiply it by the transition probability matrix shown in part A. The resulting availability figures (note these are the same as those shown in Exhibit 3.6) appear at the bottom of the columns: A1 = 71, A2 = 22, B1 = 140, and B2 = 22. The remainder of the current workforce (80) is forecast to exit and will not be available at T+1.

Limitations of Markov Analysis. Markov Analysis is an extremely useful way to capture the underlying workings of an internal labor market and then use the results to forecast future HR availabilities. It is, however, subject to some limitations that must be kept in mind.[18]

The first and most fundamental limitation is that of sample size, or the number of current workforce employees in each job category/level. As a rule, it is desirable to have 20 or more employees in each job category/level. Since this number serves as the denominator in the calculation of transition probabilities, with small sample sizes there can be substantial differences in the values of transition probabilities, even though the numerators used in their calculation are not that different (e.g., 2/10 = .20 and 4/10 = .40). Thus, transition probabilities based on small samples yield unstable estimates of future availabilities.

A second limitation of Markov Analysis is that it does not detect multiple moves by employees between T and T+1; it only classifies employees and counts their movement according to their beginning (T) and ending (T+1) job category/level, ignoring any intermittent moves. To minimize the number of undetected multiple moves, therefore, it is necessary to keep the time interval relatively short, probably no more than two years.

A third limitation pertains to the job category/level combinations created to serve as the unit of analysis. These must be meaningful to the organization for the HRP purposes of both forecasting and action planning. Thus, extremely broad categories (e.g., managers or clericals) and categories without any level designations should be avoided. Note that this recommendation may conflict somewhat with HRP for affirmative action purposes, as discussed later.

Finally, the transition probabilities reflect only gross, average employee movement and not the underlying causes of the movement. Stated differently, all employees in a job category/level are assumed to have an equal probability of movement. This is unrealistic because organizations take many factors into account (e.g., seniority, performance appraisal results, and KSAOs) when making movement decisions about employees. Because of these factors, the probabilities of movement may vary among specific employees.

Replacement and Succession Planning

Replacement and succession planning focus on identifying individual employees who will be considered for promotion, along with thorough assessment of their current capabilities and deficiencies, coupled with training and development plans to erase any deficiencies. The focus is thus on both the quantity and the quality of HR availability. Through replacement and succession planning the organization constructs internal talent pipelines that ensure steady and known flows of qualified employees to higher levels of responsibility and impact. Replacement planning precedes succession planning, and the organization may choose to stop at just replacement planning rather than proceeding into the more complex succession planning.[19]

Replacement and succession planning can occur at any and all levels of the organization. They are most widely used at the management level, starting with the chief executive officer and extending downward to the other officers or top managers. They can also be used throughout the entire management team, including the identification and preparation of individuals for promotion into the entry management level. They may also be used for linchpin positions—ones that are critical to organization effectiveness (such as senior scientists in the research and development function of a technology-driven organization) but not necessarily housed within the management structure.

Replacement Planning. Replacement planning focuses on identifying individual employees who will be considered for promotion and thoroughly assessing their current capabilities and deficiencies. Training and development plans to improve the fit between capabilities and requirements are also developed. The focus is thus on both the quantity and the quality of HR availability. The results of replacement planning are shown on a replacement chart, an example of which is shown in Exhibit 3.10. The chart is based on the previous sales–customer service unit in Exhibit 3.6. The focus is on replacement planning for sales managers (A2) from the ranks of sales associates (A1), as part of the organization's "grow your own," promotion-from-within HR strategy. The top part of the chart indicates the organization unit and jobs covered by replacement planning, as well as the minimum criteria for promotion eligibility. The next part shows the actual replacement chart information for the incumbent department manager (Woo) and the two eligible sales associates (Williams and Stemke) in the menswear department at the Cloverdale store. The key data are length of service, overall performance rating, and the promotability rating. When the incumbent sales manager (Woo) is promoted to group sales manager, both sales associates will be in the promotion pool. Williams will likely get the position because of her "ready now" promotability rating. Given his relatively short length of service and readiness for promotion in less than one year, Stemke is probably considered a "star" or a "fast tracker" whom the organization will want to promote rapidly. Similar replacement charts could be developed for all departments in the store and for all hierarchical levels up to and including store manager. Replacement chart data could then be aggregated across stores to provide a corporate composite of talent availability.

The process of replacement planning has been greatly accelerated by human resources information systems (HRISs). Many HRISs make it possible to keep data on KSAOs for each employee based on job history, training, and outside education. Software also allows organizations to create lists of employees who are ready to move into specific positions, and to assess potential risks that managers or leaders will leave the organization. The ability to keep track of employees across the organization by standardized inventories of skill sets means that staffing managers will be able to compare a variety of individuals for new job assignments quickly and consistently. A large database of candidates also makes it possible to seek out passive internal job candidates who aren't actively looking for job changes but might be willing to take new positions if offered. Many organizations that use integrated database systems that track candidates across a variety of locations report that they are able to consider a larger pool of candidates than they would with a paper-based system. Some HRISs automatically alert HR when key positions become open, and thus the process of finding a replacement can get under way quickly. The development of comprehensive replacement planning software is typically quite expensive, with costs reaching hundreds of thousands of dollars. The software is probably most useful for large organizations that are able to capitalize on the costs of a large system. However, smaller organizations may find it possible to create their own simpler databases of skills within the organization as a means of facilitating the internal replacement process.[20]

EXHIBIT 3.10   Replacement Chart Example

Organizational Unit: Merchandising—Soft Goods
Replacement for: Department Sales Manager (A2)
Pipelines for Replacement: Department Sales (A1)—preferred; External Hire—last resort
Minimum Eligibility Requirements: Two years' full-time sales experience; overall performance rates of "exceeds expectation"; promotability rating of "ready now" or "ready in < 1 yr."

Department: Menswear
Store: Cloverdale

Incumbent Manager	**Years in Job**	**Overall Performance Rating**		
Seng Woo	7	X Exceeds expectations	____ Meets expectations	____ Below expectations
Promote to		**Promotability Rating**		
Group Sales Manager		X Ready now	____ Ready in < 1 yr.	____ Ready in 1–2 yrs. ____ Not promotable

Replacement	**Years in Job**	**Overall Performance Rating**		
Shantara Williams	8	X Exceeds expectations	____ Meets expectations	____ Below expectations
Promote to		**Promotability Rating**		
Sales Manager		X Ready now	____ Ready in < 1 yr.	____ Ready in 1–2 yrs. ____ Not promotable

Replacement	**Years in Job**	**Overall Performance Rating**		
Lars Stemke	2	X Exceeds expectations	____ Meets expectations	____ Below expectations
Promote to		**Promotability Rating**		
Sales Manager		____ Ready now	X Ready in < 1 yr.	____ Ready in 1–2 yrs. ____ Not promotable

Succession Planning.   Succession plans build on replacement plans and directly tie into leadership development. The intent is to ensure that candidates for promotion will have the specific KSAOs and general competencies required for success in the new job. The key to succession planning is assessing each promotable employee for KSAO or competency gaps, and where there are gaps, creating employee training and development plans that will close the gap. A survey conducted by the Society for Human Resource Management showed that over half of HR professionals indicated that their organization had implemented some form of succession planning.[21]

Continuing the example from replacement planning, Exhibit 3.11 shows a succession plan for the two promotable sales associates. The organization has developed a set of general leadership competencies for all managers, and for each management position (such as sales manager) it indicates which of those competencies are required for promotion, in addition to the minimum eligibility require-

EXHIBIT 3.11   Succession Plan Example

Organizational Unit: Merchandising–Soft Goods
Department: Menswear
Position to Be Filled: Sales Manager (A2)
Leadership Competencies Required
- Plan work unit activities
- Budget preparation and monitoring
- Performance management of sales associates

Eligible Replacements	Promotability Ratings	Competency Gaps	Development Plans
S. Williams	Ready now	Budget prep	Now completing in-house training course
L. Stemke	Ready in < 1 year	Plan work	Shadowing sales manager
		Budget prep	Starting in-house training course
		Perf. mgt.	Serving as sales manager 10 hours per week
			Taking course on performance management at university extension

ments. It is the focus on these competencies, and the development plans to instill them in promotion candidates lacking them, that differentiates replacement and succession planning.

It can be seen that Williams, who is "ready now," has no leadership competency gaps, with the possible exception of an in-house training course on budget preparation and monitoring, which she is currently completing. Stemke, while having "star" potential, must undertake development work. When he completes that work successfully, he will be promoted to sales manager as soon as possible. Alternatively, he might be placed in the organization's acceleration pool. This pool contains hotshots like Stemke from within the organization who are being groomed for management positions generally, and for rapid acceleration upward, rather than progressing through the normal promotion paths.

It should be noted that replacement and succession planning require managers' time and expertise to conduct, both of which the organization must be willing to provide to those managers. Replacement and succession planning software might be helpful in this regard. Moreover, there must be effective performance appraisal and training and development systems in place to support replacement and succession planning. For example, overall performance and promotability ratings, plus assessment of competency gaps and spelling out development plans, could occur annually as part of the performance appraisal process conducted by management. In addition to identifying the skills needed immediately, succession plans should also identify skills needed in the future. Finally, making promotability and development assessments requires managers to make tough and honest decisions. A study of successful succession management in several Fortune 500 organizations concluded that "succession management is possible only in an organizational culture that encourages candor and risk taking at the executive level. It depends on a willingness to differentiate individual performance and a corporate culture in which the truth is valued more than politeness."[22]

An example of successful succession planning is the system used by Wellpoint Health Network in California, which has 16,500 employees and 50 million members throughout many subsidiaries such as Blue Cross of California.[23] The plan covers 600 managers in the top five levels of management, which Wellpoint thought was necessary to handle the multiple job shifts set in motion by filling a high-level vacancy. An HRP system was used to catalog detailed information about managers—including performance and promotability ratings, major accomplishments, and career goals. The system allows for organization-wide identification of eligible candidates for each management position. A unique feature is "challenge sessions," in which managers review one another's staffs, looking for hidden candidates who might have been overlooked by the immediate supervisor. Succession planning and performance appraisal are combined into one annual process where the manager rates the person's performance, core competencies, and promotability. These data are placed in an online (secure website) résumé, along with other KSAO information such as education, language skills, and past experiences.

Special training programs are undertaken when serious competency gaps are discovered. Use of the succession planning system has had good results. When a very senior manager left the organization, filling his position and the four other vacancies that occurred through musical chairs was done internally. Wellpoint was able to fill all the positions quickly and saved about $1 million on what an executive search firm would have charged to conduct external searches. More generally, the system allowed for 86% of management vacancies to be filled from within, saved $21 million in external recruitment and new hire training, and reduced the time to fill management vacancies from 60 to 35 days.

Reconciliation and Gaps

The reconciliation and gap determination process is best examined by means of an example. Exhibit 3.12 presents intact the example in Exhibit 3.6. Attention is now directed to the reconciliation and gaps column. It represents the results of bringing together requirements and availability forecasts with the results of external and internal environmental scanning. Gap figures must be decided on and entered into the column, and the likely reasons for the gaps need to be identified.

Let's first consider job category/level A1. A relatively large shortage is projected due to a mild expansion in requirements coupled with a substantial drop in availabilities. This drop is not due to an excessive exit rate but to losses through promotions and job transfers (refer back to the availability forecast in Exhibit 3.9).

For A2, decreased requirements coupled with increased availabilities lead to a projected surplus. Clearly, changes in current staffing policies and procedures will have to be made to stem the availability tide, such as a slowdown in the promotion rate into A2 from A1, or to accelerate the exit rate, such as through an early retirement program.

Turning to B1, note that a huge shortage is forecast. This is due to a major surge in requirements and a substantial reduction in availabilities. To meet the shortage, the organization could increase the transfer of employees from A1. While this would worsen the already-projected shortage in A1, it might be cost effective and would beef up the external staffing for A1 to cover the exacerbated shortage. Alternately, a massive external staffing program could be developed and undertaken for B1 alone. Or, a combination of internal transfers and external staffing for both A1 and B1 could be attempted. To the extent that external staffing becomes a candidate for consideration, this will naturally spill over into other HR activities, such as establishing starting-pay levels for A1 and B1. Finally, a very different strategy would be to develop and implement a major retention program for employees in customer service.

For B2 there is a small projected shortage. This gap is so small, however, that for all practical purposes it can be ignored. The HRP process is too imprecise to warrant concern over such small gap figures.

EXHIBIT 3.12 Operational Format and Example for Human Resource Planning

Organizational Unit: Sales and Customer Service

Job Category and Level	Current Workforce	Forecast for Workforce— One Year		Reconciliation and Gaps	Action Planning
		Requirements	Availabilities		
A1 (Sales)	100	110	71	−39 (shortage)	Recruitment Selection
A2 (Sales manager)	20	15	22	+7 (surplus)	Employment Retention
B1 (Customer service representative)	200	250	140	−110 (shortage)	Compensation Training and development
B2 (Customer service manager)	15	25	22	−3 (shortage)	
	335	400	255	−145 (shortage)	

In short, the reconciliation and gap phase of HRP involves coming to grips with projected gaps and the likely reasons for them. Quite naturally, thoughts about future implications begin to creep into the process. Even in the simple example shown, it can be seen that considerable action will have to be contemplated and undertaken to respond to the forecasting results for the organizational unit. That will involve mixtures of external and internal staffing, with compensation as another likely HR ingredient. Through action planning these possibilities become real.

STAFFING PLANNING

After the process of staffing planning is complete, it is time to move toward the development of specific plans for staffing. This is a vital phase of the planning process, in which staffing objectives are developed and alternative staffing activities are generated. The objectives are the targets the organization establishes to determine how many employees will be needed and in which job categories. The activities are the specific methods, including recruiting and selection strategies that will be used to meet these objectives. We devote special attention in this section to one of the most critical decisions made during staffing planning: Should the organization use a core workforce or a flexible workforce, or should parts of the workforce be outsourced?

Staffing Planning Process

Staffing Objectives

Staffing objectives are derived from identified gaps between requirements and availabilities. Thus, they involve objectives responding to both shortages and surpluses. They may require the establishment of quantitative and qualitative targets.

Quantitative targets should be expressed in head count or FTE form for each job category/level and will be very close in magnitude to the identified gaps. Indeed, to the extent that the organization believes in the gaps as forecast, the objectives will be identical to the gap figures. A forecast shortage of 39 employees in A1, for example, should be transformed into a staffing objective of 39 accessions (or something close to it) to be achieved by the end of the forecasting time interval. Exhibit 3.13 illustrates these points. For each cell, enter a positive number for head-count additions and a negative number for head-count subtractions.

Qualitative staffing objectives refer to the qualities of people in KSAO-type terms. For external staffing objectives, these may be stated in terms of averages, such as average education level for new hires and average scores on ability tests. Internal staffing objectives of a qualitative nature may also be established. These may reflect desired KSAOs in terms of seniority, performance appraisal record over a period of years, types of on- and off-the-job training, and so forth.

EXHIBIT 3.13   Setting Numerical Staffing Objectives

Job Category and Level	Gap	Objectives					Total
		New Hires	Promotions	Transfers	Demotions	Exits	
A1	−39	52	−6	−3	0	−4	+39
A2	+7	0	+2	−8	0	−1	−7
B1	−110	+140	−5	−3	−2	−20	+110
B2	−3	+2	+4	−1	0	−2	+3

NOTE: The objective is to close each gap exactly.

The results of replacement and succession planning, or something similar to that, will be very useful to have as well.

Generating Alternative Staffing Activities

With quantitative and, possibly, qualitative objectives established, it is necessary to begin identifying possible ways of achieving them. At the beginning stages of generating alternatives, it is wise to not prematurely close the door on any of them. Exhibit 3.14 provides an excellent list of the full range of options available for initial consideration in dealing with employee shortages and surpluses.

As shown in the exhibit, both short- and long-term options for shortages, involving a combination of staffing and workload management, are possible. Short-term options include utilizing current employees better (through more overtime, productivity increases, and buybacks of vacation and holidays), outsourcing work to other organizations (subcontracts, transfer work out), and acquiring additional employees on a short-term basis (temporary hires and assignments). Long-term options include staffing up with additional employees (recall former employees, transfer in employees from other work units, and add new permanent hires), enhancing skills (retrain), and pushing work on to other organizations (transfer work out).

Assessing and Choosing Alternatives

As should be apparent, a veritable smorgasbord of alternative staffing activities are available to address staffing gaps. Each of these alternatives needs to be assessed systematically to help decision makers choose from among them.

The goal of such assessment is to identify one or more preferred activities. A preferred activity offers the highest likelihood of attaining the staffing objective within the time limit established, at the least cost or tolerable cost, and with the

EXHIBIT 3.14   Staffing Alternatives to Deal With Employee Shortages and Surpluses

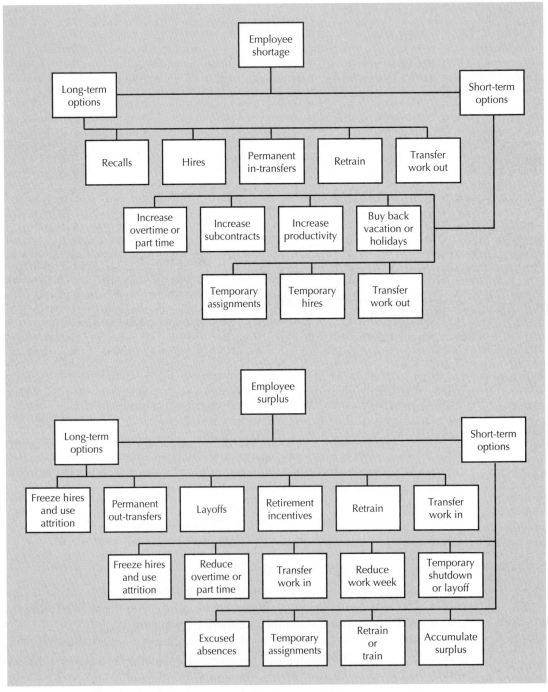

fewest negative side effects. A wide variety of metrics are available to assess potential activities. First, a common set of assessment criteria (e.g., time for completion, cost, and probability of success) should be identified and agreed on. Second, each alternative should be assessed according to each of these criteria. In this way, all alternatives will receive equal treatment, and tendencies to jump at an initial alternative will be minimized.

All of these alternatives must be considered within the broader context of how the organization creates and structures its workforce. This involves the key strategic issue of core versus flexible workforce usage. Many of the staffing activity alternatives are more applicable to one type of workforce than another.

Core Workforce

A core workforce, defined as regular full-time and part-time employees of the organization, forms the bulk of most organizations' workforces. The key advantages of a core workforce are stability, continuity, and predictability. The organization can depend on its core workforce and build strategic plans based on it. Several other advantages also accrue to the organization from using a core workforce. The regularity of the employment relationship fosters a sense of commitment and shared purpose toward the organization's mission. Also, the organization maintains the legal right to control employees working in its behalf, in terms of both work process and expected results, rather than having to divide or share that right with organizations providing a flexible workforce, such as temporary employment agencies. Finally, the organization can directly control how it acquires its workforce and the qualifications of those it employs through the management of its own staffing systems. By doing so, the organization may build not only a highly qualified workforce but also one more likely to be retained, thus lessening pressure to continually restaff the organization.

Several disadvantages of a core workforce also exist. The implied permanence of the employment relationship "locks in" the organization's workforce, with a potential loss of staffing flexibility to rapidly increase, reduce, or redeploy its workforce in response to changing market conditions and project life cycles. Reducing the core workforce, in particular, can be very costly in terms of severance pay packages, low morale, and damage to the organization's reputation as a good employer. Additionally, the labor costs of the core workforce may be greater than that of the flexible workforce due to (1) higher wages, salaries, and benefits for the core workforce, and (2) the fixed nature of these labor costs, relative to the more variable costs associated with a flexible workforce. By using a core workforce, the organization incurs numerous legal obligations—particularly taxation and employment law compliance—that could be fully or partially avoided through use of flexible workforce providers, which would be the actual employer. Finally, use of a core workforce may deprive the organization of new technical and administrative knowledge that could be infused into it by use of flexible workers such as programmers and consultants.

Consideration of these numerous advantages and disadvantages needs to occur separately for various jobs and organizational units covered by the HR plan. In this way, usage of a core workforce proceeds along selective, strategic lines. Referring back to the original example in Exhibit 3.6, staffing planners should do a unique core workforce analysis for the sales and customer service unit, and within that unit, for both sales and customer service jobs at the entry and managerial levels. The analysis may result in a decision to use only full-time core workers for the managerial jobs, both full-time and part-time core workers for sales jobs, and a combination of full-time core customer service representatives augmented by both full-time and part-time temporary customer service representatives during peak sales periods. Once the job and work unit locations of the core workers have been determined, specific staffing planning for effective acquisition must occur. This involves planning of recruitment, selection, and employment activities; these topics will be covered in subsequent chapters. However, one overarching issue needs to be addressed very early on because of its pervasive implications for all of these staffing activities. The issue is staffing philosophy.

Staffing Philosophy

In conjunction with the staffing planning process, the organization's staffing philosophy should be reviewed. Weighed in conjunction with the organization's staffing strategies, the results of this review help shape the direction and character of the specific staffing systems implemented. The review should focus on the following issues: internal versus external staffing, equal employment opportunity and affirmative action (EEO/AA) practices, and applicant reactions.

The relative importance to the organization of external or internal staffing is a critical matter because it directly shapes the nature of the staffing system, as well as sends signals to applicants and employees alike about the organization as an employer. Exhibit 3.15 highlights the advantages and disadvantages of external and internal staffing. Clearly there are trade-offs to consider in deciding the optimal internal-external staffing mix. The point regarding time to reach full productivity warrants special comment. Any new hire, either internal or external, will require time to learn the new job and reach a full productivity level. It is suggested that internal new hires have the advantage here. This reflects an assumption that internal new hires require relatively little orientation time and may have received special training and development to prepare them for the new job. This specific advantage for internal new hires, however, needs to be weighed in tandem with the other advantages and disadvantages of each type of new hire.

In terms of EEO/AA, the organization must be sure to consider or develop a sense of importance attached to being an EEO/AA-conscious employer and the commitment it is willing to make in incorporating EEO/AA elements into all

EXHIBIT 3.15 Staffing Philosophy: Internal Versus External Staffing

	Advantages	Disadvantages
Internal	• Positive employee reactions to promotion from within • Quick method to identify job applicants • Less expensive • Less time required to reach full productivity	• No new KSAOs into the organization • May perpetuate current underrepresentation of minorities and women • Small labor market to recruit from • Employees may require more training time
External	• Brings in employees with new KSAOs • Larger number of minorities and women to draw from • Large labor market to draw from • Employees may require less training time	• Negative reaction by internal applicants • Time-consuming to identify applicants • Expensive to search external labor market • More time required to reach full productivity

phases of the staffing system. Attitudes toward EEO/AA can range all the way from outright hostility and disregard to benign neglect to aggressive commitment and support. As should be obvious, the stance that the organization adopts will have major effects on its operational staffing system, as well as on job applicants and employees.

As a final point about staffing philosophy, planners must continue to bear in mind that staffing is an interaction involving both the organization and job applicants as participants. Just as organizations recruit and select applicants, so, too, do applicants recruit and select organizations (and job offers). Through their job search strategies and activities, applicants exert major influence on their own staffing destinies. Once the applicant opts into the organization's staffing process, he or she is confronted with numerous decisions about whether to continue on or withdraw from further consideration. This process of self-selection is inherent to any staffing system. During staffing planning, those within the organization must constantly consider how the applicant will react to the staffing system and its components, and whether they want to encourage or discourage applicant self-selection.

Flexible Workforce

The two major components of the flexible workforce are temporary employees provided by a staffing firm and independent contractors. Planning for usage of the flexible workforce must occur in tandem with core workforce planning; hence, it should begin with a review of the advantages and disadvantages of a flexible workforce.[24] The key advantage is staffing flexibility. The flexible workforce may be used for adjusting staffing levels quickly in response to changing technological or consumer demand conditions and to ebbs and flows of orders for products and services. Other flexibility advantages are the ability to quickly staff new areas or projects and the ability to fill in for core workers absent due to illness, vacations, and holidays. Relative to the core workforce, the flexible workforce may also present labor cost advantages in the form of lower pay and benefits, more variable labor costs, and reduced training costs. It should be noted, however, that the temporary workforce provider shoulders many of these costs and simply passes them on to the organization through the fees it charges for its services. Another advantage is possibly being relieved of many tax and employment law obligations, since flexible workers are often not considered employees of the organization. For temporary employees, however, the organization may be considered a coemployer subject to some legal obligations, especially pertaining to EEO. An emerging advantage is that the flexible workforce, especially in the professional and technical ranks, may be an important source of new knowledge about organizational best practices and new skills not present in the core workforce, especially "hot skills" in high market demand. In a related vein, organizations use temporary or interim top executives to fill in until a permanent hire is found and on board, to spur change, and to launch special projects requiring their expertise.[25] Finally, usage of a flexible workforce relieves the organization of the need to design and manage its own staffing systems, since this is done by the flexible workforce provider. An added advantage here is that the organization might use flexible workers on a tryout basis, much like a probationary period, and then hire into its core workforce those who turn out to be a solid person/job match. Many temporary workers are "temp-to-perm," meaning that the organization will hire them permanently if they perform successfully in the temporary role. Such an arrangement is usually negotiated up front with the staffing services company.

These numerous advantages must be weighed against several potential disadvantages. Most important is the legal loss of control over flexible workers because they are not employees of the organization. Thus, although the organization has great flexibility in initial job assignments for flexible workers, it is very limited in the amount of supervision and performance management it can conduct for them. Exacerbating the situation is that frictions between core and flexible workers may also arise. Core workers, for example, may feel that flexible workers lack knowledge and experience, are just "putting in time," receive the easy job assignments, and do not act like committed team players. Also, flexible workers may lack familiarity with equipment, policies, procedures, and important customers; such deficiencies may be compounded by a lack of training in specific job requirements. Finally, it should be remembered that the quality of the flexible workforce will depend heavily on the quality of the staffing and training systems used by the provider of the flexible workers. The organization may end up with flexible but poorly qualified workers.

If the review of advantages and disadvantages of flexible workers confirms the strategic choice to use them in staffing, plans must be developed for the organization units and jobs in which they will be used, and for how they will be acquired. Acquisition plans normally involve the use of staffing firms and independent contractors, both of which perform the traditional staffing activities for the organization. Hence, in contrast to the substantial and sustained staff planning that must occur for the core workforce, planning for the flexible workforce is primarily a matter of becoming knowledgeable about these potential sources and lining them up in advance of when they are actually needed.

Staffing Firms

Recall that staffing firms (also called temporary help agencies) are the legal employers of the workers being supplied, though matters of coemployment may arise. Hence, the staffing firm conducts recruitment, selection, training, compensation, performance appraisal, and retention activities for the flexible workers. The firm is also responsible for their on-site supervision and management, as well as all payrolling and the payment of legally required insurance premiums. For such services the firm charges the organization a general fee for its labor costs (wages and benefits) plus a markup percentage of labor costs (usually 40%–50%) to cover these services' costs plus provide a profit. There may be additional charges for specially provided services, such as extra testing or background checks, or skill training. Temp-to-perm workers may be hired away from the firm (with its permission and for a special fee) by the organization to become regular employees in the core workforce. For larger clients the firm may provide an on-site manager to help the organization plan its specific staffing needs, supervise and appraise the performance of the temporary workers, handle discipline and complaints, and facilitate firm–organization relations. With such additional staffing services, the firm functions increasingly like a staffing partner rather than just a staffing supplier.

Use of a staffing firm requires advance planning, rather than a panicky phone call to a firm at the moment of staffing need. In addition to becoming aware of firms that might be accessed, it is wise to become familiar with their characteristics and services. Shown in Exhibit 3.16 are descriptions of the various factors and issues to become knowledgeable about for any firm.

When the organization chooses a firm, both parties should enter into a formal written agreement. The agreement should cover such matters as specific services to be provided, costs, steps to ensure that the flexible workers are employees of the firm (such as having an on-site manager for them), and the process for terminating the firm–organization relationship. It is best to have legal counsel prepare/review the agreement.

The organization may decide to establish its own in-house staffing firm. When this is done, the employees of the firm may even be employees of the organization. Managers thus have readily available flexible workers to whom they can turn, without having to go through all the planning steps mentioned above.

Independent Contractors

An independent contractor (IC) provides specific task and project assistance to the organization, such as maintenance, bookkeeping, advertising, programming, and consulting. The IC can be a single individual (self-employed, freelancer) or an employer with its own employees. Neither the IC nor its employees are intended to be employees of the organization utilizing the IC's services, and care should be taken to ensure that the IC is not treated as an employee (see Chapter 2).[26]

As with staffing firms, the organization must take the initiative to identify and check out ICs for possible use in advance of when they are actually needed. It is desirable to solicit and examine references from past or current clients of the IC. Also, as much as possible the organization should seek to determine how the IC staffs, trains, and compensates its employees. This could occur during a preliminary get-together meeting with the IC. In these ways, the organization will have cultivated and screened ICs prior to when they are actually needed.

It is recommended that the IC and the organization prepare and enter into a written agreement between them. In general, the agreement should clarify the nature and scope of the project and contain language that reinforces the intent to have the IC function as such, rather than as an employee. For example, the agreement should refer to the parties as "firm" and "contractor," describe the specific work to be completed, specify that payment will be for completion of the project (rather than time worked), make the IC responsible for providing all equipment and supplies, exclude the IC from any of the organization's benefits, and ensure that the IC is responsible for paying all legally required taxes. Preparation of such an agreement might require the assistance of legal counsel.

EXHIBIT 3.16   Factors to Consider When Choosing a Staffing Firm

Factor	Issues
Agency and Its Reputation	How long in business; location; references from clients available.
Types of Workers Provided	What occupation and KSAO levels; how many available.
Planning and Lead Time	Does agency help client plan staffing levels and needs; how quickly can workers be provided.
Services Provided	
Recruitment	What methods are used; how targeted and truthful is recruitment process.
Selection	What selection techniques are used to assess KSAOs.
Training	What types of training, if any, are provided before workers are placed with client.
Wages and Benefits	How are wages determined; what benefits are provided.
Orientation	How does the agency prepare workers for assignment with client; does agency have an employee handbook for its workers.
Supervision	How does agency supervise its workers on site of client; does agency provide on-site manager.
Temp-to-Perm	Does agency allow client to hire its temporary workers as permanent employees.
Client Satisfaction	How does agency attempt to gauge client satisfaction with services, workers, costs.
Worker Effectiveness	
Punctuality and Attendance	Does the agency monitor these; what is its record with previous clients.
Job Performance	Is it evaluated; how are the results used.
Retention	How long do workers remain on an assignment voluntarily; how are workers discharged by the agency.
Cost	
Markup	What is the percentage over base wage charged to client (often it is 50% to cover benefits, overhead, profit margin).
For Special Services	What services cost extra beyond the markup (e.g., temp-to-perm), and what are those costs.

Outsourcing

Outsourcing of work functions can be defined as the transfer of a business process to an external organization. This is a more drastic step than simply using ICs or temporary employees. The primary difference is that when processes are outsourced, the organization expects to receive a completely finished product from the external source. This means the organization does not hire, direct, or control the way in which work is performed; rather, it only receives the end result of the work. Within the HR department, it has become the norm for organizations to completely outsource payroll tasks, meaning that data from the organization are sent to a third-party vendor that will assess taxes and withholdings and take care of either directly depositing or sending out paychecks for employees.[27]

Organizations outsource for a variety of reasons. An obvious reason for outsourcing of manufacturing and routine information-processing tasks is the availability of less expensive labor on the global market. Often, specialized vendors can achieve economies of scale for routine tasks that are performed across a variety of organizations. Organizations will also outsource functions that have highly cyclical demand so that they do not have to make major capital outlays and go through the cost of hiring and training permanent workers to perform tasks that may not be needed in the future. Sometimes organizations will outsource functions that require specific expertise that cannot be economically generated in-house. Smaller organizations that require legal services, for example, often choose to hire an external law firm rather than establishing their own pool of legal specialists. As we have noted, many organizations also outsource routine business functions, such as having payroll or benefits administration tasks completed by third-party vendors.

One variant of outsourcing is termed "offshoring," which means that products or services are provided by an external source outside the country where the organization's core operations take place.[28] The outsourcing of manufacturing to lower-wage countries has a long history, and this practice is likely to continue unabated. For example, in the computer industry it is common for large companies to have many subcomponent electronic parts manufactured by third-party vendors overseas, with final assembly of products performed domestically. Many companies have also outsourced routine computer programming and telephone help services to third-party providers in India because of the availability of a highly skilled labor force that typically draws only a fraction of the wages paid in North America. Offshoring is no longer limited to just blue- and pink-collar jobs. There has been a dramatic increase in offshoring white-collar technical and professional work in the initial years of the twenty-first century, fueled by improvements in global education, an increasingly positive climate for business in China and India, and increased demand for products and services in multinational organizations.

The decision to outsource is likely to be very controversial.[29] Outsourcing is usually done for activities that have low added value for the organization. Normal transactional or procedural work that is easily replicated is likely to be outsourced. High-value-added operations that are core to the organization's business strategy almost certainly should not be outsourced. Although most managers are certainly aware that it is unwise to outsource work that is fundamental to a business's core operations, there are still many cases where organizations have discovered, too late, that they have outsourced work that should have been done internally. Additionally, offshoring has been the focus of media and political scrutiny. Extremely low wages and dangerous working conditions provided by external partners in foreign countries have created a backlash against certain companies that have offshored manufacturing jobs. Negative press about poor working conditions in overseas "sweatshops" has been especially prominent in the clothing industry. The import of children's toys tainted with lead made by outsourced manufacturing labor in overseas factories has been a major financial and media debacle for several American toy makers. When outsourcing, an organization needs to make certain that it is not losing too much control over its major work processes. Just because a business process has been outsourced does not mean that the organization has lost the responsibility (and this sometimes includes legal liability) for the actions of external partners.

DIVERSITY PLANNING

Diversity programs arise out of a recognition that the labor force is becoming more demographically and culturally diverse. Diversity planning in staffing requires developing a strategy to recruit and select a diverse group of employees. Another major focus of diversity programs is the assimilation and adaptation of a diverse workforce.

To foster workforce diversity and to help strengthen the diversity–organizational effectiveness link, organizations have designed and implemented a wide variety of diversity initiatives and programs. Many of these initiatives involve staffing, as a diverse workforce must be actively identified, acquired, deployed, and retained. Most organizations supplement the staffing component of their diversity initiatives with many other programs, including diversity training for managers and employees to heighten awareness and acceptance of diversity, mentoring relationships, work/life balance actions such as flexible work schedules, team building, and special career- and credential-building job assignments.

Demography of the American Workforce

In part, organizations need to take diversity into account because the workforce has become more diverse. There has been a massive shift in the makeup of the American workforce over the past 30 years.[30] Once excluded from large portions of the workforce, women now make up half of the labor force, along with making up a majority of university graduates. There has also been a dramatic increase in the ethnic and racial diversity of the workforce. Immigration into the United States has brought large numbers of Latinos and Asians, and the progress of civil rights legislation has removed previous barriers to employment faced by African Americans. Legislation and technology have combined to make accommodations that allow the entry of individuals with disabilities into the workforce more feasible. Finally, the age diversity of the workforce has increased over time, as greater numbers of individuals continue working into their sixties and seventies.

These shifts in the makeup of the workforce have permanently altered the requirements for successful HR management. Surveys conducted by the Society for Human Resource Management suggest that managers are especially concerned about the loss of skills due to the retirement of baby boomers, increases in medical expenses that arise as the workforce ages, and employee elder-care responsibilities.[31] A host of other issues have been identified as arising from demographic changes, including providing work-life benefits for dual-career couples and developing multilingual training materials for workers who primarily speak a language other than English.

Business Case for Diversity

There is a strong impetus for effectively managing a diverse workforce. In fact, many argue that above and beyond the ethical need to treat all employees fairly and with respect, there is a financial imperative to manage diversity effectively.[32] As we noted in the introductory chapter, there are two ways organizations can address issues related to diversity. In passive diversity planning, the organization reviews all policies and practices to ensure there is no discrimination on the basis of race, religion, national origin, gender, disability status, or age. In active diversity planning, the organization goes a step further by encouraging underrepresented minorities to apply for positions, actively recruiting from a variety of sources that are likely to be seen by underrepresented groups, and providing additional training and mentoring to encourage the advancement of underrepresented groups.

There are certain advantages to an active diversity management strategy. Specific advantages suggested by diversity advocates include expanded talent pools associated with recruitment from among all demographic groups, a diverse workforce that better understands the needs of a diverse customer base, diversity enhancing the creativity and problem-solving effectiveness of work teams, and diversity programs boosting job satisfaction among underrepresented groups, thus reducing costly absenteeism and turnover. At the same time, there are costs associated with these active diversity efforts that must be considered, as additional recruiting, selection, and training programs do not come for free. Empirical evidence suggests that despite the conceptual advantages of having more diverse points of view in work groups, demographically diverse teams are not more effective than more homogenous teams. Active diversity efforts that are specifically directed to some groups of employees and not others may also unintentionally send a message to members of the demographic majority that they are less welcome in the organization. Therefore, an organization needs to carefully consider how to engage in active diversity planning and select the right mix of passive and active strategies to maximize organizational effectiveness.

Planning for Diversity

Whether an organization adopts an active or passive diversity strategy, there are several ways that workforce diversity should be taken into account in the staffing planning process. First and foremost, top management must state that diversity goals are important and will be measured.[33] Clear communications regarding diversity strategies should be made, and updated frequently, to remind employees of the importance of nondiscrimination for the organization's mission.

Many recruiting activities can help enhance the diversity of the workforce. One such activity is to advertise positions in media sources that target a variety of demographic groups.[34] Organizations that wish to increase the diversity of their workforce may also consider recruiting at colleges, universities, and other institutions that have large numbers of underrepresented minorities. These efforts can have a major impact on employee attitudes. Studies show that women and minorities prefer to work at companies that show a commitment to diversity in their recruiting efforts. Internally, organizational promotion efforts should target qualified members of underrepresented minority groups, possibly supplemented with mentoring programs to overcome gaps in skills.[35]

There are also techniques that can incorporate diversity into the selection process. Requirements that might lead to lower representation of traditionally underrepresented groups should be considered carefully, and eliminated when they are not absolutely necessary for job performance. Additionally, efforts to incorporate objective standards for judging candidate qualifications and policies that encourage nondiscrimination have been shown to diminish the extent of discrimination in the hiring process.[36]

Unfortunately, evidence suggests that many organizations do not take demographic shifts in the workplace into account when developing staffing plans. Programs to help dual-career couples manage work and child-care arrangements are implemented in a rather scattered fashion, with some organizations doing little to recognize the needs of such families. Other organizations have failed to adequately address the needs of employees with disabilities, even though disability rights advocates note that most accommodations are relatively inexpensive and do not affect core job tasks. A survey of over 700 organizations found that 77% of companies had not analyzed projected retirement rates of their workforce or had done so to only a limited extent.[37] Similarly, data show that about a third of employers report that they do not have enough programs for the recruitment and training of older workers.[38]

Research shows that diversity-oriented practices, including targeted recruitment, inclusion of women and African Americans on the top management team, work/family accommodations, the creation of AAPs, and diversity councils, can increase the racial and gender diversity of the organization's entire managerial workforce.[39] The effects of such practices on the composition of the nonmanagerial workforce are not well known, nor have the effects of these practices on organizational performance been documented.

It should be remembered that myriad staffing laws and regulations also apply to diversity initiatives, so the legal ramifications of any diversity-oriented policies and procedures should be considered.

LEGAL ISSUES

The major legal issues in HR and staffing planning are AAPs and diversity programs. AAPs originate from many sources—voluntary employer efforts, court-imposed remedies for discriminatory practices, conciliation or consent agreement, and requirements as a federal contractor. Regardless of the source, all AAPs seek to rectify the effects of past employment discrimination by increasing the representation of certain groups (minorities, women, and individuals with disabilities) in the organization's workforce. This is to be achieved through establishing and actively pursuing hiring and promotion goals for these groups. As described above, diversity programs are undertaken for competitive reasons, rather than as a legal response to discrimination. However, diversity programs may share components with AAPs.

This section describes the general content of AAPs, discusses the affirmative action requirements for federal contractors under AAP regulations, and provides some general indications as to the legality of AAPs and diversity programs.

Affirmative Action Plans

AAPs are organization-specific plans that, as noted above, have a legal origin and basis. They preceded diversity programs, which organizations typically undertake for strategic business reasons rather than legal ones. Often, however, the structure and content of AAPs and diversity programs are very similar. While AAPs are organization specific, they all share a common architecture composed of three major components—availability analysis of women and minorities, placement (hiring and promotion) goals derived from comparing availability with incumbency (percentages of women and minority employees), and action-oriented programs for meeting the placement goals. These components, and accompanying details, are spelled out in the federal regulations put forth and enforced by the Office of Federal Contract Compliance Programs (OFCCP).

Affirmative Action Programs Regulations

All but very small federal contractors must develop and implement AAPs according to the OFCCP's affirmative action regulations (*www.dol.gov/ofccp*). Below are a summary of those regulations and a sample of an AAP for small employers from the OFCCP website. The contractor must develop a separate AAP for each of its establishments with more than 50 employees. With advance approval from the

OFCCP, the contractor may sidestep separate establishment plans by developing a functional plan that covers employees in discrete functional or business units, even though in different locations. All employees must be included in either AAP. The description that follows is for an establishment plan and is based on the EEO-1 form previously required. The currently required EEO-1 form is shown in Chapter 13. The OFCCP has not yet provided guidance on how to use the new EEO-1 form for AAP.

Organization Profile.   An organization profile depicts the staffing pattern within an establishment. It provides a profile of the workforce at the establishment, and it assists in identifying units in which women or minorities are underrepresented. The profile may be done through either an organizational display or a workforce analysis. The latter requires a showing of job titles, while the former does not. Key elements in both approaches are a showing of organizational structure of lines of progression (promotion) among jobs or organization units, the total number of job incumbents, the total number of male and female incumbents, and the total number of male and female minority incumbents in each of the following groups: Blacks, Hispanics, Asians/Pacific Islanders, and American Indians/Alaskan Natives.

Job Group Analysis.   Jobs with similar content, wage rates, and opportunities (e.g., promotion, training) must be combined into job groups, and each group must include a list of job titles. Small establishments (fewer than 150 employees) may use as job groups the nine categories on the EEO-1 form: officials and managers, professionals, technicians, sales, office and clerical, craft workers (skilled), operatives (semiskilled), laborers (unskilled), and service workers. The percentage of minorities and the percentage of women (determined in the previous step) employed in each job group must be indicated.

Availability Determination.   The availability of women and minorities must be determined separately for each job group. At a minimum, the following two factors should be considered when determining availability:

1. The percentage of minorities or women with requisite skills in the reasonable recruitment area
2. The percentage of minorities or women among those promotable, transferable, and training with the organization

Current census data, job service data, or other data should be consulted to determine availability. When there are multiple job titles in a job group, with different availability rates, a composite availability figure for the group must be calculated. This requires summing weighted availability estimates for the job titles.

Exhibit 3.17 shows an example of availability determination for a single job group (officials and managers) based on the EEO-1 form. Listed on the left are the two availability factors that must be considered. Shown next are the raw statistic

EXHIBIT 3.17   Determining Availability of Minorities and Women

Job Group: 1	Raw Statistics		Value Weight	Weighted Statistics		Source of Statistics	Reason for Weighting
	Female	Minority		Female	Minority		
1. Percentage of minorities or women with requisite skills in the reasonable recruitment area	41.8%	9.4%	50.0%	20.9%	4.7%	2000 Census Data The reasonable recruitment area for this job group is the St. Louis, MO–IL metropolitan statistical area (MSA).	50% of placement into this job group is made from external hires.
2. Percentage of minorities or women among those promotable, transferable, and trainable within the contractor's organization	53.3%	26.7%	50.0%	26.7%	13.4%	The group of promotable employees in job group 2	50% of placement into this job group is made from internal promotions.
Totals:			100%	47.6%	18.1%	<Final Factor	

SOURCE: Sample Affirmative Action Program for Small Employers, 2004, *www.dol.gov/ofccp.*

availability estimates for females and minorities (summed across the four minority groups) for each of the two availability factors (refer to the "Source of Statistics" column to see the sources of data for these estimates). Next, the value weights represent an estimate of the percentages of the total females and minorities available according to each availability factor (50% for each group). The weighted statistics represent the raw statistics multiplied by the value weight (e.g., 41.8% × .50 = 20.9%). A summing of the weighted statistics yields the total availability estimate percentages (47.6% for female, 18.1% for minority).

Comparison of Incumbency With Availability. For each job group, the percentages of women and minority incumbents must be compared with their availability. When the percentage employed is less than would reasonably be expected by the availability percentage, a placement goal must be established.

Exhibit 3.18 compares incumbency with availability for eight job groups, including the officials and managers group (job group 1). The comparisons are shown separately for females and minorities. Where incumbency is less than availability, it may be decided to establish a placement goal. In job group 1, it was concluded that the differences between availability and incumbency percentages for both females and minorities were sufficient to warrant placement goals (47.6% for females and 18.1% for minorities). Note that an incumbency percentage less than an availability percentage does not automatically trigger a placement goal (e.g., females in job group 5).

How does the organization decide whether to set a placement goal for females or minorities in a job group? The OFCCP permits some latitude. One possibility is to set a placement goal whenever incumbency is less than availability, on the theory that any differences between availability and incumbency represent underutilization of females and minorities. A second possibility is based on the theory that some differences in percentages are due to chance, so some amount of tolerance of differences is permissible. The rule of thumb is 80% tolerance. This means that if the ratio of incumbency percentage to availability percentage is greater than 80%, no placement goal is needed. If the ratio is less than 80%, a placement goal must be set. The 80% rule was followed in Exhibit 3.18. Though the incumbency percentage for females was less than the availability percentage in both job groups 1 and 5, the difference was less than 80% in only job group 1, triggering a placement goal just for that group.

Placement Goals. If called for, an annual placement goal at least equal to the availability percentage for women or minorities must be established for the job group. Placement goals may not be rigid or inflexible quotas; quotas are expressly forbidden. Placement goals do not require hiring a person who lacks the qualifications to perform the job successfully, or hiring a less qualified person in preference to a more qualified one.

EXHIBIT 3.18   Determining Affirmative Action Goals: Comparing Incumbency With Availability and Annual Placement Goals

Job Group	Female Incumbency	Female Availability	Establish Goal? Yes/No	If Yes, Goal for Females	Minority Incumbency	Minority Availability	Establish Goal? Yes/No	If Yes, Goal for Minorities
1	0.0%	47.6%	Yes	47.6%	11.1%	18.1%	Yes	18.1%
2	45.5%	43.8%	No		18.2%	8.2%	No	
4	20.0%	34.5%	Yes	34.5%	0.0%	12.4%	Yes	12.4%
5	83.3%	87.7%	No		43.3%	27.6%	No	
6	9.3%	5.5%	No		34.9%	23.2%	No	
7	10.0%	6.3%	No		30.0%	37.5%	No	
8	6.3%	19.1%	Yes	19.1%	37.5%	26.3%	No	

NOTE: The 80% rule of thumb was followed in declaring underutilization and establishing goals when the actual employment of minorities or females is less than 80% of their availability. If the female/minority incumbency percent (%) is less than the female/minority availability percent (%) and the ratio of incumbency to availability is less than 80%, a placement goal should be included in the appropriate "If Yes" column.

SOURCE: Sample Affirmative Action Program for Small Employers, 2004, *www.dol.gov/ofccp.*

Designation of Responsibility. An official of the organization must be designated as responsible for the implementation of the AAP.

Identification of Problem Areas. The organization must evaluate the following:

1. Problems of minority or female utilization or distribution in each job group
2. Personnel activity (applicant flow, hires, terminations, and promotions) and other personnel actions for possible selection disparities
3. Compensation systems for possible gender-, race-, or ethnicity-based disparities
4. Selection, recruitment, referral, and other procedures to see if they result in disparities in employment or advancement of minorities or women

Action-Oriented Programs. Where problem areas have been identified, the organization must develop and execute action-oriented programs to correct problem areas and attain placement goals. Specific examples of these programs are shown in Exhibit 3.19.

Internal Audit and Reporting. An auditing system must be developed that periodically measures the effectiveness of the total AAP.

Legality of AAPs and Diversity Programs

AAPs have been controversial since their inception, and there have been many challenges to their legality. Questions of legality involve complex issues of constitutionality, statutory interpretations, differences in the structure of the AAPs being challenged in the courts, claims that affirmative action goals represent hiring quotas, and, very importantly, differences in the amount of weight actually being placed on race or gender in the ultimate selection decisions being made about job applicants.

Despite these problems, it is possible to provide several conclusions and recommendations regarding affirmative action. AAPs in general are legal in the eyes of the Supreme Court. However, to be acceptable, an AAP should be based on the following guidelines:[40]

1. The plan should have as its purpose the remedying of specific and identifiable effects of past discrimination.
2. There should be definite underutilization of women and/or minorities currently in the organization.
3. Regarding nonminority and male employees, the plan should not unsettle their legitimate expectations, not result in their discharge and replacement with minority or women employees, and not create an absolute bar to their promotion.

EXHIBIT 3.19 **Examples of Action-Oriented Programs for an AAP**

1. Conducting annual analyses of job descriptions to ensure they accurately reflect job functions;

2. Reviewing job descriptions by department and job title using performance criteria;

3. Making job descriptions available to recruiting sources and to all members of management involved in the recruiting, screening, selection, and promotion processes;

4. Evaluating the total selection process to ensure freedom from bias through:

   a. Reviewing job applications and other pre-employment forms to ensure information requested is job related;

   b. Evaluating selection methods that may have a disparate impact to ensure that they are job related and consistent with business necessity;

   c. Training in EEO for management and supervisory staff;

5. Using techniques to improve recruitment and increase the flow of minority and female applicants:

   a. Include the phrase "Equal Opportunity/Affirmative Action Employer" in all printed employment advertisements;

   b. Place help-wanted advertisements, when appropriate, in local minority news media and women's interest media;

   c. Disseminate information on job opportunities to organizations representing minorities, women, and employment development agencies when job opportunities occur;

   d. Encourage all employees to refer qualified applicants;

   e. Actively recruit at secondary schools, junior colleges, and colleges and universities with predominantly minority or female enrollment; and

   f. Request employment agencies to refer qualified minorities and women.

6. Hiring a statistical consultant to perform a self-audit of compensation practices; and

7. Ensuring that all employees are given equal opportunity for promotion:

   a. Post promotional opportunities;

   b. Offer counseling to assist employees in identifying promotional opportunities, training and educational programs to enhance promotions and opportunities for job rotation or transfer; and

   c. Evaluate job requirements for promotion.

SOURCE: Adapted from Sample Affirmative Action Program for Small Employers, 2010, *www.dol.gov/ofccp*.

4. The plan should be temporary and should be eliminated once affirmative action goals have been achieved.[41]

5. All candidates for positions should be qualified for those positions.

6. The plan should include organizational enforcement mechanisms as well as a grievance procedure.

Court rulings on the constitutionality of federal and state government AAPs suggest that even more strict guidelines than these may be necessary. Insofar as these programs are concerned, racial preferences are subject to strict constitutional scrutiny. They may be used only when there is specific evidence of identified discrimination, when the remedy has been narrowly tailored to only the identified discrimination, when only those who have suffered discrimination may benefit from the remedy, and when other individuals will not carry an undue burden, such as job displacement, from the remedy. Lesser scrutiny standards may apply for gender preferences.[42] Some states have even banned the use of AAPs by government employers, contractors, and educational institutions.[43]

Turning to diversity programs, the EEOC states the following about how they differ from AAPs, as well as their permissibility:

> Diversity and affirmative action are related concepts, but the terms have different origins and legal connotations. Workforce diversity is a business management concept under which employers voluntarily promote an inclusive workplace. Employers that value diversity create a culture of respect for individual differences in order to "draw talent and ideas from all segments of the population" and thereby potentially gain a "competitive advantage in the increasingly global economy." Many employers have concluded that a diverse workforce makes a company stronger, more profitable, and a better place to work, and they implement diversity initiatives for competitive reasons rather than in response to discrimination, although such initiatives may also help to avoid discrimination.
>
> Title VII permits diversity efforts designed to open up opportunities to everyone. For example, if an employer notices that African Americans are not applying for jobs in the numbers that would be expected given their availability in the labor force, the employer could adopt strategies to expand the applicant pool of qualified African Americans such as recruiting at schools with high African American enrollment. Similarly, an employer that is changing its hiring practices can take steps to ensure that the practice it selects minimizes the disparate impact on any racial group. For example, an employer that previously required new hires to have a college degree could change this requirement to allow applicants to have a college degree or two years of relevant experience in the field. A need for diversity efforts may be prompted by a change in the population's racial demographics, which could reveal an underrepresentation of certain racial groups in the work force in comparison to the current labor pool.[44]

EEO and Temporary Workers

The EEOC has provided guidance on coverage and responsibility requirements for temporary employment agencies (and other types of staffing firms) and their client organizations.[45] When both the agency and the client exercise control over the temporary employee and both have the requisite number of employees, they are considered employers and jointly liable under the Civil Rights Act, Age Discrimination in Employment Act (ADEA), Americans With Disabilities Act (ADA), and the Equal Pay Act. It should be noted that these laws also apply to individuals placed with organizations through welfare-to-work programs. The agency is obligated to make referrals and job assignments in a nondiscriminating manner, and the client may not set discriminatory job referral and job assignment criteria. The client must treat the temporary employees in a nondiscriminatory manner; if the agency knows this is not happening, the agency must take any corrective actions within its control. There are substantial penalties for noncompliance (e.g., back pay, front pay, and compensatory damages) that may be obtained from either the agency or the client, or both. There is special guidance for ADA-related issues.

SUMMARY

External forces shape the conduct and outcomes of HRP. The key forces and trends that emerge are economic conditions, labor markets, technology, and labor unions.

HRP is described as a process and set of activities undertaken to forecast future HR requirements and availabilities, resulting in the identification of likely employment gaps (shortages and surpluses). Action plans are then developed for addressing the gaps. Before HRP begins, initial decisions must be made about its comprehensiveness, planning time frame, job categories and levels to be included, how to "count heads," and the roles and responsibilities of line and staff (including HR) managers.

A variety of statistical and judgmental techniques may be used in forecasting. Those used in forecasting requirements are typically used in conjunction with business and organization planning. For forecasting availabilities, techniques must be used that take into account the movements of people into, within, and out of the organization, on a job-by-job basis. Here, manager judgment, Markov Analysis, and replacement and succession planning are suggested as particularly useful techniques.

Staffing planning is a form of action planning. It is shown to generally require setting staffing objectives, generating alternative staffing activities, and assessing and choosing from among those alternatives. A fundamental alternative involves the use of core or flexible workforces, as identified in staffing strategy. Plans must be developed for acquiring both types of workforces. Advantages and disadvantages of each type are provided; these should first be reviewed to reaffirm strategic choices about their use. Following that, planning can begin. For the core workforce, this first involves matters of staffing philosophy that will guide the planning of recruitment, selection, and employment activities. For the flexible workforce, the organization should establish early contact with the providers of the flexible workers (i.e., staffing firms and independent contractors). Organizational leaders should also consider the advantages and disadvantages of outsourcing some jobs at this point.

Changes in the demographic makeup of the workforce suggest that organizations need to take employee diversity into account in the planning process. Activities to address a diverse workforce include recruiting, selection, training, development, and retention.

AAPs are an extension and application of general HR and staffing planning. AAPs have several components. The Affirmative Action Programs Regulations, which apply to federal contractors, specify requirements for these components. The legality of AAPs has been clearly established, but the courts have fashioned limits to their content and scope. To clarify how EEO laws apply to temporary employees and agencies, the EEOC has issued specific guidance.

DISCUSSION QUESTIONS

1. What are ways that the organization can ensure that KSAO deficiencies do not occur in its workforce?
2. What are the types of experiences, especially staffing-related ones, an organization will be likely to have if it does not engage in HR and staffing planning?
3. Why are decisions about job categories and levels so critical to the conduct and results of HRP?
4. What are the advantages and disadvantages of doing succession planning for all levels of management, instead of just top management?
5. What is meant by reconciliation, and how can it be useful as an input to staffing planning?
6. What criteria would you suggest using for assessing the staffing alternatives shown in Exhibit 3.14?
7. What problems might an organization encounter in creating an AAP that it might not encounter in regular staffing planning?

ETHICAL ISSUES

1. Does an organization have any ethical responsibility to share with all of its employees the results of its forecasting of HR requirements and availabilities? Does it have any ethical responsibility to not do this?
2. Identify examples of ethical dilemmas an organization might confront when developing an AAP.

APPLICATIONS

Markov Analysis and Forecasting

The Doortodoor Sports Equipment Company sells sports clothing and equipment for amateur, light sport (running, tennis, walking, swimming, badminton, and golf) enthusiasts. It is the only company in the nation that does this on a door-to-door basis, seeking to bypass the retail sporting goods store and sell directly to the customer. Its salespeople have sales kits that include both sample products and a full-line catalog they can use to show and discuss with customers. The sales function is composed of full-time and part-time salespeople (level 1), assistant sales managers (level 2), and regional sales managers (level 3).

The company has decided to study the internal movement patterns of people in the sales function, as well as to forecast their likely availabilities in future time periods. The results will be used to help identify staffing gaps (surpluses and shortages) and to develop staffing strategy and plans for future growth.

To do this, the HR department first collected data for 2010 and 2011 to construct a transition probability matrix, as well as the number of employees for 2012 in each job category. It then wanted to use the matrix to forecast availabilities for 2013. The following data were gathered:

		Transition Probabilities (2010–11)					Current (2012)
Job Category	Level	SF	SP	ASM	RSM	Exit	No. Employees
Sales, Full-time (SF)	1	.50	.10	.05	.00	.35	500
Sales, Part-time (SP)	1	.05	.60	.10	.00	.25	150
Ass't. Sales Mgr. (ASM)	2	.05	.00	.80	.10	.05	50
Region. Sales Mgr. (RSM)	3	.00	.00	.00	.70	.30	30

Use these data to answer the following questions:

1. Describe the internal labor market of the company in terms of job stability (staying in same job), promotion paths and rates, transfer paths and rates, demotion paths and rates, and turnover (exit) rates.

2. Forecast the numbers available in each job category in 2013.

3. Indicate potential limitations to your forecasts.

Deciding Whether to Use Flexible Staffing

The Kaiser Manufacturing Company (KMC) has been in existence for over 50 years. Its main products are specialty implements for use in both the crop and dairy herd sides of the agricultural business. Products include special attachments for tractors, combines, discers, and so on, and add-on devices for milking and feeding equipment that enhance the performance and safety of the equipment.

KMC has a small corporate office plus four manufacturing plants (two in the Midwest and two in the South). It has a core workforce of 725 production workers, 30 clerical workers, 32 professional and engineering workers, and 41 managers. All employees are full time, and KMC has never used either part-time or temporary workers. It feels very strongly that its staffing strategy of using only a core workforce has paid big dividends over the years in attracting and retaining a committed and highly productive workforce.

Sales have been virtually flat at $175 million annually since 2008. At the same time, KMC has begun to experience more erratic placement of orders for its products, making sales less predictable. This appears to be a reflection of more turbulent weather patterns, large swings in interest rates, new entrants into the specialty markets, and general uncertainty about the future direction and growth of the agricultural industry. Increased unpredictability in sales has been accompanied by steadily rising labor costs. This is due to KMC's increasingly older workforce, as well as shortages of all types of workers (particularly production workers) in the immediate labor markets surrounding the plants.

Assume you are the HR manager responsible for staffing and training at KMC. You have just been contacted by a representative of the Flexible Staffing Services (FSS) Company, Mr. Tom Jacoby. Mr. Jacoby has proposed meeting with you and the president of KMC, Mr. Herman Kaiser, to talk about FSS and how it might be of service to KMC. You and Mr. Kaiser agree to meet with Mr. Jacoby. At that meeting, Mr. Jacoby makes a formal presentation to you in which he describes the services, operation, and fees of FSS and highlights the advantages of using a more flexible workforce. During that meeting, you learn the following from Mr. Jacoby.

FSS is a recent entrant into what is called the staffing industry. Its general purpose is to furnish qualified employees to companies (customers) on an as-needed basis, thus helping the customer implement a flexible staffing strategy. It furnishes employees in four major groups: production, clerical, technical, and professional/managerial. Both full-time and part-time employees are available in each of these groups. Employees may be furnished to the customer on a strictly temporary basis ("temps") or on a "temp-to-perm" basis in which the employees convert from being temporary employees of FSS to being permanent employees of the customer after a 90-day probationary period.

For both the temp and temp-to-perm arrangements, FSS offers the following services. In each of the four employee groups it will recruit, select, and hire people to work for FSS, which will in turn lease them to the customer. FSS performs all recruitment, selection, and employment activities. It uses a standard selection system for all applicants, composed of an application blank, reference checks, drug testing, and a medical exam (given after making a job offer). It also offers customized selection plans in which the customer chooses from among a set of special skill tests, a personality test, an honesty test, and background investigations. Based on the standard and/or custom assessments, FSS refers to the customer what it views as the top candidates. FSS tries to furnish two people for every vacancy, and the customer chooses from between the two.

New hires at FSS receive a base wage that is similar to the market wage, as well as close to the wage of the customer's employees with whom they will be directly working. In addition, new hires receive a paid vacation (one week for every six months of employment, up to four weeks), health insurance (with a 25% employee co-pay), and optional participation in a 401(k) plan. FSS performs and pays for all payroll functions and deductions. It also pays the premiums for workers' compensation and unemployment compensation.

FSS charges the customer as follows. There is a standard fee per employee furnished of 1.55 $\times$ base wage $\times$ hours worked per week. The 1.55 is labeled "markup"; it covers all of FSS's costs (staffing, insurance, benefits, and administration) plus a profit margin. On top of the standard fee is an additional fee for customized selection services. This fee ranges from .50 to .90 $\times$ base wage $\times$ hours worked per week. Finally, there is a special one-time fee for temp-to-perm employees (a one-month pay finder's fee), payable after the employee has successfully completed the 90-day probationary period and transferred to being an employee of the customer.

Mr. Jacoby concludes his presentation by stressing three advantages of flexible staffing as provided by FSS. First, use of FSS employees on an as-needed basis will give KMC greater flexibility in its staffing to match fluctuating product demand, as well as movement from completely fixed labor costs to more variable labor costs. Second, FSS provides considerable administrative convenience, relieving KMC of most of the burden of recruitment, selection, and payrolling. Finally, KMC will experience considerable freedom from litigation (workers' comp, EEO, torts) since FSS and not KMC will be the employer.

After Mr. Jacoby's presentation, Mr. Kaiser tells you he is favorably impressed, but that the organization clearly needs to do some more thinking before it embarks on the path of flexible staffing and the use of FSS as its provider. He asks you to prepare a brief preliminary report including the following:

1. A summary of the possible advantages and disadvantages of flexible staffing
2. A summary of the advantages and disadvantages of using FSS as a service provider

3. A summary of the type of additional information you recommend gathering and using as part of the decision-making process

TANGLEWOOD STORES CASE

The planning chapter explained how organizations can integrate their strategic goals and administrative data to determine staffing needs. The planning case will illustrate how Tanglewood implements these activities.

The Situation

The process of planning involves a combination of forecasting labor needs, comparing these needs with labor availabilities, and determining where gaps exist. Data from Tanglewood's historical hiring practices are provided to assist you in developing these estimates. Beyond developing objectives for the number of individuals to be hired, you will need to consider the demographic composition of the workforce to ensure that the company's commitment to diversity is maintained. This is an extension of the affirmative action discussion in the textbook.

Your Tasks

You will first complete a forecast of HR availabilities. Due to the strong emphasis on corporate culture at Tanglewood, you will also consider whether it should move toward the use of a flexible workforce strategy. You will also estimate the representation of women and minorities in several job categories as part of affirmative action planning. The background information for this case, and your specific assignment, can be found at *www.mhhe.com/heneman7e.*

ENDNOTES

1. K. Klemmer, "Job Openings and Hires Decline in 2008," *Monthly Labor Review*, May 2009, pp. 32–44.
2. T. A. Lacey and B. Wright, "Occupational Employment Projections to 2018," *Monthly Labor Review*, May 2009, pp. 86–125.
3. Lacey and Wright, "Occupational Employment Projections to 2018."
4. A. Spitz-Oener, "Technical Change, Job Tasks, and Rising Educational Demands: Looking Outside the Wage Structure," *Journal of Labor Economics*, 2006, 24, pp. 235–270.
5. Society for Human Resource Management, *Critical Skills Needs and Resources for the Changing Workforce* (Alexandria, VA: author, 2008).
6. M. Toossi, "Labor Force Projections to 2018: Older Workers Staying More Active," *Monthly Labor Review*, Nov. 2009, pp. 30–51; P. L. Rones, R. E. Ilg, and J. M. Garner, "Trends in Hours of Work Since the Mid-1970s," *Monthly Labor Review*, Apr. 1997, pp. 3–14; J. Schramm, *SHRM Workplace Forecast* (Alexandria, VA: Society for Human Resource Management, 2008); P. J. Kiger, "With Baby Boomers Graying, Employers Are Urged to Act Now to Avoid Skills

Shortages," *Workforce Management*, 2005, 84(13), pp. 52–54; J. F. Stinson, Jr., "New Data on Multiple Job Holding Available From the CPS," *Monthly Labor Review*, Mar. 1997, pp. 3–8; Manpower Inc., *Employment Outlook Survey: United States* (Milwaukee, WI: author, 2007).

7. T. Minton-Eversole and K. Gurchiek, "New Workers Not Ready for Prime Time," *HR Magazine*, Dec. 2006, pp. 28–34.

8. M. Rich, "Factory Jobs Return, but Employers Find Skills Shortage," *New York Times Online*, July 1, 2010.

9. M. J. Handel, "Skills Mismatch in the Labor Market," *Annual Review of Sociology*, 2003, 29, pp. 135–165.

10. BMP Forum and Success Factors, *Performance and Talent Management Trend Survey 2007* (San Mateo, CA: author, 2007).

11. Bureau of Labor Statistics, "Employed and Unemployed Full- and Part-Time Workers by Age, Race, Sex and Hispanic or Latino Ethnicity," Dec. 2007 (*www.bls.gov*).

12. US Department of Labor, "Workers on Flexible and Shift Schedules in May 2004," *News*, July 1, 2005.

13. T. Dunne, L. Foster, J. Haltiwanger, and K. R. Troske, "Wage and Productivity Dispersion in United States Manufacturing: The Role of Computer Investment," *Journal of Labor Economics*, 2004, 22, pp. 397–429; Spitz-Oener, "Technical Change, Job Tasks, and Rising Educational Demands: Looking Outside the Wage Structure."

14. US Department of Labor, "Union Members in 2006," *News,* Jan. 25, 2007.

15. G. Chaison, "Union Membership Attrition," *Monthly Labor Review*, Jan. 2010, pp. 74–76.

16. C. R. Greer, *Strategic Human Resource Management*, second ed. (Upper Saddle River, NJ: Prentice Hall, 2001); International Personnel Management Association, *Workforce Planning Guide for Public Sector Human Resource Professionals* (Alexandria, VA: author, 2002); D. W. Jarrell, *Human Resource Planning* (Englewood Cliffs, NJ: Prentice Hall, 1993); J. W. Walker, *Human Resource Strategy* (New York: McGraw-Hill, 1992).

17. F. Callocchia, "How HR Can Be Seen, Heard, and Valued," *Canadian HR Reporter*, Dec. 14, 2009, p. 35.

18. H. G. Heneman III and M. H. Sandver, "Markov Analysis in Human Resource Administration: Applications and Limitations," *Academy of Management Review*, 1977, 2, pp. 535–542.

19. J. A. Conger and R. M. Fuller, "Developing Your Leadership Pipeline," *Harvard Business Review*, Dec. 2003, pp. 76–84; International Public Management Association–Human Resources, *Succession Planning* (Alexandria, VA: author, 2003); S. J. Wells, "Who's Next?" *HR Magazine*, Nov. 2003, pp. 45–50.

20. E. Frauenheim, "Software Products Aim to Streamline Succession Planning," *Workforce Management*, Jan. 2006 (*www.workforce.com/archive/feature/24/24/94/242496.php?*).

21. S. Fegley, *2006 Succession Planning* (Alexandria, VA: Society for Human Resource Management, 2006).

22. Conger and Fuller, "Developing Your Leadership Pipeline," p. 84.

23. P. J. Kiger, "Succession Planning Keeps WellPoint Competitive," *Workforce*, Apr. 2002, pp. 50–55.

24. S. F. Matusik and C.W.L. Hill, "The Utilization of Contingent Work, Knowledge Creation, and Competitive Advantage," *Academy of Management Review*, 1998, 23, pp. 680–697; Society for Human Resource Management, *Alternative Staffing Survey* (Alexandria, VA: author, 2000); C. V. von Hippel, S. L. Mangum, D. B. Greenberger, R. L. Heneman, and J. D. Skoglind, "Temporary Employment: Can Organizations and Employees Both Win?" *Academy of Management Executive*, 1997, 11, pp. 93–104.

25. G. Weber, "Temps at the Top," *Workforce*, Aug. 2004, pp. 27–31; M. Frase-Blunt, "Short Term Executives," *HR Magazine*, June 2004, pp. 110–114.

26. J. Brown, "Contingent Workers: Employing Nontraditional Workers Requires Strategy," *IPMA-HR News*, June 2004, pp. 9–11; A. Davis-Blake and P. P. Hui, "Contracting for Knowledge-Based Competition," in S. E. Jackson, M. A. Hitt, and A. S. DeNisi (eds.), *Managing Knowledge for Sustained Competitive Advantage* (San Francisco: Jossey-Bass, 2003), pp. 178–206.

27. D. Arthur, *Recruiting, Interviewing, Selecting, and Orienting New Employees*, fourth ed. (New York: Arthur Associates Management Consultants Limited, 2006); E. Esen, *Human Resource Outsourcing Survey Report* (Alexandria, VA: Society for Human Resource Management, 2004); J. Schramm, *Workplace Forecast, 2005–2006* (Alexandria, VA: Society for Human Resource Management, 2006).

28. P. Babcock, "America's Newest Export: White-Collar Jobs," *HR Magazine*, Apr. 2004, pp. 50–57; B. Tai and N. R. Lockwood, *Outsourcing and Offshoring HR Series Part I* (Alexandria, VA: Society for Human Resource Management, 2006); R. J. Moncarz, M. G. Wolf, and B. Wright, "Service-Providing Occupations, Offshoring, and the Labor Market," *Monthly Labor Review*, Dec. 2008, pp. 71–86.

29. M. Belcourt, "Outsourcing—The Benefits and the Risks," *Human Resource Management Review*, 2006, 16, pp. 269–279; B. M. Testa, "Tales of Backshoring," *Workforce Management*, Dec. 2007 (*www.workforce.com/section/09/feature/25/27/70/index.html*); A. Fox, "The Ins and Outs of Customer Contact Centers," *HR Magazine Online*, May 2010.

30. L. Lieber, "Changing Demographics Will Require Changing the Way We Do Business," *Employment Relations Today*, Fall 2009, pp. 91–96; A. Fox, "At Work in 2020," *HR Magazine Online*, Jan. 1, 2010.

31. J. Schram, *SHRM Workplace Forecast* (Alexandria, VA: Society for Human Resource Management, 2006).

32. E. Esen, *2005 Workforce Diversity Practices* (Alexandria, VA: Society for Human Resource Management, 2005).

33. Society for Human Resource Management, *2007 State of Workplace Diversity Management* (Alexandria, VA: author, 2007).

34. D. R. Avery, "Reactions to Diversity in Recruitment Advertising: Are the Differences Black and White?" *Journal of Applied Psychology*, 2003, 88, pp. 672–679; D. R. Avery and P. F. McKay, "Target Practice: An Organizational Impression Management Approach to Attracting Minority and Female Job Applicants," *Personnel Psychology*, 2006, 59, pp. 157–187.

35. S. B. Welch, "Diversity as Business Strategy: Company Faced Racial Tensions Head On," *Workforce Management Online*, Apr. 2009; L. Lieber, "Changing Demographics Will Require Changing the Way We Do Business."

36. J. M. Sacco, C. R. Scheu, A. M. Ryan, and N. Schmitt, "An Investigation of Race and Sex Similarity Effects in Interviews: A Multilevel Approach to Relational Demography," *Journal of Applied Psychology*, 2003, 88, pp. 852–865; J. C. Ziegert and P. J. Hanges, "Employment Discrimination: The Role of Implicit Attitudes, Motivation, and a Climate for Racial Bias," *Journal of Applied Psychology*, 2005, 90, pp. 553–562.

37. P. J. Kiger, "Few Employers Addressing Impact of Aging Workforce," *Workforce Management*, Jan. 2010, pp. 6–7.

38. A. Nancherla, "Getting to the Foundation of Talent Management," *T + D*, Feb. 2010, p. 20.

39. M.E.A. Jayne and R. Dipboye, "Leveraging Diversity to Improve Business Performance: Research Findings and Recommendations for Organizations," *Human Resource Management*, 2004, 43, pp. 409–424; A. Kalev, F. Dobins, and E. Kelley, "Best Practices or Best Guesses?

Assessing the Efficacy of Corporate Affirmative Action and Diversity Policies," *American Sociological Review*, 2006, 71, pp. 589–617; N. R. Lockwood and J. Victor, *Recruiting for Workplace Diversity: A Business Strategy* (Alexandria, VA: Society for Human Resource Management, 2007).

40. D. D. Bennett-Alexander and L. B. Pincus, *Employment Law for Business*, sixth ed. (Burr-Ridge, IL: Irwin McGraw-Hill, 2009), p. 245; C. R. Gullett, "Reverse Discrimination and Remedial Affirmative Action in Employment," *Public Personnel Management*, 2000, 29(1), pp. 107–118; T. Johnson, "Affirmative Action as a Title VII Remedy: Recent U.S. Supreme Court Decisions, Racial Quotas and Preferences," *Labor Law Journal*, 1987, 38, pp. 574–581; T. Johnson, "The Legal Use of Racial Quotas and Gender Preferences by Public and Private Employers," *Labor Law Journal*, 1989, 40, pp. 419–425; D. J. Walsh, *Employment Law for Human Resource Practice*, second ed. (Mason, OH: Thompson Higher Education, 2007).

41. For an example of eliminating an AAP once affirmative action goals have been achieved, see A. R. McIlvaine, "Court: Boston Must Hire White Firefighters," *Human Resource Executive*, Feb. 2004, p. 13.

42. R. T. Seymour and B. B. Brown, *Equal Employment Law Update* (Washington, DC: Bureau of National Affairs, 1997), pp. 23-553 to 23-558.

43. M. P. Crockett and J. B. Thelen, "Michigan's Proposal 2: Affirmative Action Law Shifts at the State Level," *Legal Report*, Society for Human Resource Management, July/Aug. 2007, pp. 5–8.

44. EEOC Compliance Manual, 2006 (*www.eeoc.gov/policy/docs/race-color.html*).

45. Equal Employment Opportunity Commission, *EEOC Policy Guidance on Temporary Workers* (Washington, DC: author, 1997); Equal Employment Opportunity Commission, *Enforcement Guidance: Application of the ADA to Contingent Workers Placed by Temporary Agencies and Other Staffing Firms* (Washington, DC: author, 2000).

CHAPTER FOUR

Job Analysis and Rewards

Learning Objectives and Introduction
  Learning Objectives
  Introduction

Changing Nature of Jobs

Job Requirements Job Analysis
  Overview
  Job Requirements Matrix
  Job Descriptions and Job Specifications
  Collecting Job Requirements Information

Competency-Based Job Analysis
  Nature of Competencies
  Collecting Competency Information

Job Rewards
  Types of Rewards
  Employee Value Proposition
  Collecting Job Rewards Information

Job Analysis for Teams

Legal Issues
  Job Relatedness and Court Cases
  Essential Job Functions

Summary

Discussion Questions

Ethical Issues

Applications

LEARNING OBJECTIVES AND INTRODUCTION

Learning Objectives

- Know the difference between a job description and a job specification
- Learn about methods for collecting job requirements
- Understand why competency-based job analysis has grown in prominence
- Learn about methods for collecting competencies
- Recognize the types of rewards associated with jobs
- Learn how job analysis is done for team-based work
- Become familiar with the legal issues surrounding job analysis

Introduction

Once the planning process is complete, the next step in developing an effective, strategic staffing system is to develop a thorough understanding of the jobs to be filled. The process of studying and describing the specific requirements for a job is called job analysis. Anyone who has ever looked for a job is familiar with a traditional job description that lists the major tasks, duties, and responsibilities of a job. Such descriptions are just part of the wealth of information collected during the job analysis process. As we will see later in the book, job analysis information can be used for identifying recruiting pools, designing selection tools, and assessing and improving employee performance.

At first blush, describing a job may seem to be a straightforward enough task. However, there are some important considerations that will determine which techniques should be employed for collecting this information. In many cases, a traditional task-based job analysis is sufficient to cover both the operational and legal requirements of an organization's staffing strategy. In other cases, it will make more sense to focus on a general set of KSAOs (knowledge, skill, ability, and other characteristics) that span a wide variety of jobs in the organization. The choice of techniques will depend on both the nature of the jobs involved and the organization's plans for the future.

The chapter begins with a description of the changing nature of jobs, a force that has changed the nature of job analysis and all other staffing activities. Then, methods for performing job analysis are discussed. The first approach, job requirements job analysis, is guided by the job requirements matrix, which includes tasks, KSAOs, and job context. Next, competency-based job analysis is described. This comparatively new approach to job analysis starts from the organization's mission and goals and then develops a list of the general KSAOs that will help the organization meet these needs. Attention then turns to job rewards, including both intrinsic and extrinsic rewards that jobs may provide to employees. Finally, legal issues pertaining to job analysis are treated.

CHANGING NATURE OF JOBS

Jobs are the building blocks of an organization, in terms of both job content and the hierarchical relationships that emerge among them. They are explicitly designed and aligned in ways that enhance the production of the organization's goods and services. Job analysis thus must be considered within the broader framework of the design of jobs, for it is through their design that jobs acquire their requirements and rewards.

Jobs are constantly evolving. They are born out of organizational need, grow in scope and responsibilities as the needs grow, and, sometimes, die when the needs change.[1] At one time, all airlines had the job of flight engineer, whose role was to monitor air-to-ground communications and to watch and control certain aircraft systems during flight. Cockpits were designed so that the flight engineer sat at a panel behind the pilot and copilot. However, as computer technology advanced, the job of flight engineer became obsolete and virtually disappeared from commercial aviation. Such is the case with a surprising number of jobs. Every year scores of jobs are created and an equal number of others are eliminated. This is one of the reasons for the growth in competency-based job analysis, which is seen as a more flexible alternative to traditional job analysis.

Job analysis may be defined as the process of studying jobs in order to gather, analyze, synthesize, and report information about job requirements. Note in this definition that job analysis is an overall process as opposed to a specific method or technique. A job requirements job analysis seeks to identify and describe the specific tasks, KSAOs, and job context for a particular job. This type of job analysis is the most thoroughly developed and the most commonly used by organizations. A second type of job analysis, competency-based, attempts to identify and describe job requirements in the form of general KSAOs required across a range of jobs; task and work context requirements are of little concern. Interpersonal skills, for example, might be identified as a competency for sales and customer service jobs; leadership is a likely competency requirement for managerial jobs. Competency-based job analysis is more recent in origin, though it has some similarities to job requirements job analysis.

The traditional way of designing a job is to identify and define its elements and tasks precisely and then incorporate them into a job description. This task core includes virtually all tasks associated with the job, and from it a fairly inclusive list of KSAOs will flow. Thus defined, there are clear lines of demarcation between jobs in terms of both tasks and KSAOs, and there is little overlap between jobs on either basis. Each job also has its own set of extrinsic and intrinsic rewards. Such job design is marked by formal organization charts, clear and precise job descriptions and specifications, and well-defined relationships between jobs in terms of mobility (promotion and transfer) paths. Also, traditional jobs are very static, with little or no change occurring in tasks or KSAOs.

Certain terms are used frequently in discussions of traditional jobs. Definitions and examples of some of the key terms are provided in Exhibit 4.1. The terms are presented in a logically descending hierarchy, starting with job family and job category and proceeding downward through job, position, task dimension, task, and element.

One challenge to this traditional perspective is that jobs are constantly evolving. Generally, these changes are not so radical that a job ceases to exist (like the job of flight engineer), and they are often due to technological or workload changes. An excellent example of such an evolving job is that of secretary. Traditional or core tasks associated with the job include typing, filing, taking dictation, and answering phones. However, in nearly all organizations the job has evolved to include new tasks such as word processing, managing multiple projects, creating spreadsheets, purchasing supplies and office technology, and gathering information on the Internet. These task changes led to new KSAO requirements such as planning and coordination skills and knowledge of spreadsheet software. Accompanying these changes is a change in job title to that of "administrative assistant." Note that jobs may also evolve due to changing organization and technology requirements, as well as employee-initiated changes through a process of job crafting.

Another challenge to the traditional view is the need for flexibility. Flexible jobs have frequently changing task and KSAO requirements. Sometimes these changes are initiated by the job incumbent who constantly adds and drops (or passes off) new assignments or projects in order to work toward moving targets of oppor-

EXHIBIT 4.1   Terminology Commonly Used in Describing Jobs

Term	Definition
Job family	A grouping of jobs, usually according to function (e.g., production, finance, human resources, marketing)
Job category	A grouping of jobs according to generic job title or occupation (e.g., managerial, sales, clerical, maintenance), within or across job families
Job	A grouping of positions that are similar in their tasks and task dimensions
Position	A grouping of tasks/dimensions that constitute the total work assignment of a single employee; there are as many positions as there are employees
Task dimension	A grouping of similar types of tasks, sometimes called "duty," "area of responsibility," or "key results area"
Task	A grouping of elements to form an identifiable work activity that is a logical and necessary step in the performance of a job
Element	The smallest unit into which work can be divided without analyzing separate motions, movements, and mental processes

tunity. Other times the task changes may be dictated by changes in production schedules, client demands, or technology. Many small-business owners, general managers of start-up strategic business units, and top management members perform such flexible jobs.

A third factor that has changed the traditional view of job design and analysis is the need for new general skills or competencies. Two important new skills or competencies are teamwork and engagement. We discuss team-based job analysis toward the end of the chapter. As for engagement, job analysis typically focuses on skills and abilities to a greater degree than motivational factors. As more and more organizations emphasize employee engagement—or the degree to which an employee identifies with and has enthusiasm for his or her work—our analysis of jobs needs to take motivational factors into account. As Jack Welch stated, "[no] company, small or large, can win over the long run without energized employees who believe in the [firm's] mission and understand how to achieve it."[2] A large-scale study of 7,939 business units supports Welch's assertion that organizations whose employees reported above-average levels of engagement performed significantly better (63% of such organizations had above-average levels of performance) than those whose employees were below average on engagement (37% of such organizations had above-average levels of performance).[3]

Measures of engagement reflect innate psychological characteristics that are usually not subjects of job analysis. For example, Dell assesses employee engagement with items such as, "Considering everything, Dell is the right place for me." Intuit measures engagement with statements like, "I am proud to work for Intuit." Because engagement is inherently one of the KSAO "other" characteristics, there is very little research into how engagement can be factored into job analysis. One way to incorporate engagement is to consider it a general competency in competency-based job analysis, a method we cover later in the chapter. As one reviewer of the engagement literature suggests, "Identify those candidates who are best-suited to the job and your organization's culture."[4]

JOB REQUIREMENTS JOB ANALYSIS

Overview

As noted earlier, job requirements job analysis identifies the tasks, KSAOs, and context for a job. Job requirements job analysis yields information helpful in the recruitment, selection, and employment domains in such activities as communicating job requirements to applicants, developing selection plans for KSAOs to focus on when staffing a job, identifying appropriate assessment methods to gauge applicants' KSAOs, establishing hiring qualifications, and complying with relevant laws and regulations. Competency-based job analysis results will be helpful primarily in identifying a common set of general KSAOs in which all applicants must be proficient, regardless of the specific job for which they are applying.

Effective staffing definitely requires job requirements information, and possibly competency information, for each of the types of jobs described above. Traditional and evolving jobs readily lend themselves to this, as their requirements are generally well known and unlikely to change, except gradually. For idiosyncratic, flexible, team-based, and telework jobs, job analysis is more difficult and problematic. The requirements for these jobs may frequently be changing, difficult to pinpoint, and even unknown because they depend heavily on how the job incumbent defines them. Due to the often ambiguous and fluid nature of these jobs, the organization may focus on analyzing and defining them in terms of competencies rather than specific tasks and KSAOs. Recent developments in job analysis encourage raters to explicitly describe potential changes in future job requirements in an effort to adapt to these jobs.[5]

Job analysis and the information it provides thus serve as basic input to the totality of staffing activities for an organization. In this sense, job analysis is a support activity to the various functional staffing activities. Indeed, without thorough and accurate information about job requirements and/or competencies, the organization is greatly hampered in its attempts to acquire a workforce that will be effective in terms of human resource (HR) outcomes such as performance, satisfaction, and retention. Job analysis thus is the foundation upon which successful staffing systems are constructed.

A framework depicting job requirements job analysis is shown in Exhibit 4.2. As can be seen, the job analysis begins by identifying the specific tasks and job context for a particular job.[6] After these have been identified, the KSAOs necessary for performing these tasks within the work context are inferred. For example, after identifying the task of "developing and writing monthly sales and marketing plans" for a sales manager's job, the job analysis would proceed by inferring which KSAOs would be necessary to perform this task. The task might require knowledge of intended customers, arithmetic skills, creative ability, and willingness and availability to travel frequently to various organizational units. No particular job context factors, such as physical demands, may be relevant to performance of this task or to its required KSAOs. The task and job context information are recorded in a job description, whereas the KSAO requirements are placed into a job specification. In practice, these are often contained within a single document.

Job Requirements Matrix

The job requirements matrix shows the key components of job requirements job analysis, each of which must be explicitly considered for inclusion in any job requirements job analysis. Completion of the cell entries in the matrix represents the information that must be gathered, analyzed, synthesized, and expressed in usable written form.

A completed job requirements matrix, a portion of which is shown in Exhibit 4.3 for the job of administrative assistant, serves as the basic informational source or

EXHIBIT 4.2   Job Requirements Approach to Job Analysis

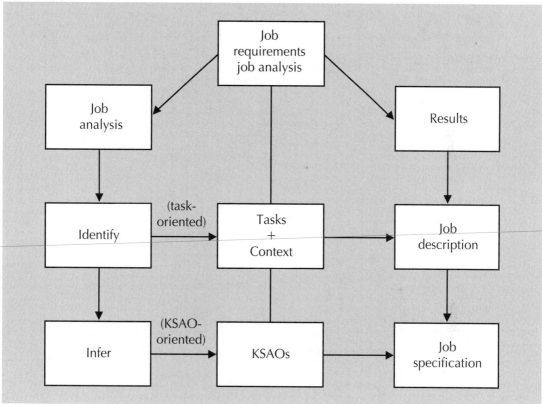

document for any job in terms of its requirements. The resultant information serves as a basic input and guide to all subsequent staffing activities.

Referring to Exhibit 4.3, five specific tasks identified via job analysis are listed. Note that only a portion of the total tasks for the job is shown. In turn, these have been categorized into two general task dimensions—supervision and word processing. Their importance to the overall job is indicated with the percentage of time spent on each—30% and 20%, respectively. For each task dimension and its specific tasks, several KSAOs have been inferred to be necessary for performance. The nature of these KSAOs is presented, along with a 1–5 rating of how important each KSAO is for performance of the task dimension. At the bottom of the matrix are indications of job context factors pertaining to work setting (indoors), privacy of work area (cubicle), attire (business clothes), body positioning (mostly sitting and standing), and physical work conditions (no environmental or job hazards).

EXHIBIT 4.3   Portion of Job Requirements Matrix for Job of Administrative Assistant

Tasks			KSAOs	
Specific Tasks	Task Dimensions	Importance (% time spent)	Nature	Importance to Tasks (1–5 rating)
1. Arrange schedules with office assistant/volunteers to ensure that office will be staffed during prescribed hours	A. Supervision	30%	1. Knowledge of office operations and policies	4.9
2. Assign office tasks to office assistant/volunteers to ensure coordination of activities	A. Supervision		2. Ability to match people to tasks according to their skills and hours of availability	4.6
			3. Skill in interaction with diverse people	2.9
			4. Skill in determining types and priorities of tasks	4.0
3. Type/transcribe letters, memos, and reports from handwritten material or dictated copy to produce final copy, using word processor	B. Word processing	20%	1. Knowledge of typing formats	3.1
			2. Knowledge of spelling and punctuation	5.0
			3. Knowledge of graphics display software	2.0
4. Prepare graphs and other visual material to supplement reports, using word processor	B. Word processing		4. Ability to proofread and correct work	5.0
5. Proofread typed copy and correct spelling, punctuation, and typographical errors in order to produce high-quality materials	B. Word processing		5. Skill in use of WordPerfect (most current version)	4.3
			6. Skill in creating visually appealing and understandable graphs	3.4

Job Context: Indoors, cubicle, business clothes, mostly sitting and standing, no environmental or job hazards.

Task Statements

Job analysis begins with the development of task statements. Task statements are objectively written descriptions of the major tasks an employee performs in a job. They serve as the building blocks for the remainder of the job requirements job analysis. The statements are made in simple declarative sentences.

Ideally, each task statement will show several things:

1. What the employee does, using a specific action verb at the start of the task statement
2. To whom or what the employee does what he or she does, stating the object of the verb
3. What is produced, indicating the expected output of the verb
4. What equipment, materials, tools, or procedures are used

Use of the sentence analysis technique is very helpful for writing task statements that conform to these four requirements. Exhibit 4.4 shows an example of the technique for several tasks from very different jobs.

In addition to the preceding four requirements, there are several other suggestions for effectively writing task statements. First, use specific action verbs that have only one meaning. Examples of verbs that do not conform to this suggestion include "supports," "assists," and "handles."

Second, focus on recording tasks, as opposed to specific elements that compose a task. This requires the use of considerable judgment because the distinction between a task and an element is relative and often fuzzy. Note that most jobs can be adequately described within a range of 15–25 task statements. A task statement list exceeding this range is a warning that it may be too narrow in terms of activities defined.

Third, do not include minor or trivial activities in task statements; focus only on major tasks and activities. An exception to this recommendation occurs when a so-called minor task is judged to have great importance to the job (see the following discussion).

Fourth, ensure that the list of task statements is reliable.[7] A good way to do this is to have two or more people (analysts) independently evaluate the task statement list in terms of both inclusiveness and clarity. Close agreement between people signifies high reliability. If there is disagreement, the nature of the disagreement can be discussed and the task statements can be appropriately modified.

Task Dimensions

Task statement lists may be maintained in list form and subsequently incorporated into the job description. Often, however, it is useful to group sets of task statements into task dimensions and then attach a name to each such dimension. Other terms for task dimensions are "duties," "accountability areas," "responsibilities," and "performance dimensions."

EXHIBIT 4.4   Use of the Sentence Analysis Technique for Task Statements

Sentence Analysis Technique			
What does the worker do?		Why does the worker do it? What gets done?	What is the final result or technological objective?
Worker action		Purpose of the worker actions	Materials, products, subject matter, and/or services
(Worker function)	(Work devices, people, or information)	(Work field)	(MPSMS)
Verb	Direct object	Infinitive phrase	
		Infinitive	Object of the infinitive
Sets up *(setting up)*	various types of metal-working machines *(work device)*	to machine *(machining)*	metal aircraft parts. *(material)*
Persuades *(persuading)*	customers *(people)*	to buy *(merchandising)*	automobiles. *(product)*
Interviews *(analyzing)*	clients *(people)*	to assess *(advising–counseling)*	skills and abilities. *(subject matter)*
Drives *(driving–operating)*	bus *(work device)*	to transport *(transporting)*	passengers. *(service)*

SOURCE: Vocational Rehabilitation Institute, *A Guide to Job Analysis* (Menomonie, WI: University of Wisconsin-Stout, 1982), p. 8.

A useful way to facilitate the grouping process is to create a task dimension matrix. Each column in the matrix represents a potential task dimension, and a label is tentatively attached to it. Each row in the matrix represents a particular task statement. Cell entries in the matrix represent the assignment of task statements to task dimensions (the grouping of tasks). The goal is to have each task statement assigned to only one task dimension.

Several things should be kept in mind about task dimensions. First, their creation is optional and should occur only if they will be useful. Second, there are many different grouping procedures, ranging from straightforward judgmental ones to highly sophisticated statistical ones.[8] For most purposes, a simple judgmental process is sufficient, such as having the people who participated in the creation of the task statements also create the groupings as part of the same exercise. As a rule, there should be four to eight dimensions, depending on the number of task statements, regardless of the specific grouping procedure used. Third, it is important that the grouping procedure yield a reliable set of task dimensions acceptable to managers, job incumbents, and other organizational members.

Importance of Tasks/Dimensions

Rarely are all tasks/dimensions of a job thought to be of equal weight or importance. It is generally felt that these differences must be captured, expressed, and incorporated into job information, especially the job description. Normally, assessments of importance are made just for task dimensions, though it is certainly possible to make them for individual tasks as well.

Before actual weighting can occur, two decisions must be made: (1) the specific attribute to be assessed in terms of importance must be decided (e.g., time spent on the task/dimension), and (2) whether the attribute will be measured in categorical terms (e.g., essential or nonessential) or continuous terms (e.g., percent of time spent, 1–5 rating of importance). Exhibit 4.5 shows examples of the results of these two decisions in terms of commonly used importance attributes and their measurement.

Once these decisions are made, it is possible to proceed with assessing or weighting the tasks/dimensions in terms of importance. If the tasks/dimensions are not explicitly assessed in such a manner, they will end up being weighted equally by default.

KSAOs

KSAOs are inferred or derived from knowledge of the tasks and task dimensions themselves. The inference process requires that the analysts think explicitly in specific cause-and-effect terms. For each task or dimension, the analyst must in essence ask, "Exactly which KSAOs do I think will be necessary for (will cause) performance on this task or dimension?" Then the analyst should ask, "Why do I

EXHIBIT 4.5 Examples of Ways to Assess Task/Dimension Importance

A. **Relative Time Spent**

For each task/dimension, rate the amount of time you spend on it, relative to all other tasks/dimensions of your job.

1	2	3	4	5
Very small amount		Average amount		Very large amount

B. **Percentage (%) Time Spent**

For each task/dimension, indicate the percentage (%) of time you spend on it (percentages must total to 100%).

Dimension _____   % Time spent _____

C. **Importance to Overall Performance**

For each task/dimension, rate its importance to your overall job performance.

1	2	3	4	5
Minor importance		Average importance		Major importance

D. **Need for New Employee Training**

Do new employees receive a standard, planned course of training for performance of this task, other than a customary job orientation?

_____ Yes

_____ No

---

think this?" in order to think through the soundness of the inferential logic. Discussions among analysts about these questions are encouraged.

When asking and answering these questions, it is useful to keep in mind what is meant by the terms "knowledge," "skill," "ability," and "other characteristics." It is also helpful to refer to research results that help us better understand the nature and complexity of these concepts. As described below, these results have been synthesized to create the Occupational Information Network, or O*NET (see *www.onetcenter.org*).

Knowledge. Knowledge is a body of information (conceptual, factual, procedural) that can be applied directly to the performance of tasks. It tends to be quite focused or specific in terms of job, organization, or occupation. O*NET can assist the analyst in identifying and writing statements of knowledge requirements. It provides definitions of 33 knowledges that might generally be necessary, in varying levels, in occupations. Exhibit 4.6 lists these knowledges. The definitions of the knowledges provided by O*NET are available in print and online. For example, "sales and marketing" knowledge is defined as "knowledge of principles and methods involved in showing, promoting, and selling products or services; this includes marketing strategies and tactics, product demonstration and sales techniques, and sales control systems."[9] Use of O*NET knowledges and their definitions is a

EXHIBIT 4.6   Knowledges Contained in O*NET

- Business and management
  Administration and management
  Clerical
  Economics and accounting
  Sales and marketing
  Customer and personal service
  Personnel and human resources
- Manufacturing and production
  Production and processing
  Food production
- Engineering and technology
  Computers and electronics
  Engineering and technology
  Design
  Building and construction
  Mechanical
- Mathematics and science
  Mathematics
  Physics
  Chemistry
  Biology
  Psychology
  Sociology and anthropology
  Geography

- Health services
  Medicine and dentistry
  Therapy and counseling
- Education and training
  Education and training
- Arts and humanities
  English language
  Foreign language
  Fine arts
  History and archaeology
  Philosophy and theology
- Law and public safety
  Public safety and security
  Law, government, and jurisprudence
- Communications
  Telecommunications
  Communications and media
- Transportation
  Transportation

Source: Adapted from N. G. Peterson, M. D. Mumford, W. C. Borman, P. R. Jeanneret, E. A. Fleishman, and K. Y. Levin (eds.), *O*NET Final Technical Report, Vol. 1* (Salt Lake City: Utah Department of Workforce Services, 1997), pp. 4-1 to 4-26. ©Utah Department of Workforce Services on behalf of US Department of Labor.

helpful starting point in preparing knowledge statements. As the knowledges are intended for general occupations, they will probably have to be supplemented with more job-specific statements crafted by the job analyst. When doing so, analysts should be particularly wary of using global or shorthand terms such as "knowledge of accounting principles." Here, it would be better to indicate which accounting principles are being utilized and why each is necessary for task performance.

Skill. Skill refers to an observable competence for working with or applying knowledge to perform a particular task or a closely related set of tasks. A skill is not an enduring characteristic of the person; it depends on experience and practice. Skill requirements are directly inferred from observation or knowledge of tasks performed.

Considerable research has been devoted to identifying particular job-related skills and to organizing them into taxonomies. Job analysts should begin the skills inference process by referring to the results of this research.

An excellent example of such useful research is found in O*NET.[10] O*NET identifies and defines 46 skills applicable across the occupational spectrum. Exhibit 4.7 lists these skills. The first 10 are basic skills involving acquiring and conveying information; the remaining 36 are cross-functional skills used to facilitate task performance. The definitions provided by O*NET are available in print and online. For example, the basic skill "reading comprehension" is defined as "understanding written sentences and paragraphs in work-related documents"; the cross-functional skill "negotiation" is defined as "bringing others together and trying to reconcile differences." Reference to these 46 skills is a good starting point for the job analyst. More specific skills may need to be identified and described for the particular job being analyzed. An excellent example in this regard is computer-related skills such as use of spreadsheets and databases, use of software such as Microsoft Word, and various types of programming.

Ability. An ability is an underlying, enduring trait of the person that is useful for performing a range of tasks. It differs from a skill in that it is less likely to change over time and that is applicable across a wide set of tasks encountered in many different jobs. Four general categories of abilities are commonly recognized: cognitive, psychomotor, physical, and sensory. O*NET contains a complete taxonomy of these four categories, shown in Exhibit 4.8. Definitions (not shown) accompany the abilities in print and online. The ability "oral expression," for example, is defined as "the ability to communicate information and ideas in speaking so others will understand." As another example, "dynamic flexibility" is "the ability to quickly and repeatedly bend, stretch, twist, or reach out with the body, arms and/or legs."[11]

Other Characteristics. "Other characteristics" is a catchall category for factors that do not fit neatly into the knowledge, skills, and abilities categories. Despite

---

EXHIBIT 4.7   Skills Contained in O*NET

Basic Skills

- Content
  Reading comprehension
  Active listening
  Writing
  Speaking
  Mathematics
  Science

- Process
  Critical thinking
  Active learning
  Learning strategies
  Monitoring

Cross-Functional Skills

- Social skills
  Social perceptiveness
  Coordination
  Persuasion
  Negotiation
  Instructing
  Service orientation
- Complex problem-solving skills
  Problem identification
  Information gathering
  Information organization
  Synthesis/reorganization
  Idea generation
  Idea evaluation
  Implementation planning
  Solution appraisal
- Resource management skills
  Time management
  Management of financial resources
  Management of material resources
  Management of personnel resources

- Technical skills
  Operations analysis
  Technology design
  Equipment selection
  Installation
  Programming
  Equipment maintenance
  Troubleshooting
  Repairing
  Testing
  Operation monitoring
  Operation and control
  Product inspection
- Systems skills
  Visioning
  Systems perception
  Identification of downstream
    consequences
  Identification of key causes
  Judgment and decision making
  Systems evaluation

Source: Adapted from N. G. Peterson, M. D. Mumford, W. C. Borman, P. R. Jeanneret, E. A. Fleishman, and K. Y. Levin (eds.), *O*NET Final Technical Report, Vol. 1* (Salt Lake City: Utah Department of Workforce Services, 1997), pp. 3-1 to 3-36. ©Utah Department of Workforce Services on behalf of US Department of Labor.

the catchall nature of these requirements, they are very important for even being able to enter into the employment relationship (legal requirements), being present to perform the job (availability requirements), and having values consistent with organizational culture and values (character requirements). Numerous examples of these factors are shown in Exhibit 4.9. Care should be taken to ensure that these

EXHIBIT 4.8 Abilities Contained in O*NET

Cognitive Abilities
- Verbal abilities
  - Oral comprehension
  - Written comprehension
  - Oral expression
  - Written expression
- Idea generation and reasoning abilities
  - Fluency of ideas
  - Originality
  - Problem sensitivity
  - Deductive reasoning
  - Inductive reasoning
  - Information ordering
  - Category flexibility
- Quantitative abilities
  - Mathematical reasoning
  - Number facility
- Memory
  - Memorization
- Perceptual abilities
  - Speed of closure
  - Flexibility of closure
  - Perceptual speed
- Spatial abilities
  - Spatial organization
  - Visualization
- Attentiveness
  - Selective attention
  - Time sharing

Psychomotor Abilities
- Fine manipulative abilities
  - Arm-hand steadiness
  - Manual dexterity
  - Finger dexterity
- Control movement abilities
  - Control precision
  - Multilimb coordination
  - Response orientation
  - Rate control

- Reaction time and speed abilities
  - Reaction time
  - Wrist-finger dexterity
  - Speed of limb movement

Physical Abilities
- Physical strength abilities
  - Static strength
  - Explosive strength
  - Dynamic strength
  - Trunk strength
- Endurance
  - Stamina
- Flexibility, balance, and coordination
  - Extent flexibility
  - Dynamic flexibility
  - Gross body coordination
  - Gross body equilibrium

Sensory Abilities
- Visual abilities
  - Near vision
  - Far vision
  - Visual color discrimination
  - Night vision
  - Peripheral vision
  - Depth perception
  - Glare sensitivity
- Auditory and speech abilities
  - Hearing sensitivity
  - Auditory attention
  - Sound localization
  - Speech recognition
  - Speech clarity

SOURCE: Adapted from N. G. Peterson, M. D. Mumford, W. C. Borman, P. R. Jeanneret, E. A. Fleishman, and K. Y. Levin (eds.), *O*NET Final Technical Report, Vol. 2* (Salt Lake City: Utah Department of Workforce Services, 1997), pp. 9-1 to 9-26. ©Utah Department of Workforce Services on behalf of US Department of Labor.

EXHIBIT 4.9   Examples of Other Job Requirements

Legal Requirements
Possession of license (occupational, driver's, etc.)
Citizen or legal alien?
Geographic residency (e.g., within city limits for public employees)
Security clearance

Availability Requirements
Starting date
Work site locations
Hours and days of week
Travel
Attendance and tardiness

Character Requirements
Moral
Work ethic
Background
Conscientiousness
Honesty and integrity

factors truly are job requirements, as opposed to whimsical and ill-defined preferences of the organization.

KSAO Importance

As suggested in the job requirements matrix, the KSAOs of a job may differ in their weight or contribution to task performance. Hence, their relative importance must be explicitly considered, defined, and indicated. Failure to do so means that all KSAOs will be assumed to be of equal importance by default.

As with task importance, deriving KSAO importance requires two decisions. First, what will be the specific attribute(s) on which importance is judged? Second, will the measurement of each attribute be categorical (e.g., required-preferred) or continuous (e.g., 1–5 rating scale)? Examples of formats for indicating KSAO importance are shown in Exhibit 4.10. O*NET uses a 1–5 rating scale format and also provides actual importance ratings for many jobs.

Job Context

As shown in the job requirements matrix, tasks and KSAOs occur within a broader job context. A job requirements job analysis should include consideration of the job context and the factors that are important in defining it. Such consideration is necessary because these factors may have an influence on tasks and KSAOs; further,

EXHIBIT 4.10   Examples of Ways to Assess KSAO Importance

A.   **Importance to (acceptable) (superior) task performance**

1 = minimal importance
2 = some importance
3 = average importance
4 = considerable importance
5 = extensive importance

B.   **Should the KSAO be assessed during recruitment/selection?**

☐ Yes
☐ No

C.   **Is the KSAO required, preferred, or not required for recruitment/selection?**

☐ Required
☐ Preferred
☐ Not required (obtain on job and/or in training)

information about the factors may be used in the recruitment and selection of job applicants. For example, the information may be given to job applicants to provide them a realistic job preview during recruitment, and consideration of job context factors may be helpful in assessing likely person/organization fit during selection.

O*NET contains a wide array of job and work context factors useful for characterizing occupations.[12] Consider the O*NET classification of physical work conditions: setting, attire, body positioning, environmental conditions, and job hazards. Within each of these categories are numerous specific facets; these are shown in Exhibit 4.11. The job analyst should use a listing such as this to identify the relevant job context factors and include them in the job requirements matrix.

O*NET also contains work context factors pertaining to interpersonal relationships (communication, types of role relationships, responsibility for others, and conflictual contact with others) and to structural job characteristics (criticality of position, routine versus challenging work, and pace and scheduling). These factors might also be considered in the job analysis.

Job Descriptions and Job Specifications

As previously noted, it is common practice to express the results of job requirements job analysis in written job descriptions and job specifications. Referring back to the job requirements matrix, note that its sections pertaining to tasks and job context are similar to a job description, and the section dealing with KSAOs is similar to a job specification.

EXHIBIT 4.11   Job Context (Physical Work Conditions) Contained in O*NET

Work Setting
- How frequently does this job require the worker to work:
    Indoors, environmentally controlled
    Indoors, not environmentally controlled
    Outdoors, exposed to all weather conditions
    Outdoors, under cover
    In an open vehicle or operating open equipment
    In an enclosed vehicle or operating enclosed equipment
- Privacy of work area
- Physical proximity

Work Attire
- How often does the worker wear:
    Business clothes
    A special uniform
    Work clothing
    Common protective or safety attire
    Specialized protective or safety attire

Body Positioning
- How much time in a usual work period does the worker spend:
    Sitting
    Standing
    Climbing ladders, scaffolds, poles, and so on
    Walking or running
    Kneeling, stooping, crouching, or crawling
    Keeping or regaining balance
    Using hands to handle, control, or feel objects, tools, or controls
    Bending or twisting the body
    Making repetitive motions

Environmental Conditions
- How often during a usual work period is the worker exposed to the following conditions:
    Sounds and noise levels that are distracting and uncomfortable
    Very hot or very cold temperatures
    Extremely bright or inadequate lighting conditions
    Contaminants
    Cramped work space that requires getting into awkward positions
    Whole body vibration

Job Hazards
- How often does this job require the worker to be exposed to the following hazards:
    Radiation
    Diseases/infections
    High places
    Hazardous conditions
    Hazardous equipment
    Hazardous situation involving likely cuts, bites, stings, or minor burns

SOURCE: Adapted from N. G. Peterson, M. D. Mumford, W. C. Borman, P. R. Jeanneret, E. A. Fleishman, and K. Y. Levin (eds.), *O*NET Final Technical Report, Vol. 2* (Salt Lake City: Utah Department of Workforce Services, 1997), pp. 7-1 to 7-35. ©Utah Department of Workforce Services on behalf of US Department of Labor.

There are no standard formats or other requirements for either job descriptions or job specifications. In terms of content, however, a job description should include the following: job family, job title, job summary, task statements and dimensions, importance indicators, job context indicators, and the date that the job analysis was conducted. A job specification should include job family, job title, job summary, KSAOs (separate section for each), importance indicators, and date conducted. An example of a combined job description/specification is shown in Exhibit 4.12.

Collecting Job Requirements Information

Job analysis involves consideration of not only the types of information (tasks, KSAOs, and job context) to be collected but also the methods, sources, and processes to be used for such collection. These issues are discussed next, and as will be seen, there are many alternatives to choose from for developing an overall job analysis system for any particular situation. Potential inaccuracies and other limitations of the alternatives will also be pointed out.[13]

Methods

Job analysis methods represent procedures or techniques for collecting job information. Many specific techniques and systems have been developed and named (e.g., Functional Job Analysis, Position Analysis Questionnaire [PAQ]). Rather than discuss each technique separately, we will concentrate on the major generic methods that underlie all specific techniques and applications. Many excellent descriptions and discussions of the specific techniques are available.[14]

Prior Information.   For any job, there is usually some prior information available that could and should be consulted. Indeed, this information should routinely be searched for and used as a starting point for a job analysis.

Many possible organizational sources of job information are available, including current job descriptions and specifications, job-specific policies and procedures, training manuals, and performance appraisals. Externally, job information may be available from other employers, as well as trade and professional associations. Both the Society for Human Resource Management (SHRM; *www.shrm.org*) and the International Public Management Association for Human Resources (IPMA-HR; *www.ipma-hr.org*) provide sample job descriptions online.

Finally there is O*NET (*www.onetcenter.org*). O*NET contains extensive research-based taxonomies in several categories: occupational tasks, knowledges, skills, abilities, education and experience/training, work context, organizational context, occupational interests and values, and work styles.[15] Additionally, O*NET contains ratings of the specific factors within each category for many occupations, and ratings for additional occupations are continually being added. For example, occupational and importance ratings of the specific knowledges, skills, and abilities shown in Exhibits 4.6, 4.7, and 4.8 are provided. The job analyst could use

EXHIBIT 4.12   Example of Combined Job Description/Specification

FUNCTIONAL UNIT: CHILDREN'S REHABILITATION
JOB TITLE: REHABILITATION SPECIALIST
DATE: 12/5/11

JOB SUMMARY

Works with children with disabilities and their families to identify developmental strengths and weaknesses, develop rehabilitation plans, deliver and coordinate rehabilitation activities, and evaluate effectiveness of those plans and activities.

PERFORMANCE DIMENSIONS AND TASKS   **Time Spent (%)**

1. Assessment   **10%**

Administer formal and informal motor screening and evaluation instruments to conduct assessments. Perform assessments to identify areas of strengths and need.

2. Planning   **25%**

Collaborate with parents and other providers to directly develop the individualized family service plan. Use direct and consultative models of service in developing plans.

3. Delivery   **50%**

Carry out individual and small-group motor development activities with children and families. Provide service coordination to designated families. Work with family care and child care providers to provide total services. Collaborate with other staff members and professionals from community agencies to obtain resources and specialized assistance.

4. Evaluation   **15%**

Observe, interpret, and report on client to monitor individual progress. Assist in collecting and reporting intervention data in order to prepare formal program evaluation reports. Write evaluation reports to assist in developing new treatment strategies and programs.

JOB SPECIFICATIONS

1. License: License to practice physical therapy in the state

2. Education: B.S. in physical or occupational therapy required; M.S. preferred

3. Experience: Prefer (not required) one year experience working with children with disabilities and their families

4. Skills: Listening to and interacting with others (children, family members, coworkers)
Developing treatment plans
Organizing and writing reports using Microsoft Word

JOB CONTEXT: Indoors, office, business clothes, no environmental or job hazards.

these ratings as benchmarks against which to compare specific importance ratings he or she determines for a specific job. For example, if the analyst was developing importance ratings of knowledges, skills, and abilities for the job of registered nurse in a particular hospital, the compiled ratings could be compared with the O*NET ratings for the same occupation. Reasonable similarity between the two sets of ratings would help confirm the analyst's accuracy. There are also statistical techniques that link O*NET KSAO ratings for a job to specific selection tools, like standardized literacy tests.[16]

Obvious advantages of O*NET are its flexibility (it can be applied to many different types of jobs) and, in particular, its ease of use.[17] The ready availability of prior job information needs to be balanced with some possible limitations. First, there is the general issue of completeness. Prior information is usually deficient in some important areas of job requirements, as in evolving or nontraditional types of jobs. Therefore, sole reliance on prior information should be avoided. A second limitation is that there will be little indication of exactly how the information was collected and, relatedly, how accurate it is. These limitations suggest that while prior information should be the starting point for job analysis, it should not be the stopping point.

Observation. Simply observing job incumbents performing the job is an excellent way to learn about tasks, KSAOs, and context. It provides a thoroughness and richness of information unmatched by any other method. It is also the most direct form of gathering information because it does not rely on intermediary information sources, as would be the case with other methods (e.g., interviewing job incumbents and supervisors).

The following potential limitations to observation should be kept in mind. First, observation is most appropriate for jobs with physical (as opposed to mental) components and ones with relatively short job cycles (i.e., amount of time required to complete job tasks before repeating them). Second, the method may involve substantial time and cost. Third, the ability of the observer to do a thorough and accurate analysis is open to question; it may be necessary to train observers prior to the job analysis. Fourth, the method will require coordination with, and approval from, many people (e.g., supervisors and incumbents). Finally, the incumbents being observed may distort their behavior during observation in self-serving ways, such as making tasks appear more difficult or time-consuming than they really are.

Interviews. Interviewing job incumbents and others, such as their managers, has many potential advantages. It respects the interviewee's vast source of information about the job. The interview format allows the interviewer to explain the purpose of the job analysis and how the results will be used, thus enhancing likely acceptance of the process by the interviewees. It can be structured in format to ensure standardization of collected information.

As with any job analysis method, the interview is not without potential limitations. It is time-consuming and costly, and this may cause the organization to skimp on it in ways that jeopardize the reliability and content validity of the information gathered. The interview, not providing anonymity, may lead to suspicion and distrust on the part of interviewees. The quality of the information obtained, as well as interviewee acceptance, depends on the skill of the interviewer. The interviewers should thus be carefully selected and trained. Finally, the success of the interview also depends on the skills and abilities of the interviewee, such as the person's verbal communication skills and the ability to recall tasks performed.

Task Questionnaire.   A typical task questionnaire contains a lengthy list of task statements that cut across many different job titles and is administered to incumbents (all or samples of them) in these job titles. For each task statement, the respondent is asked to indicate (1) whether the task applies to the respondent's job (respondents should always be given a DNA [does not apply] option) and (2) task importance (e.g., a 1–5 scale rating difficulty or time spent).

A questionnaire-based job analysis tool known as the PAQ is perhaps the single most popular specific job analysis method. The PAQ consists of 300 items and is completed by job incumbents. The items are sorted into six major divisions: (1) information input (e.g., use of written materials), (2) mental processes (e.g., use of reasoning and problem solving), (3) work output (e.g., use of keyboard devices), (4) interpersonal activities (e.g., serving/catering), (5) work situation and job context (e.g., working in low temperatures), and (6) miscellaneous aspects (e.g., irregular hours). After the employees evaluate how well each of the 300 items applies to their jobs, the completed questionnaires are scored by computer and a report is generated that provides scores for the divisions (and more finely grained subdivisions).[18]

The advantages of task questionnaires are numerous. They are standardized in content and format, thus yielding a standardized method of information gathering. They can obtain considerable information from large numbers of people. They are economical to administer and score, and the availability of scores creates the opportunity for subsequent statistical analysis. Additionally, task questionnaires are (and should be) completed anonymously, thus enhancing respondent participation, honesty, and acceptance.

The development of task questionnaires like the PAQ across a variety of organizations has also facilitated the development of linkages between task dimensions and required KSAOs. Some of these developments have involved a technique called synthetic validation, which helps determine the types of selection tools that will be most appropriate for a job.[19] As the databases linking task dimensions to KSAOs have increased in size and scope over time, it has become increasingly possible to know which selection predictors are most appropriate for a given job without having to resort to a local validation study, as will be discussed in Chapter 7.

A task questionnaire is potentially limited in certain ways. The most important limitation pertains to task statement content. Care must be taken to ensure that the questionnaire contains task statements of sufficient content relevance, representativeness, and specificity. This suggests that if a tailor-made questionnaire is to be used, considerable time and resources must be devoted to its development to ensure accurate inclusion of task statements. If a preexisting questionnaire (e.g., the PAQ) is considered, prior to its use the task statement content should be assessed relative to the task content of the jobs to be analyzed.

A second limitation of task questionnaires pertains to potential respondent reactions. Respondents may react negatively if they feel the questionnaire does not contain task statements covering important aspects of their jobs. Respondents may also find completion of the questionnaire to be tedious and boring; this may cause them to commit rating errors. Interpretation and understanding of the task statements may be problematic for respondents who have reading and comprehension skill deficiencies.

A third limitation is that questionnaires such as the PAQ assume that the incumbent is reasonably intelligent, experienced in the job, and sufficiently educated to evaluate the items. To the extent incumbents are less intelligent, lack experience, or have little education, the familiar dictum "garbage in, garbage out" may apply.

Committee or Task Force. Job analysis is often guided by an ad hoc committee or task force. Members of this group typically include job experts—both managers and employees—as well as an HR representative. They may conduct a number of activities, including (1) reviewing existing information and gathering sample job descriptions, (2) interviewing job incumbents and managers, (3) overseeing the administration of job analysis surveys and analyzing the results, (4) writing task statements, grouping them into task dimensions, and rating the importance of the task dimensions, and (5) identifying KSAOs and rating their importance. A committee or task force brings considerable job analysis expertise to the process, facilitates reliability of judgment through conversation and consensus building, and enhances acceptance of the final results.

Combined Methods. Only in rare instances does a job analysis involve use of only a single method. Much more likely is a hybrid, eclectic approach that uses multiple methods. This makes job analysis a more complicated process to design and administer than what is implied by a description of each of the methods alone.

Criteria for Choice of Methods. Some explicit choices regarding methods of job analysis need to be made. One set of choices involves deciding whether to use or not use a particular method of information collection. An organization must decide, for example, whether to use an off-the-shelf method or its own particular method that is suited to its own needs and circumstances. A second set of choices involves how to blend together a set of methods that will be used in varying ways and degrees in the actual job analysis. Some criteria for guidance in such decisions are shown in Exhibit 4.13.

Sources to Be Used

Choosing sources of information involves considering who will be used to provide the information sought. While this matter is not entirely independent of job analysis methods (e.g., use of a task questionnaire normally requires use of job incumbents as the source), it is treated this way in the sections that follow.

Job Analyst.   A job analyst is someone who, by virtue of job title and training, is available and suited to conduct job analyses and to guide the job analysis process. The job analyst is also "out of the loop," being neither manager nor incumbent of the jobs analyzed. Thus, the job analyst brings a combination of expertise and neutrality to the work.

Despite such advantages and appeals, reliance on a job analyst as the job information source is not without potential limitations. First, the analyst may be perceived as an outsider by incumbents and supervisors, a perception that may result in questioning the analyst's job knowledge and expertise, as well as trustworthiness. Second, the job analyst may, in fact, lack detailed knowledge of the jobs to be analyzed, especially in an organization with many different job titles. Lack of knowledge may cause the analyst to bring inaccurate job stereotypes to the analysis process. Finally, having specially designated job analysts (either employees or outside consultants) tends to be expensive.

Job Incumbents.   Job incumbents seem like a natural source of information to be used in job analysis, and indeed they are relied on in most job analysis systems. The major advantage to working with incumbents is their familiarity with tasks, KSAOs, and job context. In addition, job incumbents may become more accepting of the job analysis process and its results through their participation in it.

Some skepticism should be maintained about job incumbents as a source of workplace data, as is true for any source. They may lack the knowledge or insights necessary to provide inclusive information, especially if they are probationary or part-time employees. Some employees may also have difficulty describing the tasks involved in their job or being able to infer and articulate the underlying KSAOs necessary for the job. There are also concerns about job incumbents not responding to job analysis surveys; most studies show that fewer than half of job incumbents voluntarily respond to job analysis surveys. Response rates are lower among lower-level employees and those with less education.[20] Another potential limitation of job incumbents as an information source pertains to their motivation to be a willing and accurate source. Feelings of distrust and suspicion may greatly hamper employees' willingness to function capably as sources. For example, incumbents may intentionally fail to report certain tasks as part of their job so that those tasks are not incorporated into the formal job description. Or, incumbents

EXHIBIT 4.13 **Criteria for Guiding Choice of Job Analysis Methods**

Method	Sources	Advantages and Disadvantages
Prior information	Current job descriptions Training manuals Performance appraisals O*NET	Readily available Inexpensive External sources may not match jobs in your organization Focus is on how jobs have been done previously, not how they will be done in the future
Observation	Trained job analysts or HR professionals watch incumbents perform the job	Thorough, rich information Does not rely on intermediary information sources Not appropriate for jobs that are largely mental in character Incumbents may behave differently if they know they're being observed
Interviews	HR professionals discuss job requirements with job incumbents and managers	Takes the incumbent's knowledge of the position into account Time-consuming and costly Quality depends on the knowledge and ability of the interviewee and skill of the interviewer
Task questionnaire	Job incumbents, managers, and HR professionals fill in a standardized form with questions regarding job	Standardized method across a variety of jobs Can combine information from large numbers of incumbents quickly Developing questionnaires can be expensive and time-consuming Requires that incumbents are capable of completing the instruments accurately
Committee or task force	Managers, representatives from HR, and employees meet to discuss job descriptions	Brings expertise of a variety of individuals into the process Increases reliability of the process Enhances acceptance of the final product Significant investment of staff time

may deliberately inflate the importance ratings of tasks in order to make the job appear more difficult than it actually is.

Supervisors.   Supervisors are excellent sources for use in job analysis. They not only supervise employees performing the job to be analyzed but also have played a major role in defining it and in adding/deleting job tasks (as in evolving and flexible jobs). Moreover, because supervisors ultimately have to accept the resulting descriptions and specifications for jobs they supervise, including them as a source is a good way to ensure such acceptance.

Subject Matter Experts.   Often, job analysts, job incumbents, and supervisors are called subject matter experts (SMEs). Other individuals may also be used as SMEs. These people bring particular expertise to the job analysis process, an expertise not thought to be available through standard sources. Though the exact qualifications for being designated an SME are far from clear, examples of sources so designated include previous jobholders (e.g., recently promoted employees), private consultants, customer/clients, and citizens-at-large for some public sector jobs (e.g., superintendent of schools for a school district). Whatever the sources of SMEs, a common requirement is that they have recent, firsthand knowledge of the job being analyzed.[21]

Combined Sources.   Combinations of sources, like combinations of methods, are likely to be used in a typical job analysis. This is desirable because, as noted previously, each source has some potentially unique insight to contribute to job analysis, as well as some limitations. Pooling these sources and the information they provide will likely result in an accurate and acceptable job analysis.

Job Analysis Process

Collecting job information through job analysis requires development and use of an overall process. Unfortunately, there is no set or best process to be followed; the process has to be tailor-made to suit the specifics of the situation in which it occurs. Many key issues must be dealt with in the construction and operation of the process.[22] Each of these is briefly commented on next.

Purpose.   The purpose(s) of job analysis should be clearly identified and agreed on. Since job analysis is a process designed to yield job information, the organization should ask exactly what job information is desired and why. Here, it is useful to refer back to the job requirements matrix to review the types of information that can be sought and obtained in a job requirements job analysis. Management must decide exactly what types of information are desired (task statements, task dimensions, and so forth) and in what format. Once the desired output and the results of job analysis have been determined, the organization can then plan a process that will yield the desired results.

Scope.   The issue of scope involves which job(s) to include in the job analysis. Decisions about actual scope should be based on consideration of (1) the importance of the job to the functioning of the organization, (2) the number of job applicants and incumbents, (3) whether the job is entry level and thus subject to constant staffing activity, (4) the frequency with which job requirements (both tasks and KSAOs) change, and (5) the amount of time that has lapsed since the previous job analysis.

Internal Staff or Consultant.   The organization may use its own staff to conduct the job analysis or it may procure external consultants. This is a difficult decision because it involves not only the obvious consideration of cost but also many other considerations. Exhibit 4.14 highlights some of these concerns and the trade-offs involved.

Organization and Coordination.   Any job analysis project, whether conducted by internal staff or external consultants, requires careful organization and coordination. Two key steps help ensure that this is achieved. First, an organizational member should be appointed as project manager for the total process (if consultants are used, they should report to this project manager). The project manager should be assigned overall responsibility for the total project, including its organization and control. Second, the roles and relationships for the various people involved in the project—HR staff, project staff, line managers, and job incumbents—must be clearly established.

Communication.   Clear and open communication with all concerned will facilitate the job analysis process. Some employees will liken job analysis to an invasive, exploratory surgical procedure, which, in turn, naturally raises questions in their minds about its purpose, process, and results. These questions and concerns need to be anticipated and addressed forthrightly.

Work Flow and Time Frame.   Job analysis involves a mixture of people and paper in a process in which they can become entangled very quickly. The project manager should develop and adhere to a work flowchart that shows the steps to be followed in the conduct of the job analysis. This should be accompanied by a time frame showing critical completion dates for project phases, as well as a final deadline.

Analysis, Synthesis, and Documentation.   Once collected, job information must be analyzed and synthesized through the use of various procedural and statistical means. These should be planned in advance and incorporated into the work-flow and time-frame requirements. Likewise, provisions need to be made for

EXHIBIT 4.14   Factors to Consider in Choosing Between Internal Staff and Consultants for Job Analysis

Internal Staff	Consultant
Cost of technical or procedural failure is low	Cost of technical or procedural failure is high
Project scope is limited	Project scope is comprehensive and/or large
Need for job data ongoing	Need for job data is a one-time, isolated event
There is a desire to develop internal staff skills in job analysis	There is a need for assured availability of each type and level of job analysis skill
Strong management controls are in place to control project costs	Predictability of project cost can depend on adhering to work plan
Knowledge of organization's norms, "culture," and jargon are critical	Technical innovativeness and quality are critical
Technical credibility of internal staff is high	Leverage of external "expert" status is needed to execute project
Process and products of the project are unlikely to be challenged	Process and products of the project are likely to be legally, technically, or politically scrutinized
Rational or narrative job analysis methods are desired	Commercial or proprietary job analysis methods are desired
Data collected are qualitative	Data collection methods are structured, standardized, and/or quantitative

SOURCE: D. M. Van De Vort and B. V. Stalder, "Organizing for Job Analysis," in S. Gael (ed.), *The Job Analysis Handbook for Business, Industry and Government.* Copyright © 1988 by John Wiley & Sons, Inc. Reprinted by permission of John Wiley & Sons, Inc.

preparation of written documents, especially job descriptions and job specifications, and their incorporation into relevant policy and procedure manuals.

Maintenance of the System.   Job analysis does not end with completion of the project. Rather, mechanisms must be developed and put into place to maintain the job analysis and information system over time. This is critical because the system will be exposed to numerous influences requiring response and adaptation. Examples include (1) changes in job tasks and KSAOs—additions, deletions, and modifications, (2) job redesign, restructuring, and realignment, and (3) creation of new jobs. In short, job analysis must be thought of and administered as an ongoing organizational process.

Example of Job Analysis Process.   Because of the many factors involved, there is no best or required job analysis process. Rather, the process must be designed to fit each particular situation. Exhibit 4.15 shows an example of the job analysis process with a narrow scope, namely, for a single job—that of administrative assistant (secretary). This was a specially conducted job analysis that used multiple methods (prior information, observation, and interviews) and multiple sources (job analyst, job incumbents, and supervisors). A previous job holder (SME) conducted the job analysis, and it took about 20 hours over a 30-day period to conduct and prepare a written job description as the output of the process.

COMPETENCY-BASED JOB ANALYSIS

A recently emerging view of job requirements comes from the concepts of competency and competency models. These concepts are closely akin to KSAOs in some respects and a substantial extension of KSAOs in other respects. They are an innovative and potentially fruitful approach to the identification, definition, and establishment of job requirements. Discussed below are the nature of competencies and the collection of competency information.

Nature of Competencies

A competency is an underlying characteristic of an individual that contributes to job or role performance and to organizational success.[23] Competencies specific to a particular job are the familiar KSAO requirements established through job requirements job analysis. Competency requirements may extend beyond job-specific ones to those of multiple jobs, general job categories, or the entire organization. These competencies are much more general or generic KSAOs, such as technical expertise or adaptability. A competency model is a combination of the several competencies deemed necessary for a particular job or role. Usage of competencies and competency models in staffing reflects a desire to (1) connote job requirements in ways that extend beyond the specific job itself, (2) design and implement staffing programs focused around competencies (rather than just specific jobs) as a way of increasing staffing flexibility in job assignments, and (3) make it easier to adapt jobs to a changing organizational context.

Despite the strong similarities between competencies and KSAOs, there are two notable differences. First, competencies may be job spanning, meaning that they contribute to success in multiple jobs. Members of a work team, for example, may each hold specific jobs within the team but may be subject to job-spanning

EXHIBIT 4.15   Example of Job Requirements Job Analysis

1. Meet with manager of the job, discuss project → 2. Gather existing job information from O*NET, current job description, observation of incumbents → 3. Prepare tentative set of task statements →

4. Review task statement with incumbents and managers; add, delete, rewrite statements → 5. Finalize task statements, get approval from incumbents and managers → 6. Formulate task dimensions, assign tasks to dimension, determine % time spent (importance) for each dimension →

7. Infer necessary KSAOs, develop tentative list → 8. Review KSAOs with incumbents and managers; add, delete, and rewrite KSAOs → 9. Finalize KSAOs, get approval from incumbents and manager →

10. Develop job requirements matrix and/or job description in usable format →11. Provide matrix or job description to parties (e.g., incumbents, manager, HR department) →12. Use matrix or job description in staffing activities, such as communicating with recruits and recruiters, developing the selection plan

competency requirements, such as adaptability and teamwork orientation. Such requirements ensure that team members will interact successfully with one another and will even perform portions of others' jobs if necessary. As another example, competency requirements may span jobs within the same category, such as sales jobs or managerial jobs. All sales jobs may have product knowledge as a competency requirement, and all managerial jobs may require planning and results orientation. Such requirements allow for greater flexibility in job placements and job assignments within the category.

Second, competencies can contribute not only to job performance but also to organizational success. These are very general competencies applicable to, and required for, all jobs. They serve to align requirements for all jobs with the mission and goals of the organization. A restaurant, for example, may have "customer focus" as a competency requirement for all jobs as a way of indicating that servicing the needs of its customers is a key component of all jobs.

Competency Example

An illustration of the competency approach to job requirements is shown in Exhibit 4.16. The Green Care Corporation produces several lawn maintenance products. The organization is in a highly competitive industry. To survive and grow, it has as its core mission product innovation and product reliability; its goals are to achieve annual 10% growth in revenues and 2% growth in market share. To help fulfill its mission and goals, the organization has established four general (strategic) workforce competencies—creativity/innovation, technical expertise, customer focus, and results orientation. These requirements are part of every job in the organization. At the business unit (gas lawn mowers) level, the organization has also established job-specific and job-spanning requirements. Some jobs, such as design engineer, are traditional or slowly evolving jobs and, as such, have only job-specific KSAO or competency requirements. Because the products are assembled via team processes, jobs within the assembly team (such as engine assembler or final assembler) have both job-specific and job-spanning competency requirements. The job-spanning competencies—team orientation, adaptability, and communication—are general and behavioral. They are necessary because of task interdependence between engine assembly and final assembly jobs and because employees may be shifted between the two jobs in order to cover sudden employee shortages due to unscheduled absences and to maintain smooth production flows. Each job in the business unit thus has four general competency requirements, multiple job-specific competency requirements, and, where appropriate, job-spanning competency requirements.

Organization Usage

Organizations have increasingly developed competency models and have used them as the underpinnings of several HR applications.[24] Research indicates that

EXHIBIT 4.16   Examples of Competencies

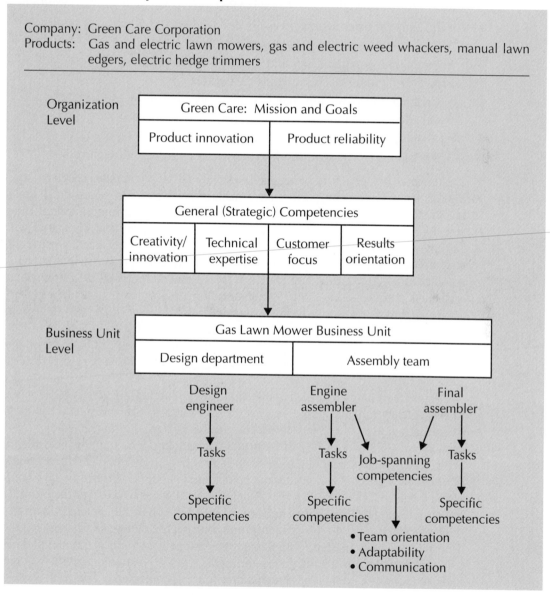

Company: Green Care Corporation
Products: Gas and electric lawn mowers, gas and electric weed whackers, manual lawn edgers, electric hedge trimmers

Organization Level

Green Care: Mission and Goals
Product innovation | Product reliability

General (Strategic) Competencies
Creativity/ innovation | Technical expertise | Customer focus | Results orientation

Business Unit Level

Gas Lawn Mower Business Unit
Design department | Assembly team

Design engineer → Tasks → Specific competencies

Engine assembler → Tasks → Specific competencies

Final assembler → Tasks → Specific competencies

Job-spanning competencies
• Team orientation
• Adaptability
• Communication

the experimentation is occurring in organizations of all sizes, but especially in large ones. The three key strategic HR reasons for doing competency modeling are to (1) create awareness and understanding of the need for change in business, (2) enhance the skill levels in the workforce, and (3) improve teamwork and coordination. Most of the emphasis has been on establishing general competencies, as illustrated by the "Great Eight" competencies used in one framework:[25]

- Leading (initiates action, gives direction)
- Supporting (shows respect, puts people first)
- Presenting (communicates and networks effectively)
- Analyzing (thinks clearly, applies expertise)
- Creating (thinks broadly, handles situations creatively)
- Organizing (plans ahead, follows rules)
- Adapting (responds to change, copes with setbacks)
- Performing (focuses on results, shows understanding of organization)

Competency models are being used for many HR applications, especially staffing, career development, performance management, and compensation. Pertaining to staffing, one important application is in HR and staffing planning. Here, workforce requirements are specified in competency terms and compared with current workforce competency levels to identify competency gaps. Such comparisons may be particularly appropriate in replacement and succession planning. Another important staffing application is in external and internal selection, where applicants are assessed not only for job-specific competencies but also for general competencies. For external hiring, competency-based interviews with applicants are conducted to gauge general competencies as a key factor in selection decisions and then in job placement decisions for those hired. For promotion decisions, competency-based interviews are used in conjunction with supervisory assessments of promotability.[26]

Despite their many potential applications to various staffing activities, adoption of competency models should be undertaken cautiously since research has identified many potential barriers to success in their usage. Prominent among these barriers are (1) a lack of buy-in from top management, who may be unwilling to apply the competency model to themselves or see its usefulness, (2) the readiness of employees generally to accept the competency model and learn the new competency behaviors required by the model, (3) conflicts as to whether there should be separate models for separate units of the organization and the relative emphases to be placed on general, job-spanning, and job-specific competencies, and (4) the time and resources needed to implement the competency model, train employees in its usage, and maintain and update the model. On the positive side, research does indicate that when raters are trained in how to use a competency approach and are given detailed information upon which to base their ratings, competency-based approaches can be valid and accurate.[27]

Collecting Competency Information

Techniques and processes for collecting competency information are continually developing.[28] General competencies at the organization (strategic) level are likely to be established by top management, with guidance from strategic HR managers. At a minimum, effective establishment of general competency requirements would seem to demand the following. First, it is crucial that the organization establish its mission and goals prior to determining competency requirements; this will help ensure that general competencies are derived from knowledge of mission and goals, much as job-specific competencies are derived from previously identified job tasks. Second, the general competencies should be truly important at all job levels so that their usage as job requirements will focus and align all jobs with the organization's mission and goals. This principle also holds in the case where, instead of general competency requirements at the organization level, there are general competency requirements at the strategic business unit or subunit level. Third, all general competencies should have specific behavioral definitions, not just labels. These definitions provide substance, meaning, and guidance to all concerned.

For job-spanning competencies, these definitions will necessarily be more task specific. To ensure effective identification and definition, several tasks should be undertaken. First, it is crucial to know the major tasks for which the competencies are to be established, meaning that some form of job analysis should occur first. For now, the organization will have to craft that process since we lack prototypes or best-practice examples as guidance. Second, SMEs familiar with all the jobs or roles to which the competencies will apply should be part of the process. Third, careful definition of the competencies will be necessary. Acquiring definitions from other organizations, consultants, or O*NET will be useful here.

A final cautionary note is that the collection and usage of competencies beyond job-specific ones will occur in uncharted legal waters. Recalling the legal standard of job-relatedness for staffing practices that cause adverse impact, will staffing practices and decisions based on general competencies be construed as job related? Will it be a defensible argument to say that although a particular competency requirement may not strongly contribute to job success, it is necessary for organizational success? Such questions will inevitably arise; to address them, the organization should conduct a thorough process for establishing competency requirements using the suggestions above as a starting point.

JOB REWARDS

In the person/job match model, jobs are composed of requirements and rewards. The focus so far in this chapter has been on job requirements vis-à-vis the discussion of job analysis. Attention now turns to job rewards. Providing and using rewards is a key staffing strategy for motivating several HR outcomes—applicant attraction, employee performance, and employee retention in particular. Successfully matching rewards provided with rewards desired will be critical in attaining the HR outcomes. Doing so first requires specifying the types of rewards potentially available and desired.

Types of Rewards

Organizations and jobs provide a wide variety of rewards. It is common to classify each reward as either extrinsic or intrinsic in nature. Extrinsic rewards are tangible factors external to the job itself that are explicitly designed and granted to employees by representatives of the organization (e.g., pay, benefits, work schedule, advancement, job security). Intrinsic rewards are the intangibles that are more internal to the job itself and experienced by the employee as an outgrowth of actually doing the job and being a member of the organization (e.g., variety in work duties, autonomy, feedback, coworker and supervisor relations).[29]

Employee Value Proposition

The totality of rewards, both extrinsic and intrinsic, associated with the job constitutes the employee value proposition (EVP).[30] The EVP is akin to the "package" or "bundle" of rewards provided to employees and to which employees respond by joining, performing, and remaining with the organization. It is the "deal" or "bargain" struck between the organization and the employee, first as a promise to the prospective employee, later as a reality to the actual new employee, and later still as a new deal as the EVP changes due to reward improvements and/or internal job changes by the employee. The EVP thus functions like a glue that binds the employee and the organization, with the employee providing certain behaviors (attraction, performance, retention, and so forth) in exchange for the EVP.

The challenge to the organization is to create EVPs for various employee groups that, on average, are both attractive and affordable (how to create an individual EVP in the form of a formal job offer to a prospective employee is considered in Chapter 12). No reward, extrinsic or intrinsic, is costless, so the organization must figure out what it can afford as it creates its EVPs. Regardless of cost, however, the rewards must also be attractive to those for whom they are intended, so attraction and cost must be considered jointly when developing EVPs. The dual affordable-attractive requirements for EVPs may create some potential problems: wrong magnitude, wrong mix, or not distinctive.[31]

Wrong magnitude refers to a package of rewards that is either too small or too great monetarily. To the prospective or current employee, too small a package may be viewed as simply inadequate, noncompetitive, or an insult, none of which are desirable perceptions to be creating. Such perceptions may arise very early in the applicant's job search, before the organization is even aware of the applicant, due to word-of-mouth information from others (e.g., former applicants or employees) or information obtained about the organization, such as through its print or electronic recruitment information. Alternatively, too small a package may not become an issue until fairly late in the job search process, as additional bits of reward package information become known to the applicant. Regardless of when the too-small perceptions emerge, they can be deal killers that lead the person to self-select out of consideration for the job, turn down the job, or quit. While too-small packages may be unattractive, they often have the virtue of being affordable for the organization.

Too large a package creates affordability problems for the organization. Those problems may not surface immediately, but long term they can threaten the organization's financial viability and possibly even its survival. Affordability problems may be particularly acute in service-providing organizations, where employee compensation costs are a substantial percentage of total operating costs.

Wrong mix refers to a situation in which the composition of the rewards package is out of sync with the preferences of prospective or current employees. A package that provides excellent retirement benefits and long-term performance incentives to a relatively young and mobile workforce, for example, is most likely a wrong mix. Its attraction and retention power in all likelihood is minimal. It might also be relatively expensive to provide.

Not distinctive refers to individual rewards packages that are viewed as ho-hum in nature. They have no uniqueness or special appeal that would either win or retain employees. They do not signal anything distinctive about the organization or give the job seeker or employee any special reason to think the "deal" is one that simply cannot be passed up or given up.

In short, creating successful EVPs is a challenge, and the results can have important implications for workforce attraction, retention, and cost. To create successful EVPs, the organization should seek to systematically collect information about rewards that are important or unimportant to employees.

Collecting Job Rewards Information

Unlike job analysis as a mechanism for collecting job requirements information, mechanisms for collecting job rewards information are more fragmentary. Nonetheless, several things can be done, all of which seek to provide data about the importance of rewards to employees—which rewards they most and least prefer. Armed with knowledge about employee preferences, the organization can begin to build EVPs that are of the right magnitude, mix, and distinctiveness. One approach for collecting job rewards information is to gauge the preferences of the organization's own employees. A different approach is to learn about employee preferences, and actual rewards provided, in other organizations.

Within the Organization

To learn about employee reward preferences within the organization, interviews with employees, or more formal surveys, might be used.

Interviews With Employees.   The interview approach requires decisions about who will guide the process, interview content, sampling confidentiality, data recording and analysis, and reporting of the results. The following are a few suggestions to guide each of those decisions. First, a person with special expertise in the employee interview process should guide the total process. This could be a person within the HR department, a person outside HR with the expertise (such as in marketing research), or an outside consultant. The person guiding the process may be the only interviewer; if not, he or she should carefully select and train those who will do the interviews, including supervising a dry run of the interview.

Second, the interviews should be structured and guided. The major content areas and specific questions should be decided in advance, tested on a small sample of employees as to their clarity and wording, and then placed in a formal interview protocol to be used by the interviewer. An example of potential questions is shown in Exhibit 4.17. Note that the major content areas covered in the interview are rewards offered, reward magnitude, reward mix, and reward distinctiveness.

Third, employees from throughout the organization should be part of the sample. In small organizations, it might be possible to include all employees; in larger organizations, random samples of employees will be necessary. When sampling, it is important to include employees from all job categories, organizational units, and organizational levels.

Fourth, it is strongly recommended that the interviews be treated as confidential and that the responses of individuals be seen only by those recording and analyz-

---

EXHIBIT 4.17 **Examples of Reward Preferences Interview Questions**

Rewards to Offer
- Are there any rewards you wish the organization would provide now?
- Looking ahead, are there any rewards you hope the organization will provide?

Reward Magnitude
- Overall, do you think the level of pay and benefits is too much, too little, or about right compared to other jobs like yours?
- Overall, do you think the reward intangibles are too much, too little, or about right compared to other jobs like yours?
- Would you be willing to pay the cost of certain rewards to ensure the organization continues to provide them?

Reward Mix
- Would you prefer the mix of pay and benefits shift more toward pay, benefits, or stay the same?
- What are the two most important rewards to you?
- What rewards are irrelevant to you?

Rewards Distinctiveness
- Which rewards that you receive are you most likely to tell others about?
- Which of our rewards really stand out to you? To job applicants?
- What rewards could we start offering that would be unique?

ing the data. At the same time, it would be useful to gather (with their permission) interviewees' demographic information (e.g., age, gender) and organizational information (e.g., job title, organizational unit) since this will permit breakouts of responses during data analysis. Such breakouts will be very useful in decisions about whether to create separate EVPs for separate employee groups or organizational units.

Fifth, interviewees' responses should be recorded rather than trusted to the memory of the interviewer. The preferred way to record responses is for the interviewer to take notes. Verbatim electronic recording of responses will likely threaten the interviewees' sense of confidentiality, plus require subsequent costly transcription. The response data will need to be analyzed with an eye toward capturing major themes in the data, such as the most and least important rewards and the rewards that the employees could do without. These findings can then be incorporated into a report that will be presented to organizational representatives.

Surveys of Employees.   A survey of employees should proceed along the same lines, following many of the same recommendations, as for an employee interview process. The biggest difference will be the mechanism for gathering the data—namely, a written set of questions with response scales rather than a verbally administered set of questions with open-ended responses. To construct the survey, a listing of the rewards to be included on the survey must be developed. These could be chosen from a listing of the organization's current extrinsic rewards, plus some questions about intrinsic rewards. For response scales, it is common to use a 1 (very unimportant) to 5 (very important) rating format. An example of a partial employee reward preferences survey is shown in Exhibit 4.18.

As with interviews, it is recommended that a person with special expertise guide the project, that the survey content be specially constructed (rather than canned), that sampling include employees throughout the organization, that employees be assured of confidentiality, that thorough analysis of results be undertaken, and that reports of findings be prepared for organizational representatives.

Which to Use?   Should the organization opt to use interviews or surveys or both? The advantages of an interview are numerous: it is of a personal nature; employees are allowed to respond in their own words; it is possible to create questions that probe preferences about reward magnitude, mix, and distinctiveness; and a very rich set of data is obtained that provides insights beyond mere rating scale responses. On the downside, interviews are costly to schedule and conduct, data analysis is messy and time-consuming, and statistical summaries and analysis of the data are difficult. Surveys are easier to administer (especially online), and they permit statistical summaries and analyses that are very helpful in interpreting responses. The biggest downsides to surveys are the lack of richness of data and the difficulty in constructing questions that tap into employees' preferences about reward magnitude, mix, and distinctiveness.

EXHIBIT 4.18   Examples of Reward Preferences Survey Questions

	Very Unimportant		Neither Important nor Unimportant		Very Important
Extrinsic Rewards					
Base pay	1	2	3	4	5
Incentive pay	1	2	3	4	5
Overtime pay	1	2	3	4	5
Health insurance	1	2	3	4	5
Promotion opportunities	1	2	3	4	5
Job security	1	2	3	4	5
Intrinsic Rewards					
Using my skills	1	2	3	4	5
Doing significant tasks	1	2	3	4	5
Deciding how to do my job	1	2	3	4	5
Getting feedback from job	1	2	3	4	5
Trust in management	1	2	3	4	5
Communications from management	1	2	3	4	5

Assuming adequate resources and expertise, a combined interview and survey approach would be best. This would allow the organization to capitalize on the unique strengths of each approach, as well as offset some of the weaknesses of each.

A final cautionary note is that both interviews and surveys of current employees miss out on two other groups from whom reward preference information would be useful. The first group is departing or departed employees, who may have left due to dissatisfaction with the EVP. In Chapter 14, the exit interview is discussed as a procedure for learning about this group. The second group is job applicants. Presumably the organization could conduct interviews and surveys with this group, but that could be administratively challenging (especially with Internet applicants). Also, applicants might feel they are "tipping their hand" to the organization in terms of what they desire or would accept in a job offer. The more common way to learn about applicant reward preferences is from surveys of employees outside the organization, who might represent the types of applicants the organization will encounter.

Outside the Organization

Other Employees.   Data on the reward preferences of employees outside the organization are available from surveys of employees in other organizations. To the extent these employees are similar to the organization's own applicants and employees, the data will likely provide a useful barometer of preferences. An example is the Job Satisfaction survey conducted by the SHRM. It administered an online survey to a national random sample of 600 employees. The employees rated the importance of 21 extrinsic and intrinsic rewards to their overall satisfaction on a 1–5 (very unimportant to very important) scale. The percentage of employees rating each reward as "very important" is shown in Exhibit 4.19.

Possibly reflecting employee anxiety surrounding the poor economic conditions in 2010, job security was ranked as the top aspect of satisfaction. Next came the extrinsic reward of "benefits," which was closely followed by intrinsic rewards of "opportunities to use skills and abilities" and "the work itself." Note that relationships with supervisors, recognition, and communication were all rated highly.

Not shown in Exhibit 4.19 are two other important findings. First, a sample of HR professionals was asked to predict the importance that employees attached to the rewards, and the HR professionals' predictions did not correspond all that closely to the actual employee ratings. A second finding was that there were some differences in reward importance as a function of employee age, tenure, gender, and industry; these differences, however, were relatively small.

Organizational Practices. A less direct way to assess the importance of rewards to employees is to examine the actual rewards that other organizations provide their employees. The assumption here is that these organizations are attuned to their employees' preferences and try to provide rewards that are consistent with them. Since pay and benefits loom large in most employees' reward preferences, it is particularly important to become knowledgeable of other organizations' pay and benefit practices to assist in the development of the EVP.

The best single source of pay and benefit information comes from the National Compensation Survey, conducted by the Bureau of Labor Statistics within the Department of Labor (*www.bls.gov*). The pay part of the survey reports average pay for employees, broken out by occupation, private-public sector, organization size, and geographic area. Another feature of the pay part is occupational leveling, in which pay rates for jobs with dissimilar occupation and job titles may be compared with one another because they share common job content. The benefits part of the survey presents detailed data about the percentage of employees who have access to a benefit or the average benefit provision. Data about the following benefits are provided: retirement, health care coverage (medical, dental, and vision) and required employee contributions, short- and long-term disability, paid holidays, paid vacation, paid jury duty leave, paid military leave, assistance for child care, adoption assistance, long-term-care insurance, flexible workplace, employer-provided PC for home use, and subsidized commuting. The data are broken out by white collar, blue collar, and service occupations; full time–part time; union–nonunion; average wage greater or less than $15/hour; organization size; goods–service producing; and geographic area.

EXHIBIT 4.19   "Very Important" Aspects of Employee Job Satisfaction (Employees)

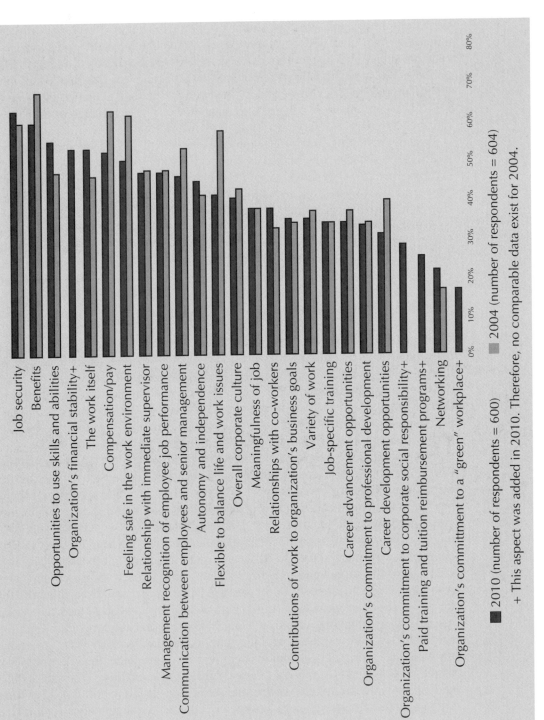

■ 2010 (number of respondents = 600)   ■ 2004 (number of respondents = 604)

+ This aspect was added in 2010. Therefore, no comparable data exist for 2004.

SOURCE: Society for Human Resource Management, *2010 Employee Job Satisfaction* (Alexandria, VA: Author), p. 7; E. Essen, *Job Satisfaction Series* (Alexandria, VA: Society for Human Resource Management, 2004), p. 156. Used with permission.

Another important source of information about benefits is the Society for Human Resource Management Annual Benefits Survey (*www.shrm.org*). It provides very detailed information about specific benefits provided in each of the following areas: family friendliness, housing and relocation, health care and wellness, personal services, financial, business travel, leave, and other benefits. The data are broken out by organization size.

JOB ANALYSIS FOR TEAMS

More and more work is being done in work teams. A work team is an interdependent collection of employees who share responsibility for achieving a specific goal. Examples of such goals include developing a product, delivering a service, winning a game, conducting a process, developing a plan, or making a joint decision.

Teams, and thus team-based jobs, occur in multiple forms. Teams are often formed around projects, such as to develop or launch a new product or manage an existing project or brand, or as part of a task force to address some critical issue or crisis. Other teams are designed to absorb management functions so that the teams themselves manage and supervise the work to be done.

No matter its form or function, every team is composed of two or more employees and has an identifiable collection of tasks to perform. Usually, these tasks are grouped into specific clusters, and each cluster constitutes a position or job. A project management team, for example, may have separate jobs and job titles for budget specialists, technical specialists, coordinators, and field staff. Each of these jobs may be traditional, evolving, flexible, or idiosyncratic.

An example of a project team is the group that developed Motorola's Razr phone, the first flat-profile cell phone on the market (which led competitors to scramble to follow suit). Work on the Razr was done with a specially formed team that comprised employees from Motorola's downtown Chicago innovation lab (known as "Moto City") and from its Libertyville, Illinois, research and development facility. Other companies such as Fisher-Price, Procter & Gamble, and Boeing have made considerable use of project teams and innovation labs to create new products and bring them to market quickly.[32]

Another type of team, one that encompasses elements of all the above team types, is the global virtual team.[33] Such a team is composed of members who are geographically dispersed, are from multiple cultures, and are working in collaboration electronically. These teams are often assigned temporary, critical tasks such as globally developing new products, setting up and overseeing offshore facilities, conducting global audits, and managing brands.

While teams differ in many respects, two differences are very important in terms of their job analysis and staffing implications. Many team members perform multiple jobs (rather than a single job). In such cases, staffing must emphasize recruitment and selection for both job-specific KSAOs and job-spanning KSAOs.

Another term used to connote job-spanning KSAOs is "competencies." Many of these job-spanning KSAOs involve flexibility, adaptability, and the ability to quickly learn skills that will facilitate performing, and switching between, multiple jobs.[34]

As an example of the above points, a product development team may include mechanical engineers, computer-assisted design specialists, product safety experts, and marketing specialists. Each team member will likely perform only one of these jobs, and thus staffing these jobs will be targeted toward job-specific KSAOs. As a different example, a team responsible for assembly of lawn mower engines may require different members to perform different jobs at any particular moment, but it may also require each member to be (or become) proficient in all phases of engine assembly. Staffing this team will require acquisition of team members who have both job-specific and job-spanning KSAOs.

The second important difference between teams regarding staffing is the degree of task interdependence among team members. The greater the task interdependence, the greater the importance of KSAOs pertaining to interpersonal qualities (e.g., communicating, collaborating, and resolving conflicts) and team self-management qualities (e.g., setting group goals, inspecting each other's work). Thus, task interdependence brings behaviorally oriented KSAOs to the forefront of job requirements for team-based jobs.

LEGAL ISSUES

Job analysis plays a crucial role in establishing the foundations for staffing activities, and that role continues from a legal perspective. Job analysis becomes intimately involved in court cases involving the job relatedness of staffing activities. It also occupies a prominent position in the Uniform Guidelines on Employee Selection Procedures (UGESP). Additionally, the Americans With Disabilities Act (ADA) requires that the organization determine the essential functions of each job, and job analysis can play a pivotal role in that process. The job requirements matrix and its development are very relevant to these issues.

Job Relatedness and Court Cases

In equal employment opportunity and affirmative action (EEO/AA) court cases, the organization is confronted with the need to justify its challenged staffing practices as being job related. Common sense suggests that this requires the organization to conduct some type of job analysis to identify job requirements. If the case involves an organization's defense of its selection procedures, the UGESP require conducting a job analysis. In addition, specific features or characteristics of the job analysis make a difference in the organization's defense. Specifically, an examination of court cases indicates that for purposes of legal defensibility the organization should conform to the following recommendations:

1. "Job analysis must be performed and must be for the job for which the selection instrument is to be utilized.
2. Analysis of the job should be in writing.
3. Job analysts should describe in detail the procedure used.
4. Job data should be collected from a variety of current sources by knowledgeable job analysts.
5. Sample size should be large and representative of the jobs for which the selection instrument is used.
6. Tasks, duties, and activities should be included in the analysis.
7. The most important tasks should be represented in the selection device.
8. Competency levels of job performance for entry-level jobs should be specified.
9. Knowledge, skills, and abilities should be specified, particularly if a content validation model is followed."[35]

These recommendations are consistent with our view of job analysis as the basic foundation for staffing activities. Moreover, even though these recommendations were made many years ago, there is little reason to doubt or modify any of them on the basis of more recent court cases.

Essential Job Functions

Recall that under the ADA, the organization must not discriminate against a qualified individual with a disability who can perform the "essential functions" of the job, with or without reasonable accommodation. This requirement raises three questions: What are essential functions? What is evidence of essential functions? What is the role of job analysis?

Essential Functions

The ADA employment regulations provide the following statements about essential functions:

1. "The term essential functions refers to the fundamental job duties of the employment position the individual with a disability holds or desires. The term essential function does not include the marginal functions of the position; and
2. A job function may be considered essential for any of several reasons, including but not limited to the following:
    • The function may be essential because the reason the position exists is to perform the function;

- The function may be essential because of the limited number of employees available among whom the performance of that job function can be distributed; and/or
- The function may be highly specialized so that the incumbent in the position is hired for his or her expertise or ability to perform the particular function."

Evidence of Essential Functions

The employment regulations go on to indicate what constitutes evidence that any particular function is in fact an essential one. That evidence includes, but is not limited to, the following:

1. The employer's judgment as to which functions are essential
2. Written job descriptions, prepared before advertising the job or interviewing applicants for the job
3. The amount of time spent on the job performing the function
4. The consequences of not requiring the incumbent to perform the function
5. The terms of a collective bargaining agreement
6. The work experience of past incumbents in the job
7. The current work experience of incumbents in similar jobs

Role of Job Analysis

What role(s) might job analysis play in identifying essential functions and establishing evidence of their being essential? The employment regulations are silent on this question. However, the Equal Employment Opportunity Commission (EEOC) has provided substantial and detailed assistance to organizations to deal with this and many other issues under the ADA.[36] The specific statements regarding job analysis and essential functions of the job are shown in Exhibit 4.20.

Examination of the statements in Exhibit 4.20 suggests the following. First, while job analysis is not required by law as a means of establishing the essential functions of a job, it is strongly recommended. Second, the job analysis should focus on tasks associated with the job. Where KSAOs are studied or specified, they should be derived from an explicit consideration of their probable links to the essential tasks. Third, with regard to tasks, the focus should be on the tasks themselves and the outcome or results of the tasks, rather than the methods by which they are performed. Finally, the job analysis should be useful in identifying potential reasonable accommodations.[37]

EXHIBIT 4.20   Job Analysis and Essential Functions of the Job

Job Analysis and the Essential Functions of a Job

The ADA does not require that an employer conduct a job analysis or any particular form of job analysis to identify the essential functions of a job. The information provided by a job analysis may or may not be helpful in properly identifying essential job functions, depending on how it is conducted.

The term "job analysis" generally is used to describe a formal process in which information about a specific job or occupation is collected and analyzed. Formal job analysis may be conducted by a number of different methods. These methods obtain different kinds of information that is used for different purposes. Some of these methods will not provide information sufficient to determine if an individual with a disability is qualified to perform "essential" job functions.

For example: One kind of formal job analysis looks at specific job tasks and classifies jobs according to how these tasks deal with data, people, and objects. This type of job analysis is used to set wage rates for various jobs; however, it may not be adequate to identify the essential functions of a *particular* job, as required by the ADA. Another kind of job analysis looks at the kinds of knowledge, skills, and abilities that are necessary to perform a job. This type of job analysis is used to develop selection criteria for various jobs. The information from this type of analysis sometimes helps to measure the importance of certain skills, knowledge and abilities, but it does not take into account the fact that people with disabilities often can perform essential functions using other skills and abilities.

Some job analysis methods ask current employees and their supervisors to rate the importance of general characteristics necessary to perform a job, such as "strength," "endurance," or "intelligence," without linking these characteristics to *specific* job functions or specific tasks that are part of a function. Such general information may not identify, for example, whether upper body or lower body strength is required, or whether muscular endurance or cardiovascular endurance is needed to perform a particular job function. Such information, by itself, would not be sufficient to determine whether an individual who has particular limitations can perform an essential function with or without an accommodation.

As already stated, the ADA does not require a formal job analysis or any particular method of analysis to identify the essential functions of a job. A small employer may wish to conduct an informal analysis by observing and consulting with people who perform the job, or have previously performed it, and their supervisors. If possible, it is advisable to observe and consult with several workers under a range of conditions, to get a better idea of all job functions and the different ways they may be performed. Production records and workloads also may be relevant factors to consider.

(continued)

EXHIBIT 4.20 Continued

To identify essential job functions under the ADA, a job analysis should focus on the purpose of the job and the importance of actual job functions in achieving this purpose. Evaluating importance may include consideration of the frequency with which a function is performed, the amount of time spent on the function, and the consequences if the function is not performed. The analysis may include information on the work environment (such as unusual heat, cold, humidity, dust, toxic substances, or stress factors). The job analysis may contain information on the manner in which a job currently is performed, but should not conclude that ability to perform the job in that manner is an essential function, unless there is no other way to perform the function without causing undue hardship. A job analysis will be most helpful for purposes of the ADA if it focuses on the results or outcome of a function, not solely on the way it customarily is performed.

For example:

- An essential function of a computer programmer job might be described as "ability to develop programs that accomplish necessary objectives," rather than "ability to manually write programs." Although a person currently performing the job may write these programs by hand, that is not the essential function, because programs can be developed directly on the computer.
- If a job requires mastery of information contained in technical manuals, this essential function would be "ability to learn technical material," rather than "ability to read technical manuals." People with visual and other reading impairments could perform this function using other means, such as audiotapes.
- A job that requires objects to be moved from one place to another should state this essential function. The analysis may note that the person in the job "lifts 50-pound cartons to a height of 3 or 4 feet and loads them into truck-trailers 5 hours daily," but should not identify the "ability to manually lift and load 50-pound cartons" as an essential function unless this is the only method by which the function can be performed without causing an undue hardship.

A job analysis that is focused on outcomes or results also will be helpful in establishing appropriate qualification standards, developing job descriptions, conducting interviews, and selecting people in accordance with ADA requirements. It will be particularly helpful in identifying accommodations that will enable an individual with specific functional abilities and limitations to perform the job.

SOURCE: Equal Employment Opportunity Commission, *Technical Assistance Manual for the Employment Provisions (Title I) of the Americans With Disabilities Act* (Washington, DC: author, 1992), pp. II-18 to II-20.

SUMMARY

Organizations design and use various types of jobs—as jobs change and evolve, new design approaches are sometimes needed. All design approaches result in job content in the form of job requirements and rewards. Job analysis is described as the process used to gather, analyze, synthesize, and report information about job content. The job requirements approach to job analysis focuses on job-specific tasks, KSAOs, and job context. Competency-based job analysis seeks to identify more general KSAOs that apply across jobs and roles.

The job requirements approach is guided by the job requirements matrix. The matrix calls for information about tasks and task dimensions, as well as their importance. In a parallel fashion, it requires information about KSAOs required for the tasks, plus indications about the importance of those KSAOs. The final component of the matrix deals with numerous elements of the job context.

When gathering the information called for by the job requirements matrix, the organization is confronted with a multitude of choices. Those choices are shown to revolve around various job analysis methods, sources, and processes. The organization must choose from among these; all have advantages and disadvantages associated with them. The choices should be guided by a concern for the accuracy and acceptability of the information being gathered.

A very new approach to identifying job requirements is competency-based job analysis. This form of job analysis seeks to identify general competencies (KSAOs) necessary for all jobs because the competencies support the organization's mission and goals. Within work units, other general competencies (job-spanning KSAOs) may also be established that cut across multiple jobs. Potential techniques and processes for collecting competency information were suggested.

Jobs offer a variety of rewards, both extrinsic and intrinsic. The totality of these rewards constitutes the EVP. To help form EVPs, it is necessary to collect information about employee reward preferences and rewards given to employees at other organizations. Numerous techniques for doing this are available.

As team-based jobs continue to expand, our approaches to job analysis need to expand too. In particular, both job-specific and job-spanning KSAOs need to be emphasized, as does the focus on interpersonal qualities.

From a legal perspective, job analysis is very important in creating staffing systems and practices that comply with EEO/AA laws and regulations. The employer must ensure (or be able to show) that its practices are job related. This requires not only conducting a job requirements job analysis but also using a process that itself has defensible characteristics. Under the ADA, the organization must identify the essential functions of the job. Though this does not require a job analysis, the organization should strongly consider it as one of the tools to be used. Over time, we will learn more about how job analysis is treated under the ADA.

DISCUSSION QUESTIONS

1. Identify a team-based job situation. What are examples of job-spanning KSAOs required in that situation?
2. How should task statements be written, and what sorts of problems might you encounter in asking a job incumbent to write these statements?
3. Would it be better to first identify task dimensions and then create specific task statements for each dimension, or should task statements be identified first and then used to create task dimensions?
4. What would you consider when trying to decide what criteria (e.g., percentage of time spent) to use for gathering indications about task importance?
5. What are the advantages and disadvantages of using multiple methods of job analysis for a particular job? Multiple sources?
6. What are the advantages and disadvantages of identifying and using general competencies to guide staffing activities?
7. Referring back to Exhibit 4.19, why do you think HR professionals were not able to very accurately predict the importance of many rewards to employees? What are the implications for creating the EVP?

ETHICAL ISSUES

1. It has been suggested that ethical conduct be formally incorporated as a general competency requirement for any job within the organization. Discuss the pros and cons of this suggestion.
2. Assume you are assisting in the conduct of job analysis as an HR department representative. You have encountered several managers who want to delete certain tasks and KSAOs from the formal job description that have to do with employee safety, even though they clearly are job requirements. How should you handle this situation?

APPLICATIONS

Conducting a Job Requirements or Job Rewards Job Analysis

Job analysis is defined as "the process of studying jobs in order to gather, synthesize, and report information about job content." Based on the person/job match model, job content consists of job requirements (tasks and KSAOs) and job rewards (extrinsic and intrinsic). The goal of a job requirements job analysis is to produce the job requirements matrix.

Choose a job you want to study and conduct either a job requirements or job rewards job analysis. Write a report of your project that includes the following sections:

1. The Job—What job (job title) did you choose to study and why?
2. The Methods Used—What methods did you use (prior information, observation, interviews, task questionnaires, committee, combinations of these), and exactly how did you use them?
3. The Sources Used—What sources did you use (job analyst, job incumbent, supervisor, SMEs, or combinations of these), and exactly how did you use them?
4. The Process Used—How did you go about gathering, synthesizing, and reporting the information? Refer back to Exhibit 4.15 for an example.
5. The Matrix—Present the actual job requirements matrix.

Maintaining Job Descriptions

The InAndOut, Inc., company provides warehousing and fulfillment services (order receiving and filling) to small publishers of books with small print runs (number of copies of a book printed). After the books are printed and bound at a printing facility, they are shipped to InAndOut for handling. The books are initially received by handlers who unload them from the trucks, place them on pallets, and move them via forklifts and conveyors to their assigned storage space in the warehouse. The handlers also retrieve books and take them to the shipping area when orders are received. The shippers package the books, place them in cartons, and load them onto delivery trucks (to take to air or ground transportation providers). Book orders are taken by customer service representatives via printed, phone, or electronic (e-mail, fax) forms. New accounts are generated by marketing representatives, who also service existing accounts. Order clerks handle all the internal paperwork. All these employees report to either the supervisor of operations or the supervisor of customer service, who in turn reports to the general manager.

The owner and president of InAndOut, Inc., Alta Fossom, is independently wealthy and delegates all day-to-day management matters to the general manager, Marvin Olson. Alta requires, however, that Marvin clear any new ideas or initiatives with her before taking action. The company is growing and changing rapidly, along with adding many new, and often larger, accounts. Publishers are demanding more services and faster order fulfillment. Information technology is constantly being upgraded, and new machinery (forklifts, computer-assisted conveyor system) is being utilized. The workforce is growing in size to meet the business growth. There are now 37 employees, and Marvin expects to hire another 15–20 new employees within the next year.

Job descriptions for the company were originally written by a consultant about eight years ago. They have never been revised and are hopelessly outdated. The job of marketing representative doesn't even have a job description, because the job was created only five years ago. As general manager, Marvin is responsible for all HR management matters, but he has little time to devote to them. To get a better grip on HR responsibilities, Marvin has hired you as a part-time HR intern. He has a gut feeling that the job descriptions need to be updated or, in some cases, created, and has assigned this project to you. Since Marvin has to clear new projects with Alta, he wants you to prepare a brief proposal that he can take to her for approval and that suggests the following:

1. Reasons why it is important to update and write new job descriptions
2. An outline of a process for doing this that will yield a set of thorough, current job descriptions
3. A process to be used in the future for periodically reviewing and updating job descriptions

Marvin wants to meet with you and discuss each of these points. He wants the proposal to contain specific suggestions and ideas. What exactly would you suggest to Marvin?

ENDNOTES

1. P. Bobko, P. L. Roth, and M. A. Buster, "A Systematic Approach for Assessing the Currency of Job Analytic Information," *Public Personnel Management*, 2008, 37, pp. 261–277.
2. J. Welch and S. Welch, "How Healthy Is Your Company?" *Business Week*, May 8, 2006, p. 126.
3. J. K. Harter, F. L. Schmidt, and T. L. Hayes, "Business-Unit-Level Relationship Between Employee Satisfaction, Employee Engagement, and Business Outcomes: A Meta-Analysis," *Journal of Applied Psychology*, 2002, 87, pp. 268–279.
4. Bobko, Roth, and Buster, "A Systematic Approach for Assessing the Currency of Job Analytic Information."
5. R. J. Vance, *Employee Engagement and Commitment* (Alexandria, VA: Society for Human Resource Management, 2006), pp. 1, 13; Harter, Schmidt, and Hayes, "Business-Unit-Level Relationship Between Employee Satisfaction, Employee Engagement, and Business Outcomes: A Meta-Analysis."
6. For excellent overviews and reviews, see M. T. Brannick, E. L. Levine, and F. P. Morgeson, *Job and Work Analysis* (Thousand Oaks, CA: Sage, 2007); S. Gael (ed.), *The Job Analysis Handbook for Business, Industry and Government*, Vols. 1 and 2 (New York: Wiley, 1988); R. D. Gatewood and H. S. Feild, *Human Resource Selection*, fifth ed. (Orlando, FL: Harcourt, 2001), pp. 267–363; P. Sackett and R. Laczo, "Job and Work Analysis," in W. Borman, D. Ilgen, and R. Klimoski (eds.), *Handbook of Psychology: Industrial and Organizational Psychology*, Vol. 12 (New York: Wiley, 2003), pp. 21–37.
7. E. T. Cornelius III, "Practical Findings From Job Analysis Research," in Gael (ed.), *The Job Analysis Handbook for Business, Industry and Government*, Vol. 1, pp. 48–70.
8. C. J. Cranny and M. E. Doherty, "Importance Ratings in Job Analysis: Note on the Misinterpretation of Factor Analysis," *Journal of Applied Psychology*, 1988, 73, pp. 320–322.
9. D. P. Costanza, E. A. Fleishman, and J. C. Marshall-Mies, "Knowledges: Evidence for the Reliability and Validity of the Measures," in N. G. Peterson, M. D. Mumford, W. C. Borman,

P. R. Jeanneret, E. A. Fleishman, and K. Y. Levin (eds.), *O*NET Final Technical Report, Vol. 1* (Salt Lake City: Utah Department of Workforce Services, 1997), pp. 4-1 to 4-26.

10. M. D. Mumford, N. G. Peterson, and R. A. Childs, "Basic and Cross-Functional Skills: Evidence for Reliability and Validity of the Measures," in Peterson et al., *O*NET Final Technical Report, Vol. 1*, pp. 3-1 to 3-36.

11. E. A. Fleishman, D. P. Costanza, and J. C. Marshall-Mies, "Abilities: Evidence for the Reliability and Validity of the Measures," in Peterson et al., *O*NET Final Technical Report, Vol. 2*, pp. 9-1 to 9-26.

12. M. H. Strong, P. R. Jeanneret, S. M. McPhail, and B. R. Blakley, "Work Context: Evidence for the Reliability and Validity of the Measures," in Peterson et al., *O*NET Final Technical Report, Vol. 2*, pp. 7-1 to 7-35.

13. F. P. Morgeson, K. Delaney-Klinger, M. S. Mayfield, P. Ferrara, and M. A. Campion, "Self-Presentations Processes in Job Analysis: A Field Experiment Investigating Inflation in Abilities, Tasks, and Competencies," *Journal of Applied Psychology*, 2004, 89, pp. 674–686.

14. For detailed treatments, see Brannick, Levine, and Morgeson, *Job Work Analysis*; Gael (ed.), *The Job Analysis Handbook for Business, Industry and Government*, pp. 315–468; Gatewood and Feild, *Human Resource Selection*, pp. 267–363; M. Mader-Clark, *The Job Description Handbook* (Berkeley, CA: Nolo, 2006).

15. Peterson et al., *O*NET Final Technical Report, Vols. 1, 2, 3*; N. G. Peterson, M. D. Mumford, W. C. Borman, P. R. Jeanneret, E. A. Fleishman, K. Y. Levin, M. A. Campion, M. S. Mayfield, F. S. Morgeson, K. Pearlman, M. K. Gowing, A. R. Lancaster, M. B. Silver, and D. M. Dye, "Understanding Work Using the Occupational Information Network: Implications for Research and Practice," *Personnel Psychology*, 2001, 54, pp. 451–492.

16. C. C. LaPolice, G. W. Carter, and J. W. Johnson, "Linking O*NET Descriptors to Occupational Literacy Requirements Using Job Component Validation," *Personnel Psychology*, 2008, 61, pp. 405–441.

17. R. Reiter-Palmon, M. Brown, D. L. Sandall, C. B. Buboltz, and T. Nimps, "Development of an O*NET Web-Based Job Analysis and Its Implementation in the U.S. Navy," *Human Resource Management Review*, 2006, 16, pp. 294–309.

18. Brannick, Levine, and Morgeson, *Job and Work Analysis*.

19. T. A. Stetz, J. M. Beaubien, M. J. Keeney, and B. D. Lyons, "Nonrandom Response and Variance in Job Analysis Surveys: A Cause for Concern?" *Public Personnel Management*, 2008, 37, pp. 223–241.

20. P.D.G. Steel and J. D. Kammeyer-Mueller, "Using a Meta-Analytic Perspective to Enhance Job Component Validation," *Personnel Psychology*, 2009, 62, pp. 533–552; P.D.G. Steel, A. I. Huffcutt, and J. D. Kammeyer-Mueller, "From the Work One Knows the Worker: A Systematic Review of the Challenges, Solutions, and Steps to Creating Synthetic Validity," *International Journal of Selection and Assessment*, 2006, 14, pp. 16–36.

21. R. G. Jones, J. I. Sanchez, G. Parameswaran, J. Phelps, C. Shop-taugh, M. Williams, and S. White, "Selection or Training? A Two-fold Test of the Validity of Job-Analytic Ratings of Trainability," *Journal of Business and Psychology*, 2001, 15, pp. 363–389; D. M. Truxillo, M. E. Paronto, M. Collins, and J. L. Sulzer, "Effects of Subject Matter Expert Viewpoint on Job Analysis Results," *Public Personnel Management*, 2004, 33(1), pp. 33–46.

22. See Brannick, Levine, and Morgeson, *Job and Work Analysis*; Gael (ed.), *The Job Analysis Handbook for Business, Industry and Government*, pp. 315–390; Gatewood and Feild, *Human Resource Selection*, pp. 267–363.

23. J. S. Schippman, "Competencies, Job Analysis, and the Next Generation of Modeling," in J. C. Scott and D. H. Reynolds (eds.), *Handbook of Workplace Assessment* (San Francisco: Jossey-Bass, 2010), pp. 197–231; M. Harris, "Competency Modeling: Viagraized Job Analysis

or Impotent Imposter?" *The Industrial-Organizational Psychologist*, 1998, 36(2), pp. 37–41; R. L. Heneman and G. E. Ledford, Jr., "Competency Pay for Professionals and Managers in Business: A Review and Implications for Teachers," *Journal of Personnel Evaluation in Education*, 1998, 12, pp. 103–122; J. S. Schippman, R. A. Ash, M. Battista, L. Carr, L. D. Eyde, B. Hesketh, J. Kehoe, K. Pearlman, E. P. Prien, and J. I. Sanchez, "The Practice of Competency Modeling," *Personnel Psychology*, 2000, 53, pp. 703–740.

24. Schippman, "Competencies, Job Analysis, and the Next Generation of Modeling."
25. D. Bartram, "The Great Eight Competencies: A Criterion-Centric Approach to Validation," *Journal of Applied Psychology*, 2007, 90, pp. 1185–1203.
26. Schippman et al., "The Practice of Competency Modeling."
27. D. Rahbar-Daniels, M. L. Erickson, and A. Dalik, "Here to Stay: Taking Competencies to the Next Level," *WorldatWork Journal*, 2001, First Quarter, pp. 70–77.
28. Schippman et al., "The Practice of Competency Modeling."
29. F. H. Borgen, "Occupational Reinforcer Patterns," in Gael (ed.), *The Job Analysis Handbook for Business, Industry and Government*, Vol. 2, pp. 902–916; R. V. Dawis, "Person-Environment Fit and Job Satisfaction," in C. J. Cranny, P. C. Smith, and E. F. Stone (eds.), *Job Satisfaction* (New York: Lexington, 1992); C. T. Kulik and G. R. Oldham, "Job Diagnostic Survey," in Gael (ed.), *The Job Analysis Handbook for Business, Industry and Government*, Vol. 2, pp. 936–959; G. Ledford, P. Mulvey, and P. LeBlanc, *The Rewards of Work* (Scottsdale, AZ: WorldatWork/ Sibson, 2000).
30. E. E. Ledford and M. I. Lucy, *The Rewards of Work* (Los Angeles, CA: Sibson Consulting, 2003).
31. Ledford and Lucy, *The Rewards of Work*, p. 12.
32. "'Mosh Pits' of Creativity," *Business Week*, Nov. 7, 2005, pp. 98–100.
33. M. Harvey, M. M. Novicevic, and G. Garrison, "Challenges to Staffing Global Virtual Teams," *Human Resource Management Review*, 2004, 14, pp. 275–294.
34. Brannick, Levine, and Morgeson, *Job and Work Analysis*.
35. D. E. Thompson and T. A. Thompson, "Court Standards for Job Analysis in Test Validation," *Personnel Psychology*, 1982, 35, pp. 865–874.
36. Equal Employment Opportunity Commission, *Technical Assistance Manual on the Employment Provisions (Title 1) of the Americans With Disabilities Act* (Washington, DC: author, 1992), pp. II-19 to II-21.
37. K. E. Mitchell, G. M. Alliger, and R. Morgfopoulos, "Toward an ADA-Appropriate Job Analysis," *Human Resource Management Review*, 1997, 7, pp. 5–26; F. Lievens, J. I. Sanchez, and W. De Corte, "Easing the Inferential Leap in Competency Modelling: The Effects of Task-Related Information and Subject Matter Expertise," *Personnel Psychology*, 2001, 57, pp. 847–879; F. Lievens and J. I. Sanchez, "Can Training Improve the Quality of Inferences Made by Raters in Competency Modeling: A Quasi-Experiment," *Journal of Applied Psychology*, 2007, 92, pp. 812–819.

The Staffing Organizations Model

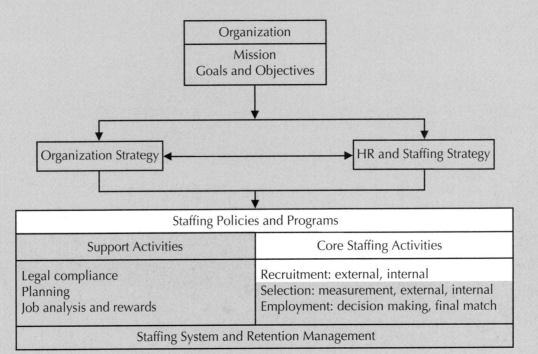

PART THREE

Staffing Activities: Recruitment

CHAPTER FIVE
External Recruitment

CHAPTER SIX
Internal Recruitment

CHAPTER FIVE

External Recruitment

Learning Objectives and Introduction
Learning Objectives
Introduction

Recruitment Planning
Organizational Issues
Administrative Issues
Recruiters

Strategy Development
Open Versus Targeted Recruitment
Recruitment Sources
Recruiting Metrics

Searching
Communication Message
Communication Medium

Applicant Reactions
Reactions to Recruiters
Reactions to the Recruitment Process
Reactions to Diversity Issues

Transition to Selection

Legal Issues
Definition of a Job Applicant
Affirmative Action Programs
Electronic Recruitment
Job Advertisements
Fraud and Misrepresentation

Summary

Discussion Questions

Ethical Issues

Applications

Tanglewood Stores Case

LEARNING OBJECTIVES AND INTRODUCTION

Learning Objectives

- Be able to engage in effective recruitment planning activities
- Understand the difference between open and targeted recruitment
- Utilize a variety of recruitment sources
- Evaluate recruiting based on established metrics
- Create a persuasive communication message
- Learn about a variety of recruitment media
- Recognize how applicant reactions influence the effectiveness of a recruiting plan

Introduction

External recruitment is the process of identifying and attracting job applicants from outside the organization. An effective recruiting process is the cornerstone of an effective staffing system. If the recruiting system works, high-quality applicants will be attracted to the organization, the best candidates will be available for selection and eventual hiring, and the organization will have a much easier time reaching its strategic staffing goals. Conversely, if recruiting fails to attract enough qualified applicants, none of the other components of the staffing system can function properly—after all, you can't hire people who don't apply.

In external recruiting, the organization is trying to sell itself to potential applicants, so many principles from marketing are applied to improve recruiting yields. Over the course of this chapter you'll learn about the advantages and disadvantages of recruiting methods such as corporate websites, employee referrals, college job fairs, and many others. You'll also learn how recruiters choose from three types of messages—realistic, employment brand, or targeted—to attract the right types of candidates.

The recruitment process begins with a planning phase during which both organizational and administrative issues, as well as those pertaining to recruiters, are addressed. Next, a recruitment strategy for finding qualified applicants is formed. Following the formation of a strategy, the message to be communicated to job applicants is established, along with the medium that will be used to convey the message. Special consideration must be given to applicant reactions to recruiters and the recruitment process in undertaking each of these phases of the external recruitment process. Close attention must also be given to legal issues. This includes consideration of the definition of job applicant, disclaimers, targeted recruitment, electronic recruitment, job advertisements, and fraud and misrepresentation.

RECRUITMENT PLANNING

Before identifying and attracting applicants to the organization, two issues must be resolved. First, organizational plans must be made to coordinate the identification and attraction of applicants. Second, administrative issues, such as the number of contacts to be made, the recruiters to be used, and the budget to be spent, need to be considered to ensure that there are adequate resources to conduct a successful recruitment campaign.

Organizational Issues

The recruitment process in an organization can be organized in a variety of ways. It can be coordinated in-house or by an external recruitment agency. An organization can do its own recruiting or cooperate with other organizations in a recruitment alliance. Authority to recruit may be centralized or decentralized in the organization.

In-House Versus External Recruitment Agency

Most organizational recruiting is done in-house. Smaller organizations may rely on external recruitment agencies rather than an in-house function, as smaller organizations may not have the staff or budget to run their own recruitment functions. Organizations with low turnover rates may also prefer to use external recruitment agencies, as they recruit so infrequently it doesn't make sense to have their own recruitment function.

External recruitment agencies are growing in number. Some agencies, such as the Elaine R. Shepherd Company, provide full-scale recruitment services ranging from identifying recruitment needs to advertising for applicants and checking references. Others, such as American Classified Services, Inc., simply perform one recruitment activity. Although these services are expensive, the costs may be justified for organizations without a recruitment function or for employers with infrequent vacancies.

Large organizations and organizations that recruit frequently should have their own in-house recruitment function. This helps ensure that recruitment costs are minimized, recruitment searches are consistent from opening to closing, and the specific needs of the organization are being met.

Centralized Versus Decentralized Recruitment

An organization can centralize or decentralize the recruitment of external job applicants. In a centralized recruitment function, one central group coordinates the recruitment activities, usually human resources (HR) professionals in the corporate offices. In a decentralized recruitment system, individual business units or individual managers coordinate the recruitment activities. Although the ultimate hiring decision resides in the business unit, most organizations centralize the administrative activities associated with recruiting and screening applicants.

One advantage to a centralized recruitment function is that efforts are not duplicated. For example, when recruiting at a school, only one advertisement is placed, rather than multiple ads for multiple business units. Another advantage is that a centralized approach ensures that policy is being interpreted consistently across business units. For example, GM centralized its recruiting system to convey a consistent message to applicants.[1] Along these same lines, a centralized function helps ensure compliance with relevant laws and regulations. Another factor that facilitates centralized recruiting is the growth in staffing software (see Chapter 13).

Some organizations, however, prefer decentralized recruitment functions. Case studies suggest that research and development departments, for example, often develop specialized recruiting practices to attract talent. These strategies are more focused on university recruiting and emphasize projects that are likely to interest highly educated and intrinsically motivated researchers.[2] One advantage to decentralized recruitment is that when there are fewer people to recruit, recruitment can take place more quickly than when a centralized approach is used. Also, the recruitment search may be more responsive to the business unit's specific needs because those involved with recruitment may be closer to the day-to-day operations of the business unit than are their corporate counterparts.

Administrative Issues

In the planning stage of recruitment, attention must be given to administrative issues as well as organizational issues. Many organizations use human resources information systems (HRISs) to integrate the filing of requisitions, to develop recruitment budgets, and to process flows.

Requisitions

A requisition is a formal document that authorizes the filling of a job opening, indicated by the signatures of top management. Supervisors are seldom given discretion to authorize the filling of job openings. Top managers, rather than supervisors, are more likely to be familiar with staffing planning information for the entire organization; thus, their approval is needed to ensure that recruitment activities are coordinated with staffing planning activities.

An example of a requisition is shown in Exhibit 5.1. A well-developed requisition clearly specifies both the quantity and the quality (knowledge, skill, ability, and other characteristics [KSAOs]) of labor to be hired. Hence, each requisition will list the number of openings per job and the minimum qualifications an applicant must have. Qualifications should be based on a job analysis or competency system.

Timing

Two factors that drive the decision of when to look for job applicants are lead time concerns and time sequence concerns. As staffing managers have been increasingly

EXHIBIT 5.1 Personnel Requisition

Position title	Division	Department	Department #
Salary/grade level	Work hours	Location	Reports to

Position eligible for the following incentive programs ☐ Sales commission ☐ Key contributor ☐ Production incentive ☐ Other (specify) ☐ Management incentive ☐ _____	Budgeted ☐ Replacement for: _____ ☐ Yes Transfer/term date_____ ☐ No ☐ Addition to staff

POSITION OVERVIEW

Instructions: (1) Complete Parts I, II, and III. (2) Attach position description questionnaire (if available) or complete reverse side.

I. POSITION PURPOSE: Briefly state in one or two sentences the primary purpose of this position.

II. POSITION QUALIFICATIONS: List the *minimum* education, formal training, and experience required to perform this position.

III. SPECIAL SKILLS: List the specialized clerical, administrative, technical, or managerial skills needed to perform this position.

Do current or previous incumbents possess these qualifications and skills? If no, please describe the reason for these requirements when hiring for this position.

APPROVALS	**FOR HUMAN RESOURCES USE ONLY**
Party responsible for conducting second interview	Posting date_____ Advertising date _____
	Req number _____ Job number _____
_____ Hiring supervisor/manager Date	Acceptance date _____Start date _____
_____ Next approval level Date	New employee_____
_____ Human resources approval Date	Source _____

SOURCE: Reprinted with permission from United Health Care Corporation.

called on to show concrete results for their work, the importance of documenting the time to fill requisitions has grown.

Lead Time Concerns.   Although managers would like to fill each position immediately on approval of the requisition, this is not possible, as recruiters handle a large number of vacancies at any one time. It is possible, however, to minimize the delay in filling vacancies by planning for openings well in advance of their actual occurrence. Effective planning requires that top management prioritize job openings so they can be filled in the order that best meets the needs of the business. It also requires that recruiters be fully prepared to conduct the search. Therefore, they must be aware of the deadlines for placing ads in the appropriate periodicals, and they should be knowledgeable about the availability of labor in the marketplace. With the growth of Internet recruiting, much hiring is now continuous.[3] For example, Starbucks keeps a list of job openings on its website (*www.starbucks.com*) that is continually updated.

Time Sequence Concerns.   In a successful recruitment program, the steps involved in the process are clearly defined and sequenced in a logical order. A staffing flowchart should be used to organize all components of the recruitment process. The sequence of recruitment activities will affect the amount of time needed to fill job vacancies.

A very useful set of indicators for time sequence concerns is known as time-lapse statistics. These statistics provide data on the average length of time between various phases in the recruitment process. Organizations should routinely collect these data in order to assist managers in planning when vacancies are to be filled (see Chapter 13).

Number of Contacts

The pool of applicants almost always needs to be larger than the number of vacant positions. Some applicants may no longer be interested in the position by the time they are contacted, and others may not be qualified.

It is very difficult to determine the exact number of contacts needed to fill a particular vacancy. However, historical data are very useful in establishing the targeted number of contacts. If careful records are kept, yield ratios can be calculated to summarize the historical data and guide decisions about the number of contacts to make. A yield ratio expresses the relationship of applicant inputs to outputs at various decision points. For example, if 90 people were contacted (as identified by the number of résumés submitted) to fill one position, the yield ratio would be 90:1. To fill two identical positions, it would be necessary to contact 180 applicants, on the basis of the historical yield ratio of 90:1.

Types of Contacts

The types of contacts to be made depend on two factors. First, it is essential that the qualifications needed to perform the job are clearly established. This is done through the process of job analysis, which results in the job requirements matrix or competency system. The more clearly these requirements are specified, the smaller the number of applicants who must be contacted to yield a successful candidate.

Second, the organization must be aware of where prospective applicants search for employment opportunities and what it will take to attract them to the organization. One consistent finding in the research is that job seekers are more likely to find out about jobs through friends and family than through employment agencies. Another consistent finding is that job seekers rely heavily on advertisements.

Some organizations spend very few resources identifying contacts and actively soliciting applicants from these sources. For example, grocery stores will often fill a vacancy by simply posting the job opening in their store window. Other organizations, however, are very proactive in making their presence known in the community. They do this by becoming involved with educational institutions through scholarships, adopt-a-school programs, mentorships, equipment grants, internships, and career planning services. NASA has programs to help educate teachers, students, and administrators on the application of science and math.[4] These approaches will likely build goodwill toward an organization in the community and, as a result, foster informal contacts with job applicants.

Research has shown that greater employer involvement with prospective applicants is likely to improve the image of the organization. In turn, a better image of the organization is likely to result in prospective applicants pursuing employment with the organization.[5]

Recruitment Budget and Return on Investment

The recruitment process is a very expensive component of organizational staffing. Costs include staff time developing a recruiting message, website development and administration, advertising, time spent making personal contacts and following up with potential candidates, and bringing candidates on-site. Because recruiting is such an expensive proposition, it is vital for HR to track both the costs and returns of its recruiting practices.[6] The use of applicant tracking systems makes it easier for leaders to estimate metrics from a variety of recruiting practices.

The high costs of recruitment also point to the importance of establishing a well-developed recruitment budget. An example of a recruitment budget is shown in Exhibit 5.2. Two issues need to be addressed in establishing a recruitment budget. First, a top-down or bottom-up procedure can be used to gather the information needed to formulate the budget. With a top-down approach, top management sets the budget for recruitment activities on the bases of the business plan for the organization and projected revenues. With a bottom-up approach, the budget for recruitment activities is set on the basis of the specific needs of each business

EXHIBIT 5.2   **Example of a Recruitment Budget for 500 New Hires**

Administrative Expenses

Staff	32,000
Supplies	45,000
Equipment	10,000
	$87,000

Recruiter Expenses

Salaries	240,000
Benefits	96,000
Expenses	150,000
	$486,000

Candidate Expenses

Travel	320,000
Lodging	295,000
Fees	50,000
Relocation	150,000
	$815,000

Total Recruitment Expenses

87,000 + 486,000 + 815,000 = $1,388,000

Total Cost per Hire

$1,388,000/500 new hires = $2,776

unit. The former approach works well when the emphasis is on controlling costs. The latter approach works better when commitment to the budget by business unit heads is the goal.

A second issue is deciding whether to charge recruitment costs to business unit users. That is, should recruitment expenses be charged to HR or to the business unit using HR services? Most organizations charge the HR department. One reason for this may be to encourage each business unit to use the recruitment services of the HR group. However, in organizations where HR is charged, business unit users may not be as concerned about minimizing recruitment costs.

Once a budget is in place and the recruiting techniques are implemented, the organization should take the additional step of assessing the effectiveness of various techniques. Applicant tracking systems make it possible to assess how many individuals are attracted and hired through each source. An applicant tracking system, usually in the form of a computer database, helps identify which recruiting sources lead applicants to the organization. For example, it is possible to determine how many candidates learned about the job opening from media advertisements, the organization's website, campus visits and job fairs, employee referrals, or other sources. It is also possible to track how many candidates are hired from each source. From this information on the number of applicants and hires, coupled with budget figures, it is possible to calculate the cost per applicant (total media cost divided by number of applicants) and the cost per hire (total media cost divided by number of hires). Cost-effective methods for attracting candidates can then become the focal part of the organization's recruiting strategy, and those that have lower returns on investment can be eliminated.

Development of a Recruitment Guide

A recruitment guide is a formal document that details the process to be followed to attract applicants to a job. It should be based on the organization's staffing flow-charts, if available. Included in the guide are details such as the time, money, and staff required to fill the job as well as the steps to be taken to do so. An example of a recruitment guide is shown in Exhibit 5.3.

Although a recruitment guide takes time to produce—time that may be difficult to find in the face of an urgent requisition to be filled—it is an essential document. It clarifies expectations for both the recruiter and the requesting department as to what will be accomplished, what the costs will be, and who will be held account-able for the results. It also clarifies the steps that need to be taken in order to ensure that they are all followed in a consistent fashion and in accordance with organiza-tion policy as well as relevant laws and regulations. In short, a recruitment guide safeguards the interests of the employer, the applicant, and the recruiter.

Process Flow and Record Keeping

Before deciding where and how to look for applicants, it is essential that the orga-nization prepare for the high volume of data that accompanies the filling of vacan-cies. This high volume of data results from the use of multiple sources to identify candidates (e.g., advertisements, walk-ins, employment agencies), the need to cir-culate the applicant's credentials to multiple parties (e.g., hiring managers, HR), and the need to communicate with candidates regarding the status of their applica-tion. If process flow and record-keeping issues are not addressed before the recruit-ment search, the organization may become overwhelmed with correspondence that is not dealt with in a timely and professional manner; in turn, the organization may lose well-qualified applicants.

To manage the process flow and record-keeping requirements, an information system must be created for recruitment efforts. An effective system allows the can-didate, the hiring manager, and HR representatives to know the candidate's status at any time. The information system tracks the applicant's file as it flows through the organization's recruitment process. The information system can also periodi-cally issue reports on how timely and accurately the applicant information is being processed.

EXHIBIT 5.3   Recruitment Guide for Director of Claims

Position: Director, Claims Processing

Reports to: Senior Director, Claims Processing

Qualifications: 4-year degree in business;
8 years' experience in health care, including 5 in claims, 3 of which should be in management

Relevant labor market: Regional Midwest

Timeline: week of 1/17: Conduct interviews with qualified applicants
2/1/11: Targeted hire date

Activities to undertake to source well-qualified candidates:

Regional newspaper advertising

Post job opening on company website

Request employee referrals

Contact regional health and life insurance associations

Call HR departments of regional health and life insurance companies to see if any are outplacing any middle managers

Contact, if necessary, executive recruiter to further source candidates

Staff members involved:

HR Recruiting Manager
Sr. Director, Claims Processing
V.P. Human Resources
Potential peers and direct reports

Budget:

$3,000–$5,000

The process of managing data and records has been transformed by online applications.[7] Indeed, one might characterize it as a double-edged sword. On the one hand, data entry and record maintenance are facilitated in that applications are immediately transferred into a searchable standardized database. Online applications often permit candidate screening by checking qualifications and administering online skills tests. This can greatly reduce the time spent weeding out résumés sent in by unqualified candidates. On the other hand, online applications generate much more data, including applications from individuals who are poorly motivated to join the organization or are obviously unqualified for the position; thus, there are many more data to wade through. To facilitate combing through all this information, many web-based recruiting systems have integrated screening tools to eliminate unqualified applicants early in the process.

As the applicant progresses through the hiring process, additional record keeping is required, such as who has reviewed the file, how long each individual has had the file to be reviewed, what decision has been reached (e.g., reject, invite for a visit, conduct a second interview), and what step needs to be taken next (e.g., arrange for a flight and accommodations, schedule an interview). Throughout the process, communications with the applicant must also be tracked so that the applicant knows whether his or her credentials will receive further review and whether he or she needs to take any additional steps to secure employment.

Even when an applicant is rejected for a position, there are record-keeping responsibilities. The applicant's file should be stored in the event that another search arises that requires someone with the applicant's qualifications. Such storage should be for a maximum of one year (see "Legal Issues," at the end of the chapter).

Recruiters

Selecting Recruiters

Many studies have been conducted to assess desirable characteristics of recruiters. Reviews of these studies indicate that an ideal recruiter would possess the following characteristics: strong interpersonal skills; knowledge about the organization, jobs, and career-related issues; technology skills (e.g., knowing how to mine databases, Internet recruiting); and enthusiasm about the organization and job candidates.[8] These characteristics represent a start on developing a set of KSAOs to select recruiters.

Recruiters used by organizations come from a variety of sources, including HR professionals, line managers, and employees. Each of these sources has some distinct advantages and disadvantages relative to the list of desirable characteristics for recruiters. HR professionals may be very knowledgeable about career development issues and enthusiastic about the organization, but they may lack detailed knowledge regarding specific job responsibilities. Line managers may have detailed knowledge about the organization and the jobs that they supervise, but they may not be particularly knowledgeable about career development opportunities. Similarly, employees may have an in-depth understanding of their own jobs but not have much knowledge of the larger organization. Thus, there is no single ideal source to draw recruiters from, and all recruiters need training to compensate for inevitable shortcomings.

Training Recruiters

Many recruiters who come from areas outside HR do not have any specialized training in HR. While training recruiters is essential, very few recruiters ever receive any training. According to current organizational practices, recruiters should receive training in the following areas: interviewing skills, job analysis, interpersonal aspects of recruiting, laws and regulations, forms and reports, organization and job characteristics, and recruitment targets.[9] Beyond these traditional areas, it is critical that recruiters receive training in some nontraditional areas: technology skills, marketing skills, working with other departments, and ethics.

First, in terms of technology skills, though access to large recruiting websites like *Monster.com* is to be expected, it must be recognized that many recruiters are mining these sites. Thus, recruiters must be instructed on accessing niche sites that specialize in a particular candidate cohort, accessing personal web pages, and even scanning through corporate websites.

Second, recruiters must be trained in marketing and sales techniques.[10] Some of these techniques are very simple, such as surfing résumé sites to get a leg up on the competition. Recruiters also need to be trained on how to be more creative in identifying candidates. For example, in tight labor markets, some recruiters will stake out airports, temples and churches, and health clubs. One recruiter even flies from airport to airport just to search the airport clubs for potential recruits. More generally, recruiters need instruction on how to sell their jobs to candidates. Recruiters can be trained on how to do market research, how to find job candidates in the market, and how to identify what candidates want. In developing their marketing skills, recruiters can be shown how to link up with other departments, such as marketing and public relations. Recruiters may be able to collaborate with marketing efforts to achieve a brand image that not only sells products to customers but sells the organization to prospective hires as well.

Finally, in their efforts to recruit more creatively, recruiters need training on ethical issues in recruitment. Is it ethical for a recruiter to recruit at a competitor's place of business? In parking lots? At weddings or funerals? Some recruiters will even lie to applicants in an effort to lure them. To ensure that recruiters behave ethically, standards should be developed and recruiters should be trained on these standards.[11]

STRATEGY DEVELOPMENT

Once the recruitment planning phase is complete, the next phase is the development of a strategy. In essence, strategy development helps assess those issues that are fundamental to the organization: open versus targeted recruitment, recruitment sources, and recruiting metrics. Each of these issues will be addressed in turn.

Open Versus Targeted Recruitment

One of the most difficult aspects of recruitment is knowing where to look for applicants. In theory, the pool of potential job applicants is the eligible labor force (i.e., employed, unemployed, discouraged workers, new labor force entrants, and labor force reentrants). In practice, the organization must narrow down this vast pool into segments or strata of workers believed to be the most desirable applicants for the organization. To do so, organizations can use open or targeted recruitment methods.

Open Recruitment

With an open recruitment approach, organizations cast a wide net to identify potential applicants for specific job openings. Very little effort is made in segmenting the market into applicants with the most desirable KSAOs. This approach is very passive in that anyone can apply for an opening, and all who apply for a position are considered, regardless of their qualifications. An advantage of the open recruitment method is that applicants often see it as being "fair" in that everyone has the opportunity to apply. Open recruitment helps ensure that a diverse set of applicants—including people with disabilities, minorities, teens, former retirees, veterans, and other overlooked employee groups—are given a fair shot at being considered. Another advantage of open recruitment is that it is useful—perhaps even essential—when large numbers of applicants must be hired. The disadvantage to this approach is that very large numbers of applications must be considered, and it is possible that qualified applicants may be overlooked in the process. Unfortunately, with the growth of web-based recruiting, many employers have found that open recruiting yields too many applicants, making it very time-consuming to review all the résumés and other application materials.[12]

Targeted Recruitment

A targeted recruitment approach is one whereby the organization identifies segments in the labor market where qualified candidates are likely to be. Often, this is done to find applicants with specific characteristics pertinent to person/job or person/organization match.

Following is a list of some of the targeted recruitment groups (of course, these categories are not mutually exclusive):

- *Key KSAO shortages*—the objective here is to identify applicants with specific new areas of knowledge or "hot" skills
- *Workforce diversity gaps*—often, one must go beyond open recruitment to reach diverse groups and make special efforts
- *Passive job seekers or noncandidates*—sometimes excellent candidates can be found in "trailing spouses" or other dual-career couples
- *Former military personnel*—especially those newly discharged with key competencies such as leadership
- *Employment discouraged*—long-term unemployed, homemakers, welfare recipients, teenagers, people with disabilities

- *Reward seekers*—those who are attracted to the organization's employee value proposition, which might offer benefits such as flexible work schedules and fully paid health care
- *Former employees*—those with good track records while they were employees
- *Reluctant applicants*—some individuals may have an interest in an organization but are conflicted; research shows that flexible work arrangements may help attract such conflicted individuals[13]

Making the Choice

The choice between open and targeted recruitment is important, as it dictates recruiting methods and sources. This is not to suggest that they necessarily achieve different goals. Targeted recruitment can achieve the same ends of inclusion as open recruitment, though by a different mechanism. Whereas open recruitment achieves inclusiveness by encouraging everyone to apply, targeted recruitment may actually seek out particular groups. In theory, open and targeted recruitment can be used in combination. For example, an organization may encourage all applications by posting jobs on its website and advertising broadly, while still making special efforts to reach certain populations. Of course, by seeking out one group, one may in a way exclude another from the same consideration. So, before targeted recruitment is undertaken, the organization needs to carefully consider the groups to target, as well as the job skills necessary to perform the job(s) in question. Similarly, before open recruitment is selected, the organization needs to decide whether it is prepared to handle and fairly consider the large number of applications that may flow in.

Recruiting experts say it is not necessary to use just one strategy.[14] Organizations might choose a very open strategy for jobs that are not core to their performance, such as clerical and administrative functions, but then use a much more targeted approach for employees who need highly specific KSAOs. Accenture Consulting, for example, suggests that retailers identify the most critical segments of the workforce, analyze the performance of the most successful employees, and then target the recruiting to attract employees sharing relevant characteristics with star performers in these high-leverage positions. For less critical positions, a less resource-intensive process might be advisable. Exhibit 5.4 reviews the advantages of open and targeted recruitment and suggests when each approach is appropriate.

Recruitment Sources

When conducting a search for applicants, employers, fortunately, do not have to identify each possible job applicant. Instead, there are institutions in our economy where job seekers congregate. Moreover, these institutions often act as intermediaries between the applicant and the employer to ensure that a match takes place.

EXHIBIT 5.4   Choosing Between Open and Targeted Recruiting

	Technique	Advantages	Best When
Open	Advertising positions with a message appealing to a wide variety of job seekers in a variety of media outlets that will reach the largest possible audience	Ensures that a diverse set of applicants are contacted and considered Lower resource and personnel cost per applicant located	Large numbers of applicants are required; pre-entry qualifications are not as important
Targeted	Focusing advertising and recruiting efforts by tailoring message content to attract segments of the labor market with specific KSAOs or demographic characteristics	Narrows the pool of potential applicants, allowing the organization to concentrate efforts on the most qualified Facilitates a more personal approach to each applicant	The organization needs specific skill sets that are in short supply; hiring for high-leverage positions

These institutions are called recruitment sources or methods in staffing. Some are very conventional and have been around for a long time. Others are more innovative and have less of a track record.

Applicant Initiated

It is a common practice for employers to accept applications from job applicants who physically walk into the organization to apply for a job or who send in résumés. The usual point of contact for unsolicited walk-ins or résumé senders is the receptionist in smaller organizations and the employment office in larger organizations. When applications are accepted, a contact person who is responsible for processing such applicants needs to be assigned. Additionally, space must be created for walk-ins to complete application blanks and preemployment tests, hours must be established when applicants can apply for jobs, and procedures must be in place to ensure that data from these individuals are entered into the applicant flow process. If walk-ins or résumé senders are treated like intruders, they may communicate a very negative image about the organization in the community.

Unsolicited applications are increasingly being sent electronically. The primary transmission portal for electronic applications is via an organization's website. Organizations need to make sure that these applications don't get lost in the system. They need to be regularly forwarded to recruiters or decision makers, and those who apply need to be contacted about the status of their application. Organizations that receive large numbers of electronic applications will narrow the pool of applicants by scanning the résumés for keywords or by requiring all applicants to complete standardized preemployment questionnaires. Although surveys reveal that most employers believe their websites do a better job of attracting applicants than do job boards,[15] many of these websites do not live up to their potential. Many have been likened to little more than post office boxes where applicants can send their résumés. Many applicants receive no more than an automated reply, or the organization has résumé uploading tools that do not function properly.[16] A study of the best practices of the websites of 140 high-profile organizations indicates seven features of high-impact websites:

1. A site layout that is easily navigated and provides information about the organization's culture
2. A "job cart" function that allows prospective applicants to search and apply for multiple positions within the organization
3. Résumé builders where applicants can easily submit their education, background, and experience
4. Detailed information on career opportunities
5. Clear graphics
6. Personal search engines that allow applicants to create profiles in the organization's database and update the data later
7. Self-assessment inventories to help steer college graduates toward appealing career paths

The website can serve as a make-or-break recruiting opportunity for many organizations.[17] In addition to the principles of website design listed above, it is wise to emphasize the organization's employment brand by providing information about the organization's history, culture, and benefits of employment. Research has shown that organizations can successfully convey cultural messages through their websites by describing organizational policies, showing pictures, and including testimonials. Effective websites also permit users to customize the information they receive by asking questions about their preferences and providing relevant information.

The look and customization of an organization's website often determine whether job seekers submit an application. To assess job seeker preferences, consultants from Brass Ring watch applicants go through the process of visiting organization websites, with the applicants describing their thought processes aloud. The consultants' research indicates that recruits are often frustrated by complex application systems, especially those that require them to enter the same data multiple times. To keep potential applicants from feeling disconnected from the online recruiting process, it is advisable to keep in touch with them at every stage of the process. To speed things up, some organizations inform applicants immediately if there is a mismatch between the information they have provided and the job requirements, so that they can know immediately that they are not under consideration. Quickly eliminating unacceptable candidates also allows recruiters to respond more quickly to applicants who do have sufficient KSAOs. A review of online job solicitation found that the best website advertising offered special features to potential applicants, including opportunities to check where they are in the hiring process, examples of a typical "day in the life" at an organization, and useful feedback to applicants regarding their potential fit with the organization and job early in the process.

Many organizations have taken these suggestions to heart and are working to improve the functionality of their online recruiting efforts. For example, Red Lobster's recruiting site was revised as part of a comprehensive half-year effort to better leverage the organization's brand-based recruiting strategy. To facilitate exploring work options, candidates are directed through several job options on the basis of their level of experience and are provided detailed descriptions and requirements for each position before they apply. Comparing multiple jobs parallels the format many job seekers might be familiar with from e-commerce sites; essentially, applicants can "shop" for jobs. By encouraging potential applicants to carefully consider a variety of work options, there should be better eventual person/job match. Research also shows that candidates prefer organizational websites that allow them to customize the information they receive. Candidates considering many jobs might self-select out of jobs that are not really of interest to them, which might help reduce the applicant pool to a set of more interested, qualified candidates and also reduce turnover down the line.

Employee Referrals

Employees currently working for an employer are a valuable source for finding job applicants.[18] The employees can refer people they know to their employer for consideration. Most estimates suggest that referrals are one of the most commonly used recruiting methods. The vast majority of organizations accept referrals, though only about half have formal programs. In some organizations, a cash bonus is given to employees who refer job candidates who prove to be successful on the job for a given period of time. Most bonuses range from a few hundred dollars to $1,000. To ensure adequate returns on bonuses for employee referrals, it is essential that a good performance appraisal system is in place to measure the performance of the referred new hire. There also needs to be a good applicant tracking system to ensure that new hire performance is maintained over time before a bonus is offered. Other organizations use more creative incentives. Lands' End, based in Dodgeville, Wisconsin, offers a drawing for each employee referral. The winner receives a free trip to a Green Bay Packers football game.

Referral programs have many potential advantages, including low cost per hire, high-quality hires, decreased hiring time, and an opportunity to strengthen bonds with current employees. Research also shows that individuals hired through referrals are less likely to leave.

Employee referral programs may fail to work for any number of reasons. Current employees may lack the motivation or ability to make referrals. Additionally, employees sometimes don't realize the importance of recruitment to the organization. As a result, the organization may need to encourage employee participation by providing special rewards and public recognition along with bonuses for successful referrals. And finally, employees may not be able to match people with jobs, because they do not know about vacancies or the requirements needed to fill them. Hence, employees must regularly be notified of job vacancies and their requirements.

Employee Networks

Though networks are not a formal referral program, many organizations use them to identify potential hires. They can be one's own network of personal contacts, or they can be formal programs that keep an active database of professional contacts.

Another way of finding applicants is through social networking, where friends or acquaintances are used to connect those looking for applicants to those looking for jobs. Many recruiters have turned to social networking websites such as Twitter, Jobster, LinkedIn, and Facebook as sources for finding qualified job candidates.[19] The number of individuals using these sites has increased dramatically in recent years, especially among younger workers, making it difficult to obtain reliable data on just how many individuals are using these sites at any specific time. There are a number of advantages to using social networking sites. Because many of the connections between users are based on professional background or shared work experiences, networking sites often provide access to groups of potential employees with specific skill sets. Some social networking websites geared toward professionals encourage users to indicate the industry and area in which they work. Recruiters can set up their own profile pages with these websites, encouraging potential applicants to apply by making personal contacts. By accessing the social networks of those already employed in the organization, it is possible to locate passive candidates who are already employed and not necessarily looking for a new job. In fields where the unemployment rate is very low, such as engineering, health care, and information technology (IT), these passive candidates may be the primary source of potential applicants. As with traditional referrals, a key advantage of using electronic networks is that employers can use their current employees as aids in the recruiting process. However, some recruiters find that these networking sites are not very efficient, because of the large number of passive candidates who are not interested in alternative employment offers. Organizations can face troubling legal and ethical quandaries when using social networking sites, because candidates' personal information, such as marital status, health status, or demographics, is often publicly available on personal pages. The long-range prospects of these networking sites will no doubt continue to change over time.

Advertisements

A convenient way to attract job applicants is to place an ad in newspapers and trade journals, along with placing a banner ad on the Internet. Job openings can also be advertised on the radio or on television. Cable television channels sometimes have job shows. Advertisements can be very costly and need to be monitored closely for yield. Using marketing data on audience demographics, employers can diversify their applicant pool by placing ads in media outlets that reach a variety of applicant populations. Research suggests that applicants react more positively to ads that reflect their own demographic group, which should be taken into account when developing a media campaign.[20] By carefully monitoring the results of each ad, the organization can make a more informed decision as to which ads should be run in the future. To track ads, each should be coded. Then, as résumés come into the organization in response to the ad, they can be recorded according to the codes, and the yield for that ad can be calculated.

Coding an ad is a very straightforward process. For example, in advertising for a vice president of HR, ads may be placed in a variety of HR periodicals, such as *HR Magazine*, and business publications, such as the *Wall Street Journal*. To track responses sent, applicants are asked to respond to Employment Department A for *HR Magazine* or Employment Department B for the *Wall Street Journal*, depending on where they saw the ad. As résumés arrive, those addressed to Department A are coded as responses from *HR Magazine*, and those addressed to Department B are coded as responses from the *Wall Street Journal*.

Employment Websites

Employment websites have evolved from their original function as job boards and database repositories of jobs and résumés to become fully featured recruiting and screening centers.[21] For employers that pay a fee, many employment websites provide services like targeted advertising, video advertising, preemployment screening examinations, and applicant tracking. For job seekers, there are resources to facilitate exploring different career paths, information about the communities where jobs are offered, and access to message boards where current and former employees can sound off on the culture and practices of different organizations.

Millions of job seekers submit their résumés to employment websites every year, and there were at least 40,000 job sites online in 2007. Although it is difficult to obtain precise data on the use of employment websites, some recent estimates suggest that they are second only to referrals as a source of new hires. More than half of the résumés Microsoft receives are over the Internet. On the other hand, research suggests that solicitations for employment from electronic bulletin boards are seen as especially low in credibility and informativeness relative to organization websites or face-to-face meetings at campus placement offices. Therefore, these methods should not be used without having some supporting practices that involve more interpersonal contact.[22]

One difficulty in the use of the Internet in recruiting is that many sites specifically designed for recruitment become defunct. Conversely, new employment websites come online on a nearly daily basis. Thus, one cannot assume that the sites an organization has used in the past will be the best options in the future, or that they will even exist. Any attempt to summarize the current state of the Internet job posting board scene needs to be taken with a grain of salt, since the landscape for Internet recruiting is shifting very rapidly. Another difficulty with Internet recruiting is the growing problem of identity theft, where fake jobs are posted online in order to obtain vital information on a person or to extract a fake fee.

Posting Jobs on General Employment Websites.   Most readers of this book are likely familiar with the biggest employment websites, so it is easy to forget that as recently as 1994 such sites for recruiting were seen as a risky proposition that might not have any future. Since that time, a few early movers and larger entrants have grabbed the lion's share of the market. Three of the biggest employment websites are *Monster.com*, *CareerBuilder.com*, and *HotJobs.com*, which collectively are estimated to be responsible for a large portion of external Internet hires. *Monster.com*, which employers can access at *www.hiring.monster.com*, estimated in 2007 that it had over 73 million résumés in its database, and over a million job postings. *CareerBuilder.com*, which employers can access at *www.careerbuilder. com*, similarly estimates that there are over 21 million unique visitors per month, and one million jobs posted at any given time.

General employment websites are not limited to simple advertising, as noted earlier. Services are rapidly evolving for these sites, and many now offer the ability to create and approve job requisitions online, manage recruiting tasks, track the progress of open positions and candidates, and report on recruiting metrics like time to hire, cost per hire, and equal employment opportunity (EEO). Several of the larger employment websites have developed extensive cross-listing relationships with local newspapers, effectively merging the advantages of local media in terms of credibility and name recognition with the powerful technological advances and large user base of employment websites.[23]

Posting Jobs on Niche Employment Websites.   Although there are advantages to open recruitment, as described earlier, it is also possible to conduct a more targeted web-based recruitment effort through niche employment websites.[24] These sites focus on specific occupations (there are employment websites for jobs ranging from nurses to geologists to metal workers), specific industries (sports, chemicals, transportation, human services), and specific locations (cities, states, or regions often have their own sites). Increasingly, employment websites are targeting blue-collar jobs as well. If recruiters want to find examples of niche job sites for a specific occupation, they simply do an Internet search of "employment websites" coupled with the occupation of interest. Although any one niche job board is unlikely to have a huge number of posters, collectively these more specific websites have been estimated to account for two-thirds of Internet hiring. Experienced recruiters claim that the audience for niche employment websites is often more highly qualified and interested in specific jobs than are applicants from more general job sites.

Niche job sites have also been developed that cater to specific demographic groups, including boards dedicated to women, African Americans, and Hispanics. Organizations that want to improve the diversity of their work sites or that are under an affirmative action plan (AAP) should consider posting in a variety of such specialized employment websites as part of their search strategy. Survey data suggest that applicants believe that companies that advertise on these targeted websites are more positively disposed toward workforce diversity, further serving to enhance the usefulness of diversity-oriented advertising.[25]

Searching Web-Based Databases.   As opposed to actively posting jobs online, another (but not mutually exclusive) means of recruiting on the web is to search for applicants without ever having posted a position. Under this process, applicants submit their résumés online, which are then forwarded to employers when they meet the employer's criteria. Such systems allow searching the databases according to various search criteria, such as job skills, years of work experience, education, major, grade-point average, and so forth. It costs applicants anywhere from nothing to $200 or more to post their résumé or other information on the databases. For organizations, there is always a cost. The exact nature of the cost depends on both the database(s) to which the organization subscribes and the services requested. More databases allow organizations to search according to Boolean logic. For example, a recruiter interested in locating résumés of prospective HR managers for a Miami-based manufacturing facility might type "human resources + Miami + manufacturing."

Advantages and Disadvantages of Employment Websites.   Web-based recruiting offers many advantages to employers. No other method reaches as many people as quickly as posting a job on a website. This advantage is particularly important when filling large numbers of positions, when the labor market is national or international, or when the unique nature of the necessary qualifications requires casting a wide net. Furthermore, using employment websites provides faster access to candidates. Most employers have résumés in their system within 24 hours of receipt, and their searchable databases facilitate access to candidates with desired qualifications. It is commonly argued that Internet recruiting presents cost advantages, and if one is comparing the cost of an ad in the *Los Angeles Times* with the price for access to an online database, this is no doubt true. Finally, there is administrative convenience. Many individuals in the same organization can access the database, and it eliminates much "paper pushing."

Some of the past limitations of web-based recruiting—specifically, that the vast majority of applicants were in the technology area and that most web users were white males—seem to be improving. On the other hand, recruiting on the web is not a magical solution for matching applicants to employers. Despite claims to the contrary, decision makers need to be involved in the process. In fact, some large organizations have created new positions for individuals to manage the Internet sites and databases. It is important to remember that no matter what lofty promises a system makes for screening out undesirable applicants, the system is only as good as the search criteria, which generally make fairly rough cuts (e.g., based on years of experience, educational background, broad areas of expertise). Like all sources, employment websites must be evaluated against other alternatives to ensure that they are delivering on their considerable promise, and employers must remember that, for the time being, it is unlikely that the web can be the sole source for recruiting applicants. The costs of employment websites must be weighed against the benefits, including the number of qualified applicants, the relative quality of these applicants, and other criteria such as offer acceptance rates and turnover.

Colleges and Placement Offices

Colleges are a source of people with specialized skills for professional positions. Most colleges have a placement office or officer who is in charge of ensuring that a match is made between the employer's interests and the graduating student's interests. Research has shown that campus recruiting efforts are seen as more informative and credible than organization websites or electronic bulletin boards.[26] In fact, recruiting experts found that members of the tech-savvy millennial generation are reluctant to use social networking and other Internet job search tools, and that they prefer campus career placement offices to find jobs.[27]

In most cases, the placement office is the point of contact with colleges. It should be noted, however, that not all students use the services of the placement office. Students sometimes avoid placement offices because they believe they will be competing against the very best students and will be unlikely to receive a job offer. Additional points of contact for students at colleges include professors, department heads, professional fraternities, honor societies, recognition societies, and national professional societies. Organizations sometimes overlook small colleges as a recruitment source because the small number of students does not make it seem worth the effort to visit. In order to present a larger number of students to choose from, some small colleges have banded together in consortia. For example, the Oregon Liberal Arts Placement Consortium provides a centralized recruitment source for nine public and private small colleges and universities. It is essential that appropriate colleges and universities be selected for a visit.

A difficult choice for the employer is deciding which colleges and universities to target for recruiting efforts. Some organizations focus their efforts on schools with the best return on investment and invest in those programs more heavily. Other organizations, especially large organizations with relatively high turnover, find they need to cast a much broader net. In the end, the decision of breadth versus depth comes down to the number of individuals who need to be hired, the recruiting budget, and a strategic decision about whether to invest deeply in a few programs or more broadly in more programs. Some factors to consider when deciding which colleges and universities to target include the following:[28]

1. Past experiences with students at the school—including the quality of recent hires (measured in terms of performance and turnover), offer acceptance rates, skills, experience, and training in the areas where job openings exist—should be factored in.

2. Rankings of school quality. *U.S. News and World Report*, *The Gorman Report*, and *Peterson's Guide* are comprehensive rankings of colleges and universities and various degree programs. *Business Week*, the *Wall Street Journal*, and the *Financial Times* rank business schools. Applicants recruited from highly ranked programs almost always come at a premium, so organizations need to make sure they are getting a good return on their investment.

3. The costs of recruiting at a particular school must be assessed. Colleges and universities that are nearby often mean substantially fewer resources expended on travel (both for recruiters traveling to the school and for bringing applicants in for interviews).

There are several ways an organization can establish a high-quality relationship with a school. A critical task is to establish a good relationship with the placement director. Although most placement directors are eager to make the organization's recruitment process productive and pleasant, there are many aspects where they exert additional influence over the success of the organization's recruitment of high-quality graduates (e.g., informal discussions with students about good employers, alerting recruiters to impressive candidates). Another way to establish a high-quality relationship with a school is to maintain a presence. This presence can take various forms, and organizations are increasingly becoming more creative and aggressive in establishing relationships with universities and their students. Some investment banks, consulting firms, and other companies shell out $500,000 and more per school to fund career seminars, gifts for students, and fancy dinners. Ernst & Young built a study room at Columbia University, and GE sponsored an e-commerce lab at the University of Connecticut.[29] Other companies are using nonconventional approaches. UPS hired massage therapists to give students massages at job fairs. Ford allowed students to test-drive Fords and Jaguars. Dow held crayfish boils.

Of course, relationship building is not just about doling out money, and smaller organizations are not likely to have the resources. Beyond building a good relationship with the placement director and providing financial support, recruiters should build relationships with other key people, such as associate deans, other placement office staff, key faculty, and members of student organizations. It is also important to keep in touch with these people beyond the day or week the recruiter visits campus. Finally, care must be taken to obtain permission for all activities. One dot-com organization was banned from a prestigious MBA program for offering students signing bonuses of BMWs, among other nonconventional ploys, without alerting career services of its plans.[30]

Employment Agencies

A source of nonexempt employees and lower-level exempt employees is employment agencies. These agencies contact, screen, and present applicants to employers for a fee. The fee is contingent on successful placement of a candidate with an employer and is a percentage of the candidate's starting salary (usually around 25%). During difficult economic periods, employers cut back on the use of these agencies or attempt to negotiate lower fees in order to contain costs.

Care must be exercised in selecting an employment agency. It is a good idea to check references, as allegations abound regarding the shoddy practices of some agencies. A poor agency may, for example, flood the organization with résumés of both qualified and unqualified applicants. A good agency will screen out unqualified applicants and not attempt to dazzle the organization with a large volume of résumés. Poor agencies may misrepresent the organization to the candidate and the candidate to the organization. Misrepresentation may take place when the agency is only concerned about a quick placement (and fee) and pays no regard to the costs of poor future relationships with clients. A good agency will be in business for the long run and not misrepresent information and invite turnover. Poor agencies may pressure managers to make decisions when they are uncertain or not ready, and they may go around the HR staff in the organization to negotiate special deals with individual managers. These so-called special deals may result in paying higher fees than agreed on with HR and overlooking qualified minorities and women. A good agency will not pressure managers, make special deals, or avoid the HR staff. Finally, it is important to have a signed contract in place where mutual rights and responsibilities are laid out.

Executive Search Firms

For higher-level professional positions or jobs with salaries of $100,000 and higher, executive search firms, or "headhunters," may be used. Like employment agencies, these firms contact, screen, and present résumés to employers. The difference between employment agencies and search firms lies in two primary areas: (1) search firms typically deal with higher-level positions than those of employment agencies, and (2) search firms are more likely to operate on the basis of a retainer than on a contingency. Search firms that operate on a retainer are paid regardless of whether a successful placement is made. The advantage of operating this way, from the hiring organization's standpoint, is that it aligns the interests of the search firm with those of the organization. Thus, search firms operating on retainer do not feel compelled to put forward candidates just so their contingency fee can be paid. Moreover, a search firm on retainer may be less likely to give up if the job is not filled in a few weeks. Of late, business has been slow for executive search firms, partly due to the moderate economic growth and the bustling online recruiting business. Thus, companies have been able to negotiate smaller fees (retainers or contingencies).[31]

When contracting with a search firm on a contingency or retainer basis, organizations cannot take a completely hands-off approach to the recruitment process; they need to keep tabs on the progress of the search and, if necessary, "light a fire" under the search firm. To expedite the search process, some organizations are going online. *Monster.com*'s website has an area that caters to executives. A disadvantage of most online databases is that they do not include passive candidates—executives who may be highly qualified for the position but are not actively looking. Some companies, such as Direct Search of the United States, sell internal corporate telephone directories to organizations and search firms looking for executives. This practice is, of course, controversial, but it appears to be legal, as a copyright on a directory generally covers only artwork and unique design features. For more information about executive recruiters, see *www.kennedypub.com*. Kennedy Information publishes an annual list of thousands of recruiters and their specialties.

Increasingly, executive search firms are getting into the appraisal business, where an organization pays the search firm to provide an assessment of the organization's top executives. On one level this makes sense, since executive search firms are in the assessment business. The problem is that since the executive assessment pays much less than the retainer or contingency fees for hiring an executive, the search firms have an incentive to pronounce top executives substandard so as to justify bringing in an outsider. This is exactly what happened with a top executive search firm whose executive recruiters negatively evaluated an executive, only to recommend hiring an outsider, for which the recruiters were compensated handsomely. Given these inherent conflicts of interest, organizations should avoid using the same search firm to hire new executives and to appraise its existing executive team.[32]

Professional Associations and Meetings

Many technical and professional organizations meet around the country at least once a year. Many of these groups run a placement service for their members, and some may charge a fee to recruit at these meetings. This source represents a way to attract applicants with specialized skills or professional credentials. Also, some meetings are an opportunity to attract women and minorities. For example, the National Society of Black Engineers holds an annual meeting where employers can meet with large numbers of qualified job candidates at a single location and time.[33] In addition to having placement activities at annual conventions, professional associations may also have a placement function throughout the year. For example, it is a common practice in professional association newsletters to advertise both positions available and interested applicants. Others may have a computerized job and applicant bank.

Social Service Agencies

All states have an employment or job service. These services are funded by employer-paid payroll taxes and are provided by the state to help secure employment for those seeking it, particularly those currently unemployed. Typically, these services refer low- to middle-level employees to employers. For jobs to be filled properly, the hiring organization must maintain a close relationship with the employment service. Job qualifications need to be clearly communicated to ensure that proper screening takes place by the agency. Positions that have been filled must be promptly reported to the agency so that résumés are not sent for closed positions. The federal Job Corps program is another option. Job Corps is designed to help individuals between 16 and 24 years of age obtain employment. The program targets individuals with lower levels of education and prepares them for entry-level jobs through a combination of work ethic training and general job skills. For employers, Job Corps can provide specialized training, prescreening of applicants, and tax benefits. Some agencies in local communities may also provide outplacement assistance for the unemployed who cannot afford it. Applicants who use these services may also be listed with a state employment service. Community agencies may also offer counseling and training.

The US Department of Labor has provided funding for states to develop one-stop career centers that will provide workers with various programs, benefits, and opportunities related to finding jobs. The centers' emphasis is on providing customer-friendly services that reach large segments of the population and are fully integrated with state employment services. These centers now offer a variety of skills certification programs, such as the National Work Readiness Credential and the National Career Readiness Certificate, which are highly sought after by employers.[34] For example, when Honda decided to build its Odyssey plant in Alabama, part of the deal was that the state would establish a close partnership with Honda to recruit and train employees.[35] Nissan has established similar relationships with the states of Mississippi and Tennessee. The state of Illinois provides customized applicant screening and referral to employers so efficiently that some employers, such as Jewel Companies (a grocery store chain), use the service as an extension of their HR department.[36]

Outplacement Services

Some organizations retain an outplacement firm to provide assistance to employees who are losing their jobs. Outplacement firms usually offer job seekers assistance in the form of counseling and training to help facilitate a good person/job match. Most large outplacement firms have job banks, which are computerized listings of applicants and their qualifications. Registration by employers to use these job banks is usually free.

Larger organizations experiencing a downsizing may have their own internal outplacement function and perform the activities traditionally found in external outplacement agencies. They may also hold in-house job fairs. An in-house function saves on the costs of using an external outplacement firm and helps build the morale of those employees who remain with the organization and are likely to be affected by their friends' loss of jobs.

Job Fairs

Professional associations, schools, employers, the military, and other interested organizations hold career or job fairs to attract job applicants. Typically, the sponsors of a job fair will meet in a central location with a large facility in order to provide information, collect résumés, and screen applicants. Often, there is a fee for employers to participate. Job fairs may provide both short- and long-term gains. In the short run, the organization may identify qualified applicants. In the long run, it may be able to enhance its visibility in the community, which, in turn, may improve its image and ability to attract applicants for jobs.

For a job fair to yield a large number of applicants, it must be advertised well in advance. Moreover, advertisements may need to be placed in specialized publications likely to attract minorities and women. To attract quality candidates from all those in attendance, the organization must be able to differentiate itself from all the other organizations competing for applicants at the job fair. Items such as mugs and key chains with the company logo can be distributed to remind the applicants of employment opportunities at a particular organization. An even better promotion may be to provide attendees at the fair with assistance in developing their résumés and cover letters.

One strength of job fairs is also a weakness—although a job fair enables the organization to reach many people, the typical job fair has around 1,600 applicants vying for the attention of about 65 employers. Given the ratio of 25 applicants for every employer, the typical contact with an applicant is probably shallow. In response, some employers instead (or also) devote their resources to information sessions geared toward a smaller group of specially qualified candidates. During these sessions, the organization presents information about itself, including its culture, work environment, and career opportunities. Small gifts and brochures are also typically given out. One recent research study showed that applicants who were favorably impressed by an organization's information session were significantly more likely to pursue employment with the organization. Other studies show that job fairs that allow for interpersonal interactions between job seekers and organization representatives are seen as especially informative by job seekers. Thus, both applicants and employers find information sessions a valuable alternative, or complement, to job fairs.[37]

Increasingly, job fairs are being held online, with preestablished time limits. One online recruiting site held a job fair that included 240 participating companies. In these virtual job fairs, recruiters link up with candidates through chat rooms.

Co-ops and Internships

Students currently attending school are sometimes available for part-time work. Two part-time working arrangements are co-ops and internships. Under a co-op arrangement, the student works with one employer on an alternating quarter basis. In one quarter the student works full time, and in the next quarter the student attends school full time. Under an internship arrangement, the student has a continuous period of employment with an employer for a specified period of time. These approaches allow an organization to not only obtain services from a part-time employee for a short period of time but also assess the person for a full-time position after graduation. One manager experienced in working with interns commented, "Working with them is one of the best talent-search opportunities available to managers."[38] In turn, interns have better employment opportunities as a result of their experiences.

Internships and co-op assignments can take a variety of forms. One type of assignment is to have the student perform a part of the business that occurs periodically. For example, some amusement parks that operate only in the summer in northern climates may have a large number of employees who need to be hired and trained in the spring. A student with a background in HR could perform these hiring and training duties. Increasingly, colleges and universities are giving students college credit for—in some cases, even instituting a requirement for—working as a part of their professional degree.[39] A student in social work, for example, might be required to work in a welfare office for a summer. Occasionally, experience shows that some internships and co-op assignments do not provide these meaningful experiences that build on the qualifications of the student. Research shows that school-to-work programs often do not provide high utility to organizations in terms of benefit-cost ratios. Thus, organizations need to evaluate co-ops and internships not only in terms of quality for the student but in terms of the cost-benefit economic perspective as well.[40]

Meaningful experiences benefit both the organization and the student. The organization gains from the influence of new ideas the student has been exposed to in his or her curriculum, and the student gains from the experience of having to apply concepts while facing the realities of organizational constraints. For both parties to gain, a learning contract must be developed and signed by the student, the student's advisor, and the corporate sponsor. The learning contract becomes, in essence, a job description to guide the student's activities. Also, it establishes the criteria by which the student's performance is assessed for purposes of grading by the academic advisor and for purposes of successful completion of the project for the organization. In the absence of a learning contract, internships can result in unrealistic expectations by the corporate sponsor, which, in turn, can result in disappointment when these unspoken expectations are not met.[41]

To secure the services of students, organizations can contact the placement offices of high schools, colleges, universities, and vocational technology schools. Also, teachers, professors, and student chapters of professional associations can be contacted to obtain student assistance. Placement officials can provide the hiring organization with the policies that need to be followed for placements, while teachers and professors can give guidance on the types of skills students could bring to the organization and the organizational experiences the students would benefit from the most.

Alternative Sources

Several innovative sources might also be experimented with, particularly for purposes of widening the search.

Interest Groups. There are many associations that help facilitate the interests of their members. Two such groups are the American Association for Retired Persons (AARP) and the National Association for the Advancement of Colored People (NAACP). For example, when Home Depot was anticipating 35,000 new jobs, it partnered with AARP to help fill some of these positions.[42]

Real Estate Agents. Some real estate agents now offer employment services for trailing partners. When one person in a relationship must relocate to further a career, the real estate agent may also help the trailing partner find a new job.

Alternative Media Outlets. Although most recruiters are familiar with the advantages of Internet, radio, television, and print advertising, there are other media outlets that have been explored less frequently that might offer a recruiter a competitive advantage for attracting candidates. For example, BNSF Railway finds that advertising for jobs in movie theaters is an effective way to reach a diverse group of candidates who might not otherwise consider working in the rail industry. The BNSF Railway recruiting method is notable for its use of movie theater advertisements to stimulate initial interest in employment opportunities, coupled with a website follow-up to provide more information about open positions. In another unusual example of innovative media recruiting, the US Army has used a very popular online video game called *America's Army* to draw in thousands of recruits.[43]

Talent Pipeline.   Some organizations develop a talent pipeline that includes individuals who may not take a job immediately but may be attracted into the organization in the future. Managing an organization's talent pipeline means establishing effective relationships even before positions open up. Some organizations try to develop an early relationship with incoming college freshmen in hopes that they will consider the organization as a potential employer when they graduate. Organizations that engage in large-scale collaborative research and development efforts with universities also cultivate relationships with faculty, with the hope of eventually luring them into private sector work. Many organizations establish folders or databases of high-potential individuals who are either still receiving an education or work for other companies who have demonstrated potential, and then send materials to these individuals regularly about potential career prospects within the organization. For example, United Health Group maintains interest among high-potential employees by conducting exploratory interviews, sending routine e-mails about openings, and conducting seminars.[44]

Former Employees.   Former employees can be an ideal source of future applicants, either by recruiting them to come back to the organization or by asking them to provide referrals. As return employees, they will know the organization, its jobs, and its culture, and will also be well known to those inside the organization. This will cut down on orientation costs and also means that they can get into the flow of work more quickly. As referral sources, they can convey their personal observations to other job seekers, and thus those who decide to apply will be better informed. Using former employees as a recruiting source naturally means that the organization must remain on good terms with departing employees and keep channels of communication open after employees leave. Many organizations that undergo cyclical layoffs or downsizing in lean times might also seek to rehire those who were laid off previously when the organization returns to an expansionary strategy.[45]

Recruiting Metrics

Each recruiting source has strengths and weaknesses. Determining the best method for an organization entails assessing the costs and benefits of each method and then selecting the optimal combination of sources to meet the organization's strategic needs. Exhibit 5.5 provides an overview of the metrics that might be expected for the categories of recruiting activities, along with issues considered relevant to each source. Conclusions for the number and types of applicants drawn by each method are informed by a number of studies comparing recruiting sources.[46] Although broad generalizations can be made regarding quantity, quality, cost, and impact on HR outcomes for different recruiting methods, each organization's unique labor market situation will need to be considered since the

EXHIBIT 5.5   Potential Recruiting Metrics for Different Sources

Recruiting Source	Quantity	Quality	Costs	Impact on HR
Applicant initiated	Contingent on how widely the company's brand is known	Highly variable KSAO levels if no skill requirements are posted	Application processing and clerical staff time	Higher training costs, lower performance, higher turnover
Employee referrals	Generates a small number of applicants	Better fit because current employees will inform applicants about the culture	Signing bonuses are sometimes provided to increase quantity	Higher performance, higher satisfaction, lower turnover, lower diversity
Employee networks	Potentially a large number of individuals, depending on employee use of networks	Depends on whether networks are made up of others with similar skills and knowledge	Time spent searching through networks and soliciting applications	Potentially similar results to referrals, although results are unknown
Advertisements	Large quantity for general media ads, fewer applicants for specialized media outlets	Highly variable KSAO levels; can specify required skills in advertisement to limit applicant pool	Development of advertisement, media source costs	Lower job performance, higher turnover; can increase diversity
Employment websites	Often opens to very large pool, although niche sites have a more narrow pool	Can provide specific keywords to limit applications to those with specific KSAOs	Subscription fees or user fees from database services	Good tracking data, potentially lower satisfaction, and higher turnover
Colleges and placement offices	About 50 individuals can be contacted at each university per day	High levels of job-relevant human capital, usually screened on the basis of cognitive ability, little work experience	Time costs of establishing relationships, traveling to college locations	Initial training and development for inexperienced workers; can increase average KSAO levels
Employment agencies	Many applicants for lower-level jobs, fewer applicants available for managerial or executive positions	Applicants will be prescreened; organizations are often able to try out candidates as temps prior to hiring	Fees charged by employment agencies	Reduced costs of screening candidates, improved person/job match

(continued)

EXHIBIT 5.5 Continued

Recruiting Source	Quantity	Quality	Costs	Impact on HR
Executive search firms	Only a small number of individuals will be contacted	Search firms will carefully screen applicants, usually experienced candidates	Fees for executive searches can be more than half of the applicant's annual salary	Reduced staff time required because the search firm finds applicants; very high costs for firms
Professional associations and meetings	Comparatively few candidates will be identified for each job opening	Those attending professional meetings will be highly engaged and qualified	Cost of attending meetings and direct interviewing with staff can be very high	Superior performance, although those seeking jobs at meetings may be "job hoppers"
Social service agencies	There are usually a limited number of individuals available, although this varies by skill level	Applicants may have had difficulty finding jobs through other routes because of lack of skills	Often there are direct financial incentives for hiring from these agencies	Potentially greater training costs, higher levels of diversity
Outplacement services	A limited number of individuals available	Applicants are typically experienced workers, although there may be questions about why they were laid off	Registration for employers is typically free	Lower training costs because of experience; effects on job performance unknown
Job fairs	About 40 applicants can be contacted per recruiter per day	Often draws in individuals with some knowledge of the company or industry	Advertising and hosting costs are considerable, although this is an efficient way to screen many candidates	Higher levels of diversity if targeted to diverse audiences; effects on performance, satisfaction unknown
Co-ops and internships	Only a small number of interns can be used in most organizations	High levels of formal educational preparation, but few interns will have work experience	Cost of paid interns can be very high; unpaid interns are a huge cost savings although they often require staff time	Those who are hired will be prescreened, and should have higher performance and lower turnover

meta-analytic evidence shows considerable variety in the effects of recruiting variables on applicant attraction.

Sufficient Quantity

The more broadly transmitted the organization's search methods, the more likely it is that a large number of individuals will be attracted to apply. Other methods of recruiting naturally tend to be more focused and will draw a comparatively small number of applicants. While some broad recruiting methods such as advertising and Internet postings are able to reach thousands of individuals, it might be to an organization's advantage not to attract too many applicants, because of the costs associated with processing all the applications.

Sufficient Quality

Recruiting methods that link employers to a database of employees with exceptional skills will enable an employer to save money on screening and selection processes. But if the search is too narrow, the organization will likely be engaged in a long-term process of looking.

Cost

The costs of any method of recruiting are the direct expenses involved in contacting job seekers and processing their applications. Some sources, such as radio advertisements, search firms, and sophisticated website portals that customize information and provide employees with feedback, are quite expensive to develop. These methods may be worth the cost if the organization needs to attract a large number of individuals, if KSAOs for a job are in short supply, or if the job is crucial to the organization's success. On the other hand, organizations that need fewer employees or that require easily found KSAOs discover that lower-cost methods like applicant-initiated recruiting or referrals are sufficient to meet their needs. Some fee-based services, like employment agencies, are able to process applications inexpensively because the pool of applicants is prescreened for relevant KSAOs.

Impact on HR Outcomes

A considerable amount of research has been conducted on the effectiveness of various recruitment sources and can be used as a starting point for which sources are likely to be effective. Research has defined effectiveness as the impact of recruitment sources on increased employee satisfaction, job performance, diversity, and retention. Evidence suggests that, overall, referrals and job trials are likely to attract employees who have a better understanding of the organization and its culture, and therefore they tend to result in employees who are more satisfied, more productive, and less likely to leave. Conversely, sources like newspaper advertising and employment agencies can produce employees who are less satisfied and productive. Any general conclusions regarding the effectiveness of recruitment sources should be tempered by the fact that the location of an organization, the compensation and benefits packages provided, the type of workers, and the typical applicant experience and education levels may moderate the efficacy of these practices.

SEARCHING

Once the recruitment planning and strategy development phases are completed, it is time to actively conduct the search. Searching for candidates first requires developing a message and then selecting a medium to communicate that message. Both phases are considered in turn.

Communication Message

Types of Messages

The communication message to applicants can focus on conveying realistic, employment brand, or targeted information.

Realistic Recruitment Message.   A realistic recruitment message portrays the organization and the job as they really are, rather than describing what the organization thinks job applicants want to hear. Organizations continue to describe themselves to applicants in overly positive terms, overstating desired values such as risk taking and understating undesirable values such as rules orientation. Some would argue this is not the best message to send applicants on moral or practical grounds. While hyping the benefits of joining up may work for the army, where recruits are obligated to remain for three to five years, employees generally have no such obligation.

A very well-researched recruitment message is known as a realistic job preview (RJP).[47] According to this practice, job applicants are given a "vaccination" by being told verbally, in writing, or on videotape what the actual job is like.[48] An example of the numerous attributes in an RJP for the job of elementary school teacher is shown in Exhibit 5.6. Note that the attributes are quite specific and that they are both positive and negative. Information like this "tells it like it is" to job applicants.

After receiving the vaccination, job applicants can decide whether they want to work for the organization. The hope with the RJP is that job applicants will self-select into or out of the organization. By selecting into the organization, the applicant may be more committed to working there than he or she might otherwise have been. When an applicant self-selects out, the organization does not face the costs associated with recruiting, selecting, training, and compensating an employee, only to then have him or her leave because the job did not meet his or her expectations.

EXHIBIT 5.6   Example of Job Attributes in an RJP for Elementary School Teachers

Positive Job Attributes
Dental insurance is provided
Innovative teaching strategies are encouraged
University nearby for taking classes
Large support staff for teachers

Negative Job Attributes
Salary growth has averaged only 2% in past three years
Class sizes are large
The length of the school day is long
Interactions with community have not been favorable

A great deal of research has been conducted on the effectiveness of RJPs, which appear to lead to somewhat higher job satisfaction and lower turnover. This appears to be true because providing applicants with realistic expectations about future job characteristics helps them better cope with job demands once they are hired. RJPs also appear to foster the belief in employees that their employer is concerned about them and honest with them, which leads to higher levels of organizational commitment.

RJPs may lead applicants to withdraw from the recruitment process, although a recent review suggests that they have little effect on such attrition. This may appear to be great news to employers interested in using RJPs: Providing applicants with realistic information provides employers with more satisfied and committed employees while still maintaining applicant interest in the position. Where the situation may become problematic is when one considers the type of applicant "scared away" by the realistic message. It appears plausible that the applicants most likely to be dissuaded by the realistic message are high-quality applicants, because they have more options. In fact, research suggests that the negative effects of RJPs on applicant attraction are particularly strong for high-quality applicants (those whose general qualifications are especially strong) and those with direct experience or familiarity with the job.

Although RJPs appear to have both weakly positive consequences (slightly higher job satisfaction and lower turnover among new hires) and negative consequences (slightly reduced ability to hire high-quality applicants), these outcomes have been found to be affected by a number of factors. A review of 40 studies on the effectiveness of RJPs suggested they have weak effects, but to some extent these effects were affected by a number of factors. The following recommendations can be gleaned from these findings:

- RJPs presented very early in the recruitment process are less effective in reducing posthire turnover than those presented just before or just after hiring.

- Posthire RJPs lead to higher posthire levels of job performance than do RJPs presented before hiring.
- Verbal RJPs tend to reduce turnover more than written or videotaped RJPs.
- RJPs are less likely to lead to turnover when the organization "restricts" turnover for a period of time after the RJP (with contracts, above-market salaries, etc.).

In general, these findings suggest that RJPs should be given verbally (rather than in writing or by showing a video) and that it is probably best to reserve their use for later in the recruiting process (RJPs should not be part of the initial exposure of the organization to applicants).[49]

Employment Brand Message.   Organizations wishing to portray an appealing message to potential applicants may develop an employment brand to attract applicants. An employment brand is a "good-company tag" that places the image of "being a great place to work" or "employer of choice" in the minds of job candidates. An organization's employment brand is closely tied to its product market image. And like general product awareness, the more "customers" (in this case, potential applicants) are aware of an organization's employment brand, the more interested they are in pursuing a job.[50] Organizations that are well known by potential applicants may not need to engage in as much advertising for their jobs. Big-name organizations that market well-known products, such as Microsoft, Apple, Sony, and Disney, often have many more applicants than they need for most openings. Organizations with lower profiles may have to actively advertise their employment brand to bring in more applicants. One of the best ways for smaller organizations to emphasize their unique brand is to emphasize their most attractive attributes. Experts in corporate branding also encourage employers to compare their own organizational employment offerings with the competition to see how they are unique, and then highlight these unique advantages in organizational recruiting messages. Under a branding strategy, the US Marine Corps emphasized the Marines as an elite group of warriors rather than focusing on the financial advantages of enlistment, which had been done in the past.

One way to enhance an employment brand is to be named to *Fortune's 100 Best Companies to Work For* list. Being named to this list communicates to applicants that the organization treats its employees fairly, has employees who like their jobs, and offers good benefits. Obviously, this can be an enormous recruiting asset. Southwest Airlines, a longtime member of the list, enjoys 80 applicants for every opening.

Beyond reputation, another employment brand may be value or culture based. For example, GE has long promoted its high performance expectations in order to attract achievement-oriented applicants seeking commensurate rewards. Organization websites are often used to convey information regarding an organization's culture and emphasize the employment brand. Most organizational websites provide information regarding the organization's history, culture, diversity, benefits, and specific job information under a "careers" heading. It is informative to look through a series of these organizational websites to see how organizations cater to applicants. For example, Merck's corporate website shows an organization that conveys a message of professional development and social responsibility, whereas Goldman Sachs emphasizes performance and success, and Coca-Cola emphasizes global opportunities and fun.

There are several possible benefits to branding. Of course, establishing an attractive employment brand may help attract desired applicants to the organization. Moreover, having an established brand may help retain employees who were attracted to the brand to begin with. Research suggests that identifiable employment brands may breed organizational commitment on the part of newly hired employees.[51] Employment brands associated with empowerment and high compensation have been shown to be especially attractive to applicants.[52]

Research shows that having an employment brand can attract applicants to an organization, even beyond job and organizational attributes. Evidence also suggests that employers are most able to get their brand image out when they engage in early recruitment activities such as advertising or generating publicity about the organization.[53]

Targeted Message.　One way to improve upon matching people with jobs is to target the recruitment message to a particular audience. Different audiences may be looking for different rewards from an employer. This would appear to be especially true of special applicant populations, such as teenagers, older workers, welfare recipients, people with disabilities, homeless individuals, veterans, and displaced homemakers, who may have special needs. Older workers, for example, may be looking for employers that can meet their financial needs (e.g., supplement Social Security), security needs (e.g., retraining), and social needs (e.g., place to interact with people). College students appear to be attracted to organizations that provide rewards and promotions on the basis of individual rather than group performance. Also, most college students prefer to receive pay in the form of a salary rather than in the form of incentives.[54]

Choice of Messages

The different types of messages—realistic, branded, and targeted—are not likely to be equally effective under the same conditions. Which message to convey depends on the labor market, vacancy characteristics, and applicant characteristics.

The three types of messages are summarized in Exhibit 5.7. If the labor market is tight and applicants are difficult to come by, realism may not be an effective message, because to the extent that applicants self-select out of the applicant pool, fewer are left for an employer to choose from. Hence, if the employment objective is simply to fill job slots in the short run and worry about turnover later, a realistic message will have counterproductive effects. Obviously, then, when applicants are abundant and turnover is an immediate problem, a realistic message is appropriate.

In a tight labor market, branded and targeted messages are likely to be more effective in attracting job applicants. Attraction is strengthened, as there are inducements in applying for a job. In addition, individual needs are more likely to

EXHIBIT 5.7   Comparing Types of Messages

	Information Conveyed	Applicant Reactions	Potential Drawback	Best For
Realistic	Both positive and negative aspects of a job and organization are described	Some applicants self-select out; those who remain will have a better understanding of the job and will be less likely to leave	The best potential applicants may be more likely to leave	Loose labor markets or when turnover is costly
Branded	An appealing description is developed based on marketing principles, emphasizing unique features of the organization	Positive view of the organization, increased intention to apply for jobs, and better prehire information about benefits of the job	Overly positive message may result in employee dissatisfaction after hire	Tight labor markets or for higher-value jobs
Targeted	Advertising themes are designed to attract a specific set of employees	Better fit between application message and specific applicant groups	May dissuade applicants who aren't interested in the work attributes featured in the message from applying	Specific KSAOs, or seeking a specific type of applicant

be perceived as met by a prospective employer. Hence, the applicant is more motivated to apply to organizations with an attractive or targeted message than those without. During loose economic times when applicants are plentiful, the branded or targeted approaches may be more costly than necessary to attract an adequate supply of labor. Also, they may set up false expectations concerning what life will be like on the job, and thus lead to turnover.

Job applicants will know more about the characteristics of highly visible jobs versus those of less visible jobs. For example, service sector jobs, such as that of cashier, are highly visible to people, and thus it may be redundant to give a realistic message. Other jobs, such as an outside sales position, are far less visible to people. These jobs may seem glamorous (e.g., sales commissions) to prospective applicants who fail to see the less glamorous aspects of the job (e.g., a lot of travel and paperwork).

Some jobs seem to be better suited to special applicant groups, and hence a targeted approach may work well. For example, older employees may have social needs that can be well met by a job that requires a lot of public contact. Organizations, then, can take advantage of the special characteristics of jobs to attract applicants.

The value of the job to the organization also has a bearing on the selection of an appropriate recruitment message. Inducements for jobs of higher value or worth to the organization are easier to justify in a budgetary sense than inducements for jobs of lower worth. The job may be of such importance to the organization that it is willing to pay a premium through inducements to attract well-qualified candidates.

Some applicants are less likely than others to be influenced in their attitudes and behaviors by the recruitment message. One study showed that a realistic message is less effective for those with considerable previous job experience.[55] A targeted message does not work very well if the source is seen as not being credible.[56] Highly experienced candidates are more likely to be persuaded by high-quality, detailed advertisements than are less experienced candidates.[57] Inducements may not be particularly effective with applicants who do not have a family or who have considerable wealth.

Communication Medium

Not only is the message itself an important part of the recruitment process, so, too, is the selection of a medium to communicate the message. The most common recruitment media are recruitment brochures, videos and videoconferencing, advertisements, direct contact, and online services.

Effective communication media are high in richness and credibility. Rich media channels allow for timely personal feedback and a variety of methods for conveying messages (e.g., visual images, text, figures and charts), and they are customized to each respondent's specific needs. Credible media channels transmit information that is honest, accurate, and thorough. Research has shown that respondents will have more positive images of organizations that transmit information that is rich and credible.[58] If the information is seen as coming directly from the employees, rather than from the organization's recruiting offices, the message will likely be seen as more honest and unbiased. Experts on advertising also advise recruiters to remember that they need to constantly promote their brand to potential employees, because sheer repetition and consistency of a promotional message increase its effectiveness.

Word of Mouth

One of the most powerful methods for communicating about a potential job opportunity is one that organizations cannot directly control: word of mouth.[59] This refers to the informal information regarding an organization's reputation, employment practices, and policies that can exert a powerful impact on job seekers' impressions of an employer. Because word of mouth usually comes from individuals who do not have a vested interest in "selling" the job, the messages are likely to be seen as more credible. The fact that job seekers can ask and have questions answered also makes word of mouth a very rich source of information. Some word of mouth is no longer conveyed face to face, as blogs and social networking sites can also be used to communicate information about employers.

How can organizations control word of mouth? One technique is to carefully cultivate relationships with current employees, recognizing that the way they are treated will come to influence the ways that other potential applicants believe they will be treated. This means making certain that jobs are as intrinsically and extrinsically satisfying for the current workforce as possible. Organizations should also make conscious efforts to shape the perception of their employment brand by using online testimonials from current employees. These testimonials act as a sort of virtual equivalent of word of mouth. Although job seekers will likely be somewhat skeptical of any information on a corporate website, a testimonial from someone who works at the organization is still likely to be more persuasive than a conventional sales pitch.

Recruitment Brochures

A recruitment brochure is usually sent or given directly to job applicants. Information in the brochure may be very detailed, and hence, the brochure may be lengthy. A brochure not only covers information about the job but also communicates information about the organization and its location. It may include pictures in addition to written narrative in order to illustrate various aspects of the job, such as the city in which the organization is located and actual coworkers. These various means of demonstrating the features of the organization enhance the richness of this recruiting technique.

The advantage of a brochure is that the organization controls who receives a copy. Also, it can be lengthier than an advertisement. A disadvantage is that it can be quite costly to develop. And because it is obviously a sales pitch made by the organization, it might be seen as less credible.

A successful brochure possesses (1) a unique theme or point of view relative to other organizations in the same industry and (2) a visual distinctiveness in terms of design and photographs. A good format for the brochure is to begin with a general description of the organization, including its history and culture (values, goals, "brand"). A description of the hiring process should come next, followed by a characterization of pay/benefits and performance reviews. Finally, the brochure should conclude with contact information.

Videos and Videoconferencing

A video can be used along with the brochure, but it should not simply replicate the brochure. The brochure should be used to communicate general information, and the video should be used to communicate the culture and climate of the organization. Professional Marketing Services, Inc., in Milwaukee, Wisconsin, helps organizations develop a profile of themselves. As part of the profile, the organization can highlight characteristics of the city in which it resides, such as the climate, housing market, school systems, churches, performing arts, spectator sports, nightlife, and festivals. Video presentations can also be made interactive so that the job seeker can submit an application electronically, request additional information, or even arrange an interview.

Another form of communicating with job applicants is known as videoconferencing.[60] Rather than meet in person with applicants, organizational representatives meet with applicants face to face on a monitor, in separate locations. Online services such as Skype can also be used for videoconferencing. The technology needed for videoconferencing was expensive in the past, but the costs have decreased in recent years. Moreover, this technology makes it possible for the organization to screen applicants at multiple or remote locations without actually having to travel to those locations. The result is that a one-time investment in videoconference technology can ultimately result in a net cost savings, as the expenses associated with travel are eliminated. Many college placement offices now have the equipment for videoconferencing.

Advertisements

Given the expense of advertising in business publications, ads are much shorter and to the point than recruitment brochures. Unfortunately, because of the short duration of most advertisements, they typically cannot provide rich information. As a general rule, the higher the circulation of the publication, the greater the cost of advertising in it.

Ads appear in a variety of places other than business publications. Ads can be found in local, regional, and national newspapers; on television and radio; and in bargain shoppers, door hangers, direct mail, and welcome wagons. Advertisements can thus be used to reach a broad market segment. There are many different types of ads:[61]

1. *Classified advertisements.* These ads appear in alphabetical order in the "Help Wanted" section of the newspaper. Typically, they allow for very limited type and style selection and are usually only one newspaper column in width. These ads are used most often for quick résumé solicitation for low-level jobs at a low cost. Most large and medium-sized newspapers now place their classified ads online, potentially reaching many more prospective job candidates. Although there has been a major shift toward the use of electronic recruiting, surveys suggest that print ads remain a significant presence in the recruiting of hourly workers.

2. *Classified display ads.* A classified display ad allows more discretion in the type that is used and its location in the paper. A classified display ad does not have to appear in alphabetical order and can appear in any section of the newspaper. The cost of these ads is moderate; they are often used to announce openings for professional and managerial jobs. An example of a classified display ad is shown in Exhibit 5.8.

3. *Display ads.* These ads allow for freedom of design and placement in a publication. Thus, they are very expensive and begin to resemble recruitment brochures. These ads are typically used when an employer is searching for a large number of applicants to fill multiple openings.

4. *Online ads.* More and more, employers are choosing to place ads on the Internet. These ads can take several forms. One form is a clickable banner ad that appears on websites visited by likely prospects. Another form of advertising of sorts was reviewed earlier—posting positions using online websites such as *Monster.com*. Still other employers set up user accounts on social networking websites.

5. *Radio and television ads.* Organizations that advertise on the radio or on television purchase a 30- or 60-second time slot to advertise openings in specific job categories. Choice of stations and broadcast times will target specific audiences. For example, a classical music radio station will likely draw in different applicants than would a contemporary pop music radio station; an all-sports network will draw in different applicants than would a cooking program. Radio and television stations often have detailed demographic information available to potential advertisers. Some recruiting experts propose that advertising through a variety of community radio stations or cable access television programs is an ideal way to improve workforce diversity. The advantage of radio and television advertisements is their reach. Individuals who are already searching for jobs generally read help wanted ads, whereas those who are not currently looking for jobs are more likely to hear radio and television ads. Being able to expand the potential job pool to include those

EXHIBIT 5.8   Classified Display Ad for Human Resource Generalist

HUMAN RESOURCE GENERALIST

ABC Health, a leader in the health care industry, currently has a position available for an experienced **Human Resource Generalist.**

This position will serve on the human resources team, which serves as a business partner with our operational departments. Our team prides itself on developing and maintaining progressive and impactful human resources policies and programs.

Qualified candidates for this position will possess a bachelor's degree in business with an emphasis on human resource management, or a degree in a related field, such as industrial psychology. In addition, a minimum of three years of experience as a human resource generalist is required. This experience should include exposure to at least four of the following functional areas: compensation, employment, benefits, training, employee relations, and performance management.

In return for your contributions, we offer a competitive salary as well as comprehensive, flexible employee benefits. If you meet the qualifications and our opportunity is attractive to you, please forward your résumé and salary expectations to:

Human Resource Department
ABC Health
P.O. Box 123
Pensacola, FL 12345
An Equal Opportunity/Affirmative Action Employer

who are not actively looking for work can be a real advantage in a tight labor market.

Organizational Websites

The web is unique in that it may function as both a recruitment source and a recruitment medium. When a web page only serves to communicate information about the job or organization to potential applicants, it serves as a recruitment medium. However, when a web page attracts actual applicants, particularly when applicants are allowed to apply online, it also functions as a recruitment source.

It may not be an overstatement to conclude that organizational websites have become the single most important medium through which organizations communicate with potential applicants. Nearly every large organization has a careers page on its website, and many small organizations have company and point-of-contact information for job seekers. Websites are a powerful means of not only communicating information about jobs but also reaching applicants who otherwise would not bother (or know how or where) to apply. Thus, care must be taken to ensure that the organizational website is appealing to potential job candidates.

The three core attributes driving the appeal of an organizational website are engagement, functionality, and content. First, the website must be vivid and attractive to applicants. Some experts have noted that in recruiting websites, engagement often takes a back seat. Second, while engagement is important, at the same time the website must be functional, meaning that it is quick to load, easily navigated, and interactive. A website that is overly complex may be vivid, but it will only generate frustration if it is hard to decipher or slow to load. Third, an organizational website must convey the information prospective applicants want to see, including current position openings, job requirements, and steps for applying. Finally, it is important to remember that communication with an applicant shouldn't end with his or her online application. Apple's website, for example, allows applicants to track the status of their application for 90 days after they apply. Procter and Gamble does the same thing (online is the only way applicants can apply), using a process eased by software that automatically scores its online applications. These technological advances may not be feasible for every website, but applicants still need to be informed about the status of their application.[62]

One way to ensure that the website meets these requirements is to test it with "naïve" users—people who are not from the organization's IT department or recruiting staff. It is critical that the number of clicks is minimized, that the online application process is clear, and that animation and color are used effectively to engage the prospective applicant. However, it is important not to overdo it. When *Coach.com*, a leather retailer, removed flash graphics from its website, page visits increased by 45%.[63]

Of course, there is more to designing an organizational website than just the three attributes discussed above. Exhibit 5.9 provides a thorough list of factors to keep in mind when designing a website for organizational recruitment.

Direct Contact

In contrast to the methods of brochures, videos, websites, and advertising, some organizations contact respondents directly to enhance recruiting outcomes. The two most common media for direct contact are telephone messages and e-mail. These techniques are much more personal than the other methods of recruiting because the applicants are specifically approached by the organization. Personal contacts are likely to be seen as more credible by respondents. In addition, messages delivered through direct contact often allow respondents to ask personally relevant questions, which obviously should enhance the richness of the information.

However, in the age of spamming, it is important to remember that most individuals will regard mass e-mailings or automated telephone messages with even less enthusiasm than that for junk mail. To make the most out of e-mail recruitment, the messages should be highly personal, reflecting an understanding of the candidate's

---
EXHIBIT 5.9 **Factors for Designing Organizational Websites**

1. *Keep it simple*—surveys reveal that potential job candidates are overwhelmed by complex, difficult-to-navigate websites; never sacrifice clarity for "jazziness"—remember, a good applicant is there for the content, not for the bells and whistles.
2. *Make access easy; web page and links should be easy to download*—studies reveal that individuals will not wait more than eight seconds for a page to download, so that four-color page that looks great will backfire if it takes the user, working from a modem, too much time to download it (also make sure that the link to the recruiting site on the home page is prominently displayed).
3. *Provide an online application form*—increasingly, potential candidates expect to be able to submit an application online; online forms are not only desired by candidates, organizations can load them directly into searchable databases.
4. *Provide information about company culture*—allow applicants to self-select out if their values clearly do not match those of your organization.
5. *Include selected links to relevant websites*—the words "selected" and "relevant" are key here; things to include might be a cost-of-living calculator and a career advice area.
6. *Make sure necessary information is conveyed to avoid confusion*—clearly specify job title, location, etc., so applicants know the job for which they are applying and, if there are several jobs, they don't apply for the wrong job.
7. *Keep information current*—make sure position information is updated regularly (e.g., weekly).
8. *Evaluate and track the results*—periodically evaluate the performance of the website on the basis of various criteria (number of hits, number of applications, application/hits ratio, quality of hires, cost of maintenance, user satisfaction, time to hire, etc.).

unique qualifications. Providing a working response e-mail address or telephone number that allows respondents to ask questions about the job opening will also help increase the yield for the direct contact method. However, personalization and customized responding to questions obviously will increase the cost per individual contacted, so the trade-offs in terms of cost must be considered.

APPLICANT REACTIONS

An important source of information in designing and implementing an effective recruitment system is applicant reactions. Both attitudinal and behavioral reactions to components of the recruitment system are important. Components of this system that have been studied include the recruiter and the recruitment process.

Reactions to Recruiters

Considerable research has been conducted and carefully reviewed on the reactions of job applicants to the behavior and characteristics of recruiters.[64] The data collected have been somewhat limited by the fact that they focus primarily on reactions to college rather than noncollege recruiters. Despite this limitation, several key themes emerge in the literature.

First, though the recruiter does indeed influence job applicant reactions, he or she does not have as much influence on them as do actual characteristics of the job. Applicants' interest in a job is strongly predicted by the work environment, the organization's image, and the location. This indicates that the recruiter cannot be viewed as a substitute for a well-defined and well-communicated recruitment message showing the actual characteristics of the job. Just having good recruiters is not enough to attract applicants to the organization.

Second, the influence of the recruiter is more likely to be felt in the attitudes rather than in the behaviors of the job applicant. That is, an applicant who has been exposed to a talented recruiter is more likely to walk away with a favorable impression of the recruiter than to accept a job on the basis of the interaction with a recruiter. This attitudinal effect is important, however, as it may lead to good publicity for the organization. In turn, good publicity may lead to a larger applicant pool to draw from in the future.

Third, demographic characteristics of the recruiter do not have much impact on applicant reactions. Respondents are largely indifferent regarding interviewer gender and function.

Fourth, two behaviors of the recruiter seem to have the largest influence on applicant reactions. The first is the level of warmth that the recruiter shows toward the job applicant. Warmth can be expressed by being enthusiastic, personable, empathetic, and helpful in dealings with the candidate. The second behavior is being knowledgeable about the job. This can be conveyed by being well versed with the job requirements matrix and the job rewards matrix. Finally, recruiters who show interest in the applicant are viewed more positively.

Reactions to the Recruitment Process

Only some administrative components of the recruitment process have been shown to have an impact on applicant reactions.[65] Research suggests that above all else, applicants want a system that is fair. First, job applicants are more likely to have favorable reactions to the recruitment process when the screening devices used to narrow the applicant pool are seen as job related. That is, the process that is used should be closely related to the content of the job as spelled out in the job requirements matrix. Applicants also see recruiting processes as more fair if they have an opportunity to perform or demonstrate their ability to do the job.

Second, delay times in the recruitment process do indeed have a negative effect on applicants' reactions. In particular, when long delays occur between the applicant's expression of interest and the organization's response, the applicant forms negative reactions about the organization but not about himself or herself. For example, with a long delay between an on-site visit and a job offer, an applicant is more likely to believe that something is wrong with the organization rather than with his or her personal qualifications. This is especially true of the better-qualified candidate, who is likely to act on these feelings by accepting another job offer.

Third, the influence of the recruiter on the applicant is more likely to occur in the initial rather than the latter stages of the recruitment process. In the latter stages, actual characteristics of the job carry more weight in the applicant's decision. At the initial screening interview, the recruiter may be the applicant's only contact with the organization. Later in the process, the applicant is more likely to have additional information about the job and organization. Hence, the credibility of the recruiter is most critical on initial contact with applicants.

Finally, though little research is available, the increasing use of the Internet in recruitment, and that it is often the applicant's first exposure to an organization, suggests that applicants' reactions to an organization's website will increasingly drive their reactions to the recruitment process.

Indeed, studies reveal that applicants are able to locate more relevant jobs on the Internet than in traditional sources such as print media. Moreover, applicants generally like the Internet, provided some provisos are kept in mind. As with general recruiting, perhaps the most important factor is the degree and speed of follow-up; delays greatly harm the image of the recruiting organization, so organizations need to make sure that online applications are followed up. Also, research shows that job seekers are more satisfied with organization websites when specific job information is provided and security provisions are taken to preserve the confidentiality of the information submitted. One key assurance is that the organization will not share résumés with vendors that will spam applicants with various solicitations.[66]

Reactions to Diversity Issues

In addition to tailoring messages to reach employees with specific KSAO profiles, some organizations also target specific underrepresented groups, such as women and racioethnic minorities. Such efforts are among the most effective, and the least controversial, elements of AAPs. One of the most common methods for increasing the diversity of applicant pools is to advertise in publications targeted at women and minorities. Surveys of job seekers show that women and minorities are especially interested in working for employers that endorse diversity through policy statements and in recruiting materials. Advertisements depicting groups of diverse employees are seen as more attractive to women and racioethnic minorities, which is probably why most organizations depict workforce diversity prominently in their recruiting materials. Effective depiction of diversity should take job functions into account as well; diversity advertisements that fail to show women and minorities in positions of organizational leadership send a negative message about the diversity climate at an organization.[67]

Some organizations are also aiming to increase the age diversity of the workforce by targeting older workers. Many traditional recruiting methods, like campus recruiting and job fairs, draw in a primarily younger workforce. However, as noted in Chapter 3, there has been an increase in the proportion of the workforce over 50 years of age that is likely to persist. These older workers are often highly qualified and experienced, and thus attractive candidates for recruiting, but a different targeted approach is required to bring them in. Mature workers are attracted by flexible schedules, health and pension benefits, and part-time opportunities, so the presence of such programs should be noted in recruiting advertisements.

TRANSITION TO SELECTION

Once a job seeker has been identified and attracted to the organization, the organization needs to prepare the person for the selection process. In preparation, applicants need to be made aware of the next steps in the hiring process and what will be required of them. If the recruiting organization overlooks this transition step, it may lose qualified applicants who mistakenly think that delays between steps in the hiring process indicate that the organization is no longer interested in them or who are fearful that they "didn't have what it takes" to successfully compete in the next steps.

The city of Columbus, Ohio, has done an excellent job preparing job seekers from external recruitment sources to apply for the position of firefighter. To become a firefighter, an applicant must pass a series of physical ability exams in which he or she must go through an obstacle course, carry heavy equipment up stairs, and complete a number of other timed physical exercises. Many applicants have never encountered these types of tests before and are afraid that they don't have the physical ability to successfully complete them.

To prepare job seekers and applicants for these tests, videotapes were developed that give instructions for taking the tests and actually show a firefighter taking the tests. The videos are shown to those who have applied for the position, and they are also shown on public access television for those who are thinking about applying for the job. The city of Columbus also provides upper-body strength training, as this is a stumbling point for some job applicants in the selection process.

This example indicates that to successfully prepare people for the transition to selection, organizations should consider reviewing the selection method instructions with the applicants, showing them actual samples of the selection method and providing them with practice or training if necessary. These steps should be followed not just for physical ability tests but for all selection methods in the hiring process that are likely to be unfamiliar to applicants or uncomfortable for them.

LEGAL ISSUES

External recruitment practices are subject to considerable legal scrutiny and influence. During recruitment there is ample room for the organization to exclude certain applicant groups (e.g., minorities, women, and people with disabilities), as well as deceive in its dealings with applicants. Various laws and regulations seek to limit these exclusionary and deceptive practices.

Legal issues regarding several of the practices are discussed in this section. These include definition of job applicants, AAPs, electronic recruitment, job advertisements, and fraud and misrepresentation.

Definition of a Job Applicant

Both the Equal Employment Opportunity Commission (EEOC) and the Office of Federal Contract Compliance Programs (OFCCP) require the organization to keep applicant records. Exactly what is a job applicant and what records should be kept? It is necessary to provide guidance on the answer to this question in terms of traditional hard-copy applicants and in terms of electronic applicants.

Hard-Copy Applicants

The original (1979) definition of an applicant by the EEOC is in the Uniform Guidelines on Employee Selection Procedures (UGESP). It reads as follows: "The precise definition of the term 'applicant' depends on the user's recruitment and selection procedures. The concept of an applicant is that of a person who has indicated an interest in being considered for hiring, promotion, or other employment opportunities. This interest may be expressed by completing an application form, or might be expressed orally, depending on the employer's practice."

This definition was created prior to the existence of the electronic job application. It remains in force for hard-copy applications. Because it is so open ended, it could create a substantial record-keeping burden for the organization since any contact with the organization by a person might count as an application for enforcement purposes. Hence, it is advisable for the organization to formulate and strictly adhere to written application policies and procedures that are communicated to organizational representatives and to all persons acting as though they are job applicants. Several suggestions for doing this follow.

First, require a written application from all who seek to be considered, and communicate this policy to all potential applicants. Inform people who apply by other means that they must submit a written application in order to be considered. If this policy is not defined, virtually anyone who contacts the organization or expresses interest by any means could be considered an applicant. Second, require that the applicant indicate the precise position applied for, and establish written minimum qualifications for each position. This way, the organization can legitimately refuse to consider as applicants those who do not meet these requirements. Third, establish a definite period for which the position will remain open, communicate this clearly to applicants, and do not consider those who apply after the deadline. Also, do not keep applications on hold or on file for future consideration. Fourth, return unsolicited applications through the mail. Finally, keep track of applicants who drop out of the process due to lack of interest or acceptance of another job. Such suggestions will help the organization limit the number of "true" applicants and reduce record keeping while also fostering legal compliance.[68]

Internet Applicants

The OFCCP regulations (the Internet Applicant rule) provide a definition of an Internet applicant for federal contractors, as well as establish record-keeping requirements.[69] The EEOC has not yet provided a definition of an Internet applicant, though it is in the process of developing one.

According to the OFCCP, an individual must meet all four of the following criteria to be considered an Internet applicant:

- The individual submits an expression of interest in employment through the Internet or related electronic data technologies.
- The employer considers the individual for employment in a particular position.
- The individual's expression of interest indicates that the individual possesses the basic qualifications for the position.
- At no point in the employer's selection process prior to receiving an offer of employment from the employer does the individual remove himself or herself from further consideration or otherwise indicate that he or she is no longer interested in the position.

"Internet or related electronic data technologies" includes electronic mail/e-mail, résumé databases, job banks, electronic scanning technology, applicant tracking system/applicant service providers, applicant screeners, and résumé submission by fax. Mobile and hand-held devices such as cell and smart phones are also likely included. "Basic qualifications for the position" are those established in advance and advertised to potential applicants. They must be noncomparative across applicants, objective (e.g., BS in biology), and relevant to performance in the specific position.

The employer must keep records of the following:

- All expressions of interest submitted through the Internet and contacts made with the job applicant

- Internal résumé databases—including date of entry, the position for which each search was made, the date of the search, and the search criteria used
- External résumé databases—position for which each search was made, the date of the search, search criteria used, and the records for each person who met the basic qualifications for the position

The OFCCP regulations also require the employer to make every reasonable effort to gather race/gender/ethnicity data from both traditional and Internet applicants. The preferred method for doing so is voluntary self-disclosure, such as through tear-off sheets on an application form, postcards, short forms to request the information, or as part of an initial telephone screen. Observation may also be used.

The employer must keep records relating to adverse impact calculations for Internet applicants and for all test takers.

Affirmative Action Programs

As discussed in Chapter 2, AAP regulations from the OFCCP require that the organization identify problem areas impeding EEO and undertake action-oriented programs to correct these problem areas and achieve the placement (hiring and promotion) goals. The regulations say little else specifically about recruitment activities. Based on former (now expired) regulations, however, the OFCCP offered considerable guidance to the organization for its recruitment actions:

- Update job descriptions and ensure their accuracy.
- Widely circulate approved job descriptions to hiring managers and recruitment sources.
- Carefully select and train all personnel included in staffing.
- Reach out to organizations prepared to refer women and minority applicants, such as the Urban League, state employment (job) services, National Organization for Women, sectarian women's groups, and so forth.
- Conduct formal briefings, preferably on organization premises, for representatives from recruiting sources.
- Encourage women and minority employees to refer job applicants.
- Include women and minorities on the HR department staff.
- Actively participate in job fairs.
- Actively recruit at secondary schools and community colleges with predominantly minority and female enrollment.
- Use special employment programs, such as internships, work/study, and summer jobs.

- Include minorities and women in the planning and production of recruitment brochures.
- Expand help-wanted advertising to include female and minority news media.

Taken in total, the OFCCP suggestions indicate that organizations with AAPs should undertake targeted recruitment programs using recruitment staff trained in affirmative action recruiting.

Electronic Recruitment

Technology has flooded the recruitment process for both the organization and job applicants. Numerous legal issues arise.

Access

The use of electronic recruitment technologies has the potential to create artificial barriers to employment opportunities.[70] It assumes that potential applicants have access to computers and the skills necessary to apply online. These may be poor assumptions, especially for some racial minorities and the economically disadvantaged. To guard against legal challenge and to ensure accessibility, the organization might do several things. One action is to supplement online recruitment with other widely used sources of recruitment, such as newspaper advertisements or other sources that organizational experience indicates are frequently used by women and minorities. Alternately, online recruitment and application could be restricted to certain jobs that have strong computer-related KSAO requirements. Applicants in all likelihood will have easy access to computers and online recruitment, as well as the skills necessary to successfully navigate and complete the application.

Another access issue is the use of recruitment software that conducts résumé searches within an applicant database using keyword search criteria. Staffing specialists or hiring managers often specify the search criteria to use, and they could select non-job-related criteria that cause adverse impact against women, minorities, or people with disabilities. Examples of such criteria include preferences for graduation from elite colleges or universities, age, and physical requirements. To guard against such a possibility, the organization should set only job-related KSAO requirements, restrict the search criteria to those KSAOs, and train recruiters in the appropriate specification and use of search criteria.

People With Disabilities

The OFCCP provides specific regulations for people with disabilities.[71] If the employer routinely offers applicants various methods (including online) of applying for a job and all are treated equally, that may be sufficient for compliance purposes. If only an online application system is used, however, the online system must be made accessible to all. Examples here include making the organization's website compatible with screen readers and using assistive technology and adaptive software.

The regulations also indicate that the employer is obligated to provide reasonable accommodation to the applicant, if requested. Examples include the following:

- Making job vacancy application information available in Braille and responding to job inquiries via telecommunications devices for the deaf (TDDs) or use of the telephone relay system
- Providing readers, interpreters, or similar assistance during the application process
- Extending the time limit for completing an online examination
- Making testing locations fully accessible to those with mobility impairments

Video Résumés

Video résumés can reveal protected class characteristics (e.g., race, sex, color, and disability) about applicants that can easily enter into the screening decision by recruiters and managers, resulting in illegal discrimination.[72] To guard against this possibility, the organization needs to take certain steps. First, create specific KSAO requirements against which applicants can be screened. Second, redesign the initial screening process so that only the applicant's résumé or application is reviewed. Third, disallow video résumés or only allow them later in the hiring process. Fourth, provide training to recruiters and managers on how to evaluate applicants' video résumé information against the job's KSAOs and on the need for great care in not allowing protected class information to enter into their evaluations of applicants.

Social Networks

Recruiters might be tempted to troll for and access private information placed on social networks such as Facebook, LinkedIn, and Twitter. Information about potential job applicants is thus obtained outside of a traditional, carefully constructed recruitment/application process. Problems may arise.[73]

Social networks may contain applicant pools of limited diversity, creating adverse impact possibilities. Another problem is the quality and legality of information obtained. Legally protected characteristics are readily available, ranging from demographics to marital status, citizenship, and sexual orientation. On top of that, applicant information may not be accurate or job related, and it may even be maliciously planted. Finally, use of the information may run afoul of state/local statutes prohibiting the consideration of lawful off-duty conduct by the applicant (e.g., smoking, drinking, medical use of marijuana, political activity).

How might the organization proceed down this new, evolving legal path? One option is to simply not use social networks in recruitment. Another option is to use them, but with constraints. Examples include requiring that social networks only be used in combination with other recruitment tools and resources, using only clearly job-related (KSAO relevant) information from the network, and providing training to recruiters and hiring managers about social network usage and record-keeping requirements under the Internet Applicant rule.

Job Advertisements

Job advertising that indicates preferences or limitations for applicants based on legally protected characteristics is generally prohibited (see Chapter 2). Questions continually arise as to exceptions or less blatant forms of advertising, as the following examples indicate.[74]

Title VII permits indicating preferences based on sex, religion, or national origin (but not race or color) if they are bona fide occupational qualification (BFOQs). The organization should be sure about the legality and validity of any BFOQ claims before conducting such advertising. Use of gender-specific job titles such as waitress or repairman, however, generally should be avoided.

Using the phrase "women and minorities are encouraged to apply" in a job advertisement is okay because it is an inclusive effort to generate the largest pool of qualified applicants. An indication that the organization is "seeking" a particular type of applicant (e.g., stay-at-home moms), however, is not permitted, because it connotes a preference for a particular group rather than an encouragement to apply.

Regarding age preferences, advertisements cannot limit or deter potential older applicants from seeking a position. It is permissible, however, to show a preference for older workers, using phrases such as "over age 60," "retirees," or "supplement your pension."

These examples show that the line between permissible and prohibited ad content is quite murky. The organization thus should monitor the construction and content of all its job advertisements.

Fraud and Misrepresentation

Puffery, promises, half-truths, and even outright lies are all encountered in recruitment under the guise of selling the applicant on the job and the organization. Too much of this type of selling can be legally dangerous. When it occurs, under workplace tort law, applicants may file suit claiming fraud or misrepresentation.[75] Claims may cite false statements of existing facts (e.g., the nature and profitability of the employer's business) or false promises of future events (e.g., promises about terms and conditions of employment, pay, promotion opportunities, and geographic location). It does not matter if the false statements were made intentionally (fraud) or negligently (misrepresentation). Both types of statements are a reasonable basis for a claim by an applicant or newly hired employee.

To be successful in such a suit, the plaintiff must demonstrate that

1. A misrepresentation occurred.
2. The employer knew, or should have known, about the misrepresentation.
3. The plaintiff relied on the information to make a decision or take action.
4. The plaintiff was injured because of reliance placed on the statements made by the employer.[76]

Though these four requirements may appear to be a stiff set of hurdles for the plaintiff, they are by no means insurmountable, as many successful plaintiffs can attest. Avoidance of fraud and misrepresentation claims in recruitment requires straightforward action by the organization and its recruiters. First, provide applicants with the job description and specific, truthful information about the job rewards. Second, be truthful about the nature of the business and its profitability. Third, avoid specific promises about future events regarding terms and conditions of employment or business plans and profitability. Finally, make sure that all recruiters follow these suggestions when they recruit job applicants.

SUMMARY

The objective of the external recruitment process is to identify and attract qualified applicants to the organization. To meet this objective, the organization must conduct recruitment planning. At this stage, attention must be given to both organizational issues (e.g., centralized versus decentralized recruitment function) and administrative issues (e.g., size of the budget). Particular care needs to be taken in selecting and training recruiters.

The next stage in external recruitment is the development of a strategy. The strategy should consider open versus targeted recruitment, recruitment sources, and the choice of sources. Multiple sources should be used to identify specific applicant populations. There are trade-offs involved with any source used to identify applicants; thus the source should be carefully reviewed prior to using it.

The next stage is to develop a message to give to the job applicants and to select a medium to convey that message. The message may be realistic, branded, or targeted. There is no one best message; it depends on the characteristics of the labor market, the job, and the applicants. The message can be communicated through brochures, videos, advertisements, voice messages, videoconferencing, online services, radio, or e-mail, each of which has strengths and weaknesses.

Applicants are influenced by characteristics of recruiters and the recruitment process. Through proper attention to these characteristics, the organization can help provide applicants with a favorable recruitment experience. That experience can be continued by carefully preparing applicants for the selection process.

Recruitment practices and decisions come under intense legal scrutiny because of their potential for discrimination at the beginning of the staffing process. The legal definition of a job applicant creates record-keeping requirements for the organization that, in turn, have major implications for the design of the entire recruitment process. Affirmative Action Program Regulations likewise affect the entire recruitment process, prodding the organization to set targeted placement goals for women and minorities and to be aggressive in recruitment outreach actions. Electronic recruitment has the potential to create legal quagmires, including lack of access to online application and recruitment by some disadvantaged applicants; résumé searches of databases using keyword search criteria that may be exclusionary of women, minorities, and people with disabilities; websites that are not screen-reader friendly for those who are visually impaired; and video résumés that reveal protected class characteristics to recruiters and hiring managers. Job advertisements may not contain applicant preferences regarding protected characteristics such as age and gender. Finally, recruitment communication with applicants must be careful to avoid false statements or promises, lest problems of fraud and misrepresentation arise.

DISCUSSION QUESTIONS

1. List and briefly describe each of the administrative issues that needs to be addressed in the planning stage of external recruiting.
2. List 10 sources of applicants that organizations turn to when recruiting. For each source, identify needs specific to the source, as well as pros and cons of using the source for recruitment.
3. In designing the communication message to be used in external recruiting, what kinds of information should be included?
4. What are the advantages of conveying a realistic recruitment message as opposed to portraying the job in a way that the organization thinks that job applicants want to hear?
5. What strategies are organizations using to ensure that they are able to attract women and underrepresented racioethnic groups?

ETHICAL ISSUES

1. Many organizations adopt a targeted recruitment strategy. For example, some organizations have targeted workers 50 years of age and older in their recruitment efforts, which includes advertising specifically in media outlets

frequented by older individuals. Other organizations target recruitment messages at women, minorities, or those with the desired skills. Do you think targeted recruitment systems are fair? Why or why not?

2. Most organizations have job boards on their web page where applicants can apply for jobs online. What ethical obligations, if any, do you think organizations have to individuals who apply for jobs online?

APPLICATIONS

Improving a College Recruitment Program

The White Feather Corporation (WFC) is a rapidly growing consumer products organization that specializes in the production and sales of specialty household items such as lawn furniture cleaners, spa (hot tub) accessories, mosquito and tick repellents, and stain-resistant garage floor paints. The organization has 400 exempt employees and 3,000 nonexempt employees, almost all of whom are full time. In addition to its corporate office in Clucksville, Arkansas, the organization has five plants and two distribution centers at various rural locations throughout the state.

Two years ago WFC created a corporate HR department to provide centralized direction and control for its key HR functions—planning, compensation, training, and staffing. In turn, the staffing function is headed by the senior manager of staffing, who receives direct reports from three managers: the manager of nonexempt employment, the manager of exempt employment, and the manager of EEO/AA. Marianne Collins, the manager of exempt employment, has been with WFC for 10 years and has grown with the organization through a series of sales and sales management positions. She was chosen for her current position as a result of WFC's commitment to promotion from within, as well as her broad familiarity with the organization's products and customers. When Marianne was appointed, her key area of accountability was defined as college recruitment, with 50% of her time to be devoted to it.

In her first year, Marianne developed and implemented WFC's first-ever formal college recruitment program. Working with the HR planning person, WFC decided there was a need for 40 college graduate new hires by the end of the year. They were to be placed in the production, distribution, and marketing functions; specific job titles and descriptions were to be developed during the year. Armed with this forecast, Marianne began the process of recruitment planning and strategy development. The result was the following recruitment process.

Recruitment was to be conducted at 12 public and private schools throughout the state. Marianne contacted the placement office at each school and set up a one-day recruitment visit. All visits were scheduled during the first week in May. The placement office at each school set up 30-minute interviews (16 at each school) and made sure that applicants completed and had on file a standard application form.

To visit the schools and conduct the interviews, Marianne selected three young, up-and-coming managers (one each from production, distribution, and marketing) to be the recruiters. Each manager was assigned to four of the schools. Since none of the managers had any recruiting experience, Marianne conducted a recruitment briefing for them. During that briefing she reviewed the overall recruitment (hiring) goal, provided a brief rundown on each of the schools, and explained the specific tasks the recruiters were to perform. Those tasks were to pick up the application materials of the interviewees at the placement office prior to the interviews, review the materials, conduct the interviews in a timely manner (the managers were told they could ask any questions they wanted to that pertained to qualifications for the job), and at the end of the day complete an evaluation form on each applicant. The form asked for a 1–7 rating of overall qualifications for the job, written comments about strengths and weaknesses, and a recommendation of whether to invite the person for a second interview in Clucksville. These forms were to be returned to Marianne, who would review them and decide which people to invite for a second interview.

After the campus interviews were conducted, problems began to surface. Placement officials at some of the schools contacted Marianne and lodged several complaints. Among those complaints were that (1) one of the managers failed to pick up the application materials of the interviewees; (2) none of the managers were able to provide much information about the nature of the jobs they were recruiting for, especially jobs outside their own functional area; (3) the interviewers got off schedule early on, so applicants were kept waiting and others had shortened interviews as the managers tried to make up time; (4) none of the managers had any written information describing the organization and its locations; (5) one of the managers asked female applicants very personal questions about marriage plans, use of drugs and alcohol, and willingness to travel with male coworkers; (6) one of the managers talked incessantly during the interviews, leaving the interviewees little opportunity to present themselves and their qualifications; and (7) none of the managers were able to tell interviewees when they might be contacted regarding a second interview. In addition to these complaints, Marianne had difficulty getting the managers to complete and turn in their evaluation forms (they claimed they were too busy, especially after being away from the job for a week). From the reports she did receive, Marianne extended invitations to 55 of the applicants for a second interview. Of these, 30 accepted the invitation. Ultimately, 25 people were given job offers, and 15 accepted.

To put it mildly, the first-ever college recruitment program was a disaster for WFC and Marianne. In addition to her embarrassment, Marianne was asked to meet with her boss and the president of WFC to explain what went wrong and to receive "guidance" from them as to their expectations for next year's recruitment program. Marianne subsequently learned that she would receive no merit pay increase for the year and that the three managers all received above-average merit increases.

To turn things around for the second year of college recruitment, Marianne realized that she needed to engage in a thorough process of recruitment planning and strategy development. As she began this undertaking, her analysis of past events led her to conclude that one of her key mistakes was to naïvely assume that the three managers would actually know how to be good recruiters and were motivated to do the job effectively. Marianne first decided to use 12 managers as recruiters, assigning one to each of the 12 campuses. She also decided that more than a recruitment briefing was needed. She determined that an intensive, one-day training program must be developed and given to the managers prior to the beginning of the recruitment "season."

You work in HR at another organization in Clucksville and are a professional acquaintance of Marianne's. Knowing that you have experience in both college recruiting and training, Marianne calls you for some advice. She asks you if you would be willing to meet and discuss the following questions:

1. What topics should be covered in the training program?
2. What materials and training aids will be needed for the program?
3. What skills should the trainees actually practice during the training?
4. Who should conduct the training?
5. What other changes might have to be made to ensure that the training has a strong impact on the managers and that during the recruitment process they are motivated to use what they learned in training?

Internet Recruiting

Selma Williams is a recruiter for Mervin/McCall-Hall (MMH), a large publisher of educational textbooks (K–12 and college). Fresh out of college, Selma has received her first big assignment at MMH, and it is a tough one—develop an Internet recruitment strategy for the entire organization. Previously, MMH had relied on the traditional recruitment methods—college recruiting, word of mouth, newspaper advertisements, and search firms. As more and more of MMH's textbook business is connected to the web, however, it became clear to Selma's boss, Jon Beerfly, that MMH needs to consider upgrading its recruitment process. Accordingly, after Selma had acclimated herself to MMH and had worked on a few smaller recruitment projects (including doing a fair amount of recruiting at college campuses in the past three months), Jon described her new assignment to her, concluding, "Selma, I really don't know much about this. I'm going to leave it to you to come up with a set of recommendations about what we ought to be doing. We just had a new intern come into the office for a stint in HR, and I'm going to assign this person to you to help on this project." Assume that you are the intern.

At your first meeting, you and Selma discuss many different issues and agree that regardless of whatever else is done, MMH must have a recruitment area on the corporate website. After further discussion, Selma gives you several assignments toward this objective:

1. Look at three to five corporate websites that have a recruitment area and note their major features, strengths, and weaknesses (see Exhibit 5.7).
2. Interview three to five students who have used the recruitment area on a corporate website and ask them what they most liked and disliked about the recruitment areas.
3. Prepare a brief report that (a) summarizes your findings from assignments #1 and #2 and (b) recommends the design features that you and Selma will develop for inclusion in the MMH website.

TANGLEWOOD STORES CASE

You have just learned about many of the major methods organizations use to encourage individuals to apply for vacancies. The recruiting case will provide an opportunity to see how staffing managers can use organizational data to resolve an internal dispute regarding which recruiting methods work best. In addition, the assignment will demonstrate how contextual factors can bring out different strengths of the various recruiting methods.

The Situation

Tanglewood is engaged in a process of centralization. Previously, each individual store made most of the staffing decisions, but the corporate offices would like to see more consistency. They also believe that the stores can learn a great deal by comparing their experiences across locations. You are provided data from Tanglewood's recruiting outcomes from four geographic regions. These data are supplemented with narrative reports from the organization's managerial focus groups pertaining to the fit between applicants and the unique requirements of Tanglewood's culture.

Your Tasks

You will assess the information about recruitment sources and the recruitment process provided by four divisions of Tanglewood Stores. You will then recommend which methods of recruiting are most likely to be successful, and also recommend whether the organization should use open or targeted recruiting. Once you have determined the best course of action, you will create a recruitment guide for the organization like the one presented in Exhibit 5.3. Finally, you will develop recruiting messages by considering the message and the medium by which information will be provided. The background information for this case, and your specific assignment, can be found at *www.mhhe.com/heneman7e*.

ENDNOTES

1. M. N. Martinez, "Recruiting Here and There," *HR Magazine*, Sept. 2002, pp. 95–100.

2. P. O. Ángel and L. S. Sánchez, "R&D Managers' Adaptation of Firms' HRM Practices," *R&D Management*, 2009, 39, pp. 271–290.

3. "Cutting Corners to the Best Candidates," *Weddle's*, Oct. 5, 2004 (*www.weddles.com*).

4. I. J. Shaver, "Innovative Techniques Lure Quality Workers to NASA," *Personnel Journal*, Aug. 1990, pp. 100–106.

5. R. D. Gatewood, M. A. Gowen, and G. Lautenschlager, "Corporate Image, Recruitment Image, and Initial Job Choice Decisions," *Academy of Management Journal*, 1993, 36(2), pp. 414–427.

6. J. Whitman, "The Four A's of Recruiting Help Enhance Search for Right Talent," *Workforce Management Online*, Nov. 2009 (*www.workforce.com*).

7. D. Dahl, "Recruiting: Tapping the Talent Pool . . . Without Drowning in Résumés," *Inc.*, Apr. 2009, pp. 121–122.

8. J. A. Breaugh and M. Starkee, "Research on Employee Recruitment: So Many Studies, So Many Questions," *Journal of Management*, 2000, 26, pp. 405–434; R. E. Thaler-Carter, "In-House Recruiters Fill a Specialized Niche," *HR Magazine*, Apr. 1998, pp. 72–78.

9. S. L. Rynes and J. W. Boudreau, "College Recruiting Practices in Large Organizations: Practice, Evaluation, and Research Implications," *Personnel Psychology*, 1986, 39(3), pp. 286–310; S. A. Carless and A. Imber, "The Influence of Perceived Interviewer and Job and Organizational Characteristics on Applicant Attraction and Job Choice Intentions: The Role of Applicant Anxiety," *International Journal of Selection and Assessment*, 2007, 15, pp. 359–371.

10. J. Sullivan, "Becoming a Great Recruiter," in N. C. Burkholder, P. J. Edwards, and L. Sartain (eds.), *On Staffing* (Hoboken, NJ: Wiley, 2004), pp. 6–67.

11. C. Patton, "Recruiter Attack," *Human Resource Executive*, Nov. 2000, pp. 106–109; E. Zimmerman, "Fight Dirty Hiring Tactics," *Workforce*, May 2001, pp. 30–34.

12. D. H. Freedman, "The Monster Dilemma," *Inc.*, May 2007, pp. 77–78; J. Barthold, "Waiting in the Wings," *HR Magazine*, Apr. 2004, pp. 89–95; A. M. Chaker, "Luring Moms Back to Work," *New York Times*, Dec. 30, 2003, pp. D1–D2; B. McConnell, "Hiring Teens? Go Where They Are Hanging Out," *HR-News*, June 2002, p. 16; J. Mullich, "They Don't Retire Them, They Hire Them," *Workforce Management*, Dec. 2003, pp. 49–57; R. Rodriguez, "Tapping the Hispanic Labor Pool," *HR Magazine*, Apr. 2004, pp. 73–79; C. Wilson, "Rehiring Annuitants," *IPMA-HR News*, Aug. 2003, pp. 1–6.

13. B. L. Rau and M. M. Hyland, "Role Conflict and Flexible Work Arrangements: The Effects on Applicant Attraction," *Personnel Psychology*, 2002, 55, pp. 111–136.

14. F. Hansen, "Recruiting the Closer: Dealing With a Deal Maker," *Workforce Management Online*, Oct. 2007 (*www.workforce.com/archive/feature/25/18/58/index.php*).

15. R. T. Cober, D. J. Brown, P. E. Levy, and J. H. Shalhoop, *HR Professionals' Attitudes Toward and Use of the Internet for Employee Recruitment*, Executive Report, University of Akron and Society for Human Resource Management Foundation, 2003.

16. K. Maher, "Online Job Hunting Is Tough. Just Ask Vinnie," *Wall Street Journal*, June 24, 2003, pp. B1, B10; S. Taylor, "Clearing the Path," *Staffing Management*, Oct. 2008 (*www.shrm.org/publications/staffingmanagementmagazine*).

17. G. Ruiz, "Studies Examine the Online Job Hunting Experience," *Workforce Management Online*, July 2006 (*www.workforce.com/archive/feature/24/45/31/index.php*); D. G. Allen, R. V. Mahto, and R. F. Otondo, "Web-based Recruitment: Effects of Information, Organizational Brand, and Attitudes Toward a Web Site on Applicant Attraction," *Journal of Applied Psychology*, 2007, 92, pp. 1696–1708; P. W. Braddy, A. W. Meade, J. J. Michael, and J. W. Fleenor, "Internet Recruiting: Effects of Website Content on Viewers' Perception of Organizational Culture," *International Journal of Selection and Assessment*, 2009, 17, pp. 19–34; B. R. Dineen and R. A. Noe, "Effects of Customization on Application Decisions and Applicant Pool Characteristics in a Web-based Recruitment Context," *Journal of Applied Psychology*, 2009, 94, pp. 224–234.

18. I. Weller, B. C. Holtom, W. Matiaske, and T. Mellewigt, "Level and Time Effects of Recruitment Sources on Voluntary Employee Turnover," *Journal of Applied Psychology*, 2009, 94, pp. 1146–1162; S. Overman, "Use the Best to Find the Rest," *Staffing Management Magazine*, June 2008 (*www.shrm.org/publications/staffingmanagementmagazine*).

19. T. Cote and T. Armstrong, "Why Tweeting Has Become an Ad Agency's Main Job-Posting Strategy," *Workforce Management Online*, May 2009 (*www.workforce.com/section/06/feature/26/41/30*); F. Hansen, "Using Social Networking to Fill the Talent Acquisition Pipeline," *Workforce Management Online*, Dec. 2006 (*www.workforce.com/archive/feature/24/60/64/index.php*); E. Frauenheim, "Company Profile: Recruiters Get LinkedIn in Search of Job Candidates," *Workforce Management Online*, Nov. 2006 (*www.workforce.com/archive/feature/24/58/49/index.php*).

20. D. R. Avery, "Reactions to Diversity in Recruitment Advertising: Are the Differences Black and White?" *Journal of Applied Psychology*, 2003, 88, pp. 672–679; D. R. Avery and P. F. McKay, "Target Practice: An Organizational Impression Management Approach to Attracting Minority and Female Job Applicants," *Personnel Psychology*, 2006, 59, pp. 157–187.

21. Freedman, "The Monster Dilemma," pp. 77–78; R. Zeidner, "Companies Tell Their Stories in Recruitment Videos," *HR Magazine*, Dec. 2007, p. 28; J. Borzo, "Taking on the Recruiting Monster," *Fortune Small Business*, May 2007, p. 89; E. Frauenheim, "Logging Off Job Boards," *Workforce Management*, June 2009, pp. 25–29.

22. D. M. Cable and K.Y.T. Yu, "Managing Job Seekers' Organizational Image Beliefs: The Role of Media Richness and Media Credibility," *Journal of Applied Psychology*, 2006, 91, pp. 828–840.

23. G. Ruiz, "Newspapers, Job Boards Step Up Partnerships," *Workforce Management*, Dec. 11, 2006, pp. 17–18.

24. P. Babcock, "Narrowing the Pool: Employers Ponder Worth of Niche Job Sites, and Many Take the Plunge," *SHRM Online HR Technology Focus Area*, May 2007 (*www.shrm.org/outsourcing/library*).

25. Avery and McKay, "Target Practice: An Organizational Impression Management Approach to Attracting Minority and Female Job Applicants."

26. Cable and Yu, "Managing Job Seekers' Organizational Image Beliefs: The Role of Media Richness and Media Credibility."

27. S. Overman, "Do Your Hiring Homework," *Staffing Management Magazine*, Jan. 1, 2009 (*www.shrm.org/publications/staffingmanagementmagazine*).

28. J. Flato, "Key Success Factors for Managing Your Campus Recruiting Program: The Good Times and Bad," in Burkholder, Edwards, and Sartain (eds.), *On Staffing*, pp. 219–229; J. Floren, "Constructing a Campus Recruiting Network," *EMT*, Spring 2004, pp. 29–31; C. Joinson, "Red Hot College Recruiting," *Employment Management Today*, Oct. 4, 2002 (*www.shrm.org/emt*); J. Mullich, "College Recruitment Goes for Niches," *Workforce Management*, Feb. 2004 (*www.workforce.com*).

29. A. Sanders, "We Luv Booz," *Forbes*, Jan. 24, 2000, p. 64; M. Schneider, "GE Capital's E-Biz Farm Team," *Business Week*, Nov. 27, 2000, pp. 110–111.

30. S. Grabczynski, "Nab New Grads by Building Relationships With Colleges," *Workforce*, May 2000, pp. 98–103; R. Buckman, "What Price a BMW? At Stanford, It May Only Cost a Resume," *Wall Street Journal*, Aug. 19, 2000, p. A1.

31. D. L. McLain, "Headhunters Edge Toward Consulting," *Wall Street Journal*, May 5, 2002, pp. B4–18; S. J. Wells, "Slow Times for Executive Recruiting," *HR Magazine*, Apr. 2003, pp. 61–68.

32. L. Gomes, "Executive Recruiters Face Built-In Conflict Evaluating Insiders," *Wall Street Journal*, Oct. 14, 2002, p. B1.

33. Deutsch, Shea, and Evans, *Human Resources Manual* (New York: author, 1992–1993).

34. D. Cadrain, "Admit One," *Staffing Management Magazine*, July 2009 (*www.shrm.org/publications/staffingmanagementmagazine*).

35. R. J. Grossman, "Made From Scratch," *HR Magazine*, Apr. 2002, pp. 44–52.

36. L. Q. Doherty and E. N. Sims, "Quick, Easy Recruitment Help—From a State?" *Workforce*, May 1998, pp. 35–42.

37. D. Aberman, "Smaller, Specialized Recruiting Events Pay Off in Big Ways," *EMA Today*, Winter 1996, pp. 8–10; T. A. Judge and D. M. Cable, "Role of Organizational Information Sessions in Applicant Job Search Decisions," Working paper, Department of Management and Organizations, University of Iowa; Cable and Yu, "Managing Job Seekers' Organizational Image Beliefs: The Role of Media Richness and Media Credibility."

38. S. Armour, "Employers Court High School Teens," *Arizona Republic*, Dec. 28, 1999, p. E5; C. Hymowitz, "Make a Careful Search to Fill Internships: They May Land a Star," *Wall Street Journal*, May 23, 2000, p. B1; "In a Tight Job Market, College Interns Wooed," *IPMA News*, Nov. 2000, p. 22.

39. P. J. Franks, "Well-Integrated Learning Programs," in Burkholder, Edwards, and Sartain (eds.), *On Staffing*, pp. 230–238.

40. L. J. Bassi and J. Ludwig, "School-to-Work Programs in the United States: A Multi-Firm Case Study of Training, Benefits, and Costs," *Industrial and Labor Relations Review*, 2000, 53, pp. 219–239.

41. G. Beenen and D. M. Rousseau, "Getting the Most From Internships: Promoting Intern Learning and Job Acceptance," *Human Resource Management*, 2010, 49, pp. 3–22.

42. C. Johansson, "Retailer Shops for Older Employees," *Wisconsin State Journal*, June 7, 2004, p. C8.

43. J. Pont, "Online, In-house," *Workforce Management*, May 2005, pp. 49–51.

44. S. Overman, "Keep Hot Prospects on Tap," *Staffing Management*, Jan. 2007, pp. 19–21.

45. P. Weaver, "Tap Ex-Employees' Recruitment Potential," *HR Magazine*, July 2006, pp. 89–91.

46. D. S. Chapman, K. L. Uggerslev, S. A. Carroll, K. A. Piasentin, and D. A. Jones, "Applicant Attraction to Organizations and Job Choice: A Meta-Analytic Review of the Correlates of Recruiting Outcomes," *Journal of Applied Psychology*, 2005, 90, pp. 928–944; M. A. Zottoli and J. P. Wanous, "Recruitment Source Research: Current Status and Future Directions," *Human Resource Management Review*, 2000, 10, pp. 353–382.

47. S. L. Premack and J. P. Wanous, "A Meta-Analysis of Realistic Job Preview Experiments," *Journal of Applied Psychology*, 1985, 70, pp. 706–719; J. M. Phillips, "Effects of Realistic Job Previews on Multiple Organizational Outcomes: A Meta-Analysis," *Academy of Management Journal*, 1998, 41, pp. 673–690.

48. J. P. Wanous, *Recruitment, Selection, Orientation, and Socialization of Newcomers*, second ed. (Reading, MA: Addison-Wesley, 1992).

49. R. D. Bretz, Jr., and T. A. Judge, "Realistic Job Previews: A Test of the Adverse Self-Selection Hypothesis," *Journal of Applied Psychology*, 1998, 83, pp. 330–337; D. M. Cable, L. Aiman-Smith, P. W. Molvey, and J. R. Edwards, "The Sources and Accuracy of Job Applicants' Beliefs About Organizational Culture," *Academy of Management Journal*, 2000, 43, pp. 1076–1085; Y. Ganzach, A. Pazy, Y. Ohayun, and E. Brainin, "Social Exchange and Organizational Commitment: Decision-Making Training for Job Choice as an Alternative to the Realistic Job Preview," *Personnel Psychology*, 2002, 55, pp. 613–637; P. W. Hom, R. W. Griffeth, L. E. Palich, and J. S. Bracker, "An Exploratory Investigation Into Theoretical Mechanisms Underlying Realistic Job Previews," *Personnel Psychology*, 1998, 51, pp. 421–451; B. M. Meglino, E. C. Ravlin, and A. S. DeNisi, "A Meta-Analytic Examination of Realistic Job Preview Effectiveness: A Test of Three Counter-Intuitive Propositions," *Human Resource Management Review*, 2000, 10, pp. 407–434.
50. C. J. Collins, "The Interactive Effects of Recruitment Practices and Product Awareness on Job Seekers' Employer Knowledge and Application Behaviors," *Journal of Applied Psychology*, 2007, 92, pp. 180–190; C. J. Collins and C. K. Stevens, "The Relationship Between Early Recruitment-Related Activities and the Application Decisions of New Labor-Market Entrants: A Brand Equity Approach to Recruitment," *Journal of Applied Psychology*, 2002, 87, pp. 1121–1133; P. J. Kiger, "Talent Acquisition Special Report: Burnishing the Brand," *Workforce Management*, Oct. 22, 2007, pp. 39–45.
51. Corporate Leadership Council, *The Employment Brand: Building Competitive Advantage in the Labor Market* (Washington, DC: author, 1999); E. Silverman, "Making Your Mark," *Human Resource Executive*, Oct. 16, 2004, pp. 32–36; M. Spitzmüller, R. Hunington, W. Wyatt, and A. Crozier, "Building a Company to Attract Talent," *Workspan*, July 2002, pp. 27–30.
52. R. K. Agrawal and P. Swaroop, "Effect of Employer Brand Image on Application Intentions of B-School Undergraduates," *VISION*, 2009, 13(3), pp. 41–49.
53. Collins and Stevens, "The Relationship Between Early Recruitment-Related Activities and the Application Decisions of New Labor-Market Entrants: A Brand Equity Approach to Recruitment"; F. Lievens and S. Highhouse, "The Relation of Instrumental and Symbolic Attributes to a Company's Attractiveness as an Employer," *Personnel Psychology*, 2003, 56, pp. 75–102.
54. R. H. Bretz and T. A. Judge, "The Role of Human Resource Systems in Job Applicant Decision Processes," *Journal of Management*, 1994, 20, pp. 531–551; D. Cable and T. Judge, "Pay Preferences and Job Search Decisions: A Person-Organization Fit Perspective," *Personnel Psychology*, 1994, 47, pp. 648–657; T. J. Thorsteinson, M. A. Billings, and M. C. Joyce, "Matching Recruitment Messages to Applicant Preferences," Poster presented at 16th annual conference of the Society for Industrial and Organizational Psychology, San Diego, 2001.
55. R. J. Vandenberg and V. Scarpello, "The Matching Model: An Examination of the Processes Underlying Realistic Job Previews," *Journal of Applied Psychology*, 1990, 75(1), pp. 60–67.
56. D. R. Ilgen, C. D. Fisher, and M. S. Taylor, "Consequences of Individual Feedback on Behavior in Organizations," *Journal of Applied Psychology*, 1979, 64, pp. 349–371.
57. H. J. Walker, H. S. Field, W. F. Giles, and J. B. Bernerth, "The Interactive Effects of Job Advertisement Characteristics and Applicant Experience on Reactions to Recruitment Messages," *Journal of Occupational and Organizational Psychology*, 2008, 81, pp. 619–638.
58. Cable and Yu, "Managing Job Seekers' Organizational Image Beliefs: The Role of Media Richness and Media Capability."
59. G. van Hoye and F. Lievens, "Social Influences on Organizational Attractiveness: Investigating If and When Word of Mouth Matters," *Journal of Applied Social Psychology*, 2007, 37, pp. 2024–2047; G. van Hoye, "Nursing Recruitment: Relationship Between Perceived Employer

Image and Nursing Employees' Recommendations," *Journal of Advanced Nursing*, 2008, 63, pp. 366–375; H. J. Walker, H. S. Field, W. F. Giles, A. A. Armenakis, and J. B. Bernerth, "Displaying Employee Testimonials on Recruitment Websites: Effects of Communication Media, Employee Race, and Job Seeker Race on Organizational Attraction and Information Credibility," *Journal of Applied Psychology*, 2009, 94, pp. 1354–1364.

60. E. Baker and J. Demps, "Videoconferencing as a Tool for Recruiting and Interviewing," *Journal of Business and Economics Research*, 2009, 7(10), pp. 9–14.

61. G. Ruiz, "Print Ads See Resurgence as Hiring Source," *Workforce Management*, Mar. 26, 2007, pp. 16–17.

62. R. T. Cober, D. J. Brown, and P. E. Levy, "Form, Content, and Function: An Evaluative Methodology for Corporate Employment Web Sites," *Human Resource Management*, 2004, 43, pp. 201–218; R. T. Cober, D. J. Brown, P. E. Levy, A. B. Cobler, and K. M. Keeping, "Organizational Web Sites: Web Site Content and Style as Determinants of Organizational Attraction," *International Journal of Selection and Assessment*, 2003, 11, pp. 158–169.

63. "A 'Shopper Friendly' Web Site," *Weddle's*, Oct. 2002, p. 1; "KISS Your Web Site Visitors," *Weddle's*, Apr. 2002, p. 1.

64. S. L. Rynes, "Recruitment, Job Choice, and Post-Hire Decisions," in M. D. Dunnette and L. M. Hough (eds.), *Handbook of Industrial and Organizational Psychology*, Vol. 2 (Palo Alto, CA: Consulting Psychologists Press, 1991), pp. 399–444; J. L. Scott, "Total Quality College Relations and Recruitment Programs: Students Benchmark Best Practices," *EMA Journal*, Winter 1995, pp. 2–5; J. P. Wanous, *Organizational Entry*, second ed. (Reading, MA: Addison-Wesley, 1992).

65. D. S. Chapman, K. L. Uggerslev, S. A. Carroll, K. A. Piasentin, and D. A. Jones, "Applicant Attraction to Organizations and Job Choice: A Meta-Analytic Review of the Correlates of Recruiting Outcomes," *Journal of Applied Psychology*, 2005, 90, pp. 928–944; W. R. Boswell, M. V. Roehling, M. A. Le Pine, and L. M. Moynihan, "Individual Job-Choice Decisions and the Impact of Job Attributes and Recruitment Practices: A Longitudinal Field Study," *Human Resource Management*, 2003, 42, pp. 23–37; A. M. Ryan, J. M. Sacco, L. A. McFarland, and S. D. Kriska, "Applicant Self-Selection: Correlates of Withdrawal From a Multiple Hurdle Process," *Journal of Applied Psychology*, 2000, 85, pp. 163–179; Rynes, "Recruitment, Job Choice, and Post-Hire Decisions"; S. L. Rynes, "Who's Selecting Whom? Effects of Selection Practices in Applicant Attitudes and Behaviors," in N. Schmitt, W. Borman, and Associates (eds.), *Personnel Selection in Organizations* (San Francisco: Jossey-Bass, 1993), pp. 240–276; S. L. Rynes, R. D. Bretz, and B. Gerhart, "The Importance of Recruitment and Job Choice: A Different Way of Looking," *Personnel Psychology*, 1991, 44, pp. 487–521; M. S. Taylor and T. J. Bergmann, "Organizational Recruitment Activities and Applicant Reactions to Different Stages of the Recruiting Process," *Personnel Psychology*, 1988, 40, pp. 261–285.

66. B. Dineen, S. R. Ash, and R. A. Noe, "A Web of Applicant Attraction: Person-Organization Fit in the Context of Web-Based Recruitment," *Journal of Applied Psychology*, 2002, 87, pp. 723–734; D. C. Feldman and B. S. Klaas, "Internet Job Hunting: A Field Study of Applicant Experiences With On-Line Recruiting," *Human Resource Management*, 2002, 41, pp. 175–192; K. Maher, "The Jungle," *Wall Street Journal*, July 18, 2002, p. B10; D. L. Van Rooy, A. Alonso, and Z. Fairchild, "In With the New, Out With the Old: Has the Technological Revolution Eliminated the Traditional Job Search Process?" *International Journal of Selection and Assessment*, 2003, 11, pp. 170–174.

67. P. F. McKay and D. R. Avery, "What Has Race Got to Do With It? Unraveling the Role of Racio-ethnicity in Job Seekers' Reactions to Site Visits," *Personnel Psychology*, 2006, 59, pp. 395–429; Avery, "Reactions to Diversity in Recruitment Advertising: Are the Differences Black and White?"; Avery and McKay, "Target Practice: An Organizational Impression Management Approach to Attracting Minority and Female Job Applicants."

68. R. H. Glover and R. A. Schwinger, "Defining an Applicant: Maintaining Records in the Electronic Age," *Legal Report*, Society for Human Resource Management, Summer 1996, pp. 6–8; G. P. Panaro, *Employment Law Manual*, second ed. (Boston: Warren Gorham Lamont, 1993), pp. I-51 to I-57.

69. OFCCP, "Frequently Asked Questions About the Internet Applicant Rule," periodically updated (*www.dol.gov/ofccp/regs/compliance/faqs/empefaqs.htm*), accessed 3/18/2010; V. J. Hoffman and G. M. Davis, "OFCCP's Internet Applicant Definition Requires Overhaul of Recruitment and Hiring Policies," *Legal Report*, Society for Human Resource Management, Jan./Feb. 2006; D. Reynolds, "OFCCP Guidance on Defining a Job Applicant in the Internet Age: The Final Word?" *The Industrial/Organizational Psychologist*, 2006, 43(3), pp. 107–113.

70. J. Arnold, "Online Job Sites: Convenient but Not Accessible to All," Society for Human Resource Management, July 31, 2007 (*www.shrm.org/hrtx/library_published/nonIC/CMS_022275.asp*).

71. OFCCP, "Frequently Asked Questions About Disability Issues Related to Online Application Systems," periodically updated (*www.dol.gov/ofccp/regs/compliance/faqs/empefaqs.htm*), accessed 3/18/10.

72. K. Gurchiek, "Video Resumes Spark Curiosity, Questions," *HR Magazine*, May 2007, pp. 28–30; J. McGregor, "Because of That Video Resume," *Business Week*, June 11, 2007, p. 12.

73. J. Deschenaux, "Attorney: Using Social Networking Sites for Hiring May Lead to Discrimination Claims" (*www.shrm.org/legalissues/employmentlawarea/pages*), accessed 3/23/2010; K. A. Gray, "Searching for Candidate Information," (*www.hreonline.com/HRE/story.jsp?storyID=327202146*), accessed 1/29/2010; F. Hansen, "Discriminatory Twist in Networking Sites Puts Recruiters in Peril" (*www.workforce.com/archive/feature/26/68/67/index.php*), accessed 2/23/2010.

74. EEOC, "Title VII and ADEA: Job Advertisements" (3/8/2008) and "ADEA: Job Advertisements Seeking Older Workers" (7/11/2007), informal discussion letters (*www.eeoc.gov/eeoc/foia/letters/index.cfm*), accessed 7/28/2010.

75. R. M. Green and R. J. Reibstein, *Employer's Guide to Workplace Torts* (Washington, DC: Bureau of National Affairs, 1992), pp. 40–61, 200, 254–255.

76. A. G. Feliu, *Primer on Individual Employee Rights* (Washington, DC: Bureau of National Affairs, 1992), p. 270.

CHAPTER SIX

Internal Recruitment

Learning Objectives and Introduction
  Learning Objectives
  Introduction

Recruitment Planning
  Organizational Issues
  Administrative Issues
  Timing

Strategy Development
  Closed, Open, and Hybrid Recruitment
  Recruitment Sources
  Recruiting Metrics

Communication Message and Medium
  Communication Message
  Communication Medium

Applicant Reactions

Transition to Selection

Legal Issues
  Affirmative Action Programs Regulations
  Bona Fide Seniority Systems
  The Glass Ceiling

Summary

Discussion Questions

Ethical Issues

Applications

LEARNING OBJECTIVES AND INTRODUCTION

Learning Objectives

- Be able to engage in effective internal recruitment planning activities
- Apply concepts of closed, open, and hybrid recruitment to the internal recruiting process
- Recognize which recruitment sources are available for internal candidates
- Evaluate internal recruiting based on established metrics
- Be able to evaluate communication messages for internal selection
- Recognize how applicant reactions influence the effectiveness of a recruiting plan
- Understand how affirmative action plans are implemented for internal recruiting

Introduction

Internal recruitment is the process of identifying and attracting current employees for open jobs. Internal recruits have numerous advantages: they already know the organization's culture, they have already developed relationships with coworkers, and they may require less training than external hires. The nearly ubiquitous presence of internal labor markets underscores the importance of effective internal recruiting. One survey of 725 human resource (HR) professionals found that as a result of recruiting, selection, training, and development costs, organizations are increasingly looking internally to staff positions.[1] A majority of those surveyed reported that managing their internal talent pool was either a high (45.6%) or very high (27.7%) strategic priority in their organization. The development of internal talent was seen as one of the top talent management tasks (63% of respondents), even more so than the acquisition of talent (49.4% of respondents).

Unfortunately, despite the imperative placed on improving talent management, this survey also showed that only 25.7% of organizations have a formal talent management strategy, and only 13.8% of small businesses have a formal talent management system. This relatively limited implementation of effective formal talent management systems means there is much room for improvement. At the same time, a poorly managed internal talent management system can lead to accusations of favoritism, bias, or discrimination. Great care must be taken to ensure that any internal recruiting system is seen as fair.

The first step in the internal recruiting process is recruitment planning. The second step is developing a strategy for where, how, and when to look. Knowing where to look requires an understanding of open, closed, and hybrid internal recruitment systems. Knowing how to look requires an understanding of job postings, intranets and intraplacement, a talent management system, nominations, in-house temporary pools, replacement and succession plans, and career development centers.

Knowing when to look requires an understanding of lead time and time sequence concerns. The third step consists of the communication message and medium for notification of the job vacancy. The fourth step in the process is developing a job posting system and providing applicants with an understanding of the selection process and how to best prepare for it. The fifth step in the process is the consideration of legal issues. Specific issues to be addressed include Affirmative Action Programs Regulations, bona fide seniority systems, and the glass ceiling.

RECRUITMENT PLANNING

Before identifying and attracting internal applicants to vacant jobs, attention must be directed to organizational and administrative issues that facilitate the effective matching of those applicants with available positions.

Organizational Issues

Just as the external labor market can be divided into segments or strata of workers believed to be desirable job applicants, so, too, can the internal labor market of an organization. This division is often done informally inside organizations. For example, managers might talk about the talented pool of managerial trainees this year and refer to some of them as "high-potential employees." As another example, people in the organization talk about their "techies," an internal collection of employees with the technical skills needed to run the business.

At a more formal level, organizations must create a structured set of jobs for their employees and paths of mobility for them to follow as they advance in their careers. To do this, organizations create internal labor markets. Each internal labor market has two components: mobility paths and mobility policies. Mobility paths depict the paths of mobility between jobs. Mobility policies cover the operational requirements needed to move people between jobs.

Mobility Paths

A mobility path consists of possible employee movements within the internal labor market structure. Mobility paths are determined by many factors, including workforce, organization, labor union, and labor market characteristics. Mobility paths are of two types: hierarchical and alternative. Both types determine who is eligible for a new job in the organization.

Hierarchical Mobility Paths.   Examples of hierarchical mobility paths are shown in Exhibit 6.1. As can be seen, the emphasis is primarily on upward mobility in the organization. Due to their upward nature, hierarchical mobility paths are often labeled promotion ladders. This label implies that each job is a step toward the top of the organization. Employees often see upward promotions as prizes because of

EXHIBIT 6.1   Hierarchical Mobility Paths

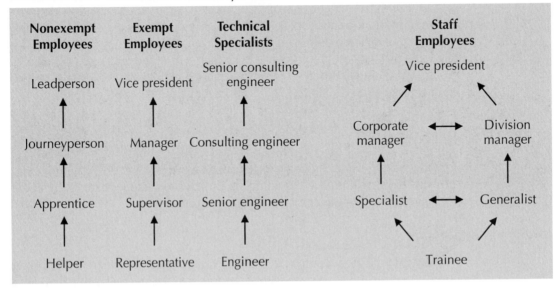

the promotions' desirable characteristics. Employees receive these prizes as they compete against one another for job vacancies. For example, a promotion might lead to a higher rate of pay, and a transfer may result in a move to a better work location. Research has shown that these competitions may be contested, as opportunities for upward advancement are limited in most organizations.[2]

An exception to the primarily upward mobility in the promotion ladders in Exhibit 6.1 shows the lateral moves that sometimes occur for the staff member who has both generalist and specialist experience as well as corporate and division experience. This staff member is considered more well-rounded and better able to work within the total organization. Experience as a specialist gives the person familiarity with technical issues that arise. Experience as a generalist gives the employee a breadth of knowledge about many matters in the staffing function. Corporate experience provides a policy and planning perspective, whereas division experience provides greater insight on day-to-day operational matters.

Hierarchical mobility paths make it very easy, from an administrative vantage point, to identify where to look for applicants in the organization. For promotion, one looks at the next level down in the organizational hierarchy, and for transfer, looks over. Although such a system is straightforward to administer, it is not very flexible and may inhibit matching the best person to the job. For example, the best person for the job may be two levels down and in another division from the vacant job. It is very difficult to locate such a person under a hierarchical mobility path.

Alternative Mobility Paths.   Examples of alternative mobility paths are shown in Exhibit 6.2. The emphasis here is on movement in the organization in any direction—up, down, and side to side. Employee movement is emphasized to ensure that each employee is continuously learning and that he or she can make the greatest contribution to the organization. This is in direct contrast to the hierarchical promotion ladder, where the goal is for each person to achieve a position with ever-higher status. Many organizations have shifted to alternative mobility paths for two reasons: (1) there is the need to be flexible given global and technological changes, and (2) slower organizational growth has made it necessary to find alternative ways to utilize employees' talents. Parallel tracks allow for employees to specialize in technical work or management work and advance within either. Historically, technical specialists had to shift away from technical work to managerial work if they wanted to receive higher-status job titles and pay. In other words, a technical specialist was a dead-end job. Under a parallel track system, job titles and salaries of technical specialists are elevated to be commensurate with their managerial counterparts.

With a lateral track system, there may be no upward mobility at all. The individual's greatest contribution to the organization may be to stay at a certain level for an extended period of time while serving in a variety of capacities, as shown in Exhibit 6.2.

EXHIBIT 6.2   Alternative Mobility Paths

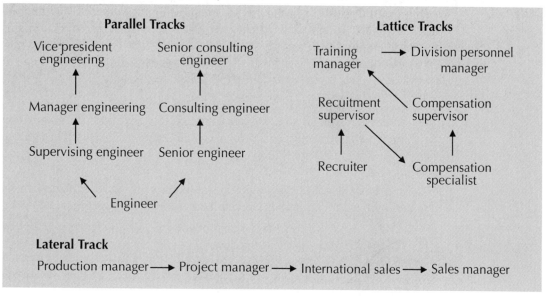

A lattice mobility path has upward, lateral, and even downward movement. For example, a recruiter may be promoted to a recruitment supervisor position, but to continue to contribute to the organization, the person may need to take a lateral step to become knowledgeable about all the technical details in compensation. After mastering these details, the person may then become a supervisor again, this time in the compensation area rather than in recruitment. From a previous organization, the person may have experience in training and be ready to move to training manager without training experience internal to the organization. Finally, the person may make a lateral move to manage all the HR functions in a division (recruitment, compensation, and training) as a division personnel manager.

Some organizations have abandoned career structures altogether. In these team-based kinds of jobs, employees do not have traditional jobs but are "bonded" together with other employees, depending on the project. In this structure, employees are essentially entrepreneurial consultants, and the organization facilitates their activities. One example of such a cellular organization is TCG, based in Sydney, Australia. TCG partners with other organizations to provide computer assistance. TCG employees work on projects according to their expertise, and they are rewarded based on the success of the project. These rewards may involve assignment to larger projects in the future, which is a form of promotion.[3]

The downside to alternative mobility paths is that they are very difficult to administer. Neat categories of where to look do not exist to the same degree as with hierarchical mobility paths. On the positive side, however, talented inside candidates who may not have been identified within a hierarchical system are identified because of the flexibility of the system.

When upward mobility is limited in an organization, as in those using alternative mobility paths, special steps need to be taken to ensure that work remains meaningful to employees. If steps are not taken, the organization with limited promotional opportunities risks turnover of good employees. Examples of steps to make work more meaningful include the following:

1. *Alternative reward systems.* Rather than basing pay increases on promotions, pay increases can be based on an individual's knowledge and skill acquisition and contribution to the organization as a team member. Research has shown that these programs are successful at encouraging employees to develop job-relevant skills.[4]

2. *Team building.* Greater challenge and autonomy in the workplace can be created by having employees work in teams where they are responsible for all aspects of work involved in providing a service or product, including self-management.

3. *Counseling.* Workshops, self-directed workbooks, and individual advising can be used to ensure that employees have a well-reasoned plan for movement in the organization.

4. *Alternative employment.* Arrangements can be made for employee leaves of absence, sabbaticals, and consulting assignments to ensure that workers remain challenged and acquire new knowledge and skills.

Mobility Policies

Mobility paths show the relationships among jobs, but they do not show the rules by which people move between jobs. These rules are specified in written policies, which must be developed and should specify eligibility criteria.

Development. A well-defined mobility path policy statement is needed for both hierarchical and alternative mobility paths and has the following characteristics:

1. The intent of the policy is clearly communicated.
2. The policy is consistent with the philosophy and values of top management.
3. The scope of the policy, such as coverage by geographic region, employee groups, and so forth, is clearly articulated.
4. Employees' responsibilities and opportunities for development are clearly defined.
5. Supervisors' responsibilities for employee development are clearly stated.
6. Procedures are clearly described, such as how employees will be notified of openings, deadlines, and data to be supplied; how requirements and qualifications will be communicated; how the selection process will work; and how job offers will be made.
7. Rules regarding compensation and advancement are included.
8. Rules regarding benefits and benefit changes as they relate to advancement are included.

Employees are likely to see a well-articulated and well-executed mobility path policy as fair. A poorly developed or nonexistent policy is likely to lead to employee claims of favoritism and discrimination.

Eligibility Criteria. An important component of an effective mobility policy is a listing of the criteria by which the organization will decide who is eligible to be considered for a vacancy in a mobility path. In essence, these criteria restrict eligibility for recruitment to certain individuals. Usually these criteria are based on the amount of seniority, level of experience, KSAOs (knowledge, skill, ability, and other characteristics), or job duties required. For example, to be considered for an international assignment, the applicant may be required to have been with the organization a certain length of time, have experience in a functional area where there is a vacancy, be proficient in a foreign language, and be interested in performing new duties. These criteria need to be made very clear in the policy, otherwise unqualified people will apply and be disappointed when they are not considered.

Also, the organization may be flooded with the paperwork and processing of applicants who are not eligible.

Administrative Issues

Mobility paths and mobility policies must be established as part of the planning process, and so, too, must administrative matters. Administrative matters include requisitions, coordination, the budget, and the recruitment guide.

Requisitions

As we noted in Chapter 5, a requisition is a formal authorization by higher-level management to fill a job opening. Requiring a formal requisition for any opening to be filled makes it easier to confirm that fair and objective procedures are followed consistently throughout the internal recruitment process. Requisitions are especially important for internal recruiting because it is more likely that supervisors will have a personal relationship with candidates under consideration. Without formal requisitions, it is far too easy for managers to make promises or "cut deals" with favored employees that run contrary to organizational objectives. By specifying the characteristics of successful applicants for internal positions prior to the recruiting process, it is easier to ensure that internal movements are made consistent with organizational standards and goals. Documenting that consistent, business-related policies are followed for internal mobility also helps ensure that the system is legally defensible.

Coordination

Internal and external recruitment efforts need to be coordinated and synchronized via the organization's staffing philosophy (see Chapter 3). If this is not done, disastrous results can occur. For example, if independent searches are conducted internally and externally, two people may be hired for one vacancy. If only an external recruitment search is conducted, the morale of current employees may suffer if they feel that they have been passed over for a promotion. If only an internal recruitment search is conducted, the person hired may not be as qualified as someone from the external market. Because of these possibilities, internal *and* external professionals must work together with the line manager to coordinate efforts before the search for candidates begins.

To coordinate activities, policies need to be created that specify the number and types of candidates sought internally and the number and types of candidates sought externally. External recruiters should stay in frequent contact with internal placement professionals.

Budget

An organization's internal recruitment budgeting process should closely mirror that for external recruitment. The cost per hire may, however, differ between internal and external recruitment. The fact that internal recruitment targets candidates already working for the organization does not mean that the cost per hire is necessarily less than the cost per hire for external recruitment. Sometimes internal recruitment can be more costly than external recruitment because the methods involved in internal recruitment can be quite expensive. For example, when internal candidates are considered for the job but not hired, they need to be counseled on what to do to further develop their careers to become competitive for the position the next time it is vacant. When an external candidate is rejected, a simple and less costly rejection letter usually suffices.

Recruitment Guide

As with external recruitment, internal recruitment activities involve the development of a recruitment guide, a formal document that details the process to be followed to attract applicants to a vacant job. Included in the plan are details such as the time, money, and staff activities required to fill the job, as well as the steps to be taken to fill the vacancy created by the internal candidate leaving to take the new job. An example of an internal recruitment guide is shown in Exhibit 6.3.

Timing

A final strategic consideration an organization must make is determining when to look for internal candidates. As with external recruitment, consideration involves calculation of lead time and time sequence concerns.

Lead Time Concerns

A major difference between internal and external recruitment is that internal recruitment not only fills vacancies but also creates them. Each time a vacancy is filled with an internal candidate, a new vacancy is created in the spot vacated by the internal candidate.

As a result of this difference, it is incumbent on the organization to do HR planning along with internal recruitment. This planning involves elements of succession planning (see Chapter 3) and is essential for effective internal recruitment.

Internal and external lead time considerations also differ because in an internal market, the employer can actively participate in identifying and developing knowledge and skills of the pool of eligible internal employees. Strategic talent management means that the organization identifies crucial skills that will be needed for future positions and begins cultivating these skills in the workforce well in advance.[5] By proactively developing needed skills in advance, the organization will be able to significantly reduce the lead time to fill positions with very specific KSAO requirements.

Time Sequence Concerns

As previously noted, it is essential that internal and external recruitment activities be properly coordinated. This is especially true with the timing and sequencing

EXHIBIT 6.3 Internal Recruitment Guide

Position Reassignments Into New Claims Processing Center

Goal: Transfer all qualified medical claims processors and examiners from one company subsidiary to the newly developed claims processing center. Terminate those who are not well qualified for the new positions and whose existing positions are being eliminated.

Assumptions: That all employees have been notified that their existing positions in company subsidiary ABC are being eliminated and they will be eligible to apply for positions in the new claims processing center.

Hiring responsibility: Manager of Claims Processing and Manager of Claims Examining.

Other resources: Entire human resource department staff.

Time frames:
Positions posted internally on April 2, 2012
Employees may apply until April 16, 2012
Interviews will be scheduled/coordinated during week of April 19, 2012
Interviews will occur during the week of April 26, 2012
Selections made and communicated by last week in May
Total number of available positions: 60

Positions available and corresponding qualification summaries:

6 claims supervisors—4-year degree with 3 years of claims experience, including 1 year of supervisory experience.

14 claims data entry operators—6 months of data entry experience. Knowledge of medical terminology helpful.

8 hospital claims examiners—12 months of claims data entry/processing experience. Knowledge of medical terminology necessary.

8 physician claims examiners—12 months of claims data entry/processing experience. Knowledge of medical terminology necessary.

8 dental claims examiners—12 months of claims data entry/processing experience and 6 months of dental claims examining experience. Knowledge of dental terminology necessary.

8 mental health claims examiners—12 months of claims data entry/processing experience and 6 months of mental health claims experience. Knowledge of medical and mental health terminology necessary.

8 substance abuse claims examiners—12 months of claims data entry/processing experience and 6 months of substance abuse experience. Knowledge of medical terminology necessary.

Transfer request guidelines: Internal candidates must submit internal transfer requests and an accompanying cover page listing all positions for which they are applying, in order of preference. Internal candidates may apply for no more than five positions.
Transfer requests must be complete and be signed by the employee and the employee's supervisor.

Candidate qualification review process: Transfer requests from internal candidates will be reviewed on a daily basis. Those not qualified for any positions for which they applied will be notified by phone that day, due to the large volume of requests.

(continued)

EXHIBIT 6.3   Continued

All transfer requests and accompanying cover pages will be filed by the position to which they refer. If internal candidates applied for more than one position, their transfer packet will be copied so that one copy is in each position folder.

Once all candidate qualifications have been received and reviewed, each candidate's transfer packet will be copied and transmitted to the managers for review and interview selection. Due to the large number of candidates, managers will be required to interview only those candidates with the best qualifications for the available positions. Managers will notify human resources with the candidates with whom they would like interviews scheduled. Whenever possible, the manager will interview the candidate during one meeting for all of the positions applied and qualified for.

Selection guidelines: Whenever possible, the best-qualified candidates will be selected for the available positions.

The corporation has committed to attempting to place all employees whose positions are being eliminated. Managers reserve the right to not select employees currently on disciplinary probationary periods. Employees should be slotted in a position with a salary grade comparable to their current salary grade. Employees' salaries shall not be reduced due to the involuntary nature of the job reassignment.

Notification of nonselection: Candidates not selected for a particular position will be notified by electronic message.

Selection notifications: Candidates selected for a position will be notified in person by the human resource staff and will be given a confirmation letter specifying starting date, position, reporting relationship, and salary.

of events that must be carefully laid out for both recruitment and placement personnel. Many organizations start with internal recruitment followed by external recruitment to fill a vacancy. Issues to be addressed include how long the internal search will take place, whether external recruitment can be done concurrently with internal recruitment, and who will be selected if an internal candidate and an external candidate with relatively equal KSAOs are identified.

STRATEGY DEVELOPMENT

After organizational and administrative issues have been covered in the planning phase of internal recruitment, an organization must develop a strategy to locate viable internal job applicants. It must consider where to look, how to look, and when to look.

Closed, Open, and Hybrid Recruitment

The strategy for where to look must be conducted within the constraints of the general eligibility criteria for mobility. Within these constraints, a knowledge of closed, open, and hybrid systems is required.

Closed Internal Recruitment System

Under a closed internal recruitment system, employees are not made aware of job vacancies. The only people made aware of promotion or transfer opportunities are those who oversee placement in the HR department, line managers with vacancies, and contacted employees. Exhibit 6.4 shows how a vacancy is typically filled under a closed system.

A closed system is very efficient. There are only a few steps to follow, and the time and cost involved are minimal. However, a closed system is only as good as the files showing candidates' KSAOs. If the files are inaccurate or out of date, qualified candidates may be overlooked. Thus, maintaining accurate human resource information systems (HRISs) that track KSAOs regularly is vital.

Open Internal Recruitment System

Under an open internal recruitment system, employees are made aware of job vacancies. Usually this is accomplished by a job posting and bidding system. Exhibit 6.5 shows the typical steps followed in filling a vacancy under an open internal recruitment system.

An open system gives employees a chance to measure their qualifications against those required for advancement. It helps minimize the possibility that supervisors

EXHIBIT 6.4   Closed Internal Recruitment System

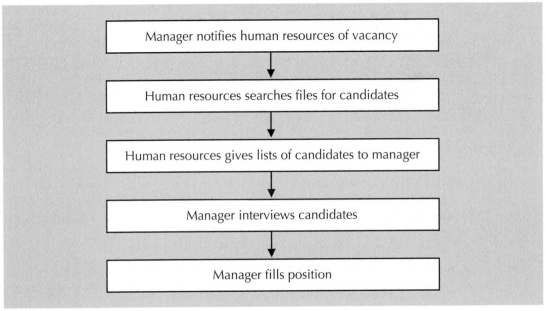

EXHIBIT 6.5   Open Internal Recruitment System

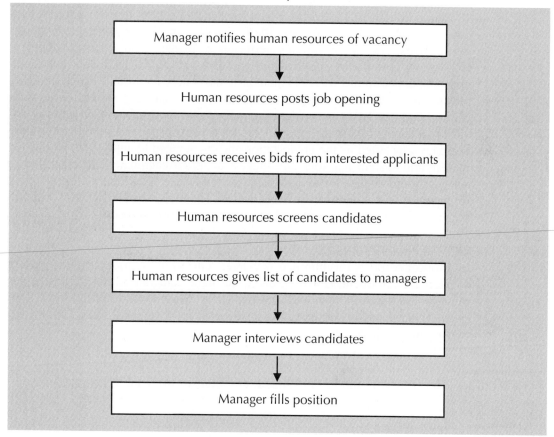

will select favorite employees for promotion or transfer, and it often uncovers hidden talent.

An open system may, however, create unwanted competition among employees for limited advancement opportunities. It is a very lengthy and time-consuming process to screen all candidates and provide them with feedback. Employee morale may decrease among those who do not advance.

Hybrid System of Internal Recruitment

Under a hybrid system, both open and closed steps are followed at the same time. Job vacancies are posted, and the HR department conducts a search outside the job posting system. Both systems are used to cast as wide a net as possible. The large applicant pool is then narrowed down by KSAOs, seniority eligibility, demographics, and availability of applicants.

Merico Hotels uses a hybrid system that includes both training and developing promising employees for specific higher-level positions alongside job posting methods.[6] The organization's performance management system encourages employees to specify their potential internal career tracks and indicate which developmental opportunities will help them progress. Those identified as high-potential receive special training within a formal succession planning system. When jobs come open, they are posted via an internal job vacancy software program developed specifically by Merico, and employees who are especially qualified for these openings are alerted by the organization and encouraged to apply.

A hybrid system has four advantages: qualified candidates are identified in advance, a thorough search is conducted, people have equal opportunity to apply for postings, and hidden talent is uncovered. The major disadvantage of a hybrid system is that it entails a very time-consuming and costly process.

Criteria for Choice of System

In an ideal world with unlimited resources, one would choose a hybrid system of internal recruitment. However, due to resource constraints, most organizations must choose between open and closed systems. Several criteria need to be thoroughly considered before selecting an internal recruitment system. Exhibit 6.6 reviews these criteria.

EXHIBIT 6.6   Choosing Among Open, Closed, and Hybrid Internal Recruiting

Technique	Advantages	Best When
Open	Identifies more candidates, including those who might be overlooked in a closed system Makes rules and regulations explicit and open to all employees Sometimes required by labor agreements	Issues exist about perceived fairness; hidden talent might be overlooked
Closed	Less expensive in terms of search costs Offers a quicker response Less cumbersome when only a select few meet the minimum requirements	Managers need the new candidate to start immediately; jobs require a very narrow and specialized set of KSAOs
Hybrid	Finds a large number of candidates Everyone has an opportunity to apply	There are adequate resources to run such a hybrid system; jobs are especially key to organizational success

Although the choice of system is important, with the advent of staffing software (see Chapter 13), bridges among these systems may be built so as to take advantage of the best features of each.

Recruitment Sources

Once it has been specified where and how in the organization individuals are likely to be found, several major methods can be used to identify them: job postings, intranet and intraplacement, a talent management system, nominations, replacement and succession plans, career development centers, and in-house temporary pools.

Job Postings

A job posting is very similar to the advertisement used in external recruitment. It spells out the duties and requirements of the job and tells how applicants can apply. Its content should be based on the job requirements matrix. A job posting begins when a job vacancy occurs. A position announcement is then posted through a bulletin board, newsletter, e-mail, or intranet (see subsequent section). In this step, organizations must decide whether to first limit the posting or advertise it throughout the organization. If the first posting is limited to a department, location, or work area and the job is not filled, it should be posted more broadly. Applicants respond to job postings using a bid sheet like the one shown in Exhibit 6.7.

At Home Depot, job openings are listed on computer kiosks in break rooms. Employees can view these job postings during breaks or before or after shifts. If an employee is interested in one of the jobs, he or she can take a computerized test for the opening at the kiosk. If the employee makes the cut, his or her application is forwarded. If the employee fails, the supervisor is notified and the employee may be offered training so he or she can compete successfully for the position in the future.[7]

Even advanced job posting systems have some problems in administration. Examples of such difficulties include situations where employees believe that someone has been selected before the job was posted (a "bagged" job), cumbersome systems where managers and HR personnel are overwhelmed with résumés of unqualified candidates, and criticisms that the HR department is not doing an effective job of screening candidates for positions.

Some of these problems again point to the critical importance of the job requirements matrix. A good job posting system will clearly define the requisite KSAOs needed to perform the job. By having a job requirements matrix, employees, HR staff, and managers can do a more effective and efficient job of screening.

Another important issue with posting systems is feedback. Not only do employees need to know whether they have received the job, but those who do not receive the job need to be made aware of *why* they did not. Providing this feedback serves

Although a number of different models for implementing talent management systems exist, there are a few key processes common to most. The first stage of the process is identifying the KSAOs required for all jobs in the organization. This information can be obtained from job descriptions and job specifications. The complete set of KSAOs required across the organization will then be compiled into a master list. The current workforce will need to be assessed for its competence in this set of KSAOs, usually as an adjunct to routine performance evaluations. When positions come open, managers make a query to the talent management system to determine which employees are ready to come into open positions. A process should be in place to make regular comprehensive examinations of the changing nature of KSAO requirements throughout the organization. Information from these analyses can then be used as a springboard for developing comprehensive plans for training and development experiences.

There has been such a strong integration of database software for talent management systems that when staffing managers refer to talent management systems, they are often talking about the specific HRIS that is used to facilitate tracking KSAOs in the workforce. While these database applications offer great promise for coordinating information, many managers find operating talent management systems challenging. Most of the problems in implementing the systems in practice do not come from a lack of technology but from an excess of technology that cannot be understood by line managers. A few principles should be borne in mind when developing or evaluating a user-friendly talent management system:

- Keep the format for entering data as simple as possible.
- Have an easy method for updating basic information with each performance evaluation cycle.
- Make it easy to perform database queries.
- Provide varied formats for obtaining reports.
- Ensure that information is confidential.
- Make it possible to perform statistical analyses using relational databases.
- Integrate data with other HR files.

Nominations

Nominations for internal candidates to apply for open positions can be solicited from potential supervisors and peers. These individuals are an excellent source of names of internal candidates, as they are familiar with what is required to be successful in the position. They can help establish the criteria for eligibility and then, through their contacts in the organization, search for eligible candidates. Self-nominations are also very useful in that they ensure that qualified candidates are not inadvertently overlooked using other applicant searching methods.

Self-nomination is an especially important consideration in the internal recruitment of minorities and women.

Using employees to refer potential hires to the organization is a common method of looking for candidates in external recruitment. Though it has not been used much in internal recruitment, more organizations are using employees' referrals to staff positions internally. One system that helps organizations do this is CareerRewards. CareerRewards uses web-based software that rewards employees who refer other employees within the organization for open positions. Employees log onto their company's CareerRewards site and make referrals. If a referral is hired, the employee is rewarded (rewards differ from company to company). There are other providers of internal referral systems.[11] Regardless of what system is used, as with external recruitment, employee referral programs used internally may need to rely on formal programs that recognize employees who actively participate in making referrals. Moreover, they need to be educated on eligibility requirements to ensure that qualified personnel are referred.

In-House Temporary Pools

In-house temporary pools are not only important to the temporary staffing of organizations, but also an excellent source of permanent internal employment. Unlike employees hired through external staffing agencies, those employed through in-house temporary pools are legally treated as employees. Therefore, the full legal liability for these employees falls exclusively on the employer. There are a number of advantages to using in-house temporary employees.[12] Internal temporary employees require less orientation to the organization than external hires. Staffing agencies typically charge an employer an hourly fee for each temporary employee. But with an internal system, because the employer does not have to pay an hourly fee to an external agency, the cost savings can be applied to higher levels of compensation and benefits. It is also easier for an organization to ensure the quality and person/organization fit for employees from an in-house pool relative to a pool of external hires. Temporary employment can also serve as an "audition" for full-time employment, allowing the temporary employees to try out a number of positions until the employee and the organization agree on a good person/job match. Carroll County, Maryland, set up an in-house temporary pool to deal with absences, vacations, and vacancies. Rather than relying on costly temporary agencies, Carroll County has five entry-level employees who fill in wherever needed. The city of Little Rock, Arkansas, has a similar program.[13] In health care, it is common to have "float" staff who are assigned to different units regularly, depending on the organization's needs. Substitute teachers are staffed in a similar manner. Such employees must be adaptable to different situations, and the organization must ensure that there is sufficient work for the employees. Also, extra training may be needed for these employees since they are expected to have a broad range of skills in their repertoire.

Replacement and Succession Plans

A critical source of internal recruitment is provided by the results of replacement and succession planning. Most succession plans include replacement charts (see Chapter 3), which indicate positions and who is scheduled to fill those slots when they become vacant. Replacement charts usually also indicate when the individual will be ready for the assignment. Succession plans are organized by position and list the skills needed for the prospective position (i.e., "for the employee to be promoted into this position from her current position, she needs to develop the following skills"). Dow Chemical's succession plan, for example, includes a list of "now ready" candidates; where there are jobs with similar competencies, it clusters roles and lists candidates for these roles as well. Dow has formal succession plans for 50–60 jobs that are identified as critical corporate roles and also has plans for another 200–300 jobs that are identified as needing continuity.

It is critical that succession planning be future oriented, lest the organization plan be based on historical competencies that fail to meet new challenges. Software exists to assist organizations with succession planning. Saba Succession is a succession planning package that interfaces with an organization's HRIS to provide replacement charts and competency libraries that allow an organization to identify developmental activities and assignments for individuals in the replacement charts. Many Fortune 500 companies use Saba Succession.

CEO succession has always been an important issue for organizations, but never more so than today. The need for employee development has heightened as an increasing proportion of the workforce is approaching retirement. There is a very strong concern among career development specialists that the mass retirement of baby boomers will lead to a loss of organizational memory and knowledge built up with experience. Having strong succession planning techniques that will enable the more recently hired workforce to acquire knowledge from its experienced coworkers before moving into managerial positions is one way to minimize the impact of mass retirements. For example, at Bristol-Myers Squibb, a talent management program has been developed that provides employees with feedback on how to learn from great managers and leaders, and widely announces internal promotions with descriptions of the demonstrated leadership skills that led to the promotion being granted.[14] Many large, successful corporations lack clear succession plans. The problem may be even more severe in Asia, where many large conglomerates and family-owned businesses are run by aging chief executives without a clear succession plan in place.[15]

The key to avoiding potential fiascoes is to have a succession plan for CEOs. However, a poll of 518 organizations indicated that only 42% have a formal succession plan in place. According to a study by the National Association of Corporate Directors, a succession plan should begin with a thorough job analysis and a listing of the characteristics and behaviors of a successful CEO.[16] The organization should not leave it to the CEO to identify a successor. CEOs are typically not trained or experienced in staffing, and they may have selfish motives in appointing a successor. Or, they may avoid appointing a successor altogether, thus keeping themselves in the job. Therefore, the board must be deeply involved in the selection process. Boards also need to realize that the succession process should begin well before the CEO departs; in fact, it should be a continuous process.

Career Development Centers

To facilitate internal transfers, many organizations have an internal office of career development that helps employees explore career options available within the organization.[17] Career development centers provide employees with opportunities to take interest inventories, assess their personal career goals, and interview with representatives across the organization. The goal of career development centers is twofold. First, employees learn about themselves and have a chance to think about what they really want to achieve in their careers. Second, employers have a chance to explain the career options within the organization and develop methods to structure internal career paths that match the interests of their employees. Surveys conducted in numerous organizations consistently demonstrate that employees are more satisfied when their employers provide them with ample communication and opportunities for internal advancement—an interactive career development center can do both.[18]

The interest inventories provided in career development centers often take the form of multiple-choice questionnaires that ask employees to indicate their preferred work activities. For example, respondents might be asked whether they prefer tasks that involve analytical processes like analyzing financial data or more social tasks like motivating a group of workers. After completing these surveys, employees compare their work preferences with the profiles of activities in a variety of jobs. Career development counselors can help talk employees through their thoughts and concerns about job options. Ideally, these career development inventories, coupled with careful analysis of KSAOs, will be paired with job analysis information to improve the person/job match. If employees lack the required KSAOs, career development counselors can suggest developmental work experiences or training opportunities.

Any assessment of career development centers needs to take the organization's bottom line into account.[19] Having full-time career development staff is a significant cost for any organization, and it is unlikely that small or medium-sized organizations will find it cost effective to develop a comprehensive career development center. For smaller organizations, it is more advisable to develop smaller-scale informal initiatives based on personal interactions. Smaller organizations can make use of some career development tools by bringing in external career coaches or consultants to work with individuals who are especially interested in career development within the organization. To reduce costs, employees could take their career development profiles and receive initial feedback through web-based surveys. These electronic survey options save money by reducing staff needs, and employees will not need to go to the career development offices to receive initial counseling.

Although career development centers are complicated to develop and expensive to maintain, they do offer organizations an opportunity to help employees learn about a large spectrum of careers. By providing employees with a clear sense of how they can direct their own careers, it is hoped that job satisfaction will increase and thus lead to increased retention. Because of the cost of career development services, it is especially important to keep track of the return on investment for these services.

Recruiting Metrics

As with external recruiting sources, each internal recruiting source has strengths and weaknesses. Exhibit 6.8 provides an overview of the metrics that might be expected for the categories of recruiting activities, along with issues considered relevant to each source. There is far less research on the costs and benefits of internal recruiting techniques, so our comments here are necessarily somewhat speculative; it is likely that each organization will need to consider its unique needs even more thoroughly than it would when selecting external recruiting methods.

Sufficient Quantity

Because the organization's pool of employees will necessarily be smaller than the general labor market, most internal recruiting methods will have far lower quantity yields. Techniques that permit job postings and intranets will likely produce far more candidates for promotion and advancement than will succession plans.

Sufficient Quality

The degree to which the organization utilizes its own internal information on candidate qualifications and job performance to narrow the pool will determine how qualified the applicants will be. Most organizations that have internal recruiting systems have a huge advantage in assessing applicant characteristics over organizations that use external recruiting systems, so the ability of each source to draw in qualified internal candidates should capitalize on the additional capacity to carefully observe candidates. Regular performance appraisals of all employees, coupled with talent management systems to track KSAOs, are a vital part of an effective internal recruiting system.

EXHIBIT 6.8   **Potential Recruiting Metrics for Different Sources**

Recruiting Method	Quantity	Quality	Costs	Impact on HR
Job posting	Often will be the company's entire workforce	Because all employees will be able to apply, quality is variable	Staff time to develop the recruiting message	May reduce turnover, reduced time to full performance
Intranet and intraplacement	Similar to job posting, although will weed out those who don't like the job characteristics	Better than job postings because applicants have more customized advance knowledge	Sophisticated interface systems will cost more in development time	May reduce turnover, reduced time to full performance
Talent management system	Identifies knowledge, skills, and abilities across all employees	High; preselection of applicants based on identified skill sets	Maintenance of databases can be very time and resource intensive	Higher performance, reduced downtime, reduced training costs
Nominations	Limited to those who receive positive appraisals by supervisors or coworkers	If supervisors make accurate assessments, will be very good person/job match	Many companies keep routine records of employee performance	Can actively identify those who will be good performers and target identified training needs
In-house temporary pools	Based on organization's need for temporary staff coverage	Higher quality if in-house temps receive better benefits than what external staffing firms provide	Start-up costs can be significant; reduces payments to external agencies	More accountability relative to external agencies; increased internal flexibility
Replacement and succession plans	A small number of select workers seen as having high potential	Able to assess skill sets very carefully and consider configurations	HRIS start-up costs, data entry, and checking	Reduces gaps in leadership, protects against shocks due to turnover, reduced turnover
Career development centers	The set of employees who are interested in career development	Assesses employee KSAOs and preferences	Start-up costs, cost of staff, system maintenance	Significant reduction in turnover, increased match between KSAOs and work requirements

Cost

Internal recruitment methods have a completely different set of costs than external recruitment methods. In some ways, internal recruitment can be far less expensive than external recruitment because the organization's own internal communication systems can usually be utilized. It costs very little to send an e-mail to all qualified staff informing them of job opportunities or to post job advertisements on either a physical or electronic bulletin board. However, more sophisticated systems, such as a corporate intranet or comprehensive talent management systems, take more personnel resources to set up and maintain. Career development centers are very costly propositions, and only organizations with considerable internal placement needs will find them cost effective.

Impact on HR Outcomes

Very little research has been done on the effectiveness of various internal recruitment sources. Thus, it is imperative that organizational leaders consider how their internal recruiting systems are impacting turnover rates, job performance, and diversity. Despite the lack of research, it should be easier to monitor these outcomes directly, because it is easier to directly measure the applicant pool contacted through internal methods. From anecdotal observations, some preliminary conclusions can be drawn regarding the advantages of internal placement. There is some evidence that internal career opportunities can reduce turnover intentions. Internal recruitment methods may reduce the time it takes for employees to reach full performance once placed, because they will already be familiar with the organization and may know more about the job in question than would an external hire. Any costs of internal recruitment should be compared against the costs of external recruiting, and the replacement of the employee who takes an internal position should also be taken into account.

COMMUNICATION MESSAGE AND MEDIUM

Once the planning and strategy development phases have been conducted, it is time to conduct the search. As with external recruitment, the search for internal recruits is activated with a requisition. Once the requisition has been approved, the message and medium must be developed to communicate the vacancy to applicants.

Communication Message

As with external recruitment, the message to be communicated can be realistic, targeted, or branded. A realistic message portrays the job as it really is, including positive and negative aspects. A targeted message points out how the job matches the needs of the applicant. A branded message emphasizes the value, culture, and identity of the unit so as to attract applicants who fit the brand label.

Realistic messages can be communicated using a technique like a realistic job preview (RJP). This technique needs to be carefully applied for internal recruitment because, as a result of their already being a member of the organization, applicants may have an accurate picture of the job. Hence, an RJP may not be needed. It should not, however, be automatically assumed that all internal candidates have accurate information about the job and organization. Hence, RJPs are appropriate for internal applicants when they move to an unknown job, a newly created job, or a new geographic area, including an international assignment.

Targeted messages along with inducements are likely to attract experienced internal employees. Targeted messages about the desirability of a position and the actual rewards should come directly from the job rewards matrix. The hiring manager needs to clearly communicate factual information in the job rewards matrix, rather than offers of elaborate rewards that the manager may not be able to provide.

Communication Medium

The actual method or medium used to communicate job openings internally may be a job posting, other written documents, potential supervisors and peers, or informal systems. In a job posting, the duties and requirements of the job should be clearly defined, as should the eligibility requirements. To ensure consistency and fair treatment, job postings are usually coordinated by the HR department.

Other written documents used to communicate a vacancy may include a description of the organization and its location as well as a description of the job. A brochure or video can also be created to show and describe what the organization and its location are really like. This message may be very important to the applicant, who may, for example, be asked to relocate to a new geographic area or to accept an international assignment.

Potential supervisors and peers can be used to describe to the internal applicant how the position he or she is considering fits into the larger organizational picture. Supervisors are knowledgeable about how the position fits with the strategic direction of the organization. Hence, they can communicate information regarding the expansion or contraction of the business unit within which the organization resides. Moreover, supervisors can convey the mobility paths and requirements for future movement by applicants within the business unit, should they be hired. Peers can supplement these supervisory observations by giving candidates a realistic look at what actually happens by way of career development.

Informal systems exist in organizations where organizational members communicate with one another about job vacancies to be filled internally in the absence of verifiable information. The problem with "word of mouth," the "grapevine," or "hall talk" is that it can be a highly selective, inaccurate, and haphazard method of communicating information. It is selective because, by accident or design, not all employees hear about vacant jobs. Talented personnel, including minorities and women, may thus be overlooked. It is inaccurate because it relies on second- or thirdhand information; important details, such as actual job requirements and rewards, are omitted or distorted as they are passed from person to person. Informal methods are also haphazard in that there is no regular communication channel specifying set times for communicating job information. As a result of these problems, informal systems are not to be encouraged.

APPLICANT REACTIONS

A glaring omission in the research literature is a lack of attention paid to studying the reactions of applicants to the internal recruitment process. This lapse stands in stark contrast to the quantity of research conducted on reactions to the external recruitment process. One notable exception in the internal recruitment process is the study of perceived fairness. Given limited opportunities for promotion and transfer, issues of fairness often arise over mobility decisions within an organization. Issues of fairness can be broken down into the categories of distributive and procedural justice. Distributive justice refers to how fair the employee perceives the actual decision to be (e.g., promote or not promote). Procedural justice refers to how fair the employee perceives the process (e.g., policies and procedures) that leads to the promotion or transfer decision to be. Reviews of the evidence suggest that procedures may be nearly as great a source of dissatisfaction to employees as decisions.[20] In some organizations, dissatisfaction arises because there is no formal policy regarding promotion and transfer opportunities. In other organizations, there may be a formal policy, but it may not be closely followed. In yet other organizations, it may be who you know rather than what you know that serves as the criterion for advancement. Finally, in some organizations there is outright discrimination against women and minorities. All these examples are violations of procedural justice and are likely to be perceived as unfair.

TRANSITION TO SELECTION

As with external recruitment, once a job seeker has been identified and attracted to a new job, the organization needs to prepare the person for the selection process. It should not be assumed that just because job seekers come from inside the organization they will automatically know and understand the selection procedures. With the rapid advances being made in selection methods, the applicant may be unaware of new methods being used that are different from those used to hire the applicant to a previous job. Even if the same selection methods are being used, the applicant may need to be refreshed on the process, as much time may have elapsed between the current and previous selection decisions.

An example of an organization that has done an excellent job of preparing internal job seekers to become applicants is the Public Works Agency for the county of Sacramento, California.[21] The county uses a panel of interviewers together, rather than a series of individual interviews, to make selection decisions. For many lower-level employees in the maintenance department, this approach was a first-time experience. Consequently, they were apprehensive about this process because they had no previous experience with the internal selection process. In response to this situation, the HR group initially conducted training classes to describe the process to applicants. But as this was a very time-consuming process for the staff, they replaced the classroom training with videos. One major component of the video was the preparation required prior to the panel interview. Instructions here included appropriate dress and materials to review. Another major component of the video depicted what happens to the applicant during the panel interview. This component included instructions on types of questions that would be asked, the process to be followed, and dos and don'ts in answering the panel interview questions. A final component of the video was testimonials from previous exam takers who became managers. They explain from an organizational perspective what the organization is looking for, as well as provide study tips and strategies.

LEGAL ISSUES

The mobility of people within the organization, particularly upward, has long been a matter of equal employment opportunity/affirmative action (EEO/AA) concern. The workings of the internal labor market rely heavily on internal recruitment activities. As with external recruitment, internal recruitment activities can operate in exclusionary ways, resulting in unequal promotion opportunities, rates, and results for certain groups of employees, particularly women and minorities. The Affirmative Action Programs Regulations specifically address internal recruitment as part of the federal contractor's affirmative action plan (AAP). Seniority systems are likewise subject to legal scrutiny, particularly regarding what constitutes a bona fide system under the law. More recently, promotion systems have been studied as they relate to the glass ceiling effect and the kinds of barriers that have been found to stifle the rise of minorities and women upward in organizations.

Affirmative Action Programs Regulations

Regulations on Affirmative Action Programs from the Office of Federal Contract Compliance Programs (OFCCP) require promotion placement goals where there are discrepancies between percentages of minorities and women employed and available internally in job groups. Accompanying these goals must be an identification of problem areas and action-oriented programs to correct these areas. As in the case of external recruitment, the regulations are virtually silent on indications of specific steps the organization might take to correct promotion system problems. Previous (now expired) regulations provided many useful ideas.

Suggestions include the following:

- Post or otherwise announce promotion opportunities.
- Make an inventory of current minority and female employees' academic, skill, and experience levels.
- Initiate necessary remedial job training and work-study programs.
- Develop and implement formal employee evaluation programs.
- Make certain that "worker specifications" have been validated on job performance–related criteria (neither minority nor female employees should be required to possess higher qualifications than those of the lowest qualified incumbent).
- When apparently qualified minority or female employees are passed over for upgrading, require supervisory personnel to submit written justification.
- Establish formal career counseling programs to include attitude development, education aid, job rotation, buddy systems, and similar programs.
- Review seniority practices and seniority clauses in union contracts to ensure such practices or clauses are nondiscriminatory and do not have a discriminatory effect.

As can be seen, the previous regulations contained a broad range of suggestions for reviewing and improving promotion systems. In terms of recruitment itself, the previous regulations appeared to favor developing KSAO-based information about employees as well as an open promotion system characterized by job posting and cautious use of seniority as a basis for governing upward mobility.

Bona Fide Seniority Systems

Title VII (see Chapter 2) explicitly permits the use of bona fide seniority systems as long as they are not the result of an intention to discriminate. This position presents the organization with a serious dilemma. Past discrimination in external staffing may have resulted in a predominantly white male workforce. A change to a nondiscriminatory external staffing system may increase the presence of women and minorities within an organization, but they will still have less seniority than the white males. If eligibility for promotion is based on seniority and/or if seniority is an actual factor considered in promotion decisions, those with less seniority will have a lower incidence of promotion. Thus, the seniority system will have an adverse impact on women and minorities, even though there is no current intention to discriminate. Is such a seniority system bona fide?

Two points are relevant here. First, the law doesn't define "seniority system." Generally, however, any established system that uses length of employment as a basis for making decisions (such as promotion decisions) is interpreted as a seniority system. Promotions based on ad hoc judgments about which candidates are "more experienced," however, would not likely be considered a bona fide seniority system.[22] Seniority systems can and do occur outside the context of a collective bargaining agreement.

Second, current interpretation is that, in the absence of a discriminatory intent, virtually any seniority system is likely to be bona fide, even if it causes adverse impact.[23] This interpretation incentivizes the organization not to change its current seniority-based practices or systems. Other pressures, such as the Affirmative Action Program Regulations or a voluntary AAP, create an incentive to change in order to eliminate the occurrence of adverse impact in promotion. The organization thus must carefully consider exactly what its posture will be toward seniority practices and systems within the context of its overall AAP.

Under the Americans With Disabilities Act (ADA) there is potential conflict between needing to provide reasonable accommodation to an employee (such as job reassignment) and provisions of the organization's seniority system (such as bidding for jobs on the basis of seniority). According to the Supreme Court, it will ordinarily be unreasonable (undue hardship) for a reassignment request to prevail over the seniority system unless the employee can show some special circumstances that warrant an exception.

The Glass Ceiling

The "glass ceiling" is a term used to characterize strong but invisible barriers to promotion in the organization, particularly to the highest levels, for women and minorities. Evidence demonstrating the existence of a glass ceiling is substantial. The overall labor force is 74% white and 54% male. At the very top in large corporations, senior-level managers are overwhelmingly white males. As one goes down the hierarchy and across industries, a more mixed pattern of data emerges. Equal Employment Opportunity Commission (EEOC) data show that on a nationwide basis, the percentage of women who are officials and managers has increased to a present-day 36.4%. In some industries, particularly health care, department stores, legal services, and banking, the percentage of women managers is substantially higher, ranging from 47% to 77%. In other industries, such as manufacturing, trucking, and architectural/engineering services, the percentage of women managers is much lower (13%–18%).[24] Unfortunately, similar kinds of data for minorities are not available, though few doubt a general underrepresentation of minorities in managerial roles as well. Thus, the closer to the top of the hierarchy, the thicker the glass in the ceiling. At lower levels, the glass becomes much thinner. Across industries, there are substantial variations in this pattern.

Where glass ceilings exist, there are two important questions to ask: What are the reasons for a lack of upward mobility and representation for minorities and women at higher levels of the organization? What changes need to be made, especially staffing-related ones, to help shatter the glass ceiling?

Barriers to Mobility

An obvious conclusion from such data is that there are barriers to mobility, many of them originating within the organization. The Federal Glass Ceiling Commission conducted a four-year study of glass ceilings and barriers to mobility. It identified many barriers: lack of outreach recruitment practices, lack of mentoring training in revenue-generating areas, and lack of access to critical developmental assignments; initial selection for jobs in staff areas outside the upward pipeline to top jobs; biased performance ratings; little access to informal networks; and harassment by colleagues.[25] Added to this list should be another important barrier, namely, child rearing and domestic responsibilities that create difficult work/life balance choices.

An instructive illustration of these barriers, particularly the internal ones, comes from a 21-company study of men and women in sales careers.[26] The study found that 41% of women and 45% of men were eager to move into management, but the women were much less optimistic of their chances of getting promoted. Whereas the sales forces studied were 26% female, only 14% of sales managers were female. The study portrayed "a survivalist culture where career paths are more like obscure jungle trails and where most women say they experience sexual harassment." The study also found "recruiters' use of potentially discriminatory screening tests, managers' negative stereotypes about women, women's lack of access to career-boosting mentors and networks, and difficulty entertaining customers in traditional ways such as fishing and golf outings." Saleswomen were also highly dependent on their mostly male managers for job and territory assignments, which were often based on stereotypes about willingness to travel, relocate, and work long hours.

Overcoming Barriers

It is generally recognized that multiple actions, many of them beyond just staffing-system changes, will be needed to overcome barriers to mobility. Exhibit 6.9 shows a listing of such actions, many of which are consistent with recommendations of the Glass Ceiling Commission.[27]

In terms of specific staffing practices that may help eliminate the glass ceiling, we offer the following suggestions. Barriers to upward mobility can be addressed and removed, at least in part, through internal recruitment activities. Internal recruitment planning needs to involve the design and operation of internal labor markets that facilitate the identification and flows of people to jobs throughout the organization. This may very well conflict with seniority-based practices or seniority systems, both of which are likely to be well entrenched. Organizations simply have to make hard and clear choices about the role(s) that seniority will play in promotion systems.

In terms of recruitment strategy, where to look for employees looms as a major factor in potential change. The organization must increase its scanning capabilities

EXHIBIT 6.9   Ways to Improve Advancement for Women and Minorities

Examine the Organizational Culture
- Review HR policies and practices to determine if they are fair and inclusive.
- Examine the organization's informal culture: look at subtle behaviors, traditions, and norms that may work against women.
- Discover men's and women's perceptions about the organization's culture, their career expectations, and what drives their intentions to stay or leave.
- Identify the organization's best practices that support women's advancement.

Drive Change Through Management Commitment
- Support top-management commitment to talent management, including women in senior positions.
- Ensure that diversity (including women in senior positions) is a key business measurement for success that is communicated to all employees by top management.
- Require line management accountability for advancement of women by incorporating it in performance goals.
- Train line managers to raise awareness and understand barriers to women's advancement.

Foster Inclusion
- Establish and lead a change-management diversity program for managers and employees.
- Affirm diversity inclusion in all employment brand communications.
- Develop a list of women for succession planning.
- Develop and implement retention programs for women.

Educate and Support Women in Career Development
- Emphasize the importance of women acquiring line management experience.
- Encourage mentoring via informal and formal programs.
- Acknowledge successful senior-level women as role models.
- Support the development and utilization of women's networks inside and outside the organization.
- Create and implement leadership development programs for women, including international assignments, if applicable.

Measure for Change
- Monitor the impact of recruiting strategies designed to attract women to senior levels of the organization.
- Track women's advancement in the organization (hiring, job rotation, transfers, international assignments, promotions).
- Determine who gets access to leadership and management training and development opportunities.
- Evaluate differences between salary of men and women at parallel levels within the organization.
- Measure women's turnover against men's.
- Explore reasons why women leave the organization.

Source: Adapted from N. Lockwood, *The Glass Ceiling* (Alexandria, VA: Society for Human Resource Management, 2004), pp. 8–9. Used with permission.

and horizons to identify candidates to promote throughout the organization. In particular, this requires looking across functions for candidates, rather than merely promoting within an area (from sales to sales manager to district manager, for example). Candidates should thus be recruited through both hierarchical and alternative career paths.

Recruitment sources have to be more open and accessible to far-ranging sets of candidates. Informal, word-of-mouth, and "good old boy" sources do not suffice. Job posting and other recruitment strategies that encourage openness of vacancy notification and candidate application will become necessary.

Recruitment changes must be accompanied by many other changes.[28] Top male managers need to fully understand that women executives differ from them in what they perceive to be the major barriers to advancement. Research suggests that women executives are more likely to see an exclusionary climate (male stereotyping and preconceptions of women, exclusion from informal networks, and inhospitable corporate culture) as a critical barrier, whereas top male managers are more likely to point to experience deficiencies (lack of significant general management and line experience, not being in the pipeline long enough) as the culprit. Hence, top management must take steps to not only create better experience-generating opportunities for women, but also develop and foster a more inclusive climate for women, such as through mentoring and providing access to informal networks. To encourage such changes and improve advancement results for women and minorities, managers must be held formally accountable for their occurrence.

An example of a far-reaching diversity initiative to expand the internal diversity pipeline is the "Championing Change for Women: An Integrated Strategy" program at Safeway, a retail grocery giant. A focal point is the Retail Leadership Development (RLD) program, a formal full-time career development program for entry-level grocery store employees to prepare them for moving up into the management ranks (90% of store managers and above come through the program). The program has a particular focus on women and people of color. Employees apply for the program by taking a retail knowledge and skill exam. Those who complete the program are immediately assigned to a store as an assistant manager—the stepping stone to further advancement. To support the advancement program, all managers attend a managing diversity workshop, receive additional on-the-job education, and have access to a toolkit to help them incorporate diversity discussions into their staff meetings. Managers are evaluated in part on their success in meeting diversity goals, and bonus money is riding on that success. Every manager is also expected to serve as a mentor, helping mentees acquire the KSAOs necessary for continued advancement. Other elements of the program include strong support and participation from the CFO, women's leadership network groups (for black, Asian, Hispanic, and LGBT employees), modification of a requirement to relocate in order to gain experience, and work/life balance initiatives for employees with and without children. Since the program was initiated, the number of women who qualified for and completed the RLD program rose 37%, and the number of women store managers increased by 42% (31% for white women and 92% for women of color).[29]

In summary, solutions to the glass ceiling problem require myriad points of attack. First, women and minorities must have visibility and support at top levels—from the board of directors, the CEO, and senior management. That support must include actions to eliminate prejudice and stereotypes. Second, women and minorities must be provided the job opportunities and assignments that will allow them to develop the depth and breadth of KSAOs needed for ascension to, and success in, top management positions. These developmental experiences include assignments in multiple functions, management of diverse businesses, line management experience with direct profit-loss and bottom-line accountability, diverse geographic assignments, and international experience. Naturally, the relative importance of these experiences will vary according to type and size of the organization. Third, the organization must provide continual support for women and minorities to help ensure positive person/job matches. Included here are mentoring, training, and flexible work hour systems. Fourth, the organization must gear up its internal recruitment to aggressively and openly track and recruit women and minority candidates for advancement. Finally, the organization must develop and use valid methods of assessing the qualifications of women and minority candidates (see Chapters 8 and 9).[30]

SUMMARY

The steps involved in the internal recruitment process—planning, strategy development, and communication—closely parallel those in the external recruitment process. With internal recruitment, the search is conducted inside rather than outside the organization. Where both internal and external searches are conducted, they need to be coordinated with each other.

The planning stage requires that the applicant population be identified. Doing so requires an understanding of mobility paths in the organization and mobility path policies. To get access to the internal applicant population, attention must be devoted in advance of the search to requisitions, number and types of contacts, the budget, development of a recruitment guide, and timing.

In terms of strategy development, a closed, open, or hybrid system can be used to decide where to look. How to look requires a knowledge of recruitment sources, such as job postings, intranet and intraplacement, nominations, a talent management system, in-house temporary pools, replacement and succession plans, and career development centers. Just as with external recruitment, there are multiple criteria to be considered in choosing internal sources.

When searching for candidates, the message to be communicated can be realistic, targeted, or branded. Which approach is best to use depends on the applicants, job, and organization. The message is usually communicated with a job posting.

It should, however, be supplemented with other media, including other written documents and potential peers' and supervisors' input. Informal communication methods with information that cannot be verified or that is incomplete are to be discouraged.

The organization needs to provide the applicant with assistance for the transition to selection. This assistance requires that the applicant be made fully aware of the selection process and how to best prepare for it. Taking this step, along with providing well-developed job postings and clearly articulated mobility paths and policies in the organization, should help applicants see the internal recruitment system as fair.

Internal recruitment activities have long been the object of close legal scrutiny. Past and current regulations make several suggestions regarding desirable promotion system features. The relevant laws permit bona fide seniority systems, as long as they are not intentionally used to discriminate. Seniority systems may have the effect of impeding promotions for women and minorities because these groups have not had the opportunity to accumulate an equivalent amount of seniority to that of white males. The glass ceiling refers to invisible barriers to upward advancement, especially to the top levels, for minorities and women. Studies of promotion systems indicate that internal recruitment practices contribute to this barrier. As part of an overall strategy to shatter the glass ceiling, changes are now being experimented with for opening up internal recruitment. These include actions to eliminate stereotypes and prejudices, training and developmental experiences, mentoring, aggressive recruitment, and use of valid selection techniques.

DISCUSSION QUESTIONS

1. Traditional career paths emphasize strict upward mobility within an organization. How does mobility differ in organizations with innovative career paths? List three innovative career paths discussed in this chapter, describing how mobility occurs in each.

2. A sound promotion policy is important. List the characteristics necessary for an effective promotion policy.

3. Compare and contrast a closed internal recruitment system with an open internal recruitment system.

4. What information should be included in the targeted internal communication message?

5. Exhibit 6.9 contains many suggestions for improving the advancement of women and minorities. Choose the three suggestions you think are most important and explain why.

ETHICAL ISSUES

1. MDN, Inc., is considering two employees for the job of senior manager. An internal candidate, Julie, has been with MDN for 12 years and has received very good performance evaluations. The other candidate, Raoul, works for a competitor and has valuable experience in the product market into which MDN wishes to expand. Do you think MDN has an obligation to promote Julie? Why or why not?

2. Do organizations have an ethical obligation to have a succession plan in place? If no, why not? If so, what is the ethical obligation, and to whom is it owed?

APPLICATIONS

Recruitment in a Changing Internal Labor Market

Mitchell Shipping Lines is a distributor of goods on the Great Lakes. It also manufactures shipping containers used to store the goods while in transit. The name of the subsidiary that manufactures those containers is Mitchell-Cole Manufacturing, and the president and CEO is Zoe Brausch.

Brausch is in the middle of converting the manufacturing system from an assembly line to autonomous work teams. Each team will be responsible for producing a separate type of container and will have different tools, machinery, and manufacturing routines for its particular type of container. Members of each team will have the job title "assembler," and each team will be headed by a permanent "leader." Brausch would like all leaders to come from the ranks of current employees, in terms of both the initial set of leaders and the leaders in the future as vacancies arise. In addition, she wants to discourage employee movement across teams in order to build team identity and cohesion. The current internal labor market, however, presents a formidable potential obstacle to her internal staffing goals.

In the long history of the container manufacturing facility, employees have always been treated like union employees even though the facility is nonunion. Such treatment was desired many years ago as a strategy to remain nonunion. It was management's belief that if employees were treated like union employees, there should be no need for employees to vote for a union. A cornerstone of the strategy is use of what everyone in the facility calls the "blue book." The blue book looks like a typical labor contract, and it spells out all terms and conditions of employment. Many of those terms apply to internal staffing and are very typical of traditional mobility systems found in unionized work settings. Specifically, internal transfers and promotions are governed by a facility-wide job posting system. A vacancy is posted throughout the facility and remains open for 30 days; an exception to this is identified entry-level jobs that are filled only externally. Any employee with two or more years of seniority is eligible to bid for any posted vacancy; employees with less seniority may also bid, but they are considered only when no two-year-plus employees apply or are chosen. Internal applicants are assessed by the hiring manager and a representative from the HR department. They review applicants' seniority, relevant experience, past performance appraisals, and other special KSAOs. The blue book requires that the most senior employee who meets the desired qualifications receive the transfer or promotion. Thus, seniority is weighted heavily in the decision.

Brausch is worried about this current internal labor market, especially for recruiting and choosing team leaders. These leaders will likely be required to have many KSAOs that are more important than seniority, and KSAOs likely to not even be positively related to seniority. For example, team leaders will need to have advanced computer, communication, and interpersonal skills. Brausch thinks these skills will be critical for team leaders to have, and that they will more likely be found among junior rather than senior employees. Brausch is in a quandary. She asks for your responses to the following questions:

1. Should seniority be eliminated as an eligibility standard for bidding on jobs—meaning the two-year-plus employees would no longer have priority?

2. Should the job posting system simply be eliminated? If so, what should replace it?

3. Should a strict promotion-from-within policy be maintained? Why or why not?

4. How could career mobility paths be developed that would allow across-team movement without threatening team identity and cohesion?

5. If a new internal labor market system is to be put in place, how should it be communicated to employees?

Succession Planning for a CEO

Lone Star Bank, based in Amarillo, is the fourth largest bank in Texas. The president and CEO, Harry "Tex" Ritter, has been with the company for 30 years, the last 12 in his current position as president and CEO. The last three years have been difficult for Lone Star, as earnings have been below average for the industry, and shareholders have grown increasingly impatient. Last month's quarterly earnings report was the proverbial last straw for the board. Particularly troublesome was Ritter's failure to invest enough of Lone Star's assets in higher-yielding investments. Though banks are carefully regulated in terms of their investment strategies, Ritter's investment strategy was conservative even for a bank.

In a meeting last week, the board decided to allow Ritter to serve out the last year of his contract and then replace him. An attractive severance package was hastily put together; when it was presented to Ritter, he agreed to its terms and conditions. Although the board feels it has made a positive step, it is unsure how to identify a successor. When they met with Ritter, he indicated that he thought the bank's senior vice president of operations, Bob Bowers, would be an able successor. Some members of the board think they should follow Ritter's suggestion because he knows the inner workings of the bank better than anyone on the board. Others are not sure what to do.

1. How should Lone Star go about finding a successor to Ritter? Should Bowers be recruited to be the next CEO?
2. How should other internal candidates be identified and recruited?
3. Does Lone Star need a succession plan for the CEO position? If so, how would you advise the board in setting up such a plan?
4. Should Lone Star have a succession plan in place for other individuals at the bank? If so, why and for whom?

ENDNOTES

1. BMP Forum and Success Factors, *Performance and Talent Management Trend Survey 2007* (San Mateo, CA: author, 2007).
2. W. T. Markham, S. L. Harlan, and E. J. Hackett, "Promotion Opportunity in Organizations: Causes and Consequences," in K. M. Rowland and G. R. Ferris (eds.), *Research in Personnel and Human Resources Management* (Greenwich, CT: JAI Press, 1987), pp. 223–287.
3. B. R. Allred, C. C. Snow, and R. E. Miles, "Characteristics of Managerial Careers in the 21st Century," *Academy of Management Executive*, 1998, 10, pp. 17–27.
4. E. C. Dierdorff and E. A. Surface, "If You Pay for Skills, Will They Learn? Skill Change and Maintenance Under a Skill-Based Pay System," *Journal of Management*, 2008, 34, pp. 721–743.
5. D. G. Collings and K. Mellahi, "Strategic Talent Management: A Review and Research Agenda," *Human Resource Management Review*, 2009, 19, pp. 304–313.
6. R. Fisher and R. McPhail, "Internal Labour Markets as a Strategic Tool," *The Service Industries Journal*, Oct. 2010, pp. 1–16.
7. E. R. Silverman, "Break Requests," *Wall Street Journal*, Aug. 1, 2000, p. B1.
8. L. W. Kleinman and K. J. Clark, "Users' Satisfaction With Job Posting," *Personnel Administrator*, 1984, 29(9), pp. 104–110.
9. M. Frase-Blunt, "Intranet Fuels Internal Mobility," *EMT*, Spring 2004, pp. 16–21; L. G. Klaff, "New Internal Hiring Systems Reduce Cost and Boost Morale," *Workforce Management*, July 2004, pp. 17–20; C. Waxer, "Inside Jobs," *Human Resource Executive*, Sept. 2004, pp. 36–41; S. Overman, "Keep Hot Prospects on Tap," *Staffing Management*, Jan. 2007, pp. 19–21.
10. US Office of Personnel Management, *Human Capital Assessment and Accountability Framework* (Washington, DC: author, 2005); A. Gakovic and K. Yardley, "Global Talent Management at HSBC," *Organization Development Journal*, 2007, 25, pp. 201–206; E. Frauenheim, "Talent

Management Keeping Score With HR Analytics Software," *Workforce Management*, May 21, 2007, pp. 25–33; K. Oakes, "The Emergence of Talent Management," *T + D*, Apr. 2006, pp. 21–24.

11. B. Calandra, "Reeling Them In," *Human Resource Executive*, May 16, 2000, pp. 58–62; "You've Got Friends," *HR Magazine*, Aug. 2001, pp. 49–55.

12. N. Glube, J. Huxtable, and A. Stanard, "Creating New Temporary Hire Options Through In-House Agencies," *Staffing Management Magazine*, June 2002 (*www.shrm.org/hrdisciplines/staffingmanagement/Articles/Pages/CMS_000353.aspx*).

13. P. Lindsay, "Personnel Services: An Innovative Alternative to Temporary Staffing Problems," *IPMA-HR News*, Dec. 2003, p. 19; "Temporary or Contingent Workers," *IPMA-HR News*, June 2004, p. 7.

14. E. Goldberg, "Why You Must Build Management Capability," *Workforce Management Online*, Nov. 2007 (*www.workforce.com/archive/feature/25/22/23/index.php?ht=*); M. Toosi, "Labor Force Projections to 2014: Retiring Boomers," *Monthly Labor Review*, 2005, 128(11), pp. 25–44; P. J. Kiger, "With Baby Boomers Graying, Employers Are Urged to Act Now to Avoid Skills Shortages," *Workforce Management*, 2005, 84(13), pp. 52–54.

15. S. McBride, "In Corporate Asia, a Looming Crisis Over Succession," *Wall Street Journal*, Aug. 7, 2003, pp. A1, A6.

16. National Association of Corporate Directors, *The Role of the Board in Corporate Succession* (Washington, DC: author, 2006).

17. F. Anseel and F. Lievens, "An Examination of Strategies for Encouraging Feedback Interest After Career Assessment," *Journal of Career Development*, 2007, 33, pp. 250–268; T. F. Harrington and T. A. Harrigan, "Practice and Research in Career Counseling and Development—2005," *Career Development Quarterly*, 2006, 55, pp. 98–167.

18. T. Minton-Eversole, "Continuous Learning—in Many Forms—Remains Top Recruiting, Retention Tool," *SHRM Online Recruiting & Staffing Focus Area*, Feb. 2006 (*www.shrm.org*); Society for Human Resource Management, *2007 Job Satisfaction* (Alexandria, VA: author, 2007).

19. I. Speizer, "The State of Training and Development: More Spending, More Scrutiny," *Workforce Management*, May 22, 2006, pp. 25–26.

20. D. K. Ford, D. M. Truxillo, and T. N. Bauer, "Rejected but Still There: Shifting the Focus in Applicant Reactions to the Promotional Context," *International Journal of Selection and Assessment*, Dec. 2009, pp. 402–416.

21. "Panic or Pass—Preparing for Your Oral Board Review," *IPMA News*, July 1995, p. 2.

22. D. J. Walsh, *Employment Law for Human Resource Practice*, second ed. (Mason, OH: Thompson Higher Education, 2007), p. 207.

23. Bureau of National Affairs, *Fair Employment Practices* (Arlington, VA: author, 2007), pp. 421:161–166.

24. Equal Employment Opportunity Commission, *Glass Ceilings: The Status of Women as Officials and Managers in the Private Sector* (Washington, DC: author, 2004).

25. Federal Glass Ceiling Commission, "Good for Business: Making Full Use of the Nation's Human Capital—Fact-Finding Report of the Federal Glass Ceiling Commission," *Daily Labor Report*, Bureau of National Affairs, Mar. 17, 1995, Special Supplement, p. S6.

26. S. Shellenberger, "Sales Offers Women Fairer Pay, but Bias Lingers," *Wall Street Journal*, Jan. 24, 1995, p. B1.

27. Federal Glass Ceiling Commission, "Good for Business: Making Full Use of the Nation's Human Capital," p. S19.

28. P. Digh, "The Next Challenge: Holding People Accountable," *HR Magazine*, Oct. 1998, pp. 63–69; B. R. Ragins, B. Townsend, and M. Mattis, "Gender Gap in the Executive Suite: CEOs and Female Executives Report on Breaking the Glass Ceiling," *Academy of Management Executive*, 1998, 12, pp. 28–42.
29. A. Pomeroy, "Cultivating Female Leaders," *HR Magazine*, Feb. 2007, pp. 44–50.
30. K. L. Lyness and D. E. Thompson, "Climbing the Corporate Ladder: Do Male and Female Executives Follow the Same Route?" *Journal of Applied Psychology*, 2000, 85, pp. 86–101; S. J. Wells, "A Female Executive Is Hard to Find," *HR Magazine*, June 2001, pp. 40–49; S. J. Wells, "Smoothing the Way," *HR Magazine*, June 2001, pp. 52–58.

The Staffing Organizations Model

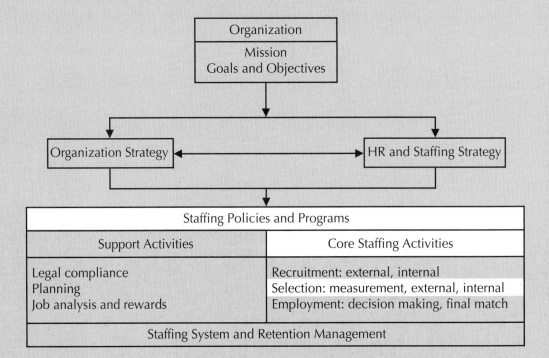

PART FOUR

Staffing Activities: Selection

CHAPTER SEVEN
Measurement

CHAPTER EIGHT
External Selection I

CHAPTER NINE
External Selection II

CHAPTER TEN
Internal Selection

CHAPTER SEVEN

Measurement

Learning Objectives and Introduction
    Learning Objectives
    Introduction

Importance and Use of Measures

Key Concepts
    Measurement
    Scores
    Correlation Between Scores

Quality of Measures
    Reliability of Measures
    Validity of Measures
    Validation of Measures in Staffing
    Validity Generalization
    Staffing Metrics and Benchmarks

Collection of Assessment Data
    Testing Procedures
    Acquisition of Tests and Test Manuals
    Professional Standards

Legal Issues
    Determining Adverse Impact
    Standardization
    Best Practices

Summary

Discussion Questions

Ethical Issues

Applications

Tanglewood Stores Case I

Tanglewood Stores Case II

LEARNING OBJECTIVES AND INTRODUCTION

Learning Objectives

- Define measurement and understand its use and importance in staffing decisions
- Understand the concept of reliability and review the different ways reliability of measures can be assessed
- Define validity and consider the relationship between reliability and validity
- Compare and contrast the two types of validation studies typically conducted
- Consider how validity generalization affects and informs validation of measures in staffing
- Review the primary ways assessment data can be collected

Introduction

In staffing, measurement is a process used to gather and express information about people and jobs in numerical form. Measurement is critical to staffing because, as far as selection decisions are concerned, a selection decision can only be as effective as the measures on which it is based.

The first part of this chapter presents the process of measurement in staffing decisions. After showing the vital importance and uses of measurement in staffing activities, three key concepts are discussed. The first concept is that of measurement itself, along with the issues raised by it—standardization of measurement, levels of measurement, and the difference between objective and subjective measures. The second concept is that of scoring and how to express scores in ways that help in their interpretation. The final concept is that of correlations between scores, particularly as expressed by the correlation coefficient and its significance. Calculating correlations between scores is a very useful way to learn even more about the meaning of scores.

What is the quality of the measures used in staffing? How sound an indicator of the attributes measured are they? Answers to these questions lie in the reliability and validity of the measures and the scores they yield. There are multiple ways of doing reliability and validity analysis; these methods are discussed in conjunction with numerous examples drawn from staffing situations. As these examples show, the quality of staffing decisions (e.g., who to hire or reject) depends heavily on the quality of measures and scores used as inputs to these decisions. Some organizations rely only on common staffing metrics and benchmarks—what leading organizations are doing—to measure effectiveness. Though benchmarks have their value, reliability and validity are the real keys in assessing the quality of selection measures.

An important practical concern involved in the process of measurement is the collection of assessment data. Decisions about testing procedures (who is qualified to test applicants, what information should be disclosed to applicants, and how to assess applicants with standardized procedures) need to be made. The collection of assessment data also includes the acquisition of tests and test manuals. This process will vary depending on whether paper-and-pencil or computerized selection measures are utilized. Finally, in the collection of assessment data, organizations need to attend to professional standards that govern their proper use.

Measurement concepts and procedures are directly involved in legal issues, particularly equal employment opportunity and affirmative action (EEO/AA) issues. This requires collection and analysis of applicant flow and stock statistics. Also reviewed are methods for determining adverse impact, standardization of measures, and best practices as suggested by the Equal Employment Opportunity Commission (EEOC).

IMPORTANCE AND USE OF MEASURES

Measurement is one of the key ingredients for, and tools of, staffing organizations. Indeed, it is virtually impossible to have any type of systematic staffing process that does not use measures and an accompanying measurement process.

Measures are methods or techniques for describing and assessing attributes of objects that are of concern to us. Examples include tests of applicants' KSAOs (knowledge, skill, ability, and other characteristics), evaluations of employees' job performance, and applicants' ratings of their preferences for various types of job rewards. These assessments of attributes are gathered through the measurement process, which consists of (1) choosing an attribute of concern, (2) developing an operational definition of the attribute, (3) constructing a measure of the attribute (if no suitable measure is available) as it is operationally defined, and (4) using the measure to actually gauge the attribute.

Results of the measurement process are expressed in numbers or scores—for example, applicants' scores on an ability test, employees' performance evaluation rating scores, or applicants' ratings of rewards in terms of their importance. These scores become the indicators of the attribute. Through the measurement process, the initial attribute and its operational definition are transformed into a numerical expression of the attribute.

KEY CONCEPTS

This section covers a series of key concepts in three major areas: measurement, scores, and correlation between scores.

Measurement

In the preceding discussion, the essence of measurement and its importance and use in staffing were described. It is important to define the term "measurement" more formally and explore implications of that definition.

Definition

Measurement may be defined as the process of assigning numbers to objects to represent quantities of an attribute of the objects.[1] Exhibit 7.1 depicts the general process of the use of measures in staffing, along with an example for the job of

EXHIBIT 7.1   Use of Measures in Staffing

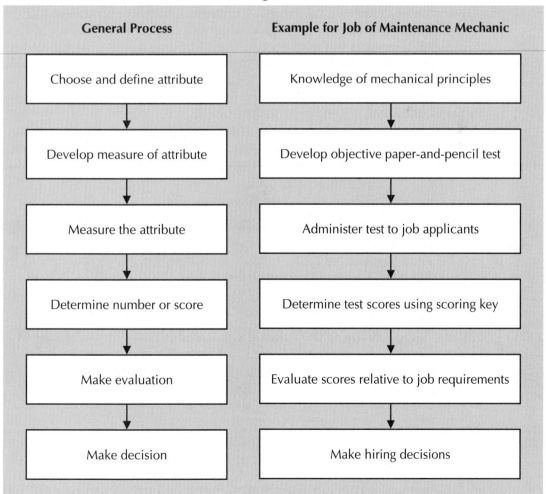

General Process	Example for Job of Maintenance Mechanic
Choose and define attribute	Knowledge of mechanical principles
Develop measure of attribute	Develop objective paper-and-pencil test
Measure the attribute	Administer test to job applicants
Determine number or score	Determine test scores using scoring key
Make evaluation	Evaluate scores relative to job requirements
Make decision	Make hiring decisions

maintenance mechanic. The first step in measurement is to choose and define an attribute (also called a construct) to be measured. In the example, this is knowledge of mechanical principles. Then, a measure must be developed for the attribute so that it can physically be measured. In the example, a paper-and-pencil test is developed to measure mechanical knowledge, and this test is administered to applicants. Once the attribute is physically measured, numbers or scores are determined (in the example, the mechanical test is scored). At that point, the applicants' scores are evaluated (which scores meet the job requirements), and a selection decision can be made (e.g., hire a maintenance mechanic).

Of course, in practice, this textbook process is often not followed explicitly, and thus selection errors are more likely. For example, if the methods used to determine scores on an attribute are not explicitly determined and evaluated, the scores themselves may be incorrectly determined. Similarly, if the evaluation of the scores is not systematic, each selection decision maker may put his or her own spin on the scores, thereby defeating the purpose of careful measurement. The best way to avoid these problems is for all those involved in selection decisions to go through each step of the measurement process depicted in Exhibit 7.1, apply it to the job(s) in question, and reach agreement at each step of the way.

Standardization

The hallmark of sound measurement practice is standardization.[2] Standardization is a means of controlling the influence of outside or extraneous factors on the scores generated by the measure and ensuring that, as much as possible, the scores obtained reflect the attribute measured.

A standardized measure has three basic properties:

1. The content is identical for all objects measured (e.g., all job applicants take the same test).
2. The administration of the measure is identical for all objects (e.g., all job applicants have the same time limit on a test).
3. The rules for assigning numbers are clearly specified and agreed on in advance (e.g., a scoring key for the test is developed before it is administered).

These seemingly simple and straightforward characteristics of standardization of measures have substantial implications for the conduct of many staffing activities. These implications will become apparent throughout the remainder of this text. For example, assessment devices, such as the employment interview and letters of reference, often fail to meet the requirements for standardization, and organizations must undertake steps to make them more standardized.

Levels of Measurement

There are varying degrees of precision in measuring attributes and in representing differences among objects in terms of attributes. Accordingly, there are different levels or scales of measurement.[3] It is common to classify any particular measure as falling into one of four levels of measurement: nominal, ordinal, interval, or ratio.

Nominal.   With nominal scales, a given attribute is categorized, and numbers are assigned to the categories. With or without numbers, however, there is no order or level implied among the categories. The categories are merely different, and none is higher or lower than the others. For example, each job title could represent a different category, with a different number assigned to it: managers = 1, clericals = 2, sales = 3, and so forth. Clearly, the numbers do not imply any ordering among the categories.

Ordinal.   With ordinal scales, objects are rank ordered according to how much of the attribute they possess. Thus, objects may be ranked from best to worst or from highest to lowest. For example, five job candidates, each of whom has been evaluated in terms of overall qualification for the job, might be rank ordered from 1 to 5, or highest to lowest, according to their job qualifications.

Rank orderings only represent relative differences among objects; they do not indicate the absolute levels of the attribute. Thus, the rank ordering of the five job candidates does not indicate exactly how qualified each of them is for the job, nor are the differences in their ranks necessarily equal to the differences in their qualifications. The difference in qualifications between applicants ranked 1 and 2 may not be the same as the difference between those ranked 4 and 5.

Interval.   Like ordinal scales, interval scales allow us to rank order objects. However, the differences between adjacent points on the measurement scale are now equal in terms of the attribute. If an interval scale is used to rank order the five job candidates, the differences in qualifications between those ranked 1 and 2 are equal to the differences between those ranked 4 and 5.

In many instances, the level of measurement falls somewhere between an ordinal and interval scale. That is, objects can be clearly rank ordered, but the differences between the ranks are not necessarily equal throughout the measurement scale. In the example of the five job candidates, the difference in qualifications between those ranked 1 and 2 might be slight compared with the distance between those ranked 4 and 5.

Unfortunately, this in-between level of measurement is characteristic of many of the measures used in staffing. Though it is not a major problem, it does signal the need for caution in interpreting the meaning of differences in scores among people.

Ratio.   Ratio scales are like interval scales in that there are equal differences between scale points for the attribute being measured. In addition, ratio scales have a logical or absolute true zero point. Because of this, how much of the attribute each object possesses can be stated in absolute terms.

Normally, ratio scales are involved in counting or weighing things. There are many such examples of ratio scales in staffing. Assessing how much weight a candidate can carry over some distance for physically demanding jobs such as firefighting or general construction is an example. Perhaps the most common example is counting how much previous job experience (general or specific) job candidates have had.

Objective and Subjective Measures

Frequently, staffing measures are described as being either objective or subjective. Often, the term "subjective" is used in disparaging ways ("I can't believe how subjective that interview was; there's no way they can rate me fairly on the basis of it"). Exactly what is the difference between so-called objective and subjective measures?

The difference, in large part, pertains to the rules used to assign numbers to the attribute being assessed. With objective measures, the rules are predetermined and usually communicated and applied through some sort of scoring key or system. Most paper-and-pencil tests are considered objective. The scoring systems in subjective measures are more elusive and often involve a rater or judge who assigns the numbers. Many employment interviewers fall into this category, especially those with an idiosyncratic way of evaluating people's responses, one that is not known or shared by other interviewers.

In principle, any attribute can be measured objectively or subjectively, and sometimes both are used. Research shows that when an attribute is measured by both objective and subjective means, there is often relatively low agreement between scores from the two types of measures. A case in point pertains to the attribute of job performance. Performance may be measured objectively through quantity of output, and it may be measured subjectively through performance appraisal ratings, yet these two types of measures correlate only weakly with each other.[4] Undoubtedly, the raters' lack of sound scoring systems for rating job performance was a major contributor to the lack of obtained agreement.

It thus appears that whatever type of measure is used to assess attributes in staffing, serious attention should be paid to the scoring system or key. In a sense, this requires nothing more than having a firm knowledge of exactly what the organization is trying to measure. This is true for both paper-and-pencil (objective) measures and judgmental (subjective) measures, such as the employment interview. It is simply another way of emphasizing the importance of standardization in measurement.

Scores

Measures yield numbers or scores to represent the amount of the attribute being assessed. Scores are thus the numerical indicator of the attribute. Once scores have been derived, they can be manipulated in various ways to give them even greater meaning and to better describe characteristics of the objects being scored.[5]

Central Tendency and Variability

Assume that a group of job applicants was administered a test of their knowledge of mechanical principles. The test is scored using a scoring key, and each applicant receives a score, known as a raw score. These are shown in Exhibit 7.2.

Some features of this set of scores may be summarized through the calculation of summary statistics. These pertain to central tendency and variability in the scores and are also shown in Exhibit 7.2.

The indicators of central tendency are the mean, the median, and the mode. Since it was assumed that the data were interval level data, it is permissible to compute

---

EXHIBIT 7.2   Central Tendency and Variability: Summary Statistics

Data		Summary Statistics
Applicant	**Test Score (X)**	
A	10	A. Central tendency
B	12	Mean ($\bar{X}$) = 338/20 = 16.9
C	14	Median = middle score = 17
D	14	Mode = most frequent score = 15
E	15	
F	15	B. Variability
G	15	Range = 10 to 24
H	15	Standard deviation (SD) =
I	15	
J	17	$\sqrt{\dfrac{\Sigma\,(X-\bar{X})^2}{n-1}} = 3.52$
K	17	
L	17	
M	18	
N	18	
O	19	
P	19	
Q	19	
R	22	
S	23	
T	24	

Total (Σ) = 338

N = 20

all three indicators of central tendency. Had the data been ordinal, the mean should not be computed. For nominal data, only the mode would be appropriate.

The variability indicators are the range and the standard deviation. The range shows the lowest to highest actual scores for the job applicants. The standard deviation shows, in essence, the average amount of deviation of individual scores from the average score. It summarizes the amount of spread in the scores. The larger the standard deviation, the greater the variability, or spread, in the data.

Percentiles

A percentile score for an individual is the percentage of people scoring below the individual in a distribution of scores. Refer again to Exhibit 7.2, and consider applicant C. That applicant's percentile score is in the 10th percentile (2/20 × 100). Applicant S is in the 90th percentile (18/20 × 100).

Standard Scores

When interpreting scores, it is natural to compare individuals' raw scores with the mean, that is, to ask whether scores are above, at, or below the mean. But a true understanding of how well an individual did relative to the mean takes into account the amount of variability in scores around the mean (the standard deviation). That is, the calculation must be "corrected" or controlled for the amount of variability in a score distribution to accurately present how well a person scored relative to the mean.

Calculation of the standard score for an individual is the way to accomplish this correction. The formula for calculation of the standard score, or Z, is as follows:

$$Z = \frac{X - \overline{X}}{SD}$$

Applicant S in Exhibit 7.2 had a raw score of 23 on the test; the mean is 16.9 and the standard deviation is 3.52. Substituting into the above formula, applicant S has a Z score of 1.7. Thus, applicant S scored about 1.7 standard deviations above the mean.

Standard scores are also useful for determining how a person performed, in a relative sense, on two or more tests. For example, assume the following data for a particular applicant:

	Test 1	Test 2
Raw score	50	48
Mean	48	46
SD	2.5	.80

On which test did the applicant do better? To answer that, simply calculate the applicant's standard scores on the two tests. The Z score on test 1 is .80, and the Z score on test 2 is 2.5. Thus, while the applicant got a higher raw score on test 1 than on test 2, the applicant got a higher Z score on test 2 than on test 1. Viewed in this way, it is apparent that the applicant did better on the second of the two tests.

Correlation Between Scores

Frequently in staffing there are scores on two or more measures for a group of individuals. One common occurrence is to have scores on two (or often, more than two) KSAO measures. For example, there could be a score on the test of knowledge of mechanical principles and also an overall rating of the applicant's probable job success based on the employment interview. In such instances, it is logical to ask whether there is some relation between the two sets of scores. Is there a tendency for an increase in knowledge test scores to be accompanied by an increase in interview ratings?

As another example, an organization may have scores on a particular KSAO measure (e.g., the knowledge test) and on a measure of job performance (e.g., performance appraisal ratings) for a group of individuals. Is there a correlation between these two sets of scores? If there is, this would provide some evidence about the probable validity of the knowledge test as a predictor of job performance. This evidence would help the organization decide whether to incorporate the use of the test into the selection process for job applicants.

Investigation of the relationship between two sets of scores proceeds through the plotting of scatter diagrams and through calculation of the correlation coefficient.

Scatter Diagrams

Assume two sets of scores for a group of people—scores on a test and scores on a measure of job performance. A scatter diagram is simply the plot of the joint distribution of the two sets of scores. Inspection of the plot provides a visual representation of the type of relationship that exists between the two sets of scores. Exhibit 7.3 provides three different scatter diagrams for the two sets of scores. Each X represents a test score and job performance score combination for an individual.

Example A in Exhibit 7.3 suggests very little relationship between the two sets of scores. Example B shows a modest relationship between the scores, and example C shows a somewhat strong relationship between the two sets of scores.

Correlation Coefficient

The relationship between two sets of scores may also be investigated through calculation of the correlation coefficient. The symbol for the correlation coefficient is r. Numerically, r values can range from $r = -1.0$ to $r = 1.0$. The larger the absolute value of r, the stronger the relationship. When an r value is shown without a (plus or minus) sign, the value is assumed to be positive.

EXHIBIT 7.3 Scatter Diagrams and Corresponding Correlations

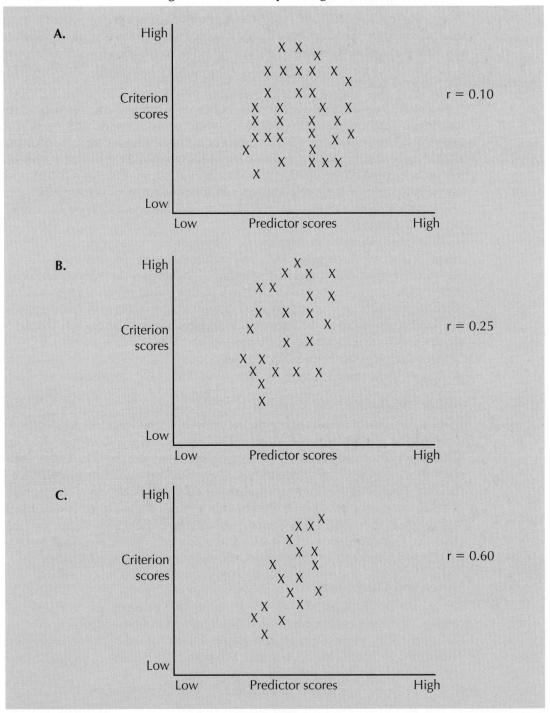

Naturally, the value of r bears a close resemblance to the scatter diagram. As a demonstration of this, Exhibit 7.3 also shows the approximate r value for each of the three scatter diagrams. The r in example A is low (r = .10), the r in example B is moderate (r = .25), and the r in example C is high (r = .60).

Calculation of the correlation coefficient is straightforward. An example of this calculation and the formula for r are shown in Exhibit 7.4. In the exhibit are two sets of scores for 20 people. The first set is the test scores for the 20 individuals in Exhibit 7.2. The second set of scores is an overall job performance rating (on a 1–5 rating scale) for these people. As can be seen from the calculation, there is a correlation of r = .58 between the two sets of scores. The resultant value of r succinctly summarizes both the strength of the relationship between the two sets of scores and the direction of the relationship. Despite the simplicity of its calculation, there are several notes of caution to sound regarding the correlation.

EXHIBIT 7.4   Calculation of Product-Moment Correlation Coefficient

Person	Test Score (X)	Performance Rating (Y)	(X²)	(Y²)	(XY)
A	10	2	100	4	20
B	12	1	144	1	12
C	14	2	196	4	28
D	14	1	196	1	14
E	15	3	225	9	45
F	15	4	225	16	60
G	15	3	225	9	45
H	15	4	225	16	60
I	15	4	225	16	60
J	17	3	289	9	51
K	17	4	289	16	68
L	17	3	289	9	51
M	18	2	324	4	36
N	18	4	324	16	72
O	19	3	361	9	57
P	19	3	361	9	57
Q	19	5	361	25	95
R	22	3	484	9	66
S	23	4	529	16	92
T	24	5	576	25	120
	$\Sigma X = 338$	$\Sigma Y = 63$	$\Sigma X^2 = 5948$	$\Sigma Y^2 = 223$	$\Sigma XY = 1109$

$$r = \frac{N\Sigma XY - (\Sigma X)(\Sigma Y)}{\sqrt{[N\Sigma X^2 - (\Sigma X)^2][N\Sigma Y^2 - (\Sigma Y)^2]}} = \frac{20(1109) - (338)(63)}{\sqrt{[20(5948) - (338)^2][20(223) - (63)^2]}} = .58$$

First, the correlation does not connote a proportion or percentage. An r = .50 between variables X and Y does not mean that X is 50% of Y or that Y can be predicted from X with 50% accuracy. The appropriate interpretation is to square the value of r, for r^2, and then say that the two variables share that percentage of common variation in their scores. Thus, the proper interpretation of r = .50 is that the two variables share 25% ($.5^2 \times 100$) common variation in their scores.

Second, the value of r is affected by the amount of variation in each set of scores. Other things being equal, the less variation there is in one or both sets of scores, the smaller the calculated value of r will be. At the extreme, if one set of scores has no variation, the correlation will be r = .00. That is, for there to be a correlation, there must be variation in both sets of scores. The lack of variation in scores is called the problem of restriction of range.

Third, the formula used to calculate the correlation in Exhibit 7.4 is based on the assumption that there is a linear relationship between the two sets of scores. This may not always be a good assumption; something other than a straight line may best capture the true nature of the relationship between scores. To the extent that two sets of scores are not related in a linear fashion, use of the formula for calculation of the correlation will yield a value of r that understates the actual strength of the relationship.

Finally, the correlation between two variables does not imply causation between them. A correlation simply says how two variables covary or correlate; it says nothing about one variable necessarily causing the other one.

Significance of the Correlation Coefficient

The statistical significance refers to the likelihood that a correlation exists in a population, based on knowledge of the actual value of r in a sample from that population. Concluding that a correlation is indeed statistically significant means that there is most likely a correlation in the population. That means if the organization were to use a selection measure based on a statistically significant correlation, the correlation is likely to be significant when used again to select another sample (e.g., future job applicants).

More formally, r is calculated in an initial group, called a sample. From this piece of information, the question arises whether to infer that there is also a correlation in the *population*. To answer this, compute the t value of our correlation using the following formula,

$$t = \frac{r}{\sqrt{(1-r^2)/n-2}}$$

where r is the value of the correlation, and n is the size of the sample.

A t distribution table in any elementary statistics book shows the significance level of r.[6] The significance level is expressed as p < some value, for example, p < .05. This p level tells the probability of concluding that there is a correlation in the population when in fact there is not a relationship. Thus, a correlation with p < .05 means there are fewer than 5 chances in 100 of concluding that there is a relationship in the population when in fact there is not. This is a relatively small probability and usually leads to the conclusion that a correlation is indeed statistically significant.

It is important to avoid concluding that there is a relationship in the population when in fact there is not. Therefore, one usually chooses a fairly conservative or stringent level of significance that the correlation must attain before one can conclude that it is significant. Typically, a standard of p < .05 or less (another common standard is p < .01) is chosen. The actual significance level (based on the t value for the correlation) is then compared with the desired significance level, and a decision is reached as to whether the correlation is statistically significant. Here are some examples:

Desired Level	Actual Level	Conclusion About Correlation
p < .05	p < .23	Not significant
p < .05	p < .02	Significant
p < .01	p < .07	Not significant
p < .01	p < .009	Significant

Although statistical significance is important in judging the usefulness of a selection measure, caution should be exercised in placing too much weight on this. With very large sample sizes, even very small correlations will be significant, and with very small samples, even strong correlations will fail to be significant. The absolute size of the correlation matters as well.

QUALITY OF MEASURES

Measures are developed and used to gauge attributes of objects. Results of measures are expressed in the form of scores, and various manipulations may be done to them. Such manipulations lead to better understanding and interpretation of the scores, and thus the attribute represented by the scores.

In staffing, for practical reasons, the scores of individuals are treated as if they were, in fact, the attribute itself rather than merely indicators of the attribute. For example, scores on a mental ability test are interpreted as being synonymous with how intelligent individuals are. Or, individuals' job performance ratings from their supervisors are viewed as indicators of their true performance.

Treated in this way, scores become a major input to decision making about individuals. For example, scores on the mental ability test are used and weighted heavily to decide which job applicants will receive a job offer. Or, performance ratings may serve as a key factor in deciding which individuals will be eligible for an internal staffing move, such as a promotion. In these and numerous other ways, management uses these scores to guide the conduct of staffing activities in the organization. This is illustrated through such phrases as "Let the numbers do the talking," "We manage by the numbers," and "Never measured, never managed."

The quality of the decisions made and the actions taken are unlikely to be any better than the quality of the measures on which they are based. Thus, there is a lot at stake in the quality of the measures used in staffing. Such concerns are best viewed in terms of reliability and validity of measures.[7]

Reliability of Measures

Reliability of measurement refers to the consistency of measurement of an attribute.[8] A measure is reliable to the extent that it provides a consistent set of scores to represent an attribute. Rarely is perfect reliability achieved, because of the occurrence of measurement error. Reliability is thus a matter of degree.

Reliability of measurement is of concern both within a single time period in which the attribute is being measured and between time periods. Moreover, reliability is of concern for both objective and subjective measures. These two concerns help create a general framework for better understanding reliability.

The key concepts for the framework are shown in Exhibit 7.5. In the exhibit, a single attribute, "A" (e.g., knowledge of mechanical principles), is being measured. Scores (ranging from 1 to 5) are available for 15 individuals. A is being measured in time period 1 (T_1) and time period 2 (T_2). In each time period, A may be measured objectively, with two test items, or subjectively, with two raters. The same two items or raters are used in each time period. (In reality, more than two items or raters would probably be used to measure A, but for simplicity, only two are used here.) Each test item or rater in each time period is a submeasure of A. There are thus four submeasures of A—designated X_1, X_2, Y_1, and Y_2—and four sets of scores. In terms of reliability of measurement, the concern is with the consistency or similarity in the sets of scores. This requires various comparisons of the scores.

Comparisons Within T_1 or T_2

Consider the four sets of scores as coming from the objective measure, which used test items. Comparing sets of scores from these items in either T_1 or T_2 is called internal consistency reliability. The relevant comparisons are X_1 and Y_1, and X_2 and Y_2. It is hoped that the comparisons will show high similarity, because both items are intended to measure A within the same time period.

Now treat the four sets of scores as coming from the subjective measure, which relied on raters. Comparisons of these scores involve what is called interrater

EXHIBIT 7.5   Framework for Reliability of Measures

	Scores on Attribute A							
	Objective (Test Items)				Subjective (Raters)			
	Time 1		Time 2		Time 1		Time 2	
Person	X_1	Y_1	X_2	Y_2	X_1	Y_1	X_2	Y_2
A	5	5	4	5	5	5	4	5
B	5	4	4	3	5	4	4	3
C	5	5	5	4	5	5	5	4
D	5	4	5	5	5	4	5	5
E	4	5	3	4	4	5	3	4
F	4	4	4	3	4	4	4	3
G	4	4	3	4	4	4	3	4
H	4	3	4	3	4	3	4	3
I	3	4	3	4	3	4	3	4
J	3	3	5	3	3	3	5	3
K	3	3	2	3	3	3	2	3
L	3	2	4	2	3	2	4	2
M	2	3	4	3	2	3	4	3
N	2	2	1	2	2	2	1	2
O	1	2	3	2	1	2	3	2

NOTE: X_1 and X_2 are the same test item or rater; Y_1 and Y_2 are the same test item or rater. The subscript "1" refers to T_1, and the subscript "2" refers to T_2.

reliability. The relevant comparisons are the same as with the objective measure scores, namely, X_1 and Y_1, and X_2 and Y_2. Again, it is hoped that there will be high agreement between the raters, because they are focusing on a single attribute at a single moment in time.

Comparisons Between T_1 and T_2

Comparisons of scores between time periods involve assessment of measurement stability. When scores from an objective measure are used, this is referred to as test–retest reliability. The relevant comparisons are X_1 and X_2, and Y_1 and Y_2. To the extent that A is not expected to change between T_1 and T_2, there should be high test–retest reliability.

When subjective scores are compared between T_1 and T_2, the concern is with intrarater reliability. Here, the same rater evaluates individuals in terms of A in two different time periods. To the extent that A is not expected to change, there should be high intrarater reliability.

In summary, reliability is concerned with consistency of measurement. There are multiple ways of treating reliability, depending on whether scores from a measure are being compared for consistency within or between time periods and depending on whether the scores are from objective or subjective measures. These points are summarized in Exhibit 7.6. Ways of computing agreement between scores will be covered shortly, after the concept of measurement error is explored.

Measurement Error

Rarely will any of the comparisons among scores discussed previously yield perfect similarity or reliability. Indeed, none of the comparisons in Exhibit 7.6 visually shows complete agreement among the scores. The lack of agreement among the scores may be due to the occurrence of measurement error. This type of error represents "noise" in the measure and measurement process. Its occurrence means that the measure did not yield perfectly consistent scores, or so-called true scores, for the attribute.

The scores actually obtained from the measure thus have two components to them, a true score and measurement error. That is,

$$\text{actual score} = \text{true score} + \text{error}$$

The error component of any actual score, or set of scores, represents unreliability of measurement. Unfortunately, unreliability is a fact of life for the types

---

EXHIBIT 7.6 Summary of Types of Reliability

	Compare scores within T_1 or T_2	Compare scores between T_1 and T_2
Objective measure (test items)	Internal consistency	Test–retest
Subjective measure (raters)	Interrater	Intrarater

of measures used in staffing. To help understand why this is the case, the various types or sources of error that can occur in a staffing context must be explored. These errors may be grouped under the categories of deficiency error and contamination error.[9]

Deficiency Error. Deficiency error occurs when there is failure to measure some portion or aspect of the attribute assessed. For example, if knowledge of mechanical principles involves gear ratios, among other things, and our test does not have any items (or an insufficient number of items) covering this aspect, the test is deficient. As another example, if an attribute of job performance is "planning and setting work priorities," and the raters fail to rate people on that dimension during their performance appraisal, the performance measure is deficient.

Deficiency error can occur in several related ways. First, the attribute may have been inadequately defined in the first place. Thus, the test of knowledge of mechanical principles may fail to address familiarity with gear ratios because it was never included in the initial definition of mechanical principles. Or, the performance measure may fail to require raters to rate their employees on "planning and setting work priorities" because this attribute was never considered an important dimension of their work.

A second way that deficiency error occurs is in the construction of measures used to assess the attribute. Here, the attribute may be well defined and understood, but there is a failure to construct a measure that adequately gets at the totality of the attribute. This is akin to poor measurement by oversight, which happens when measures are constructed in a hurried, ad hoc fashion.

Deficiency error also occurs when the organization opts to use whatever measures are available because of ease, cost considerations, sales pitches and promotional claims, and so forth. The measures so chosen may turn out to be deficient.

Contamination Error. Contamination error represents the occurrence of unwanted or undesirable influence on the measure and on individuals for whom the measure is being used. These influences muddy the scores and make them difficult to interpret.

Sources of contamination abound, as do examples of them. Several of these sources and examples are shown in Exhibit 7.7, along with some suggestions for how they might be controlled. These examples show that contamination error is multifaceted, making it difficult to minimize and control.

Calculation of Reliability Estimates

Numerous procedures are available for calculating actual estimates of the degree of reliability of measurement.[10] The first two of these (coefficient alpha and interrater agreement) assess reliability within a single time period. The other two procedures (test–retest and intrarater agreement) assess reliability between time periods.

EXHIBIT 7.7   Sources of Contamination Error and Suggestions for Control

Source of Contamination	Example	Suggestion for Control
Content domain	Irrelevant material on test	Define domain of test material to be covered
Standardization	Different time limits for same test	Have same time limits for everyone
Chance response tendencies	Guessing by test taker	Impossible to control in advance
Rater	Rater gives inflated ratings to people	Train rater in rating accuracy
Rating situation	Interviewees are asked different questions	Ask all interviewees the same questions

Coefficient Alpha.   Coefficient alpha may be calculated in instances in which there are two or more items (or raters) for a particular attribute. Its formula is

$$\alpha = \frac{n\,(\bar{r})}{1 + \bar{r}\,(n-1)}$$

where $\bar{r}$ is the average intercorrelation among the items (raters) and n is the number of items (raters). For example, if there are five items (n = 5), and the average correlation among those five items is $\bar{r}$ = .80, coefficient alpha is .95.

It can be seen from the formula and the example that coefficient alpha depends on just two things—the number of items and the amount of correlation between them. This suggests two basic strategies for increasing the internal consistency reliability of a measure—increase the number of items and increase the amount of agreement between the items (raters). It is generally recommended that coefficient alpha be at least .80 for a measure to have an acceptable degree of reliability.

Interrater Agreement.   When raters serve as the measure, it is often convenient to talk about interrater agreement, or the amount of agreement among them. For example, if members of a group or panel interview independently rate a set of job applicants on a 1–5 scale, it is logical to ask how much they agreed with one another.

A simple way to determine this is to calculate the percentage of agreement among the raters. An example of this is shown in Exhibit 7.8.

There is no commonly accepted minimum level of interrater agreement that must be met in order to consider the raters sufficiently reliable. Normally, a fairly

EXHIBIT 7.8   Calculation of Percentage Agreement Among Raters

Person (ratee)	Rater 1	Rater 2	Rater 3
A	5	5	2
B	3	3	5
C	5	4	4
D	1	1	5
E	2	2	4

$$\% \text{ Agreement} \quad \frac{\text{\# agreements}}{\text{\# agreements} + \text{\# disagreements}} \times 100$$

% Agreement
Rater 1 and Rater 2 = 4/5 = 80%
Rater 1 and Rater 3 = 0/5 = 0%
Rater 2 and Rater 3 = 1/5 = 20%

high level should be set—75% or higher. The more important the end use of the ratings, the greater the agreement required should be. Critical uses, such as hiring decisions, demand very high levels of reliability, well in excess of 75% agreement.

Test–Retest Reliability.   To assess test–retest reliability, the test scores from two different time periods are correlated through calculation of the correlation coefficient. The r may be calculated on total test scores, or a separate r may be calculated for scores on each item. The resultant r indicates the stability of measurement—the higher the r, the more stable the measure.

Interpretation of the r value is made difficult by the fact that the scores are gathered at two different points in time. Between those two time points, the attribute being measured has an opportunity to change. Interpretation of test–retest reliability thus requires some sense of how much the attribute may be expected to change, and what the appropriate time interval between tests is. Usually, for very short time intervals (hours or days), most attributes are quite stable, and a large test–retest r (r = .90 or higher) should be expected. Over longer time intervals, it is usual to expect much lower r's, depending on the attribute being measured. For example, over six months or a year, individuals' knowledge of mechanical principles might change. If so, there will be lower test–retest reliabilities (e.g., r = .50).

Intrarater Agreement.   To calculate intrarater agreement, scores that the rater assigns to the same people in two different time periods are compared. The calculation could involve computing the correlation between the two sets of scores, or it could involve using the same formula as for interrater agreement (see Exhibit 7.8).

Interpretation of intrarater agreement is made difficult by the time factor. For short time intervals between measures, a fairly high relationship is expected (e.g., r = .80, or percentage agreement = 90%). For longer time intervals, the level of reliability may reasonably be expected to be lower.

Implications of Reliability

The degree of reliability of a measure has two implications. The first of these pertains to interpreting individuals' scores on the measure and the standard error of measurement. The second implication pertains to the effect that reliability has on the measure's validity.

Standard Error of Measurement. Measures yield scores, which in turn are used as critical inputs for decision making in staffing activities. For example, in Exhibit 7.1 a test of knowledge of mechanical principles was developed and administered to job applicants. The applicants' scores were used as a basis for making hiring decisions.

The discussion of reliability suggests that measures and scores will usually have some amount of error in them. Hence, scores on the test of knowledge of mechanical principles most likely reflect both true knowledge and error. Since only a single score is obtained from each applicant, the critical issue is how accurately that particular score indicates the applicant's true level of knowledge of mechanical principles alone.

The standard error of measurement (SEM) addresses this issue. It provides a way to state, within limits, a person's likely score on a measure. The formula for the SEM is

$$SEM = SD_x \sqrt{1 - r_{xx}}$$

where SD_x is the standard deviation of scores on the measure and r_{xx} is an estimate of the measure's reliability. For example, if $SD_x = 10$ and $r_{xx} = .75$ (based on coefficient alpha), SEM = 5.

With the SEM known, the range within which any individual's true score is likely to fall can be estimated. This range is known as a confidence interval or limit. There is a 95% chance that a person's true score lies within ±2 SEM of his or her actual score. Thus, if an applicant received a score of 22 on the test of knowledge of mechanical principles, the applicant's true score is most likely to be within the range of 22 ± 2(5), or 12–32.

Recognition and use of the SEM allow for care in interpreting people's scores, as well as differences between individuals in terms of their scores. For example, using the preceding data, if the test score for applicant 1 is 22 and the score for applicant 2 is 19, what should be made of the difference between the two applicants? Is applicant 1 truly more knowledgeable of mechanical principles than applicant 2?

The answer is probably not. This is because of the SEM and the large amount of overlap between the two applicants' intervals (12–32 for applicant 1, and 9–29 for applicant 2).

In short, there is not a one-to-one correspondence between actual scores and true scores. Most measures used in staffing are sufficiently unreliable, meaning that small differences in scores are probably due to error of measurement and should be ignored.

Relationship to Validity.   The validity of a measure is defined as the degree to which it measures the attribute it is supposed to be measuring. For example, the validity of the test of knowledge of mechanical principles is the degree to which it measures that knowledge. There are specific ways to investigate validity, and these are discussed in the next section. Here, it simply needs to be recognized that the reliability with which an attribute is measured has direct implications for the validity of the measure.

The relationship between the reliability and the validity of a measure is

$$r_{xy} \leq \sqrt{r_{xx}}$$

where r_{xy} is the validity of the measure and r_{xx} is the reliability of the measure. For example, it had been assumed previously that the reliability of the test of knowledge of mechanical principles was $r = .75$. The validity of that test thus cannot exceed $\sqrt{.75} = 86$.

Thus, the reliability of a measure places an upper limit on the possible validity of a measure. It should be emphasized that this is only an upper limit. A highly reliable measure is not necessarily valid. Reliability does not guarantee validity; it only makes validity possible.

Validity of Measures

The validity of a measure is defined as the degree to which it measures the attribute it is intended to measure.[11] Refer back to Exhibit 7.1, which involved the development of a test of knowledge of mechanical principles that was to be used in selecting job applicants. The validity of this test is the degree to which it truly measures the attribute or construct "knowledge of mechanical principles."

Judgments about the validity of a measure occur through the process of gathering data and evidence about the measure to assess how it was developed and whether accurate inferences can be made from scores on the measure. This process can be illustrated in terms of concepts pertaining to accuracy of measurement and accuracy of prediction. These concepts may then be used to demonstrate how validation of measures occurs in staffing.

Accuracy of Measurement

How accurate is the test of knowledge of mechanical principles? This question asks for evidence about the accuracy with which the test portrays individuals' true levels of that knowledge. This is akin to asking about the degree of overlap between the attribute being measured and the actual measure of the attribute.

Exhibit 7.9 shows the concept of accuracy of measurement in Venn diagram form. The circle on the left represents the construct "knowledge of mechanical principles," and the circle on the right represents the actual test of knowledge of mechanical principles. The overlap between the two circles represents the degree of accuracy of measurement for the test. The greater the overlap, the greater the accuracy of measurement.

Notice that perfect overlap is not shown in Exhibit 7.9. This signifies the occurrence of measurement error with the use of the test. These errors, as indicated in the exhibit, are the errors of deficiency and contamination previously discussed.

So how does accuracy of measurement differ from reliability of measurement since both are concerned with deficiency and contamination? There is disagreement among people on this question. Generally, the difference may be thought of

EXHIBIT 7.9   Accuracy of Measurement

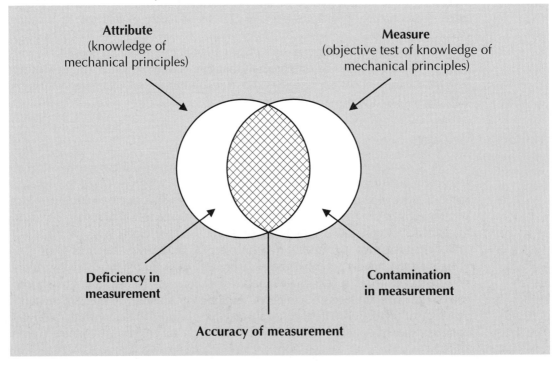

as follows. Reliability refers to consistency among the scores on the test, as determined by comparing scores as previously described. Accuracy of measurement goes beyond this to assess the extent to which the scores truly reflect the attribute being measured—the overlap shown in Exhibit 7.9. Accuracy requires reliability, but it also requires more by way of evidence. For example, accuracy requires knowing something about how the test was developed. Accuracy also requires some evidence concerning how test scores are influenced by other factors—for example, how do test scores change as a result of employees attending a training program devoted to providing instruction in mechanical principles? Accuracy thus demands greater evidence than reliability.

Accuracy of Prediction

Measures are often developed because they provide information about people that can be used to make predictions about them. In Exhibit 7.1, the knowledge test was to be used to help make hiring decisions, which are actually predictions about which people will be successful at a job. Knowing something about the accuracy with which a test predicts future job success requires examining the relationship between scores on the test and scores on some measure of job success for a group of people.

Accuracy of prediction is illustrated in the top half of Exhibit 7.10. Where there is an actual job success outcome (criterion) to predict, the test (predictor) will be used to predict the criterion. Each person is classified as high or low on the predictor and high or low on the criterion, based on predictor and criterion scores. Individuals falling into cells A and C represent correct predictions, and individuals falling into cells B and D represent errors in prediction. Accuracy of prediction is the percentage of total correct predictions and can range from 0% to 100%.

The bottom half of Exhibit 7.10 shows an example of the determination of accuracy of prediction using a selection example. The predictor is the test of knowledge of mechanical principles, and the criterion is an overall measure of job performance. Scores on the predictor and criterion measures are gathered for 100 job applicants and are dichotomized into high or low scores on each. Each individual is placed into one of the four cells. The accuracy of prediction for the test is 70%.

Validation of Measures in Staffing

In staffing, there is concern with the validity of predictors in terms of both accuracy of measurement and accuracy of prediction. It is important to have and use predictors that accurately represent the KSAOs to be measured, and those predictors need to be accurate in their predictions of job success. The validity of predictors is explored through the conduct of validation studies.

Two types of validation studies are typically conducted. The first of these is criterion-related validation, and the second is content validation. A third type of validation study, known as construct validation, involves components of reliability,

EXHIBIT 7.10 Accuracy of Prediction

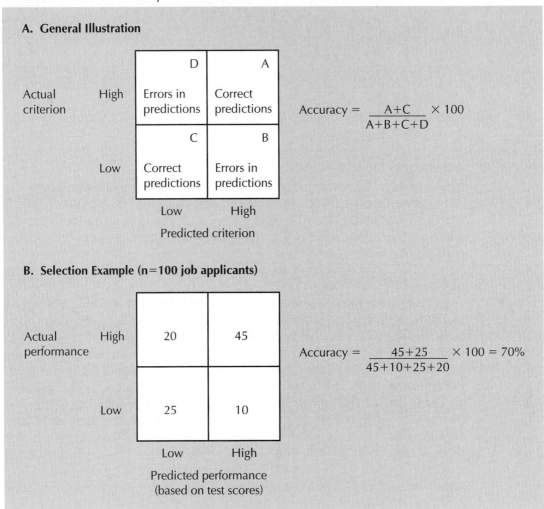

A. General Illustration

Actual criterion — High

	D	A
	Errors in predictions	Correct predictions
	C	B
Low	Correct predictions	Errors in predictions

Low   High

Predicted criterion

$$\text{Accuracy} = \frac{A+C}{A+B+C+D} \times 100$$

B. Selection Example (n=100 job applicants)

Actual performance — High

20	45
25	10

Low   High

Predicted performance
(based on test scores)

$$\text{Accuracy} = \frac{45+25}{45+10+25+20} \times 100 = 70\%$$

criterion-related validation, and content validation. Each component is discussed separately in this book, and thus no further reference is made to construct validation.

Criterion-Related Validation

Exhibit 7.11 shows the components of criterion-related validation and their usual sequencing.[12] The process begins with job analysis. Results of job analysis are fed into criterion and predictor measures. Scores on the predictor and criterion are

EXHIBIT 7.11   Criterion-Related Validation

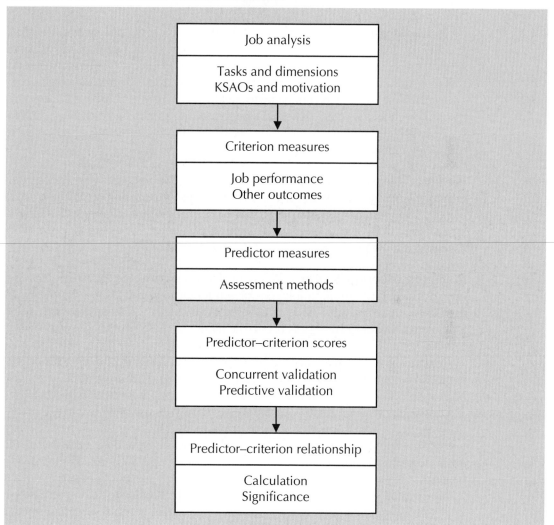

obtained for a sample of individuals; the relationship between the scores is then examined to make a judgment about the predictor's validity.

Job Analysis.   Job analysis is undertaken to identify and define important tasks (and broader task dimensions) of the job. The KSAOs and motivation thought to be necessary for performance of these tasks are then inferred. Results of the process of identifying tasks and underlying KSAOs are expressed in the form of the job requirements matrix. The matrix is a task × KSAO matrix; it shows the tasks required and the relevant KSAOs for each task.

Criterion Measures. Measures of performance on tasks and task dimensions are needed. These may already be available as part of an ongoing performance appraisal system, or they may have to be developed. However these measures are gathered, it is critical that they be as free from measurement error as possible.

Criterion measures need not be restricted to performance measures. Others may be used, such as measures of attendance, retention, safety, and customer service. As with performance-based criterion measures, these alternative criterion measures should also be as error-free as possible.

Predictor Measure. The predictor measure is the measure whose criterion-related validity is being investigated. Ideally, it taps into one or more of the KSAOs identified in job analysis. Also, it should be the type of measure most suitable to assess the KSAOs. Knowledge of mechanical principles, for example, is probably best assessed with some form of written, objective test.

Predictor–Criterion Scores. Predictor and criterion scores must be gathered from a sample of current employees or job applicants. If current employees are used, a concurrent validation design is used. Alternately, if job applicants are used, a predictive validation design is used. The nature of these two designs is shown in Exhibit 7.12.

Concurrent validation definitely has some appeal. Administratively, it is convenient and can often be done quickly. Moreover, results of the validation study will be available soon after the predictor and criterion scores have been gathered.

Unfortunately, some serious problems can arise with use of a concurrent validation design. One problem is that if the predictor is a test, current employees may not be motivated in the same way that job applicants would be in terms of the desire to perform well. Yet, it is future applicants for whom the test is intended to be used.

In a related vein, current employees may not be similar to, or representative of, future job applicants. Current employees may differ in terms of demographics such as age, race, sex, disability status, education level, and previous job experience. Hence, it is by no means certain that the results of the study will generalize to future job applicants. Also, some unsatisfactory employees will have been terminated, and some high performers may have been promoted. This leads to restriction of range on the criterion scores, which in turn will lower the correlation between the predictor and criterion scores.

Finally, current employees' predictor scores may be influenced by the amount of experience and/or success they have had in their current job. For example, scores on the test of knowledge of mechanical principles may reflect not only that knowledge but also how long people have been on the job and how well they have per-

EXHIBIT 7.12   Concurrent and Predictive Validation Designs

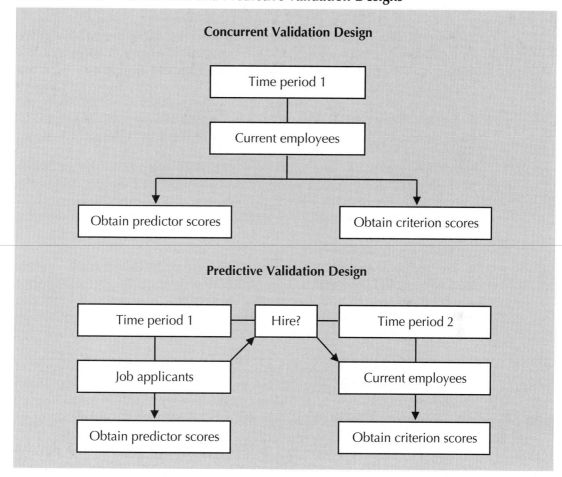

formed it. This is undesirable because one wants predictor scores to be predictive of the criterion rather than a result of it.

Predictive validation overcomes the potential limitations of concurrent validation since the predictor scores are obtained from job applicants. Applicants will be motivated to do well on the predictor, and they are more likely to be representative of future job applicants. Applicants' scores on the predictor cannot be influenced by success and/or experience on the job, because the scores are gathered prior to their being on the job.

Predictive validation is not without potential limitations, however. It is neither administratively easy nor quick. Moreover, results will not be available immediately, as some time must lapse before criterion scores can be obtained. Despite these limitations, predictive validation is considered the more sound of the two designs.

Predictor–Criterion Relationship.   Once predictor and criterion scores have been obtained, the correlation r, or some variation of it, must be calculated. The value of r is then referred to as the validity of the scores on the predictor. For example, if an r = .35 was found, the predictor would be referred to as having a validity of .35. Then, the practical and statistical significance of the r should be determined. Only if the r meets desired levels of practical and statistical significance should the predictor be considered valid and thus potentially usable in the selection system.

Illustrative Study.   A state university civil service system covering 20 institutions sought to identify predictors of job performance for clerical employees. The clerical job existed within different schools (e.g., engineering, humanities) and nonacademic departments (e.g., payroll, data processing). The goal of the study was to have a valid clerical test in two parallel forms that could be administered to job applicants in one hour.

The starting point was to conduct a job analysis, the results of which would be used as the basis for constructing the clerical tests (predictors) and the job performance ratings (criteria). Subject matter experts (SMEs) used job observation and previous job descriptions to construct a task-based questionnaire that was administered to clerical incumbents and their supervisors throughout the system. Task statements were rated in terms of importance, frequency, and essentialness (if it was essential for a newly hired employee to know how to do this task). Based on statistical analysis of the ratings' means and standard deviations, 25 of the 188 task statements were retained as critical task statements. These critical task statements were the key input to the identification of key KSAOs and the dimension of job performance.

Analysis of the 25 critical task statements indicated there were five KSAO components of the job: knowledge of computer hardware and software, ability to follow instructions and prioritize tasks, knowledge and skill in responding to telephone and reception scenarios, knowledge of English language, and ability to file items in alphabetical order. A test was constructed to measure these KSAOs as follows:

- Computer hardware and software—17 questions
- Prioritizing tasks—18 questions
- Route and transfer calls—14 questions
- Record messages—20 questions
- Give information on the phone—20 questions
- Correct sentences with errors—22 questions
- Identify errors in sentences—71 questions

- Filing—44 questions
- Typing—number of questions not reported

To develop the job performance (criterion) measure, a behavioral performance rating scale (1–7 rating) was constructed for each of the nine areas, ensuring a high content correspondence between the tests and the performance criteria they sought to predict. Scores on these nine scales were summed to yield an overall performance score.

The nine tests were administered to 108 current clerical employees to obtain predictor scores. A separate score on each of the nine tests was computed, along with a total score for all tests. In addition, total scores on two short (50-question) forms of the total test were created (Form A and Form B).

Performance ratings of these 108 employees were obtained from their supervisors, who were unaware of their employees' test scores. The performance ratings were summed to form an overall performance rating. Scores on each of the nine tests, on the total test, and on Forms A and B of the test were correlated with the overall performance ratings.

Results of the concurrent validation study are shown in Exhibit 7.13. It can be seen that seven of the nine specific tests had statistically significant correlations with overall performance (filing and typing did not). Total test scores were

EXHIBIT 7.13   Clerical Test Concurrent Validation Results

Test	Correlation With Overall Performance
Computer software and hardware	.37**
Prioritize tasks	.29*
Route and transfer calls	.19*
Record messages	.31**
Give information on phone	.35**
Correct sentences with errors	.32**
Identify errors in sentences	.44**
Filing	.22
Typing	.10
Total test	.45**
Form A	.55**
Form B	.49**

NOTE: *$p < .05$, **$p < .01$

SOURCE: Adapted from J. E. Pynes, E. J. Harrick, and D. Schaefer, "A Concurrent Validation Study Applied to a Secretarial Position in a State University Civil Service System," *Journal of Business and Psychology*, 1997, 12, pp. 3–18.

significantly correlated with overall performance, as were scores on the two short forms of the total test. The sizes of the statistically significant correlations suggest favorable practical significance of the correlations as well.

Content Validation

Content validation differs from criterion-related validity in one important respect: no criterion measure is used in content validation. Thus, predictor scores cannot be correlated with criterion scores as a way of gathering evidence about a predictor's validity. Rather, a judgment is made about the probable correlation, had there been a criterion measure. For this reason, content validation is frequently referred to as judgmental validation.[13]

Content validation is most appropriate, and most likely to be found, in two circumstances: (1) when there are too few people to form a sample for purposes of criterion-related validation, and (2) when criterion measures are not available, or they are available but are of highly questionable quality. At an absolute minimum, an n = 30 is necessary for criterion-related validation.

Exhibit 7.14 shows the two basic steps in content validation: conducting a job analysis and choosing or developing a predictor. These steps are commented on next. Comparing the steps in content validation with those in criterion-related validation (see Exhibit 7.11) shows that the steps in content validation are part of criterion-related validation. Because of this, the two types of validation should be thought of as complementary, with content validation being a subset of criterion-related validation.

Job Analysis.   As with criterion-related validation, content validation begins with job analysis, which, in both cases, is undertaken to identify and define tasks and

---

EXHIBIT 7.14   Content Validation

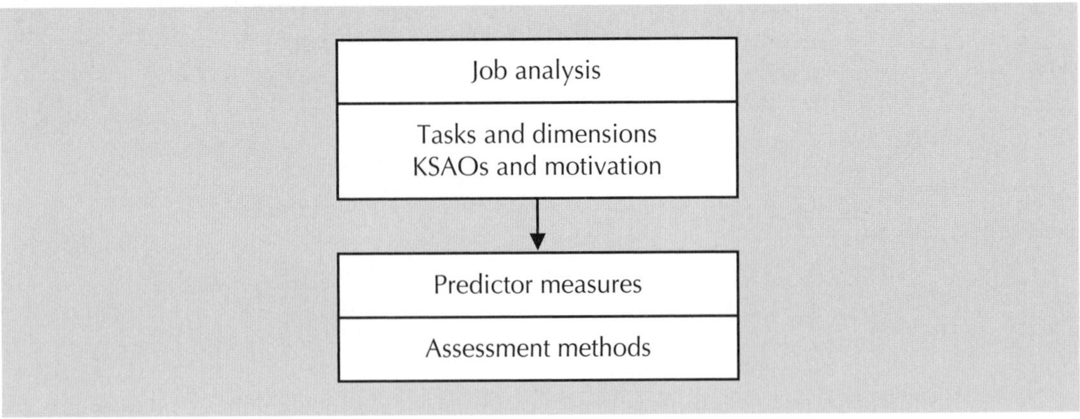

task dimensions and to infer the necessary KSAOs and motivation for those tasks. Results are expressed in the job requirements matrix.

Predictor Measures. Sometimes the predictor will be one that has already been developed and is in use. An example here is a commercially available test, interviewing process, or biographical information questionnaire. Other times, such a measure will not be available. This occurs frequently in the case of job knowledge, which is usually very specific to the particular job involved in the validation.

Lacking a readily available or modifiable predictor means that the organization will have to construct its own predictors. At this point, the organization has built predictor construction into the predictor validation process. Now, content validation and the predictor development processes occur simultaneously. The organization becomes engaged in test construction, a topic beyond the scope of this book.[14]

A final note about content validation emphasizes the importance of continually paying attention to the need for reliability of measurement and standardization of the measurement process. Though these are always matters of concern in any type of validation effort, they are of paramount importance in content validation. The reason for this is that without an empirical correlation between the predictor and the criterion, only the likely r can be judged. It is important, in forming that judgment, to pay considerable attention to reliability and standardization.

Illustrative Study. The Maryland Department of Transportation sought to develop a series of assessment methods for identifying supervisory potential among candidates for promotion to a first-level supervising position anywhere within the department. The content validation process and outputs are shown in Exhibit 7.15. As shown in the exhibit, job analysis was first conducted to identify and define a set of performance dimensions and then infer the KSAOs necessary for successful performance in those dimensions. Several SMEs met to develop a tentative set of task dimensions and underlying KSAOs. The underlying KSAOs were in essence general competencies required of all first-level supervisors, regardless of work unit within the department. Their results were sent to a panel of experienced human resource (HR) managers within the department for revision and finalization. Three assessment method specialists then set about developing a set of assessments that would (1) be efficiently administered at locations throughout the state, (2) be reliably scored by people at those locations, and (3) emphasize the interpersonal skills important for this job. As shown in Exhibit 7.15, five assessment methods were developed: multiple-choice in-basket exercise, structured panel interview, presentation exercise, writing sample, and training and experience evaluation exercise.

Candidates' performance on the exercises was to be evaluated by specially chosen assessors at the location where the exercises were administered. To ensure that candidates' performance was skillfully observed and reliably evaluated by the

EXHIBIT 7.15   Content Validation Study

Job Analysis: First-Level Supervisor—Maryland Department of Transportation

Seven performance dimensions and task statements:
   Organizing work; assigning work; monitoring work; managing consequences; counseling, efficiency reviews, and discipline; setting an example; employee development

Fourteen KSAOs and definitions:
   Organizing; analysis and decision making; planning; communication (oral and written); delegation; work habits; carefulness; interpersonal skill; job knowledge; organizational knowledge; toughness; integrity; development of others; listening

Predictor Measures: Five Assessment Methods

Multiple-choice in-basket exercise
   (assume role of new supervisor and work through in-basket on desk)
Structured panel interview
   (predetermined questions about past experiences relevant to the KSAOs)
Presentation exercise
   (make presentation to a simulated work group about change in their work hours)
Writing sample
   (prepare a written reprimand for a fictitious employee)
Training and experience evaluation exercise
   (give examples of training and work achievements relevant to certain KSAOs)

SOURCE: Adapted from M. A. Cooper, G. Kaufman, and W. Hughes, "Measuring Supervisory Potential," *IPMA News,* December 1996, pp. 8–18. Reprinted with permission of *IPMA News,* published by the International Personnel Management Association (IPMA; *www.ipma-hr.org*).

assessors, an intensive training program was developed. The program provided both a written user's manual and specific skill training.

Validity Generalization

In the preceding discussions of validity and validation, an implicit premise is being made that validity is situation specific, and therefore validation of predictors must occur in each specific situation. All of the examples involve specific types of measures, jobs, individuals, and so forth. Nothing is said about generalizing validity across those jobs and individuals. For example, if a predictor is valid for a particular job in organization A, would it be valid for the same type of job in organization B? Or is validity specific to the particular job and organization?

The situation-specific premise is based on the following scenario, which has its origins in findings from decades of previous research. Assume that 10 criterion-related validation studies have been conducted. Each study involves various predictor measures of a common KSAO attribute (e.g., general mental ability) and various criterion measures of a common outcome attribute (e.g., job performance). The predictor will be designated x, and the criterion will be designated y. The studies are conducted in different situations (types of jobs, types of organizations), and they involve different samples (with different sample sizes [n]). In each study, the reliability of the predictor (r_{xx}) and the criterion (r_{yy}), as well as the validity coefficient (r_{xy}), is calculated. These results are provided in Exhibit 7.16. At first blush, the results, because of the wide range of r_{xy} values, would seem to support situational specificity. These results suggest that while, on average, there seems to be some validity to x, the validity varies substantially from situation to situation.

The concept of validity generalization questions this premise.[15] It says that much of the variation in the r_{xy} values is due to the occurrence of a number of "artifacts"—methodological and statistical differences across the studies (e.g., differences in reliability of x and y). If these differences were controlled statistically, the variation in values would shrink and converge toward an estimate of the

EXHIBIT 7.16   Hypothetical Validity Generalization Example

Study	Sample Size n	Validity r_{xy}	Reliability Predictor (x) r_{xx}	Reliability Criterion (y) r_{yy}	Corrected Validity r_c
Birch, 2011	454	.41	.94	.94	.44
Cherry, 1990	120	.19	.66	.76	.27
Elm, 1978	212	.34	.91	.88	.38
Hickory, 2009	37	−.21	.96	.90	−.23
Locust, 2000	92	.12	.52	.70	.20
Maple, 1961	163	.32	.90	.84	.37
Oak, 1948	34	.09	.63	.18	.27
Palm, 2007	202	.49	.86	.92	.55
Pine, 1984	278	.27	.80	.82	.33
Walnut, 1971	199	.18	.72	.71	.25

true validity of x. If that true r is significant (practically and statistically), one can indeed generalize validity of x across situations. Validity thus is not viewed as situation specific.

Indeed, the results in the exhibit reveal that the average (weighted by sample size) uncorrected validity is $\bar{r}_{xy} = .30$, and the average (weighted by sample size) validity corrected for unreliability in the predictor and criterion is $\bar{r}_{xy} = .36$. In this example, fully two-thirds (66.62%) of the variance in the correlations was due to study artifacts (differences in sample size and differences in reliability of the predictor or the criterion). Put another way, the variability in the correlations is lower once they are corrected for artifacts, and the validities do generalize.

An enormous amount of evidence supporting the validity generalization premise has accumulated. Some experts argue that validity generalization reduces or even eliminates the need for an organization to conduct its own validation study. If validity generalization shows that a selection measure has a statistically significant and practically meaningful correlation with job performance, the reasoning goes, why go to the considerable time and expense to reinvent the wheel (to conduct a validation study when evidence clearly supports use of the measure in the first place)? There are two caveats to keep in mind in accepting this logic. First, organizations or specific jobs (for which the selection measure in question is intended) can sometimes be unusual. To the extent that the organization or job was not reflected in the validity generalization effort, the results may be inapplicable to the specific organization or job. Second, validity generalization efforts, while undoubtedly offering more evidence than a single study, are not perfect. For example, validity generalization results can be susceptible to "publication bias," where test vendors may report only statistically significant correlations. Although procedures exist for correcting this bias, they assume evidence and expertise usually not readily available to an organization.[16] Thus, as promising as validity generalization is, we think organizations, especially if they think the job in question differs from comparable organizations, may still wish to conduct validation studies of their own.

A particular form of validity generalization that has proved useful is meta-analysis. Returning to Exhibit 7.16, meta-analysis reveals that the average correlation between x and y (i.e., $\bar{r}_{xy}$) is $\bar{r}_{xy} = .36$, that most of the variability in the correlations is due to statistical artifacts (and not due to true substantive differences in validity across studies), and that the validity appears to generalize. Meta-analysis is very useful in comparing the relative validity of selection measures, which is precisely what we do in Chapters 8 and 9.

Staffing Metrics and Benchmarks

For some time now, HR as a business area has sought to prove its value through the use of metrics, or quantifiable measures that demonstrate the effectiveness (or ineffectiveness) of a particular practice or procedure. Staffing is no exception. Fortunately, many of the measurement processes described in this chapter represent excellent metrics. Unfortunately, most HR managers, including many in staffing, may have limited (or no) knowledge of job analysis, validation, and measurement. The reader of this book can "show his or her stuff" by educating other organizational members about these metrics in an accessible and nonthreatening way. The result may be a more rigorous staffing process, producing higher levels of validity, and kudos for you.

Many who work in staffing are likely more familiar with another type of metric, namely, those produced by benchmarking. Benchmarking is a process where organizations evaluate their practices (in this case, staffing practices) against those used by industry leaders. Some commonly used benchmarks include cost per hire, forecasted hiring, and vacancies filled. Traditionally, most benchmarking efforts have focused on quantity of employees hired and cost. That situation is beginning to change. For example, Reuters and Dell are tracking "quality of hire," or the performance levels of those hired. Eventually, if enough organizations track such information, they can form a consortium so they can benchmark off one another's metrics for both quantity and quality.[17]

More generally, the Society for Human Resource Management (SHRM) regularly offers conferences and mini-conferences on staffing that provide benchmarks of current organizational practices. At a recent SHRM conference, Robyn Corr, VP of global staffing for Starbucks, discussed the company's approach to staffing, including how Starbucks hires over 300 employees every day.

Such benchmarks can be a useful means of measuring important aspects of staffing methods or the entire staffing process. However, they are no substitute for the other measurement principles described in this chapter, including reliability and validity. Reliability, validity, utility, and measurement principles are more enduring, and more fundamental, metrics of staffing effectiveness.

COLLECTION OF ASSESSMENT DATA

In staffing decisions, the process of measurement is put into practice by collecting assessment data on external or internal applicants. To this point in this chapter, we have discussed how selection measures can be evaluated. To be sure, thorough evaluation of selection measures is important. Selection decision makers must be knowledgeable about how to use the assessment data that have been collected; otherwise the potential value of the data will lie dormant. On the other hand, to put these somewhat theoretical concepts to use in practice, selection decision makers must know how to collect the assessment data. Otherwise, the decision maker may find himself or herself in the unenviable "big hat, no cattle" situation—knowing how to analyze and evaluate assessment data but not knowing where to find the data in the first place.

In collecting assessment data, if a predictor is purchased, support services are needed. Consulting firms and test publishers can provide support for scoring of tests. Also necessary is legal support to ensure compliance with laws and regulations. Validity studies are important to ensure the effectiveness of the measures. Training on how to administer the predictor is also needed.

Beyond these general principles, which apply no matter what assessment data are collected, there is other information that the selection decision maker must know about the tangible process of collecting assessment data. Collection of data with respect to testing procedures, tests and test manuals, and professional standards is discussed.

Testing Procedures

Regardless of whether paper-and-pencil or computerized tests are given, certain guidelines need to be kept in mind.

Qualification

Predictors cannot always be purchased by any firm that wants to use them; many test publishers require the purchaser to have certain expertise to properly use the test. For example, they may want the user to hold a PhD in a field of study related to the test and its use. For smaller organizations, this means hiring the consulting services of a specialist to use a particular test.

Security

Care must be taken to ensure that correct answers for predictors are not shared with job applicants in advance of administration of the predictor. Any person who has access to the predictor answers should be fully trained and should sign a predictor security agreement. Also, applicants should be instructed not to share information about the test with fellow applicants. Alternative forms of the test should be considered if the security of the test is in question.

Not only should the predictor itself be kept secure, but also the results of the predictor in order to ensure the privacy of the individual. The results of the predictor should be used only for the intended purposes and by persons qualified to interpret them. Though feedback can be given to the candidate concerning the results, the individual should not be given a copy of the predictor or the scoring key.

Standardization

Finally, it is imperative that all applicants be assessed with standardized procedures. This means that not only should the same or a psychometrically equivalent predictor be used, but individuals should take the test under the same circumstances. The purpose of the predictor should be explained to applicants, and they should be put at ease, held to the same time requirements to complete the predictor, and take the predictor in the same location.

Internet-Based Test Administration

Increasingly, selection measures are being administered on the Internet. For example, job applicants for hourly positions at Kmart, Albertson's, and the Sports Authority take an electronic assessment at in-store kiosks. The test vendor, Unicru, forwards the test scores on to selection decision makers. Some organizations may develop their own tests and administer them online.

In general, research suggests that web-based tests work as well as paper-and-pencil tests, as long as special care is taken to ensure that the actual applicant is the test taker and that the tests are validated in the same manner as other selection measures. Some organizations, however, in their rush to use such tests, fail to validate them. The results can be disastrous. The Transportation Security Administration (TSA) has been criticized for its "inane" online test. Many questions on the test were obvious to a grade-school student. For example, one question was: Why is it important to screen bags for improvised explosive devices (IEDs)?

a. The IED batteries could *leak and damage* other passenger bags.
b. The wires in the IED could *cause a short* to the aircraft wires.
c. IEDs can cause *loss of lives*, property and aircraft.
d. The *ticking timer* could worry other passengers.

Obviously, the correct answer is "c." The TSA farmed out the test to a vendor without asking for validation evidence. The TSA's justification was, "We administered the test the way we were told to [by the vendor]." Thus, Internet-based testing can work well and has many advantages, but organizations need to ensure that the tests are rigorously developed and validated.[18]

Acquisition of Tests and Test Manuals

The process of acquiring tests and test manuals, whether digital versions or print versions, requires some start-up costs in terms of the time and effort required to contact test publishers. Once the selection decision maker is on an e-mail or mailing list, however, he or she can stay up to date on the latest developments.

Publishers of selection tests include Wonderlic (*www.wonderlic.com*), Consulting Psychologists Press (*www.cpp-db.com*), Institute for Personality and Ability Testing (*www.ipat.com*), Psychological Assessment Resources (*www.parinc.com*), Hogan Assessment Systems (*www.hoganassessments.com*), and Psychological Services, Inc. (*www.psionline.com*). All these organizations have information on their websites that describes the products available for purchase.

Most publishers provide sample copies of the tests and a user's manual that selection decision makers may consult before purchasing the test. Test costs vary widely depending on the test and the number of times the test is given. One test that can be scored by the selection decision maker, for example, costs $100 for testing

25 applicants and $200 for testing 100 applicants. Another test that comes with a scoring system and interpretive report costs from $25 each for testing 5 applicants to $17 each for testing 100 applicants. Discounts are available for testing larger numbers of applicants.

Any test worth using will be accompanied by a professional user's manual (whether in print or online). This manual should describe the development and validation of the test, including validity evidence in selection contexts. A test manual should also include administration instructions, scoring instructions or information, interpretation information, and normative data. All of this information is crucial to make sure that the test is appropriate and that it is used in an appropriate (valid, legal) manner. Avoid using a test that has no professional manual, as it is unlikely to have been validated. Using a test without a proven track record is akin to hiring an applicant sight unseen. The *Wonderlic Personnel Test User's Manual* is an excellent example of a professional user's manual. It contains information about various forms of the *Wonderlic Personnel Test* (see Chapter 9), how to administer the test and interpret and use the scores, validity and fairness of the test, and various norms by age, race, gender, and so on. The SHRM has launched the SHRM Testing Center, whereby SHRM members can review and receive discounts on more than 200 web-based tests.[19]

Professional Standards

Revised in 2003 by the Society for Industrial and Organizational Psychology (SIOP) and approved by the American Psychological Association (APA), the *Principles for the Validation and Use of Personnel Selection Procedures* is a guidebook that provides testing standards for use in selection decisions. It covers test choice, development, evaluation, and use of personnel selection procedures in employment settings. Specific topics covered include the various ways selection measures should be validated, how to conduct validation studies, which sources can be used to determine validity, generalizing validation evidence from one source to another, test fairness and bias, how to understand worker requirements, data collection for validity studies, ways in which validity information can be analyzed, the appropriate uses of selection measures, and an administration guide.

Principles was developed by many of the world's leading experts on selection, and therefore any selection decision maker would be well advised to consult this important document, which is written in practical, nontechnical language. This guidebook is free and can be ordered from SIOP by visiting its website (*www.siop. org*).

A related set of standards has been promulgated by the APA. Formulated by the Joint Committee on Testing Practices, *The Rights and Responsibilities of Test Takers: Guidelines and Expectations* enumerates 10 rights and 10 responsibilities of test takers. One of the rights is for the applicant to be treated with courtesy, respect, and impartiality. Another right is to receive prior explanation for the purpose(s) of the testing. One responsibility is to follow the test instructions as given. In addition to enumerating test-taker rights and responsibilities, the document also provides guidelines for organizations administering the tests. For example, the standards stipulate that organizations should inform test takers about the purpose of the test. This document is available online at *www.apa.org/science/programs/testing/rights. aspx*. Organizations testing applicants should consult these guidelines to ensure that these rights are provided wherever possible.

LEGAL ISSUES

Staffing laws and regulations, particularly EEO/AA laws and regulations, place great reliance on the use of measurement concepts and processes. Three key topics are determining adverse impact, standardization of measurement, and best practices suggested by the EEOC.

Determining Adverse Impact

In Chapter 2, adverse (disparate) impact was introduced as a way of determining whether staffing practices were having potentially illegal impacts on individuals because of race, sex, and so forth. Such a determination requires the compilation and analysis of statistical evidence, primarily applicant flow and applicant stock statistics.

Applicant Flow Statistics

Applicant flow statistical analysis requires the calculation of selection rates (proportions or percentages of applicants hired) for groups and the subsequent comparison of those rates to determine whether they are significantly different from one another. This may be illustrated by taking the example from Exhibit 2.5:

	Applicants	Hires	Selection Rate
Men	50	25	.50 or 50%
Women	45	5	.11 or 11%

This example shows a sizable difference in selection rates between men and women (.50 as opposed to .11). Does this difference indicate adverse impact? The Uniform Guidelines on Employee Selection Procedures (UGESP) speak directly to this question. Several points need to be made regarding the determination of disparate impact analysis.

First, the UGESP require the organization to keep records that will permit calculation of such selection rates, also referred to as applicant flow statistics. These statistics are the primary vehicle by which compliance with the law (Civil Rights Act) is judged.

Second, the UGESP require calculation of selection rates (1) for each job category, (2) for both external and internal selection decisions, (3) for each step in the selection process, and (4) by race and sex of applicants. To meet this requirement, the organization must keep detailed records of its staffing activities and decisions. Such record keeping should be built directly into the organization's staffing system routines.

Third, comparisons of selection rates among groups in a job category for purposes of compliance determination should be based on the 80% rule in the UGESP, which states that "a selection rate for any race, sex or ethnic group which is less than four-fifths (4/5) (or eighty percent) of the rate for the group with the highest rate will generally be regarded by federal enforcement agencies as evidence of adverse impact, while a greater than four-fifths rate will generally not be regarded by federal enforcement agencies as evidence of adverse impact."

If this rule is applied to the previous example, the group with the highest selection rate is men (.50). The rate for women should be within 80% of this rate, or .40 (.50 × .80 = .40). Since the actual rate for women is .11, this suggests the occurrence of adverse impact.

Fourth, the 80% rule is truly only a guideline. Note the use of the word "generally" in the rule with regard to differences in selection rates. Also, the 80% rule goes on to provide for other exceptions, based on sample size considerations and issues surrounding statistical and practical significance of difference in selection rates. Moreover, there are many other technical measurement and legal issues in determining whether adverse impact is occurring. Examples include deciding exactly who is considered an applicant, and whether it is meaningful to pool applicant counts for different minority groups into a "total minority" group. Best practice recommendations for handling such issues are available.[20]

Applicant Stock Statistics

Applicant stock statistics require the calculation of the percentages of women and minorities in two areas: (1) employed, and (2) available for employment in the population. These percentages are compared to identify disparities. This is referred to as utilization analysis.

To illustrate, the example from Exhibit 2.5 is shown here:

	Employed	Availability
Nonminority	90%	70%
Minority	10%	30%

It can be seen that 10% of employees are minorities, whereas their availability is 30%. A comparison of these two percentages suggests an underutilization of minorities.

Utilization analysis of this sort is an integral part of not only compliance assessment but also affirmative action plans (AAPs). Indeed, utilization analysis is the starting point for the development of AAPs. This may be illustrated by reference to the Affirmative Action Programs Regulations.

The regulations require the organization to conduct a formal utilization analysis of its workforce. That analysis must be (1) conducted by job group, and (2) done separately for women and minorities. Though calculation of the numbers and percentages of persons employed is relatively straightforward, determination of their availability is not. The regulations require that the availabilities take into account at least the following factors: (1) the percentage of women or minorities with requisite skills in the recruitment area, and (2) the percentage of women or minorities among those promotable, transferable, and trainable within the organization. Accurate measurement and/or estimation of availabilities that take into account these factors is difficult.

Despite these measurement problems, the regulations require comparison of the percentages of women and minorities employed with their availability. When the percentage of minorities or women in a job group is less than would reasonably be expected given their availability, underutilization exists and placement (hiring and promotion) goals must be set. Thus, the organization must exercise considerable discretion in the determination of adverse impact through the use of applicant stock statistics. It would be wise to seek technical and/or legal assistance for conducting utilization analysis (see also "Affirmative Action Plans" in Chapter 3).

Standardization

A lack of consistency in treatment of applicants is one of the major factors contributing to the occurrence of discrimination in staffing. This is partly due to a lack of standardization in measurement, in terms of both what is measured and how it is evaluated or scored.

An example of inconsistency in what is measured is that the type of background information required of minority applicants may differ from that required of nonminority applicants. Minority applicants may be asked about credit ratings and criminal conviction records, while nonminority applicants are not. Or, the type of interview questions asked of male applicants may be different from those asked of female applicants.

Even if information is consistently gathered from all applicants, it may not be evaluated the same for all applicants. A male applicant who has a history of holding several different jobs may be viewed as a career builder, while a female with the same history may be evaluated as an unstable job-hopper. In essence, different scoring keys are being used for men and women applicants.

Reducing, and hopefully eliminating, such inconsistency requires a straightforward application of the three properties of standardized measures discussed previously. Through standardization of measurement comes consistent treatment of applicants, and with it, the possibility of lessened adverse impact.

Best Practices

Based on its long and in-depth involvement in measurement and selection procedures, the EEOC provides guidance to employers in the form of several best practices for testing and selection.[21] These practices apply to a wide range of tests and selection procedures, including cognitive and physical ability tests, sample job tasks, medical inquiries and physical exams, personality and integrity tests, criminal and credit background checks, performance appraisals, and English proficiency tests. The best practices are the following:

- Employers should administer tests and other selection procedures without regard to race, color, national origin, sex, religion, age (40 or older), or disability.
- Employers should ensure that employment tests and other selection procedures are properly validated for the positions and purposes for which they are used. The test or selection procedure must be job-related and its results appropriate for the employer's purpose. While a test vendor's documentation supporting the validity of a test may be helpful, the employer is still responsible for ensuring that its tests are valid under the UGESP (discussed in Chapter 9).
- If a selection procedure screens out a protected group, the employer should determine whether there is an equally effective alternative selection procedure that has less adverse impact and, if so, adopt the alternative procedure. For example, if the selection procedure is a test, the employer should determine whether another test would predict job performance but not disproportionately exclude the protected group.
- To ensure that a test or selection procedure remains predictive of success in a job, employers should keep abreast of changes in job requirements and should update the test specifications or selection procedures accordingly.
- Employers should ensure that tests and selection procedures are not adopted casually by managers who know little about these processes. A test or selection procedure can be an effective management tool, but no test or selection procedure should be implemented without an understanding of its effectiveness and limitations for the organization, its appropriateness for a specific job, and whether it can be appropriately administered and scored.

Note that these best practices apply to virtually all selection procedures or tools, not just tests. They emphasize the need for fair administration of these tools, the importance of the procedures being job related, usage of alternative valid selection procedures that have less adverse impact, and the updating of job requirements (KSAOs) and selection tools. In addition, casual usage of selection tools by uninformed managers is to be avoided.

SUMMARY

Measurement, defined as the process of using rules to assign numbers to objects to represent quantities of an attribute of the objects, is an integral part of the foundation of staffing activities. Standardization of the measurement process is sought. This applies to each of the four levels of measurement: nominal, ordinal, interval, and ratio. Standardization is also sought for both objective and subjective measures.

Measures yield scores that represent the amount of the attribute being measured. Scores are manipulated in various ways to aid in their interpretation. Typical manipulations involve central tendency and variability, percentiles, and standard scores. Scores are also correlated to learn about the strength and direction of the relationship between two attributes. The significance of the resultant correlation coefficient is then assessed.

The quality of measures involves issues of reliability and validity. Reliability refers to consistency of measurement, both at a moment in time and between time periods. Various procedures are used to estimate reliability, including coefficient alpha, interrater and intrarater agreement, and test–retest. Reliability places an upper limit on the validity of a measure.

Validity refers to accuracy of measurement and accuracy of prediction, as reflected by the scores obtained from a measure. Criterion-related and content validation studies are conducted to help learn about the validity of a measure. In criterion-related validation, scores on a predictor (KSAO) measure are correlated with scores on a criterion (HR outcome) measure. In content validation, there is no criterion measure, so judgments are made about the content of a predictor relative to the HR outcome it is seeking to predict. Traditionally, results of validation studies were treated as situation specific, meaning that the organization ideally should conduct a new and separate validation study for any predictor in any situation in which the predictor is to be used. Recently, however, studies have suggested that the validity of predictors may generalize across situations, meaning that the requirement of conducting costly and time-consuming validation studies in each specific situation could be relaxed. Staffing metrics such as cost per hire and benchmarks, representing how leading organizations staff positions, can be useful measures. But they are no substitutes for reliability and validity.

Various practical aspects of the collection of assessment data were described. Decisions about testing procedures and the acquisition of tests and test manuals require the attention of organizational decision makers. The collection of assessment data and the acquisition of tests and test manuals vary depending on whether paper-and-pencil or computerized selection measures are utilized. Finally, organizations need to attend to professional standards that govern the proper use of the collection of assessment data.

Measurement is also said to be an integral part of an organization's EEO/AA compliance activities. When adverse impact is found, changes in measurement practices may be legally necessary. These changes will involve movement toward standardization of measurement and the methods for determining adverse impact.

DISCUSSION QUESTIONS

1. Imagine and describe a staffing system for a job in which no measures are used.
2. Describe how you might go about determining scores for applicants' responses to (a) interview questions, (b) letters of recommendation, and (c) questions about previous work experience.
3. Give examples of when you would want the following for a written job knowledge test: (a) a low coefficient alpha (e.g., $\alpha = .35$), and (b) a low test–retest reliability.
4. Assume you gave a general ability test, measuring both verbal and computational skills, to a group of applicants for a specific job. Also assume that because of severe hiring pressures, you hired all of the applicants, regardless of their test scores. How would you investigate the criterion-related validity of the test?
5. Using the same example as in question four, how would you go about investigating the content validity of the test?
6. What information does a selection decision maker need to collect in making staffing decisions? What are the ways in which this information can be collected?

ETHICAL ISSUES

1. Do individuals making staffing decisions have an ethical responsibility to know measurement issues? Why or why not?
2. Is it unethical for an employer to use a selection measure that has high empirical validity but lacks content validity? Explain.

APPLICATIONS

Evaluation of Two New Assessment Methods for Selecting Telephone Customer Service Representatives

The Phonemin Company is a distributor of men's and women's casual clothing. It sells exclusively through its merchandise catalog, which is published four times per year to coincide with seasonal changes in customers' apparel tastes. Customers may order merchandise from the catalog via mail or over the phone. Currently, 70% of orders are phone orders, and the organization expects this to increase to 85% within the next few years.

The success of the organization is obviously very dependent on the success of the telephone ordering system and the customer service representatives (CSRs) who staff the system. There are currently 185 CSRs; that number should increase to about 225 CSRs to handle the anticipated growth in phone order sales. Though the CSRs are trained to use standardized methods and procedures for handling phone orders, there are still seemingly large differences among them in their job performance. The CSRs' performance is routinely measured in terms of error rate, speed of order taking, and customer complaints. The top 25% and lowest 25% of performers on each of these measures differ by a factor of at least three (e.g., the error rate of the bottom group is three times as high as that of the top group). Strategically, the organization knows that it could substantially enhance CSR performance (and ultimately sales) if it could improve its staffing "batting average" by more accurately identifying and hiring new CSRs who are likely to be top performers.

The current staffing system for CSRs is straightforward. Applicants are recruited through a combination of employee referrals and newspaper ads. Because turnover among CSRs is so high (50% annually), recruitment is a continuous process at the organization. Applicants complete a standard application blank, which asks for information about education and previous work experience. The information is reviewed by the staffing specialist in the HR department. Only obvious misfits are rejected at this point; the others (95%) are asked to have an interview with the specialist. The interview lasts 20–30 minutes, and at the conclusion the applicant is either rejected or offered a job. Due to the tightness of the labor market and the constant presence of vacancies to be filled, 90% of the interviewees receive job offers. Most of those offers (95%) are accepted, and the new hires attend a one-week training program before being placed on the job.

The organization has decided to investigate fully the possibilities of increasing CSR effectiveness through sounder staffing practices. In particular, it is not pleased with its current methods of assessing job applicants; it feels that neither the application blank nor the interview provides the accurate and in-depth assessment of the KSAOs that are truly needed to be an effective CSR. Consequently, it engaged the services of a consulting firm that offers various methods of KSAO assessment, along with validation and installation services. In cooperation with the HR staffing specialist, the consulting firm conducted the following study for the organization.

A special job analysis led to the identification of several specific KSAOs likely to be necessary for successful performance as a CSR. Three of these (clerical speed, clerical accuracy, and interpersonal skills) were singled out for further consideration because of their seemingly high impact on job performance. Two new methods of assessment, provided by the consulting firm, were chosen for experimentation. The first was a paper-and-pencil clerical test assessing clerical speed and accuracy. It was a 50-item test with a 30-minute time limit. The second was a brief work sample that could be administered as part of the interview process. In the work sample, the applicant must respond to four different phone calls: from a customer irate about an out-of-stock item, from a customer wanting more product information about an item than was provided in the catalog, from a customer who wants to change an order placed yesterday, and from a customer with a routine order to place. Using a 1–5 rating scale, the interviewer rates the applicant on tactfulness (T) and concern for customers (C). The interviewer is provided with a rating manual containing examples of exceptional (5), average (3), and unacceptable (1) responses by the applicant.

A random sample of 50 current CSRs were chosen to participate in the study. At Time 1 they were administered the clerical test and the work sample; performance data were also gathered from company records for error rate (number of errors per 100 orders), speed (number of orders filled per hour), and customer complaints (number of complaints per week). At Time 2, one week later, the clerical test and the work sample were readministered to the CSRs. A member of the consulting firm sat in on all the interviews and served as a second rater of CSRs' performance

Results for Clerical Test

	Time 1	Time 2
Mean score	31.61	31.22
Standard deviation	4.70	5.11
Coefficient alpha	.85	.86
Test–retest r		.92**
r with error rate	−.31**	−.37**
r with speed	.41**	.39**
r with complaints	−.11	−.08
r with work sample (T)	.21	.17
r with work sample (C)	.07	.15

Results for Work Sample (T)

	Time 1	Time 2
Mean score	3.15	3.11
Standard deviation	.93	1.01
% agreement (raters)	88%	79%
r with work sample (C)	.81**	.77**
r with error rate	−.13	−.12
r with speed	.11	.15
r with complaints	−.37**	−.35**

Results for Work Sample (C)

	Time 1	Time 2
Mean score	2.91	3.07
Standard deviation	.99	1.10
% agreement (raters)	80%	82%
r with work sample (T)	.81**	.77**
r with error rate	−.04	−.11
r with speed	.15	.14
r with complaints	−.40**	−.31**

(Note: ** means that r was significant at $p < .05$)

on the work sample at Time 1 and Time 2. It is expected that the clerical test and work sample will have positive correlations with speed and negative correlations with error rate and customer complaints.

Based on the description of the study and the results above,

1. How do you interpret the reliability results for the clerical test and work sample? Are they favorable enough for Phonemin to consider using them "for keeps" in selecting new job applicants?

2. How do you interpret the validity results for the clerical test and work sample? Are they favorable enough for Phonemin to consider using them "for keeps" in selecting new job applicants?

3. What limitations in the above study should be kept in mind when interpreting the results and deciding whether to use the clerical test and work sample?

Conducting Empirical Validation and Adverse Impact Analysis

Yellow Blaze Candle Shops provides a full line of various types of candles and accessories such as candleholders. Yellow Blaze has 150 shops in shopping malls and strip malls throughout the country. Over 600 salespeople staff these stores, each of which has a full-time manager. Staffing the manager's position, by policy, must occur by promotion from within the sales ranks. The organization is interested in trying to improve its identification of salespeople most likely to be successful store managers. It has developed a special technique for assessing and rating the suitability of salespeople for the manager's job.

To experiment with this technique, the regional HR department representative met with the store managers in the region to review and rate the promotion suitability of each manager's salespeople. They reviewed sales results, customer service orientation, and knowledge of store operations for each salesperson, and then assigned a 1–3 promotion suitability rating (1 = not suitable, 2 = may be suitable, 3 = definitely suitable) on each of these three factors. A total promotion suitability (PS) score, ranging from 3 to 9, was then computed for each salesperson.

The PS scores were gathered, but not formally used in promotion decisions, for all salespeople. Over the past year, 30 salespeople have been promoted to store manager. Now it is time for the organization to preliminarily investigate the validity of the PS scores and to see if their use might lead to the occurrence of adverse impact against women or minorities. Each store manager's annual overall performance appraisal rating, ranging from 1 (low performance) to 5 (high performance), was used as the criterion measure in the validation study. The following data were available for analysis:

Employee ID	PS Score	Performance Rating	Sex M/F	Minority Status (M = Minority, NM = Nonminority)
11	9	5	M	NM
12	9	5	F	NM
13	9	1	F	NM
14	9	5	M	M
15	8	4	F	M
16	8	5	F	M
17	8	4	M	NM
18	8	5	M	NM
19	8	3	F	NM
20	8	4	M	NM
21	7	5	F	M
22	7	3	M	M
23	7	4	M	NM
24	7	3	F	NM
25	7	3	F	NM
26	7	4	M	NM

Employee ID	PS Score	Performance Rating	Sex M/F	Minority Status (M = Minority, NM = Nonminority)
27	7	5	M	M
28	6	4	F	NM
29	6	4	M	NM
30	6	2	F	M
31	6	3	F	NM
32	6	3	M	NM
33	6	5	M	NM
34	6	5	F	NM
35	5	3	M	NM
36	5	3	F	M
37	5	2	M	M
38	4	2	F	NM
39	4	1	M	NM
40	3	4	F	NM

Based on the above data, calculate:

1. Average PS scores for the whole sample, males, females, nonminorities, and minorities.
2. The correlation between PS scores and performance ratings, and its statistical significance ($r = .37$ or higher is needed for significance at $p < .05$).
3. Adverse impact (selection rate) statistics for males and females, and nonminorities and minorities. Use a PS score of 7 or higher as a hypothetical passing score (the score that might be used to determine who will or will not be promoted).

Using the data, results, and description of the study, answer the following questions:

1. Is the PS score a valid predictor of performance as a store manager?
2. With a cut score of 7 on the PS, would its use lead to adverse impact against women? Against minorities? If there is adverse impact, does the validity evidence justify use of the PS anyway?
3. What are the limitations of this study?
4. Would you recommend that Yellow Blaze use the PS score in making future promotion decisions? Why or why not?

TANGLEWOOD STORES CASE I

Identifying the methods that select the best employees for the job is indisputably one of the central features of the organizational staffing process. The measurement chapter described statistical methods for assessing the relationship between organizational hiring practices and important outcomes. The case will help you see exactly how these data can be analyzed in an employment setting, and it will show how the process differs depending on the job being analyzed.

The Situation

As you read in the recruiting case, Tanglewood has a history of very divergent staffing practices among stores, and it is looking to centralize its operations. For most stores, the only information collected from applicants is an application blank with education level and prior work experience. After the applicant undergoes a brief unstructured interview with representatives from the operations and HR departments, store managers make a hiring decision. Many managers have complained that the result of this system is that many individuals are hired who have little understanding of Tanglewood's position in the retail industry and whose personalities are completely wrong for the company's culture. To improve its staffing system, Tanglewood has selected certain stores to serve as prototypes for an experimental selection system that includes a much more thorough assessment of applicant qualifications.

Your Tasks

The case considers concurrent validation evidence from the existing hiring system for store associates as well as predictive validation evidence from the proposed hiring system. You will determine whether the proposed selection system represents a real improvement in the organization's ability to select associates who will perform well. Your willingness to generalize the results to other stores will also be assessed. An important ancillary activity in this case is ensuring that you communicate your statistical analyses in a way that is easy for a nonexpert to comprehend. Finally, you will determine whether there are any other outcomes you would like to assess with the new staffing materials, such as the potential for adverse impact and the reactions of store managers to the new system. The background information for this case, and your specific assignment, can be found at *www.mhhe.com/heneman7e.*

TANGLEWOOD STORES CASE II

Adverse Impact

One of the most significant equal employment opportunity concerns for any organization is when a large class of employees gathers together to declare that they have been discriminated against. In this case, you will assess a complaint of adverse impact proposed by the nonwhite employees of Tanglewood in Northern California.

The Situation

This case revolves around analyzing data on the promotion pipeline at Tanglewood Stores and trying to decide if there is a glass ceiling in operation. As you saw in the introduction and planning case, Tanglewood's top management is deeply concerned about diversity, and they want to ensure that the promotion system does not discriminate. They have provided you with background data that will help you assess the situation.

Your Tasks

Using the information in this chapter, you will assess the proportional representation of women and minorities by analyzing concentration statistics and promotion rates. As in the measurement and validation case, an important activity in this case is ensuring that you communicate your statistical analyses in a way that is easy for management to comprehend. After making these assessments, you will provide specific recommendations to the organization regarding elements of planning, culture change, and recruiting. The background information for this case, and your specific assignment, can be found at *www.mhhe.com/heneman7e*.

ENDNOTES

1. E. F. Stone, *Research Methods in Organizational Behavior* (Santa Monica, CA: Goodyear, 1978), pp. 35–36.
2. F. G. Brown, *Principles of Educational and Psychological Testing* (Hinsdale, IL: Dryden, 1970), pp. 38–45.
3. Stone, *Research Methods in Organizational Behavior*, pp. 36–40.
4. W. H. Bommer, J. L. Johnson, G. A. Rich, P. M. Podsakoff, and S. B. McKenzie, "On the Interchangeability of Objective and Subjective Measures of Employee Performance: A Meta-Analysis," *Personnel Psychology*, 1995, 48, pp. 587–606; R. L. Heneman, "The Relationship Between Supervisory Ratings and Results-Oriented Measures of Performance: A Meta-Analysis," *Personnel Psychology*, 1986, 39, pp. 811–826.

5. This section draws on Brown, *Principles of Educational and Psychological Testing*, pp. 158–197; L. J. Cronbach, *Essentials of Psychological Testing*, fourth ed. (New York: Harper and Row, 1984), pp. 81–120; N. W. Schmitt and R. J. Klimoski, *Research Methods in Human Resources Management* (Cincinnati: South-Western, 1991), pp. 41–87.

6. J. T. McClave and P. G. Benson, *Statistics for Business and Economics*, third ed. (San Francisco: Dellan, 1985).

7. For an excellent review, see Schmitt and Klimoski, *Research Methods in Human Resources Management*, pp. 88–114.

8. This section draws on E. G. Carmines and R. A. Zeller, *Reliability and Validity Assessment* (Beverly Hills, CA: Sage, 1979).

9. D. P. Schwab, "Construct Validity in Organization Behavior," in B. Staw and L. L. Cummings (eds.), *Research in Organizational Behavior* (Greenwich, CT: JAI Press, 1980), pp. 3–43.

10. Carmines and Zeller, *Reliability and Validity Assessment*; J. M. Cortina, "What Is Coefficient Alpha? An Examination of Theory and Application," *Journal of Applied Psychology*, 1993, 78, pp. 98–104; Schmitt and Klimoski, *Research Methods in Human Resources Management*, pp. 89–100.

11. This section draws on R. D. Arvey, "Constructs and Construct Validation," *Human Performance*, 1992, 5, pp. 59–69; W. F. Cascio, *Applied Psychology in Personnel Management*, fourth ed. (Englewood Cliffs, NJ: Prentice-Hall, 1991), pp. 149–170; H. G. Heneman III, D. P. Schwab, J. A. Fossum, and L. Dyer, *Personnel/Human Resource Management*, fourth ed. (Homewood, IL: Irwin, 1989), pp. 300–329; N. Schmitt and F. J. Landy, "The Concept of Validity," in N. Schmitt, W. C. Borman, and Associates, *Personnel Selection in Organizations* (San Francisco: Jossey-Bass, 1993), pp. 275–309; Schwab, "Construct Validity in Organization Behavior"; S. Messick, "Validity of Psychological Assessment," *American Psychologist*, Sept. 1995, pp. 741–749.

12. Heneman, Schwab, Fossum, and Dyer, *Personnel/Human Resource Management*, pp. 300–310.

13. I. L. Goldstein, S. Zedeck, and B. Schneider, "An Exploration of the Job Analysis-Content Validity Process," in Schmitt, Borman, and Associates, *Personnel Selection in Organizations*, pp. 3–34; Heneman, Schwab, Fossum, and Dyer, *Personnel/Human Resource Management*, pp. 311–315; D. A. Joiner, *Content Valid Testing for Supervisory and Management Jobs: A Practical/Common Sense Approach* (Alexandria, VA: International Personnel Management Association, 1987); P. R. Sackett and R. D. Arvey, "Selection in Small N Settings," in Schmitt, Borman, and Associates, *Personnel Selection in Organizations*, pp. 418–447.

14. R. S. Barrett, "Content Validation Form," *Public Personnel Management*, 1992, 21, pp. 41–52; E. E. Ghiselli, J. P. Campbell, and S. Zedeck, *Measurement Theory for the Behavioral Sciences* (San Francisco: W. H. Freeman, 1981).

15. F. Schmidt and J. Hunter, "History, Development, Evolution, and Impact of Validity Generalization and Meta-Analysis Methods, 1975–2001," in K. R. Murphy (ed.), *Validity Generalization: A Critical Review* (Mahwah, NJ: Erlbaum, 2003), pp. 31–65; K. R. Murphy, "Synthetic Validity: A Great Idea Whose Time Never Came," *Industrial and Organizational Psychology*, 2010, 3(3), pp. 356–359; K. R. Murphy, "Validity, Validation and Values," *Academy of Management Annals*, 2009, 3, pp. 421–461.

16. M. A. McDaniel, H. R. Rothstein, and D. L. Whetzel, "Publication Bias: A Case Study of Four Test Vendors," *Personnel Psychology*, 2006, 59, pp. 927–953.

17. C. Winkler, "Quality Check: Better Metrics Improve HR's Ability to Measure—and Manage—the Quality of Hires," *HR Magazine*, May 2007, pp. 93–98; Society for Human Resource Management, *SHRM Human Capital Benchmarking Study* (Alexandria, VA: author, 2005).

18. J. A. Naglieri, F. Drasgow, M. Schmit, L. Handler, A. Prifitera, A. Margolis, and R. Velasquez, "Psychological Testing on the Internet," *American Psychologist*, Apr. 2004, 59, pp. 150–162;

R. E. Ployhart, J. A. Weekley, B. C. Holtz, and C. Kemp, "Web-Based and Paper-and-Pencil Testing of Applicants in a Proctored Setting: Are Personality, Biodata, and Situational Judgment Tests Comparable?" *Personnel Psychology*, 2003, 56, pp. 733–752; S. Power, "Federal Official Faults TSA Screener Testing as 'Inane,'" *Wall Street Journal*, Oct. 9, 2003, pp. B1–B2.

19. See the Society for Human Resource Management Testing Center (*www.shrm.org/Templates Tools/AssessmentResources/SHRMTestingCenter/Pages/index.aspx*).

20. D. B. Cohen, M. G. Aamodt, and E. M. Dunleavy, "Technical Advisory Committee Report on Best Practices in Adverse Impact Analysis," Center for Corporate Equality, 2010 (*www.cceq. org*), accessed 10/5/10.

21. Equal Employment Opportunity Commission, "Employment Tests and Selection Procedures," 2008 (*www.eeoc.gov/policy/docs/factemployment_procedures.html*), accessed 6/29/10.

CHAPTER EIGHT

External Selection I

Learning Objectives and Introduction
Learning Objectives
Introduction

Preliminary Issues
The Logic of Prediction
The Nature of Predictors
Development of the Selection Plan
Selection Sequence

Initial Assessment Methods
Résumés and Cover Letters
Application Blanks
Biographical Information
Reference and Background Checks
Initial Interview
Choice of Initial Assessment Methods

Legal Issues
Disclaimers
Reference Checks
Background Checks: Credit and Criminal
Preemployment Inquiries
Bona Fide Occupational Qualifications

Summary

Discussion Questions

Ethical Issues

Applications

LEARNING OBJECTIVES AND INTRODUCTION

Learning Objectives

- Understand how the logic of prediction guides the selection process
- Review the nature of predictors—how selection measures differ
- Understand the process involved in developing a selection plan, and the selection sequence
- Learn about initial assessment methods and understand how these methods are optimally used in organizations
- Evaluate the relative effectiveness of initial assessment methods to determine which work best, and why
- Review the legal issues involved in the use of initial assessment methods, and understand how legal problems can be avoided

Introduction

External selection—one of the more practically important and heavily researched areas of staffing—refers to the assessment and evaluation of external job applicants. A variety of assessment methods are used. Preliminary issues that guide the use of these assessment methods will be discussed. These issues include the logic of prediction, the nature of predictors, development of the selection plan, and the selection sequence.

Initial assessment methods are used to select candidates from among the initial job applicants. Those methods that will be reviewed are résumés and cover letters, application blanks, biographical information, letters of recommendation, reference and background checks, and initial interviews. The factors that should guide the choice of initial assessment methods will be reviewed. These include frequency of use, cost, reliability, validity, utility, applicant reactions, and adverse impact.

The use of assessment methods requires a firm understanding of legal issues—including the use of disclaimers and the legal complexities surrounding reference and background checks. The most important of these details will be reviewed. Finally, bona fide occupational qualifications (BFOQs) are particularly relevant to initial assessment because such qualifications are usually assessed during the initial stages of selection. The legal issues involved in establishing such qualifications will be reviewed.

PRELIMINARY ISSUES

Many times, selection is equated with one event, namely, the interview. Nothing could be further from the truth if the best possible person/job match is to be made. For this to be achieved, a series of well-thought-out activities needs to take place.

Hence, selection is a process rather than an event. It is guided by a logic that determines the steps that need to be taken. The logic applies to all predictors that might be used, even though they differ in terms of several characteristics. Actual implementation of the logic of prediction requires that predictors be chosen through development of a selection plan. Implementation also requires creation of a selection sequence, which is an orderly flow of people through the stages of applicant, candidate, finalist, and offer receiver.

The Logic of Prediction

In Chapter 1, the selection component of staffing was defined as the process of assessing and evaluating people for purposes of determining the likely fit between the person and the job. This process is based on the logic of prediction, which holds that indicators of a person's degree of success in past situations should be predictive of how successful he or she will likely be in new situations. Application of this logic to selection is illustrated in Exhibit 8.1.

A person's knowledge, skills, abilities, and other characteristics (KSAOs) and motivation are the product of experiences of past job, current job, and nonjob situations. During selection, the organization identifies, assesses, and evaluates samples of these KSAOs and motivation. The results constitute the person's overall qualifications for the new situation or job. These qualifications are then used to predict how successful the person is likely to be in that new situation or job regarding the human resource (HR) outcomes. The logic of prediction works in practice if the organization accurately identifies and measures qualifications relative to job requirements, and if those qualifications remain stable over time so that the person carries them over to the new job.

An example of how this logic can be followed in practice comes from a national communications organization with sales volume in the billions of dollars.[1] The organization was interested in improving on the prediction of job success (sales

EXHIBIT 8.1   The Logic of Prediction

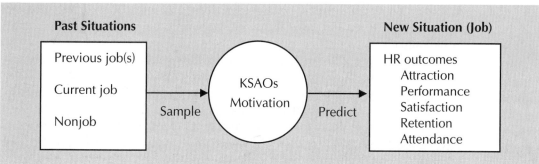

volume) for its salespeople, whose sales figures had stagnated. To do so, it constructed what it labeled a "sales competency blueprint," or selection plan, to guide development of a new selection process. The blueprint depicted the KSAOs that needed to be sampled from previous jobs in order to predict sales success in a telemarketing sales job. The blueprint was based on a thorough job analysis in which subject matter experts (SMEs) identified the KSAOs thought necessary to be a successful telemarketer (e.g., knowledge of the product, how it was developed, and how it compared with the competitors' products). A structured interview was developed to sample the extent to which applicants for telemarketing sales jobs had acquired the necessary KSAOs. In turn, the interview was used in selection to predict the likely success of applicants for the job.

The logic of prediction shown in Exhibit 8.1 demonstrates how critical it is to carefully scrutinize the applicant's past situation when making selection decisions. For example, in selecting someone for a police officer position, the success of the applicant in a previous security guard position might be considered a relevant predictor of the likelihood that the applicant will succeed in the police officer position. Alternatively, the fact that the person was previously successful as a homemaker might be viewed as totally irrelevant. Surprisingly, considering the homemaker role to be irrelevant might well be an incorrect assessment. Research shows that there is a close correspondence between the role of homemaker and the police officer position. Specifically, thorough job analysis showed that both jobs rely heavily on troubleshooting and emergency handling skills. Hence, in the absence of a sound job analysis, many qualified applicants may inadvertently be overlooked even though they have some of the characteristics needed to perform the job. Non-job experience in the home, in the community, and in other institutions may be as valuable as or more valuable than previous employment experiences.

Job titles such as homemaker are not nearly specific enough for making selection decisions. Similarly, the fact that someone has a certain number of years of experience usually does not provide sufficient detail to make selection decisions. What counts, and what is revealed through job analysis, is the specific types of experiences required and the level of successfulness at each. Similarly, whether someone was paid for employment is not relevant. What counts is the quality of the experience as it relates to success in the new job. In short, the logic of prediction indicates that a point-to-point comparison needs to be made between requirements of the job to be filled and the qualifications applicants have acquired from a variety of past situations.

The logic of prediction is important to not only selection but also recruitment. One study showed that applicant reactions to selection procedures were determined in part by the job relatedness of the selection procedure. If applicants see the selection process as job related, which should occur if the logic of prediction is used, they are more likely to view the selection process as being fair.[2] Applicants who view the selection procedure as fair are more likely to accept a job offer and/or encourage others to apply for a job in the organization.

Finally, the logic of prediction means separating recruitment from selection. For example, many organizations use employee referrals to identify prospective hires (recruitment), to select among those who have applied (selection), or both. Though there is nothing wrong with using referrals, how they are evaluated as a recruitment device will differ from how they are evaluated as a selection measure (often in the form of references).

The Nature of Predictors

As will be seen shortly, many types of predictors, ranging from interviews to reference checks, are used in external selection. They can be differentiated from one another in terms of content and form.

Content

The substance or content of what is being assessed with a predictor varies considerably and may range from a sign to a sample to a criterion.[3] A sign is a predisposition of the person that is thought to relate to performance on the job. Personality as a predictor is a good example here. If personality is used as a predictor, the prediction is that someone with a certain personality (e.g., abrasive) will demonstrate certain behaviors (e.g., rude to customers) leading to certain results on the job (e.g., failure to make a sale). As can be seen, a sign is very distant from actual on-the-job results. A sample is closer than a sign to actual on-the-job results. Observing a set of interactions between a sales applicant and a customer to see if a sale is made is an example of a sample. The criterion is very close to the actual job performance, such as sales during a probationary period for a new employee.

Form

The form or design of the predictor may vary along several different lines.

Speed Versus Power.   A person's score on some predictors is based on the number of responses completed within a certain time frame, for example, the number of bench presses an individual completes in a given period of time. This is known as a speed test. A power test, on the other hand, presents individuals with items of increasing difficulty. For example, a power test of numerical ability may begin with addition and subtraction, move on to multiplication and division, and conclude with complex problem-solving questions. A speed test is used when speed of work is an important part of the job, and a power test is used when the correctness of the response is essential to the job. Of course, some tests (see the *Wonderlic Personnel Test* in Chapter 9) can be both speed and power tests, in which case few individuals would finish.

Paper and Pencil Versus Performance.   Many predictors are of the paper-and-pencil variety; applicants are required to fill out a form, write an answer, or complete multiple-choice items. Other predictors are performance tests, where the applicant is asked to manipulate an object or equipment. Timing running backs for the NFL in the 40-yard dash is a performance test. Paper-and-pencil tests are frequently used when psychological abilities are required to perform the job; performance tests are used when physical and social skills are required to perform the job.

Objective Versus Essay.   An objective paper-and-pencil predictor uses either multiple-choice questions or true/false questions. These tests should be used to measure knowledge in specific areas. Another form of a predictor is an essay, where the respondent provides a written answer. Essays are best used to assess written communication, problem-solving, and analytical skills.[4]

Oral Versus Written Versus Computer.   Responses to predictor questions can be spoken, written, or entered into a computer or other electronic communication device. When conducting interviews, some organizations listen to oral responses, read written responses, or read computer printouts of typed-in responses to assess applicants. As with all predictors, the appropriate form depends on the nature of the job. If the job requires a high level of verbal skill, oral responses should be solicited. If the job requires a large amount of writing, written responses should be required. If the job requires constant interaction with the computer, applicants should use a computer to enter their responses.[5]

Development of the Selection Plan

To translate the results of a job analysis into the actual predictors to be used for selection, a selection plan must be developed. A selection plan describes which predictor(s) will be used to assess the KSAOs required to perform the job. The recommended format for a selection plan, and an example of such a plan for the job of secretary, is shown in Exhibit 8.2. A selection plan can be established in three steps. First, the KSAOs are written in the left-hand column. This list comes directly from the job requirements matrix. Second, for each KSAO, a "yes" or "no" is written to show whether it needs to be assessed in the selection process. Sometimes the answer is no because the applicant will acquire the KSAO once on the job (e.g., knowledge of company policies and procedures). Third, possible methods of assessment are listed for the required KSAOs, and the specific method to be used for each is indicated.

Although selection plans are costly and time-consuming to develop, organizations are increasingly finding that the benefits of developing a selection plan outweigh the costs. As a result, it is and should be a required step in the selection process. Barnett Bank in Jacksonville, Florida, uses a selection plan or "niche testing" to select tellers and customer service representatives. It found that an essential KSAO for both positions was the ability to make judgments when interacting with

EXHIBIT 8.2   Selection Plan Format and Example for Secretarial Position

Major KSAO Category	Necessary for Selection? (Y/N)	WP	CT	DB	LTR	TEF	ML	EM	TM	Inter-view
1. Ability to follow oral directions/ listening skills	Y			X					X	
2. Ability to read and understand manuals/guidelines	Y	X	X	X	X	X	X	X		
3. Ability to perform basic arithmetic operations	Y			X		X				
4. Ability to organize	Y			X	X	X	X			
5. Judgments/priority setting/decision-making ability	Y			X						
6. Oral communication skills	Y				X					X
7. Written communication skills	Y		X		X			X		
8. Interpersonal skills	Y									X
9. Typing skills	Y	X	X		X	X				
10. Knowledge of word processing, graphics, database, and spreadsheet software	Y	X	X	X	X	X				
11. Knowledge of company policies and procedures	N									
12. Knowledge of basic personal computer operations	Y	X	X	X	X	X		X		
13. Knowledge of how to use basic office machines	N									
14. Flexibility in dealing with changing job demands	Y						X	X	X	
15. Knowledge of computer software	Y	X	X	X	X	X	X	X		
16. Ability to attend to detail and accuracy	Y	X	X	X	X	X	X	X	X	

WP = Word processing test, CT = Correction test, DB = Database exam, LTR = Letter, TEF = Travel expense form, ML = Mail log, EM = Electronic mail messages, and TM = Telephone messages.

SOURCE: Adapted from N. Schmitt, S. Gilliland, R. S. Landis, and D. Devine, "Computer-Based Testing Applied to Selection of Secretarial Positions," *Personnel Psychology*, 1993, 46, pp. 149–165.

the public. For this KSAO, a niche test was developed in which applicants watch actual dealings with the public on video and then determine the appropriate course of action. Their responses are graded and used to predict their likelihood of success in either position.

Selection Sequence

Usually, a series of decisions are made about job applicants before they are selected. These decisions are depicted in Exhibit 8.3. The first decision is whether initial applicants who have applied for the job become candidates or are rejected. A candidate is someone who possesses the minimum qualifications to be considered for further assessment but has not yet received an offer.

EXHIBIT 8.3   Assessment Methods by Applicant Flow Stage

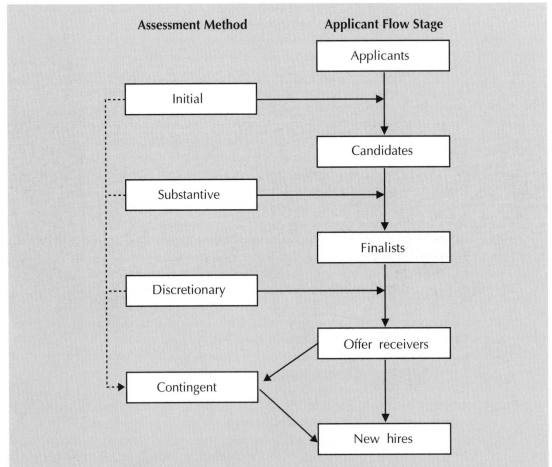

Initial assessment methods are used to choose candidates (these will be discussed later in this chapter). The second decision is to determine which candidates become finalists. A finalist is someone who meets all the minimum qualifications and whom the organization considers fully qualified for the job. Substantive assessment methods, discussed in Chapter 9, are used to select finalists. The third decision is to determine which finalist receives the job offer. Offer receivers are those finalists to whom the organization extends an offer of employment. Discretionary methods, also discussed in Chapter 9, are used to select these individuals. Contingent methods are sometimes used, meaning the job offer is subject to certain qualifications, such as the offer receiver passing a medical exam or drug test. Use of contingent methods, in particular drug testing and medical exams, will be reviewed in Chapter 9. Finally, some offer receivers become new hires when they decide to join the organization.

INITIAL ASSESSMENT METHODS

Initial assessment methods, also referred to as preemployment inquiries, are used to minimize the costs associated with substantive assessment methods by reducing the number of people assessed. Predictors typically used to screen candidates from applicants include application blanks, biographical information, reference reports, and initial interviews. Each of these initial assessment methods will be described in turn. Using meta-analysis results, the average validity (i.e., $\bar{r}$) of each method is also provided if possible. Then, a general evaluation is presented to help guide decisions about which initial assessment methods to use.

Résumés and Cover Letters

The first introduction of the applicant to the organization is often a cover letter and résumé. The applicant controls the introduction in regard to the amount, type, and accuracy of information provided. As a result, résumés and cover letters always need to be verified with other predictors, such as background checks, to ensure that there are accurate and complete data across all job applicants with which to make informed selection decisions.

One major issue with résumés as a selection tool is the volume that organizations must process. Some organizations make few provisions for how to file and organize résumés as they filter in, and for how to store them once a hiring decision is made. Most organizations are well advised to produce and maintain an electronic copy of résumés received, both to ease sharing of information among selection decision makers and to track applicants should any questions (legal or otherwise) arise once the applicant is hired.

Employers can outsource résumé collection to résumé-tracking services. Many services not only scan résumés but also score them and place a percentage next to the applicant's name that reflects the number of criteria his or her résumé meets. Though such methods have powerful time- and cost-saving advantages, there are disadvantages, such as rejection of résumés that the software could not read (e.g., those on colored paper or that use special formatting like bullets) and applicants who try to beat the system by loading their résumés with every conceivable skill that appears in the advertisement. Despite these drawbacks, the efficiencies of such services make them particularly attractive for organizations facing large volumes of résumés.

The vast majority of large employers, and even many medium-size employers, encourage submission of résumés via e-mail or through online forms on the organization's website. For example, on the Toys "R" Us website, applicants can search an online database for openings and then apply either by completing an online form or, for managerial positions, by attaching their résumé to an e-mail message.

Even if applicants submit an electronic résumé to an employer, they need to make sure it is electronically scan-ready. This means applicants should avoid unusual fonts and formatting. With today's résumés, form definitely should follow function. Moreover, applicants should use nouns to describe noteworthy aspects of their background ("nonprofit," "3.75 GPA," "environmental science experience," etc.), as opposed to the traditional emphasis on action verbs ("managed," "guided," etc.), because nouns are more likely to be identified as keywords in scanning software. If the résumé is likely to be scanned, the applicant should build it around such keywords that will be the focus of the scan.

Video Résumés

Video résumés are getting considerable attention in the business press. Sites like *WorkBlast.com* help applicants put together video résumés where the applicants talk about their qualifications directly to the camera or in a simulated interview. Lucy Cherkasets sent a video résumé to organizations in the New York area that had openings she was interested in. "I used it to apply for the jobs I wanted the most," she said. She is now working as an HR manager for LaForce & Stevens, a public relations firm in Manhattan.

While the topic of video résumés is fashionable, few employers have any experience with them, and there is no research on their effectiveness. Although a survey indicated that many hiring managers would view a video résumé, a majority (58%) of those admitted they would do so out of "sheer curiosity." As one career advisor noted, "Most employers don't have much direct familiarity with them yet. Folks are still trying to figure out where the video résumé falls in the calculus in applicant selection." Some employers refuse to view video résumés for fear of introducing subjective biasing factors (appearance, race, or a disability) into their decisions. Other job applicants have submitted video résumés only to be the subject of ridicule by their potential employers. Aleksey Vayner, a finance major at

Yale, sent a video résumé to bank giant UBS, only to have it posted on blogs and be mocked by others.[6]

Thus, while video résumés are receiving a lot of attention in the press, the pitfalls involved for employers and applicants, for the time being at least, might cause them to be considered more of a fad than the wave of the future.

Résumé Issues

Résumés have the advantage of allowing the applicant to control information presented to employers. In evaluating résumés, employers should be aware of fabrications and distortions. Applicants, meanwhile, will want to know how to get their résumés noticed. We consider each of these issues and how to address them below.

Résumé Fabrications and Distortions. Because résumés are prepared by applicants and follow no set-in-stone form, and because applicants want to present themselves in a favorable light, distortions are a significant problem. David J. Edmondson, CEO of RadioShack, was fired after a newspaper investigation revealed that he padded his résumé with two degrees he never earned, from a university he never attended. Edmondson is not alone. In any given year, it seems the career of some CEO, athletic coach, or public official is derailed by a false statement the individual made on his or her résumé—often years ago. ResumeDoctor, an online company that assists applicants in preparing résumés, checked the accuracy of applicants' résumés posted on its website and found that nearly half (42.7%) had "significant inaccuracies." A background checking agency found that 56% of résumés contained a falsehood of some kind.[7]

Like the truth, résumés come in various degrees of accuracy, ranging from small, unintentional mistakes to outright fabrications. Some degree of what we might call "fudging" is commonplace. For example, Ellie Strauss's two more recent full-time jobs lasted less than six months. Ellie represented these as freelance jobs, under the heading "Senior Project Manager," to make them look like contract positions. Some might call this deception. Others might call it creative marketing or tailoring. Whatever you call it, résumé padding happens a lot. People even fudge their education for wedding announcements. The *New York Times* had to print a correction because a bride indicated she graduated from the University of Pennsylvania and received a doctorate in neuroscience from the University of Southern California, neither of which was true.[8] If people will lie on a wedding announcement, imagine what they will do on a résumé!

According to one survey, the three biggest areas of distortion or misinformation are the following:[9]

1. Inflated titles
2. Inaccurate dates to cover up job-hopping or employment gaps
3. Half-finished degrees, inflated education, or "purchased" degrees

The best way to combat résumé fraud or fudging is to conduct careful background checks. Also, applying a "smell" test to any suspicious information is a wise policy. For example, in light of the false information submitted by coaches, colleges are scrutinizing résumés much more closely. On the University of Louisville's athletic department application forms, a warning has been inserted: "If a discrepancy is found after the background check, the employee is subject to dismissal." In short, the best protection against résumé fraud is for the hiring organization to do its homework.[10]

Getting a Résumé Noticed.　The conscientious job seeker may wonder how to best prepare a résumé. Although there are as many theories on the ingredients of a perfect résumé as there are résumé readers, a few general guidelines may be helpful. First, realize that typos and other minor mistakes can kill your chances. A survey revealed that 84% of hiring managers exclude applicants from further consideration with two typographical errors on their résumé; 47% of these managers exclude applicants with just a single error. Second, customize your résumé to the position if at all possible (try to address how your background, skills, and accomplishments fit the specific job requirements). Third, although résumés are getting somewhat longer, recognize that brevity is highly valued among hiring managers—many of whom refuse to read résumés that are longer than two pages, and some won't read those that are longer than a page. Third, as we noted above, be factual and truthful. Where judgment is required, err on the side of accuracy. As one expert put it, "People are lying when they don't have to." Most hiring managers understand that no résumé is perfect. And even if being truthful hurts you in the short run, better to pay the price now rather than later, when you might have an entire career at stake. Finally, though taking care to be truthful, a résumé is no time to underplay your accomplishments. Do not just list your job duties; identify your accomplishments as well. Consider your impact on your division or group: What would not have happened had you not been there? What are you proudest of? Can you identify your own strengths from your performance review? Did you demonstrate skills during college that you might describe? The global head of recruiting for Accenture says he looks for evidence of teamwork skills in hiring: "I'd have to put the ability to work in a team environment toward the very top of what we look for," he says. Since most college students do some of their work in teams, why not list that as a skill acquired?[11]

Evaluation.　Almost no research exists on the validity and reliability of résumés and cover letters, nor is there information on their costs or adverse impact. A review did indicate relatively low validity for applicant self-reports of grades, class standing, and test scores, but this does not address other information—such as self-reported work experience—often provided in applications and résumés. This situation is unfortunate given the pervasive use of résumés and cover letters in certain types of jobs, especially entry-level management, professional, and technical positions. Thus, organizations using résumés and cover letters in selection should carefully evaluate their effectiveness and make sure to independently verify information they are using in hiring decisions.[12]

Application Blanks

Most application blanks request in written form the applicant's background in regard to educational experiences, training, and job experiences. This information is often on the résumé as well and may seem unnecessarily duplicated. This is not the case. An application can be used to verify the data presented on the résumé and can also be used to obtain data omitted on the résumé, such as employment dates. The major advantage of application blanks over résumés is that the organization, rather than the applicant, dictates what information is presented. As a result, information critical to success on the job is less likely to be omitted by the applicant or overlooked by the reviewer of the résumé. The major issue with application blanks is to make sure that information requested is critical to job success, following the logic of prediction discussed earlier.

A sample application blank is provided in Exhibit 8.4. As with most application blanks, the major sections are personal information, employment desired, educational background, special interests and abilities, work experience, and suggested references. The only information sought from the application blank should be KSAOs that can be demonstrated as relevant to the job. This not only avoids wasting the organization's and the applicant's time but also protects the employer from charges of unfair discrimination (see "Legal Issues" at the end of this chapter). Note the disclaimer statement at the bottom of the application blank. It provides certain legal protections to the organization, which are discussed in "Legal Issues." Asking applicants to sign a disclaimer may also decrease the incentive to distort or falsify information.

Educational Requirements

Special care needs to be taken in wording items on an application blank when soliciting information about educational experiences and performance.[13] Following are several particularly important areas pertaining to educational requirement information on application blanks.

Level of Education. Level of education or degree is one element of educational performance used to predict job performance. Often, level of education is measured by the attainment of a degree. Despite its pervasive use, it is not clear that level of education is a truly useful selection measure. Some economists and sociologists question its importance, and a meta-analysis suggested that the correlation between education and task performance was relatively small (across all measures of task performance, $\bar{r}_{xy} = .10$).[14]

EXHIBIT 8.4 Application for Employment

PERSONAL INFORMATION

DATE _____

NAME _____

SOCIAL SECURITY
NUMBER _____

             LAST   FIRST   MIDDLE

PRESENT ADDRESS _____
                      STREET   CITY   STATE   ZIP

PERMANENT ADDRESS _____
                      STREET   CITY   STATE   ZIP

PHONE NO. _____ ARE YOU 18 YEARS OR OLDER? Yes ☐ No ☐

ARE YOU PREVENTED FROM LAWFULLY BECOMING EMPLOYED
IN THIS COUNTRY BECAUSE OF VISA OR IMMIGRATION STATUS? Yes ☐ No ☐

EMPLOYMENT DESIRED

POSITION _____

DATE YOU
CAN START _____

SALARY
DESIRED _____

ARE YOU EMPLOYED NOW? _____

IF SO MAY WE INQUIRE
OF YOUR PRESENT EMPLOYER? _____

APPLIED TO THIS COMPANY BEFORE? _____ WHERE? _____ WHEN? _____

REFERRED BY _____

EDUCATION

	NAME AND LOCATION	NO. OF YEARS ATTENDED	DID YOU GRADUATE?	SUBJECTS STUDIED
GRAMMAR SCHOOL				
HIGH SCHOOL (GED)				
COLLEGE				
OTHER				

(continued)

EXHIBIT 8.4 Continued

GENERAL

SUBJECTS OF SPECIAL STUDY
_____

SPECIAL SKILLS
_____

ACTIVITIES: (CIVIC, ATHLETIC, ETC.)
_____

U.S. MILITARY OR NAVAL SERVICE	RANK	PRESENT MEMBERSHIP IN NATIONAL GUARD OR RESERVES

FORMER EMPLOYERS (LIST BELOW LAST 3 EMPLOYERS, STARTING WITH THE LAST ONE FIRST)

DATE	NAME & ADDRESS	SALARY	POSITION	REASON FOR LEAVING
FROM				
TO				
FROM				
TO				
FROM				
TO				

REFERENCES (GIVE THE NAMES OF 3 PERSONS NOT RELATED TO YOU)

	NAME	ADDRESS	BUSINESS	YEARS ACQUAINTED
1				
2				
3				

"I certify that all the information submitted by me on this application is true and complete, and I understand that if any false information, omissions, or misrepresentations are discovered, my application may be rejected and, if I am employed, my employment may be terminated at any time. In consideration of my employment, I agree to conform to the company's rules and regulations, and I agree that my employment and compensation can be terminated, with or without cause, and with or without notice, at any time, at either my or the company's option. I also understand and agree that the terms and conditions of my employment may be changed, with or without cause, and with or without notice, at any time by the company. I understand that no company representative, other than its president, and only when in writing and signed by the president, has any authority to enter into any agreement for employment for any specific period of time, or to make any agreement contrary to the foregoing."

DATE	SIGNATURE

Grade Point Average.   Classroom grades are measured using a grade point average (GPA). Care should be exercised in the interpretation of GPA information. For example, a GPA in one's major in college may be different (usually higher) from one's GPA for all classes. Grades also vary widely by field (e.g., grades in engineering tend to be lower than in other fields). Further, a GPA of 3.5 may be good at one school but not at another. Research suggests that the validity of GPA in predicting job performance may be as high as the mid .30s. College grades are no more valid than high school grades, and grades are most valid in predicting early job performance. Although there is variability from employer to employer, evidence indicates that GPA does not play a large role in most recruiters' evaluations. GPAs tend to have adverse impact against minorities, and, as with all selection measures with adverse impact, the validity evidence must be balanced against adverse impact implications.[15]

Quality of School.   Much has been said and written about the quality of various educational programs. For example, *U.S. News and World Report* annually publishes the results of a survey showing ratings of school quality (or prestige, depending on the faith you have in such ratings).[16]

Graduates from prestigious universities are commanding wage premiums for MBA degrees in particular, but also educational degrees in general. Sixty percent of corporate recruiters cite the reputation of the school as the top reason for recruiting at a particular university. As one article concluded, "It's not necessarily what you learn in an MBA program, but where you learn it."[17]

Major Field of Study.   The more specialized the knowledge requirements of a particular position, the more important an applicant's major field of study is likely to be as a predictor. An English major may do very well as an editor but may be unsuccessful as a physician. It should also be noted that choice of major does not guarantee that a certain number or type of classes have been taken. The number and type of classes needed for a major or minor vary from school to school and need to be carefully scrutinized to ensure comparability across majors. The relationship between field of study and job performance is very difficult to assess; therefore, no conclusive validity evidence is available.

Extracurricular Activities.   The usefulness of extracurricular activities as a predictor depends on the job. Being a field hockey player may have little relevance to being a successful manager. However, being elected captain of a hockey team may indeed be a sign of leadership qualities needed to be a successful manager. Information about extracurricular activities taken from an application blank must be relevant to the job in question. Evidence suggests that participation in extracurricular activities demonstrates interpersonal skills, indicating that it may be more valid for jobs with a heavy social component.[18]

Training and Experience Requirements

Many past experiences predictive of future performance do not take place in a classroom. Instead, they come from life experiences in other institutions, which, fortunately, can also be captured on an application blank. A great deal of weight is often put on training and experience requirements on the theory that actions speak louder than words. Experienced surgeons tend to make better surgeons, for example. A study found that the mortality rate of procedures was about twice as high for inexperienced surgeons as for experienced surgeons. As with other jobs, though, the benefits of experience tend to be at the low levels of experience. Beyond a certain level, added experience doesn't help much. The drawback of putting too much emphasis on previous work experience, however, is that the amount of experience and training an applicant has may be overstated. Also, applicants with high potential may be overlooked because they have not had the opportunity to gain the training or experience needed.

Various methods can be used to measure training and experience. Since training and experience information is not directly equivalent across applicants, all methods require the judgment of selection decision makers. These decision makers render judgments about how to classify and weight different levels of experience. An approach termed the "behavioral consistency method" has shown the highest degree of validity because it focuses on determining the quality of an applicant's previous training and experience. One of the means by which the behavioral consistency method determines quality is by asking applicants to complete a supplemental application wherein they describe their most significant accomplishments relative to a list of key job behaviors. Due to their involved nature, however, behavioral consistency ratings are time-consuming and expensive to administer, and they require the applicant to possess some degree of analytical ability and writing skills. Thus, the choice of weighting methods rests on a trade-off between accuracy and ease and cost of administration.[19]

Licensing, Certification, and Job Knowledge

Many professions and occupations require or encourage people to demonstrate mastery of a certain body of knowledge. Such mastery is commonly measured by two distinct methods: licensure and certification. A license is required of people by law to perform an activity, whereas a certification is voluntary in the sense that it is not mandated by law (though an individual employer may require it). The purpose of a license is to protect the public interest, whereas the purpose of a certification is to identify an individual who has met a minimum standard of proficiency. Licensing exams and certification exams are usually developed by SMEs in conjunction with testing specialists. Licensure and certification are to be distinguished from job knowledge tests. While licensure and certification demonstrate mastery of a general body of knowledge applicable to many organizations, job knowledge tests assess a specific body of knowledge within a particular organization. Job knowledge tests are usually used in the public sector as an initial screening device. In the private sector, they are used primarily for promotion purposes. Although mentioned here, job knowledge tests will be covered in detail in Chapter 9.

The actual use of licensing and certification requirements depends on whether they are used as an initial or a contingent assessment method. As an initial method, licensing and certification requirements are used to eliminate applicants who fail to possess these credentials. For example, a car repair shop electing to hire only certified mechanics might initially screen out individuals who fail to have the proper certification. When licensing and certification requirements are used as a contingent method, the selection process proceeds on the assumption that the applicant has the requisite credentials (or will have them by the time of hire). This is then verified after an initial offer decision has been made. For example, rather than verifying that each applicant for a nursing position possesses a valid state license, a hospital may assess applicants on the assumption that they have a valid license and then verify this assumption after a contingent job offer has been made. Thus, the difference between using licensing and certification requirements as initial or contingent assessment methods depends on when the information is considered in the selection process.

Increasingly, organizations are using voluntary professional certification as a method of verifying competence in various occupations. There are more than 1,000 professional certifications. Most of these voluntary certifications are issued on the basis of experience and education. The vast majority of certifications also require examinations.

There are several practical problems or limitations in using licensing and certification requirements in selection. First, one cannot assume that simply because an applicant has a license or certification he or she is qualified for the position. That assumption places full confidence in the licensing and certification standards of the professional organization. Licensing and certification requirements vary greatly in their rigor, and one should not accept on faith that the fulfillment of those requirements ensures professional competency. Moreover, even if the requirements did perfectly measure professional competence, because licenses and certifications are issued to those passing some minimum threshold, they do not discriminate between the minimally qualified and the exceptionally well qualified.

A second difficulty with licensing and certification requirements is that, like job titles, there has been significant proliferation. This is particularly true with certifications. For example, among financial advisors are certified financial planners (CFPs), certified financial analysts (CFAs), certified investment management analysts (CIMAs), chartered financial consultants (ChFCs), chartered retirement planning counselors (CRPCs), and so forth. Indeed, more than 100 such titles are used by financial professionals. No central regulator monitors these titles, and the growth in financial services certifications seems to have done little to prevent the myriad mistakes and malfeasances that contributed to the recent financial crisis that decimated Wall Street and Main Street alike. If selection decision makers wish to require certification, they need to research the types and meanings of certifications that may exist for a job.

Finally, there are practice effects with repeated tries at a licensing or certification exam, and the effects may be quite strong. One study of medical professionals found that for one certification exam, second-time examinees improved their scores by .79 standard deviations. For another exam, the average gain was .48 standard deviations. Translating the gain from the first exam (.79SD) into a standard normal distribution, this would mean that someone who scored at the 34th percentile the first time out would be expected to score at the 66th percentile on the second try. For the second exam (.48SD), the improvement would be from the 34th percentile to the 53rd percentile. Unlike some standardized tests, where scores may be reported for each time the test is taken, there generally is no way for a selection decision maker to know how many times an applicant has taken a licensing or certification exam (nor can one determine a test taker's exact score).

We are not arguing that selection decision makers should ignore licensing and certification requirements. They are important—even necessary—for many jobs. However, selection decision makers need to be informed consumers for those areas where they require licensure and certification, and supplement licensure and certification with other information to ascertain knowledge and competency.[20]

Weighted Application Blanks

Not all of the information contained on an application blank is of equal value to the organization in making selection decisions. Depending on the organization and job, some information predicts success on the job better than other information. Procedures have been developed that help weight application blank information by the degree to which the information differentiates between high- and low-performing individuals.[21] This scoring methodology is referred to as a weighted application blank and is useful not only in making selection decisions but also in developing application blanks. The statistical procedures involved help the organization discern which items should be retained for use in the application blank and which should be excluded, depending on how well they predict performance.

Evaluation of Application Blanks

Evidence suggests that scored evaluations of the unweighted application blank are not particularly valid predictors of job performance (average validity ranges from $\bar{r} = .10$ to $\bar{r} = .20$).[22] This is not surprising given the rudimentary information collected in application blanks. Another factor that may undermine the validity of application blanks is distortion. Evidence suggests that about one-third of the investigations into the backgrounds of applicants suggested that misrepresentation occurred on the application blank. Subsequent studies have suggested that the most common questions that are misrepresented include previous salary, education, tenure on previous job, and reasons for leaving previous job. Some individuals even go beyond misrepresentation to outright invention. One study revealed that 15% of supposedly previous employers of applicants indicated that the individual had never worked for them.[23] Thus, application information that is weighted heavily in selection decisions should be verified.

The validity evidence for weighted application blanks is much more positive.[24] In a sense, this would almost have to be true since items in the weighted application blank are scored and weighted according to their ability to predict job performance. Thus, as long as *some* of the items are predictive, the scoring and weighting schemes embedded in the weighted application blank will ensure that the overall score is predictive. Because the process used to develop the weighted application blank is time-consuming and expensive, more cost-benefit studies need to be conducted. Is the validity worth the cost? Unfortunately, there is little recent research on the weighted application blank, so answering this question is difficult.

The relatively poor validity of unweighted application blanks also should not be taken as an indication that they are useless in selection decisions. Unweighted application blanks are a very inexpensive means of collecting basic information on job applicants. Most organizations use unweighted application blanks only for initial screening decisions (to rule out applicants who are obviously unqualified for the job). As long as application blanks are used in this context (and not relied on to a significant degree in making substantive hiring decisions), they can be a useful method of making initial decisions about applicants. Thus, it is not necessarily appropriate to condemn unweighted application blanks based on a criterion for which they are rarely used.

Biographical Information

Biographical information, often called biodata, is personal history information on an applicant's background and interests. Results from a biodata survey provide a general description of a person's life history. The principal assumption behind the use of biodata is the axiom "The best predictor of future behavior is past behavior." These past behaviors may reflect ability or motivation.

Like application blanks, biographical information blanks ask applicants to report on their background. Responses to both of these questionnaires can provide useful information in making initial selection decisions about applicants. Unlike application blanks, however, biographical information can also be fruitfully used for substantive selection decisions. In fact, if scores on a biodata inventory are predictive of subsequent job performance (which, as we will see, is often the case), it may be somewhat limiting to use biodata scores only for initial assessment decisions. Thus, although biographical information is as much a substantive assessment method as it is an initial assessment method, because it shares many similarities with application blanks, we have included it in this section. Nevertheless, it should also be considered in deliberations about which substantive assessment methods are to be used.

Biographical information has some similarities to background tests (see the section on reference and background checks). Biodata and background checks are similar in that both look into an applicant's past. However, the two types of selection methods differ in their general purpose and measurement. First, whereas a background check is often used to turn up any "buried bones" in an applicant's background, biodata is used to predict future performance. Second, whereas reference checks are conducted through checks of records and conversations with references, biodata information is collected by survey. Thus, biodata inventories and background checks are distinct methods of selection that must be considered separately.

The type of biographical information collected varies a great deal from inventory to inventory and often depends on the job. For example, a biographical survey for executives might focus on career aspirations, accomplishments, and disappointments. A survey for blue-collar workers might focus on training and work experience. A biodata inventory for federal government workers might focus on school and educational experiences, work history, skills, and interpersonal relations. As can be seen from these examples, most biodata surveys consider individual accomplishments, group accomplishments, disappointing experiences, and stressful situations.[25] The domains in which these attributes are studied often vary from job to job but can range from childhood experiences to educational or early work experiences to current hobbies or family relations.

Measures

Typically, biographical information is collected in a questionnaire that applicants complete. Exhibit 8.5 provides example biodata items. As can be seen, the items are quite diverse. It has been suggested that each biodata item can be classified according to 10 criteria:

- *History* (does the item describe an event that occurred in the past or a future or hypothetical event?)
- *Externality* (does the item address an observable event or an internal event such as values or judgments?)
- *Objectivity* (does the item focus on reporting factual information or subjective interpretations?)
- *Firsthandedness* (does the item seek information that is directly available to the applicant rather than an evaluation of the applicant's behavior by others?)
- *Discreteness* (does the item pertain to a single, unique behavior or a simple count of events as opposed to summary responses?)
- *Verifiability* (can the accuracy of the response to the item be confirmed?)

EXHIBIT 8.5 Examples of Biodata Items

1. In college, my grade point average was:
   a. I did not go to college or completed less than two years
   b. Less than 2.50
   c. 2.50 to 3.00
   d. 3.00 to 3.50
   e. 3.50 to 4.00

2. In the past five years, the number of different jobs I have held is:
   a. More than five
   b. Three–five
   c. Two
   d. One
   e. None

3. The kind of supervision I like best is:
   a. Very close supervision
   b. Fairly close supervision
   c. Moderate supervision
   d. Minimal supervision
   e. No supervision

4. When you are angry, which of the following behaviors most often describes your reaction:
   a. Reflect on the situation for a bit
   b. Talk to a friend or spouse
   c. Exercise or take a walk
   d. Physically release the anger on something
   e. Just try to forget about it

5. Over the past three years, how much have you enjoyed each of the following (use the scale at right below):
   a. ____ Reading   1 = Very much
   b. ____ Watching TV   2 = Some
   c. ____ Home improvements   3 = Very little
   d. ____ Music   4 = Not at all
   e. ____ Outdoor recreation

6. In most ways is your life close to ideal?
   a. Yes
   b. No
   c. Undecided or neutral

- *Controllability* (does the item address an event that the applicant controlled?)
- *Equal accessibility* (are the events or experiences expressed in the item equally accessible to all applicants?)
- *Job relevance* (does the item solicit information closely tied to the job?)
- *Invasiveness* (is the item sensitive to the applicant's right to privacy?)[26]

Most selection tests simply score items in a predetermined manner and add the scores to arrive at a total score. These total scores form the basis of selection decisions made about applicants. With most biodata inventories, the process of making decisions on the basis of responses to items is considerably more complex. Essentially, the development of a biodata inventory is a bit of a fishing expedition where current employees are given many items to complete and the inventory used for future hiring decisions is based on those items—and the specific responses within items or questions—that seem to discriminate between high performers and low performers.

Google developed its biodata inventory by first asking its employees 300 questions and then correlating employee responses to their job performance. Once it isolated items that predicted the job performance of current employees, Google asked applicants a smaller set of questions that ranged from the age when an applicant first got excited about computers to whether the applicant has ever turned a profit at his or her own side business.[27]

Evaluation of Biodata

Research conducted on the reliability and validity of biodata is quite positive.[28] Responses tend to be fairly reliable (test–retest coefficients range from .60 to .90). More important, past research suggests that biodata inventories are valid predictors of job performance. A number of meta-analyses have been conducted, and the average validity has ranged from $\bar{r}_{xy} = .32$ to $\bar{r}_{xy} = .37$.[29]

In addition to job performance, biodata scores appear to predict turnover (individuals with a past history of job changes are more likely to turn over) and student academic performance (biodata scores of incoming college freshmen predicted their subsequent college GPAs).[30]

Despite the quite positive validity evidence, biodata does have some important limitations. First, because biodata inventories are developed and scored on the basis of a particular job and sample, it has commonly been argued that the validity of a particular inventory in one organization is unlikely to generalize to another organization. Although this issue has not been conclusively resolved in the literature, prudent practice would suggest that organizations regularly validate their biodata inventory.[31]

Second, there is some concern about faking. Not only might applicants be motivated to fake their responses to biodata questions, but many responses are impossible to verify (e.g., "Did you collect coins or stamps as a child?"). Research also suggests, though, that faking can be reduced in a couple of ways: by using items that are more objective and verifiable, and by warning applicants against faking.[32]

Third, applicants and managers do not react positively to biodata. The inventories often comprise more than 100 items, and most research suggests that applicants do not see the questions as job related. Neither, apparently, do HR managers. A survey of 255 HR professionals revealed that, among various selection measures, biodata beat only a "personal hunch" in terms of its perceived validity.[33]

Despite these limitations, it is important to keep in mind that biodata does have impressive validity and that its use is appropriate when it is carefully validated and when the aforementioned limitations are addressed.

Reference and Background Checks

Background information about job applicants can come not only from the applicant but also from people familiar with the applicant (e.g., employers, creditors, and neighbors). Organizations often solicit this information on their own or use the services of agencies that specialize in investigating applicants. Background information solicited from others consists of letters of recommendation, reference checks, and background checks.

Letters of Recommendation

A very common reference check in some settings (e.g., academic institutions) is to ask applicants to have letters of recommendation written for them. There are two major problems with this approach. First, these letters may do little to help the organization discern the more-qualified applicants from the less-qualified applicants. The reason for this is that only very poor applicants are unable to arrange for positive letters about their accomplishments. Second, most letters are not structured or standardized, meaning the data the organization receives from the letter writers are not consistent across organizations. For example, a letter about one applicant may concern the applicant's educational qualifications, whereas a letter about another applicant may focus on work experience. Comparing the qualifications of applicants A and B under these circumstances is like comparing apples and oranges.

The problem with letters of recommendation is demonstrated dramatically in one study that showed there was a stronger correlation between two letters written by one person for two applicants than between two people writing letters for the same person.[34] This finding indicates that letters of recommendation have more to do with the letter writer than with the person being written about. In fact, one study revealed that letter writers who had a dispositional tendency to be positive wrote consistently more favorable letters than letter writers with a tendency to be critical or negative.[35]

Such problems indicate that organizations should downplay the weight given to letters unless a great deal of credibility and accountability can be attached to the letter writer's comments. Also, a structured form should be provided so that each writer provides the same information about each applicant.

Another way to improve on letters of recommendation is to use a standardized scoring key, as shown in Exhibit 8.6. Using this method, categories of KSAOs are established and become the scoring key (shown at the bottom of the exhibit). The adjectives in the letter are underlined and classified into the appropriate category. The number of adjectives used in each category constitutes the applicant's score.

EXHIBIT 8.6   Scoring Letters of Recommendation

Dear Personnel Director:

Mr. John Anderson asked that I write this letter in support of his application as assistant manager and I am pleased to do so. I have known John for six years as he was my assistant in the accounting department.

John always had his work completed accurately and promptly. In his years here, he never missed a deadline. He is very detail oriented, alert in finding errors, and methodical in his problem-solving approach. Interpersonally, John is a very friendly and helpful person.

I have great confidence in John's ability. If you desire more information, please let me know.

MA _0_   CC _2_   DR _6_   U _0_   V _0_

Dear Personnel Director:

Mr. John Anderson asked that I write this letter in support of his application as assistant manager and I am pleased to do so. I have known John for six years as he was my assistant in the accounting department.

John was one of the most popular employees in our agency as he is a friendly, outgoing, sociable individual. He has a great sense of humor, is poised, and is very helpful. In completing his work, he is independent, energetic, and industrious.

I have great confidence in John's ability. If you desire more information, please let me know.

MA _0_   CC _2_   DR _0_   U _5_   V _3_

Key   MA = mental ability
CC = consideration-cooperation
DR = dependability-reliability
U = urbanity
V = vigor

SOURCE: M. G. Aumodt, D. A. Bryan, and A. J. Whitcomb, "Predicting Performance With Letters of Recommendation," *Public Personnel Management*, 1993, 22, pp. 81–90. Reprinted with permission of *Public Personnel Management*, published by the International Personnel Management Association.

Reference Checks

With reference checking, a spot check is made on the applicant's background. Usually the person contacted is the immediate supervisor of the applicant or is in the HR department of current or previous organizations with which the applicant has had contact. Surveys reveal that 96% of organizations conduct reference checks. A roughly equal number conduct the checks in-house (by HR) versus a third-party vendor. The most common information sought is on criminal background and verification of employment eligibility, former employers, dates of previous employment, and former job titles.[36] Exhibit 8.7 provides a sample reference request. Although this reference request was developed for checking references by mail, the questions contained in the request could easily be adapted for use in checking references via telephone.

Both of the problems that occur with letters of recommendation occur with reference checks as well. An even more significant concern, however, is the reluctance of organizations to give out the requested information because they fear a lawsuit on the grounds of invasion of privacy or defamation of character. Recall that the survey results reported above indicated that 96% of employers always check references. The same survey indicated that 93% of employers refuse to provide reference information for fear of being sued. As one executive stated, "There's a dire need for better reference information but fear of litigation keeps employers from providing much more than name, rank, and serial number."[37] As a result of employers' reluctance to provide reference information, reference checkers claim to receive inadequate information roughly half of the time. To a large degree, this concern over providing even rudimentary reference information is excessive—less than 3% of employers have had legal problems with reference checks (see "Legal Issues" at the end of this chapter). If every organization refused to provide useful reference information, a potentially important source of applicant information could lose its value.

It is still the case that most reference checking is done over the telephone. There is evidence, though, that this situation is changing. Increasingly, employers are mining networking websites such as Facebook, MySpace, and LinkedIn, not only to find out more about an applicant but also to locate references to contact. T-Mobile, for example, regularly mines "public" information on applicants' profile pages. These networking websites have "changed everything" about how T-Mobile conducts reference checks, according to one hiring manager.[38] No matter the source or method used to gather the information, it is critical that the questions be job related and that the same information is asked about all applicants. When properly structured and job relevant, references can have moderate levels of validity.[39]

Background Checks

How would you feel if you found out that the organization you are hoping to join was investigating your traffic record and moral character? How would you feel if

EXHIBIT 8.7   Sample Reference Request

TO BE COMPLETED BY APPLICANT

NAME (PRINT):   SOCIAL SEC. NUMBER:

I have made application for employment at this company. I request and authorize you to release all information requested below concerning my employment record, reason for leaving your employ, or my education. I hereby release my personal references, my former employers and schools, and all individuals connected therewith, from all liability for any damage whatsoever for furnishing this information.

SIGNATURE _____ DATE _____

SCHOOL REFERENCE
DATES ATTENDED
FROM: TO: GRADUATED?   YES☐   NO ☐
DEGREE AWARDED:

EMPLOYMENT REFERENCE
POSITION HELD: EMPLOYMENT DATES:

IMMEDIATE SUPERVISOR'S NAME

REASON FOR LEAVING   DISCHARGED   ☐   RESIGNED ☐   LAID OFF ☐

FORMER EMPLOYER OR SCHOOL—Please complete the following. Thank you.

IS THE ABOVE INFORMATION CORRECT?   YES ☐   NO ☐

If not, give correct information: _____

_____

PLEASE CHECK
                    EXCEL. GOOD   FAIR   POOR   COMMENTS:

ATTITUDE   _____   _____ _____ _____
QUALITY OF WORK   _____   _____ _____ _____
COOPERATION   _____   _____ _____ _____
ATTENDANCE   _____   _____ _____ _____

WOULD YOU RECOMMEND FOR EMPLOYMENT?   YES   ☐   NO ☐

ADDITIONAL COMMENTS

_____

_____

an organization did *not* investigate the backgrounds of guards to be selected for the gun storage depot of the US military base near your home? More and more organizations are thoroughly checking applicants' backgrounds even when security is not a particular issue.

Although background checking may seem to be a very invasive procedure, such checks have increased dramatically in the past 10 years. A recent survey indicated that nearly three in four organizations now perform background checks, a percentage that has steadily increased over time.[40] There are several reasons for this. First, after the September 11, 2001, terrorist attacks, more organizations became concerned about security issues. Second, some ethical lapses, and many instances of workplace violence, might be avoided by background checks. For example, consider the case of Wal-Mart. In two separate incidents in South Carolina, Wal-Mart employees were accused of sexually assaulting young girls. Both of the accused employees had past criminal convictions for sexually related offenses. In response, Wal-Mart instituted criminal background checks on all of its employees.[41] A third reason behind the growing use of background checks is legal protection against responsibility for malfeasance, and defense against claims of negligent hiring (which we review under "Reference Checks" in "Legal Issues" at the end of the chapter).

A fourth, and perhaps the most important, reason underlying the increasing use of background checks is technological. As public records have become more accessible, both legally (with so-called Sunshine laws) and practically (many local and state governments post criminal records online), and as credit checking has increased, it has become far easier to perform background checks. Moreover, scores of organizations now provide background checks, with the fee determined by the scope of information desired. Bed Bath & Beyond uses Sterling to conduct its background checks, FedEx uses Infomart, and Jackson Hewitt uses IdentityPi.com. Other large background checking services include USIS, ChoicePoint, ADP, and First Advantage. Background checks cost anywhere from $5 to $1,000 per hire, depending on the type of position and the information sought. Most background checks cost around $25 per applicant.

Background checks identify more problems than one might think. Additionally, the consequences of failing to conduct a background check are quite serious. In many cases, subsequent malfeasance could have been prevented by a background check. Take, for example, Nick Leeson, the "rogue trader" responsible for the demise of Barings Bank. Britain's Securities and Futures Authority had discovered that Leeson lied on his application regarding a civil court judgment of unpaid debts. When hiring Leeson, Barings's Singapore branch never checked into his credit history, nor was his history discovered by the Singapore stock exchange. At Barings's Singapore office, Leeson made unauthorized speculative trades and creatively hid his mounting losses. The losses eventually accumulated to $1.3 billion, bankrupting the oldest bank in London.[42]

In many industries, the percentage of applicants identified to have some problem (e.g., a criminal record or a discrepancy in past employment or education) is surprisingly high. According to one source, more than half (51.7%) of the applicants in the nonprofit industry had significant discrepancies between their self-reported and their actual employment history, and nearly half (48.9%) of the applicants in the construction industry had a major motor vehicle violation (involving license suspension).[43]

Background checks do have limitations. First, the records can be wrong or misinterpreted. For example, sometimes peoples' identities get mixed up. Unless someone has an unusual name, there are probably many others in the population with the same name. Sometimes the records contain misleading information. Johnnie Ulrigg was denied a job in Missoula, Montana, because his background check turned up a list of probation violations. He later learned that several counties in the state list failure to pay a traffic ticket as a probation violation. It took Ulrigg two years to clear his record. Second, because background checks have become more commonplace, they can place a seemingly permanent bar on the reemployment of reformed criminals. Peter Demain was sentenced to six years for possessing 21 pounds of marijuana. While in prison, he was so adept in the prison kitchen that he quickly rose to head baker. Once out of prison, though, Demain was unable to find a job at bagel shops, coffeehouses, grocery stores, and bakeries. Is it fair for reformed criminals, no matter how long ago or the nature of the offense, to be banned from employment?[44] Such questions are difficult to answer.

Finally, many labor unions have historically resisted background checking. In 2007, Major League Baseball owners clashed with the umpires union about background checks.[45] Conversely, in 2010, the Air Line Pilots Association, which represents UPS pilots, backed increased use of background checks.[46]

One way to ameliorate some of these problems is to limit background checks to information that is job related (it may be difficult to establish that a spotty credit history is important to jobs that mostly involve manual labor) and to use multiple sources to verify problems for exclusionary information (i.e., if an applicant is to be excluded because of what a background check uncovered, it would be prudent to independently verify the information).

Evaluation of Recommendations, References, and Background Checks

The empirical data that exist on the validity of reference checks suggest that their validity is low to moderate. A meta-analysis of a number of studies revealed that the validity coefficients of reference data ranged from $\bar{r} = .16$ to $\bar{r} = .26$. Another study suggested that when reference reports are structured (the same questions were asked about every applicant), their validity was $\bar{r} = .25$. To some degree, the validity depends on who is providing the information. If it is the personnel officer, a coworker, or a relative, the information is not very valid. On the other hand, reference reports from supervisors and acquaintances are somewhat more valid.

The information from personnel officers may be less valid because they are less knowledgeable about the applicant (their past employee); the reports of coworkers and relatives probably are less valid because these individuals are positively biased toward the applicant.

Although references do not have high validity, we need to take a cost-benefit approach. In general, the quality of the information may be low, but in the few cases where reference information changes a decision, the payoff can be significant. An executive with the US Postal Service once told one of the authors that many of the acts of violence by Postal Service employees would have been avoided if a thorough background check had been conducted. Thus, since references are a relatively cheap method of collecting information on applicants, screening out the occasional unstable applicants or, in a few cases, learning something new and important about an applicant may make reference checks a good investment. As with unweighted application blanks, though, using reference checks requires employers to turn elsewhere to obtain suitable information for making final decisions about applicants.

Finally, because they are difficult to quantify, we do not have validity evidence for letters of recommendation and background checks. However, this does not mean that they (especially background checks) lack utility.

Initial Interview

The initial interview occurs very early in the initial assessment process and is often the applicant's first personal contact with the organization and its staffing system. At this point, applicants are relatively undifferentiated to the organization in terms of KSAOs. The initial interview begins the process of necessary differentiation, a sort of "rough cut."

The purpose of the initial interview is, and should be, to screen out the most obvious cases of person/job mismatches. To do this, the interview should focus on an assessment of KSAOs that are absolute requirements for the applicant. Examples of such minimum levels of qualifications for the job include certification and licensure requirements and necessary (not just preferred) training and experience requirements.

These assessments may be made from information gathered from written means (e.g., application blank or résumé) and from the interview. Care should be taken to ensure that the interviewer focuses only on this information as a basis for decision making. Evaluations of personal characteristics of the applicant (e.g., race or sex), as well as judgments about an applicant's personality (e.g., "She seems very outgoing and just right for this job"), are to be avoided. Indeed, to ensure that this focus happens, some organizations (e.g., civil service agencies) have eliminated the initial interview altogether and make the initial assessment from the written information provided by the applicant.

One of the limitations of the initial interview is that it is perhaps the most expensive method of initial assessment. One way to dramatically reduce costs is to conduct video or computer interviews, which we cover next.

Video and Computer Interviews

With the growth of videoconferencing software, it is increasingly easy—and inexpensive—to conduct initial screening interviews from any two locations with Internet access. As long as both parties have their computers connected to the Internet, the conversation is free. Skype, which has more than 500 million registered accounts, has become a common platform for conducting computer-based initial interviews.

When the University of Pittsburgh Medical Center screened candidates for various management position openings, it used Skype to conduct the initial interviews. "We see a ton of value in it," noted Matt Rimer, director of talent acquisition for the medical center. "I, personally, have done a few Skype interviews here recently. I've found them to be very productive interactions with the candidates."

Larger companies often use a more customized platform to conduct initial interviews. HireVue, a Salt Lake City online video interview company, counts Dish Network, CDW, and Oracle among its customers. The advantage of providers such as HireVue, or competitors such as GreenJobInterview.com, is that they allow interviews to be securely stored, shared with others in the organization, and accompanied by ratings and comments.[47]

One of the advantages of video-based interviews is that they can dramatically lower the cost of initial interviews. This is particularly true for employers that wish to interview only a few applicants at a given location. Another advantage is that the interviews can be arranged on short notice (no travel and no schedule rearrangements). Of course, disadvantages of these interviews are that they do not permit face-to-face contact and that the quality of the video connection can, at times, be poor. The effects of these limitations on validity and applicant reactions are unknown.

Another form of video interviews takes the process a step further. Computer-based interviews utilize software that asks applicants questions (e.g., "Have you ever been terminated for stealing?") or presents realistic scenarios (e.g., an irate customer on the screen) while recording applicants' responses. These responses are forwarded to selection decision makers for use in initial screening. The software can also be configured to inform applicants about job duties and requirements. It can even track how long it takes an applicant to answer each question. Retailers are beginning to use computerized interviews on-site, where applicants walk into a store, enter a kiosk, and submit information about their work habits and experiences. As before, though, the accuracy of these high-tech interviews as compared with the old standby, the person-to-person variety, is unclear. The same holds true for how applicants will react to these relatively impersonal methods.

Evaluation of Initial Interview

Whether high-tech or traditional, the interview has benefits and limitations. Nearly all of the research evaluating the interview in selection has considered it a substantive method (see "Structured Interview" in Chapter 9). Thus, there is little evidence about the usefulness of the initial interview. However, organizations using the initial interview in selection are likely to find it more useful by following a few guidelines:

1. Ask questions that assess the most basic KSAOs identified by job analysis. This requires separating what is required from what is preferred.
2. Stick to basic, qualifying questions suitable for making rough cuts (e.g., "Have you completed the minimum certification requirements to qualify for this job?") rather than subtle, subjective questions more suitable for substantive decisions (e.g., "How would this job fit within your overall career goals?"). Remember, the purpose of the initial interview is closer to cutting with a saw than operating with a scalpel. Ask only the most fundamental questions now, and leave the fine-tuning for later.
3. Keep interviews brief. Most interviewers make up their minds quickly, and given the limited usefulness and the type of information collected, a long interview (e.g., 45–60 minutes) is unlikely to add much over a shorter one (15–30 minutes).
4. As with all interviews, the same questions should be asked of all applicants, and equal employment opportunity (EEO) compliance must be monitored.

Choice of Initial Assessment Methods

As described, a wide range of initial assessment methods are available to organizations to help reduce the applicant pool to bona fide candidates. A range of formats is available as well. Fortunately, with so many choices available to organizations, research results are available to help guide choices of methods to use. This research has been reviewed many times and is summarized in Exhibit 8.8. In the exhibit, each initial assessment method is rated according to several criteria. Each of these criteria will be discussed in turn.

Use

Use refers to how frequently the surveyed organizations use each predictor. Use is probably an overused criterion in deciding which selection measures to adopt. Benchmarking—basing HR decisions on what other companies are doing—is a predominant method of decision making in all areas of HR, including staffing. However, is this a good way to make decisions about selection methods? Although it is always comforting to do what other organizations are doing, relying on information from other organizations assumes that they know what they are doing. Just because many organizations use a selection measure does not necessarily make it a

EXHIBIT 8.8   Evaluation of Initial Assessment Methods

Predictors	Use	Cost	Reliability	Validity	Utility	Applicant Reactions	Adverse Impact
Level of education	High	Low	Moderate	Low	Low	?	Moderate
Grade point average	Moderate	Low	Moderate	Moderate	?	?	?
Quality of school	?	Low	Moderate	Low	?	?	Moderate
Major field of study	?	Low	Moderate	Moderate	?	?	?
Extracurricular activity	?	Low	Moderate	Moderate	?	?	?
Training and experience	High	Low	High	Moderate	Moderate	?	Moderate
Licensing and certification	Moderate	Low	?	?	?	?	?
Weighted application blanks	Low	Moderate	Moderate	Moderate	Moderate	?	?
Biographical data	Low	High	High	High	High	Negative	Moderate
Letters of recommendation	Moderate	Low	?	Low	?	?	?
Reference checks	High	Moderate	Low	Low	Moderate	Mixed	Low
Background checks	Moderate	High	?	?	?	Mixed	Moderate
Résumés and cover letters	Moderate	Low	Moderate	?	?	Moderate	?
Initial interview	High	Moderate	Low	Low	?	Positive	Moderate

good idea for a particular organization. Circumstances differ from organization to organization. Perhaps more important, many organizational decision makers (and HR consultants) either lack knowledge about the latest findings in HR research or have decided that such findings are not applicable to their organization. It is also difficult to determine whether a successful organization that uses a particular selection method is successful because it uses this method or is successful for some other reason. Thus, from a research standpoint, there may be a real strategic advantage in relying on "effectiveness" criteria (e.g., validity, utility, and adverse impact) rather than worrying about the practices of other organizations.

Another reason to have a healthy degree of skepticism about the use criterion is that there is a severe lack of timely and broad surveys of selection practices (i.e., coverage of many industries and regions in the United States). The Bureau of National Affairs (BNA) has conducted broad surveys of selection practices, but the most recent was in 1988. Other surveys of selection practices are available, but they generally cover only a single selection practice (e.g., drug testing) or lack adequate scope or breadth. In providing conclusions about the use of various selection methods in organizations, we are forced to make judgment calls concerning which survey to rely on. In the case of some selection measures (e.g., application blanks), there is little reason to believe the BNA figures have changed much. With other predictors, the use figures have shown a fair degree of volatility and change from year to year. Thus, in classifying the use of assessment methods, we rely on the most recent surveys that achieve some degree of breadth. For purposes of classifying the predictors, high use refers to use by more than two-thirds of organizations, moderate is use by one-third to two-thirds of organizations, and low use refers to use by less than one-third of organizations.

Now that we've issued these caveats about the use criterion, Exhibit 8.8 reveals clear differences in the use of various methods of initial assessment. The most frequently used methods of initial assessment are education level, training and experience, reference checks, and initial interview. These methods are considered, to some degree, in selection decisions for most types of positions. Grade point average, licensing and certification requirements, letters of recommendation, background checks, and résumés and cover letters have moderate levels of use. All of these methods are widely used in filling some types of positions but infrequently used in filling many others. The least widely used initial assessment methods are weighted application blanks and biographical information. It is relatively unusual for organizations to use these methods for initial screening decisions. There are no reliable figures on the use of quality of school, major field of study, and extracurricular activity in initial selection decisions; thus, their use could not be estimated.

Cost

Cost refers to expenses incurred in using the predictor. Although most of the initial assessment methods may seem relatively cost-free since the applicant provides the information on his or her own time, this is not entirely accurate. For most initial assessment methods, the major cost associated with each selection measure is administration. Consider an application blank. It is true that applicants complete application blanks on their own time, but someone must be present to hand out applications, answer inquiries in person and over the phone about possible openings, and collect, sort, and forward applications to the appropriate person. Then the selection decision maker must read each application, perhaps make notes about an applicant, weed out the clearly unacceptable applicants, and then make decisions about candidates. Thus, even for the least expensive methods of initial assessment, costs associated with their use are far from trivial.

On the other hand, utility research has suggested that costs do not play a large part in evaluating the financial benefit of using particular selection methods. This becomes readily apparent when one considers the costs of hiring a poor performer. For example, a secretary who performs one standard deviation below average (16th percentile, if performance is normally distributed) may cost the organization $8,000 in lost productivity per year. This person is likely to remain on the job for more than one year, multiplying the costs. Considered in this light, spending an extra few hundred dollars to accurately identify good secretaries is an excellent investment. Thus, although costs need to be considered in evaluating assessment methods, more consideration should be given to the fact that valid selection measures pay off handsomely and will return many times their cost.

As can be seen in Exhibit 8.8, the least costly initial assessment methods include information that can be obtained from application blanks (level of education, grade point average, quality of school, major field of study, extracurricular activity, training and experience, licensing and certification) and information provided by the applicant (letters of recommendation, résumés, and cover letters). Initial assessment methods of moderate cost include weighted application blanks, reference checks, and initial interviews. Biographical information and background checks are relatively expensive assessment methods.

Reliability

Reliability refers to consistency of measurement. As was noted in Chapter 7, reliability is a requirement for validity, so it would be very difficult for a predictor with low reliability to have high validity. By the same token, it is unlikely that a valid predictor would have low reliability. Unfortunately, the reliability information on many initial assessment methods is lacking in the literature. Some researchers have investigated distortion of applicant-reported information (application blanks and résumés). One study found that 20% of applicants distorted nearly half of the items on application blanks. Other studies have suggested that one-third of application blanks contain some inaccuracies.[48] Thus, it is probably reasonable to infer that applicant-supplied information in application blanks and résumés is of moderate reliability. The reliability of reference checks appears to be relatively low. In terms of training and experience evaluations, while distortion can occur if the applicant supplies training and experience information, interrater agreement in evaluating this information is quite high.[49] Biographical information also generally has high reliability. The initial interview, like most unstructured interviews, probably has a relatively low level of reliability.

Validity

Validity refers to the strength of the relationship between the predictor and job performance. Low validity ranges from about .00 to .15, moderate validity ranges from about .16 to .30, and high validity is .31 and above. As might be expected, most initial assessment methods have moderate to low validity because they are used only for making rough cuts among applicants rather than for final decisions. Perhaps the two most valid initial assessment methods are biodata and training and experience requirements; their validity can range from moderate to high.

Utility

Utility refers to the monetary return associated with using the predictor, relative to its cost. According to researchers and decision makers, when comparing the utility of selection methods, validity appears to be the most important consideration.[50] In short, it would be very unusual for a valid selection method to have low utility. Thus, as can be seen in Exhibit 8.8, high, moderate, and low validities tend to directly correspond to high, moderate, and low utility values, respectively. Question marks predominate this column in the exhibit because relatively few studies have directly investigated the utility of these methods. However, based on the argument that validity should be directly related to utility, it is likely that high validity methods will also realize large financial benefits to organizations that choose to use them. Research does indicate that training and experience requirements have moderate (or even high) levels of utility, and reference checks have moderate levels of utility.

Applicant Reactions

Applicant reactions refers to the favorability of applicants' reactions to the predictor. Applicant reactions has been suggested as an important criterion because applicants who feel positively about selection methods and the selection process might be more inclined to join or recommend an organization, and have more positive attitudes toward the organization once hired. Some have argued, however, that evidence suggesting that applicant reactions matter is scarce. One review concluded, "Evidence for a relationship between applicant perceptions and actual behavioral outcomes was meager and disappointing."[51]

Research suggests that whatever their centrality to the selection process, selection measures that are perceived as job related, present applicants with an opportunity to perform, are administered consistently, and provide applicants with feedback about their performance are likely to generate favorable applicant reactions. Moreover, a meta-analysis of 26 studies revealed that explanations justifying the use of selection measures shape applicant perceptions of fairness of the selection process and their affective reactions to the organization.[52] Although research on applicants' reactions to specific selection procedures is lacking, evidence has been accumulating and suggests that applicants react more positively to some initial assessment methods, such as interviews, résumés, and reference checks, than to others, such as biodata or background checks.[53]

Adverse Impact

Adverse impact refers to the possibility that a disproportionate number of protected-class members may be rejected using this predictor. Several initial assessment methods have moderate degrees of adverse impact against women and/or minorities, including level of education, quality of school, training and experience, biographical information, and the initial interview. Reference and background checks appear to have moderate adverse impact.

LEGAL ISSUES

Initial assessment methods are subject to numerous laws, regulations, and other legal considerations. Five major matters of concern pertain to using disclaimers, conducting reference checks, conducting background (credit and criminal) checks, making preemployment inquiries, and making BFOQ claims.

Disclaimers

During the initial stages of contact with job applicants, it is important for the organization to protect itself legally by clearly identifying rights it wants to maintain. This involves the use of disclaimers. Disclaimers are statements (usually written) that provide or confer explicit rights to the employer as part of the employment contract and that are shown to job applicants. The organization needs to decide (or reevaluate) which rights it wants to retain and how these will be communicated to job applicants.

Three areas of rights are usually suggested for possible inclusion in a disclaimer policy: (1) employment-at-will (right to terminate the employment relationship at any time, for any reason), (2) verification consent (right to verify information provided by the applicant), and (3) false statement warning (right to not hire, terminate, or discipline prospective employee for providing false information to the employer). An example of a disclaimer statement covering these three areas is shown at the bottom of the application blank in Exhibit 8.4. Disclaimer language must be clear, understandable, and conspicuous to the applicant or employee.[54]

Reference Checks

Reference checking creates a legal quagmire for organizations. Current or former employers of the job applicant may be reluctant to provide a reference (especially one with negative information about the applicant) because they fear the applicant may file a defamation suit against them. On the other hand, failure to conduct a reference check opens up the organization to the possibility of a negligent hiring suit. To deal with such problems and obtain thorough, accurate information, the following suggestions are offered.

First, gather as much information as possible directly from the applicant, along with a verification consent. In this way, use of reference providers and information demands on them are minimized.

Second, be sure to obtain written authorization from the applicant to check references. The applicant should sign a blanket consent form for this purpose. Also, the organization could prepare a request-for-reference form that the applicant would give to the person(s) being asked to provide a reference (see Exhibit 8.7).

Third, specify the type of information being requested and obtain the information in writing. The information should be specific, factual, and job related in content; do not seek health or disability information.

Fourth, be wary of (or even prohibit) treating as references information given by others about applicants from online social networking websites. Questions about accuracy, job-relatedness, and confidentiality abound for such information. Also, develop a policy about whether your own employees can make recommendations about their current or former colleagues on these sites.

Fifth, limit access to reference information to those making selection decisions.

Finally, check relevant state laws about permissible and impermissible reference-check practices. Also, determine whether your organization is covered by state reference immunity laws, which provide some degree of immunity from civil liability to organizations that in good faith provide information about the job performance and professional conduct of former or current employees. Organizations in these states (currently 39) may be more willing to request and provide reference information.[55]

Background Checks: Credit and Criminal

Credit Checks

The first legal requirement for the organization is to comply with the federal Fair Credit Reporting Act (FCRA; see Chapter 2). The FCRA governs the gathering and use of background information on applicants and employees (*www.ftc.gov*). Its requirements apply to both consumer reports and investigative consumer reports. Consumer reports are prepared from accessible databases by a consumer reporting agency and bear on the person's creditworthiness and standing, character, general reputation, personal information, and mode of living. Investigative consumer reports are a subset of consumer reports; they obtain information about the applicant's or employee's general reputation, character, personal characteristics, and mode of living via personal interviews with friends, neighbors, or business associates.

Before obtaining a consumer report, the organization must (1) give the applicant clear notice in writing that a report may be obtained and used in hiring or promotion procedures, and (2) obtain the applicant's written authorization to seek the report. These notification requirements do not apply to an organization conducting a third-party investigation of suspected employee misconduct. The consumer reporting agency may not furnish a consumer report to the organization unless the organization certifies to the agency that it has given the required notice and received authorization. Before taking any adverse action, such as denial of employment, based in whole or part on the report received, the organization must wait a reasonable amount of time and then provide the applicant with a copy of the report and a written description of his or her consumer rights put forth by the Federal Trade Commission. After taking an adverse action, the organization must (1) notify (by written, oral, or electronic means) the applicant of the adverse action, (2) provide the name, address, and phone number of the consumer reporting agency to the applicant, and (3) provide notice of the applicant's right to obtain a free copy of the report from the agency and to dispute the accuracy and completeness of the report. The organization is not required to inform the applicant which information in the report led to the adverse action, but it must inform the applicant that the agency had no part in the decision.

Another legal requirement for the organization is to comply with the state and local laws that govern background checks. This should include the state/locale in which the individual being investigated resides, the reporting agency conducts business, and the requesting organization is incorporated and conducts business.[56]

Credit checking is coming under heightened legal scrutiny and likely regulation. Reasons for this include (1) credit report errors, (2) blanket usage of hiring bars for applicants with credit problems, regardless of type of job and job requirements, (3) lack of evidence supporting credit checks as a valid predictor of job performance or theft and embezzlement, and (4) possible adverse impact, especially against minorities.

Here are suggestions for navigating these difficult legal waters. Do credit checks only for jobs with financial and legal responsibilities, such as tellers, auditors, senior executives, and law enforcement. Be able to explain for each of these jobs exactly why a credit check is necessary, and allow applicants to explain any unfavorable credit information. Be sure to watch for the development of new credit checking laws and regulations, especially at the state level. The Illinois Employer Credit Privacy Act, for example, prohibits employers from inquiring about or using a credit history or report from applicants and employees, except for certain positions.[57] Finally, remember to comply with the provisions of the FCRA.

Criminal Checks

Criminal background checks are generally an attempt to head off potential problems of workplace violence, theft, and fraud. The FCRA and state and local laws govern these checks. Some organizations have a general "no felons" hiring policy, while others have a more job-specific hiring bar policy. While it is generally permissible to gather both arrest and conviction records of applicants, only conviction records may be used in the hiring decisions for certain jobs, such as those involving public safety or contact with children.

It is often noted that there is a lack of empirical validity evidence showing that criminal checks are actually predictive of violence, theft, and fraud. On top of this, the Equal Employment Opportunity Commission (EEOC) indicates that conviction usage has an adverse impact against black men due to their higher conviction rate than other groups. So the EEOC is of the opinion that convictions should not be used in hiring decisions without a business necessity justification in situations of likely adverse impact. To pursue this justification the employer must consider (1) the nature and gravity of the offense, (2) the time that has passed since conviction/completion of sentence, and (3) the nature of the job assignment. It is likely that the EEOC will issue more formal regulations on criminal checks and adverse impact.

States are also placing restrictions on criminal check usage. Pennsylvania allows refusal to hire only when the job is related to the crime. In New York, refusal to hire must take into account job responsibilities, time since the crime was committed, applicant's age at the time of the crime, and seriousness of the offense. There may also be exemptions for arrest/conviction usage. Washington, for example, exempts law enforcement agencies, state agencies, school districts, and organizations that have a direct responsibility for the supervision, care, or treatment of children, mentally ill persons, or other vulnerable adults.[58]

These factors suggest that the organization should decide on a job-by-job basis whether to seek a criminal background check, carefully communicate to the background screening firm exactly what information it wishes to receive, and decide in advance exactly how it will use that information.

Preemployment Inquiries

The term "preemployment inquiry" (PI), as used here, pertains to both content and method of assessment. Regarding content, PI refers to applicants' personal and background data. These data cover such areas as demographics (race, color, religion, sex, national origin, and age), physical characteristics (disability, height, and weight), family and associates, residence, economic status, and education. The information could be gathered by any method; most frequently, it is gathered with an initial assessment method, particularly the application blank, biodata questionnaire, or preliminary interview. At times, PIs may also occur as part of an unstructured interview.

PIs have been singled out for particular legal (equal employment opportunity and affirmative action [EEO/AA]) attention at both the federal and state levels. The reason for this is that PIs have great potential for use in a discriminatory manner early on in the selection process. Moreover, research continually finds that organizations make inappropriate and illegal PIs. One study, for example, found that out of 48 categories of application blank items, employers used an average of 5.4 inadvisable items on their application blanks for customer service jobs.[59] It is thus critical to understand the laws and regulations surrounding the use of PIs.

Federal Laws and Regulations

The laws and their interpretation indicate that it is illegal to use PI information that has a disparate impact based on a protected characteristic (race, color, etc.), unless such disparate impact can be shown to be job related and consistent with business necessity. The emphasis here is on the potentially illegal use of the information rather than on its collection per se.

EEOC Guide to Preemployment Inquiries.   The EEOC guide provides the principles given above, along with specific guidance (dos and don'ts) on PIs regarding race, color, religion, sex, national origin, age, height and weight, marital status, number of children, provisions for child care, English language skill, educational requirements, friends or relatives working for the employer, arrest records, conviction records, discharge from military service, citizenship, economic status, and availability for work on weekends or holidays (*www.eeoc.gov/employers/index.cfm*).

Americans With Disabilities Act Regulations.   There appears to be a fine line between permissible and impermissible information that may be gathered, and between appropriate and inappropriate methods for gathering it, under the Americans With Disabilities Act (ADA). To help employers, the EEOC has developed specific enforcement guidance on these matters (*www.eeoc.gov/employers/index.cfm*).

The general thrust of the guidance is that the organization may not ask disability-related questions and may not conduct medical examinations until after it makes a conditional job offer to a person. Once that offer is made, however, the organization may ask disability-related questions and conduct medical examinations so long as this is done for all entering employees in the job category. When such questions or exams screen out a person with a disability, the reason for rejection must be job related and consistent with business necessity. A person may be rejected for safety reasons if the person provides a direct threat of substantial harm to himself or herself or others. We will have more to say about the legality of medical examinations in the next chapter.

More specific guidance is provided for the preoffer stage as follows. Disability-related questions cannot be asked, meaning questions that (1) inquire whether a person has a disability, (2) are likely to elicit information about a disability, or (3) are closely related to asking about a disability. Along with these general prohibitions, it is impermissible to ask applicants whether they will need reasonable accommodation to perform the functions of the job or can perform major life activities (e.g., lifting, walking), to ask about lawful use of drugs, to ask about workers' compensation history, or to ask third parties (e.g., former employers, references) questions that cannot be asked of the applicant.

Alternatively, before the offer is made, it is permissible to ask:

- Whether the applicant can perform the job, with or without reasonable accommodation
- The applicant to describe or demonstrate how he or she would perform the job (including any needed reasonable accommodation)
- Whether the applicant will need reasonable accommodation for the hiring process (unless there is an obvious disability or the applicant discloses a disability)
- The applicant to provide documentation of a disability if requesting reasonable accommodation for the hiring process
- Whether the applicant can meet the organization's attendance requirement
- The applicant for certifications and licenses
- About the applicant's current illegal use of drugs (but not past addiction)
- About the applicant's drinking habits (but not alcoholism)

State Laws and Regulations

There is a vast cache of state laws and regulations pertaining to PIs.[60] These requirements vary substantially among the states. They are often more stringent and inclusive than federal laws and regulations. The organization thus must become familiar with and adhere to the laws for each state in which it is located.

An example of Ohio state law regarding PIs is shown in Exhibit 8.9. Notice how the example points out both lawful and unlawful ways of gathering PI information.

Bona Fide Occupational Qualifications

Title VII of the Civil Rights Act explicitly permits discrimination on the basis of sex, religion, or national origin (but not race or color) if it can be shown to be a BFOQ "reasonably necessary to the normal operation" of the business. The Age Discrimination in Employment Act (ADEA) contains a similar provision regarding age. These provisions thus permit outright rejection of applicants because of their sex, religion, national origin, or age, as long as the rejection can be justified under the "reasonably necessary" standard. Exactly how have BFOQ claims by employers fared? When are BFOQ claims upheld as legitimate? Several points are relevant to understanding the BFOQ issue.

EXHIBIT 8.9   **Ohio Preemployment Inquiry Guide**

INQUIRIES BEFORE HIRING	LAWFUL	UNLAWFUL*
1. NAME	Name.	Inquiry into any title which indicates race, color, religion, sex, national origin, handicap, age, or ancestry.
2. ADDRESS	Inquiry into place and length at current address.	Inquiry into any foreign addresses which would indicate national origin.
3. AGE	Any inquiry limited to establishing that applicant meets any minimum age requirement that may be established by law.	A. Requiring birth certificate or baptismal record before hiring. B. Any inquiry which may reveal the date of high school graduation. C. Any other inquiry which may reveal whether applicant is at least 40 and less than 70 years of age.
4. BIRTHPLACE, NATIONAL ORIGIN, OR ANCESTRY		A. Any inquiry into place of birth. B. Any inquiry into place of birth of parents, grandparents, or spouse. C. Any other inquiry into national origin or ancestry.
5. RACE OR COLOR		Any inquiry which would indicate race or color.
6. SEX		A. Any inquiry which would indicate sex. B. Any inquiry made of members of one sex, but not the other.

(continued)

EXHIBIT 8.9   Continued

INQUIRIES BEFORE HIRING	LAWFUL	UNLAWFUL*
7. HEIGHT AND WEIGHT	Inquiries as to ability to perform actual job requirements.	Being a certain height or weight will not be considered to be a job requirement unless the employer can show that no employee with the ineligible height or weight could do the work.
8. RELIGION— CREED		A. Any inquiry which would indicate or identify identify religious denomination or custom. B. Applicant may not be told any religious identity or preference of the employer. C. Request pastor's recommendation or reference.
9. HANDICAP	Inquiries necessary to determine applicant's ability to substantially perform specific job without significant hazard.	A. Any inquiry into past or current medical conditions not related to position applied for. B. Any inquiry into worker's compensation or similar claims.
10. CITIZENSHIP	A. Whether a U.S. citizen. B. If not, whether applicant intends to become one. C. If U.S. residence is legal. D. If spouse is citizen. E. Require proof of citizenship after being hired. F. Any other requirement mandated by the Immigration Reform and Control Act of 1986, as amended.	A. If native-born or naturalized. B. Proof of citizenship before hiring. C. Whether parents or spouse are native-born or naturalized.
11. PHOTOGRAPHS	May be required after hiring for identification.	Require photograph before hiring.

(continued)

▬▬▬▬
EXHIBIT 8.9 Continued

INQUIRIES BEFORE HIRING	LAWFUL	UNLAWFUL*
12. ARREST AND CONVICTIONS	Inquiries into *conviction* of specific crimes related to qualifications for the job applied for.	Any inquiry which would reveal arrests without convictions.
13. EDUCATION	A. Inquiry into nature and extent of academic, professional, or vocational training. B. Inquiry into language skills such as reading and writing of foreign languages, if job-related.	A. Any inquiry which would reveal the nationality or religious affiliation of a school. B. Inquiry as to what mother tongue is or how foreign language ability was acquired.
14. RELATIVES	Inquiry into name, relationship, and address of person to be notified in case of emergency.	Any inquiry about a relative which would be unlawful if made about the applicant.
15. ORGANIZATIONS	Inquiry into membership in professional organizations and offices held, excluding any organization, the name or character of which indicates the race, color, religion, sex, national origin, handicap, age, or ancestry of its members.	Inquiry into every club and organization where membership is held.
16. MILITARY SERVICE	A. Inquiry into service in U.S. Armed Forces when such service is a qualification for the job. B. Require military discharge certificate after being hired.	A. Inquiry into military service in armed service of any country but U.S. B. Request military service records. C. Inquiry into type of discharge.
17. WORK SCHEDULE	Inquiry into willingness or ability to work required work schedule.	Any inquiry into willingness or ability to work any particular religious holidays.

(continued)

EXHIBIT 8.9   Continued

INQUIRIES BEFORE HIRING	LAWFUL	UNLAWFUL*
18. MISCELLANEOUS	Any question required to reveal qualifications for the job applied for.	Any non-job-related inquiry which may elicit or attempt to elicit any information concerning race, color, religion, sex, national origin, handicap, age, or ancestry of an applicant for employment or membership.
19. REFERENCES	General personal and work references which do not reveal the race, color, religion, sex, national origin, handicap, age, or ancestry of the applicant.	Request references specifically from clergy or any other persons who might reflect race, color, religion, sex, national origin, handicap, age, or ancestry of applicant.

I. Employers acting under bona fide Affirmative Action Programs or acting under orders of Equal Employment law enforcement agencies of federal, state, or local governments may make some of the prohibited inquiries listed above to the extent that these inquiries are required by such programs or orders.

II. Employers having federal defense contracts are exempt to the extent that otherwise prohibited inquiries are required by federal law for security purposes.

III. Any inquiry is prohibited although not specifically listed above, which elicits information as to, or which is not job-related and may be used to discriminate on the basis of race, color, religion, sex, national origin, handicap, age, or ancestry in violation of law.

*Unless bona fide occupational qualification is certified in advance by the Ohio Civil Rights Commission.

Source: Ohio Civil Rights Commission, 1989.

The burden of proof is on the employer to justify any BFOQ claim, and it is clear that the BFOQ exception is to be narrowly construed. Thus, it does not apply to the following:[61]

- Refusing to hire women because of a presumed difference in comparative HR outcomes (e.g., women are lower performers, have higher turnover rates)
- Refusing to hire women because of personal characteristic stereotypes (e.g., women are less aggressive than men)
- Refusing to hire women because of the preferences of others (customers or fellow workers)

To amplify on the above points, an analysis of BFOQ claims involving sex reveals four types of justifications usually presented by the employer: (1) inability to perform the work, (2) personal contact with others that requires the same sex, (3) customers' preference for dealing with one sex, and (4) pregnancy or fertility protection concerns.[62]

Inability to Perform

The general employer claim here is that one gender (usually women) is unable to perform the job due to job requirements such as lifting heavy weights, being of a minimum height, or working long hours. The employer must be able to show that the inability holds for most, if not all, members of the gender. Moreover, if it is possible to test the required abilities for each person, then that must be done rather than having a blanket exclusion from the job based on sex.

Same-Sex Personal Contact

Due to a job requirement of close personal contact with other people, the employer may claim that employees must be the same sex as those people with whom they have contact. This claim has often been made, but not always successfully defended, for the job of prison guard. Much will depend on an analysis of just how inhospitable and dangerous the work environment is (e.g., minimum security versus maximum security prisons). Same-sex personal conflict claims have been successfully made for situations involving personal hygiene, health care, and rape victims. In short, the permissibility of these claims depends on a very specific analysis of the job requirements matrix (including the job context portion).

Customer Preference

Organizations may argue that customers prefer members of one sex, and this preference must be honored in order to serve and maintain the continued patronage of the customer. This claim might occur, for example, for the job of salesperson in women's sportswear. Another example, involving religion, is a refusal to hire people who wear turbans or hijabs, due to a fear that customers will not want to interact with them. Usually, customer preference claims cannot be successfully defended by the employer.

Pregnancy or Fertility

Exclusion of pregnant applicants could be a valid BFOQ claim, particularly in jobs where the risk of sudden incapacitation due to pregnancy poses threats to public safety (e.g., airline attendant). A threat to fertility of either sex generally cannot be used as a basis for sustaining a BFOQ claim. For example, an employer's fetal protection policy that excluded women from jobs involving exposure to lead in the manufacture of batteries was held to not be a permissible BFOQ.[63]

The discussion and examples here should make clear that BFOQ claims involve complex situations and considerations. The organization should remember that the burden of proof is on it to defend BFOQ claims. BFOQ provisions in the law are and continue to be construed very narrowly. The employer thus must have an overwhelming preponderance of argument and evidence on its side in order to make and successfully defend a BFOQ claim.

SUMMARY

This chapter reviewed the processes involved in external selection and focused specifically on methods of initial assessment. Before candidates are assessed, it is important to base assessment methods on the logic of prediction and to use selection plans. The logic of prediction focuses on the requisite correspondence between elements in applicants' past situations and KSAOs critical to success on the job applied for. The selection plan involves the process of detailing the required KSAOs and indicating which selection methods will be used to assess each KSAO. The selection sequence is the means by which the selection process is used to narrow down the initial applicant pool to candidates, then finalists, and, eventually, job offer receivers.

Initial assessment methods are used during the early stages of the selection sequence to reduce the applicant pool to candidates for further assessment. The methods of initial assessment were reviewed in some detail; they include résumés and cover letters, application blanks, biographical data, letters of recommendation, reference and background checks, and initial interviews. Initial assessment methods differ widely in their usefulness. The means by which these methods can be evaluated for potential use include frequency of use, cost, reliability, validity, utility, applicant reactions, and adverse impact.

Legal issues need to be considered in making initial assessments about applicants. The use of disclaimers as a protective mechanism is critical. Also, three areas of initial assessment that require special attention are reference and background checking, preemployment inquiries, and BFOQs.

DISCUSSION QUESTIONS

1. A selection plan describes the predictor(s) that will be used to assess the KSAOs required to perform the job. What are the three steps to follow in establishing a selection plan?
2. In what ways are the following three initial assessment methods similar and in what ways are they different: application blanks, biographical information, and reference and background checks?
3. Describe the criteria by which initial assessment methods are evaluated. Are some of these criteria more important than others?
4. Some methods of initial assessment appear to be more useful than others. If you were starting your own business, which initial assessment methods would you use and why?
5. How can organizations avoid legal difficulties in the use of preemployment inquiries in initial selection decisions?

ETHICAL ISSUES

1. Is it wrong to pad one's résumé with information that, while not an outright lie, is an enhancement? For example, would it be wrong to term one's job "maintenance coordinator" when in fact one simply emptied garbage cans?
2. Do you think employers have a right to check into applicants' backgrounds? Even if there is no suspicion of misbehavior? Even if the job poses no security or sensitivity risks? Even if the background check includes driving offenses and credit histories?

APPLICATIONS

Reference Reports and Initial Assessment in a Start-Up Company

Stanley Jausneister owns a small high-tech start-up company called BioServer-Systems (BSS). Stanley's company specializes in selling web server space to clients. The server space that Stanley markets runs from a network of personal computers. This networked configuration allows BSS to more efficiently manage its server space and provides greater flexibility to its customers, who often want weekly or even daily updates of their websites. The other innovation Stanley brought to BSS is special security encryption software protocols that make the BSS server space nearly impossible for hackers to access. This flexibility is particularly attractive to organizations that need to manage large, security-protected databases with multiple points of access. Stanley has even been contacted by the government, which is interested in using BSS's systems for some of its classified intelligence.

Due to its niche, BSS has experienced rapid growth. In the past year, BSS hired 12 programmers and 2 marketers, as well as a general manager, an HR manager, and other support personnel. Before starting BSS, Stanley was a manager with a large pharmaceutical firm. Because of his industry connections, most of BSS's business has been with drug and chemical companies.

Yesterday, Stanley received a phone call from Lee Rogers, head of biotechnology for Mercelle-Poulet, one of BSS's largest customers. Lee is an old friend, and he was one of BSS's first customers. Lee had called to express concern about BSS's security. One area of Mercelle-Poulet's biotech division is responsible for research and development on vaccines for various bioterrorist weapons such as anthrax and the plague. Because the research and development on these vaccines require the company to develop cultures of the biological weapons themselves, Lee has used BSS to house information for this area. A great deal of sensitive information is housed on BSS's servers, including in some cases the formulas used in developing the cultures.

Despite the sensitivity of the information on BSS's servers, given BSS's advanced software, Stanley was very surprised to hear Lee's concern about security. "It's not your software that worries me," Lee commented, "it's the people running it." Lee explained that last week a Mercelle-Poulet researcher was arrested for attempting to sell certain cultures to an overseas client. This individual had been dismissed from a previous pharmaceutical company for unethical behavior, but this information did not surface during the individual's background check. This incident not only caused Lee to reexamine Mercelle-Poulet's background checks, but also made him think of BSS, as certain BSS employees have access to Mercelle-Poulet's information.

Instantly after hearing Lee's concern, Stanley realized he had a problem. Like many small employers, BSS did not do thorough background checks on its employees. It assumed that the information provided on the application was accurate and generally only called the applicant's previous employer (often with ineffective results). Stanley realized he needed to do more, not only to keep Lee's business but to protect his company and customers.

1. What sort of background testing should BSS conduct on its applicants?
2. Is there any information BSS should avoid obtaining for legal or EEO reasons?

3. How can BSS know that its background testing programs are effective?

4. In the past, BSS has used the following initial assessment methods: application blank, interviews with Stanley and other BSS managers, and a follow-up with the applicant's former employer. Beyond changes to its background testing program, would you suggest any other alterations to BSS's initial assessment process?

Developing a Lawful Application Blank

Consolidated Trucking Corporation, Inc. (CTCI) is a rapidly growing short-haul (local) firm within the greater Columbus, Ohio, area. It has grown primarily through the acquisitions of numerous small, family-owned trucking companies. Currently it has a fleet of 150 trucks and over 250 full-time drivers. Most of the drivers were hired initially by the firms that CTCI acquired, and they accepted generous offers to become members of the CTCI team. CTCI's expansion plans are very ambitious, but they will be fulfilled primarily from internal growth rather than additional acquisitions. Consequently, CTCI is now faced with the need to develop an external staffing system that will be geared up to hire 75 new truckers within the next two years.

Terry Tailgater is a former truck driver for CTCI who was promoted to truck maintenance supervisor, a position he has held for the past five years. Once CTCI's internal expansion plans were finalized, the firm's HR director (and sole member of the HR department), Harold Hornblower, decided he needed a new person to handle staffing and employment law duties. Harold promoted Terry Tailgater to the job of staffing manager. One of Terry's major assignments was to develop a new staffing system for truck drivers.

One of the first projects Terry undertook was to develop a new, standardized application blank for the job of truck driver. To do this, Terry looked at the many different application blanks the current drivers had completed for their former companies. (These records were given to CTCI at the time of acquisition.) The application blanks showed that a large amount of information was requested and that the specific information sought varied among the application forms. Terry scanned the various forms and made a list of all the questions the forms contained. He then decided to evaluate each question in terms of its probable lawfulness under federal and state (Ohio) laws. Terry wanted to identify and use only lawful questions on the new form he is developing.

On the next page is the list of questions Terry developed, along with columns labeled "probably lawful" and "probably unlawful." Assume that you are Terry and are deciding on the lawfulness of each question. Place a check mark in the appropriate column for each question and prepare a justification for its mark as "probably lawful" or "probably unlawful."

Questions Terry Is Considering Including on Application Blank

Question About	Probably Lawful	Probably Unlawful
Birthplace	_____	_____
Previous arrests	_____	_____
Previous felony convictions	_____	_____
Distance between work and residence	_____	_____
Domestic responsibilities	_____	_____
Height	_____	_____
Weight	_____	_____
Previous work experience	_____	_____
Educational attainment	_____	_____
High school favorite subjects	_____	_____
Grade point average	_____	_____
Received workers' compensation in past	_____	_____
Currently receiving workers' compensation	_____	_____
Child care arrangements	_____	_____
Length of time on previous job	_____	_____
Reason for leaving previous job	_____	_____
Age	_____	_____
Sex	_____	_____
Home ownership	_____	_____
Any current medical problems	_____	_____
History of mental illness	_____	_____
OK to seek references from previous employer?	_____	_____
Have you provided complete/truthful information?	_____	_____
Native language	_____	_____
Willing to work on Easter and Christmas	_____	_____
Get recommendation from pastor/priest	_____	_____

ENDNOTES

1. G. J. Myszkowski and S. Sloan, "Hiring by Blueprint," *HR Magazine*, May 1991, pp. 55–58.
2. J. W. Smither, R. R. Reilly, R. E. Millsap, K. Pearlman, and R. Stoffey, "Applicant Reactions to Selection Procedures," *Personnel Psychology*, 1993, 46, pp. 49–76.
3. P. F. Wernimont and J. P. Campbell, "Signs, Samples, and Criteria," *Journal of Applied Psychology*, 1968, 52, pp. 372–376.
4. State of Wisconsin, Chapter 134, *Evaluating Job Content for Selection*, Undated.
5. State of Wisconsin, *Evaluating Job Content for Selection*.
6. A. Ellin, "Lights! Camera! It's Time to Make a Résumé," *New York Times*, Apr. 21, 2007, pp. B1, B6; K. Gurchiek, "Video Résumé Use Rises, but So Do Big Questions," *SHRM Online*, Apr. 12, 2007, pp. 1–2; M. J. de la Merced, "Student's Video Résumé Gets Attention (Some of It Unwanted)," *New York Times*, Oct. 21, 2006, pp. B1, B6.
7. R. Strauss, "When the Résumé Is Not to Be Believed," *New York Times*, Sept. 12, 2006, p. 2; K. J. Winstein and D. Golden, "MIT Admissions Dean Lies on Résumé in 1979, Quits," *New York Times*, Apr. 27, 2007, pp. B1, B2; M. Villano, "Served as King of England, Said the Résumé," *New York Times*, Mar. 19, 2006, p. BU9.
8. "Editor's Note," *New York Times*, Mar. 21, 2004, p. ST13.
9. "Resume Fraud," *Gainesville Sun*, Mar. 5, 2006, pp. 5G, 6G.
10. "Getting Jail Time for This Resume Lie?" *Netscape Careers & Jobs*, Mar. 18, 2004 (*www.channels.netscape.com/ns/careers*); "Lying on Your Resume," *Netscape Careers & Jobs*, Mar. 18, 2004 (*www.channels.netscape.com/ns/careers*); K. Maher, "The Jungle," *Wall Street Journal*, May 6, 2003, p. B5; E. Stanton, "If a Résumé Lies, Truth Can Loom Large," *Wall Street Journal*, Dec. 29, 2002, p. B48; T. Weir, "Colleges Give Coaches' Résumés Closer Look," *USA Today*, May 28, 2002, p. C1.
11. "Survey Finds a Single Resume Typo Can Ruin Job Prospects," *IPMA-HR Bulletin*, Sept. 15, 2006, p. 1; C. Soltis, "Eagle-Eyed Employers Scour Résumés for Little White Lies," *Wall Street Journal*, Mar. 21, 2006, p. B7; D. Mattioli, "Standing Out in a Sea of CVs," *Wall Street Journal*, Jan. 16, 2007, p. B8; D. Mattioli, "Hard Sell on 'Soft' Skills Can Primp a Resume," *Wall Street Journal*, May 15, 2007, p. B6.
12. N. R. Kuncel, M. Credé, and L. L. Thomas, "The Validity of Self-Reported Grade Point Averages, Class Ranks, and Test Scores: A Meta-Analysis and Review of the Literature," *Review of Educational Research*, 2005, 75, pp. 63–82.
13. A. Howard, "College Experiences and Managerial Performance," *Journal of Applied Psychology*, 1986, 71, pp. 530–552; R. Merritt-Halston and K. Wexley, "Educational Requirements: Legality and Validity," *Personnel Psychology*, 1983, 36, pp. 743–753.
14. C. Murray, *Real Education: Four Simple Truths for Bringing America's Schools Back to Reality* (New York: Crown Forum, 2008); T. H. Ng and D. C. Feldman, "How Broadly Does Education Contribute to Job Performance?" *Personnel Psychology*, 2009, 62, pp. 89–134.
15. A. E. McKinney, K. D. Carlson, R. L. Meachum, N. C. D'Angelo, and M. L. Connerley, "Recruiters' Use of GPA in Initial Screening Decisions: Higher GPAs Don't Always Make the Cut," *Personnel Psychology*, 2003, 56, pp. 823–845; P. L. Roth, C. A. BeVier, F. S. Switzer, and J. S. Schippman, "Meta-Analyzing the Relationship Between Grades and Job Performance," *Journal of Applied Psychology*, 1996, 81, pp. 548–556; P. L. Roth and P. Bobko, "College Grade Point Average as a Personnel Selection Device: Ethnic Group Differences and Potential Adverse Impact," *Journal of Applied Psychology*, 2000, 85, pp. 399–406.
16. F. P. Morgeson and J. D. Nahrgang, "Same as It Ever Was: Recognizing Stability in the *Business-Week* Rankings," *Academy of Management Learning & Education*, 2008, 7, pp. 26–41.

17. S. Jaschik, "The B-School Hierarchy," *New York Times*, Apr. 25, 2004, pp. 36–40; J. Merritt, "What's an MBA Really Worth?" *BusinessWeek*, Sept. 22, 2003, pp. 90–102; J. Pfeffer and C. T. Fong, "The End of Business Schools? Less Success Than Meets the Eye," *Academy of Management Learning and Education*, 2002, 1(1), pp. 78–95.

18. R. S. Robin, W. H. Bommer, and T. T. Baldwin, "Using Extracurricular Activity as an Indicator of Interpersonal Skill: Prudent Evaluation or Recruiting Malpractice?" *Human Resource Management*, 2002, 41(4), pp. 441–454.

19. R. A. Ash, "A Comparative Study of Behavioral Consistency and Holistic Judgment Methods of Job Applicant Training and Work Experience Evaluation," *Public Personnel Management*, 1984, 13, pp. 157–172; M. A. McDaniel, F. L. Schmidt, and J. E. Hunter, "A Meta-Analysis of the Validity of Methods for Rating Training and Experience in Personnel Selection," *Personnel Psychology*, 1988, 41, pp. 283–314; R. Tomsho, "Busy Surgeons Are Good for Patients," *Wall Street Journal*, Nov. 28, 2003, p. B3.

20. M. R. Raymond, S. Neustel, and D. Anderson, "Retest Effects on Identical and Parallel Forms in Certification and Licensure Testing," *Personnel Psychology*, 2007, 60, pp. 367–396; J. D. Opdyke, "'Wait, Let Me Call My ChFC,'" *Wall Street Journal*, Jan. 28, 2006, pp. B1, B3; J. McKillip and J. Owens, "Voluntary Professional Certifications: Requirements and Validation Activities," *The Industrial-Organizational Psychologist*, July 2000, pp. 50–57.

21. G. W. England, *Development and Use of Weighted Application Blanks* (Dubuque, IA: W.M.C. Brown, 1961).

22. J. E. Hunter and R. F. Hunter, "Validity and Utility of Alternative Predictors of Job Performance," *Psychological Bulletin*, 1984, 96, pp. 72–98.

23. I. L. Goldstein, "The Application Blank: How Honest Are the Responses?" *Journal of Applied Psychology*, 1974, 59, pp. 491–494.

24. G. W. England, *Development and Use of Weighted Application Blanks*, revised ed. (Minneapolis: University of Minnesota Industrial Relations Center, 1971).

25. C. J. Russell, J. Mattson, S. E. Devlin, and D. Atwater, "Predictive Validity of Biodata Items Generated From Retrospective Life Experience Essays," *Journal of Applied Psychology*, 1990, 75, pp. 569–580.

26. F. A. Mael, "A Conceptual Rationale for the Domain and Attributes of Biodata Items," *Personnel Psychology*, 1991, 44, pp. 763–792.

27. S. Hansell, "Google Answer to Filling Jobs Is an Algorithm," *New York Times*, Jan. 3, 2007, pp. A1, C9.

28. J. S. Breaugh, "The Use of Biodata for Employee Selection: Past Research and Future Directions," *Human Resource Management Review*, 2009, 19, pp. 219–231; C. M. Harold, L. A. McFarland, and J. A. Weekley, "The Validity of Verifiable and Non-verifiable Biodata Items: An Examination Across Applicants and Incumbents," *International Journal of Selection and Assessment*, 2006, 14, pp. 336–346.

29. J. E. Hunter and R. F. Hunter, "Validity and Utility of Alternative Predictors of Job Performance"; R. R. Reilly and G. T. Chao, "Validity and Fairness of Some Alternative Selection Procedures," *Personnel Psychology*, 1982, 35, pp. 1–62.

30. B. J. Becton, M. C. Matthews, D. L. Hartley, and D. H. Whitaker, "Using Biodata to Predict Turnover, Organizational Commitment, and Job Performance in Healthcare," *International Journal of Selection and Assessment*, 2009, 17, pp. 189–202; N. Schmitt, J. Keeney, F. L. Oswald, T. J. Pleskac, A. Q. Billington, R. Sinha, and M. Zorzie, "Prediction of 4-year College Student Performance Using Cognitive and Noncognitive Predictors and the Impact on Demographic Status of Admitted Students," *Journal of Applied Psychology*, 2009, 94, pp. 1479–1497.

31. K. D. Carlson, S. Sculten, F. L. Schmidt, H. Rothstein, and F. Erwin, "Generalizable Biographical Data Validity Can Be Achieved Without Multi-Organizational Development and Keying," *Personnel Psychology*, 1999, 52, pp. 731–755; J. S. Breaugh, "The Use of Biodata for Employee Selection: Past Research and Future Directions."

32. N. Schmitt, F. L. Oswald, B. H. Kim, M. A. Gillespie, L. J. Ramsay, and T. Yoo, "Impact of Elaboration on Socially Desirable Responding and the Validity of Biodata Measures," *Journal of Applied Psychology*, 2003, 88, pp. 979–988.

33. N. Anderson, J. F. Salgado, and U. R. Hülsheger, "Applicant Reactions in Selection: Comprehensive Meta-Analysis into Reaction Generalization versus Situational Specificity," *International Journal of Selection and Assessment*, 2010, 18, pp. 291–304; A. Furnham, "HR Professionals' Beliefs About, and Knowledge of, Assessment Techniques and Psychometric Tests," *International Journal of Selection and Assessment*, 2008, 16, pp. 300–305.

34. J. C. Baxter, B. Brock, P. C. Hill, and R. M. Rozelle, "Letters of Recommendation: A Question of Value," *Journal of Applied Psychology*, 1981, 66, pp. 296–301.

35. T. A. Judge and C. A. Higgins, "Affective Disposition and the Letter of Reference," *Organizational Behavior and Human Decision Processes*, 1998, 75, pp. 207–221.

36. M. E. Burke, "2004 Reference Check and Background Testing," *Society for Human Resource Management*, 2005; P. J. Taylor, K. Pajo, G. W. Cheung, and P. Stringfield, "Dimensionality and Validity of a Structured Telephone Reference Check Procedure," *Personnel Psychology*, 2004, 57, pp. 745–772.

37. J. Click, "SJRM Survey Highlights Dilemmas of Reference Checks," *HR News*, July 1995, p. 13.

38. A. Athavaley, "Job References You Can't Control," *Wall Street Journal*, Sept. 27, 2007, pp. D1, D2.

39. Taylor et al., "Dimensionality and Validity of a Structured Telephone Reference Check Procedure."

40. S. Hananel, "Some Job-Screening Tactics Challenged as Illegal," MSNBC, Oct. 12, 2010 (*www.msnbc.msn.com/id/38664839*), accessed 1/28/11.

41. A. Zimmerman, "Wal-Mart to Probe Job Applicants," *Wall Street Journal*, Aug. 12, 2004, pp. A3, B6.

42. H. Drummond, *The Dynamics of Organizational Collapse: The Case of Barings Bank* (London: Routledge, 2007).

43. "Employers Increase Use of Background Checks," *USA Today*, Apr. 26, 2007, p. 1B; T. Minton-Eversole, "More Background Screening Yields More 'Red Tape,'" *SHRM News*, July 2007, pp. 1–5.

44. K. Maher, "The Jungle," *Wall Street Journal*, Jan. 20, 2004, p. B8; A. Zimmerman and K. Stringer, "As Background Checks Proliferate, Ex-Cons Face Jobs Lock," *Wall Street Journal*, Aug. 26, 2004, pp. B1, B3.

45. L. Schwarz, "Baseball and Umpires Clash Over Background Checks," *New York Times*, Aug. 7, 2007, p. C15.

46. A. Levin, "Unions: Safety Bar Set Lower for Cargo Planes," *USA Today*, Nov. 5, 2010, p. 1A.

47. M. Harding, "Companies Turning to Web Conferencing for Employment Interviews," *Pittsburgh Tribune Review*, Apr. 20, 2010, p. 1.

48. Goldstein, "The Application Blank: How Honest Are the Responses?"; W. Keichel, "Lies on the Resume," *Fortune*, Aug. 23, 1982, pp. 221–222, 224; J. N. Mosel and L. W. Cozan, "The Accuracy of Application Blank Work Histories," *Journal of Applied Psychology*, 1952, 36, pp. 365–369.

49. R. A. Ash and E. L. Levine, "Job Applicant Training and Work Experience Evaluation: An Empirical Comparison of Four Methods," *Journal of Applied Psychology*, 1985, 70, pp. 572–576.

50. G. P. Latham and G. Whyte, "The Futility of Utility Analysis," *Personnel Psychology*, 1994, 47, pp. 31–46.

51. P. R. Sackett and F. Lievens, "Personnel Selection," *Annual Review of Psychology*, 2008, 59, pp. 419–450; U. R. Hülsheger and N. Anderson, "Applicant Perspectives in Selection: Going Beyond Preference Reactions," *International Journal of Selection and Assessment*, 2009, 17, pp. 335–345; F. P. Morgeson and A. M. Ryan, "Reacting to Applicant Perspectives Research: What's Next?" *International Journal of Selection and Assessment*, 2009, 17, pp. 431–437.

52. J. P. Hausknecht, D. V. Day, and S. C. Thomas, "Applicant Reactions to Selection Procedures: An Updated Model and Meta-Analysis," *Personnel Psychology*, 2004, 57, pp. 639–683; D. M. Truxillo, T. E. Bodner, M. Bertolino, T. N. Bauer, and C. A. Yonce, "Effects of Explanations on Applicant Reactions: A Meta-Analytic Review," *International Journal of Selection and Assessment*, 2009, 17, pp. 346–361.

53. Anderson, Salgado, and Hülsheger, "Applicant Reactions in Selection: Comprehensive Meta-Analysis Into Reaction Generalization Versus Situational Specificity."

54. G. P. Panaro, *Employment Law Manual,* second ed. (Boston: Warren Gorham Lamont, 1993), pp. 1-29 to 1-42; M. G. Danaher, "Handbook Disclaimer Dissected," *HR Magazine*, Feb. 2007, p. 116; D. J. Walsh, *Employment Law for Human Resource Practice* (Mason, OH: Thompson Higher Education, 2007).

55. J. E. Bahls, "Available Upon Request," *HR Magazine Focus*, Jan. 1999, p. 206; Panaro, *Employment Law Manual,* pp. 2-101 to 2-106; M. E. Burke and L. A. Weatherly, *Getting to Know the Candidate: Providing Reference Checks* (Alexandria, VA: Society for Human Resource Management, 2005); S. Z. Hable, "The Trouble With Online References," *Workforce Management Online*, Feb. 2010, accessed 6/22/10.

56. T. B. Stivarius, J. Skonberg, R. Fliegel, R. Blumberg, R. Jones, and K. Mones, "Background Checks: Four Steps to Basic Compliance in a Multistate Environment," *Legal Report*, Society for Human Resource Management, Mar.–Apr. 2003.

57. K. McNamera, "Bad Credit Derails Job Search," *Wall Street Journal*, Mar. 16, 2010, p. D6; R. Mauer, "Federal Lawmakers, Enforcers Set Sights on Background Screening," Society for Human Resource Management, Legal Issues, accessed 3/9/10; Employment Screening Resources, *ESR Newsletter and Legal Update*, Oct. 2009, pp. 1–2; *ESR Newsletter and Legal Update*, Aug. 2010, pp. 1–2.

58. F. Hanson, "Burden of Proof," *Workforce Management*, Feb. 2010, pp. 27–33; F. Hanson, "Blaming Clients in Background Check Lawsuits," *Workforce Management*, July 2010, pp. 8–9; J. Greenwald, "Ex-Convicts in Workforce Pose Liability Problems," *Workforce Management Online*, Sept. 15, 2009, accessed 3/12/10.

59. J. C. Wallace and S. J. Vadanovich, "Personal Application Blanks: Persistence and Knowledge of Legally Inadvisable Application Blank Items," *Public Personnel Management*, 2004, 33, pp. 331–349.

60. Bureau of National Affairs, *Fair Employment Practices* (Washington, DC: author, periodically updated), 454: whole section.

61. Bureau of National Affairs, *Fair Employment Practices*, pp. 421:352–356.

62. N. J. Sedmak and M. D. Levin-Epstein, *Primer on Equal Employment Opportunity* (Washington, DC: Bureau of National Affairs, 1991), pp. 36–40.

63. Bureau of National Affairs, *Fair Employment Practices,* pp. 405:6941–6943.

CHAPTER NINE

External Selection II

Learning Objectives and Introduction
   Learning Objectives
   Introduction

Substantive Assessment Methods
   Personality Tests
   Ability Tests
   Emotional Intelligence Tests
   Performance Tests and Work Samples
   Situational Judgment Tests
   Integrity Tests
   Interest, Values, and Preference Inventories
   Structured Interview
   Choice of Substantive Assessment Methods

Discretionary Assessment Methods

Contingent Assessment Methods
   Drug Testing
   Medical Exams

Legal Issues
   Uniform Guidelines on Employee Selection Procedures
   Selection Under the Americans With Disabilities Act
   Drug Testing

Summary

Discussion Questions

Ethical Issues

Applications

Tanglewood Stores Case

LEARNING OBJECTIVES AND INTRODUCTION

Learning Objectives

- Distinguish among initial, substantive, and contingent selection
- Review the advantages and disadvantages of personality and cognitive ability tests
- Compare and contrast work sample and situational judgment tests
- Understand the advantages of structured interviews and how interviews can be structured
- Review the logic behind contingent assessment methods and how they are administrated
- Understand the ways in which substantive and contingent assessment methods are subject to various legal rules and restrictions

Introduction

The previous chapter reviewed preliminary issues surrounding external staffing decisions made in organizations, including the use of initial assessment methods. This chapter continues the discussion of external selection by discussing in some detail substantive assessment methods. The use of discretionary and contingent assessment methods, collection of assessment data, and legal issues will also be considered. In a real sense, substantive and contingent assessment are the heart of staffing decisions, where the "rubber meets the road." This is because substantive and contingent selection are the highlight of actual hiring decisions. Done well, and the stage is set for effective organizational staffing. Done poorly, and it is difficult, if not impossible, to staff successfully.

Whereas initial assessment methods are used to reduce the applicant pool to candidates, substantive assessment methods are used to reduce the candidate pool to finalists for the job. Thus, the use of substantive methods is often more involved than the use of initial methods. Numerous substantive assessment methods will be discussed in depth, including various tests (personality, ability, emotional intelligence, performance/work samples, situational judgment, and integrity); interest, values, and preference inventories; structured interviews; and assessment for team environments. The average validity (i.e., $\bar{r}_{xy}$) of each method and the criteria used to choose among methods will be reviewed.

Discretionary assessment methods are used in some circumstances to separate those who receive job offers from the list of finalists. The applicant characteristics that are assessed when using discretionary methods are sometimes very subjective. Several of the characteristics most commonly assessed by discretionary methods will be reviewed.

Contingent assessment methods are used to make sure that tentative offer recipients meet certain qualifications for the job. Although any assessment method can be used as a contingent method (e.g., licensing/certification requirements, background checks), perhaps the two most common contingent methods are drug tests and medical exams. These procedures will be reviewed.

All forms of assessment decisions require the collection of assessment data. The procedures used to make sure this process is properly conducted will be reviewed. In particular, several issues will be discussed, including support services, training requirements in using various predictors, maintaining security and confidentiality, and the importance of standardized procedures.

Finally, many important legal issues surround the use of substantive, discretionary, and contingent methods of selection. The most important of these issues will be reviewed. Particular attention will be given to the Uniform Guidelines on Employee Selection Procedures (UGESP) and staffing requirements under the Americans With Disabilities Act (ADA).

SUBSTANTIVE ASSESSMENT METHODS

Organizations use initial assessment methods to make rough cuts among applicants, weeding out the obviously unqualified. Conversely, substantive assessment methods are used to make more precise decisions about applicants—among those who meet minimum qualifications for the job, who are the most likely to be high performers if hired? Because substantive methods are used to make fine distinctions among applicants, the nature of their use is somewhat more involved than initial assessment methods. As with initial assessment methods, however, substantive assessment methods are developed using the logic of prediction outlined in Exhibit 8.1 and the selection plan shown in Exhibit 8.2. Predictors typically used to select finalists from the candidate pool include personality tests; ability tests; emotional intelligence tests; performance tests and work samples; situational judgment tests; integrity tests; interest, values, and preference inventories; structured interviews; and team assessments. Each of these predictors is described next in some detail.

Personality Tests

At one time, personality tests were not perceived as a valid selection method.[1] Today, however, most researchers reach much more positive conclusions about the role of personality tests in predicting job performance.[2] Mainly, this is due to the widespread acceptance of a major taxonomy of personality, often called the Big Five. The Big Five are used to describe behavioral (as opposed to emotional or cognitive) traits that may capture up to 75% of an individual's personality.

The Big Five factors are *extraversion* (tendency to be sociable, assertive, active, upbeat, and talkative), *agreeableness* (tendency to be altruistic, trusting, sympathetic, and cooperative), *conscientiousness* (tendency to be purposeful, determined, dependable, and attentive to detail), *emotional stability* (disposition to be calm, optimistic, and well adjusted), and *openness to experience* (tendency to be imaginative, attentive to inner feelings, intellectually curious, and independent). The Big Five are very stable over time, and evidence suggests that roughly 50% of the variance in the Big Five traits appears to be inherited.[3]

Measures of Personality

Although personality can be measured in many ways, for personnel selection, the most common measures are self-report surveys. Several survey measures of the Big Five traits are used in selection. The *International Personality Item Pool* (IPIP) contains several Big Five measures. Exhibit 9.1 provides sample items from the IPIP. The IPIP has the advantage of being nonproprietary and therefore free to use. The *Personal Characteristics Inventory* (PCI) is a self-report measure of the Big Five that asks applicants to report their agreement or disagreement (using a "strongly disagree" to "strongly agree" scale) with 150 sentences.[4] The measure takes about 30 minutes to complete and has a fifth- to sixth-grade reading level. Another commonly used measure of the Big Five is the *NEO Personality Inventory* (NEO), of which there are several versions that have been translated into numerous languages.[5] A third alternative is the *Hogan Personality Inventory* (HPI), which is also based on the Big Five typology. Responses to the HPI can be scored to yield measures of employee reliability and service orientation.[6] All of these measures have shown validity in predicting job performance in various occupations.

Traditionally, personality tests were administered to applicants on-site, with a paper-and-pencil survey. Nowadays, many surveys are administered online, which is cheaper for the organization and more convenient for the applicant. However, because most online testing is unmonitored, there are three potential problems: (1) test security might be compromised (e.g., test items posted on a blog), (2) applicants may find it easier to cheat or be more motivated to cheat online, and (3) applicants may not tolerate long online personality tests. There are no silver bullet remedies to these problems. Because each of these problems is less of an issue with paper-and-pencil tests, organizations may be well advised to use that format where feasible.

Where traditional paper-and-pencil personality testing is infeasible, several steps can be taken to ameliorate the problems with online testing. First, experts recommend keeping online personality tests as brief as possible. If the test takes more than 20 minutes, applicants may grow impatient. Second, it is important to assign applicants identification codes, to collect basic background data, and to break the test into sections. These steps increase accountability (lessening the odds of faking) and ensure that if the applicant loses the Internet connection while taking the test, the portions completed will not be lost. Third, the probability of

---

EXHIBIT 9.1   Sample Items Measuring Big Five Personality Dimensions

Please rate how accurately each statement describes you on a scale from 1="to no extent" to 5="to a very great extent."

Extraversion

Am quiet around strangers.

Take charge.

Am skilled in handling social situations.

Agreeableness

Have a soft heart.

Insult people. (reverse scored)

Have a good word for everyone.

Conscientiousness

Am always prepared.

Pay attention to details.

Am exacting in my work.

Emotional Stability

Am relaxed most of the time.

Seldom feel blue.

Have frequent mood swings. (reverse scored)

Openness to Experience

Have a vivid imagination.

Love to think up new ways of doing things.

Try to avoid complex people. (reverse scored)

SOURCE: *International Personality Item Pool (ipip.ori.org).*

faking can be reduced by following some of the steps outlined shortly. These steps are especially important for online testing. Finally, many experts recommend the use of "item banking" (variation in specific items used to measure each trait) to enhance test security; to further reduce faking, inform test takers that their online scores will be verified with a paper-and-pencil test should they advance further in the selection process.[7]

Evaluation of Personality Tests

Many comprehensive reviews of the validity of personality tests have been published. Nearly all of the recent reviews focus on the validity of the Big Five.[8] Although there are some inconsistencies across reviews, the results can be summarized in Exhibit 9.2. As the exhibit shows, each of the Big Five traits has advantages

EXHIBIT 9.2 **Implications of Big Five Personality Traits at Work**

Big Five Trait	Advantages	Disadvantages
Conscientiousness	• Better overall job performers • Higher levels of job satisfaction • More likely to emerge as leaders • Fewer "deviant" work behaviors • Higher retention (lower turnover)	• Lower adaptability
Emotional stability	• Better overall job performers • Higher levels of job satisfaction • More effective leaders • Higher retention (lower turnover)	• Less able to identify threats • More likely to engage in high-risk behaviors
Extraversion	• Perform better in sales • More likely to emerge as leaders • Higher levels of job satisfaction	• Higher absenteeism • More accidents
Agreeableness	• More valued as team members • More "helping" behaviors • Fewer "deviant" work behaviors	• Lower career success • Less able to cope with conflict • Give more lenient ratings
Openness	• Higher creativity • More effective leaders • More adaptable	• Less committed to employer • More "deviant" work behaviors • More accidents

and disadvantages. However, the traits differ in the degree to which they are a mixed blessing. Specifically, whereas the disadvantages of agreeableness and openness appear to offset their advantages, the advantages of conscientiousness, emotional stability, and, to some degree, extraversion outweigh the disadvantages. These three traits also happen to have the strongest correlates with overall job performance. Conscientiousness and emotional stability, in particular, appear to be useful across a wide range of jobs. Thus, in general, the personality traits of conscientiousness, emotional stability, and extraversion—in that order—appear to be the most useful for selection contexts. Of course, in certain situations—such as where adaptability or creativity may be highly valued, or where cooperative relations are crucial—openness and agreeableness may be important to assess as well.

Today there is widespread acceptance regarding the validity and utility of personality tests in personnel selection. This does not mean that the area is free of its critics, however. A few researchers continue to argue that personality traits are not useful selection tools.[9] Here we evaluate three of the most important criticisms of the use of personality tests in selection decisions: the validities are trivial, faking undermines their usefulness, and applicants react negatively to them.

Trivial Validities. One set of critics has argued that the validities of personality traits are so small as to border on the trivial, rendering them of limited usefulness as selection devices. These researchers note, "Why are we now suddenly looking at personality as a valid predictor of job performance when the validities still haven't changed and are still close to zero?"[10] While this is an extreme position, it does contain a grain of truth: the validities are far from perfect. For example, our best estimate of the validity of conscientiousness in predicting overall job performance is $\bar{r}_{xy}$ = .23. By no means would this be labeled a strong validity (though, in fairness, we are not aware of any personality researchers who have done so). Does this mean that the validity of personality measures, though, are trivial? We do not believe so, for five reasons.

First, because applicants can complete an entire Big Five inventory in less than 30 minutes in most selection situations, the entire Big Five framework is used, or at least more than a single trait is assessed. So, it is important to look at the multiple correlations between the set of Big Five traits and criteria such as job performance. For example, the multiple correlations between the Big Five and criteria such as overall job performance and leadership is roughly r = .50. This is hardly trivial.[11]

Second, as with any selection measure, one can find situations in which a personality trait does not predict job performance. Even though personality tests generalize across jobs, this doesn't mean they will work in every case. And sometimes when they work and when they don't is counterintuitive. For example, evidence suggests that conscientiousness and positive self-concept work well in predicting player success in the NFL but not so well in predicting the performance of police officers.[12] Organizations need to perform their own validation studies to ensure that the tests are working as hoped. In general, personality is more predictive of performance in jobs that have substantial autonomy, meaning that individuals have discretion in deciding how—and how well—to do their work.[13]

Third, the Big Five do not exhaust the set of potentially relevant personality traits. Research suggests, for example, that a trait termed proactive personality (degree to which people take action) predicts performance and career success, even controlling for the Big Five traits.[14] Another trait, termed core self-evaluations (a reflection of individuals' self-confidence and self-worth), has also been linked to job performance. The Core Self-Evaluations Scale is shown in Exhibit 9.3. Research indicates that core self-evaluations are predictive of job performance, and the Core Self-Evaluations Scale appears to have validity equivalent to that of conscientiousness. A further advantage of this measure is that it is nonproprietary (free).[15]

Fourth, personality is not intended to be a stand-alone selection tool. In nearly all cases it is part of a selection battery consisting of other substantive selection measures. No reasonable person would recommend that applicants be hired solely

EXHIBIT 9.3   The Core Self-Evaluations Scale

Instructions: Below are several statements about you with which you may agree or disagree. Using the response scale below, indicate your agreement or disagreement with each item by placing the appropriate number on the line preceding that item.

1	2	3	4	5
Strongly Disagree	Disagree	Neutral	Agree	Strongly Agree

1.____I am confident I get the success I deserve in life.
2.____Sometimes I feel depressed. (r)
3.____When I try, I generally succeed.
4.____Sometimes when I fail, I feel worthless. (r)
5.____I complete tasks successfully.
6.____Sometimes I do not feel in control of my work. (r)
7.____Overall, I am satisfied with myself.
8.____I am filled with doubts about my competence. (r)
9.____I determine what will happen in my life.
10.____I do not feel in control of my success in my career. (r)
11.____I am capable of coping with most of my problems.
12.____There are times when things look pretty bleak and hopeless to me. (r)

Note: r = reverse-scored (for these items, 5 is scored 1, 4 is scored 2, 2 is scored 4, and 1 is scored 5).

SOURCE: T. A. Judge, A. Erez, J. E. Bono, and C. J. Thoresen, "The Core Self-Evaluations Scale: Development of a Measure," *Personnel Psychology*, 2003, 56, pp. 303–331.

on the basis of scores on a personality test. But by the same token, personality measures do appear to add to the validity of other selection measures.[16]

Finally, recent evidence suggests that personality validities may be nonlinear. One study found that in two samples, the validities of conscientiousness and emotional stability in predicting job performance were nonlinear, such that there were diminishing returns to increasing levels of these traits (extremely conscientious employees don't necessarily perform better than highly conscientious employees). Thus, correlation coefficients (which assume linearity) may understate the true validity of personality tests. Practically, when choosing between two applicants, it may make sense to consider where they are on the distribution of each trait.[17]

Faking.   Another frequent criticism of personality measures is that they are "fakeable," meaning applicants will distort their responses to increase their odds of being hired. This concern is apparent when one considers personality items (see

Exhibits 9.1 and 9.3) and the nature of the traits. Few individuals would want to describe themselves as disagreeable, neurotic, unconscientious, and unconfident. Furthermore, since answers to these questions are nearly impossible to verify (e.g., imagine trying to verify whether an applicant prefers reading a book to watching television), the possibility of "faking good" is quite real. This then leads to the perverse outcome that the applicants most likely to be hired are those who enhanced their responses (faked) the most.

There is a voluminous literature on faking. The results of this literature can be summarized as follows. First, there is little doubt that some faking or enhancement does occur. Studies suggest that applicants consistently score higher on socially desirable personality traits (like conscientiousness, emotional stability, and agreeableness) than do current employees (in most situations, there is no reason to believe that applicants should score more favorably on personality tests than employees—if anything, the reverse would be expected). Also, when individuals are informed that their scores matter (might be used in selection decisions), their scores on personality tests increase.[18]

But what is the outcome of this enhancement? Does the fact that some applicants fake their responses destroy the validity of personality measures in selection? Interestingly, the answer to this question appears to be quite clearly no. In short, though applicants do try to look good by enhancing their responses to personality tests, it seems clear that such enhancement does not significantly detract from the validity of the tests. Why might this be the case? Evidence suggests that socially desirable responding, or presenting oneself in a favorable light, doesn't end once someone takes a job. So, the same tendencies that cause someone to present himself or herself in a somewhat favorable light on a personality test also help him or her do better on the job.[19]

Because faking does not appear to undermine personality validities, some of the proposed solutions to faking may be unnecessary or may cause more problems than they solve. For example, some have proposed correcting applicant scores for faking. However, the literature is quite clear that such corrections do not improve the validity of personality measures.[20] Another proposed solution—using forced-choice personality measures, where applicants must evaluate themselves as either, say, conscientious or emotionally stable—also appears to be fraught with considerable problems.[21] The third possible method of reducing faking—warning applicants that their scores will be verified—appears to reduce faking (by as much as 30%) without undermining validities.[22]

A final possibility is to use other reports of personality. One might have individuals who have worked with an applicant report on the applicant's personality. The upside of observer reports appears to be noteworthy in that most research suggests that observer ratings of personality outperform self-reports when predicting job performance.[23] If one is using observer reports of personality, however, it is important to attend to information security concerns. One should ensure that the observer nominated by the applicant actually completes the assessment and that the observer is asked to be objective in the assessment. Also, to the extent possible, multiple observer ratings should be used, as it greatly improves reliability and, thus, validity.

Negative Applicant Reactions. Finally, it is important to evaluate personality tests not only in terms of their validity but also from the applicant's perspective. From an applicant's standpoint, the subjective and personal nature of the questions asked in these tests may cause questions about their validity and concerns about invasiveness. In fact, the available evidence concerning applicants' perceptions of personality tests suggests that they are viewed relatively negatively compared with other selection measures. To some degree, applicants who react the most negatively are those who believe they have scored the worst.[24] But in general, applicants do not perceive personality measures to be as face-valid as other selection measures. Thus, while personality tests—when used properly—do have validity, this validity does not seem to translate into favorable applicant perceptions. More research is needed into the ways that these tests could be made more acceptable to applicants.

Ability Tests

Ability tests are measures that assess an individual's capacity to function in a certain way. There are two major types of ability tests: aptitude and achievement. Aptitude tests look at a person's innate capacity to function, whereas achievement tests assess a person's learned capacity to function. In practice, these types of abilities are often difficult to separate. Thus, it is not clear that this is a productive, practical distinction for ability tests used in selection.

Surveys reveal that between 15% and 20% of organizations use some sort of ability test in selection decisions, although there is some reason to believe use is increasing.[25] Organizations that use ability tests do so because they assume the tests assess a key determinant of employee performance. Without a certain level of ability, innate or learned, performance is unlikely to be acceptable, regardless of motivation. Someone may try extremely hard to do well in a very difficult class (e.g., calculus) but will not succeed unless he or she has the ability to do so (e.g., mathematical aptitude).

There are four major classes of ability tests: cognitive, psychomotor, physical, and sensory/perceptual.[26] As these ability tests are quite distinct, each will be considered separately below. Because most of the research attention—and public controversy—has focused on cognitive ability tests, they are discussed in considerable detail.

Cognitive Ability Tests

Cognitive ability tests refer to measures that assess abilities involved in thinking (including perception), memory, reasoning, verbal and mathematical abilities, and the expression of ideas. Is cognitive ability a general construct or does it have a number of specific aspects? Research shows that measures of specific cognitive abilities, such as verbal, quantitative, reasoning, and so on, appear to reflect general intelligence (sometimes referred to as GMA [general mental ability], IQ, or "g").[27] One of the facts that best illustrate this finding is the relatively high correlations among scores on measures of specific facets of intelligence. Someone who scores well on a measure of one specific ability is more likely to score well on measures of other specific abilities. In other words, general intelligence causes individuals to have similar scores on measures of specific abilities.

Measures of Cognitive Ability.   Many cognitive ability tests measure both specific cognitive abilities and general mental ability. Many test publishers offer an array of tests. The Psychological Corporation sells the *Employee Aptitude Survey*, a test of 10 specific cognitive abilities (e.g., verbal comprehension, numerical ability, numerical and verbal reasoning, and word fluency). Each of these specific tests is sold separately and takes no more than five minutes to administer to applicants. Each of the 10 specific tests is sold in packages of 25 for about $44 per package. The Psychological Corporation also sells the *Wonderlic Personnel Test*, perhaps the most widely used test of general mental ability for selection decisions. The Wonderlic is a 12-minute, 50-item test. Items range in type from spatial relations to numerical problems to analogies. Exhibit 9.4 provides examples of items from one of the Wonderlic forms. In addition to being a speed (timed) test, the Wonderlic is also a power test—the items get harder as the test progresses (very few individuals complete all 50 items). The Wonderlic has been administered to more than 2.5 million applicants, and normative data are available from a database of more than 450,000 individuals. Cost of the Wonderlic ranges from about $1.50 to $3.50 per applicant, depending on whether the organization scores the test itself. Costs of other cognitive ability tests are similar. Although cognitive ability tests are not entirely costless, they are among the least expensive of any substantive assessment method.

There are many other tests and test publishers in addition to those reviewed above. Before deciding which test to use, organizations should seek out a reputable testing firm. An association of test publishers has been formed with bylaws to help ensure this process.[28] It is also advisable to seek out the advice of researchers or testing specialists, many of whom are members of the American Psychological Association or the American Psychological Society.

Evaluation of Cognitive Ability Tests.   The findings regarding general intelligence have had profound implications for personnel selection. A number of meta-analyses have been conducted on the validity of cognitive ability tests. Although the validities found in these studies have fluctuated to some extent, the most comprehensive reviews have estimated the "true" validity of measures of

EXHIBIT 9.4   Sample Cognitive Ability Test Items

Look at the row of numbers below. What number should come next?

| 8 | 4 | 2 | 1 | 1/2 | 1/4 | ? |

Assume the first 2 statements are true. Is the final one: (1) true, (2) false, (3) not certain?
The boy plays baseball. All baseball players wear hats. The boy wears a hat.

One of the numbered figures in the following drawing is most different from the others. What is the number in that drawing?

A train travels 20 feet in 1/5 second. At this same speed, how many feet will it travel in three seconds?

How many of the six pairs of items listed below are exact duplicates?

3421	1243
21212	21212
558956	558956
10120210	10120210
612986896	612986896
356471201	356571201

The hours of daylight and darkness in SEPTEMBER are nearest equal to the hours of daylight and darkness in

| (1) June | (2) March | (3) May | (4) November |

SOURCE: Reprinted with permission from C. F. Wonderlic Personnel Test, Inc., *1992 Catalog: Employment Tests, Forms, and Procedures* (Libertyville, IL: author, 1992).

general cognitive ability to be roughly $\bar{r}_{xy} = .50$.[29] The conclusions from these meta-analyses are dramatic:

1. Cognitive ability tests are among the most valid, if not *the* most valid, methods of selection.

2. Cognitive ability tests appear to generalize across all organizations, all job types, and all types of applicants; thus, they are likely to be valid in virtually any selection context.

3. Organizations using cognitive ability tests in selection enjoy large economic gains compared with organizations that do not use them.

4. Cognitive ability tests appear to generalize across cultures, with validities in Europe at least as high as those in the United States.

5. Beyond job performance, cognitive ability predicts other important criteria, including health-conscious behaviors (such as exercise), occupational prestige, income, steeper career success trajectories, and lower turnover.[30]

These conclusions are not simply esoteric speculations from the ivory tower. They are based on hundreds of studies of hundreds of organizations employing hundreds of thousands of workers. Thus, whether an organization is selecting engineers, customer service representatives, or meat cutters, general mental ability is likely the single most valid method of selecting among applicants. A large-scale quantitative review of the literature suggested relatively high average validities for many occupational groups:[31]

Manager, $\bar{r}_{xy} = .53$
Clerk, $\bar{r}_{xy} = .54$
Salesperson, $\bar{r}_{xy} = .61$
Protective professional, $\bar{r}_{xy} = .42$
Service worker, $\bar{r}_{xy} = .48$
Trades and crafts, $\bar{r}_{xy} = .46$
Elementary industrial worker, $\bar{r}_{xy} = .37$
Vehicle operator, $\bar{r}_{xy} = .28$
Sales clerk, $\bar{r}_{xy} = .27$

These results show that cognitive ability tests have some degree of validity for all types of jobs. The validity is particularly high for complex jobs (e.g., manager, engineer), but even for simple jobs the validity is positive. The same review also revealed that cognitive ability tests have very high degrees of validity in predicting training success—$\bar{r}_{xy} = .37$ for vehicle operators to $\bar{r}_{xy} = .87$ for protective professionals. This is due to the substantial learning component of training and the obvious fact that smart people learn more and adapt more readily to changing job conditions.[32]

Whereas cognitive ability tests are more valid for jobs of medium complexity (e.g., police officers, salespeople) and high complexity (e.g., computer programmers, pilots), they are even valid for jobs of relatively low complexity (e.g., bus driver, factory worker). Why are cognitive ability tests predictive even for relatively simple jobs where intelligence would not appear to be an important attribute? The fact is that some degree of intelligence is important for *any* type of job. The validity of cognitive ability tests even seems to generalize to performance on and of athletic teams (see Exhibit 9.5). Additionally, one study found that college basketball teams high in cognitive ability performed better than teams low in cognitive ability.[33] Thus, cognitive ability may be unimportant to performance in some jobs, but if this is true, we have yet to find them.

EXHIBIT 9.5   Cognitive Ability Testing in the NFL

As ardent football fans know, each year the NFL holds a draft to select college players for its teams. As part of that draft, potential draftees go through a "combine" where their skills are tested: they bench press, they run, they jump through hoops (literally), and they complete an intelligence test (the *Wonderlic Personnel Test*). Although the test has its critics, it continues to be used by NFL teams.

Although players for all positions take the Wonderlic, NFL teams pay particular attention to quarterbacks' scores because of the importance of decision making and memory for that position (an NFL playbook is quite extensive).

Here's a select sample of how some NFL quarterbacks scored on the Wonderlic (scores for some NFL quarterbacks, like Matt Cassel, Troy Smith, and Jon Kitna, were unavailable):

30 and higher (very intelligent)
Ryan Fitzpatrick: 48, Alex Smith: 40, Eli Manning: 39, Matthew Stafford: 38, Tony Romo: 37, Sam Bradford: 36, Aaron Rodgers: 35, Tom Brady: 33, Matt Ryan: 32, Brian Brohm: 32, Matt Schaub: 30, Philip Rivers: 30

25–29 (intelligent)
Matt Hasselbeck: 29, Marc Bulger: 29, Peyton Manning: 28, Drew Brees: 28, Mark Sanchez: 28, Joe Flacco: 27, Jason Campbell: 27, Josh Freeman: 27, Jay Cutler: 26, Carson Palmer: 26, Kyle Orton: 26, Colt McCoy: 25, Shaun Hill: 25, Ben Roethlisberger: 25

20–24 (above average)
Jimmy Clausen: 23, Chad Henne: 22, Brett Favre: 22, Tim Tebow: 22, Michael Vick: 20

Less than 20 (average to below average)
Derek Anderson: 19, Bruce Gradkowski: 19, Vince Young: 16, Donovan McNabb: 16, David Garrard: 14, Seneca Wallace: 12

It's clear that NFL quarterbacks are smart—they score well above average relative to the US population (the population average is 19). Do differences among the quarterbacks predict success? Judging from the recent seasons, it's not clear. In the past several seasons, there was not a strong correlation between Wonderlic scores and quarterback ratings (a composite index assessing quarterback performance). On the other hand, if you take an average of the Wonderlic scores of the quarterbacks for the past seven Super Bowl winners, you get a rather lofty average of 30.

Of course, like all selection methods, cognitive ability tests have their limits. George Young, general manager of the New York Giants, was the individual responsible for convincing the NFL to use the Wonderlic. He recalled a game where a defensive lineman with a low test score went up against an offensive lineman with a high score. According to Young, "The defensive lineman told the offensive lineman, 'Don't worry. After I hit you a few times, you'll be just as dumb as I am.'"

SOURCES: M. Mirabile, "NFL Quarterback Wonderlic Scores" (*www.macmirabile.com/Wonderlic.htm*); E. Thompson, "Wonderlic Scores of 2010 NFL Starting Quarterbacks and NFL Draft QB Prospects," *Palm Beach Post*, Mar. 10, 2010, (*www.palmbeachpost.com/sports*); J. Saraceno, "Who Knows if This Longhorn Is Short on IQ," *USA Today*, Mar. 1, 2006, p. 2C; B. Plaschke and E. Almond, "Has the NFL Become a Thinking Man's Game?" *Los Angeles Times*, Apr. 21, 1995.

Why do cognitive ability tests work so well in predicting job performance? Research has shown that most of the effect of cognitive ability tests is due to the fact that intelligent employees learn more on the job and thus have greater job knowledge. As we noted earlier, evidence also suggests that intelligent employees adapt better to changing job conditions, an important skill in many workplaces.[34]

Another important issue in understanding the validity of cognitive ability tests is the nature of specific versus general abilities. Historically, evidence has suggested that specific abilities add little to the prediction of job performance beyond the general factor. Recently, however, this conclusion has been challenged. Researchers in one study argued that specific abilities are sometimes more important than GMA, and another research study suggested that specific cognitive abilities may matter to certain narrow criteria (e.g., perceptual accuracy may predict the degree to which an editor spots errors).[35] Thus, while GMA is the most important predictor of job performance in nearly every situation, there may be situations in which specific abilities are important.

Potential Limitations. If cognitive ability tests are so valid and cheap, why don't more organizations use them? One of the main reasons is concern over the adverse impact and fairness of these tests. In terms of adverse impact, regardless of the type of measure used, cognitive ability tests have severe adverse impact against minorities. Specifically, blacks on average score 1 standard deviation below whites, and Hispanics on average score .72 standard deviations below whites. This means that only 10% of blacks score above the average score for whites.[36] Historically, this led to close scrutiny—and sometimes rejection—of cognitive ability tests by the courts. The issue of fairness of cognitive ability tests has been hotly debated and heavily researched. One way to think of fairness is in terms of accuracy of prediction of a test. If a test predicts job performance with equal accuracy for two groups, such as whites and blacks, then most people would say the test is fair. The problem is that even though the test is equally accurate for both groups, the average test score may be different between the two groups. When this happens, use of the test will cause some degree of adverse impact. This causes a dilemma: Should the organization use the test because it is an accurate and unbiased predictor, or should it not be used because it would cause adverse impact?

Research shows that cognitive ability tests are equally accurate predictors of job performance for various racial and ethnic groups.[37] But research also shows that blacks and Hispanics score lower on such tests than whites. Thus, the dilemma noted above is a real one for the organization. It must decide whether to (1) use the cognitive ability test and experience the positive benefits of using an accurate predictor, (2) not use the cognitive ability test, to avoid adverse impact, and substitute a different measure that has less adverse impact, or (3) use the cognitive ability test in conjunction with other predictors that do not have adverse impact, thus lessening adverse impact overall. Unfortunately, current research does not offer clear guidance on which approach is best. Research suggests that while using other selection measures in conjunction with cognitive ability tests reduces the adverse impact of cognitive ability tests, it by no means eliminates it.[38]

Although the apparent trade-off between diversity and validity is not likely to disappear anytime soon, there have been three positive developments in the cognitive ability testing area. First, one study suggests that tests constructed in an open-ended manner—where the test taker writes in a response—reduces differences in test scores between blacks and whites by 39% while producing equivalent levels of validity, compared with traditional multiple-choice tests. Evidence suggests that open-ended tests reduce group differences because they generate more positive reactions from minority test takers (minority test takers are more likely to see open-ended tests as fair and are more motivated to do well on them). Second, some research suggests the negative effects of cognitive ability testing on diversity can be mitigated by recruiting—by targeted recruiting not only for diversity but also for cognitive ability and personality (e.g., by announcing in recruiting materials that one is looking for smart, diverse, and conscientious applicants).[39] Finally, some evidence suggests that the gap in test scores between whites and blacks is narrowing, perhaps by as much as 10%. Though controversy exists over this issue, if it is true, it would mean that future employers may still face a validity-diversity trade-off, but the trade-off would be less severe.[40]

Another aspect of using cognitive ability tests in selection is concern over applicant reactions. Research on how applicants react to cognitive ability tests is scant and somewhat mixed. One study suggested that 88% of applicants for managerial positions perceived the Wonderlic as job related.[41] Another study, however, demonstrated that applicants thought companies had little need for information obtained from a cognitive ability test.[42] Perhaps one explanation for these conflicting findings is the nature of the test. One study characterized eight cognitive ability tests as either concrete (vocabulary, mathematical word problems) or abstract (letter sets, quantitative comparisons) and found that concrete cognitive ability test items were viewed as job related while abstract test items were not.[43] Thus, while applicants may have mixed reactions to cognitive ability tests, concrete items are less likely to be objectionable. In general, applicants perceive cognitive ability tests to be more valid than personality tests but less valid than interviews or work samples.[44]

Conclusion. In sum, cognitive ability tests are one of the most valid selection measures across jobs; they also predict learning and training success, and predict retention.[45] But they also have some troubling side effects, notably that applicants aren't wild about the tests and that the tests have substantial adverse impact against minorities.

A recent survey of 703 members of the main professional association in which cognitive ability tests are used generated some interesting findings. Among the experts, there were several areas of consensus:[46]

1. Cognitive ability is measured reasonably well by standardized tests.
2. General cognitive ability will become increasingly important in selection as jobs become more complex.
3. The predictive validity of cognitive ability tests depends on how performance is defined and measured.
4. The complex nature of job performance means that cognitive ability tests need to be supplemented with other selection measures.
5. There is more to intelligence than what is measured by a standard cognitive ability test.

Given such prominent advantages and disadvantages, cognitive ability tests are here to stay. But so is the controversy over their use.

Other Types of Ability Tests

Following the earlier classification of abilities into cognitive, psychomotor, physical, and sensory/perceptual, and having just reviewed cognitive ability tests, we now consider the other types of ability tests.

Psychomotor Ability Tests.   Psychomotor ability tests measure the correlation of thought with bodily movement. Involved here are processes such as reaction time, arm-hand steadiness, control precision, and manual and digit dexterity. An example of testing for psychomotor abilities is the test used by the city of Columbus, Ohio, to select firefighters. The test mimics coupling a hose to a fire hydrant, and it requires a certain level of processing with psychomotor abilities to achieve a passing score. Some tests of mechanical ability are psychomotor tests. The *MacQuarrie Test for Mechanical Ability* is a 30-minute test that measures manual dexterity. Seven subtests require tracing, tapping, dotting, copying, and so on.

Physical Abilities Tests.   Physical abilities tests measure muscular strength, cardiovascular endurance, and movement quality.[47] An example of a test that requires all three is the test given to firefighters in the city of Milwaukee, Wisconsin. The test measures upper-body strength (bench press, a lat pulldown, and grip strength pressure), abdominal strength (sit-ups), aerobic endurance (five-minute step tests), and physical mobility (roof ladder placement).[48]

Physical abilities tests are becoming increasingly common to screen out individuals susceptible to repetitive stress injuries, such as carpal tunnel syndrome. One company, Devilbiss Air Power, found that complaints of repetitive stress injuries dropped from 23 to 3 after it began screening applicants for repetitive strain.[49] Physical abilities tests may also be necessary for equal employment opportunity (EEO) reasons.[50] Although female applicants typically score 1.5 standard deviations lower than male applicants on a physical abilities test, the distributions of scores for male and female applicants overlap considerably. Therefore, all applicants must be given a chance to pass requirements and not be judged as a class. Another reason to use physical abilities tests for appropriate jobs is to avoid injuries on the job. Well-designed tests will screen out applicants who have applied for positions that are poorly suited to their physical abilities. Thus, fewer injuries should result. In fact, one study using a concurrent validation approach on a sample of railroad workers found that 57% of all injury costs were due to the 26% of current employees who failed the physical abilities test.[51]

When carefully conducted for appropriate jobs, physical abilities tests can be highly valid. One comprehensive study reported average validities of $\bar{r} = .39$ for warehouse workers to $\bar{r} = .87$ for enlisted army men.[52] Applicant reactions to these sorts of tests are unknown.

Sensory/Perceptual Abilities Tests.   Sensory/perceptual abilities tests assess the ability to detect and recognize environmental stimuli. An example of a sensory/perceptual ability test is a flight simulator used as part of the assessment process for airline pilots. Some tests of mechanical and clerical ability can be considered measures of sensory/perceptual ability, although they take on characteristics of cognitive ability tests. For example, the most commonly used mechanical ability test is the *Bennett Mechanical Comprehension Test*, which contains 68 items that measure an applicant's knowledge of the relationship between physical forces and mechanical objects (e.g., how a pulley operates, how gears function). In terms of clerical tests, the most widely known is the *Minnesota Clerical Test*. This timed test consists of 200 items in which the applicant is asked to compare names or numbers to identify matching elements. For example, an applicant might be asked (needing to work under time constraints) to check the pairs of numbers in the following list for the set that is the same:

109485_____	104985
456836_____	456836
356823_____	536823
890940_____	890904
205837_____	205834

These tests of mechanical and clerical ability and others like them have reliability and validity data available that suggest they are valid predictors of performance within their specific area.[53] The degree to which these tests add validity over general intelligence, however, is not known.

Job Knowledge Tests.   Job knowledge tests attempt to directly assess an applicant's ability to comprehend job requirements. Although generally not marketed as cognitive ability tests per se, not surprisingly, job knowledge test scores tend to correlate highly with cognitive ability test scores.

Job knowledge tests can be of two kinds. One type asks questions that directly assess knowledge of the duties involved in a particular job. For example, an item from a job knowledge test for an oncology nurse might be, "Describe the five oncological emergencies in cancer patients." The other type of job knowledge test focuses on the level of experience with, and corresponding knowledge about, critical job tasks and tools/processes necessary to perform the job. The state of Wisconsin uses an *Objective Inventory Questionnaire* to evaluate applicants on the basis of their experience with tasks, duties, tools, technologies, and equipment that are relevant to a particular job.[54]

There has been less research on the validity of job knowledge tests than on other ability tests. One study, however, provided relatively strong support for the validity of job knowledge tests. A meta-analytic review of 502 studies indicated that the "true" validity of job knowledge tests in predicting job performance is .45. These validities were found to be higher for complex jobs and when job and test content were similar.[55]

Emotional Intelligence Tests

Increasingly, researchers argue that measures of cognitive intelligence miss an important piece of the abilities puzzle, namely, social or emotional intelligence. More and more, organizations are using measures of emotional intelligence (EI) in selection decisions. We consider EI by answering four questions: (1) What is EI? (2) How is EI measured? (3) How valid is EI? and (4) What are the criticisms of EI?

What Is Emotional Intelligence?

One of the most prominent EI researchers defines EI as "the ability to monitor one's own and others' feelings, to discriminate among them, and to use this information to guide one's thinking and action."[56] Thus, EI may be broken down into the following components:

- *Self-awareness:* Good at recognizing and understanding one's own emotions
- *Other awareness:* Good at recognizing and understanding others' emotions
- *Emotion regulation:* Good at making use of or managing this awareness

It's not hard to understand that this concept is important. Wouldn't nearly every employee be more effective if he or she could readily sense what he or she was feeling (and why), sense what others were feeling, and manage his or her own—and others'—emotions?

How Is Emotional Intelligence Measured?

Although there are many variants, EI has mainly been measured in two ways. First, some EI measures are very similar to items contained in a personality test, and, indeed, one review found that such EI items are strongly related to personality, especially to emotional stability and conscientiousness. Second, other EI measures are more ability-focused. For example, some measures involve describing the emotional qualities of certain sounds and images. While these measures bear less similarity to personality measures, they have been criticized for having poor reliability and for their content validity (one measure asks test takers to identify the emotions of colors). Somewhat troubling is the fact that the two types of measures do not appear to assess the same construct. One review revealed that personality-like and ability measures only correlated r = .14.[57]

Of the two types of EI measures, the former—the personality-like variety—is more common. Exhibit 9.6 contains items from a nonproprietary (i.e., free) personality-like EI measure.

How Valid Is Emotional Intelligence?

Evidence suggests that EI is modestly related to job performance. A recent meta-analysis suggests that of the various dimensions of EI, emotion regulation had the highest correlation with job performance, $\overline{r}_{xy} = .18$. This same study found that once individual differences related to EI (cognitive ability, conscientiousness, and emotional stability) were controlled, the relationship between emotion recognition and job performance dropped to .08.[58] Thus, one could conclude that EI has a relatively small and unique effect on job performance, though the effects may be higher with some measures of EI and in certain situations (e.g., jobs that are emotionally demanding).

What Are the Criticisms of Emotional Intelligence?

It's safe to say that EI has proved to be a controversial measure—many criticisms have been offered.[59] First, many researchers have focused on measuring EI, or

---

EXHIBIT 9.6   Sample Items Measuring Emotional Intelligence

Self-awareness
  Generally, I find it difficult to know exactly what emotion I'm feeling.
  I'm generally aware of my emotions as I experience them.

Other awareness
  I often find it difficult to see things from another person's viewpoint.
  I'm normally able to "get into someone's shoes" and experience their emotions.

Emotion regulation
  I usually find it difficult to regulate my emotions.
  I'm usually able to influence the way other people feel.

SOURCE: A. Cooper and K. V. Petrides, "A Psychometric Analysis of the Trait Emotional Intelligence Questionnaire–Short Form (TEIQue-SF) Using Item Response Theory," *Journal of Personality Assessment*, 2010, 92(5), pp. 449–457.

seeing how well EI predicts performance (often to disappointing effect), without paying sufficient attention to what EI might uniquely predict. To understand this, one has to work from the criterion backward. Shouldn't EI better predict empathetic behavior on the part of social workers than predict whether a bank teller's cash drawer will balance?[60] Second, for many researchers, it's not clear what EI is. Is it really a form of intelligence? Most of us wouldn't think that being self-aware or sensitive to others' emotions is a matter of intellect. Beyond this definitional ambiguity, different EI researchers have studied a dizzying array of concepts—including emotion recognition, self-awareness, empathy, self-control, interpersonal skills, stress management, well-being, and self-discipline. One reviewer noted, "The concept of EI has now become so broad and the components so variegated that . . . it is no longer even an intelligible concept."[61] Finally, some critics argue that because EI is so closely related to intelligence and personality, once you control for these factors, EI has nothing unique to offer. We noted earlier evidence showing that controlling for personality and cognitive ability does indeed detract from the validity of EI.[62]

Still, among consulting firms and in the popular press, EI is wildly popular. For example, one organization's promotional materials for an EI measure claimed, "EI accounts for more than 85 percent of star performance in top leaders."[63] To say the least, it's hard to validate this statement with the research literature.

Summary

Although few would deny that emotional awareness and regulation are important for many jobs, EI has proved hard to measure in a way that is valid. Weighing the arguments for and against EI, it's still too early to tell whether the concept is useful. It *is* clear, though, that more and more organizations are using EI measures in selection decisions. If an organization wishes to use an EI measure in selection decisions, we urge a certain amount of caution. At the very least, it should be restricted to jobs with exceptional emotional demands, and the construct and empirical validity of the EI measure used should be investigated before it is used in actual selection decisions.

Performance Tests and Work Samples

Performance tests are mechanisms to assess actual performance rather than underlying capacity or disposition. As such, they are more akin to samples rather than signs of work performance. For example, Chrysler asks applicants for its assembly-line jobs to try assembling auto parts, and applicants for executive-level positions undergo a "day in the life" simulation in which they play the role of plant manager, a process that has been followed by Hyundai and Mitsubishi.[64] Exhibit 9.7 provides examples of performance tests and work samples for a variety of jobs. As can be seen in the exhibit, the potential uses of these selection measures are quite broad in terms of job content and skill level.

EXHIBIT 9.7   Examples of Performance Tests and Work Samples

Professor
Teaching a class while on a campus interview
Reading samples of an applicant's research
Mechanic
Repairing a particular problem on a car
Reading a blueprint
Clerical
Typing test
Proofreading
Cashier
Operating a cash register
Counting money and totaling a balance sheet
Manager
Performing a group problem-solving exercise
Reacting to memos and letters
Airline Pilot
Pilot simulator
Rudder control test
Taxi Cab Driver
Driving test
Street knowledge test
TV Repair Person
Repairing a broken television
Finger and tweezer dexterity test
Police Officer
Check police reports for errors
Shooting accuracy test
Computer Programmer
Programming and debugging test
Hardware replacement test

Types of Tests

Performance Test Versus Work Sample.   A performance test measures what the person actually does on the job. The best examples of performance tests are internships, job tryouts, and probationary periods. Although probationary periods have their uses when one cannot be completely confident in an applicant's ability to perform a job, they are no substitute for a valid prehire selection process. Discharging a probationary employee and finding a replacement is expensive and has numerous legal issues.[65] A work sample is designed to capture parts of the job, for example, a drill press test for machine operators and a programming test for computer programmers.[66] A performance test is more costly to develop than a work sample, but it is usually a better predictor of job performance.

Motor Versus Verbal Work Samples. A motor work sample test involves the physical manipulation of things. Examples include a driving test and a clothes-making test. A verbal work sample test involves a problem situation requiring language skills and interaction with people. Examples include role-playing tests that simulate contact with customers, and an English test for foreign teaching assistants.

High- Versus Low-Fidelity Tests. A high-fidelity test uses realistic equipment and scenarios to simulate the actual tasks of the job. Therefore, it elicits actual responses encountered in performing the task.[67] A good example of a high-fidelity test is one used in the petroleum industry to select truck drivers. The test is on the computer and mimics all the steps taken to load and unload fuel from a tanker to a fuel reservoir at a service station.[68] It is not a test of perfect high fidelity, because fuel is not actually unloaded. It is, however, a much safer test because the dangerous process of fuel transfer is simulated rather than performed. Another example of an organization that uses a high-fidelity test is Station Casino. Most of Station Casino's applicants (more than 800 per week) are customers, so the casino starts off with a very short high-fidelity test (five minutes behind a bank-type counter); applicants then pass through successive simulations, such as assembling a jigsaw puzzle in a group, to assess teamwork skills.[69]

A low-fidelity test simulates the task in a written or verbal description and elicits a written or verbal response rather than an actual response. An example of a low-fidelity test is describing a work situation to job applicants and asking them what they would do in that particular situation. In one study, seven organizations in the telecommunications industry used a written low-fidelity test for the position of manager.[70] Low-fidelity work samples bear many similarities to some types of structured interviews, and in some cases they may be indistinguishable (see "Structured Interview" section).

Work sample tests are becoming more innovative and are increasingly being used for customer service positions. For example, Aon Consulting has developed a web-based simulation called REPeValuator in which applicants assume the role of a customer service specialist. In the simulation, the applicant takes phone calls, participates in Internet chat, and responds to e-mails. The test takes 30 minutes to complete and costs $20 per applicant. The test provides scores on rapport, problem solving, communication, empathy, and listening skills.[71] Another interesting work sample test resembles a job tryout, except that the applicant is not hired or compensated. One small business took a promising applicant on a sales call. In this case, although the applicant looked perfect on paper, the sales call revealed troubling aspects to the applicant's behavior and she wasn't hired.[72] Finally, some technology organizations are hosting "coding competitions" at colleges, where in return for a hefty prize (first-place awards can be as high as $50,000) and a job offer, students can try to develop software or solve a programming problem. The organization gets a chance to spread its brand name and a crack at hiring the best applicants, who have just proved themselves.[73]

Computer Interaction Performance Tests Versus Paper-and-Pencil Tests. As with ability testing, the computer has made it possible to measure aspects of work that are not possible to measure with a paper-and-pencil test. The computer can capture the complex and dynamic nature of work. This is especially true in work where perceptual and motor performance are required.

An example of how the computer can be used to capture the dynamic nature of service work comes from Suntrust Bank. Suntrust has applicants perform some of the same tasks its tellers perform, such as looking up account information and entering customer data. The candidates' reactions to the scenarios, both mental (e.g., comprehension, coding, and calculation) and motor (e.g., typing speed and accuracy), are assessed.[74]

The computer can also be used to capture the complex and dynamic nature of management work. On video, Accu Vision shows the candidate actual job situations likely to be encountered. In turn, the candidate selects a behavioral option in response to each situation. The response is entered into the computer and scored according to what it demonstrates of the skills needed to successfully perform as a manager.[75]

Evaluation

Research indicates that performance or work sample tests have a high degree of validity in predicting job performance. One meta-analysis of a large number of studies suggested that the average validity was $\bar{r} = .54$ in predicting job performance.[76] Because performance tests measure the entire job and work samples measure a part of the job, they also have a high degree of content validity. Thus, when one considers the high degree of empirical and content validity, work samples are perhaps the most valid method of selection for many types of jobs.

Performance tests and work samples have other advantages as well. Research indicates that these measures are widely accepted by applicants as being job related. One study found that no applicants complained about performance tests but that 10%–20% complained about other selection procedures.[77] A study of American workers in a Japanese automotive plant concluded that work sample tests are best able to accommodate cross-cultural values and therefore are well suited for selecting applicants in international joint ventures. Another possible advantage of performance tests and work samples is that they have low degrees of adverse impact, though some evidence suggests that they may have more adverse impact than is commonly thought.[78]

Work samples do have several limitations. The costs of the realism embedded in work samples are high. The closer a predictor comes to simulating actual job performance, the more expensive it becomes to use it. Actually having people perform the job, as with an internship, may require paying a wage. Using videos and computers adds costs as well. As a result, performance tests and work samples are among the most expensive means of selecting workers; their costs are amplified when one considers the lack of generalizability of such measures. Probably more than any other selection method, performance tests and work samples are tied to the specific job at hand. This means that a different test, based on a thorough analysis of the job, will need to be developed for each job. While their validity may well be worth the cost, in some circumstances the costs of work samples may be prohibitive. One means of mitigating the administrative expense associated with performance tests or work samples is to use a two-stage selection process whereby the full set of applicants is reduced using relatively inexpensive tests. Once the initial cut is made, performance tests or work samples can be administered to the smaller group of applicants who demonstrated minimum competency levels on the first-round tests.[79]

Finally, most performance tests and work samples assume that the applicant already possesses the knowledge, skill, ability, and other characteristics (KSAOs) necessary to do the job. If substantial training is involved, applicants will not be able to perform the work sample effectively, even though with adequate training they could be high performers. Thus, if substantial on-the-job training is involved and some or many of the applicants would require this training, work samples simply will not be feasible.

Situational Judgment Tests

A hybrid selection procedure that takes on some of the characteristics of an ability test (especially a job knowledge test) and some of the aspects of a work sample is the situational judgment test. These tests place applicants in hypothetical job-related situations where they are asked to choose a course of action from several alternatives. For example, applicants for a 911 operator position may listen to a series of phone calls and then are asked to choose the best response from a series of multiple-choice alternatives. Or, applicants to be a member of a project team may be confronted with a scenario in which the team is in conflict and the applicant must choose a method to resolve the conflict. Exhibit 9.8 provides two examples of situational judgment test items.

As one can see, there are similarities among situational judgment tests and job knowledge tests and work samples, so much so that the main differentiation in the type of situational judgment test reflects whether the test assesses knowledge (more similar to job knowledge tests) or behavioral tendency (more similar to work samples). There are also distinctions among situational judgment tests and

---

EXHIBIT 9.8 Examples of Situational Judgment Test Items

Retail Industry Manager
You are the assistant manager of a large department store. One weekend day while you are in charge of the store a customer seeks to return a pair of tennis shoes. The employee in charge of the customer service department refused to accept the return. The customer asked to speak to the manager, and so the employee paged you. Upon meeting the customer—who is clearly agitated—you learn that the customer does not have a receipt, and, moreover, you see that the shoes are clearly well worn. When you ask the customer why she is returning the shoes, she tells you that she has bought many pairs of shoes from your store, and in the past they have "held up much better over time than these." You recognize the shoes as a brand that your store has stocked, so you have no reason to believe the customer is lying when she says that she bought them from your store. Still, the shoes have clearly been worn for a long time. Should you:
  a. Issue a refund to the customer
  b. Check with your boss—the store manager—when he is at the store on Monday
  c. Deny a refund to the customer, explaining that the shoes are simply too worn to be returned
  d. Inform the customer of the current sale prices on comparable tennis shoes

Park Ranger
You are a park ranger with the National Park Service, stationed in Yellowstone National Park. One of your current duties is to scout some of the park's more obscure trails to look for signs of lost hikers, to detect any malfeasance, and to inspect the conditions of the trails. It is mid-September, and you're inspecting one of the more remote trails in the Mount Washburn area to determine whether it should be closed for the season. When you set out on your hike, the forecast called for only a slight chance of snow, but midway through your hike, an early fall blizzard has struck. For a time you persisted on, but later you took refuge under a large lodgepole pine tree. Although the storm is now abating, it is near dark. Which of the following would be your best course of action?
  a. Stay put until help comes
  b. Reverse course and hike back to the ranger station
  c. Once the clouds clear, locate the North Star, and hike north to the nearest ranger station
  d. Use your matches to build a fire, and hike back in the morning

job knowledge tests and work samples. A job knowledge test more explicitly taps the content of the job (areas that applicants are expected to know immediately upon hire), whereas situational judgment tests are more likely to deal with future hypothetical job situations. Furthermore, job knowledge tests are less "holistic" than situational judgment tests in that the latter are more likely to include video clips and other more realistic material. Situational judgment tests differ from work samples in that the former presents applicants with multiple-choice responses to the scenarios, whereas in the latter, applicants actually engage in behavior that is observed by others.

The principal argument in favor of situational judgment tests is to capture the validity of work samples and cognitive ability tests in a way that is cheaper than work samples and that has less adverse impact than cognitive ability tests. How well are these aims achieved? A recent meta-analysis of the validity of situational judgment tests indicated that such tests are reasonably valid correlates of job performance ($\bar{r}_{xy}$ = .26).[80] Research also suggests that situational judgment tests have less (but not zero) adverse impact against minorities.[81] Furthermore, video-based situational judgment tests appear to generate positive applicant reactions.[82]

One possible limitation of situational judgment tests is that while they are easier to administer than work sample tests, and have less adverse impact and more positive applicant reactions than cognitive ability tests, they are not as valid as work sample tests or job knowledge tests. Moreover, because situational judgment tests are generally significantly correlated with cognitive ability ($\bar{r}_{xy}$ = .32) and personality (especially conscientiousness, $\bar{r}_{xy}$ = .27), there is reason to worry about whether they have incremental validity beyond cognitive ability and personality. Some studies have shown that they do.[83] However, other studies have shown little or no incremental validity.[84] In the aforementioned meta-analysis, the average incremental validity contributed by situational judgment tests over cognitive ability and personality tests was only Δr = .02. As the authors note, this is not the last word on the incremental validity of situational judgment tests. However, given the recent attention focused on situational judgment tests, one might well wonder, "Where's the beef?"

If situational judgment tests are used, three important decisions must be made. First, there is the issue of format. The two main formats of situational judgment tests are written and video. With video tests, applicants first view a video clip that typically involves a role-play episode (e.g., an employee whom the applicant is assumed to supervise asks for advice about a personal matter) and then are asked to choose from a list of responses. Some evidence suggests that video-based situational judgment tests have less adverse impact than written ones and may have higher levels of incremental validity.[85]

Second, there is the issue of scoring. Although general scoring schemes are often developed so that responses can be quickly recorded and scores computed, care needs to be taken in developing the scoring scheme. Generally, the more knowledge the scorer has about the specific requirements of the job, the more valid situational judgment test scores will be.[86]

Third, another issue that must be considered is which constructs should be measured. Of course, job analysis should be the guide here: Constructs that job analysis has suggested are important to perform the job should be assessed. More generally, research indicates that some constructs measured by situational judgment tests appear to be more valid than others. Specifically, research indicates that situational judgment tests that measure leadership, personal initiative, and team-work tend to best predict job performance. That may be because these constructs are not well measured by other means (i.e., situational judgment tests measure these important aspects distinctly well).[87]

Integrity Tests

When asked to identify the qualities desired in ideal job applicants, employers routinely put honesty and integrity at the top of their list. In a recent survey, college recruiters were asked to rate the importance of various skills/qualities in job candidates on a 1 = *not important* to 5 = *extremely important* scale. The following skills/qualities were the six most highly rated:[88]

1. Honesty/integrity	4.7
2. Communication skills (oral and written)	4.7
3. Interpersonal skills (relates well to others)	4.5
4. Motivation/initiative	4.5
5. Strong work ethic	4.5
6. Teamwork skills	4.5

Clearly, integrity is an important quality in applicants; integrity tests are designed to tap this important attribute.

Integrity tests are paper-and-pencil or computerized tests that attempt to assess an applicant's honesty and moral character. They are alternatives to other methods—such as polygraph (so-called lie detector) tests or interviewer evaluations—that attempt to ascertain an applicant's honesty and morality. For most employers, polygraph tests are prohibited by law. Even if they were legal, polygraphs are so invasive that negative applicant reactions would weigh against their use in most situations. Interviewer evaluations of applicant integrity are, of course, not illegal, but they are unreliable as a method of detecting dishonesty, as dishonesty is very hard to detect. Even experts such as FBI agents, judges, and psychologists scarcely perform above chance in detecting lying. A review of 108 studies revealed that people detect lies at a rate that is only 4.2% better than chance.[89] For these reasons, integrity tests are seen as a superior alternative to polygraph tests and interviews, and indeed the use of integrity tests in selection decisions has grown dramatically in the past decade. The tests are especially likely to be used where theft, safety, or malfeasance is an important concern. For example, retail organizations lose an estimated $19 billion per year to employee theft, and it might surprise you to learn that theft due to employees accounts for roughly half (46.8%) of all inventory shrinkage—much greater than that attributed to shoplifting (31.6%).[90] The promise of integrity testing is that it will weed out those most prone to these counter-productive work behaviors.[91]

Measures

There are two major types of integrity tests: clear purpose (sometimes called overt) and general purpose (sometimes called veiled purpose or personality-oriented). Exhibit 9.9 provides examples of items from both types of measures. Clear purpose tests directly assess employee attitudes toward theft. Such tests often consist of two sections: (1) questions of antitheft attitudes (see items 1 and 2 in Exhibit 9.9), and (2) questions about the frequency and degree of involvement in theft or other counterproductive activities (see items 3 and 4 in Exhibit 9.9).[92] General or veiled purpose integrity tests assess employee personality with the idea that personality influences dishonest behavior (see items 5–8 in Exhibit 9.9). The most commonly used clear purpose or overt integrity tests are the *Personnel Selection Inventory*, the *Reid Report*, and the *Stanton Survey*. The most commonly used general or veiled purpose tests are the *Personnel Reaction Blank*, the *PDI Employment Survey*, and the *Reliability Scale of the Hogan Employment Inventory*.[93]

Some have suggested that integrity represents a sixth personality factor, something unique from the Big Five traits.[94] However, most researchers believe that scores on integrity tests reflect a broad or "compound" personality trait that is a combination of several Big Five personality traits. Specifically, integrity test scores appear to reflect conscientiousness, agreeableness, and emotional stability.[95] Regardless of which aspects of personality integrity tests measure, it appears that they predict workplace deviance or counterproductive behaviors better than any of the individual Big Five traits.

EXHIBIT 9.9   Sample Integrity Test Questions

Clear Purpose or Overt Test Questions

1. Do you think most people would cheat if they thought they could get away with it?
2. Do you believe a person has a right to steal from an employer if he or she is unfairly treated?
3. Did you ever write a check knowing there was not enough money in the bank?
4. Have you ever stolen anything?

Veiled Purpose or Personality-Based Test Questions

5. Would you rather go to a party than read a newspaper?
6. How often do you blush?
7. Do you almost always make your bed?
8. Do you like to take chances?

Validity of Integrity Tests

A major meta-analysis of more than 500,000 people and more than 650 individual studies suggests that integrity tests have surprising levels of validity.[96] The principal findings from this study are the following:

1. Both clear and general purpose integrity tests are valid predictors of counterproductive behaviors (actual and admitted theft, dismissals for theft, illegal activities, absenteeism, tardiness, and workplace violence). The average validity for clear purpose measures ($\bar{r} = .55$) was higher than for general purpose ($\bar{r} = .32$).
2. Both clear and general purpose tests are valid predictors of job performance ($\bar{r} = .33$ and $\bar{r} = .35$, respectively).
3. Limiting the analysis to estimates using a predictive validation design and actual detection of theft lowers the validity to $\bar{r} = .13$.
4. Integrity tests have no adverse impact against women or minorities and are relatively uncorrelated with intelligence. Thus, integrity tests demonstrate incremental validity over cognitive ability tests and reduce the adverse impact of cognitive ability tests.

Results from this comprehensive study suggest that organizations would benefit from using integrity tests for a wide array of jobs. Since most of the individual studies included in the meta-analysis were conducted by test publishers (who have an interest in finding good results), however, organizations using integrity tests should consider conducting their own validation studies.

Criticisms and Concerns

Faking. One of the most significant concerns with the use of integrity tests is the obvious possibility that applicants might fake their responses. Consider answering the questions in Exhibit 9.9. Now consider answering these questions in the context of applying for a job that you want. It seems more than plausible that applicants might distort their responses in such a context (particularly given that most of the answers would be impossible to verify). This possibility becomes a real concern when one considers the prospect that the individuals most likely to "fake good" (people behaving dishonestly) are exactly the type of applicants organizations would want to weed out.

Embedded within the issue of faking are three questions: (1) Can integrity tests be faked? (2) Do applicants fake or enhance their responses to integrity tests? and (3) Does faking harm the validity of the tests, such that a "perverse inversion" occurs where those who get high scores are those who have the least integrity (fake the most)?

First, it is clear that applicants can fake their scores when instructed or otherwise sufficiently motivated to do so, just as they can with personality tests. Studies that compare individuals who are asked to respond honestly with those who are told to "fake good" reveal that, unsurprisingly, integrity test scores in the "fake condition" situation are higher.

Second, a problem with interpreting whether applicants *can* fake is that it doesn't tell us whether they indeed *do* fake. After all, job applicants certainly aren't told to "fake good" when completing employment tests, and many applicants may not purposely enhance their responses out of moral reasons (they feel it would be wrong to enhance) or practical reasons (they believe enhancements would be detected). Unfortunately, there is much less evidence on this second question. As one review noted, "A generally unanswered question is whether job applicants actually do fake on integrity tests."[97]

Finally, in terms of whether faking matters, if faking was pervasive, integrity test scores would either have no validity in predicting performance from applicant scores or have *negative* validity (honest applicants reporting worse scores than dishonest applicants). The fact that validity was positive for applicant samples suggests that if faking does occur, it does not severely impair the predictive validity of integrity tests. It has been suggested that dishonest applicants do not fake more than honest applicants, because they believe that everyone is dishonest and therefore they are reporting only what everyone else already does. No matter what the reason, it does seem clear that if faking is a problem, it is not sufficient enough to undermine the validity of the tests.

Misclassification and Stigmatization.   Some object to integrity tests on the basis of applicants being misclassified as dishonest.[98] In a sense, this is an odd objection in that all selection procedures involve misclassification of individuals because all selection methods are imperfect (having validities less than 1.0). We think the larger issue is the possible stigmatization of applicants who are thought to be dishonest due to their test scores. These problems can be avoided with proper procedures for maintaining the security and confidentiality of test scores (which, of course, should be done in any case).

Negative Applicant Reactions.   A meta-analysis compared applicant reactions to 10 selection procedures, including interviews, work samples, cognitive ability tests, and integrity tests. The results revealed that applicants react negatively to integrity tests—indeed, their favorability ratings were lower than all methods except graphology (handwriting analysis).[99] It is likely that applicants react quite differently to various kinds of integrity test questions, and that applicants' negative reactions might be mollified with explanations and administrative instructions. Unfortunately, there is little published research on these issues.

Interest, Values, and Preference Inventories

Interest, values, and preference inventories attempt to assess the activities individuals prefer to do both on and off the job. This is in comparison with predictors that measure whether the person can do the job. However, just because a person can do a job does not guarantee success on the job. If the person does not want to do the job, that individual will fail, regardless of ability. Although interests seem important, they have not been used very much in human resource (HR) selection.

Standardized tests of interests, values, and preferences are available. Many of these measure vocational interests (e.g., the type of career that would motivate and satisfy someone) rather than organizational interests (e.g., the type of job or organization that would motivate and satisfy someone). The two most widely used interest inventories are the *Strong Vocational Interest Blank* (SVIB) and the *Myers-Briggs Type Inventory* (MBTI). Rather than classify individuals along continuous dimensions (e.g., someone is more or less conscientious than another), both the SVIB and the MBTI classify individuals into distinct categories based on their responses to the survey. With the MBTI, individuals are classified into 16 types that have been found to be related to the Big Five personality characteristics discussed earlier.[100] Example interest inventory items are provided in Exhibit 9.10. The SVIB classifies individuals into six categories (realistic, investigative, artistic, social, enterprising, and conventional) that match jobs that are characterized in a corresponding manner. Both of these inventories are used extensively in career counseling in high school, college, and trade schools.

Past research has suggested that interest inventories are not valid predictors of job performance. In past research, the average validity of interest inventories in predicting job performance was estimated to be roughly $\bar{r}_{xy} = .10$. However, a more recent review of more than 400 studies suggested more positive conclusions.[101] Specifically, vocational interests organized by Holland's six occupational types (realistic, investigative, artistic, social, enterprising, and conventional) predicted various criteria (investigative scores were positively related to task performance; artistic scores negatively so), though these validities were not strong (less than .20 in all cases).

Even if interest inventories are modest predictors of performance, this does not mean that they are invalid for all purposes. Research clearly suggests that when individuals' interests match those of their occupation, they are happier with their jobs and are more likely to remain in their chosen occupation.[102] Thus, although interest inventories fail to predict job performance, they do predict occupational choices and job satisfaction levels. Undoubtedly, one of the reasons why vocational interests are poorly related to job performance is because the interests are tied to the occupation rather than the organization or the job.

Research suggests that while interest inventories play an important role in vocational choice, their role in organizational selection decisions is limited. However, a more promising way of considering the role of interests and values in the staffing process is to focus on person/organization fit.[103] As was discussed in Chapter 1, person/organization fit argues that it is not the applicants' characteristics alone that influence performance but rather the interaction between the applicants' characteristics and those of the organization. For example, an individual with a strong inter-

---

EXHIBIT 9.10   Sample Items From Interest Inventory

1. Are you usually:
   (a) A person who loves parties
   (b) A person who prefers to curl up with a good book?

2. Would you prefer to:
   (a) Run for president
   (b) Fix a car?

3. Is it a higher compliment to be called:
   (a) A compassionate person
   (b) A responsible person?

4. Would you rather be considered:
   (a) Someone with much intuition
   (b) Someone guided by logic and reason?

5. Do you more often:
   (a) Do things on the "spur of the moment"
   (b) Plan out all activities carefully in advance?

6. Do you usually get along better with:
   (a) Artistic people
   (b) Realistic people?

7. With which statement do you most agree?
   (a) Learn what you are, and be such.
   (b) Ah, but a man's reach should exceed his grasp, or what's a heaven for?

8. At parties and social gatherings, do you more often:
   (a) Introduce others
   (b) Get introduced?

est in social relations at work may perform well in an organization that emphasizes cooperation and teamwork, but the same individual might do poorly in an organization whose culture is characterized by independence or rugged individualism. Thus, interest and value inventories may be more valid when they consider the match between applicant values and organizational values (person/organization fit).[104]

Structured Interview

The structured interview is a very standardized, job-related method of assessment. It requires careful and thorough construction, as described in the sections that follow. It is instructive to compare the structured job interview with an unstructured or psychological interview. This comparison will serve to highlight the differences between the two.

A typical unstructured interview has the following characteristics:

- It is often unplanned, informal, and quick, and the interviewer often spends little time preparing for it.
- Rather than being based on the requirements of the job, questions are based on interviewer "hunches" or "pet questions" in order to psychologically diagnose applicant suitability.
- It consists of casual, open-ended, or subjective questioning (e.g., "Tell me a little bit about yourself").
- It has obtuse questions (e.g., "What type of animal would you most like to be, and why?").
- It has highly speculative questions (e.g., "Where do you see yourself 10 years from now?").
- The interviewer makes a quick, and final, evaluation of the candidate (often in the first couple of minutes).

Despite its continued prevalence—it remains the most widely used substantive selection procedure—research shows that organizations clearly pay a price for using the unstructured interview, namely, lower reliability and validity.[105] Interviewers using the unstructured interview are unable to agree among themselves in their evaluation of job candidates and cannot predict the job success of candidates with any degree of consistent accuracy.

Over the years, research has unraveled the reasons why the unstructured interview does not work well and what factors need to be changed to improve reliability and validity. Sources of error or bias in the unstructured interview include the following:[106]

- Reliability of the unstructured interview is relatively low. Interviewers base their evaluations on different factors, have different hiring standards, and differ in the degree to which their actual selection criteria match their intended criteria.
- Applicant physical attractiveness has consistently been shown to predict interviewer evaluations.
- Negative information receives more weight than positive information in the interview. Research suggests it takes more than twice as much positive information as negative information to change an interviewer's initial impression of an applicant. As a result, the unstructured interview has been labeled a "search for negative evidence."
- Interviewers tend to make snap decisions—people's first impressions form after only 1/10 of one second, and the majority of interviewers make their decisions after the first few minutes of the interview.
- Interviewers place weight on superficial background characteristics such as names and the presence of accents. One study found that when responding

to actual employment ads in Boston and Chicago, fictitious applicants with the first names of Allison and Brad were twice as likely to receive interview invitations than individuals with the first names of Kenya and Hakim, even though the résumés were otherwise identical.

- Evaluations from unstructured interviews are particularly affected by applicant impression management and nonverbal behavior.
- Similarity effects—where applicants who are similar to the interviewer with respect to race, gender, or other characteristics receive higher ratings—also exist.
- Poor recall by interviewers often plagues unstructured interviews. One study demonstrated this by giving managers an exam based on factual information after watching a 20-minute videotaped interview. Some managers got all 20 questions correct, but the average manager got only half right.

Thus, the unstructured interview is not very valid, and research has identified the reasons why. The structured interview is an attempt to eliminate the biases inherent in unstructured formats by standardizing the process.

Characteristics of Structured Interviews

There are numerous hallmarks of structured interviews. Some of the more prominent characteristics are the following: (1) questions are based on job analysis, (2) the same questions are asked of each candidate, (3) the response to each question is numerically evaluated, (4) detailed anchored rating scales are used to score each response, and (5) detailed notes are taken, particularly focusing on interviewees' behaviors.[107]

There are two principal types of structured interviews: situational and experience based. Situational interviews assess an applicant's ability to project what his or her behavior would be in future hypothetical situations.[108] The assumption behind the use of the situational interview is that the goals or intentions individuals set for themselves are good predictors of what they will do in the future.

Experience-based or job-related interviews assess past behaviors that are linked to the prospective job. The assumption behind the use of experience-based interviews is the same as that for the use of biodata: past behavior is a good predictor of future behavior. It is assumed that applicants who are likely to succeed have demonstrated success with past job experiences similar to the experiences they would encounter in the prospective job. An example of an experience-based interview is the *Patterned Behavior Description Interview*, which collects four types of experiential information during the interview: (1) credentials (objective verifiable information about past experiences and accomplishments), (2) experience descriptions (descriptions of applicant's normal job duties, capabilities, and responsibilities), (3) opinions (applicant's thoughts about his or her strengths, weaknesses, and self-perceptions), and (4) behavior descriptions (detailed accounts of actual events from the applicant's job and life experiences).[109]

Situational and experience-based interviews have many similarities. Generally, both are based on the critical incidents approach to job analysis, where job behaviors especially important to (as opposed to typically descriptive of) job performance are considered. Also, both approaches attempt to assess applicant *behaviors* rather than feelings, motives, values, or other psychological states. Finally, both methods have substantial reliability and validity evidence in their favor.

On the other hand, situational and experience-based interviews have important differences. The most obvious difference is that situational interviews are future oriented ("what *would* you do if?"), whereas experience-based interviews are past oriented ("what *did* you do when?"). Also, situational interviews are more standardized in that they ask the same questions of all applicants, while many experience-based interviews place an emphasis on discretionary probing based on responses to particular questions. Presently, there is little basis to guide decisions about which of these two types of structured interviews should be adopted. However, one factor to consider is that experience-based interviews may only be relevant for individuals who have had significant job experience. It does not make much sense to ask applicants what they did in a particular situation if they have never been in that situation. Another relevant factor is complexity of the job. Situational interviews fare worse than experience-based interviews when the job is complex. This may be because it is hard to simulate the nature of complex jobs.

Evaluation

Traditionally, the employment interview was thought to have a low degree of validity. Recently, however, evidence for the validity of structured (and even unstructured) interviews has been much more positive. Meta-analyses have suggested the following conclusions:[110]

1. The average validity of interviews is $\bar{r} = .37$.
2. Structured interviews are more valid ($\bar{r} = .31$) than unstructured interviews ($\bar{r} = .23$).
3. The literature on whether situational or experience-based interviews are more valid is not consistent. The largest meta-analysis found that situational interviews were more valid ($\bar{r} = .35$) than experience-based interviews ($\bar{r} = .28$). However, a more recent meta-analysis found the opposite.
4. Panel interviews may be *less* valid ($\bar{r} = .22$) than individual interviews ($\bar{r} = .31$).

Given the advantages of structured interviews, their lack of use is perplexing— whereas 99% of organizations indicate they use the interview in selection, only slightly more than half (55%) claim to use a structured interview. As one review concluded, "Structured interviews are infrequently used in practice." Like all of us, selection decision makers show considerable inertia and continue to use the unstructured interview because they always have, and because they favor expediency over quality. Thus, a cycle of past practice generating continued use needs to be broken by changing the climate. The best way to do this is to educate decision makers about the benefits of structured interviews.[111]

Applicants tend to react very favorably to the interview, whether it is structured or not. Research suggests that most applicants believe the interview is an essential component of the selection process, and most view the interview as the most suitable measure of relevant abilities. As a result, applicants have rated the interview as more job related than any other selection procedure.[112]

The interview appears to have moderate adverse impact against minorities—more than personality tests but considerably less than cognitive ability tests.[113]

Structuring an interview requires that organizations follow a systematic and standardized process. For illustration purposes, we describe development of a situational interview.

Constructing a Structured Interview

The structured interview, by design and conduct, standardizes and controls for sources of influence on the interview process and the interviewer. The goal is to improve interview reliability and validity beyond that of the unstructured interview. Research shows that this goal can be achieved; doing so requires following each of these steps: consult the job requirements matrix, develop the selection plan, develop the structured interview plan, select and train interviewers, and evaluate effectiveness. Each of these steps is elaborated on next.

The Job Requirements Matrix and Selection Plan

The starting point for the structured interview is the job requirements matrix. It identifies the tasks and KSAOs that define the job requirements around which the structured interview is constructed and conducted.

Because the selection plan flows from the KSAOs identified in the job requirements matrix, it helps identify which KSAOs are necessary to assess during selection and whether the structured interview is the preferred method of assessing them.

Is the KSAO Necessary?   Some KSAOs must be brought to the job by the candidate, and others can be acquired on the job (through training and/or job experience). The bring-it/acquire-it decision must be made for each KSAO, and it should be guided by the importance indicator(s) for the KSAOs in the job requirements matrix.

Is the Structured Interview the Preferred Method?   It must be decided whether the structured interview is the preferred method of assessing each KSAO necessary for selection. Several factors should be considered when making this decision. The structured interview is probably best suited for assessing only the more interpersonal or face-to-face skills and abilities, such as communication and interpersonal skills.

An example of a selection plan for the job of sales associate in a retail clothing store is shown in Exhibit 9.11. While there were five task dimensions for the job in the job requirements matrix (customer service, use of machines, use of customer service outlets, sales and departmental procedures, and cleaning and maintenance), the selection plan is shown only for the dimension of customer service.

Note in the exhibit that the customer service dimension has several required KSAOs. However, only some of these will be assessed during selection, and only some of those will be assessed by the structured interview. The method of assessment is thus carefully targeted to the KSAO to be assessed.

The Structured Interview Plan

Development of the structured interview plan proceeds along three sequential steps: construction of interview questions, construction of benchmark responses for the questions, and weighting of the importance of the questions. The output of this process for the sales associate job is shown in Exhibit 9.12 and is referred to in the discussion that follows.

Constructing Questions.   One or more questions must be constructed for each KSAO targeted for assessment by the structured interview. Care must be taken to ensure that the questions reflect a sampling of the candidate's behavior, as revealed by past situations (behavioral description) or what the candidate reports would be his or her behavior in future situations (situational). The questions ask, in essence, "What have you done in this situation?" and "What would you do if you were in this situation?"

The key to constructing both types of questions is to create a scenario relevant to the KSAO in question and to ask the candidate to respond to it by way of answering

---

EXHIBIT 9.11   Partial Selection Plan for Job of Retail Store Sales Associate

KSAO	Necessary for Selection?	Method of Assessment
Task Dimension: Customer Service		
1. Ability to make customer feel welcome	Yes	Interview
2. Knowledge of merchandise to be sold	Yes	Written test
3. Knowledge of location of merchandise in store	No	None
4. Skill in being cordial with customers	Yes	Interview
5. Ability to create and convey ideas to customers ...	Yes	Interview

EXHIBIT 9.12   Structured Interview Questions, Benchmark Responses, Rating Scale, and Question Weights

Job: Sales Associate
Task Dimension: Customer Service

Question	Rating Scale 1	2	3	4	5	Rating	×	Weight	=	Score
Question No. One (KSAO 1) A customer walks into the store. No other salespeople are around to help the person, and you are busy arranging merchandise. What would you do if you were in this situation?	Keep on arranging merchandise		Keep working, but greet the customer		Stop working, greet customer, and offer to provide assistance	5		1		5
Question No. Two (KSAO 4) A customer is in the fitting room and asks you to bring her some shirts to try on. You do so, but by accident bring the wrong size. The customer becomes irate and starts shouting at you. What would you do if you were in this situation?	Tell customer to "keep her cool"		Go get correct size		Apologize, go get correct size	3		1		3
Question No. Three (KSAO 5) A customer is shopping for the "right" shirt for her 17-year-old granddaughter. She asks you to show her shirts that you think would be "right" for her. You do this, but the customer doesn't like any of them. What would you do if you were in this situation?	Tell customer to go look elsewhere		Explain why you think your choices are good ones		Explain your choices, suggest gift certificate as alternative	5		2		10
										18

a question. If one plans on considering applicants with limited prior experience, future-oriented or situational questions should be favored over behavioral description questions, since not all applicants will have been in the situation previously.

Exhibit 9.12 shows three questions for the KSAOs to be assessed by the interview, as determined by the initial selection plan for the job of sales associate in a retail store. As can be seen, all three questions present very specific situations that a sales associate is likely to encounter. The content of all three questions is clearly job relevant, a logical outgrowth of the process that began with the development of the job requirements matrix.

Developing Benchmark Responses and Rating Scales.   The interviewer must somehow evaluate or judge the quality of the candidate's response to the interview questions. Prior development of benchmark responses and corresponding rating scales will provide firm guidance to the interviewer in doing this task. Benchmark responses represent qualitative examples of the types of candidate responses that the interviewer may encounter. They are located on a rating scale (usually 1–5 or 1–7 rating scale points) to represent the level or "goodness" of the response.

Exhibit 9.12 contains benchmark responses, positioned on a 1–5 rating scale, for each of the three interview questions. Note that all the responses are quite specific and that some answers are better than others. These responses represent judgments on the part of the organization as to the desirability of behaviors its employees could engage in.

Weighting Responses.   Each candidate will receive a total score for the structured interview. It thus must be decided whether each question is of equal importance in contributing to the total score. If so, the candidate's total interview score is simply the sum of the scores on the individual rating scales. If some questions are more important than others in assessing candidates, those questions receive greater weight. The more important the question, the greater its weight relative to the other questions.

Exhibit 9.12 shows the weighting decided on for the three interview questions. The first two questions receive a weight of 1, and the third question receives a weight of 2. The candidate's assigned ratings are multiplied by their weights and then summed to determine a total score for this particular task dimension. In the exhibit, the candidate receives a score of 18 (5 + 3 + 10 = 18) for customer service. The candidate's total interview score would be the sum of the scores on all the dimensions.

Selection and Training of Interviewers

Some interviewers are more accurate in their judgments than others. In fact, several studies have found significant differences in interviewer validity and that even in structured interviews many interviewers form lasting early impressions.[114] Thus, rather than asking, "How valid is the interview?" it might be more appropriate to ask, "Who is a valid interviewer?" Answering this question requires selecting interviewers with characteristics that will enable them to make accurate decisions about applicants. Little research is available regarding the factors that should guide selection of interviewers. Perhaps not surprisingly, cognitive ability has been linked to accuracy in evaluating others. It would also be possible to design an interview simulation where prospective interviewers are asked to analyze jobs to determine applicant KSAOs, preview applications, conduct hypothetical interviews, and evaluate applicants.

Interviewers will probably need training in the structured interview process, as it may be quite different from what they have encountered and/or used. Training is a way of introducing them to the process, and it is another means of increasing the validity of structured interviews. Logical program content areas to be covered as part of the training are the following:

- Problems with the unstructured interview
- Advantages of the structured interview
- Development of the structured interview
- Use of note taking and elimination of rating errors
- Actual practice in conducting the structured interview

Research on whether interviewer training works is inconsistent. One review concluded that the evidence regarding the ability of training programs to reduce rating errors showed that these programs "have achieved at best mixed results."[115] However, a more recent study revealed that an interviewer training program was effective, in no small part because it increased the degree to which a structured format was followed.[116] Given that interviewers tend not to use structured formats, this is a key advantage.

Evaluating Effectiveness

As with any assessment device, there is a constant need to learn more about the reliability, validity, and utility of the structured interview. This is particularly so because of the complexity of the interview process. Thus, evaluation of the structured interview's effectiveness should be built into the process.

Selection for Team Environments

Decades ago, when companies such as W. L. Gore and General Foods used work teams, it was news. Nowadays, of course, teams are pervasive. One of the main reasons organizations have turned to teams is that they feel teams are more flexible and responsive to changing events. They may also believe that teams operate more efficiently than individuals working alone. Or, they may wish to make teamwork a part of their culture as a way to democratize themselves and increase employee motivation.[117]

There are as many types of teams as there are configurations of individuals. However, teams can be clustered into four categories:[118] (1) problem-solving teams, or teams where members share ideas or offer suggestions on how work processes can be improved (though they rarely have the authority to unilaterally implement any of their suggested actions), (2) self-managed work teams, where groups of typically 10–15 employees perform highly related or interdependent jobs and take on many of the responsibilities of their former supervisors, (3) cross-functional teams, or teams made up of employees from roughly the same hierarchical level but from different work areas or functions, and (4) virtual teams, or teams that use computers to tie together physically dispersed members in order to achieve a common goal or work on a single project.

No matter the reason for the existence of teams, or the type of team involved, teamwork means revisiting the way work is done in an organization, which necessarily affects how positions are staffed.

The first step in understanding the proper steps for selection in team-based environments is to understand the requirements of the job. This involves determining the knowledge, skills, and abilities (KSAs) required for teamwork. For example, to be effective in a teamwork assignment, an employee may need to demonstrate *interpersonal KSAs* (consisting of conflict resolution, collaborative problem solving, and communication KSAs) and *self-management KSAs* (consisting of goal setting and performance management KSAs, and planning and task coordination KSAs).

One means of incorporating team-based KSAs into the existing selection process has been developed.[119] Exhibit 9.13 provides some sample items from the 35-item test. This test has been validated against three criteria (teamwork performance, technical performance, and overall performance) in two studies.[120] The teamwork test showed substantial validity in predicting teamwork and overall performance in one of the studies, but no validity in predicting any of the criteria in the other study. (It is not clear why the teamwork test worked well in one study and not in the other.) It should be noted that tests are not the only method of measuring teamwork KSAs. Other methods of assessment that some leading companies have used in selecting team members include structured interviews, assessment centers, personality tests, and biographical inventories.[121] For example, one research study developed and validated a situational judgment test to assess team role orientation. One scenario from the situational judgment test is paraphrased below:

> Assume the role of a sales team member at a bookstore. The bookstore has been experiencing rapidly declining sales, and the team was tasked with finding solutions to the problem. During the meeting, the discussion became heated when one team member blamed the problem on the two new sales representatives. One of the new sales representatives reacted angrily to the accusation and made accusations of his own. The other new sales representative simply stared at the floor. How would you respond?

Applicants choose one of four responses, the best of which was: "Remind the two sales reps that personal attacks are not appropriate and that the team should

---

EXHIBIT 9.13   Example Items Assessing Teamwork KSAs

1. Suppose that you find yourself in an argument with several coworkers about who should do a very disagreeable but routine task. Which of the following would likely be the most effective way to resolve this situation?
   A.   Have your supervisor decide, because this would avoid any personal bias.
   B.   Arrange for a rotating schedule so everyone shares the chore.
   C.   Let the workers who show up earliest choose on a first-come, first-served basis.
   D.   Randomly assign a person to do the task and don't change it.

2. Your team wants to improve the quality and flow of the conversations among its members. Your team should:
   A.   Use comments that build on and connect to what others have said.
   B.   Set up a specific order for everyone to speak and then follow it.
   C.   Let team members with more to say determine the direction and topic of conversation.
   D.   Do all of the above.

3. Suppose you are presented with the following types of goals. You are asked to pick one for your team to work on. Which would you choose?
   A.   An easy goal to ensure the team reaches it, thus creating a feeling of success.
   B.   A goal of average difficulty so the team will be somewhat challenged, but successful without too much effort.
   C.   A difficult and challenging goal that will stretch the team to perform at a high level, but attainable so that effort will not be seen as futile.
   D.   A very difficult, or even impossible goal so that even if the team falls short, it will at least have a very high target to aim for.

SOURCE: M. J. Stevens and M. A. Campion, "The Knowledge, Skill, and Ability Requirements for Teamwork: Implications for Human Resource Management," *Journal of Management*, 1994, 20, pp. 503–530. With permission from Elsevier Science.

focus on the future solutions." This study revealed that scores on the test were correlated r = .30 with team role performance in a sample of 82 production and maintenance teams.[122]

Another important decision in team member selection is who should make the hiring decisions. In many cases, team assessments are made by members of the self-directed work team in deciding who becomes a member of the group. An example of an organization following this procedure is South Bend, Indiana–based I/N Tek, a billion-dollar steel-finishing mill established in a joint venture between the United States' Inland Steel and Japan's Nippon Steel. Employees in self-directed work teams, along with managers and HR professionals, interview candidates as a final step in the selection process. This approach is felt to lead to greater satisfaction with the results of the hiring process because employees have a say in which person is selected to be part of the team.[123]

Thus, staffing processes and methods in team environments require modifications from the traditional approaches to selection. Before organizations go to the trouble and expense of modifying these procedures, however, it would be wise to examine whether the team initiatives are likely to be successful. Many teams fail because they are implemented as an isolated practice.[124] Thus, before overhauling selection practices in an effort to build teams, care must be taken to ensure the proper context for these environments in the first place.

Choice of Substantive Assessment Methods

As with the choice of initial assessment methods, a large amount of research has been conducted on substantive assessment methods that can help guide organizations in the appropriate methods to use. Reviews of this research, using the same criteria that were used to evaluate initial assessment methods, are shown in Exhibit 9.14. Specifically, the criteria are use, cost, reliability, validity, utility, applicant reactions, and adverse impact.

Use

As can be seen in Exhibit 9.14, there are no widely used (at least two-thirds of all organizations) substantive assessment methods. Structured interviews, emotional intelligence tests, and performance tests and work samples have moderate degrees of use. The other substantive methods are only occasionally or infrequently used by organizations.

Cost

The costs of substantive assessment methods vary widely. Some methods can be purchased from vendors quite inexpensively (personality tests; ability tests; emotional intelligence tests; interest, values, and preference inventories; integrity tests)—often for less than $2 per applicant. (Of course, the costs of administering and scoring the tests must be factored in.) Some methods, such as team assessments, can vary in price depending on whether the organization develops the measure itself or purchases it from a vendor. Other methods, such as structured interviews, performance tests and work samples, and situational judgment tests, generally require extensive time and resources to develop; thus, these measures are the most expensive substantive assessment methods.

Reliability

The reliability of all the substantive assessment methods is moderate or high. Generally, this is true because many of these methods have undergone extensive development efforts by vendors. However, whether an organization purchases an assessment tool from a vendor or develops it independently, the reliability of the

EXHIBIT 9.14   Evaluation of Substantive Assessment Methods

Predictors	Use	Cost	Reliability	Validity	Utility	Applicant Reactions	Adverse Impact
Personality tests	Low	Low	High	Moderate	?	Negative	Low
Ability tests	Low	Low	High	High	High	Negative	High
Emotional intelligence tests	Moderate	Low	High	Low	?	?	Low
Performance tests and work samples	Moderate	High	High	High	High	Positive	Low
Situational judgment tests	Low	High	Moderate	Moderate	?	Positive	Moderate
Integrity tests	Low	Low	High	High	High	Negative	Low
Interest, values, and preference inventories	Low	Low	High	Low	?	?	Low
Structured interviews	Moderate	High	Moderate	High	?	Positive	Mixed
Team assessments	Low	Moderate	?	?	?	Positive	?

method must be investigated. Just because a vendor claims a method is reliable does not necessarily mean it will be so within a particular organization.

Validity

Like cost, the validity of substantive assessment methods varies a great deal. Some methods, such as interest, values, and preference inventories, have demonstrated little validity in past research. As was noted when reviewing these measures, however, steps can be taken to increase their validity. Emotional intelligence tests also have relatively low validity, though there is reason to believe the tests are improving. Some methods, such as personality tests and structured interviews, have at least moderate levels of validity. Some structured interviews have high levels of validity, but the degree to which they add validity beyond cognitive ability tests remains in question. Finally, ability tests, performance tests and work samples, and integrity tests have high levels of validity. Integrity tests are moderate to high predictors of job performance; their validity in predicting other important job behaviors (counterproductive work behaviors) appears to be stronger.

Utility

As with initial assessment methods, the utility of most substantive assessment methods is unknown. A great deal of research has shown that the utility of ability tests (in particular, cognitive ability tests) is quite high. Performance tests and work samples and integrity tests also appear to have high levels of utility.

Applicant Reactions

Research is just beginning to emerge concerning applicant reactions to substantive assessment methods. From the limited research that has been conducted, however, applicants' reactions to substantive assessment methods appear to depend on the particular method. Relatively abstract methods that require an applicant to answer questions not directly tied to the job (i.e., questions on personality tests, most ability tests, and integrity tests) seem to generate negative reactions from applicants. Thus, research tends to suggest that applicants view personality, ability, and integrity tests unfavorably. Methods that are manifestly related to the job for which applicants are applying appear to generate positive reactions. Thus, research suggests that applicants view performance tests and work samples and structured interviews favorably. Little is known for how applicants react to emotional intelligence tests.

Adverse Impact

A considerable amount of research has been conducted on adverse impact of some substantive assessment methods. In particular, research suggests that personality tests, emotional intelligence tests, performance tests and work samples, and integrity tests have little adverse impact against women or minorities. In the past, interest, values, and preference inventories had substantial adverse impact against women, but this problem has been corrected. Conversely, ability tests have a high degree of adverse impact. In particular, cognitive ability tests have substantial adverse impact against minorities, while physical ability tests have significant adverse impact against women. The adverse impact of structured interviews was denoted as mixed. Furthermore, since even structured interviews have an element of subjectivity to them, the potential always exists for interviewer bias to enter into the process.

A comparison of Exhibits 8.8 and 9.14 is instructive. In general, both the validity and the cost of substantive assessment procedures are higher than those of initial assessment procedures. As with the initial assessment procedures, the economic and social impacts of substantive assessment procedures are not well understood. Many initial assessment methods are widely used, whereas most substantive assessment methods have moderate or low degrees of use. Thus, many organizations rely on initial assessment methods to make substantive assessment decisions. This is unfortunate, because, with the exception of biographical data, the validity of substantive assessment methods is higher. This is especially true of the initial interview relative to the structured interview. At a minimum, organizations need to supplement the initial interview with structured interviews. Better yet, organizations should strongly consider using ability, performance, personality, and work sample tests along with either interview.

DISCRETIONARY ASSESSMENT METHODS

Discretionary assessment methods are used to separate those who receive job offers from the list of finalists. Sometimes discretionary methods are not used, because all finalists may receive job offers. When used, discretionary assessment methods are typically highly subjective and rely heavily on the intuition of the decision maker. Thus, factors other than KSAOs may be assessed. Organizations intent on maintaining strong cultures may wish to consider assessing the person/organization match at this stage of the selection process.

Another interesting method of discretionary assessment that focuses on person/organization match is the selection of people on the basis of likely organizational citizenship behavior.[125] With this approach, finalists not only must fulfill all the requirements of the job but also are expected to fulfill some roles outside the requirements of the job, called organizational citizenship behaviors. These behaviors include things like doing extra work, helping others at work, covering for a sick coworker, and being courteous.

Discretionary assessments should involve use of the organization's staffing philosophy regarding equal employment opportunity and affirmative action (EEO/AA) commitments. Here, the commitment may be to enhance the representation of minorities and women in the organization's workforce, either voluntarily or as part of an organization's affirmative action plans and programs (AAPs). At this point in the selection process, the demographic characteristics of the finalists may be given weight in the decision about to whom the job offer will be extended. Regardless of how the organization chooses to make its discretionary assessments, they should never be used without being preceded by initial and substantive methods.

CONTINGENT ASSESSMENT METHODS

As was shown in Exhibit 8.3, contingent methods are not always used, depending on the nature of the job and legal mandates. Virtually any selection method can be used as a contingent method. For example, a health clinic may verify that an applicant for a nursing position possesses a valid license after a tentative offer has been made. Similarly, a defense contractor may perform a security clearance check on applicants once initial, substantive, and discretionary methods have been exhausted. While these methods may be used as initial or contingent methods, depending on the preferences of the organization, two selection methods, drug testing and medical exams, should be used exclusively as contingent assessment methods for legal compliance. When drug testing and medical exams are used, considerable care must be taken in their administration and evaluation.

Drug Testing

More than 70% of substance abusers hold jobs, and substance abuse has been identified as a major cause of workplace violence, accidents, absenteeism, and increased health care costs. A workplace study revealed that the average drug user was 3.6 times more likely to be involved in an accident, received 3 times the average level of sick benefits, was 5 times more likely to file a workers' compensation claim, and missed 10 times as many work days as nonusers.[126] One comprehensive study found that over an 11-year period, approximately 50 train accidents were attributed to workers under the influence of drugs or alcohol. These accidents resulted in 37 people killed, 80 injured, and the destruction of property valued at $34 million. A National Transportation Safety Board study found that 31% of all fatal truck accidents were due to alcohol or drugs.[127]

As a result of the manifold problems caused by drug use, many employers have drug testing programs to screen out drug users. Drug testing grew dramatically throughout the 1980s and 1990s, though there is reason to believe that its growth has peaked. A study by the American Management Association found that drug testing in the workplace peaked in 1996, when 81% of employers screened workers and applicants, and then declined steadily to 62% in 2004 (it was up slightly, to 66%, by 2006).[128]

One of the reasons drug testing has declined is shown in Exhibit 9.15: drug tests do not catch many people.[129] Far and away, the highest positive test rate is for marijuana, and it is only 2.54%—meaning that only 2.54% of applicants tested positive for marijuana. Overall, only 3.8% tested positive (the positive results in the exhibit add up to more than 3.8% because some applicants tested positive for more than one drug). The 3.8% positive rate means that if an organization tested 100 applicants, only about 4 would fail the test (i.e., test positive). The positive rate has dropped over time—indeed, the largest provider of employer drug testing says that positive tests are at a 17-year low. The decline is probably due to a combination of factors, including lower drug use in the population and the deterrent effect of the

EXHIBIT 9.15 **Percent of Applicants Testing Positive by Drug Category**

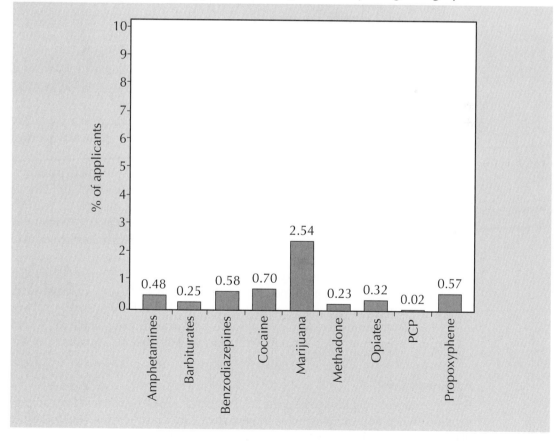

SOURCE: *Amphetamines Use Declined Significantly Among U.S. Workers in 2005, According to Quest Diagnostics' Drug Testing Index*, Quest Diagnostics Incorporated, 2006.

drug tests themselves (if an individual has used drugs recently and is aware that the organization tests for drugs, he or she won't apply). It may also reflect applicants "gaming" the tests (diluting, adulterating, or substituting samples); though, as we note shortly, if properly conducted, drug tests are difficult to fake.

Types of Tests

A variety of tests may be used to ascertain substance abuse. The major categories of tests are the following:[130]

1. *Body fluids.* Both urine and blood tests can be used. Urine tests are by far the most frequently used method of detecting substance abuse. There are different types of measures for each test. For example, urine samples can be measured using the enzyme-multiplied immunoassay technique or the gas chromatography/spectrometry technique. The latest innovation in drug testing uses a strip that is dipped into a urine sample (similar to a home pregnancy test), allowing organizations to test applicants and receive results on the spot.
2. *Hair analysis.* Samples of hair are analyzed using the same techniques as those used to measure urine samples. Chemicals remain in the hair as it grows, so it can provide a longer record of drug use. Hair analysis is more expensive than urinalysis.
3. *Pupillary reaction test.* The reaction of the pupil to light is assessed. The pupils will react differently when the applicant is under the influence of drugs than when the applicant is drug-free.
4. *Performance tests.* Hand-eye coordination is assessed to see if there is impairment compared with the standard drug-free reactions. One of the limitations of performance tests in a selection context is that there may be no feasible means of establishing a baseline against which performance is compared. Thus, performance tests are usually more suitable for testing employees than applicants.
5. *Integrity test.* Many integrity tests contain a section with 20 or so items that ask applicants about past and present drug use (e.g., "I only drink at work when things get stressful") as well as attitudes toward drug use (e.g., "How often do you think the average employee smokes marijuana on the job?"). Of course, such tests are susceptible to denial or deliberate falsification.

Administration

For the results of drug tests to be accurate, precautions must be taken in their administration. When collecting samples to be tested, care must be exercised to ensure that the sample is authentic and not contaminated. The US Department of Health and Human Services has established specific guidelines that must be followed by federal agencies (and are good guidelines to follow in the private sector as well).[131]

The testing itself must be carefully administered. Large labs process thousands of samples each day. Hence, human error can occur in the detection process. Also, false-positive results can be generated due to cross-reactions. This means that a common compound (e.g., poppy seeds) may interact with the antibodies and mistakenly identify a person as a substance abuser. Prescription medications may also affect drug test results. One new complicating factor in evaluating drug test results is the use of adulterants that mask the detection of certain drugs in the system. Although most adulterants can be tested, not all are easily detected, and many firms are unaware they can ask drug companies to test for adulterants.

For the testing to be carefully administered, two steps need to be taken. First, care must be taken in the selection of a reputable drug testing firm. Various certification programs, such as the College of American Pathologists and the National Institute for Drug Abuse (NIDA), exist to ensure that accurate procedures are followed. More than 50 drug testing laboratories have been certified by NIDA. Second, positive drug tests should always be verified by a second test to ensure reliability.

What does a well-conducted drug testing program look like?[132] Samples are first submitted to screening tests, which are relatively inexpensive ($25–$45 per applicant) but yield many false positives (test indicates drug use when none occurred) due to the cross-reactions described above. Confirmatory tests are then used, which are extremely accurate but more expensive. Error rates for confirmatory tests with reputable labs are very low. To avoid false positives, most organizations have nonzero cutoff levels for most drugs. Thus, if a mistake does occur, it is much more likely to be a false negative (testing negative when in fact drug use did occur) than a false positive. Thus, some applicants who occasionally use drugs may pass a test, but it is very rare for an individual who has never used the drug to fail the test—assuming the two-step process described above is followed. Exhibit 9.16 outlines the steps involved in a well-designed drug testing program. In this example:

- Applicants are advised in advance of testing.
- All applicants are screened by urine testing.
- Prescreening is done in-house; positives are referred to an independent lab.
- A strict chain of custody is followed.
- Verified positive applicants are disqualified.
- Disqualified applicants cannot reapply for two years.

The Other Drugs: Smoking and Alcohol

Increasingly, employers are banning smokers from hiring consideration. World-renowned Cleveland Clinic, for example, now bans hiring of smokers. (About half

EXHIBIT 9.16   Example of an Organizational Drug Testing Program

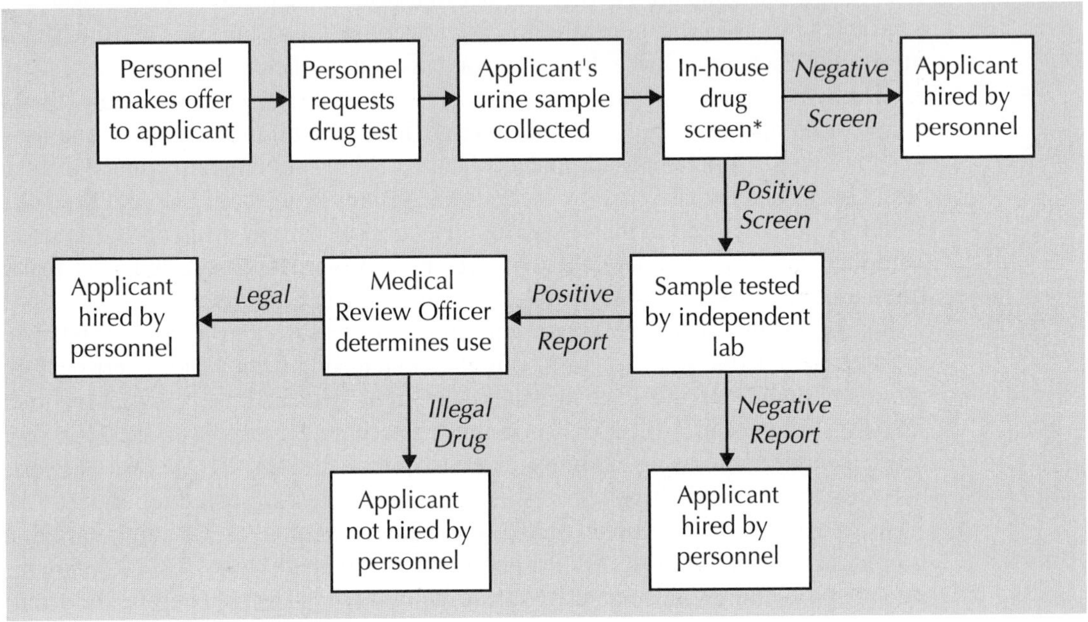

of US states prohibit rejecting applicants on the basis of smoking.) Union Pacific, a railroad that operates in 23 states, screens job candidates for smoking not by a nicotine test but by another method. "We will not process applications of people who indicate they are smokers," commented Kathryn Blackwell, a Union Pacific manager. Because smoking has been linked to higher health care costs, increased accident claims, and absenteeism, such policies may be justified. On the other hand, employers need to have arguments and evidence to support such policies: you have to "make the business case," as one expert noted. Thus, regardless of how smokers are screened out, employers who do so need to ensure that their policies comply with federal, state, and local regulations.[133]

As for alcohol, few employers test applicants for alcohol use for two reasons. First, because alcohol use is legal, and far more socially accepted than use of other mood-altering drugs, most employers have no desire to test applicants for alcohol; doing so would exclude large numbers of applicants. A second reason alcohol testing is infrequently used is because alcohol remains in the system for only a day. Some organizations that do test for alcohol are using a test called EtG. The advantage of this test is that rather than scanning for the presence of alcohol, EtG scans for a by-product of the metabolization of alcohol, ethyl glucuronide, which remains in the system for about 80 hours. To date, the only organizations using the EtG test are those that prohibit or restrict alcohol use in certain jobs (e.g., some health care positions, transportation jobs), and for those with applicants who have had former alcohol problems but now claim to be sober.[134]

Evaluation

It is commonly believed that drug testing results in a large number of false positives. But if the proper procedures are followed, drug test results are extremely accurate and error rates are very low. Accuracy of the test, however, is not the same as its validity in predicting important job criteria. The most accurate drug test in the world will be a poor investment if it cannot be established that substance abuse is related to employee behaviors such as accidents, absenteeism, tardiness, impaired job performance, and so on.

Although more research on the validity of drug testing programs is needed, some organizations are conducting research on the deleterious effects of substance abuse. The US Postal Service conducted an evaluation of its drug testing program using applicants who applied for positions in 21 sites over a six-month period.[135] A quality control process revealed that the drug testing program was 100% accurate (zero false positives and false negatives). Ten percent of applicants tested positive for drug use (for the purposes of the study, applicants were hired without regard to their test scores). Of those positive tests, 65% were for marijuana, 24% were for cocaine, and 11% were for other drugs. It found higher absenteeism for drug users and higher dismissal rates for cocaine users. Drug use was not related to accidents or injuries. A cost-benefit analysis suggested that full implementation of the program would save the Postal Service several million dollars per year in lower absenteeism and turnover rates.

The validity of performance and psychological drug tests is not well established. As with integrity tests, a major concern is faking, but an advantage of psychological drug tests is that applicants are likely to perceive them as less intrusive. Of those organizations that drug test, few rely on physical or psychological tests.

In considering the validity of drug tests, one should not assume that the logical criterion against which the tests are validated is job performance. Typically, the criterion of job performance is central to evaluating the validity of most selection measures, yet drug tests have not been validated against job performance. Thus, it is far from clear that drug tests do a good job of discerning good performers from poor performers. Drug tests do appear to predict other work behaviors, however, including absenteeism, accidents, and other counterproductive behavior. For the purposes for which they are suited, then, validity of drug tests can be concluded to be high.

Finally, as with other assessment methods, two other criteria against which drug testing should be evaluated are adverse impact and applicant reactions. The adverse impact of drug testing is not universally accepted, but the Postal Service study indicated that drug testing programs did have a moderate to high degree of adverse impact against black and Hispanic applicants. Research on applicant reactions to drug tests shows that if applicants perceive a need for drug testing, they are more likely to find such a program acceptable.[136] Thus, organizations that do a good job explaining the reasons for the tests to applicants are more likely to find that applicants react favorably to the program.

Recommendations for Effective Drug Testing Programs

Though drug testing may have peaked, it is likely to continue as one of the most commonly used selection methods, especially among large employers. In an effort to make organizations' drug testing programs as accurate and effective as possible, six recommendations are outlined as follows:

1. Emphasize drug testing in safety-sensitive jobs as well as positions where the link between substance abuse and negative outcomes (e.g., as was the case with the Postal Service study described earlier) has been documented.
2. Use only reputable testing laboratories, and ensure that strict chain of custody is maintained.
3. Ask applicants for their consent and inform them of test results; provide rejected applicants with the opportunity to appeal.
4. Use retesting to validate positive samples from the initial screening test.
5. Ensure that proper procedures are followed to maintain the applicant's right to privacy.
6. Review the program and validate the results against relevant criteria (accidents, absenteeism, turnover, and job performance); conduct a cost-benefit analysis of the program, as a very small number of detections may cause the program to have low utility.

Medical Exams

Medical exams are often used to identify potential health risks in job candidates. Care must be taken to ensure that medical exams are used only when a compelling reason to use them exists. This is to ensure that individuals with disabilities unrelated to job performance are not screened out. As a result of these sorts of potential abuses, the use of medical exams is strictly regulated by the ADA (discussed later in this chapter).

Although many organizations use medical exams, they are not particularly valid, because the procedures performed vary from doctor to doctor.[137] Also, medical exams are not always job related.[138] Finally, the emphasis is usually on short-term rather than long-term health. One way to make medical exams more reliable and therefore valid is to ensure that the exam is based on job-related medical standards (i.e., the exam focuses on the specific diseases and health conditions that prohibit adequate functioning on specific jobs or clusters of tasks). Such an approach should not only improve content validity (because it is job related) but also improve reliability because it standardizes the diagnosis across physicians.

LEGAL ISSUES

This section discusses three major legal issues. The first of these is the UGESP, a document that addresses the need to determine whether a selection procedure is causing adverse impact, and if so, the validation requirements for the procedure. The second issue is selection in conformance with the ADA as pertains to reasonable accommodation to job applicants and the use of medical tests. The final issue is that of drug testing for job applicants.

Uniform Guidelines on Employee Selection Procedures

The UGESP are a comprehensive set of federal regulations specifying requirements for the selection systems of organizations covered under the Civil Rights Acts and under E.O. 11246 (see *www.access.gpo.gov/nara/cfr/waisidx_09/29cfr1607_09. html* for the full text of the UGESP). There are four major sections to the UGESP, namely, general principles, technical standards, documentation of impact and validity evidence, and definitions of terms. Each of these sections is summarized next. An excellent review of the UGESP in terms of court cases and examples of acceptable and unacceptable practices is available and should be consulted. The organization should also consult research that reviews how the UGESP have been interpreted, criticized, and used since their passage.[139]

General Principles

1. *Summary.* The organization must keep records that allow it to determine whether its selection procedures are causing adverse impact in employment decisions. If no adverse impact is found, the remaining provisions of the UGESP generally do not apply. If adverse impact is found, the organization must either validate the selection procedure(s) causing the adverse impact or take steps to eliminate the adverse impact (such as stopping use of the procedure or using an alternate selection procedure that has less adverse impact).
2. *Scope.* The scope of the UGESP is very broad in that the guidelines apply to selection procedures used as the basis for any employment decisions. Employment decisions include hiring, promotion, demotion, and retention. A selection procedure is defined as "any measure, combination of measures, or procedure used as a basis for any employment decision." The procedures include "the full range of assessment techniques from traditional paper-and-pencil tests, performance tests, training programs, or probationary periods and physical, educational, and work experience requirements through informal or casual interviews and unscored application forms."
3. *Discrimination defined.* In general, any selection procedure that has an adverse impact is discriminatory unless it has been shown to be valid. There is a separate section for procedures that have not been validated.

4. *Suitable alternative selection procedures.* When a selection procedure has adverse impact, consideration should be given to the use of any suitable alternative selection procedures that may have lesser adverse impact.
5. *Information on adverse impact.* The organization must keep impact records by race, sex, and ethnic group for each of the job categories shown on the EEO-1 form (see Chapter 13).
6. *Evaluation of selection rates.* For each job or job category, the organization should evaluate the results, also known as the "bottom line," of the total selection process. The purpose of the evaluation is to determine whether there are differences in selection rates that indicate adverse impact. If adverse impact is not found, the organization usually does not have to take additional compliance steps, such as validation of each step in the selection process. If overall adverse impact is found, the individual components of the selection process should be evaluated for adverse impact.
7. *Adverse impact and the four-fifths rule.* To determine whether adverse impact is occurring, the organization should compute and compare selection rates for race, sex, and ethnic groups. A selection rate that is less than four-fifths (or 80%) of the rate for the group with the highest rate is generally regarded as evidence of adverse impact. There are exceptions to this general rule, based on sample size (small sample) considerations and on the extent to which the organization's recruitment practices have discouraged applicants disproportionately on grounds of race, sex, or ethnic group.
8. *General standards for validity studies.* There are three types of acceptable validity studies: criterion related, content, and construct. Numerous provisions pertain to standards governing these validity studies, as well as the appropriate use of selection procedures.
9. *Procedures that have not been validated.* This section discusses the use of alternative selection procedures to eliminate adverse impact. It also discusses instances in which validation studies cannot or need not be performed.
10. *Affirmative action.* Use of validated selection procedures does not relieve the employer of any affirmative action obligation it may have. The employer is encouraged to adopt and implement voluntary AAPs.

Technical Standards

This section contains a lengthy specification of the minimum technical standards that should be met when conducting a validation study. Separate standards are given for each of the three types of validity (criterion-related, content, construct) studies.

Documentation of Impact and Validity Evidence

For each job or job category, the employer is required to keep detailed records on adverse impact and, where adverse impact is found, evidence of validity. Detailed record-keeping requirements are provided.

There are two important exceptions to these general requirements. First, a small employer (fewer than 100 employees) does not have to keep separate records for each job category, but only for its total selection process across all jobs. Second, records for race or national origin do not have to be kept for groups constituting less than 2% of the labor force in the relevant labor area.

Definitions

This section defines terms (25 total) used throughout the UGESP.

Summary

The UGESP make substantial demands on an organization and its staffing systems. Those demands exist to ensure organizational awareness of the possibility of adverse impact in employment decisions. When adverse impact is found, the UGESP provide mechanisms (requirements) for coping with it. The UGESP thus should occupy a place of prominence in any covered organization's EEO/AA policies and practices.

Selection Under the Americans With Disabilities Act

The ADA, as interpreted by the Equal Employment Opportunity Commission (EEOC), creates substantial requirements and suggestions for compliance pertaining to external selection.[140] The general nature of these is identified and commented on next.

General Principles

Two major, overarching principles pertain to selection. The first principle is that it is unlawful to screen out individuals with disabilities, unless the selection procedure is job related and consistent with business necessity. The second principle is that a selection procedure must accurately reflect the KSAOs being measured, and not impaired sensory, manual, or speaking skills, unless those impaired skills are the ones being measured by the procedure.

The first principle is obviously very similar to principles governing selection generally under federal laws and regulations. The second principle is important because it cautions the organization to be sure that its selection procedures do not inadvertently and unnecessarily screen out applicants with disabilities.

Access to Job Application Process

The organization's job application process must be accessible to individuals with disabilities. Reasonable accommodation must be provided to enable all persons to apply, and applicants should be provided assistance (if needed) in completing the application process. Applicants should also be told about the nature and content of the selection process. This allows them to request reasonable accommodation to testing, if needed, in advance.

Reasonable Accommodation to Testing

In general, the organization may use any kind of test in assessing job applicants. These tests must be administered consistently to all job applicants for any particular job.

A very important provision of testing pertains to the requirement to provide reasonable accommodation if requested by an applicant to take the test. The purpose of this requirement is to ensure that the test accurately reflects the KSAO being measured, rather than an impairment of the applicant. Reasonable accommodation, however, is not required for a person with an impaired skill if the purpose of that test is to measure that skill. For example, the organization does not have to provide reasonable accommodation on a manual dexterity test to a person with arthritis in the fingers and hands if the purpose of the test is to measure manual dexterity.

Numerous types of reasonable accommodation can be made, and there is organizational experience and research in providing reasonable accommodation.[141] Examples include substituting an oral test for a written one (or vice versa); providing extra time to complete a test; scheduling rest breaks during a test; administering tests in large print, in Braille, or by reader; and using assistive technologies to adapt computers, such as a special mouse or screen magnifier.

Inquiries About Disabilities

Virtually all assessment tools and questions are affected by the ADA. A summary of permissible and impermissible practices is shown in Exhibit 9.17. Note that permissibility depends on the assessment tool, whether the tool is being used for an external applicant or employee, and whether the tool is being used prehire (like most selection procedures) or after a conditional offer has been made. Also note the many stipulations governing usage. Another useful source of information is "Job Applicants and the Americans With Disabilities Act" (*www.eeoc.gov/facts/jobapplicant.html*).

Medical Examinations: Job Applicants

Substantial regulations surround medical exams, both before and after a job offer. Prior to the offer, the organization may not make medical inquiries or require medical exams of an applicant. The job offer, however, may be conditional, pending the results of a medical exam.

Postoffer, the organization may conduct a medical exam. The exam must be given to all applicants for a particular job, not just individuals with a known or suspected disability. Whereas the content of the exam is not restricted to being only job related, the reasons for rejecting an applicant on the basis of the exam must be job related. A person may also be rejected if exam results indicate a direct threat to the health and safety of the applicant or others such as employees or customers. This rejection must be based on reasonable medical judgment, not a simple judgment that the applicant might or could cause harm. Each applicant must be assessed individually in order to determine whether the applicant's impairment

EXHIBIT 9.17   Inquiries About Disabilities

Type	What Inquiries Can Be Made About Disabilities?		
	External Applicant (Pre-Offer Stage)	External Applicants (Post-Conditional Offer Stage)	Employees
AA data (self-ID and requests)	Yes	Yes	Yes
Physical exam	No	Yes (C, D)	Yes (B, E)
Psychological exam	No	Yes (C, D)	Yes (B, E)
Health questionnaire	No	Yes (C, D)	Yes (B, E)
Work comp history	No	Yes (C, D)	Yes (B, E)
Physical agility test	Yes (A, C)	Yes (A, C)	Yes (A, C)
Drug test	Yes	Yes	Yes
Alcohol test	No	Yes (B, D)	Yes (B, E)
Specific questions (oral and written):			
About existence of a disability, its nature	Yes	Yes (A, C)	Yes (B, E)
About ability to perform job-related functions (essential and nonessential)	Yes	Yes	Yes
About smoking (but not allergic to it)	Yes	Yes	Yes
About history of illegal drug use	No	Yes (B, D)	Yes (B, E)
Specific requests:			
Describe how you would perform job-related functions (essential and nonessential) with or without reasonable accommodation	Yes (D, F)	Yes (C, D)	Yes (B, E)
Provide evidence of not currently using drugs	Yes	Yes	Yes

A. If given to all similarly situated applicants/employees
B. If job related and consistent with business necessity
C. If only job-related criteria consistent with business necessity are used afterwards to screen out/ exclude the applicant, at which point reasonable accommodation must be considered.
D. If all entering employees in the same job category are subjected to it and subjected to same qualification standard
E. But only for the following purposes:
    a. To determine fitness for duty (still qualified or still able to perform essential functions)
    b. To determine reasonable accommodation
    c. To meet requirements imposed by federal, state, or local law (DOT, OSHA, EPA, etc.)
    d. To determine direct threat
F. Can be requested of a particular individual if the disability is known and may interfere with or prevent performance of a job-related function.

SOURCE: S. K. Willman, "Tips for Minimizing Abuses Under the Americans With Disabilities Act," *Legal Report*, Society for Human Resource Management, Jan.–Feb. 2003, p. 8. Used with permission.

creates a significant risk of harm and cannot be accommodated through reasonable accommodation. Results of medical exams are to be kept confidential, held separate from the employee's personnel file, and released only under very specific circumstances.

It may be difficult to determine whether something is a medical examination and thus subject to the above requirements surrounding its use. The EEOC defines a medical examination as "a procedure or test that seeks information about an individual's physical or mental impairments or health."[142] The following factors are suggestive of a selection procedure that would be considered a medical examination:

- It is administered by a health care professional and/or someone trained by such a professional.
- It is designed to reveal an impairment of physical or mental health.
- It is invasive (e.g., requires drawing blood, urine, or breath).
- It measures the applicant's physiological responses to performing a task.
- It is normally given in a medical setting and/or medical equipment is used.
- It tests for alcohol consumption.

Though closely allied with medical examinations, several types of tests fall outside the bounds of medical examinations; these may be used preoffer. These include physical agility tests, physical fitness tests, vision tests, drug tests for current illegal use of controlled substances, and tests that measure honesty, tastes, and habits.

A gray area involves the use of psychological tests, such as personality tests. They are considered medical if they lead to identifying a medically recognized mental disorder or impairment, such as those in the American Psychiatric Association's *Diagnostic and Statistical Manual of Mental Disorders*. Future regulations and court rulings may help clarify which types of psychological tests are medical exams.

Medical Examinations: Current Employees

This enforcement guidance applies to employees generally, not just employees with disabilities.[143] An employee who applies for a new (different) job with the same employer should be treated as an applicant for a new job and thus subject to the provisions described above for job applicants. An individual is not an applicant where she or he is entitled to another position with the same employer (e.g., because of seniority or satisfactory performance in her or his current position) or when returning to a regular job after being on temporary assignment in another job. Instead, these individuals are considered employees.

For employees, the employer may make disability-related inquiries and require medical examinations only if they are job related and consistent with business necessity. Any information obtained, or voluntarily provided by the employee, is a confidential medical record. The record may only be shared in limited circumstances with managers, supervisors, first aid and safety personnel, and government officials investigating ADA compliance. Generally, a disability-related inquiry or medical examination is job related and consistent with business necessity when the employer has a reasonable belief, based on objective evidence, that (1) an employee's ability to perform essential job functions will be impaired by a medical condition or (2) an employee will pose a direct threat due to a medical condition.

A medical examination for employees is defined the same way as for job applicants. Examples of disability-related inquiries include the following:

- Asking an employee whether she or he was disabled (or ever had a disability) or how she or he became disabled, or asking about the nature or severity of an employee's disability
- Asking an employee to provide medical documentation regarding her or his disability
- Asking an employee's coworkers, family members, doctor, or another person about the employee's disability
- Asking about an employee's genetic information
- Asking about an employee's prior workers' compensation history
- Asking if an employee is taking any medication or drugs or has done so in the past
- Asking an employee broad information that is likely to elicit information about a disability

Drug Testing

Drug testing is permitted to detect the use of illegal drugs. The law, however, is neutral as to its encouragement.

UGESP

The UGESP do not apply to the ADA or its regulations. This means that the guidance and requirements for employers' selection systems under the Civil Rights Act may or may not be the same as those required for compliance with the ADA.

Drug Testing

Drug testing is surrounded by an amalgam of laws and regulations at the federal and state levels. Special law for the Department of Transportation requires alcohol and drug testing for transportation workers in safety-sensitive jobs.[144] The organization should seek legal and medical advice to determine whether it should do drug testing, and if so, what the nature of the drug testing program should be. Beyond that, the organization should require and administer drug tests on a contingency (postoffer) basis only, to avoid the possibility of obtaining and using medical information illegally. For example, positive drug test results may occur because of the presence of a legal drug, and using these results preoffer to reject a person would be a violation of the ADA.

SUMMARY

This chapter continued the discussion of proper methods and processes to be used in external selection. Specifically, substantive, discretionary, and contingent assessment methods were discussed, as well as collection of assessment data and pertinent legal issues.

Most of the chapter discussed various substantive methods, which are used to separate finalists from candidates. As with initial assessment methods, substantive assessment methods should always be based on the logic of prediction and the use of selection plans. The substantive methods that were reviewed include personality tests; ability tests; emotional intelligence tests; performance tests and work samples; situational judgment tests; integrity tests; interest, values, and preference inventories; structured interviews; and assessment for team environments. As with initial assessment methods, the criteria used to evaluate the effectiveness of substantive assessment methods are frequency of use, cost, reliability, validity, utility, applicant reactions, and adverse impact. In general, substantive assessment methods show a marked improvement in reliability and validity over initial assessment methods. This is probably due to the stronger relationship between the sampling of the applicant's previous situations and the requirements for success on the job.

Discretionary selection methods are somewhat less formal and more subjective than other selection methods. When discretionary methods are used, two judgments are important: will the applicant be a good organization "citizen," and do the values and goals of this applicant match those of the organization?

Though discretionary methods are subjective, contingent assessment methods typically involve decisions about whether applicants meet certain objective requirements for the job. The two most common contingent methods are drug testing and medical exams. Particularly in the case of drug testing, the use of contingent methods is relatively complex from an administrative and legal standpoint.

Regardless of predictor type, attention must be given to the proper collection and use of predictor information. In particular, support services need to be established, administrators with the appropriate credentials need to be hired, data need to be kept private and confidential, and administration procedures must be standardized.

Along with administrative issues, legal issues need to be considered as well. Particular attention must be paid to regulations that govern permissible activities by organizations. Regulations include those in the UGESP and the ADA.

DISCUSSION QUESTIONS

1. Describe the similarities and differences between personality tests and integrity tests. When is each warranted in the selection process?
2. How would you advise an organization considering adopting a cognitive ability test for selection?
3. Describe the structured interview. What are the characteristics of structured interviews that improve on the shortcomings of unstructured interviews?
4. What are the most common discretionary and contingent assessment methods? What are the similarities and differences between the use of these two methods?
5. What is the best way to collect and use drug-testing data in selection decisions?
6. How should organizations apply the general principles of the UGESP to practical selection decisions?

ETHICAL ISSUES

1. Do you think it's unethical for employers to select applicants on the basis of measures such as "Dislike loud music" and "Enjoy wild flights of fancy" even if the scales that such items measure have been shown to predict job performance? Explain.
2. Cognitive ability tests are one of the best predictors of job performance, yet they have substantial adverse impact against minorities. Do you think it's fair to use such tests? Why or why not?

APPLICATIONS

Assessment Methods for the Job of Human Resources Director

Nairduwel, Inoalot, and Imslo (NII) is a law firm specializing in business law. Among other areas, it deals in equal employment opportunity law, business litigation, and workplace torts. The firm has more than 50 partners and approximately 120 employees. It does business in three states and has law offices in two major metropolitan areas. The firm has no federal contracts.

NII plans to expand into two additional states with two major metropolitan areas. One of the primary challenges accompanying this ambitious expansion plan is how to staff, train, and compensate the individuals who will fill the positions in the new offices. Accordingly, the firm wishes to hire an HR director to oversee the recruitment, selection, training, performance appraisal, and compensation activities accompanying the business expansion, as well as supervise the HR activities in the existing NII offices. The newly created job description for the HR director is listed in the accompanying exhibit.

The firm wishes to design and then use a selection system for assessing applicants that will achieve two objectives: (1) create a valid and useful system that will do a good job of matching applicant KSAOs to job requirements, and (2) be in compliance with all relevant federal and state employment laws.

The firm is considering numerous selection techniques for possible use. For each method listed below, decide whether you would or would not use it in the selection process and state why.

1. A job knowledge test specifically designed for HR professionals that focuses on an applicant's general knowledge of HR management
2. A medical examination and drug test at the beginning of the selection process in order to determine if applicants are able to cope with the high level of stress and frequent travel requirements of the job and are drug-free
3. A paper-and-pencil integrity test
4. A structured behavioral interview that would be specially designed for use in filling only this job
5. A general cognitive ability test
6. Personal Characteristics Inventory
7. A set of interview questions that the firm typically uses for filling any position:
   a. Tell me about a problem you solved on a previous job.
   b. Do you have any physical impairments that would make it difficult for you to travel on business?
   c. Have you ever been tested for AIDS?
   d. Are you currently unemployed, and if so, why?
   e. This position requires fresh ideas and energy. Do you think you have those qualities?
   f. What is your definition of success?
   g. What kind of sports do you like?
   h. How well do you work under pressure? Give me some examples.

Exhibit

Job Description for Human Resources Director

JOB SUMMARY

Performs responsible administrative work managing personnel activities. Work involves responsibility for the planning and administration of HRM programs, including recruitment, selection, evaluation, appointment, promotion, compensation, and recommended change of status of employees, and a system of communication for disseminating information to workers. Works under general supervision, exercising initiative and independent judgment in the performance of assigned tasks.

TASKS

1. Participates in overall planning and policy making to provide effective and uniform personnel services.
2. Communicates policy through organization levels by bulletin, meetings, and personal contact.
3. Supervises recruitment and screening of job applicants to fill vacancies. Supervises interviewing of applicants, evaluation of qualifications, and classification of applications.
4. Supervises administration of tests to applicants.
5. Confers with supervisors on personnel matters, including placement problems, retention or release of probationary employees, transfers, demotions, and dismissals of permanent employees.
6. Initiates personnel training activities and coordinates these activities with work of officials and supervisors.
7. Establishes effective service rating system and trains unit supervisors in making employee evaluations.
8. Supervises maintenance of employee personnel files.
9. Supervises a group of employees directly and through subordinates.
10. Performs related work as assigned.

JOB SPECIFICATIONS

1. *Experience and Training*
   Should have considerable experience in area of HRM administration. Six years minimum.

2. *Education*
   Graduation from a four-year college or university, with major work in human resources, business administration, or industrial psychology. Master's degree in one of these areas is preferable.

3. *Knowledge, Skills, and Abilities*
Considerable knowledge of principles and practices of HRM, including staffing, compensation, training, and performance evaluation.

4. *Responsibility*
Supervises the human resource activities of six office managers, one clerk, and one assistant.

Choosing Among Finalists for the Job of Human Resources Director

Assume that NII, after weighing its options, decided to use the following selection methods to assess applicants for the HR director job: résumé, cognitive ability test, job knowledge test, structured interview, and questions (f) and (g) from the list of generic interview questions.

NII advertised for the position extensively, and out of a pool of 23 initial applicants, it was able to come up with a list of three finalists. Shown in the accompanying exhibit are the results from the assessment of the three finalists using these selection methods. In addition, information from an earlier résumé screen is included for possible consideration. For each finalist, you are to decide whether you would be willing to hire the person and why.

Exhibit

Results of Assessment of Finalists for Human Resources Director Position

	Finalist 1— Lola Vega	Finalist 2— Sam Fein	Finalist 3— Shawanda Jackson
Résumé	GPA 3.9/Cornell University B.S. Human Resource Mgmt. 5 years' experience in HRM • 4 years in recruiting	GPA 2.8/SUNY Binghamton B.B.A. Finance 20 years' experience in HRM • Numerous HR assignments • Certified HR professional	GPA 3.2/Auburn University B.B.A. Business and English 8 years' experience in HRM • 3 years HR generalist • 4 years compensation analyst
	No supervisory experience	15 years' supervisory experience	5 years' supervisory experience

	Finalist 1— Lola Vega	Finalist 2— Sam Fein	Finalist 3— Shawanda Jackson
Cognitive ability test	90% correct	78% correct	84% correct
Knowledge test	94% correct	98% correct	91% correct
Structured Int. (out of 100 pts)	85	68	75
Question (f)	Ability to influence others	To do things you want to do	Promotions and earnings
Question (g)	Golf, shuffleboard	Spectator sports	Basketball, tennis

TANGLEWOOD STORES CASE

In our second chapter on external selection, you read how structured interviews are developed. However, following these steps is more complex than you might think. By using the procedures described in the chapter, you will better understand the challenges posed in developing a good structured interview. You will also be able to see the advantages of using a structured protocol.

The Situation

Tanglewood is looking to revise its method for selecting department managers. Currently, external candidates are assessed by an application blank and an unstructured interview. Neither of these methods is satisfactory to the organization, and it would like to use your knowledge of structured interviews to help design a more reliable, valid selection procedure.

Your Tasks

First, you should carefully examine the job description for the position in Appendix A and then create a selection plan as shown in Exhibit 9.11. Then, you will write situational and experience-based interview questions designed to assess candidates' knowledge, skills, and abilities for the department manager position, like those in Exhibit 9.12. After writing up these initial questions and behavioral rating scales, you will try them out on a friend to see how he or she reacts to the questions as either an applicant or an interviewer. Based on the comments of your "test subject," you will revise the content of the questions and make recommendations on the process to be followed in conducting the interview. The background information for this case, and your specific assignment, can be found at *www.mhhe.com/ heneman7e.*

ENDNOTES

1. L. M. Hough, "The 'Big Five' Personality Variables—Construct Confusion: Description Versus Prediction," *Human Performance*, 1992, 5, pp. 139–155.

2. R. M. Guion and R. F. Gottier, "Validity of Personality Measures in Personnel Selection," *Personnel Psychology*, 1965, 18, pp. 135–164.

3. P. T. Costa, Jr., and R. R. McCrae, "Four Ways Five Factors Are Basic," *Personality and Individual Differences*, 1992, 13, pp. 653–665.

4. M. K. Mount and M. R. Barrick, *Manual for the Personal Characteristics Inventory* (Iowa City, IA: authors, 1995).

5. P. T. Costa, Jr., and R. R. McCrae, *Revised NEO Personality Inventory (NEO-PI-R) and NEO Five-Factor (NEO-FFI) Inventory Professional Manual* (Odessa, FL: Psychological Assessment Resources, 1992).

6. J. Hogan and R. Hogan, "How to Measure Employee Reliability," *Journal of Applied Psychology*, 1989, 74, pp. 273–279.

7. N. T. Tippins, J. Beaty, F. Drasgow, W. M. Gibson, K. Pearlman, D. O. Segall, and W. Shepherd, "Unproctored Internet Testing in Employment Settings," *Personnel Psychology*, 2006, 59, pp. 189–225; S. Overman, "Online Screening Saves Time and Money," *Staffing Management*, July–Sept. 2005, pp. 18–22.

8. Exhibit 9.2 and the review here are based on C. M. Berry, D. S. Ones, and P. R. Sackett, "Interpersonal Deviance, Organizational Deviance, and Their Common Correlates: A Review and Meta-Analysis," *Journal of Applied Psychology*, 2007, 92, pp. 410–424; C. Viswesvaran, J. Deller, and D. S. Ones, "Personality Measures in Personnel Selection: Some New Contributions," *International Journal of Selection and Assessment*, 2007, 15, pp. 354–358; N. M. Dudley, K. A. Orvis, J. E. Lebiecki, and J. M. Cortina, "A Meta-Analytic Investigation of Conscientiousness in the Prediction of Job Performance: Examining the Intercorrelations and the Incremental Validity of Narrow Traits," *Journal of Applied Psychology*, 2006, 91, pp. 40–57; D. S. Ones, C. Viswesvaran, and S. Dilchert, "Personality at Work: Raising Awareness and Correcting Misconceptions," *Human Performance*, 2005, 18, pp. 389–404; M. G. Rothstein and R. D. Goffin, "The Use of Personality Measures in Personnel Selection: What Does Current Research Support?" *Human Resource Management Review*, 2006, 16, pp. 155–180.

9. For a review of these criticisms and responses to them, see F. P. Morgeson, M. A. Campion, R. L. Dipboye, J. R. Hollenbeck, K. Murphy, and N. Schmitt, "Reconsidering the Use of Personality Tests in Personnel Selection Contexts," *Personnel Psychology*, 2007, 60, pp. 683–729; D. S. Ones, S. Dilchert, C. Viswesvaran, and T. A. Judge, "In Support of Personality Assessment in Organizational Settings," *Personnel Psychology*, 2007, 60, pp. 995–1027; R. P. Tett and N. D. Christiansen, "Personality Tests at the Crossroads: A Response to Morgeson, Campion, Dipboye, Hollenbeck, Murphy, and Schmitt (2007)," *Personnel Psychology*, 2007, 60, pp. 967–993.

10. Morgeson et al., "Reconsidering the Use of Personality Tests in Personnel Selection Contexts," p. 694.

11. Ones, Dilchert, Viswesvaran, and Judge, "In Support of Personality Assessment in Organizational Settings"; M. R. Barrick, M. K. Mount, and T. A. Judge, "Personality and Performance at the Beginning of the New Millennium: What Do We Know and Where Do We Go Next?" *International Journal of Selection & Assessment*, 2001, 9, pp. 9–30.

12. G. V. Barrett, R. F. Miguel, J. M. Hurd, S. B. Lueke, and J. A. Tan, "Practical Issues in the Use of Personality Tests in Police Selection," *Public Personnel Management*, 2003, 32, pp. 497–517;

V. M. Mallozzi, "This Expert in Scouting Athletes Doesn't Need to See Them Play," *New York Times*, Apr. 25, 2004, pp. SP3, SP7.

13. M. R. Barrick and M. K. Mount, "Autonomy as a Moderator of the Relationships Between the Big Five Personality Dimensions and Job Performance," *Journal of Applied Psychology*, 1993, 78, pp. 111–118.

14. D. Chan, "Interactive Effects of Situational Judgment Effectiveness and Proactive Personality on Work Perceptions and Work Outcomes," *Journal of Applied Psychology*, 2006, 91, pp. 475–481; J. A. Thompson, "Proactive Personality and Job Performance: A Social Capital Perspective," *Journal of Applied Psychology*, 2005, 90, pp. 1011–1017; S. E. Seibert, M. L. Kraimer, and J. M. Crant, "What Do Proactive People Do? A Longitudinal Model Linking Proactive Personality and Career Success," *Personnel Psychology*, 2001, 54, pp. 845–874.

15. T. A. Judge and J. E. Bono, "Relationship of Core Self-Evaluations Traits—Self-Esteem, Generalized Self-Efficacy, Locus of Control, and Emotional Stability—With Job Satisfaction and Job Performance: A Meta-Analysis," *Journal of Applied Psychology*, 2001, 86, pp. 80–92; T. A. Judge, A. Erez, J. E. Bono, and C. J. Thoresen, "The Core Self-Evaluations Scale: Development of a Measure," *Personnel Psychology*, 2003, 56, pp. 303–331.

16. S. A. Birkeland, T. M. Manson, J. L. Kisamore, M. T. Brannick, and M. A. Smith, "A Meta-Analytic Investigation of Job Applicant Faking on Personality Measures," *International Journal of Selection and Assessment*, 2006, 14, pp. 317–335; S. Stark, O. S. Chernyshenko, and F. Drasgow, "Examining Assumptions About Item Responding in Personality Assessment: Should Ideal Point Methods Be Considered for Scale Development and Scoring?" *Journal of Applied Psychology*, 2006, 91, pp. 25–39.

17. H. Le, I. Oh, S. B. Robbins, R. Ilies, E. Holland, and P. Westrick, "Too Much of a Good Thing: Curvilinear Relationships Between Personality Traits and Job Performance," *Journal of Applied Psychology*, 2011, 96, pp. 113–133; D. L. Whetzel, M. A. McDaniel, A. P. Yost, and N. Kim, "Linearity of Personality-Performance Relationships: A Large-Scale Examination," *International Journal of Selection and Assessment*, 2010, 18(3), pp. 310–320.

18. Rothstein and Goffin, "The Use of Personality Measures in Personnel Selection: What Does Current Research Support?"

19. J. E. Ellingson, D. B. Smith, and P. R. Sackett, "Investigating the Influence of Social Desirability on Personality Factor Structure," *Journal of Applied Psychology*, 2001, 86, pp. 122–133; D. B. Smith and J. E. Ellingson, "Substance Versus Style: A New Look at Social Desirability in Motivating Contexts," *Journal of Applied Psychology*, 2002, 87, pp. 211–219.

20. N. Schmitt and F. L. Oswald, "The Impact of Corrections for Faking on the Validity of Noncognitive Measures in Selection Settings," *Journal of Applied Psychology*, 2006, 91, pp. 613–621.

21. E. D. Heggestad, M. Morrison, C. L. Reeve, and R. A. McCloy, "Forced-Choice Assessments of Personality for Selection: Evaluating Issues of Normative Assessment and Faking Resistance," *Journal of Applied Psychology*, 2006, 91, pp. 9–24; S. Dilchert, D. S. Ones, C. Viswesvaran, and J. Deller, "Response Distortion in Personality Measurement: Born to Deceive, yet Capable of Providing Valid Self-Assessments?" *Psychology Science*, 2006, 48, pp. 209–225.

22. S. A. Dwight and J. J. Donovan, "Do Warnings Not to Fake Reduce Faking?" *Human Performance*, 2003, 16, pp. 1–23; J. Hogan, P. Barrett, and R. Hogan, "Personality Measurement, Faking, and Employment Selection," *Journal of Applied Psychology*, 2007, 92, pp. 1270–1285; J. E. Ellingson, P. R. Sackett, and B. S. Connelly, "Personality Assessment Across Selection and Development Contexts: Insights Into Response Distortion," *Journal of Applied Psychology*, 2007, 92, pp. 386–395.

23. R. D. Zimmerman, M. Triana, and M. R. Barrick, "Predictive Criterion-Related Validity of Observer Ratings of Personality and Job-Related Competencies Using Multiple Raters and

Multiple Performance Criteria," *Human Performance*, 2010, 23(4), pp. 361–378; C. M. Berry, P. R. Sackett, and V. Tobares, "A Meta-Analysis of Conditional Reasoning Tests of Aggression," *Personnel Psychology*, 2010, 63(2), pp. 361–384; R. E. Johnson, A. L. Tolentino, O. B. Rodopman, and E. Cho, "We (Sometimes) Know Not How We Feel: Predicting Job Performance With an Implicit Measure of Trait Affectivity," *Personnel Psychology*, 2010, 63(1), pp. 197–219; I. Oh and C. M. Berry, "The Five-Factor Model of Personality and Managerial Performance: Validity Gains Through the Use of 360 Degree Performance Ratings," *Journal of Applied Psychology*, 2009, 94(6), pp. 1498–1513.

24. J. P. Hausknecht, D. V. Day, and S. C. Thomas, "Applicant Reactions to Selection Procedures: An Updated Model and Meta-Analysis," *Personnel Psychology*, 2004, 57, pp. 639–683; "Workers Question Validity of Personality Tests," *Staffing Management*, Jan.–Mar. 2007, p. 11.

25. A. Wolf and A. Jenkins, "Explaining Greater Test Use for Selection: The Role of HR Professionals in a World of Expanding Regulation," *Human Resource Management Journal*, 2006, 16(2), pp. 193–213.

26. E. A. Fleishman and M. E. Reilly, *Handbook of Human Abilities* (Palo Alto, CA: Consulting Psychologists Press, 1992).

27. C. L. Reeve and N. Blacksmith, "Identifying g: A Review of Current Factor Analytic Practices in the Science of Mental Abilities," *Intelligence*, 2009, 37(5), pp. 487–494.

28. C. F. Wonderlic, Jr., "Test Publishers Form Association," *Human Resource Measurements* (Supplement to the Jan. 1993 *Personnel Journal*), p. 3.

29. L. S. Gottfredson, "Societal Consequences of the g Factor in Employment," *Journal of Vocational Behavior*, 1986, 29, pp. 379–410; J. F. Salgado, N. Anderson, S. Moscoso, C. Bertua, F. de Fruyt, and J. P. Rolland, "A Meta-Analytic Study of General Mental Ability Validity for Different Occupations in the European Community," *Journal of Applied Psychology*, 2003, 88, pp. 1068–1081.

30. T. A. Judge, R. Ilies, and N. Dimotakis, "Are Health and Happiness the Product of Wisdom? The Relationship of General Mental Ability to Educational and Occupational Attainment, Health, and Well-Being," *Journal of Applied Psychology*, 2010, 95(3), pp. 454–468; M. A. Maltarich, A. J. Nyberg, and G. A. Reilly, "A Conceptual and Empirical Analysis of the Cognitive Ability–Voluntary Turnover Relationship," *Journal of Applied Psychology*, 2010, 95(6), pp. 1058–1070.

31. J. E. Hunter, "Cognitive Ability, Cognitive Aptitudes, Job Knowledge, and Job Performance," *Journal of Vocational Behavior*, 1986, 29, pp. 340–362.

32. J.W.B. Lang and P. D. Bliese, "General Mental Ability and Two Types of Adaptation to Unforeseen Change: Applying Discontinuous Growth Models to the Task-Change Paradigm," *Journal of Applied Psychology*, 2009, 94(2), pp. 411–428; M. J. Ree and J. A. Earles, "Predicting Training Success: Not Much More Than g," *Personnel Psychology*, 1991, 44, pp. 321–332.

33. P. M. Wright, G. McMahan, and D. Smart, "Team Cognitive Ability as a Predictor of Performance: An Examination of the Role of SAT Scores in Determining NCAA Basketball Team Performance," Working paper, Department of Management, Texas A&M University.

34. Hunter, "Cognitive Ability, Cognitive Aptitudes, Job Knowledge, and Job Performance"; F. L. Schmidt and J. E. Hunter, "Development of a Causal Model of Processes Determining Job Performance," *Current Directions in Psychological Science*, 1992, 1, pp. 89–92.

35. J.W.B. Lang, M. Kersting, U. R. Hülsheger, and J. Lang, "General Mental Ability, Narrower Cognitive Abilities, and Job Performance: The Perspective of the Nested-Factors Model of Cognitive Abilities," *Personnel Psychology*, 2010, 63(3), pp. 595–640; M. K. Mount, I. Oh, and M. Burns, "Incremental Validity of Perceptual Speed and Accuracy Over General Mental Ability," *Personnel Psychology*, 2008, 61(1), pp. 113–139.

36. P. L. Roth, C. A. BeVier, P. Bobko, F. S. Switzer, and P. Tyler, "Ethnic Group Differences in Cognitive Ability in Employment and Educational Settings: A Meta-Analysis," *Personnel Psychology*, 2001, 54, pp. 297–330.

37. See P. R. Sackett and W. Shen, "Subgroup Differences on Cognitive Tests in Contexts Other Than Personnel Selection," in J. L. Outtz (ed.), *Adverse Impact: Implications for Organizational Staffing and High Stakes Selection* (New York: Routledge/Taylor & Francis, 2010), pp. 323–346; C. L. Reeve and J. E. Charles, "Survey of Opinions on the Primacy of g and Social Consequences of Ability Testing: A Comparison of Expert and Non-Expert Views," *Intelligence*, 2008, 36(6), pp. 681–688.

38. W. F. Cascio, R. Jacobs, and J. Silva, "Validity, Utility, and Adverse Impact: Practical Implications from 30 Years of Data," in Outtz (ed.), *Adverse Impact: Implications for Organizational Staffing and High Stakes Selection*, pp. 271–288; P. Bobko, P. L. Roth, and D. Potosky, "Derivation and Implications of a Meta-Analytic Matrix Incorporating Cognitive Ability, Alternative Predictors, and Job Performance," *Personnel Psychology*, 1999, 52, pp. 561–589; A. M. Ryan, R. E. Ployhart, and L. A. Friedel, "Using Personality to Reduce Adverse Impact: A Cautionary Note," *Journal of Applied Psychology*, 1998, 83, pp. 298–307.

39. B. D. Edwards and W. Arthur, Jr., "An Examination of Factors Contributing to a Reduction in Subgroup Differences on a Constructed-Response Paper-and-Pencil Test of Scholastic Achievement," *Journal of Applied Psychology*, 2007, 92, pp. 794–801; D. A. Newman and J. S. Lyon, "Recruitment Efforts to Reduce Adverse Impact: Targeted Recruiting for Personality, Cognitive Ability, and Diversity," *Journal of Applied Psychology*, 2009, 94(2), pp. 298–317.

40. W. T. Dickens and J. R. Flynn, "Black Americans Reduce the IQ Gap," *Psychological Science*, 2006, 17, pp. 913–920; J. P. Rushton and A. R. Jensen, "The Totality of Available Evidence Shows the Race IQ Gap Still Remains," *Psychological Science*, 2006, 17, pp. 921–922. See also E. Hunt and J. Carlson, "Considerations Relating to the Study of Group Differences in Intelligence," *Perspectives on Psychological Science*, 2007, 2, pp. 194–213.

41. T. A. Judge, D. Blancero, D. M. Cable, and D. E. Johnson, "Effects of Selection Systems on Job Search Decisions," Paper presented at the Tenth Annual Conference of the Society for Industrial and Organizational Psychology, Orlando, FL, 1995.

42. S. L. Rynes and M. L. Connerley, "Applicant Reactions to Alternative Selection Procedures," *Journal of Business and Psychology*, 1993, 7, pp. 261–277.

43. J. P. Hausknecht, D. V. Day, and S. C. Thomas, "Applicant Reactions to Selection Procedures: An Updated Model and Meta-Analysis," *Personnel Psychology*, 2004, 57(3), pp. 639–683; J. W. Smither, R. R. Reilly, R. E. Millsap, K. Pearlman, and R. W. Stoffey, "Applicant Reactions to Selection Procedures," *Personnel Psychology*, 46, pp. 49–76.

44. Hausknecht, Day, and Thomas, "Applicant Reactions to Selection Procedures: An Updated Model and Meta-Analysis."

45. S. M. Gully, S. C. Payne, and K.L.K. Koles, "The Impact of Error Training and Individual Differences on Training Outcomes: An Attribute-Treatment Interaction Perspective," *Journal of Applied Psychology*, 2002, 87, pp. 143–155; J. P. Hausknecht, C. O. Trevor, and J. L. Farr, "Retaking Ability Tests in a Selection Setting: Implications for Practice Effects, Training Performance, and Turnover," *Journal of Applied Psychology*, 2002, 87, pp. 243–254; J. F. Salgado, N. Anderson, and S. Moscoso, "International Validity Generalization of GMA and Cognitive Abilities: A European Community Meta-Analysis," *Personnel Psychology*, 2003, 56, pp. 573–605.

46. K. R. Murphy, B. E. Cronin, and A. P. Tam, "Controversy and Consensus Regarding Use of Cognitive Ability Testing in Organizations," *Journal of Applied Psychology*, 2003, 88, pp. 660–671.

47. J. Hogan, "Physical Abilities," in M. D. Dunnette and L. M. Hough (eds.), *Handbook of Industrial and Organizational Psychology*, Vol. 2 (Palo Alto, CA: Consulting Psychologists Press, 1991), pp. 753–831.

48. N. Henderson, M. W. Berry, and T. Malic, "Field Measures of Strength and Fitness Predict Firefighter Performance on Physically Demanding Tasks," *Personnel Psychology*, 2007, 60, pp. 431–473.

49. R. Britt, "Hands and Wrists Are Thrust Into the Hiring Process," *New York Times*, Sept. 21, 1997, p. 11.

50. M. A. Campion, "Personnel Selection for Physically Demanding Jobs: Review and Recommendations," *Personnel Psychology*, 1987, 36, pp. 527–550.

51. T. A. Baker, "The Utility of a Physical Test in Reducing Injury Costs," Paper presented at the Ninth Annual Meeting of the Society for Industrial and Organizational Psychology, Nashville, TN, 1995.

52. B. R. Blakley, M. A. Quinones, M. S. Crawford, and I. A. Jago, "The Validity of Isometric Strength Tests," *Personnel Psychology*, 1994, 47, pp. 247–274.

53. E. E. Ghiselli, "The Validity of Aptitude Tests in Personnel Selection," *Personnel Psychology*, 1973, 61, pp. 461–467.

54. Wisconsin Department of Employment Relations, *Developing Wisconsin State Civil Service Examinations and Assessment Procedures* (Madison, WI: author, 1994).

55. D. M. Dye, M. Reck, and M. A. McDaniel, "The Validity of Job Knowledge Measures," *International Journal of Selection and Assessment*, 1993, 1, pp. 153–157.

56. P. Salovey and D. Grewal, "The Science of Emotional Intelligence," *Current Directions in Psychological Science*, 2005, 14, p. 281; J. D. Mayer, P. Salovey, and D. R. Caruso, "Emotional Intelligence: New Ability or Eclectic Traits?" *American Psychologist*, 2008, 63(6), pp. 503–517.

57. D. L. Van Rooy, D. S. Whitman, and C. Viswesvaran, "Emotional Intelligence: Additional Questions Still Unanswered," *Industrial and Organizational Psychology*, 2010, 3(2), pp. 149–153.

58. D. L. Joseph and D. A. Newman, "Emotional Intelligence: An Integrative Meta-Analysis and Cascading Model," *Journal of Applied Psychology*, 2010, 95(1), pp. 54–78.

59. M. Zeidner, G. Matthews, and R. D. Roberts, "Emotional Intelligence in the Workplace: A Critical Review," *Applied Psychology: An International Review*, 2004, 53, pp. 371–399.

60. S. Kaplan, J. Cortina, and G. A. Ruark, "Oops . . . We Did It Again: Industrial-Organizational's Focus on Emotional Intelligence Instead of on Its Relationships to Work Outcomes," *Industrial and Organizational Psychology*, 2010, 3(2), pp. 171–177.

61. E. A. Locke, "Why Emotional Intelligence Is an Invalid Concept," *Journal of Organizational Behavior*, 2005, 26, p. 426; C. Cherniss, "Emotional Intelligence: Toward Clarification of a Concept," *Industrial and Organizational Psychology*, 2010, 3(2), pp. 110–126; S. Côté, "Taking the 'Intelligence' in Emotional Intelligence Seriously," *Industrial and Organizational Psychology*, 2010, 3(2), pp. 127–130.

62. Joseph and Newman, "Emotional Intelligence: An Integrative Meta-Analysis and Cascading Model."

63. F. J. Landy, "Some Historical and Scientific Issues Related to Research on Emotional Intelligence," *Journal of Organizational Behavior*, 2005, 26, p. 421.

64. E. White, "Walking a Mile in Another's Shoes," *Wall Street Journal*, Jan. 16, 2006, p. B3.

65. R. Miller, "The Legal Minefield of Employment Probation," *Benefits and Compensation Solutions*, 1998, 21, pp. 40–43.

66. J. J. Asher and J. A. Sciarrino, "Realistic Work Sample Tests: A Review," *Personnel Psychology*, 1974, 27, pp. 519–533.

67. S. J. Motowidlo, M. D. Dunnette, and G. Carter, "An Alternative Selection Procedure: A Low-Fidelity Simulation," *Journal of Applied Psychology*, 1990, 75, pp. 640–647.
68. W. Arthur, Jr., G. V. Barrett, and D. Doverspike, "Validation of an Information Processing-Based Test Battery Among Petroleum-Product Transport Drivers," *Journal of Applied Psychology*, 1990, 75, pp. 621–628.
69. J. Cook, "Sure Bet," *Human Resource Executive*, Jan. 1997, pp. 32–34.
70. Motowidlo, Dunnette, and Carter, "An Alternative Selection Procedure: A Low-Fidelity Simulation."
71. "Making a Difference in Customer Service," *IPMA News*, May 2002, pp. 8–9.
72. P. Thomas, "Not Sure of a New Hire? Put Her to a Road Test," *Wall Street Journal*, Jan. 2003, p. B7.
73. S. Greengard, "Cracking the Hiring Code," *Workforce Management*, June 2004 (*www.workforce.com/archive/article/23/74/45.php*).
74. C. Winkler, "Job Tryouts Go Virtual," *HR Magazine*, Sept. 2006, pp. 131–134.
75. Electronic Selection Systems Corporation, *Accu Vision: Assessment Technology for Today, Tomorrow, and Beyond* (Maitland, FL: author, 1992).
76. J. E. Hunter and R. F. Hunter, "Validity and Utility of Alternative Predictors of Job Performance," *Psychological Bulletin*, 1984, 96, pp. 72–98.
77. W. Cascio and W. Phillips, "Performance Testing: A Rose Among Thorns?" *Personnel Psychology*, 1979, 32, pp. 751–766.
78. P. Bobko, P. L. Roth, and M. A. Buster, "Work Sample Tests and Expected Reduction in Adverse Impact: A Cautionary Note," *International Journal of Selection and Assessment*, 2005, 13, pp. 1–24.
79. K. A. Hanisch and C. L. Hulin, "Two-Stage Sequential Selection Procedures Using Ability and Training Performance: Incremental Validity of Behavioral Consistency Measures," *Personnel Psychology*, 1994, 47, pp. 767–785.
80. M. A. McDaniel, N. S. Hartman, D. L. Whetzel, and W. L. Grubb, "Situational Judgment Tests, Response Instructions, and Validity: A Meta-Analysis," *Personnel Psychology*, 2007, 60, pp. 63–91.
81. D. L. Whetzel, M. A. McDaniel, and N. T. Nguyen, "Subgroup Differences in Situational Judgment Test Performance: A Meta-Analysis," *Human Performance*, 2008, 21, pp. 291–309.
82. F. Lievens and P. R. Sackett, "Video-Based Versus Written Situational Judgment Tests: A Comparison in Terms of Predictive Validity," *Journal of Applied Psychology*, 2006, 91, pp. 1181–1188.
83. McDaniel et al., "Situational Judgment Tests, Response Instructions, and Validity: A Meta-Analysis"; D. Chan and N. Schmitt, "Situational Judgment and Job Performance," *Human Performance*, 2002, 15, pp. 233–254; J. A. Weekley and C. Jones, "Further Studies of Situational Tests," *Personnel Psychology*, 1999, 52, pp. 679–700; J. Clevenger, G. M. Pereira, D. Wiechmann, N. Schmitt, and V. S. Harvey, "Incremental Validity of Situational Judgment Tests," *Journal of Applied Psychology*, 2001, 86, pp. 410–417.
84. M. S. O'Connell, N. S. Hartman, M. A. McDaniel, W. L. Grubb, and A. Lawrence, "Incremental Validity of Situational Judgment Tests for Task and Contextual Job Performance," *International Journal of Selection and Assessment*, 2007, 15, pp. 19–29.
85. Lievens and Sackett, "Video-Based Versus Written Situational Judgment Tests: A Comparison in Terms of Predictive Validity."
86. S. J. Motowidlo and M. E. Beier, "Differentiating Specific Job Knowledge from Implicit Trait Policies in Procedural Knowledge Measured by a Situational Judgment Test," *Journal of Applied Psychology*, 2010, 95(2), pp. 321–333.

87. M. S. Christian, B. D. Edwards, and J. C. Bradley, "Situational Judgment Tests: Constructs Assessed and a Meta-Analysis of Their Criterion-Related Validities," *Personnel Psychology*, 2010, 63(1), pp. 83–117; R. Bledow and M. Frese, "A Situational Judgment Test of Personal Initiative and Its Relationship to Performance," *Personnel Psychology*, 2009, 62(2), pp. 229–258.

88. "Employers Cite Communication Skills, Honesty/Integrity as Key for Job Candidates," *IPMA-HR Bulletin*, Mar. 23, 2007, p. 1.

89. M. G. Aamodt and H. Custer, "Who Can Best Catch a Liar? A Meta-Analysis of Individual Differences in Detecting Deception," *The Forensic Examiner*, Spring 2006, pp. 6–11.

90. R. C. Hollinger, "2006 National Retail Security Survey Final Report," Survey Research Project, University of Florida (downloaded January 8, 2008, from *http://web.crim.ufl.edu/research/srp/srp.html*).

91. C. M. Berry, D. S. Ones, and P. R. Sackett, "Interpersonal Deviance, Organizational Deviance, and Their Common Correlates: A Review and Meta-Analysis," *Journal of Applied Psychology*, 2007, 92, pp. 410–424.

92. P. R. Sackett and J. E. Wanek, "New Developments in the Use of Measures of Honesty, Integrity, Conscientiousness, Dependability, Trustworthiness, and Reliability for Personnel Selection," *Personnel Psychology*, 1996, 49, pp. 787–829.

93. C. M. Berry, P. R. Sackett, and S. Wiemann, "A Review of Recent Developments in Integrity Test Research," *Personnel Psychology*, 2007, 60, pp. 271–301.

94. B. Marcus, K. Lee, and M. C. Ashton, "Personality Dimensions Explaining Relations Between Integrity Tests and Counterproductive Behavior: Big Five, or One in Addition?" *Personnel Psychology*, 2007, 60, pp. 1–34.

95. D. S. Ones, C. Viswesvaran, and S. Dilchert, "Personality at Work: Raising Awareness and Correcting Misconceptions," *Human Performance*, 2005, 18, pp. 389–404.

96. D. S. Ones, C. Viswesvaran, and F. L. Schmidt, "Comprehensive Meta-Analysis of Integrity Test Validities: Findings and Implications for Personnel Selection and Theories of Job Performance," *Journal of Applied Psychology* (monograph), 1993, 78, pp. 531–537.

97. Berry, Sackett, and Wiemann, "A Review of Recent Developments in Integrity Test Research."

98. R. J. Karren and L. Zacharias, "Integrity Tests: Critical Issues," *Human Resource Management Review*, 2007, 17, pp. 221–234.

99. Hausknecht, Day, and Thomas, "Applicant Reactions to Selection Procedures: An Updated Model and Meta-Analysis."

100. R. R. McCrae and P. T. Costa, Jr., "Reinterpreting the Myers-Briggs Type Indicator From the Perspective of the Five-Factor Model of Personality," *Journal of Personality*, 1989, 57, pp. 17–40.

101. C. H. Van Iddekinge, D. J. Putka, and J. P. Campbell, "Reconsidering Vocational Interests for Personnel Selection: The Validity of an Interest-Based Selection Test in Relation to Job Knowledge, Job Performance, and Continuance Intentions," *Journal of Applied Psychology*, 2011, 96(1), pp. 13–33.

102. M. Assouline and E. I. Meir, "Meta-Analysis of the Relationship Between Congruence and Well-Being Measures," *Journal of Vocational Behavior*, 1987, 31, pp. 319–332.

103. See B. Schneider, H. W. Goldstein, and D. B. Smith, "The ASA Framework: An Update," *Personnel Psychology*, 1995, 48, pp. 747–773.

104. D. M. Cable, "The Role of Person-Organization Fit in Organizational Entry," Unpublished doctoral dissertation, Cornell University, Ithaca, NY, 1995.

105. R. W. Eder and M. Harris (eds.), *The Employment Interview Handbook* (Thousand Oaks, CA: Sage, 1999).

106. M. Hosoda, E. F. Stone-Romero, and G. Coats, "The Effects of Physical Attractiveness on Job-Related Outcomes: A Meta-Analysis of Experimental Studies," *Personnel Psychology*, 2003,

56, pp. 431–462; M. R. Barrick, J. A. Shaffer, and S. W. DeGrassi, "What You See May Not Be What You Get: Relationships Among Self-Presentation Tactics and Ratings of Interview and Job Performance," *Journal of Applied Psychology*, 2009, 94, pp. 1394–1411; "Survey Finds Employers Form Opinions of Job Interviewees Within 10 Minutes," *IPMA-HR Bulletin*, Apr. 21, 2007, p. 1; M. Bertrand and S. Mullainathan, "Are Emily and Greg More Employable Than Lakisha and Jamal? A Field Experiment on Labor Market Discrimination," *American Economic Review*, 2004, 94, pp. 991–1013; S. L. Purkiss, P. L. Perrewé, T. L. Gillespie, B. T. Mayes, and G. R. Ferris, "Implicit Sources of Bias in Employment Interview Judgments and Decisions," *Organizational Behavior and Human Decision Processes*, 2006, 101, pp. 152–167.

107. M. A. Campion, D. K. Palmer, and J. E. Campion, "A Review of Structure in the Selection Interview," *Personnel Psychology*, 1997, 50, pp. 655–702.

108. G. P. Latham, L. M. Saari, E. D. Pursell, and M. A. Campion, "The Situational Interview," *Journal of Applied Psychology*, 1980, 65, pp. 422–427; S. D. Maurer, "The Potential of the Situational Interview: Existing Research and Unresolved Issues," *Human Resource Management Review*, 1997, 7, pp. 185–201.

109. A. I. Huffcutt, J. N. Conurey, P. L. Roth, and U. Klehe, "The Impact of Job Complexity and Study Design on Situational and Behavior Description Interview Validity," *International Journal of Selection and Assessment*, 2004, 12, pp. 262–273.

110. M. A. McDaniel, D. L. Whetzel, F. L. Schmidt, and S. D. Maurer, "The Validity of Employment Interviews: A Comprehensive Review and Meta-Analysis," *Journal of Applied Psychology*, 1994, 79, pp. 599–616; Huffcutt et al., "The Impact of Job Complexity and Study Design on Situational and Behavior Description Interview Validity."

111. K. I. van der Zee, A. B. Bakker, and P. Bakker, "Why Are Structured Interviews So Rarely Used in Personnel Selection?" *Journal of Applied Psychology*, 2002, 87, pp. 176–184; F. Lievens and A. De Paepe, "An Empirical Investigation of Interviewer-Related Factors That Discourage the Use of High Structure Interviews," *Journal of Organizational Behavior*, 2004, 25, pp. 29–46; N. Smith, "Using Structured Interviews to Increase Your Organization's Hiring Investments," *HR Weekly*, Oct. 2006, pp. 1–3.

112. Hausknecht, Day, and Thomas, "Applicant Reactions to Selection Procedures: An Updated Model and Meta-Analysis."

113. A. I. Huffcutt and P. L. Roth, "Racial Group Differences in Interview Evaluations," *Journal of Applied Psychology*, 1998, 83, pp. 179–189.

114. C. H. Van Iddekinge, C. E. Sager, J. L. Burnfield, and T. S. Heffner, "The Variability of Criterion-Related Validity Estimates Among Interviewers and Interview Panels," *International Journal of Selection and Assessment*, 2006, 14, pp. 193–205; M. R. Barrick, B. W. Swider, and G. L. Stewart, "Initial Evaluations in the Interview: Relationships With Subsequent Interviewer Evaluations and Employment Offers," *Journal of Applied Psychology*, 2010, 95, pp. 1163–1172.

115. M. Harris, "Reconsidering the Employment Interview: A Review of Recent Literature and Suggestions for Future Research," *Personnel Psychology*, 1989, 42, pp. 691–726.

116. D. S. Chapman and D. I. Zweig, "Developing a Nomological Network for Interview Structure: Antecedents and Consequences of the Structured Selection Interview," *Personnel Psychology*, 2005, 58, pp. 673–702.

117. S. P. Robbins and T. A. Judge, *Organizational Behavior*, thirteenth ed. (Upper Saddle River, NJ: Prentice-Hall, 2008).

118. Robbins and Judge, *Organizational Behavior*.

119. M. J. Stevens and M. A. Campion, "The Knowledge, Skill, and Ability Requirements for Teamwork: Implications for Human Resource Management," *Journal of Management*, 1994, 20, pp. 503–530.

120. M. J. Stevens, "Staffing Work Teams: Testing for Individual-Level Knowledge, Skill, and Ability Requirements for Teamwork," Unpublished doctoral dissertation, Purdue University, West Lafayette, IN, 1993.

121. R. S. Wellens, W. C. Byham, and G. R. Dixon, *Inside Teams* (San Francisco: Jossey-Bass, 1995).

122. T. V. Mumford, C. H. Van Iddekinge, F. P. Morgeson, and M. A. Campion, "The Team Role Test: Development and Validation of a Team Role Knowledge Situational Judgment Test," *Journal of Applied Psychology*, 2008, 93(2), pp. 250–267.

123. S. M. Colarelli and A. L. Boos, "Sociometric and Ability-Based Assignment to Work Groups: Some Implications for Personnel Selection," *Journal of Organizational Behavior Management*, 1992, 13, pp. 187–196; M. Levinson, "When Workers Do the Hiring," *Newsweek*, June 21, 1993, p. 48.

124. B. Dumaine, "The Trouble With Teams," *Fortune*, Sept. 5, 1994, pp. 86–92.

125. W. C. Borman and S. J. Motowidlo, "Expanding the Criterion Domain to Include Elements of Contextual Performance," in N. Schmitt, W. Borman, and Associates (eds.), *Personnel Selection in Organizations* (San Francisco: Jossey-Bass, 1993), pp. 71–98.

126. "Why Worry About Drugs and Alcohol in the Workplace?" Facts for Employers, American Council for Drug Education, 2007 (*www.acde.org/employer/DAwork.htm*).

127. Smithers Institute, "Drug Testing: Cost and Effect," *Cornell/Smithers Report*, Vol. 1 (Ithaca, NY: Cornell University, 1992), pp. 1–5.

128. "U.S. Corporations Reduce Levels of Medical, Drug and Psychological Testing of Employees," American Management Association, 2007 (*www.amanet.org/press/archives/reduce.htm*).

129. *Amphetamines Use Declined Significantly Among U.S. Workers in 2005, According to Quest Diagnostics' Drug Testing Index*, Quest Diagnostics Incorporated, 2006.

130. L. Paik, "Organizational Interpretations of Drug Test Results," *Law & Society Review*, Dec. 2006, pp. 1–28.

131. *Mandatory Guidelines and Proposed Revisions to Mandatory Guidelines for Federal Workplace Drug Testing Programs*, Department of Health and Human Services, Substance Abuse and Mental Health Services Administration, 2004.

132. S. Overman, "Debating Drug Test ROI," *Staffing Management*, Oct.–Dec. 2005, pp. 19–22.

133. S. Overman, "Refusing to Hire Candidates Who Test Positive for Nicotine May Help Reduce Health Care Costs. But Is It Worth It? *Staffing Management*, Jan. 1, 2008 (*www.shrm.org/Publications/StaffingManagementMagazine*), accessed 1/28/2011.

134. K. Helliker, "A Test for Alcohol—and Its Flaws," *Wall Street Journal*, Aug. 12, 2006, pp. A1, A6.

135. J. Normand, S. D. Salyards, and J. J. Mahoney, "An Evaluation of Preemployment Drug Testing," *Journal of Applied Psychology*, 1990, 75, pp. 629–639.

136. J. M. Crant and T. S. Bateman, "An Experimental Test of the Impact of Drug-Testing Programs on Potential Job Applicants' Attitudes and Intentions," *Journal of Applied Psychology*, 1990, 75, pp. 127–131; K. R. Murphy, G. C. Thornton III, and D. H. Reynolds, "College Students' Attitudes Toward Employee Drug Testing Programs," *Personnel Psychology*, 1990, 43, pp. 615–631.

137. E. A. Fleishman, "Some New Frontiers in Personnel Selection Research," *Personnel Psychology*, 1988, 41, pp. 679–701.

138. M. A. Campion, "Personnel Selection for Physically Demanding Jobs: Review and Recommendations," *Personnel Psychology*, 1983, 36, pp. 527–550.

139. W. F. Cascio and H. Aquinis, "The Federal Uniform Guidelines on Employee Selection Procedures: An Update on Selected Issues," *Review of Public Personnel Administration*, 2001, 21, pp. 200–218; C. Daniel, "Separating Law and Professional Practice From Politics: The Uniform

Guidelines Then and Now," *Review of Public Personnel Administration*, 2001, 21, pp. 175–184; A.I.E. Ewoh and J. S. Guseh, "The Status of the Uniform Guidelines on Employee Selection Procedures: Legal Developments and Future Prospects," *Review of Public Personnel Administration*, 2001, 21, pp. 185–199; G. P. Panaro, *Employment Law Manual*, second ed. (Boston: Warren Gorham Lamont, 1993), pp. 3-28 to 3-82.

140. Equal Employment Opportunity Commission, *Technical Assistance Manual of the Employment Provisions (Title 1) of the Americans With Disabilities Act* (Washington, DC: author, 1992), pp. 51–88; J. G. Frierson, *Employer's Guide to the Americans With Disabilities Act* (Washington, DC: Bureau of National Affairs, 1992); D. L. Stone and K. L. Williams, "The Impact of the ADA on the Selection Process: Applicant and Organizational Issues," *Human Resource Management Review*, 1997, 7, pp. 203–231.

141. L. Daley, M. Dolland, J. Kraft, M. A. Nester, and R. Schneider, *Employment Testing of Persons With Disabling Conditions* (Alexandria, VA: International Personnel Management Association, 1988); L. D. Eyde, M. A. Nester, S. M. Heaton, and A. V. Nelson, *Guide for Administering Written Employment Examinations to Persons With Disabilities* (Washington, DC: US Office of Personnel Management, 1994).

142. Equal Employment Opportunity Commission, *ADA Enforcement Guidance: Preemployment Disability Related Questions and Medical Examinations* (Washington, DC: author, 1995).

143. Equal Employment Opportunity Commission, *Enforcement Guidance on Disability-Related Inquiries and Medical Examinations of Employees Under the Americans With Disabilities Act* (Washington, DC: author, 2001).

144. J. E. Balls, "Dealing With Drugs: Keep It Legal," *HR Magazine*, Mar. 1998, pp. 104–116; A. G. Feliu, *Primer on Employee Rights* (Washington, DC: Bureau of National Affairs, 1998), pp. 137–166.

CHAPTER TEN

Internal Selection

Learning Objectives and Introduction
Learning Objectives
Introduction

Preliminary Issues
The Logic of Prediction
Types of Predictors
Selection Plan

Initial Assessment Methods
Talent Management/Succession Systems
Peer Assessments
Self-Assessments
Managerial Sponsorship
Informal Discussions and Recommendations
Choice of Initial Assessment Methods

Substantive Assessment Methods
Seniority and Experience
Job Knowledge Tests
Performance Appraisal
Promotability Ratings
Assessment Centers
Interview Simulations
Promotion Panels and Review Boards
Choice of Substantive Assessment Methods

Discretionary Assessment Methods

Legal Issues
Uniform Guidelines on Employee Selection Procedures
The Glass Ceiling

Summary

Discussion Questions

Ethical Issues

Applications

LEARNING OBJECTIVES AND INTRODUCTION

Learning Objectives

- Compare how the logic of prediction applies to internal vs. external selection decisions
- Evaluate the relative advantages and disadvantages of the five initial assessment methods used in internal selection
- Consider the merits and pitfalls of using seniority and experience for internal selection decisions
- Describe the main features of assessment centers
- Understand the advantages and disadvantages of using assessment centers for internal selection decisions
- Evaluate the relative advantages and disadvantages of the seven substantive assessment methods used in internal selection

Introduction

Internal selection refers to the assessment and evaluation of employees from within the organization as they move from job to job via transfer and promotion systems. Internal selection is of considerable practical value to an organization because one nearly always knows one's own employees better than external applicants, and effective internal selection decisions can motivate valued employees in any organization.

Preliminary issues we will discuss to guide the use of these assessment methods include the logic of prediction, the nature of predictors, and the development of a selection plan. Initial assessment methods are used to select internal candidates from among the internal applicants. Methods that will be reviewed include talent management/succession systems, peer assessments and self-assessments, managerial sponsorship, and informal discussions and recommendations. The criteria that should be used to choose among these methods will be discussed.

Substantive assessment methods are used to select internal finalists from among the internal candidates. Various methods will be reviewed, including seniority and experience, job knowledge tests, performance appraisal, promotability ratings, assessment centers, interview simulations, and promotion panels and review boards. The criteria used to choose among the substantive assessment methods will also be discussed.

Discretionary assessment methods are used to select offer recipients from among the finalists. The factors on which these decisions are based, such as equal employment opportunity and affirmative action (EEO/AA) concerns, whether the finalist had previously been a finalist, and second opinions about the finalist by others in the organization, will be considered.

All of these assessment methods require a large amount of data to be collected. Accordingly, attention must be given to support services, the required expertise needed to administer and interpret predictors, security, privacy and confidentiality, and the standardization of procedures. Also, the use of internal selection methods requires a clear understanding of legal issues.

PRELIMINARY ISSUES

The Logic of Prediction

The logic of prediction, described in Chapter 8, is equally relevant to the case of internal selection. Specifically, indicators of internal applicants' degree of success in past situations should be predictive of their likely success in new situations. Past situations importantly include previous jobs, as well as the current one, held by the applicant with the organization. The new situation is the internal vacancy the applicant is seeking via the organization's transfer or promotion system.

There may also be similarities between internal and external selection in terms of the effectiveness of selection methods. As you may recall from Chapters 8 and 9, three of the most valid external selection measures are biographical data, cognitive ability tests, and work samples. These methods also have validity in internal selection decisions. Personality measures have been found to be a valid predictor in selecting top corporate leaders. Research indicates that cognitive ability is strongly predictive of long-term job performance and advancement. Finally, work samples are valid predictors of advancement.[1] In this chapter we focus on processes and methods of selection that are unique to promotion and transfer decisions. However, in considering these methods and processes, it should be remembered that many of the techniques of external selection may be relevant as well.

Although the logic of prediction and the likely effectiveness of selection methods are similar for external and internal selection, in practice there are several potential advantages of internal over external selection. In particular, the data collected on internal applicants in their previous jobs often provide greater depth, relevance, and verifiability than the data collected on external applicants. This is because organizations usually have much more detailed and in-depth information about internal candidates' previous job experiences.

Along with depth and relevance, another positive aspect of the nature of predictors for internal selection is variability. Rather than simply relying on the opinion of one person as to the suitability of an internal candidate for the job, multiple assessments may be solicited, such as from other supervisors and peers. By pooling opinions, it is possible to get a more complete and accurate picture of a candidate's qualifications.

While internal selection has important advantages over external selection, two factors can derail the logic of prediction. First, impression management and organizational politics can play important roles in who gets promoted in organizations. Although impression management also plays a role in external hiring (especially in employment interviews), internal "apple polishers" have a much greater opportunity to work their magic, with more targets for their influence and over a longer period of time, than external candidates. Thus, decision makers selecting internal candidates need to make sure they are not being "played" by internal candidates. A second factor that can undermine the logic of prediction for internal selection is title inflation. A recent study revealed that the job responsibilities of nearly half (46%) of recently promoted executives remained roughly the same after their new titles. Although there may be no great harm in such title inflation, the newly promoted, with no corresponding change in pay or responsibilities, should see these "promotions" for what they are. Being given a title of "process change manager" may mean little more than words.[2]

Types of Predictors

The distinctions made between types of predictors used in external selection are also applicable to types of internal predictors. One important difference to note between internal and external predictors pertains to content. There is usually greater depth and relevance to the data available on internal candidates. That is, the organization can go to its own files or managers to get reports on the applicants' previous experiences.

Selection Plan

Often it seems that internal selection is done on the basis of "who you know" rather than relevant knowledge, skill, ability, and other characteristics (KSAOs). Managers tend to rely heavily on the subjective opinions of previous managers who supervised the internal candidate. When asked why they rely on these subjective assessments, the answer is often, "Because the candidate has worked here for a long time, and I trust the supervisor's feel for the candidate."

Decision errors often occur when relying on subjective feelings for internal selection decisions. For example, in selecting managers to oversee engineering and scientific personnel in organizations, it is sometimes felt that those internal job candidates with the best technical skills will be the best managers. This is not always the case. Some technical wizards are poor managers and vice versa. Sound internal selection procedures need to be followed to guard against this error. A sound job analysis will show that both technical and managerial skills need to be assessed with well-crafted predictors.

Feel, hunch, gut instinct, intuition, and the like do not substitute for well-developed predictors. Relying solely on others' "feelings" about the job applicant may result in lowered hiring standards for some employees, discrimination against protected-class employees, and decisions with low validity. Therefore, it is imperative that a selection plan be used for internal as well as external selection. As described in Chapter 8, a selection plan lists the predictors to be used for assessment of each KSAO.

INITIAL ASSESSMENT METHODS

The internal recruitment process may generate a large number of applications for vacant positions. This is especially true when an open recruitment system (where jobs are posted for employees to apply) rather than a closed recruitment system is used. Given the time and cost of rigorous selection procedures, organizations use initial assessment methods to screen out applicants who do not meet the minimum qualifications needed to become a candidate. Initial assessment methods for internal recruitment typically include the following predictors: talent management/ succession systems, peer evaluations, self-assessments, managerial sponsorship, and informal discussions and recommendations. Each of these predictors will be discussed in turn, followed by a general evaluation of all predictors.

Talent Management/Succession Systems

Most organizations have a desire to internally select, or promote from within, for both informational and motivational reasons. The reasons are, respectively, that one knows one's employees better than external applicants and that valued employees may be motivated, and retained, based on an expectation of future promotions. However, a major problem with internal selection, especially for medium-sized and large organizations, is finding out which employees have the desired skills. This is where talent management/succession systems come into play.

Talent management/succession systems—sometimes called human capital management—keep an ongoing organizational record of the skills, talents, and capabilities of an organization's employees to inform human resource (HR) decisions. Talent management/succession systems can be used to attain many goals, including performance management, recruitment needs analysis, employee development, and compensation and career management. However, one of the primary goals of such systems is to facilitate internal selection decisions by keeping an organized, up-to-date record of employee skills, talents, and capabilities.

As logical as talent management/succession systems seem, a recent survey of large multinationals revealed that less than half had such a system in place. Organizations may not use a talent management system for two reasons. First, it may be perceived as too costly. However, the cost of a talent management/succession system should be considered against the cost of *not* using a system: What are the costs of making selection decisions based on incomplete knowledge of the skills and capabilities of current employees? Second, the expertise to develop a system may not be available.

This problem can be mitigated by working with a vendor that specializes in talent management software. Talent management/succession software is often integrated within a vendor's human resource information systems (HRISs). For example, the two largest HRIS providers—SAP and Oracle/Peoplesoft—include talent management systems in the HRIS packages they market to organizations.

Whether developed internally or purchased from a vendor, a good talent management/succession system includes the KSAOs held by each employee in the organization. The KSAOs are organized by skill categories such as education/experience, intangible talents such as leadership accomplishments and potential, and ratings of managerial competencies or talents. An effective talent management/succession system also includes the employee's current position, along with any future positions that the employee is capable of occupying. Additionally, a good talent management system also summarizes the data so that a skills audit can be generated to ascertain unit- or organization-wide talent shortages. Indianapolis-based pharmaceutical giant Eli Lilly does this on a quarterly basis.

One of the problems with talent management/succession systems is that they often quickly become outdated. For it to be useful (rather than simply another bureaucratic form to complete), managers must systematically enter the latest skills acquired by employees into the database as soon as they are developed. Another limitation is that the KSAOs are often rather general or generic. For a talent management/succession system to be successful, it must be specific, be actively maintained and updated, be aligned with an organization's strategies (so as to anticipate future talent needs), and be used when internal selection decisions are made.[3]

Peer Assessments

Assessments by peers or coworkers can be used to evaluate the promotability of an internal applicant. A variety of methods can be used, including peer ratings, peer nominations, and peer rankings.[4] Examples of all three are shown in Exhibit 10.1.

As can be seen in Exhibit 10.1, whereas peers are used to make promotion decisions in all three methods of peer assessments, the format of each is different. With peer ratings, readiness to be promoted is assessed using a rating scale for each peer. The person with the highest rating is deemed most promotable. Peer nominations rely on voting for the most promotable candidates. Peers receiving the greatest number of votes are the most promotable. Finally, peer rankings rely on a rank ordering of peers. Those peers with the highest rankings are the most promotable.

Peer assessments have been used extensively in the military over the years and to a lesser degree in industry. A virtue of peer assessments is that they rely on raters who presumably are very knowledgeable of the applicants' KSAOs due to their day-to-day contact with them. A possible downside to peer assessments, however, is that they may encourage friendship bias. Also, they may undermine morale in a work group by fostering a competitive environment.

EXHIBIT 10.1 **Peer Assessment Methods**

Peer Rating

On a scale of 1–5, please rate the following employees for the position of manager as described in the job requirements matrix:

	Not Promotable		Promotable in One Year		Promotable Now
	1	2	3	4	5
Jean	1	2	3	4	5
John	1	2	3	4	5
Andy	1	2	3	4	5
Herb	1	2	3	4	5

Peer Nominations

Please place an X next to the employee who is most promotable to the position of manager as described in the job requirements matrix:

Joe	_____
Nishant	_____
Carlos	_____
Suraphon	_____
Renee	_____

Peer Ranking

Please rank order the following employees from the most promotable (1) to the least promotable (5) for the position of manager as described in the job requirements matrix:

Ila	_____
Karen	_____
Phillip	_____
Yi-Chan	_____
Kimlang	_____

Another possible problem is that the criteria by which assessments are made are not always made clear. For peer assessments to work, the KSAOs needed for successful performance in the position the peer is being considered for should be spelled out in advance. To do so, a job requirements matrix should be used.

A probable virtue of peer assessments is that peers are more likely to feel that the decisions reached are fair since they had an input into the decision. The decision is thus not seen as a "behind the back" maneuver by management. Therefore, peer assessments are used more often with open rather than closed systems of internal recruitment.

Self-Assessments

Job incumbents can be asked to evaluate their own skills as a basis for determining promotability. This procedure is sometimes used with open recruitment systems. An example of this approach is shown in Exhibit 10.2. Caution must be exercised in using this process for selection, as it may raise the expectations of those rating themselves that they will be selected. As one VP of HR noted, "Some people think

---

EXHIBIT 10.2   Self-Assessment Form Used for Application in Job Posting System

SUPPLEMENTAL QUESTIONNAIRE

This supplemental questionnaire will be the principal basis for determining whether or not you are highly qualified for this position. You may add information not identified in your SF-171 or expand on that which is identified. You should consider appropriate work experience, outside activities, awards, training, and education for each of the items listed below.

1. Knowledge of the Bureau of Indian Affairs' mission, organization, structure, policies, and functions, as they relate to real estate.
2. Knowledge of technical administrative requirements to provide technical guidance in administrative areas, such as personnel regulations, travel regulations, time and attendance requirements, budget documents, Privacy Act, and Freedom of Information Act, etc.
3. Ability to work with program directors and administrative staff and ability to apply problem-solving techniques and management concepts; ability to analyze facts and problems and develop alternatives.
4. Ability to operate various computer programs and methodology in the analysis and design of automated methods for meeting the information and reporting requirements for the division.
5. Knowledge of the bureau budget process and statistical profile of all field operations that impact in the Real Estate Services program.

On a separate sheet of paper, address the above items in narrative form. Identify the vacancy announcement number across the top. Sign and date your Supplemental Questionnaire.

Source: Department of the Interior, Bureau of Indian Affairs. Form BIA-4450 (4/22/92).

a lot more highly of their skills and talent" than is warranted. Employees' supervisors should encourage upward mobility (not "hoard" talent), but they also need to ensure that employees are realistic in their self-assessments.[5]

Managerial Sponsorship

Increasingly, organizations are relying on higher-ups to identify and develop the KSAOs of those at lower levels in the organization. Historically, the higher-up has been the person's immediate supervisor. Today, however, the higher-up may be a person at a higher level of the organization who does not have direct responsibility for the person being rated. Higher-ups are sometimes labeled coaches, sponsors, or mentors, and their roles are defined in Exhibit 10.3. Some organizations have formal mentorship programs where employees are assigned coaches, sponsors, and mentors. In other organizations, these matches may naturally occur, often progressing from coach to sponsor to mentor as the relationship matures. Regardless of the formality of the relationship, these individuals are often given considerable influence in promotion decisions.

EXHIBIT 10.3   Employee Advocates

Coach

- Provides day-to-day feedback
- Diagnoses and resolves performance problems
- Creates opportunities for employees using existing training programs and career development programs

Sponsor

- Actively promotes person for advancement opportunities
- Guides person's career rather than simply informing them of opportunities
- Creates opportunities for people in decision-making capacities to see the skills of the employee (e.g., lead a task force)

Mentor

- Becomes personally responsible for the success of the person
- Available to person on and off the job
- Lets person in on "insider" information
- Solicits and values person's input

SOURCE: Reprinted with permission from Dr. Janina Latack, PhD, Nelson O'Connor & Associates/Outplacement International, Phoenix/Tucson.

Important, too, is the developmental nature of these relationships. Sponsors are in a position to not only internally select candidates whom they sponsor but also give these individuals valuable developmental experiences that make them viable candidates in the future. Research shows that employees working with sponsors who provide them with challenging developmental experiences earn higher promotability ratings after those experiences. Mentors, too, may provide "psychosocial" support for employees—by being a sounding board, a source of interpersonal support, or a confidante—and, indeed, this form of support may be the clearest consequence of mentoring.[6]

Informal Discussions and Recommendations

Not all promotion decisions are made on the basis of formal HR policy and procedures. For many promotions, much or all of the decision process occurs outside normal channels, through informal discussions and recommendations. For example, Celeste Russell, vice president of HR for Good Times Entertainment, a New York home video and direct marketing company, invites employees out for coffee. "It's like a sales call," she says. Although such informal discussions are a common means of internal selection decisions, especially in small companies, they may have limited validity because they are quite subjective. Although Russell prides herself on knowing the names of employees' pets and other personal information, it seems likely the personal and subjective nature of these conversations compromises her ability to make internal selection decisions relative to "cold and hard" data such as skills, accomplishments, abilities, and so forth. Such is the case with many, if not most, informal approaches to selection.[7]

Choice of Initial Assessment Methods

As was discussed, there are several formal and informal methods of initial assessment available to screen internal applicants to produce a list of candidates. Research has been conducted on the effectiveness of each method, which will now be presented to help determine which initial assessment methods should be used. The reviews of this research are summarized in Exhibit 10.4.

In Exhibit 10.4, the same criteria are applied to evaluate the effectiveness of these predictors as were used to evaluate the effectiveness of predictors for external selection. Cost refers to expenses incurred in using the predictor. Reliability refers to the consistency of measurement. Validity refers to the strength of the relationship between the predictor and job performance. Low validity ranges from about .00 to .15, moderate validity ranges from about .16 to .30, and high validity is .31 and above. Utility refers to the monetary return, minus costs, associated with using the predictor. Adverse impact refers to the possibility that a disproportionate number of women and minorities are rejected using this predictor. Finally, applicant reactions refers to the likely impact on applicants.

EXHIBIT 10.4 Evaluation of Initial Assessment Methods

Predictors	Use	Cost	Reliability	Validity	Utility	Applicant Reactions	Adverse Impact
Self-nominations	Low	Low	Moderate	Moderate	?	Mixed	?
Talent management/ succession systems	High	High	Moderate	Moderate	?	?	?
Peer assessments	Low	Low	High	High	?	Negative	?
Managerial sponsorship	Low	Moderate	?	?	?	Positive	?
Informal methods	High	Low	?	?	?	Mixed	?

Two points should be made about the effectiveness of initial internal selection methods. First, talent management/succession systems and informal methods are used extensively, suggesting that many organizations continue to rely on closed rather than open internal recruitment systems. Certainly this is a positive procedure when administrative ease is of importance. However, it must be noted that talented applicants may be overlooked in these approaches. Also, there may be a discriminatory impact on women and minorities.

The second point is that peer assessment methods are very promising in terms of reliability and validity. They are not frequently used, but more organizations should consider using them as a screening device. Perhaps this will take place as organizations continue to decentralize decision making and empower employees to make business decisions historically made only by the supervisor.

SUBSTANTIVE ASSESSMENT METHODS

The internal applicant pool is narrowed down to candidates using the initial assessment methods. A decision as to which internal candidates will become finalists is usually made using the following substantive assessment methods: seniority and experience, job knowledge tests, performance appraisal, promotability ratings, assessment centers, interview simulations, and review boards. After each of these methods is discussed, an evaluation is made.

Seniority and Experience

At first blush the concepts of seniority and experience may seem the same. In reality, however, they are quite different. Seniority typically refers to length of service or tenure with the organization, department, or job. For example, company seniority is measured as length of continuous employment in an organization—the difference between the present date of employment and the date of hire. Thus, seniority is a purely quantitative measure that has nothing to do with the type or quality of job experiences.

Conversely, experience generally has a broader meaning. While seniority may be one aspect of experience, experience also reflects *type* of experience. Two employees working at the same company for 20 years may have the same level of seniority but very different levels of experience if one employee has performed a number of different jobs, worked in different areas of the organization, enrolled in various training programs, and so on. Thus, experience includes not only length of service in the organization or in various positions in the organization but also the kinds of activities undertaken in those positions. So, although seniority and experience are often considered synonymous, they are quite different. And as we will see in the following discussion, these differences have real implications for internal selection decisions.

Use and Evaluation

Seniority and experience are among the most prevalent methods of internal selection. Most unionized companies place heavy reliance on seniority over other KSAOs for advancement, and most union contracts stipulate that seniority be considered in promotion decisions. Indeed, research suggests that seniority matters more to the wages and advancement of union workers than nonunion workers. In policy, nonunion organizations claim to place less weight on seniority than other factors in making advancement decisions. In practice, however, at least one study showed that regardless of the wording in policy statements, heavy emphasis is still placed on seniority in nonunion settings. Research has shown that seniority is more likely to be used for promotions in small, unionized, and capital-intensive companies.[8]

Seniority and experience are widely used methods of internal selection decisions for many reasons. First, organizations believe that direct experience in a job content area reflects an accumulated stock of KSAOs necessary to perform the job. In short, experience may be content valid because it reflects on-the-job experience. Second, seniority and experience information is easily obtained. Furthermore, unions believe that reliance on objective measures such as seniority and experience protects the employee from capricious treatment and favoritism. Finally, promoting experienced or senior individuals is socially acceptable because it is seen as rewarding loyalty.

Due to these reasons, moving from a seniority-based system is not easy, particularly in union environments. When former Washington, DC, mayor Adrian Fenty and former schools chancellor Michelle Rhee attempted to reduce the weight placed on seniority in teacher hiring, promotion, and pay decisions, they were met with fierce resistance from teachers and teachers' unions.[9]

In evaluating seniority and experience as methods of internal selection, it is important to return to our earlier distinction between the two concepts. A meta-analysis of 350 empirical studies revealed that seniority (organizational tenure) was rather weakly related to task performance ($\bar{r}_{xy} = .10$), helping behavior at work ($\bar{r}_{xy} = .08$), work creativity ($\bar{r}_{xy} = .06$), and work counterproductive behavior ($\bar{r}_{xy} = -.07$).[10]

As compared with seniority, evidence for the validity of experience is more positive. A large-scale review of the literature has shown that experience is moderately related to job performance.[11] Research suggests that experience is predictive of job performance in the short run but is followed by a plateau during which experience loses its ability to predict job performance. It appears that most of the effect of experience on performance is because experienced employees have greater job knowledge. However, while experience may result in increased performance due to greater job knowledge, it does not remedy performance difficulties due to low ability; initial performance deficits of low-ability employees are not remedied by increased experience over time.[12] Thus, while experience is more likely to be related to job performance than seniority, neither ranks among the most valid predictors for internal selection decisions.

Several conclusions drawn from the research evidence about the use of seniority and experience in internal selection decisions seem appropriate:

1. Experience is a more valid method of internal selection than seniority (although unionized employers may have little choice but to use seniority).
2. Experience is better suited to predict short-term rather than long-term potential.
3. Experience is more likely to be content valid if the past or present jobs are similar to the future job.
4. Employees seem to expect that promotions will go to the most senior or experienced employee, so using seniority or experience for promotions may yield positive reactions from employees.
5. Experience is unlikely to remedy initial performance difficulties of low-ability employees.

Job Knowledge Tests

Job knowledge measures one's mastery of the concepts needed to perform certain work. Job knowledge is a complex concept that includes elements of both ability (capacity to learn) and seniority (opportunity to learn). It is usually measured with a paper-and-pencil test. To develop a paper-and-pencil test to assess job knowledge, the content domain from which test questions will be constructed must be clearly identified. For example, a job knowledge test used to select sales managers from salespeople must identify the specific knowledge necessary for being a successful sales manager.

Federal Express developed an innovative video-based job knowledge test to be used as part of its promotion system.[13] The interactive test assesses employees' ability to deal with customers. The test is based on job analysis data derived from the critical tasks necessary to deliver high levels of customer service. The test, termed QUEST (Quality Using Electronic Systems Training), presents employees with a menu of modules on CD-ROM (e.g., delivering packages, defensive driving). A 90% competency level on the test is the expectation for minimum performance—and subsequent promotability. This suggests that such assessments could fruitfully be used in internal selection decisions when promoting employees into customer-sensitive positions. The greater the employee's portfolio of customer skills, the better the employee should be able to help Federal Express meet its customer service goals.

Although job knowledge is not a well-researched method of either internal or external employee selection, it holds great promise as a predictor of job

performance. This is because it reflects an assessment of previous experiences of an applicant and an important KSAO, namely, cognitive ability.[14]

Performance Appraisal

One possible predictor of future job performance is past job performance. This assumes, of course, that elements of the future job are similar to the past job. Data on employees' previous performance are routinely collected as part of the performance appraisal process and thus available for use in internal selection.

One advantage of performance appraisals over other internal assessment methods is that they are readily available in many organizations. Another desirable feature is that they probably capture both ability and motivation. Hence, they offer a very complete look at the person's qualifications for the job. Care must still be taken in using performance appraisals, because there is not always a direct correspondence between the requirements of the current job and the requirements of the position applied for. Performance appraisals should only be used as predictors when job analysis indicates a close relationship between the current job and the position applied for.

For example, performance in a highly technical position (e.g., scientist, engineer) may require certain skills (e.g., quantitative skills) that are required in both junior- and senior-level positions. Thus, using the results of the performance appraisal of the junior position is appropriate in predicting the performance in the senior position. It is not, however, appropriate to use the results of the performance appraisal for the junior-level technical job to predict performance in a job requiring a different set of skills (e.g., planning, organizing, and staffing), such as that of manager.

Although there are some advantages to using performance appraisal results for internal selection, they are far from perfect predictors. They are subject to many influences that have nothing to do with the likelihood of success in a future job.[15]

The well-known "Peter Principle"—that individuals rise to their lowest level of incompetence—illustrates another limitation of using performance appraisal as a method of internal staffing decisions.[16] The argument behind the Peter Principle is that if organizations promote individuals on the basis of their past performance, the only time that people stop being promoted is when they perform poorly in the job into which they were last promoted. Thus, over time, organizations will have internally staffed positions with individuals who are incompetent. In fact, the authors have data from a Fortune 100 company showing that less than one-fifth of the variance in an employee's current performance rating can be explained by the performance ratings of the previous three years. Thus, although past performance may have some validity in predicting future performance, the relationship may not be overly strong.

This is not to suggest that organizations should abandon using performance ratings as a factor in internal staffing decisions. Rather, the validity of using per-

EXHIBIT 10.5   Questions to Ask in Using Performance Appraisal as a Method of Internal Staffing Decisions

- Is the performance appraisal process reliable and unbiased?
- Is present job content representative of future job content?
- Have the KSAOs required for performance in the future job(s) been acquired and demonstrated in the previous job(s)?
- Is the organizational or job environment stable such that what led to past job success will lead to future job success?

formance appraisal as an internal selection method may depend on a number of considerations. Exhibit 10.5 provides several questions that should be used in deciding how much weight to place on performance appraisal as a means of making internal selection decisions. Answering yes to these questions suggests that past performance may be validly used in making internal selection decisions.

An advance over simple use of performance ratings is to review past performance records more thoroughly, including an evaluation of various dimensions of performance that are particularly relevant to job performance (where the dimensions are based on job analysis results). For example, a study of police officer promotions used a pool of six supervisors to score officers on four job-relevant police officer performance dimensions—supervisory-related education and experience, disciplined behavior, commendatory behavior, and reliability—with the goal of predicting future performance. Results of the study indicated that using ratings of past performance records was an effective method of promoting officers.[17] Such a method might be adapted to other positions and provide a useful means of incorporating past performance data into a more valid prediction of future potential.

Promotability Ratings

In many organizations, an assessment of promotability (assessment of potential for a higher-level job) is made at the same time that performance appraisals are conducted. Replacement and succession planning frequently use both types of assessments (see Chapter 3).

Promotability ratings are useful not only from a selection perspective but also from a recruitment perspective. By discussing what is needed to be promotable, employee development may be encouraged as well as coupled with organizational sponsorship of the opportunities needed to develop. In turn, the development of new skills in employees increases the internal recruitment pool for promotions.

Caution must be exercised in using promotability ratings as well. If employees receive separate evaluations for purposes of performance appraisal, promotability, and pay, the possibility exists of employees receiving mixed messages. For example, it is difficult to understand why one receives an excellent performance rating and a solid pay raise, but at the same time is rated as not promotable. Care must be taken to show employees the relevant judgments being made in each assessment. In this example, it must be clearly indicated that promotion is based not only on past performance but also on skill acquisition and opportunities for advancement.

Assessment Centers

An elaborate method of employee selection, primarily used internally and for higher-level jobs, is an assessment center. An assessment center is a collection of predictors used to forecast success. It is used for higher-level jobs because of the high costs involved in conducting the center. The assessment center can be used to select employees for lower-level jobs as well, though this is rarely done.

The theory behind assessment centers is relatively straightforward. Concern is with predicting an individual's behavior and effectiveness in critical roles, usually managerial. Since these roles require complex behavior, multiple KSAOs will predict those behaviors. Hence, there is a need to carefully identify and assess those KSAOs; multiple methods, as well as multiple assessors, will be required. The result should be higher validity than could be obtained from a single assessment method or assessor.

As with any sound selection procedure, the assessment center predictors are based on job analysis to identify KSAOs and aid in the construction of content-valid methods of assessment for those KSAOs. As a result, a selection plan must be developed when using assessment centers. An example of such a selection plan is shown in Exhibit 10.6.

Characteristics of Assessment Centers

Whereas specific characteristics vary from situation to situation, assessment centers generally have some common characteristics. Job candidates usually participate in an assessment center for a period of days rather than hours. Most assessment centers last two to three days, but some may be as long as five days. As we describe shortly, a big part of assessment centers is simulations, where employees participate in exercises and trained assessors evaluate their performance. Assessors are usually line managers, but sometimes psychologists are used as well. The average ratio of assessors to assessees ranges from 1:1 to 4:1.

The participants in the center are usually managers who are being assessed for higher-level managerial jobs. Normally, they are chosen to participate by other organization members, such as their supervisor. Often selection is based on an employee's current level of job performance.

At the conclusion of the assessment center, the participants are evaluated by the assessors. Typically, this involves the assessor examining all the information gathered about each participant. The information is then translated into a series

EXHIBIT 10.6 Selection Plan for an Assessment Center

KSAO	Writing Exercise	Speech Exercise	Analysis Problem	In-Basket		Leadership Group Discussion	
				Tent.	Final	Management Problems	City Council
Oral communications					X	X	X
Oral presentation		X				X	
Written communications	X		X	X	X		
Stress tolerance				X	X	X	X
Leadership					X	X	
Sensitivity			X	X	X	X	X
Tenacity				X	X	X	
Risk taking			X	X	X	X	X
Initiative			X	X	X	X	X
Planning & organization			X	X	X	X	X
Management control			X	X	X		
Delegation				X	X		
Problem analysis			X	X	X	X	X
Decision making			X	X	X	X	X
Decisiveness			X	X	X	X	X
Responsiveness			X	X	X	X	X

Source: Department of Employment Relations, State of Wisconsin.

of ratings on several dimensions of managerial jobs. Typical dimensions assessed include communications (written and oral), leadership and human relations, planning, problem solving, and decision making. In evaluating these dimensions, assessors are trained to look for critical behaviors that represent highly effective or ineffective responses to the exercise situations in which participants were placed. There may also be an overall assessment rating that represents the bottom-line evaluation for each participant. Assessment center dimensions are relatively highly correlated with one another, though evidence suggests that the dimensions do add to the prediction of performance beyond the overall score.[18] Exhibit 10.7 provides a sample rating form.

A variety of exercises are used at a center. Experts argue that the simulation is the key to an assessment center, though exactly how future performance is simulated varies from assessment center to assessment center.[19]

Although many assessment centers contain written tests and interviews—and thus may include some of the external selection techniques we discussed in Chapters 8 and 9—the simulation exercises are the heart of assessment centers. The most frequently used exercises are the in-basket exercise, group discussion, and case analysis. Each of these exercises will be briefly described.

In-Basket Exercise. The most commonly used assessment center exercise is the in-basket (according to one study, 82% of assessment centers use it). The in-basket (sometimes called "inbox") usually contains memoranda, reports, phone messages, and letters that require a response. When this in-basket material is presented to a candidate, he or she is asked to respond to the items by prioritizing them, drafting responses, scheduling meetings, and so forth. It is a timed exercise, and usually the candidate has two to three hours to respond. Even when used alone, the in-basket exercise seems to forecast ascendancy, one of the key criteria of assessment centers.[20]

Group Discussion. In a group discussion, a small group of candidates is given a problem to solve. The problem is one they would likely encounter in the higher-level position for which they are applying. As the candidates work on the problem, assessors sit around the perimeter of the group and evaluate how each candidate behaves in an unstructured setting. They look for skills such as leadership and communication. Roughly 60% of assessment centers include a group discussion. Some group discussion exercises assign candidates specific roles to play; others are "leaderless" in that no one is assigned a particular role. An example of the former is where participants are part of a project team and each participant assumes a role (IT, HR, marketing, etc.). An example of the latter is a "lost in the wilderness" exercise, where a group of individuals is presented a scenario in which they are lost and have a few resources on which they can survive and find their way home. Both assigned-role and leaderless group discussions assess the skills of leadership, judgment, persuasive oral communication, teamwork, and interpersonal sensitivity.

EXHIBIT 10.7   Sample Assessment Center Rating Form

Participant Name: _____

Personal Qualities:
    1. Energy   _____
    2. Risk taking   _____
    3. Tolerance for ambiguity   _____
    4. Objectivity   _____
    5. Reliability   _____

Communication Skills:
    6. Oral   _____
    7. Written   _____
    8. Persuasion   _____

Human Relations:
    9. Teamwork   _____
    10. Flexibility   _____
    11. Awareness of social environment   _____

Leadership Skills:
    12. Impact   _____
    13. Autonomy   _____

Decision-Making Skills:
    14. Decisiveness   _____
    15. Organizing   _____
    16. Planning   _____

Problem-Solving Skills:
    17. Fact finding   _____
    18. Interpreting information   _____

Overall Assessment Rating:

Indication of potential to perform
effectively at the next level is:
    Excellent   _____
    Good   _____
    Moderate   _____
    Low   _____

Case Analysis. Cases of actual business situations can also be presented to the candidates. Each candidate is asked to provide a written analysis of the case, describing the nature of the problem, likely causes, and recommended solutions. Not only are the written results evaluated but the candidate's oral report is scored as well. The candidates may be asked to give an oral presentation to a panel of managers and to respond to their questions, comments, and concerns. Case analyses are used in roughly half of all assessment centers.

Validity and Effective Practices

A study of 27 validity studies revealed that the correlation between the assessment center overall assessment rating (OAR) and job performance was reasonably positive ($\bar{r}_{xy} = .28$).[21] Another advantage of assessment centers is that they appear to have little or no adverse impact against women and minorities. Indeed, one recent study of nearly 2,000 managers found that female candidates generally performed better than male candidates. Finally, analyses based on meta-analytic data suggest that assessment centers add incremental validity over personality and cognitive ability.[22]

On the other hand, research has uncovered several problems with assessment centers. First, the construct validity of assessment center evaluations is often questioned. Research has shown that there are much stronger exercise and assessor effects than there are dimension effects, meaning that there is much higher agreement within exercises and within assessors than there is within dimensions. In short, assessment center dimensions do not show much construct validity, calling into question the content of what is being assessed in assessment centers. As one reviewer of the literature noted, "Assessment centers (ACs), as they are often designed and implemented, do not work as they are intended to work and probably never will." Two reasons why dimensional effects tend to be weak are (1) halo effects in assessors' ratings (if an assessor thinks an assessee is a strong candidate, it spills over onto ratings on other dimensions), and (2) assessee behavior tends to be consistent across situations (and thus across exercises and dimensions). These pieces of evidence do not mean assessment centers utterly lack construct validity, but the evidence does suggest that more research is needed as to what constructs are uniquely captured with assessment centers.[23]

One of the biggest limitations of assessment centers is their cost. The nature of the individualized assessment and the requirement of multiple assessors make them cost-prohibitive for many organizations. One way some organizations are mitigating the costs is through other, related assessments. The organizations videotape assessees' performance so that assessors can evaluate their performance when convenient. This saves coordination and travel costs. A practice that results in even greater cost savings is to use situational judgment tests, where assessees are given various exercises in written, video, or computerized form. A meta-analysis of 45 studies suggested that the validity of a situational judgment test composite score ($\bar{r}_{xy} = .28$) was identical to the validity of assessment centers.[24]

Another way to reduce the costs of the assessment center is to use computerized assessments. One research study reported favorable results for a computerized assessment center simulation that asked assessees to prioritize information, formulate e-mail correspondences, make decisions about hypothetical simulations, and engage in strategic planning.[25] Another means of reducing costs is to use off-the-shelf assessments provided by vendors. For example, Assessment Center Exercises (AC-ESX) is a vendor that sells more than 150 assessment center exercises, including instructions on how to train assessors, administer the exercises, and score responses. The exercises include the three most common exercises noted above, as well as scheduling exercises, interview simulations, and fact-finding exercises. While using such off-the-shelf products may save money, it is critical that assessors have proper training. Without the right training, the resulting assessment or score derived from the assessment may be so scattershot as to be useless.

There is little research that has examined participant reactions to assessment centers, though professional guidelines recommend that assessee reactions be included in the process. However, it is commonly noted that assessment centers are stressful to participants, and the unfavorable feedback that often results from participation is particularly taxing to assessees. This does mean, however, that assessment centers always or even generally generate negative reactions from assesses. It is true that assessment centers are stressful and often provide applicants with sobering feedback. Evidence also suggests, though, that assessees quickly recover from either positive or negative initial reactions from assessment center participation. It is, perhaps, more important what happens *after* the assessment center (whether the assessee was promoted; whether the feedback proved helpful) than what happened *during* the assessment center.[26]

Assessment for Global Assignments

When assessment centers were developed, little thought was given to the prospect of using assessment data to forecast job success in a foreign environment. As globalization continues, however, organizations are increasingly promoting individuals into positions overseas. A survey indicated that 80% of midsize and large companies send professionals abroad, and many plan on increasing this percentage. Because overseas assignments present additional demands on an employee beyond the typical skills and motivations required to perform a job in the host country, staffing overseas positions presents special challenges for employers. Indeed, one study revealed that cultural factors were much more important to success in an overseas assignment than were technical skills factors. Although many competencies are important to expatriate success, such as family stability/support and language skills, the most important competency is cultural adaptability and flexibility.

One means of predicting success in overseas assignments is a personality test. For example, employees who respond positively to items such as, "It is easy for me to strike up conversations with people I do not know" or "I find it easy to put myself in other people's positions" may better navigate the challenges of overseas assignments. Personnel Decisions International developed a personality test designed to assess whether employees will be successful in overseas assignments. The company reports a positive relationship between scores on the test and success in overseas assignments. Another tool is simulations or interviews designed to simulate conditions overseas or typical challenges that arise.[27] As one can see, bringing these methods together may make the assessment process for global assignments closely resemble an assessment center.

Interview Simulations

An interview simulation simulates the oral communication required on the job. It is sometimes used in an assessment center, but less frequently than in-baskets, leaderless group discussions, and case analysis. It is also used as a predictor separate from the assessment center. There are several different forms of interview simulations.[28]

Role-Play

With a role-play, the job candidate is placed in a simulated situation where he or she must interact with a person at work, such as the boss, a subordinate, or a customer. The interviewer or another individual plays one role, and the job candidate plays the role of the person in the position applied for. So, for example, in selecting someone to be promoted to a supervisory level, the job candidate may be asked to role-play dealing with a difficult employee.

Fact Finding

In a fact-finding interview, the job candidate is presented with a case or problem with incomplete information. The candidate's job is to solicit from the interviewer or a resource person the additional facts needed to resolve the case. If one was hiring someone to be an EEO manager, one might present him or her with a case where adverse impact is suggested, and then evaluate the candidate according to what data he or she solicits to confirm or disconfirm adverse impact.

Oral Presentations

In many jobs, presentations need to be made to customers, clients, or even boards of directors. To select someone to perform this role, an oral presentation can be required. This approach would be useful, for example, to see what sort of "sales pitch" a consultant might make or to see how an executive would present his or her proposed strategic plan to a board of directors.

Given the importance of interpersonal skills in many jobs, it is unfortunate that not many organizations use interview simulations. This is especially true with internal selection, where the organization knows if the person has the right credentials (e.g., company experiences, education, and training) but may not know if the person has the right interpersonal chemistry to fit in with the work group. Interview simulations allow for a systematic assessment of this chemistry rather than relying on the instinct of the interviewer. To be effective, these interviews need to be structured and evaluated according to observable behaviors identified in the job analysis as necessary for successful performance.

Promotion Panels and Review Boards

In the public sector, it is a common practice to use a panel or board of people to review the qualifications of candidates. Frequently, a combination of both internal and external candidates are being assessed. The panel or board typically consists of job experts, HR professionals, and representatives from constituencies in the community that the board represents. Having a board such as this to hire public servants, such as school superintendents or fire and police officials, offers two advantages. First, as with assessment centers, there are multiple assessors with which to ensure a complete and accurate assessment of the candidate's qualifications. Second, by participating in the selection process, constituents are likely to be more committed to the decision reached. This buy-in is particularly important for community representatives with whom the job candidate will interact. It is hoped that by having a say in the process, they will be less likely to voice objections once the candidate is hired.

Choice of Substantive Assessment Methods

Along with research on initial assessment methods, research has also been conducted on substantive assessment methods. The reviews of this research are summarized in Exhibit 10.8. The same criteria are applied to evaluating the effectiveness of these predictors as were used to evaluate the effectiveness of initial assessment methods.

An examination of Exhibit 10.8 indicates that there is no single best method of narrowing down the candidate list to finalists. What is suggested, however, is that some predictors are more likely to be effective than others. In particular, job knowledge tests, promotability ratings, and assessment centers have a strong record in terms of reliability and validity in choosing candidates. A very promising development for internal selection is the use of job knowledge tests. The validity of these tests appears to be substantial, but unfortunately, few organizations use them for internal selection purposes.

The effectiveness of several internal selection predictors (case analysis, interview simulations, and panels and review boards) is not known at this stage.

EXHIBIT 10.8   Evaluation of Substantive Assessment Methods

Predictors	Use	Cost	Reliability	Validity	Utility	Applicant Reactions	Adverse Impact
Seniority	High	Low	High	Low	?	?	High
Experience	High	Low	High	Moderate	High	Positive	Mixed
Job knowledge tests	Low	Moderate	High	High	?	?	?
Performance appraisal	Moderate	Moderate	?	Moderate	?	?	?
Promotability ratings	Low	Low	High	High	?	?	?
Assessment center	Low	High	High	High	High	?	?
In-basket exercise	Low	Moderate	Moderate	Moderate	High	Mixed	Mixed
Leaderless group discussion	Low	Low	Moderate	Moderate	?	?	?
Case analysis	Low	Low	?	Moderate	?	?	?
Global assignments	High	Moderate	?	?	?	?	?
Interview simulations	Low	Low	?	?	?	?	?
Panels and review boards	Low	?	?	?	?	?	?

Interview simulations appear to be a promising technique for jobs requiring public contact skills. All of them need additional research. Other areas in need of additional research are the utility, applicant reactions, and adverse impact associated with all the substantive assessment methods.

DISCRETIONARY ASSESSMENT METHODS

Discretionary methods are used to narrow down the list of finalists to those who will receive job offers. Sometimes all finalists will receive offers, but other times there may not be enough positions to fill for each finalist to receive an offer. As with external selection, discretionary assessments are sometimes made on the basis of organizational citizenship behavior and staffing philosophy regarding EEO/AA.

Two areas of discretionary assessment differ from external selection and need to be considered in deciding job offers. First, previous finalists who do not receive job offers do not simply disappear. They may remain with the organization in hopes of securing an offer the next time the position is open. At the margin, this may be a factor in decision making because being bypassed a second time may create a disgruntled employee. As a result, a previous finalist may be given an offer over a first-time finalist, all other things being equal.

Second, multiple assessors are generally used with internal selection. That is, not only can the hiring manager's opinion be used to select who will receive a job offer but so can the opinions of others (e.g., previous manager, top management) who are knowledgeable about the candidate's profile and the requirements of the current position. As a result, in deciding which candidates will receive job offers, evaluations by people other than the hiring manager may be accorded substantial weight in the decision-making process.

LEGAL ISSUES

From a legal perspective, methods and processes of internal selection are to be viewed in the same way as those of external selection. The laws and regulations do not distinguish between them. Consequently, most of the legal influences on internal selection have already been treated in Chapters 8 and 9. There are, however, some brief comments to be made about internal selection legal influences. Those influences are the Uniform Guidelines on Employee Selection Procedures (UGESP) and the glass ceiling.

Uniform Guidelines on Employee Selection Procedures

The UGESP define a "selection procedure" in such a way that virtually any selection method, be it used in an external or internal context, is covered by the requirements of the UGESP. Moreover, the UGESP apply to any "employment decision," which explicitly includes promotion decisions.

When there is adverse impact in promotions, the organization is given the option of justifying it through the conduct of validation studies. These are primarily criterion-related or content validity studies. Ideally, criterion-related studies with predictive validation designs will be used, as has been partially done in the case of assessment centers. Unfortunately, this places substantial administrative and research demands on the organization that are difficult to fulfill most of the time. Consequently, content validation appears to be a better bet for validation purposes.

Many of the methods of assessment used in internal selection attempt to gauge KSAOs and behaviors directly associated with a current job that are felt to be related to success in higher-level jobs. Examples include seniority, performance appraisals, and promotability ratings. These are based on current, as well as past, job content. Validation of these methods, if legally necessary, likely occurs along content validation lines. The organization thus should pay particular and close attention to the validation and documentation requirements for content validation in the UGESP.

The Glass Ceiling

In Chapter 6, the nature of the glass ceiling was discussed, as well as staffing steps to remove it from organizational promotion systems. Most of that discussion centered on internal recruitment and supporting activities that could be undertaken. Surprisingly, selection methods used for promotion assessment are rarely mentioned in literature on the glass ceiling.

This is a major oversight. Whereas the internal recruitment practices recommended may enhance the identification and attraction of minority and women candidates for promotion, effectively matching them to their new jobs requires applying internal selection processes and methods. The Equal Employment Opportunity Commission's (EEOC's) policy on nondiscriminatory promotions is (1) the KSAOs to be assessed must be job related and consistent with business necessity, and (2) there must be uniform and consistently applied standards across all promotion candidates.[29] How might the organization operate its internal selection system to comply with EEOC policy?

The first possibility is for greater use of selection plans. As discussed in Chapter 8, these plans lay out the KSAOs required for a job, which KSAOs are necessary to bring to the job (as opposed to being acquired on the job), and of those necessary, the most appropriate method of assessment for each. Such a plan forces an organization to conduct job analysis, construct career ladders or KSAO lattices, and consider alternatives to many of the traditional methods of assessment used in promotion systems.

A second suggestion is for the organization to back away from use of these traditional methods of assessment as much as possible, in ways consistent with the selection plan. This means a move away from casual, subjective methods such as supervisory recommendation, typical promotability ratings, quick reviews of personnel files, and informal recommendations. In their place should be more formal, standardized, and job-related assessment methods. Examples here include assessment centers, promotion review boards or panels, and interview simulations.

A final suggestion is for the organization to pay close attention to the types of KSAOs necessary for advancement, and undertake programs to impart these KSAOs to aspiring employees. These developmental actions might include key job and committee assignments, participation in conferences and other networking opportunities, mentoring and coaching programs, and skill acquisition in formal training programs. Internal selection methods would then be used to assess proficiency on these newly acquired KSAOs, in accordance with the selection plan.

SUMMARY

The selection of internal candidates follows a process very similar to the selection of external candidates. The logic of prediction is applied, and a selection plan is developed and implemented.

One important area where internal and external selection methods differ is in the nature of the predictor. Predictors used for internal selection tend to have greater depth and more relevance and are better suited for verification. As a result, different types of predictors are used for internal selection decisions than for external selection decisions.

Initial assessment methods are used to narrow down the applicant pool to a set of qualified candidates. Approaches used are talent management/succession systems, peer assessments, self-assessments, managerial sponsorship, and informal discussions and recommendations. Of these approaches, none is particularly strong in predicting future performance. Hence, consideration should be given to using multiple predictors to verify the accuracy of any one method. These results also point to the need to use substantive as well as initial assessment methods in making internal selection decisions.

Substantive assessment methods are used to select finalists from the list of candidates. Predictors used to make these decisions include seniority and experience, job knowledge tests, performance appraisals, promotability ratings, assessment centers, interview simulations, and panels and review boards. Of this set of predictors, job knowledge tests, promotability ratings, and assessment centers work well. Organizations need to give greater consideration to the latter three predictors to supplement traditional seniority and experience.

Although very costly, the assessment center seems to be very effective. This is because it is grounded in behavioral science theory and the logic of prediction. In particular, samples of behavior are analyzed, multiple assessors and predictors are used, and predictors are developed on the basis of job analysis.

Internal job applicants have the potential for far greater access to selection data than do external job applicants due to their physical proximity to the data. As a result, procedures must be implemented to ensure that manual and computer files with sensitive data are kept private and confidential.

Two areas of legal concern for internal selection decisions are the UGESP and the glass ceiling. In terms of the UGESP, particular care must be taken to ensure that internal selection methods are valid if adverse impact is occurring. To minimize glass ceiling effects, organizations should make greater use of selection plans and more objective internal assessment methods, as well as help impart the KSAOs necessary for advancement.

DISCUSSION QUESTIONS

1. Explain how internal selection decisions differ from external selection decisions.
2. What are the differences among peer ratings, peer nominations, and peer rankings?
3. Explain the theory behind assessment centers.
4. Describe the three different types of interview simulations.
5. Evaluate the effectiveness of seniority, assessment centers, and job knowledge as substantive internal selection procedures.
6. What steps should be taken by an organization that is committed to shattering the glass ceiling?

ETHICAL ISSUES

1. Given that seniority is not a particularly valid predictor of job performance, do you think it's unethical for a company to use it as a basis for promotion? Why or why not?
2. Vincent and Peter are sales associates and are up for promotion to sales manager. In the last five years, on a 1 = poor to 5 = excellent scale, Vincent's average performance rating was 4.7 and Peter's was 4.2. In an assessment center that was meant to simulate the job of sales manager, on a 1 = very poor to 10 = outstanding scale, Vincent's average score was 8.2 and Peter's was 9.2. Other things being equal, who should be promoted? Why?

APPLICATIONS

Changing a Promotion System

Bioglass, Inc. specializes in sales of a wide array of glass products. One area of the company, the commercial sales division (CSD), specializes in selling high-tech mirrors and microscope and photographic lenses. Sales associates in CSD are responsible for selling the glass products to corporate clients. In CSD there are four levels of sales associates, ranging in pay from $28,000 to $76,000 per year. There are also four levels of managerial positions in CSD; those positions range in pay from $76,000 to $110,000 per year (that's what the division president makes).

Tom Caldwell has been a very effective sales associate. He has consistently demonstrated good sales techniques in his 17 years with Bioglass and has a large and loyal client base. Over the years, Tom has risen from the lowest level of sales associate to the highest. He has proved himself successful at each stage. An entry- (first-) level management position in CSD opened up last year, and Tom was a natural candidate. Although several other candidates were given consideration, Tom was the clear choice for the position.

However, once in the position, Tom had a great deal of difficulty being a manager. He was not accustomed to delegating and rarely provided feedback or guidance to the people he supervised. Although he set goals for himself, he never set performance goals for his workers. Morale in Tom's group was low, and group performance suffered. The company felt that demoting Tom back to sales would be disastrous for him and present the wrong image to other employees; firing such a loyal employee was considered unacceptable. Therefore, Bioglass decided to keep Tom where he was but never promote him again. It was also considering enrolling Tom in some expensive managerial development programs to enhance his management skills.

Meanwhile, Tom's replacement, although successful at the lower three levels of sales associate positions, was having a great deal of difficulty with the large corporate contracts that the highest-level sales associates must service. Two of Tom's biggest clients had recently left Bioglass for a competitor. CSD was confused about how such a disastrous situation had developed when they seemed to make all the right decisions.

Based on this application and your reading of this chapter, answer the following questions:

1. What is the likely cause of CSD's problems?
2. How might CSD, and Bioglass more generally, make better promotion decisions in the future? Be specific.
3. In general, what role should performance appraisals play in internal selection decisions? Are there some cases in which they are more relevant than others? Explain.

Promotion From Within at Citrus Glen

Mandarine "Mandy" Pamplemousse is vice president of HR for Citrus Glen, a juice producer based in south Florida that supplies orange and grapefruit juice to grocery stores, convenience stores, restaurants, and food processors throughout the

United States. Citrus Glen has been growing rapidly over the last few years, leading Mandy to worry about how to hire and promote enough qualified individuals to staff the ever-expanding array of positions within the company.

One of the ways Mandy has been able to staff positions internally is by contracting with Staffing Systems International (SSI), a management consulting firm based in Charlotte, North Carolina. When positions open up at Citrus Glen that are appropriate to staff internally, Mandy sends a group of candidates for the position up to SSI to participate in its assessment center. The candidates return from SSI three days later, and a few days after that, SSI sends Mandy the results of the assessment with a recommendation. Though Mandy has never formally evaluated the accuracy of the promotions, it is her feeling that the process is pretty accurate. Of course, for $5,500 per candidate, Mandy thought, it *should* be accurate.

A few days ago, Mandy was hosting Thanksgiving, and her brother-in-law, Vin Pomme, joined them. Vin is a doctoral student in industrial psychology at Ohio International University. After Thanksgiving dinner, while Mandy, Vin, and their family were relaxing on her lanai and enjoying the warm Florida sunshine, Mandy was talking to Vin about her difficulties in promoting from within and the cost of SSI's assessment process. Vin quickly realized that SSI was using an assessment center. He was also aware of research suggesting that once one takes an applicant's personality and cognitive ability into account, assessment center scores may contribute little additional validity. Given the high cost of assessment centers, he reasoned, one must wonder whether this "incremental" validity (the validity that assessment centers contribute beyond the validity provided by personality and cognitive ability tests) would prove cost effective. After Vin conveyed these impressions to Mandy, she felt that after the holidays she would reexamine Citrus Glen's internal selection processes.

Questions

1. Drawing from concepts presented in Chapter 7 ("Measurement"), how could Mandy more formally evaluate SSI's assessment process, as well as the alternative presented to her by Vin?

2. Construct a scenario in which you think Mandy should continue her business relationship with SSI. On the other hand, if Mandy decides on an alternative assessment process, what would that process be? How would she evaluate whether that process was effective?

3. Citrus Glen has considered expanding its operations into the Caribbean and Latin America. One of Mandy's concerns is how to staff such positions. If Citrus Glen does expand its operations to different cultures, how should Mandy go about staffing such positions? Be specific.

ENDNOTES

1. A. Howard and D. W. Bray, "Predictions of Managerial Success Over Long Periods of Time: Lessons From the Management Progress Study," in K. E. Clark and M. B. Clark (eds.), *Measures of Leadership* (West Orange, NJ: Leadership Library of America, 1990), pp. 113–130; C. J. Russell, "Selecting Top Corporate Leaders: An Example of Biographical Information," *Journal of Management*, 1990, 16, pp. 73–86; J. S. Schippman and E. P. Prien, "An Assessment of the Contributions of General Mental Ability and Personality Characteristics to Management Success," *Journal of Business and Psychology*, 1989, 3, pp. 423–437.

2. "Nearly Half of Newly-Promoted Executives Say Their Responsibilities Are Same," *IPMA-HR Bulletin*, Dec. 22, 2006, p. 1.

3. E. E. Lawler, "Make Human Capital a Source of Competitive Advantage," *Organizational Dynamics*, 2009, 38(1), pp. 1–7; R. Burbach and T. Royle, "Talent on Demand? Talent Management in the German and Irish Subsidiaries of a US Multinational Corporation," *Personnel Review*, 2010, 39(4), pp. 414–431; A. McDonnell, R. Lamare, and P. Gunnigle, "Developing Tomorrow's Leaders—Evidence of Global Talent Management in Multinational Enterprises," *Journal of World Business*, 2010, 45(2), pp. 150–160.

4. J. J. Kane and E. E. Lawler, "Methods of Peer Assessment," *Psychological Bulletin*, 1978, 85, pp. 555–586.

5. L. Grensing-Pophal, "Internal Selections," *HR Magazine*, Dec. 2006, p. 75.

6. I. E. De Pater, A.E.M. Van Vianen, M. N. Bechtoldt, and U. Klehe, "Employees' Challenging Job Experiences and Supervisors' Evaluations of Promotability," *Personnel Psychology*, 2009, 62(2), pp. 297–325; J. D. Kammeyer-Mueller and T. A. Judge, "A Quantitative Review of Mentoring Research: Test of a Model," *Journal of Vocational Behavior*, 2008, 72, pp. 269–283.

7. C. Patton, "Standout Performers: HR Professionals Are Testing Unconventional Strategies for Finding Employees With Leadership Potential," *Human Resource Executive*, Aug. 1, 2005, pp. 46–49.

8. N. Williams, "Seniority, Experience, and Wages in the UK," *Labour Economics*, 2009, 16, pp. 272–283.

9. B. Turque, "Top Teachers Have Uneven Reach in District," *Washington Post*, November 14, 2010, pp. M1–M2.

10. T.W.H. Ng and D. C. Feldman, "Organizational Tenure and Job Performance," *Journal of Management*, 2010, 36(5), pp. 1220–1250.

11. M. A. Quinones, J. K. Ford, and M. S. Teachout, "The Relationship Between Work Experience and Job Performance: A Conceptual and Meta-Analytic Review," *Personnel Psychology*, 1995, 48, pp. 887–910; P. E. Tesluk and R. R. Jacobs, "Toward an Integrated Model of Work Experience," *Personnel Psychology*, 1998, 51, pp. 321–355.

12. F. L. Schmidt, J. E. Hunter, and A. N. Outerbridge, "Joint Relation of Experience and Ability With Job Performance: Test of Three Hypotheses," *Journal of Applied Psychology*, 1988, 73, pp. 46–57.

13. W. Wilson, "Video Training and Testing Supports Customer Service Goals," *Personnel Journal*, 1994, 73, pp. 47–51.

14. F. L. Schmidt and J. E. Hunter, "Development of a Causal Model of Processes Determining Job Performance," *Current Directions in Psychological Science*, 1992, 1, pp. 89–92.

15. K. R. Murphy and J. M. Cleveland, *Performance Appraisal: An Organizational Perspective* (Boston: Allyn and Bacon, 1991).

16. L. J. Peter and R. Hull, *The Peter Principle* (New York: William Morrow, 1969).

17. G. C. Thornton III and D. M. Morris, "The Application of Assessment Center Technology to the Evaluation of Personnel Records," *Public Personnel Management*, 2001, 30, pp. 55–66.

18. W. Arthur, Jr., E. A. Day, T. L. McNelly, and P. S. Edens, "A Meta-Analysis of the Criterion-Related Validity of Assessment Center Dimensions," *Personnel Psychology*, 2003, 56, pp. 125–154.

19. D. A. Joiner, "Assessment Center: What's New?" *Public Personnel Management*, 2003, 31, pp. 179–185.

20. B. B. Gaugler, D. B. Rosenthal, G. C. Thornton III, and C. Bentson, "Meta-Analysis of Assessment Center Validity," *Journal of Applied Psychology*, 1987, 72, pp. 493–511.

21. E. Hermelin, F. Lievens, and I. T. Robertson, "The Validity of Assessment Centres for the Prediction of Supervisory Performance Ratings: A Meta-Analysis," *International Journal of Selection and Assessment*, 2007, 15, pp. 405–411.

22. J. P. Meriac, B. J. Hoffman, D. J. Woehr, and M. S. Fleisher, "Meta-Analysis of the Incremental Criterion-Related Validity of Dimension Ratings," *Journal of Applied Psychology*, 2008, 93(5), pp. 1042–1052; S. Dilchert and D. S. Ones, "Assessment Center Dimensions: Individual Differences Correlates and Meta-Analytic Incremental Validity," *International Journal of Selection and Assessment*, 2009, 17(3), pp. 254–270.

23. A. M. Gibbons and D. E. Rupp, "Dimension Consistency as an Individual Difference: A New (Old) Perspective on the Assessment Center Construct Validity Debate," *Journal of Management*, 2009, 35(5), pp. 1154–1180; C. E. Lance, "Why Assessment Centers Do Not Work the Way They Are Supposed To," *Industrial and Organizational Psychology*, 2008, 1, pp. 84–97; B. S. Connelly, D. S. Ones, A. Ramesh, and M. Goff, "A Pragmatic View of Assessment Center Exercises and Dimensions," *Industrial and Organizational Psychology*, 2008, 1, pp. 121–124.

24. M. S. Christian, B. D. Edwards, and J. C. Bradley, "Situational Judgment Tests: Constructs Assessed and a Meta-Analysis of Their Criterion-Related Validities," *Personnel Psychology*, 2010, 63(1), pp. 83–117.

25. F. Lievens, E. Van Keer, and E. Volckaert, "Gathering Behavioral Samples Through a Computerized and Standardized Assessment Center Exercise: Yes, It Is Possible," *Journal of Personnel Psychology*, 2010, 9(2), pp. 94–98.

26. D. E. Krause and G. C. Thornton III, "A Cross-Cultural Look at Assessment Center Practices: Survey Results From Western Europe and North America," *Applied Psychology: An International Review*, 2009, 58(4), pp. 557–585; I. J. van Emmerik, A. B. Bakker, and M. C. Euwema, "What Happens After the Developmental Assessment Center? Employees' Reactions to Unfavorable Performance Feedback," *Journal of Management Development*, 2008, 27(5), pp. 513–527; N. Anderson and V. Goltsi, "Negative Psychological Effects of Selection Methods: Construct Formulation and an Empirical Investigation Into an Assessment Center," *International Journal of Selection and Assessment*, 2006, 14(3), pp. 236–255.

27. J. E. Abueva, "Return of the Native Executive," *New York Times*, May 17, 2000, pp. B1, B8; P. Caligiuri and W. F. Cascio, "Sending Women on Global Assignments," *WorldatWork*, Second Quarter 2001, pp. 34–41; J. A. Hauser, "Filling the Candidate Pool: Developing Qualities in Potential International Assignees," *WorldatWork*, Second Quarter 2000, pp. 26–33; M. Mukuda, "Global Leaders Wanted . . . Apply Within," *Workspan*, Apr. 2001, pp. 36–41; C. Patton, "Match Game," *Human Resource Executive*, June 2000, pp. 36–41.

28. G. C. Thornton III, *Assessment Centers in Human Resource Management* (Reading, MA: Addison-Wesley, 1992).

29. EEOC Compliance Manual—Section 15 (*www.eeoc.gov/policy/docs/race-color.html*); J. A. Segal, "Land Executives, Not Lawsuits," *HR Magazine*, Oct. 2006, pp. 123–130.

The Staffing Organizations Model

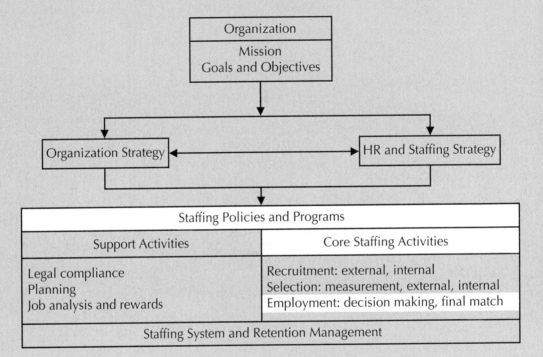

PART FIVE

Staffing Activities: Employment

CHAPTER ELEVEN
Decision Making

CHAPTER TWELVE
Final Match

CHAPTER ELEVEN

Decision Making

Learning Objectives and Introduction
Learning Objectives
Introduction

Choice of Assessment Method
Validity Coefficient
Face Validity
Correlation With Other Predictors
Adverse Impact
Utility

Determining Assessment Scores
Single Predictor
Multiple Predictors

Hiring Standards and Cut Scores
Description of the Process
Consequences of Cut Scores
Methods to Determine Cut Scores
Professional Guidelines

Methods of Final Choice
Random Selection
Ranking
Grouping
Ongoing Hiring

Decision Makers
Human Resource Professionals
Managers
Employees

Legal Issues
Uniform Guidelines on Employee Selection Procedures
Diversity and Hiring Decisions

Summary

Discussion Questions

Ethical Issues

Applications

Tanglewood Stores Case

LEARNING OBJECTIVES AND INTRODUCTION

Learning Objectives

- Be able to interpret validity coefficients
- Estimate adverse impact and utility of selection systems
- Learn about methods for combining multiple predictors
- Establish hiring standards and cut scores
- Evaluate various methods of making a final selection choice
- Understand the roles of various decision makers in the staffing process
- Recognize the importance of diversity concerns in the staffing process

Introduction

The preceding chapters described a variety of techniques that organizations can use to assess candidates. However, collecting data on applicants does not ultimately lead to a straightforward conclusion about who should be selected. Should interviews take precedence over standardized ability tests? Should job experience be the primary focus of selection decisions, or will organizations make better choices if experience ratings are supplemented with data on personality? What role should experience and education have in selection? In this chapter, we'll discuss how this information can be used to make decisions about who will ultimately be hired. As we will see, subjective factors often enter into the decision process. Having methods to resolve any disputes that arise in the process of evaluating candidates in advance can greatly facilitate efficient decision making and reduce conflict among members of the hiring committee.

When it comes to making final decisions about candidates, it is necessary to understand the nature of the organization and the jobs being staffed. Organizations that have strong cultures and heavy needs for customer service might put a stronger emphasis on candidate personality and values. For jobs with a stronger technical emphasis, it makes more sense to evaluate candidates on the basis of demonstrated knowledge and skills. Throughout this chapter, you'll want to consider how your own organization's strategic goals factor into staffing decision making.

The process of translating predictor scores into assessment scores is broken down into a series of subtopics. First, techniques for using single predictors and multiple predictors are discussed. The process used to determine minimum standards (a.k.a. "cut scores") will be described, as well as the consequences of cut scores and methods to determine cut scores. Methods of final choice must be considered to determine who from among the finalists will receive a job offer. For all the preceding decisions, consideration must be given to who should be involved in the decision process. Finally, legal issues should also guide the decision making.

Particular consideration will be given to the Uniform Guidelines on Employee Selection Procedures (UGESP) and to the role of diversity considerations in hiring decisions.

CHOICE OF ASSESSMENT METHOD

In our discussions of external and internal selection methods, we listed multiple criteria to consider when deciding which method(s) to use (e.g., validity, utility). Some of these criteria require more amplification, specifically validity, correlation with other predictors (newly discussed here), adverse impact, and utility.

Validity Coefficient

Validity refers to the relationship between predictor and criterion scores. Often this relationship is assessed using a correlation (see Chapter 7). The correlation between predictor and criterion scores is known as a validity coefficient. The usefulness of a predictor is determined on the basis of the practical significance and statistical significance of its validity coefficient. As was noted in Chapter 7, reliability is a necessary condition for validity. Selection measures with questionable reliability will have questionable validity.

Practical Significance

Practical significance refers to the extent to which the predictor adds value to the prediction of job success. It is assessed by examining the sign and the magnitude of the validity coefficient.

Sign.   The sign of the validity coefficient refers to the direction of the relationship between the predictor and the criterion. A useful predictor is one where the sign of the relationship is positive or negative and is consistent with the logic or theory behind the predictor.

Magnitude.   The magnitude of the validity coefficient refers to its size. It can range from 0 to 1.00, where a coefficient of 0 is least desirable and a coefficient of 1.00 is most desirable. The closer the validity coefficient is to 1.00, the more useful the predictor. Predictors with validity coefficients of 1.00 are not to be expected, given the inherent difficulties in predicting human behavior. Instead, as shown in Chapters 8 and 9, validity coefficients for current assessment methods range from 0 to about .60. Any validity coefficient above 0 is better than random selection and may be somewhat useful. Validities above .15 are moderately useful, and validities above .30 are highly useful.

Statistical Significance

Statistical significance, as assessed by probability or p values (see Chapter 7), is another factor that should be used to interpret the validity coefficient. If a validity coefficient has a reasonable p value, chances are good that it would yield a similar validity coefficient if the same predictor was used with different sets of job applicants. That is, a reasonable p value indicates that the method of prediction, rather than chance, produced the observed validity coefficient. Convention has it that a reasonable level of significance is p < .05. This means there are fewer than 5 chances in 100 of concluding there is a relationship in the population of job applicants when, in fact, there is not.

Caution must be exercised in using statistical significance as a way to gauge the usefulness of a predictor. Research has clearly shown that nonsignificant validity coefficients may simply be due to the small samples of employees used to calculate the validity coefficient. Rejecting the use of a predictor solely on the basis of a small sample may lead to rejecting a predictor that would have been quite acceptable had a larger sample of employees been used to test for validity.[1] These concerns over significance testing have led some researchers to recommend the use of "confidence intervals," for example, showing that one can be 90% confident that the true validity is no less than .30 and no greater than .40.[2]

Face Validity

Face validity concerns whether the selection measure appears valid to the applicant. Face validity is potentially important to selection decision making in general, and choice of selection methods in particular, if it affects applicant behavior (willingness to continue in the selection process, performance, and turnover once hired). Judgments of face validity are closely associated with applicant reactions.[3]

Correlation With Other Predictors

If a predictor is to be considered useful, it must add value to the prediction of job success. To add value, it must add to the prediction of success above and beyond the forecasting powers of current predictors. In general, a predictor is more useful if it has a smaller correlation with other predictors and a higher correlation with the criterion.

To assess whether the predictor adds anything new to forecasting, a matrix showing all the correlations between the predictors and the criteria should always be generated. If the correlations between the new predictor and the existing predictors are higher than the correlations between the new predictor and the criterion, the new predictor is not adding much that is new. There are also relatively straightforward techniques, such as multiple regression, that take the correlation among predictors into account.[4]

Predictors are likely to be highly correlated with one another when their domain of content is similar. For example, both biodata and application blanks may focus on previous training received. Thus, using both biodata and application blanks as predictors may be redundant, and neither one may augment the other much in predicting job success.

Adverse Impact

A predictor discriminates between people in terms of the likelihood of their success on the job. A predictor may also discriminate by screening out a disproportionate number of minorities and women. To the extent that this happens, the predictor has adverse impact, and it may result in legal problems. As a result, when the validity of alternative predictors is the same and one predictor has less adverse impact than the other predictor, the one with less adverse impact should be used.

A very difficult judgment call arises when one predictor has high validity and high adverse impact while another predictor has low validity and low adverse impact. From the perspective of accurately predicting job performance, the former predictor should be used. From an equal employment opportunity and affirmative action (EEO/AA) standpoint, the latter predictor is preferable. Balancing the trade-offs is difficult and requires use of the organization's staffing philosophy regarding EEO/AA. Later in this chapter we consider some possible solutions to this important problem.

Utility

Utility refers to the expected gains to be derived from using a predictor. Expected gains are of two types: hiring success and economic.

Hiring Success Gain

Hiring success refers to the proportion of new hires who turn out to be successful on the job. Hiring success *gain* refers to the increase in the proportion of successful new hires that is expected to occur as a result of adding a new predictor to the selection system. If the current staffing system yields a success rate of 75% for new hires, how much of a gain in this success rate will occur by adding a new predictor to the system? The greater the expected gain, the greater the utility of the new predictor. This gain is influenced not only by the validity of the new predictor (as already discussed) but also by the selection ratio and base rate.

Selection Ratio. The selection ratio is simply the number of people hired divided by the number of applicants (sr = number hired / number of applicants). The lower the selection ratio, the more useful the predictor. When the selection ratio is low, the organization is more likely to be selecting successful employees.

If the selection ratio is low, then the denominator is large or the numerator is small. Both conditions are desirable. A large denominator means that the organization is reviewing a large number of applicants for the job. The chances of identifying a successful candidate are much better in this situation than when an organization hires the first available person or reviews only a few applicants. A small numerator indicates that the organization is being very stringent with its hiring standards. The organization is hiring people likely to be successful rather than hiring anyone who meets the most basic requirements for the job; it is using high standards to ensure that the very best people are selected.

Base Rate.   The base rate is defined as the proportion of current employees who are successful on some criterion or human resource (HR) outcome (br = number of successful employees / number of employees). A high base rate is desired for obvious reasons. A high base rate may come about from the organization's staffing system alone or in combination with other HR programs, such as training and compensation.

When considering possible use of a new predictor, one issue is whether the proportion of successful employees (i.e., the base rate) will increase as a result of using the new predictor in the staffing system. This is the matter of hiring success gain. Dealing with it requires simultaneous consideration of the organization's current base rate and selection ratio, as well as the validity of the new predictor.

The Taylor-Russell tables help address this issue. An excerpt is shown in Exhibit 11.1.

EXHIBIT 11.1   Excerpt From the Taylor-Russell Tables

A.

Validity	Base Rate = .30 Selection Ratio	
	.10	.70
.20	43%	33
.60	77	40

B.

Validity	Base Rate = .80 Selection Ratio	
	.10	.70
.20	89%	83
.60	99	90

SOURCE: H. C. Taylor and J. T. Russell, "The Relationship of Validity Coefficients to the Practical Effectiveness of Tests in Selection," *Journal of Applied Psychology*, 1939, 23, pp. 565–578.

The cells in the tables show the percentage of new hires who will turn out to be successful. This is determined by a combination of the validity coefficient for the new predictor, the selection ratio, and the base rate. The top matrix (A) shows the percentage of successful new hires when the base rate is low (.30), the validity coefficient is low (.20) or high (.60), and the selection ratio is low (.10) or high (.70). The bottom matrix (B) shows the percentage of successful new hires when the base rate is high (.80), the validity coefficient is low (.20) or high (.60), and the selection ratio is low (.10) or high (.70). Two illustrations show how these tables may be used.

The first illustration has to do with the decision whether to use a new test to select computer programmers. Assume that the current test has a validity coefficient of .20. Also assume that a consulting firm has approached the organization with a new test that has a validity coefficient of .60. Should the organization purchase and use the new test?

At first blush, the answer might seem to be yes, because the new test has a substantially higher level of validity. This initial reaction, however, must be gauged in the context of the selection ratio and the current base rate. If the current base rate is .80 and the current selection ratio is .70, then, as can be seen in matrix B of Exhibit 11.1, the new selection procedure will only result in a hiring success gain from 83% to 90%. The organization may already have a very high base rate due to other facets of HR management it does quite well (e.g., training, rewards). Hence, even though it has validity of .20, the base rate of its current predictor is already .80.

On the other hand, if the existing base rate of the organization is .30 and the existing selection ratio is .10, the organization should strongly consider the new test. As shown in matrix A of Exhibit 11.1, the hiring success gain will go from 43% to 77% with the addition of the new test.

A second illustration using the Taylor-Russell tables has to do with recruitment in conjunction with selection. Assume that the validity of the organization's current predictor, a cognitive ability test, is .60. Also assume that a new college recruitment program has been very aggressive. As a result, there is a large swell in the number of applicants, and the selection ratio has decreased from .70 to .10. The organization must decide whether to continue the college recruitment program.

An initial reaction may be that the program should be continued because of the large increase in applicants generated. As shown in matrix A of Exhibit 11.1, this answer would be correct if the current base rate is .30. By decreasing the selection ratio from .70 to .10, the hiring success gain increases from 40% to 77%. On the other hand, if the current base rate is .80, the organization may decide not to continue the program. The hiring success increases from 90% to 99%, which may not justify the very large expense associated with aggressive college recruitment campaigns.

The point of these illustrations is that when confronted with the decision of whether to use a new predictor, the decision depends on the validity coefficient, base rate, and selection ratio. They should not be considered independent of one another. HR professionals should carefully record and monitor base rates and selection ratios. Then, when management asks whether they should use a new predictor, the HR professionals can respond appropriately. The Taylor-Russell tables may be used for any combination of validity coefficient, base rate, and selection ratio values. The values shown in Exhibit 11.1 are excerpts for illustration only; when other values need to be considered, the original tables should be consulted to provide the appropriate answers.

Economic Gain

Economic gain refers to the bottom-line or monetary impact of a predictor on the organization. The greater the economic gain the predictor produces, the more useful the predictor. Considerable work has been done over the years on assessing the economic gain associated with predictors. The basic utility formula used to estimate economic gain is shown in Exhibit 11.2.

At a general level, this formula works as follows. Economic gains derived from using a valid predictor versus random selection (the left-hand side of the equation) depend on two factors (the right-hand side of the equation). The first factor (the entry before the subtraction sign) is the revenue generated by hiring productive employees using the new predictor. The second factor (the entry after the subtraction sign) is the costs associated with using the new predictor. Positive economic gains are achieved when revenues are maximized and costs are minimized. Revenues are maximized by using the most valid selection procedures. Costs are

---

EXHIBIT 11.2 Economic Gain Formula

$\Delta U \ (T \times N_n \times r_{xy} \times SD_y \times \bar{Z}_s) - (N_a \times C_y)$
Where:
ΔU = expected dollar value increase to the organization using the predictor versus random selection
T = average tenure of employees in position
N_n = number of people hired
r_{xy} = correlation between predictor and job performance
SD_y = dollar value of job performance
$\bar{Z}_s$ = average standard predictor score of selected group
N_a = number of applicants
C_y = cost per applicant

Source: Adapted from C. Handler and S. Hunt, "Estimating the Financial Value of Staffing-Assessment Tools," *Workforce Management*, Mar. 2003 (*www.workforce.com*).

minimized by using the predictors with the least costs. To estimate actual economic gain, values are entered into the equation for each of the variables shown. Values are usually generated by experts in HR research relying on the judgments of experienced line managers.

Several variations on this formula have been developed. For the most part, these variations require consideration of additional factors such as assumptions about tax rates and applicant flows. In all these models, the most difficult factor to estimate is the dollar value of job performance, which represents the difference between productive and nonproductive employees in dollar value terms. A variety of methods have been proposed, ranging from manager estimates of employee value to percentages of compensation (usually 40% of base pay).[5] Despite this difficulty, economic gain formulas represent a significant way of estimating the economic gains that may be anticipated with the use of a new (and valid) predictor.

Limitations With Utility Analysis

Although utility analysis can be a powerful method to communicate the bottom-line implications of using valid selection measures, it is not without its limitations. Perhaps the most fundamental concern among researchers and practitioners is that utility estimates lack realism because of the following:

1. Virtually every organization uses multiple selection measures, yet existing utility models assume that the decision is whether to use a single selection measure rather than selecting applicants by chance alone.[6]
2. Many important variables are missing from the model, such as EEO/AA concerns and applicant reactions.[7]
3. The utility formula is based on many assumptions that are probably overly simplistic, including that validity does not vary over time;[8] that nonperformance criteria such as attendance, trainability, applicant reactions, and fit are irrelevant;[9] and that applicants are selected in a top-down manner and all job offers are accepted.[10]

Perhaps as a result of these limitations, several factors indicate that utility analysis may have a limited effect on managers' decisions about selection measures. For example, a survey of managers who stopped using utility analysis found that 40% did so because they felt that utility analysis was too complicated, whereas 32% discontinued use because they believed that the results were not credible.[11] Other studies have found that managers' acceptance of utility analysis is low; one study found that reporting simple validity coefficients was more likely to persuade HR decision makers to adopt a particular selection method than was reporting utility analysis results.[12]

These criticisms should not be taken as arguments that organizations should ignore utility analysis when evaluating selection decisions. However, decision makers are much less likely to become disillusioned with utility analysis if they are informed consumers and realize some of the limitations inherent in such analyses. Researchers have the responsibility of better embedding utility analysis in the strategic context in which staffing decisions are made, while HR decision makers have the responsibility to use the most rigorous methods possible to evaluate their decisions.[13] By being realistic about what utility analysis can and cannot accomplish, the potential to fruitfully inform staffing decisions will increase.

DETERMINING ASSESSMENT SCORES

Single Predictor

Using a single predictor in selection decisions makes the process of determining scores easy. In fact, scores on the single predictor *are* the final assessment scores. Thus, concerns over how to combine assessment scores are not relevant when a single predictor is used in selection decisions. Although using a single predictor has the advantage of simplicity, there are some obvious drawbacks. First, few employers would feel comfortable hiring applicants on the basis of a single attribute. In fact, almost all employers use multiple methods in selection decisions. A second and related reason for using multiple predictors is that utility increases as the number of valid predictors used in selection decisions increases. In most cases, using two valid selection methods will result in more effective selection decisions than using a sole predictor. For these reasons, although basing selection decisions on a single predictor is a simple way to make decisions, it is rarely the best one.

Multiple Predictors

Given the less-than-perfect validities of predictors, most organizations use multiple predictors in making selection decisions. With multiple predictors, decisions must be made about combining the resultant scores. These decisions can be addressed through consideration of compensatory, multiple hurdles, and combined approaches.

Compensatory Model

With a compensatory model, scores on one predictor are simply added to scores on another predictor to yield a total score. This means that high scores on one predictor can compensate for low scores on another. For example, if an employer is using an interview and grade point average (GPA) to select a person, an applicant with a low GPA who does well in the interview may still get the job.

The advantage of a compensatory model is that it recognizes that people have multiple talents and that many different constellations of talents may produce success on the job. The disadvantage of a compensatory model is that, at least for some jobs, the level of proficiency for specific talents cannot be compensated for by other proficiencies. For example, a firefighter requires a certain level of strength that cannot be compensated for by intelligence.

In terms of using the compensatory model to make decisions, four procedures may be followed: clinical prediction, unit weighting, rational weighting, and multiple regression. The four methods differ from one another in terms of the manner in which predictor scores (raw or standardized) are weighted before being added together for a total or composite score.

Exhibit 11.3 illustrates these procedures. In all four methods, raw scores are used to determine a total score. Standard scores (see Chapter 7) may need to be used rather than raw scores if each predictor variable uses a different method of measurement or is measured under different conditions. Differences in weighting methods are shown in the bottom part of Exhibit 11.3, and a selection system consisting of interviews, application blanks, and recommendations is shown in the top part. For simplicity, assume that scores on each predictor range from 1 to 5. Scores on these three predictors are shown for three applicants.

Clinical Prediction.   In the clinical prediction approach in Exhibit 11.3, note that managers use their expert judgment to arrive at a total score for each applicant. That final score may or may not be a simple addition of the three predictor scores shown in the exhibit. Hence, applicant A may be given a higher total score than applicant B even though simple addition shows that applicant B had one more point (4 + 3 + 4 = 11) than applicant A (3 + 5 + 2 = 10).

Frequently, clinical prediction is done by initial screening interviewers or hiring managers. These decision makers may or may not have "scores" per se, but they have multiple pieces of information on each applicant, and they make a decision on the applicant by taking everything into account. In initial screening decisions, this summary decision is whether the applicant gets over the initial hurdle and passes on to the next level of assessment. For example, when making an initial screening decision on an applicant, a manager at a fast-food restaurant might subjectively combine his or her impressions of various bits of information about the applicant on the application form. A hiring manager for a professional position might focus on a finalist's résumé and answers to the manager's interview questions to decide whether to extend an offer to the finalist.

The advantage to the clinical prediction approach is that it draws on the expertise of managers to weight and combine predictor scores. In turn, managers may be more likely to accept the selection decisions than if a mechanical scoring rule (e.g., add up the points) was used. Many managers believe that basing decisions on their experiences, rather than on mechanical scoring, makes them better at judging which applicants will be successful.[14] The problem with this approach is that the reasons for the weightings are known only to the manager. Also, clinical predictions have generally been shown to be less accurate than mechanical decisions; although there are times when using intuition and a nuanced approach is necessary or the only option. In general, one is well advised to heed former GE CEO Jack

EXHIBIT 11.3   Raw Scores for Applicants on Three Predictors

	Predictors		
Applicant	Interview	Applicant Blank	Recommendation
A	3	5	2
B	4	3	4
C	5	4	3

Clinical Prediction
$P_1, P_2, P_3 \rightarrow$ Subjective assessment of qualifications
Example: Select applicant A based on "gut feeling" for overall qualification level.

Unit Weighting
$P_1 + P_2 + P_3 =$ Total score
Example: All predictor scores are added together.
Applicant A = 3 + 5 + 2 = 10
Applicant B = 4 + 3 + 4 = 11
Applicant C = 5 + 4 + 3 = 12

Rational Weighting
$w_1 P_1 + w_2 P_2 + w_3 P_3 =$ Total score
Example: Weights are set by manager judgment at $w_1 = .5$, $w_2 = .3$, $w_3 = .2$
Applicant A = (.5 × 3) + (.3 × 5) + (.2 × 2) = 3.4
Applicant B = (.5 × 4) + (.3 × 3) + (.2 × 4) = 3.7
Applicant C = (.5 × 5) + (.3 × 4) + (.2 × 3) = 4.3

Multiple Regression
$a + b_1 P_1 + b_2 P_2 + b_3 P_3 =$ Total score
Example: Weights are set by statistical procedures at $b_1 = .09$, $b_2 = .6$, $b_3 = .2$
Applicant A = .09 + (.9 × 3) + (.6 × 5) + (.2 × 2) = 6.19
Applicant B = .09 + (.9 × 4) + (.6 × 3) + (.2 × 4) = 6.29
Applicant C = .09 + (.9 × 5) + (.6 × 4) + (.2 × 3) = 7.59

Welch's advice for making hiring decisions: "Fight like hell against . . . using your gut. Don't!"[15]

Unit Weighting.   With unit weighting, each predictor is weighted the same at a value of 1.00. As shown in Exhibit 11.3, the predictor scores are simply added together to get a total score. So, the total scores for applicants A, B, and C are 10, 11, and 12, respectively. The advantage to unit weighting is that it is a simple and straightforward process and makes the importance of each predictor explicit to decision makers. The problem with this approach is that it assumes each predictor contributes equally to the prediction of job success, which often is not the case.

Rational Weighting. With rational weighting, each predictor receives a differential rather than equal weighting. Managers and other subject matter experts (SMEs) establish the weights for each predictor according to the degree to which each is believed to predict job success. These weights (w) are then multiplied by each raw score (P) to yield a total score, as shown in Exhibit 11.3.

For example, the predictors are weighted .5, .3, and .2 for the interview, application blank, and recommendation, respectively. This means managers think interviews are the most important predictors, followed by application blanks, and then recommendations. Each applicant's raw score is multiplied by the appropriate weight to yield a total score. For example, the total score for applicant A is (.5)3 + (.3)5 + (.2)2 = 3.4.

The advantage to this approach is that it considers the relative importance of each predictor and makes this assessment explicit. The downside, however, is that it is an elaborate procedure that requires managers and SMEs to agree on the differential weights to be applied.

To make the process of rational weighting simpler, some organizations are turning to computer-aided decision tools. Williams Insurance Service utilizes a program called ChoiceAnalyst to make it easier for hiring managers to integrate information on a variety of candidate characteristics into a single score.[16] Recruiters select the predictor constructs that will be used to judge applicants, and provide decision weights for how important they think each construct should be in making a final choice. Scores on a variety of predictor measures are entered into the software, which produces a rank ordering of candidates. One advantage of these software-based solutions is that they can be explicitly developed to consider a variety of managerial preferences and assess how differences in perceptions of predictor importance can lead to differences in final hiring decisions.

Multiple Regression. Multiple regression is similar to rational weighting in that the predictors receive different weights. With multiple regression, however, the weights are established on the basis of statistical procedures rather than on judgments by managers or other SMEs. The statistical weights are developed from (1) the correlation of each predictor with the criterion, and (2) the correlations among the predictors. As a result, regression weights provide optimal weights in the sense that they will yield the highest total validity.

The calculations result in a multiple regression formula like the one shown in Exhibit 11.3. A total score for each applicant is obtained by multiplying the statistical weight (b) for each predictor by the predictor (P) score and summing these along with the intercept value (a). As an example, assume the statistical weights are .9, .6, and .2 for the interview, application blank, and recommendation, respectively, and that the intercept is .09. Using these values, the total score for applicant A is .09 + (.9)3 + (.6)5 + (.2)2 = 6.19.

Multiple regression offers the possibility of a higher degree of precision in the prediction of criterion scores than do the other methods of weighting. Unfortunately, this level of precision is realized only under a certain set of circumstances. In particular, for multiple regression to be more precise than unit weighting, there must be a small number of predictors, low correlations between predictor variables, and a large sample that is similar to the population that the test will be used on.[17] Many selection settings do not meet these criteria, so in these cases consideration should be given to unit or rational weighting, or to alternative regression-based weighting schemes that have been developed—general dominance weights or relative importance weights.[18] In situations where these conditions are met, however, multiple regression weights can produce higher validity and utility than the other weighting schemes.

Choosing Among Weighting Schemes. Choosing among the different weighting schemes is important because how various predictor combinations are weighted is critical in determining the usefulness of the selection process. Despite the limitations of regression weighting schemes noted above, one analysis of actual selection measures revealed that when scores on cognitive ability and integrity tests were combined by weighting them equally, the total validity increased to .65, an increase of 27.6% over the validity of the cognitive ability test alone.[19] When scores were weighted according to multiple regression, however, the increase in validity became 28.2%. While these results do not prove that multiple regression weighting is a superior method in all circumstances, they do help illustrate that the choice of the best weighting scheme is consequential and likely depends on answers to the most important questions about clinical, unit, rational, and multiple regression schemes (in that order):

- Do selection decision makers have considerable experience and insight into selection decisions, and is managerial acceptance of the selection process important?
- Is there reason to believe that each predictor contributes relatively equally to job success?
- Are there adequate resources to use relatively involved weighting schemes such as rational weights or multiple regression?
- Are the conditions under which multiple regression is superior (relatively small number of predictors, low correlations among predictors, and large sample) satisfied?

Answers to these questions—and the importance of the questions themselves—will go a long way toward deciding which weighting scheme to use. We should also note that while statistical weighting is more valid than clinical weighting,

556 PART FIVE Staffing Activities: Employment

the combination of both methods may yield the highest validity. One study indicated that regression-weighted predictors were more valid than clinical judgments, but clinical judgments contributed uniquely to performance controlling for regression-weighted predictors. This suggests that both statistical and clinical weighting might be used. Thus, the weighting schemes are not necessarily mutually exclusive.[20]

Multiple Hurdles Model

With a multiple hurdles approach, an applicant must earn a passing score on each predictor before advancing in the selection process. Such an approach is taken when each requirement measured by a predictor is critical to job success. Passing scores are set using the methods to determine cut scores (discussed in the next section). Unlike the compensatory model, the multiple hurdles model does not allow a high score on one predictor to compensate for a low score on another predictor.

Many organizations use multiple hurdles selection systems to both reduce the cost of selecting applicants and make the decision-making process more tractable in the final selection stage. It would be very inefficient to process all the possible information the organization might collect on a large number of candidates, so some candidates are screened out relatively early in the process. Typically, the first stage of a selection process screens the applicant pool down to those who meet some minimal educational or years of experience requirement. Collecting information on such requirements is fairly inexpensive for organizations and can usually be readily quantified. After this stage, the pool of remaining applicants might be further reduced by administering relatively inexpensive standardized tests to those who passed the initial screen. This will further reduce the pool of potential candidates, allowing the organization to devote more resources to interviewing finalists and having them meet with managers at the organization's headquarters. This is the selection stage. There are many variations in how the multiple hurdles model can be implemented, and the exact nature of the "screen" vs. "select" measures will vary based on the job requirements.

Combined Model

For jobs where some but not all requirements are critical to job success, a combined method may be used involving both the compensatory and the multiple hurdles models. The process starts with the multiple hurdles model and ends with the compensatory method.

An example of the combined approach for the position of recruitment manager is shown in Exhibit 11.4. The selection process starts with two hurdles that applicants must pass in succession: the application blank and the job knowledge test. Failure to clear either hurdle results in rejection. Applicants who pass receive an interview and have their references checked. Information from the interview and

EXHIBIT 11.4   Combined Model for Recruitment Manager

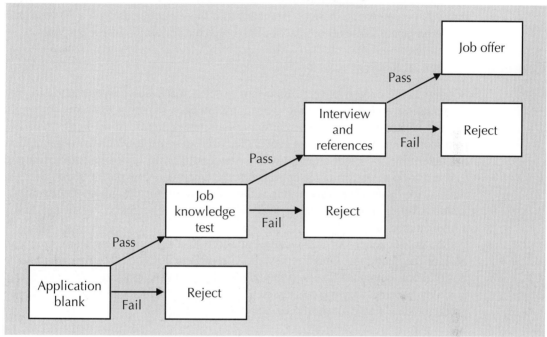

the references is combined in a compensatory manner. Those who pass are offered jobs, and those who do not pass are rejected.

HIRING STANDARDS AND CUT SCORES

Hiring standards or cut scores address the issue of what constitutes a passing score. The score may be a single score from a single predictor or a total score from multiple predictors. To address this, a description of the process and the consequences of cut scores are presented. Then, methods that may be used to establish the actual cut score are described. These techniques include minimum standards, top-down hiring, and banding.

Description of the Process

Once one or more predictors have been chosen for use, a decision must be made as to who advances in the selection process. This decision requires that one or more cut scores be established. A cut score is the score that separates those who advance in the process (e.g., applicants who become candidates) from those who are rejected. For example, assume a test is used on which scores may range from 0 to 100 points. A cut score of 70 means that those applicants with a 70 or higher would advance, while all others would be rejected for employment purposes.

Consequences of Cut Scores

Setting a cut score is a very important process, as it has consequences for the organization and the applicant. The consequences of cut scores are shown in Exhibit 11.5, which contains a summary of a scatter diagram of predictor and criterion scores. The horizontal line shows the criterion score at which the organization has determined whether an employee is successful or unsuccessful—for example, a 3 on a 5-point performance appraisal scale where 1 is low performance and 5 is high performance. The vertical line is the cut score for the predictor—for example, a 3 on a 5-point interview rating scale where 1 reveals no chance of success and 5 a high chance of success.

The consequences of setting the cut score at a particular level are shown in each of the quadrants. Quadrants A and C represent correct decisions, which have positive consequences for the organization. Quadrant A applicants are called true positives because they were assessed as having a high chance of success using the predictor and would have succeeded if hired. Quadrant C applicants are called

---

EXHIBIT 11.5   Consequences of Cut Scores

Criterion	Predictor Cut Score	
	D	A
Successful	False negatives	True positives
	C	B
Unsuccessful	True negatives	False positives
		Predictor
	No hire	Hire

true negatives because they were assessed as having little chance for success and, indeed, would not be successful if hired.

Quadrants D and B represent incorrect decisions, which have negative consequences to the organization and affected applicants. Quadrant D applicants are called false negatives because they were assessed as not being likely to succeed, but had they been hired, they would have been successful. Not only was an incorrect decision reached, but a person who would have done well was not hired. Quadrant B applicants are called false positives. They were assessed as being likely to succeed, but would have ended up being unsuccessful performers. Eventually, these people would need to receive remedial training, be transferred to a new job, or even be terminated.

How high or low a cut score is set has a large impact on the consequences shown in Exhibit 11.5, and trade-offs are always involved. Compared with the moderate cut score in the exhibit, a high cut score results in fewer false positives but a larger number of false negatives. Is this a good, bad, or inconsequential set of outcomes for the organization? The answer depends on the job open for selection and the costs involved. If the job is an astronaut position for NASA, it is essential that there be no false positives. The cost of a false positive may be the loss of human life.

Now consider the consequences of a low cut score, relative to the one shown in Exhibit 11.5. There are fewer false negatives and more true positives, but more false positives are hired. In organizations that gain competitive advantage in their industry by hiring the very best, this set of consequences may be unacceptable. Alternatively, for EEO/AA purposes it may be desirable to have a low cut score so that the number of false negatives for minorities and women is minimized.

In short, when setting a cut score, attention must be given to the consequences, as they can be very serious. As a result, different methods of setting cut scores have been developed to guide decision makers. These will now be reviewed.[21]

Methods to Determine Cut Scores

Three methods may be used to determine cut scores: minimum competency, top-down, and banding. Each of these is described below, along with professional guidelines for setting cut scores.

Minimum Competency

Using the minimum competency method, the cut score is set on the basis of the minimum qualifications deemed necessary to perform the job. SMEs usually establish the minimum competency score. This approach is often needed in situations where the first step in the hiring process is the demonstration of minimum skill requirements. Exhibit 11.6 illustrates the use of cut scores in selection. The scores of 25 applicants on a particular test are listed. Using the minimum competency method, the cut score is set at the level at which applicants who score below the line are deemed unqualified for the job. In this case, a score of 75 was determined

EXHIBIT 11.6   Use of Cut Scores in Selection Decisions

Rank	Test Score	Minimum Competency		Top-Down			Banding*
1	100	100		100	1st	choice	100
2	98	98		98	2nd	choice	98
3	97	97		97	3rd	choice	97
4	96	96		96	4th	choice	96
T5	93	93		95	5th	choice	93
T5	93	93		95	5th	choice	93
7	91	91		91	''		91
T8	90	90		90	''		90
T8	90	90		90	''		90
10	88	88	Qualified	88	''		88
11	87	87		87	''		87
T12	85	85		85	''		85
T12	85	85		85	''		85
14	83	83		83	''		83
15	81	81		81	''		81
16	79	79		79	''		79
T17	77	77		77	''		77
T17	77	77		77	''		77
19	76	76		76	''		76
20	75	75	Min. competency	75	''		75
21	74	74		74	21st	choice	74
22	71	71	Unqualified	71	22nd	choice	71
23	70	70		70	23rd	choice	70
24	69	69		69	24th	choice	69
25	65	65		65	25th	choice	65

*All scores within brackets are treated as equal; choice of applicants within brackets (if necessary) can be made on the basis of other factors, such as EEO/AA considerations.

to be the minimum competency level necessary. Thus, all applicants who scored below 75 are deemed unqualified and rejected, and all applicants who scored 75 or above are deemed at least minimally qualified. Finalists and ultimately offer receivers can then be chosen from among these qualified applicants on the basis of other criteria.

A variation of the minimum competency approach is hiring the first acceptable candidate. It is often used when candidates come to the attention of the hiring person sequentially, one at a time, rather than having a total pool of candidates from which to choose the finalists. It is also used when the organization is desperate for "warm bodies" and willing to hire anyone who meets some threshold. Although at times a rush to hire is understandable, the consequences can be most unfortunate. In one case, due to the difficulty of finding telemarketers, a home mortgage call center had a policy of hiring the first acceptable candidate. The hiring manager at this call center overheard a newly hired employee tell a customer, "If I had a rate as high as yours, I'd slit my wrists, then climb to the top of the highest building and jump off."[22] So, while hiring the first acceptable candidate may seem necessary, it is far from an ideal hiring strategy and the costs may not be revealed until it is too late.

Another variant on the minimum competency approach is to impose a sort of *maximum* competency on overqualified applicants. The assumption here is that the job will not be sufficiently rewarding, and the overqualified employee will quickly quit. Evidence suggests that employees who perceive themselves to be overqualified for their jobs report lower levels of job satisfaction and higher intentions to leave.[23] This may be because individuals who feel that they are overqualified believe that they deserve a better job and that their present work does not sufficiently challenge them. Employers can use tactics like increasing employee empowerment to alleviate these feelings among overqualified employees and therefore allow the organization to retain individuals who have exceptional levels of skills.[24] Managers should exercise caution before automatically rejecting individuals who appear to be overqualified. Sometimes people are interested in a job for reasons unknown to the hiring manager. There are also legal dangers, as many apparently overqualified applicants are over 40. As one manager said, "I think it's a huge mistake not to take a second look at overqualified candidates. Certainly there are valid reasons to reject some candidates, but it shouldn't be a blanket response."[25]

Top-Down

Another method of determining the level at which the cut score should be set is to simply examine the distribution of predictor scores for applicants and set the cut score at the level that best meets the demands of the organization. These demands might include the number of vacancies to be filled and EEO/AA requirements. This top-down method of setting cut scores is illustrated in Exhibit 11.6. As the exhibit shows, under top-down hiring, cut scores are established by the number of applicants that need to be hired. Once that number has been determined, applicants are selected from the top based on the order of their scores until the number desired is reached. The advantage of this approach is that it is easy to administer. It also minimizes judgment required because the cut score is determined on the basis of the demand for labor. The big drawback is that validity is often not established prior to the use of the predictor. Also, there may be overreliance on the use of a single predictor and cut score, while other potentially useful predictors are ignored.

A well-known example of a top-down method is the Angoff method.[26] In this approach, SMEs set the minimum cut scores needed to proceed in the selection process. These experts go through the content of the predictor (e.g., test items) and determine which items the minimally qualified person should be able to pass. Usually 7–10 SMEs (e.g., job incumbents, managers) are used, and they must agree on the items to be passed. The cut score is the sum of the number of items that must be answered correctly.

There are several problems with this particular approach and the subsequent modifications to it. First, it is a time-consuming procedure. Second, the results are dependent on the SMEs. It is a very difficult matter to get members of the organization to agree on who "the" SMEs are. Which SMEs are selected may have a bearing on the actual cut scores developed. Finally, it is unclear how much agreement there must be among SMEs when they evaluate test items. There may also be judgmental errors and biases in how cut scores are set. If the Angoff method is used, it is important that SMEs are provided with a common definition of minimally competent test takers, and that SMEs are encouraged to discuss their estimates. Each of these steps has been found to increase the reliability of the SME.[27]

Banding and Other Alternatives to Top-Down Selection

The traditionally selected cut score method is the top-down approach. For both external hiring and internal promotions, the top-down method will yield the highest validity and utility. This method has been criticized, however, for ignoring the possibility that small differences between scores are due to measurement error. Another criticism of the top-down method is its potential for adverse impact, particularly when cognitive ability tests are used. As we noted in Chapter 9, there is perhaps no greater paradox in selection than the fact that the single most valid selection measure (cognitive ability tests) is also the measure with the most adverse impact. The magnitude of the adverse impact is such that, on a standard cognitive ability test, if half the white applicants are hired, only 16% of the black applicants would be expected to be hired.[28]

One suggestion for reducing the adverse impact of top-down hiring is to use different norms for minority and majority groups; thus, hiring decisions are based on normatively defined (rather than absolute) scores. For example, a black employee who achieved a score of 75 on a test where the mean of all black applicants was 50 could be considered to have the same normative score as a white applicant who scored a 90 on a test where the mean for white applicants was 60. However, this "race norming" of test scores, which was a common practice in the civil service and among some private employers, is expressly forbidden by the Civil Rights Act of 1991. As a result, another approach, termed "banding," has been promulgated.

Banding refers to the procedure whereby applicants who score within a certain score range or band are considered to have scored equivalently. A simple banding procedure is provided in Exhibit 11.6. In a 100-point test, all applicants who score within the band of 10-point increments are considered to have scored equally. For example, all applicants who score 91 and above could be assigned a score of 9, those who score 81–90 are given a score of 8, and so on. (In essence, this is what is done when letter grades are assigned based on exam scores.) Hiring within bands could then be done at random or, more typically, could be based on race or sex in conjunction with other factors (e.g., seniority or experience). Banding might reduce the adverse impact of selection tests because such a procedure tends to reduce differences between higher- and lower-scoring groups (as is the case with whites and minorities on cognitive ability tests). In practice, band widths are usually calculated on the basis of the standard error of measurement.

Research suggests that banding procedures result in substantial decreases in the adverse impact of cognitive ability tests, while, under certain conditions, the losses in terms of utility are relatively small. Various methods of banding have been proposed, but the differences between these methods are relatively unimportant.[29]

Perhaps the major limitation with banding is that it sacrifices validity, especially when the selection measure is reliable. Because the standard error of the difference between test scores is partly a function of the reliability of the test, when test reliability is low, band widths are wider than when the reliability of the test is high. For example, if the reliability of a test is .80, at a reasonable level of confidence, nearly half the scores on a test can be considered equivalent.[30] Obviously, taking scores on a 100-point test and lumping applicants into only two groups wastes a great deal of important information on applicants (it is unlikely that an applicant who scores a 51 on a valid test will perform the same on the job as an applicant who scores 99). Therefore, if the reliability of a test is even moderately high, the validity and utility decrements that result from banding become quite severe. There is also evidence that typical banding procedures overestimate the width of bands, which of course exacerbates the problem.[31]

The scientific merit of test banding is hotly debated.[32] It is unlikely that we could resolve here the myriad ethical and technical issues underlying its use. Organizations considering the use of banding in personnel selection decisions must weigh the pros and cons carefully, including the legal issues (a review of lawsuits concerning banding found that it was generally upheld by the courts[33]). In the end, however, there may be a values choice to be made: to optimize validity (to some detriment to diversity) or to optimize diversity (with some sacrifice in validity). As one review noted, though "there is extensive evidence supporting the validity [of cognitive tests], adverse impact is unlikely to be eliminated as long as one assesses" cognitive abilities in the selection process.[34]

In an effort to resolve this somewhat pessimistic trade-off, some researchers have developed nonlinear models that attempt to find optimal solutions that maximize validity and diversity. One effort produced a statistical algorithm that attempts to achieve an optimal trade-off between validity and adverse impact by differentially weighting the selection measures. Although such algorithms may reduce the price to be paid in the values (between optimizing validity and diversity), the silver bullet solution remains elusive.[35]

EXHIBIT 11.7   Professional Guidelines for Setting Cutoff Scores

1. It is unrealistic to expect that there is a single "best" method of setting cutoff scores for all situations.
2. The process of setting a cutoff score (or a critical score) should begin with a job analysis that identifies relative levels of proficiency on critical knowledge, skills, abilities, or other characteristics.
3. The validity and job relatedness of the assessment procedure are crucial considerations.
4. How a test is used (criterion-referenced or norm-referenced) affects the selection and meaning of a cutoff score.
5. When possible, data on the actual relation of test scores to outcome measures of job performance should be considered carefully.
6. Cutoff scores or critical scores should be set high enough to ensure that minimum standards of job performance are met.
7. Cutoff scores should be consistent with normal expectations of acceptable proficiency within the workforce.

SOURCE: W. F. Cascio, R. A. Alexander, and G. V. Barrett, "Setting Cutoff Scores: Legal, Psychometric, and Professional Issues and Guidelines," *Personnel Psychology*, 1988, 41, pp. 21–22. Used with permission.

Professional Guidelines

Much more research is needed on systematic procedures that are effective in setting optimal cut scores. In the meantime, a sound set of professional guidelines for setting cut scores is shown in Exhibit 11.7.

METHODS OF FINAL CHOICE

The discussion thus far has been on decision rules that can be used to narrow down the list of people to successively smaller groups that advance in the selection process from applicant to candidate to finalist. How does the organization determine which finalists will receive job offers? Discretionary assessments about the finalists must be converted into final choice decisions. The methods of final choice are the mechanisms by which discretionary assessments are translated into job offer decisions.

Methods of final choice include random selection, ranking, and grouping. Examples of each of these methods are shown in Exhibit 11.8 and are discussed here.

Random Selection

With random selection, each finalist has an equal chance of being selected. The only rationale for selecting a person is the "luck of the draw." For example, the

---

EXHIBIT 11.8   Methods of Final Choice

Random	Ranking	Grouping
Casey Keisha Buster Lyn Aung — Pick one Meg Luis	1. Keisha 2. Meg 3. Buster 4. Lyn Aung 5. Casey 6. Luis	Keisha Meg] Top choices Buster Lyn Aung] Acceptable Casey Luis] Last resorts

six names from Exhibit 11.8 could be put in a hat and the finalist drawn out and tendered a job offer. This approach has the advantage of being quick. Also, with random selection, one cannot be accused of favoritism, because everyone has an equal chance of being selected. The disadvantage to this approach is that discretionary assessments are simply ignored.

Ranking

With ranking, finalists are ordered from the most desirable to the least desirable based on results of discretionary assessments. As shown in Exhibit 11.8, the person ranked 1 (Keisha) is the most desirable, and the person ranked 6 (Luis) is the least desirable. It is important to note that desirability should be viewed in the context of the entire selection process. When this is done, persons with lower levels of desirability (e.g., ranks of 3, 4, and 5) should not be viewed necessarily as failures. Job offers are extended to people on the basis of their rank ordering, with the person ranked 1 receiving the first offer. Should that person turn down the job offer or suddenly withdraw from the selection process, finalist number 2 receives the offer, and so on.

The advantage of ranking is that it indicates the relative worth of each finalist for the job. It also provides a set of backups should one or more of the finalists withdraw from the process.

Backup finalists may decide to withdraw from the process to take a position elsewhere. Although ranking gives the organization a cushion if the top choices withdraw from the process, it does not mean that the process of job offers can proceed at a leisurely pace. Immediate action needs to be taken with the top choices in case they decide to withdraw and there is a need to go to backups. This is especially true in tight labor markets, where there is a strong demand for the services of people on the ranking list.

Grouping

With the grouping method, finalists are banded together into rank-ordered categories. In Exhibit 11.8, the finalists are grouped according to whether they are top choices, acceptable, or last resorts. The advantage of this method is that it permits ties among finalists, thus avoiding the need to assign a different rank to each person. The disadvantage is that decisions still have to be made from among the top choices. These decisions might be based on factors such as probability of each person accepting the offer.

Ongoing Hiring

In some organizations, the hiring process is continuous, meaning that there is never a final list of candidates to be selected. Instead, an organization that has continuous needs for employees in a variety of positions might continuously collect résumés from interested parties, and then when positions open up, call in for interviews everyone who passes the minimum qualifications for open jobs. In many ways, this is like the method of hiring the first acceptable candidate, described under the minimum competency approach. Jobs with very high turnover rates, like entry-level retail and food service positions, are typically staffed in this way. The advantage of an ongoing hiring method is that it generates a large quantity of applicants who can start in a relatively short period of time, which can be very important for organizations that frequently replace staff. The disadvantage of this system is that it seldom allows for careful consideration of the best possible candidates from a set of qualified applicants.

DECISION MAKERS

A final consideration in decision making for selection is who should participate in the decisions. That is, who should determine the process to be followed (e.g., establishing cut scores), and who should determine the outcome (e.g., who gets the job offer)? The answer is that both HR professionals and line managers must play a role. Although the two roles are different, both are critical to the organization. Employees may play certain roles as well.

Human Resource Professionals

As a general rule, HR professionals should have a high level of involvement in the processes used to design and manage the selection system. They should be consulted in matters such as which predictors to use and how to best use them. In particular, they need to orchestrate the development of policies and procedures in the staffing areas covered. These professionals have or know where to find the technical expertise needed to develop sound selection decisions. Also, they have the knowledge to ensure that relevant laws and regulations are being followed. Finally, they can also represent the interests and concerns of employees to management.

Although the primary role HR professionals should play is in terms of the process, they should also have some involvement in determining who receives job offers. One obvious area where this is true is with staffing the HR function. A less obvious place where HR professionals can play an important secondary role is in terms of providing input into selection decisions made by managers.

HR professionals may be able to provide some perception on applicants that is not always perceived by line managers. For example, they may be able to offer some insight on the applicants' people skills (e.g., communications, teamwork). HR professionals are sensitive to these issues because of their training and experience. They may have data to share on these matters as a result of their screening interviews, knowledge of how to interpret paper-and-pencil instruments (e.g., personality test), and interactions with internal candidates (e.g., serving on task forces with the candidates).

The other area where HR professionals may contribute to outcomes is in terms of initial assessment methods. Many times, HR professionals are, and should be, empowered to make initial selection decisions, such as who gets invited into the organization for administration of the next round of selection. Doing so saves managers time in which to carry out their other responsibilities. Also, HR professionals can ensure that minorities and women applicants are actively solicited and not excluded from the applicant pool for the wrong reasons.

Managers

As a general rule, a manager's primary involvement in staffing is in determining who is selected for employment. Managers are the SMEs of the business, and they are thus held accountable for the success of the people hired. They are far less involved in determining the processes followed to staff the organization, because they often do not have the time or expertise to do so. The average manager can also be expected to have no knowledge of staffing research whatsoever, though that doesn't mean he or she is uninterested in learning.[36]

Although they may not play a direct role in establishing process, managers can and should be periodically consulted by HR professionals on process issues. They should be consulted because they are the consumers of HR services. As such, they should be allowed to provide input into the staffing process to ensure that it is meeting their needs in making the best possible person/job matches.

An additional benefit of allowing management a role in process issues is that as a result of their involvement, managers may develop a better understanding of why HR professionals prescribe certain practices. When they are not invited to be part of the process to establish staffing policy and procedures, line managers may view HR professionals as obstacles to hiring the right person for the job.

It should also be noted that the degree of managers' involvement usually depends on the type of assessment decisions made. Decisions made using initial assessment methods are usually delegated to the HR professional, as just discussed. Decisions made using substantive assessment methods usually involve some degree of input from the manager. Decisions made using discretionary methods are usually the direct responsibility of the manager. As a general rule, the extent of managerial involvement in determining outcomes should only be as great as management's knowledge of the job. If managers are involved in hiring decisions for jobs with which they are not familiar, legal, measurement, and morale problems are likely to be created.

Employees

Traditionally, employees have not been considered part of the decision-making process in staffing. But this tradition is slowly changing. For example, in team assessment approaches (see Chapter 8), employees may have a voice in both process and outcomes. That is, they may have ideas about how selection procedures are established and make decisions about, or provide input into, who gets hired. Involvement in the team approach is encouraged because it may give employees a sense of ownership of the work process and help them better identify with organizational goals. Also, it may result in selecting members who are more compatible with the goals of the work team. Google includes line managers and peers in the hiring process. Its consensus-based hiring process is seen as a valuable way to get a variety of perspectives on the fit between applicants and the organization.[37] In order for employee involvement to be effective, employees need to be provided with staffing training just as managers are (see Chapter 9).

LEGAL ISSUES

One of the most important legal issues in decision making is that of cut scores or hiring standards. These scores or standards regulate the flow of individuals from applicant to candidate to finalist to new hire. Throughout this flow, adverse impact may occur. When it does, the UGESP come into play. In addition, the organization could form a multipronged strategy for increasing workforce diversity.

Uniform Guidelines on Employee Selection Procedures

If the use of cut scores does not lead to adverse impact in decision making, the UGESP are essentially silent on the issue of cut scores. The discretion exercised by the organization as it makes its selection decisions is thus unconstrained legally. If adverse impact is occurring, the UGESP become directly applicable to decision making.

Under conditions of adverse impact, the UGESP require the organization to either eliminate its occurrence or justify it through the conduct of validity studies and the careful setting of cut scores:

> Where cutoff scores are used, they should normally be set as to be reasonable and consistent with normal expectations of acceptable proficiency within the workforce. Where applicants are ranked on the basis of properly validated selection procedures and those applicants scoring below a higher cutoff score than appropriate in light of such expectations have little or no chance of being selected for employment, the higher cutoff score may be appropriate, but the degree of adverse impact should be considered.

This provision suggests that the organization should be cautious in general about setting cut scores that are above those necessary to achieve acceptable proficiency among those hired. In other words, even with a valid predictor, the organization should be cautious that its hiring standards are not so high that they create needless adverse impact. This is particularly true with ranking systems. Use of random methods—or to a lesser extent, grouping methods—would help overcome this particular objection to ranking systems.

Whatever cut score procedure is used, the UGESP also require that the organization be able to document its establishment and operation. Specifically, the UGESP say that "if the selection procedure is used with a cutoff score, the user should describe the way in which normal expectations of proficiency within the workforce were determined and the way in which the cutoff score was determined."

The UGESP also suggest two options to eliminate adverse impact, rather than to justify it as in the validation and cut score approach. One option is use of "alternative procedures." Here, the organization uses an alternative selection procedure that causes less adverse impact (e.g., work sample instead of a written test) but has roughly the same validity as the procedure it replaces.

The other option is that of affirmative action. The UGESP do not relieve the organization of any affirmative action obligations it may have. Also, the UGESP strive to "encourage the adoption and implementation of voluntary affirmative action programs" for organizations that do not have any affirmative action obligations.

Diversity and Hiring Decisions

There has been considerable controversy and litigation over the issue of whether it is permissible for a legally protected characteristic such as race or gender to enter into a staffing decision at all, and if so, under exactly what circumstances. At the crux of the matter is whether staffing decisions should be based solely on a person's qualifications or on qualifications and the protected characteristic. It is argued that allowing the protected characteristic to receive some weight in the decision would serve to create a more diverse workforce, which many public and private organizations claim is something they have a compelling interest in and responsibility to do (refer back to Chapter 3 and the discussion of affirmative action).

It can be concluded that unless the organization is under a formal affirmative action plan (AAP), protected characteristics (e.g., race, sex, and religion) should not be considered in selection decision making. This conclusion is consistent with Equal Employment Opportunity Commission (EEOC) policy that the organization should use job-related hiring standards and that the same selection techniques and weights must be used for all people.[38]

How should the organization proceed, especially if it wants to not only comply with the law but also increase the diversity of its workforce? Several things might be done. First, carefully establish KSAOs (knowledge, skill, ability, and other characteristics) for jobs so that they are truly job related; as part of that process, attempt to establish some job-related KSAOs that may correlate with protected characteristics, such as diversity in experience and customer contacts. For example, a KSAO for the job of marketing manager might be "substantial contacts within diverse racial and ethnic communities." Both white and nonwhite applicants could potentially meet this requirement, increasing the chances of recruiting and selecting a person of color for the job. Second, use recruitment (both external and internal) as a tool for attracting a more qualified and diverse applicant pool. Third, use valid methods of KSAO assessment derived from a formal selection plan. Fourth, avoid clinical or excessively subjective prediction in making the assessment and deriving a total assessment or score for candidates. Instead, establish and use the same set of predictors and weights for them to arrive at the final assessment. Fifth, provide training in selection decision making for hiring managers and staffing managers. Content of the training should focus on overcoming usage of stereotypes, learning how to gather and weight predictor information consistently for all candidates, and looking for red flags about acceptance or rejection based on vague judgments about the candidate being a "good fit." Sixth, use a diverse group of hiring and staffing managers to gather and evaluate KSAO information, including a diverse team to conduct interviews. Finally, monitor selection decision making and challenge those decision makers who reject candidates who would enhance diversity to demonstrate that the reasons for rejection are job related.

When the organization is under an AAP, either voluntary or court imposed, the above recommendations are still appropriate. Attempts to go even further and provide a specific "plus" to protected characteristics should not be undertaken without a careful examination and opinion of whether this would be legally permissible.

SUMMARY

The selection component of a staffing system requires that decisions be made in several areas. The critical concerns are deciding which predictors (assessment methods) to use, determining assessment scores and setting cut scores, making final decisions about applicants, considering who within the organization should help make selection decisions, and complying with legal guidance.

In deciding which assessment methods to use, consideration should be given to the validity coefficient, face validity correlation with other predictors, adverse impact, utility, and applicant reactions. Ideally, a predictor would have a validity coefficient with large magnitude and significance, high face validity, low correlations with other predictors, little adverse impact, and high utility. In practice, this ideal situation is hard to achieve, so decisions about trade-offs are necessary.

How assessment scores are determined depends on whether a single predictor or multiple predictors are used. In the case of a single predictor, assessment scores are simply the scores on the predictor. With multiple predictors, a compensatory, multiple hurdles, or combined model must be used. A compensatory model allows a person to compensate for a low score on one predictor with a high score on another predictor. A multiple hurdles model requires that a person achieve a passing score on each successive predictor. A combined model uses elements of both the compensatory and multiple hurdles models.

In deciding who earns a passing score on a predictor or a combination of predictors, cut scores must be set. When doing so, the consequences of setting different levels of cut scores should be considered, especially those of assessing some applicants as false positives or false negatives. Approaches to determining cut scores include minimum competency, top-down, and banding methods. Professional guidelines were reviewed on how best to set cut scores.

Methods of final choice involve determining who will receive job offers from among those who have passed the initial hurdles. Several methods of making these decisions were reviewed, including random selection, ranking, and grouping. Each has advantages and disadvantages.

Multiple individuals may be involved in selection decision making. HR professionals play a role primarily in determining the selection process to be used and in making selection decisions based on initial assessment results. Managers play a role primarily in deciding whom to select during the final choice stage. Employees are becoming part of the decision-making process, especially in team assessment approaches.

A basic legal issue is conformance with the UGESP, which provide guidance on how to set cut scores in ways that help minimize adverse impact and allow the organization to fulfill its EEO/AA obligations. In the absence of an AAP, protected class characteristics must not enter into selection decision making. That prohibition notwithstanding, organizations can take numerous steps to increase workforce diversity.

DISCUSSION QUESTIONS

1. Your boss is considering using a new predictor. The base rate is high, the selection ratio is low, and the validity coefficient is high for the current predictor. What would you advise your boss and why?
2. What are the positive consequences associated with a high predictor cut score? What are the negative consequences?
3. Under what circumstances should a compensatory model be used? When should a multiple hurdles model be used?
4. What are the advantages of ranking as a method of final choice over random selection?
5. What roles should HR professionals play in staffing decisions? Why?
6. What guidelines do the UGESP offer to organizations when it comes to setting cut scores?

ETHICAL ISSUES

1. Do you think companies should use banding in selection decisions? Defend your position.
2. Is clinical prediction the fairest way to combine assessment information about job applicants, or are the other methods (unit weighting, rational weighting, and multiple regression) fairer? Why?

APPLICATIONS

Utility Concerns in Choosing an Assessment Method

Randy May is a 32-year-old airplane mechanic for a small airline based on Nantucket Island, Massachusetts. Recently, Randy won $2 million in the New England lottery. Because Randy is relatively young, he decided to invest his winnings in a business to create a future stream of earnings. After weighing many investment options, Randy chose to open up a chain of ice cream shops in the Cape Cod area. (As it turns out, Cape Cod and the nearby islands are short of ice cream shops.) Based on his own budgeting, Randy figured he had enough cash to open shops on each of the two islands (Nantucket and Martha's Vineyard) and two shops in small towns on the Cape (Falmouth and Buzzards Bay). Randy contracted with a local builder and the construction/renovation of the four shops is well under way.

The task that is occupying Randy's attention now is how to staff the shops. Two weeks ago, he placed advertisements in three area newspapers. So far, he has received 100 applications. Randy has done some informal HR planning and figures he needs to hire 50 employees to staff the four shops. Being a novice at this, Randy is unsure how to select the 50 people he needs to hire. Randy consulted his friend Mary, who owns the lunch counter at the airport. Mary told Randy that she used interviews to get "the most knowledgeable people possible" and recommended it to Randy because her people had "generally worked out well." While Randy greatly respected Mary's advice, on reflection several questions came to mind. Does Mary's use of the interview mean that it meets Randy's requirements? How could Randy determine whether his chosen method of selecting employees was effective or ineffective?

Confused, Randy also sought the advice of Professor Ray Higgins, from whom Randy took an HR management course while getting his business degree. After learning of the situation and offering his consulting services, Professor Higgins suggested that Randy choose one of two selection methods (after paying Professor Higgins's consulting fees, he cannot afford to use both methods). The two methods Professor Higgins recommended are the interview (as Mary recommended) and a work sample test that entails scooping ice cream and serving it to a customer. Randy estimates that it would cost $100 to interview an applicant and $150 per applicant to administer the work sample. Professor Higgins told Randy that the validity of the interview is $r = .30$ while the validity of the work sample is $r = .50$. Professor Higgins also informed Randy that if the selection ratio is .50, the average score on the selection measure of those applicants selected is $z = .80$ (.80 standard deviations above the mean). Randy plans to offer employees a wage of $6 per hour. (Over the course of a year, this would amount to a $12,000 salary.)

Based on the information presented above, Randy would really appreciate it if you could help him answer the following questions:

1. How much money would Randy save using each selection method?
2. If Randy can use only one method, which should he use?
3. If the number of applicants increases to 200 (more applications are coming in every day), how will your answers to questions 1 and 2 change?
4. What limitations are inherent in the estimates you have made?

Choosing Entrants Into a Management Training Program

Come As You Are, a convenience store chain headquartered in Fayetteville, Arkansas, has developed an assessment program to promote nonexempt employees into its management training program. The minimum entrance requirements for the program are five years of company experience, a college degree from an accredited university, and a minimum acceptable job performance rating (3 or higher on a 1–5 scale). Anyone interested in applying for the management program can enroll in the half-day assessment program, where the following assessments are made:

1. Cognitive ability test
2. Integrity test
3. Signed permission for background test
4. Brief (30-minute) interview by various members of the management team
5. Drug test

At the Hot Springs store, 11 employees have applied for openings in the management training program. The selection information on the candidates is provided in the exhibit on the next page. (The scoring key is provided at the bottom of the exhibit.) It is estimated that three slots in the program are available for qualified candidates from the Hot Springs location. Given this information and what you know about external and internal selection, as well as staffing decision making, answer the following questions:

1. How would you go about deciding whom to select for the openings? In other words, without providing your decisions for the individual candidates, describe how you would weigh the various selection information to reach a decision.
2. Using the decision-making process from the previous question, which three applicants would you select for the training program? Explain your decision.
3. Although the data provided in the exhibit reveal that all selection measures were given to all 11 candidates, would you advise Come As You Are to continue to administer all the predictors at one time during the half-day assessment program? Or, should the predictors be given in a sequence so that a multiple hurdles or combined approach could be used? Explain your recommendation.

TANGLEWOOD STORES CASE

The cases you have considered up to this point have involved making aggregated decisions about a large number of applicants. After gathering relevant information, there is still the important task of determining how to combine this information to arrive at a set of candidates. This case combines several concepts from the chapters on selection and decision making.

EXHIBIT

Predictor Scores for 11 Applicants to Management Training Program

Name	Company Experience	College Degree	Performance Rating	Cognitive Ability Test	Integrity Test	Background Test	Interview Rating	Drug Test
Radhu	4	Yes	4	9	6	OK	6	P
Merv	12	Yes	3	3	6	OK	8	P
Marianne	9	Yes	4	8	5	Arrest '95	4	P
Helmut	5	Yes	4	5	5	OK	4	P
Siobhan	14	Yes	5	7	8	OK	8	P
Galina	7	No	3	3	4	OK	6	P
Raul	6	Yes	4	7	8	OK	2	P
Frank	9	Yes	5	2	5	OK	7	P
Osvaldo	10	Yes	4	10	9	OK	3	P
Byron	18	Yes	3	3	7	OK	6	P
Aletha	11	Yes	4	7	6	OK	5	P
Scale	Years	Yes–No	1–5	1–10	1–10	OK–Other	1–10	P–F

The Situation

Tanglewood is faced with a situation in which 11 qualified applicants have advanced to the candidate stage for the job of store manager. These individuals have submitted résumés, completed several standardized tests similar to those described in the case on measurement, and engaged in initial interviews. There is considerable debate among the regional management staff that is responsible for selecting store managers about which of these candidates are best qualified to make it to the finalist stage, and they have asked you to help them reach a more informed decision.

Your Tasks

You will select the top candidates for the finalist pool by using various combinations of the predictors. The methods for combining predictors will include clinical prediction, unit weighting, rational weighting, and a multiple hurdles model. In your answers you will provide detailed descriptions of how you made decisions and also assess how comfortable you are with the results. You will also describe what you think are appropriate minimal cut scores for each of the predictors. The background information for this case, and your specific assignment, can be found at *www.mhhe.com/heneman7e.*

ENDNOTES

1. F. L. Schmidt and J. E. Hunter, "Moderator Research and the Law of Small Numbers," *Personnel Psychology*, 1978, 31, pp. 215–232.
2. J. Cohen, "The Earth Is Round (p <.05)," *American Psychologist*, 1994, 49, pp. 997–1003; F. L. Schmidt, "Statistical Significance Testing and Cumulative Knowledge in Psychology: Implications for Training of Researchers," in A. E. Kazdin, *Methodological Issues and Strategies in Clinical Research*, third ed. (Washington, DC: American Psychological Association, 2003), pp. 437–460.
3. J. P. Hausknecht, D. V. Day, and S. C. Thomas, "Applicant Reactions to Selection Procedures: An Updated Model and Meta-Analysis," *Personnel Psychology*, 2004, 57, pp. 639–683.
4. L. G. Grimm and P. R. Yarnold, *Reading and Understanding Multivariate Statistics* (Washington, DC: American Psychological Association, 1995).
5. C. Handler and S. Hunt, "Estimating the Financial Value of Staffing-Assessment Tools," *Workforce Management*, Mar. 2003 (*www.workforce.com*); J. Sullivan, "The True Value of Hiring and Retaining Top Performers," *Workforce Management*, Aug. 2002 (*www.workforce.com*).
6. M. C. Sturman and T. A. Judge, "Utility Analysis for Multiple Selection Devices and Multiple Outcomes," Working paper, Cornell University, 1994.
7. J. Hersch, "Equal Employment Opportunity Law and Firm Profitability," *Journal of Human Resources*, 1991, 26, pp. 139–153.
8. G. V. Barrett, R. A. Alexander, and D. Doverspike, "The Implications for Personnel Selection of Apparent Declines in Predictive Validities Over Time: A Critique of Hulin, Henry, and Noon," *Personnel Psychology*, 1992, 45, pp. 601–617; C. L. Hulin, R. A. Henry, and S. L. Noon, "Adding a Dimension: Time as a Factor in Predictive Relationships," *Psychological Bulletin*, 1990,

107, pp. 328–340; C. T. Keil and J. M. Cortina, "Degradation of Validity Over Time: A Test and Extension of Ackerman's Model," *Psychological Bulletin*, 2001, 127, pp. 673–697.

9. J. W. Boudreau, M. C. Sturman, and T. A. Judge, "Utility Analysis: What Are the Black Boxes, and Do They Affect Decisions?" in N. Anderson and P. Herriot (eds.), *Assessment and Selection in Organizations* (Chichester, England: Wiley, 1994), pp. 77–96.

10. K. M. Murphy, "When Your Top Choice Turns You Down," *Psychological Bulletin*, 1986, 99, pp. 133–138; F. L. Schmidt, M. J. Mack, and J. E. Hunter, "Selection Utility in the Occupation of US Park Ranger for Three Modes of Test Use," *Journal of Applied Psychology*, 1984, 69, pp. 490–497.

11. T. H. Macan and S. Highhouse, "Communicating the Utility of Human Resource Activities: A Survey of I/O and HR Professionals," *Journal of Business and Psychology*, 1994, 8, pp. 425–436.

12. K. C. Carson, J. S. Becker, and J. A. Henderson, "Is Utility Really Futile? A Failure to Replicate and an Extension," *Journal of Applied Psychology*, 1998, 83, pp. 84–96; J. T. Hazer and S. Highhouse, "Factors Influencing Managers' Reactions to Utility Analysis: Effects of SDy Method, Information Frame, and Focal Intervention," *Journal of Applied Psychology*, 1997, 82, pp. 104–112; G. P. Latham and G. Whyte, "The Futility of Utility Analysis," *Personnel Psychology*, 1994, 47, pp. 31–46; G. Whyte and G. Latham, "The Futility of Utility Analysis Revisited: When Even an Expert Fails," *Personnel Psychology*, 1997, 50, pp. 601–610.

13. C. J. Russell, A. Colella, and P. Bobko, "Expanding the Context of Utility: The Strategic Impact of Personnel Selection," *Personnel Psychology*, 1993, 46, pp. 781–801.

14. S. Highhouse, "Stubborn Reliance on Intuition and Subjectivity in Employee Selection," *Industrial and Organizational Psychology*, 2008, 1, pp. 333–342.

15. J. Sawyer, "Measurement and Predictions, Clinical and Statistical," *Psychological Bulletin*, 1966, 66, pp. 178–200; D. Westen and J. Weinberger, "When Clinical Description Becomes Statistical Prediction," *American Psychologist*, 2004, 59, pp. 595–613; J. Welch and S. Welch, "Hiring Wrong—and Right," *Business Week*, Jan. 29, 2007, p. 102.

16. "ChoiceAnalyst Software Makes Hiring Decisions Easier on the Brain," *Recruiter*, Mar. 3, 2010, p. 12.

17. R. E. McGrath, "Predictor Combination in Binary Decision Making Scenarios," *Psychological Assessment*, 2008, 20, pp. 195–205.

18. J. M. LeBreton, M. B. Hargis, B. Griepentrog, F. L. Oswald, and R. E. Ployhart, "A Multidimensional Approach for Evaluating Variables in Organizational Research and Practice," *Personnel Psychology*, 2007, 60, pp. 475–498.

19. D. S. Ones, F. L. Schmidt, and K. Yoon, "Validity of an Equally-Weighted Composite of General Mental Ability and a Second Predictor," and "Predictive Validity of General Mental Ability Combined With a Second Predictor Based on Standardized Multiple Regression," Working papers, University of Iowa, Iowa City, 1996.

20. Y. Ganzach, A. N. Kluger, and N. Klayman, "Making Decisions From an Interview: Expert Measurement and Mechanical Combination," *Personnel Psychology*, 2000, 53, pp. 1–20.

21. W. F. Cascio, R. A. Alexander, and G. V. Barrett, "Setting Cutoff Scores: Legal, Psychometric, and Professional Issues and Guidelines," *Personnel Psychology*, 1988, 41, pp. 1–24.

22. J. Bennett, "Scientific Hiring Strategies Are Raising Productivity While Reducing Turnover," *Wall Street Journal*, Feb. 10, 2004, p. B7.

23. W. R. Johnson, P. C. Morrow, and G. J. Johnson, "An Evaluation of Perceived Overqualification Scales Across Work Settings," *Journal of Psychology*, 2002, 136, pp. 425–441; D. C. Maynard, T. A. Joseph, and A. M. Maynard, "Underemployment, Job Attitudes, and Turnover Intentions," *Journal of Organizational Behavior*, 2006, 27, pp. 509–536.

24. B. Erdogan and T. N. Bauer, "Perceived Overqualification and Its Outcomes: The Moderating Role of Empowerment," *Journal of Applied Psychology*, 2009, 94, pp. 557–565.

25. S. J. Wells, "Too Good to Hire?" *HR Magazine*, Oct. 2004, pp. 48–54.

26. W. H. Angoff, "Scales, Norms, and Equivalent Scores," in R. L. Thorndike (ed.), *Educational Measurement* (Washington, DC: American Council on Education, 1971), pp. 508–600; R. E. Biddle, "How to Set Cutoff Scores for Knowledge Tests Used in Promotion, Training, Certification, and Licensing," *Public Personnel Management*, 1993, 22, pp. 63–79.

27. J. P. Hudson, Jr., and J. E. Campion, "Hindsight Bias in an Application of the Angoff Method for Setting Cutoff Scores," *Journal of Applied Psychology*, 1994, 79, pp. 860–865; G. M. Hurtz and M. A. Auerbach, "A Meta-Analysis of the Effects of Modifications to the Angoff Method on Cutoff and Judgment Consensus," *Educational and Psychological Measurement*, 2003, 63, pp. 584–601.

28. P. R. Sackett and S. L. Wilk, "Within-Group Norming and Other Forms of Score Adjustment in Preemployment Testing," *American Psychologist*, 1994, 49, pp. 929–954.

29. K. R. Murphy, K. Osten, and B. Myors, "Modeling the Effects of Banding in Personnel Selection," *Personnel Psychology*, 1995, 48, pp. 61–84.

30. K. R. Murphy," Potential Effects of Banding as a Function of Test Reliability," *Personnel Psychology*, 1994, 47, pp. 477–495.

31. P. Bobko, P. L. Roth, and A. Nicewander, "Banding Selection Scores in Human Resource Management Decisions: Current Inaccuracies and the Effect of Conditional Standard Errors," *Organizational Research Methods*, 2005, 8, pp. 259–273.

32. W. F. Cascio, I. L. Goldstein, and J. Outtz, "Social and Technical Issues in Staffing Decisions," in H. Aguinis (ed.), *Test-Score Banding in Human Resource Selection: Technical, Legal, and Societal Issues* (Westport, CT: Praeger, 2004), pp. 7–28; K. R. Murphy, "Conflicting Values and Interests in Banding Research and Practice," in Aguinis (ed.), *Test-Score Banding in Human Resource Selection: Technical, Legal, and Societal Issues*, pp. 175–192; F. Schmidt and J. E. Hunter, "SED Banding as a Test of Scientific Values in I/O Psychology," in Aguinis (ed.), *Test-Score Banding in Human Resource Selection: Technical, Legal, and Societal Issues*, pp. 151–173.

33. C. A. Henle, "Case Review of the Legal Status of Banding," *Human Performance*, 2004, 17, pp. 415–432.

34. P. R. Sackett, N. Schmitt, J. E. Ellingson, and M. B. Kabin, "High-Stakes Testing in Employment, Credentialing, and Higher Education," *American Psychologist*, 2001, 56, pp. 302–318.

35. W. De Corte, F. Lievens, and P. R. Sackett, "Combining Predictors to Achieve Optimal Trade-Offs Between Selection Quality and Adverse Impact," *Journal of Applied Psychology*, 2007, 92, pp. 1380–1393; H. Aguinis and M. A. Smith, "Understanding the Impact of Test Validity and Bias on Selection Errors and Adverse Impact in Human Resource Selection," *Personnel Psychology*, 2007, 60, pp. 165–190.

36. M. D. Nowicki and J. G. Rosse, "Managers' Views of How to Hire: Building Bridges Between Science and Practice," *Journal of Business and Psychology*, 2002, 17, pp. 157–170.

37. "Google Goes for Consensus in Hiring," *Recruiter*, Apr. 28, 2010, p. 5.

38. D. D. Bennett-Alexander and L. P. Hartman, *Employment Law for Business*, sixth ed. (New York: McGraw-Hill-Irwin, 2009), pp. 207–243; R. K. Robinson, G. M. Franklin, and R. E. Wayland, *Employment Regulation in the Workplace* (Aramonk, NY: M. E. Sharpe, 2010), pp. 182–212; US Equal Employment Opportunity Commission, "EEOC Compliance Manual," 2006 (*www.eeoc. gov/policy/docs/race-color.html*), accessed 7/27/10.

CHAPTER TWELVE

Final Match

Learning Objectives and Introduction
Learning Objectives
Introduction

Employment Contracts
Requirements for an Enforceable Contract
Parties to the Contract
Form of the Contract
Disclaimers
Contingencies
Other Employment Contract Sources
Unfulfilled Promises

Job Offers
Strategic Approach to Job Offers
Job Offer Content

Job Offer Process
Formulation of the Job Offer
Presentation of the Job Offer
Timing of the Offer
Job Offer Acceptance and Rejection
Reneging

New Employee Orientation and Socialization
Orientation
Socialization
Examples of Programs

Legal Issues
Employment Eligibility Verification
Negligent Hiring
Employment-at-Will

Summary

Discussion Questions

Ethical Issues

Applications

LEARNING OBJECTIVES AND INTRODUCTION

Learning Objectives

- Learn about the requirements for an enforceable contract
- Recognize issues that might arise in the employment contract process
- Understand how to make strategic job offers
- Plan for the steps of formulating and presenting a job offer
- Know how to establish a formal employment relationship
- Develop effective plans for new employee orientation and socialization
- Recognize potential legal issues involving final matches

Introduction

In the previous chapter, we described how to reduce the initial applicant pool to a smaller set of candidates and identify one or more job finalists. In this chapter we move to the next stage—the process of actually hiring the individuals who have been selected. A final match occurs when the offer receiver and the organization have determined that there is sufficient overlap between the person's knowledge, skill, ability, and other characteristics (KSAOs) and the job's requirements and rewards. Once the decision to enter the employment relationship has been made, the organization and the candidate become bound through mutual agreement on the terms and conditions of employment.

The central theme of this chapter is setting the stage for a legally sound employment relationship. Organizations often get into legal trouble when they fail to understand the contractual nature of many employment relationships. As we show, careless promises or guarantees made during the job offer can come back to haunt an organization when it needs to alter the employment relationship later. This chapter also discusses the process of convincing promising job finalists to take the job offer, and developing the grounds of the relationship that will persist throughout this individual's employment.

Knowledge of employment contract concepts and principles is central to understanding the final match. This chapter begins with an overview of such material, emphasizing the essential requirements for establishing a legally binding employment contract. A strategic approach to job offers is then presented, followed by a discussion of the major components of a job offer and points to address in it. Through the job offer process, these terms and conditions are proposed, discussed, negotiated, modified, and, ultimately, agreed on. The process, therefore, is frequently complex, requiring planning by those responsible for it. Once agreement on the terms and conditions of employment has been reached, the final match process is completed, and the formal employment relationship is established. To phase the new hire into his or her job, it is vital to develop appropriate techniques for orienting and socializing the newcomer. The chapter concludes with a discussion of specific legal issues that pertain not only to the establishment of the employment contract but also to potential long-term consequences of that contract that must be considered at the time it is established.

EMPLOYMENT CONTRACTS

The establishment and enforcement of employment contracts is a very complex and constantly changing undertaking. Covered next are some very basic, yet subtle, issues associated with this undertaking. It is crucial to understand the elements that compose a legally enforceable contract and to be able to identify the parties to the contract (employees or independent contractors, third-party representatives), the form of the contract (written, oral), disclaimers, fulfillment of other conditions, reneging on an offer or acceptance, and other sources (e.g., employee handbooks) that may also constitute a portion of the total employment contract.

Requirements for an Enforceable Contract

Three basic elements are required for a contract to be legally binding and enforceable: offer, acceptance, and consideration.[1] If any one of these is missing, there is no binding contract.

Offer

The offer is usually made by the employer. It is composed of the terms and conditions of employment desired and proposed by the employer. The terms must be clear and specific enough to be acted on by the offer receiver. Vague statements and offers are unacceptable (e.g., "Come to work for me right now; we'll work out the details later"). The content of newspaper ads for the job and general written employer material, such as a brochure describing the organization, are probably also too vague to be considered offers. Both the employer and the offer receiver should have a definite understanding of the specific terms being proposed.

Acceptance

To constitute a contract, the offer must be accepted on the terms as offered. Thus, if the employer offers a salary of $50,000 per year, the offer receiver must either accept or reject that term. Acceptance of an offer on a contingency basis does not constitute an acceptance. If the offer receiver responds to the salary offer of $50,000 by saying, "Pay me $52,500, and I'll come to work for you," this is not an acceptance. Rather, it is a counteroffer, and the employer must now either formally accept or reject it.

The offer receiver must also accept the offer in the manner specified in the offer. If the offer requires acceptance in writing, for example, the offer receiver must accept it in writing. Or, if the offer requires acceptance by a certain date, it must be accepted by that date.

Consideration

Consideration entails the exchange of something of value between the parties to the contract. Usually, it involves an exchange of promises. The employer offers or promises to provide compensation to the offer receiver in exchange for labor, and the offer receiver promises to provide labor to the employer in exchange for compensation. The exchange of promises must be firm and of value, which is usually quite straightforward. Occasionally, consideration can become an issue. For example, if the employer makes an offer to a person that requires a response by a certain date, and then does not hear from the person, there is no contract, even though the employer thought that they "had a deal."

Parties to the Contract

Two issues arise regarding the parties to the contract: whether the employer is entering into a contract with an employee or with an independent contractor, and whether an outsider or third party can execute or otherwise play a role in the employment contract.[2]

Employee or Independent Contractor

Individuals are acquired by the organization as either employees or independent contractors. Both of these terms have definite legal meanings that should be reviewed (see Chapter 2) before entering into a contractual relationship. The organization should be clear in its offer whether the relationship being sought is that of employer–employee or employer–independent contractor. Care should be taken to avoid misclassifying the offer receiver as an independent contractor when in fact the receiver will be treated practically as an employee (e.g., subject to specific direction and control by the employer). Such a misclassification can result in substantial tax and other legal liability problems for the organization. Staffing experts anticipate that many organizations seeking to enhance flexibility will seek to expand the number of independent contractors they work with. Therefore, understanding how to maintain the distinction between an employee and an independent contractor will be of great importance.

Third Parties

Often, someone other than the employer or the offer receiver speaks on their behalf in the establishment or modification of employment contracts. These people serve as agents for the employer and the offer receiver. For the employer, this may mean the use of outsiders such as employment agencies, executive recruiters, or search consultants; it also usually means the use of one or more employees, such as the human resource (HR) department representative, the hiring manager, higher-level managers, and other managers within the organization. For the offer receiver, it may mean the use of a special representative, such as a professional agent for an athlete or an executive. These possibilities raise three important questions for the employer.

First, who, if anyone, speaks for the offer receiver? This is usually a matter of checking with the offer receiver as to whether any given person is indeed authorized to be a spokesperson, and what, if any, limits have been placed on that person regarding terms that may be discussed and agreed on with the employer.

Second, who is the spokesperson for the employer? In the case of its own employees, the employer must recognize that from a legal standpoint, any of them could be construed as speaking for the employer. Virtually anyone could thus suggest and agree to contract terms, knowingly or unknowingly. This means that the employer should formulate and enforce explicit policies as to who is authorized to speak on its behalf.

Third, exactly what is that person authorized to say? Here, the legal concept of apparent authority is relevant. If the offer receiver believes that a person has the authority to speak for the employer, and there is nothing to indicate otherwise, that person has the apparent authority to speak for the employer. In turn, the employer may be bound by what that person says and agrees to, even if the employer did not grant express authority to do so to this person. It is thus important for the organization to clarify to both the offer receiver and the designated spokespersons what the spokesperson is authorized to discuss and agree to without approval from other organizational members.

Form of the Contract

Employment contracts may be written, oral, or a combination of the two.[3] All may be legally binding and enforceable. Within this broad parameter, however, are numerous caveats and considerations.

Written Contracts

As a general rule, the law favors written contracts over oral ones. This alone should lead an organization to use only written contracts whenever possible.

A written contract may take many forms, and all may be legally enforceable. Examples of a written document that may be construed as a contract include a letter of offer and acceptance (the usual example), a statement on a job application blank (such as an applicant voucher to the truthfulness of information provided), internal job posting notices, e-mail messages, and statements in employee handbooks or other personnel manuals. The more specific the information and statements in such documents, the more likely they are to be considered employment contracts.

Unintended problems may arise with these documents. They may be interpreted as enforceable contracts even though that was not their intent (perhaps the intent was merely informational). Or, statements on a given term or condition of employment may contradict one another in various documents.

An excellent illustration of these kinds of problems involves the issue of employment-at-will. Assume an employer wishes to be, as a matter of explicit policy, a strict at-will employer. That desire may be unintentionally undercut by written documents that imply something other than an employment-at-will relationship. For example, correspondence with an applicant may talk of "continued employment after you complete your probationary period." This statement might be legally interpreted as creating something other than a strict at-will employment relationship. To further muddy the waters, the employee handbook may contain an explicit at-will statement, thus contradicting the policy implied in the correspondence with the applicant.

Care must thus be taken to ensure that all written documents accurately convey only the intended meanings regarding terms and conditions of employment. To this end, the following suggestions should be heeded:[4]

- Before putting anything in writing, ask, Does the company mean to be held to this?
- Choose words carefully; where appropriate, avoid using words that imply binding commitment.
- Make sure all related documents are consistent with one another.
- Always have a second person, preferably a lawyer, review what another has written.
- Form the habit of looking at the entire hiring procedure and consider any writings within that context.

Oral Contracts

While oral contracts may be every bit as binding as written contracts, there are two notable exceptions that support placing greater importance on written contracts.

The first exception is the one-year rule, which comes about in what is known as the statute of frauds.[5] Under this rule, a contract that cannot be performed or fulfilled within a one-year interval is not enforceable unless it is in writing. Thus, oral agreements for any length greater than one year are not enforceable. Because of this rule, the organization should not make oral contracts that are intended to last more than one year.

The second exception involves the concept of parole evidence, which pertains to oral promises made about the employment relationship.[6] Legally, parole evidence (e.g., the offer receiver's claim that "I was promised that I wouldn't have to work on weekends") may not be used to enforce a contract if it is inconsistent with the terms of a written agreement. Thus, if the offer receiver's letter of appointment explicitly stated that weekend work was required, the oral promise of not having to work weekends would not be enforceable.

Note, however, in the absence of written statements to the contrary, oral statements may indeed be enforceable. In the preceding example, if the letter of appointment was silent on the issue of weekend work, the oral promise of no weekend work might well be enforceable.

More generally, oral statements are more likely to be enforceable as employment contract terms in the following situations:[7]

- When there is no written statement regarding the term (e.g., weekend work) in question
- When the term is quite certain ("You will not have to work on weekends," as opposed to, "Occasionally, we work weekends around here")
- When the person making the oral statement is in a position of authority to do so (e.g., the hiring manager as opposed to a coworker)
- The more formal the circumstances in which the statement was made (the manager's office as opposed to around the bar or dinner table as part of a recruiting trip)
- The more specific the promise ("You will work every other Saturday from 8:00 to 5:00," as opposed to, "You may have to work from 8:00 to the middle of the afternoon on the weekends, but we'll try to hold that to a minimum")

As this discussion makes clear, from a legal perspective, oral statements are a potential minefield in establishing employment contracts. They obviously cannot be avoided (the employer and the applicant have to speak to each other), and they may serve other legitimate and desired outcomes, such as providing realistic recruitment information to job applicants. Nonetheless, the organization should use oral statements with extreme caution and alert all members to its policies regarding their use. As further protection, the organization should include in its written offer that, by accepting the offer, the employee agrees the organization has made no other promises than those contained in the written offer.

Disclaimers

A disclaimer is a statement (oral or written) that explicitly limits an employee right and reserves that right for the employer.[8] Disclaimers are often used in letters of appointment, job application blanks, and employee handbooks.

A common, and increasingly important, employee "right" that is being limited through the use of a disclaimer is that of job security. Here, through its policy of employment-at-will, the employer explicitly makes no promise of any job security and reserves the right to terminate the employment relationship at its own will. The following is an example of such a disclaimer that survived legal challenge:

In consideration of my employment, I agree to conform to the rules and regulations of Sears, Roebuck and Company, and recognize that employment and compensation can be terminated, with or without cause, and with or without notice, at any time, at the option of either the company or myself. I understand that no store manager or representative of Sears, Roebuck and Company, other than the president or vice-president of the company, has any authority to enter into any agreement for employment for any specified period of time, or to make any agreement contrary to the foregoing.[9]

An employment-at-will disclaimer should appear in the job offer letter. It should also appear on the application blank, along with two other disclaimers (see Chapter 8). First, there should be a statement of consent by the applicant for the organization to check provided references, along with a waiver of the right to make claims against them for anything they said. Second, there should be a so-called false statement warning, indicating that any false statement, misleading statement, or material omission may be grounds for dismissal.

Disclaimers are generally enforceable. They can thus serve as an important component of employment contracts. Their use should be guided by the following set of recommendations:[10]

1. They should be clearly stated and conspicuously placed in appropriate documents.
2. The employee should acknowledge receipt and review of the document and the disclaimer.
3. The disclaimer should state that it may be modified only in writing and by whom.
4. The terms and conditions of employment, including the disclaimer, as well as limits on their enforceability, should be reviewed with offer receivers and employees.

It would be wise to obtain legal counsel for drafting language for all disclaimers.

Contingencies

The employer may wish to make a job offer that is contingent on certain other conditions being fulfilled by the offer receiver.[11] Examples of such contingencies include (1) passage of a particular test, such as a licensure exam (e.g., CPA or bar exam), (2) passage of a medical exam, including alcohol/drug/screening tests, (3) satisfactory background and reference checks, and (4) proof of employability under the Immigration Reform and Control Act (IRCA).

Though contingencies to a contract are generally enforceable, contingencies to an employment contract (especially those involving any of the preceding examples) are exceedingly complex and may be made only within defined limits. For this reason, contingencies should not be used in employment contracts without prior legal counsel.

Other Employment Contract Sources

As alluded to previously, employment contract terms may be established through multiple sources, not just the letters of job offer and acceptance. Such establishment may be the result of both intentional and unintentional acts by the employer. Moreover, these terms may come about not only when the employment relationship is first established but also during the course of the employment relationship.[12]

The employer thus must constantly be alert to the fact that terms and conditions of employment may come into being and be modified through a variety of employment contract sources. Sources worth reiterating here are employee handbooks (and other written documents) and oral statements made by employer representatives. Job advertisements and job descriptions are generally not considered employment contracts.

In the case of employee handbooks, the employer must consider whether statements in them are legally enforceable or merely informational. While there is legal opinion on both sides of this question, handbooks are increasingly being considered as a legally enforceable part of the employment contract. To avoid this occurrence, the employer may wish to place an explicit disclaimer in the handbook that states the intent to provide only information to employees and that the employer will not be bound by any of the statements contained in the handbook.

In the case of oral statements, their danger and the need for caution in their use have already been addressed. Oral statements may present legal problems and challenges when made not only at the time of the initial employment contract but also throughout the course of the employment relationship. Of particular concern here are oral promises made to employees regarding future events, such as job security ("Don't worry, you will always have a place with us") or job assignments ("After training, you will be assigned as the assistant manager at our new store"). With oral statements, there is thus a constant need to be careful regarding the messages being delivered to employees, as well as who delivers those messages.

Unfulfilled Promises

Since the staffing process in general, and the job offer process in particular, involve making promises to offer receivers about terms and conditions of employment, it is important for the organization to (1) not make promises it is unwilling to keep, and (2) be sure that promises made are actually kept. Unfulfilled promises may spur the disappointed person to pursue a legal action against the organization. Three types of claims might be pursued.[13]

The first claim is that of breach of contract, and it may be pursued for both written and oral promises. The employee has to show that both parties intended to be legally bound by the promise and that it was specific enough to establish an actual oral agreement. The second claim is that of promissory estoppel. Here, even if there is no enforceable oral contract, employees may claim that they relied on promises made by the organization, to their subsequent detriment, since the actual or presumed job offer was withdrawn (such withdrawal is known as reneging). Examples of detrimental effects include resigning from one's current employer, passing up other job opportunities, relocating geographically, and incurring expenses associated with the job offer. When the offer receiver experiences such detrimental reliance, the person may sue the employer for compensatory damages; actual hiring of the person is rarely sought. The final claim is that of fraud, where the employee claims the organization made promises it had no intention of keeping. Employees may legally pursue fraud claims and seek both compensatory and punitive damages.

JOB OFFERS

A job offer is an attempt by the organization to induce the offer receiver into the establishment of an employment relationship. Assuming that the offer is accepted and that consideration is met, the organization and the offer receiver will have established their relationship in the form of a legally binding employment contract. That contract is the culmination of the staffing process. The contract also signifies that the person/job match process has concluded and that the person/job match is now about to become a reality. That reality, in turn, becomes the start of, and foundation for, subsequent employee effectiveness on the various HR outcomes. For these reasons, the content and extension of the job offer become critical final parts of the overall staffing process.

This section discusses a strategic approach to job offers, along with the numerous factors that should be considered in the determination of the content of job offers. Then the actual content of job offers is discussed, along with some of the complexities associated with it.

Strategic Approach to Job Offers

The organization has considerable discretion in the content of the offers that it puts together to present to finalists. Rather than hastily crafting job offers, often in the heat of the hiring moment and with a desire to fill the vacancy now, it is better to think a bit more strategically as to job offer content. Such an approach has a better possibility of serving the interests of both the organization and the finalists and not locking them into a contract either will come to regret. Another benefit of the strategic approach is that it will help the organization decide whether there will be a standard offer for all finalists or whether enhanced offers will be possible for some finalists, and the circumstances that will give rise to such offers.

Shown in Exhibit 12.1 is the strategic approach to job offers, or the employee value proposition (EVP). Recall from Chapter 4 that the EVP is the total package of extrinsic and intrinsic rewards that the offered job will provide to the finalist if the job offer is accepted. Technically, the job offer is not the same as the EVP, because it is difficult to reduce to writing in the job offer letter the nature of the intrinsic rewards that will be provided, and because a job offer contains information in addition to job rewards (e.g., starting date, date the offer lapses, and disclaimers). Nonetheless, the major thrust and purpose of the job offer is to convey to the finalist the nature of the rewards "deal" being promised if the offer is accepted. First and foremost, the job offer must be a compelling one—an EVP the finalist will find enticing and difficult to turn down. The offer thus must present a package of rewards with the right combination of magnitude, mix, and distinctiveness to be compelling to the offer receiver.

Exhibit 12.1 indicates that labor market conditions, organization needs, applicant needs, and legal issues are forces to consider in the creation of job offers. As to labor markets, the simple availability of potential offer receivers needs to be considered, for there may be shortages that will require the organization to sweeten the deal if it is to fill vacancies. Coupled with that is consideration of the overall tightness or looseness of the labor market. Tight labor markets will serve to exacerbate limited supply availability, for applicants in the limited supply pool will likely have many job offer alternatives. On the other hand, with plentiful supply and a

EXHIBIT 12.1   Strategic Approach to Job Offers

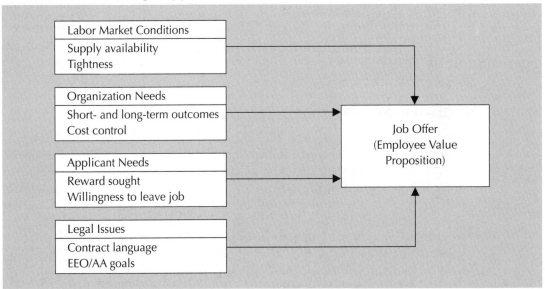

loose labor market, the organization will be in a position to provide standard offers, and ones that are lower in cost.

The organization has multiple needs it must seek to identify and fulfill in the formation of the employment relationship. Some of these are short-term outcomes—such as filling vacancies quickly or at any cost. To what extent does the organization want to respond to such pressures? The answer will clearly shape the content of job offers. Long-term outcomes such as the likely performance level of the new employee, the extent to which the employee fits in with the organization and work unit, the promotion success of the employee, and employee job satisfaction and retention all need to be considered. To what extent does the organization wish to craft job offers that are likely to enhance these longer-term outcomes? Finally, cost control must come into play. All job offers, if accepted, will cost the organization, so how much is it willing to spend? And is the organization willing to spend more for finalists that it thinks will more likely deliver the short-term and/or long-term outcomes it seeks?

In terms of applicant needs, the organization must seek to identify the rewards likely sought by applicants. Here, it is useful to consider the full range of rewards possible and to gather information about reward preferences of applicants (see Chapter 4). Strategically, it will be helpful to identify some rewards with a distinctiveness that may be particularly alluring. For example, in the case of over-the-road (long distance) truck drivers, common driver complaints (and causes of turnover) were long stretches on the road without a return home, and cramped and inhospitable quarters ("It's like being in a kennel," one driver said). This knowledge led trucking companies to make changes in the nature of the EVP, such as changing routes to provide less time away from home and equipping cabs with televisions, microwaves, and closets to provide a friendlier work environment. In addition, the magnitude of some extrinsic rewards was increased. The mileage rate paid was increased (drivers are paid by the mile), and health insurance and pension coverage were provided or enhanced.[14] Such job offer improvements required strategic information gathering and analysis, plus extended lead times to implement them.

Coupled with the assessment of applicant needs should be an assessment of the finalists' willingness to leave their current jobs. If the finalist is relatively willing, or even eager to leave, the job offer may not need to be as compelling in magnitude, mix, or distinctiveness. On the other hand, if the finalist is satisfied with the current job and current geographic location, the need to craft a compelling offer rises dramatically. Basically, such offers must provide an EVP that stirs in the finalist a dissatisfaction with the current job and boosts the willingness to change locations, both by pointing out positive features of the new location and by minimizing the costs of making the move.

Finally, legal issues come into play. The contract language will need to be reviewed for clarity and completeness of rewards promised and other terms of the offer, and for consistency with organizational employment policies, especially those with a legal basis. In addition, a review of the organization's equal employment opportunity and affirmative action (EEO/AA) policies, and progress toward hiring and promotion goals, should be made as the offer is being constructed. Being behind on these goals might well signal a need for more aggressive job offers.

Job Offer Content

The organization has considerable latitude in the terms and conditions of employment that it may offer to people. That latitude, of course, should be exercised within the organization's particular applicant attraction strategy, as well as the rewards generally available and shown in the job rewards matrix.

With some degree of latitude in terms and conditions offered for almost any job, it is apparent that job offers should be carefully constructed. There are definite rewards that can, and for the most part should, be addressed in any job offer. Moreover, the precise terms or content of the offer to any given finalist requires careful forethought. What follows is a discussion of the types of rewards to address, as well as some of their subtleties and complexities.

Starting Date

Normally, the organization controls when the employment relationship begins. To do so, it must provide a definite starting date in its offer. If it does not, acceptance and consideration of the offer occur at the time the new hire actually begins work. Normally, the starting date is one that allows the offer receiver at least two weeks to provide notification of resignation to a current employer.

Duration of Contract

Employment contracts may be of a fixed term (i.e., have a definite ending date) or an indeterminate term (i.e., have no definite ending date). The decision about duration is intimately related to the employment-at-will issue.

A fixed-term contract provides certainty to both the new hire and the organization regarding the length of the employment relationship. Both parties decide to and must abide by an agreed-on term of employment. The organization can then (according to common law) terminate the contract prior to its expiration date for "just cause" only. Determination and demonstration of just cause can be a complicated legal problem for the organization.

Most organizations are unwilling to provide such employment guarantees. They much prefer an employment-at-will relationship, in which either party may terminate the employment relationship at any time without having to demonstrate just cause.[15] Should the organization decide to have indeterminate-term employment contracts, it should carefully state in its written offer that the duration is indeterminate and that it may be terminated by either party at any time, for any reason. Because of the overriding importance of this issue, all wording should be approved at the highest organizational level.

A compromise between a fixed-term and an indefinite-term provision is to have a contract provision that states the employment relationship is for an indefinite term, that the employer may terminate the agreement at any time for good cause, and that either the employer or the employee may terminate the contract on 30 days' (or some other time period) written notice. Such a provision protects the employee against arbitrary, immediate termination, and protects the employer against a sudden and unanticipated loss of an employee.[16]

Compensation

Compensation is the most important reward the organization has to offer in its attraction strategy. It is a multifaceted reward that may be presented to the offer receiver in many forms. Sometimes it consists of a standard pay rate and benefits package, which must be simply accepted or rejected. Other times the offer may be more tailor-made, often negotiated in advance.

It should be remembered that job seekers carry with them a set of pay preferences and expectations that shape how they respond to the compensation components of the job offer. For example, a study of engineering and hotel administration soon-to-graduate job seekers found that they would respond more favorably to a pay package that had (1) a high, fixed rate of pay that was not contingent on the success of the organization, (2) pay pegged to a particular job rather than the number of skills they possessed, (3) pay raises based on individual rather than group performance, and (4) a flexible, as opposed to standard, benefits package.[17]

The compensation portion of the job offer should thus be carefully thought out and planned in advance. This pertains to starting pay, variable pay, and benefits.

Starting Pay: Flat Rate.   In flat-rate job offers, all persons are offered an identical rate of pay, and variance from this is not permitted. Starting pay is thus offered on a "take it or leave it" basis.

Use of flat rates is appropriate in many circumstances, such as the following examples:

- Jobs for which there is a plentiful supply of job applicants
- Where applicants are of quite similar KSAO quality
- Where there is a desire to avoid creating potential inequities in starting pay among new employees

Note that under some circumstances, use of flat rates may be mandatory. Examples here include pay rates under many collective bargaining agreements and for many jobs covered by civil service laws and regulations.

Starting Pay: Differential Rates.   Organizations often opt out of flat rates, despite their simplicity, and choose differential starting pay rates. In general, this occurs under three sets of circumstances.

First, there are situations where the organization thinks there are clear qualitative (KSAO) differences among finalists. Some finalists are thus felt to be worth more than others, and starting pay differentials are used in recognizing this. A good example here involves new college graduates. Research clearly shows that differences in major and previous work experience lead to starting pay differentials among new graduates.[18] Another example involves differences in starting pay for MBA graduates that reflect the quality of the MBA program from which they graduated. On the assumption that graduates from the elite programs (top 25 nationally ranked schools) represent better "raw business talent" than the mass of graduates from other schools, the elite-program graduates are receiving starting pay offers about twice the amount of other program graduates ($120,000 versus $60,000). A final example is paying a premium for applicants with bilingual language skills. The city of Los Angeles provides a bilingual pay premium to ensure that city services are accessible to non-English speakers. New hires (and current employees) who are required to speak, write, or interpret a language other than English receive a 5.5% bilingual premium.[19]

The second situation occurs when the organization is concerned about attraction outcomes, almost regardless of applicant KSAO differences. Here, the organization is under intense pressure to acquire new employees and fill vacancies promptly. To accomplish these outcomes, flexibility in starting pay rate offers is used to respond to finalists' demands, to sweeten offers, and to otherwise impress applicants with an entrepreneurial spirit of wheeling and dealing. Hence, the organization actively seeks to strike a bargain with the offer receiver, and differential starting pay rates are a natural part of the attraction package.

The third situation involves geographic pay differentials. For organizations with multiple facilities in different geographic areas, the starting pay rate for any particular job may need to vary because of average pay differentials across geographic areas. For example, for the job of HR manager, which has an average national rate of $88,500, pay varies from $57,300 in Montana to $103,500 in Delaware.[20] Clearly, starting pay must take into account geographic pay variation.

Use of differential starting pay rates requires attention to several potential problems.[21] One problem is that offer receivers, though similarly qualified, may have different pay "mix" preferences. Some offer receivers may place higher (or lower) value on salary than on stock options or benefits, leading them to demand higher (or lower) salaries. The organization must decide how much it is willing to provide offer receivers salary trade-offs for other forms of compensation. A second problem, often heightened by the first one, is that issues of fairness and internal equity among employees may arise when there is too much discretion in the range of starting salaries that exist. Naturally, similarly qualified employees receiving wide differences in starting pay is a guaranteed recipe for perceived pay inequities, and paying new hires starting salaries that exceed those of current "leapfrogged" employees also fuels the perceived inequity flames. Finally, research shows that starting pay expectations are often lower among female than male applicants. A survey of 1,600 undergraduate and graduate students found that the average starting pay expectation for men was $55,950, compared to $49,190 for women. If these expectations shape salary negotiations and acceptances, the average starting pay for women will be lower than that for men, and "catch up" for women may be difficult since raises are usually a percentage of one's salary. These represent potential salary discrimination issues confronting the organization.

For such reasons, whenever differential rates of starting pay are used, the organization must carefully consider what is permissible and within bounds. At times, the organization may choose to provide minimal guidance to managers making the offers. Often, however, there is a need for some constraints on managers. These constraints may specify when differential starting pay offers may be made and where within a pay range starting pay rates must fall. Exhibit 12.2 contains examples of such starting pay policies.

Variable Pay: Short Term.   Short-term variable pay may be available on jobs, and if so, the organization should address this in the job offer.

Prior to the job offer, the organization should determine whether there should be variable pay. This is a major issue that transcends staffing per se, but it does have important implications for the likely effectiveness of staffing activities.

Consider an organization with sales jobs, a classic example of a situation in which incentive or commission pay systems might be used. The mere presence/absence of such a pay plan will likely affect the motivation/job rewards part of the

---

EXHIBIT 12.2   Example of Starting Pay Policies

The Wright Company

The following policies regarding starting pay must be adhered to:

1. No person is to be offered a salary that is below the minimum, or above the midpoint, of the salary range for the job.
2. Generally, persons with reasonable qualifications should be offered a salary within the first quartile (bottom 25%) of the salary range for the job.
3. Salary offers above the first quartile, but not exceeding the midpoint, may be made for exceptionally well-qualified persons, or when market conditions dictate.
4. Salary offers should be fair in relation to other offers made and to the salaries paid to current employees.
5. Salary offers below the first quartile may be made without approval; offers at or above the first quartile must be approved in advance by the manager of compensation.
6. Counteroffers may not be accepted without approval of the manager of compensation.

matching process. Different "breeds of cats" may be attracted to jobs providing incentive plans as opposed to those that do not.

More generally, research shows that the use of short-term incentive pay is quite common, with almost 90% of private sector, 76% of partnerships, and 44% of public sector organizations offering incentive pay plans of various sorts. Of these organizations, 95% provide cash payments via individual incentive pay and bonuses, based on financial, customer service, production, goal attainment, efficiency, and cost reduction measures. Two of the major reasons these organizations provide for such short-term incentive offerings are to compete for qualified employees and to retain employees.[22] Usage of these types of incentive systems is increasing.[23]

If there are to be short-term variable pay plans, the organization should communicate this in the offer letter. Beyond that, the organization should carefully consider how much detail about such plans, including payout formulas and amounts, to include in the job offer. The more specific the information, the less flexibility the organization will have in the operation or modification of the plan.

Variable Pay: Long Term. Long-term variable pay plans provide employees ownership opportunity and the opportunity to increase their income as the value of the organization increases. Applicable only in the private sector, the most commonly used long-term variable pay plan is stock options—either an incentive stock option or a nonqualified stock option.[24] A stock option is a right to purchase a share of stock for a predetermined price at a later date; there is both a time span during which the right may be exercised (e.g., 10 years) and a waiting period before the employee is eligible (vested) to make purchases (e.g., 1 year). Incentive stock option plans provide special tax treatment for the employee, primarily regarding capital gains when the employee sells the purchased stock (hopefully at a net gain), but these plans place many statutory restrictions on employers. Nonqualified stock options do not have to meet statutory requirements like those of incentive stock option plans, thus providing the organization greater flexibility in granting options. But nonqualified options do not qualify for special tax treatment for the employee, whereas the organization can receive a tax deduction for the corporation expense of the stock options.

Though stock options provide potential incentive value to offer receivers, some may prefer cash in the form of base pay or short-term variable pay incentives. In addition, stock options only have actual value to the recipient if the value of the stock appreciates beyond the purchase price and if the employee remains eligible to participate in the plan—such as through remaining with the organization for a specified time period.

The use of stock options has been waning. In its place are numerous other long-term variable pay plans—performance options, stock appreciation rights, stock grants, restricted stock, delayed issuance awards, employee stock ownership, and employee stock purchase. Each of these types of plans has both strong and weak points, and careful analysis of the objectives sought (e.g., employee retention) should occur prior to its use and presentation to job offer receivers.[25] As with short-term variable pay plans, the job offer letter should mention the right or requirement to participate in these plans, but not go into too much detail about them.

Inclusion of stock options or other types of long-term variable pay in the job offer requires considerable care and expertise. Experts should draft the actual language in the offer, and the organization should take special steps to ensure that the offer receiver actually understands what is being offered.

Benefits.   Normally there is a fixed benefits package for a job, and it is offered to all offer receivers. Examples include health insurance and retirement and work/life plans. When a fixed or standard benefits package is offered, the offer letter should not spell out all of the specific benefit provisions. Rather, it should state that the employee will be eligible to participate in the benefit plans maintained by the organization, as provided in written descriptions of these plans. In this way, the job offer letter does not inadvertently make statements or promises that contradict or go beyond the organization's actual benefits plan.

Sometimes the offer may provide not only standard benefits but also additional custom-made benefits or other perquisites, known as "perks." These deal sweeteners may be offered to all potential new hires in a job category, or they may be tailor-made to the preferences of the individual offer receiver. In other instances, they may be offered in direct response to requests or demands from the offer receiver. The number and value of perks offered (or demanded) vary with the degree of difficulty in successfully attracting new hires. Perks are most likely provided to top executives, managers, and professionals. The set of perks used by organizations is almost endless. Commonly used perks are shown in Exhibit 12.3. More exotic perks used for enticing executive stars to relocate include providing a family clothing allowance, moving pet horses, covering a housekeeper's medical insurance, paying children's tuition at private schools, and reimbursing for financial counseling services and tax preparation.

EXHIBIT 12.3   Examples of Perquisites

• First-class air travel	• Specially equipped computer
• Paid meals	• Fax machine at home
• Country club membership	• Adoption assistance
• Automobile	• Corporate plane
• Cell phone	• Housing supplement
• Tuition reimbursement	• Interest-free loans
• Pay-off of student loans	• Assistance in selling home

Whether to offer perks, which ones, and to whom are perplexing issues. Although they may have definite applicant enticement appeal, they increase hiring costs, raise numerous tax issues, and may cause feelings of inequity and jealousy among other employees.

Hours. Statements regarding hours of work should be carefully thought out and worded. For the organization, such statements will affect staffing flexibility and cost. In terms of flexibility, a statement such as "Hours of work will be as needed and scheduled" provides maximum flexibility. Designation of work as part time, as opposed to full time, may affect cost because the organization may provide restricted, if any, benefits to part-time employees.

Factors other than just number of hours may also need to be addressed in the job offer. If there are to be any special arrangements for work hours, these need to be clearly spelled out. Examples include, "Weekend work will not be required of you," and "Your hours of work will be from 7:30 to 11:30 a.m. and 1:30 to 5:30 p.m." Overtime hours requirements and overtime pay, if applicable, could also be addressed.

Hiring Bonuses. Hiring, signing, or "up-front" bonuses are one-time payments offered and subsequently paid upon acceptance of the offer. Typically, the bonus is in the form of an outright cash grant; the bonus may also be in the form of a cash advance against future expected earnings. Top executives are likely to receive not only a cash bonus but also restricted stock and/or stock options.

For recent college graduates, hiring bonuses range from $1,000 to $10,000, with an average of $3,568. Roughly half (46.4%) of college recruiters say they use hiring bonuses to recruit college graduates.[26]

Generally, as labor markets tighten and employee shortages increase, hiring bonuses become more prevalent and of larger size. For example, in information technology (IT), hiring bonuses are the norm, with 65% of IT employers offering them. However, hiring bonuses can happen at all job levels, including nondegree jobs such as fast-food workers, butchers, bartenders, hairstylists, and pizza cooks.[27] The converse is also true, with looser labor markets and employee surpluses leading to smaller or disappearing hiring bonuses.

In addition to simply helping attract highly desired individuals (monetary flattery), hiring bonuses can help offset something the offer receiver may give up by changing jobs, such as a pending pay raise or a promotion. Also, hiring bonuses might be a useful way to persuade people to move to rural areas or to offset relocation costs or a higher cost of living. Finally, use of a hiring bonus might help in avoiding a permanent elevation in base pay, thus holding down labor costs.

Offers of hiring bonuses should be used judiciously, or they will lose their particular distinctiveness as part of the EVP, as well as lead to other problems. For example, while it is desirable to be flexible as to the use and amount of hiring bonuses, it is necessary to carefully monitor them so that they do not get out of control. Also, it is important to avoid getting into overly spirited hiring bonus bidding wars with competitors—the other rewards of the job need to be emphasized in addition to the bonus. Another danger is that hiring bonuses might give rise to feelings of jealousy and inequity, necessitating retention bonuses if existing employees learn of the bonuses being given to new hires. To avoid this possibility, hiring bonuses should be confidential.[28] Another potential problem is that bonus recipients may be tempted to "take the money and run," and their performance motivation may be lessened because their bonus money is not contingent on their job performance. Debra Ortega, vice president (VP) of HR at Huntington Hospital in Pasadena, California, stopped using hiring bonuses for exactly that reason. "Although sign-on bonuses are common in our industry because of the labor shortages, we find that the practice can almost encourage job hopping from bonus to bonus," she said.

To address these problems, the organization may place restrictions on the bonus payment, paying half up front and the other half after some designated time period, such as 6 or 12 months; another option is to make payment of a portion or all of the bonus contingent on meeting certain performance goals within a designated time period. Such payment arrangements should help other employees see the hiring bonus as not a total "freebie" and should encourage only serious and committed offer receivers to accept the offer. Although such "clawbacks" are awkward, and some employers have had difficulties enforcing such agreements, they are generally necessary in some form because the very labor markets in which bonuses are most likely to be used (tight labor markets) are the same markets in which job-hopping is very easy to do.[29]

Relocation Assistance.   Acceptance of the offer may require a geographic move and entail relocation costs for the offer receiver. The organization may want to provide assistance to conduct the move, as well as totally or partially defray moving costs. Thus, a relocation package may include assistance with house hunting, guaranteed purchase of the applicant's home, a mortgage subsidy, actual moving cost reimbursement, and a cost-of-living adjustment if the move is to a higher-cost area. To simplify things, a lump-sum relocation allowance may be provided, thus reducing record keeping and other paperwork.[30]

Recently, relocation has become even more difficult in dual-career circumstances.[31] With both people working, it may be necessary to move both the offer receiver and the accompanying partner. Such a move may entail employing both people or providing job search assistance to the accompanying partner. The problem is likely to grow in magnitude.

Hot Skill Premiums.   A hot skill premium is a temporary pay premium added to the regular base pay to account for a temporary market escalation in pay for certain skills in extreme shortage. Hiring bonuses are also frequently used to attract in-demand talent. The job offer should clearly indicate the amount of base pay that constitutes the premium, the length of time the premium will be in effect, and the mechanism by which the premium will be halted or phased out. Before offering such premiums, it is wise to recognize that there will likely be pressure to maintain rather than discontinue the premium and that careful communication with the offer receiver about the temporary nature of the premium will be necessary.[32]

Severance Packages.   Terms and conditions that the organization states the employee is entitled to upon departure from the organization constitute a severance package. Content of the package typically includes one or two weeks of pay for every year of service, earned vacation and holiday pay, extended health insurance coverage and premium payment, and outplacement assistance in finding a new job.[33] What is the organization willing to provide?

In pondering this question, a few points should be borne in mind. Severance packages for top executives are usually expected and provided, and their provisions can be quite complex. Lower-level managers and nonmanagers also appear to be aware of and expect severance packages. In other words, job applicants are considering these packages as part of the EVP. This expectation is probably due to a realization of how marketable their KSAOs are, as well as increased concerns about job security and layoff protection. Unmet severance expectations may translate into demands by candidates for a severance package to be included in their job offer, or a refusal to even consider a job offer that does not provide some form of severance benefit.[34]

Other thorny issues surround these packages. When does an employee become eligible for the package? Will severance be granted for voluntary or involuntary termination, or both? If involuntary, are there exceptions, such as for unacceptable job performance or misconduct? Questions such as these illustrate the need to very carefully craft the terms that will govern the package and define its contents.

Restrictions on Employees

In some situations, the organization may want to place certain restrictions on employees to protect its own interests. These restrictions should be known, and agreed to, by the new employee at the time of hire. Thus, they should be incorporated into the job offer and resultant employment contract. Because of the potential complexities in these restrictions and the fact that they are subject to state contract laws, legal counsel should be sought to guide the organization in drafting appropriate contract language. Several types of restrictions are possible.[35]

One form of restriction involves so-called confidentiality clauses that prohibit current or departing employees from the unauthorized use or disclosure of confidential information during or after employment. Confidential information is any information not made public and that gives the organization an advantage over its competitors. Examples of such information include trade secrets, customer lists, secret formulas, manufacturing processes, marketing and pricing plans, and business forecasts. It will be necessary to spell out, in some degree, exactly what information the organization considers confidential, as well as the time period after employment for which confidentiality must be maintained.

Another restriction, known as a noncompete agreement, seeks to keep departed employees from competing against the organization. For example, former Microsoft VP Kai-Fu Lee signed a noncompete agreement when he first joined Microsoft. When Lee left Microsoft to run a Google research facility in China, Microsoft sued Google and Lee for violating his noncompete agreement. Google and Microsoft eventually settled out of court, but the case showed that not all noncompete agreements are enforceable. For example, some states (Alabama, California, Georgia, Montana, Nebraska, North Dakota, Oklahoma, and Texas) do not favor noncompetes. If an employee signs a noncompete agreement in a state that allows them, but relocates to a state that disfavors them, the employer may be out of luck—which is exactly what happened to Convergys Corp. when an employee signed a noncompete agreement with Convergys in Ohio and then moved to work for a competitor in Georgia, which bars such agreements.[36]

More generally, noncompete agreements cannot keep departed employees from practicing their trade or profession completely or indefinitely, for this would in essence restrict the person from earning a living in a chosen field. Accordingly, the noncompete agreement must be carefully crafted in order to be enforceable. The agreement should probably not be a blanket statement that applies to all employees; rather, the agreement should apply to those employees who truly could turn into competitors, such as high-level managers, scientists, and technical staff. Also, the agreement must be limited in time and geography. The time should be of short duration (less than two years), and the area should be limited to the geographic area of the organization's competitive market. For example, the VP of sales for an insurance agency with locations in two counties of a state might have a noncompete agreement that prohibits working with any other agencies within the two counties, and the solicitation of the agency's policyholders, for one year.

A final type of restriction is the "golden handcuff," or payback agreement. The intent of this restriction is to retain new hires for some period of time and to financially discourage them from leaving the organization, particularly soon after they have joined. A typical golden handcuff will require the employee to repay (in full or pro rata) the organization for any up-front payments made at the time of hire if the employee departs within the first year of employment. These payments might include hiring bonuses, relocation expenses, tuition reimbursements, or any other financial hiring lures. Executive pay packages might contain even more restrictions designed to tie the executive to the organization for an extended period of time. Annual bonuses might be deferred for two or three years and be contingent on the executive not leaving during that time, or an executive may forfeit accrued pension benefits if he or she departs before a particular date.

Other Terms and Conditions

Job offers are by no means restricted to the terms and conditions discussed so far. Virtually any terms and conditions may be covered and presented in a job offer, provided they are legally permissible. Hence, the organization should carefully and creatively think of other terms it may wish to offer. None of these other possible terms should be offered, however, unless the organization is truly willing to commit itself to them as part of a legally binding contract.

The organization should also give careful thought to the possible use of contingencies, which, as mentioned previously, are terms and conditions that the applicant must fulfill before the contract becomes binding (e.g., passage of a medical exam). As was noted, inclusion of these contingencies should not be done without prior knowledge and understanding of their potential legal ramifications (e.g., in the case of a medical exam, potential factors to consider under the Americans With Disabilities Act [ADA]).

Acceptance Terms

The job offer should specify terms of acceptance required of the offer receiver. For reasons previously noted regarding oral contracts, acceptances should normally be required in writing only. The receiver should be required to accept or reject the offer in total, without revision. Any other form of acceptance is not an acceptance, merely a counteroffer. Finally, the offer should specify the date, if any, by which it will lapse. A lapse date is recommended so that certainty and closure are brought to the offer process.

Sample Job Offer Letter

A sample job offer letter is shown in Exhibit 12.4 that summarizes and illustrates the previous discussion and recommendations regarding job offers. This letter should be read and analyzed for purposes of becoming familiar with job offer letters, as well as gaining an appreciation for the many points that need to be addressed in such a letter. Remember that, normally, whatever is put in the job offer letter, once accepted by the receiver, becomes a binding employment contract. Examples of more complex job offer letters, more relevant to executives, might also be consulted.

JOB OFFER PROCESS

Besides knowing the types of issues to address in a job offer, it is equally important to understand the total job offer process. The content of any specific job offer must be formulated within a broad context of considerations. Once these have been taken into account, the specific offer must be developed and presented to the finalist. Following this, there will be matters to address in terms of either acceptance

---

EXHIBIT 12.4   Example of Job Offer Letter

The Wright Company

Mr. Vern Markowski
152 Legion Lane
Clearwater, Minnesota

Dear Mr. Markowski:

We are pleased to offer you the position of Human Resource Specialist, beginning March 1, 2011. Your office will be located here in our main facility at Silver Creek, Minnesota.

This offer is for full-time employment, meaning you will be expected to work a minimum of 40 hours per week. Weekend work is also expected, especially during peak production periods.

You will receive a signing bonus of $2,500, half payable on March 1, 2011, and the other half on August 1, 2011, if you are still an employee of the company. Your starting pay will be $3,100 per month. Should you complete one year of employment, you will then participate in our managerial performance review and merit pay process. You will be eligible to participate in our benefit plans as provided in our written descriptions of those plans.

Should you choose to relocate to the Silver Creek area, we will reimburse you for one house/apartment hunting trip for up to $1,000. We will also pay reasonable and normal moving expenses up to $7,500, with receipts required.

It should be emphasized that we are an employment-at-will employer. This means that we, or you, may terminate our employment relationship at any time, for any reason. Only the president of the Wright Company is authorized to provide any modification to this arrangement.

This offer is contingent on (a) your receiving certification as a professional in human resources (PHR) from the Human Resource Certification Institute prior to March 1, 2011, and (b) your passing a company-paid and -approved medical exam prior to March 1, 2011.

We must have your response to this offer by February 1, 2011, at which time the offer will lapse. If you wish to accept our offer as specified in this letter, please sign and date at the bottom of the letter and return it to me (a copy is enclosed for you). Should you wish to discuss these or any other terms prior to February 1, 2011, please feel free to contact me.

Sincerely yours,

Mary Kaiser
Senior Vice President, Human Resources

I accept the employment offer, and its terms, contained in this letter. I have received no promises other than those contained in this letter.

_____   _____
Signed   Date

or rejection of the offer. Finally, there will be an occasional need to deal with the unfortunate issue of reneging, either by the organization or by the offer receiver.

Formulation of the Job Offer

When the organization puts together a specific job offer, several factors should be explicitly considered: knowledge of the terms and conditions offered by competitors, applicant truthfulness about KSAOs and reward information provided, the receiver's likely reaction to the offer, and policies on negotiation of job offer content with the offer receiver.

Knowledge of Competitors

The organization competes for labor within labor markets. The job offer must be sensitive to the labor demand and supply forces operating, for these forces set the overall parameters for job offers to be extended.

On the demand side, this requires becoming knowledgeable about the terms and conditions of job contracts offered and provided by competitors. Here, the organization must confront two issues: exactly who are the competitors, and exactly what terms and conditions are they offering for the type of job for which the hiring organization is staffing?

Assume the hiring organization is a national discount retailer, and it is hiring recent (or soon-to-be) college graduates for the job of management trainee. It may identify as competitors other retailers at the national level (e.g., Sears), as well as national discount retailers (e.g., Target, Wal-Mart, and Kmart). There may be fairly direct competitors in other industries as well (e.g., banking, insurance) that typically place new college graduates in training programs.

Once such competitors are identified, the organization needs to determine, if possible, what terms and conditions they are offering. This may be done through formal mechanisms such as performing salary surveys, reading competitors' ads and websites, or consulting with trade associations. Information may be gathered informally as well, such as through telephone contacts with competitors, and conversations with actual job applicants, who have firsthand knowledge of competitors' terms.

The organization may quickly acquire salary information through the use of free online salary sites (e.g., *salary.com*, *glassdoor.com*, and *salaryexpert.com*) or ones that charge fees (e.g., *towers.com*, *haygroup.com*). Listings of the sites and discussions of their advantages and disadvantages are available.[37] Generally, the user should be cautious in his or her use of these data, being careful to assess salary survey characteristics such as sample nature and size, currency of data, definitions of terms and job descriptions, and data presentation. It should also be remembered that a job seeker can and will access these data, making this individual a very knowledgeable "shopper" and negotiator.

Through all the above mechanisms, the organization becomes "marketwise" regarding its competitors. Invariably, however, the organization will discover that for any given term or condition, a range of values will be offered. For example, starting pay might range from $30,000 to $40,500 per year, and the length of the training program may vary from three months to two years. The organization will thus need to determine where within these ranges it wishes to position itself in general, as well as for each particular offer receiver.

On the labor supply side, the organization will need to consider its needs concerning both labor quantity and quality (KSAOs and motivation). In general, offers need to be attractive enough that they yield the head count required. Moreover, offers need to take into account the KSAOs each specific receiver possesses and what these specific KSAOs are worth in terms and conditions offered the person. This calculation is illustrated in Exhibit 12.2, which shows an example of an organization's policies regarding differential starting pay offers among offer receivers. Such differential treatment, and all the issues and questions it raises, applies to virtually any other term or condition as well.

Applicant Truthfulness

Throughout the recruitment and selection process, information about KSAOs and other factors (e.g., current salary) is being provided by the applicant. Initially, this information is gathered as part of the assessment process, whose purpose is to determine which applicants are most likely to provide a good fit with job requirements and rewards. For applicants who pass the hurdles and are to receive job offers, the information that has been gathered may very well be used to decide the specific terms and conditions to include in a job offer. Just how truthful or believable is this information? The content and cost of job offers depend on how the organization answers this question.

There is little solid evidence on the degree of applicant truthfulness. However, there are some anecdotal indications that lack of truthfulness by applicants may be a problem, especially for current salary, salary history, job title, and job duties and accomplishments.

Consider the case of starting pay. Quite naturally, the organization may wish to base its starting pay offer on what the offer receiver's pay is currently. Will the person be truthful or deceitful in reporting current salary? Indications are that deceit may be common. People may embellish or enhance not only their reported salaries but also their KSAOs to provide an artificially high base or starting point for the organization as it prepares its job offer. A production analyst earning $55,000 did this and obtained a new job at $150,000, with a company car and a country club membership also included in the package.[38]

To combat such deceit by applicants, organizations are increasingly verifying all applicant information, including salary, and may go to extremes to do so. At the executive level, for example, some organizations now require people to provide copies of their W-2 income forms. The organization should not act on finalist-provided information in the preparation of job offers unless it is willing to assume, or has verified, that the information is accurate.

Likely Reactions of Offer Receivers

Naturally, the terms and conditions to be presented in an offer should be based on some assessment of the receiver's likely reaction to it. Will the receiver jump at it, laugh at it, or respond somewhere in between?

One way to gauge likely reactions to the offer is to gather information about various preferences from the offer receiver during the recruitment/selection process. Such preliminary discussions and communications will help the organization construct an offer that is likely to be acceptable. At the extreme, the process may lead to almost simultaneous presentation and acceptance of the offer. Another way to assess likely reactions to offers from offer receivers is to conduct research on reward importance to employees and applicants (see Chapter 4).

Policies on Negotiations and Initial Offers

Before making job offers, the organization should decide whether it will negotiate on them. In essence, the organization must decide whether its first offer to a person will also be its final offer. If there will be room for negotiation, the style of negotiation should also be determined.

To help make this decision, it is useful to consider what components of the salary and benefits part of the offer are considered open to negotiation by organizations. An example of such data, based on a survey of 418 HR professionals in organizations of all sizes, is shown in Exhibit 12.5. It can be seen that salary is almost uniformly considered negotiable. A majority also considers the following components negotiable: payment for relocation costs, flexible work schedules, and early salary reviews with the possibilities for increases. The openness to negotiation of other components trails off from there.

Several considerations should also be kept in mind when formulating strategies and policies for making job offers. First, remember that job offers occur for both external and internal staffing. For external staffing, the job offer is intended to convert the offer receiver into a new hire. For internal staffing, the job offer is being made to induce the employee to accept a new job assignment or to attempt to retain the employee by making a counteroffer to an offer the employee has received from another organization. These separate types of job offers (new hires, new assignment, and retention) will likely require separate job offer strategies and policies.

Second, consider fully the costs of the offer receiver not accepting the job offer. Are there other equally qualified individuals available as backup offer receivers? How long can the organization afford to let a position remain vacant? How will current employees feel about job offers being rejected—will they, too, feel rejected,

EXHIBIT 12.5 Negotiable Components of Salary and/or Benefits According to HR Professionals

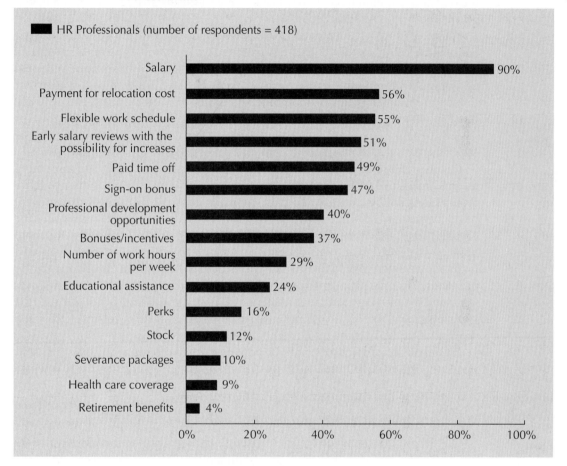

HR Professionals (number of respondents = 418)

Salary	90%
Payment for relocation cost	56%
Flexible work schedule	55%
Early salary reviews with the possibility for increases	51%
Paid time off	49%
Sign-on bonus	47%
Professional development opportunities	40%
Bonuses/incentives	37%
Number of work hours per week	29%
Educational assistance	24%
Perks	16%
Stock	12%
Severance packages	10%
Health care coverage	9%
Retirement benefits	4%

SOURCE: E. Esen, *Job Negotiation Survey Findings: A Study by SHRM and CareerJournal.com* (Alexandria, VA: Society for Human Resource Management, 2004), p. 9. Used with permission.

or will they feel that something they are unaware of is amiss in the organization? Will those next in line to receive an offer feel like second-class citizens or choices of desperation and last resort? Answers to such questions often suggest it may be desirable to negotiate (up to a point) with the offer receiver.

Third, recognize that many people to whom you will be making offers may in turn be seeking and receiving counteroffers from their current employer. Although counteroffers are less likely in a poor economy, many organizations do seek to keep their employees by making counteroffers even during down times.[39] Hence, the organization should recognize that any offer it makes may lead to a bidding war of sorts with other organizations.

Fourth, a currently employed offer receiver normally incurs costs for leaving and will expect a "make whole" offer from the organization. Often these costs can amount to 20%–30% of the offer receiver's current base pay. In addition to relocation or higher commuting costs, the offer receiver may forfeit employer contribution to a retirement plan, vacation time and holidays, various perks, and so forth. In addition, there may be waiting periods before the offer receiver is eligible for various benefits, leading to opportunity costs of lost coverage and possibly paying the costs (e.g., health insurance premiums) out of pocket until coverage begins.

Finally, job seekers are often quite sophisticated in formulating and presenting their demands to the organization. They will know what it truly costs them to leave their current job and will frame their demands accordingly. They will be aware of the particular KSAOs that they have to offer, make these acutely known to the organization, and demand a high price for them. The terms demanded (or more politely, proposed) may focus not only on salary but on myriad other possibilities, including vacation time, a flexible work schedule to help balance work and family pressures, guaranteed expenditures on training and development, higher employer matching to a 401(k) retirement plan, and so on. In short, unless it is illegal, it is negotiable, and the organization must be prepared to handle demands from job seekers on virtually every term and condition of employment.

Presumably, each term or condition contained in an offer is a mini-offer in itself. For each term or condition, therefore, the organization must decide the following:

- Whether it will negotiate on this term or condition
- If it negotiates, what are its lower and (especially) upper bounds

Once these questions have been answered, the organization may determine its posture regarding the presentation of the initial offer to the receiver. There are three basic strategies to choose from: lowball, competitive, and best shot.

Lowball. The lowball strategy involves offering the lower bounds of terms and conditions to the receiver. Advantages of this strategy include getting acceptances from desperate or unknowledgeable receivers, minimizing initial employment costs, and leaving plenty of room to negotiate upward. Dangers of the lowball strategy include failing to get any acceptances, driving people away from and out of the finalist pool, developing an unsavory reputation among future potential applicants, and creating inequities and hard feelings that the reluctant accepter may carry into the organization, which may then influence postemployment attraction outcomes such as retention. This strategy is often adopted during periods of economic downturn, when applicants have relatively few alternatives.[40]

Competitive.   With a competitive strategy, the organization prepares an offer that it feels is "on the market," neither too high nor too low. The competitive strategy should yield a sufficient number of job offer acceptances overall, though not all of the highest-quality (KSAO) applicants. This strategy leaves room for subsequent negotiation, should it be necessary. Competitive offers are unlikely to offend or excite the receiver, and they probably will not have negative consequences for postemployment outcomes.

Best Shot.   With the best-shot strategy, the organization goes for broke and gives a high offer, one right at the upper bounds of feasible terms and conditions. Accompanying this offer is usually a statement to the receiver that this is indeed the organization's best shot, thus leaving little or no room for negotiation. These offers should enhance both preemployment attraction outcomes (e.g., filling vacancies quickly) and postemployment outcomes (e.g., job satisfaction). Best-shot offers obviously increase employment costs. They also leave little or no room for negotiation or for sweetening the offer. Finally, they may create feelings of inequity or jealousy among current employees.

None of these initial offer strategies is inherently superior. But the organization does need to choose which type to generally use. It could also choose to tailor a strategy to fit the finalist pursued, as well as other circumstances. For example, the best-shot strategy may be chosen (1) for high-quality finalists, (2) when there are strong competitive hiring pressures from competitors, (3) when the organization is pressured to fill vacancies quickly, and (4) as part of an aggressive EEO/AA recruitment program.

Policies for how negotiations will be conducted should also be discussed in advance. After the initial offer is made—either lowball, competitive, or best shot—the job offer maker will have to know what style of negotiation is appropriate. Research has generally suggested that individuals are more satisfied with a give-and-take negotiation than a hardline "take it or leave it" approach.[41] In other words, offer receivers may be more satisfied with their offer if they feel as though they have a chance to move the initial figure somewhat. This argues against setting in stone all components of the job offer in advance. A nonconfrontational tone may also generate more positive outcomes down the road. Research also suggests that individuals who are more satisfied with their job negotiation process and outcomes are more satisfied with their subsequent compensation and jobs in general, and have lower intentions to leave a year later.[42]

Presentation of the Job Offer

Presentation of the offer may proceed along many different paths. The precise path chosen depends on the content of the offer, as well as factors considered in formulating the offer. To illustrate, two extreme approaches to presenting the job offer—the mechanical approach and the sales approach—are detailed.

Mechanical Approach

The mechanical approach relies on simple one-way communication from the organization to the offer receiver. Little more than a standard, or "form," written offer is sent to the person. The organization then awaits a response. Little or no input about the content of the offer is received from the person, and after the offer has been made, there is no further communication with the person. If the person rejects the offer, another form letter acknowledging receipt of the rejection is sent. Meanwhile, the offer process is repeated anew, without modification, for a different receiver. Although there are obvious disadvantages to such an approach, it is highly efficient and inexpensive.

Sales Approach

The sales approach treats the job offer as a product that must be developed and sold to the customer (i.e., receiver). There is active interaction between the organization and the receiver as the terms and conditions are developed and incorporated into an offer package. Informal agreement unfolds between the receiver and the organization, and reduction of that agreement into an actual job offer is a mere formality. After the formal offer has been presented, the organization continues to have active communication with the receiver. In this way, the organization can be alert to possible glitches that occur in the offer process and can continue to sell the job to the receiver. The sales approach is much more expensive and time-consuming, but it may have a higher chance of the receiver accepting the offer.

As the mechanical and sales approaches to job offer presentation make clear, the organization has considerable discretion in how it delivers the offer. When developing its job offer presentation process, the organization should be ever mindful of the strategic job offer process (Exhibit 12.1) and its emphasis on labor market conditions, organization and applicant need, and legal issues, all as factors affecting applicant attraction outcomes.

Timing of the Offer

Another issue that must be considered in the process of presenting an offer is the timing of the offer. In general, organizations will want to deliver the offer as quickly as possible after a final decision has been reached. Post-interview delays in communication with candidates have been linked to negative perceptions of the organization.[43] Research has also demonstrated that organizations that make offers more quickly are more likely to have their offers accepted.[44] This same research has shown that individuals who accept these quicker offers have similar levels of performance and turnover relative to those who received later offers. In sum, it appears that organizations can increase acceptance rates and reduce vacancy times if they make offers in a timely manner.

Job Offer Acceptance and Rejection

Ultimately, of course, job offers are accepted and rejected. How this happens and how it is handled are often as important as the outcomes themselves.

Provided next are some general suggestions and recommendations about acceptances and rejections. These are intended to serve as advice about additional practices and issues involved in the job offer process.

Acceptance

When the offer receiver accepts a job offer, the organization should do two important things. First, it should check the receiver's actual acceptance to ensure that it has been accepted as required in the offer. Thus, the acceptance should not come in the form of a counteroffer or with any other contingencies attached to it. Also, the acceptance should occur in the manner required (normally in writing), and it should arrive on or before the date specified.

Second, the organization must maintain contact with the new hire. Initially, this means acknowledging receipt of the acceptance. Additional communication may also be appropriate to further "cement the deal" and build commitment to the new job and organization. Examples of such continued communication include soon-to-be coworkers calling and offering congratulations to the new hire, sending work materials and reports to the new hire to help phase the person into the new job, and inviting the new hire to meetings and other activities prior to that person's starting date.

Rejection

The organization may reject the finalist, and the finalist may reject the organization.

By the Organization.   Depending on the decision-making process used, the acceptance of an offer by one person means that the organization will have to reject others. This should be done promptly and courteously. Moreover, the organization should keep records of those it rejects. This is necessary for legal purposes (e.g., applicant flow statistics) and for purposes of building and maintaining a pool of potential applicants that the organization may wish to contact about future vacancies.

The content of the rejection message (usually a letter) is at the discretion of the organization. Most organizations opt for short and vague content that mentions a lack of fit between the applicant's KSAOs and the job's requirements. Providing more specific reasons for rejection should only be done with caution. The reasons provided should be candid and truthful, and they should match the reasons recorded and maintained on other documents by the organization.

By the Offer Receiver.   When the receiver rejects the job offer, the organization must decide whether to accept the rejection or extend a new offer to the person. If the organization's position on negotiations has already been determined, as ideally it should, the organization simply needs to carry out its plan to either extend a new offer or move on to the next candidate.

The organization should accept the rejection in a prompt and courteous manner. Moreover, records should be kept of these rejections, for the same reasons they are kept when rejection by the organization occurs.

Reneging

Occasionally, and unfortunately, reneging occurs. Organizations rescind offers extended, and receivers rescind offers accepted. Solid evidence on reneging, and exactly why it occurs, is lacking. Sometimes reneging is unavoidable. The organization may experience a sudden downturn in business conditions, which causes planned-on jobs to evaporate. Or, the offer receiver may experience sudden changes in circumstances requiring reneging, such as a change in health status.

As an example of reneging, consider the case of Ford Motor Company, which extended offers of employment as assemblers to hundreds of individuals in its Oakville plant in Ontario, Canada.[45] A sudden drop in demand for vehicles led Ford to withdraw these job offers soon after they had been made. As a result, the individuals who had lost their offers brought a class-action lawsuit, claiming that they had faced considerable economic difficulties as a result of this repudiation of the employment agreement. Economic damages included lost wages for individuals who had terminated work at another employer in anticipation of these jobs with Ford. In addition to the legal concerns, there are also reputational concerns that come with reneging. As word of the Oakville plant problems spreads, Ford may anticipate problems in staffing future positions because applicants will be worried about the company's tendency to keep its word.

While some reneging by the organization may be necessary, we believe that the organization can and should take steps to lessen its occurrence. If these steps are insufficient, we believe the organization should take other actions to handle reneging. Examples of these actions are shown in Exhibit 12.6. They represent attempts to be fair to the offer receiver while still representing the interests of the organization.

For the offer receiver, high standards of fairness are also required. The receiver should not be frivolous and should not go through the application process just "for the experience." Nor should the receiver accept an offer as a way of extracting a counteroffer out of his or her current employer. Indeed, organizations should be aware that some people to whom they make job offers will receive such counteroffers, and this should be taken into account during the time the offer is initially formulated and presented. Finally, the receiver should carefully assess the probable fit for the person/job match prior to accepting an offer.

EXHIBIT 12.6   Organization Actions to Deal With Reneging

A. To Lessen the Occurrence of Reneging

Extend offers only for positions known to exist and be vacant.
Require top management approval of all reneging.
Conduct thorough assessments of finalists prior to job offer.
Honor outstanding offers but make no new ones.
Discourage offer receiver from accepting offer.
Defer starting date and provide partial pay in interim.
Keep offer open but renegotiate or reduce salary and other economic items.
Stagger new hire starting dates to smooth out additions to payroll.

B. To Handle Reneging

Communicate honestly and quickly with offer receiver.
Provide consolation or apology package (e.g., hiring bonus, three months salary).
Pay for any disruption costs (e.g., relocation).
Hire as consultant (independent contractor), convert to employee later.
Guarantee priority over other applicants when future vacancies occur.

NEW EMPLOYEE ORIENTATION AND SOCIALIZATION

Establishment of the employment relationship through final match activities does not end a concern with the person/job match. Rather, that relationship must now be nurtured and maintained over time to ensure that the intended match becomes and remains effective. The new hires become newcomers, and their initial entry into the job and organization should be guided by orientation and socialization activities. Orientation and socialization may be concurrent, overlapping activities that occur for the newcomer. Orientation is typically more immediate, while socialization is more long term.

Despite the importance of a quality orientation program, many organizations do not invest substantial resources into helping new employees get on board.[46] A survey conducted by Harris Interactive found that only 29% of employers give managers training in techniques to facilitate orientation for newcomers, and 15% leave the process of getting new employees on board entirely in the hands of the hiring manager. Experts agree that this short-sighted approach can be very costly, as turnover rates for new hires tend to be much higher than for established employees. Programs that continue to challenge and develop employees are an especially important element in effective orientation and socialization processes.

As an example of a comprehensive "onboarding" program, new employees at Sun Microsystems have jettisoned the typical orientation program that involves filling out mountains of paperwork.[47] Instead, new employees learn about the company through an interactive video game. When they arrive at their desks, new hires receive welcome notes and other company-themed paraphernalia. There are also opportunities to join online social networks to form relationships with established employees. Filing forms must be accomplished during orientation, of course, but the entire process has been integrated with the company's human resource information systems, and hiring managers can guide employees through a checklist of requirements relatively quickly and efficiently. This level of attention and guidance is certainly not typical—many companies still engage in minimal, low-cost efforts to facilitate newcomer engagement—but Sun believes that the returns for the system are well worth the expenditures.

It should be remembered that the newcomer is likely entering a situation of uncertainties and unknowns. Research indicates that how the organization reduces these will have an important impact on how well the newcomer adapts to the job and remains with the organization. Several factors have been identified as influencing the likely effectiveness of orientation and socialization:[48]

- Providing realistic recruitment information about job requirements and rewards (orientation begins before the job does)
- Clarifying for the newcomer job requirements and knowledge and skills to be acquired
- Socializing for the newcomer to learn sources of influence in the organization and to develop friendships
- Integrating the newcomer into the work unit and team
- Providing more information about job rewards to newcomers
- Conducting active mentoring for the newcomer

Elaboration on these points, as well as many examples, is provided below.

Orientation

Orientation requires considerable advanced planning in terms of topics to cover, development of materials for the newcomer, and scheduling of the myriad activities that contribute to an effective program. Often, the HR department is responsible for the design and conduct of the orientation, and it will seek close coordination of actual orientation activities and schedules with the newcomer's supervisor. This is also the organization's first opportunity to welcome new hires and to emphasize the opportunities it can provide.

Exhibit 12.7 contains a far-ranging set of suggested topics of information for an orientation program, delivery of which is accomplished via written materials,

EXHIBIT 12.7   New Employee Orientation Guidelines

Before the Employee Arrives

- Notify everyone in your unit that a new person is starting and what the person's job will be; ask the other staff members to welcome the new employee and encourage their support
- Prepare interesting tasks for the employee's first day
- Provide new employee with a copy of the job description, job performance standards, organization chart, and your department's organization chart
- Enroll the employee in any necessary training programs
- Make sure the employee's work location is available, clean, and organized
- Make sure a copy of the appropriate personnel policy manual or contract is available for the employee
- Have a benefits information package available
- If possible, identify a staff member to act as a buddy for the first week
- Put together a list of key people the employee should meet and interview to get a broader understanding of their roles
- Arrange for a building pass, parking pass, and IDs if necessary
- Draft a training plan for the new employee's first few months

First Day on the Job

- Give a warm welcome and discuss the plan for the first day
- Tour the employee's assigned work space
- Explain where rest rooms, vending machines, and break areas are located
- Provide required keys
- Arrange to have lunch with the new employee
- Tour the building and immediate area and introduce the new employee to other staff members
- Introduce the new employee to the person you've identified as a mentor (if appropriate)
- Review job description
- Review the department's (or office's) organizational chart
- Review your office's policies and procedures involving working hours, telephone, e-mail and Internet use, office organization, office resources, and ethics

During the First Week

- Review employee work area to ensure needed equipment is in place
- Set up a brief meeting with the employee and the assigned buddy to review the first week's activities (if appropriate)
- Schedule meeting with human resources office to complete required paperwork, review personnel policies and procedures, learn about benefits, obtain credentials, and explain other policies and procedures

(continued)

EXHIBIT 12.7   Continued

Within the First Month of Employment

- Meet with employee to review:
    - ❑ Job description
    - ❑ Performance standards
    - ❑ Work rules
    - ❑ Organization structure
    - ❑ Health and safety
    - ❑ Benefits overview

Within Six Months of Starting

- Revisit performance standards and work rules
- Schedule performance appraisal meeting

SOURCE: Based on "Guide to Managing Human Resources: New Employee Orientation," Human Resources, University of California, Berkeley (*http://hrweb.berkeley.edu/guide/orient.htm*).

online services, training programs, meetings with various people, and visual inspection. Note that these activities are spaced out rather than concentrated in just the first day of work for the newcomer. An effective orientation program will foster an understanding of the organization's culture and values, help the new employee understand his or her role and how he or she fits into the total organization, and help the new employee achieve objectives and shorten the learning curve.

Some organizations see the orientation program as a crucial part of their culture formation process.[49] For example, Accenture Consulting puts new employees through a two-week orientation at headquarters, followed by an additional two-week "New Joiner Orientation" program. During the orientation program, new employees learn about the company's methods for interacting with clients, go through mock client engagement sessions, make presentations to clients, and implement systems to solve client problems. As a follow-up, each new hire has a career counselor who reinforces orientation materials in the workplace and helps the new employee throughout his or her career. Although this extensive orientation program is costly, representatives from the organization argue that it has helped them create a unified culture among employees who work in offices around the world. Some experts argue that in addition to making sure the first few weeks are successful, organizations should conduct routine follow-up sessions with new employees throughout the first year of employment as a means of enhancing newcomer engagement and retention. This extended check-in period bridges the gap between orientation and socialization.

Socialization

Socialization of the newcomer is a natural extension of orientation activities. Like orientation, the goal of socialization is to achieve effective person/job and person/organization matches. Whereas orientation focuses on the initial and immediate aspects of newcomer adaptation, socialization emphasizes helping the newcomer fit into the job and organization over time. The emphasis is on the long haul, seeking to gain newcomers' adaptation in ways that will make them want to be successful, long-term contributors to the organization.[50] Research has shown that when socialization programs are effective, they facilitate new employee adjustment by increasing employees' role clarity (clarify job duties and performance expectations), by enhancing their self-efficacy (their belief that they can do the job), and by fostering their social acceptance (making employees believe that they are valued members of the team).[51]

To increase new employees' role clarity, self-efficacy, and social acceptance, two key issues should be addressed in developing and conducting an effective socialization process. First, what are the major elements or contents of socialization that should occur? Second, how can the organization best deliver those elements to the newcomer?

Content

While the content of the socialization process should obviously be somewhat job- and organization-specific, several components are likely candidates for inclusion. From the newcomer's perspective, these are the following:[52]

1. *People*—meeting and learning about coworkers, key contacts, informal groups and gatherings, and networks; becoming accepted and respected by these people as "one of the gang"
2. *Performance proficiency*—becoming very familiar with job requirements; mastering tasks; having impacts on performance results; and acquiring necessary KSAOs for proficiency in all aspects of the job
3. *Organization goals and values*—learning of the organization's goals; accepting these goals and incorporating them into my line of sight for performance proficiency; learning about values and norms of desirable behavior (e.g., working late and on weekends; making suggestions for improvements)
4. *Politics*—learning about how things really work; becoming familiar with key players and their quirks; taking acceptable shortcuts; schmoozing and networking
5. *Language*—learning special terms, buzzwords, and acronyms; knowing what not to say; learning the jargon of people in my trade or profession
6. *History*—learning about the origins and growth of the organization; becoming familiar with customs, rituals, and special events; understanding the origins of my work unit and the backgrounds of people in it

Many of these topics overlap with the possible content of an orientation program, suggesting that orientation and socialization programs be developed in tandem so that they are synchronized and seamless as the newcomer passes from orientation into socialization.

Delivery

Helping to socialize the newcomer should be the responsibility of several people. First, the newcomer's supervisor should be personally responsible for socializing the newcomer, particularly in terms of performance proficiency and organization goals and values. The supervisor is intimately familiar with and the "enforcer" of these key elements of socialization. It is important that the newcomer and the supervisor communicate directly, honestly, and formally about these elements.

Peers in the newcomer's work unit or team are promising candidates for assisting in socialization. They can be most helpful in terms of politics, language, and history, drawing on their own accumulated experiences and sharing them with the newcomer. They can also make their approachability and availability known to the newcomer when he or she wants to ask questions or raise issues in an informal manner.

To provide a more formal information and support system to the newcomer, but one outside a chain of command, a mentor or sponsor may be assigned to (or chosen by) the newcomer. The mentor functions as an identifiable point of contact for the newcomer, as well as someone who actively interacts with the newcomer to provide the inside knowledge, savvy, and personal contacts that will help the newcomer settle into the current job and prepare for future job assignments. Mentors can also play a vital role in helping shatter the glass ceiling of the organization.

Given the advances in computer technology and the increasing geographic dispersion of an organization's employees, organizations might be tempted to conduct their orientation programs online. Web-based recruiting tools make it easy to track and monitor new hires, provide new hires with an online tour complete with streaming video, provide mandatory training, and automate processes like signing up for insurance, e-mail addresses, and security badges.[53] Though some of this may be necessary, depending on the job, research suggests that socialization programs are less effective when conducted entirely online—both in the eyes of the employees and in the eyes of their supervisors. As would be expected, when compared with in-person programs, online socialization programs do a particularly poor job of socializing employees to the personal aspects of the job and organization, such as organizational goals and values, politics, and how to work well with others.[54]

Finally, the HR department can be very useful to the socialization process. Its representatives can help establish formal, organization-wide socialization activities such as mentoring programs, special events, and informational presentations. Also, representatives may undertake development of training programs on socialization topics for supervisors and mentors. Representatives might also work closely, but informally, with supervisors and coach them in how to become successful social- izers of their own newcomers.

Examples of Programs

The Sonesta Hotels chain developed a formal program to help newcomers adapt to their jobs during their first 100 days. After 30 days the hotel site HR director meets with the newcomer to see whether his or her expectations are being met and whether he or she has the resources needed to do the job. At 60 days the newcomer participates in a program called the Booster, which focuses on developing cus- tomer service and communication skills. Then at the end of 90 days the newcomer meets with the supervisor to do performance planning for the rest of the year. In addition, managers are encouraged to take the newcomer and the rest of the depart- ment out to lunch during the first month.[55]

The president and CEO of Southcoast Hospitals Group in Fall River, Massachu- setts, decided to develop an "owner's manual" about himself that was to be given to the new VP of performance improvement that he was recruiting for. The one-page manual gave tips to the new VP on how to work for the president. It was developed on the basis of self-assessment and feedback from colleagues and direct reports. These people began using the completed manual immediately in their interactions with the president. The manual was given to the finalist for the VP job two days before the job offer was actually extended. The finalist took the job and com- mented on how helpful the manual was in saving him time figuring out what the president thinks of things.[56]

The National City Corporation in Cleveland, a bank and financial services orga- nization, experienced high turnover among newcomers within the first 90 days on the job. These early-exiting employees were referred to as "quick quits" in the HR department. To combat this problem, a program called Early Success was designed for entry-level, nonexempt newcomers. Newcomers attend a series of custom-made training programs that provide them the necessary knowledge and skills. Examples of the programs are Plus (overview of the organization's objec- tives, employee benefits, and brand); People, Policies, and Practices (augment the employee handbook and reinforce the organization as an employer of choice); and Top-Notch Customer Care (focus on customer service delivery and how to be a team player). Another component of the program is a buddy system that matches a newcomer with a peer; buddies then attend workshops to learn coaching skills. Finally, the hiring managers of the newcomers also attend workshops on such top- ics as how to select a buddy for the newcomer, how to communicate and create a supportive work environment, and how to help the newcomer assume more job responsibilities and achieve career goals. The program has reduced turnover 50% and improved attendance 25%, saving over $1.6 million per year.[57]

LEGAL ISSUES

The employment contract establishes the actual employment relationship and the terms and conditions that will govern it. In the process of establishing it, the organization must deal with certain obligations and responsibilities. These pertain to (1) employing only those people who meet the employment requirements under the IRCA, (2) avoiding the negligent hiring of individuals, and (3) maintaining the organization's posture toward employment-at-will. Each of these is discussed in turn.

Employment Eligibility Verification

Under the IRCA (see Chapter 2), the organization must verify each new employee's identity and employment eligibility (authorization). The verification cannot begin until after the job offer has been accepted. Specific federal regulations detail the requirements and methods of compliance (*www.uscis.gov*).

For each new employee, the employer must complete the I-9 form. Section One, seeking employment information, must be completed no later than the first day of employment. Section Two, requiring the employer to examine evidence of the employee's identity and employment eligibility, must be completed within three business days of the date employment begins. Both identity and employment eligibility must be verified. Form I-9 shows the only documents that may be used for verification. Some documents (e.g., US passport) verify both identity and eligibility; other documents verify only identity (e.g., state-issued driver's license or ID card) or eligibility (e.g., original Social Security card or birth certificate).

E-Verify is an Internet-based system that allows the employer to determine employment eligibility and the validity of social security numbers, based on the I-9 information. The information is checked against federal databases, usually yielding results in a few seconds. E-Verify verifies only employment eligibility, not immigration status. Federal contractors and subcontractors, along with employers in some states, are required to use E-Verify. Other employers may voluntarily participate in E-Verify. Users must first complete an E-Verify tutorial and pass a mastery test. Employers may not use E-Verify to prescreen applicants or selectively verify only some new employees.

I-9 records should be retained for three years after the date of hire or one year after the date of employment ends, whichever is later. Use of paper or electronic systems or a combination of these is permitted, as are electronic signatures. Employees must be given a copy of the record if they request it.

Finally, since the IRCA prohibits national origin or citizenship discrimination, it is best not to ask for proof of employment eligibility before making the offer. The reason for this is that many of the identity and eligibility documents contain personal information that pertains to national origin and citizenship status, and such personal information might be used in a discriminatory manner. As a further matter of caution, the organization should not refuse to make a job offer to a person based on that person's foreign accent or appearance.

Negligent Hiring

Negligent hiring is a claim made by an injured party (coworker, customer, client, or the general public) against the employer. The claim is that an injury was the result of the employer hiring a person it knew, or should have known, was unfit and posed a threat of risk. In short, negligent hiring is a failure to exercise "due diligence" in the selection and hiring of employees.[58] Injuries may include violence, physical damage, bodily or emotional injury, death, and financial loss. Elderly patients in a long-term-care facility, for example, may suffer injury from a health care attendant due to overmedication or failure to provide adequate food and water. Or, an accountant might divert funds from a client's account into his or her own personal account.

What should the organization do to minimize negligent hiring occurrences? Following are several straightforward recommendations.[59] First, staffing any job should be preceded by a thorough analysis that identifies all the KSAOs required by the job. Failure to identify or otherwise consider KSAOs prior to the final match is not likely to be much of a defense in a negligent hiring lawsuit.

Second, particular attention should be paid to the O part of KSAOs, such as licensure requirements, criminal records, references, unexplained gaps in employment history, and alcohol and illegal drug usage. Of course, these should be derived separately for each job rather than applied identically to all jobs.

Third, methods for assessing these KSAOs that are valid and legal must be used. This is difficult to do in practice because of lack of knowledge about the validity of some predictors, or their relatively low levels of validity. Also, difficulties arise because of legal constraints on the use of preemployment inquiries, credit checks, and background checks (see Chapter 8).

Fourth, require all applicants to sign disclaimer statements allowing the employer to check references and otherwise conduct background investigations. In addition, have the applicant sign a statement indicating that all provided information is true and that the applicant has not withheld requested information.

Fifth, apply utility analysis to determine whether it is worthwhile to engage in the preceding recommendations to try to avoid the (usually slight) chance of a negligent hiring lawsuit. Such an analysis will undoubtedly indicate great variability among jobs in terms of how many resources the organization wishes to invest in negligent hiring prevention.

Finally, when in doubt about a finalist and whether to extend a job offer, do not proceed until those doubts have been resolved. Acquire more information from the finalist, verify existing information more thoroughly, and seek the opinions of others on whether to proceed with the job offer.

Employment-at-Will

As discussed in this chapter and in Chapter 2, employment-at-will involves the right of either the employer or the employee to unilaterally terminate the employment relationship at any time, for any legal reason. In general, the employment relationship is at-will, and usually the employer wishes it to remain that way. Hence, during the final match (and even before), the employer must take certain steps to ensure that its job offers clearly establish the at-will relationship. These steps are merely a compilation of points already made regarding employment contracts and employment-at-will.

First, ensure that job offers are for an indeterminate time period, meaning that they have no fixed term or specific ending date. Second, include in the job offer a specific disclaimer stating that the employment relationship is strictly at-will. Third, review all written documents (e.g., employee handbook, application blank) to ensure that they do not contain any language that implies anything but a strictly at-will relationship. Finally, take steps to ensure that organizational members do not make any oral statements or promises that would serve to create something other than a strictly at-will relationship.[60]

SUMMARY

During the final match, the offer receiver and the organization move toward each other through the job offer/acceptance process. They seek to enter into the employment relationship and become legally bound to each other through an employment contract.

Knowledge of employment contract principles is central to understanding the final match. The most important principle pertains to the requirements for a legally enforceable employment contract (offer, acceptance, and consideration). Other important principles focus on the identity of parties to the contract, the form of the contract (written or oral), disclaimers by the employer, contingencies, reneging by the organization or the offer receiver, other sources that may also specify terms and conditions of employment (e.g., employee handbooks), and unfulfilled promises.

Job offers are designed to induce the offer receiver to join the organization. Offers should be viewed and used strategically by the organization. In that strategy, labor market conditions, organization and applicant needs, and legal issues all converge to shape the job offer and EVP.

Job offers may contain virtually any legal terms and conditions of employment. Generally, the offer addresses terms pertaining to starting date, duration of contract, compensation, hours, special hiring inducements (if any), other terms (such as contingencies), and acceptance of the offer.

The process of making job offers can be complicated, involving a need to think through multiple issues before making formal offers. Offers should take into account the content of competitors' offers, potential problems with applicant truthfulness, likely reactions of the offer receiver, and the organization's policies on negotiating offers. Presentation of the offer can range from a mechanical process all the way to a major sales job. Ultimately, offers are accepted and rejected, and all offer receivers should receive prompt and courteous attention during these events. Steps should be taken to minimize reneging by either the organization or the offer receiver.

Acceptance of the offer marks the beginning of the employment relationship. To help ensure that the initial person/job match starts out and continues to be effective, the organization should undertake both orientation and socialization activities for newcomers.

From a legal perspective, the organization must be sure that the offer receiver is employable according to provisions of the IRCA. Both identity and eligibility for employment must be verified. The potential negligent hiring of individuals who, once on the job, cause harm to others (employees or customers) is also of legal concern. Those so injured may bring suit against the organization. The organization can take steps to help minimize the occurrence of negligent hiring lawsuits. There are limits on these steps, however, such as the legal constraints on the gathering of background information about applicants. Finally, the organization should have its posture, policies, and practices regarding employment-at-will firmly developed and aligned. Numerous steps can be taken to help achieve this.

DISCUSSION QUESTIONS

1. If you were the HR staffing manager for an organization, what guidelines might you recommend regarding oral and written communication with job applicants by members of the organization?

2. If the same job offer content is to be given to all offer receivers for a job, is there any need to use the strategic approach to job offers? Explain.

3. What are the advantages and disadvantages of the sales approach in the presentation of the job offer?

4. What are examples of orientation experiences you have had as a new hire that have been particularly effective (or ineffective) in helping to make the person/job match happen?

5. What are the steps an employer should take to develop and implement its policy regarding employment-at-will?

ETHICAL ISSUES

1. A large financial services organization is thinking of adopting a new staffing strategy for entry into its management training program. The program will provide the trainees all the knowledge and skills they need for their initial job assignment after training. The organization has therefore decided to do college recruiting at the end of the recruiting season. It will hire those who have not been fortunate enough to receive any job offers, pay them a salary 10% below market, and provide no other inducements such as a hiring bonus or relocation assistance. The organization figures this strategy and EVP will yield a high percentage of offers accepted, low cost per hire, and considerable labor cost savings due to below-market salaries. Evaluate this strategy from an ethical perspective.

2. An organization has a staffing strategy in which it hires 10% more employees than it actually needs in any job category in order to ensure its hiring needs are met. It reasons that some of the new hires will renege on the accepted offer and that the organization can renege on some of its offers, if need be, in order to end up with the right number of new hires. Evaluate this strategy from an ethical perspective.

APPLICATIONS

Making a Job Offer

Clean Car Care (3Cs) is located within a western city of 175,000 people. The company owns and operates four full-service car washes in the city. The owner of 3Cs, Arlan Autospritz, has strategically cornered the car wash market, with his only competition being two coin-operated car washes on the outskirts of the city. The unemployment rate in the city and surrounding area is 3.8%, and it is expected to go somewhat lower.

Arlan has staffed 3Cs by hiring locally and paying wage premiums (above market wages) to induce people to accept job offers and to remain with 3Cs. Hiring occurs at the entry level only, for the job of washer. If they remain with 3Cs, washers have the opportunity to progress upward through the ranks, going from washer to shift lead person to assistant manager to manager of one of the four car wash facilities. Until recently, this staffing system worked well for Arlan. He was able to hire high-quality people, and a combination of continued wage premiums and promotion opportunities meant he had relatively little turnover (under 30% annually). Every manager at 3Cs, past or present, had come up through the ranks. But that is now changing with the sustained low unemployment and the new hires, who just naturally seem more turnover-prone. The internal promotion pipeline is thus drying up, since few new hires are staying with 3Cs long enough to begin climbing the ladder.

Arlan has a vacancy for the job of manager at the north-side facility. Unfortunately, he does not think any of his assistant managers are qualified for the job, and he reluctantly concluded that he has to fill the job externally.

A vigorous three-county recruitment campaign netted Arlan a total of five applicants. Initial assessments resulted in four of those being candidates, and two candidates became finalists. Jane Roberts is the number-one finalist, and the one to whom Arlan has decided to extend the offer. Jane is excited about the job and told Arlan she will accept an offer if the terms are right. Arlan is quite certain Jane will get a counteroffer from her company. Jane has excellent supervisory experience in fast-food stores and a light manufacturing plant. She is willing to relocate, a move of about 45 miles. She will not be able to start for 45 days, due to preparing for the move and the need to give adequate notice to her present employer. As a single parent, Jane wants to avoid work on either Saturday or Sunday each week. The number-two finalist is Betts Cook. Though she lacks the supervisory experience that Jane has, Arlan views her as superior to Jane in customer service skills. Jane told Arlan she needs to know quickly if she is going to get the offer, since she is in line for a promotion at her current company and she wants to begin at 3Cs before being offered and accepting the promotion.

Arlan is mulling over what kind of an offer to make to Jane. His three managers make between $28,000 and $35,000, with annual raises based on a merit review conducted by Arlan. The managers receive one week of vacation the first year, two weeks of vacation for the next four years, and three weeks of vacation after that. They also receive health insurance (with a 20% employee co-pay on the premium). The managers work five days each week, with work on both Saturday and Sunday frequently occurring during peak times. Jane currently makes $31,500, receives health insurance with no employee co-pay, and has one week of vacation (she is due to receive two weeks shortly, after completing her second year with the company). She works Monday through Friday, with occasional work on the weekends. Betts earns $34,500, receives health insurance fully paid by her employer, and has one week of vacation (she is eligible for two weeks in another year). Weekend work, if not constant, is acceptable to her.

Arlan is seeking input from you on how to proceed. Specifically, he wants you to:

1. Recommend whether Jane should receive a best-shot, competitive, or lowball offer, and why.
2. Recommend other inducements beyond salary, health insurance, vacation, and schedule that might be addressed in the job offer, and why.
3. Draft a proposed job offer letter to Jane, incorporating your recommendations from items 1 and 2 above, as well as other desired features that should be part of a job offer letter.

Evaluating a Hiring and Variable Pay Plan

Effective Management Solutions (EMS) is a small, rapidly growing management consulting company. EMS has divided its practice into four areas: management systems, business process improvement, human resources, and quality improvement. Strategically, EMS has embarked on an aggressive revenue growth plan, seeking a 25% revenue increase in each of the next five years for each of the four practice areas. A key component of its plan involves staffing growth, since most of EMS's current entry-level consultants (associates) are at peak client loads and cannot take on additional clients; the associates are also at peak hours load, working an average of 2,500 billable hours per year.

Staffing strategy and planning have resulted in the following information and projections. Each practice area currently has 25 associates, the entry-level position and title. Each year, on average, each practice area has five associates promoted to senior associate within the area (there are no promotions or transfers across areas, due to differing KSAO requirements), and five associates leave EMS, mostly to go to other consulting firms. Replacement staffing thus averages 10 new associates in each practice area, for a total of 40 per year. To meet the revenue growth goals, each practice area will need to hire 15 new associates each year, or a total of 60. A total of 100 associate new hires will thus be needed each year (40 for replacement and 60 for growth).

Currently, EMS provides each job offer receiver a generous benefits package plus what it deems to be a competitive salary that is nonnegotiable. About 50% of such offers are accepted. Most of those who reject the offer are the highest-quality applicants; they take jobs in larger, more established consulting firms that provide somewhat below-market salaries but high-upside monetary potential through various short-term variable-pay programs, plus rapid promotions.

Faced with these realities and projections, EMS recognizes that its current job offer practices need to be revamped. Accordingly, it has asked Manuel Rodriguez, who functions as a one-person HR "department" for EMS, to develop a job offer proposal for the EMS partners to consider at their next meeting. The partners tell Rodriguez they want a plan that will increase the job offer acceptance rate, slow down the outflow of associates to other firms, and not create dissatisfaction among the currently employed associates.

In response, Rodriguez developed the proposed hiring and variable pay (HVP) program. It has as its cornerstone varying monetary risk/reward packages through a combination of base and short-term variable (bonus) pay plans. The specifics of the HVP program are as follows:

- The offer receiver must choose one of three plans to be under, prior to receiving a formal job offer. The plans are high-risk, standard, and low-risk.
- The high-risk plan provides a starting salary from 10% to 30% below the market average and participation in the annual bonus plan, with a bonus range from 0% to 60% of current salary.

- The standard plan provides a starting salary of 10% below the market average and participation in the annual bonus plan, with a bonus range from 0% to 20% of current salary.
- The low-risk plan provides a starting salary that is 5% above the market average and no participation in the annual bonus plan.
- The average market rate will be determined by salary survey data obtained by HR.
- The individual bonus amount will be determined by individual performance on three indicators: number of billable hours, number of new clients generated, and client-satisfaction survey results.
- The hiring manager will negotiate the starting salary for those in the high-risk and standard plans, based on likely person/job and person/organization fit and on need to fill the position.
- The hiring manager may also offer a "hot skills" premium of up to 10% of initial starting salary under all three plans—the premium will lapse after two years.
- Switching plans is permitted only once every two years.
- Current associates may opt into one of the new plans at their current salary.

Evaluate the HVP program as proposed, answering the following questions:

1. If you were an applicant, would the HVP program be attractive to you? Why or why not? If you were an offer receiver, which of the three plans would you choose, and why?
2. Will the HVP program likely increase the job offer acceptance rate? Why or why not?
3. Will the HVP program likely reduce turnover? Why or why not?
4. How will current associates react to the HVP program, and why?
5. What issues and problems will the HVP plan create for HR? For the hiring manager?
6. What changes would you make in the HVP program, and why?

ENDNOTES

1. M. W. Bennett, D. J. Polden, and H. J. Rubin, *Employment Relationships: Law and Practice* (New York: Aspen, 2004), pp. 3-3 to 3-4; A. G. Feliu, *Primer on Individual Employee Rights*, second ed. (Washington, DC: Bureau of National Affairs, 1996), pp. 7–29; G. P. Panaro, *Employment Law Manual* (Boston, MA: Warren, Gorham and Lamont, 1993), pp. 4-2 to 4-4; Society for Human Resource Management, "How to Create an Offer Letter Without Contractual Implications," Sept. 15, 2010 (*www.shrm.org/templatestools/howtoguides/pages/howtocreateanofferletter.aspx*).
2. Panaro, *Employment Law Manual*, pp. 4-61 to 4-63; D. Cadrain, "Coming to Terms," *Staffing Management Magazine*, Oct. 2009 (*www.shrm.org/publications/staffingmanagementmagazine/EditorialContent/Pages/1009cadrain.aspx*).

3. Bennett, Polden, and Rubin, *Employment Relationships: Law and Practice*, pp. 3-22 to 3-23; Panaro, *Employment Law Manual*, pp. 4-5 to 4-60.

4. Panaro, *Employment Law Manual*, pp. 4-18 to 4-19; Society for Human Resource Management, "How to Create an Offer Letter Without Contractual Implications."

5. Feliu, *Primer on Individual Employee Rights*, pp. 23–25; Panaro, *Employment Law Manual*, pp. 4-30 to 4-31.

6. Feliu, *Primer on Individual Employee Rights*, pp. 26–28.

7. Feliu, *Primer on Individual Employee Rights*, pp. 48–51.

8. Bennett, Polden, and Rubin, *Employment Relationships: Law and Practice*, pp. 3-30 to 3-32; Feliu, *Primer on Individual Employee Rights*, pp. 22–25.

9. Feliu, *Primer on Individual Employee Rights*, p. 24.

10. Feliu, *Primer on Individual Employee Rights*, p. 26.

11. Panaro, *Employment Law Manual*, pp. 4-66 to 4-136.

12. Bennett, Polden, and Rubin, *Employment Relationships: Law and Practice*, pp. 3-24 to 3-34; Feliu, *Primer on Individual Employee Rights*, pp. 39–50; Society for Human Resource Management, "How to Create an Offer Letter Without Contractual Implications."

13. J. A. Segal, "An Offer They Couldn't Refuse," *HR Magazine*, Apr. 2001, pp. 131–144.

14. A. W. Matthews, "Wanted: 400,000 Long Distance Truck Drivers," *Wall Street Journal*, Sept. 11, 1997, p. B1; R. Romell, "Truckers in the Driver's Seat," *Milwaukee Journal Sentinel*, Nov. 30, 1997, p. 1D.

15. Bennett, Polden, and Rubin, *Employment Relationships: Law and Practice*, pp. 2-11 to 2-49.

16. D. S. Fortney and B. Nuterangelo, "Written Employment Contracts: When? How? Why?" *Legal Report*, Society for Human Resource Management, Spring 1998, pp. 5–8.

17. D. M. Cable and T. A. Judge, "Pay Preferences and Job Search Decisions: A Person–Organization Fit Perspective," *Personnel Psychology*, 1994, 47, pp. 317–348.

18. P. D. Gardner, *Recruiting Trends 2000–2001* (East Lansing, MI: Michigan State University Student Services, 2000).

19. S. Nasar, "A Top MBA Is a Hot Ticket as Pay Climbs," *New York Times*, Aug. 2, 1998, p. B1; E. Price, "Paying for Bilingual Skills: Job Requirement or Added Value?" *International Personnel Management Association News*, Feb. 1997, p. 10.

20. O*NET OnLine (*www.onetonline.org*).

21. Y. J. Dreazen, "When #$%+! Recruits Earn More," *Wall Street Journal*, July 25, 2000, p. B1; K. J. Dunham, "Back to Reality," *Wall Street Journal*, Apr. 12, 2001, p. R5; M. Gasser, N. Flint, and R. Tan, "Reward Expectations: The Influence of Race, Gender, and Type of Job," *Journal of Business and Psychology*, 2000, 15, pp. 321–329; E. R. Silverman, "Great Expectations," *Wall Street Journal*, July 25, 2000.

22. Society for Human Resource Management, *Strategic Compensation Survey* (Alexandria, VA: author, 2000), pp. 35–47.

23. E. E. Lawler III, "Pay Practices in Fortune 1000 Companies," *WorldatWork Journal*, 2003, Fourth Quarter, pp. 45–53.

24. M. A. Jacobs, "The Legal Option," *Wall Street Journal*, Apr. 12, 2001, p. R9; Society for Human Resource Management, *Strategic Compensation Survey*, pp. 48–57.

25. B. Jones, M. Staubus, and D. N. Janich, "If Not Stock Options, Then What?" *Workspan*, Fall 2003, pp. 26–32; R. Simon, "With Options on the Outs, Alternatives Get a Look," *Wall Street Journal*, Apr. 28, 2004, p. D2.

26. "Employers Say Increased Competition Not Likely to Translate Into Signing Bonuses for New College Graduates," *IPMA-HR Bulletin*, Dec. 1, 2006, p. 1.

27. F. Hansen, "Smarter About Hiring Bonuses," *Workforce Management*, Mar. 27, 2006, pp. 39–42.

28. Hansen, "Smarter About Hiring Bonuses"; J. R. Bratkovich and J. Ragusa, "The Perils of the Signing Bonus," *Employment Management Today*, Spring 1998, pp. 22–25.
29. L. Morsch, "Return of the Signing Bonus?" Sept. 24, 2007 (*www.careerbuilder.com*).
30. L. G. Klaff, "Tough Sell," *Workforce Management*, Nov. 2003, pp. 47–50; J. S. Lublin, "The Going Rate," *Wall Street Journal*, Jan. 11, 2000, p. B14.
31. J. S. Lublin, "As More Men Become 'Trailing Spouses,' Firms Help Them Cope," *Wall Street Journal*, Apr. 13, 1993, p. A1.
32. J. Barthiaume and L. Culpepper, "Hot Skills: Most Popular Compensation Strategies for Technical Expertise," Jan. 14, 2008 (*www.shrm.org/hrdisciplines/compensation/articles/pages/popular compensationstrategies.aspx*).
33. J. S. Lublin, "You Should Negotiate a Severance Package—Even Before the Job Starts," *Wall Street Journal*, May 1, 2001, p. B1.
34. C. Patton, "Parting Ways," *Human Resource Executive*, May 20, 2002, pp. 50–51.
35. T. D. Egler, "A Manager's Guide to Employment Contracts," *HR Magazine*, May 1996, pp. 28–33; J. J. Meyers, D. V. Radack, and P. M. Yenerall, "Making the Most of Employment Contracts," *HR Magazine*, Aug. 1998, pp. 106–109; D. R. Sandler, "Noncompete Agreements," *Employment Management Today*, Fall 1997, pp. 14–19; S. G. Willis, "Protect Your Firm Against Former Employees' Actions," *HR Magazine*, Aug. 1997, pp. 117–122.
36. A. Smith, "Noncompetes Can Be Tough to Enforce When Former Employees Move," *HR News*, Apr. 10, 2006 (*www.shrm.org/hrnews*).
37. M. Orgel, "Web Sites That Provide Salary Help," *Wall Street Journal*, Oct. 16, 2008, p. D5.
38. J. A. Lopez, "The Big Lie," *Wall Street Journal*, Apr. 21, 1993, pp. R6–R8.
39. M. Himmelberg, "Counteroffers Grow More Commonplace," *Knight-Ridder Tribune Business News*, Feb. 6, 2007, p. 1.
40. J. S. Lublin, "How to Handle the Job Offer You Can't Afford," *Wall Street Journal*, Dec. 2, 2008, p. B9; J. Sammer, "Money Matters in the Hiring Process," *HR Magazine*, Sept. 2009, pp. 93–95.
41. S. Kwon and L. R. Weingart, "Unilateral Concessions From the Other Party: Concession Behavior, Attributions, and Negotiation Judgments," *Journal of Applied Psychology*, 2004, 89, 263–278.
42. J. R. Curhan, H. A. Elfenbein, and G. J. Kilduff, "Getting Off on the Right Foot: Subjective Value Versus Economic Value in Predicting Longitudinal Job Outcomes From Job Offer Negotiations," *Journal of Applied Psychology*, 2009, 94, pp. 524–534.
43. D. S. Chapman and J. Webster, "Toward an Integrated Model of Applicant Reactions and Job Choice," *International Journal of Human Resource Management*, 2006, 17, pp. 1032–1057.
44. W. J. Becker, T. Connolly, and J. E. Slaughter, "The Effect of Job Offer Timing on Offer Acceptance, Performance, and Turnover," *Personnel Psychology*, 2010, 63, pp. 223–241.
45. T. Stefanik, "Ford Hit With Class-Action Lawsuit After Backing out of 100s of Jobs," *Canadian HR Reporter*, Mar. 8, 2010, p. 5.
46. K. Gurchiek, "Many Employers Wing Support of New Hires," *HR News*, Sept. 18, 2007 (*www.shrm.org/publications/hrnews/Pages/CMS_023039.aspx*).
47. L. G. Klaff, "New Emphasis on First Impressions," *Workforce Management Online*, Mar. 2008 (*www.workforce.com/section/11/feature/25/41/58*).
48. J. Kammeyer-Mueller and C. Wanberg, "Unwrapping the Organizational Entry Process: Disentangling Multiple Antecedents and Their Pathways to Adjustment," *Journal of Applied Psychology*, 2003, 88, pp. 779–794; M. J. Lankau and T. A. Scanduva, "An Investigation of Personal Learning in Mentoring Relationships: Content, Antecedents, and Consequences," *Academy of Management Journal*, 2002, 45, pp. 779–790; E. W. Morrison, "Newcomer Relationships: The Role of Social Network Ties During Socialization," *Academy of Management Journal*, 2002, 45,

pp. 1149–1160; T. N. Bauer, T. Bodner, B. Erdogan, D. M. Truxillo, and J. S. Tucker, "Newcomer Adjustment During Organizational Socialization: A Meta-Analytic Review of Antecedents, Outcomes, and Methods," *Journal of Applied Psychology*, 2007, 92, pp. 707–721.

49. J. Marquez, "Connecting a Virtual Workforce," *Workforce Management*, Sept. 22, 2008, pp. 23–25; F. Hansen, "Onboarding for Greater Engagement," *Workforce Management Online*, Oct. 2008 (*www.workforce.com*).

50. C. L. Adkins, "Previous Work Experience and Organizational Socialization: A Longitudinal Examination," *Academy of Management Journal*, 1995, 38, pp. 839–862.

51. Bauer et al., "Newcomer Adjustment During Organizational Socialization: A Meta-Analytic Review of Antecedents, Outcomes, and Methods."

52. G. T. Chao, A. M. O'Leary-Kelly, S. Wolf, H. J. Klein, and P. D. Gardner, "Organizational Socialization: Its Content and Consequences," *Journal of Applied Psychology*, 1994, 79, pp. 730–743.

53. A. D. Wright, "Experts: Web-Based Onboarding Can Aid Employee Retention," Society for Human Resource Management, July 14, 2008 (*www.shrm.org/hrdisciplines/technology/articles/pages/web-basedonboardingaidsretention.aspx*).

54. M. J. Wesson and C. I. Gogus, "Shaking Hands With a Computer: An Examination of Two Methods of Organizational Newcomer Orientation," *Journal of Applied Psychology*, 2005, 90, pp. 1018–1026.

55. J. Mullich, "They're Hired: Now the Real Recruiting Begins," *Workforce Management Online*, Feb. 9, 2004 (*www.workforce.com*).

56. J. S. Lublin, "Job Candidates Get Manual From Boss: How to Handle Me," *Wall Street Journal*, Jan. 7, 2003, p. B1.

57. M. Hammers, "Optimas Award Financial Impact: National City Corporation," *Workforce Management Online*, Feb. 9, 2004 (*www.workforce.com*).

58. USLegal, "Negligent Hiring Law and Legal Definition" (*definitions.uslegal.com/n/negligent-hiring*), accessed 9/13/10; S. Smith, "Negligent Hiring" (*sideroad.com/Human_Resources/negligent_hiring.html*), accessed 9/13/10; R. K. Robinson, G. M. Franklin, and R. F. Wayland, "Employment Regulation in the Workplace" (Armonk, NY: M. E. Sharpe, 2010), pp. 334–336.

59. Bureau of National Affairs, "Recruiting Exposure to Negligent Hiring Suits Requires Preventive Action, Practitioner Says," *Daily Labor Report*, June 18, 1998, p. C1; F. Hansen, "Taking 'Reasonable Action' to Avoid Negligent Hiring Claims," *Workforce Management*, Dec. 11, 2006, pp. 31–33.

60. Bennett, Polden, and Rubin, *Employment Relationships: Law and Practice*, pp. 2-1 to 2-65.

The Staffing Organizations Model

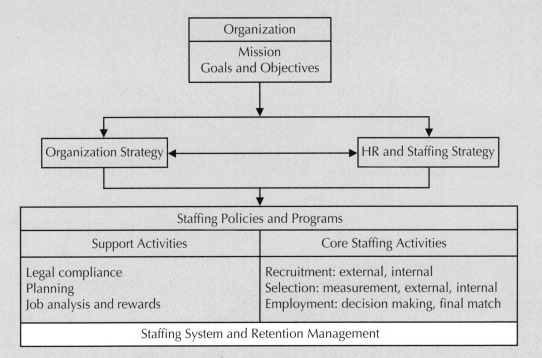

PART SIX

Staffing System and Retention Management

CHAPTER THIRTEEN
Staffing System Management

CHAPTER FOURTEEN
Retention Management

CHAPTER THIRTEEN

Staffing System Management

Learning Objectives and Introduction
  Learning Objectives
  Introduction

Administration of Staffing Systems
  Organizational Arrangements
  Jobs in Staffing
  Policies and Procedures
  Human Resource Information Systems
  Outsourcing

Evaluation of Staffing Systems
  Staffing Process
  Staffing Process Results
  Calculating Staffing Metrics
  Customer Satisfaction

Legal Issues
  Record Keeping and Privacy
  EEO Report
  Legal Audits
  Training for Managers and Employees
  Dispute Resolution

Summary

Discussion Questions

Ethical Issues

Applications

LEARNING OBJECTIVES AND INTRODUCTION

Learning Objectives

- Recognize the importance of effective policies and procedures for staffing
- Understand the importance of concrete, fair policies and procedures in selection
- Evaluate the advantages and disadvantages of outsourcing staffing processes
- Understand how to evaluate the various results of staffing processes
- Develop metrics for the measurement of staffing systems
- Recognize the legal issues involving record keeping and applicant/employee privacy
- Plan for effective dispute resolution

Introduction

Up to this point, we have covered how organizations plan for effective staffing system implementation, recruit candidates, evaluate candidates, select from candidates, and make a final match. We now take a step back from these operational issues and evaluate whether an overall staffing system is functioning effectively. Staffing systems involve complex processes and decisions that require organizational direction, coordination, and evaluation. Most organizations must create mechanisms for managing their staffing system and its components. Management of staffing systems requires consideration of both administration and evaluation, as well as legal issues.

The evaluation of the effectiveness of a staffing system as a whole has become a central issue for human resource (HR) managers. An increased push for accountability in all areas of HR that began over 20 years ago has become a permanent feature of the organizational landscape. Staffing managers who are successfully adapting to this environment focus on analytics, which demonstrate relationships between a variety of staffing functions and organizational performance.[1]

The chapter starts by describing how the staffing function operates within the HR department of many organizations. The role and nature of staffing policies and procedures in administering the staffing function are explained, as is the use of human resource information systems (HRISs) to enhance efficient operation of staffing systems. Next, a discussion of ways to evaluate the effectiveness of the staffing function is presented. Various results of the staffing process are examined to gauge the effectiveness of staffing systems. Compilation and analysis of staffing system costs are also suggested as an evaluation technique. Last, assessment of customer (hiring manager, applicant) satisfaction is presented as an important approach to the evaluation of staffing systems. Legal issues surround the management of staffing systems. Partly, this involves matters of compiling various records and reports and of conducting legal audits of staffing activities. Also discussed are training for managers and employees, and mechanisms for dispute resolution.

ADMINISTRATION OF STAFFING SYSTEMS

Organizational Arrangements

Organizational arrangements refers to how the organization structures itself to conduct HR and staffing activities, often within the HR department. The arrangements vary considerably, and both organization size and type (integrated or multiple business) make a difference in the arrangement used.

Consider the following data from the US Census Bureau on organization size (*www.census.gov*). The vast majority of organizations (5.9 million) have fewer than 100 employees, and those organizations employ about 36% of total employees. At the other extreme, only 18,000 organizations have 500+ employees, and they employ about 50% of total employees. In between are about 89,000 organizations, each one employing between 100 and 499 employees.[2]

In organizations with fewer than 100 employees (regardless of the organization's purpose), research suggests that staffing is most likely to be conducted by the owner, the president, or the work unit manager. Only a small percentage (13%) of these organizations have an HR department that is responsible for staffing. Among these small organizations, staffing activities are quite varied in terms of establishing job requirements, recruitment sources, recruitment communication techniques, selection methods, decision making, and job offers. The presence of an HR department leads these organizations to adopt staffing practices different from those without an HR department.[3]

As organization size increases, so does the likelihood of there being an HR department and a unit within it responsible for staffing. But the exact configuration of the HR department and staffing activities will depend on whether the organization is composed of business units pursuing a common business product or service (an integrated business organization) or a diverse set of products or services (a multiple-business organization).[4] Because of its diversity, the multiple-business organization will likely not try to have a major, centralized corporate HR department. Rather, it will have a small corporate HR department, with a separate HR department within each business unit. In this arrangement, staffing activities will be quite decentralized, with some guidance and expertise from the corporate HR department.

In an integrated business organization, there will likely be a highly centralized HR department at the corporate level, with a much smaller HR presence at the plant or site level. As pertains to staffing, such centralization creates economies of scale and consistency in staffing policies and processes, as well as hiring standards and new hire quality.

Sun Trust Bank in Atlanta provides an excellent example of an organization that moved from a decentralized to a centralized HR function and created a new corporate employment department to manage staffing throughout its 1,200 branches.[5] Previously, Sun Trust had operated with 28 regional charters, and each region had its own HR department and staffing function. This created a muddle of inconsistency in technologies, services, and expertise, as well as quality of its job candidates. Through centralization, the bank sought to achieve greater consistency, along with a common vision and strategic focus, while still allowing some flexibility in operation among the regions. HR managers from the regional HR departments who had served as generalists were moved into specialist roles, some of them in the new employment department, with the assistance of considerable training in new policies and procedures. Job descriptions, qualifications, and recruitment strategies were standardized, and competency models were created to identify ideal candidates' personality traits, interests, and skills. Also, standardized guidelines, checklists, and candidate evaluation tools were developed. Some latitude was allowed for individual banks and staffing managers, such as decisions on how and when to recruit within their own territory. It appears as though the centralization has worked well. The new head of the HR function said, "We tried to balance the push-pull between the corporate vision and the real-world banking realities. We did not want one side or the other to hold all the cards. . . . The bank managers unanimously say they are now getting better candidates and our new, more precise recruiting system has enabled us to reduce advertising and sourcing expenditures, while increasing the amount of assessments on each candidate. So in effect we end up spending less but getting more." In addition, turnover in full-time teller positions decreased, the average time to fill a position dropped, and the average cost to fill a nonexempt position was reduced.

A more detailed example of a centralized organizational arrangement for an integrated-business, multiplant manufacturing organization is shown in Exhibit 13.1. At the corporate level, the HR department is headed by the vice president (VP) of HR. Reporting to the VP are directors of employment and equal employment opportunity/affirmative action (EEO/AA), compensation and benefits, training and development, labor relations, and HR information systems. These directors, along with the VP, formulate and coordinate HR strategy and policy, as well as manage their own functional units.

The director of employment and EEO/AA has three direct reports: the managers of exempt, nonexempt, and EEO/AA employment areas. Each manager, in turn, is responsible for the supervision of specialists and assistants. The manager of exempt employment, for example, handles external and internal staffing for managerial and professional jobs. Two specialists (a college recruiter and an internal placement specialist) and an administrative assistant are in this unit. The manager of nonexempt employment is responsible for external and internal staffing for hourly employees. Reporting to this manager are four specialists (a recruiter, an interviewer, a testing specialist, and a consultant) and two administrative assistants.

EXHIBIT 13.1   Example of HR Department and Employment (Staffing) Function

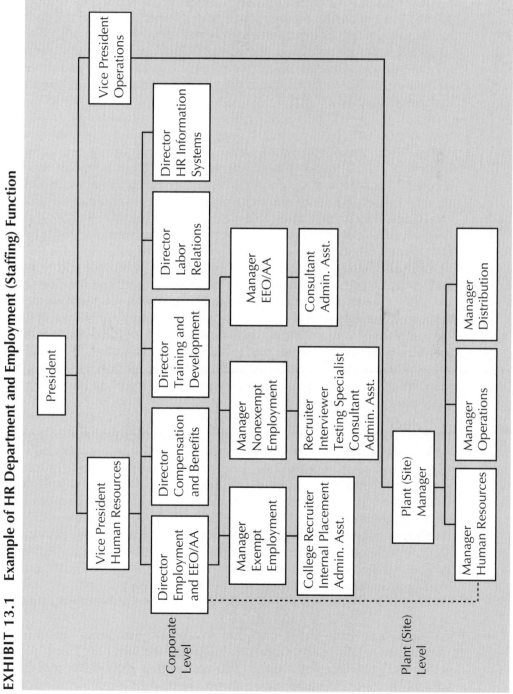

The EEO/AA manager has a consultant and an administrative assistant as direct reports. The consultants are individuals who serve in liaison roles with the line managers of units throughout the organization when hiring is occurring. Functioning as internal customer service representatives to these managers, the consultants help the managers understand corporate employment policies and procedures, determine specific staffing needs, handle special staffing problems and requests, and answer questions.

At the plant level, a single HR manager and an administrative assistant perform all HR activities, including staffing. This HR manager is a true generalist and works closely with the plant manager on all issues involving people concerns. Regarding staffing, the dotted line shows that the HR manager has an indirect reporting relationship to the director of employment and EEO/AA, as well as to the other corporate-level HR directors (not shown). These directors will work with the HR manager to develop policies and programs (including staffing) that are consistent with corporate strategy and are also tailor-made to the particular needs and workforce of the plant.

This example shows staffing to be a critical area within the HR department, and research confirms this importance. For example, the staffing function typically receives a greater percentage of the total HR department budget than any other function, averaging about 20% of the total budget. A study of HR departments in large organizations found that the focus on recruitment and selection activities had increased significantly over the past several years, more so than for any other HR activity.[6] Salaries for people in the staffing function are comparable to those in other HR functions. Increasingly, employees in all HR areas are becoming eligible for short-term incentives and bonuses.[7]

Those employed within the staffing function must work closely with members of all the other HR function areas. For example, staffing members must coordinate their activities with the compensation and benefits staff in developing policies on the economic components of job offers, such as starting pay, hiring bonuses, and special perks. Staffing activities must also be closely coordinated with the training and development function. This will be needed to identify training needs for external, entry-level new hires, as well as for planning transfer and promotion-enhancing training experiences for current employees. The director of labor relations will work with the staffing area to determine labor contract language pertaining to staffing issues (e.g., promotions and transfers) and to help resolve grievances over staffing procedures and decisions. Record keeping, staffing software, and EEO/AA statistics requirements will be worked out with the director of HR information systems.

Note that although staffing activities are concentrated within the HR department, members of any specific organizational unit for which staffing is occurring will (and should) also play a role in the overall staffing process. The unit manager will submit the hiring authorization request; work closely with HR in developing the knowledge, skill, ability, and other characteristics (KSAOs) required/preferred for the vacant position; and actively participate in making discretionary assessments and job offers. Other members of the unit may provide input to the unit manager on KSAOs sought, formally meet and interact with candidates for recruiting and attracting purposes, and provide input to the unit manager on their preferences about who should receive the job offer. In team-based work units, team members may play an even more active role in all phases of the staffing process. Each organization needs to work out arrangements for staffing that best fit its own staffing strategy and preferences of organizational members.

Jobs in Staffing

Jobs in staffing are quite varied. In the private sector, most are housed within the HR department (corporate and plant or office site levels). In the public sector, they are found within the central personnel or HR office, as well as in various specified agencies such as transportation or human services.

The types and scope of tasks and responsibilities in staffing jobs are also varied. Some jobs are specialist ones, involving a functional specialty such as interviewing, recruiting, or college relations. These are often entry-level jobs as well. Other jobs may have a more generalist flavor to them, particularly in smaller organizations or smaller units (plant or office) of a larger organization. In such units, one person may handle all staffing-related activities. At higher organizational levels, both specialist and generalist jobs are found. Examples of specialist positions include test development and validation, executive assessment, and affirmative action. Generalists usually have broader managerial responsibilities that cut across specialties; the job of staffing manager is one example.

Exhibit 13.2 provides job descriptions for two staffing jobs at Science Applications International Corporation (SAIC), taken from the SAIC website (*www.saic.com*). The junior recruiter/HR generalist is an entry-level staffing job, and the corporate manager of staffing (western region) is a generalist, corporate-level staffing job. SAIC is a Fortune 500, employee-owned research and engineering organization with offices in over 150 cities worldwide.

Entry into staffing jobs normally occurs at the specialist rank in the areas of recruiting and interviewing, in both private and public organizations. Staffing of these jobs may come from the new hire ranks of the organization. It may also come from an internal transfer from a management training program, from a line management job, or from another HR function. In short, there is no fixed point or method of entry into staffing jobs.

Mobility within staffing jobs may involve both traditional and nontraditional career tracks. In a traditional track, the normal progression is from entry-level specialist up through the ranks to staffing manager, with assignments at both the corporate and operating unit levels. A nontraditional track might involve entry into a staffing specialist job, lateral transfer after a year to another functional HR area,

EXHIBIT 13.2   Staffing Jobs at Science Applications International Corporation

A. Junior Recruiter/HR Generalist

Job Description:
Performs technical and administrative recruiting for the Pacific Programs Division. Recruits for several different locations throughout the Pacific to include Hawaii, Alaska, Guam, California, Korea, and Japan. Responsibilities include job requisition tracking, job posting and ad placement, pre-screening candidates, coordinating with hiring manager on scheduling and conducting interviews and conducting reference checks. Secondary responsibility includes performing HR Generalist job duties which may include benefits, compensation and employee relations.

Education:
Bachelor's degree preferred.

Required Skills:
One to three years of recruiting experience. Ability to establish effective working relationships with peers, applicants and hiring managers. Must project a positive professional image through written and verbal communication and must be able to work independently with minimal supervision. Must be proficient in MS Office (Word, Excel, Power Point). Some travel may be required.

Desired Skills:
Recruiting for technical positions to include systems engineers, software engineers and systems administrators. Experience working with Resumix or other automated recruitment and staffing tools.

Job Category: Human Resources   **Ref. No:**
Location: Honolulu, Hawaii, US
Contact:

Part Time or Temporary: Full-time (1st shift)

Must be able to obtain clearance level: Secret

SAIC is an Equal Opportunity/Affirmative Action Employer

B. Corporate Manager of Staffing—Western Region (San Diego Based)

Job Description:
The incumbent provides strategic staffing support to HR managers, recruiters and generalists within SAIC Western Region. Analyzes, develops, implements and evaluates the effectiveness of employment process addressing the business needs of Sectors and Groups within the Western Region, while meeting legal and corporate compliance requirements. Coordinates College Relations and College Recruitment activities, including advertising strategies, within the Region. Develops and coordinates Regional print and Internet advertising strategies, diversity and professional recruiting processes, employee referral programs, student internships and the collection of employment metrics. Develops and implements tools and processes to improve

(continued)

EXHIBIT 13.2 Continued

ROI [Return on Investment] by optimizing recruiting strategies. Will be required to travel to meet business needs supporting any incumbent captures, acquisitions, outsourcing, and other engagements with critical hiring needs. The incumbent will have a dual reporting relationship to the Corporate Staffing Director and Director of HR, Western Region. Directly supervises regional service center recruiting and administrative staff. In addition, responsible for ensuring all recruiters receive timely training and refresher courses for Applicant Tracking Information System (e.g., Resumix) operations. Will develop and lead a team of superusers, providing user support and development, upgrade, implementation requirements, and some vendor relations.

Education:
BA/BS in a relevant field plus a minimum of 10 years of experience, with a minimum of 3 years in a supervisory capacity required. Masters degree in HR or a related area is desirable.

Required Skills:
Must have supervisory experience leading a successful high volume recruiting team in a tight labor market. Experience with electronic applicant tracking systems required, Resumix preferred. Must be well organized with excellent interpersonal skills. Must be a team player with outstanding persuasive, negotiation, and motivational skills. Must possess the ability to manage a team and achieve results through influence, without the benefit of direct management authority. Must possess the proven ability to facilitate the exchange of information through leadership of meetings, and in the development and delivery of effective training and information sessions. Must be knowledgeable of EEO, labor laws and immigration compliance practices.

Desired Skills:
Prefer experience with managing IT industry high volume recruiting programs.

Job Category: Human Resources   **Ref. No:**
Location: San Diego, California, US
Contact:

Part Time or Temporary: Full-time (1st shift)
SAIC is an Equal Opportunity/Affirmative Action Employer

SOURCE: Science Applications International Corporation. Used with permission.

rotation into an entry-level supervisory position, advancement within the supervisory ranks, and then promotion to the job of staffing manager. In short, there is often no established upward mobility track. One should expect the unexpected.

A person who advances beyond or outside the staffing function will be in a good position to advance to the highest levels of HR (director or VP). At these levels, job occupants have typically held varied assignments, including working outside HR in managerial or professional capacities. This work has been in a diverse set of areas, including customer service, operations, finance, sales/marketing, and HR consulting.[8]

Jobs in staffing (and other areas of HR) are becoming increasingly more customer focused and facilitative in nature. As staffing activities become more decentralized and subject to line management control, holders of staffing jobs will exist to provide requested services and act as consultants to the service requesters. This will be a challenge, because many of those newly responsible for staffing (line managers and team leaders) will be untrained and inexperienced in staffing matters.

Increasing numbers of staffing jobs are found in staffing firms. Staffmark is a large, diversified staffing firm with offices nationwide (*www.staffmark.com*). It offers services such as supplemental staffing (short and long term), supplemental to direct staffing, direct hire, executive search, on-site managed programs, national multisite workforce management, and training programs. Exhibit 13.3 provides a job description for the entry-level job of staffing specialist for Staffmark. More advanced jobs include senior staffing specialist, direct hire recruiter, on-site staffing supervisor, and staffing manager. Individuals in on-site staffing roles work directly with the client's HR department to conduct all phases of staffing. Use of such specialists occurs when the client lacks staffing expertise or is seeking to hire large numbers of new employees quickly.[9]

Another new type of staffing job is that of chief talent officer or VP for talent acquisition. Organizations that are critically dependent on talent, such as those in technology and entertainment, and that need to conduct specialized talent searches outside the mainstream of normal staffing processes are creating such positions. One organization, America Online, went even further and created a special talent acquisition department of 35 people who conduct both external and internal searches. It is suggested that such individuals have a background in recruiting, understand accountability in organizations, possess some marketing experience to help sell the organization and build relationships, and can think "outside the box" and devise a strategic vision for recruits and their roles within the organization.[10]

Policies and Procedures

It is highly desirable to have written policies and procedures to guide the administration of staffing systems. Understanding the importance of policies and procedures first requires definition of these terms.

A policy is a selected course or guiding principle. It is an objective to be sought through appropriate actions. For example, the organization might have a promotion-from-within policy as follows: "It is the intent of XXX organization to fill from within all vacancies above the entry level, except in instances of critical, immediate need for a qualified person unavailable internally." This policy makes it clear that promotion from within is the desired objective; the only exception is in the absence of an immediately available, qualified current employee.

EXHIBIT 13.3   Staffing Job at Staffmark

Job Title: Staffing Specialist

Job Summary:
This position is responsible for taking complete and accurate job orders and identifying and placing temporary associates on temporary assignments or direct placement with client companies according to specified job orders and requirements and identifying business development opportunities through penetration of existing accounts.

Essential Duties and Responsibilities:
1. Carries out such functions as identifying qualified applicants, conducting screening interviews, administering tests, checking references, and evaluating applicant qualifications.
2. Hires qualified temporary associates and establishes appropriate pay rates for temporary associates based on skills, abilities, and experience.
3. Makes job offer to associate explaining full job description, term of assignment, pay rate, benefits.
4. Obtains complete and accurate information from clients placing job orders and matches best temporary associate to the client job order. May quote and explain base rates to client.
5. Determines appropriate client placement of qualified associates (may be through skill marketing) and conducts basic associate orientation.
6. Monitors associate activity at client, e.g. track attendance, performance, etc.
7. Maintains current, accurate data in the computer of client activity and associate inventory.
8. Conducts regular service calls (retail accounts <$500,000) to assigned clients to ensure quality service, identify any problems, and obtain feedback.
9. Completes quality control procedures including check-in calls and follow-up calls on completed job orders.
10. Completes accurate payroll processing for temporary associates.
11. Follows and communicates all safety rules and regulations as established by Staffmark to associates.
12. Ensures worker's compensation claims are properly filed.
13. Under the supervision of management, will counsel associates and handle conflict resolution.
14. At the direction of Branch Manager, will record drug testing results and follow drug testing policy.
15. Performs telephone marketing and recruiting in order to identify suitable temporary associates for current and prospective clients.
16. Represents the company in a professional manner at various professional, academic, and/or civic activities as requested.

(continued)

EXHIBIT 13.3 **Continued**

Other Duties and Responsibilities:
1. Occasionally, may be given responsibility for handling worker's compensation or unemployment compensation hearings.
2. Needs to be available for on-call duty after hours and on weekends.
3. May require shift work.

Note: Additional responsibilities not listed here may be assigned at times.

Supervisory Responsibilities:
Supervises temporary associates including monitoring extension or completion of assignments, addressing problems or concerns of temporary associates, coaching, counseling, and taking corrective action with temporary associates. Terminates temporary associates when appropriate. Does not have responsibility for supervising internal Staffmark employees.

Required Competencies:
Utilizes independent judgment and exhibits sound reasoning. Has a working knowledge of Staffmark's unemployment compensation and worker's compensation filing process.

Required Qualifications:
To perform this job successfully, an individual must be able to perform each essential duty satisfactorily. The requirements listed below are representative of the knowledge, skill, and/or ability required. Reasonable accommodations may be made to enable individuals with disabilities to perform the essential functions.

Education and/or Experience:
High school diploma or general education degree (GED); or one to three months' related experience and/or training; or equivalent combination of education and experience.

Language Skills:
Ability to read and interpret documents such as safety rules, operating and maintenance instructions, and procedure manuals. Ability to write routine reports and correspondence. Ability to speak effectively before groups of customers or employees of organization.

Mathematical Skills:
Ability to add, subtract, multiply, and divide in all units of measure, using whole numbers, common fractions, and decimals. Ability to compute rate, ratio, and percent and to draw and interpret bar graphs.

Reasoning Ability:
Ability to apply common sense understanding to carry out detailed but uninvolved written or oral instructions. Ability to deal with problems involving a few concrete variables in standardized situations.

(continued)

EXHIBIT 13.3   Continued

Computer Skills:
Microsoft Word, Microsoft Outlook, Caldwell, Excel, Powerpoint, and Internet.

Certificates, Licenses, Registrations:
Must have current, valid driver's license. Position requires travel to and from client companies and civic events.

Physical Demands:
The physical demands described here are representative of those that must be met by an employee to successfully perform the essential functions of this job. Reasonable accommodations may be made to enable individuals with disabilities to perform the essential functions.

While performing the duties of this job, the employee is regularly required to sit; use hands to finger, handle, or feel; and talk or hear. The employee is frequently required to walk and reach with hands and arms. The employee is occasionally required to stand; climb or balance and stoop, kneel, crouch, or crawl. The employee must frequently lift and/or move up to 10 pounds and occasionally lift and/or move up to 25 pounds. Specific vision abilities required by this job include close vision, distance vision, color vision, peripheral vision, depth perception and ability to adjust focus.

Work Environment:
The work environment characteristics described here are representative of those an employee encounters while performing the essential functions of this job. Reasonable accommodations may be made to enable individuals with disabilities to perform the essential functions. While performing the duties of this job, the employee is occasionally exposed to wet and/or humid conditions; moving mechanical parts; outside weather conditions; extreme cold and extreme heat. The noise level in the work environment is usually moderate. On occasion, duties may require the wearing of proper safety equipment in areas where such equipment is required.

Needs to be available for on-call duty after hours and on weekends. May require shift work.

SOURCE: Staffmark. Used with permission.

A procedure is a prescribed routine or way of acting in similar situations. It provides the rules that govern a particular course of action. To carry out the promotion-from-within policy, for example, the organization may follow specific procedures for listing and communicating the vacancy, identifying eligible applicants, and assessing the qualifications of the applicants.

Policies and procedures can improve the strategic focus of the staffing area. When there are clearly articulated systems of policies and procedures, it is possible to consider the meaning and function of the entire system at a strategic level. On the other hand, poorly thought out or inconsistent policies and procedures result in HR managers spending an inordinate amount of time playing catch-up or "putting out fires," as inconsistent behavior across organizational units inevitably leads to employee complaints. Without clear staffing policies, managers scramble to develop solutions to recruiting or selection needs at the last minute. Dealing with these routine breakdowns in procedures leaves less time to consult organizational goals or consider alternatives. The final result is inefficiency and wasted time.

The existence of policies and procedures can also greatly enhance the perceived justice of staffing activities. Research conducted in a wide variety of organizations has consistently shown that employees perceive organizational decision making as most fair when decisions are based on facts rather than social influence or personal biases, when decision-making criteria are clearly communicated, and when the process is consistently followed across all affected individuals.[11] The use of well-articulated policies and procedures can increase perceived justice considerably if they meet all of the requirements for perceived justice. There are bottom-line implications: employee perceptions of organizational justice have been linked to increased intention to pursue a job in the recruiting context, increased intention to accept a job in the selection context, increased satisfaction and commitment for job assignments, and decreased intention to sue a former employer in the layoff context.[12]

Human Resource Information Systems

Staffing activities generate and use considerable information. Job descriptions, application materials, résumés, correspondence, applicant profiles, applicant flow and tracking, and reports are examples of the types of information that are necessary ingredients for the operation of a staffing system. Naturally, problems regarding what types of information to generate, along with how to file, access, and use it, will arise when managing a staffing system. Addressing and solving these problems have important implications for paperwork burdens, administrative processing costs, and speed in filling job vacancies. Thus, management of a staffing system involves management of an HRIS.

Most organizations with a sufficient number of employees to warrant a dedicated HR department have integrated the function with HRISs. Many vendors have developed specialized HRIS interfaces that can track the critical processes and outcomes involved in staffing, as shown in Exhibit 13.4. The features listed in the exhibit are meant to be illustrative rather than exhaustive; new functionality is continually being added to HRISs. Providing hard data on staffing system outcomes can increase the credibility of staffing services in organizations. The increased availability of data on staffing processes following from the use of HRISs means that organizations will also be able to accurately track the efficacy of policies and procedures. Staffing policies that do not show returns on investments can be

EXHIBIT 13.4   Human Resources Information Systems for Staffing Tasks

Staffing Task	HRIS Functionality
Legal compliance	EEO data analysis and reports Policy and procedure writing guides Statistical analysis for demonstrating job relatedness
Planning	Tracking historical demand for employees Forecasting workforce supply Replacement and succession planning
Job analysis	Database of job titles and responsibilities Database of competencies across jobs Compare job descriptions with O*Net
External recruitment and selection	Job posting reports Time-to-fill hiring requisitions Applicant logs, status, and tracking reports Recruitment source effectiveness Electronic résumé routing Keyword scanning of applications New hire reports (numbers, qualifications, assignments) Validation of selection systems
Internal recruitment and selection	Employee succession planning Intranet for job postings Skills databases Tracking progress through assessment centers Job performance reports Individual development plans
Final match	Tracking job acceptance rates Contract development Tracking employee socialization progress
Staffing system management	System cost reports Return on investments Record-keeping functions
Retention	Collection and analysis of job satisfaction data Track differences in turnover rates across locations and time Document performance management and/or progressive discipline

eliminated, whereas those that show positive results can be expanded. Organizations that have outsourced staffing functions should also be aware of the information provided by HRISs and should ensure that they are receiving accurate and comprehensive reports from their vendor's HRIS database. Organizations considering outsourcing options should request historical data showing the efficacy of staffing systems in other organizations before committing resources toward any particular vendor. If an outsourcing service provider cannot provide these data, this may be a sign that it does not communicate well or may not be very rigorous about evaluating the quality of its services.

Web-based staffing management systems are also available from application service providers (ASPs) or software-as-a-service (SaaS) providers. With such systems, the vendor provides both the hardware (e.g., servers, scanners) and the software, as well as day-to-day management of the system. Recruiters and hiring managers access the system through a web browser. One example of such a system was the Enterprise system from Brass Ring, Inc. (*www.brassring.com*). The system posted job openings to job boards and other websites. It accepted all forms of résumés (paper, fax, e-mail, and web-based), scanned and coded them, and stored them in a relational database on a secure server. In addition to résumé information, a talent record may have included information pertaining to work samples, background checks, test scores, training, certification, performance reviews, and references. The hiring manager or recruiter could access the database to submit job requisitions, perform literal and conceptual searches based on specified KSAOs, schedule interviews, conduct correspondence with applicants, forward résumés to others, track the search status of current applicants, track current employee KSAOs, and conduct various recruitment reports, such as average cost per hire for each recruitment source used and EEO compliance.

Several trends continue to alter the landscape of HRISs.[13] One growing trend is the development of systems that allow frontline managers and employees to access their HR records and engage with the system directly rather than working through a centralized HR system. These processes are already being implemented to facilitate internal staffing functions. Employee self-service pages can be used to help employees stay up to date with skills needed in the organization through succession management plans, find training that will help them prepare for higher-level positions, and submit applications when positions come open. The increased availability of web-based solutions will also make it easier for even small employers with limited resources to provide a full suite of automated HRIS solutions for staffing.

Social networking applications for information sharing, mirroring Facebook or Twitter, have become much more common elements in HRISs. Social networking applications have been particularly popular elements of employee orientation or "onboarding" programs because they allow newcomers to quickly interact with established employees.

Effectiveness

Surveys of organizations' experiences with new staffing technologies and case studies of their adoption, implementation, and operation provide a comprehensive overview of how well the technologies are working.[14] What emerges from the data is a very "mixed bag" of evidence, with numerous positive and negative experiences being reported.

When assessing HRISs for staffing tasks, HR managers need to carefully consider their needs and goals for the entire HRIS today and in the future.[15] Some of the key factors that differentiate HRISs include whether the system is hosted on-site or as SaaS on a remote server run by an HRIS provider, the degree and nature of custom reporting provided by the HRIS, the ability to generate reports that integrate a variety of HR functions, and the degree to which systems for recruiting, selection, record keeping, orientation, benefits, and compensation are integrated with one another. Other factors to consider include how long the service provider has been in business, how often it upgrades its system, how many other customers the provider has, who those clients are, and, of course, costs. The sheer complexity of deciding which HRIS to use means that the decision is seldom made by a single individual; rather, the decision is made by joint committees made up of executives, members of the HR staff, and information technology professionals.

Staffing technologies may have a multitude of positive and negative effects. Many of these effects extend beyond process improvement (e.g., speed of staffing) and cost reduction. While these two potential advantages are very important, they need to be considered within the context of other potential advantages, and especially the myriad potential disadvantages. The organization should proceed with caution and due diligence in deciding whether to use new staffing technologies, evaluating products and vendors, establishing service agreements with vendors, and conducting planning prior to implementation. It is also clear that even once the staffing technologies are implemented, monitoring and system improvement will need to be periodically undertaken.

Outsourcing

Outsourcing refers to contracting out work to a vendor or third-party administrator. In Chapter 3 we discussed outsourcing work for noncore organizational processes. Here we consider the case when certain staffing functions are outsourced. Examples of specific staffing activities that are outsourced include a search for temporary employees, an executive search, drug testing, skill testing, background checks, job fairs, employee relocation, assessment centers, and affirmative action planning. Other examples continue to emerge. For example, on-demand recruiting services provide short-term assistance in conducting executive searches, but payment for these services is based on a fixed fee or time rate, rather than on a percentage of the new hire's salary.[16] A number of factors that influence the decision of whether to outsource are reviewed in Exhibit 13.5. Outsourcing decisions require consideration of organizational strategy, size, and the skills required. As you can see, the decision about whether to outsource is not an all-or-nothing proposition. Some staffing functions are more easily outsourced, so most organizations use outsourcing for some tasks but not for others.

One of the benefits of outsourcing is that it frees the internal HR department from performing day-to-day administrative activities that could be more efficiently managed by an external organization. A survey of HR representatives showed that the major advantages of outsourcing include access to superior information from specialists, access to technology and services that are difficult to implement internally, and general cost reduction.[17] By eliminating the day-to-day work of maintaining staffing systems, it is possible to dedicate more energy to analyzing and improving the effectiveness of the staffing system as a whole. Because specialized staffing firms work with the same processes all the time, they can develop spe-

---

EXHIBIT 13.5   **Comparing Outsourced vs. In-House Staffing**

	Outsourced	In-House
Strategy	Staffing functions not linked to core organizational competencies	Staffing functions linked to core organizational competencies
Size	Small organizations, organizations without a centralized HR function, or organizations with continual hiring needs	Large organizations where economies of scale will pay off or for executive selection tasks where knowledge of the organization is crucial
Skills required	General human capital, such as that easily obtained through education	Firm-specific human capital, such as knowledge of organizational policies or specific personality traits
Examples	• Recruiting packaging employees in a small warehouse • Screening registered nurses for a long-term-care facility • Developing a website for automatically screening entry-level candidates • Providing temporary employees for a highly cyclical manufacturing organization	• Recruiting creative talent for an advertising firm • Selecting members of the organization's executive team • Providing employee orientation • Recruiting and selecting employees for a large retail organization • Recruiting and selecting individuals for an interdependent work team

cialized, highly efficient systems that can deliver results more quickly and more cheaply than an organization's in-house staffing services. An external staffing firm will have more resources to keep up with developments in its area. For example, a firm that specializes in EEO compliance will always have the latest information regarding court decisions and changing precedents.

These advantages of outsourcing should always be weighed against the potential downfalls of outsourcing too many staffing functions or outsourcing functions too rapidly. Experts in this area warn that the expected benefits will not materialize if the decision to outsource is not accompanied by a complete transformation of the way HR is delivered.[18] Organizations that outsource should hold external providers accountable by keeping track of staffing metrics, especially since specialized staffing firms should have access to better systems for managing and reporting staffing data. Someone inside the organization should have final, bottom-line accountability for any outsourced services. In many organizations, there is resistance to outsourcing, and employees may feel that the company is treating them impersonally if questions or concerns about employment are directed to an external vendor. Thus, if employees have complaints or concerns about staffing services, they should be able to discuss their concerns with someone inside the organization who can respond to them.

It is worth noting that staffing is not one of the first activities most organizations outsource. The same surveys noted earlier demonstrate that the most commonly outsourced HR services are payroll and pension plans. It is also more common for organizations to outsource their recruiting function than selection. This makes sense when one considers the comparative advantages of internal and outsourced services: most organizations do not have much access to the external labor market, so a specialized staffing firm can provide superior recruiting. But the choice of who will or will not work in an organization is often made from a complex assessment of fit with the job and work group that would be more accurately made by internal HR representatives.

An emerging type of vendor is the professional employer organization (PEO), formerly referred to as an employee leasing firm. It is similar to a staffing firm, but unlike a staffing firm, a PEO provides a wider range of HR services and has a long-term commitment to the client. Under a typical arrangement, the client organization enters into a contractual relationship with a PEO to conduct some or all HR activities and functions. The client and the PEO are considered coemployers of record. A PEO is particularly appealing to small employers because it can provide special HR expertise and technical assistance, conduct the administrative activities and transactions of an HR department, provide more affordable employee benefits, meet legal obligations (payroll, withholding, workers' compensation, and unemployment insurance), and manage legal compliance. PEOs are licensed in many states.[19]

Some organizations are experimenting with total outsourcing of the staffing function. An example is Kellogg's (cereal and convenience foods), which selected a single vendor to handle its entire staffing process. Kellogg's worked with the vendor at the outset to develop a staffing strategy and fit it into the vendor's staffing technology, implement the total staffing solution, and then modify the system to fix any problems. Assessment and hiring of finalists, however, remained in the hands of the hiring manager. Within three years, the vendor was filling over 95% of available jobs at Kellogg's.[20]

Consider the example of Charmant, a moderate-sized organization (130 employees) that was seeking to update its outmoded HRISs.[21] Like most organizations of this size, Charmant has a relatively small HR department, consisting of only two individuals. Its systems were old and poorly integrated, required a great deal of redundant work to access information from multiple systems (e.g., recruiting, performance management, benefits, and payroll were completely separate applications), and had a user interface that was difficult to understand. Through a relationship with a specialized software provider, it was able to obtain a seamless integration of all its HR systems, which simultaneously reduced the amount of staff time required for routine HR processes while increasing access to data for decision making. The new system made it possible to update records for payroll and benefits simultaneously when new employees were hired or employees left, which made managing head count and related HR functions more straightforward. Using an external vendor helped facilitate the posting of internal jobs with recruiting providers like Monster and also made conducting background checks easier. In sum, tasks that this medium-sized organization's HR representatives could not complete as readily, especially information systems integration, were performed by an external vendor, thereby allowing in-house HR individuals to concentrate more of their time on core business operations. This example demonstrates how outsourcing for specific HR services can facilitate in-house staffing effectiveness for organizations that do not have resources to devote to a large HR department.

At the outset, it is important to remember that the agreement (often called a service-level agreement, or SLA) with the vendor is almost always negotiable, and that flaws in the negotiating stage are responsible for many problems that may subsequently occur in the relationship. Using some form of legal or consulting assistance might be desirable, especially for the organization that has little or no staffing outsourcing experience.

There are many issues to discuss and negotiate. Awareness of these factors and advance preparation with regard to the organization's preferences and requirements are critical to a successful negotiation with a potential vendor. The factors include the actual staffing services sought and provided, client control rights (e.g., monitoring of the vendor's personnel and the software to be used), fees and other costs, guaranteed improvements in service levels and cost savings, benchmarking metrics and performance reviews, and willingness to hire the organization's own employees to provide expertise and coordination. On top of these factors, the choice of vendor should take into account the vendor's past track record and familiarity with the organization's industry.[22]

EVALUATION OF STAFFING SYSTEMS

Evaluation of staffing systems refers to the effectiveness of the total system. The evaluation should focus on the operation of the staffing process, the results and costs of the process, and the satisfaction of customers of the staffing system.

Staffing Process

The staffing process establishes and governs the flow of employees into, within, and out of the organization. Evaluation of the process itself requires a mapping out of the intended process, identifying any deviations from the intended process, and planning corrective actions to reduce or eliminate the deviations. The intent of such an evaluation is to ensure standardization of the staffing process, remove bottlenecks in operation, and improve speed of operation.

Standardization refers to the consistency of operation of the organization's staffing system. Use of standardized staffing systems is desirable for several reasons. First, standardization ensures that the same KSAO information is gathered from all job applicants, which, in turn, is a key requirement for reliably and validly measuring these KSAOs. Second, standardization ensures that all applicants receive the same information about job requirements and rewards. Thus, all applicants can make equally informed evaluations of the organization. Third, standardization will enhance applicants' perceptions of the procedural fairness of the staffing system and of the decisions made about them by the organization. Having applicants feel they were treated fairly and got a "fair shake" can reap substantial benefits for the organization. Applicants will speak favorably of their experience and the organization to others, they may seek employment with the organization in the future (even if rejected), they may be more likely to accept job offers, and they may become organizational newcomers with a very upbeat frame of mind as they begin their new jobs. Finally, standardized staffing systems are less likely to generate legal challenges by job applicants; if standardized staffing systems are challenged, they are more likely to successfully withstand the challenge.

Mapping out the staffing process involves constructing a staffing flowchart. The staffing flowchart shown in Exhibit 13.6 depicts the staffing system of a medium-sized (580 employees) high-tech printing and lithography company. It shows the actual flow of staffing activities, and both organization and applicant decision points, from the time a vacancy occurs until the time it is filled with a new hire.

A detailed inspection of the chart reveals the following information about the organization's staffing system:

1. It is a generic system used for both entry-level and higher-level jobs.
2. For higher-level jobs, vacancies are first posted internally (thus showing a recruitment philosophy emphasizing a commitment to promotion from within). Entry-level jobs are filled externally.

EXHIBIT 13.6   Staffing Flowchart for Medium-Sized Printing Company

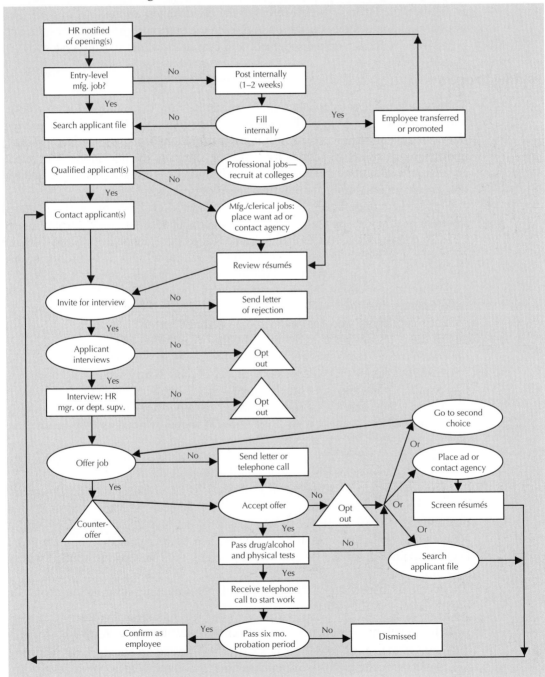

3. External recruitment sources (colleges, newspaper ads, and employment agencies) are used only if the current applicant file yields no qualified applicants.

4. Initial assessments are made using biographical information (application blanks, résumés), and the results of these assessments determine who will be interviewed.

5. Substantive assessments are made through the interview(s) conducted by the HR manager and the hiring supervisor, and the results of these assessments determine who receives the job offer.

6. The applicant may counteroffer, and acceptance of the final offer by the applicant is conditional on passing drug/alcohol and physical tests.

7. The new hire undergoes a six-month probationary employment period before becoming a so-called permanent employee.

A more fine-grained analysis is then conducted to indicate the specific steps and actions that should be taken throughout the staffing process. For example, it can be seen in Exhibit 13.6 that non-entry-level manufacturing jobs are posted internally, so the more fine-grained analysis would describe the job posting process—content of the posting, timing of the posting, mechanisms for circulating and displaying the posting, and the person responsible for handling the posting. As another example, the staffing process involves contacting qualified applicants, inviting them for an interview, and interviewing them. The more fine-grained analysis would identify the amount of time between the initial contact and completion of interviews, who conducts the interview, and the nature/content of the interview (such as a structured, situational interview). After the fine-grained analysis is complete, there would be a detailed specification of the staffing process in flow terms, along with specific events, actions, and timing that should occur over the course of the process.

Once the staffing process has been mapped out, the next step is to check for any deviations that have occurred. This will require an analysis of some past staffing "transactions" with job applicants, following what was done and what actions were taken as the applicants entered and flowed through the staffing system. All identified deviations should be recorded. It might be found, for example, that the content of the job postings did not conform to specific requirements for listing tasks and necessary KSAOs, or that interviews were not being conducted within the required one-week period from date of first contact with a qualified applicant, or that interviewers were conducting unstructured interviews rather than the required structured, situational interview.

The next step is to analyze all discovered deviations and determine the reason(s) for their occurrence. The final step is to make changes in the staffing system in order to reduce deviations, enhance standardization, and remove bottlenecks.

Staffing Process Results

In the past it was commonly argued that most of the processes involved in staffing were too subjective or difficult to quantify. As a result, staffing managers could not provide representatives from finance and accounting with the hard cost-effectiveness data they were looking for. Fortunately, a dramatic increase in the availability and functionality of database software in recent years means that staffing system effectiveness can be assessed much more readily. HRISs can catalog and quickly display recruiting, hiring, retention, and job performance data. HR scholars have developed standardized metrics based on these sources of information that can help staffing managers communicate the business case for staffing services across the organization.[23]

Exhibit 13.7 provides a flowchart for using metrics to evaluate and update staffing processes. The first stage of the process is assessing the organization's needs and strategic goals at the job, work unit, and organization levels. This stage was covered in organizational planning. Once organizational priorities are established, a set of policies and procedures designed to achieve these ends is developed. The next stage is to measure the outcomes of the staffing system. Consulting staffing system metrics will then serve as the basis for assessing future organizational needs, priorities, and goals, and will also be used to revise staffing system policies and procedures. After measurements have been obtained, they should be compared with benchmark figures. These benchmarks can be obtained from split sample techniques, longitudinal techniques, or external benchmarking, which we will cover shortly. This strategic planning and evaluation process is an essential component of staffing system management. If there are no attempts to monitor and check the outcomes of staffing systems, it is likely that systems that may have been effective in the past will remain in place long after they have failed to obtain desired results. Of course, there is no guarantee that HR programs will prove to be effective when put to the test; experienced managers who have used staffing system metrics often find that new staffing systems may not represent a significant improvement.

EXHIBIT 13.7   Staffing Process Results Evaluation Flowchart

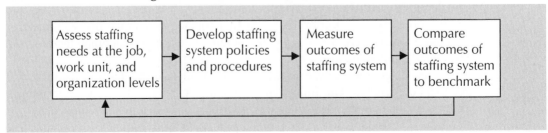

One method for evaluating the efficacy of staffing programs is to use the scientific technique of split samples.[24] As an example, a split sample analysis might begin with the premise that a new recruiting program will affect operational outcomes by attracting more qualified employees, improving the organization's ability to respond to staffing requisitions quickly, and reducing long-range turnover. The specific metrics for this proposed program include measures of employee qualifications, time-to-hire for position openings taken from the organization's HRIS, and unit turnover rates. In a split sample analysis, the target employee population is split in half, and the new HR program is initiated with only one of these halves. In this case, perhaps one region of a national chain would serve as the experimental group for the new recruiting program. Their outcomes will be compared with the rest of the organization, which would not use the new recruiting program. After the program has had an opportunity to work, representatives from HR can compare the metrics from the experimental sample with areas of the company where the new recruiting system was not employed. The split sample technique is not just useful for evaluating new programs. To assess the effectiveness of an existing program, it is always possible to selectively discontinue the program in one location or business unit while maintaining it in another section. If the temporary elimination of a costly program does not appreciably alter business outcomes, it may be wise to eliminate the program permanently.

If it is not possible to use the split sample technique because the workforce does not have geographically or operationally distinct units, it is still possible to use metrics to assess the efficacy of proposed system changes. Staffing managers can compare long-run data on a single business unit's effectiveness before and after a change has been initiated. This is called a longitudinal design, or simply put, a measure of change. To make valid inferences, benchmark data should be taken over a long period of time so that changes in staffing metrics can be reliably attributed to the program implementation rather than just routine variability in organizational performance.

A final strategy for assessing the effectiveness of HR programs is to compare organizational results with external benchmarks. The Society for Human Resource Management (SHRM) has developed a number of guidelines for developing and interpreting staffing metrics. Its website provides a number of benchmarking studies every year, including surveys that outline the use and perceived efficacies ranging across a number of practices, such as retention initiatives, e-recruiting, and diversity management. More detailed metrics can also be obtained from SHRM surveys of human capital benchmarks. Learning what other organizations are doing may not always be especially informative for determining the effectiveness of these policies and procedures for the organization. Many practices that work in one context may not be as useful in another context, and the research on HR bundling suggests that policies need to be implemented into a comprehensive system rather than just implementing individual practices in isolation. So, although it is helpful to have some benchmark information, any new policies should be investigated for how well they are working in one's own organization.

The use of scientific methods with data from HRISs can help investigate whether common assumptions about staffing are supported in an organization.[25] For example, Thrivenet financial managers had assumed that new hires who had substantial prior experience in the industry were less likely to leave in their first year, but analysis of HR metrics showed that the exact opposite was true. Managers at Metropolitan Life assumed that there was no common profile of individuals who were most likely to succeed in their organization, but they found that they could identify future high performers by looking at the variety of job experiences employees had in the company. Although managers at the food service company Wawa Inc. suspected that hourly wage rates were influencing turnover among clerks, analysis of their staffing data found that part-time workers were more prone to turnover than full-time employees. This led the company to change its staffing mix to include a higher proportion of full-timers than it had previously. As these examples illustrate, HR metrics and associated analytics can be powerful tools for testing and refining beliefs about the effectiveness of a variety of practices related to staffing.

Over the course of the staffing process it is possible to develop quantitative indicators that show how effectively and efficiently the staffing system is operating. For example, how many applicants does a given vacancy attract on average? Or, what percentage of job offers are accepted? What is the average number of days it takes to fill a vacancy? What percentage of new hires remain with the organization for one year posthire? Answers to such questions can be determined by tracking and analyzing applicant flows through the staffing pipeline.

In Exhibit 13.8 we offer some suggestions for the types of financial and process data that might be most useful for assessing the effectiveness of staffing systems overall. These suggestions are based on established research on best practices in the field. Following from several other writers, we divided the outcomes into four key categories: cost, timeliness, outcomes, and reactions. For each category, we present some representative metrics that might be useful, although there are many other measurable outcomes that might be relevant depending on an organization's goals.

Exhibit 13.9 shows the required layout for this tracking and analysis, as well as some staffing process results that may be easily calculated. In part A, the steps in the staffing process start with the announcement of a vacancy and run through a sequential flow of selection, job offer, offer acceptance, start as new hire, and retention. A timeline shows the average number of days to complete each step. For illustration purposes, it is assumed that 25 vacancies attracted 1,000 applicants who proceeded through the staffing process. Ultimately, all 25 vacancies were filled, and these new hires were tracked to see how many remained with the organization for six months and one year posthire.

EXHIBIT 13.8 Common Staffing Metrics

	Cost	Timeliness	Outcomes	Reactions
Staffing system	Staffing budget Staffing-to-employee ratios Staffing expenses for full-time equivalents (FTEs)	Time to respond to requests	Evaluation of employee readiness for strategic goals	Communication Satisfaction with services provided
Recruiting	Advertising expenses Cost per applicant	Recruits per week	Number of recruits	Applicant quality
Selection	Test costs per candidate Interview expenses Cost per candidate	Time to hire Days to fill	Competence Workforce diversity	Candidate quality Satisfaction with tests
Final match	Training costs per hire Cost per hire	Days to start Time-to-perform	Number of positions filled Job performance	New employee satisfaction
Retention	Exit interview expenses Replacement costs	Timely response to external offers	Voluntary separation rate Involuntary separation rate	Employee job satisfaction

In part B of Exhibit 13.9 are staffing process results indicators, also referred to as metrics, along with their calculations using data from the example. The first indicator is applicants per vacancy, which averaged 40. This is an indication of the effectiveness of recruitment activities to attract people to the organization. The second indicator is the yield ratio; it indicates the percentage of people who moved on to one or more of the next steps in the staffing process. For example, the percentage of applicants who became candidates is 20%; the percentage of job offers accepted is 83.3%. The third indicator, time lapse (or cycle time), shows the average amount of time lapsed between each step in the staffing process. It can be seen that the average days to fill a vacancy is 44. The final indicator is retention rate; the six-month retention rate for new hires is 80%, and the one-year rate fell to 52%.

These types of metrics are very useful barometers for gauging the pulse of the staffing flow. They have an objective, bottom-line nature that can be readily communicated to managers and others in the organization. These types of data are also very useful for comparative purposes. For example, the relative effectiveness and efficiency of staffing systems in two different units of the organization could

EXHIBIT 13.9 **Evaluation of Staffing Process and Results: Example**

A. Staffing Process Example

No. of vacancies filled = 25

Process step	Vacancy announced (1)	Applicants (2)	Candidates (3)	Finalists (4)	Offer receiver (5)	Offer acceptance (6)	Start as new hire (7)	On the job	
								Six months (8)	One Year (9)
No. of people	0	1,000	200	125	30	25	25	20	13
Process time Avg. no. of days	0	14	21	28	35	42	44		

B. Staffing Process Results

Applicants/Vacancy = 1,000/25 = 40

Yield ratio: candidates/applicant = 20%; new hires/applicant = 2.5%; offers accepted/received = 83.3%

Time lapse: avg. days to offer = 35; avg. days to start = 44 (cycle time)

Retention rate: $\dfrac{\text{on job six months}}{\text{new hires}}$ = 80% for six months; $\dfrac{\text{on job one year}}{\text{new hires}}$ = 52% for first year be assessed by comparing their respective yield ratios and so forth. Additionally, the metrics of one staffing system could be compared over time. Such time-based comparisons are useful for tracking trends in effectiveness and efficiency. These comparisons are also used to help judge how well changes in staffing practices have worked to improve staffing process performance.

Increasingly, organizations are emphasizing time to fill vacancies as a key indicator of staffing effectiveness, because the shorter the vacancy time, the less the employee contribution forgone. Vacancies in sales jobs, for example, often mean lost sales and revenue generation, so shortening the time to fill means lessening the revenue forgone. Filling vacancies more quickly has led organizations to develop "speed hiring" and continuous hiring programs, in which they redesign their staffing systems to eliminate any excessive delays or bottlenecks in the process.[26]

Surveys of organizational practice in calculating staffing metrics should be consulted to learn about the many nuances involved.[27]

Calculating Staffing Metrics

We have already outlined methods for assessing the costs and benefits of staffing policies and procedures. Below we present more specific methods for calculating these metrics.[28] Number of positions filled is a straightforward count of the number of individuals who accepted positions during the fiscal year. These data are collected for both internal and external candidates. Time to fill openings is estimated by assessing the number of days it takes for a job requisition to result in a job acceptance by a candidate. Hiring cost estimates are the sum of advertising, agency fees, employee referrals, travel costs for applicants and staff, relocation costs, and pay and benefits for recruiters. Hiring cost estimates are often indexed by dividing by the number of positions filled. As we noted in the chapters on recruiting, these cost estimates may be subdivided in a number of ways to get a better idea of which portions of the staffing process are comparatively more expensive. Turnover rates are also often used as staffing metrics. The annual turnover rate is estimated by dividing the number of separations per month by the average number of individuals employed each month and then taking the sum of these average month rates. Turnover rates are often differentiated based on whether they represent voluntary or involuntary turnover, which we cover in the next chapter. Other cost data, and how to calculate them, are also available.[29]

Another staffing metric is the staffing cost or efficiency ratio.[30] It takes into account that recruiting applicants for jobs with a higher compensation level might cost more due to such costs as executive search fees, recruitment advertising, relocation, and so forth. The formula is total staffing cost ratio = total staffing costs / total compensation recruited. Though the cost per hire may be greater for one job category than for another, their staffing cost ratios may be the same. This is illustrated in Exhibit 13.10. If just cost per hire is considered, it appears that recruitment for the repair job is more effective than for the sales manager job. But by also

EXHIBIT 13.10   Comparison of Cost per Hire and Staffing Cost Ratio

Job Category	New Hires	Staffing Cost	Cost per Hire	Compensation per Hire	Staffing Cost Ratio
Repair	500	$500,000	$1,000	$20,000	5%
Sales Manager	100	$300,000	$3,000	$60,000	5%

calculating the staffing cost ratio, it can be seen that recruitment is at the same level of efficiency for both job categories. That is, recruitment for each source is incurring the same relative expense to "bring in" the same amount of compensation via new hires.

Customer Satisfaction

Staffing systems, by their very nature, influence users of them. Such users can be thought of as customers of the system. Two of the key customers are managers and job applicants. Managers look to the staffing system to provide them the right numbers and types of new hires to meet their own staffing needs. Job applicants expect the staffing system to recruit, select, and make employment decisions about them in ways that are fair and legal. For both sets of customers, therefore, it is important to know how satisfied they are with the staffing systems that serve them. Customer satisfaction can reinforce the usage of current staffing practices. Customer dissatisfaction, alternately, may serve as a trigger for needed changes in the staffing system and help pinpoint the nature of those changes.

Customer satisfaction with staffing systems is of fairly recent origin as an organizational concern. Rarely in the past were managers and job applicants even thought of as customers, and rarer yet were systematic attempts made to measure their customer satisfaction as a way of evaluating the effectiveness of staffing systems. Recently, that has begun to change. Described next are examples of measures of customer satisfaction for managers and job applicants.

Managers

The state of Wisconsin Department of Employment Relations houses the Division of Merit Recruitment and Selection (DMRS), which is the central agency responsible for staffing the state government. Annually, it helps the 40 state agencies fill about 4,000 vacancies through hiring and promoting. Managers within these agencies are customers of the DMRS and its staffing systems.

To help identify and guide needed staffing system improvements, the DMRS decided to develop a survey measure of managers' satisfaction with staffing services. Through the use of focus groups, managers' input on the content of the survey was solicited. The final survey contained 53 items that were grouped into five areas: communication, timeliness, candidate quality, test quality, and service focus. Examples of the survey items are shown in Exhibit 13.11.

The survey was administered via internal mail to 645 line and HR managers throughout the agencies. Statistical analyses provided favorable psychometric evidence supporting usage of the survey. Survey results served as a key input to implementation of several initiatives to improve staffing service delivery. These initiatives led to increases in the speed of filling vacancies, elimination of paperwork, higher reported quality of job applicants, and positive applicant reactions to the staffing process.[31]

Job Applicants

As with managers, it is best to develop a tailor-made survey for job applicants, one that reflects the specific characteristics of the staffing system being used and the types of contacts and experiences job applicants will have with it. Consultation of a staffing flowchart (Exhibit 13.6) would be helpful in this regard. If possible, the survey should be given to three different applicant groups: candidates who were rejected, candidates who accepted a job offer, and candidates who declined a job offer. Examples of questions that might be included in the survey are in Exhibit 13.12. Separate analysis of responses from each group should be done. Online assistance in survey design, survey administration, and analysis of results is available from SurveyMonkey (*www.surveymonkey.com*) and Zoomerang (*www.zoomerang.com*). Many web-based recruiting systems provide applicants with surveys or open-ended text boxes where they can share their reactions to the recruiting process. Because these systems provide immediate feedback to the organization, it may be possible to make real-time improvements to a recruiting drive.

LEGAL ISSUES

Record Keeping and Privacy

In staffing systems, substantial information is generated, used, recorded, and disclosed. Numerous legal constraints and requirements surround staffing information. These pertain to record keeping and privacy concerns.

Record Keeping

The organization creates a wide range of information during staffing and other HR activities. Examples include personal data (name, address, date of birth, dependents, etc.), KSAO information (application blank, references, test scores, etc.),

EXHIBIT 13.11   Examples of Survey Items for Assessing Managers' Satisfaction With Staffing Services

Communication: How well are you kept informed on the staffing process?

How satisfied are you with:

1. The clarity of instructions and explanation you receive on the staffing process
2. Your overall understanding of the steps involved in filling a vacancy
3. The amount of training you receive in order to effectively participate in the total staffing process

Timeliness: How do you feel about the speed of recruitment, examination, and selection services?

How satisfied are you with the time required to:

1. Obtain central administrative approval to begin the hiring process
2. Score oral and essay exams, achievement history questionnaires, or other procedures involving scoring by a panel of raters
3. Hire someone who has been interviewed and selected

Candidate Quality: How do you feel about the quality (required knowledges and skills) of the job candidates?

How satisfied are you with:

1. The number of people you can interview and select from
2. The quality of candidates on new register
3. Your involvement in the recruitment process

Test Quality: How do you feel about the quality of civil service exams (tests, work samples, oral board interviews, etc.)?

How satisfied are you with:

1. Your involvement in exam construction
2. The extent to which the exams assess required KSAOs
3. The extent to which the exams test for new technologies used on the job

Service Focus: To what extent do you believe your personnel/staffing representatives are committed to providing high-quality service?

How satisfied are you with:

1. The accessibility of a staffing person
2. The expertise and competence of the staffing representative
3. Responses to your particular work unit's needs

SOURCE: H. G. Heneman III, D. L. Huett, R. J. Lavigna, and D. Ogsten, "Assessing Managers' Satisfaction With Staffing Services," *Personnel Psychology*, 1995, 48, pp. 170–173. © *Personnel Psychology*, 1995. Used with permission.

EXHIBIT 13.12   Sample Job Applicant's Satisfaction Survey Questionnaire

1. What prompted you to apply to Organization X?

   ____ company website   ____ advertisement   ____ employee referral
   ____ job fair   ____ campus recruitment   ____ other (indicate)

2. Was the information you got from this source valuable?

   ____ very   ____ somewhat   ____ no

3. Please indicate your level of agreement with each of the following on the 1–5 scale, where 1 = strongly disagree and 5 = strongly agree

	strongly disagree			strongly agree	
The applicant process was easy to use.	1	2	3	4	5
I received a prompt response to my application.	1	2	3	4	5
My first interview was promptly scheduled.	1	2	3	4	5
My first interview covered all my qualifications.	1	2	3	4	5
The test I took was relevant to the job.	1	2	3	4	5
The test process was fair.	1	2	3	4	5
I received prompt feedback about my test scores.	1	2	3	4	5
I always knew where I stood in the selection process.	1	2	3	4	5
My interview with the hiring manager was thorough.	1	2	3	4	5
The hiring manager represented Organization X well.	1	2	3	4	5
I was treated honestly and openly.	1	2	3	4	5
Overall, I am satisfied with the selection process.	1	2	3	4	5
I would recommend Organization X to others as a place to work.	1	2	3	4	5

4. Please describe what you liked most about your experience seeking a job with Organization X.

5. Please describe what you liked least about your experience seeking a job with Organization X.

medical information, performance appraisal and promotability assessments, and changes in employment status (promotion, transfers, etc.). Why should records of such information be created?

Records should be created and maintained for two major legal purposes in staffing. First, they are necessary for legal compliance. Federal, state, and local laws specify what information should be kept, and for how long. Second, having records allows the organization to provide documentation to justify staffing decisions or to defend these decisions against legal challenge. For example, performance appraisal and promotability assessments might be used to explain to employees why they were or were not promoted. Or, these same records might be used as evidence in a legal proceeding to show that promotion decisions were job related and unbiased.

It is strongly recommended that two sets of records be created. These records can be kept in paper or electronic form. The first set should be the individual employee's personnel file. It should comprise only documents that relate directly to the job and the employee's performance of it. To determine which documents to place in the personnel file, ask if it is a document on which the organization could legally base an employment decision. If the answer is "no," "probably no," or "unsure," the document should not be placed in the employee's personnel file. The second set of records should contain documents that cannot be used in staffing decisions. Examples include documents pertaining to medical information (both physical and mental), equal employment opportunity (e.g., information about protected characteristics such as age, sex, religion, race, color, national origin, and disability), and information about authorization to work (e.g., I-9 forms).[32]

Any document that is to be placed in an employee's personnel file should be reviewed before it becomes part of that record. Examine the document for incomplete, inaccurate, or misleading information, as well as potentially damaging notations or comments about the employee. All such information should be completed, corrected, explained, or, if necessary, eliminated. Remember that any document in the personnel file is a potential court exhibit that may work either for or against the employer's defense of a legal challenge.[33]

Federal EEO/AA laws contain general record-keeping requirements. Though the requirements vary somewhat from law to law, major subject areas for which records are to be kept (if created) are shown in Exhibit 13.13. Requirements by the Office of Federal Contract Compliance Programs (OFCCP) are broader than those shown, and records must be maintained for at least two years.

The various laws also have requirements about length of retention of records. As a general rule, most records must be kept for a minimum of one year from the date a document is made or a staffing action is taken, whichever is later. Exceptions to the one-year requirements all provide for even longer retention periods. If a charge of discrimination is filed, the records must be retained until the matter is resolved.

EXHIBIT 13.13   Federal Record-Keeping Requirements

Records that should be kept include the following:

- Applications for employment (hire, promote, or transfer)
- Reasons for refusal to hire, promote, or transfer
- Tests and test scores, plus other KSAO information
- Job orders submitted to labor unions and employment agencies
- Medical exam results
- Advertisements or other notices to the public or employees about job openings and promotion opportunities
- Requests for reasonable accommodation
- Impact of staffing decisions on protected groups (adverse impact statistics)
- Records related to filing of a discrimination charge

All records should be kept for a minimum of one year.

Privacy Concerns

The organization must observe legal requirements governing employees' and others' access to information in personnel files, as well as guard against unwarranted disclosure of the information to third-party requesters (e.g., other employers). Information access and disclosure matters raise privacy concerns under both constitutional and statutory law.[34]

Several states have laws guaranteeing employees reasonable access to their personnel files. The laws generally allow the employee to review and copy pertinent documents; some documents such as letters of reference or promotion plans for the person may be excluded from access. The employee may also have a right to seek to correct erroneous information in the file. Where there is no state law permitting access, employees are usually allowed access to their personnel file only if the organization has a policy permitting it. Disclosure of information in personnel files to third parties is often regulated as well, requiring such procedures as employees' written consent for disclosure.

At the federal level, numerous laws and regulations restrict access to and disclosure of employee personnel information. An example here is the Americans With Disabilities Act (ADA) and its provisions regarding the confidentiality of medical information. There is, however, no general federal privacy law covering private employees. Public employees' privacy rights are protected by the Privacy Act of 1974.

EEO Report

Under the Civil Rights Act and Affirmative Action Programs Regulations, private employers with more than 100 employees (50 for federal contractors) are required to file an annual report with the Equal Employment Opportunity Commission (EEOC). The basis of the report is the revised EEO-1 form, especially the section requesting employment data, shown in Exhibit 13.14.[35] Data are to be reported for combinations of job categories and race/ethnicity classifications. The data may be gathered from organization records, visual inspection, or a self-report. Detailed instructions and questions and answers are available online (*www.eeoc.gov*). They cover issues such as definitions of job categories and race/ethnicity classification, and data collection. While the report is to be included in the federal contractor's affirmative action plan (AAP), the OFCCP has not yet provided guidance on how to incorporate the data from the revised EEO-1 form into availability determination, establishment of placement goals, identification of problem areas, or development of action-oriented programs (see Chapter 3). The EEOC has a web-based system for reporting and will accept paper forms only if the employer does not have Internet access.

Legal Audits

It is highly desirable to periodically conduct audits or reviews of the organization's degree of compliance with laws and regulations pertaining to staffing. The audit forces the organization to study and specify what in fact its staffing practices are and to compare these current practices against legally desirable and required practices. Results can be used to identify potential legal trouble spots and to map out changes in staffing practices that will serve to minimize potential liability and reduce the risk of lawsuits being filed against the organization. Note that development of AAPs and reports includes a large audit and review component. They do not, however, cover the entire legal spectrum of staffing practices, nor do they require sufficient depth of analysis of staffing practices in some areas. For these reasons, AAPs and reports are not sufficient as legal audits, though they are immensely important and useful inputs to a legal audit.

The audit could be conducted by the organization's own legal counsel. Alternately, the HR department might first conduct a self-audit and then review its findings with legal counsel. Conducting an audit after involvement in employment litigation is also recommended.[36]

Training for Managers and Employees

Training for managers and employees in employment law and compliance requirements is not only a sound practice but increasingly a defense point for the organization in employment litigation. The following statement illustrates this: "Recent judicial and agency activity make clear that training is no longer a discretionary

EXHIBIT 13.14   Employer Information Report EEO-1 Form

Job Categories	Number of Employees (Report employees in only one category)														
	Race/Ethnicity														
	Hispanic or Latino		Not-Hispanic or Latino												Total Col A–N
			Male						Female						
	Male	Female	White	Black or African American	Native Hawaiian or other Pacific Islander	Asian	American Indian or Alaska Native	Two or more races	White	Black or African American	Native Hawaiian or other Pacific Islander	Asian	American Indian or Alaska Native	Two or more races	
	A	B	C	D	E	F	G	H	I	J	K	L	M	N	O
Executive/Senior Level Officials and Managers 1.1															
First/Mid-Level Officials and Managers 1.2															
Professionals 2															
Technicians 3															
Sales Workers 4															
Administrative Support Workers 5															
Craft Workers 6															
Operatives 7															
Laborers and Helpers 8															
Service Workers 9															
TOTAL 10															
PREVIOUS YEAR TOTAL 11															

HR activity—it is essential. The question is not whether your company is going to provide it, but how long will it have to suffer the costly consequences of neglect. A carefully crafted, effectively executed, methodically measured, and frequently fine-tuned employment practices training program for managers and employees is a powerful component of a strategic HRD (human resource development) plan that aligns vital corporate values with daily practices. The costs of neglect are serious. The benefits are compelling and fundamental to long-term success. . . . Adequate, effective, and regularly scheduled employment law and practices training is now the rule, not the exception."[37] The constantly changing employment law landscape reinforces the need for training. New laws, regulations, and court rulings can all redefine permissible and impermissible staffing practices.[38]

Though the requirements for employment law training are still developing, it appears as though there are several desirable components to be incorporated into it: (1) the training should be for all members of the organization; (2) basic harassment and discrimination training should be given immediately to new employees, managers should receive additional training, and refresher training should occur periodically and when special circumstances arise, such as a significant change in policy or practice; (3) the trainers should have special expertise in employment law and practice; (4) the training content should be substantive and cover EEO practices in several staffing areas—such as recruitment, hiring, succession planning, and promotion—as pertains to the numerous EEO laws and regulations; training in other areas of HR, such as compensation and benefits, should also be provided; and (5) the training materials should also be substantive, incorporate the organization's specific harassment and discrimination policies, and allow for both information presentation and active practice by the participants.[39] Trainees should learn which EEO actions they can implement on their own and which actions should be referred to the HR department. Finally, the training should be matched with diversity initiatives to avoid an overly legalistic perspective.[40]

Dispute Resolution

Employment laws and regulations naturally lead to claims of their violation by job applicants and employees. If the claim is filed with an external agency, such as the EEOC, the dispute resolution procedures described in Chapter 2 (Laws and Regulations section) are applied. In the case of the EEOC, by providing mediation as an alternative dispute resolution (ADR) procedure (*www.eeoc.gov*), it seeks to settle disputes quickly and without formal investigation and litigation. The EEOC provides, without a fee, a trained mediator to help the employer and the job applicant (or employee) reconcile their differences and reach a satisfactory resolution. The process is confidential, any records or notes are destroyed at its conclusion, and nothing that is revealed may be used subsequently in investigation or litigation should the dispute not be resolved.

For claims of discrimination (or other grievances) made internally, the organization will likely offer some form of ADR to resolve the dispute. Exhibit 13.15 shows the numerous approaches to ADR that might be used.

Sometimes new hires are required as part of an employment contract to sign a provision waiving their protected rights under civil rights laws to file or participate in a proceeding against the organization and to instead use only a specified ADR system to resolve complaints. The EEOC has issued guidance indicating that such waiver provisions are null and void, and that their existence cannot stop the EEOC from enforcing the law.[41] The EEOC may pursue a discrimination claim even when the employee has signed an ADR waiver.

The Special Case of Arbitration

With arbitration as the ADR procedure, the employer and the job applicant (or employee) agree in advance to submit their dispute to a neutral third-party arbitrator, who will issue a final and binding decision. Such arbitration agreements usually include statutory discrimination claims, meaning that the employee agrees to not pursue charges of discrimination against the employer by any means (e.g., lawsuit) except arbitration. The courts have ruled that such arbitration agreements generally are legally permissible and enforceable. However, such agreements do not serve as a bar to pursuit by the EEOC of a discrimination claim seeking victim-specific relief.

The arbitration agreement and process must meet many specific, suggested standards in order to be enforceable.[42] For example, the agreement must be "knowing

---

EXHIBIT 13.15 Alternative Dispute Resolution Approaches

Approach	Description
Negotiation	Employer and employee discuss complaint with goal of resolving complaint.
Fact finding	A neutral person, from inside or outside the organization, investigates a complaint and develops findings that may be the basis for resolving the complaint.
Peer review	A panel of employees and managers work together to resolve the complaint.
Mediation	A neutral person (mediator) from within or outside the organization helps the parties negotiate a mutually acceptable agreement. Mediator is trained in mediation methods. Settlement is not imposed.
Arbitration	A neutral person (arbitrator) from within or outside the organization conducts formal hearing and issues a decision that is binding on the parties.

and voluntary," meaning that it is clearly written, obvious as to purpose, and presented to the employee as a separate document for a signature. Other suggested standards include the following:

- The arbitrator must be a neutral party.
- The process should provide for more than minimal discovery (presentation of evidence).
- The same remedies as permitted by the law should be allowed.
- The employee should have the right to hire an attorney, and the employer should reimburse the employee a portion of the attorney's fees.
- The employee should not have to bear excessive responsibility for the cost of the arbitrator.
- The types of claims (e.g., sex discrimination, retaliation) subject to arbitration should be indicated.
- The arbitrator should issue a written award.

These points are complex, indicating that legal counsel should be sought prior to use of arbitration agreements.

SUMMARY

The multiple and complex set of activities collectively known as a staffing system must be integrated and coordinated throughout the organization. Such management of the staffing system requires both careful administration and evaluation, as well as compliance with legal mandates.

To manage the staffing system, the usual organizational arrangement in all but very small organizations is to create an identifiable staffing or employment function and place it within the HR department. That function then manages the staffing system at the corporate and/or plant and office levels. Numerous types of jobs, both specialist and generalist, are found within the staffing function. Entry into these jobs, and movement among them, is very fluid and does not follow any set career mobility path.

The myriad staffing activities require staffing policies to establish general staffing principles and procedures to guide the conduct of those activities. Lack of clear policies and procedures can lead to misguided and inconsistent staffing practices, as well as potentially illegal ones. Staffing technology can help achieve these consistencies and aid in improving staffing system efficiency. Electronic systems are increasingly being used to conduct a wide range of staffing tasks; they have a mixed bag of advantages and disadvantages. Outsourcing of staffing activities is also being experimented with as a way of improving staffing system operation and results.

Evaluation of the effectiveness of the staffing system should proceed along several fronts. First is assessment of the staffing system from a process perspective. Here, it is desirable to examine the degree of standardization (consistency) of the process, as well as a staffing flowchart in order to identify deviations in staffing practice and bottlenecks. The results of the process according to indicators such as yield ratios and time lapse (cycle time), along with the costs of staffing system operation, should also be estimated. Finally, the organization should consider assessing the satisfaction of staffing system users, such as managers and job applicants.

Various laws require maintenance of numerous records and protection of privacy. It is desirable to periodically conduct a legal audit of all the organization's staffing activities. This will help identify potential legal trouble spots that require attention. Employment law training for managers and employees is increasingly becoming necessary. Methods for addressing employment disputes, known as ADRs, should be explored.

DISCUSSION QUESTIONS

1. What are the advantages of having a centralized staffing function, as opposed to letting each manager be totally responsible for all staffing activities in his or her unit?

2. What are examples of staffing tasks and activities that cannot or should not be simply delegated to a staffing information system?

3. What are the advantages and disadvantages of outsourcing an entire staffing system to a vendor?

4. In developing a report on the effectiveness of a staffing process for entry-level jobs, what factors would you address and why?

5. How would you try to get individual managers to be more aware of the legal requirements of staffing systems and to take steps to ensure that they themselves engaged in legal staffing actions?

ETHICAL ISSUES

1. It has been suggested that the use of staffing technology and software is wrong because it dehumanizes the staffing experience, making it nothing but a mechanical process that treats applicants like digital widgets. Evaluate this assertion.

2. Since there are no standard ways of creating staffing process results and cost metrics, is there a need for some sort of oversight of how these data are calculated, reported, and used within the organization? Explain.

APPLICATIONS

Learning About Jobs in Staffing

The purpose of this application is to have you learn in detail about a particular job in staffing currently being performed by an individual. The individual could be a staffing job holder in the HR department of a company or public agency (state or local government), a nonprofit agency, a staffing firm, an employment agency, a consulting firm, or the state employment (job) service. The individual may be someone who performs staffing tasks full time, such as a recruiter, interviewer, counselor, employment representative, or employment manager. Or, the individual may be someone who performs staffing duties as part of the job, such as the HR manager in a small company or an HR generalist in a specific plant or site.

Contact the job holder and arrange for an interview with that person. Explain that the purpose of the interview is for you to learn about the person's job in terms of job requirements (tasks and KSAOs) and job rewards (both extrinsic and intrinsic). To prepare for the interview, review the examples of job descriptions for staffing jobs in Exhibits 13.2 and 13.3, obtain any information you can about the organization, and then develop a set of questions to ask the job holder. Either before or at the interview, be sure to obtain a copy of the job holder's job description if one is available. Based on the written and interview information, prepare a report of your investigation. The report should cover the following:

1. The organization's products and services, size, and staffing (employment) function
2. The job holder's job title, and why you chose that person's job to study
3. A summary of the tasks performed by the job holder and the KSAOs necessary for the job
4. A summary of the extrinsic and intrinsic rewards received by the job holder
5. Unique characteristics of the job that you did not expect to be part of the job

Evaluating Staffing Process Results

The Keepon Trucking Company (KTC) is a manufacturer of custom-built trucks. It does not manufacture any particular truck lines, styles, or models. Rather, it builds trucks to customers' specifications; these trucks are used for specialty purposes such as snow removal, log hauling, and military cargo hauling. One year ago, KTC received a new, large order that would take three years to complete and required the external hiring of 100 new assemblers. To staff this particular job, the HR department manager of nonexempt employment hurriedly developed and implemented a special staffing process for filling these new vacancies. Applicants were recruited from three sources: newspaper ads, employee referrals, and a local employment agency. All applicants generated by these methods were subjected to a common selection and decision-making process. All offer receivers were given the same terms and conditions in their job offer letters and were told there was no room for any negotiation. All vacancies were eventually filled.

After the first year of the contract, the manager of nonexempt employment, Dexter Williams, decided to pull together some data in an attempt to determine how well the staffing process for the assembler jobs had worked. Since he had not originally planned on doing any evaluation, Dexter was able to retrieve only the following data to help him with his evaluation:

Exhibit
Staffing Data for Filling the Job of Assembler

Recruitment Source	Applicants	Offer Receivers	Start as New Hires	Remaining at Six Months
Newspaper ads				
No. apps.	300	70	50	35
Avg. no. days	30	30	10	
Employee referral				
No. apps.	60	30	30	27
Avg. no. days	20	10	10	
Employment agency				
No. apps.	400	20	20	8
Avg. no. days	40	20	10	

1. Determine the yield ratios (offer receivers/applicants, new hires/applicants), time lapse or cycle times (days to offer, days to start), and retention rates associated with each recruitment source.
2. What is the relative effectiveness of the three sources in terms of yield ratios, cycle times, and retention rates?
3. What are some possible reasons for the fact that the three sources differ in their relative effectiveness?
4. What would you recommend that Dexter do differently in the future to improve his evaluation of the staffing process?

ENDNOTES

1. T. H. Davenport, J. Harris, and J. Shapiro, "Competing on Talent Analytics," *Harvard Business Review*, Oct. 2010, pp. 52–58.

2. US Census Bureau, "Statistics About Business Size (Including Small Business) From the US Census Bureau" (*www.census.gov/epcd/www/smallbus.html*), accessed 1/28/11.

3. H. G. Heneman III and R. A. Berkley, "Applicant Attraction Practices and Outcomes Among Small Businesses," *Journal of Small Business Management*, Jan. 1999, pp. 53–74.

4. E. E. Lawler III and A. A. Mohrman, *Creating a Strategic Human Resources Organization* (Stanford, CA: Stanford University Press, 2003), pp. 15–20.

5. M. Hammers, "Sun Trust Bank Combines 28 Recruiting and Screening Systems Into One," *Workforce Management*, Dec. 3, 2003 (*www.workforce.com*).

6. Lawler and Mohrman, *Creating a Strategic Human Resources Organization*, p. 33.

7. J. Vocino, "HR Compensation Continues to Rise," *HR Magazine*, Nov. 2004, pp. 72–88.

8. Mercer Human Resource Consulting, *Transforming HR for Business Results* (New York: author, 2004), p. 9.

9. A. Rosenthal, "Hiring Edge," *Human Resource Executive*, Apr. 2000, pp. 96–98.

10. J. S. Arthur, "Title Wave," *Human Resource Executive*, Oct. 2000, pp. 115–118; K. J. Dunham, "Tapping Talent," *Wall Street Journal*, Apr. 10, 2001, p. B14.

11. J. A. Colquitt, "On the Dimensionality of Organizational Justice: A Construct Validation of a Measure," *Journal of Applied Psychology*, 2001, 86, pp. 386–400; J. A. Colquitt, D. E. Conlon, M. J. Wesson, C. O. Porter, and N. K. Yee, "Justice at the Millennium: A Meta-Analytic Review of 25 Years of Organizational Justice Research," *Journal of Applied Psychology*, 2001, 86, pp. 425–445.

12. R. E. Ployhart and A. M. Ryan, "Toward an Explanation of Applicant Reactions: An Examination of Organizational Justice and Attribution Frameworks," *Organizational Behavior and Human Decision Processes*, 1997, 72, pp. 308–335; D. M. Truxillo, T. N. Bauer, M. A. Campion, and M. E. Paronto, "Selection Fairness Information and Applicant Reactions: A Longitudinal Field Study," *Journal of Applied Psychology*, 2002, 87, pp. 1020–1031; T. N. Bauer, D. M. Truxillo, R. J. Sanchez, J. Craig, P. Ferrara, and M. A. Campion, "Applicant Reactions to Selection: Development of the Selection Procedural Justice Scale (SPJS)," *Personnel Psychology*, 2001, 54, pp. 387–419; S. W. Gilliland, "Effects of Procedural and Distributive Justice on Reactions to a Selection System," *Journal of Applied Psychology*, 1994, 79, pp. 691–701; C. W. Wanberg, L. W. Bunce, and M. B. Gavin, "Perceived Fairness of Layoffs Among Individuals Who Have Been Laid Off: A Longitudinal Study," *Personnel Psychology*, 1999, 52, pp. 59–84; J. Brockner, S. L. Grover, and M. D. Blonder, "Predictors of Survivors' Job Investment Following Layoffs: A Field Study," *Journal of Applied Psychology*, 1988, 73, pp. 436–442.

13. H. Williams, "e-HR 2010: Key HR Software Developments Ahead," *Personnel Today*, Dec. 1, 2009, p. 10; Anonymous, "What Are the Latest Trends in HR Applications Adoption," *HR Focus*, Dec. 2009, pp. 10–11; E. Frauenheim, "Core HR Technology Takes Center Stage," *Workforce Management*, Oct. 2007 (*www.workforce.com*).

14. Brass Ring, Inc. "Measuring the Value of a Talent Management System," Jan. 7, 2005 (*www.brassring.com*); P. Buckley, K. Minette, D. Joy, and J. Michaels, "The Use of an Automated Employment Recruiting and Screening System for Temporary Professional Employees: A Case Study," *Human Resource Management*, 2004, 43, pp. 233–241; D. Chapman and J. Webster, "The Use of Technologies in the Recruiting, Screening, and Selection Processes for Job Candidates," *International Journal of Selection and Assessment*, 2003, 11, pp. 113–120; S. Greengard, "Seven Myths About Recruiting Technology," *Workforce Management*, Aug. 10, 2004

(*www.workforce.com*); J. W. Jones and K. D. Dages, "Technology Trends in Staffing and Assessment, A Practical Note," *International Journal of Selection and Assessment*, 2003, 11, pp. 247–252.

15. B. Roberts, "How to Get Satisfaction from SAAS," *HR Magazine*, Apr. 2010 (*www.shrm.org/publications/hrmagazine*); L. Grensing-Pophal, "Mission: Organized HR!" *Credit Union Management*, Oct. 2008, pp. 36–39; E. Frauenheim, "Talent Tools Still Essential," *Workforce Management*, Apr. 2009, pp. 20–26.

16. M. Frase-Blunt, "A Recruiting Spigot," *HR Magazine*, Apr. 2003, pp. 71–79.

17. WorldatWork, *The State of Human Resources Outsourcing: 2004–2005* (Scottsdale, AZ: author, 2005); E. Zimmerman, "B of A and Big-Time Outsourcing," *Workforce Management*, Apr. 2001, pp. 51–54; B. E. Rosenthal, "How to Outsource Everything in HR," *SHRM HR Outsourcing Library*, Aug. 2006 (*www.shrm.org*).

18. E. Van Slyke, "Laying the Groundwork for HR Outsourcing," *Workforce Management*, Jan. 2010 (*www.workforce.com*); P. Meskanik, "Critical Success Factors for Recruiting Process Outsourcing," *Oil and Gas Journal*, Jan. 1, 2009, pp. 8–11.

19. B. S. Klaas, J. McClendon, T. Gainey, and H. Yang, *HR Outsourcing in Small and Medium Enterprises: A Field Study of the Use and Impact of Professional Employer Organizations* (Alexandria, VA: Society for Human Resource Management Foundation, 2004).

20. B. Siegel, "Outsourced Recruiting," in N. C. Burkholder, P. J. Edwards, and L. Sartain (eds.), *On Staffing* (Hoboken, NJ: Wiley, 2004), pp. 116–132.

21. J. Harney, "Integrating Payroll With Benefits Administration Transforms HR for Charmant," *Outsourcing Journal*, Dec. 2007 (*www.outsourcing-journal.com/dec2007-hr.html*).

22. P. Babcock, "Slicing Off Pieces of HR," *HR Magazine*, July 2004, pp. 71–76; J. C. Berkshire, "Seeking Full Partnership," *HR Magazine*, July 2004, pp. 89–96; D. Dell, *HR Outsourcing* (New York: The Conference Board, 2004); E. Esen, *Human Resource Outsourcing* (Alexandria, VA: Society for Human Resource Management, 2004); S. Greengard, "Pulling the Plug," *Workforce Management*, July 2004, pp. 43–46; R. J. Grossman, "Sticker Shock," *HR Magazine*, July 2004, pp. 79–86; T. Starner, "Measuring Success," *Human Resource Executive*, Oct. 16, 2004, pp. 49–50.

23. S. Overman, "Staffing Management: Measure What Matters," *Staffing Management Magazine*, Oct. 1, 2008 (*www.shrm.org/publications/staffingmanagementmagazine*); B. Roberts, "Analyze This!" *HR Magazine*, Oct. 1, 2009 (*www.shrm.com/publications/hrmagazine*); J. Fitz-enz, *The ROI of Human Capital: Measuring the Economic Value of Employee Performance* (New York: AMACOM, 2000); J. E. Edwards, J. C. Scott, and N. S. Raju, *The Human Resources Program-Evaluation Handbook* (Thousand Oaks, CA: Sage Publications, 2003); M. A. Huselid, B. E. Becker, and R. W. Beatty, *The Workforce Scorecard: Managing Human Capital to Execute Strategy* (Boston: Harvard Business School Press, 2005); Society for Human Resource Management, *SHRM Human Capital Benchmarking Study* (Alexandria, VA: author, 2007).

24. J. Sullivan, "HR's Burden of Proof," *Workforce Management*, Jan. 2007, p. 26; I. L. Goldstein and Associates, *Training and Development in Organizations* (San Francisco: Jossey-Bass, 1991).

25. Roberts, "Analyze This!"; B. Roberts, "How to Put Analytics on Your Side," *HR Magazine*, Oct. 1, 2010 (*www.shrm.com/publications/hrmagazine*).

26. L. Micco, "Lockheed Wins the Best Catches," *Employment Management Association Today*, Spring 1997, pp. 18–20; E. R. Silverman, "The Fast Track," *Human Resource Executive*, Oct. 1998, pp. 30–34.

27. L. Klutz, *Time to Fill/Time to Start: 2002 Staffing Metrics Survey* (Alexandria, VA: Society for Human Resource Management, 2003).

28. Fitz-enz, *The ROI of Human Capital: Measuring the Economic Value of Employee Performance*; Society for Human Resource Management, *SHRM Human Capital Benchmarking Study*.

29. Society for Human Resource Management, *2002 SHRM/EMA Staffing Metrics Study* (Alexandria, VA: author, 2003); Staffing.Org, *2003 Recruiting Metrics and Performance Benchmark Report* (Willow Grove, PA: author, 2003).

30. K. Burns, "Metrics Are Everything: Why, What and How to Choose," in Burkholder, Edwards, and Sartain (eds.), *On Staffing*, pp. 364–371.

31. H. G. Heneman III, D. L. Huett, R. J. Lavigna, and D. Ogsten, "Assessing Managers' Satisfaction With Staffing Service," *Personnel Psychology*, 1995, 48, pp. 163–173.

32. H. P. Coxson, "The Double-Edged Sword of Personnel Files and Employee Records," *Legal Report*, Society for Human Resource Management, 1992; Warren Gorham Lamont, *How Long Do We Have to Keep These Records?* (Boston: author, 1993).

33. Coxson, "The Double-Edged Sword of Personnel Files and Employee Records."

34. M. W. Finkin, *Privacy in Employment Law*, third ed. (Washington, DC: BNA Books, 2009), pp. 650–657; International Personnel Management Association, "Employee Privacy and Record-keeping—I and II," *IPMA News*, Aug. and Sept. 1998, pp. 16–18.

35. V. J. Hoffman, "Equal Opportunity Reporting: New Requirements, New Best Practices," *Legal Report*, Society for Human Resource Management, July–Aug. 2006 (*www.shrm.org/hrresources/lrpt_published/CMS_018229.asp#P-10_0*); R. Zeidner, "EEO-1 Changes," *HR Magazine*, May 2006, pp. 61–64.

36. J. W. Janove, "It's Not Over, Even When It's Over," *HR Magazine*, Feb. 2004, pp. 123–131.

37. W. K. Turner and C. S. Thrutchley, "Employment Law and Practices Training: No Longer the Exception—It's the Rule," *Legal Report*, Society for Human Resource Management, July–Aug. 2002, p. 1.

38. A. Smith, "Managerial Training Needed as Hiring Resumes," (*www.shrm.org/legalissues/federalresources/pages/managerialtraininghiring.aspx*), accessed 3/16/10; D. G. Bower, "Don't Cut Legal Compliance Training," *Workforce Management*, Feb. 2009 (*www.workforce.com*).

39. S. K. Williams, "The New Law of Training," *HR Magazine*, May 2004, pp. 115–118.

40. J. A. Segal, "Unlimited Check-Writing Authority for Supervisors?" *HR Magazine*, Feb. 2007, pp. 119–124; J. C. Ramirez, "A Different Bias," *Human Resource Executive*, May 16, 2006, pp. 37–40.

41. Equal Employment Opportunity Commission, *EEOC Enforcement Guidance on Non-Waivable Employee Rights Under EEOC Enforcement Statutes* (Washington, DC: author, 1997).

42. M. E. Bruno, "The Future of ADR in the Workplace," *Compensation and Benefits Review*, Nov.–Dec. 2001, pp. 46–59; C. Hirschman, "Order in the Hear," *HR Magazine*, July 2001, pp. 58–64; L. P. Postol, "To Arbitrate Employment Disputes or Not, That Is the Question," *Legal Report*, Society for Human Resource Management, Sept.–Oct. 2001, pp. 5–8.

CHAPTER FOURTEEN

Retention Management

Learning Objectives and Introduction
    Learning Objectives
    Introduction

Turnover and Its Causes
    Nature of the Problem
    Types of Turnover
    Causes of Turnover

Analysis of Turnover
    Measurement
    Reasons for Leaving
    Costs and Benefits

Retention Initiatives: Voluntary Turnover
    Current Practices and Deciding to Act
    Desirability of Leaving
    Ease of Leaving
    Alternatives

Retention Initiatives: Discharge
    Performance Management
    Progressive Discipline

Retention Initiatives: Downsizing
    Weighing Advantages and Disadvantages
    Staffing Levels and Quality
    Alternatives to Downsizing
    Employees Who Remain

Legal Issues
    Separation Laws and Regulations
    Performance Appraisal

Summary

Discussion Questions

Ethical Issues

Applications

Tanglewood Stores Case

LEARNING OBJECTIVES AND INTRODUCTION

Learning Objectives

- Be able to differentiate among the types and causes of employee turnover
- Recognize the different reasons employees leave their jobs
- Evaluate the costs and benefits of turnover
- Learn about the variety of techniques companies use to limit turnover
- See how performance management and progressive discipline limit discharge turnover
- Understand how companies manage downsizing
- Recognize a variety of legal issues that affect separation policies and practices

Introduction

Even the best recruiting and selection system in the world will be of little value to an organization if the new employees leave their jobs soon after being hired. Therefore, the establishment of effective systems for retaining employees is a crucial part of the staffing process. While some loss of employees is both inevitable and desirable, retention management seeks to ensure that the organization is able to keep enough employees with important knowledge, skill, ability, and other characteristics (KSAOs) to generate future success.

From a strategic perspective, some turnover of employees is actually good. For example, when an employee who lacks strategic competencies leaves, an opportunity arises to find a more suitable replacement. On the other hand, if a highly productive employee with unique skills leaves, the organization may have trouble finding a suitable replacement. In this case, turnover can severely limit the organization's ability to achieve strategic goals. Therefore, throughout the chapter we will highlight how turnover is a complex phenomenon with both positive and negative aspects.

The chapter begins with a look at three types of turnover—voluntary, discharge, and downsizing. Retention management must be based on a thorough analysis of these three types of turnover. Analyses include measuring turnover, determining employees' reasons for leaving, and assessing the costs and benefits of turnover. Attention then turns to retention initiatives. As we will see, organizations often encourage retention by focusing on the extrinsic nature of jobs; this involves enacting policies like generous compensation plans, matching job offers from competitors, developing unique benefits programs, and providing incentives for long-term service. Organizations can also improve the intrinsic quality of jobs by providing more satisfying working conditions, improving the social nature of interactions with coworkers, and ensuring that supervisors engage in effective and motivational leadership behaviors. Next, we discuss how to reduce employee discharges through both performance management and progressive discipline initiatives. Although layoffs are generally avoided in most organizations, at times downsizing is necessary; thus, we will discuss some strategies for effectively and ethically reducing head count. The final topic involves the myriad laws and regulations pertaining to employee separation from the organization.

TURNOVER AND ITS CAUSES

Nature of the Problem

The focus of this book so far has been on acquiring and deploying people in ways that contribute to organizational effectiveness. Attention now shifts to retaining employees as another part of staffing that can contribute to organizational effectiveness. Although turnover is often seen as a detriment to organizational performance, there are several positive, functional outcomes. An extremely important part of employee retention strategy and tactics thus must involve careful assessment of both retention costs and benefits and the design of retention initiatives that provide positive benefits at reasonable cost to the organization. Moreover, retention strategies and tactics must focus not only on how many employees are retained but exactly who is retained. Both within and between jobs and organization levels, some employees are "worth" more than others in terms of their contributions to job and organizational effectiveness. Another important matter for the retention agenda is thus making special efforts to retain what we call "high-value" employees.

Retention must be tackled realistically, however, since some amount of employee turnover is inevitable.[1] People constantly move out of organizations voluntarily, and organizations shed employees as well. The Department of Labor estimates that employees between the ages of 18 and 44 have held an average of 11 jobs, and among employees aged 33–38, 58% of jobs lasted less than two years. While job-hopping decreases and median tenure increases with age, some amount of turnover persists throughout workers' careers. In some industries, high voluntary turnover is a continual fact of life and cost of doing business. Turnover among sit-down restaurant managers, for example, hovers around 50% annually year after year. It is not clear that even costly retention initiatives, such as substantial pay level increases or converting managers to franchisees, can reduce this turnover. A final example is that in 2009, the Department of Labor estimates there were over 28,000 mass layoffs (those involving 50 or more employees), creating nearly 3 million unemployed workers. This was a relatively high number of mass layoffs due to generally poor economic conditions that year.

When people voluntarily leave an organization, they do so for a variety of reasons, only some of which are potentially avoidable (controllable) by the organization. Sound retention management thus must be based on a gathering and analysis of employees' reasons for leaving. Specific retention initiatives must be tailor-made to address these reasons and hopefully neutralize them to take them out of play, but in a cost-effective way. Against this backdrop we now turn to a more detailed discussion of types of turnover and their causes.

Types of Turnover

There are many different types of employee turnover. Exhibit 14.1 provides a basic classification of these types.[2] It can be seen that turnover is either voluntary (initiated by the employee) or involuntary (initiated by the organization).

Voluntary

Voluntary turnover is broken down into avoidable and unavoidable turnover. Avoidable turnover is that which potentially could have been prevented by certain organization actions, such as a pay raise or a new job assignment. Unavoidable turnover represents employee quits that the organization probably could not have prevented, such as people who quit and withdraw from the labor force through retirement or by returning to school. Other examples of unavoidable turnover are people who quit due to dual career problems, pursuit of a new and different career, health problems that require taking a different type of job, child-care and elder-care responsibilities, or leaving the country. The line of demarcation between avoidable and unavoidable turnover is fuzzy and depends on decisions by the organization as to exactly what types of voluntary turnover it thinks it could potentially prevent.

A further line of demarcation involves just avoidable turnover, in which the organization explicitly chooses to either try to prevent or not try to prevent employees from quitting. As shown in Exhibit 14.1, the organization will try to prevent high-value employees from quitting—those employees with high job performance, strong KSAOs, key intellectual capital, high promotion potential, high training and development invested in them, and high experience and who are difficult to replace. The organization is less likely to try to retain low-value employees.

Involuntary

Involuntary turnover is split into discharge and downsizing types. Discharge turnover is aimed at the individual employee, due to discipline and/or job performance problems. Downsizing turnover typically targets groups of employees and is also known as a reduction in force (RIF). It occurs as part of an organizational restructuring or cost-reduction program to improve organizational effectiveness and increase shareholder value (stock price). RIFs may occur as permanent or temporary layoffs for the entire organization, or as part of a plant or site closing or relocation. RIFs may also occur as the result of a merger or acquisition, in which some employees in the combined workforces are viewed as redundant in the positions they hold. It is important to recognize that even though the organization is considering terminating employees through discharge and downsizing, it can take many steps to lessen or eliminate discharges or downsizing, thereby having positive employee-retention impacts.

EXHIBIT 14.1   Types of Employee Turnover

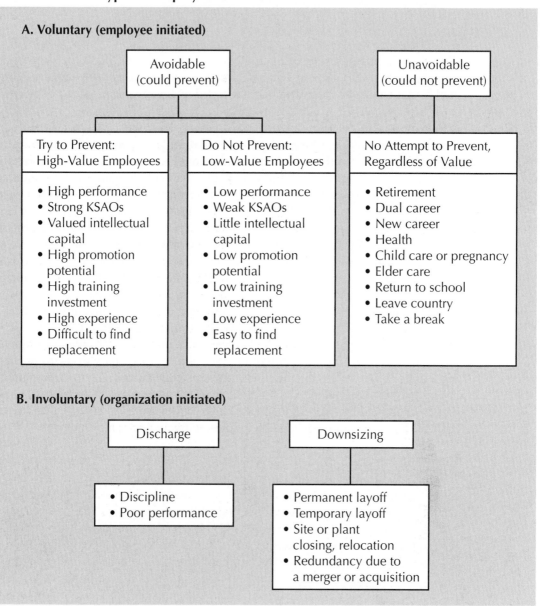

A. Voluntary (employee initiated)

Avoidable (could prevent)		Unavoidable (could not prevent)

Try to Prevent: High-Value Employees	Do Not Prevent: Low-Value Employees	No Attempt to Prevent, Regardless of Value
• High performance • Strong KSAOs • Valued intellectual capital • High promotion potential • High training investment • High experience • Difficult to find replacement	• Low performance • Weak KSAOs • Little intellectual capital • Low promotion potential • Low training investment • Low experience • Easy to find replacement	• Retirement • Dual career • New career • Health • Child care or pregnancy • Elder care • Return to school • Leave country • Take a break

B. Involuntary (organization initiated)

Discharge	Downsizing
• Discipline • Poor performance	• Permanent layoff • Temporary layoff • Site or plant closing, relocation • Redundancy due to a merger or acquisition

The different types of turnover have different underlying causes, leading the organization to think very selectively in terms of the different types of retention strategies and tactics it wishes to deploy. It is first necessary to explore the underlying causes of turnover, since knowledge of those causes is necessary for developing and implementing retention strategies and tactics.

Causes of Turnover

Separate models of turnover causes are presented for each of the three turnover types that the organization may seek to influence with its retention strategies and tactics. These are voluntary, discharge, and downsizing turnover.

Voluntary Turnover

Through considerable research, various models of voluntary turnover have been developed and tested.[3] The model shown in Exhibit 14.2 is a distillation of that research.

EXHIBIT 14.2   Causes (Drivers) of Voluntary Turnover

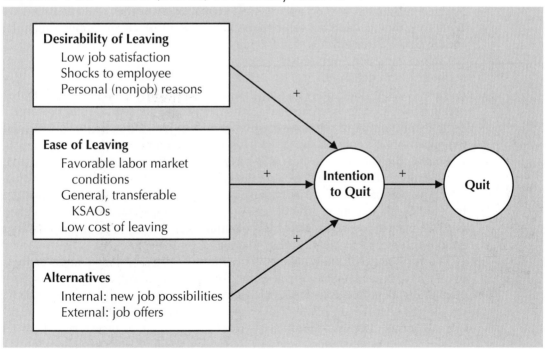

NOTE: The relative importance of the drivers and how they interact to determine the decision to quit vary across situations.

The employee's intention to quit depends on three general factors: the perceived desirability of leaving, the perceived ease of leaving, and alternatives available to the employee. The perceived desirability of leaving is often an outgrowth of a poor person/job or person/organization match. One form of the mismatch may be a difference between the rewards provided by the job and the rewards desired by the employee, leading to job dissatisfaction. In addition to mismatches, certain shocks may occur to the employee that trigger a more impulsive intention to quit, such as finding out that the organization is being acquired and one's job might be eliminated. Interpersonal conflicts with coworkers or supervisors are another type of shock that could lead to turnover. Finally, employees may find it desirable to leave for personal, nonjob reasons that are unavoidable.

The perceived ease of leaving represents a sense of lack of barriers to leaving and the likelihood of finding a new job. Labor market conditions, specifically the tightness or looseness of the labor market, are important for the employee in helping to frame an intention to quit. Tight labor markets fuel the intention-to-quit flames, and loose labor markets douse the flames. The flames may also be doused by the employee's knowing that many of his or her KSAOs are specific and only useful to the current employer. Ease of leaving may also be heightened by a low cost of leaving, such as not having to give up valuable benefits, because none were provided by the organization. In short, the ease of leaving will be higher when labor market conditions provide plentiful job opportunities with other organizations, when the employee possesses KSAOs that are transferable to other organizations, and when the departure is not a very costly proposition for the employee. Employees who are highly embedded in their jobs, organizations, and communities are less likely to leave. Some of the factors that increase embeddedness can be influenced by the organization, such as interpersonal relationships with supervisors and coworkers or levels of training in company-specific human capital. Other factors are beyond the organization's control, such as ties to the local community.[4]

Finally, the intention to quit will depend on other job alternatives available to the employee within and outside the organization. Specifically, the availability of promotion, transfer, and relocation alternatives may lessen or eliminate the employee's intentions to quit, even though the employee is very dissatisfied with the current job. Also, actual or potential receipt of a job offer from another employer represents a clear external alternative for the employee.

The final stage of the turnover process is the formation of intention to turnover, which is accompanied by a search for alternatives. Job searching has been empirically identified as a close correlate of turnover. However, employers should not assume that it is too late to make efforts to keep an employee who is seeking another job. Directly addressing what changes would be necessary to keep an employee is a good strategy in this case. Many employees who are looking for alternative jobs would be willing to stay with their current employers if their jobs were sufficiently modified.

The model in Exhibit 14.2 illustrates both avoidable and unavoidable turnover. Retention initiatives must be directed toward the avoidable types of turnover: turnover due to job dissatisfaction, employee possession of general and transferable KSAOs, a low cost of leaving, the availability of other job opportunities within the organization, and the employee's receipt of a job offer.

Discharge Turnover

Discharge turnover is due to extremely poor person/job matches, particularly the mismatch between job requirements and KSAOs. One form of the mismatch involves the employee failing to follow rules and procedures. These requirements range from the relatively minor (e.g., dress code violations, horseplay) to the very serious (e.g., bringing a firearm to work). Often it is the cumulative effect of multiple incidents that results in the discharge.

The other form of discharge turnover involves unacceptable job performance. Here, the KSAO–job requirements mismatch is severe. In fact, the employee's performance is so deficient that the organization has decided that it is intolerable and the only solution is termination.

Downsizing Turnover

Downsizing turnover reflects a staffing level mismatch in which the organization is, or is projected to be, overstaffed. In other words, the head count available exceeds the head count required. Overstaffing may be due to (1) a lack of forecasting and planning, (2) inaccuracies in forecasting and planning, (3) unanticipated changes in labor demand and/or labor supply, or (4) downturns in the economy. For example, optimistic forecasts of demand for products and services that do not materialize may lead to overstaffing, as may sudden unanticipated downturns in demand that create sudden excess head count. Or, an increasing looseness in the labor market may reduce the ease of movement, causing fewer employees to leave the organization—an unanticipated decrease in the voluntary turnover rate and thus an increase in workforce head count available. Quite naturally, these types of demand/supply imbalances create strong downsizing pressure on the organization to which it must respond.

ANALYSIS OF TURNOVER

Analysis of turnover requires that the three types of turnover be measured and benchmarked, that specific reasons for employees' leaving be identified, and that costs and benefits of each type of turnover be assessed.

Measurement

Formula

Since turnover involves the discrete action of leaving or staying with the organization, it is expressed as the proportion or percentage of employees who leave the organization in some time period. Thus:

$$\text{turnover rate} = \frac{\text{number of employees leaving}}{\text{average number of employees}} \times 100$$

Use of this formula to calculate turnover rates will require data on, and decisions about, the following: (1) what is the time period of interest (e.g., month, year), (2) what is an employee that "counts" (e.g., full time only? part time? seasonal?), and (3) how to calculate the average number of employees over the time period, such as straight or weighted average.

Breakouts and Benchmarks

Analysis and interpretation of turnover data are aided by making breakouts of the data according to various factors, including (1) type of turnover: voluntary (avoidable and unavoidable) or involuntary (discharge and downsizing); (2) type of employee (e.g., exempt–nonexempt, demographics, KSAOs, and performance level); (3) job category; and (4) geographic location. Such breakouts help in identifying how much variation in turnover there is around the overall average and pockets of the most and least severe turnover. Such data are the foundation for development of strategic retention initiatives. Human resources information systems (HRISs) are designed to process and track employee departures, so data are often readily available regarding when, where, and even why employee turnover is occurring.

It is also useful to benchmark turnover data in order to have comparative statistics that will aid in interpretation of the organization's turnover data. One benchmark is internal, looking at the trends in the organization's own turnover data over time. Such trend analysis is very useful for identifying where turnover problems are worsening or improving and for evaluating the effectiveness of retention initiatives. Internal benchmarking requires a commitment to a sustained data collection process.

The other form of benchmarking is external, in which the organization compares its own data with the current rates and turnover trends of other organizations. One major external benchmarking source is the data from the Job Openings and Labor Turnover Survey (JOLTS), collected and published by the US Department of Labor (*www.bls.gov/jlt*). The JOLTS is conducted monthly among 16,000 business establishments and provides data on total employment, job openings, hires, quits, layoffs and discharges, and other separations. Exhibit 14.3 provides representative

EXHIBIT 14.3 Data From Job Openings and Labor Turnover Survey

Annual	Hires	Quits	Layoffs and Discharges	Other Terminations
2002	45.9%	24.8%	17.9%	3.6%
2003	44.5%	22.6%	18.4%	3.5%
2004	46.9%	24.2%	17.8%	3.4%
2005	48.2%	26.2%	17.0%	3.3%
2006	47.7%	26.7%	15.8%	3.6%
2007	46.1%	25.5%	16.4%	3.2%
2008	41.1%	22.7%	17.9%	2.9%
2009	37.2%	16.8%	21.2%	3.0%

NOTE: Percentages of total nonfarm employment.

data from the JOLTS for the period between 2002 and 2009. On the website, the data are broken down by region and industry but not by occupation.

Reasons for Leaving

It is important to ascertain, record, and track the various reasons why employees leave an organization. These data are essential for measuring and analyzing turnover. At a minimum, the exit of each employee should be classified as a voluntary, discharge, or downsizing exit, thus permitting the calculation of turnover rates. To learn more about the specific reasons underlying exit decisions, however, more in-depth probing of employee motivations is necessary. Tools for conducting such probing are exit interviews, postexit surveys, and employee satisfaction surveys.[5] All three tools can be used to help gauge whether the decision to leave was voluntary, and if so, the specific reasons—thus allowing a determination of avoidable or unavoidable turnover.

Exit Interviews

Exit interviews are formally planned and conducted interviews with departing employees. In addition to helping learn the employee's reasons for leaving, exit interviews are used to explain such things as rehiring rights, benefits, and confidentiality agreements. Because of the major implication of a potentially inaccurate measurement, the organization should not dramatically alter its retention strategies on the basis of any one interview. Rather, the overall pattern of results that emerges over many interviews should be used.

It is important to ensure that exit interviews are conducted carefully. Research suggests that there are differences between the reasons for turnover that employees provide in exit interviews and the reasons employees provide in anonymous surveys.[6] Departing employees are reluctant to complain about their former employers because they don't want to burn any bridges or jeopardize future references. In response, employees may claim that they are leaving for higher pay, when in fact they are leaving because of poor working conditions or interpersonal conflicts with supervisors or coworkers.

The following are suggestions for conducting an appropriate interview that will hopefully elicit truthful information from the interviewee: (1) the interviewer should be a neutral person (normally someone from the human resources [HR] department or an external consultant) who has been trained in how to conduct exit interviews; (2) the training should cover how to put the employee at ease and explain the purposes of the interview, how to follow the structured interview format and avoid excessive probing and follow-up questions, the need for taking notes, and how to end the interview on a positive note; (3) there should be a structured interview format that contains questions about unavoidable and avoidable reasons for leaving, and for the avoidable category, the questions should focus on desirability of leaving, ease of leaving, and job alternatives (Exhibit 14.4 contains an example of structured exit interview questions, with questions focused on these three aspects); (4) the interviewer should prepare for each exit interview by reviewing the interview format and the interviewee's personnel file; (5) the interview should be conducted in a private place, before the employee's last day; and (6) the interviewee should be told that the interview is confidential and that only aggregate results will be used to help the organization better understand why employees leave and to possibly develop new retention initiatives. The organization must decide whether to conduct exit interviews with all departing employees or only those who are leaving voluntarily. The advantage of including all departing employees is that it expands the sample from which information is drawn, and even employees leaving involuntarily can provide useful information. Conducting the interview before an employee's last day can sometimes bring up issues that, if addressed, could prevent the interviewee from leaving. For example, if an exit interview reveals that an employee is only leaving for higher pay, the organization can make a counteroffer.

Postexit Surveys

To minimize departing employees' concerns about confidentiality in exit interviews and possible employer retaliation, postexit surveys might be used. It is recommended that the survey cover the same areas as the exit interview and that the survey be sent shortly after the employee's last day. Many organizations have found that online exit surveys are a convenient, inexpensive method to collect data. Online data are easily compiled into statistical reports and might be compared with other data on performance to facilitate a focus on the reasons why productive employees leave.

EXHIBIT 14.4   Examples of Exit Interview Questions

1. Current job title _____ Department/work unit _____
2. Length of time in current job _____ Length of time with organization _____
3. Are you leaving for any of the following reasons?
   retirement _____ dual career _____ new career _____ health _____
   child care or pregnancy _____ elder care _____ return to school _____
   leave the country _____ take a break _____
4. Do you have another job lined up? _____ New employer _____
5. What aspects of your new job will be better than current job? _____
6. Before deciding to leave did you check the possibility of
   job transfer _____ promotion _____ relocation _____
7. Was it easy to find another job? _____ Why? _____
8. Did many of your current skills fit with your new job? _____
9. What aspects of your job have been most satisfying? _____
   least satisfying? _____
10. What could the company have done to improve your job satisfaction? _____
11. How satisfactory has your job performance been since your last review? _____
12. What are things the company or your manager could have done to help you improve your performance? _____
13. If you could have had a different manager, would you have been more likely to stay with the company? _____
14. Are you willing to recommend the company to others as a place to work? _____
15. Would you be willing to hire back with the company? _____
16. Is there anything else you would like to tell us about your decision to leave the company? _____

Employee Satisfaction Surveys

Since employee job dissatisfaction (desirability of leaving) is known to be a potent predictor of voluntary turnover, conducting job satisfaction surveys is a good way to discover the types of job rewards that are most dissatisfying to employees and might therefore become reasons for leaving. Conducting job satisfaction surveys has the advantage of learning from all employees (at least those who respond to the survey), rather than just those who are leaving. Satisfaction survey results also give the organization information it can use to hopefully preempt turnover by making changes that will increase job satisfaction. Designing, conducting, analyzing, and interpreting results from these surveys require substantial organizational resources and should only be undertaken with the guidance of a person explicitly trained in job satisfaction survey techniques. Oftentimes a consultant is retained for this purpose. Online surveys allow managers to quickly and conveniently collect information from geographically dispersed employees.

Costs and Benefits

Costs, both financial and nonfinancial in nature, and benefits may be estimated for each of the three turnover types. Most involve actual costs or benefits, though some are potential, depending on how events transpire. Some of the costs and benefits may be estimated financially, a useful and necessary exercise. Such financial analysis must be supplemented with a careful consideration of the other costs and benefits to arrive at a reasonable estimate of the total costs and benefits of turnover. It may well turn out that the nonfinancial costs and benefits outweigh the financial ones in importance and impact for the development of retention strategies and tactics.

Voluntary Turnover

Voluntary turnover can be extremely expensive for organizations. Research consistently shows that organizations with high turnover have a low stock price, a low return on investment, low revenues, and other low financial returns.[7] Exhibit 14.5 shows the major types of costs and benefits that can occur when an employee leaves the organization.[8] An assessment of these costs and benefits could be used in the case of an employee who is threatening to leave for avoidable reasons; the assessment will help determine whether a retention attempt should be made, and if so, how far the organization is willing to go in that attempt. Or, at the aggregate level, the costs and benefits assessment could be developed for the work or business unit, division, or total organization. The results could be used to communicate with top management about the nature and severity of employee turnover and to help develop retention strategies and tactics.

Exhibit 14.5 shows that on the cost side there are separation, replacement, and training costs, both financial and nonfinancial. The financial costs mainly involve the cost of people's time, cost of materials and equipment, cash outlays, and productivity losses. The other costs are less discernible and harder to estimate but may entail large negative impacts on organizational effectiveness, such as loss of clients. On the benefits side, a number of positive things may occur, including finding a higher-quality, less-expensive replacement for the departing employee(s).

Accurate cost and benefit calculations require diligence and care in development, particularly those involving people's time. To estimate time costs, it is necessary to know the average amount of time each person spends in the specific activity, plus each person's compensation (pay rate plus benefits). Consider the case of an exit interview, a separation cost. Assume that (1) the staffing manager spends one hour conducting the interview and writing up a brief summary for the voluntary turnover data file, (2) the staffing manager's salary is $46,000 ($23/hour) and the employee's salary is $50,000 ($25/hour), and (3) benefits are 30% of pay ($6.90/hour for

---

EXHIBIT 14.5   Voluntary Turnover: Costs and Benefits

I. Separation Costs
  A. Financial Costs
  - HR staff time (e.g., exit interview, payroll, benefits)
  - Manager's time (e.g., retention attempts, exit interview)
  - Accrued paid time off (e.g., vacation, sick pay)
  - Temporary coverage (e.g., temporary employee; overtime for current employees)

  B. Other Costs
  - Production and customer service delays or quality decreases
  - Lost or unacquired clients
  - Leaves—goes to competitor or forms competitive business
  - Contagion—other employees decide to leave
  - Teamwork disruptions
  - Loss of workforce diversity

II. Replacement Costs
  - Staffing costs for new hire (e.g., cost-per-hire calculations)
  - Hiring inducements (e.g., bonus, relocation, perks)
  - Hiring manager and work-unit employee time
  - Orientation program time and materials
  - HR staff induction costs (e.g., payroll, benefits enrollment)

III. Training Costs
  - Formal training (trainee and instruction time, materials, equipment)
  - On-the-job training (supervisor and employee time)
  - Mentoring (mentor's time)
  - Socialization (time of other employees, travel)
  - Productivity loss (loss of production until full proficient employee)

IV. Benefits
  - Replacement employee better performer and organization citizen than last employee
  - New KSAO and motivation infusion to organization
  - Opportunity to restructure work unit
  - Savings from not replacing employee
  - Vacancy creates transfer or promotion opportunity for others
  - Replacement less expensive in salary and seniority-based benefits

the staffing manager and $7.50/hour for the employee). The time cost of the exit interview is $62.40. At the aggregate level, if the staffing manager conducts 100 exit interviews annually, and the average pay rate of those interviewed is $20/hour, the annual time cost of exit interviews is $5,590 (staffing manager pay = $2,300 and benefits = $690; employee's pay = $2,000 and benefits = $600).

Materials and equipment costs are likely to be most prevalent in replacement and training costs. Recruitment brochures and testing materials, orientation program materials, and induction materials such as benefits enrollment forms all add to staffing costs. Formal training may involve the use of both materials and equipment that must be costed. Cash outlays include paying for (1) the departing employee's accrued but unused paid time off, (2) possible temporary coverage for the departed employee, and (3) hiring inducements for the replacement employee.

On the benefits side, the primary immediate benefit is the labor cost savings from not having the departing employee on the payroll. This will save the organization labor costs until a permanent replacement is hired (if ever). The organization will also save on labor costs if a temporary replacement at a lower pay rate can fill the position until a permanent replacement is acquired. The hired permanent replacement may be hired at a lower wage or salary than the departing employee, resulting in additional pay and benefit savings. The other benefits shown in Exhibit 14.5 are less tangible but potentially very important in a longer-run sense of improved work-unit and organizational effectiveness.

Exhibit 14.6 shows the cost estimates for a single incident of voluntary turnover for a hypothetical industrial supplies organization that employs 40 salespeople who receive $20/hour on average and bring in approximately $8,000,000 in total annual sales. The three categories of the turnover and replacement process (separation, replacement, and training) are described in terms of their time costs, materials and equipment costs, and other costs.

Separation costs include the time of the employees who process turnover ($25 + $15) and the former employee's manager ($120). There is also accrued time off paid to the departing individual ($160). Replacement costs include both a temporary fill-in and a permanent replacement. It takes an average of four weeks to find a permanent replacement. During these four weeks (160 hours), a temporary replacement is hired from a staffing firm for $15/hour plus a 33.3% markup. While this temporary employee is paid less than the average salesperson, temporary salespeople typically make $2,000 less in sales over the four-week period. A permanent new hire receives an average of $15/hour for the first six months of employment until he or she gets up to speed ($5/hour less × 960 hours = $4,800 in savings). Each new hire costs $4,500, and newcomers receive a hiring bonus of $3,000 and a laptop computer worth $2,000. Each new salesperson's manager typically has an additional three hours devoted to orienting the newcomer, along with an eight-hour organizational orientation session.

Training costs include the materials and equipment required for the program ($1,000), two weeks (80 hours) of paid time in the class, and the instructor's pay (100 hours). Additionally, an experienced salesperson acts as a mentor during the transition period, averaging one hour per week over the course of a year. It takes the new permanent replacement 24 weeks (24 weeks × 40 hours = 960 hours) to reach the average sales proficiency of $200,000; this means that $50,000 in sales is lost during this period. Overall, the estimated total other costs for this organization

EXHIBIT 14.6 Example of Financial Cost Estimates for One Voluntary Turnover

	Time		Materials and Equipment ($)	Other Costs ($)
	Hours	Cost ($)		
A. Separation Costs				
Staffing manager	1	25		
HR staff	1	15		
Employee's manager	3	120		
Accrued paid time off	160	2,400		
Processing			30	
B. Replacement Costs				
Temporary replacement				
Compensation difference	160	(800)		
Staffing manager	1	25		
Employee's manager	1	40		
Staffing firm fee (markup)				800
Permanent replacement				
Compensation difference	960	(4,800)		
Cost-per-hire				4,500
Hiring bonus				3,000
Laptop computer				2,000
Employee's manager	3	120		
Orientation	8	160		
C. Training Costs				
Training program			1,000	
Trainee	80	1,200		
Instructor	100	1,600		
Mentor	52	1,040		
Productivity/sales loss				
Permanent replacement				50,000
Temporary replacement				2,000
D. Total Costs		1,145	1,030	62,300

for a single salesperson turnover incident come to $62,300. The data for this organization also suggest that time costs and material costs are a fairly trivial contribution to the total expense of turnover. Lost productivity makes up 81% of the cost of turnover (i.e., 52,000 / 64,475 = 81%). This figure will, of course, vary considerably depending on the job under consideration.

It should be recognized that turnover cost estimates require considerable judgment and guesstimates. Nonetheless, this example illustrates that many turnover costs are hidden in (1) the time demands placed on the many employees who must handle the separation, replacement, and training activities, and (2) the sales or productivity losses experienced. Such costs might be offset, at least in part, through the acquisition of less-expensive temporary and permanent replacement employees, at least for a while. Also note that when turnover costs for a single employee loss are aggregated to an annual level for multiple losses, the costs can be substantial. In this example, if the sales unit experienced just a 20% annual voluntary turnover rate, it would lose eight employees at a total cost of $519,000, or 6.5% of annual sales.

Discharge

In the case of an employee discharge, some of the costs and benefits are the same as for voluntary turnover. Exhibit 14.7 shows that separation, replacement, and training costs are still incurred. There may be an additional separation cost for a contract buyout of guarantees (salary, benefits, and perks) made in a fixed-term contract. Such buyouts are common for high-level executives and public sector leaders such as school superintendents. These guarantees are negotiated and used to make the hiring package more attractive and to reduce the financial risk of failure for the new hire. Such guarantees can drive up the costs of discharge substantially, reinforcing the need for careful selection decisions followed by support to help the new hire become a successful performer who will remain with the organization for at least the full term of the contract.

It is the other costs that are potentially very large. A discharge is usually preceded by the manager and others spending considerable time, often unpleasant and acrimonious, with the employee, seeking to change the person's behavior through progressive discipline or performance management activities. The discharge may be followed by a lawsuit, such as a claim that the discharge was tainted by discrimination based on the race or sex of the dischargee. The time costs for handling the matter, and the potential cash outlays required in a settlement or court-imposed remedy, can be substantial.[9] In short, compared with voluntary turnover, discharge is a more costly, and unpleasant, type of turnover to experience. Moreover, in unionized settings, discharge problems may pose a serious threat to labor–management relations.

Against these often large costs are many potential benefits. First and foremost is that the organization will be rid of a truly low-value employee whose presence has

---

EXHIBIT 14.7   Discharge: Costs and Benefits

I. Separation Costs

A. Financial Costs

- Same as for voluntary turnover plus possible contract buyout (salary, benefits, perks)

B. Other Costs

- Manager and HR staff time handling problem employee
- Grievance, alternative dispute resolution
- Possibility of lawsuit, loss of lawsuit, settlement or remedy
- Damage to harmonious labor–management relations

II. Replacement Costs

- Same as for voluntary turnover

III. Training Costs

- Same as for voluntary turnover

IV. Benefits

- Departure of low-value employee
- High-value employee replacement possibility
- Reduced disruption for manager and work unit
- Improved performance management and disciplinary skills

---

caused considerable disruption, ineffective performance, and possibly declines in organizational effectiveness. A following benefit is the opportunity to replace this person with a high-quality new hire who will hopefully turn out to be a high-value employee. A side benefit of a discharge experience is that many members of the organization will gain improved disciplinary and performance management skills, and the HR department's awareness of the need for better discipline and performance management systems may be heightened and lead to these necessary changes.

Downsizing

Downsizing costs are concentrated in separation costs for a permanent RIF since there will presumably be no replacement hiring and training. These costs are shown in Exhibit 14.8, along with potential benefits.[10] The major economic cost areas are time costs, cash outlays for various severance and buyout packages, and increased

EXHIBIT 14.8 Downsizing: Costs and Benefits

I. Separation Costs

A. Financial Costs

- HR staff time in planning and implementing layoff
- Managers' time in handling layoff
- Accrued paid time off (e.g., vacation, sick pay)
- Early retirement package
- Voluntary severance package (e.g., one week pay/year of service, continued health insurance, outplacement assistance)
- Involuntary severance package
- Contract buyouts for fulfillment of guarantees
- Higher unemployment insurance premiums
- Change in control (CIC) guarantees for key executives during a merger or acquisition

B. Other Costs

- Shareholder value (stock price) may not improve
- Loss of critical employees and KSAOs
- Inability to respond quickly to surges in product and service demand; restaffing delays and costs
- Contagion—other employees leave
- Threat to harmonious labor–management relations
- Possibility of lawsuit, loss of lawsuit, costly settlement or remedy
- Decreased morale, increased feelings of job insecurity
- Difficulty in attracting new employees

II. Benefits

- Lower payroll and benefit costs
- Increased production and staffing flexibility
- Ability to relocate facilities
- Improved promotion and transfer opportunities for stayers
- Focus on core businesses, eliminate peripheral ones
- Spread risk by outsourcing activities to other organizations
- Flatten organization hierarchy—especially among managers
- Increase productivity

unemployment compensation insurance premiums. The time costs involve both HR staff and managers' time in planning, implementing, and handling the RIF.

Severance costs may take numerous forms. First, employees can be paid for accrued time off. Second, early retirement packages may be offered to employees as an inducement to leave early. Third, employees ineligible for early retirement may be offered a voluntary severance package as an inducement to leave without being laid off. A typical severance package includes one week's pay for each year of service, continued health insurance coverage and premium payment, and out-placement assistance. More generous terms may be provided to key executives, such as two weeks' pay for each year of service and a lump-sum exit bonus. A danger with both early retirement and voluntary severance packages is that their provisions may turn out to be so attractive that more employees take them and leave than had been planned for in the RIF.

If the early retirement and voluntary severance packages do not adequately induce a sufficient number of employees to leave, the organization may also institute an involuntary RIF with a severance package, oftentimes not as generous as the voluntary package offered. It is customary to inform employees of the content of both the voluntary and involuntary packages at the time the RIF is announced so they may decide which to take. Some employees may decide to take their chances by not accepting the voluntary package and gambling that they won't be laid off (and if they are, being willing to live with the involuntary severance package).

Some employees may receive special severance consideration. For those on a fixed-term contract, a contract buyout will be necessary. Others, usually key executives, may have change in control (CIC) clauses in their contracts that must be fulfilled if there is a merger or acquisition; CICs are also known as "golden parachutes." In addition to the terms in typical severance packages, a CIC may provide for immediate vesting of stock options, a retirement payout sweetener or buyout, bonus payments, continuation of all types of insurance for an extended time period, and maintenance of various perks.

Severance costs can be considerable. The Wall Street securities firm Merrill Lynch and Company reduced its workforce 14% over a two-year period as part of a restructuring effort. About 15,000 employees were cut, at a severance cost of $1.2 billion ($80,000 per employee).[11]

Other costs of downsizing shown in Exhibit 14.8 may also be considerable. Shareholder value (stock price) may not improve, suggesting the stock market views the probable effectiveness of the restructuring as low. There will be a critical talent loss and an inability to respond quickly to the need for workforce additions to cover new demand surges. And a reputation for job instability will create added difficulties in attracting new employees. Terminated employees may pursue legal avenues, claiming, for example, that decisions about whom to lay off were tainted by age discrimination. Employees who survive the job cuts may have damaged morale and may fear even more cuts, which may harm performance and cause them to look for another job with a more secure organization. Finally, as with discharges, downsizing may place great strains on labor–management harmony.

Against this backdrop of heavy costs are many potential benefits. There will in fact be lower payroll and benefits costs. The organization may gain production and staffing flexibility, an ability to outsource parts of the business that are not mission critical, and opportunities to redesign and relocate facilities. The restructuring may also entail a flattening of the organization hierarchy by eliminating management layers, leading to increased speed in decision making and productivity boosts. Finally, new promotion and transfer opportunities may open up as the restructuring leads to the hoped-for rebound in organizational effectiveness.

Summary

Despite their many potential benefits, voluntary turnover, discharges, and downsizing are typically costly propositions. Time costs, materials costs, performance and revenue losses, severance costs, legal costs, and so forth can create substantial cost challenges and risks for the organization. Potentially even more important are the human costs of frayed relationships, critical talent losses, performance declines, disruptive discipline, the contagion effect of other employees leaving along with the departing employee, and the risk of not being able to locate, attract, and hire high-quality replacements.

The organization must carefully weigh these costs and benefits generally for each type of turnover, as well as specifically for separate employee groups, job categories, and organizational units. Clear cost-benefit differences in turnover will likely emerge from these more fine-grained analyses. Such analyses will help the organization better understand its turnover, determine where and among whom turnover is most worrisome, and learn how to fashion tailor-made retention strategies and tactics.

RETENTION INITIATIVES: VOLUNTARY TURNOVER

For most organizations, of the three types of turnover, voluntary turnover is the most prevalent and the one they choose to focus on in the continual "war for talent." Described below are examples of retention initiatives undertaken by organizations. These are vast in number, but little is known about how organizations actually decide to act on a turnover problem and go forth with one or more retention initiatives. To fill this void, a retention decision process is described that will help the organization more systematically and effectively pursue the right retention initiatives. Based on the causes of turnover model (Exhibit 14.2), ways to influence the three primary turnover drivers—desirability of leaving, ease of leaving, and alternatives—are suggested for retention initiatives.

Current Practices and Deciding to Act

Turnover analysis does not end with the collection and analysis of data. These activities are merely a precursor to the critical decision of whether to act to solve a perceived turnover problem, and if so, how to intervene to attack the problem and ultimately assess how effective the intervention was. Presented first are some examples of organization retention initiatives that illustrate the breadth and depth of attempts to address retention concerns. Then a systematic decision process for retention initiatives is provided as a framework to help with deciding whether to act. Such decision guidance is necessary given the complexity of the retention issue and the lack of demonstrated best practices for improving retention.

What Do Organizations Do?

Several descriptive surveys provide glimpses of the actions that organizations take to address retention. These examples come mostly from relatively large organizations, so what happens in small organizations is more of an unknown. Nonetheless, the data provide interesting illustrations of organization tenacity and ingenuity, along with a willingness to commit resources, in their approaches to retention.

SHRM Survey. The Society for Human Resource Management (SHRM) surveyed HR professionals in 432 organizations nationwide on the reasons for turnover.[12] The top 10 reasons, and the percentage of HR professionals citing each, were as follows: career opportunity elsewhere (51%), better compensation elsewhere (50%), dissatisfaction with potential for career development at the organization (31%), burnout from current job (23%), poor management (16%), conflict with supervisors (16%), difficulty balancing work/life issues (14%), not feeling appreciated (14%), ready for a new experience (13%), and better benefits package elsewhere (13%). It is interesting to compare HR managers' responses with those provided by employees in this same survey. The responses of line managers and other employees were typically very similar to those provided by HR managers, although the line managers and employees thought turnover was also often driven by being ready for new experiences and boredom with an old job, neither of which was highlighted as a major driver of turnover by HR managers. It is not entirely clear why there was this inconsistency in opinions between the HR managers and the other employees, but it should be noted that most research supports the perspective of employees, showing that employees who are dissatisfied with their work assignments are considerably more likely to quit.

What do these organizations do about retention problems and threats? Exhibit 14.9 shows the perceived most and least effective retention practices.

Although few intrinsic rewards were mentioned in the SHRM survey, this does not mean that such rewards do not reduce turnover in the aggregate. In fact, research generally suggests that there is a strong relationship between job enrichment efforts from organizations and employee satisfaction. Employee perceptions that their jobs provide them with high levels of intrinsic satisfiers are consistently related to job satisfaction across multiple studies.[13] In addition, research suggests that individuals who hold jobs that are intrinsically satisfying are less likely to leave.[14]

EXHIBIT 14.9   Most and Least Effective Retention Initiatives

Most Effective Retention Initiatives
- Competitive merit increases/salary adjustments
- Career development opportunities
- Promoting qualified employees
- Competitive merit increases
- Increasing health care benefits
- Offering schedules conducive to work/life balance
- Bonuses

Least Effective Retention Initiatives
- Telecommuting
- Child care
- Early eligibility for benefits
- Stock options
- Miscellaneous competitive benefits

WorldatWork Survey.   WorldatWork conducts regular surveys of HR managers regarding the implementation and success of retention initiatives. A survey conducted with a sample of 649 respondents in 2007 focused on benefits and work/life programs.[15] Paid vacation and medical benefits were both very widely used, and both were seen as extremely effective tools for improving retention. Deferred compensation plans, such as defined benefit pensions, were also rated as highly effective in reducing turnover. Not many organizations offered flextime and telecommuting, but those that did believe that these flexible work options increased retention. Although a large number of organizations provided flexible spending accounts for child care, HR managers did not see this as an especially effective retention tool.

The 100 Best Companies.   Each year *Fortune* magazine publishes the report "The 100 Best Companies to Work For."[16] Organizations apply to be on the list, and their score is based on randomly chosen employees' responses to the Great Place to Work Trust Index survey and an evaluation of a Culture Audit. Winners are ranked in order according to their final score, and brief descriptions are provided about the number of US employees (including the percentages of women and minorities), job growth, annual number of job applicants and voluntary turnover rate, average number of employee training hours, entry-level salary for production and for professional employees, revenues, and what makes the organization stand out.

Unfortunately, the study does not provide specific information on patterns of usage and effectiveness of retention initiatives among the 100 organizations. However, comments about what makes the organization stand out provide intriguing tidbits as to special practices that might enhance retention. SAS, which was the top-rated organization for 2010, provides employees with an impressive array of perquisites, including gourmet cafeterias, laundry and dry-cleaning facilities, concierge services, car washing and oil changes, massage therapists, and inexpensive on-site child-care services. The company boasts a 2% annual turnover rate, compared with an industry average turnover rate of 22%. *Fortune* also previously highlighted Capital One's Future of Work project as a retention tool. This program aims to increase satisfaction and decrease stress by providing employees with a laptop computer with wireless Internet capability, a BlackBerry handheld computer, and an iPod, all of which promote flexible scheduling. All these forms of technology allow employees to work away from the office, and open-space floor plans for regional offices allow employees to work at different desks, booths, couches, or wherever is convenient for that day. Capital One provides employees with opportunities to use this technology to access internal quarterly company reports and to take distance learning courses from top business schools. The reader should consult the 100 Best Companies results each year to gain glimpses such as these into what organizations are doing to make themselves attractive to job applicants and employees, which may aid in retention enhancement.

Retention Bundles. The retention initiatives up to this point have been described in terms of individual practices, such as either providing rewards linked to tenure or matching offers from other organizations. This should not be taken to suggest that retention initiatives should be offered in isolation. To be effective, retention practices need to be integrated into a comprehensive system, or as a "bundle" of practices. As an example, research has shown that the best performers are least likely to quit when an organization both rewards performance with higher compensation *and* widely communicates its compensation practices. Focusing on only compensation or communication did not have these effects—the procedures are much more effective as a bundle.[17] One study grouped steel minimills into those that used a bundle of commitment-oriented staffing practices (including programs to foster social relationships, employee participation, and general training) as opposed to minimills that used control-oriented practices (including programs that focused on reducing employment costs through minimal investment in employee programs). Turnover was two times higher in control-oriented organizations relative to commitment-oriented organizations.[18] A study examining a more diverse set of firms focused on an alternative effective set of bundles, including extensive recruiting, careful use of validated selection strategies, attitude assessments, incentive compensation, organizational communication, and use of formal job analysis procedures. Each standard deviation increase in the use of this bundle of high-performance work practices resulted in a 7% decrease in the turnover rate relative to the average turnover rates.[19]

In practical terms, managers need to examine all the characteristics in the work environment that might lead to turnover and address them in a comprehensive manner. Organizations with strong investments in their staffing methods may find their investments are lost if they do not support this strategy with an equally strong commitment to providing newcomers with sufficient orientation material to adjust to their new jobs. Organizations that provide numerous benefits in a poorly integrated fashion may similarly find that the intended effects are lost if managers and employees believe that the programs fail to address their needs.

Specific Retention Initiatives.   To further illustrate policies that organizations might adopt to control turnover, Exhibit 14.10 summarizes practices from a number of organizations that have been able to significantly improve retention outcomes.[20] One noteworthy feature of these programs is the use of both extrinsic and intrinsic rewards.

Decision Process

Exhibit 14.11 provides a suggested decision process that can help navigate the complex trade-offs inherent in developing retention initiatives.

The first question—do we think turnover is a problem?—requires consideration and analysis of several types of data. It is necessary to judge whether the turnover rate(s) are increasing and/or high relative to internal and external benchmarks such as industry or direct competitor data. If turnover is relatively high or getting higher, this is cause for concern. Additional information is necessary, such as whether managers are complaining about retention problems, whether mostly high-value employees are leaving, and whether there are demographic disparities among those who leave. If these indicators also show trouble signs, turnover is likely a problem. The final analysis should involve the type of costs/benefits described earlier. Even though turnover may be high, in the final analysis it is only a problem if its costs are judged to exceed the benefits.

The second question—how might we attack the problem?—requires consideration of desirability of leaving, ease of leaving, and alternative turnover causes. Also, within each of these areas, which specific factors is it possible to change? In Exhibit 14.11, for desirability of leaving it shows that increasing job satisfaction, improving organizational justice, and improving the social environment are possible, but it is likely not possible to change personal shocks or personal reasons for leaving. Likewise, for ease of leaving it is possible to provide organization-specific KSAOs and to increase the cost of leaving for the employee.

Question three—what do we need to decide?—crosses the boundary from consideration to possible implementation. First to be decided are specific numerical turnover (retention) goals in the form of desired turnover rates. Retention programs without retention goals are bound to fail. Then it must be decided whether the goals and retention programs will be across the board, targeted to specific organization units and employee groups, or applied to both. Examples of targeted

EXHIBIT 14.10   Retention Initiative Examples

Organization	Initiative	Results
Cedant	Flexible working schedule and work/life balance program designed around employee survey feedback	Annual turnover decreased from approximately 30% to less than 10%
Deloitte	Develop "mass career customization," which allows employees to customize their workload to suit their needs	Dramatic reduction in turnover of top-performing employees
Fleet Bank	Career growth opportunities and ensuring that employees are able to establish long-term relationships with their managers	Turnover fell by 40% among salaried employees and by 25% among hourly employees
Outback Steakhouse	Provide adequate information on job characteristics prior to hiring, extensive opportunities for employee voice	Turnover rates at approximately half of industry norms
SAP Americas	Increase communication regarding the organization's strategic direction and goals, provide rewards for retention, improve supervisor–employee relationship	Voluntary annual turnover rates fell from 14.9% to 6.1%
UPS	Provide well-above-market wages, ample vacation time, free health insurance, and pension	Typical annual turnover rate of 1.8%
Wegman's	Provide a comprehensive menu of health care benefits far above industry norms	Turnover rates at approximately 60% of industry norms

groups include certain job categories in which turnover is particularly troublesome, women and minorities, and first-year employees (newcomers)—a group that traditionally experiences high turnover. Next to be considered is if and how high-value employees will be treated. Many organizations develop special retention initiatives for high-value employees on top of other retention programs, and it will have to be decided whether to follow this path of special treatment for such employees.[21] Having identified organizational units, targeted groups, and high-value employees (and established turnover goals for them), the retention program specifics must be designed. These may be general (across-the-board) initiatives applicable to all employees, or they may be targeted ones. For each such initiative, it must then be

EXHIBIT 14.11   Decision Process for Retention Initiatives

Do We Think Turnover Is a Problem?	How Might We Attack the Problem?	What Do We Need to Decide?	Should We Proceed?	How Should We Evaluate the Initiatives?

• Turnover high or increasing relative to internal and external benchmarks
• Managers complain about retention problems
• High-value employees are leaving
• Demographic disparities among those who leave
• Overall costs exceed benefits of turnover
	• Lower desirability of leaving?
	  Increase job satisfaction—yes
	  Decrease shocks—no
	  Personal reasons—no
	  Improve organizational justice—yes
	  Improve social environment at work—yes
	• Lower ease of leaving?
	  Change market conditions—no
	  Provide organization-specific KSAOs—yes
	  Make leaving more costly—yes
	• Change alternatives?
	  Promotion and transfers—yes
	  Respond to job offers—yes
		• Turnover goals
		• Targeted to units and groups
		• High-value employees
		• General and targeted retention initiatives
		• Lead, match, or lag the market
		• Supplement or supplant
		• HR and managers' roles
			• Feasibility
			• Probability of success
			• Timing
			• Costs
				• Lower proportion of turnover if avoidable
				• Turnover low or decreasing compared with benchmarks
				• Fewer complaints about retention problems
				• Fewer high-value employees leaving
				• Reduced demographic disparities
				• Lower costs relative to benefits

decided how to position the organization's initiatives relative to the marketplace. Will it seek to lead, match, or lag the market? For example, will base pay on average be higher than the market average (lead), be the same as the market average (match), or be lower than the market average (lag)? Likewise, will new variable pay plans try to outdo competitors (e.g., more favorable stock option plan) or simply match them? Adding to the complexity of the decision process is the delicate issue of whether new retention initiatives will supplement (add on to) or supplant (replace) existing rewards and programs. If the latter, the organization should be prepared for the possibility of employee backlash against what employees may perceive as "take backs" of rewards they currently have and must give up. Finally, the respective rules of HR and individual managers will have to be worked out, and this may vary among the retention initiatives. If the initiative involves responding to job offers, for example, line managers may demand a heavy or even exclusive hand in making them. Alternatively, some initiatives may be HR driven; examples here include hours of work and variable pay plans.

Should we proceed? is question four in the decision process. It will depend on judgments about feasibility, such as ease of implementation. Judgments about probability of success will also enter in, and having specific turnover (retention) goals will be immensely helpful in making the decision. Finally, matters of timing should enter in. Even if judged to be feasible and a likely success, a retention program may not be launched immediately. Other HR problem areas and initiatives may have emerged and taken on a higher priority. Or, turnover problems may have lost urgency because looser labor markets may have intervened to reduce turnover at the very time the retention initiatives were being planned. The cost of these initiatives will also be a major consideration.

The final question—how should we evaluate the initiatives?—should be considered *before* any plan is implemented. Answers will provide focus to the design of the intervention and agreed-upon criteria on which to later judge intervention effectiveness. Ideally, the same criteria that led to the conclusion that turnover was a problem (question one) will be used to determine whether the chosen solution actually works (question five).

Desirability of Leaving

Employees' desire to leave depends on their job satisfaction, shocks they experience, and personal (nonjob) reasons. Of these, only job satisfaction can usually be meaningfully influenced by the organization. So the first strategy for improving retention is to improve job satisfaction. The myriad examples of retention initiatives used by organizations described above mostly represent attempts to improve job satisfaction through delivery of various rewards to employees.

It is critical to understand that merely throwing more or new rewards at employees is not a sound retention initiative. Which rewards are chosen, and how they are delivered to employees, will determine how effective they are in improving job satisfaction. Accordingly, guidelines for reward choice and delivery are also described. Exhibit 14.12 summarizes the guidelines for increasing job satisfaction and retention.

As discussed in Chapter 4, a variety of extrinsic and intrinsic rewards can be brought to bear on the question of job satisfaction. Rather than reiterating these specific rewards here, we instead discuss the manner in which organizations can provide both categories of rewards consistent with the best practices identified by research and experience.

One important point must be borne in mind for both intrinsic and extrinsic rewards. The person/job match model emphasizes that job satisfaction results from a match between the rewards desired by employees and the rewards provided by the job. Employee reward preferences may be assessed at all stages of the staffing process by (1) asking applicants what attracted them to the organization, (2) asking current employees about the most important sources of job satisfaction, and (3) assessing reasons for turnover during exit interviews. It is also important to provide rewards large enough to be meaningful to the recipient. For example, an employee earning $50,000 who receives a gross 4% raise of $2,000 will realize a raise of 2.8% if inflation and taxes combined are at 30%. Such a net raise may not be very meaningful.

Extrinsic Rewards

To have attraction and retention power, extrinsic rewards must be unique and unlikely to be offered by competitors. Surveys of employees consistently show that inadequate compensation and benefits are extremely powerful drivers of employee turnover decisions.[22] The organization must benchmark against its competitors to

---

EXHIBIT 14.12 Guidelines for Increasing Job Satisfaction and Retention

A. Extrinsic Rewards

- Reward must be meaningful and unique.
- Reward must match individual preferences.
- Link rewards to retention behaviors.
- Link reward to performance.

B. Intrinsic Rewards

- Assign employees to jobs that meet their needs for work characteristics.
- Provide clear communications with employees.
- Design fair reward allocation systems.
- Ensure supervisors provide a positive environment.
- Provide programs to enhance work/life balance.

determine what others are offering. Base pay levels are an important component in this process. Organizations may attempt to lead the market by providing wages above the market level. This leader strategy allows the organization to attract a higher-quality workforce, provides a workforce that is very satisfied with its pay, and minimizes the attractiveness of alternatives because employees cannot find comparable salaries elsewhere. This market leader strategy can be pursued for any reward and can be tailored to particular employee and industry demands. For example, an organization that is a seasonal employer in the recreation and tourism industry may concede pay leadership and lead with benefits such as free use of equipment (e.g., boats, bikes), clothing at cost, and free passes for use of facilities. A survey of 1,223 employed adults also revealed that employee benefits were a key driver of employee retention. In particular, 40% of respondents indicated that 401(k) matching decreased their odds of turnover; health care coverage and competitive salary also topped the list.[23] Surveys also suggest that in a down economy, many employees see benefits like health insurance as a vital part of their personal safety net.[24]

Rewards can be even more powerfully attached to employee retention if they explicitly take seniority into account. For example, employees who have been with the organization longer may receive more vacation hours, career advancement opportunities, and increased job security. A more subtle way of rewarding employee retention is to make the reward contingent on the person's base pay level. Base pay levels typically increase over time through a combination of promotions and merit pay increases. Defined benefit retirement plans, for example, typically calculate retirement pay as some percentage (say, 50%) of the average person's three highest years of pay multiplied by years of service. Specific retention bonuses are also used to encourage longer-term relationships.

Rewards can also be linked to employee job performance. Organizations with a strong performance management culture thrive on high performance expectations, coupled with large rewards (e.g., base pay raises, bonuses, commissions, and stock options) for high performers. Because lesser performers receive lower wages in these organizations, they are more likely to leave, whereas superior performers are more likely to stay.[25] Organizations may even more specifically target key performers by providing special retention bonuses, new job assignments, and additional perks if it appears that top performers are likely to leave.[26]

Intrinsic Rewards

The intrinsic rewards described in Exhibit 4.19 should not be overlooked. There is consistent evidence that employee dissatisfaction with the intrinsic quality of their jobs is strongly related to turnover.[27]

Improving the work environment involves assigning employees to jobs that better meet their intrinsic-reward preferences. For example, employees with high needs for skill variety could be assigned to more complex jobs or projects within a work unit, or employees with high autonomy needs could be assigned to supervisors with a very "hands-off" style of leadership. Job redesign can also improve the work environment. To increase skill variety, managers may broaden the scope of tasks and responsibility for longer-term employees, allowing for personal growth on the job. Job rotation programs also help reduce perceived monotony on the job. Some organizations combine intrinsic and extrinsic rewards through the development of formal knowledge- and skill-based plans. In these plans, specific knowledge or skills are designated as critical, and employees receive a predetermined increase in base pay for demonstrated proficiency or acquisition of the knowledge or skill. For example, many school districts provide teachers with increases in their base compensation level for receiving master's degrees. Enhancing job autonomy might be facilitated by establishing formal performance goals for the job while giving employees minimal direction or oversight for the methods required to achieve these goals. A survey of over 700 nursing managers found that higher levels of training and development opportunities were associated with lower levels of establishment-level turnover.[28] Similar methods for improving task identity, task significance, and feedback should also be considered.

One of the closest correlates of employee commitment is the perception that the organization treats its employees fairly and provides them with support. Two forms of justice are necessary.[29] Distributive justice refers to perceptions that the individual reward levels are consistent with employee contributions to the organization. Procedural justice refers to perceptions that the process for allocating rewards and punishments is administered consistently, follows well-defined guidelines, and is free from bias. A sense that these justice principles have been violated can create dissatisfaction and may result in turnover or a lawsuit.

A crucial component to increasing employees' perception of justice is clear communication. Communication must begin early in the staffing process by providing employees with honest information about their job conditions. Evidence suggests that employees who receive adequate information regarding job conditions perceive their employers as more honest and may be less likely to leave.[30] If reward systems are to increase satisfaction, employees must know why the system was developed, the mechanics of the system, and the payouts to be expected. Such knowledge and understanding require continuous communication. Research shows that a very common form of employee dissatisfaction with reward systems is a failure to understand them, or actual misinformation about them.[31] Any retention initiative designed to increase job satisfaction must have a solid communication component. On a broader level, communication regarding the organization's strategic direction can reduce turnover. Surveys at SAP Software indicated that employees who felt that the organization had a clear vision for the future and believed that top management supported them were more likely to report that they were engaged in their work.[32]

Justice perceptions are also strongly influenced by reward system design. Distributive justice requires that there be a rational and preferably measurable basis for reward decisions. Seniority-based rewards score high here because many employees believe seniority is a legitimate way to distinguish employees, and because it can be objectively measured. Objective measures of job performance, such as sales figures, are also likely to be accepted as legitimate. Rewards based on managerial performance reviews may be more problematic if employees question the legitimacy of the performance measurement system, or if they believe that these rewards create divisive comparisons among employees. When managerial reviews are part of the rewards process, the procedures involved in the review should be clearly communicated to employees. The importance of system fairness has been demonstrated in many contexts. Although much of the research on justice has been conducted in the United States and Canada, studies from China, Korea, Japan, and Pakistan have also shown that perceived justice increases job satisfaction and decreases turnover intentions.[33]

It is said that employees don't quit their jobs, they quit their bosses. Thus, interpersonal compatibility or chemistry between the employee and the supervisor can be a critical part of the employee's decision to stay or leave. The same could be said for coworkers. Employees who believe that they fit with the social environment in which they work are more likely to see their jobs as a source of significant social rewards. The resultant sense of camaraderie with the supervisor and coworkers may make them reluctant to leave the organization. Research confirms that individuals whose coworkers are searching for alternative jobs will increase their own job search.[34]

The supervisor is also a source of justice perceptions because of his or her role as a direct source of reward or punishment.[35] The supervisor functions as an intermediary between the employee and the organization's compensation and promotion systems. This is because the supervisor decides the process for assessing employees, as well as the amount of rewards to be provided on the basis of these assessments. The supervisor also serves as a key communication conduit regarding reward systems. If supervisors communicate the purpose and mechanics of the system, employees will be able to understand the process of reward distribution and what they need to do to receive rewards in the future. Supervisors who treat subordinates with respect and concern can also help reduce turnover.

Supervisors and coworkers in the social setting can also engage in abusive or harassing behaviors that are threatening or discomforting to the employees. Research suggests that employees who believe that their supervisors are abusive are more likely to leave.[36] Examples of abusive supervisor behavior that are frequently cited in surveys include "tells me my thoughts and feelings are stupid," "puts me down in front of others," and "tells me I'm incompetent." More extreme behaviors, such as sexual harassment, have even stronger negative impacts on an employee's desire to remain on the job. Turnover due to interpersonal conflicts at work tends to come especially quickly; many employees who have such conflicts will bypass the process of searching for and considering alternative jobs and will instead quit immediately. Employees who are isolated from others in their racial, ethnic, or gender group are more likely to leave, whereas pro-diversity workplace climates tend to reduce turnover intentions.

For many employees, trying to balance work tasks with their personal lives contributes to stress, dissatisfaction, and a desire to leave.[37] Therefore, many organizations hoping to reduce turnover have developed programs to help employees integrate their work and nonwork lives. These work/life balance programs allow employees to take time off from work if needed, create flexible scheduling options, and facilitate opportunities to work from remote locations. Many organizations have made family-friendly benefits and flexible work arrangements centerpieces of their retention strategies, and surveys suggest that making efforts to help employees balance their work and family lives can pay off in terms of lower turnover. For example, a survey of 393 professional-level employees demonstrated that individuals who made use of telework options experienced lower levels of work exhaustion and had lower intentions to leave. Data from 3,504 individuals who responded to the National Study of the Changing Workforce found that employees who had access to family-friendly work benefits experienced less stress and had lower turnover intentions relative to employees who did not have access to these benefits. A survey of over 200 HR professionals found that 67% of respondents believed that flexible work arrangements had a positive impact on employee retention. Despite evidence supporting their use, it should be remembered that these work/life programs do not come without costs. Restructuring the workforce can disrupt productivity and may require investments in new technology to facilitate off-site work. Research has also shown that some employees who choose not to take advantage of telework options resent their coworkers who are not in the office regularly, and this resentment can lead to increased intention to leave.

Individual Dispositions

Although organizations often try to influence turnover rates by providing intrinsically and extrinsically satisfying working conditions, a growing body of evidence suggests that some employees are more likely to quit because of their personality dispositions. In other words, some people are just more prone to quit than others. We have already noted that a variety of tools like standardized tests and interviews can be used to identify the characteristics of job applicants. Organizations that are especially concerned about turnover might consider assessing applicants' propensity to voluntarily quit as part of their selection system.

One approach to identifying individuals who are likely to quit is by explicitly asking applicants how often they have changed jobs and what their intentions are regarding staying in their current jobs. Although the effects are not large, these types of biodata questions are related to turnover rates.[38] Another approach to identifying employees with high turnover propensity is to assess conscientiousness, agreeableness, and emotional stability, as some research has shown that individuals high in these traits are less likely to quit.[39]

Ease of Leaving

The decision process (Exhibit 14.11) indicates two points of attack on ease of leaving—providing organization-specific training and increasing the cost of leaving. The third possible factor, changing labor market conditions, cannot be influenced and represents a variable that will continuously influence the organization's voluntary turnover.

Organization-Specific Training

Training and development activities provide KSAOs to employees that they did not possess when they entered the organization as new hires. Training and development seek to increase labor quality in ways that enhance employees' effectiveness. As shown previously, training represents a substantial investment (cost) that evaporates when an employee leaves the organization.

The organization may invest in training to provide KSAOs that vary along a continuum of general to organization specific. The more general the KSAOs, the more transferable they are to other organizations, thus increasing the likelihood they improve the employee's marketability and raise the probability of leaving. Organization-specific KSAOs are not transferable, and possession of them does not improve employee marketability. Hence, it is possible to lower the employee's ease of leaving by providing, as much as possible, only organization-specific training content that has value only as long as the employee remains with the organization.

This strategy needs to be coupled with a selection strategy in which any general KSAOs required for the job are assessed and selected on so that they will not have to be invested in once the employee is on the job. For example, applicants for an entry-level sales job might be assessed and selected for general sales competencies such as written and verbal communication and interpersonal skills. Those hired may then receive more specialized training in such areas as product knowledge, specific software, and knowledge of territories. To the extent such organization-specific KSAOs become an increasingly large proportion of the employee's total KSAO package over time, they help restrict the employee's mobility.

This strategy entails some risk. It assumes the general KSAOs are available and affordable among applicants. It also assumes these applicants will not be dissuaded if they learn about the organization-specific training and development they will receive.

Increased Cost of Leaving

Driving up the cost of leaving is a way to make it less easy to leave. Providing above-market pay and benefits is one way to do this since employees will have a hard time finding better-paying jobs elsewhere. Any form of deferred compensation, such as deferred bonuses, will also raise the cost of leaving since the compensation will be lost if the employee leaves before he or she is eligible to receive it.

Retention bonuses might also be used. Normally, these are keyed to high-value employees whose loss would wreak organizational havoc. Such may be the case during mergers and acquisitions, when retention of key managers is essential to a smooth transition. For example, when TransWorld Airlines (TWA) sold itself to American Airlines, TWA had a plan to pay retention bonuses of 15% to 30% of annual salaries to 100 key managers. The bonuses were paid in three phases over a one-year period. In addition, a separate $500,000 discretionary fund was used to pay other people retention bonuses.[40]

Another long-term way to make leaving costly is to locate the organization's facilities in an area where it is the dominant employer and other amenities (housing, schools, and health care) are accessible and affordable. This may entail location in the outer rings of suburban areas or relatively small and rural communities. Once employees move to and settle into these locations, the cost of leaving is high because of the lack of alternative jobs within the area and a need to make a costly geographic shift in order to obtain a new job.

Alternatives

In confronting outside alternatives available to employees, the organization must fashion ways to make even better internal alternatives available and desirable. Two key ways to do this involve internal staffing and responding to outside job offers.

Internal Staffing

The nature and operation of internal staffing systems have already been explored. It is important to reiterate that open systems serve as a safety valve, retention-wise, in that employees are encouraged to look internally for new job opportunities and managers benefit by seeking internal candidates rather than going outside the organization. The organization should also think of ways outside the realm of its traditional internal staffing systems to provide attractive internal alternatives to its employees.

For example, Mercer Management Consulting has developed a rotational externship program for some of its consultants. These consultants are allowed to take on a full-time operational role for a client for 6 to 24 months, rather than handle multiple clients. The consultant gets the satisfaction of seeing a project through to completion and gains valuable operating experience. It is hoped that these consultants will return to Mercer at the end of the project, following the "if you love something, set it free" saying. Another example is a temporary internal transfer system used by Interbrand Group, Inc., a unit of Omnicom Group, Inc. Certain high-performance employees are offered short-term transfers to any of its 26 offices worldwide. The lateral moves last from three months to one year. The transfers allow employees to make a change in their lives without quitting their jobs.[41] Illustrating this point, a study of 205 individuals employed in diverse work settings found that those who were unhappy with their work environments did not translate this dissatisfaction into an intention to leave if they believed that there were opportunities for mobility within their organization. In a sense, one could say that these dissatisfied individuals saw internal transfers as a way to quit a disliked job, but without the costs to the employer that typically come with turnover.[42]

Response to Job Offers

When employees receive an outside job offer or are on the verge of receiving one, they clearly have a solid job alternative in hand. How should the organization respond, if at all, in order to make itself the preferred alternative?

The organization should confront this dilemma with a policy that has been carefully thought through in advance. This will help prevent some knee-jerk, potentially regrettable actions being taken on the spot when an employee brings forth a job offer and wants to use it for leverage.

First, the organization should decide whether it will respond to job offers. Some organizations choose not to, thereby avoiding bidding wars and counteroffer games. Even if the organization successfully retained the employee, the employee may now lack commitment to the organization, and other employees may resent the special retention deal that was cut. Other organizations choose to respond to job offers, not wanting to automatically close out an opportunity to at least respond to, and hopefully retain, the employee. Other times, job offers are welcomed because they help the organization sort out who its stars are and what kinds of offer packages it may have to give other recruits in order to persuade them to join the organization. One organization pays $1,000 "notification bonuses" to employees who disclose receiving an outside offer so that it can learn its content and have the option of being able to respond to it.[43] The price for such an openness to outside offers is that it may encourage employees to actively solicit them in order to try to squeeze a counteroffer out of the organization, thus improving the "deal."

The second major policy issue is for which employees will the organization respond to outside offers. Will it be for all employees or only select ones; if the latter, which ones? Here, the focus should likely be on high-value employees.

A third set of policy issues pertains to who will put together the counteroffer and what approval process must be followed. While individual managers will likely want wide latitude over these issues, the HR function will need to be an important player for cost-control purposes, as well as for ensuring procedural and distributive justice overall.

RETENTION INITIATIVES: DISCHARGE

Performance Management

Many organizations use performance management to help ensure that the initial person/job match made during staffing yields an effectively performing employee, to facilitate employee performance improvement and competency growth, and to detect and hopefully remedy performance problems. Performance management systems focus most of their attention on planning, enabling, appraising, and rewarding employee performance.[44] Having a performance management system in place, however, also allows the organization to systematically detect and treat performance problems that employees exhibit before those problems become so harmful and intractable that discharge is the only recourse. The discharge prevention possibilities of a performance management system make it another important retention initiative to use within an overall retention program. Also, a sound performance management system can be very useful in helping an organization successfully defend itself against legal challenges to discharges that do occur.

Exhibit 14.13 portrays the performance management process. Organization strategy drives work-unit plans, which in turn become operational and doable for employees through a four-stage process. Stage one—performance planning—involves setting performance goals for each employee and identifying specific competencies the employee will be evaluated on. In stage two—performance execution—the focus is on the employee actually performing the job. Assistance to the employee could or should be made in the form of resources to aid in job performance, coupled with coaching and feedback from the employee's manager, peers, and others. To be effective, performance feedback should be provided frequently and should always be accompanied by specific suggestions for improvement. At the end of the performance period, such as a quarter or a year, stage three begins and a formal performance review is conducted, usually by the manager. In this stage, the employee's success in reaching established goals is assessed, ratings of the employee's competencies are made, written comments are developed to explain ratings and provide suggestions for performance improvement, and feedback of the assessment is provided to the employee. Collectively, these actions are known as performance appraisal. In stage four, the information developed during the performance review is used to help make decisions that will affect the employee. These decisions will likely pertain to pay raises and to training and career plans. They may also pertain to formal identification of performance problems, where the employee has shown, or is headed toward, unacceptable performance. In reality, this process is ongoing, with each decision leading to a new cycle of performance planning.

The design, implementation, and operation of a performance management system is a complex undertaking, and the specific ways that the four stages are carried out vary among organizations.[45] For our purposes here, the performance management system depicted in Exhibit 14.13 shows how such a system can be a critical retention tool for the organization when it is confronted with employees with severe performance problems that place them on the cusp of termination.

Specifically, it may be decided that an employee has severe performance problems (stage four), and this can set in motion a focused performance-improvement process throughout the next performance management cycle. The process of performance counseling and discipline can be conceptualized in six stages, as shown in Exhibit 14.14. It is important for managers to consider different types of per-

EXHIBIT 14.13 Performance Management Process

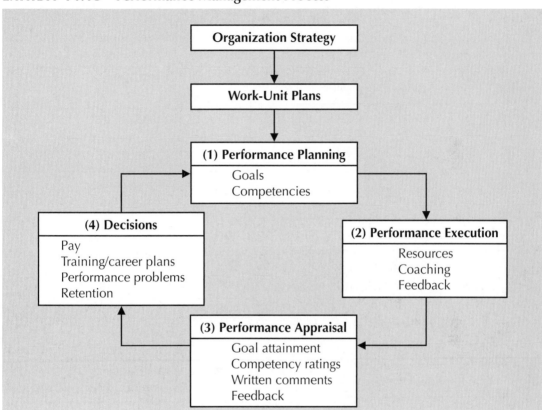

formance problems when developing a counseling and disciplinary plan, because each dimension requires different responses. The model in Exhibit 14.14 breaks job performance into three categories.[46] Task performance includes the completion of job tasks that are specifically included in the job description. Citizenship reflects the psychological and social environment of work created by employees, which might be only indirectly reflected in written job descriptions but is important for maintaining a smoothly functioning work group. Counterproductivity represents actions that directly violate organizational rules or that undermine performance. The first imperative for managers is to continually monitor employee performance and identify problems. Next, managers should determine why employee performance has become unacceptable. This process should involve the employees' input as well. If problems are occurring because of a lack of knowledge or skills, it may be possible to use corrective action based on training or counseling; problems involving lack of motivation or negative attitudes require the use of rewards and

EXHIBIT 14.14 **Performance Counseling and Disciplinary Processes**

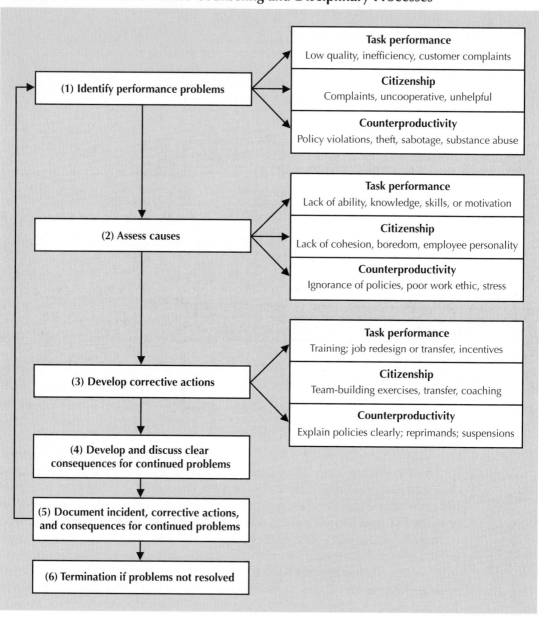

punishments, and problems involving personality or lack of ability may require reassignment to a different job. Regardless of which corrective actions are taken, employees need to be clearly informed about the consequences for continued failure to perform adequately, and the entire counseling and disciplinary process needs to be documented. It is hoped that performance will improve, but if not, the organization will need to consider the possibility of terminating employment.

Manager Training and Rewards

A successful performance management system requires many components. Probably none are more critical than training and rewards for the managers who will use the performance management system with employees in their work units.[47]

Performance management requires managers to possess a complex set of knowledges and skills, particularly for the performance execution and performance appraisal stages. Training for managers is essential to provide them these requisites to being effective performance managers. Examples of training content include purposes of performance management, policies and procedures of the performance management system, appraisal forms and how to complete them, keeping records of employee performance incidents, rating accuracy, coaching techniques, finding and providing resources, methods of providing feedback, goal setting, and legal compliance requirements. It is especially important to stress exactly why and how performance management is to be used as a retention initiative that seeks to prevent discharge through intensive performance improvement attempts.

Managers must also be provided incentives for using these new knowledges and skills to effectively conduct performance management. At a minimum it will be necessary to formally make performance management part of the manager's job during the performance planning stage; the manager's own performance appraisal results will depend on how well he or she practices performance management.

Another important part of training should be concerned with employee termination. Here, managers must come to understand that a decision to discharge an employee for performance problems falls outside the normal performance management process (Exhibit 14.13) and is not a decision that can or should be made by the individual manager alone. Terminations require separate procedural and decision-making processes.[48] These could also be covered as part of a regular performance management training program, or a separate program devoted to termination could be conducted.

Progressive Discipline

Employee discipline pertains to behavioral conduct problems that violate rules, procedures, laws, and professional and moral standards.[49] Discipline may also come into play for employees with performance problems. Progressive discipline has a series of penalties for misconduct that increase in severity if the misconduct is repeated, starting with an informal warning and going all the way up to termination. In progressive discipline, employees are given notice of their misconduct and are provided the opportunity (and often the assistance) to change their behavior; termination is a last resort.

Progressive discipline systems are rooted in major principles of fairness and justice that can be summarized in the following five requirements for a progressive discipline system: (1) give employees notice of the rules of conduct and misconduct, (2) give employees notice of the consequences of violating the rules, (3) provide equal treatment for all employees, (4) allow for full investigation of the alleged misconduct and defense by the employee, and (5) provide employees the right to appeal a decision.[50]

Actions to Take

Several things can be done to address the fairness requirements. First, establish what constitutes misconduct and the penalties for misconduct. The penalties start with an oral warning and progress through a written warning, suspension, and termination. Second, provide training to employees and managers so that they are aware of the types of misconduct, penalties, investigation and documentation requirements, and appeal rights. Third, work with managers to ensure that there is consistency of treatment (no favoritism) of employees, meaning that similar misconduct results in similar penalties for all employees. Finally, establish an appeals procedure, if one is not already in place, in which employees may challenge disciplinary actions.

Documentation by the manager is critical in all but the least severe instances of misconduct (e.g., first-time minor offense with an oral warning).[51] Thus, the manager must investigate allegations of misconduct, gather evidence, write down what happened, and keep records of what was learned. Allegations of tardiness, for example, might involve inspection of time cards and interviews with other employees. The time cards and interview notes should then be kept as part of the documentation record. Employees should have the right to see all documentation and provide written documentation in self-defense.

Performance problems could be incorporated into, or dovetailed with, the progressive discipline system.[52] Here, it would be wise (if possible) to first adhere to the normal performance management cycle so that correction of performance deficiencies is done in a consultative way between the employee and the manager, and the manager assumes major responsibility for providing resources to the employee, as well as for attentive coaching and feedback. If performance improvement is not forthcoming, then shifting to the progressive discipline system will be necessary. For very serious performance problems, it may be necessary for the manager to address them with an expedited performance management cycle, coupled with a clear communication to the employee that failure to correct performance problems could lead immediately to the beginning of formal disciplinary actions.

Employee termination is the final step in progressive discipline, and ideally it would never be necessary. Rarely, if ever, will this be the case. The organization thus must be prepared for the necessity of conducting terminations. Termination processes, guidelines, training for managers, and so forth must be developed and implemented. Considerable guidance is available to help the organization in this regard.[53]

RETENTION INITIATIVES: DOWNSIZING

Downsizing involves reducing the organization's staffing levels through layoffs (RIFs). Many factors contribute to layoff occurrences: decline in profits, restructuring of the organization, substitution of the core workforce with a flexible workforce, obsolete job or work unit, mergers and acquisitions, loss of contracts and clients, technological advances, productivity improvements, shortened product life cycles, and financial markets that favor downsizing as a positive organizational action.[54] While downsizing obviously involves the elimination of jobs and employees, it also encompasses several retention matters that involve balancing the advantages and disadvantages of downsizing, staffing levels and quality, alternatives to layoffs, and dealing with employees who remain after downsizing.

Weighing Advantages and Disadvantages

Downsizing has multiple advantages (benefits) and disadvantages (costs); refer back to Exhibit 14.8 for a review. A thoughtful consideration of these makes it clear that if downsizing is to be undertaken, it should be done with great caution. It is usually not an effective "quick fix" to financial performance problems confronting the organization.

Moreover, research suggests that the presumed and hoped-for benefits of downsizing may not be as great as they might seem.[55] For example, one study looked at how employment level changes affected profitability and stock returns of 537 organizations over a 14-year period. Downsizing did not significantly improve profitability, though it did produce somewhat better stock returns. Organizations that combined downsizing with asset restructuring fared better. Another study looked at the incidence of downsizing across the regional sales offices of a large financial services organization and found that layoffs ranged from 0% to 29% of the workforce, with an average of 7%. It was also found that the amount of downsizing had a significant negative impact on sales offices' profitability, productivity, and customer satisfaction. Additional research has found that downsizing has negative impacts on employee morale and health, workgroup creativity and communication, and workforce quality.[56]

In short, downsizing is not a panacea for poor financial health. It has many negative impacts on employees and should be combined with a well-planned total restructuring if it is to be effective. Such conclusions suggest the organization should carefully ponder whether it should downsize; if so, by how much and which employees it should seek to retain.

Staffing Levels and Quality

Reductions in staffing levels should be mindful of retention in at least two ways. First, enthusiasm for a financial quick fix needs to be tempered by a realization that, once lost, many downsized employees may be unlikely to return later if economic circumstances improve. The organization will then have to engage in costly restaffing, as opposed to potentially less costly and quicker retention initiatives. At a minimum, therefore, the organization should consider alternatives to downsizing simultaneously with downsizing planning. Such an exercise may well lead to less downsizing and greater retention.

Staffing level reductions should also be thought of in selective or targeted terms, rather than across the board. Such a conclusion is a logical outgrowth of HR planning, through which it is invariably discovered that the forecasted labor demand and supply figures lead to differing HR head-count requirements across organizational units and job categories. Indeed, it is possible that some units or job categories may be confronting layoffs while others will actually be hiring. Such an occurrence is increasingly common in organizations.[57]

If cuts are to be made, who should be retained? Staffing quality and employee acceptance concerns combine to produce some alternatives to choose from. The first alternative would be to retain the most senior employees in each work unit. Such an approach explicitly rewards these employees, thus likely enhancing long-run retention efforts by signaling job security commitments to long-term employees. On the downside, the most senior employees may not be the best performers, and looking ahead, the most senior employees may not have the necessary qualifications for job requirement changes that will be occurring as part of the restructuring process.

A second alternative would be to make performance-based retention decisions.[58] Employees' current and possibly past performance appraisals would be consulted in each work unit. The lowest-performing employees would be designated for layoff. This approach seeks to retain the highest-quality employees, those whose performance contributes most to organizational effectiveness. It may meet with less employee acceptance than the first alternative because of perceived injustice in the performance appraisal process. It also assumes that the current crop of best performers will continue to be so in the future, even though job requirements might change. Legal challenges may also arise, as discussed later.

A third alternative focuses on retaining high-value employees and laying off low-value employees (refer back to Exhibit 14.1). Here, multiple criteria of value are used, rather than a single criterion such as seniority or performance, though both of these value indicators would likely be included in a value assessment of employees. Recognition of multiple indicators of value is more encompassing in terms of employees' likely future contributions to organizational effectiveness, and because of this it may also meet with high employee acceptance. Use of this approach, however, requires a complex and potentially burdensome process. Indeed, the process is directly akin to an internal selection system in which the value indicators must be identified, assessed, scored, and weighted to come up with a composite value score for each employee that would then be used as the basis for the retention decision. Cut scores would probably be required.

Alternatives to Downsizing

A no-layoffs or guaranteed employment policy as an organization strategy is the most dramatic alternative to downsizing. No-layoff strategies require considerable organization and HR planning, along with a commitment to a set of programs necessary for successfully implementing the strategy. The strategies also require a gamble and a bet that, if lost, could severely damage employee loyalty and trust. During the deep recession of 2007–2009, many employers that had previously pursued a no-layoff strategy abandoned these policies and significantly reduced their workforces.[59]

Other organizations are unwilling to make a no-layoff guarantee but pursue layoff minimization through many different programs. Exhibit 14.15 provides an example, based on a survey of 663 organizations. It can be seen that multiple steps were taken as alternatives to layoffs, headed by attrition (not replacing employees who leave), employment freezes, and nonrenewal of contract workers. A series of direct and indirect pay changes (e.g., salary reduction, early retirement) also played some role in their layoff minimization. Other actions are also possible, such as temporary layoff with some proportion of pay and benefits continued, substitution of stock options for bonuses, conversion of regular employees to independent contractors, temporary assignments at a reduced time (and pay) commitment, and off-site employees who temporarily work at home on a reduced time (and pay) basis.[60]

Employees Who Remain

Employees who remain either in their prelayoff job or in a redeployed job after a downsizing must not be ignored. Doing otherwise creates a new retention problem—survivors who are stressed and critical of the downsizing process. One survey of workers employed at 318 companies found that 81% reported customer service had declined, 77% reported more errors and mistakes being made, and 64% reported that their coworkers' productivity had declined. The survey authors attributed these negative results to layoff survivor stress,[61] which is heightened by loss of coworkers and friends, higher workloads, new locations and work hours, new and/or more responsibilities, and fear of job loss just around the corner.

EXHIBIT 14.15 Alternative Methods for Cost Minimization

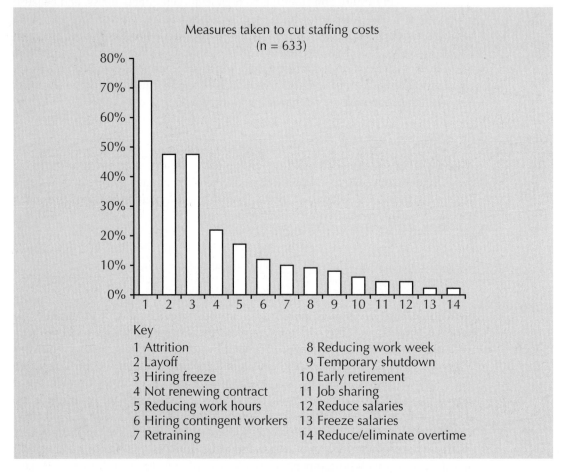

Measures taken to cut staffing costs
(n = 633)

Key

1 Attrition
2 Layoff
3 Hiring freeze
4 Not renewing contract
5 Reducing work hours
6 Hiring contingent workers
7 Retraining

8 Reducing work week
9 Temporary shutdown
10 Early retirement
11 Job sharing
12 Reduce salaries
13 Freeze salaries
14 Reduce/eliminate overtime

SOURCE: Society for Human Resource Management, *The Impact of 2008 U.S. Economy on Businesses* (Alexandria, VA: Author, 2008). Used by permission.

These examples of "survivor sickness" suggest a need to anticipate and attack it directly within downsizing planning. Experts recommend that organizations take active steps to reduce survivor stress. This can include active communication, involving the current workforce in redesigning jobs to accommodate lower staffing levels, and discussing career-related issues.[62] Unless steps are taken to help survivors plan for and adjust to the new realities they will confront, heightened job dissatisfaction seems inevitable. In turn, voluntary turnover may spike upward, further increasing the cost of downsizing.[63]

There are numerous examples of organizations that took steps to soften the blow of layoffs. When Circuit City announced plans to liquidate all of its stores in 2009, the organization took extraordinary steps to ensure that employees had assistance in their search for new jobs. Staff members established contacts with other organizations to help downsized employees find new jobs.[64] The organization also hosted résumé-writing and interviewing workshops for former associates. When HOK had to lay off a portion of its workforce, it offered transfers to other locations and held multiple training sessions with managers to teach them how to openly communicate about the layoffs with their employees.[65] As another example, following a steep drop in demand for products during a recession, Piper Aircraft moved to a four-day workweek, which reduced employee compensation by 20%.[66]

LEGAL ISSUES

Retention initiatives are closely intertwined with the occurrence of employee separations since the result of an unsuccessful retention initiative is the voluntary or involuntary separation of the employee from the organization. The organization's retention initiatives thus must be guided in part by the laws and regulations governing separations. A brief overview of these is provided. Then a detailed look at the role of performance appraisal in separation is presented since a thrust of this chapter was on performance-based retention.

Separation Laws and Regulations

A desire to provide protection and safeguards to employees leaving the organization, especially for discharge and downsizing, has led to myriad laws and regulations governing the separation process.[67] These include the following:

- Public policy restrictions on employment-at-will
- Employment discrimination laws and regulations
- Affirmative action requirements
- Employment contract principles
- Labor contract provisions
- Civil service laws and regulations
- Negligent supervision and retention
- Advanced warning about plant closings
- Severance agreements

A basic tenet underlying restrictions on employee separation is the need for fair and consistent treatment of employees. Included here are concerns for ensuring procedural fairness and having legitimate bases for separations, such as merit, seniority, or performance. The organization should be thoroughly familiar with these numerous laws and regulations, and their underlying principles, as it designs and administers its separation initiatives.

Performance Appraisal

Organizations often favor retention and separation systems and decisions being driven by employee performance. Laws and regulations generally uphold or even encourage such a role for performance. However, the law as interpreted also insists that the performance appraisals, and the performance appraisal system generally, be fairly and equitably applied to employees undergoing separation. Interpretations come about from a combination of court decisions and governmental regulations that have evolved around the issue of performance appraisal in practice.

Based on these decisions and regulations, numerous specific suggestions have been put forth to guide the organization in the design and use of its performance appraisal (or management) system:[68]

- Appraisal criteria should be job related, specific, and communicated in advance to the employee.
- The manager (rater) should receive training in the overall performance appraisal process and in how to avoid common rating errors.
- The manager should be familiar with the employee's job description and actual performance.
- There should be agreement among different raters in their evaluation of the employee's performance.
- Evaluations should be in writing.
- The employee should be able to review the evaluation and comment on it before it becomes final.
- The employee should receive timely feedback about the evaluation and an explanation for any outcome decision (e.g., retention or separation).
- There should be an upward review of the employee's appraisal.
- There should be an appeal system for employees dissatisfied with their evaluation.

Conforming to these recommendations will help provide (not guarantee) a fair evaluation process and help defend decisions pertaining to retention and separation. If the organization wants to manage a performance-driven retention system, it would be wise to ensure the adequacy of its performance appraisal system relative to the above recommendations.

SUMMARY

Retention management seeks to control the numbers and types of employees who leave the organization and those who remain with the organization. Employee loss occurs via voluntary turnover or involuntary turnover in the form of discharge or downsizing. Voluntary turnover is caused by a combination of perceived desirability of leaving, ease of leaving, and alternatives to one's current job. Some of these reasons are avoidable, but others are not. Avoidable turnover can also be said to occur among high- and low-value employees. Discharge occurs for performance- and discipline-related problems. Downsizing or RIF occurs because the organization is, or is projected to be, overstaffed in head-count terms.

It is important for the organization to conduct thorough analyses of its turnover. Using a simple formula, turnover rates can be calculated, both overall and broken down by types of turnover, types of employees, job categories, and geographic location. It is also useful to benchmark the organization's turnover rates internally and externally. Another form of analysis is determining reasons that people leave. This can be done via exit interviews, postexit surveys, and employee satisfaction surveys. Analysis of costs and benefits of each of the three types of turnover should also be done. The three major cost categories are separation, replacement, and training. Within each category, numerous costs, both financial and nonfinancial, may be estimated. Likewise, each type of turnover has both financial and nonfinancial benefits associated with it that must be weighed against the many costs. A thorough understanding of costs and benefits will help the organization determine where and among whom turnover is the most worrisome, and how to fashion retention strategies and tactics.

To reduce voluntary turnover, organizations engage in numerous retention initiatives centered around direct and variable pay programs, benefits, hours of work schedules, and training and development. Little is known about attempts to increase intrinsic rewards. A decision process may be followed to help decide which, if any, retention initiatives to undertake. The process follows five basic questions: Do we think turnover is a problem? How might we attack the problem? What do we need to decide? Should we proceed? How should we evaluate the programs? To influence the desirability of leaving, the organization must raise job satisfaction by providing both extrinsic and intrinsic rewards. Ease of leaving can possibly be reduced by providing organization-specific training and by increasing the costs of leaving. Finally, retention might be improved by providing more internal job alternatives to employees and by responding forcefully to other job offers they receive.

Discharges might be reduced via formal performance management and progressive discipline systems. The performance management system involves four stages—performance planning, performance execution, performance appraisal, and decisions about the employee. This helps prevent and correct performance problems. A progressive discipline system addresses behavioral conduct problems that violate rules, procedures, laws, and professional and moral standards. It has a series of penalties for misconduct that progress up to termination, which the system seeks to prevent if at all possible.

While downsizing seems to have some obvious benefits, research indicates that there are many costs as well, so the organization should carefully consider whether it really wants to downsize, and if so, by how much in terms of employee numbers and quality. Staffing levels should be achieved in a targeted way rather than across the board. From a staffing quality perspective, cuts could be based on seniority, job performance, or a more holistic assessment of who are the high-value employees the organization desires to retain. There are many alternatives to downsizing that could be pursued. Attention must be paid to employees who survive a downsizing, or they might create a new retention problem for the organization by starting to leave.

Legally, employee separation from the organization, especially on an involuntary basis, is subject to myriad laws and regulations that the organization must be aware of and incorporate into its retention strategy and tactics. If the organization wishes to base retention decisions on employees' job performance, it should recognize that laws and regulations require performance management systems to be fair and equitable to employees during separation. Based on regulations and court decisions, numerous recommendations must be followed for a performance management system to have a chance at withstanding legal challenges and scrutiny.

DISCUSSION QUESTIONS

1. For the three primary causes of voluntary turnover (desirability of leaving, ease of leaving, alternatives), might their relative importance depend on the type of employee or type of job? Explain.

2. Which of the costs and benefits of voluntary turnover are most likely to vary according to type of job? Give examples.

3. If a person said to you, "It's easy to reduce turnover—just pay people more money," what would your response be?

4. Why should an organization seek to retain employees with performance or discipline problems? Why not just fire them?

5. Discuss some potential problems with downsizing as an organization's first response to a need to cut labor costs.

ETHICAL ISSUES

1. Imagine your organization is doing exit interviews and has promised confidentiality to all who respond. You are responsible for conducting the exit interviews. Your supervisor has asked you to give her the name of each respondent so she can assess the information in conjunction with the person's supervisor. What obligation do corporate HR employees have to keep information confidential in such circumstances?

2. Firing an employee has numerous negative organizational consequences, including the discomfort of the supervisor who delivers the termination information, conflict or sabotage from the departing employee, and the poten-

tial for a lawsuit. In response, many supervisors give problem employees unpleasant work tasks, reduce their working hours, or otherwise negatively modify their jobs in hopes that problem employees will simply quit. What are the ethical issues raised by this strategy?

APPLICATIONS

Managerial Turnover: A Problem?

HealthCareLaunderCare (HCLC) is a company that specializes in picking up, cleaning, and delivering all the laundry for health care providers, especially hospitals, nursing homes, and assisted-care facilities. Basically, these health care providers have outsourced their laundry operations to HCLC. In this very competitive business, a typical contract between HCLC and a health care provider is only two years, and HCLC experiences a contract nonrenewal rate of 10%. Most nonrenewals occur because of dissatisfaction with service costs and especially quality (e.g., surgical garb that is not completely sterilized).

HCLC has 20 laundry facilities throughout the country, mostly in large metropolitan areas. Each laundry facility is headed by a site manager, and there are unit supervisors for the intake, washing, drying, inspection and repair, and delivery areas. An average of 100 nonexempt employees are employed at each site.

The operation of the facilities is technologically sophisticated and very health- and safety-sensitive. In the intake area, for example, employees wear protective clothing, gloves, and eyewear because of all the blood, tissue, and germs on laundry that comes in. The washing area is composed of huge washers in 35-foot stainless steel tunnels with screws that move the laundry through various wash cycles. Workers in this area are exposed to high temperatures and must be proficient in the operation of the computer control systems. Laundry is lifted out of the tunnels by robots and moved to the drying room area, where it is dried, ironed, and folded by machines tended by employees. In the inspection and repair area, quality inspection and assurance occurs. Laundry is inspected for germs and pinholes (in the case of surgical garb—pinholes could allow blood and fluids to come into contact with the surgeon), and employees complete repairs on torn clothing and sheets. In the delivery area, the laundry is hermetically sealed in packages and placed in delivery vans for transport.

HCLC's vice president of operations, Tyrone Williams, manages the sites—and site and unit managers—with an iron fist. Mr. Williams monitors each site with a weekly report of a set of cost, quality, and safety indicators for each of the five areas. When he spots what he thinks are problems or undesirable trends, he has a conference call with both the site manager and the area supervisor. In the decidedly one-way conversation, marching orders are delivered and are expected to be fulfilled. If a turnaround in the "numbers" doesn't show up in the next weekly report,

Mr. Williams gives the manager and the supervisor one more week to improve. If sufficient improvement is not forthcoming, various punitive actions are taken, including base pay cuts, demotions, reassignments, and terminations. Mr. Williams feels such quick and harsh justice is necessary to keep HCLC competitive and to continually drive home to all employees the importance of working "by the numbers." Fed up with this management system, many managers have opted to say "Bye-bye, numbers!" by leaving HCLC.

Recently, the issue of site and unit manager retention came up on the radar screen of HCLC's president, Roman Dublinski. Mr. Dublinski glanced at a payroll report showing that 30 of the 120 site and unit managers had left HCLC in the past year, though no reasons for leaving were given. In addition, Mr. Dublinski had received copies of a few angry resignation letters written to Mr. Williams. Having never confronted or thought about possible employee retention problems or how to deal with them, Mr. Dublinski calls you (the corporate manager of staffing) to prepare a brief written analysis that will then be used as the basis for a meeting between the two of you and the vice president of HR, Debra Angle (Ms. Angle recommended this). Address the following questions in your report:

1. Is the loss of 30 managers out of 120 in one year cause for concern?
2. What additional data should be gathered to learn more about managerial turnover?
3. What are the costs of this turnover? Might there be any benefits?
4. Are there any lurking legal problems?
5. If retention is a serious problem for HCLC, what are the main ways we might address it?

Retention: Deciding to Act

Wally's Wonder Wash (WWW) is a full-service, high-tech, high-touch car wash company owned solely by Wally Wheelspoke. Located in a midwestern city of 200,000 people (with another 100,000 in suburbs and more rural towns throughout the county), WWW currently has four facilities within the city. Wally plans to add four more facilities within the city in the next two years, and later on he plans to begin placing facilities in suburban locations and rural towns. Major competitors include two other full-service car washes (different owners), plus three touchless automatic facilities (same owner) in the city.

Wally's critical strategy is to provide the very best to customers who want and relish extremely clean and "spiffy" vehicles and to have customers feel a positive experience each time they come to WWW. To do this, WWW seeks to provide high-quality car washes and car detailing and to generate considerable repeat business through competitive prices combined with attention to customers. To make itself accessible to customers, WWW is open seven days a week, 8:00 a.m. to

8:00 p.m. Peak periods, volumewise, are after 1:00 on weekdays and from 10:00 to 5:00 on weekends. In addition, Wally uses his workforce to drive his strategy. Though untrained in HR, Wally knows that he must recruit and retain a stable, high-quality workforce if his current businesses, let alone his ambitious expansion plans, are to succeed.

WWW has a strong preference for full-time employees, who work either 7:30 to 4:00 or 11:00 to 8:00. Part-timers are used occasionally to help fill in during peak demand times and during the summer when full-timers are on vacation. There are two major jobs at WWW: attendant (washer) and custom service specialist (detailer). Practicing promotion from within, WWW promotes all specialists from the attendant ranks. There are currently 70 attendants and 20 custom service specialists at WWW. In addition, each facility has a manager. Wally has filled the manager's job by promotion from within (from either the attendant or custom service specialist ranks), but he is unsure if he will be able to continue doing this as he expands.

The job of attendant is a demanding one. Attendants vacuum vehicles from front to rear (and trunk if requested by the customer), wash and dry windows and mirrors, dry vehicles with hand towels, apply special cleaning compounds to tires, wipe down the vehicle's interior, and wash or vacuum floor mats. In addition, attendants wash and fold towels, lift heavy barrels of cleaning compounds and waxes, and perform light maintenance and repair work on the machinery. Finally, and very important, attendants consistently provide customer service by asking customers if they have special requests and by making small talk with them. A unique feature of customer service at WWW is that the attendant must ask the customer to personally inspect the vehicle before leaving to ensure that the vehicle is satisfactorily cleaned (attendants also correct any mistakes pointed out by the customer). The attendants work as a team, with each attendant expected to be able to perform all of the above tasks.

Attendants start at a base pay of $8.00/hour, with automatic $.50 raises at six months and one year. They receive a brief training from the manager before starting work. Custom service specialists start at $9.00/hour, with $.50 raises after six months and one year. Neither attendants nor custom service specialists receive performance reviews. Managers receive a salary of $27,000, plus an annual "merit" raise based on a very casual performance review conducted by Wally (whenever he gets around to it). All attendants share equally in a customer tip pool; custom service specialists receive individual tips. The benefits package is composed of (1) major medical health insurance with a 20% employee co-pay on the premium, (2) paid holidays for Christmas, Easter, July 4, and Martin Luther King, Jr.'s birthday, and (3) a generous paid sick pay plan of two days per month (in recognition of high illness rates due to extreme working conditions).

In terms of turnover, Wally has spotty and general data only. WWW experienced an overall turnover rate the past year of 65% for attendants and 20% for custom service specialists; no managers left. Though lacking data farther back, Wally thinks the turnover rate for attendants has been increasing. WWW's managers constantly complain to Wally about the high level of turnover among attendants and the problems it creates, especially in fulfilling the strong customer-service orientation for WWW. Though the managers have not conducted exit interviews, the major complaints they hear from attendants are (1) pay is not competitive relative to the other full-service car washes or many other entry-level jobs in the area, (2) training is hit-or-miss at best, (3) promotion opportunities are limited, (4) managers provide no feedback or coaching, and (5) customer complaints and mistreatment of attendants by customers are on the rise.

Wally is frustrated by attendant turnover and its threat to his customer service and expansion strategies. He calls on you for assistance in figuring out what to do about the problem. Use the decision process shown in Exhibit 14.11 to help develop a retention initiative for WWW. Address each of the questions in the process, specifically:

1. Do we think turnover is a problem?
2. How might we attack the problem?
3. What do we need to decide?
4. Should we proceed?
5. How should we evaluate the initiatives?

TANGLEWOOD STORES CASE

The final stage of the staffing process is ensuring that you are able to retain those individuals you have carefully recruited and selected. This chapter has described some of the best-documented correlates of employee turnover, including perceptions of organizational reward systems, the work environment, communication and justice, and the social environment.

The Situation

Although some retail organizations are comfortable with fairly high turnover, Tanglewood is very concerned about losing the talent and cultural knowledge of its managerial employees. The leaders of the organization are especially worried that competing retail firms have recognized the quality of Tanglewood's employee development plans and are enticing away the best store managers with large salary offers. Corporate staffing representatives have collected information regarding turnover rates and job satisfaction scores for all of its stores. In addition to the raw turnover rates, they have also provided you with data on employees who have left, including their job performance levels and exit interviews.

Your Tasks

First and foremost, Tanglewood wants you to see if turnover is a serious concern by looking at the relationship between performance and turnover. Once you have determined how much of a concern turnover is, you will investigate why employees are leaving. You will assess what the available information tells you about the reasons for turnover, and you will assess what new information Tanglewood might gather in the future to improve its understanding of why turnover occurs. Using Exhibit 14.12 as a guide, you will develop recommendations for how Tanglewood can improve retention with a combination of intrinsic and extrinsic rewards. The background information for this case, and your specific assignment, can be found at *www.mhhe.com/heneman7e*.

ENDNOTES

1. US Department of Labor, "Employee Tenure Study," *News*, Aug. 29, 2000; US Department of Labor, "Mass Layoffs in October 2001," *News*, Nov. 30, 2001; US Department of Labor, "Number of Jobs Held, Labor Market Activity, and Earnings Growth Among the Youngest Baby Boomers," *News*, Sept. 10, 2010.

2. P. W. Hom and R. W. Griffeth, *Employee Turnover* (Cincinnati, OH: South-Western, 1995), pp. 1–12; Saratoga Institute, *Human Capital Benchmarking Report* (Santa Clara, CA: author, 2001).

3. R. W. Griffeth, P. W. Hom, and S. Gaertner, "A Meta-Analysis of Antecedents and Correlates of Employee Turnover," *Journal of Management*, 2000, 26, pp. 463–488; Hom and Griffeth, *Employee Turnover*, pp. 51–107; J. D. Kammeyer-Mueller, C. R. Wanberg, T. M. Glomb, and D. A. Ahlburg, "Turnover Processes in a Temporal Context: It's About Time," *Journal of Applied Psychology*, 2005, 90, pp. 644–658; R. P. Steel and J. W. Lounsbury, "Turnover Process Models: Review and Synthesis of a Conceptual Literature," *Human Resource Management Review*, 2009, 19, pp. 271–282; P. W. Hom, L. Roberson, and A. D. Ellis, "Challenging Conventional Wisdom about Who Quits: Revelations from Corporate America," *Journal of Applied Psychology*, 2008, 93, pp. 1–34; J. G. March and H. A. Simon, *Organizations* (New York: Wiley, 1958); C. O. Trevor, "Interactions Among Actual Ease of Movement Determinants and Job Satisfaction in the Prediction of Voluntary Turnover," *Academy of Management Journal*, 2001, 44, pp. 621–638.

4. C. D. Crossley, R. J. Bennett, S. M. Jex, and L. Burnfield, "Development of a Global Measure of Job Embeddedness and Integration Into a Traditional Model of Voluntary Turnover," *Journal of Applied Psychology*, 2007, 92, pp. 1031–1042; W. S. Harman, T. W. Lee, T. R. Mitchell, W. Felps, and B. P. Owens, "The Psychology of Voluntary Employee Turnover," *Current Directions in Psychological Science*, 2007, 16, pp. 51–54; F. Niederman, M. Sumner, and C. P. Maertz, Jr., "Testing and Extending the Unfolding Model of Voluntary Turnover to IT Professionals," *Human Resource Management*, 2007, 46, pp. 331–347; C. P. Maertz and M. A. Campion, "Profiles in Quitting: Integrating Content and Process Turnover Theory," *Academy of Management Journal*, 2004, 47, pp. 566–582.

5. R. W. Griffeth and P. W. Hom, *Retaining Valued Employees* (Cincinnati, OH: South-Western, 2001), pp. 203–222; K. Fernandez, "Tie Up Loose Ends," *Staffing Management*, Jan. 2007 (*www.shrm.org/publications/staffingmanagementmagazine*); E. Agnvall, "Exit Interviews with the Click of a Mouse: Exit Interviews Go High-Tech," SHRM Online HR Technology Focus Area, Oct. 2006 (*www.shrm.org/hrdisciplines/technology/articles/pages/CMS_018960.aspx*).

6. M. A. Campion, "Meaning and Measurement of Turnover: Comparison and Recommendations for Research," *Journal of Applied Psychology*, 1991, 76, pp. 199–212; H. R. Nalbantian and A. Szostak, "How Fleet Bank Fought Employee Flight," *Harvard Business Review*, Apr. 2004, pp. 116–125; S. Wescott, "Goodbye and Good Luck," *Inc.*, Apr. 2006, pp. 40–41.

7. Z. Ton and R. S. Huckman, "Managing the Impact of Employee Turnover on Performance: The Role of Process Conformance," *Organization Science*, 2008, 16, pp. 56–68; K. M. Kacmar, M. C. Andrews, D. L. Rooy, R. C. Steilberg, and S. Cerrone, "Sure, Everyone Can Be Replaced . . . But at What Cost? Turnover as a Predictor of Unit Level Performance," *Academy of Management Journal*, 2006, 49, pp. 133–144; J. Hausknecht, C. O. Trevor, and M. J. Howard, "Unit Level Voluntary Turnover Rates and Customer Service Quality Implications of Group Cohesiveness, Newcomer Concentration, and Size," *Journal of Applied Psychology*, 2009, 94, pp. 1068–1075.

8. W. F. Cascio, *Costing Human Resources*, fourth ed. (Cincinnati, OH: South-Western, 2000), pp. 23–57; Griffeth and Hom, *Retaining Valued Employees*, pp. 10–22; R. Williams and L. Arnett, "Retaining Employees by Sticking to the Basics," *Workforce Management*, Dec. 2008 (*www.workforce.com/tools/features/081215_apqc_stickingtobasics.pdf*).

9. Cascio, *Costing Human Resources*, pp. 83–105; P. C. Gibson and K. S. Piscitelli, *Basic Employment Law Manual for Managers and Supervisors* (Chicago: Commerce Clearing House, 1997); E. E. Schuttauf, *Performance Management Manual for Managers and Supervisors* (Chicago: Commerce Clearing House, 1997).

10. J. N. Barron and D. M. Kreps, *Strategic Human Resources* (New York: Wiley, 1999), pp. 421–445; Cascio, *Costing Human Resources*, pp. 23–57; J. A. Schmidt (ed.), *Making Mergers Work* (New York: Towers, Perrin, Foster and Crosby, 2001), pp. 257–268.

11. S. Craig and J. Singer, "Merrill Confirms 9,000 Job Cuts, Earnings Charge of 2.2 Billion," *Wall Street Journal*, Jan. 10, 2002, p. C1.

12. E. Esen, *U.S. Job Recovery and Retention: Poll Findings* (Alexandria, VA: SHRM Research, 2005).

13. T. A. Judge, J. E. Bono, and E. A. Locke, "Personality and Job Satisfaction: The Mediating Role of Job Characteristics," *Journal of Applied Psychology*, 2000, 85, pp. 237–249; B. T. Loher, R. A. Noe, N. L. Moeller, and M. P. Fitzgerald, "A Meta-Analysis of the Relation of Job Characteristics to Job Satisfaction," *Journal of Applied Psychology*, 1985, 70, pp. 280–289.

14. M. A. Campion and M. M. Mitchell, "Management Turnover: Experiential Differences Between Former and Current Managers," *Personnel Psychology*, 1986, 39, pp. 57–69; Kammeyer-Mueller, Wanberg, Glomb, and Ahlburg, "Turnover Processes in a Temporal Context: It's About Time"; P. E. Spector and S. M. Jex, "Relations of Job Characteristics From Multiple Data Sources With Employee Affect, Absence, Turnover Intentions, and Health," *Journal of Applied Psychology*, 1991, 76, pp. 46–53.

15. WorldatWork, *Attraction and Retention: The Impact and Prevalence of Work-Life & Benefit Programs* (Scottsdale, AZ: author, 2007).

16. A. Fisher, "Playing for Keeps," *Fortune,* Jan. 22, 2007, pp. 85–93; D. A. Kaplan, "SAS the Best Company to Work For," *Fortune*, Feb. 8, 2010, pp. 56–64.

17. J. D. Shaw and N. Gupta, "Pay System Characteristics and Quit Patterns of Good, Average, and Poor Performers," *Personnel Psychology*, 2007, 60, pp. 903–928.

18. J. B. Arthur, "Effects of Human Resource Systems on Manufacturing Performance and Turnover," *Academy of Management Journal*, 1994, 37, pp. 670–687.

19. M. A. Huselid, "The Impact of Human Resource Management Practices on Turnover, Productivity, and Corporate Financial Performance," *Academy of Management Journal*, 1995, 38, pp. 635–672.

20. E. R. Demby, "The Insider: Benefits," *Workforce Management*, Feb. 2004, pp. 57–59; Nalbantian and Szostak, "How Fleet Bank Fought Employee Flight"; S. Overman, "Outback Steakhouse Grills Applicants, Caters to Employees to Keep Turnover Low," *SHRM News Online*, Oct. 2004 (*www.shrm.org/ema/news_published/CMS_008306.asp*); T. Rutigliano, "Tuning Up Your Talent Engine," *Gallup Management Journal*, Fall 2001, pp. 12–14; G. Strauss, "UPS' Pay, Perks Make It a Destination Job for Many," *Wall Street Journal*, Oct. 14, 2003, pp. B1–B2; E. Zimmerman, "The Joy of Flex," *The Workforce Management 2004 Optimas Awards*, pp. 4–5; J. T. Marquez, "Tailor-Made Careers," *Workforce Management*, Jan. 2010, pp. 16–21.

21. H. Axel, "Strategies for Retaining Critical Talent," *The Conference Board*, 1998, 6(2), pp. 4–18; P. Cappelli, "A Market-Driven Approach to Retaining Talent," *Harvard Business Review*, Jan.–Feb. 2000, pp. 103–111; T. Wilson, "Brand Imaging," *ACA News*, May 2000, pp. 44–48.

22. S. Miller, "What Do Employees Want? Not Always What Employers Think," Mar. 2007 (*www. shrm.org/hrdisciplines/compensation/articles/pages/cms_020601.aspx*); Williams and Arnett, "Retaining Employees by Sticking to the Basics."

23. Harris Interactive, *Working in America: The Key to Employee Satisfaction* (Rochester, NY: author, 2007).

24. M. Schoeff, "Retention Edges Cost Reduction as Benefits Objective," *Workforce Management Online*, Mar. 24, 2009 (*www.workforce.com/archive*).

25. C. O. Trevor, B. Gerhart, and J. W. Boudreau, "Voluntary Turnover and Job Performance: Curvilinearity and the Moderating Influences of Salary Growth and Promotions," *Journal of Applied Psychology*, 1997, 82, pp. 44–61; S. J. Peterson and F. Luthans, "The Impact of Financial and Nonfinancial Incentives on Business-Unit Outcomes Over Time," *Journal of Applied Psychology*, 2006, 91, pp. 156–165; Shaw and Gupta, "Pay System Characteristics and Quit Patterns of Good, Average, and Poor Performers"; J. D. Shaw, N. Gupta, and J. E. Delery, "Pay Dispersion and Work Force Performance: Moderating Effects of Incentives and Interdependence," *Strategic Management Journal*, 2002, 23, pp. 491–512; J. D. Shaw, N. Gupta, and J. E. Delery, "Alternative Conceptualizations of the Relationship Between Voluntary Turnover and Organizational Performance," *Academy of Management Journal*, 2005, 48, pp. 50–68.

26. Cappelli, "A Market-Driven Approach to Retaining Talent"; L. Gomez-Mejia and D. Balkin, *Compensation, Organizational Strategy, and Firm Performance* (Cincinnati, OH: South-Western, 1992), pp. 290–307; B. Klaas and J. McClendon, "To Lead, Lag, or Match: Estimating the Financial Impact of Pay Level Policies," *Personnel Psychology*, 1996, 49, pp. 121–140.

27. S. L. Peterson, "Managerial Turnover in U.S. Retail Organizations," *Journal of Management Development*, 2007, 26, pp. 770–789; Griffeth and Hom, *Retaining Valued Employees*, pp. 31–45; Kammeyer-Mueller, Wanberg, Glomb, and Ahlburg, "Turnover Processes in a Temporal Context: It's About Time"; Harman, Lee, Mitchell, Felps, and Owens, "The Psychology of Voluntary Employee Turnover"; Niederman, Sumner, and Maertz, "Testing and Extending the Unfolding Model of Voluntary Turnover to IT Professionals"; Maertz and Campion, "Profiles in Quitting: Integrating Content and Process Turnover Theory."

28. K. V. Rondeau, E. S. Williams, and T. H. Wagar, "Developing Human Capital: What Is the Impact on Nurse Turnover?" *Journal of Nursing Management*, 2009, 17, pp. 739–748.

29. R. Folger and R. Cropanzano, *Organizational Justice and Human Resource Management* (Thousand Oaks, CA: Sage, 1998); R. A. Postuma, C. P. Maertz, Jr., and J. B. Dworkin, "Procedural Justice's Relationship With Turnover: Explaining Past Inconsistent Findings," *Journal of Organizational Behavior*, 2007, 28, pp. 381–398.

30. G. Paré and M. Tremblay, "The Influence of High-Involvement Human Resources Practices, Procedural Justice, Organizational Commitment, and Citizenship Behaviors on Information Technology Professionals' Turnover Intentions," *Group & Organization Management*,

2007, 32, pp. 326–357; N. P. Podsakoff, J. A. LePine, and M. A. LePine, "Differential Challenge Stressor-Hindrance Stressor Relationships With Job Attitudes, Turnover Intentions, Turnover, and Withdrawal Behavior: A Meta-Analysis," *Journal of Applied Psychology*, 2007, 92, pp. 438–454.

31. S. Fournier, "Keeping Line Managers in the Know," *ACA News*, 2000, 43(3), pp. 1–3; K. D. Scott, D. Morajda, and J. W. Bishop, "Increase Company Competitiveness," *WorldatWork Journal*, 2002, 11(1), pp. 35–42.

32. Rutigliano, "Tuning Up Your Talent Engine."

33. J. Choi and C. C. Chen, "The Relationships of Distributive Justice and Compensation System Fairness to Employee Attitudes in International Joint Ventures," *Journal of Organizational Behavior*, 2007, 28, pp. 687–703; A. A. Chughtai and S. Zafar, "Antecedents and Consequences of Organizational Commitment Among Pakistani University Teachers," *Applied H.R.M. Research*, 2006, 11, pp. 39–64; T. Kim and K. Leung, "Forming and Reacting to Overall Fairness: A Cross-Cultural Comparison," *Organizational Behavior and Human Decision Processes*, 2007, 104, pp. 83–95; D. G. Allen, R. W. Griffeth, J. M. Vardaman, K. Aquino, S. Gaertner, M. Lee, "Structural Validity and Generalizability of a Referent Cognitions Model of Turnover Decisions," *Applied Psychology: An International Review*, 2009, 58, pp. 709–728.

34. W. Felps, T. R. Mitchell, D. R. Hekman, T. W. Lee, B. C. Holtom, and W. S. Harman, "Turnover Contagion: How Coworkers, Job Embeddedness and Job Search Behaviors Influence Quitting," *Academy of Management Journal*, 2009, 52, pp. 545–561.

35. J. Mayfield and M. Mayfield, "The Effects of Leader Communication on a Worker's Intent to Stay: An Investigation Using Structural Equation Modeling," *Human Performance*, 2007, 20, pp. 85–102; C. Donoghue and N. G. Castle, "Leadership Styles of Nursing Home Administrators and Their Association with Staff Turnover," *The Gerontologist*, 2009, 49, pp. 166–174; L. H. Nishii and D. M. Mayer, "Do Inclusive Leaders Help to Reduce Turnover in Diverse Groups?" *Journal of Applied Psychology*, 2009, 94, pp. 1412–1426.

36. B. J. Tepper, "Consequences of Abusive Supervision," *Academy of Management Journal*, 2000, 43, pp. 178–190; J. S. Leonard and D. I. Levine, "The Effect of Diversity on Turnover: A Large Case Study," *Industrial and Labor Relations Review*, 2006, 59, pp. 547–572; P. F. McKay, D. R. Avery, S. Toniandel, M. A. Morris, M. Hernandez, and M. R. Hebl, "Racial Differences in Employee Retention: Are Diversity Climate Perceptions the Key?" *Personnel Psychology*, 2007, 60, pp. 35–62.

37. C. A. Thompson and D. J. Prottas, "Relationships Among Organizational Family Support, Job Autonomy, Perceived Control, and Employee Well-Being," *Journal of Occupational Health Psychology*, 2006, 11, pp. 100–118; Podsakoff, LePine, and LePine, "Differential Challenge Stressor-Hindrance Stressor Relationships With Job Attitudes, Turnover Intentions, Turnover, and Withdrawal Behavior: A Meta-Analysis"; S. Aryee, V. Luk, and R. Stone, "Family-Responsive Variables and Retention-Relevant Outcomes Among Employed Parents," *Human Relations*, 1998, 51, pp. 73–87; T. D. Golden, "Avoiding Depletion in Virtual Work: Telework and the Intervening Impact of Work Exhaustion on Commitment and Turnover Intentions," *Journal of Vocational Behavior*, 2006, 69, pp. 176–187; T. Golden, "Co-workers Who Telework and the Impact on Those in the Office: Understanding the Implications of Virtual Work for Co-worker Satisfaction and Turnover Intentions," *Human Relations*, 2007, 60, pp. 1641–1667; Society for Human Resource Management, *Workplace Flexibility in the 21st Century* (Alexandria, VA: author, 2008).

38. M. R. Barrick and R. D. Zimmerman, "Reducing Voluntary, Avoidable Turnover Through Selection," *Journal of Applied Psychology*, 2005, 90, pp. 159–166; J. B. Becton, M. C. Matthews, D. L. Hartley, and D. H. Whitaker, "Using Biodata to Predict Turnover, Organizational Commit-

ment, and Job Performance in Healthcare," *International Journal of Selection and Assessment*, 2009, 17, pp. 189–202.

39. R. D. Zimmerman, "Understanding the Impact of Personality Traits on Individuals' Turnover Decisions: A Meta-Analytic Path Model," *Personnel Psychology*, 2008, 61, pp. 309–348; M. R. Barrick and R. D. Zimmerman, "Hiring for Retention and Performance," *Human Resource Management*, 2009, 48, pp. 183–206; M. R. Barrick and M. K. Mount, "Effects of Impression Management and Self-Deception on the Validity of Personality Constructs," *Journal of Applied Psychology*, 1996, 81, pp. 261–272.

40. D. J. Hanford, "Stay. Please," *Wall Street Journal*, Apr. 12, 2001, p. R8.

41. E. R. Silverman, "Mercer Tries to Keep Its Employees Through Its 'Externship' Program," *Wall Street Journal*, Nov. 7, 2000, p. B18.

42. A. R. Wheeler, V. C. Gallagher, R. L. Brover, and C. J. Sablynski, "When Person-Organization (Mis)Fit and (Dis)Satisfaction Lead to Turnover: The Moderating Role of Perceived Job Mobility," *Journal of Managerial Psychology*, 2007, 22, pp. 203–219.

43. J. S. Lublin, "In Hot Demand, Retention Czars Face Tough Job," *Wall Street Journal*, Sept. 12, 2000, p. B1.

44. M. Armstrong, *Performance Management*, second ed. (London: Kogan-Page, 2000); D. Grote, *The Complete Guide to Performance Appraisal* (New York: AMACOM, 1996); G. P. Latham and K. N. Wexley, *Increasing Productivity Through Performance Appraisal*, second ed. (Reading, MA: Addison-Wesley, 1994); Schuttauf, *Performance Management Manual for Managers and Supervisors.*

45. Grote, *The Complete Guide to Performance Appraisal*; Society for Human Resource Management, *Performance Management Survey* (Alexandria, VA: author, 2000).

46. M. Rotundo and P. R. Sackett, "The Relative Importance of Task, Citizenship, and Counterproductive Performance to Global Ratings of Job Performance: A Policy Capturing Approach," *Journal of Applied Psychology*, 2002, 87, pp. 66–80; J. W. Johnson, "The Relative Importance of Task and Contextual Performance Dimensions to Supervisor Judgments of Overall Performance," *Journal of Applied Psychology*, 2001, 86, pp. 984–996; P. R. Sackett, C. M. Berry, S. A. Wiemann, and R. M. Laczo, "Citizenship and Counterproductive Behavior: Clarifying Relations Between the Two Domains," *Human Performance*, 2006, 19, pp. 441–464; F. Lievens, J. M. Conway, and W. De Corte, "The Relative Importance of Task, Citizenship, and Counterproductive Performance to Job Performance Ratings: Do Rater Source and Team-Based Culture Matter?" *Journal of Occupational and Organizational Psychology*, 2008, 81, pp. 11–27.

47. G. A. Stoskopf, "Taking Performance Management to the Next Level," *Workspan*, Feb. 2002, pp. 26–33.

48. F. T. Coleman, *Ending the Employment Relationship Without Ending Up in Court* (Alexandria, VA: Society for Human Resource Management, 2001); Gibson and Piscitelli, *Basic Employment Law Manual for Managers and Supervisors.*

49. Gibson and Piscitelli, *Basic Employment Law Manual for Managers and Supervisors*, pp. 51–53.

50. R. R. Hastings, "Designing a Progressive Discipline Policy," 2010 (*www.shrm.org/hrdisciplines/ employeerelations/articles/Pages/designingaprogressive.aspx*); R. R. Hastings, "Is Progressive Discipline a Thing of the Past?" 2010 (*www.shrm.org/hrdisciplines/employeerelations/articles/ Pages/IsProgressiveDisciplineaThing.aspx*).

51. Schuttauf, *Performance Management Manual for Managers and Supervisors*, pp. 43–45.

52. Gibson and Piscitelli, *Basic Employment Law Manual for Managers and Supervisors*, pp. 48–53; Hastings, "Is Progressive Discipline a Thing of the Past?"

53. Coleman, *Ending the Employment Relationship Without Ending Up in Court*, pp. 51–84.

54. D. K. Datta, J. P. Guthrie, D. Basuil, and A. Pandey, "Causes and Effects of Employee Downsizing: A Review and Synthesis," *Journal of Management*, 2010, 36, pp. 281–348.

55. J. P. Guthrie and D. K. Datta, "Dumb and Dumber: The Impact of Downsizing on Firm Performance as Moderated by Industry Conditions," *Organization Science*, 2008, 19, pp. 108–123.

56. Datta, Guthrie, Basuil, and Pandey, "Causes and Effects of Employee Downsizing: A Review and Synthesis."

57. P. Barta, "In This Expansion, As Business Booms, So Do the Layoffs," *Wall Street Journal*, Mar. 13, 2000, p. A1; L. Uchitelle, "Pink Slip? Now It's All in a Day's Work," *New York Times*, Aug. 5, 2001, p. BU1.

58. A. Fox, "Prune Employees Carefully," *HR Magazine*, Apr. 2008 (*www.shrm.org/publications/hrmagazine*).

59. C. Tuna, "No Layoff Policies Crumble," *Wall Street Journal*, Dec. 29, 2008, p. B1.

60. B. Mirza, "Look at Alternatives to Layoffs," *HR News*, Dec. 29, 2008 (*www.shrm.org/hrdisciplines/businessleadership/articles/Pages/AlternativestoLayoffs.aspx*).

61. K. Gurchiek, "Layoffs Pack Punch to 'Surviving' Employees," *HR News*, Dec. 22, 2008 (*www.shrm.org/publications/hrnews/Pages/PunchtoSurvivingEmployees.aspx*).

62. Gurchiek, "Layoffs Pack Punch to 'Surviving' Employees."

63. C. O. Trevor and A. J. Nyberg, "Keeping Your Headcount When All About You Are Losing Theirs: Downsizing, Voluntary Turnover Rates, and the Moderating Role of HR Practices," *Academy of Management Journal*, 2008, 51, pp. 259–276; A. K. Mishra, K. E. Misra, and G. M. Spreitzer, "Downsizing the Company Without Downsizing Morale," *MIT Sloan Management Review*, 2009, 50(3), pp. 39–44.

64. A. Fox, "Pulling the Plug on Circuit City," *HRMagazine*, June 1, 2009 (*www.shrm.org/publications/hrmagazine/EditorialContent/Pages/0609fox.aspx*).

65. J. T. Marquez, "How HOK Builds Engagement Despite the Downturn," *Workforce Management Online*, Dec. 2009 (*www.workforce.com/section/hr-management/feature/how-hok-builds-engagement-despite-downturn*).

66. R. Zeidner, "Cutting Hours Without Increasing Risk," *HRMagazine*, Apr. 1, 2009 (*www.shrm.org/publications/hrmagazine/EditorialContent/Pages/0409zeidner.aspx*).

67. Coleman, *Ending the Employment Relationship Without Ending Up in Court*; J. G. Frierson, *Preventing Employment Lawsuits* (Washington, DC: Bureau of National Affairs, 1997); S. C. Kahn, B. B. Brown, and M. Lanzarone, *Legal Guide to Human Resources* (Boston: Warren, Gorham and Lamont, 2001), pp. 9-3 to 9-82; D. P. Twomey, *Labor and Employment Law*, eleventh ed. (Cincinnati, OH: South-Western, 2001); E. Lipsig, M. E. Dollarhide, and B. K. Seifert, *Reductions in Force in Employment Law*, second ed. (Washington, DC: BNA Books, 2010).

68. Kahn, Brown, and Lanzarone, *Legal Guide to Human Resources*, pp. 6-2 to 6-58; D. C. Martin, K. M. Bartol, and P. E. Kehoe, "The Legal Ramifications of Performance Appraisal," *Public Personnel Management*, 2000, 29, pp. 379–406; J. M. Werner and M. C. Bolino, "Explaining U.S. Courts of Appeals Decisions Involving Performance Appraisals: Accuracy, Fairness, and Validation," *Personnel Psychology*, 1997, 50, pp. 1–24; J. Marquez, "Is G.E.'s Ranking System Broken?" *Workforce Management*, June 25, 2007, pp. 1–3; M. Orey, "Fear of Firing," *Business Week*, Apr. 23, 2007, pp. 52–62.

NAME INDEX

Aamodt, M. G., 367, 498
Aberman, D., 266
Abrams, N., 84
Abueva, J. E., 536
Adkins, C. L., 630
Agnvall, E., 735
Agrawal, R. K., 267
Aguinis, H., 578
Ahlburg, D. A., 735, 736, 737
Aiman-Smith, L., 267
Alexander, D., 9
Alexander, R. A., 564, 576, 577
Allen, D. G., 265, 738
Alliger, G. M., 198
Allred, B. R., 307
Almond, E., 438
Alonso, A., 268
Altizer, C., 13
Anders, G., 40
Anderson, D., 422
Anderson, N., 423, 424, 494, 495, 536, 577
Andrews, M. C., 736
Ángel, P. O., 264
Angoff, W. H., 578
Anseel, F., 308
Aquinis, H., 500
Aquino, K., 738
Ardichvili, A., 41
Arkey, T., 61
Armenakis, A. A., 268
Armour, S., 266
Armstrong, M., 739
Armstrong, T., 265
Arnett, L., 736, 737
Arnold, J., 269
Arthur, D., 143
Arthur, J. B., 736
Arthur, J. S., 678

Arthur, W., Jr., 495, 497, 536
Arvey, R. D., 366
Aryee, S., 738
Ash, R. A., 198, 422, 423
Ash, S. R., 268
Asher, J. J., 496
Ashton, M. C., 498
Assouline, M., 498
Athavaley, A., 423
Atwater, D., 422
Auerbach, M. A., 578
Aumodt, M. G., 393
Avery, D. R., 143, 265, 269, 738
Axel, H., 737

Babcock, P., 143, 265, 679
Bahls, J. E., 424
Baker, E., 268
Baker, T. A., 496
Bakker, A. B., 499, 536
Bakker, P., 499
Baldwin, T. T., 422
Balls, J. E., 501
Barney, J. B., 40
Barrett, G. V., 492, 497, 564, 576, 577
Barrett, P., 493
Barrett, R. S., 366
Barrick, M. R., 492, 493, 499, 738, 739
Barron, J. N., 736
Barta, P., 740
Barthiaume, J., 629
Barthold, J., 264
Bartol, K. M., 740
Bartram, D., 198
Bassi, L. J., 266
Basuil, D., 740
Bateman, T. S., 500
Battista, M., 198

Bauer, T. N., 308, 424, 578, 630, 678
Baxter, J. C., 423
Beatty, R. W., 679
Beaty, J., 492
Beaubien, J. M., 197
Bechtoldt, M. N., 535
Becker, B. E., 679
Becker, J. S., 577
Becker, W. J., 629
Becton, J. B., 422, 738
Beenen, G., 266
Beier, M. E., 497
Belcourt, M., 143
Bennett, J., 577
Bennett, M. W., 83, 627, 628, 630
Bennett, R. J., 735
Bennett-Alexander, D. D., 84, 144, 578
Benson, P. G., 366
Bentson, C., 536
Bergmann, T. J., 268
Berkley, R. A., 678
Bernerth, J. B., 267, 268
Berry, C. M., 492, 494, 498, 739
Berry, M. W., 496
Bertolino, M., 424
Bertrand, M., 499
Bertua, C., 494
BeVier, C. A., 421, 495
Bezos, J., 9
Biddle, R. E., 578
Billings, M. A., 267
Billington, A. Q., 422
Birkeland, S. A., 493
Bishop, J. W., 738
Blacksmith, N., 494
Blackwell, K., 476
Blakley, B. R., 197, 496
Blancero, D., 495

Bland, T. S., 84
Bledow, R., 498
Bliese, P. D., 494
Bliss, W., 84
Blonder, M. D., 678
Blumberg, R., 424
Bobko, P., 196, 421, 495, 497, 577, 578
Bodner, T. E., 424, 630
Bohner, R. J., Jr., 84
Bolino, M. C., 740
Bommer, W. H., 365, 422
Bono, J. E., 432, 493, 736
Boos, A. L., 500
Borgen, F. H., 198
Borman, C., 157, 159–60, 163
Borman, W. C., 196, 197, 268, 366, 500
Borzo, J., 265
Boswell, W. R., 268
Boudreau, J. W., 264, 577, 737
Bowen, D. E., 41
Bower, D. G., 680
Bowers, C., 41
Bracker, J. S., 267
Braddy, P. W., 265
Bradley, J. C., 498, 536
Brainin, E., 267
Brannick, M. T., 196, 197, 198, 493
Bray, D. W., 535
Breaugh, J. A., 264
Breaugh, J. S., 422, 423
Bretz, R. D., Jr., 41, 267, 268
Bretz, R. H., 267
Britt, R., 496
Brock, B., 423
Brockner, J., 678
Brover, R. L., 739
Brown, B. B., 144, 740
Brown, D. J., 264, 268
Brown, F. G., 365
Brown, J., 143
Brown, M., 197
Bruno, M. E., 680
Brush, C. G., 41
Bryan, D. A., 393
Buboltz, C. B., 197
Buckley, P., 678

Bunce, L. W., 678
Burbach, R., 535
Burke, M. E., 423, 424
Burkholder, N. C., 40, 264, 265, 266, 679, 680
Burnfield, J. L., 499
Burnfield, L., 735
Burns, K., 680
Burns, M., 494
Buster, M. A., 196, 497
Byham, W. C., 500
Byrnes, N., 41

Cable, D. M., 265, 266, 267, 495, 498, 628
Cadrain, D., 266, 627
Calandra, B., 308
Caldwell, D. F., 41
Caligiuri, P., 536
Callocchia, F., 142
Campbell, J. P., 366, 421, 498
Campion, J. E., 499, 578
Campion, M. A., 197, 467, 492, 496, 499, 500, 678, 735, 736, 737
Cappelli, P., 29, 737
Carless, S. A., 264
Carlson, J., 495
Carlson, K. D., 421, 423
Carmines, E. G., 366
Carr, L., 198
Carroll, S. A., 266, 268
Carson, K. C., 577
Carter, G., 497
Carter, G. W., 197
Caruso, D. R., 496
Cascio, W. F., 366, 495, 497, 500, 536, 564, 577, 578, 736
Castle, N. G., 738
Cerrone, S., 736
Chaison, G., 142
Chaker, A. M., 264
Chan, D., 493, 497
Chao, G. T., 422, 630
Chapman, D. S., 266, 268, 499, 629, 678
Charles, J. E., 495
Chatman, J., 41
Chen, C. C., 738

Chernyshenko, O. S., 493
Cheung, G. W., 423
Childs, R. A., 197
Cho, E., 494
Choi, J., 738
Christian, M. S., 498, 536
Christiansen, N. D., 492
Chughtai, A. A., 738
Clark, K. E., 535
Clark, K. J., 307
Clark, M. B., 535
Cleveland, J. M., 535
Clevenger, J., 497
Click, J., 423
Coats, G., 498
Cober, R. T., 264, 268
Cobler, A. B., 268
Cohen, D. B., 367
Cohen, J., 576
Colarelli, S. M., 500
Colella, A., 577
Coleman, F. T., 739
Collings, D. G., 307
Collins, C. J., 267
Collins, M., 197
Colquitt, J. A., 678
Conger, J. A., 142
Conlon, D. E., 678
Connelly, B. S., 493, 536
Connerley, M. L., 421, 495
Connolly, T., 629
Conurey, J. N., 499
Conway, J. M., 739
Cook, J., 497
Cooper, A., 444
Cooper, M. A., 346
Cornelius, E. T., III, 196
Cortina, J. M., 366, 492, 496, 577
Costa, P. T., Jr., 492, 498
Costanza, D. P., 196, 197
Côté, S., 496
Cote, T., 265
Coxson, H. P., 680
Cozan, L. W., 423
Craig, J., 678
Craig, S., 41, 736
Cranny, C. J., 196
Crant, J. M., 493, 500

Crawford, M. S., 496
Credé, M., 421
Crockett, M. P., 144
Cronbach, L. J., 366
Cronin, B. E., 495
Cropanzano, R., 737
Crossley, C. D., 735
Crozier, A., 267
Culpepper, L., 629
Cummings, L. L., 366
Curhan, J. R., 629
Custer, H., 498

Dages, K. D., 679
Dahl, D., 264
Daley, L., 501
Dalik, A., 198
Danaher, M. G., 424
D'Angelo, N. C., 421
Daniel, C., 500
Datta, D. K., 740
Davenport, T. H., 678
Davis, G. M., 269
Davis-Blake, A., 143
Dawis, R. V., 198
Day, D. V., 494, 495, 498, 499, 576
Day, E. A., 536
De Corte, W., 198, 578, 739
De Fruyt, F., 494
DeGrassi, S. W., 499
De la Merced, M. J., 421
Delaney-Klinger, K., 197
Delery, J. E., 737
Deller, J., 492, 493
DelPo, A., 84
Demby, E. R., 737
Demps, J., 268
DeNisi, A. S., 143, 267
De Paepe, A., 499
De Pater, I. E., 535
Deschenaux, J., 269
Devlin, S. E., 422
DeWolf, M., 40
Dickens, W. T., 495
Dierdorff, E. C., 307
Digh, P., 309
Dilchert, S., 492, 493, 498, 536
Dimotakis, N., 494

Dineen, B. R., 265, 268
Dipboye, R. L., 143, 492
Dixon, G. R., 500
Dobins, F., 143
Doherty, L. Q., 266
Doherty, M. E., 196
Dolland, M., 501
Dollarhide, M. E., 740
Donoghue, C., 738
Donovan, J. J., 493
Dougherty, C., 41
Doverspike, D., 497, 576
Drasgow, F., 366, 492, 493
Dreazen, Y. J., 628
Drieband, E., 63
Drummond, H., 423
Dudley, N. M., 492
Dumaine, B., 500
Dunham, K. J., 628, 678
Dunleavy, E. M., 367
Dunne, T., 142
Dunnette, M. D., 268, 496, 497
Dwight, S. A., 493
Dworkin, J. B., 737
Dye, D. M., 197, 496
Dyer, L., 366

Earles, J. A., 494
Edens, P. S., 536
Eder, R. W., 498
Edmondson, D. J., 379
Edwards, B. D., 495, 498, 536
Edwards, J. E., 679
Edwards, J. R., 267
Edwards, P. J., 264, 266, 680
Egler, T. D., 629
Elfenbein, H. A., 629
Ellin, A., 421
Ellingson, J. E., 493, 578
Ellis, A. D., 735
England, G. W., 422
Erdogan, B., 578, 630
Erez, A., 432, 493
Erickson, M. L., 198
Erwin, F., 423
Esen, E., 41, 143, 607, 679, 736
Euwema, M. C., 536
Ewoh, A.I.E., 501
Eyde, L. D., 198, 501

Fairchild, Z., 268
Farr, J. L., 495
Fegley, S., 142
Feild, H. S., 196, 197
Feldman, D. C., 84, 268, 421, 535
Feliu, A. G., 269, 501, 627, 628
Felps, W., 735, 737, 738
Fenty, A., 516
Fernandez, K., 735
Ferrara, P., 197, 678
Ferris, G. R., 307, 499
Field, H. S., 267, 268
Fillingham, L., 30
Finkin, M. W., 680
Fisher, A., 736
Fisher, C. D., 267
Fisher, R., 307
Fitz-enz, J., 679, 680
Fitzgerald, M. P., 736
Flato, J., 265
Fleck, C., 41
Fleenor, J. W., 265
Fleisher, M. S., 536
Fleishman, E. A., 157, 159–60, 163, 196, 197, 494, 500
Fliegel, R., 424
Flint, N., 628
Floren, J., 265
Flynn, J. R., 495
Folger, R., 737
Fong, C. T., 422
Ford, D. K., 308
Ford, J. K., 535
Fortney, D. S., 628
Fossum, J. A., 366
Foster, L., 142
Fournier, S., 738
Fox, A., 143, 740
Franklin, G. M., 84, 630
Franks, P. J., 266
Frase-Blunt, M., 143, 307, 679
Frauenheim, E., 142, 265, 307–8, 678, 679
Freedman, D. H., 264, 265
Frese, M., 498
Friedel, L. A., 495
Fuller, R. M., 142
Furnham, A., 423

Gael, S., 173, 196
Gaertner, S., 735, 738
Gainey, T., 679
Gakovic, A., 307
Gallagher, V. C., 739
Ganzach, Y., 267, 577
Gardner, P. D., 628, 630
Garner, J. M., 141
Gasser, M., 628
Gatewood, R. D., 196, 197, 264
Gaugler, B. B., 536
Gavin, M. B., 678
Gerhart, B., 268, 737
Ghiselli, E. E., 366, 496
Gibbons, A. M., 536
Gibson, P. C., 736, 739
Gibson, W. M., 492
Giles, W. F., 267, 268
Gillespie, M. A., 423
Gillespie, T. L., 499
Gilliland, S. W., 678
Glomb, T. M., 735, 736, 737
Glover, R. H., 269
Glube, N., 308
Goff, M., 536
Goffin, R. D., 492
Gogus, C. I., 630
Goldberg, E., 308
Golden, D., 421
Golden, T. D., 738
Goldstein, H. W., 498
Goldstein, I. L., 422, 423, 578, 679
Goltsi, V., 536
Gomes, L., 266
Gottfredson, L. S., 494
Gottier, R. F., 492
Gowen, M. A., 264
Gowing, M. K., 197
Grabczynski, S., 266
Green, R. M., 269
Greenberger, D. B., 142
Greene, P. G., 41
Greengard, S., 497, 678, 679
Greenwald, J., 424
Greer, C. R., 142
Grensing-Pophal, L., 535, 679
Grewal, D., 496
Griepentrog, B., 577

Griffeth, R. W., 267, 735, 736, 737, 738
Grimm, L. G., 576
Grossman, R. J., 266, 679
Grote, G., 739
Grover, S. L., 678
Grubb, W. L., 497
Guerin, L., 84
Guion, R. M., 492
Gullett, C. R., 144
Gully, S. M., 495
Gunnigle, P., 535
Gupta, N., 736, 737
Gupta, R., 9
Gurchiek, K., 142, 421, 629, 740
Guseh, J. S., 501
Guthrie, J. P., 740
Gutterman, A. M., 84

Hable, S. Z., 424
Hackett, E. J., 307
Haltiwanger, J., 142
Hammers, M., 630, 678
Hananel, S., 423
Handel, M. J., 142
Handler, C., 549, 576
Handler, L., 366
Hanford, D. J., 739
Hanges, P. J., 143
Hanisch, K. A., 497
Hansell, S., 422
Hansen, F., 264, 265, 269, 628, 629, 630
Hanson, F., 424
Harding, M., 423
Hargis, M. B., 577
Harlan, S. L., 307
Harman, W. S., 735, 737, 738
Harney, J., 679
Harold, C. M., 422
Harrick, E. J., 343
Harrigan, T. A., 308
Harrington, T. F., 308
Harris, J., 678
Harris, M., 197, 498, 499
Hart, M. M., 41
Harter, J. K., 196
Hartley, D. L., 422, 738
Hartman, L. P., 84, 578

Hartman, N. S., 497
Harvey, M., 198
Harvey, V. S., 497
Hastings, R. R., 739
Hauser, J. A., 536
Hausknecht, J. P., 494, 495, 498, 499, 576, 736
Hayes, T. L., 196
Hazer, J. T., 577
Heaton, S. M., 501
Hebl, M. R., 738
Heffner, T. S., 499
Heggestad, E. D., 493
Hekman, D. R., 738
Helliker, K., 500
Henderson, J. A., 577
Henderson, N., 496
Heneman, H. G., III, 142, 366, 666, 678, 680
Heneman, R. L., 142, 198, 365
Henle, C. A., 578
Henry, R. A., 576
Hermelin, E., 536
Hernandez, M., 738
Herriot, P., 577
Hersch, J., 576
Hesketh, B., 198
Higgins, C. A., 423
Highhouse, S., 267, 577
Hill, C.W.L., 142
Hill, P. C., 423
Himmelberg, M., 629
Hitt, M. A., 143
Hoffman, B. J., 536
Hoffman, V. J., 269, 680
Hogan, J., 492, 493, 496
Hogan, R., 492, 493
Holland, E., 493
Hollenbeck, J. R., 492
Hollinger, R. C., 498
Holtom, B. C., 265, 738
Holtz, B. C., 367
Hom, P. W., 267, 735, 736, 737
Hosoda, M., 498
Hough, L. M., 268, 492, 496
Howard, A., 421, 535
Howard, M. J., 736
Huckman, R. S., 736
Hudson, J. P., Jr., 578

Huett, D. L., 666, 680
Huffcutt, A. I., 197, 499
Hughes, W., 346
Hui, P. P., 143
Hulin, C. L., 497, 576
Hull, R., 536
Hülsheger, U. R., 423, 424, 494
Hunington, R., 267
Hunt, E., 495
Hunt, S., 549, 576
Hunter, J. E., 366, 422, 494, 497,
    535, 576, 577, 578
Hunter, R. F., 422, 497
Hurd, J. M., 492
Hurtz, G. M., 578
Huselid, M. A., 679, 736
Huxtable, J., 308
Hyland, M. M., 264
Hyland-Savage, G., 9, 40
Hymowitz, C., 266

Ilg, R. E., 141
Ilgen, D. R., 196, 267
Ilies, R., 493, 494
Imber, A., 264

Jackson, S. E., 143
Jacobs, M. A., 628
Jacobs, R., 495
Jacobs, R. R., 535
Jago, I. A., 496
Janich, D. N., 628
Janove, J. W., 680
Jarrell, D. W., 142
Jaschik, S., 422
Jayne, M.E.A., 143
Jeanneret, P. R., 157, 159–60, 163,
    197
Jenkins, Wolfand A., 494
Jensen, A. R., 495
Jex, S. M., 735, 736
Johansson, C., 266
Johnson, D. E., 495
Johnson, G. J., 577
Johnson, J. L., 365
Johnson, J. W., 197, 739
Johnson, R. E., 494
Johnson, T., 144
Johnson, W. R., 577

Johnston, L., 9
Joiner, D. A., 366, 536
Joinson, C., 265
Jondle, D., 41
Jones, B., 628
Jones, C., 497
Jones, D. A., 266, 268
Jones, J. W., 679
Jones, R., 424
Jones, R. G., 197
Joseph, D. L., 496
Joseph, J., 41
Joseph, T. A., 577
Joy, D., 678
Joyce, M. C., 267
Judge, T. A., 41, 266, 267, 423,
    432, 492, 493, 494, 495, 499,
    535, 576, 577, 628, 736

Kabin, M. B., 578
Kacmar, K. M., 736
Kahn, S. C., 740
Kalev, A., 143
Kammeyer-Mueller, J. D., 197,
    535, 629, 735, 736, 737
Kane, J. J., 535
Kaplan, S., 496
Karren, R. J., 498
Kaufman, G., 346
Kazdin, A. E., 576
Keeney, J., 422
Keeney, M. J., 197
Keeping, K. M., 268
Kehoe, J., 198
Kehoe, P. E., 740
Keichel, W., 423
Keil, C. T., 577
Kelley, E., 143
Kemp, C., 367
Kersting, M., 494
Kessler, M., 41
Keynes, J. M., 29
Kiger, P. J., 141, 142, 143, 267, 308
Kilduff, G. J., 629
Kim, B. H., 423
Kim, N., 493
Kim, T., 738
Kisamore, J. L., 493
Klaas, B. S., 84, 268, 679, 737

Klaff, L. G., 629
Klayman, N., 577
Klehe, U., 499, 535
Klein, H. J., 630
Kleinman, L. W., 307
Klemmer, K., 40, 141
Klimoski, R. J., 196, 366
Kluger, A. N., 577
Klutz, L., 679
Koles, K.L.K., 495
Kraft, J., 501
Kraimer, M. L., 493
Krause, D. E., 536
Kreps, D. M., 736
Kriska, S. D., 268
Kristof, A. L., 41
Kulik, C. T., 198
Kuncel, N. R., 421
Kwon, S., 629

Lacey, T. A., 141
Laczo, R. M., 196, 739
Lamare, R., 535
Lamont, W. G., 680
Lancaster, A. R., 197
Lance, C. E., 536
Landy, F. J., 366, 496
Lang, J., 494
Lang, J.W.B., 494
Lankau, M. J., 629
Lanzarone, M., 740
LaPolice, C. C., 197
Latack, J., 512
Latham, G. P., 424, 499, 577, 739
Lautenschlager, G., 264
Lavigna, R. J., 666, 680
Lawler, E. E., III, 535, 628, 678
Lawrence, A., 497
Le, H., 493
Lebiecki, J. E., 492
LeBlanc, P., 198
LeBreton, J. M., 577
Ledford, G. E., Jr., 41, 198
Lee, K., 498
Lee, K.-F., 601
Lee, M., 738
Lee, T. W., 735, 737, 738
Leonard, B., 41
Leonard, J. S., 738

LePine, J. A., 738
LePine, M. A., 268, 738
Leung, K., 738
Levesque, L. L., 41
Levin, A., 423
Levin, K. Y., 157, 159–60, 163, 197
Levine, D. I., 738
Levine, E. L., 196, 197, 198, 423
Levin-Epstein, M. D., 424
Levinson, M., 500
Levy, P. E., 264, 268
Lewis, K. R., 41
Lieber, L., 143
Lievens, F., 198, 267, 308, 424, 497, 499, 536, 578, 739
Lindsay, P., 308
Lipsig, E., 740
Locke, E. A., 496, 736
Lockwood, N. R., 143, 144, 301
Loher, B. T., 736
Lopez, J. A., 629
Lounsbury, J. W., 735
Lublin, J. S., 41, 629, 630, 739
Ludwig, J., 266
Lueke, S. B., 492
Luk, V., 738
Luthans, F., 737
Lyness, K. L., 309
Lyon, J. S., 495
Lyons, B. D., 197

Macan, T. H., 577
Mack, M. J., 577
Mael, F. A., 422
Maertz, C. P., Jr., 735, 737
Maher, K., 264, 268, 421, 423
Mahoney, J. J., 500
Mahto, R. V., 265
Malic, T., 496
Mallozzi, V. M., 493
Maltarich, M. A., 494
Mangum, S. L., 142
Manson, T. M., 493
March, J. G., 735
Marcus, B., 498
Margolis, A., 366
Markham, W. T., 307
Marquez, J. T., 41, 630, 737, 740

Marshall-Mies, J. C., 196, 197
Martin, D. C., 740
Martinez, M. N., 264
Maryn, Lanza, 84
Maryn, M. R., 84
Matiaske, W., 265
Matthews, A. W., 628
Matthews, G., 496
Matthews, M. C., 422, 738
Mattioli, D., 421
Mattis, M., 309
Mattson, J., 422
Matusik, S. F., 142
Mauer, R., 424
Maurer, S. D., 499
Mayer, D. M., 738
Mayer, J. D., 496
Mayes, B. T., 499
Mayfield, J., 738
Mayfield, M., 738
Mayfield, M. S., 197
Maynard, A. M., 577
Maynard, D. C., 577
McAttee, S. A., 84
McBride, S., 308
McClave, J. T., 366
McClendon, J., 679, 737
McCloy, R. A., 493
McConnell, B., 264
McCoy, J., 40
McCrae, R. R., 492, 498
McDaniel, M. A., 366, 422, 493, 496, 497, 499
McDonnell, A., 535
McFarland, L. A., 268, 422
McGrath, R. E., 577
McGregor, J., 269
McIlvaine, A. R., 144
McKay, P. F., 143, 265, 269, 738
McKenzie, S. B., 365
McKillip, J., 422
McKinney, A. E., 421
McLain, D. L., 266
McMahan, G., 494
McNamera, K., 424
McNelly, T. L., 536
McPhail, R., 307
McPhail, S. M., 197
Meachum, R. L., 421

Meade, A. W., 265
Meade, K. D., 84
Meglino, B. M., 267
Meir, E. I., 498
Mellahi, K., 307
Mellewigt, T., 265
Meriac, J. P., 536
Merritt, J., 422
Merritt-Halston, R., 421
Meskanik, P., 679
Messick, S., 366
Meyers, J. J., 629
Micco, L., 679
Michael, J. J., 265
Michaels, J., 678
Midence, A. R., 84
Miguel, R. F., 492
Miles, R. E., 307
Miller, R., 496
Miller, S., 737
Millsap, R. E., 421, 495
Minette, K., 678
Minton-Eversole, T., 142, 308, 423
Mirabile, M., 438
Mirza, B., 740
Mishra, A. K., 740
Misra, K. E., 740
Mitchell, J. H., 61
Mitchell, K. E., 198
Mitchell, M. M., 736
Mitchell, T. R., 735, 737, 738
Moeller, N. L., 736
Mohrman, A. A., 678
Molvey, P. W., 267
Moncarz, R. J., 143
Mones, K., 424
Mook, J. R., 84
Morajda, D., 738
Morgeson, F. P., 196, 197, 198, 421, 424, 492, 500
Morgeson, F. S., 197
Morgfopoulos, R., 198
Morris, D. M., 536
Morris, M. A., 738
Morrison, E. W., 629
Morrison, M., 493
Morrow, P. C., 577
Morsch, L., 629
Moscoso, S., 494, 495

Mosel, J. N., 423
Moskowitz, J. A., 84
Motowidlo, S. J., 497, 500
Mount, M. K., 492, 493, 494, 739
Moynihan, L. M., 268
Muhl, C. J., 84
Mukuda, M., 536
Mullainathan, S., 499
Mullich, J., 264, 265, 630
Mulvey, P., 198
Mumford, M. D., 157, 159–60, 163, 196, 197
Mumford, T. V., 500
Murphy, K., 492
Murphy, K. M., 577
Murphy, K. R., 366, 495, 500, 535, 578
Murray, C., 421
Myors, B., 578
Myszkowski, G. J., 421

Naglieri, J. A., 366
Nahrgang, J. D., 421
Nalbantian, H. R., 736, 737
Nancherla, A., 143
Nasar, S., 628
Nathan, B. R., 41
Nelson, A. V., 501
Nester, M. A., 501
Neustel, S., 422
Newman, D. A., 495, 496
Ng, T.W.H., 421, 535
Nguyen, N. T., 497
Nicewander, A., 578
Niederman, F., 735, 737
Nimps, T., 197
Nishii, L. H., 738
Noe, R. A., 265, 268, 736
Noon, S. L., 576
Normand, J., 500
Nowicki, M. D., 578
Nuterangelo, B., 628
Nyberg, A. J., 494, 740

Oakes, K., 308
O'Connell, M. S., 497
Ogsten, D., 666, 680
Oh, I., 493, 494
Ohayun, Y., 267

Oldham, G. R., 198
O'Leary-Kelly, A. M., 630
Ones, D. S., 492, 493, 498, 536, 577
Opdyke, J. D., 422
O'Reilly, C. A., III, 41
Orey, M., 740
Ornelas, L. A., 61
Ortega, D., 599
Orvis, K. A., 492
Osten, K., 578
Oswald, F. L., 422, 423, 493, 577
Otondo, R. F., 265
Outerbridge, A. N., 535
Outtz, J. L., 495, 578
Overman, S., 265, 307, 500, 679, 737
Owens, B. P., 735, 737
Owens, J., 422

Paik, L., 500
Pajo, K., 423
Palich, L. E., 267
Palmer, D. K., 499
Panaro, G. P., 269, 424, 501, 627, 628
Pandey, A., 740
Parameswaran, G., 197
Paré, G., 737
Paronto, M. E., 197, 678
Patton, C., 264, 535, 536, 629
Payne, S. C., 495
Pazy, A., 267
Pearlman, K., 197, 198, 421, 492, 495
Pegano, J. W., 84
Pereira, G. M., 497
Perrewé, P. L., 499
Peter, L. J., 536
Peterson, N. G., 157, 159–60, 163, 196, 197
Peterson, S. J., 737
Peterson, S. L., 737
Petrides, K. V., 444
Pfeffer, J., 422
Phelps, J., 197
Phillips, J. M., 266
Phillips, W., 497
Piasentin, K. A., 266, 268
Pincus, L. B., 144

Piscitelli, K. S., 736, 739
Plaschke, B., 438
Pleskac, T. J., 422
Ployhart, R. E., 367, 495, 577, 678
Podsakoff, N. P., 738
Podsakoff, P. M., 365
Polden, D. J., 83, 627, 628, 630
Pomeroy, A., 309
Pont, J., 266
Porter, C. O., 678
Postol, L. P., 680
Postuma, R. A., 737
Potosky, D., 495
Power, S., 367
Premack, S. L., 266
Price, E., 628
Prien, E. P., 198, 535
Prifitera, A., 366
Prottas, D. J., 738
Purkiss, S. L., 499
Pursell, E. D., 499
Putka, D. J., 498
Pynes, J. E., 343

Quinones, M. A., 496, 535

Radack, D. V., 629
Ragins, B. R., 309
Rahbar-Daniels, D., 198
Raju, N. S., 679
Ramesh, A., 536
Ramirez, J. C., 680
Ramsay, L. J., 423
Rau, B. L., 264
Ravlin, E. C., 267
Raymond, M. R., 422
Reck, M., 496
Ree, M. J., 494
Reeve, C. L., 493, 494, 495
Reibstein, R. J., 269
Reilly, G. A., 494
Reilly, M. E., 494
Reilly, R. R., 421, 422, 495
Reiter-Palmon, R., 197
Reynolds, D., 269
Reynolds, D. H., 500
Rhee, M., 516
Rich, G. A., 365
Rich, M., 142

Rimer, M., 399
Robbins, S. B., 493
Robbins, S. P., 499
Roberson, L., 735
Roberts, B., 679
Roberts, R. D., 496
Robertson, I. T., 536
Robin, R. S., 422
Robinson, R. K., 84, 630
Rodopman, O. B., 494
Rodriguez, R., 264
Roehling, M. V., 268
Rolland, J. P., 494
Romell, R., 628
Rondeau, K. V., 737
Rones, P. L., 141
Rooy, D. L., 736
Rosenthal, A., 678
Rosenthal, B. E., 679
Rosenthal, D. B., 536
Rosse, J. G., 578
Roth, P. L., 196, 421, 495, 497, 499, 578
Rothstein, H. R., 366, 423
Rothstein, M. G., 492
Rotundo, M., 739
Rousseau, D. M., 266
Rowland, K. M., 307
Royle, T., 535
Rozelle, R. M., 423
Ruark, G. A., 496
Rubin, H. J., 83, 627, 628, 630
Ruiz, G., 265, 268
Rupp, D. E., 536
Rushton, J. P., 495
Russell, C., 513
Russell, C. J., 422, 535, 577
Russell, J. T., 547
Rutigliano, T., 737, 738
Ryan, A. M., 143, 268, 424, 495, 678
Rynes, S. L., 264, 268, 495

Saari, L. M., 499
Sablynski, C. J., 739
Sacco, J. M., 143, 268
Sackett, P. R., 196, 366, 424, 492, 493, 494, 495, 497, 498, 578, 739

Sadeghi, A., 40
Sager, C. E., 499
Salasko, E. R., 84
Salgado, J. F., 423, 424, 494, 495
Salovey, P., 496
Salvatore, P., 84
Salyards, S. D., 500
Sammer, J., 629
Sanchez, J. I., 197, 198
Sánchez, L. S., 264
Sanchez, R. J., 678
Sandall, D. L., 197
Sanders, A., 266
Sandler, D. R., 629
Sandver, M. H., 142
Saraceno, J., 438
Sartain, L., 264, 266, 680
Sawyer, J., 577
Saxe, I. M., 84
Scanduva, T. A., 629
Scarpello, V., 267
Schaefer, D., 343
Scheu, C. R., 143
Schippmann, J. S., 197, 198, 421, 535
Schmidt, F. L., 196, 366, 422, 423, 494, 499, 535, 576, 577, 578
Schmidt, J. A., 736
Schmit, M., 366
Schmitt, N., 143, 268, 366, 422, 423, 492, 493, 497, 500, 578
Schmitt, N. W., 366
Schneider, B., 498
Schneider, M., 266
Schneider, R., 501
Schoeff, M., 737
Schram, J., 143
Schramm, J., 94, 141, 143
Schuttauf, E. E., 736, 739
Schwab, D. P., 366
Schwarz, L., 423
Schwinger, R. A., 269
Sciarrino, J. A., 496
Scott, J. C., 679
Scott, J. L., 268
Scott, K. D., 738
Sculten, S., 423
Sedmak, N. J., 424
Segal, J. A., 536, 628, 680

Segall, D. O., 492
Seibert, S. E., 493
Seifert, B. K., 740
Seymour, R. T., 144
Shaffer, J. A., 499
Shalhoop, J. H., 264
Shapiro, J., 678
Shaver, I. J., 264
Shaw, J. D., 736, 737
Shellenberger, S., 308
Shen, W., 495
Shepherd, W., 492
Shop-taugh, C., 197
Shuster, S., 12–13
Siegel, B., 679
Silva, J., 495
Silver, M. B., 197
Silverman, E. R., 267, 307, 679, 739
Simon, H. A., 735
Simon, R., 628
Sims, E. N., 266
Singer, J., 736
Singh, J. V., 40
Sinha, R., 422
Skoglind, J. D., 142
Skonberg, J., 424
Slaughter, J. E., 629
Sloan, S., 421
Slyke, E. Van, 679
Smart, D., 494
Smith, A., 629, 680
Smith, D. B., 493, 498
Smith, M. A., 493, 578
Smith, N., 499
Smith, S., 630
Smither, J. W., 421, 495
Snow, C. C., 307
Soltis, C., 421
Spector, P. E., 736
Speizer, I., 308
Spitzmüller, M., 267
Spitz-Oener, A., 141, 142
Spletzer, J. R., 40
Spreitzer, G. M., 740
Stalder, B. V., 173
Staman, J., 84
Stanard, A., 308
Stanton, E., 421

Stark, S., 493
Starkee, M., 264
Starner, T., 679
Staubus, M., 628
Staw, B., 366
Steel, P.D.G., 197
Steel, R. P., 735
Stefanik, T., 629
Steilberg, R. C., 736
Stetz, T. A., 197
Stevens, C. K., 267
Stevens, M. J., 467, 499, 500
Stewart, G. L., 499
Stinson, J. F., Jr., 142
Stivarius, T. B., 424
Stoffey, R., 421
Stoffey, R. W., 495
Stone, D. L., 501
Stone, E. F., 365
Stone, R., 738
Stone-Romero, E. F., 498
Stoskopf, G. A., 739
Strauss, G., 737
Strauss, R., 421
Stringer, K., 423
Stringfield, P., 423
Strong, M. H., 197
Sturman, M. C., 576, 577
Sullivan, J., 264, 576, 679
Sulzer, J. L., 197
Sumner, M., 735, 737
Surface, C., 307
Swaroop, P., 267
Swider, B. W., 499
Switzer, F. S., 421, 495
Szostak, A., 736, 737

Tai, B., 143
Talan, D. M., 40
Tam, A. P., 495
Tan, J. A., 492
Tan, R., 628
Taylor, H. C., 547
Taylor, M. S., 267, 268
Taylor, P. J., 423
Teachout, M. S., 535
Tepper, B. J., 738
Tesluk, P. E., 535
Testa, B. M., 143

Tett, R. P., 492
Thaler-Carter, R. E., 264
Thelen, J. B., 144
Thomas, L. L., 421
Thomas, P., 497
Thomas, S. C., 494, 495, 498, 499, 576
Thompson, C. A., 738
Thompson, D. E., 198, 309
Thompson, J. A., 493
Thompson, T. A., 198
Thoresen, C. J., 432, 493
Thorndike, R. L., 578
Thornton, G. C., III, 500, 536
Thorsteinson, T. J., 267
Thrutchley, C. S., 680
Tippins, N. T., 492
Tobares, V., 494
Tolentino, A. L., 494
Tomsho, R., 422
Ton, Z., 736
Toniandel, S., 738
Toosi, M., 308
Toossi, M., 141
Townsend, B., 309
Tremblay, M., 737
Trevor, C. O., 495, 735, 736, 737, 740
Triana, M., 493
Troske, K. R., 142
Truxillo, D. M., 197, 308, 424, 630, 678
Tucker, J. S., 630
Tuna, C., 740
Turner, W. K., 680
Turque, B., 535
Twomey, D. P., 740
Tyler, K., 84
Tyler, P., 495

Uchitelle, L., 740
Uggerslev, K. L., 266, 268

Vadanovich, S. J., 424
Vance, R. J., 196
Vandenberg, R. J., 267
Van der Zee, K. I., 499
Van De Vort, D. M., 173
Van Emmerik, I. J., 536

Van Hoye, G., 267
Van Iddekinge, C. H., 498, 499, 500
Van Rooy, D. L., 268, 496
Van Vianen, A.E.M., 535
Vardaman, J. M., 738
Velasquez, R., 366
Victor, J., 144
Villano, M., 421
Viswesvaran, C., 492, 493, 496, 498
Vocino, J., 678
Volckaert, E., 536
Von Hippel, C. V., 142

Wagar, T. H., 737
Walker, H. J., 267, 268
Walker, J. W., 142
Wallace, J. C., 424
Walsh, D. J., 144, 308
Wanberg, C. R., 629, 735, 736, 737
Wanberg, C. W., 678
Wanek, J. E., 498
Wanous, J. P., 266, 268
Waxer, C., 307
Wayland, R. F., 84, 630
Weatherly, L. A., 424
Weaver, P., 266
Weber, G., 143
Webster, J., 629, 678
Weekley, J. A., 367, 422, 497
Weinberger, J., 577
Weingart, L. R., 629
Weir, T., 421
Welch, J., 149, 196, 552–53, 577
Welch, S., 196, 577
Welch, S. B., 143
Wellens, R. S., 500
Weller, I., 265
Wells, S. J., 142, 266, 309, 578
Werner, J. M., 740
Wernimont, P. F., 421
Wescott, S., 736
Wesson, M. J., 630, 678
Westen, D., 577
Westrick, P., 493
Wexley, K. N., 421, 739
Wheeler, A. R., 739
Whetzel, D. L., 366, 493, 497, 499

Whitaker, D. H., 422, 738
Whitcomb, A. J., 393
White, E., 496
White, S., 197
Whitman, D. S., 496
Whitman, J., 264
Whyte, G., 424, 577
Wiechmann, D., 497
Wiemann, S. A., 498, 739
Wiesen, J. P., 84
Wilk, S. L., 578
Williams, E. S., 737
Williams, H., 678
Williams, K. L., 501
Williams, M., 197
Williams, N., 535
Williams, R., 736, 737
Williams, S. K., 483, 680
Willis, S. G., 629
Wilson, C., 264

Wilson, T., 737
Wilson, W., 535
Winkler, C., 366, 497
Winstein, K. J., 421
Wisnefski, S., 41
Woehr, D. J., 536
Wolf, A., 494
Wolf, M. G., 143
Wolf, S., 630
Wonderlic, C. F., Jr., 436, 494
Wright, A. D., 630
Wright, B., 141, 143
Wright, P. M., 40, 494
Wyatt, I., 29
Wyatt, W., 267

Yang, H., 679
Yardley, K., 307
Yarnold, P. R., 576
Yee, N. K., 678

Yenerall, P. M., 629
Yonce, C. A., 424
Yoo, T., 423
Yoon, K., 577
Yost, A. P., 493
Yu, K.Y.T., 265, 266, 267

Zacharias, L., 498
Zafar, S., 738
Zedeck, S., 366
Zeidner, M., 496
Zeidner, R., 265, 680, 740
Zeller, R. A., 366
Ziegert, J. C., 143
Zimmerman, A., 423
Zimmerman, E., 679, 737
Zimmerman, R. D., 493, 738, 739
Zorzie, M., 422
Zottoli, M. A., 266
Zweig, D. I., 499

SUBJECT INDEX

Abercrombie & Fitch, 63
Abilities, 158, 160
Ability tests
  adverse impact and, 439–40,
    471, 562–63
  cognitive ability tests, 434–41
  discrimination and, 66
  external selection and, 434–43
  job knowledge tests, 442–43
  physical ability tests, 441–42
  psychomotor ability tests, 441
  sensory/perceptual ability tests,
    442
Accenture Consulting, 217, 380,
  616
Access to computers, 255
Accuracy
  of measurement, 336–37
  of prediction, 337–38
Accu Vision, 448
Acquisition staffing strategy,
  25–26
ADA. See Americans with
  Disabilities Act (ADA)
Adaptive devices, 70, 256, 482
ADEA. See Age Discrimination in
  Employment Act (ADEA)
Adverse impact
  ability tests and, 439–40, 471,
    562–63
  applicant flow statistics, 59,
    353–54
  applicant stock statistics, 59–60,
    354–55
  claims of, 58–60, 62
  concentration statistics, 59–60
  drug tests and, 477–78
  litigation process and, 62, 65
  predictors and, 546
  preemployment inquiry and, 409

substantive assessment methods
    and, 470–71
  UGESP on, 479–81, 529–30
  See also Discrimination
Advertisements
  BFOQ and, 257
  depiction of diversity in,
    250–51
  discrimination and, 67
  job seeker reliance on, 210
  legal issues, 257
  older workers and, 68, 257
  recruitment messages in,
    244–46
  in recruitment strategy, 222
  types of, 245
Affirmative action plans (AAPs)
  action-oriented programs,
    133–34
  annual placement goals, 131–32
  constitutionality of, 133, 135
  elements of, 128
  hiring decisions and, 570
  niche employment websites and,
    224
  protections for women/
    minorities, 64, 128–33
  recruitment and, 254–55
  in staffing planning, 128–33
  See also Diversity; EEO/AA
    laws
Affirmative Action Program
    regulations (OFCCP), 55, 64,
    297–98, 670
Age
  advertisements and, 257
  as BFOQ, 67
  labor force trends and, 91
  Millennial generation, 225
  See also Older workers

Age Discrimination in
    Employment Act (ADEA)
  BFOQs and, 410
  overseas US employers and, 57
  provisions of, 55, 67–68
  staffing firms and, 55, 136
Air Line Pilots Association, 397
Albertson's, 351
Alcohol tests, 476–77
Alternative dispute resolution
    (ADR), 672–74
American Association for Retired
    Persons (AARP), 232
American Classified Services, Inc.,
    206
American Management
    Association study, 472
American Psychological
    Association (APA), 32–33,
    352
Americans with Disabilities Act
    (ADA)
  confidentiality of medical
    information, 669
  employee selection, 70–71,
    481–85
  essential job functions, 189–92
  overseas US employers and, 57
  preemployment inquiry, 409–10
  provisions of, 55, 68–71
  reasonable accommodation,
    69–70, 256, 481–85
  seniority systems, 299
  staffing firms and, 51, 136
America Online, 644
America's Army (video game), 232
Angoff method, 561–62
Aon Consulting, 447
Apparent authority, 583–84
Apple, 239, 247

Applicant flow statistics, 59, 353–54
Applicant pool size, 209
Applicants
    employment websites, 222–25
    hard-copy applicants, 252–53
    Internet applicants, 253–54, 378
    legal definition of, 251–54
    mobile device applicants, 253
    networking by, 210
    record keeping and, 251–54
    surveys of, 665, 667
    truthfulness/deceit of, 605–6
    written authorization for reference checks, 406
Applicant stock statistics, 59–60, 354–55
Applicant tracking systems, 210, 212–14, 220
Applications
    disclaimer statements, 381
    educational requirements, 381, 384
    in external selection, 381–88
    job knowledge requirements, 385–87
    licensing and certification requirements, 385–87
    online applications, 210–11, 213–14, 218–20, 256
    résumés vs., 381
    training and experience requirements, 385
    unsolicited, 218–19
Application service providers (ASPs), 650
Asian Americans, in labor force, 91
Assessment Center Exercises (AC-ESX), 525
Assessment centers (ACs), 520–26
Assistive technologies, 70, 256, 482
Audits, 64, 670
Availability requirements, 161
Avon Products, Inc., 13–14

Background checks, 379, 389, 394, 396–98, 406–8
Banding, 560, 562–63

Barnett Bank, 374, 376
Base rate, 547–49
Basic skills, 92–93, 158, 159
Benchmarks, 348–49, 357, 400, 659, 690–91
    See also Measurement
Benefits, 597–98, 608, 711, 714
Bennett Mechanical Comprehension Test, 442
BFOQ. See Bona fide occupational qualification (BFOQ)
Bidding forms, 285–86
Big Five personality traits, 427–31, 453
Bilingual skills pay premiums, 594
Biodata, 388–92, 714
Blood tests, 474
BMW, 287
BNSF Railway, 232
Body positioning, in O*Net system, 163
Boeing, 187
Bona fide occupational qualification (BFOQ)
    advertisements and, 257
    age as, 67
    legal issues, 410, 415–16
    protected characteristic as, 66
Bona fide seniority systems. See Seniority/merit systems
Bonuses
    employee referral programs and, 220
    hiring bonuses, 598–600
    lump-sum exit bonuses, 701
    notification bonuses, 717
    retention bonuses, 711, 715–16
    See also Compensation
Brand messages, 239–42
Brass Ring, 219
Breach of contract claims, 588–89
Bristol-Myers Squibb, 290
Brochures, 243–44
Bureau of Labor Statistics (BLS), 29, 90–91, 185
Bureau of National Affairs (BNA), 402
Business necessity, 65, 66

Campus recruitment. See Students, recruitment of
Capital One, 705
CareerBuilder.com, 223
Career development centers, 291–92, 293, 294
CareerRewards system, 289
Cedant, 707
Central tendency in scores, 321–22
CEOs, succession planning for, 290–91
Change in control (CIC) clauses, 701
Character requirements, 161
Charmant, 654
Chief talent officers, 644
ChoiceAnalyst (software), 554
Chrysler, 445
Circuit City, 726–27
Citizenship behavior, 719–20
Civil Rights Acts (Title VII)
    ban on race norming of test scores, 562
    BFOQs and, 410, 415–16
    EEO annual report, 670
    litigation process under, 60, 62–64
    overseas US employers and, 57
    provisions of, 55–56, 64–67
    staffing firms and, 51, 136
Civil service, 77–78
Classified advertisements, 245, 246
Cleveland Clinic, 475
Clinical prediction, 552–53
Closed internal recruitment system, 282, 284
Coaches, 512–13
Coca-Cola, 240
Code of Federal Regulations (CFR), 54
Coding competitions, 447–48
Coefficient alpha calculation, 332
Cognitive abilities, in O*NET system, 160
Cognitive ability tests, 434–41, 562–63
College of American Pathologists, 475

Combined model, of hiring decisions, 556–57
Commitment-oriented organizations, 705
Common law, 53–54
Communication in recruitment messages, 237–42
Company websites, 222–23, 239–40, 246–48
    See also specific companies and websites
Compensation
    benefits, 597–98, 608, 711, 714
    bilingual skills pay premiums, 594
    bonuses, 220, 598–600, 701, 711, 715–16, 717
    deferred compensation plans, 704, 715
    differential rates, 593–95
    flat rates, 593
    geographic pay differentials, 594
    hot skill premium, 599–600
    hours of work and, 598
    incentive pay, 595–96
    in job offers, 593–600, 607
    pay expectations, 594–95
    relocation assistance, 599
    retention management, 710–11
    severance packages, 600, 701
    starting pay policies, 595
    stock options, 596–97
    variable pay, 595–97
Compensatory damages, 64, 589
Compensatory model, 551–56
Competencies, defined, 174, 188
Competency-based job analysis, 146–47, 177–79
Concentration statistics, 59–60
Conciliation, 60, 64
Confidentiality, 71, 72
Confidentiality clauses, in job offers, 600–601
Consent decree, 63–64
Consideration, in enforceable contracts, 583
Constitutional law, 54
Consulting Psychologists Press, 351

Consumer reports, 75, 406–7
Contamination error, 331–32
Contingent assessment methods, 427, 472–78
Contingent employees, 93
Continuous hiring, 209, 566, 663
Contract firms, 93
Contracts
    acceptance, 582–83, 602, 611
    with agents, 583–84
    breach of contract claims, 588–89
    change in control (CIC) clauses, 701
    consideration, 583
    contingencies, 587–88
    disclaimer statements, 586–87
    duration of, 592–93
    employee handbooks and, 584–88
    enforceability of, 582–83
    fixed-term contracts, 592–93, 698, 701
    with independent contractors, 583
    learning contracts, 231–32
    offers, 582
    oral contracts, 585–86, 588, 589
    oral statements and, 586, 588
    parties to, 583–84
    written contracts, 584–85
Control-oriented organizations, 705
Convergys Corp., 601
Co-op assignments, 231–32
Core Self-Evaluations Scale, 431–32
Core staffing activities, 24
Core workforce, 27, 117–21
    See also Flexible workforce
Correlation coefficient, 323–24, 325–27
Cost-benefit analysis
    of downsizing, 723–24
    of drug testing, 477
    of employee turnover, 694–702, 725–26
Costs
    of classified display ads, 245
    of drug testing, 475

of hiring, 663–64
of initial assessment methods, 402–3
of internal recruitment, 294
of recruitment methods, 236
of substantive assessment methods, 468
of test acquisition, 351–53
Counterproductivity, as job performance criteria, 55, 719–20
Cover letters, 377, 380–81
Credibility
    of exit interviews, 691–92
    of online applications, 222–23, 256
Credit checks, 406–7
Criminal background checks, 408
Criterion-related validation studies, 338–44
Cross-functional skills, in O*NET system, 159
Customer satisfaction surveys, 664–67
Cut scores, 557–64
    banding, 560, 562–63
    consequences of, 558–59
    minimum competency method, 559–61
    process of, 557–58
    top-down method, 561–62
    See also Scores

Decision making, in staffing process, 543–71
    adverse impact, 546
    choice of assessment method, 544–51
    continuous hiring, 566, 663
    cut scores and, 557–64
    diversity and, 569–70
    employee participation, 568
    final choice methods, 564–66
    grouping, 566
    human resource professionals and, 566
    legal issues, 568–70
    managers and, 567–68

predictors and assessment
  scores, 551–57
random selection, 564–65
ranking, 565
Taylor-Russell tables, 547–49
utility analysis, 546–51
validity coefficient, 544–45
Deferred compensation plans, 704,
  715
Deficiency error, 331
Defined benefit retirement plans,
  704, 711
Dell Computer, 149, 349
Deloitte, 707
Department of Homeland Security,
  54
Deployment, defined, 8–9
Development staffing strategy,
  25–26
Direct contact, 247–48
Direct Search of the United States,
  228
Disability, ADA definition of,
  68–69
  See also Individuals with
    disabilities
Discharge turnover, 685–87, 689,
  698–99
Disciplinary process, 719–23
Disclaimer statements, 381, 405,
  586–88, 621
Discretionary assessment methods,
  426, 471–72, 529
Discrimination
  advertisements and, 67
  age-related, 55, 57, 67–68, 136,
    410
  bona fide occupational
    qualification, 66
  disparate treatment, 58
  glass ceiling and, 299–303,
    530–31
  preferential treatment, 67
  pregnancy-related, 67, 416
  quotas, 67
  racial, 61
  seniority/merit systems and,
    66
  testing and, 66, 562

  See also Adverse impact;
    EEOC (Equal Employment
    Opportunity Commission);
    specific legislation
Disney, 239
Disparate impact, 58
  See also Adverse impact
Disparate treatment
  claims of business necessity
    and, 65
  factors of, 58
  litigation process and, 62, 64
Display ads, 245
Dispute resolution, 672–74
Distributive justice, 296, 712–13
Diversity
  in advertisements, 250–51
  business case for, 126
  constitutionality of AAPs,
    135
  hiring decisions and, 569–70
  niche employment websites and,
    224
  open recruitment and, 216
  staffing strategies for, 31,
    125–28
  turnover reduction, 714
  workforce demographics and,
    91, 125–27
  See also Racioethnic minorities;
    Women
DOL. *See* Labor Department
  (DOL)
Dow Chemical, 226, 290
Downsizing turnover, 685–87, 689,
  699–702, 723–27, 729
Drug tests, 472–78, 485–86
Duties. *See* Task dimensions

Early retirement, 14, 89, 112,
  700–701
E-commerce, 94
Economic gain formula, 549–50
Edocs, inc., 11
Education
  on application forms, 381, 384
  job demand and, 90, 94–95
  labor supply deficiencies and,
    92–93

  of women, 125
  See also Training
EEO-1 form, 129, 670, 671
EEO/AA laws
  conciliation, 60, 64
  enforcement of, 58–64
  litigation process, 60, 62–64
  provisions of, 55–56
  See also specific laws
EEOC (Equal Employment
    Opportunity Commission)
  on conviction records, 408
  dispute resolution, 672–74
  employer annual report, 670
  enforcement of laws, 58–64
  on hiring decision making, 570
  mediation program, 60
  on permissibility of diversity
    programs, 135
  on preemployment inquiry,
    409–10
  prohibited employment
    practices, 57
  on promotional systems, 530
  on retaliation evidence, 55
  on RFOA rules, 68
  settlements with, 60–61
  on staffing firms, 51
  on testing and selection, 356–57
  website, 54
  See also Uniform Guidelines
    on Employee Selection
    Procedures (UGESP)
Efficiency ratio, 663–64
Elaine R. Shepherd Company, 206
Electronic recruitment
    technologies, 255–57
Eli Lilly, 509
E-mail
  internal recruitment and, 287
  Internet applicants and, 253, 378
  recruitment messages in, 247–48
  as written contract, 584
Embezzlement, 75
Emotional intelligence (EI),
  443–45
Employee eligibility verification,
  74, 620–21
Employee handbooks, 584–88

Employee networks, 221–22
Employee Polygraph Protection
    Act (1988), 73, 75
Employee referral programs,
    220–21, 233
Employees
    abusive supervisors and, 713
    disciplinary process, 719–23
    engagement of, 149, 712
    former, 233
    head count, 100
    in-house temporary, 289–90, 293
    legal protection of, 52
    new employee orientations,
        613–17, 650
    participation in hiring decisions,
        568
    recruitment referrals by, 221–22
    socialization of, 617–19
    See also Workforce
Employee satisfaction surveys,
    693–94
Employee turnover. See Turnover
Employee value proposition
    (EVP), 180–81, 183, 590,
    598–600
Employer Credit Privacy Act
    (Illinois), 407
Employers
    AAPs for small employers,
        128–33
    American employers based
        overseas, 57
    EEO annual report, 670
    EEOC mediation program for,
        60
    legal protection of, 52
    See also Government employers;
        specific companies
Employment advertising. See
    Advertisements
Employment agencies, 227,
    583–84
Employment-at-will, 53–54,
    585–87, 592, 622
Employment contracts. See
    Contracts
Employment eligibility
    verification, 74, 620–21

Employment projections, 89–90
Employment relationship
    employment contracts, 582–89
    job offers, 589–613
    legal issues, 48–51, 620–22
    new employee orientation,
        613–17, 650
    See also specific aspects
Employment websites. See Internet
    recruitment
Engagement of employees, 149, 712
Environmental conditions, in
    O*NET system, 163
Equal employment opportunity
    laws. See EEO/AA laws;
        specific laws
Equal Pay Act, 51, 136
Ernst & Young, 226
Error in measurement, 330–32,
    334–35
Essential job functions, job
    analysis and, 189–92
EtG tests, 476–77
Ethical issues
    recruiters and, 215
    SHRM code of ethics, 32
    staffing practices, 31–34
    student recruitment, 227
E-Verify, 74, 620–21
EVP. See Employee value
    proposition (EVP)
Executive Order 11246, 55–56, 64,
    73, 479
Executive order agencies, 53
Executive search firms, 227–28
Exit interviews, 691–93
Experience, 385, 515–17
External recruitment, 205–59
    applicant reactions, 248–51
    applicant tracking systems, 210,
        212–14
    background checks, 379, 389,
        394, 396–98, 406–8
    budgets, 210–12
    centralized vs. decentralized,
        206–7
    contacts, 209–10
    coordination with internal
        recruitment, 278

job requisitions, 207–8
    legal issues, 252–58
    open vs. targeted strategy,
        215–17, 218
    recruiters and, 214–15
    recruitment guides, 212–13
    recruitment messages, 237–48
    recruitment metrics, 233–37
    recruitment planning, 206–15
    recruitment sources, 217–37
    recruitment strategy, 215–37
    timing issues, 207, 209, 279
    transition to selection, 251–52
    See also Internal recruitment;
        specific recruitment sources
External selection, 370–486
    ability tests, 66, 434–43, 471,
        562–63
    applicant flow stages, 376–77
    applicant reactions, 404–5, 470
    application blanks, 381–88
    background checks, 379, 389,
        394, 396–98, 406–8
    biodata, 388–92, 714
    contingent assessment methods,
        427, 472–78
    discretionary assessment
        methods, 426, 471–72, 529
    emotional intelligence tests,
        443–45
    evaluation of methods, 400–405
    initial assessment methods, 370,
        377–405
    initial interviews, 398–400
    integrity tests, 452–55, 474
    interest/values/preferences
        inventories, 455–57
    legal issues, 381, 405–16,
        479–86
    licensing and certification
        requirements, 385–87
    logic of prediction, 371–73
    medical exams, 478
    overview, 26–27
    performance tests and work
        samples, 445–49
    personality tests, 427–34
    plan development, 374–77
    predictors, 373–74

preemployment inquiry, 408–14
reference checks, 389, 392–95,
    396–98, 406
résumés, 377–81
situational judgment tests,
    449–52, 466–67, 468, 524–25
structured interviews, 457–68
substantive assessment methods,
    426, 427–71
types of predictors, 373–74
See also Internal selection
Externships, 716
Extrinsic rewards, 180, 710–11

Facebook, 221
Face validity, 545
Fact-finding interview simulations,
    526
Fair Credit Reporting Act (FCRA),
    73, 75, 406–8
Fair enforcement practice (FEP)
    laws, 60
Fairness, 296, 372, 722
Faking
    in biodata answers, 391–92
    integrity tests and, 454–55
    on personality tests, 428–29,
        432–34
    on psychological drug tests, 477
False statement warnings, 587
Federal contractors, 72, 75, 253–54
    See also Office of Federal
        Contract Compliance
        Programs (OFCCP)
Federal Express, 517
Federal Glass Ceiling Commission,
    300
Federal laws. *See specific laws*
Federal Register, 54
Federal Trade Commission, 75,
    407
Fertility protection policies, 416
Fetal protection policies, 416
Final match stage. *See*
    Compensation; Contracts; Job
    offers
Fisher-Price, 187
Fixed-term contracts, 592–93, 698,
    701

Fleet Bank, 707
Flexible shift work, 92–93, 704, 714
Flexible spending accounts, 704
Flexible workforce
    core workforce vs., 27, 117–21
    independent contractors and,
        93, 122
    outsourcing and, 123–25
    in staffing planning, 92–93,
        120–23
    technological tools and, 705
    turnover reduction, 704
    See also Core workforce
Ford Motor Company, 226, 612
Forecasting requirements in HRP,
    96–97, 100–107
Foreign workers, 54, 74
Fortune's *100 Best Companies to
    Work For* report, 239, 704–5
Fraud and misrepresentation,
    257–58, 589
Full-time equivalents (FTEs), 100,
    114

General mental ability (GMA),
    435, 439
General Motors (GM), 207, 226,
    239
Genetic Information
    Nondiscrimination Act
    (GINA), 55
Glass ceiling, 299–303, 530–31
Global assignments, 525–26
Global virtual team, 187
Golden handcuff, 601
Golden parachutes, 701
Goldman Sachs, 21, 240
Good Times Entertainment, 513
Google, 391, 568, 601
Government employers
    bilingual skills pay premiums,
        594
    in-house temporary employees,
        289
    internal selection, 296–97
    physical ability testing, 251
    survey on managers' satisfaction
        with staffing services,
        664–65, 666

Great Eight competencies, 178
Great Place to Work Trust Index
    survey, 704
Great recession (2007–2009), 89,
    684, 725
GreenJobInterview.com, 399

H-1B visas, 74
H-2B visas, 74
Hair analysis tests, 474
Hand-eye coordination tests, 474
Hard-copy applicants, 252–53
Harassment, 713
Harris Interactive surveys, 613
Head count. *See* Workforce
Headhunters, 227–28
Health and Human Services
    Department, US, 474–75
Health care coverage, 711
Hewlett-Packard, 287
Hierarchical job levels, 99–100
Hierarchical mobility paths, 273–74
High-fidelity tests, 447
High turnover propensity, 714
Hire.com, 287
HireVue, 399
Hiring bonuses, 598–600
Hiring success gain, 546–49
Hispanic Americans, in labor force,
    91
Hogan Assessment Systems, 351
Hogan Personality Inventory
    (HPI), 428
HOK, 727
Home Depot, 232, 285
Homemaker role, 372
Honda, 229
HotJobs.com, 223
HRISs. *See* Human resource
    information systems (HRISs)
HRP. *See* Human resource
    planning (HRP)
Human capital, 7, 659
    See also Talent management
        systems
Human resource information
    systems (HRISs)
    KSAO tracking, 288
    recruitment planning and, 207

social networking applications, 650

staffing system management, 648–51

succession planning and, 290, 509

talent management and, 509

Human resource planning (HRP), 87, 95–114

elements of, 95–96

forecasting requirements, 96–97, 100–107

job categories/levels, 99–100

linkage to business strategy, 98–99

reconciliation and gap phase, 112–14

replacement plans, 107–9

roles of HR staff, 100

succession planning, 107, 110–12

time frames, 99

Human resource professionals, 566, 641–47

Hyatt, 287

Hybrid internal recruitment system, 283–84

Hyundai, 445

IBM, 28

Identity theft, 223

Immigrants, in labor force, 91

Immigration Reform and Control Act (IRCA), 73–74, 620–21

In-basket exercises, 522

Independent contractors (ICs), 50, 93, 122, 123–24, 583

Indeterminate-term contracts, 592–93

Individuals with disabilities

access to electronic recruitment methods, 255–56

ADA definition of, 68–69

affirmative action and, 128

external selection procedures and, 481–85

labor force trends and, 91

See also Americans with Disabilities Act (ADA)

In-house temporary employees, 289–90, 293

I-9 form (IRCA), 620

Inland Steel, 467–68

Institute for Personality and Ability Testing, 351

Integrity tests, 452–55, 474

I/N Tek, 467–68

Intel, 28

Interbrand Group, Inc., 716

Interest inventories, 291–92, 455–57

Internal recruitment, 272–303

applicant reactions, 296

budgets, 278–79

closed system, 282, 284

hybrid system, 283–84

job requisitions, 278

legal issues, 297–303

mobility paths, 273–78

open system, 282–84

recruitment guides, 279, 280–81

recruitment messages and, 294–96

recruitment metrics, 292–94

recruitment planning, 273–81

recruitment sources, 285–92

recruitment strategy, 281–94

succession planning and, 290–91

timing issues, 279, 281

transition to selection, 296–97

See also External recruitment; *specific recruitment sources*

Internal Revenue Service (IRS), 50

Internal selection, 505–32

assessment centers, 520–26

discretionary assessment methods, 529

evaluation of methods, 513–15, 527–29

experience, 515–17

initial assessment methods, 508–15

interview simulations, 526–27

job knowledge tests, 517–18

legal issues, 529–31

logic of prediction, 506–8

managerial sponsorship, 512–13

overview, 26–27

peer assessments, 509–11

performance appraisals, 518–19

plan development, 507–8, 520–21

promotability ratings, 519–20

promotion panels, 527

self-assessments, 511–12

seniority systems, 515–17

substantive assessment methods, 515–29

succession planning, 508–9

supervisor role in, 282–83, 288, 295, 506, 512

talent management systems, 508–9

types of predictors, 507

International Personality Item Pool (IPIP), 428

International Public Management Association for Human Resources (IPMA-HR), 164

Internet recruitment

best practices, 219–20

company websites, 222–23

continuous hiring capability via, 209

electronic résumés and, 378

e-mail and, 253, 378

employment websites, 222–25

job fairs, 231

Millennial generation and, 225

online applications, 209–11, 213–14, 218–20, 256

user satisfaction, 250

web-based databases, 224, 228

Internships, 231–32

Interpersonal conflicts, 688, 692, 713–14

Interrater agreement, 332–33

Interval scales, 319

Interviews

exit interviews, 691–93

initial interviews, 398–400

integrity tests vs., 452

in job analysis, 166–67

job rewards and, 181–84

online computer-based, 399

simulations, 526–27

See also Structured interviews

Intranets, 287, 293
Intrarater agreement, 333–34
Intrinsic rewards, 180, 703,
    710–14
Intuit, 149
Involuntary turnover
    discharge turnover, 685–87, 689,
        698–99
    downsizing turnover, 685–87,
        689, 699–702, 723–24, 729
IQ, cognitive ability tests and, 435
Item banking, 429

Jewel Companies, 229
Job analysis, 146–93
    competency-based, 146–47,
        174–79
    defined, 147, 191
    essential job functions, 189–92
    job design and, 147–49
    job requirements type, 146–47,
        149–74
    job rewards and, 179–87
    legal issues, 188–92
    O*NET and, 156–66, 179
    Position Analysis Questionnaire
        in, 167–68
    for teams, 187–88
    in validation studies, 339–40,
        344–45
Job analysts, 169, 171
Job applicants. See Applicants
Job autonomy, 711–12
Job context, in job analysis, 151,
    161–63
Job Corps program, 229
Job descriptions, 148, 162, 164–65
    See also O*NET (Occupational
        Information Network)
Job design, 147–49
Job dissatisfaction, 688–89, 693
Job fairs, 230–31
Job hazards, in O*NET system,
    163
Job incumbents, 169, 171
Job knowledge tests, 442–43,
    517–18
Job offers, 582, 589–602
    acceptance terms, 602, 611

applicant truthfulness/deceit,
    605–6
compensation, 593–600, 607
confidentiality clauses, 600–601
contract duration, 592–93
hiring bonuses, 598–600
hours of work, 598
knowledge of competitors, 604
legal issues, 591–92, 620–22
negotiation policies, 606–9
noncompete agreements, 601
payback agreements, 601
presentation of, 609–10
rejections, 611–12
relocation assistance, 599
reneging of, 589, 612–13
sample job offer letter, 602–3
strategic approach to, 589–92
timing of, 610
Job Openings and Labor Turnover
    Survey (JOLTS), 690–91
Job posting systems, 285–87, 293
Job redesign, 712
Job relatedness, in court cases,
    188–89
Job requirements job analysis,
    149–74
    competency-based vs., 146–47,
        149
    examples of, 175
    information collection methods,
        164, 166–71
    internal vs. external analysts,
        173
    job context, 151, 161–63
    job descriptions, 164–65
    job requirements matrix,
        150–52, 171
    job specifications, 164–65
    KSAOs and, 155–62
    process of, 171–74
    task dimensions, 153, 155–56
    task statements, 153, 154
Job requirements matrix
    job analysis and, 150–52, 171,
        339–40
    peer assessments and, 510
    structured interviews and,
        461–62

Job rewards, 179–87
    employee value proposition,
        180–81, 183
    extrinsic rewards, 180, 710–11
    information collection methods,
        181–87
    interviews and, 181–84
    intrinsic rewards, 180, 703,
        710–14
    retention management, 710–14
Job satisfaction, 693–94, 709–14
Job Satisfaction survey (SHRM),
    185
Job security, 586–87
Job seekers. See Applicants
Job specifications, in job analysis,
    164–65
Jobster, 221
Justice, perception of, 296, 648,
    712–14

Kellogg's, 287, 653–54
Kennedy Information, 228
Kmart, 351
Knowledge, defined, 156–58
KSAOs (knowledge, skill, ability,
    and other characteristics)
    access to electronic recruitment
        methods and, 255
    assessment centers and, 520
    behaviorally oriented type, 188
    career questionnaires and, 291
    defined, 156–61
    in external selection, 371–72,
        374–76
    general vs. specific, 30
    hiring decisions and, 570
    importance ratings, 161–62
    in job posting systems, 285, 287
    job-related résumé search terms,
        255
    job requirements job analysis
        and, 155–62
    in job requisitions, 207–8
    job-spanning type, 187–88
    labor demand and, 90–92
    legal compliance and, 47
    letters of recommendation
        scoring and, 393

negligent hiring claims and, 621
Occupational Outlook
    Handbook, 90
organization-specific, 706, 715
peer assessments and, 510
performance tests and work
    samples, 449
person/job match model, 15–17
structured interviews and,
    461–64, 466–67
talent management and, 287–88,
    509
in targeted recruitment, 215–17,
    218
in teams, 187
technological advances and, 94

Labor Department (DOL)
    Affirmative Action Program
        Regulations, 55, 64, 297–98,
        670
    Job Openings and Labor
        Turnover Survey, 690–91
    one-stop career centers, 229
    on recent mass layoffs, 684
    reinstatement of veterans, 76
    on retention, 684
    website, 55
    See also Bureau of Labor
        Statistics (BLS); Office of
        Federal Contract Compliance
        Programs (OFCCP)
Labor market conditions, 359, 590,
    688–89
Labor markets
    demand, 89–90
    employment arrangements and,
        92–93
    KSAOs in demand, 90–92
    shortages/surpluses, 29–30,
        90–92
    statistical information, 7–8
    trends, 91, 94
Labor unions
    on background checks, 397
    discharge turnover and, 698
    influence on staffing, 95
    internal selection and, 516
    spillover effect from, 95

Lands' End, 220
Lateral track system, 275
Lattice track system, 275–76
Laws and regulations, 52–54
    See also Legal compliance;
        Legal issues; specific laws
        and regulations
Layoffs, 684, 725–27
    See also Downsizing turnover
Leadership development, 11, 107,
    110–12, 290–91
Learning contracts, 231–32
Legal compliance, 47–83
    civil service laws, 77–78
    EEO/AA enforcement, 56–64
    EEO/AA provisions, 55–56
    employment relationships,
        48–51, 620–22
    federal law overview, 73–76
    laws and regulations, 51–54
    staffing and EEO/AA laws,
        64–73
    state/local laws, 76–77
    See also specific laws
Legal counsel, 37, 122, 587–88,
    600, 670, 674
Legal issues
    AAPs and, 133, 135, 254–55
    advertisements, 257
    audits, 670
    breach of contract claims, 588
    compensatory damages, 64, 589
    constitutionality of diversity
        programs, 135
    disclaimer statements, 381, 405,
        586–88, 621
    dispute resolution, 672–74
    electronic recruitment, 255–57
    employment-at-will, 585–87,
        622
    employment eligibility
        verification, 74, 620–21
    essential job functions, 189–92
    external recruitment, 252–58
    external selection, 381, 405–16,
        479–86
    fraud and misrepresentation,
        257–58
    general competencies, 179

glass ceiling and, 299–303,
    530–31
hiring decisions and, 568–70
internal recruitment, 297–303
internal selection, 529–31
job analysis and, 188–92
job applicant, defined, 251–54
job offers and, 591–92, 620–22
job relatedness, 188–89
negligent hiring claims, 621
outsourcing and, 125
privacy, 669
promissory estoppel, 589
record keeping, 665, 668–69
reference checks, 406
retention management, 727–28
seniority/merit systems,
    297–300
social networking sites, 221–22,
    256–57, 406
standardization of procedures,
    355–56
workplace tort cases, 53–54, 257
    See also Adverse impact;
        specific laws
Letters of recommendation,
    392–93
Licensing and certification
    requirements, 385–87
Lie detectors, 75
LinkedIn, 221
Litigation process
    basis of, 47–48
    consent decree, 63–64
    remedies, 64
    under Title VII, 60, 62–64
Logic of prediction, 371–73,
    506–8
Low-fidelity tests, 447

Major life activities, defined, 69
Managers
    attitudes toward HR, 99
    availability forecasts, 103–4
    hiring decisions and, 567–68
    internal selection and, 512–13
    performance management and,
        718–19, 721
    role in HRP, 100

satisfaction with staffing
services, 664–65, 666
training of, 256
See also Supervisors
Markov Analysis, 104–7
Measurement, 315–57
accuracy of, 336–37
central tendency, 321–22
coefficient alpha calculation,
332
collection of assessment data,
349–53
correlations, 323–27
defined, 317
error, 330–32, 334–35
importance of, 316, 327–28
legal issues, 353–57
levels of, 318–19
objective vs. subjective
measures, 320
reliability of, 328–35
scores, 320–23
staffing metrics and benchmarks,
348–49
standardization, 318
of turnover, 689–702
validation studies in staffing,
337–46
validity generalization, 346–48
validity of, 335–37
See also Testing and assessment
Media outlets, 222, 232–33
Mediation, 60, 672–74
Medical exams, 71, 478, 482,
484–85
Medical records, 71
Mental impairments as disability,
68–69
Mentors, 512–13
Mercer Management Consulting,
716
Merck, 240
Merit principles, 76–78
Merit systems. *See* Seniority/merit
systems
Merrill Lynch and Company,
701
Messages. *See* Recruitment
messages

Metrics
recruitment metrics, 233–37,
292–94
staffing process metrics, 348–49,
658–64
staffing system evaluation,
658–63
See also Measurement
Metropolitan Life, 660
Microsoft, 222, 239, 601
Milgard Manufacturing, Inc., 61
Millennial generation, 225
Minnesota Clerical Test, 442
Minorities. *See* Racioethnic
minorities
Misconduct, 33–34, 722
Mitsubishi, 445
Mixed motive defenses, 65–66
Mobile device applicants, 253
Mobility paths
alternative, 275–77
hierarchical, 273–74
internal recruitment and,
273–78
policies, 277–78
in staffing systems, 641, 643
Monster.com, 215, 223, 228, 654
Motorola, 28, 187
Multiple hurdles model, 556
Multiple regression, 554–55
Myers-Briggs Type Inventory
(MBTI), 456

National Association for the
Advancement of Colored
People (NAACP), 232
National Association of Corporate
Directors, 290–91
National Career Readiness
Certificate, 229
National City Corporation, 619
National Compensation Survey,
185
National Football League (NFL),
374, 431, 438
National Institute for Drug Abuse
(NIDA), 475
National Society of Black
Engineers, 229

National Study of the Changing
Workforce, 714
National Transportation Safety
Board study, 472
National Work Readiness
Credential, 229
Negligent hiring claims, 621
Negotiation policies, in job offers,
606–9
NEO Personality Inventory, 428
Networking, 210, 221–22
New employee orientations,
613–17, 650
Newspapers, online ads, 245
Niche employment websites,
223–24
Nippon Steel, 467–68
Nissan, 229
Nominal scales, 319
Nominations, for internal
recruitment, 288–89, 293
Noncompete agreements, 601

O*NET (Occupational Information
Network)
basic skills, 158, 159
cross-functional skills, 159
job analysis and, 156–66, 179
knowledge areas, 157
website, 156
Obesity, legal issues and, 69
Objective Inventory Questionnaire,
443
Observation, in job analysis, 166
Occupational Outlook Handbook,
90
Offers. *See* Job offers
Office of Federal Contract
Compliance Programs
(OFCCP), 54
affirmative action programs, 55,
64, 73, 254–55, 297–98, 670
conciliation process, 64
demographic applicant data, 254
enforcement of laws, 64
Internet applicants, defined,
253–54
record maintenance, 668
Offshoring, 28, 124–25

Older workers
    advertisements and, 68, 257
    labor force trends and, 91
    targeted messages and, 240, 251
On-call workers, 93
One-stop career centers, 229
Online ads, 245
Online application process. *See*
    Internet recruitment
Open internal recruitment system,
    282–84
Open recruitment, 215–16, 218
Opportunistic hiring, 18–19
Oracle, 287, 399, 509
Oral contracts, 585–86, 588, 589
Oral presentations, 526–27
Oral statements, employment
    contracts and, 586, 588
Ordinal scales, 319
Oregon Liberal Arts Placement
    Consortium, 225
Organizational effectiveness, 11–12
Orientations, 613–17, 650
Other characteristics, definition
    (KSAOs), 158, 161
Outback Steakhouse, 707
Outplacement firms, 230
Outsourcing
    flexible workforce and, 123–25
    overview, 26, 27–28
    of résumé-tracking services,
        377–78
    service-level agreements, 654
    of staffing functions, 650,
        651–54

Parallel track system, 275
Part-time workers, 92–93
Passive candidates, 221, 228
*Patterned Behavior Description
    Interview*, 459
Pay. *See* Compensation
Payback agreements, 601
PDI Employment Survey, 453
Peer assessments, 509–11
Penalties, 75, 721–22
Pension plans, 704, 711
PEO (professional employer
    organization), 653

Perceived justice, 648
Percentile scores, 322
Performance appraisals
    downsizing turnover, 724
    internal selection, 518–19
    laws and regulations, 728
    succession planning and, 111
Performance management
    disciplinary process, 719–23
    managerial training and rewards,
        721
    performance counseling,
        719–20
    as retention initiative, 717–21
Performance tests and work
    samples, 445–49
Permatemps, 51
Perquisites (perks), 597–98, 705
Personal Characteristics Inventory
    (PCI), 428
Personality, 373, 398, 714
Personality tests, 427–34, 453
Person/job match model
    career questionnaires and, 291
    discharge turnover, 689
    employment relationships and,
        48–49
    overview, 6, 15–17, 30
Personnel Decisions International,
    526
Personnel files, 668–69
Personnel Reaction Blank, 453
Personnel Selection Inventory, 453
Person/organization match model,
    6, 17–19, 30
Peter Principle, 518
Pfizer, 13
Physical abilities, in O*NET
    system, 160
Physical ability tests, 251, 441–42
Physical impairments as disability,
    68–69
Physical work conditions. *See* Job
    context
Piper Aircraft, 727
Planning, 87–137
    AAPs in, 128–33
    core workforce, 27, 117–21
    diversity planning, 125–28

employee shortages/surpluses,
    115–17
external influences on, 88–95
for external recruitment, 206–15
external vs. internal staffing,
    118–20
flexible workforce, 92–93,
    120–25
for internal recruitment, 273–81
legal issues, 128–36
outsourcing, 123–25
qualitative staffing objectives,
    114
quantitative targets, 114–15
staffing planning, 94–95,
    114–25
technology and, 94–95
See also Human resource
    planning (HRP); Succession
    planning
Politics in workplace, 507
Polygraph tests, 73, 75, 452
Position Analysis Questionnaire
    (PAQ), 167–68
Postexit surveys, 692
Power relationships, 52
Practical significance, 544
Prediction, logic of, 371–73, 506–8
Predictors
    in external selection, 373–74
    hiring decisions and, 551–57
    in internal selection, 507
Preemployment inquiry (PI),
    408–14
Preferential treatment, 67
Pregnancy, BFOQ exclusion and,
    416
Pregnancy Discrimination Act
    (PDA), 67
*Principles for the Validation and
    Use of Personnel Selection
    Procedures*, 352
Privacy, as legal issue, 669
Privacy Act (1974), 669
Procedural justice, 296, 712
Procedure, defined, 647
Procter & Gamble, 187, 247
Professional employer organization
    (PEO), 653

Professional Marketing Services, Inc., 244

Professional organizations, 228–29

Progressive discipline systems, 721–23

Project management teams, 187

Promises and legal issues, 588–89

Promissory estoppel, 589

Psychological Assessment Resources, 351

Psychological Corporation, 435

Psychological Services, Inc., 351

Psychomotor abilities, 160, 441

Punitive damages, 64, 589

Pupillary reaction tests, 474

Qualifications. See KSAOs (knowledge, skill, ability, and other characteristics)

QUEST (Quality Using Electronic Systems Training), 517

Quotas, 67

Race norming of test scores, 66, 562

Racioethnic minorities
  advancement opportunities, 301
  affirmative action and, 64, 128–33
  availability determination, 129–31
  cognitive ability tests and, 439–40, 562–63
  drug tests and, 477–78
  EEOC discrimination settlement, 61
  See also Affirmative action plans (AAPs); Diversity

Radio advertisements, 245

Random selection, 564–65

Ranking, 565

Ratio analysis, 101

Rational weighting, 554

Ratio scales, 319–20

Real estate agents, 232

Realistic job preview (RJP), 237–39, 240–42, 295

Reasonable accommodation, under ADA, 69–70, 256, 481–85
  See also Americans with Disabilities Act (ADA)

Reasonable factors other than age (RFOA), 68

Reconciliation and gaps in HRP, 112–14

Record keeping, 251–54, 665, 668–69

Recovering substance abusers, 69

Recruiters
  applicant reactions, 249–50
  job offers and, 583–84
  selection of, 214
  training of, 214–15, 256

Recruitment. See External recruitment; Internal recruitment

Recruitment agencies, 206

Recruitment brochures, 243–44

Recruitment guides, 212–13, 279, 280–81

Recruitment messages
  in advertisements, 244–46
  brand messages, 239–42
  on company websites, 246–48
  direct contact and, 247–48
  external recruitment and, 237–48
  internal recruitment and, 294–96
  realistic messages, 237–39, 240–42, 295
  in recruitment brochures, 243–44
  targeted messages, 240–42, 250–51, 295
  in videos and videoconferencing, 244
  word of mouth referrals and, 243, 295–96

Recruitsoft, 287

Red Lobster, 220

Reduction in force (RIF), 685, 700–701, 723

Reference checks, 389, 392–98, 406

Rehabilitation Act (1973), 55, 72

Reid Report, 453

Rejections of job offers, 611–12

Reliability of measurement
  calculation of estimates, 331–34
  error component, 330–32
  implications of, 334–35
  of initial assessment methods, 403–4
  of substantive assessment methods, 468–70
  types of, 328–30
  validity and, 335

Reliability Scale of the Hogan Employment Inventory, 453

Relocation assistance, 599

Reneging of job offers, 589, 612–13

REPeValuator test, 447

Replacement plans, 107–9, 290–91, 293

Requisitions for job openings, 207–8, 278

Responsibilities. See Task dimensions

ResumeDoctor, 379

Résumés
  electronic submission of, 378
  errors in, 380
  in external selection, 377–81
  fabrication/distortion in, 379–80
  keywords in, 378
  video presentation of, 256, 378–79

Résumé-tracking services, 377–78

Retaliation, 33, 55

Retention management, 683–730
  causes of turnover, 687–89
  cost-benefit analysis of turnover, 694–702, 725–26
  counteroffers, 717
  decision process, 706–9
  desirability of leaving, 687, 709–14
  discharge initiatives, 717–23
  downsizing initiatives, 723–27
  ease of leaving, 687–88, 715–16
  effectiveness of initiatives, 703–4
  employee satisfaction surveys, 693–94

exit interviews, 691–93
high turnover propensity, 714
internal transfers, 716–17
layoff survivors, 725–27
legal issues, 727–28
measurement of turnover,
    689–702
no-layoff guarantees, 725
overview, 10, 24–25, 27
performance management,
    717–21
progressive discipline, 721–23
reasons for leaving, 691–94
retention bonuses, 711, 715–16
retention bundles, 705–6
staffing levels and quality, 689,
    724–25
types of turnover, 685–87
voluntary turnover initiatives,
    702–17
Retraining, 94
Reuters, 349
Rewards. *See* Job rewards
RIF (reduction in force), 685,
    700–701, 723
*The Rights and Responsibilities of
    Test Takers*, 352–53
Right to sue letter, 60
RJP. *See* Realistic job preview
    (RJP)
Role-play, 526

Saba Succession, 290
Safeway, 302
Salary survey websites, 604
Sales approach, in job offers, 610
Sales techniques, for recruiters,
    215
Same-sex personal contact, as job
    requirement, 415
SAP Software, 287, 509, 712
SAS (company), 705
Scatter diagrams, 323, 324
Science Applications International
    Corporation (SAIC), 641–43
Scores
    central tendency and variability,
        321–22
    correlations between, 323–27

defined, 320–21
percentiles, 322
scatter diagrams, 323, 324
standard scores, 322–23
See also Cut scores
Selection ratio, 546–47
Self-assessment, 511–12
Seniority/merit systems
    discrimination and, 66
    internal selection, 515–17
    job rewards and, 713
    legal issues, 297–300
    principles of, 76–78
    retention management, 711
Sensory abilities, in O*NET
    system, 160
Sensory/perceptual ability tests,
    442
Sentence analysis technique, task
    statements, 154
Separation costs, 694–702, 725–26
Separation laws and regulation,
    727
Service-level agreements (SLAs),
    654
Severance packages, 600, 701
Shareholder value, 694, 700, 701
Siemens, 28
Signing bonuses, 598–600
Situational judgment tests, 449–52,
    466–67, 468, 524–25
Skill, definition (KSAOs), 158
Skype, 399
Smoking, 475–76
Socialization of new employees,
    617–19
Social networking websites
    HRISs and, 650
    job postings on, 245
    recruitment and, 221–22,
        256–57
    in reference checks, 394, 406
    See also specific websites
Social service agencies, 229
Society for Human Resource
    Management (SHRM)
    benefits data, 187
    on changing demographics, 125
    code of ethics, 32

company benchmarks, 349
Job Satisfaction survey, 185–86
online sample job descriptions,
    164
on staffing metrics, 659
on succession planning, 110
survey on retention initiatives,
    703–4
Testing Center, 352
website, 32
Society for Industrial and
    Organizational Psychology
    (SIOP), 32–33, 352
Software-as-a-service (SaaS)
    providers, 650, 651
Sonesta Hotels, 619
Sony, 239
Southcoast Hospitals Group, 619
Speed hiring, 663
Split sample analysis, 659
Sponsors, 512–13
Sports Authority, 351
Staffing firms
    fees, 121
    flexible workforce and, 93,
        121–23
    legal compliance, 136
    selection of, 123
    temporary employees, 50–51
Staffing jobs, 566, 641–47
Staffing levels
    retention management, 689,
        724–25
    staffing strategy and, 25–30
    workforce head count, 6, 14, 724
Staffing models and strategy, 6–40
    acquisition strategy, 25–26
    attract staff vs. relocate, 28
    core vs. flexible workforce, 27,
        117–21
    definition of staffing, 8–10, 48
    diversity, 31
    ethical practices, 31–34
    exceptional vs. acceptable
        workforce, 30
    external vs. internal staffing,
        26–27
    importance of, 6–9
    KSAOs, 30

organizational effectiveness and, 11
outsourcing, 26, 27–28
person/job match, 6, 15–17, 30
person/organization match, 6, 17–19, 30
as process/system, 10
retention management, 10, 27
short-term vs. long-term focus, 29–30
staffing levels, 14, 25–30
staffing organizations model, 21–25
staffing quality, 30–31
system components, 19–21
Staffing organizations model
chart of, 22
core staffing activities, 24
retention management, 24–25
staffing strategy, 21–23
support activities, 23–24
See also specific aspects
Staffing philosophy, 118–20
Staffing strategy. *See* Staffing models and strategy
Staffing system management, 636–75
calculation of staffing metrics, 663–64
components of, 19–21
customer satisfaction surveys, 664–67
effectiveness of technologies, 651
evaluation of, 655–65
HRISs, 648–51
legal issues, 665–74
organizational arrangements, 637–41
outsourcing, 650, 651–54
policies and procedures, 644, 647–48
staffing flowcharts, 655–57
staffing jobs, 641–47
staffing process metrics, 658–63
standardization of processes, 655–57
training within, 670, 672
web-based systems, 650

Staffmark, 644–47
Standard error of measurement (SEM), 334–35
Standardization
of measurement, 318
of testing procedures, 350, 355–56
Standard scores, 322–23
Stanton Survey, 453
Starbucks, 209, 349
Starting dates, in job offers, 592
State employment services, 229
State governments, 55, 57
See also Statutory law
Station Casino, 447
Statistical evidence, 59–60
Statistical significance, 545
Statute of frauds, 585
Statutory law
on access to personnel files, 269
on background checks, 406–8
basis of, 54
fair enforcement practice (FEP) law, 60
noncompete agreements, 601
on preemployment inquiry, 408–14
on reference checks, 406
on tests for smoking habits, 475–76
Stock options, 596–97
Strong Vocational Interest Blank (SVIB), 456
Structured interviews
adverse impact, 471
characteristics, 458–60
error/bias in, 458–59
evaluation of, 460–61
external selection and, 457–68
job requirements matrix and, 461–62
KSAOs and, 461–64, 466–67
in team environments, 465–68
training of interviewers, 464–65
See also Interviews
Students, recruitment of, 225–27, 231–32, 240
Subject matter experts (SMEs), 171, 179

Substance abuse
alcohol tests, 476–77
counterproductivity and, 720
drug tests, 472–78, 485–86
rights of recovering abusers, 69
types of detection tests, 474
Succession planning, 107, 110–12, 290–91, 293, 508–9
Sun Microsystems, 614
SunTrust Bank, 448, 638
Supervisors
abusive behavior by, 713–14
internal recruitment and selection, 282–83, 288, 295, 506, 512
interpersonal conflicts with, 688, 692, 713–14
in job analysis, 171
job requisitions, 207, 278
justice perceptions and, 713–14
See also Managers
SurveyMonkey, 665
Surveys
customer satisfaction surveys, 664–67
design of, 665
on downsizing, 725
on employee benefits, 711
employee satisfaction surveys, 693–94
Great Place to Work Trust Index survey, 704
Harris Interactive surveys, 613
human capital benchmark surveys, 659
of job applicants, 665, 667
Job Openings and Labor Turnover Survey, 690–91
job rewards and, 183–84
managers' satisfaction with staffing services, 664–65, 666
National Compensation Survey, 185
National Study of the Changing Workforce, 714
online exit surveys, 692
PDI Employment Survey, 453
salary survey websites, 604
Stanton Survey, 453

on telework, 714
on turnover, 712
WorldatWork surveys, 704
See also Society for Human
    Resource Management
    (SHRM)
Survivor sickness, 725–27
Sweatshops, 125

Talent management systems, 273,
    287–88, 290, 293, 508–9
Talent pipeline, 233, 273
Targeted recruitment, 215–17, 218,
    223–24, 250–51
Task dimensions, 153, 155–56
Task questionnaires, 167–68
Task statements, 153, 154
Taylor-Russell tables, 547–49
TCG, 276
Teams, 187–88, 276, 465–68, 568
Technology
    assistive, 70, 256, 482
    flexible workforce and, 705
    recruitment, 244, 255–57
    staffing planning and, 94–95
    system management and, 651
    *See also specific tools and
        software*
Telecommunications devices for
    the deaf (TDDs), 256
Television advertisements, 245–46
Telework, 70, 150, 704, 714
Temporary employees, 50–51, 136
Temporary employment agencies.
    See Staffing firms
Temporary worker visas, 74
Temp-to-perm workers, 121
Terminology, in job descriptions,
    148
Testing and assessment
    ban on race norming, 66
    best practices, 356–57
    computer vs. paper/pencil, 448
    discrimination and, 66
    faking and, 391–92, 428–29,
        432–34, 454–55, 477
    Internet-based, 351
    legal issues, 353–57
    professional standards, 352–53

qualifications of test
    administrators, 350
reasonable accommodation
    under ADA, 482–83
security of tests, 350
standardization of procedures,
    350, 355–56
start-up costs, 351–53
See also External selection;
    *specific assessment methods
    and tests*
Test-retest reliability, 333
Test-taker rights, 352–53
Thrivenet, 660
Time-lapse statistics, 209
Title inflation, 507
Title VII. *See* Civil Rights Acts
    (Title VII)
T-Mobile, 394
Torts, 53–54, 257
Toys "R" Us, 378
Training
    to conduct structured interviews,
        464–65
    costs and turnover, 695–96
    on employee termination,
        721–23
    of in-house temporary
        employees, 289–90
    organization-specific KSAOs,
        706, 715
    on performance management,
        721–23
    succession planning and,
        111–12
    video instruction, 297
Transportation Security
    Administration (TSA), 351
TransWorld Airlines (TWA), 716
Trend analysis, 101
Turnover
    analysis of, 689–702
    causes of, 687–89
    discharge turnover, 685–87, 689,
        698–99
    downsizing turnover, 685–87,
        689, 699–702, 723–24, 729
    involuntary turnover, 685–87

measurement of, 663, 689–702,
    725–26
mobility paths and, 276
RJPs and reduction of, 238
voluntary turnover, 685–89,
    694–98
See also Retention management
Twitter, 221

Undue hardship, 70
Unicru, 351
Uniformed Services Employment
    and Reemployment Rights
    Act (USERRA), 76
Uniform Guidelines on Employee
    Selection Procedures
    (UGESP)
    applicant, defined, 252
    on cut scores and adverse
        impact, 568–69
    explanation of, 55, 66
    on job analysis, 188
    on selection and adverse impact,
        479–81, 529–30
United Health Group, 233
United Parcel Service (UPS), 226,
    707
Unit weighting, 553–54
University of Pittsburgh Medical
    Center, 399
Urine tests, 474
US Army, recruitment methods,
    232
US Citizenship and Immigration
    Services, 54, 73–74, 620–21
USERRA. *See* Uniformed
    Services Employment and
    Reemployment Rights Act
    (USERRA)
US Marine Corps, 239
US Postal Service, 398, 477–78
US Small Business Administration,
    637
Utility analysis, 546–51

Vacancy time, 663
Validation studies
    concurrent validation, 340–44
    construct validation, 337–38

content validation, 344–46
criterion-related validation, 338–44
predictive validation, 340–41
Validity coefficient, 544–45
Validity generalization, 346–48
Validity of measurement
accuracy and, 336–38
assessment centers and, 524–25
in assessment methods, 544–45
face validity, 545
initial assessment methods and, 404
personality tests, 429–34
reliability and, 335
substantive assessment methods, 470, 513–14
Values inventories, 455–57
Veterans Employment and Training Service (VETS), 76
Videos and videoconferencing
initial screening interviews, 399
in recruitment, 244
résumé presentations, 256, 378–79
training videos, 297

Violence in workplace, 398, 408
Visas, 74

Wawa Inc., 660
Web-based recruitment. *See* Internet recruitment
Website design, 246–48
Wegmans, 707
Welfare-to-work programs, 91, 136
Wellpoint Health Network, 111–12
Whirlpool, 287
Williams Insurance Service, 554
W. L. Gore & Associates, 11
Women
affirmative action and, 64, 128–33
availability determination, 129–31
glass ceiling and, 299–303, 530–31
in labor force demographics, 125
pay expectations and, 594–95
See also Affirmative action plans (AAPs); Diversity
Wonderlic, 351, 352
Wonderlic Personnel Test, 352, 373, 435–36, 437, 440

Work attire, in O*NET system, 163
WorkBlast.com, 378
Workforce
demographics of, 67, 125–27
head count, 6, 14, 55, 100–103, 114, 689, 724, 729
quality of, 7
trends, 94
See also Core workforce; Flexible workforce
Workforce planning software, 101
Work/life balance, 127, 714
Workplace violence, 398, 408
Work samples, in external selection, 445–49
Work setting, in O*NET system, 163
Work teams. *See* Teams
WorldatWork surveys, 704
Written employment contracts, 584–85
See also Contracts

Yield ratios, 209

Zoomerang, 665